# HISTORY O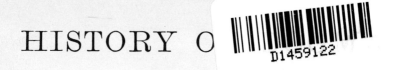

BY

## Dr. ADOLPH HARNACK

ORDINARY PROF. OF CHURCH HISTORY IN THE UNIVERSITY, AND FELLOW OF
THE ROYAL ACADEMY OF SCIENCE, BERLIN

*TRANSLATED FROM THE THIRD GERMAN
EDITION*

BY

## NEIL BUCHANAN

VOLUME II
and
VOLUME III

DOVER PUBLICATIONS, INC.

NEW YORK

Published in the United Kingdom by Constable
and Company Limited, 10 Orange Street, London
W. C. 2.

This new Dover edition, first published in 1961,
is an unabridged republication of the English translation of the third German edition that appeared
circa 1900. This Dover edition is an unaltered republication except that minor typographical errors
in Volume VII have been corrected.

The original English edition appeared as seven
separate volumes, whereas this Dover edition is
published complete in four separate volumes.

Manufactured in the United States of America

Dover Publications, Inc.
180 Varick Street
New York 14, N.Y.

# HISTORY OF DOGMA

BY

## DR. ADOLPH HARNACK

Volume II

# CONTENTS.

# DIVISION I.

---

## BOOK II.

### THE LAYING OF THE FOUNDATIONS

# CHAPTER I.

## HISTORICAL SURVEY.

THE second century of the existence of Gentile-Christian communities was characterised by the victorious conflict with Gnosticism and the Marcionite Church, by the gradual development of an ecclesiastical doctrine, and by the decay of the early Christian enthusiasm. The general result was the establishment of a great ecclesiastical association, which, forming at one and the same time a political commonwealth, school and union for worship, was based on the firm foundation of an "apostolic" law of faith, a collection of "apostolic" writings, and finally, an "apostolic" organisation. This institution was *the Catholic Church*. [1] In opposition to Gnosticism and Marcionitism, the main articles forming the estate and possession of orthodox Christianity were raised to the rank of apostolic regulations and laws, and thereby placed beyond all discussion and assault. At first the innovations introduced by this were not of a material, but of a formal, character. Hence they were not noticed by any of those who had never, or only in a vague fashion, been elevated to the feeling and idea of freedom and independence in religion.

---

[1] Aubé (Histoire des Persécutions de l'Eglise, Vol. II. 1878, pp. 1—68) has given a survey of the genesis of ecclesiastical dogma. The disquisitions of Renan in the last volumes of his great historical work are excellent, though not seldom exaggerated in particular points. See especially the concluding observations in Vol. VII. cc. 28—34. Since the appearance of Ritschl's monograph on the genesis of the old Catholic Church, a treatise which, however, forms too narrow a conception of the problem, German science can point to no work of equal rank with the French. Cf. Sohm's Kirchenrecht, Vol. I. which, however, in a very one-sided manner, makes the adoption of the legal and constitutional arrangements responsible for all the evil in the Church.

How great the innovations actually were, however, may be measured by the fact that they signified a scholastic tutelage of the faith of the individual Christian, and restricted the immediateness of religious feelings and ideas to the narrowest limits. But the conflict with the so-called Montanism showed that there were still a considerable number of Christians who valued that immediateness and freedom; these were, however, defeated. The fixing of the tradition under the title of apostolic necessarily led to the assumption that whoever held the apostolic doctrine was also essentially a Christian in the apostolic sense. This assumption, quite apart from the innovations which were legitimised by tracing them to the Apostles, meant the separation of doctrine and conduct, the preference of the former to the latter, and the transformation of a fellowship of faith, hope, and discipline into a communion "eiusdem sacramenti", that is, into a union which, like the philosophical schools, rested on a doctrinal law, and which was subject to a legal code of divine institution. [1]

The movement which resulted in the Catholic Church owes its right to a place in the history of Christianity to the victory

[1] Sohm (p. 160) declares: "The foundation of Catholicism is the divine Church law to which it lays claim." In many other passages he even seems to express the opinion that the Church law of itself, even when not represented as divine, is the hereditary enemy of the true Church and at the same time denotes the essence of Catholicism. See, e.g., p. 2: "The whole essence of Catholicism consists in its declaring legal institutions to be necessary to the Church." Page 700: "The essence of Church law is incompatible with the essence of the Church." This thesis really characterises Catholicism well and contains a great truth, if expressed in more careful terms, somewhat as follows: The assertion that there is a divine Church law (emanating from Christ, or, in other words, from the Apostles), which is necessary to the spiritual character of the Church and which in fact is a token of this very attribute, is incompatible with the essence of the Gospel and is the mark of a pseudo-Catholicism." But the thesis contains too narrow a view of the case. For the divine Church law is only one feature of the essence of the Catholic Church, though a very important element, which Sohm, as a jurist, was peculiarly capable of recognising. The whole essence of Catholicism, however, consists in the deification of tradition generally. The declaration that the empirical institutions of the Church, created for and necessary to this purpose, are apostolic, a declaration which amalgamates them with the essence and content of the Gospel and places them beyond all criticism, is the peculiarly "Catholic" feature. Now, as a great part of these institutions cannot be inwardly appropriated and cannot really amalgamate with faith and piety, it is self-evident that such portions become

over Gnosticism and to the preservation of an important part of early Christian tradition. If Gnosticism in all its phases was the violent attempt to drag Christianity down to the level of the Greek world, and to rob it of its dearest possession, belief in the Almighty God of creation and redemption, then Catholicism, inasmuch as it secured this belief for the Greeks, preserved the Old Testament, and supplemented it with early Christian writings, thereby saving—as far as documents, at least, were concerned—and proclaiming the authority of an important part of primitive Christianity, must in one respect be acknowledged as a conservative force born from the vigour of Christi-

legal ordinances, to which obedience must be rendered. For no other relation to these ordinances can be conceived. Hence the legal regulations and the corresponding slavish devotion come to have such immense scope in Catholicism, and well-nigh express its essence. But behind this is found the more general conviction that the empirical Church, as it actually exists, is the authentic, pure, and infallible creation: its doctrine, its regulations, its religious ceremonial are apostolic. Whoever doubts that renounces Christ. Now, if, as in the case of the Reformers, this conception be recognised as erroneous and unevangelical, the result must certainly be a strong detestation of "the divine Church law." Indeed, the inclination to sweep away all Church law is quite intelligible, for when you give the devil your little finger he takes the whole hand. But, on the other hand, it cannot be imagined how communities are to exist on earth, propagate themselves, and train men without regulations; and how regulations are to exist without resulting in the formation of a code of laws. In truth, such regulations have at no time been wanting in Christian communities, and have always possessed the character of a legal code. Sohm's distinction, that in the oldest period there was no "law", but only a "regulation", is artificial, though possessed of a certain degree of truth; for the regulation has one aspect in a circle of like-minded enthusiasts, and a different one in a community where all stages of moral and religious culture are represented, and which has therefore to train its members. Or should it not do so? And, on the other hand, had the oldest Churches not the Old Testament and the διατάξεις of the Apostles? Were these no code of laws? Sohm's proposition: "The essence of Church law is incompatible with the essence of the Church," does not rise to evangelical clearness and freedom, but has been formed under the shadow and ban of Catholicism. I am inclined to call it an Anabaptist thesis. The Anabaptists were also in the shadow and ban of Catholicism; hence their only course was either the attempt to wreck the Church and Church history and found a new empire, or a return to Catholicism. Hermann Bockelson or the Pope! But the Gospel is above the question of Jew or Greek, and therefore also above the question of a legal code. It is reconcilable with everything that is not sin, even with the philosophy of the Greeks. Why should it not be also compatible with the monarchical bishop, with the legal code of the Romans, and even with the Pope, provided these are not made part of the Gospel.

anity. If we put aside abstract considerations and merely look at the facts of the given situation, we cannot but admire a creation which first broke up the various outside forces assailing Christianity, and in which the highest blessings of this faith have always continued to be accessible. If the founder of the Christian religion had deemed belief in the Gospel and a life in accordance with it to be compatible with membership of the Synagogue and observance of the Jewish law, there could at least be no impossibility of adhering to the Gospel within the Catholic Church.

Still, that is only one side of the case. The older Catholicism never clearly put the question, "What is Christian?" Instead of answering that question it rather laid down rules, the recognition of which was to be the guarantee of Christianism. This solution of the problem seems to be on the one hand too narrow and on the other too broad. Too narrow, because it bound Christianity to rules under which it necessarily languished; too broad, because it did not in any way exclude the introduction of new and foreign conceptions. In throwing a protective covering round the Gospel, Catholicism also obscured it. It preserved Christianity from being hellenised to the most extreme extent, but, as time went on, it was forced to admit into this religion an ever greater measure of secularisation. In the interests of its world-wide mission it did not indeed directly disguise the terrible seriousness of religion, but, by tolerating a less strict ideal of life, it made it possible for those less in earnest to be considered Christians, and to regard themselves as such. It permitted the genesis of a Church, which was no longer a communion of faith, hope, and discipline, but a political commonwealth in which the Gospel merely had a place beside other things. [1] In ever increasing measure it invested all the forms which this secular commonwealth required with apostolic, that is, indirectly, with divine authority. This course disfigured Christianity and made a knowledge of what is Christian an obscure and difficult matter. But, in Catholicism, religion for the first time obtained a formal dogmatic system. Catholic Christi-

---

[1] In the formation of the Marcionite Church we have, on the other hand, the attempt to create a rigid œcumenical community, held together solely by religion. The Marcionite Church therefore had a founder, the Catholic has none.

anity  discovered  the  formula  which  reconciled  faith  and  knowledge.    This  formula  satisfied  humanity  for  centuries,  and  the
blessed  effects  which  it  accomplished  continued  to  operate  even
after  it  had  itself  already  become  a  fetter.

Catholic  Christianity  grew  out  of  two  converging  series  of
developments.    In  the  one  were  set  up  fixed  outer  standards
for  determining  what  is  Christian,  and  these  standards  were
proclaimed  to  be  apostolic  institutions.  The  baptismal  confession
was  exalted  to  an  apostolic  rule  of  faith,  that  is,  to  an  apostolic
law  of  faith.    A  collection  of  apostolic  writings  was  formed  from
those  read  in  the  Churches,  and  this  compilation  was  placed  on
an  equal  footing  with  the  Old  Testament.    The  episcopal  and
monarchical  constitution  was  declared  to  be  apostolic,  and  the
attribute  of  successor  of  the  Apostles  was  conferred  on  the
bishop.  Finally,  the  religious  ceremonial  developed  into  a  celebration  of  mysteries,  which  was  in  like  manner  traced  back  to
the  Apostles.    The  result  of  these  institutions  was  a  strictly
exclusive  Church  in  the  form  of  a  communion  of  doctrine,  ceremonial,  and  law,  a  confederation  which  more  and  more  gathered
the  various  communities  within  its  pale,  and  brought  about  the
decline  of  all  nonconforming  sects.  The  confederation  was  primarily  based  on  a  common  confession,  which,  however,  was  not
only  conceived  as  "law,"  but  was  also  very  soon  supplemented
by  new  standards.    One  of  the  most  important  problems  to  be
investigated  in  the  history  of  dogma,  and  one  which  unfortunately  cannot  be  completely  solved,  is  to  show  what  necessities
led  to  the  setting  up  of  a  new  canon  of  Scripture, what  circumstances  required  the  appearance  of  living  authorities  in  the
communities,  and  what  relation  was  established  between  the
apostolic  rule  of  faith,  the  apostolic  canon  of  Scripture,  and  the
apostolic  office.  The  development  ended  with  the  formation of a
clerical  class,  at  whose  head  stood  the  bishop,  who  united  in
himself  all  conceivable  powers,  as  teacher,  priest,  and  judge.
He  disposed  of  the  powers  of  Christianity,  guaranteed its purity,
and  therefore  in  every  respect  held  the  Christian  laity  in tutelage.

But  even  apart  from  the  content  which  Christianity  here
received,  this  process  in  itself represents  a  progressive  secularising
of  the  Church.    This  would  be  self-evident  enough,  even  if  it

were not confirmed by noting the fact that the process had already been to some extent anticipated in the so-called Gnosticism (See vol. I. p. 253 and Tertullian, de præscr. 35). But the element which the latter lacked, namely, a firmly welded, suitably regulated constitution, must by no means be regarded as one originally belonging and essential to Christianity. The depotentiation to which Christianity was here subjected appears still more plainly in the facts, that the Christian hopes were deadened, that the secularising of the Christian life was tolerated and even legitimised, and that the manifestations of an unconditional devotion to the heavenly excited suspicion or were compelled to confine themselves to very narrow limits.

But these considerations are scarcely needed as soon as we turn our attention to the second series of developments that make up the history of this period. The Church did not merely set up dykes and walls against Gnosticism in order to ward it off externally, nor was she satisfied with defending against it the facts which were the objects of her belief and hope; but, taking the creed for granted, she began to follow this heresy into its own special territory and to combat it with a scientific theology. That was a necessity which did not first spring from Christianity's own internal struggles. It was already involved in the fact that the Christian Church had been joined by cultured Greeks, who felt the need of justifying their Christianity to themselves and the world, and of presenting it as the desired and certain answer to all the pressing questions which then occupied men's minds.

The beginning of a development which a century later reached its provisional completion in the theology of Origen, that is, in the transformation of the Gospel into a scientific system of ecclesiastical doctrine, appears in the Christian Apologetic, as we already find it before the middle of the second century. As regards its content, this system of doctrine meant the legitimising of Greek philosophy within the sphere of the rule of faith. The theology of Origen bears the same relation to the New Testament as that of Philo does to the Old. What is here presented as Christianity is in fact the idealistic religious philosophy of the age, attested by divine revelation, made accessible to all by the incarnation of the Logos, and purified from any

connection with Greek mythology and gross polytheism. [1] A
motley multitude of primitive Christian ideas and hopes, derived
from both Testaments, and too brittle to be completely recast,
as yet enclosed the kernel. But the majority of these were
successfully manipulated by theological art, and the traditional
rule of faith was transformed into a system of doctrine, in which,
to some extent, the old articles found only a nominal place. [2]

This hellenising of ecclesiastical Christianity, by which we do
not mean the Gospel, was not a gradual process; for the truth
rather is that it was already accomplished the moment that the
reflective Greek confronted the new religion which he had
accepted. The Christianity of men like Justin, Athenagoras,
and Minucius is not a whit less Hellenistic than that of Origen.
But yet an important distinction obtains here. It is twofold.
In the first place, those Apologists did not yet find themselves
face to face with a fixed collection of writings having a title
to be reverenced as Christian; they have to do with the Old
Testament and the "Teachings of Christ" (διδάγματα Χριστοῦ).
In the second place, they do not yet regard the scientific
presentation of Christianity as the main task and as one which
this religion itself demands. As they really never enquired
what was meant by "Christian," or at least never put the
question clearly to themselves, they never claimed that their
scientific presentation of Christianity was the first proper expression of it that had been given. Justin and his contemporaries
make it perfectly clear that they consider the traditional faith
existing in the churches to be complete and pure and in itself
requiring no scientific revision. In a word, the gulf which existed

[1] The historian who wishes to determine the advance made by Græco-Roman
humanity in the third and fourth centuries, under the influence of Catholicism and
its theology, must above all keep in view the fact that gross polytheism and
immoral mythology were swept away, spiritual monotheism brought near to all,
and the ideal of a divine life and the hope of an eternal one made certain.
Philosophy also aimed at that, but it was not able to establish a community of
men on these foundations.

[2] Luther, as is well known, had a very profound impression of the distinction
between Biblical Christianity and the theology of the Fathers, who followed the
theories of Origen. See, for example, Werke, Vol. LXII. p. 49, quoting Proles:
'When the word of God comes to the Fathers, me thinks it is as if milk were
'filtered through a coal sack, where the milk must become black and spoiled."

between the religious thought of philosophers and the sum of
Christian tradition is still altogether unperceived, because that
tradition was not yet fixed in rigid forms, because no religious
utterance testifying to monotheism, virtue, and reward was as
yet threatened by any control, and finally, because the speech
of philosophy was only understood by a small minority in the
Church, though its interests and aims were not unknown to
most. Christian thinkers were therefore still free to divest of
their direct religious value all realistic and historical elements
of the tradition, while still retaining them as parts of a huge
apparatus of proof, which accomplished what was really the
only thing that many sought in Christianity, viz., the assurance that the theory of the world obtained from other sources
was the truth. The danger which here threatened Christianity
as a religion was scarcely less serious than that which had been
caused to it by the Gnostics. These remodelled tradition, the
Apologists made it to some extent inoperative without attacking
it. The latter were not disowned, but rather laid the foundation of Church theology, and determined the circle of interests
within which it was to move in the future. [1]

But the problem which the Apologists solved almost offhand,
namely, the task of showing that Christianity was the perfect
and certain philosophy, because it rested on revelation, and that
it was the highest scientific knowledge of God and the world,
was to be rendered more difficult. To these difficulties all that
primitive Christianity has up to the present transmitted to the
Church of succeeding times contributes its share. The conflict
with Gnosticism made it necessary to find some sort of solution
to the question, "What is Christian?" and to fix this answer.
But indeed the Fathers were not able to answer the question
confidently and definitely. They therefore made a selection
from tradition and contented themselves with making it binding
on Christians. Whatever was to lay claim to authority in the

[1] They were not the first to determine this circle of interests. So far as we
can demonstrate traces of independent religious knowledge among the so-called
Apostolic Fathers of the post-apostolic age, they are in thorough harmony with
the theories of the Apologists, which are merely expressed with precision and
divested of Old Testament language.

Church had henceforth to be in harmony with the rule of faith
and the canon of New Testament Scriptures. That created an
entirely new situation for Christian thinkers, that is, for those
trying to solve the problem of subordinating Christianity to the
Hellenic spirit. That spirit never became quite master of the
situation; it was obliged to accommodate itself to it. [1] The
work first began with the scientific treatment of individual
articles contained in the rule of faith, partly with the view
of disproving Gnostic conceptions, partly for the purpose of
satisfying the Church's own needs. The framework in which
these articles were placed virtually continued to be the apologetic
theology, for this maintained a doctrine of God and the world,
which seemed to correspond to the earliest tradition as much
as it ran counter to the Gnostic theses. (Melito), Irenæus, Tertullian and Hippolytus, aided more or less by tradition on the
one hand and by philosophy on the other, opposed to the Gnostic
dogmas about Christianity the articles of the baptismal confession interpreted as a rule of faith, these articles being developed
into doctrines. Here they undoubtedly learned very much from
the Gnostics and Marcion. If we define ecclesiastical dogmas
as propositions handed down in the creed of the Church, shown
to exist in the Holy Scriptures of both Testaments, and
rationally reproduced and formulated, then the men we have just
mentioned were the first to set up dogmas[2]—dogmas but no

---

[1] It was only after the apostolic tradition, fixed in the form of a comprehensive
collection, seemed to guarantee the admissibility of every form of Christianity that
reverenced that collection, that the hellenising of Christianity within the Church
began in serious fashion. The fixing of tradition had had a twofold result. On
the one hand, it opened the way more than ever before for a free and unhesitating
introduction of foreign ideas into Christianity, and, on the other hand, so far as
it really also included the documents and convictions of primitive Christianity, it
preserved this religion to the future and led to a return to it, either from scientific
or religious considerations. That we know anything at all of original Christianity
is entirely due to the fixing of the tradition, as found at the basis of Catholicism.
On the supposition—which is indeed an academic consideration—that this fixing
had not taken place because of the non-appearance of the Gnosticism which
occasioned it, and on the further supposition that the original enthusiasm had
continued, we would in all probability know next to nothing of original Christianity
to-day. How much we would have known may be seen from the Shepherd of Hermas.

[2] So far as the Catholic Church is concerned, the idea of dogmas, as individual
theorems characteristic of Christianity, and capable of being scholastically proved,

system of dogmatics. As yet the difficulty of the problem was
by no means perceived by these men either. Their peculiar
capacity for sympathising with and understanding the traditional
and the old still left them in a happy blindness. So far as
they had a theology they supposed it to be nothing more than
the explanation of the faith of the Christian multitude (yet
Tertullian already noted the difference in one point, certainly a
very characteristic one, viz., the Logos doctrine). They still
lived in the belief that the Christianity which filled their minds
required no scientific remodelling in order to be an expression
of the highest knowledge, and that it was in all respects identical with the Christianity which even the most uncultivated
could grasp. That this was an illusion is proved by many
considerations, but most convincingly by the fact that Tertullian
and Hippolytus had the main share in introducing into the
doctrine of faith a philosophically formulated dogma, viz., that
the Son of God is the Logos, and in having it made the *articulus
constitutivus ecclesiæ*. The effects of this undertaking can never
be too highly estimated, for the Logos doctrine is Greek philosophy *in nuce*, though primitive Christian views may have been
subsequently incorporated with it. Its introduction into the creed
of Christendom, which was, strictly speaking, the setting up
*of the first dogma in the Church*, meant the future conversion
of the rule of faith into a philosophic system. But in yet another
respect Irenæus and Hippolytus denote an immense advance
beyond the Apologists, which, paradoxically enough, results both
from the progress of Christian Hellenism and from a deeper
study of the Pauline theology, that is, emanates from the controversy with Gnosticism. In them a religious and realistic idea
takes the place of the moralism of the Apologists, namely, the
deifying of the human race through the incarnation of the Son
of God. The apotheosis of mortal man through his acquisition
of immortality (divine life) is the idea of salvation which was
taught in the ancient mysteries. It is here adopted as a Christian
one, supported by the Pauline theology (especially as contained
in the Epistle to the Ephesians), and brought into the closest

originated with the Apologists. Even as early as Justin we find tendencies to
amalgamate historical material and natural theology.

connection with the historical Christ, the Son of God and Son
of man (filius dei et filius hominis). What the heathen faintly
hoped for as a possibility was here announced as certain, and
indeed as having already taken place. What a message! This
conception was to become the central Christian idea of the future.
A long time, however, elapsed before it made its way into the
dogmatic system of the Church. [1]

But meanwhile the huge gulf which existed between both
Testaments and the rule of faith on the one hand, and the
current ideas of the time on the other, had been recognized
in Alexandria. It was not indeed felt as a gulf, for then either
the one or the other would have had to be given up, but as
a *problem*. If the Church tradition contained the assurance,
not to be obtained elsewhere, of all that Greek culture knew,
hoped for, and prized, and if for that very reason it was regarded as in every respect inviolable, then the absolutely indissoluble union of Christian tradition with the Greek philosophy
of religion was placed beyond all doubt. But an immense
number of problems were at the same time raised, especially
when, as in the case of the Alexandrians, heathen syncretism
in the entire breadth of its development was united with the
doctrine of the Church. The task, which had been begun by
Philo and carried on by Valentinus and his school, was now undertaken in the Church. Clement led the way in attempting a
solution of the problem, but the huge task proved too much
for him. Origen took it up under more difficult circumstances,
and in a certain fashion brought it to a conclusion. He, the
rival of the Neoplatonic philosophers, the Christian Philo, wrote
the first Christian dogmatic, which competed with the philosophic systems of the time, and which, founded on the Scriptures
of both Testaments, presents a peculiar union of the apologetic
theology of a Justin and the Gnostic theology of a Valentinus,

---

[1] It is almost completely wanting in Tertullian. That is explained by the
fact that this remarkable man was in his inmost soul an old-fashioned Christian,
to whom the Gospel was *conscientia religionis, disciplina vitæ* and *spes fidei*, and
who found no sort of edification in Neoplatonic notions, but rather dwelt on the
ideas "command", "performance", "error", "forgiveness". In Irenæus also,
moreover, the ancient idea of salvation, supplemented by elements derived from the
Pauline theology, is united with the primitive Christian eschatology.

while keeping steadily in view a simple and highly practical
aim. In this dogmatic the rule of faith is recast and that quite
consciously. Origen did not conceal his conviction that Christianity finds its correct expression only in scientific knowledge,
and that every form of Christianity that lacks theology is but
a meagre kind with no clear consciousness of its own content.
This conviction plainly shows that Origen was dealing with a
different kind of Christianity, though his view that a mere relative
distinction existed here may have its justification in the fact,
that the untheological Christianity of the age with which
he compared his own was already permeated by Hellenic
elements and in a very great measure secularised. [1] But Origen,
as well as Clement before him, had really a right to the conviction that the true essence of Christianity, or, in other words,
the Gospel, is only arrived at by the aid of critical speculation;
for was not the Gospel veiled and hidden in the canon of both
Testaments, was it not displaced by the rule of faith, was it
not crushed down, depotentiated, and disfigured in the Church
which identified itself with the people of Christ? Clement and
Origen found freedom and independence in what they recognized to be the essence of the matter and what they contrived
with masterly skill to determine as its proper aim, after an
examination of the huge apparatus of tradition. But was not
that the ideal of Greek sages and philosophers? This question
can by no means be flatly answered in the negative, and still
less decidedly in the affirmative, for a new significance was
here given to the ideal by representing it *as assured beyond
all doubt, already realised* in the person of Christ and incompatible with polytheism. If, as is manifestly the case, they found
joy and peace in their faith and in the theory of the universe
connected with it, if they prepared themselves for an eternal
life and expected it with certainty, if they felt themselves to be
perfect only through dependence on God, then, in spite of their
Hellenism, they unquestionably came nearer to the Gospel than
Irenæus with his slavish dependence on authority.

The setting up of a scientific system of Christian dogmatics, which

[1] On the significance of Clement and Origen see Overbeck, "Über die Anfänge
der patristischen Litteratur" in d. Hist. Ztschr. N. F., Vol. XII. p. 417 ff.

was still something different from the rule of faith, interpreted in an Antignostic sense, philosophically wrought out, and in some parts proved from the Bible, was a private undertaking of Origen, and at first only approved in limited circles. As yet, not only were certain bold changes of interpretation disputed in the Church, but the undertaking itself, as a whole, was disapproved. [1] The circumstances of the several provincial churches in the first half of the third century were still very diverse. Many communities had yet to adopt the basis that made them into Catholic ones; and in most, if not in all, the education of the clergy—not to speak of the laity—was not high enough to enable them to appreciate systematic theology. But the schools in which Origen taught carried on his work, similar ones were established, and these produced a number of the bishops and presbyters of the East in the last half of the third century. They had in their hands the means of culture afforded by the age, and this was all the more a guarantee of victory because the laity no longer took any part in deciding the form of religion. Wherever the Logos Christology had been adopted the future of Christian Hellenism was certain. At the beginning of the fourth century there was no community in Christendom which, apart from the Logos doctrine, possessed a purely philosophical theory that was regarded as an ecclesiastical dogma, to say nothing of an official scientific theology. But the system of Origen was a prophecy of the future. The Logos doctrine started the crystallising process which resulted in further deposits. Symbols of faith were already drawn up which contained a peculiar mixture of Origen's theology with the inflexible Antignostic *regula fidei*. One celebrated theologian, Methodius, endeavoured to unite the theology of Irenæus and Origen, ecclesiastical realism and philosophic spiritualism, under the badge of monastic mysticism. The developments of the following period therefore no longer appear surprising in any respect.

As Catholicism, from every point of view, is the result of

---

[1] Information on this point may be got not only from the writings of Origen (see especially his work against Celsus), but also and above all from his history. The controversy between Dionysius of Alexandria and the Chiliasts is also instructive on the matter.

the blending of Christianity with the ideas of antiquity,[1] so the Catholic dogmatic, as it was developed after the second or third century on the basis of the Logos doctrine, is Christianity conceived and formulated from the standpoint of the Greek philosophy of religion.[2] This Christianity conquered the old world, and became the foundation of a new phase of history in the Middle Ages. The union of the Christian religion with a definite historical phase of human knowledge and culture may be lamented in the interest of the Christian religion, which was thereby secularised, and in the interest of the development of culture which was thereby retarded (?). But lamentations become here ill-founded assumptions, as absolutely everything that we have and value is due to the alliance that Christianity and antiquity concluded in such a way that neither was able to prevail over the other. Our inward and spiritual life, which owes the least part of its content to the empiric knowledge which we have acquired, is based up to the present moment on the discords resulting from that union.

These hints are meant among other things to explain and justify[3] the arrangement chosen for the following presentation, which embraces the fundamental section of the history of Christian dogma.[4] A few more remarks are, however, necessary.

[1] The three or (reckoning Methodius) four steps of the development of church doctrine (Apologists, Old Catholic Fathers, Alexandrians) correspond to the progressive religious and philosophical development of heathendom at that period: philosophic moralism, ideas of salvation (theology and practice of mysteries), Neoplatonic philosophy, and complete syncretism.

[2] "Virtus omnis ex his causam accipit, a quibus provocatur (Tertull., de bapt. 2.)

[3] The plan of placing the apologetic theology before everything else would have much to recommend it, but I adhere to the arrangement here chosen, because the advantage of being able to represent and survey the outer ecclesiastical development and the inner theological one, each being viewed as a unity, seems to me to be very great. We must then of course understand the two developments as proceeding on parallel lines. But the placing of the former parallel before the latter in my presentation is justified by the fact that what was gained in the former passed over much more directly and swiftly into the general life of the Church, than what was reached in the latter. Decades elapsed, for instance, before the apologetic theology came to be generally known and accepted in the Church, as is shown by the long continued conflict against Monarchianism.

[4] The origin of Catholicism can only be very imperfectly described within the framework of the history of dogma, for the political situation of the Christian

1.  One special difficulty in ascertaining the genesis of the Catholic rules is that the churches, though on terms of close connection and mutual intercourse, had no real *forum publicum*, though indeed, in a certain sense, each bishop was *in foro publico*.  As a rule, therefore, we can only see the advance in the establishment of fixed forms in the shape of results, without being able to state precisely the ways and means which led to them.  We do indeed know the factors, and can therefore theoretically construct the development; but the real course of things is frequently hidden from us.  The genesis of a harmonious Church, firmly welded together in doctrine and constitution, can no more have been the natural unpremeditated product of the conditions of the time than were the genesis and adoption of the New Testament canon of Scripture.  But we have no direct evidence as to what communities had a special share in the development, although we know that the Roman Church played a leading part.  Moreover, we can only conjecture that conferences, common measures, and synodical decisions were not wanting. It is certain that, beginning with the last quarter of the second century, there were held in the different provinces, mostly in the East, but later also in the West, Synods in which an understanding was arrived at on all questions of importance to Christianity, including, e.g., the extent of the canon. [1]

2.  The degree of influence exercised by particular ecclesiastics

communities in the Roman Empire had quite as important an influence on the development of the Catholic Church as its internal conflicts.  But inasmuch as that situation and these struggles are ultimately connected in the closest way, the history of dogma cannot even furnish a complete picture of this development within definite limits.

[1]  See Tertullian, de pudic. 10: "Sed cederem tibi, si scriptura Pastoris, quæ sola moechos amat, divino instrumento meruisset incidi, si non ab omni concilio ecclesiarum etiam vestrarum inter aprocrypha et falsa iudicaretur;" de ieiun. 13: "Aguntur præterea per Græcias illa certis in locis concilia ex universis ecclesiis, per quæ et altiora quæque in commune tractantur, et ipsa repræsentatio totius nominis Christiani magna veneratione celebratur."  We must also take into account here the intercourse by letter, in which connection I may specially remind the reader of the correspondence between Dionysius, Bishop of Corinth, Euseb., H.E. IV. 23, and journeys such as those of Polycarp and Abercius to Rome. Cf. generally Zahn, Weltverkehr und Kirche während der drei ersten Jahrhunderte, 1877.

on the development of the Church and its doctrines is also
obscure and difficult to determine.  As they were compelled to
claim the sanction of tradition for every innovation they introduced, and did in fact do so, and as every fresh step they took
appeared to themselves necessary only as an explanation, it is
in many cases quite impossible to distinguish between what they
received from tradition and what they added to it of their own.
Yet an investigation from the point of view of the historian of
literature shows that Tertullian and Hippolytus were to a great
extent dependent on Irenæus.  What amount of innovation these
men independently contributed can therefore still be ascertained.
Both are men of the second generation.  Tertullian is related
to Irenæus pretty much as Calvin to Luther.  This parallel holds
good in more than one respect.  First, Tertullian drew up
a series of plain dogmatic formulæ which are not found in Irenæus and which proved of the greatest importance in succeeding
times.  Secondly, he did not attain the power, vividness, and
unity of religious intuition which distinguish Irenæus.  The truth
rather is that, just because of his forms, he partly destroyed the
unity of the matter and partly led it into a false path of development.  Thirdly, he everywhere endeavoured to give a conception
of Christianity which represented it as the divine law, whereas
in Irenæus this idea is overshadowed by the conception of the
Gospel as real redemption.  The main problem therefore resolves
itself into the question as to the position of Irenæus in the
history of the Church.  To what extent were his expositions new,
to what extent were the standards he formulated already employed
in the Churches, and in which of them? We cannot form to
ourselves a sufficiently vivid picture of the interchange of Christian
writings in the Church after the last quarter of the second century. [1]  Every important work speedily found its way into
the churches of the chief cities in the Empire.  The diffusion
was not merely from East to West, though this was the general
rule.  At the beginning of the fourth century there was in Cæsarea a Greek translation of Tertullian's Apology and a collection

---

[1] See my studies respecting the tradition of the Greek Apologists of the second
century in the early Church in the Texte und Unters. z. Gesch. der alt christl.
Litteratur, Vol. I. Part I. 2.

of Cyprian's epistles.[1] The influence of the Roman Church extended over the greater part of Christendom. Up till about the year 260 the Churches in East and West had still insome degree a common history.

3. The developments in the history of dogma within the period extending from about 150 to about 300 were by no means brought about in the different communities at the same time and in a completely analogous fashion. This fact is in great measure concealed from us, because our authorities are almost completely derived from those leading Churches that were connected with each other by constant intercourse. Yet the difference can still be clearly proved by the ratio of development in Rome, Lyons, and Carthage on the one hand, and in Alexandria on the other. Besides, we have several valuable accounts showing that in more remote provinces and communities the development was slower, and a primitive and freer condition of things much longer preserved.[2]

4. From the time that the clergy acquired complete sway over the Churches, that is, from the beginning of the second third of the third century, the development of the history of dogma practically took place within the ranks of that class, and was carried on by its learned men. Every mystery they set up therefore became doubly mysterious to the laity, for these did not even understand the terms, and hence it formed another new fetter.

---

[1] See Euseb., H.E. II. 2; VI. 43.

[2] See the accounts of Christianity in Edessa and the far East generally The Acta Archelai and the Homilies of Aphraates should also be specially examined. Cf. further Euseb., H. E. VI. 12, and finally the remains of the Latin-Christian literature of the third century—apart from Tertullian, Cyprian and Novatian—as found partly under the name of Cyprian, partly under other titles. Commodian, Arnobius, and Lactantius are also instructive here. This literature has been but little utilised with respect to the history of dogma and of the Church.

# I. *FIXING AND GRADUAL SECULARISING OF CHRISTIANITY AS A CHURCH.*

## CHAPTER II.

### THE SETTING UP OF THE APOSTOLIC STANDARDS FOR ECCLESIASTICAL CHRISTIANITY. THE CATHOLIC CHURCH. [1]

We may take as preface to this chapter three celebrated passages from Tertullian's "de præscriptione hæreticorum." In chap. 21 we find: "It is plain that all teaching that agrees with those apostolic Churches which are the wombs and origins of the faith must be set down as truth, it being certain that such doctrine contains that which the Church received from the Apostles, the Apostles from Christ, and Christ from God." In chap. 36 we read: "Let us see what it (the Roman Church) has learned, what it has taught, and what fellowship it has likewise had with the African Churches. It acknowledges one God the

---

[1] In itself the predicate "Catholic" contains no element that signifies a secularising of the Church. "Catholic" originally means Christianity in its totality as contrasted with single congregations. Hence the concepts "all communities" and the "universal Church" are identical. But from the beginning there was a dogmatic element in the concept of the universal Church, in so far as the latter was conceived to have been spread over the whole earth by the Apostles; an idea which involved the conviction that only that could be true which was found *everywhere* in Christendom. Consequently, "entire or universal Christendom," "the Church spread over the whole earth," and "the true Church" were regarded as identical conceptions. In this way the concept "Catholic" became a pregnant one, and finally received a dogmatic and political content. As this result actually took place, it is not inappropriate to speak of pre-Catholic and Catholic Christianity.

Lord, the creator of the universe, and Jesus Christ, the Son of God the creator, born of the Virgin Mary, as well as the resurrection of the flesh. It unites the Law and the Prophets with the writings of the Evangelists and Apostles. From these it draws its faith, and by their authority it seals this faith with water, clothes it with the Holy Spirit, feeds it with the eucharist, and encourages martyrdom. Hence it receives no one who rejects this institution." In chap. 32 the following challenge is addressed to the heretics: "Let them unfold a series of their bishops proceeding by succession from the beginning in such a way that this first bishop of theirs had as his authority and predecessor some one of the Apostles or one of the apostolic men, who, however, associated with the Apostles." * From the consideration of these three passages it directly follows that three standards are to be kept in view, viz., the apostolic doctrine, the apostolic canon of Scripture, and the guarantee of apostolic authority, afforded by the organisation of the Church, that is, by the episcopate, and traced back to apostolic institution. It will be seen that the Church always adopted these three standards together, that is simultaneously. [1] As a matter of fact they originated in Rome and gradually made their way in the other Churches. That Asia Minor had a share in this is probable, though the question is involved in obscurity. The three Catho-

---

* *Translator's note.* The following is Tertullian's Latin as given by Professor Harnack: Cap. 21: "Constat omnem doctrinam quæ cum ecclesiis apostolicis matricibus et originalibus fidei conspiret veritati deputandam, id sine dubio tenentem quod ecclesiæ ab apostolis, apostoli a Christo, Christus a deo accepit." Cap. 36 : "Videamus quid (ecclesia Romanensis) didicerit, quid docuerit, cum Africanis quoque ecclesiis contesserarit. Unum deum dominum novit, creatorem universitatis, et Christum Iesum ex virgine Maria filium dei creatoris, et carnis resurrectionem; legem et prophetas cum evangelicis et apostolicis litteris miscet; inde potat fidem, eam aqua signat, sancto spiritu vestit, eucharistia pascit, martyrium exhortatur, et ita adversus hanc institutionem neminem recipit." Chap. 32: "Evolvant ordinem episcoporum suorum, ita per successionem ab initio decurrentem, ut primus ille episcopus aliquem ex apostolis vel apostolicis viris, qui tamen cum apostolis perseveravit, habuerit auctorem et antecessorem."

[1] None of the three standards, for instance, were in the original of the first six books of the Apostolic Constitutions, which belong to the third century and are of Syrian origin; but instead of them the Old Testament and Gospel on the one hand, and the bishop, as the God of the community, on the other, are taken as authorities.

lic standards had their preparatory stages, (1) in short kerygmatic
creeds; (2) in the authority of the Lord and the formless
apostolic tradition as well as in the writings read in the Churches;
(3) in the veneration paid to apostles, prophets, and teachers,
or the "elders" and leaders of the individual communities.

### A. *The Transformation of the Baptismal Confession into the Apostolic Rule of Faith.*

It has been explained (vol. I. p. 157) that the idea of the
complete identity of what the Churches possessed as Christian
communities with the doctrine or regulations of the twelve
Apostles can already be shown in the earliest Gentile-Christian
literature.   In the widest sense the expression, κανὼν τῆς
παραδόσεως (canon of tradition), originally included all that was
traced back to Christ himself through the medium of the Apostles
and was of value for the faith and life of the Church, together
with everything that was or seemed her inalienable possession,
as, for instance, the Christian interpretation of the Old Testament.
In the narrower sense that canon consisted of the history and
words of Jesus.   In so far as they formed the content of faith
they were the faith itself, that is, the Christian truth; in so far
as this faith was to determine the essence of everything Christian,
it might be termed κανὼν τῆς πίστεως, κανὼν τῆς ἀληθείας (canon of
the faith, canon of the truth). [1]   But the very fact that the
extent of what was regarded as tradition of the Apostles was
quite undetermined ensured the possibility of the highest degree
of freedom; it was also still allowable to give expression to

[1] See Zahn, Glaubensregel und Taufbekenntniss in der alten Kirche in the
Zeitschrift f. Kirchl. Wissensch. u. Kirchl. Leben, 1881, Part 6, p. 302 ff., especially p. 314 ff.   In the Epistle of Jude, v. 3, mention is made of the ἅπαξ παραδοθεῖσα τοῖς ἁγίοις πίστις, and in v. 20 of "building yourselves up in your most holy
faith." See Polycarp, ep. III. 2 (also VII. 2; II. 1).   In either case the expressions
κανὼν τῆς πίστεως, κανὼν τῆς ἀληθείας, or the like, might stand for πίστις, for the faith
itself is primarily the canon; but it is the canon only in so far as it is comprehensible and plainly defined.   Here lies the transition to a new interpretation of the
conception of a standard in its relation to the faith.   Voigt has published an
excellent investigation of the concept ὁ κανὼν τῆς ἀληθείας cum synonymis.
(Eine verschollene Urkunde des antimont. Kampfes, 1891, pp. 184—205).

Christian inspiration and to the intuition of enthusiasm without
any regard to tradition.

We now know that before the violent conflict with Gnosticism
short formulated summaries of the faith had already grown out
of the missionary practice of the Church (catechising). The
shortest formula was that which defined the Christian faith as
belief in the Father, Son, and Spirit. [1] It appears to have been
universally current in Christendom about the year 150. In the
solemn transactions of the Church, therefore especially in baptism,
in the great prayer of the Lord's Supper, as well as in the
exorcism of demons, [2] fixed formulæ were used. They embraced
also such articles as contained the most important facts in the
history of Jesus. [3] We know definitely that not later than about
the middle of the second century (about 140 A.D.) the Roman
Church possessed a fixed creed, which every candidate for baptism
had to profess; [4] and something similar must also have existed

---

[1] In Hermas, Mand. I., we find a still shorter formula which only contains the
confession of the monarchy of God, who created the world, that is the formula
πιστεύω εἰς ἕνα θεὸν παντακράτορα, which did not originate with the baptismal
ceremony. But though at first the monarchy may have been the only dogma in the
strict sense, the mission of Jesus Christ beyond doubt occupied a place alongside
of it from the beginning; and the new religion was inconceivable without this.

[2] See on this point Justin, index to Otto's edition. It is not surprising that
formulæ similar to those used at baptism were employed in the exorcism of
demons. However, we cannot immediately infer from the latter what was the
wording of the baptismal confession. Though, for example, it is an established
fact that in Justin's time demons were exorcised with the words: "In the name of
Jesus Christ who was crucified under Pontius Pilate," it does not necessarily follow
from this that these words were also found in the baptismal confession. The sign
of the cross was made over those possessed by demons; hence nothing was more
natural than that these words should be spoken. Hence they are not necessarily
borrowed from a baptismal confession.

[3] These facts were known to every Christian. They are probably also alluded
to in Luke I. 4.

[4] The most important result of Caspari's extensive and exact studies is the
establishment of this fact and the fixing of the wording of the Romish Confession.
(Ungedruckte, unbeachtete und wenig beachtete Quellen z. Gesch. des Taufsymbols
u d. Glaubensregels. 3 Vols. 1866—1875. Alte u. neue Quellen zur Gesch. des
Taufsymbols u. d. Glaubensregel, 1879). After this Hahn, Bibliothek d. Symbole u.
Glaubensregeln der alten Kirche. 2 Aufl. 1877; see also my article "Apostol.
Symbol" in Herzog's R.E., 2nd. ed., as well as Book I. of the present work,
Chap. III. § 2.

in Smyrna and other Churches of Asia Minor about the year
150, in some cases, even rather earlier. We may suppose that
formulæ of similar plan and extent were also found in other
provincial Churches about this time. [1] Still it is neither probable
that all the then existing communities possessed such creeds, nor
that those who used them had formulated them in such a rigid
way as the Roman Church had done. The proclamation of the
history of Christ predicted in the Old Testament, the κήρυγμα
τῆς ἀληθείας, also accompanied the short baptismal formula
without being expressed in set terms. [2]

Words of Jesus and, in general, directions for the Christian
life were not, as a rule, admitted into the short formulated
creed. In the recently discovered "Teaching of the Apostles"
(Διδαχὴ τῶν ἀποστόλων) we have no doubt a notable attempt
to fix the rules of Christian life as traced back to Jesus through
the medium of the Apostles, and to elevate them into the
foundation of the confederation of Christian Churches; but
this undertaking, which could not but have led the development
of Christianity into other paths, did not succeed. That the
formulated creeds did not express the principles of conduct, but
the facts on which Christians based their faith, was an unavoidable necessity. Besides, the universal agreement of all earnest
and thoughtful minds on the question of Christian morals was
practically assured. [3] Objection was not taken to the principles

---

[1] This supposition is based on observation of the fact that particular
statements of the Roman Symbol, in exactly the same form or nearly so, are
found in many early Christian writings. See Patr. App. Opp. I. 2, ed. 2,
pp. 115—42.

[2] The investigations which lead to this result are of a very complicated nature
and cannot therefore be given here. We must content ourselves with remarking
that all Western baptismal formulæ (creeds) may be traced back to the Roman,
and that there was no universal Eastern creed on parallel lines with the latter.
There is no mistaking the importance which, in these circumstances, is to be
attributed to the Roman symbol and Church as regards the development of
Catholicism.

[3] This caused the pronounced tendency of the Church to the formation of
dogma, a movement for which Paul had already paved the way. The development
of Christianity, as attested, for example, by the Διδαχή, received an additional
factor in the dogmatic tradition, which soon gained the upper hand. The great
reaction is then found in monasticism. Here again the rules of morality become

of morality—at least this was not a primary consideration—for there were many Greeks to whom they did not seem foolishness, but to the adoration of Christ as he was represented in tradition and to the Church's worship of a God, who, as creator of the world and as a speaking and visible being, appeared to the Greeks, with their ideas of a purely spiritual deity, to be interwoven with the world, and who, as the God worshipped by the Jews also, seemed clearly distinct from the Supreme Being. This gave rise to the mockery of the heathen, the theological art of the Gnostics, and the radical reconstruction of tradition as attempted by Marcion. With the freedom that still prevailed Christianity was in danger of being resolved into a motley mass of philosophic speculations or of being completely detached from its original conditions. " It was admitted on all sides that Christianity had its starting-point in certain facts and sayings; but if any and every interpretation of those facts and sayings was possible, if any system of philosophy might be taught into which the words that expressed them might be woven, it is clear that there could be but little cohesion between the members of the Christian communities. The problem arose and pressed for an answer: What should be the basis of Christian union? But the problem was for a time insoluble. For there was no standard and no court of appeal. " From the very beginning, when the differences in the various Churches began to threaten their unity, appeal was probably made to the Apostles' doctrine, the words of the Lord, tradition, " sound doctrine ", definite facts, such as the reality of the human nature (flesh) of Christ, and the reality of his death and resurrection. [1] In instruction, in exhortations, and above all in opposing erroneous doctrines and moral aber-

---

the prevailing feature, and therefore the old Christian gnomic literature attains in this movement a second period of vigour. In it again dogmatics only form the background for the strict regulation of life. In the instruction given as a preparation for baptism the Christian moral commandments were of course always inculcated, and the obligation to observe these was expressed in the renunciation of Satan and all his works. In consequence of this, there were also fixed formulæ in these cases.

[1] See the Pastoral Epistles, those of John and of Ignatius; also the epistle of Jude, 1 Clem. VII.. Polycarp, ad Philipp. VII., II. 1, VI. 3, Justin.

rations, this precept was inculcated from the beginning: ἀπολίπωμεν
τὰς κενὰς καὶ ματαίας Φροντίδας, καὶ ἔλθωμεν ἐπὶ τὸν εὐκλεῆ καὶ σεμνὸν
τῆς παραδόσεως ἡμῶν κανόνα ("Let us leave off vain and foolish
thoughts and betake ourselves to the glorious and august canon of
our tradition "). But the very question was: What is sound doctrine?
What is the content of tradition? Was the flesh of Christ a
reality? etc. There is no doubt that Justin, in opposition to those
whom he viewed as pseudo-Christians, insisted on the absolute
necessity of acknowledging certain definite traditional facts and
made this recognition the standard of orthodoxy. To all appearance
it was he who began the great literary struggle for the expulsion
of heterodoxy (see his σύνταγμα κατὰ πασῶν τῶν γεγενημένων
αἱρέσεων); but, judging from those writings of his that have
been preserved to us, it seems very unlikely that he was already
successful in finding a fixed standard for determining orthodox
Christianity. [1]

The permanence of the communities, however, depended on
the discovery of such a standard. They were no longer held
together by the *conscientia religionis,* the *unitas disciplinæ,* and
the *fœdus spei.* The Gnostics were not solely to blame for that.

---

[1] In the apologetic writings of Justin the courts of appeal invariably continue
to be the Old Testament, the words of the Lord, and the communications of
prophets; hence he has hardly insisted on any other in his anti-heretical work. On
the other hand we cannot appeal to the observed fact that Tertullian also, in his
apologetic writings, did not reveal his standpoint as a churchman and opponent
of heresy; for, with one exception, he did not discuss heretics in these tractates at
all. On the contrary Justin discussed their position even in his apologetic writings;
but nowhere, for instance, wrote anything similar to Theophilus' remarks in "ad
Autol.," II. 14. Justin was acquainted with and frequently alluded to fixed formulæ
and perhaps a baptismal symbol related to the Roman, if not essentially identical
with it. (See Bornemann. Das Taufsymbol Justins in the Ztschr. f. K. G. Vol. III.
p. 1 ff.), but we cannot prove that he utilised these formulæ in the sense of Irenæus
and Tertullian. We find him using the expression ὀρθογνώμονες in Dial. 80. The
resurrection of the flesh and the thousand years' kingdom (at Jerusalem) are there
reckoned among the beliefs held by the ὀρθογνώμονες κατὰ πάντα Χριστιανοί. But
it is very characteristic of the standpoint taken up by Justin that he places between
the heretics inspired by demons and the orthodox a class of Christians to whom
he gives the general testimony that they are τῆς καθαρᾶς καὶ εὐσεβοῦς γνώμης,
though they are not fully orthodox in so far as they reject one important doctrine.
Such an estimate would have been impossible to Irenæus and Tertullian. They
have advanced to the principle that he who violates the law of faith in one point
is guilty of breaking it all.

They rather show us merely the excess of a continuous transformation which no community could escape. The gnosis which subjected religion to a critical examination awoke in proportion as religious life from generation to generation lost its warmth and spontaneity. There was a time when the majority of Christians knew themselves to be such, (1) because they had the "Spirit" and found in that an indestructible guarantee of their Christian position, (2) because they observed all the commandments of Jesus (εντολαι Ἰησοῦ). But when these guarantees died away, and when at the same time the most diverse doctrines that were threatening to break up the Church were preached in the name of Christianity, the fixing of tradition necessarily became the supreme task. Here, as in every other case, the tradition was not fixed till after it had been to some extent departed from. It was just the Gnostics themselves who took the lead in a fixing process, a plain proof that the setting up of dogmatic formulæ has always been the support of new formations. But the example set by the Gnostics was the very thing that rendered the problem difficult. Where was a beginning to be made? "There is a kind of unconscious logic in the minds of masses of men when great questions are abroad, which some one thinker throws into suitable form." [1] There could be no doubt that the needful thing was to fix what was "apostolic", for the one certain thing was that Christianity was based on a divine revelation which had been transmitted through the medium of the Apostles to the Churches of the whole earth. It certainly was not a single individual who hit on the expedient of affirming the fixed forms employed by the Churches in their solemn transactions to be apostolic in the strict sense. It must have come about by a natural process. But the confession of the Father, Son, and Spirit and the *kerygma* of Jesus Christ had the most prominent place among these forms. The special emphasising of these articles, in opposition to the Gnostic and Marcionite undertakings, may also be viewed as the result of the "common sense" of all those who clung to the belief that the Father of Jesus Christ was the creator of the world, and

---

[1] Hatch, "Organisation of the Church ", p. 96.

that the Son of God really appeared in the flesh. But that was
not everywhere sufficient, for, even admitting that about the
period between 150 and 180 A.D. all the Churches had a fixed
creed which they regarded as apostolic in the strict sense—and
this cannot be proved,—the most dangerous of all Gnostic
schools, viz., those of Valentinus, could recognise this creed,
since they already possessed the art of explaining a given text
in whatever way they chose. What was needed was an apostolic
creed *definitely interpreted;* for it was only by the aid of
a definite interpretation that the creed could be used to
repel the Gnostic speculations and the Marcionite conception of
Christianity.

In this state of matters the Church of Rome, the proceedings
of which are known to us through Irenæus and Tertullian, took,
with regard to the fixed Roman baptismal confession ascribed
to the Apostles, the following step: The Antignostic interpretation required by the necessities of the times was proclaimed
as its self-evident content; the confession, thus explained, was
designated as the "Catholic faith" ("fides catholica"), that is
the rule of truth for the faith; and its acceptance was made
the test of adherence to the Roman Church as well as to the
general confederation of Christendom. Irenæus was not the
author of this proceeding. How far Rome acted with the coöperation or under the influence of the Church of Asia Minor is a
matter that is still obscure,[1] and will probably never be determined with certainty. What the Roman community accomplished
practically was theoretically established by Irenæus[2] and Tertullian. The former proclaimed the baptismal confession, definitely interpreted and expressed in an Antignostic form, to
be the apostolic rule of truth (regula veritatis), and tried

---

[1] We can only conjecture that some teachers in Asia Minor contemporary with
Irenæus, or even of older date, and especially Melito, proceeded in like manner,
adhering to Polycarp's exclusive attitude. Dionysius of Corinth (Eusebius, H. E. IV.
23. 2, 4) may perhaps be also mentioned.

[2] Irenæus set forth his theory in a great work, adv. haeres., especially in the
third book. Unfortunately his treatise, "λόγος εἰς ἐπίδειξιν τοῦ ἀποστολικοῦ κηρύγματος", probably the oldest treatise on the rule of faith, has not been preserved
(Euseb., H. E. V. 26.)

to prove it so. He based his demonstration on the theory that this series of doctrines embodied the faith of the churches founded by the Apostles, and that these communities had always preserved the apostolic teaching unchanged (see under C).

Viewed historically, this thesis, which preserved Christianity from complete dissolution, is based on two unproved assumptions and on a confusion of ideas. It is not demonstrated that any creed emanated from the Apostles, nor that the Churches they founded always preserved their teaching in its original form; the creed itself, moreover, is confused with its interpretation. Finally, the existence of a *fides catholica*, in the strict sense of the word, cannot be justly inferred from the essential agreement found in the doctrine of a series of communities. [1] But, on the other hand, the course taken by Irenæus was the only one capable of saving what yet remained of primitive Christianity, and that is its historical justification. A *fides apostolica* had to be set up and declared identical with the already existing *fides catholica*. It had to be made the standard for judging all particular doctrinal opinions, that it might be determined whether they were admissible or not.

The persuasive power with which Irenæus set up the principle of the apostolic "rule of truth," or of "tradition" or simply of "faith," was undoubtedly, as far as he himself was concerned, based on the facts that he had already a rigidly formulated creed before him and that he had no doubt as to its interpretation. [2] The rule

---

[1] Irenæus indeed asserts in several passages that all Churches—those in Germany, Iberia, among the Celts, in the East, in Egypt, in Lybia and Italy; see I. 10. 2; III. 3. 1; III. 4. 1 sq.—possess the same apostolic *kerygma*; but "qui nimis probat nihil probat." The extravagance of the expressions shows that a dogmatic theory is here at work. Nevertheless this is based on the correct view that the Gnostic speculations are foreign to Christianity and of later date.

[2] We must further point out here that Irenæus not only knew the tradition of the Churches of Asia Minor and Rome, but that he had sat at the feet of Polycarp and associated in his youth with many of the "elders" in Asia. Of these he knew for certain that they in part did not approve of the Gnostic doctrines and in part would not have done so. The confidence with which he represented his antignostic interpretation of the creed as that of the Church of the Apostles was no doubt owing to this sure historical recollection. See his epistle to Florinus in Euseb., H. E. V. 20 and his numerous references to the "elders" in his great work. (A collection of these may be found in Patr. App. Opp. I. 3, p. 105 sq.)

of truth (also ἡ ὑπὸ τῆς ἐκκλησίας κηρυσσομένη ἀλήθεια "the truth
proclaimed by the Church;" and τὸ τῆς ἀληθείας σωμάτιον, "the
body of the truth") is the old baptismal confession well known
to the communities for which he immediately writes. (See I. 9. 4;
οὕτω δέ καὶ ὁ τὸν κανόνα τῆς ἀληθείας ἀκλινῆ ἐν ἑαυτῷ κατέχων
ὃν διὰ τοῦ βαπτίσματος εἴληφε, "in like manner he also who
retains immovably in his heart the rule of truth which he
received through baptism"); because it is this, it is apostolic, firm
and immovable.[1]

By the fixing of the rule of truth, the formulation of which
in the case of Irenæus (I. 10. 1, 2) naturally follows the arrangement of the (Roman) baptismal confession, the most important
Gnostic theses were at once set aside and their antitheses
established as apostolic. In his apostolic rule of truth Irenæus
himself already gave prominence to the following doctrines:[2]

[1] Caspari's investigations leave no room for doubt as to the relation of the rule
of faith to the baptismal confession. The baptismal confession was not a deposit
resulting from fluctuating anti-heretical rules of faith; but the latter were the explanations of the baptismal confession. The full authority of the confession itself was
transferred to every elucidation that appeared necessary, in so far as the needful
explanation was regarded as given with authority. Each momentary formula employed
to defend the Church against heresy has therefore the full value of the creed. This
explains the fact that, beginning with Irenæus' time, we meet with differently
formulated rules of faith, partly in the same writer, and yet each is declared to be
*the* rule of faith. Zahn is virtually right when he says, in his essay quoted above,
that the rule of faith is the baptismal confession. But, so far as I can judge, he has
not discerned the dilemma in which the Old Catholic Fathers were placed, and which
they were not able to conceal. This dilemma arose from the fact that the Church
needed an apostolic creed, expressed in fixed formulæ and at the same time definitely
interpreted in an anti-heretical sense; whereas she only possessed, and this not in
all churches, a baptismal confession, contained in fixed formulæ but not interpreted,
along with an ecclesiastical tradition which was not formulated, although it no
doubt excluded the most offensive Gnostic doctrines. It was not yet possible for
the Old Catholic Fathers to frame and formulate that doctrinal confession, and
they did not attempt it. The only course therefore was to assert that an elastic
collection of doctrines which were ever being formulated anew, was a fixed standard
in so far as it was based on a fixed creed. But this dilemma—we do not know
how it was viewed by opponents—proved an advantage in the end, for it enabled
churchmen to make continual additions to the rule of faith, whilst at the same time
continuing to assert its identity with the baptismal confession. We must make the
reservation, however, that not only the baptismal confession, but other fixed
propositions as well, formed the basis on which particular rules of faith were
formulated.

[2] Besides Irenæus I. 10. 1, 2, cf. 9. 1—5; 22. 1: II. 1. 1; 9. 1; 28. 1; 32. 3,

the unity of God; the identity of the supreme God with the Creator; the identity of the supreme God with the God of the Old Testament; the unity of Jesus Christ as the Son of the God who created the world; the essential divinity of Christ; the incarnation of the Son of God; the prediction of the entire history of Jesus through the Holy Spirit in the Old Testament; the reality of that history; the bodily reception (ἔνσαρκος ἀνάληψις) of Christ into heaven; the visible return of Christ; the resurrection of all flesh (ἀνάστασις πάσης σαρκὸς, πάσης ἀνθρωπότητος), the universal judgment. These dogmas, the antitheses of the Gnostic regulæ, [1] were consequently, as apostolic and therefore also as Catholic, removed beyond all discussion.

Tertullian followed Irenæus in every particular. He also interpreted the (Romish) baptismal confession, represented it, thus explained, as the *regula fidei*, [2] and transferred to the latter the attributes of the confession, viz., its apostolic origin (or origin from Christ), as well as its fixedness and completeness. [3] Like Irenæus, though still more stringently, he also endeavoured to prove that the formula had descended from Christ, that is, from the Apostles, and was incorrupt. He based his demonstration on the alleged incontestable facts that it contained the faith of those Churches founded by the Apostles, that in these communities a corruption of doctrine was inconceivable, because in them, as could be proved, the Apostles had always had successors, and that the other Churches were in communion with them (see under C). In a more definite way than Irenæus, Tertullian conceives the rule of faith as a rule for the faith, [4] as the law given

---

4: III. 1—4; 11. 1; 12. 9; 15. 1; 16. 5 sq.; 18. 3; 24. 1: IV. 1. 2; 9. 2; 20. 6; 33. 7 sq.: V. Præf. 12. 5; 20. 1.

[1] See Iren. I. 31. 3: II. Præf. 19. 8.

[2] This expression is not found in Irenæus, but is very common in Tertullian.

[3] See de præscr. 13: "Hæc regula a Christo instituta nullas habet apud nos quæstiones."

[4] See l. c. 14: "Ceterum manente forma regulæ in suo ordine quantumlibet quæras et tractes." See de virg. vol. 1.

to faith,[1] also as a "regula doctrinæ" or "doctrina regulæ" (here the creed itself is quite plainly the regula), and even simply as "doctrina" or "institutio".[2] As to the content of the *regula,* it was set forth by Tertullian in three passages.[3] It is essentially the same as in Irenæus. But Tertullian already gives prominence within the *regula* to the creation of the universe out of nothing,[4] the creative instrumentality of the

---

[1] See 1. c. 14: "Fides in regula posita est, habet legem et salutem de observatione legis," and de vir. vol. 1.

[2] See de præscr. 21: "Si hæc ita sunt, constat perinde omnem doctrinam, quæ cum illis ecclesiis apostolicis matricibus et originalibus fidei conspiret, veritati deputandum ... Superest ergo ut demonstremus an hæc nostra doctrina, cujus regulam supra edidimus, de apostolorum traditione censeatur ... Communicamus cum ecclesiis catholicis, quod nulla doctrina diversa." De præscr. 32: "Ecclesiæ, quæ licet nullum ex apostolis auctorem suum proferant, ut multo posteriores, tamen in eadem fide conspirantes non minus apostolicæ deputantur pro consanguinitate doctrinæ." That Tertullian regards the baptismal confession as identical with the *regula fidei,* just as Irenæus does, is shown by the fact that in de spectac. 4 ("Cum aquam ingressi Christianam fidem in legis suæ verba profitemur, renuntiasse nos diabolo et pompæ et angelis eius ore nostro contestamur.") the baptismal confession is the *lex.* He also calls it "sacramentum" (military oath) in ad mart. 3; de idolol. 6; de corona 11; Scorp. 4. But he likewise gives the same designation to the interpreted baptismal confession (de præscr. 20, 32; adv. Marc. IV. 5); for we must regard the passages cited as referring to this. Adv. Marc. I. 21: "regula sacramenti"; likewise V. 20, a passage specially instructive as to the fact that there can be only one regula. The baptismal confession itself had a fixed and short form (see de spectac. 4; de corona, 3: "amplius aliquid respondentes quam dominus in evangelio determinavit"; de bapt. 2: "homo in aqua demissus et inter pauca verba tinctus"; de bapt. 6, 11; de orat. 2 etc.). We can still prove that, apart from a subsequent alteration, it was the Roman confession that was used in Carthage in the days of Tertullian. In de præscr. 26 Tertullian admits that the Apostles may have spoken some things "inter domesticos", but declares that they could not be communications "quæ aliam regulam fidei superducerent."

[3] De præscr. 13; de virg. vol. 1; adv. Prax. 2. The latter passage is thus worded: "Unicum quidem deum credimus, sub hac tamen dispensatione quam οἰκονομίαν dicimus, ut unici dei sit et filius sermo ipsius, qui ex ipso processerit, per quem omnia facta sunt et sine quo factum est nihil, hunc missum a patre in virginem et ex ea natum, hominem et deum, filium hominis et filium dei et cognominatum Iesum Christum, hunc passum, hunc mortuum et sepultum secundum scripturas et resuscitatum a patre et in cœlo resumptum sedere ad dextram patris, venturum judicare vivos et mortuos; qui exinde miserit secundum promissionem suam a patre spiritum s. paracletum sanctificatorem fidei eorum qui credunt in patrem et filium et spiritum s. Hanc regulam ab initio evangelii decucurrisse."

[4] De præscr. 13.

Logos,[1] his origin before all creatures,[2] a definite theory of the Incarnation,[3] the preaching by Christ of a *nova lex* and a *nova promissio regni cœlorum,*[4] and finally also the Trinitarian economy of God.[5] Materially, therefore, the advance beyond Irenæus is already very significant. Tertullian's *regula* is in point of fact a *doctrina.* In attempting to bind the communities to this he represents them as schools.[6] The apostolic "lex et doctrina" is to be regarded as inviolable by every Christian. Assent to it decides the Christian character of the individual. Thus the Christian *disposition and life* come to be a matter which is separate from this and subject to particular conditions. In this way the essence of religion was split up—the most fatal turning-point in the history of Christianity.

But we are not of course to suppose that at the beginning of the third century the actual bond of union between all the Churches was a fixed confession developed into a doctrine, that is, definitely interpreted. This much was gained, as is clear from the treatise *de præscriptione* and from other evidence, that in the communities with which Tertullian was acquainted, mutual recognition and brotherly intercourse were made to depend on assent to formulæ which virtually coincided with the Roman baptismal confession. Whoever assented to such a formula was regarded as a Christian brother, and was entitled to the salutation of peace, the name of brother, and hospitality.[7]

[1] L. c.

[2] L. c.

[3] L. c.: "id verbum filium eius appellatum, in nomine dei varie visum a patriarchis, in prophetis semper auditum, postremo delatum ex spiritu patris dei et virtute in virginem Mariam, carnem factum," etc.

[4] L. c.

[5] Adv. Prax. 2: "Unicum quidem deum credimus, sub hac tamen dispensatione quam οἰκονομίαν dicimus, ut unici dei sit et filius sermo ipsius," etc.

[6] But Tertullian also knows of a "regula disciplinæ" (according to the New Testament) on which he puts great value, and thereby shows that he has by no means forgotten that Christianity is a matter of conduct. We cannot enter more particularly into this rule here.

[7] Note here the use of "contesserare" in Tertullian. See de præscr. 20: "Itaque tot ac tantæ ecclesiæ una est illa ab apostolis prima, ex qua omnes. Sic omnes

In so far as Christians confined themselves to a doctrinal formula which they, however, strictly applied, the adoption of this practice betokened an advance. The scattered communities now possessed a "lex" to bind them together, quite as certainly as the philosophic schools possessed a bond of union of a real and practical character [1] in the shape of certain briefly formulated doctrines. In virtue of the common apostolic *lex* of Christians the Catholic Church became a reality, and was at the same time clearly marked off from the heretic sects. But more than this was gained, in so far as the Antignostic interpretation of the formula, and consequently a "doctrine", was indeed in some measure involved in the *lex*. The extent to which this was the case depended, of course, on the individual community or its leaders. All Gnostics could not be excluded by the wording of the confession; and, on the other hand, every formulated faith leads to a formulated doctrine, as soon as it is set up as a critical canon. What we observe in Irenæus and Tertullian must have everywhere taken place in a greater or less degree; that is to say, the authority of the confessional formula must have been extended to statements not found in the formula itself.

We can still prove from the works of Clement of Alexandria that a confession claiming to be an apostolic law of faith, [2] ostensibly comprehending the whole essence of Christianity, was not set up in the different provincial Churches at one and the

prima et omnes apostolicæ, dum una omnes. Probant unitatem communicatio pacis et appellatio fraternitatis et *contesseratio* hospitalitatis, quæ iura non alia ratio regit quam eiusdem sacramenti una traditio." De præscr. 36: "Videamus, quid ecclesia Romanensis cum Africanis ecclesiis contesserarit."

[1] We need not here discuss whether and in what way the model of the philosophic schools was taken as a standard. But we may refer to the fact that from the middle of the second century the Apologists, that is the Christian philosophers, had exercised a very great influence on the Old Catholic Fathers. But we cannot say that 2. John 7—11 and Didache XI. 1 f. attest the practice to be a very old one. These passages only show that it had preparatory stages; the main element, namely, the formulated summary of the faith, is there sought for in vain.

[2] Herein lay the defect, even if the content of the law of faith had coincided completely with the earliest tradition. A man like Tertullian knew how to protect himself in his own way from this defect, but his attitude is not typical.

same time.    From this it is clearly manifest that at this period the Alexandrian Church neither possessed a baptismal confession similar to that of Rome, nor understood by "regula fidei" and synonymous expressions a collection of beliefs fixed in some fashion and derived from the apostles. [2]  Clement of Alexandria in his Stromateis appeals to the holy (divine)

---

[1]  Hegesippus, who wrote about the time of Eleutherus, and was in Rome about the middle of the second century (probably somewhat earlier than Irenæus), already set up the apostolic rule of faith as a standard.    This is clear from the description of his work in Euseb., H. E. IV. 8. 2 (ἐν πέντε συγγράμμασιν τὴν ἀπλανῆ παράδοσιν τοῦ Ἀποστολικοῦ κηρύγματος ὑπομνηματισάμενος) as well as from the fragments of this work (l.c. IV. 22. 2, 3: ὁ ὀρθὸς λόγος and § 5 ἐμέρισαν τὴν ἕνωσιν τῆς ἐκκλησίας φθοριμαίοις λόγοις κατὰ τοῦ θεοῦ; see also § 4).  Hegesippus already regarded the unity of the Church as dependent on the correct doctrine.  Polycrates (Euseb., H. E. V. 24. 6) used the expression ὁ κανὼν τῆς πίστεως in a very wide sense.    But we may beyond doubt attribute to him the same conception with regard to the significance of the rule of faith as was held by his opponent Victor  The Antimontanist (in Euseb. H. E. V. 16. 22.) will only allow that the martyrs who went to death for the κατὰ ἀλήθειαν πίστις were those belonging to the Church. The *regula fidei* is not here meant, as in this case it was not a subject of dispute. On the other hand, the anonymous writer in Eusebius, H. E. V. 28. 6, 13 understood by τὸ ἐκκλησιαστικὸν φρόνημα or ὁ κανὼν τῆς ἀρχαίας πίστεως the interpreted baptismal confession, just as Irenæus and Tertullian did.   Hippolytus entirely agrees with these (see Philosoph. Præf., p. 4. v. 50 sq. and X. 32—34).  Whether we are to ascribe the theory of Irenæus to Theophilus is uncertain. His idea of the Church is that of Irenæus (ad Autol. II. 14): δέδωκεν ὁ Θεὸς τῷ κόσμῳ κυμαινομένῳ καὶ χειμαζομένῳ ὑπὸ τῶν ἁμαρτημάτων τὰς συναγωγάς, λεγομένας δὲ ἐκκλησίας ἁγίας, ἐν αἷς καθάπερ λιμέσιν εὐόρμοις ἐν νήσοις ἁι διδασκαλίαι τῆς ἀληθείας εἰσίν... Καὶ ὥσπερ αὖ νῆσοι εἰσιν ἕτεραι πετρώδεις καὶ ἄνυδροι καὶ ἄκαρποι καὶ θηριώδεις καὶ ἀοίκητοι ἐπὶ βλάβῃ τῶν πλεόντων... οὕτως εἰσὶν αἱ διδασκαλίαι τῆς πλάνης, λέγω δὲ τῶν αἱρέσεων, αἱ ἐξαπολλύουσιν τοὺς προσιόντας αὐταῖς.

[2]  This has been contested by Caspari (Ztschr. f. Kirchl. Wissensch. 1886, Part. 7, p. 352 ff.: "Did the Alexandrian Church in Clement's time possess a baptismal confession or not"?); but his arguments have not convinced me.  Caspari correctly shows that in Clement the expression "ecclesiastical canon" denotes the summary of the Catholic faith and of the Catholic rule of conduct; but he goes on to trace the baptismal confession, and that in a fixed form, in the expression ἡ περὶ τῶν μεγίστων ὁμολογία, Strom. VII. 15. 90 (see remarks on this passage below), and is supported in this view by Voigt, l. c. p. 196 ff.  I also regard this as a baptismal confession; but it is questionable if it was definitely formulated, and the passage is not conclusive on the point.  But, supposing it to be definitely formulated, who can prove that it went further than the formula in Hermas, Mand. I. with the addition of a mere mention of the Son and Holy Spirit.  That a free *kerygma* of Christ and some other matter were added to Hermas, Mand. I. may still be proved by a reference to Orig., Comm. in Joh. XXXII. 9 (see the passage in vol. I. p. 155.).

Scriptures, to the teaching of the Lord,[1] and to the standard
tradition which he designates by a great variety of names,
though he never gives its content, because he regards the whole
of Christianity in its present condition as needing to be reconstructed by gnosis, and therefore as coming under the head of
tradition.[2] In one respect therefore, as compared with Irenæus
and Tertullian, he to some extent represents an earlier standpoint; he stands midway between them and Justin. From this
author he is chiefly distinguished by the fact that he employs
sacred Christian writings as well as the Old Testament, makes
the true Gnostic quite as dependent on the former as on the
latter and has lost that naïve view of tradition, that is, the
complete content of Christianity, which Irenæus and Tertullian
still had. As is to be expected, Clement too assigns the
ultimate authorship of the tradition to the Apostles; but it is
characteristic that he neither does this of such set purpose as
Irenæus and Tertullian, nor thinks it necessary to prove that
the Church had presented the apostolic tradition intact. But
as he did not extract from the tradition a fixed complex of
fundamental propositions, so also he failed to recognise the importance of its publicity and catholicity, and rather placed an esoteric
alongside of an exoteric tradition. Although, like Irenæus and
Tertullian, his attitude is throughout determined by opposition to the
Gnostics and Marcion, he supposes it possible to refute them
by giving to the Holy Scriptures a scientific exposition which
must not oppose the κανὼν τῆς ἐκκλησίας, that is, the Christian
common sense, but receives from it only certain guiding rules.
But this attitude of Clement would be simply inconceivable
if the Alexandrian Church of his time had already employed the fixed standard applied in those of Rome, Carthage

---

[1] ‘Η κυριακὴ διδασκαλία, e.g., VI. 15. 124; VI. 18. 165; VII. 10. 57; VII. 15. 90;
VII. 18. 165, etc.

[2] We do not find in Clement the slightest traces of a baptismal confession
related to the Roman, unless we reckon the Θεὸς παντοκράτωρ or εἰς Θ. π. as such.
But this designation of God is found everywhere and is not characteristic of the
baptismal confession. In the lost treatise on the Passover Clement expounded the
“παραδόσεις τῶν ἀρχαίων πρεσβυτέρων” which had been transmitted to him.

and Lyons.[1] Such a standard did not exist; but Clement made no distinction in the yet unsystematised tradition, even between faith and discipline, because as a theologian he was not able to identify himself with any single article of it without

---

[1] Considering the importance of the matter it is necessary to quote as copiously as possible from original sources. In Strom. IV. 15. 98, we find the expression ὁ κανὼν τῆς πίστεως; but the context shows that it is used here in a quite general sense. With regard to the statement of Paul: "whatever you do, do it to the glory of God," Clement remarks ὅσα ὑπὸ τὸν κανόνα τῆς πίστεως ποιεῖν ἐπιτέτραπται. In Strom. I. 19. 96; VI. 15. 125; VI. 18. 165; VII. 7. 41; VII. 15. 90; VII. 16. 105 we find ὁ κανὼν τῆς ἐκκλησίας (ἐκκλησιαστικός). In the first passage that canon is the rule for the right observance of the Lord's Supper. In the other passages it describes no doubt the correct doctrine, that is, the rule by which the orthodox Gnostic has to be guided in contrast with the heretics who are guided by their own desires (it is therefore parallel to the διδασκαλία τοῦ κυρίου); but Clement feels absolutely no need to mention wherein this ecclesiastical canon consists. In Strom IV. 1. 3; VI. 15. 124; VI. 15. 131; VII. 16. 94, we find the expression ὁ κανὼν τῆς ἀληθείας. In the first passage it is said: ἡ γοῦν κατὰ τὸν τῆς ἀληθείας κανόνα γνωστικῆς παραδόσεως φυσιολογία, μᾶλλον δὲ ἐποπτεία, ἐκ τοῦ περὶ κοσμογονίας ἤρτηται λόγου, ἐνθένδε ἀναβαίνουσα ἐπὶ τὸ θεολογικὸν εἶδος. Here no one can understand by the rule of truth what Tertullian understood by it. Very instructive is the second passage in which Clement is dealing with the right and wrong exposition of Scripture. He says first: παρακαταθήκη ἀποδιδομένη Θεῷ ἡ κατὰ τὴν τοῦ κυρίου διδασκαλίαν διὰ τῶν ἀποστόλων αὐτοῦ τῆς θεοσεβοῦς παραδόσεως σύνεσίς τε καὶ συνάσκησις; then he demands that the Scriptures be interpreted κατὰ τὸν τῆς ἀληθείας κανόνα, or τ. ἐκκλησ. καν.; and continues (125): κανὼν δὲ ἐκκλησιαστικὸς ἡ συνῳδία καὶ ἡ συμφωνία νόμου τε καὶ προφητῶν τῇ κατὰ τὴν τοῦ κυρίου παρουσίαν παραδιδομένῃ διαθήκῃ. Here then the agreement of the Old Testament with the Testament of Christ is described as the ecclesiastical canon. Apart from the question as to whether Clement is here already referring to a New Testament canon of Scripture, his rule agrees with Tertullian's testimony about the Roman Church: "legem et prophetas cum evangelicis et apostolicis litteris miscet." But at any rate the passage shows the broad sense in which Clement used the term "ecclesiastical canon." The following expressions are also found in Clement: ἡ ἀληθὴς τῆς μακαρίας διδασκαλίας παράδοσις (I. 1. 11), αἱ ἅγιαι παραδόσεις (VII. 18. 110), ἡ εὐκλεὴς καὶ σεμνὸς τῆς παραδόσεως κανών (all gnosis is to be guided by this, see also ἡ κατὰ τὴν θείαν παράδοσιν φιλοσοφία, I, 1. 15. I: 11. 52., also the expression ἡ θεία παράδοσις (VII. 16. 103), ἡ ἐκκλησιαστικὴ παράδοσις (VII. 16. 95), αἱ τοῦ Χριστοῦ παραδόσεις (VII. 16. 99), ἡ τοῦ κυρίου παράδοσις (VII. 17. 106 : VII. 16. 104), ἡ θεοσεβὴς παράδοσις (VI. 15. 124). Its content is not more precisely defined, and, as a rule, nothing more can be gathered from the context than what Clement once calls τὸ κοινὸν τῆς πίστεως (VII. 16. 97). Where Clement wishes to determine the content more accurately he makes use of supplementary terms. He speaks, e.g., in III. 10. 66 of the κατὰ ἀλήθειαν εὐαγγελικὸς κανών, and means by that the tradition contained in the Gospels recognised by the Church in contradistinction to that found in other gospels (IV. 4. 15 : κατὰ τὸν κανόνα τοῦ εὐαγγελίου = κατὰ τ. εὐαγγ.). In none of these formulæ is

hesitation, and because he ascribed to the true Gnostic the ability to fix and guarantee the truth of Christian doctrine. Origen, although he also attempted to refute the heretics chiefly by a scientific exegesis of the Holy Scriptures, exhibits

any notice taken of the Apostles. That Clement (like Justin) traced back the public tradition to the Apostles is a matter of course and manifest from I. 1. 11, where he gives an account of his early teachers (οἱ μὲν τὴν ἀληθῆ τῆς μακαρίας σώζοντες διδασκαλίας παράδοσιν εὐθὺς ἀπὸ Πέτρου τε καὶ Ἰακώβου, Ἰωάννου τε καὶ Παύλου τῶν ἁγίων ἀποστόλων, παῖς παρὰ πατρὸς ἐκδεχόμενος ἧκον δὴ σὺν θεῷ καὶ εἰς ἡμᾶς τὰ προγονικὰ ἐκεῖνα καὶ ἀποστολικὰ καταβησόμενοι σπέρματα). Clement does not yet appeal to a hierarchical tradition through the bishops, but adheres to the natural one through the teachers, though he indeed admits an esoteric tradition alongside of it. On one occasion he also says that the true Gnostic keeps the ἀποστολικὴ καὶ ἐκκλησιαστικὴ ὀρθοτομία τῶν δογμάτων (VII. 16. 104). He has no doubt that : μία ἡ πάντων γέγονε τῶν ἀποστόλων ὥσπερ διδασκαλία οὕτως δὲ καὶ ἡ παράδοσις (VII. 17. 108). But all that might just as well have been written in the first half of the second century. On the tracing back of the Gnosis, the esoteric tradition, to the Apostles see Hypotyp. in Euseb., H. E. II. 1. 4, Strom. VI. 15. 131: αὐτίκα διδάξαντος τοῦ σωτῆρος τοὺς ἀποστόλους ἡ τῆς ἐγγράφου ἄγραφος ἤδη καὶ εἰς ἡμᾶς διαδίδοται παράδοσις. VI. 7. 61: ἡ γνωσις δὲ αὐτή ἡ κατὰ διαδοχὰς (this is the only place where I find this expression) εἰς ὀλίγους ἐκ τῶν ἀποστόλων ἀγράφως παραδοθεῖσα κατελήλυθεν, ibid ἡ γνωστικὴ παράδοσις; VII. 10. 55: ἡ γνῶσις ἐκ παραδόσεως διαδιδομένη τοῖς ἀξίους σφᾶς αὐτοὺς τῆς διδασκαλίας παρεχομένοις οἷον παρακαταθήκη ἐγχειρίζεται. In VII. 17. 106 Clement has briefly recorded the theories of the Gnostic heretics with regard to the apostolic origin of their teaching, and expressed his doubts. That the tradition of the "Old Church", for so Clement designates the orthodox Church as distinguished from the "human congregation" of the heretics of his day, is throughout derived from the Apostles, he regards as so certain and self-evident that, as a rule, he never specially mentions it, or gives prominence to any particular article as apostolic. But the conclusion that he had no knowledge of any apostolic or fixed confession might seem to be disproved by one passage. It is said in Strom. VII. 15. 90: Μή τι οὖν, εἰ καὶ παραβαίη τις συνθήκας καὶ τὴν ὁμολογίαν παρέλθοι τὴν πρὸς ἡμᾶς, διὰ τὸν ψευσάμενον τὴν ὁμολογίαν ἀφεξόμεθα τῆς ἀληθείας καὶ ἡμεῖς, ἀλλ᾽ ὡς ἀψευδεῖν χρὴ τὸν ἐπιεικῆ καὶ μηδὲν ὧν ὑπέσχηται ἀκυροῦν κἂν ἄλλοι τινὲς παραβαίνωσι συνθήκας, οὕτως καὶ ἡμᾶς κατὰ μηδένα τρόπον τὸν ἐκκλησιαστικὸν παραβαίνειν προσήκει κανόνα καὶ μάλιστα τὴν περὶ τῶν μεγίστων ὁμολογίαν ἡμεῖς μὲν φυλάττομεν, οἱ δὲ παραβαίνουσι. But in the other passages in Clement where ὁμολογία appears it is nowhere signifies a fixed formula of confession, but always the confession in general which receives its content according to the situation (see Strom. IV. 4. 15; IV. 9. 71; III. 1. 4: ἐγκράτεια σώματος ὑπεροψία κατὰ τὴν πρὸς θεὸν ὁμολογίαν). In the passage quoted it means the confession of the main points of the true doctrine. It is possible or probable that Clement was here alluding to a confession at baptism, but that is also not quite certain. At any rate this one passage cannot prove that Clement identified the ecclesiastical canon with a formulated confession similar to or identical with the Roman, or else such identification must have appeared more frequently in his works.

an attitude which is already more akin to that of Irenæus and Tertullian than to that of Clement. In the preface to his great work, "De principiis," he prefixed the Church doctrine as a detailed apostolic rule of faith, and in other instances also he appealed to the apostolic teaching.[1] It may be assumed that in the time of Caracalla and Heliogabalus the Alexandrian Christians had also begun to adopt the principles acted upon in Rome and other communities.[2] The Syrian Churches, or at least a part of them, followed still later.[3] There can be no doubt that, from the last decades of the third century onward, one and the same confession, identical not in its wording, but in its main features, prevailed in the great confederation of Churches extending from Spain to the Euphrates and from Egypt to beyond the Alps.[4] It was the basis of the confederation, and therefore also a passport, mark of recognition, etc., for the orthodox Chris-

---

[1] De princip. l. I. præf. § 4—10., IV. 2. 2. Yet we must consider the passage already twice quoted, namely, Com. in John. XXXII. 9, in order to determine the practice of the Alexandrian Church at that time. Was this baptismal confession not perhaps compiled from Herm., Mand. I., and Christological and theological teachings, so that the later confessions of the East with their dogmatic details are already to be found here?

[2] That may be also shown with regard to the New Testament canon. Very important is the declaration of Eusebius (H. E. VI. 14) that Origen, on his own testimony, paid a brief visit to Rome in the time of Zephyrinus, "because he wished to become acquainted with the ancient Church of the Romans." We learn from Jerome (de vir. inl. 61) that Origen there became acquainted with Hippolytus, who even called attention to his presence in the church in a sermon. That Origen kept up a connection with Rome still later and followed the conflicts there with keen interets may be gathered from his works. (See Döllinger, "Hippolytus und Calixtus" p. 254 ff.) On the other hand, Clement was quite unacquainted with that city. Bigg therefore l.c. rightly remarks: "The West is as unknown to Clement as it was to his favourite Homer." That there was a formulated πίστις καὶ ὁμολογία in Alexandria about 250 A.D. is shown by the epistle of Dionysius (Euseb., H. E. VII. 8) He says of Novatian, ἀνατρέπει τὴν πρὸ λούτρου πίστιν καὶ ὁμολογίαν. Dionysius would hardly have reproduced this Roman reproach in that way, if the Alexandrian Church had not possessed a similar πίστις.

[3] The original of the Apostolic Constitutions has as yet no knowledge of the Apostolic rule of faith in the Western sense.

[4] The close of the first homily of Aphraates shows how simple, antique, and original this confession still was in outlying districts at the beginning of the fourth century. On the other hand, there were oriental communities where it was already heavily weighted with theology.

tians. The interpretation of this confession was fixed in certain ground features, that is, in an Antignostic sense. But a definite theological interpretation was also more and more enforced. By the end of the third century there can no longer have been any considerable number of outlying communities where the doctrines of the pre-existence of Christ and the identity of this pre-existent One with the divine Logos were not recognised as the orthodox belief. [1] They may have first become an "apostolic confession of faith" through the Nicene Creed. But even this creed was not adopted all at once.

B. *The designation of selected writings read in the churches as New Testament Scriptures or, in other words, as a collection of apostolic writings.* [2]

Every word and every writing which testified of the κύριος (Lord) was originally regarded as emanating from him, that is, from his spirit: "Ὅθεν ἡ κυριότης λαλεῖται ἐκεῖ Κύριός ἐστιν. (Didache IV. 1;

---

[1] Cf. the epistles of Cyprian, especially ep. 69. 70. When Cyprian speaks (69. 7) of one and the same law which is held by the whole Catholic Church, and of one *symbol* with which she administers baptism (this is the first time we meet with this expression), his words mean far more than the assertion of Irenæus that the confession expounded by him is the guiding rule in all Churches; for in Cyprian's time the intercourse of most Catholic communities with each other was so regulated that the state of things in each was to some extent really known. Cf. also Novatian, "de trinitate seu de regula fidei," as well as the circular letter of the Synod of Antioch referring to the Metropolitan Paul (Euseb., H. E. VII. 30. 6 ... ἀποστὰς τοῦ κανόνος ἐπὶ κίβδηλα καὶ νόθα διδάγματα μετελήλυθεν), and the homilies of Aphraates. The closer examination of the last phase in the development of the confession of faith during this epoch, when the apostolic confessions received an interpretation in accordance with the theology of Origen, will be more conveniently left over till the close of our description (see chap. 7 fin).

[2] See the histories of the canon by Credner, Reuss, Westcott, Hilgenfeld, Schmiedel, Holtzmann, and Weiss; the latter two, which to some extent supplement each other, are specially instructive. To Weiss belongs the merit of having kept Gospels and Apostles clearly apart in the preliminary history of the canon (see Th. L. Z. 1886. Nr. 24); Zahn, Gesch. des N. Tlichen Kanons, 2 vols, 1888 ff.; Harnack, Das Neue Test. um d. J. 200, 1889; Voigt, Eine verschollene Urkunde des antimontan. Kampfes, 1891, p. 236 ff.; Weizsäcker, Rede bei der akad. Preisvertheilung, 1892. Nov.; Köppel, Stud. u. Krit. 1891, p. 102 ff.; Barth, Neue Jahrbb. f. deutsche Theologie, 1893, p. 56 ff. The following account gives only a few aspects of the case, not a history of the genesis of the canon.

see also 1 Cor. XII. 3). Hence the contents were holy. [1] In this sense the New Testament is a "residuary product," just as the idea of its inspiration is a remnant of a much broader view. But on the other hand, the New Testament is a new creation of the Church, [2] inasmuch as it takes its place alongside of the Old—which through it has become a complicated book for Christendom,—as a Catholic and apostolic collection of Scriptures containing and attesting the truth.

Marcion had founded his conception of Christianity on a new canon of Scripture, [3] which seems to have enjoyed the same authority among his followers as was ascribed to the Old Testament in orthodox Christendom. In the Gnostic schools, which likewise rejected the Old Testament altogether or in part, Evangelic and Pauline writings were, by the middle of the second century, treated as sacred texts and made use of to confirm their theological

[1] "Holy" is not always equivalent to "possessing absolute authority." There are also various stages and degrees of "holy."

[2] I beg here to lay down the following principles as to criticism of the New Testament. (1) It is not individual writings, but the whole book that has been immediately handed down to us. Hence, in the case of difficulties arising, we must first of all enquire, not whether the title and historical setting of a book are genuine or not, but if they are original, or were only given to the work when it became a component part of the collection. This also gives us the right to assume interpolations in the text belonging to the time when it was included in the canon, though this right must be used with caution. (2) Baur's 'tendency-criticism' has fallen into disrepute; hence we must also free ourselves from the pedantry and hair-splitting which were its after effects. In consequence of the (erroneous) assumptions of the Tübingen school of critics a suspicious examination of the texts was justifiable and obligatory on their part. (3) Individual difficulties about the date of a document ought not to have the result of casting suspicion on it, when other good grounds speak in its favour; for, in dealing with writings which have no, or almost no accompanying literature, such difficulties cannot fail to arise. (4) The condition of the oldest Christianity up to the beginning of the second century did not favour literary forgeries or interpolations in support of a definite tendency. (5) We must remember that, from the death of Nero till the time of Trajan, very little is known of the history of the Church except the fact that, by the end of this time, Christianity had not only spread to an astonishing extent, but also had become vigorously consolidated.

[3] The novelty lies first in the idea itself, secondly in the form in which it was worked out, inasmuch as Marcion would only admit the authority of one Gospel to the exclusion of all the rest, and added the Pauline epistles which had originally little to do with the conception of the apostolic doctrinal tradition of the Church.

speculations. [1] On the other hand, about the year 150 the main body
of Christendom had still no collection of Gospels and Epistles possessing equal authority with the Old Testament, and, apart from Apocalypses, no new writings at all, which as such, that is, as sacred texts,
were regarded as inspired and authoritative. [2] Here we leave

[1] It is easy to understand that, wherever there was criticism of the Old Testament,
the Pauline epistles circulating in the Church would be thrust into the foreground.
The same thing was done by the Manichæans in the Byzantine age.

[2] Four passages may be chiefly appealed to in support of the opposite view, viz.,
2 Peter III. 16; Polycarp ep. 12. 1; Barn. IV. 14; 2 Clem. II. 4. But the first is
put out of court, as the second Epistle of Peter is quite a late writing. The second
is only known from an unreliable Latin translation (see Zahn on the passage:
'verba "his scripturis" suspecta sunt, cum interpres in c. II. 3 ex suis inseruerit
"quod dictum est"'), and even if the latter were faithful here, the quotation from
the Psalms prefixed to the quotation from the Epistle to the Ephesians prevents us
from treating the passage as certain evidence. As to the third passage (μήποτε, ὡς
γέγραπται, πολλοὶ κλητοὶ, ὀλίγοι δὲ ἐκλεκτοὶ εὑρεθῶμεν), it should be noted that the
author of the Epistle of Barnabas, although he makes abundant use of the evangelic
tradition, has nowhere else described evangelic writings as γραφή, and must have
drawn from more sources than the canonic Gospels. Here, therefore, we have an
enigma which may be solved in a variety of ways. It seems worth noting that
it is a saying of the Lord which is here in question. But from the very beginning
words of the Lord were equally reverenced with the Old Testament (see the Pauline
Epistles). This may perhaps explain how the author—like 2 Clem. II. 4: ἑτέρα δὲ
γραφὴ λέγει· ὅτι οὐκ ἦλθον καλέσαι δικαίους ἀλλὰ ἁμαρτωλούς—has introduced a
saying of this kind with the same formula as was used in introducing Old Testament quotations. Passages, such as Clem. XIII. 4: λέγει ὁ θεός· οὐ χάρις ὑμῖν εἰ
ἀγαπᾶτε κ.τ.λ. would mark the transition to this mode of expression. The correctness
of this explanation is confirmed by observation of the fact that the same formula
as was employed in the case of the Old Testament was used in making quotations
from early Christian apocalypses, or utterances of early Christian prophets in
the earliest period. Thus we already read in Ephesians V. 14: διὸ λέγει· ἔγειρε
ὁ καθεύδων καὶ ἀνάστα ἐκ τῶν νεκρῶν καὶ ἐπιφαύσει σοι ὁ Χριστός. That,
certainly, is a saying of a Christian prophet, and yet it is introduced with the
usual "λέγει". We also find a saying of a Christian prophet in Clem. XXIII.
(the saying is more complete in 2 Clem. XI.) introduced with the words: ἡ γραφὴ
αὕτη, ὅπου λέγει. These examples may be multiplied still further. From
all this we may perhaps assume that the trite formulæ of quotation "γραφὴ,
γέγραπται," etc., were applied wherever reference was made to sayings of the Lord
and of prophets that were fixed in writings, even when the documents in question
had not yet as a whole obtained canonical authority. Finally, we must also draw
attention to the following:—The Epistle of Barnabas belongs to Egypt; and there
probably, contrary to my former opinion, we must also look for the author of the
second Epistle of Clement. There is much to favour the view that in Egypt
*Christian* writings were treated as sacred texts, without being united into a collection
of equal rank with the Old Testament. (See below on this point.)

out of consideration that their content is a testimony of the Spirit. From the works of Justin it is to be inferred that the ultimate authorities were the Old Testament, the words of the Lord, and the communications of Christian prophets. [1] The memoirs of the Apostles (ἀπομνημονεύματα τῶν ἀποστόλων = τὰ εὐαγγέλια) owed their significance solely to the fact that they recorded the words and history of the Lord and bore witness to the fulfilment of Old Testament predictions. There is no mention whatever of apostolic epistles as holy writings of standard authority. [2] But we learn further from Justin that the Gospels as well as the Old Testament were read in public worship (Apol. I. 67) and that our first three Gospels were already in use. We can, moreover, gather from other sources that other Christian writings, early and late, were more or less regularly read in Christian meetings. [3] Such writings naturally possessed a high degree of authority. As the Holy Spirit and the Church are inseparable, everything that edifies the Church originates with the Holy Spirit, [4] which in this, as well as every other respect, is inexhaustibly rich. Here, however, two interests were predominant from the beginning, that of immediate spiritual edification and that of attesting and certifying the Christian

---

[1] See on Justin Bousset. Die Evv.—Citate Justins. Gött., 1891. We may also infer from the expression of |Hegesippus (Euseb., H. E. IV. 22. 3; Stephanus Gobarus in Photius, Bibl. 232. p. 288) that it was not Christian writings, but the Lord himself, who was placed on an equality with Law and Prophets. Very instructive is the formula: "Libri et epistolæ Pauli viri iusti" (αἱ καθ᾽ ἡμᾶς βίβλοι καὶ αἱ προσεπιτούτοις ἐπιστολαὶ Παύλου τοῦ ὁσίου ἀνδρός), which is found in the Acta Mart. Scillit. anno 180 (ed. Robinson, Texts and Studies, 1891, I. 2, p. 114 f.), and tempts us to make certain conclusions. In the later recensions of the Acta the passage, characteristically enough, is worded: "Libri evangeliorum et epistolæ Pauli viri sanctissimi apostoli" or "Quattuor evv. dom. nostri J. Chr. et epp. S. Pauli ap. et omnis divinitus inspirata scriptura."

[2] It is worthy of note that the Gnostics also, though they quote the words of the Apostles (John and Paul) as authoritative, place the utterances of the Lord on an unattainable height. See in support of this the epistle of Ptolemy to Flora.

[3] Rev. I. 3; Herm. Vis. II. 4; Dionys. Cor. in Euseb., IV. 23. 11.

[4] Tertullian, this Christian of the primitive type, still reveals the old conception of things in one passage where, reversing 2 Tim. III. 16, he says (de cultu fem. I. 3) "Legimus omnem scripturam ædificationi habilem divinitus inspirari."

*Kerygma* (ή άσΦάλεια τῶν λόγων). *The ecclesiastical canon was the result of the latter interest,* not indeed in consequence of a process of collection, for individual communities had already made a far larger compilation, [1] but, in the first instance, through selection, and afterwards, but not till then, through addition. We must not think that the four Gospels now found in the canon had attained full canonical authority by the middle of the second century, for the fact—easily demonstrable—that the texts were still very freely dealt with about this period is in itself a proof of this. [2] Our first three Gospels contain passages and corrections that could hardly have been fixed before about the year 150. Moreover, Tatian's attempt to create a new Gospel from the four shews that the text of these was not yet fixed. [3] We may remark that he was the first in whom we find the Gospel of John [4] alongside of the Synoptists, and these four the only ones recognised. From the assault of the "Alogi" on the Johannine Gospel we learn that about 160 the whole of our four Gospels had not been definitely recognised even in Asia Minor. Finally, we must refer to the Gospel of the Egyp-

---

[1] The history of the collection of the Pauline Epistles may be traced back to the first century (1 Clem. XLVII. and like passages). It follows from the Epistle of Polycarp that this native of Asia Minor had in his hands all the Pauline Epistles (quotations are made from nine of the latter; these nine imply the four that are wanting, yet it must remain an open question whether he did not yet possess the Pastoral Epistles in their present form), also 1 Peter, 1 John (though he has not named the authors of these), the first Epistle of Clement and the Gospels. The extent of the writings read in churches which Polycarp is thus seen to have had approaches pretty nearly that of the later recognised canon. Compare, however, the way in which he assumes sayings from those writings to be well known by introducing them with "εἰδότες" (I. 3; IV. 1; V. 1). Ignatius likewise shows himself to be familiar with the writings which were subsequently united to form the New Testament. We see from the works of Clement, that, at the end of the second century, a great mass of Christian writings were collected in Alexandria and were used and honoured.

[2] It should also be pointed out that Justin most probably used the Gospel of Peter among the ἀπομνημονεύματα; see Texte u. Unters. IX. 2.

[3] See my article in the Zeitschr. f. K. Gesch. Vol. IV. p. 471 ff. Zahn (Tatian's Diatessaron, 1881) takes a different view.

[4] Justin also used the Gospel of John, but it is a disputed matter whether he regarded and used it like the other Gospels.

tians, the use of which was not confined to circles outside the Church. [1]

From the middle of the second century the Encratites stood midway between the larger Christendom and the Marcionite Church as well as the Gnostic schools. We hear of some of these using the Gospels as canonical writings side by side with the Old Testament, though they would have nothing to do with the Epistles of Paul and the Acts of the Apostles. [2] But Tatian, the prominent Apologist, who joined them, gave this sect a more complete canon, an important fact about which was its inclusion of Epistles of Paul. Even this period, however, still supplies us with no testimony as to the existence of a New Testament canon in orthodox Christendom, in fact the rise of the so-called " Montanism " and its extreme antithesis, the " Alogi ", in Asia Minor soon after the middle of the second century proves that there was still no New Testament canon there; for, if such an authoritative compilation had existed, these movements could not have arisen. If we gather together all the indications and evidence bearing on the subject, we shall indeed be ready to expect the speedy appearance in the Church of a kind of Gospel canon comprising the four Gospels; [3] but we are prepared neither for this being formally placed on an equality with the Old Testament, nor for its containing apostolic writings, which as yet are only found in Marcion and the Gnostics. The canon emerges quite suddenly in an allusion of Melito of Sardis preserved by Eusebius, [4] the meaning of which is, however, still dubious; in the works of Irenæus and Tertullian; and in the so-called Muratorian Fragment. There is no direct account of its origin

[1] The Sabellians still used it in the third century, which is a proof of the great authority possessed by this Gospel in Christian antiquity. (Epiph., H. 62. 2.)

[2] Euseb., H. E. IV. 29. 5.

[3] In many regions the Gospel canon alone appeared at first, and in very many others it long occupied a more prominent place than the other canonical writings. Alexander of Alexandria, for instance, still calls God the giver of the Law, the Prophets, and the Gospels (Theodoret, I. 4).

[4] Euseb., H. E. II. 26. 13. As Melito speaks here of the ἀκρίβεια τῶν παλαιῶν βιβλίων, and of τὰ βιβλία τῆς παλαιᾶς διαθήκης, we may assume that he knows τὰ βιβλία τῆς καινῆς διαθήκης.

and scarcely any indirect; yet it already appears as something to all intents and purposes finished and complete. [1] Moreover, it emerges in the same ecclesiastical district where we were first able to show the existence of the apostolic *regula fidei*. We hear nothing of any authority belonging to the compilers, because we learn nothing at all of such persons. [2] And yet the collection is regarded by Irenæus and Tertullian as completed. A refusal on the part of the heretics to recognise this or that book is already made a severe reproach against them. Their Bibles are tested by the Church compilation as the older one, and the latter itself is already used exactly like the Old Testament. The assumption of the inspiration of the books; the harmonistic interpretation of them; the idea of their absolute sufficiency with regard to every question which can arise and every event which they record; the right of unlimited combination of passages; the assumption that nothing in the Scriptures is without importance; and, finally, the allegorical interpretation: are the immediately observable result of the creation of the canon. [3]

[1] We may here leave undiscussed the hesitancy with regard to the admissibility of particular books. That the Pastoral Epistles had a fixed place in the canon almost from the very first is of itself a proof that the date of its origin cannot be long before 180. In connection with this, however, it is an important circumstance that Clement makes the general statement that the heretics reject the Epistles to Timothy (Strom. II. 12. 52: οἱ ἀπὸ τῶν αἱρέσεων τὰς πρὸς Τιμόθεον ἀθετοῦσιν ἐπιστολάς). They did not happen to be at the disposal of the Church at all till the middle of the second century.

[2] Yet see the passage from Tertullian quoted, p. 15, note 1; see also the "receptior", de pudic. 20, the cause of the rejection of Hermas in the Muratorian Fragment and Tertull. de bapt. 17: "Quodsi quæ Pauli perperam scripta sunt exemplum Theclæ ad licentiam mulierum docendi tinguendique defendunt, sciant in Asia presbyterum, qui eam scripturam construxit, quasi titulo Pauli de suo cumulans, convictum atque confessum id se amore Pauli fecisse, loco decessisse." The hypothesis that the Apostles themselves (or the apostle John) compiled the New Testament was definitely set up by no one in antiquity and therefore need not be discussed. Augustine (c. Faustum XXII. 79) speaks frankly of "sancti et docti homines" who produced the New Testament. We can prove by a series of testimonies that the idea of the Church having compiled the New Testament writings was in no way offensive to the Old Catholic Fathers. As a rule, indeed, they are silent on the matter. Irenæus and Tertullian already treat the collection as simply existent.

[3] Numerous examples may be found in proof of all these points, especially in the writings of Tertullian, though such are already to be met with in Irenæus also. He is not yet so bold in his allegorical exposition of the Gospels as Ptole-

The probable conditions which brought about the formation of the New Testament canon in the Church, for in this case we are only dealing with probabilities, and the interests which led to and remained associated with it can only be briefly indicated here. [1]

The compilation and formation of a canon of Christian writings by a process of selection [2] was, so to speak, a kind of involuntary undertaking of the Church in her conflict with Marcion and the Gnostics, as is most plainly proved by the

mæus whom he finds fault with in this respect; but he already gives an exegesis of the books of the New Testament not essentially different from that of the Valentinians. One should above all read the treatise of Tertullian " de idololatria " to perceive how the authority of the New Testament was even by that time used for solving all questions.

[1] I cannot here enter into the disputed question as to the position that should be assigned to the Muratorian Fragment in the history of the formation of the canon, nor into its interpretation, etc. See my article "Das Muratorische Fragment und die Entstehung einer Sammlung apostolisch-katholischer Schriften" in the Ztschr. f. K. Gesch. III. p. 358 ff. See also Overbeck, Zur Geschichte des Kanons, 1880; Hilgenfeld, in the Zeitschrift f. Wissensch. Theol. 1881, part 2; Schmiedel, Art. "Kanon" in Ersch. u. Gruber's Encykl., 2 Section, Vol. XXXII. p. 309 ff.; Zahn, Kanongeschichte, Vol. II. p. 1 ff. I leave the fragment and the conclusions I have drawn from it almost entirely out of account here. The following sketch will show that the objections of Overbeck have not been without influence on me.

[2] The use of the word "canon" as a designation of the collection is first plainly demonstrable in Athanasius (ep. fest. of the year 365) and in the 59th canon of the synod of Laodicea. It is doubtful whether the term was already used by Origen. Besides, the word "canon" was not applied even to the Old Testament before the fourth century. The name "New Testament" (books of the New Testament) is first found in Melito and Tertullian. For other designations of the latter see Rönsch, Das N. T. Tertullian's p. 47 f. The most common name is "Holy Scriptures". In accordance with its main components the collection is designated as τὸ εὐαγγέλιον καὶ ὁ ἀπόστολος (evangelicæ et apostolicæ litteræ); see Tertullian, de bapt. 15: "tam ex domini evangelio quam ex apostoli litteris." The name "writings of the Lord" is also found very early. It was already used for the Gospels at a time when there was no such thing as a canon. It was then occasionally transferred to all writings of the collection. Conversely, the entire collection was named, after the authors, a collection of apostolic writings, just as the Old Testament Scriptures were collectively called the writings of the prophets. Prophets and Apostles (= Old and New Testament) were now conceived as the media of God's revelation fixed in writing (see the Muratorian Fragment in its account of Hermas, and the designation of the Gospels as "Apostolic memoirs" already found in Justin.) This grouping became exceedingly important. It occasioned

warnings of the Fathers not to dispute with the heretics about the Holy Scriptures, [1] although the New Testament was already in existence. That conflict necessitated the formation of a new Bible. The exclusion of particular persons on the strength of some apostolic standards, and by reference to the Old Testament, could not be justified by the Church in her own eyes and those of her opponents, so long as she herself recognised that there were apostolic writings, and so long as these heretics appealed to such. She was compelled to claim exclusive possession of *everything* that had a right to the name " apostolic," to deny it to the heretics, and to shew that she held it in the highest honour. Hitherto she had "contented" herself with proving her legal title from the Old Testament, and, passing over her actual origin, had dated herself back to the beginning of all things. Marcion and the Gnostics were the first who energetically pointed out that Christianity began with Christ, and that all Christianity was really to be *tested* by the apostolic preaching, that the assumed identity of Christian common sense with apostolic Christianity did not exist, and (so Marcion said) that the Apostles contradicted themselves. This opposition made it necessary to enter into the questions raised by their opponents. But, in point of content, the problem of proving the contested identity was simply insoluble, because it was endless and subject to question on every particular point. The "unconscious logic," that is the logic of self-preservation, could only prescribe an expedient. The Church had to collect everything apostolic and declare herself to be its only legal possessor. She was obliged, moreover, to amalgamate the apostolic with the canon of the Old Testament in such a way as to fix the exposition

new speculations about the unique dignity of the Apostles and did away with the old collocation of Apostles and Prophets (that is Christian prophets). By this alteration we may measure the revolution of the times. Finally, the new collection was also called "the writings of the Church" as distinguished from the Old Testament and the writings of the heretics. This expression and its amplifications shew that it was the Church which selected these writings.

[1] Here there is a distinction between Irenæus and Tertullian. The former disputed with heretics about the interpretation of the Scriptures, the latter, although he has read Irenæus, forbids such dispute. He cannot therefore have considered Irenæus' efforts as successful.

from the very first. But what writings were apostolic? From
the middle of the second century great numbers of writings
named after the Apostles had already been in circulation, and there
were often different recensions of one and the same writing. [1]
Versions which contained docetic elements and exhortations to
the most pronounced asceticism had even made their way into
the public worship of the Church. Above all, therefore, it was
necessary to determine (1) what writings were really apostolic, (2)
what form or recension should be regarded as apostolic. The
selection was made by the Church, that is, primarily, by the churches
of Rome and Asia Minor, which had still an unbroken history
up to the days of Marcus Aurelius and Commodus. In making
this choice, the Church limited herself to the writings that were
used in public worship, and only admitted what the tradition
of the elders justified her in regarding as genuinely apostolic.
The principle on which she proceeded was to reject as spurious
all writings, bearing the names of Apostles, that contained anything contradictory to Christian common sense, that is, to the
rule of faith—hence admission was refused to all books in which
the God of the Old Testament, his creation, etc., appeared to
be depreciated,—and to exclude all recensions of apostolic
writings that seemed to endanger the Old Testament and the
monarchy of God. She retained, therefore, only those writings
which bore the names of Apostles, or anonymous writings to
which she considered herself justified in attaching such names, [2]
and whose contents were not at variance with the orthodox

---

[1] The reader should remember the different recensions of the Gospels and the
complaints made by Dionysius of Corinth (in Euseb., H. E. IV. 23. 12).

[2] That the text of these writings was at the same time revised is more than
probable, especially in view of the beginnings and endings of many New Testament
writings, as well as, in the case of the Gospels, from a comparison of the canonical text with the quotations dating from the time when there was no canon. But
much more important still is the perception of the fact that, in the course of the
second century, a series of writings which had originally been circulated anony-
mously or under the name of an unknown author were ascribed to an Apostle
and were also slightly altered in accordance with this. In what circumstances or
at what time this happened, whether it took place as early as the beginning of
the second century or only immediately before the formation of the canon, is in
almost every individual case involved in obscurity; but the fact itself, of which
unfortunately the Introductions to the New Testament still know so little, is, in

creed or attested it. This selection resulted in the awkward fact that besides the four Gospels there was almost nothing but Pauline epistles to dispose of, and therefore no writings or almost none which, as emanating from the twelve Apostles, could immediately confirm the truth of the ecclesiastical *Kerygma*. *This perplexity was removed by the introduction of the Acts of the Apostles* [1] *and in some cases also the Epistles of Peter and John*, though that of Peter was not recognised at Rome at first. As a collection this group is the most interesting in the new compilation. It gives it the stamp of Catholicity, unites the Gospels with the Apostle (Paul), and, by subordinating his Epistles to the "Acta omnium apostolorum", makes them witnesses to the particular tradition that was required and divests them of every thing suspicious and insufficient. [2] The Church, however, found

---

my opinion, incontestable. I refer the reader to the following examples, without indeed being able to enter on the proof here (see my edition of the "Teaching of the Apostles" p. 106 ff). (1) The Gospel of Luke seems not to have been known to Marcion under this name, and to have been called so only at a later date. (2) The canonical Gospels of Matthew and Mark do not claim, through their content, to originate with these men; they were regarded as apostolic at a later period. (3) The so-called Epistle of Barnabas was first attributed to the Apostle Barnabas by tradition. (4) The Apocalypse of Hermas was first connected with an apostolic Hermas by tradition (Rom. XVI. 14). (5) The same thing took place with regard to the first Epistle of Clement (Philipp. IV. 3). (6) The Epistle to the Hebrews, originally the writing of an unknown author or of Barnabas, was transformed into a writing of the Apostle Paul (Overbeck zur Gesch. des Kanons, 1880), or given out to be such. (7) The Epistle of James, originally the communication of an early Christian prophet, or a collection of ancient holy addresses, first seems to have received the name of James in tradition. (8) The first Epistle of Peter, which originally appears to have been written by an unknown follower of Paul, first received its present name from tradition. The same thing perhaps holds good of the Epistle of Jude. Tradition was similarly at work, even at a later period, as may for example be recognised by the transformation of the epistle "de virginitate" into two writings by Clement. The critics of early Christian literature have created for themselves insoluble problems by misunderstanding the work of tradition. Instead of asking whether the tradition is reliable, they always wrestle with the dilemma "genuine or spurious", and can prove neither.

[1] As regards its aim and contents, this book is furthest removed from the claim to be a portion of a collection of Holy Scriptures. Accordingly, so far as we know, its reception into the canon has no preliminary history.

[2] People were compelled by internal and external evidence (recognition of their apostolicity; example of the Gnostics) to accept the epistles of Paul. But, from the Catholic point of view, a canon which comprised only the four Gospels and the

the selection facilitated by the fact that the content of the
early Christian writings was for the most part unintelligible to
the Christendom of the time, whereas the late and spurious
additions were betrayed not only by heretical theologoumena,
but also and above all by their profane lucidity. Thus arose
a collection of apostolic writings, which in extent may not have
been strikingly distinguished from the list of writings that for

Pauline Epistles, would have been at best an edifice of two wings without the
central structure, and therefore incomplete and uninhabitable. The actual novelty
was the bold insertion into its midst of a book, which, if everything is not deceptive, had formerly been only in private use, namely, the Acts of the Apostles, which
some associated with an Epistle of Peter and an Epistle of John, others with an
Epistle of Jude, two Epistles of John, and the like. There were now (1) writings
of the Lord which were at the same time regarded as ἀπομνημονεύματα of definite
Apostles; (2) a book which contained the acts and preaching of all the Apostles,
which historically legitimised Paul, and at the same time gave hints for the explanation of "difficult" passages in his Epistle; (3) the Pauline Epistles increased by
the compilation of the Pastoral ones, documents which "in ordinatione ecclesiasticæ
disciplinæ sanctificatæ erant." The Acts of the Apostles is thus the key to the
understanding of the Catholic canon and at the same time shows its novelty. In
this book the new collection had its bond of cohesion, its Catholic element (apostolic
tradition), and the guide for its exposition. That the Acts of the Apostles found
its place in the canon *faute de mieux* is clear from the extravagant terms, not at
all suited to the book, in which its appearance there is immediately hailed. It is
inserted in place of a book which should have contained the teaching and missionary acts of all the 12 Apostles; but, as it happened, such a record was not in
existence. The first evidence regarding it is found in the Muratorian fragment and
in Irenæus and Tertullian. There it is called "acta omnium apostolorum sub uno
libro scripta sunt, etc." Irenæus says (III. 14. 1): "Lucas non solum prosecutor
sed et cooperarius fuit *Apostolorum*, maxime autem Pauli", and makes use of the
book to prove the subordination of Paul to the twelve. In the celebrated passages,
de præscr. 22, 23: adv. Marc. I. 20; IV. 2—5; V. 1—3, Tertullian made a still more
extensive use of the Acts of the Apostles, as the Antimarcionite book in the canon.
One can see here why it was admitted into that collection and used against Paul
as the Apostle of the heretics. The fundamental thought of Tertullian is that no
one who fails to recognise the Acts of the Apostles has any right to recognise
Paul, and that to elevate him by himself into a position of authority is unhistorical
and absolutely unfounded fanaticism. If the διδαχὴ τῶν δώδεκα ἀποστόλων was
needed as an authority in the earlier time, a *book* which contained that authority
was required in the later period; and nothing else could be found than the work
of the so-called Luke. "Qui Acta Apostolorum non recipiunt, nec spiritus sancti
esse possunt, qui necdum spiritum sanctum possunt agnoscere discentibus missum,
sed nec ecclesiam se dicant defendere qui quando et quibus incunabulis institutum
est hoc corpus probare non habent." But the greater part of the heretics remained
obstinate. Neither Marcionites, Severians, nor the later Manicheans recognised the
Acts of the Apostles. To some extent they replied by setting up other histories of

more than a generation had formed the chief and favourite
reading in the communities. [1]  The new collection was already
exalted to a high place by the use of other writings being
prohibited either for purposes of general edification or for
theological ends. [2]  But the causes and motives which led to

Apostles in opposition to it, as was done later by a fraction of the Ebionites and
even by the Marcionites.  But the Church also was firm.  It is perhaps the most
striking phenomenon in the history of the formation of the canon that this late
book, from the very moment of its appearance, asserts its right to a place in the
collection, just as certainly as the four Gospels, though its position varied.  In Clement
of Alexandria indeed the book is still pretty much in the background, perhaps on
a level with the κήρυγμα Πέτρου, but Clement has no New Testament at all in
the strict sense of the word; see below.  But at the very beginning the book stood
where it is to-day, *i.e.*, immediately after the Gospels (see Muratorian Fragment,
Irenæus, etc.).  The parallel creation, the group of Catholic Epistles, acquired a
much more dubious position than the Acts of the Apostles, and its place was never
really settled.  Its germ is probably to be found in two Epistles of John (viz., 1st
and 3rd) which acquired dignity along with the Gospel, as well as in the Epistle
of Jude.  These may have given the impulse to create a group of narratives about
the twelve Apostles from anonymous writings of old Apostles, prophets, and teachers.
But the Epistle of Peter is still wanting in the Muratorian Fragment, nor do we
yet find the group there associated with the Acts of the Apostles.  The Epistle of
Jude, two Epistles of John, the Wisdom of Solomon, the Apocalypse of John and
that of Peter form the unsymmetrical conclusion of this oldest catalogue of the
canon.  But, all the same writings, by Jude, John, and Peter are here found side
by side; thus we have a preparation for the future arrangement made in different
though similar fashion by Irenæus and again altered by Tertullian.  The genuine
Pauline Epistles appear enclosed on the one hand by the Acts of the Apostles and
the Catholic Epistles, and on the other by the Pastoral ones, which in their way
are also "Catholic."  That is the character of the "Catholic" New Testament
which is confirmed by the earliest use of it (in Irenæus and Tertullian).  In speaking
above of the Acts of the Apostles as a late book, we meant that it was so relatively
to the canon.  In itself the book is old and for the most part reliable.

[1] There is no doubt that this was the reason why to all appearance the innovation
was scarcely felt.  Similar causes were at work here as in the case of the apostolic
rule of faith.  In the one case the writings that had long been read in the Church
formed the basis, in the other the baptismal confession.  But a great distinction is
found in the fact that the baptismal confession, as already settled, afforded an elastic
standard which was treated as a fixed one and was therefore extremely practical;
whilst, conversely, the undefined group of writings hitherto read in the Church
was reduced to a collection which could neither be increased nor diminished.

[2] At the beginning, that is about 180, it was only in practice, and not in theory,
that the Gospels and the Pauline Epistles possessed equal authority.  Moreover, the
name New Testament is not yet found in Irenæus, nor do we yet find him giving
an exact idea of its content.  See Werner in the Text. u. Unters. z. altchristl.
Lit. Gesch. Bd. VI. 2.

its being formed into a canon, that is, being placed on a footing of complete equality with the Old Testament, may be
gathered partly from the earlier history, partly from the mode
of using the new Bible and partly from the results attending
its compilation.  First, Words of the Lord and prophetic utterances, including the written records of these, had always possessed standard authority in the Church; there were therefore
parts of the collection the absolute authority of which was undoubted from the first. [1]  Secondly, what was called "Preaching
of the Apostles," "Teaching of the Apostles," etc., was likewise regarded from the earliest times as completely harmonious
as well as authoritative.  There had, however, been absolutely
no motive for fixing this in documents, because Christians supposed they possessed it in a state of purity and reproduced it
freely.  The moment the Church was called upon to fix this
teaching authentically, and this denotes a decisive revolution,
she was forced to have recourse to *writings*, whether she would
or not.  The attributes formerly applied to the testimony of
the Apostles, so long as it was not collected and committed
to writing, had now to be transferred to the written records
they had left.  Thirdly, Marcion had already taken the lead in
forming Christian writings into a canon in the strict sense of
the word.  Fourthly, the interpretation was at once fixed
by forming the apostolic writings into a canon, and placing
them on an equality with the Old Testament, as well as by
subordinating troublesome writings to the Acts of the Apostles.
Considered by themselves these writings, especially the Pauline
Epistles, presented the greatest difficulties.  We can see even
yet from Irenæus and Tertullian that the duty of accommodating
herself to these Epistles was *forced* upon the Church by Marcion
and the heretics, and that, but for this constraint, her method
of satisfying herself as to her relationship to them would hardly
have taken the shape of incorporating them with the canon. [2]

See above, p. 40, note 2.

[2] We have ample evidence in the great work of Irenæus as to the difficulties
he found in many passages of the Pauline Epistles, which as yet were almost
solely utilised as sources of doctrine by such men as Marcion, Tatian, and theologians of the school of Valentinus.  The difficulties of course still continued to be felt
in the period which followed. (See, e.g., Method, Conviv. Orat. III. 1, 2.)

This shows most clearly that the collection of writings must
not be traced to the Church's effort to create for herself a
powerful controversial weapon.  But the difficulties which the
compilation presented so long as it was a mere collection
vanished as soon as it was viewed as a *sacred* collection.  For
now the principle: "as the teaching of the Apostles was one,
so also is the tradition" (μια ή πάντων γέγονε τῶν ἀποστόλων
ὥσπερ διδασκαλία οὕτως δὲ καὶ ή παράδοσις)" was to be applied
to all contradictory and objectionable details. [1]  It was now
imperative to explain one writing by another; the Pauline Epistles, for example, were to be interpreted by the Pastoral
Epistles and the Acts of the Apostles. [2]  Now was required what
Tertullian calls the "mixture" of the Old and New Testaments, [3]
in consequence of which the full recognition of the knowledge
got from the old Bible was regarded as the first law for the
interpretation of the new.  The formation of the new collection
into a canon was therefore an immediate and unavoidable
necessity if doubts of all kinds were to be averted.  These
were abundantly excited by the exegesis of the heretics; they
were got rid of by making the writings into a canon.  Fifthly,
the early Christian enthusiasm more and more decreased in the
course of the second century; not only did Apostles, prophets,
and teachers die out, but the religious mood of the majority
of Christians was changed.  A reflective piety took the place
of the instinctive religious enthusiasm which made those who
felt it believe that they themselves possessed the Spirit. [4]  Such
a piety requires rules; at the same time, however, it is characterised by the perception that it has not the active and spontaneous character which it ought to have, but has to prove its

[1] Apollinaris of Hierapolis already regards any contradiction between the (4)
Gospels as impossible.  (See Routh, Reliq. Sacr. I. p. 150.)

[2] See Overbeck, "Ueber die Auffassung des Streites des Paulus mit Petrus in
Antiochien bei den Kirchenvätern," 1877, p. 8.

[3] See also Clement Strom. IV. 21. 124; VI. 15. 125.  The expression is also
frequent in Origen, e.g., de princip. præf. 4.

[4] The Roman Church in her letter to that of Corinth designates her own words
as the words of God (1 Clem. LIX. 1) and therefore requires obedience "τοῖς ὑφ'
ήμῶν γεγραμμένοις διὰ τοῦ ἁγίου πνεύματος" (LXIII. 2).

legitimacy in an indirect and "objective" way. The breach
with tradition, the deviation from the original state of things
is felt and recognised. Men, however, conceal from themselves
their own defects, by placing the representatives of the past
on an unattainable height, and forming such an estimate of
their qualities as makes it unlawful and impossible for those of
the present generation, in the interests of their own comfort,
to compare themselves with them. When matters reach this
point, great suspicion attaches to those who hold fast their
religious independence and wish to apply the old standards. Not
only do they seem arrogant and proud, but they also appear
disturbers of the necessary new arrangement which has its justification in the fact of its being unavoidable. This development
of the matter was, moreover, of the greatest significance for the
history of the canon. Its creation very speedily resulted in the
opinion that the time of divine revelation had gone past and
was exhausted in the Apostles, that is, in the records left by
them. We cannot prove with certainty that the canon was
formed to confirm this opinion, but we can show that it was
very soon used to oppose those Christians who professed to be
prophets or appealed to the continuance of prophecy. The influence which the canon exercised in this respect is the most
decisive and important. That which Tertullian, as a Montanist,
asserts of one of his opponents: "Prophetiam expulit, paracletum fugavit" ("he expelled prophecy, he drove away the Paraclete"), can be far more truly said of the New Testament which
the same Tertullian as a Catholic recognised. The New Testament, though not all at once, put an end to a situation where
it was possible for any Christian under the inspiration of the
Spirit to give authoritative disclosures and instructions. It likewise prevented belief in the fanciful creations with which such
men enriched the history of the past, and destroyed their pretensions to read the future. As the creation of the canon, though
not in a hard and fast way, fixed the period of the production
of sacred facts, so it put down all claims of Christian prophecy
to public credence. Through the canon it came to be acknowledged that all post-apostolic Christianity is only of a mediate
and particular kind, and can therefore never be itself a standard.

The Apostles alone possessed the Spirit of God completely and
without measure. They only, therefore, are the media of revelation, and by their word alone, which, as emanating from the
Spirit, is of equal authority with the word of Christ, all that is
Christian must be tested. [1]

The Holy Spirit and the Apostles became correlative conceptions (Tertull., de pudic. 21). The Apostles, however, were
more and more overshadowed by the New Testament Scriptures; and this was in fact an advance beyond the earlier state
of things, for what was known of the Apostles? Accordingly,
*as authors of these writings*, they and the Holy Spirit became
correlative conceptions. This led to the assumption that the
apostolic writings were inspired, that is, in the full and only
intelligible sense attached to the word by the ancients. [2] By
this assumption the Apostles, viewed as *prophets*, received a
significance quite equal to that of Old Testament writers. [3] But,
though Irenæus and Tertullian placed both parties on a level,
they preserved a distinction between them by basing the whole
authority of the New Testament on its apostolic origin, the
concept "apostolic" being much more comprehensive than that

---

[1] Tertull., de exhort. 4: "Spiritum quidem dei etiam fideles habent, sed non
omnes fideles apostoli... Proprie enim apostoli spiritum sanctum habent, qui plene
habent in operibus prophetiæ et efficacia virtutum documentisque linguarum, non
ex parte, quod ceteri." Clem. Alex. Strom. IV. 21. 135 : Ἕκαστος ἴδιον ἔχει χάρισμα
ἀπὸ θεοῦ, ὁ μὲν οὕτως, ὁ δὲ οὕτως, οἱ ἀπόστολοι δὲ ἐν πᾶσι πεπληρωμένοι; Serapion
in Euseb., H. E. VI. 12. 3 : ἡμεῖς καὶ τὸν Πέτρον καὶ τοὺς ἄλλους ἀποστόλους
ἀποδεχόμεθα ὡς Χριστόν. The success of the canon here referred to was an undoubted blessing, for, as the result of enthusiasm, Christianity was menaced with
complete corruption, and things and ideas, no matter how alien to its spirit, were
able to obtain a lodgment under its protection. The removal of this danger, which
was in some measure averted by the canon, was indeed coupled with great
disadvantages, inasmuch as believers were referred in legal fashion to a new book,
and the writings contained in it were at first completely obscured by the assumption
that they were inspired and by the requirement of an "expositio legitima."

[2] See Tertull., de virg. vol. 4, de resurr. 24, de ieiun. 15, de pudic. 12. Sufficiency is above all included in the concept "inspiration" (see for ex. Tertull., de
monog. 4: "Negat scriptura quod non notat"), and the same measure of authority
belongs to all parts (see Iren., IV. 28. 3. Nihil vacuum neque sine signo apud deum").

[3] The direct designation "prophets" was, however, as a rule, avoided. The
conflict with Montanism made it expedient to refrain from this name; but see Tertullian,
adv. Marc. IV. 24: "Tam apostolus Moyses, quam et apostoli prophetæ."

of "prophet." These men, being Apostles, that is men chosen by Christ himself and entrusted with the proclamation of the Gospel, have for that reason received the Spirit, and their writings are filled with the Spirit. To the minds of Western Christians the primary feature in the collection is its apostolic authorship. [1] This implies inspiration also, because the Apostles cannot be inferior to the writers of the Old Testament. For that very reason they could, in a much more radical way, rid the new collection of everything that was not apostolic. They even rejected writings which, in their form, plainly claimed the character of inspiration; and this was evidently done because they did not attribute to them the degree of authority which, in their view, only belonged to that which was apostolic. [2] The new canon of Scripture set up by Irenæus and Tertullian primarily professes to be nothing else than a collection of *apostolic* writings, which, as such, claim absolute authority. [3] It takes its place beside the apostolic rule of faith; and by this faithfully preserved

---

[1] Compare also what the author of the Muratorian Fragment says in the passage about the Shepherd of Hermas.

[2] This caused the most decisive breach with tradition, and the estimate to be formed of the Apocalypses must at first have remained an open question. Their fate was long undecided in the West; but it was very soon settled that they could have no claim to public recognition in the Church, because their authors had not that fulness of the Spirit which belongs to the Apostles alone.

[3] The disputed question as to whether all the acknowledged apostolic writings were regarded as canonical must be answered in the affirmative in reference to Irenæus and Tertullian, who conversely regarded no book as canonical unless written by the Apostles. On the other hand, it appears to me that no certain opinion on this point can be got from the Muratorian Fragment. In the end the Gospel, Acts, Kerygma, and Apocalypse of Peter as well as the Acts of Paul were rejected, a proceeding which was at the same time a declaration that they were spurious. But these three witnesses agree (see also App. Constit. VI. 16) that the apostolic *regula fidei* is practically the final court of appeal, inasmuch as it decides whether a writing is really apostolic or not, and inasmuch as, according to Tertullian, the apostolic writings belong to the Church alone, because she alone possesses the apostolic *regula* (de præscr. 37 ff.). The *regula* of course does not legitimise those writings, but only proves that they are authentic and do not belong to the heretics. These witnesses also agree that a Christian writing has no claim to be received into the canon merely on account of its prophetic form. On looking at the matter more closely, we see that the view of the early Church, as opposed to Montanism, led to the paradox that the Apostles were prophets in the sense of being inspired by the Spirit, but that they were not so in the strict sense of the word.

possession, the Church scattered over the world proves herself
to be that of the Apostles.

But we are very far from being able to show that such a
rigidly fixed collection of apostolic writings existed everywhere
in the Church about the year 200. It is indeed continually
asserted that the Antiochian and Alexandrian Churches had at
that date a New Testament which, in extent and authority,
essentially coincided with that of the Roman Church; but this
opinion is not well founded. As far as the Church of Antioch
is immediately concerned, the letter of Bishop Serapion (whose
episcopate lasted from about 190 to about 209), given in Eusebius
(VI. 12), clearly shows that Cilicia and probably also Antioch itself
as yet possessed no such thing as a completed New Testament.
It is evident that Serapion already holds the Catholic principle
that all words of Apostles possess the same value to the Church
as words of the Lord; but a completed collection of apostolic
writings was not yet at his disposal. [1] Hence it is very improbable that Theophilus, bishop of Antioch, who died as early
as the reign of Commodus, presupposed such a collection. Nor,
in point of fact, do the statements in the treatise "ad Autoly-
cum" point to a completed New Testament. [2] Theophilus makes
diligent use of the Epistles of Paul and mentions the evangelist
John (C.I.1.) as one of the bearers of the Spirit. But with him
the one canonical court of appeal is the Scriptures of the Old
Testament, that is, the writings of the Prophets (bearers of the
Spirit). These Old Testament Prophets, however, are continued
in a further group of "bearers of the Spirit", which we cannot
definitely determine, but which at any rate included the authors
of the four Gospels and the writer of the Apocalypse. It is
remarkable that Theophilus has never mentioned the Apostles.
Though he perhaps regards them all, including Paul, as "bearers
of the Spirit", yet we have no indication that he looked on
their *Epistles* as canonical. The different way he uses the Old

---

[1] The fragment of Serapion's letter given in Eusebius owes its interest to the
fact that it not only shows the progress made at this time with the formation of
the canon at Antioch, but also what still remained to be done.

[2] See my essay "Theophilus v. Antiochien und das N. T." in the Ztschr. f.
K. Gesch. XI. p 1 ff.

Testament and the Gospels on the one hand and the Pauline
Epistles on the other is rather evidence of the contrary. Theophilus was acquainted with the four Gospels (but we have no
reference to Mark), the thirteen Epistles of Paul (though he does
not mention Thessalonians), most probably also with the Epistle
to the Hebrews, as well as 1st Peter and the Revelation of
John. It is significant that no single passage of his betrays an
acquaintance with the Acts of the Apostles. [1]

It might certainly seem venturesome, on the basis of the
material found in Theophilus and the original document of the
first six books of the Apostolic Constitutions, to conclude that
the formation of a New Testament canon was not everywhere
determined by the same interest and therefore did not everywhere take a similar course. It might seem hazardous to
assume that the Churches of Asia Minor and Rome began by
creating a fixed canon of *apostolic* writings, which was thus
necessarily declared to be inspired, whereas other communities
applied or did not deny the notion of inspiration to a great
number of venerable and ancient writings not rigidly defined,
and did not make a selection from a stricter historical point of
view, till a later date. But the latter development not only
corresponds to the indication found in Justin, but in my opinion
may be verified from the copious accounts of Clement of
Alexandria. [2] In the entire literature of Greeks and barbarians
Clement distinguishes between profane and sacred, *i. e.,* inspired

---

[1] The most important passages are Autol. II. 9. 22: ὅθεν διδάσκουσιν ἡμᾶς αἱ
ἅγιαι γραφαὶ καὶ πάντες οἱ πνευματοφόροι, ἐξ ὧν Ἰωάννης λέγει κ.τ.λ. (follows John I. 1)
III. 12: καὶ περὶ δικαιοσύνης, ἧς ὁ νόμος εἴρηκεν, ἀκόλουθα εὑρίσκεται καὶ τὰ τῶν
προφητῶν καὶ τῶν εὐαγγελίων ἔχειν, διὰ τὸ τοὺς πάντας πνευματοφόρους ἑνὶ πνεύματι
θεοῦ λελαληκέναι; III. 13: ὁ ἅγιος λόγος—ἡ εὐαγγέλιος φωνή.; III. 14.: Ἡσαΐας—τὸ
δὲ εὐαγγέλιον—ὁ θεῖος λόγος. The latter formula is not a quotation of Epistles of
Paul viewed as canonical, but of a divine command found in the Old Testament
and given in Pauline form. It is specially worthy of note that the original of the
six books of the Apostolic Constitutions, written in Syria and belonging to the
second half of the third century, knows yet of no New Testament. In addition to
the Old Testament it has no authority but the "Gospel."

[2] There has as yet been no sufficient investigation of the New Testament of
Clement. The information given by Volkmar in Credner's Gesch. d. N.Tlichen
Kanon, p. 382 ff., is not sufficient. The space at the disposal of this manual
prevents me from establishing the results of my studies on this point. Let me at

writings. As he is conscious that all knowledge of truth is
based on inspiration, so all writings, that is all parts, paragraphs,
or sentences of writings which contain moral and religious truth
are in his view inspired.[1] This opinion, however, does not
exclude a distinction between these writings, but rather requires
it. (2) The Old Testament, a fixed collection of books, is
regarded by Clement, as a whole and in all its parts, as the
divine, that is, inspired book *par excellence*. (3) As Clement in
theory distinguishes a new covenant from the old, so also he
distinguishes the books of the new covenant from those of the
old. (4) These books to which he applies the formula "Gospel"
(τὸ ἐυαγγέλιον) and "Apostles" (δι ἀπόστολοι) are likewise
viewed by him as inspired, but he does not consider them as
forming a fixed collection. (5) Unless all appearances are
deceptive, it was, strictly speaking, only the four Gospels that
he considered and treated as completely on a level with the
Old Testament. The formula: ὁ νόμος καὶ οἱ προφῆται καὶ τὸ
ἐυαγγέλιον ("the Law and the Prophets and the Gospel") is
frequently found, and everything else, even the apostolic writings,
is judged by this group.[2] He does not consider even the
Pauline Epistles to be a court of appeal of equal value with
the Gospels, though he occasionally describes them as γραφάι.[3]

least refer to some important passages which I have collected. Strom. I. §§ 28,
100; II. §§ 22, 28, 29; III. §§ 11, 66, 70, 71, 76, 93, 108; IV. §§ 2, 91, 97, 105,
130, 133, 134, 138, 159; V. §§ 3, 17, 27, 28, 30, 31, 38, 80, 85, 86; VI. §§ 42, 44,
54, 59, 61, 66—68, 88, 91, 106, 107, 119, 124, 125, 127, 128, 133, 161, 164; VII.
§§ 1, 14, 34, 76, 82, 84, 88, 94, 95, 97, 100, 101, 103, 104, 106, 107. As to the estimate
of the Epistles of Barnabas and Clement of Rome as well as of the Shepherd, in
Clement, see the Prolegg. to my edition of the Opp. Patr. Apost.

[1] According to Strom. V. 14. 138 even the Epicurean Metrodorus uttered certain
words ἐνθέως; but on the other hand Homer was a prophet against his will. See
Pæd. I. 6. 36, also § 51.

[2] In the Pæd. the Gospels are regularly called ἡ γραφή, but this is seldom the
case with the Epistles. The word "Apostle" is used in quoting these.

[3] It is also very interesting to note that Clement almost nowhere illustrates
the parabolic character of the Holy Scriptures by quoting the Epistles, but in this
connection employs the Old Testament and the Gospels, just as he almost never
allegorises passages from other writings. 1 Cor. III. 2 is once quoted thus in
Pæd. I. 6. 49: τὸ ἐν τῷ ἀποστόλῳ ἅγιον πνεῦμα τῇ τοῦ κυρίου ἀποχρώμενον φωνῇ
λέγει. We can hardly conclude from Pæd. I. 7. 61 that Clement called Paul a
"prophet."

A further class of writings stands a stage lower than the Pauline
Epistles, viz., the Epistles of Clement and Barnabas, the Shepherd
of Hermas, etc. It would be wrong to say that Clement views
this group as an appendix to the New Testament, or as in any
sense Antilegomena. This would imply that he assumed the
existence of a fixed collection whose parts he considered of
equal value, an assumption which cannot be proved. ¹ (6) As
to certain books, such as the " Teaching of the Apostles," the
"Kerygma of Peter," etc., it remains quite doubtful what
authority Clement attributed to them. ² He quotes the Διδαχή
as γραφή. (7) In determining and estimating the sacred books of
the New Testament Clement is manifestly influenced by an
ecclesiastical tradition, for he recognises four Gospels and no
more because that was the exact number handed down. This
tradition had already applied the name " apostolic" to most
Christian writings which were to be considered as γραφαί, but
it had given the concept "apostolic" a far wider content than
Irenæus and Tertullian, ³ although it had not been able to
include all the new writings which were regarded as sacred
under this idea. (Hermas). At the time Clement wrote, the
Alexandrian *Church* can neither have held the principle
that all writings of the Apostles must be read in the Church
and form a decisive court of appeal like the Old Testament,
nor have believed that nothing but the Apostolic—using this
word also in its wider sense—has any claim to authority among
Christians. We willingly admit the great degree of freedom

---

¹ It is worthy of special note that Clem., Pæd. II. 10. 3; Strom. II. 15. 67 has
criticised an interpretation given by the author of ˌthe Epistle of Barnabas, although
he calls Barnabas an Apostle.

² In this category we may also include the Acts of the Apostles, which is
perhaps used like the κήρυγμα. It is quoted in Pæd. II. 16. 56; Strom. I. 50, 89,
91, 92, 153, 154; III. 49; IV. 97; V. 75, 82; VI. 63, 101, 124, 165.

³ The "seventy disciples" were also regarded as Apostles, and the authors of
writings the names of which did not otherwise offer a guarantee of authority were
likewise included in this category. That is to say, writings which were regarded
as valuable and which for some reason or other could not be characterised as
apostolic in the narrower sense were attributed to authors whom there was no
reason for denying to be Apostles in the wider sense. This wider use of the concept
ˌ"apostolic" is moreover no innovation. See my edition of the Didache, pp. 111—118.

and peculiarity characteristic of Clement, and freely acknowledge the serious difficulties inseparable from the attempt to
ascertain from his writings what was regarded as possessing
standard authority in the *Church*. Nevertheless it may be
assumed with certainty that, at the time this author wrote, the
content of the New Testament canon, or, to speak more
correctly, its reception in the Church and exact attributes had
not yet been finally settled in Alexandria.

The condition of the Alexandrian Church of the time may
perhaps be described as follows: Ecclesiastical custom had
attributed an authority to a great number of early Christian
writings without strictly defining the nature of this authority or
making it equal to that of the Old Testament. Whatever
professed to be inspired, or apostolic, or ancient, or edifying
was regarded as the work of the Spirit and therefore as the
Word of God. The prestige of these writings increased in
proportion as Christians became more incapable of producing
the like themselves. Not long before Clement wrote, however,
a systematic arrangement of writings embodying the early
Christian tradition had been made in Alexandria also. But,
while in the regions represented by Irenæus and Tertullian the
canon must have arisen and been adopted all at once, so to
speak, it was a slow process that led to this result in Alexandria.
Here also the principle of apostolicity seems to have been of
great importance for the collectors and editors, but it was
otherwise applied than at Rome. A conservative proceeding
was adopted, as they wished to insure as far as possible the
permanence of ancient Christian writings regarded as inspired.
In other words, they sought, wherever practicable, to proclaim
all these writings to be apostolic by giving a wider meaning
to the designation and ascribing an imaginary apostolic origin
to many of them. This explains their judgment as to the
Epistle to the Hebrews, and how Barnabas and Clement were
described by them as Apostles. [1] Had this undertaking succeeded
in the Church, a much more extensive canon would have resulted

---

[1] The formation of the canon in Alexandria must have had some connection
with the same process in Asia Minor and in Rome. This is shown not only by
each Church recognising four Gospels, but still more by the admission of

than in the West. But it is more than questionable whether it was really the intention of those first Alexandrian collectors to place the great compilation thus produced, as a New Testament, side by side with the Old, or, whether their undertaking was immediately approved in this sense by the Church. In view of the difference of Clement's attitude to the various groups within this collection of γραφαί, we may assert that in the Alexandrian *Church* of that time Gospels and Apostles were indeed ranked with the Law and the Prophets, but that this position of equality with the Old Testament was not assigned to all the writings that were prized either on the score of inspiration or of apostolic authority. The reason of this was that the great collection of early Christian literature that was inspired and declared to be apostolic could hardly have been used so much in public worship as the Old Testament and the Gospels.

Be this as it may, if we understand by the New Testament a fixed collection, equally authoritative throughout, of all the writings that were regarded as genuinely apostolic, that is, those of the original Apostles and Paul, then the Alexandrian Church at the time of Clement did not yet possess such a book; but the process which led to it had begun. She had come much nearer this goal by the time of Origen. At that period the writings included in the New Testament of the West were all regarded in Alexandria as equally authoritative, and also stood in every respect on a level with the Old Testament. The principle of apostolicity was more strictly conceived and more surely applied. Accordingly the extent of "Holy Scripture" was already limited in the days of Origen. Yet we have to thank the Alexandrian Church for giving us the seven Catholic Epistles. But, measured by the canon of the Western Church, which must have had a share in the matter, this sifting process was by no means complete. The inventive minds of scholars

thirteen Pauline Epistles. We would see our way more clearly here, if anything certain could be ascertained from the works of Clement, including the Hypotyposes, as to the arrangement of the Holy Scriptures; but the attempt to fix this arrangement is necessarily a dubious one, because Clement's "canon of the New Testament" was not yet finally fixed. It may be compared to a half-finished statue whose bust is already completely chiselled, while the under parts are still embedded in the stone.

designated a group of writings in the Alexandrian canon as
"Antilegomena." The historian of dogma can take no great interest
in the succeeding development, which first led to the canon
being everywhere finally fixed, so far as we can say that this
was ever the case. For the still unsettled dispute as to the extent
of the canon did not essentially affect its use and authority,
and in the following period the continuous efforts to establish a harmonious and strictly fixed canon were solely
determined by a regard to tradition. The results are no doubt
of great importance to Church history, because they show
us the varying influence exerted on Christendom at different
periods by the great Churches of the East and West and by
their learned men.

*Addendum.*—The results arising from the formation of a part
of early Christian writings into a canon, which was a great and
meritorious act of the Church,[1] notwithstanding the fact that it
was forced on her by a combination of circumstances, may be
summed up in a series of antitheses. (1) The New Testament, or
group of "apostolic" writings formed by selection, preserved
from destruction one part, and undoubtedly the most valuable
one, of primitive Church literature; but it caused all the rest
of these writings, as being intrusive, or spurious, or superfluous,
to be more and more neglected, so that they ultimately perished.[2]
(2) The New Testament, though not all at once, put an end
to the composition of works which claimed an authority binding
on Christendom (inspiration); but it first made possible the
production of secular Church literature and neutralised the extreme
dangers attendant on writings of this kind. By making room
for all kinds of writings that did not oppose it, it enabled the
Church to utilise all the elements of Greek culture. At the same

---

[1] No greater creative act can be mentioned in the whole history of the Church
than the formation of the apostolic collection and the assigning to it of a position
of equal rank with the Old Testament.

[2] The history of early Christian writings in the Church which were not definitely
admitted into the New Testament is instructive on this point. The fate of some
of these may be described as tragical. Even when they were not branded as
downright forgeries, the writings of the Fathers from the fourth century downwards
were far preferred to them.

time, however, it required an ecclesiastical stamp to be placed
on all the new Christian productions due to this cause.[1] (3) The
New Testament obscured the historical meaning and the historical origin of the writing contained in it, especially the Pauline
Epistles, though at the same time it created the conditions for
a thorough study of all those documents.  Although primarily
the new science of theological exegesis in the Church did more
than anything else to neutralise the historical value of the New
Testament writings, yet, on the other hand, it immediately
commenced a critical restoration of their original sense.  But,
even apart from theological science, the New Testament enabled
original Christianity to exercise here and there a quiet and
gradual effect on the doctrinal development of the Church,
without indeed being able to exert a dominant influence on the
natural development of the traditional system.  As the standard
of interpretation for the Holy Scriptures was the apostolic *regula
fidei*, always more and more precisely explained, and as that
*regula*, in its Antignostic and philosophico-theological interpretation, was regarded as apostolic, the New Testament was
explained in accordance with the conception of Christianity that
had become prevalent in the Church.  At first therefore the
spirit of the New Testament could only assert itself in certain
undercurrents and in the recognition of particular truths.  But
the book did not in the least ward off the danger of a total
secularising of Christianity.  (4) The New Testament opposed
a barrier to the enthusiastic manufacture of "facts."  But at
the same time its claim to be a collection of *inspired* writings [2]
naturally resulted in principles of interpretation (such as the
principle of unanimity, of unlimited combination, of absolute
clearness and sufficiency, and of allegorism) which were neces-

[1] See on this point Overbeck "Abhandlung über die Anfänge der patristischen
Litteratur, l.c., p. 469." Nevertheless, even after the creation of the New Testament
canon, theological authorship was an undertaking which was at first regarded as
highly dangerous. See the Antimontanist in Euseb., H. E. V. 16. 3: δεδιὼς καὶ
ἐξευλαβούμενος, μή πη δόξω πρὶν ἐπισυγγράφειν ἤ ἐπιδιατάσσεσθαι τῷ τῆς τοῦ
εὐαγγελίου καινῆς διαθήκης λόγῳ, We find similar remarks in other old Catholic
Fathers (see Clemen. Alex.).

[2] But how diverse were the expositions; compare the exegesis of Origen and
Tertullian, Scorp. 11.

sarily followed by the manufacture of new facts on the part of theological experts. (5) The New Testament fixed a time within which divine revelation ceased, and prevented any Christian from putting himself into comparison with the disciples of Jesus. By doing so it directly promoted the lowering of Christian ideals and requirements, and in a certain fashion legitimised this weakening of religious power. At the same time, however, it maintained the knowledge of these ideals and requirements, became a spur to the conscience of believers, and averted the danger of Christianity being corrupted by the excesses of en- thusiasm. (6) The fact of the New Testament being placed on a level with the Old proved the most effective means of pre- serving to the latter its canonical authority, which had been so often assailed in the second century. But at the same time it brought about an examination of the relation between the Old and New Testaments, which, however, also involved an enquiry into the connection between Christianity and pre-christian revel- ation. The immediate result of this investigation was not only a theological exposition of the Old Testament, but also a theory which ceased to view the two Testaments as of equal authority and *subordinated* the Old to the New. This result, which can be plainly seen in Irenæus, Tertullian, and Origen, led to exceedingly important consequences. [1] It gave some degree of insight into statements, hitherto completely unintelligible, in certain New Testament writings, and it caused the Church to reflect upon a question that had as yet been raised only by heretics, viz., what are the marks which distinguish Christianity from the Old Testament religion? An historical examination imperceptibly arose; but the old notion of the inspiration of the Old Testament confined it to the narrowest limits, and in fact always continued to forbid it; for, as before, appeal was constantly made to the Old Testament as a Christian book which contained all the truths of religion in a perfect form. Nevertheless the conception

---

[1] On the extent to which the Old Testament had become subordinated to the New and the Prophets to the Apostles, since the end of the second century, see the following passage from Novatian, de trinit. 29: "Unus ergo et idem spiritus qui in prophetis et apostolis, nisi quoniam ibi ad momentum, hic semper. Ceterum ibi non ut semper in illis inesset, hic ut in illis semper maneret, et ibi mediocriter distributus, hic totus effusus, ibi parce datus, hic large commodatus."

of the Old Testament was here and there full of contradictions. [1]
(7) The fatal identification of words of the Lord and words
of the Apostles (apostolical tradition) had existed before the
creation of the New Testament, though this proceeding gave it
a new range and content and a new significance. But, with
the Epistles of Paul included, the New Testament elevated the
highest expression of the consciousness of redemption into a
guiding principle, and by admitting Paulinism into the canon it
introduced a wholesome ferment into the history of the Church.
(8) By creating the New Testament and claiming exclusive possession of it the Church deprived the non-Catholic communions of
every apostolic foundation, just as she had divested Judaism of
every legal title by taking possession of the Old Testament;
but, by raising the New Testament to standard authority, she
created the armoury which supplied the succeeding period with
the keenest weapons against herself. [2]   The place of the Gospel
was taken by a book with exceedingly varied contents, which
theoretically acquired the same authority as the Gospel. Still,
the Catholic Church never became a religion " of the book ",
because every inconvenient text could be explained away by
the allegoric method, and because the book was not made use of
as the immediate authority for the guidance of Christians, this
latter function being directly discharged by the rule of faith. [3]

[1] That may be shown in all the old Catholic Fathers, but most plainly perhaps
in the theology of Origen. Moreover, the subordination of the Old Testament
revelation to the Christian one is not simply a result of the creation of the New
Testament, but may be explained by other causes; see chap. 5. If the New Testament had not been formed, the Church would perhaps have obtained a Christian
Old Testament with numerous interpolations—tendencies in this direction were not
wanting; see vol. I. p. 114 f.—and increased in extent by the admission of apocalypses.
The creation of the New Testament preserved the purity of the Old, for it removed
the need of doing violence to the latter in the interests of Christianity.

[2] The Catholic Church had from the beginning a very clear consciousness of the
dangerousness of many New Testament writings, in fact she made a virtue of
necessity in so far as she set up a theory to prove the unavoidableness of this
danger. See Tertullian, de præscr. passim, and de resurr. 63.

[3] To a certain extent the New Testament disturbs and prevents the tendency
to summarise the faith and reduce it to its most essential content. For it not only
puts itself in the place of the unity of a system, but frequently also in the place of

In practice it continued to be the rule for the New Testament
to take a secondary place in apologetic writings and disputes
with heretics. [1]   On the other hand it was regarded (1) as the
directly authoritative document for the direction of the Christian
life, [2] and (2) as the final court of appeal in all the conflicts
that arose within the sphere of the rule of faith.   It was freely
applied in the second stage of the Montanist struggle, but still
more in the controversies about Christology, that is, in the conflict
with the Monarchians.   The apostolic writings belong solely to the
Church, because she alone has preserved the apostolic doctrine
(regula).   This was declared to the heretics and therewith all
controversy about Scripture, or the sense of Scripture passages,
was in principle declined.   But within the Church herself the
Holy Scripture was regarded as the supreme and completely
independent tribunal against which not even an old tradition
could be appealed to; and the rule πολιτεύεσθαι κατὰ τὸ
εὐαγγέλιον ("live according to the Gospel") held good in every
respect.   Moreover, this formula, which is rarely replaced by
the other one, viz., κατὰ τὴν καινὴν διαθήκην ("according to the
New Testament"), shows that the words of the Lord, as in the
earlier period, continued to be the chief standard of *life and
conduct.*

a harmonious and complete creed. Hence the rule of faith is necessary as a guiding
principle, and even an imperfect one is better than a mere haphazard reliance upon
the Bible.

[1] We must not, however, ascribe that to conscious mistrust, for Irenæus and
Tertullian bear very decided testimony against such an idea, but to the acknowledgment
that it was impossible to make any effective use of the New Testament Scriptures in
arguments with educated non-Christians and heretics.  For these writings could
carry no weight with the former, and the latter either did not recognise them or
else interpreted them by different rules.  Even the offer of several of the Fathers
to refute the Marcionites from their own canon must by no means be attributed
to an uncertainty on their part with regard to the authority of the ecclesiastical canon
of Scripture.  We need merely add that the extraordinary difficulty originally felt
by Christians in conceiving the Pauline Epistles, for instance, to be analogous and equal
in value to Genesis or the prophets occasionally appears in the terminology even in
the third century, in so far as the term "divine writings" continues to be more
frequently applied to the Old Testament than to certain parts of the New.

[2] Tertullian, in de corona 3, makes his Catholic opponent say: "Etiam in
traditionis obtentu exigenda est auctoritas scripta."

C. *The transformation of the episcopal office in the Church into an apostolic office. The history of the remodelling
of the conception of the Church.* [1]

I. It was not sufficient to prove that the rule of faith was of
apostolic origin, *i.e.*, that the Apostles had set up a rule of
faith. It had further to be shown that, up to the present, the
Church had always maintained it unchanged. This demonstration
was all the more necessary because the heretics also claimed
an apostolic origin for their *regulæ*, and in different ways tried
to adduce proof that they alone possessed a guarantee of in-
heriting the Apostles' doctrine in all its purity. [2] An historical
demonstration was first attempted by the earliest of the old
Catholic Fathers. They pointed to communities of whose
apostolic origin there could be no doubt, and thought it could
not reasonably be denied that those Churches must have
preserved apostolic Christianity in a pure and incorrupt
form. The proof that the Church had always held fast by
apostolic Christianity depended on the agreement in doctrine
between the other communities and these. [3] But Irenæus as
well as Tertullian felt that a special demonstration was needed
to show that the Churches founded by the Apostles had really
at all times faithfully preserved their genuine teaching. General
considerations, as, for instance, the notion that Christianity would
otherwise have temporarily perished, or "that one event among
many is as good as none; but when one and the same feature
is found among many, it is not an aberration but a tradition"
("Nullus inter multos eventus unus est ... quod apud multos unum

1 Hatch, Organisation of the early Christian Church, 1883. Harnack, Die Lehre
der zwölf Apostel, 1884. Sohm, Kirchenrecht, Vol. I. 1892.

2 Marcion was the only one who did not claim to prove his Christianity from
traditions inasmuch as he rather put it in opposition to tradition. This disclaimer
of Marcion is in keeping with his renunciation of apologetic proof, whilst, conversely,
in the Church the apologetic proof, and the proof from tradition adduced against
the heretics, were closely related. In the one case the truth of Christianity was
proved by showing that it is the oldest religion, and in the other the truth of
ecclesiastical Christianity was established from the thesis that it is the oldest
Christianity, viz., that of the Apostles.

3 See Tertullian, de præscr. 20, 21, 32.

invenitur, non est erratum sed traditum") and similar ones which
Tertullian does not fail to mention, were not sufficient. But
the dogmatic conception that the *ecclesiæ* (or *ecclesia*) are the
abode of the Holy Spirit, [1] was incapable of making any impression on the heretics, as the correct application of this theory
was the very point in question. To make their proof more
precise Tertullian and Irenæus therefore asserted that the
Churches guaranteed the incorruptness of the apostolic inheritance,
inasmuch as they could point to a chain of "elders," or, in
other words, an "ordo episcoporum per successionem ab initio
decurrens," which was a pledge that nothing false had been
mixed up with it. [2] This thesis has quite as many aspects as
the conception of the "Elders," *e.g.*, disciples of the Apostles,
disciples of the disciples of the Apostles, bishops. It partly

---

[1] This theory is maintained by Irenæus and Tertullian, and is as old as the
association of the ἁγία ἐκκλησία and the πνεῦμα ἅγιον. Just for that reason the
distinction they make between Churches founded by the Apostles and those of
later origin is of chief value to themselves in their arguments against heretics.
This distinction, it may be remarked, is clearly expressed in Tertullian alone.
Here, for example, it is of importance that the Church of Carthage derives its
"authority" from that of Rome (de præscr. 36).

[2] Tertull., de præscr. 32 (see p. 19). Iren., III. 2. 2: "Cum autem ad eam iterum
traditionem, quæ est ab apostolis, quæ per successiones presbyterorum in ecclesiis
custoditur, provocamus eos, etc." III. 3. 1: "Traditionem itaque apostolorum in toto
mundo manifestatam in omni ecclesia adest perspicere omnibus qui vera velint
videre, et habemus annumerare eos, qui ab apostolis instituti sunt episcopi in ecclesiis et successiones eorum usque ad nos... valde enim perfectos in omnibus eos
volebant esse, quos et successores relinquebant, suum ipsorum locum magisterii
tradentes... traditio Romanæ ecclesiæ, quam habet ab apostolis, et annuntiata
hominibus fides per successiones episcoporum perveniens usque ad nos." III. 3. 4,
4. 1: "Si de aliqua modica quæstione disceptatio esset, nonne oporteret in anti-
quissimas recurrere ecclesias, in quibus apostoli conversati sunt... quid autem si
neque apostoli quidem scripturas reliquissent nobis, nonne oportebat ordinem sequi
traditionis, quam tradiderunt iis, quibus committebant ecclesias?" IV. 33. 8: "Character
corporis Christi secundum successiones episcoporum, quibus apostoli eam quæ in
unoquoque loco est ecclesiam tradiderunt, quæ pervenit usque ad nos, etc." V. 20. 1:
"Omnes enim ii valde posteriores sunt quam episcopi, quibus apostoli tradiderunt
ecclesias." IV. 26. 2: "Quapropter eis, qui in ecclesia sunt, presbyteris obaudire
oportet, his qui successionem habent ab apostolis; qui cum episcopatus successione
charisma veritatis certum secundum placitum patris acceperunt." IV. 26. 5: "Ubi
igitur charismata domini posita sunt, ibi discere oportet veritatem, apud quos est
ea quæ est ab apostolis ecclesiæ successio." The declaration in Luke X. 16 was
already applied by Irenæus (III. praef.) to the successors of the Apostles.

preserves a historic and partly assumes a dogmatic character. The former aspect appears in the appeal made to the foundation of Churches by Apostles, and in the argument that each series of successors were faithful disciples of those before them and therefore ultimately of the Apostles themselves. But no historical consideration, no appeal to the "Elders" was capable of affording the assurance sought for. Hence even in Irenæus the historical view of the case had clearly changed into a dogmatic one. This, however, by no means resulted merely from the controversy with the heretics, but was quite as much produced by the altered constitution of the Church and the authoritative position that the bishops had actually attained. The idea was that the Elders, *i.e.*, the bishops, had received "cum episcopatus successione certum veritatis charisma," that is, their office conferred on them the apostolic heritage of truth, which was therefore objectively attached to this dignity as a *charism*. This notion of the transmissibility of the charism of truth became associated with the episcopal office after it had become a monarchical one, exercising authority over the Church in all its relations;[1] and after the bishops had proved themselves the strongest supports of the communities against the attacks of the secular power and of

[1] For details on this point see my edition of the Didache, Proleg., p. 140. As the *regula fidei* has its preparatory stages in the baptismal confession, and the New Testament in the collection of writings read in the Churches, so the theory that the bishops receive and guarantee the apostolic heritage of truth has its preparatory stage in the old idea that God has bestowed on the Church Apostles, prophets, and teachers, who always communicate his word in its full purity. The functions of these persons devolved by historical development upon the bishop; but at the same time it became more and more a settled conviction that no one in this latter period could be compared with the Apostles. The only true Christianity, however, was that which was apostolic and which could prove itself to be so. The natural result of the problem which thus arose was the theory of an objective transference of the *charisma veritatis* from the Apostles to the bishops. This notion preserved the unique personal importance of the Apostles, guaranteed the apostolicity, that is, the truth of the Church's faith, and formed a dogmatic justification for the authority already attained by the bishops. The old idea that God bestows his Spirit on the Church, which is therefore the holy Church, was ever more and more transformed into the new notion that the bishops receive this Spirit, and that it appears in their official authority. The theory of a succession of prophets, which can be proved to have existed in Asia Minor, never got beyond a rudimentary form and speedily disappeared.

heresy. [1] In Irenæus and Tertullian, however, we only find the
first traces of this new theory. The old notion, which regarded
the *Churches* as possessing the heritage of the Apostles in so far
as they possess the Holy Spirit, continued to exercise a powerful
influence on these writers, who still united the new dogmatic
view with a historical one, at least in controversies with the
heretics. Neither Irenæus, nor Tertullian in his earlier writings, [2]
asserted that the transmission of the *charisma veritatis* to the
bishops had really invested them with the apostolic office in its
full sense. They had indeed, according to Irenæus, received the
"locum magisterii [apostolorum" ("place of government of the
Apostles"), but nothing more. It is only the later writings of
Tertullian, dating from the reigns of Caracalla and Heliogabalus,
which show that the bishop of Rome, who must have had
imitators in this respect, claimed for his office the full authority
of the apostolic office. Both Calixtus and his rival Hippolytus
described themselves as successors of the Apostles in the full
sense of the word, and claimed for themselves in that capacity
much more than a mere guaranteeing of the purity of Christianity.
Even Tertullian did not question this last mentioned attribute
of the bishops. [3] Cyprian found the theory already in existence,
but was the first to develop it definitely and to eradicate every

---

[1] This theory must have been current in the Roman Church before the time
when Irenæus wrote; for the list of Roman bishops, which we find in [Irenæus and
which he obtained from Rome, must itself be considered as a result of that dogmatic
theory. The first half of the list must have been concocted, as there were no
monarchical bishops in the strict sense in the first century (see my treatise : "Die
ältesten christlichen Datirungen und ̈die Anfänge einer bischöflichen Chronographie
in Rom." in the report of the proceedings of the Royal Prussian Academy of
Science, 1892, p. 617 ff). We do not know whether such lists were drawn up so
early in the other churches of apostolic origin (Jerusalem?). Not till the beginning
of the 3rd century have we proofs of that being done, whereas the Roman community, as early as Soter's time, had a list of bishops giving the duration of each
episcopate. Nor is there any evidence before the 3rd century of an attempt to invent
such a list for Churches possessing no claim to have been founded by Apostles.

[2] We do not yet find this assertion in Tertullian's treatise "de præscr."

[3] Special importance attaches to Tertullian's treatise "de pudicitia," which has
not been sufficiently utilised to explain the development of the episcopate and the
pretensions at that time set up by the Roman bishop. It shows clearly that Calixtus claimed for himself as bishop the powers and rights of the Apostles in their
full extent, and that Tertullian did not deny that the "doctrina apostolorum" was

remnant of the historical argument in its favour. The conception of the Church was thereby subjected to a further transformation.

(2) The transformation of the idea of the Church by Cyprian completed the radical changes that had been gradually taking

inherent in his office, but merely questioned the "potestas apostolorum." It is very significant that Tertullian (c. 21) sneeringly addressed him as "apostolice" and reminded him that "ecclesia spiritus, non ecclesia numerus episcoporum." What rights Calixtus had already claimed as belonging to the apostolic office may be ascertained from Hippol. Philos. IX. 11. 12. But the introduction to the Philosophoumena proves that Hippolytus himself was at one with his opponent in supposing that the bishops, as successors of the Apostles, had received the attributes of the latter: Τὰς αἱρέσεις ἕτερος οὐκ ἐλέγξει, ἢ τὸ ἐν ἐκκλησίᾳ παραδοθὲν ἅγιον πνεῦμα, οὗ τυχόντες πρότεροι οἱ ἀπόστολοι μετέδοσαν τοῖς ὀρθῶς πεπιστευκόσιν ὧν ἡμεῖς διάδοχοι τυγχάνοντες τῆς τε αὐτῆς χάριτος μετέχοντες ἀρχιερατείας τε καὶ διδασκαλίας καὶ φρουροὶ τῆς ἐκκλησίας λελογισμένοι οὐκ ὀφθαλμῷ νυστάζομεν, οὐδὲ λόγον ὀρθὸν σιωπῶμεν, κ.τ.λ. In these words we have an immense advance beyond the conception of Irenæus. This advance, of course, was first made in practice, and the corresponding theory followed. How greatly the prestige and power of the bishops had increased in the first 3rd part of the 3rd century may be seen by comparing the edict of Maximinus Thrax with the earlier ones (Euseb., H. E. VI. 28; see also the genuine Martyr. Jacobi, Mariani, etc., in Numidia c. 10 [Ruinart, Acta mart. p. 272 edit. Ratisb.])1 "Nam ita inter se nostræ religionis gradus artifex sævitia diviserat, ut laicos clericis separatos tentationibus sæculi et terroribus suis putaret esse cessuros" that is, the heathen authorities also knew that the clergy formed the bond of union in the Churches). But the theory that the bishops were successors of the Apostles, that is, possessed the apostolic office, must be considered a Western one which was very slowly and gradually adopted in the East. Even in the original of the first six books of the Apostolic Constitutions, composed about the end of the 3rd century, which represents the bishop as mediator, king, and teacher of the community, the episcopal office is not yet regarded as the apostolic one. It is rather presbyters, as in Ignatius, who are classed with the Apostles. It is very important to note that the whole theory of the significance of the bishop in determining the truth of ecclesiastical Christianity is completely unknown to Clement of Alexandria. As we have not the slightest evidence that his conception of the Church was of a hierarchical and anti-heretical type, so he very rarely mentions the ecclesiastical officials in his works and rarest of all the bishops. These do not at all belong to his conception of the Church, or at least only in so far as they resemble the English orders (cf. Pæd. III. 12. 97, presbyters, bishops, deacons, widows; Strom. VII. 1. 3; III. 12. 90, presbyters, deacons, laity; VI. 13. 106, presbyters, deacons; VI. 13. 107, bishops, presbyters, deacons; Quis dives 42, bishops and presbyters). On the other hand, according to Clement, the true Gnostic has an office like that of the Apostles. See Strom. VI. 13. 106, 107: ἔξεστιν οὖν καὶ νῦν ταῖς κυριακαῖς ἐνασκήσαντας ἐντολαῖς κατὰ τὸ εὐαγγέλιον τελείως βιώσαντας καὶ γνωστικῶς εἰς τὴν ἐκλογὴν τῶν ἀποστόλων ἐγγραφῆναι. οὗτος πρεσβύτερός ἐστι τῷ ὄντι τῆς ἐκκλησίας καὶ διάκονος ἀληθὴς τῆς τοῦ θεοῦ βουλήσεως. Here we see plainly that the servants of the earthly Church, as such, have nothing to do with the true Church and the heavenly hierarchy). Strom. VII. 9, 52 says: the true Gnostic is the mediator with God. In Strom. VI.

place from the last half of the second century.[1] In order to understand them it is necessary to go back. It was only with slowness and hesitation that the theories of the Church followed the actual changes in her history. It may be said that the idea of the Church always remained a stage behind the condition reached in practice. That may be seen in the whole course of the history of dogma up to the present day.

The essential character of Christendom in its first period was a new holy life and a sure hope, both based on repentance

14. 108; VII. 12. 77 we find the words: ὁ γνωστικὸς οὗτος συνελόντι εἰπεῖν τὴν ἀποστολικὴν ἀπουσίαν ανταναπληροῖ, κ.τ.λ. Clement could not have expressed himself in this way if the office of bishop had at that time been as much esteemed in the Alexandrian Church, of which he was a presbyter, as it was at Rome and in other Churches of the West (see Bigg l.c. 101). According to Clement the Gnostic as a teacher has the same significance as is possessed by the bishop in the West; and according to him we may speak of a natural succession of teachers. Origen in the main still held the same view as his predecessor. But numerous passages in his works and above all his own history shew that in his day the episcopate had become stronger in Alexandria also, and had begun to claim the same attributes and rights as in the West (see besides de princip. praef. 2: "servetur ecclesiastica prædicatio per successionis ordinem ab apostolis tradita et usque ad praesens in ecclesiis permanens: illa sola credenda est veritas, quæ in nullo ab ecclesiastica et apostolica discordat traditione"—so in Rufinus, and in IV. 2. 2: τοῦ κανόνος τῆς Ἰησοῦ Χριστοῦ κατὰ διαδοχὴν τ. ἀποστόλων οὐρανίου ἐκκλησίας). The state of things here is therefore exactly the same as in the case of the apostolic *regula fidei* and the apostolic canon of scripture. Clement still represents an earlier stage, whereas by Origen's time the revolution has been completed. Wherever this was so, the theory that the monarchical episcopate was based on apostolic institution was the natural result. This idea led to the assumption—which, however, was not an immediate consequence in all cases—that the apostolic office, and therefore the authority of Jesus Christ himself, was continued in the episcopate: "Manifesta est sententia Iesu Christi apostolos suos mittentis et ipsis solis potestatem a patre sibi datam permittentis, quibus nos successimus eadem potestatex ecclesiam domini gubernantes et credentium fidem baptizantes (Hartel, Opp. Cypr. I. 459).

See Rothe, Die Anfänge der christlichen Kirche und ihrer Verfassung, 1837. Köstlin, Die Katholische Auffassung von der Kirche in ihrer ersten Ausbildung in the Deutsche Zeitschrift für christliche Wissenschaft und christliches Leben, 1855. Ritschl, Entstehung der altkatholischen Kirche," 2nd ed., 1857. Ziegler, Des Irenäus Lehre von der Autorität der Schrift, der Tradition und der Kirche, 1868. Hackenschmidt, Die Anfänge des katholischen Kirchenbegriffs, 1874. Hatch—Harnack, Die Gesellschaftsverfassung der christlichen Kirche im Alterthum, 1883. Seeberg, Zur Geschichte des Begriffs der Kirche, Dorpat, 1884. Söder, Der Begriff der Katholicität der Kirche und' des Glaubens, 1881. O. Ritschl, Cyprian von Karthago und die Verfassung der Kirche, 1885. (This contains the special literature treating of Cyprian's conception of the Church). Sohm, l.c.

towards God and faith in Jesus Christ and brought about by
the Holy Spirit. Christ and the Church, that is, the Holy Spirit
and the holy Church, were inseparably connected. The Church,
or, in other words, the community of all believers, attains her
unity through the Holy Spirit. This unity manifested itself in
brotherly love and in the common relation to a common ideal
and a common hope. [1] The assembly of all Christians is realised
in the Kingdom of God, viz., in heaven; on earth Christians
and the Church are dispersed and in a foreign land. Hence,
properly speaking, the Church herself is a heavenly community
inseparable from the heavenly Christ. Christians believe that
they belong to a real super-terrestrial commonwealth, which, from
its very nature, cannot be realised on earth. The heavenly goal
is not yet separated from the idea of the Church; there is a
holy Church on earth in so far as heaven is her destination. [2]
Every individual congregation is to be an image of the heavenly Church. [3] Reflections were no doubt made on the contrast
between the empirical community and the heavenly Church
whose earthly likeness it was to be (Hermas); but these
did not affect the theory of the subject. Only the saints of
God, whose salvation is certain, belong to her, for the essential
thing is not to be called, but to be, a Christian. There
was as yet no empirical universal Church possessing an outward legal title that could, so to speak, be detached from the
personal Christianity of the individual Christian. [4] All the lofty

---

[1] See Hatch, l.c. pp. 191, 253.

[2] See vol. I. p. 150 f. Special note should be given to the teachings in the
Shepherd, in the 2nd Epistle of Clement and in the Διδαχή.

[3] This notion lies at the basis of the exhortations of Ignatius. He knows nothing
of an empirical union of the different communities into one Church guaranteed by
any law or office. The bishop is of importance only for the individual community,
and has nothing to do with the essence of the Church; nor does Ignatius view
the separate communities as united in any other way than by faith, charity, and
hope. Christ, the invisible Bishop, and the Church are inseparably connected (ad
Ephes. V. 1; as well as 2nd Clem. XIV.), and that is ultimately the same idea as
is expressed in the associating of πνεῦμα and ἐκκλησία. But every individual
community is an image of the heavenly Church, or at least ought to be.

[4] The expression "Catholic Church" appears first in Ignatius (ad Smyrn. VIII. 2):
ὅπου ἄν φανῇ ὁ ἐπίσκοπος, ἐκεῖ τὸ πλῆθος ἔστω· ὥσπερ ὅπου ἄν ᾖ Χριστὸς Ἰησοῦς,
ἐκεῖ ἡ καθολικὴ ἐκκλησία. But in this passage these words do not yet express a

designations which Paul, the so-called Apostolic Fathers, and
Justin gathered from the Old Testament and applied to the
Church, relate to the holy community which originates in heaven
and returns thither. [1]

But, in consequence of the naturalising of Christianity in the
world and the repelling of heresy, a formulated creed was made
the basis of the Church. This confession was also recognised
as a foundation of her unity and guarantee of her truth, and in
certain respects as the main one. Christendom protected itself
by this conception, though no doubt at a heavy price. To
Irenæus and Tertullian the Church rests entirely on the apostolic,
traditional faith which legitimises her. [2] But this faith itself
appeared as a *law* and aggregate of doctrines, all of which are
of equally fundamental importance, so that their practical aim
became uncertain and threatened to vanish ("fides in regula posita
est, habet legem et salutem de observatione legis").

The Church herself, however, became a union based on the
true doctrine and visible in it; and this confederation was at
the same time enabled to realise an actual outward unity by
means of the apostolic inheritance, the doctrinal confession, and
the apostolic writings. The narrower and more external character
assumed by the idea of the Church was concealed by the fact
that, since the latter half of the second century, Christians in

new conception of the Church, which represents her as an empirical commonwealth. Only the individual earthly communities exist empirically, and the universal,
*i.e.*, the whole Church, occupies the same position towards these as the bishops of
the individual communities do towards the Lord. The epithet "καθολικός" does
not of itself imply any secularisation of the idea of the Church.

[1] The expression "invisible Church" is liable to be misunderstood here, because
it is apt to impress us as a mere idea, which is certainly not the meaning attached
to it in the earliest period.

[2] It was thus regarded by Hegesippus in whom the expression "ἡ ἕνωσις τῆς
ἐκκλησίας" is first found. In his view the ἐκκλησία is founded on the ὀρθὸς λόγος
transmitted by the Apostles. The innovation does not consist in the emphasis laid
upon faith, for the unity of faith was always supposed to be guaranteed by the
possession of the one Spirit and the same hope, but in the setting up of a formulated
creed, which resulted in a loosening of the connection between faith and conduct.
The transition to the new conception of the Church was therefore a gradual one.
The way is very plainly prepared for it in 1 Tim. III. 15: οἶκος θεοῦ ἐκκλησία,
στύλος καὶ ἑδραίωμα τῆς ἀληθείας.

all parts of the world had really united in opposition to
the state and "heresy", and had found compensation for the
incipient decline of the original lofty thoughts and practical
obligations in the consciousness of forming an œcumenical and
international alliance. The designation "Catholic Church" gave
expression to the claim of this world-wide union of the same faith
to represent the true Church. [1] This expression corresponds to the
powerful position which the "great Church" (Celsus), or the

---

[1] The oldest predicate which was given to the Church and which was always
associated with it, was that of *holiness*. See the New Testament; Barn. XIV. 6; Hermas,
Vis. I. 3, 4; I. 6; the Roman symbol; Dial. 119; Ignat. ad Trall. inscr.; Theophil., ad
Autol., II. 14 (here we have even the plural, "holy churches"); Apollon. in Euseb,
H. E. V. 18. 5; Tertull., adv. Marc. IV. 13; V. 4; de pudicit. 1; Mart. Polyc. inscr.;
Alexander Hieros. in Euseb., H. E. VI. 11. 5; Clemens Alex.; Cornelius in Euseb.,
VI. 43. 6; Cyprian. But the holiness (purity) of the Church was already referred
by Hegesippus (Euseb., H. E. IV. 22. 4) to its pure doctrine: ἐκάλουν τὴν ἐκκλησίαν
παρθένον· οὔπω γὰρ ἔφθαρτο ἀκοαῖς ματαίαις. The unity of the Church according
to Hegesippus is specially emphasised in the Muratorian Fragment (line 55); see
also Hermas; Justin; Irenæus; Tertullian, de præscr. 20; Clem. Alex., Strom. VII.
17. 107. Even before Irenæus and Tertullian the *universality* of the Church was
emphasised for apologetic purposes. In so far as universality is a proof of truth,
"universal" is equivalent to "orthodox." This signification is specially clear in
expressions like: ἡ ἐν Σμύρνῃ καθολικὴ ἐκκλησία (Mart. Polyc. XVI. 2). From Irenæus,
III. 15, 2, we must conclude that the Valentinians called their ecclesiastical opponents
"Catholics." The word itself is not yet found in Irenæus, but the idea is there
(see I. 10. 2; II. 9. 1, etc., Serapion in Euseb., H. E. V. 19: πᾶσα ἡ ἐν κόσμῳ
ἀδελφότης). Καθολικός is found as a designation of the orthodox, visible Church
in Mart. Polyc. inscr.: αἱ κατὰ πάντα τόπον τῆς ἁγίας καὶ καθολικῆς ἐκκλησίας
παροικίαι; 19. 2; 16. 2 (in all these passages, however, it is probably an interpolation, as I have shown in the "Expositor" for Dec. 1885, p. 410 f.); in the
Muratorian Fragment 61, 66, 69; in the anonymous writer in Euseb., H. E. V. 16. 9.
in Tertull. frequently, *e.g.*, de præscr. 26, 30; adv. Marc. III. 22 : IV. 4; in Clem.
Alex., Strom. VII. 17. 106, 107; in Hippol. Philos. IX. 12; in Mart. Pionii 2, 9,
13, 19; in Cornelius in Cypr., epp. 49. 2; and in Cyprian. The expression "catholica
traditio" occurs in Tertull., de monog. 2, "fides catholica" in Cyprian ep. 25,
"κανὼν καθολικός" in the Mart. Polyc. rec. Mosq. fin. and Cypr. ep. 70. 1, "catholica fides et religio" in the Mart. Pionii 18. In the earlier Christian literature the
word καθολικός occurs in various connections in the following passages: in fragments
of the Peratae (Philos. V. 16), and in Herakleon, *e.g.*, in Clement, Strom. IV. 9. 71;
in Justin, Dial., 81, 102; Athenag., 27; Theophil., I. 13; Pseudojustin, de monarch. 1,
(καθολ. δόξα); Iren., III. 11, 8; Apollon. in Euseb., H. E. IV. 18. 5, Tertull., de
fuga 3; adv. Marc. II. 17; IV. 9; Clement, Strom., IV. 15. 97; VI. 6. 47; 7. 57; 8. 67.
The addition "catholicam" found its way into the symbols of the West only at a
comparatively late period. The earlier expressions for the whole of Christendom are
πᾶσαι αἱ ἐκκλησίαι, ἐκκλησίαι κατὰ πᾶσαν πόλιν, ἐκκλησίαι αἱ ἐν κόσμῳ, αἱ ὑφ' οὐρανοῦ, etc.

"old" Church (Clemens Alex.) had attained by the end of the second century, as compared with the Marcionite Church, the school sects, the Christian associations of all kinds, and the independent Christians. This Church, however, was declared to be apostolic, *i. e.*, founded in its present form by Christ through the Apostles. Through this idea, which was supported by the old enthusiastic notion that the Apostles had already proclaimed the Gospel to all the world, it came to be completely forgotten how Christ and his Apostles had exercised their ministry, and an empirical conception of the Church was created in which the idea of a holy life in the Spirit could no longer be the ruling one. It was taught that Christ received from God a law of faith, which, as a new lawgiver, he imparted to the Apostles, and that they, by transmitting the truth of which they were the depositaries, founded the one Catholic Church (Iren. III. 4. 1). The latter, being guardian of the apostolic heritage, has the assurance of possessing the Spirit; whereas all communities other than herself, inasmuch as they have not received that deposit, necessarily lack the Spirit and are therefore separated from Christ and salvation. [1]   Hence one must be a member of this Church in order to be a partaker of salvation, because in her alone one can find the creed which must be recognised as the condition of redemption. [2]   Consequently, in proportion as the faith became a doctrine of faith, the Catholic Church interposed herself as an empiric power between the individual and salvation. She became a condition of salvation;

[1]  Very significant is Tertullian's expression in adv. Val. 4 : "Valentinus de ecclesia authenticæ regulæ abrupit," (but probably this still refers specially to the Roman Church).

[2]  Tertullian called the Church *mother* (in Gal. IV. 26 the heavenly Jerusalem is called "mother"); see de orat. 2 : "ne mater quidem ecclesia præteritur", de monog. 7; adv. Marc. V. 4 (the author of the letter in Euseb., H. E. V. 2. 7, 1. 45, had already done this before him). In the African Church the symbol was thus worded soon after Tertullian's time: "credis in remissionem peccatorum et vitam æternam per sanctam ecclesiam" (see Hahn, Bibliothek der Symbole, 2nd ed. p. 29 ff.) On the other hand Clement of Alexandria (Strom. VI. 16. 146) rejected the designation of the Church, as "mother": μήτηρ δέ οὐχ, ὥς τινες ἐκδεδώκασιν, ἡ ἐκκλησία, ἀλλ᾿ ἡ θεία γνῶσις καὶ ἡ σοφία (there is a different idea in Pæd. I. 5. 21 and 6. 42: μήτηρ παρθένος· ἐκκλησίαν ἐμοὶ φίλον ἀυτὴν καλεῖν). In the Acta Justini c. 4 the faith is named "mother."

but the result was that she ceased to be a sure communion of the saved and of saints (see on this point the following chapter). It was quite a logical proceeding when about the year 220 Calixtus, a Roman bishop, started the theory that there *must* be wheat and tares in the Catholic Church and that the Ark of Noah with its clean and unclean beasts was her type.[1] The departure from the old idea of the Church appears completed in this statement. But the following facts must not be overlooked: — First, the new conception of the Church was not yet a hierarchical one. Secondly, the idea of the union and unity of all believers found here magnificent expression. Thirdly, the development of the communities into one solid Church also represents the creative power of the Christian spirit. Fourthly, through the consolidation effected in the Church by the rule of faith the Christian religion was in some measure preserved from enthusiastic extravagancies and arbitrary misinterpretation. Fifthly, in consequence of the regard for a Church founded on the doctrine of faith the specific significance of redemption by Christ, as distinguished from natural religion and that of the Old Testament, could no longer be lost to believers. Sixthly, the independence of each individual community had a wide scope not only at the end of the second but also in the third century.[2] Consequently, though the revolution which led to the Catholic Church was a result of the situation of the communities in the world in general and of the struggle with the Gnostics and Marcion in particular, and though it was a fatal error to identify the Catholic and apostolic Churches, this change did not take place without an exalting of the Christian spirit and an awakening of its self-consciousness.

But there was never a time in history when the conception of the Church, as nothing else than the visible communion of those holding the correct apostolic doctrine, was clearly grasped or exclusively emphasised. In Irenæus and Tertullian we rather find, on the one hand, that the old theory of the

---

[1] Hippol. Philos. IX. 12 p. 460.

[2] The phraseology of Irenæus is very instructive here. As a rule he still speaks of Churches (in the plural) when he means the empirical Church. It is already otherwise with Tertullian, though even with him the old custom still lingers.

Church was still to a great extent preserved and, on the other, that the hierarchical notion was already making its appearance. As to the first point, Irenæus frequently asserts that the Spirit and the Church, that is, the Christian people, are inseparable; that the Spirit in divers ways continually effects whatever she needs; that she is the totality of all true believers, that all the faithful have the rank of priests; that outside the holy Church there is no salvation, etc.; in fact these doctrines form the very essence of his teaching. But, since she was also regarded as the visible institution for objectively preserving and communicating the truth, and since the idea of the Church in contradistinction to heresy was necessarily exhausted in this as far as Irenæus was concerned, the old theories of the matter could not operate correctively, but in the end only served to glorify the earthly Catholic Church.[1] The proposition that truth is only to be found in the Church and that she and the Holy Spirit are inseparable must be understood in Irenæus as already referring to the Catholic Church in contradistinction to every other calling itself Christian.[2] As to the second point, it cannot be denied that, though Irenæus desires to maintain that the only essential part of the idea of the Church is the fact of her being the depository of the truth, he was no longer able to confine himself to this (see above). The episcopal succession and the transmission to the bishops of the *magisterium* of the Apostles were not indeed of any direct importance to his idea of the Church, but they were of consequence for the preservation of truth and therefore indirectly for the idea of the Church also. To Irenæus, however, that theory was still

---

[1] The most important passages bearing on this are II. 31. 3 : III. 24. I (see the whole section, but especially: "in ecclesia posuit deus universam operationem spiritus; cuius non sunt participes omnes qui non concurrunt ad ecclesiam ... ubi enim ecclesia, ibi et spiritus dei, et ubi spiritus dei, illic ecclesia et omnis gratia "); III. 11. 8 : στύλος καὶ στήριγμα ἐκκλησίας τὸ εὐαγγέλιον καὶ πνεῦμα ζωῆς : IV. 8. 1 : " semen Abrahæ ecclesia "., IV. 8. 3 : "omnes iusti sacerdotalem habent ordinem "; IV. 36. 2 : "ubique præclara est ecclesia; ubique enim sunt qui suscipiunt spiritum "; IV. 33. 7 : ἐκκλησία μέγα καὶ ἔνδοξον σῶμα τοῦ Χριστοῦ ; IV. 26. I sq. : V. 20. I. : V. 32. : V. 34. 3., " Levitæ et sacerdotes sunt discipuli omnes domini."

[2] Hence the repudiation of all those who separate themselves from the Catholic Church (III. 11. 9; 24. 1 : IV. 26. 2; 33. 7).

nothing more than an artificial line; but artificial lines are really
supports and must therefore soon attain the value of found-
ations.¹ Tertullian's conception of the Church was essentially
the same as that of Irenæus; but with the former the idea that
she is the outward manifestation of the Spirit, and therefore a
communion of those who are spiritual, at all times continued to
operate more powerfully than with the latter. In the last period
of his life Tertullian emphasised this theory so vigorously that
the Antignostic idea of the Church being based on the "traditio
unius sacramenti" fell into the background. Consequently we
find nothing more than traces of the hierarchical conception of
the Church in Tertullian. But towards the end of his life he
found himself face to face with a *fully developed* theory of this
kind. This he most decidedly rejected, and, in doing so,
advanced to such a conception of ecclesiastical orders, and
therefore also of the episcopate, as clearly involved him in a
contradiction of the other theory—which he also never gave
up—viz., that the bishops, as the class which transmits the rule
of faith, are an apostolic institution and therefore necessary to
the Church. ²

¹ On IV. 33. 7 see Seeberg, l.c., p. 20, who has correctly punctuated the passage,
but has weakened its force. The fact that Irenæus was here able to cite
the "antiquus ecclesiæ status in universo mundo et character corporis Christi
secundum successiones episcoporum", etc., as a second and independent item alongside of the apostolic doctrine is, however, a proof that the transition from the idea
of the Church, as a community united by a common faith, to that of a hierarchical
institution was already revealing itself in his writings.

² The Church as a communion of the same faith, that is of the same doctrine,
is spoken of in de præscr. 20; de virg. vol. 2. On the other hand we find the
ideal spiritual conception in de bapt. 6: " ubi tres, id est pater et filius et spiritus
sanctus, ibi ecclesia, quæ trium corpus est "; 8: " columba s. spiritus advolat, pacem
dei adferens, emissa de cœlis, ubi ecclesia est arca figurata"; 15: " unus deus et
unum baptismum et una ecclesia in cœlis"; de pænit. 10: " in uno et altero ecclesia
est, ecclesia vero Christus "; de orat. 28: " nos sumus veri adoratores et veri sacerdotes, qui spiritu orantes spiritu sacrificamus; " Apolog. 39; de exhort. 7: "differentiam inter ordinem et plebem constituit ecclesiæ auctoritas et honor per ordinis
consessum sanctificatus. Adeo ubi ecclesiastici ordinis non est consessus, et offers
et tinguis et sacerdos es tibi solus. Sed ubi tres, ecclesia est, licet laici" (the same
idea, only not so definitely expressed, is already found in de bapt. 17); de monog. 7:
"nos autem Iesus summus sacerdos sacerdotes deo patri suo fecit... vivit unicus
pater noster deus et mater ecclesia, .. certe sacerdotes sumus a Christo vocati " :
12; de pudic. 21: "nam et ipsa ecclesia proprie et principaliter ipse est spiritus, in

From the disquisitions of Clement of Alexandria we see how
vigorous the old conception of the Church, as the heavenly
communion of the elect and believing, still continued to be
about the year 200. This will not appear strange after what we
have already said as to Clement's views about the rule of faith,
the New Testament, and the episcopate. It is evident that his
philosophy of religion led him to give a new interpretation to
the original ideas. Yet the old form of these notions can be
more easily made out from his works than from those of Irenæus. [1]
Up to the 15th Chapter of the 7th Book of his great work, the
Stromateis, and in the Pædagogus, Clement simply speaks of
the Church in the sense of the Epistle to the Ephesians and
the Shepherd of Hermas. She is a heavenly formation, continued
in that which appears on earth as her image. Instead of
distinguishing two Churches Clement sees one, the product of
God's will aiming at the salvation of man—a Church which is
to be on earth as it is in heaven, and of which faith forms the
subjective and the Logos the objective bond of union. But,
beginning with Strom. VII. 15 (see especially 17), where he is
influenced by opposition to the heretics, he suddenly identifies
this Church with the single old Catholic one, that is, with the
visible "Church" in opposition to the heretic sects. Thus the
empirical interpretation of the Church, which makes her the
institution in possession of the true doctrine, was also completely
adopted by Clement; but as yet he employed it simply in
polemics and not in positive teachings. He neither reconciled
nor seemingly felt the contradiction in the statement that the
Church is to be at one and the same time the assembly of the
elect and the empiric universal Church. At any rate he made

quo est trinitas unius divinitatis, pater et filius et spiritus sanctus. Illam ecclesiam
congregat quam dominus in tribus posuit. Atque ita exinde etiam numerus omnis
qui in hanc fidem conspiraverint ecclesia ab auctore et consecratore censeatur. Et
ideo ecclesia quidem delicta donabit, sed ecclesia spiritus per spiritalem hominem,
non ecclesia numerus episcoporum"; de anima 11, 21. Contradictions in detail
need not surprise us in Tertullian, since his whole position as a Catholic and
as a Montanist is contradictory.

[1] The notion that the true Gnostic can attain the same position as the Apostles
also preserved Clement from thrusting the ideal conception of the Church into
the background.

as yet no unconditional acknowledgment of the Catholic Church, because he was still able to attribute independent value to Gnosis, that is, to independent piety as he understood it. [1] Consequently, as regards the conception of the Church, the mystic Gnosis exercised the same effect as the old religious enthusiasm from which in other respects it differs so much. [2] The hierarchy has still no significance as far as Clement's idea of the Church is concerned. [3] At first Origen entirely agrees with Clement in regard to this conception. He also starts with the theory that the Church is essentially a heavenly communion and a holy communion of believers, and keeps this idea constantly before him. [4] When opposing heretics, he also, like Clement, cannot help identifying her with the Catholic Church, because the latter contains the true doctrine, though he likewise

---

[1] Some very significant remarks are found in Clement about the Church which is the object of faith. See Pæd. I. 5. 18, 21 ; 6. 27 : ὡς γὰρ τὸ θέλημα τοῦ Θεοῦ ἔργον ἐστὶ καὶ τοῦτο κόσμος ὀνομάζεται, οὕτω καὶ τὸ βούλημα αὐτοῦ ἀνθρώπων ἐστὶ σωτηρία, καὶ τοῦτο ἐκκλησία κέκληται—here an idea which Hermas had in his mind (see Vol. I., p. 180. note 4) is pregnantly and excellently expressed. Strom. II. 12. 55 ; IV. 8. 66 : εἰκὼν τῆς οὐρανίου ἐκκλησίας ἡ ἐπίγειος, διόπερ εὐχόμεθα καὶ ἐπί γῆς γενέσθαι τὸ θέλημα τοῦ Θεοῦ ὡς ἐν οὐρανῷ ; IV. 26. 172 : ἡ ἐκκλησία ὑπὸ λόγου ἀπολιόρκητος ἀτυράννητος πόλις ἐπὶ γῆς, θέλημα θεῖον ἐπὶ γῆς, ὡς ἐν οὐρανῷ ; VI. 13. 106, 107 ; VI. 14. 108 : ἡ ἀνωτάτω ἐκκλησία, καθ᾿ ἥν οἱ φιλόσοφοι συνάγονται τοῦ Θεοῦ ; VII. 5. 29 : πῶς οὐ κυρίως τὴν εἰς τιμὴν τοῦ Θεοῦ κατ᾿ ἐπίγνωσιν ἁγίαν γενομένην ἐκκλησίαν ἱερὸν ἂν εἴποιμεν Θεοῦ τὸ πολλοῦ ἄξιον... ὀυ γὰρ νῦν τὸν τόπον, ἀλλὰ τὸ ἄθροισμα τῶν ἐκλεκτῶν ἐκκλησίαν καλῶ ; VII. 6. 32 ; VII. 11. 68 : ἡ πνευματικὴ ἐκκλησία. The empirical conception of the Church is most clearly formulated in VII. 17. 107 ; we may draw special attention to the following sentences : φανερὸν οἶμαι γεγενῆσθαι μίαν εἶναι τὴν ἀληθῆ ἐκκλησίαν τὴν τῷ ὄντι ἀρχαίαν, εἰς ἥν οἱ κατὰ πρόθεσιν δίκαιοι ἐγκαταλέγονται, ἑνὸς γὰρ ὄντος τοῦ Θεοῦ καὶ ἑνὸς τοῦ κυρίου... τῇ γοῦν τοῦ ἑνὸς φύσει συγκληροῦται ἐκκλησία ἡ μία, ἥν εἰς πολλὰς κατατέμνειν βιάζονται αἱρέσεις.

[2] It may, however, be noted that the old eschatological aim has fallen into the background in Clement's conception of the Church.

[3] A significance of this kind is suggested by the notion that the orders in the earthly Church correspond to those in the heavenly one ; but this idea, which afterwards became so important in the East, was turned to no further account by Clement. In his view the "Gnostics" are the highest stage in the Church. See Bigg, l.c., p. 100.

[4] De princip. IV. 2. 2 : ἡ οὐράνιος ἐκκλησία ; Hom. IX. in Exod. c. 3 : "ecclesia credentium plebs"; Hom. XI. in Lev. c. 5 ; Hom. VI. in Lev. c. 5 ; ibid. Hom. IX. : "omni ecclesiæ dei et credentium populo sacerdotium datum."; T.XIV. in Mt. c. 17 : c. Cels. VI. 48 : VI. 79 ; Hom. VII. in Lk. ; and de orat. 31 a twofold Church is distinguished

refrains from acknowledging any hierarchy.[1] But Origen is
influenced by two further considerations, which are scarcely
hinted at in Clement, but which were called forth by the
actual course of events and signified a further development in
the idea of the Church. For, in the first place, Origen saw
himself already compelled to examine closely the distinction
between the essence and the outward appearance of the Church,
and, in this process, reached results which again called in
question the identification of the Holy Church with the empiric
Catholic one (see on this point the following chapter). Secondly,
in consequence of the extraordinary extension and powerful
position attained by the Catholic Church by the time of Philip
the Arabian, Origen, giving a new interpretation to a very old
Christian notion and making use of a Platonic conception,[2]
arrived at the idea that she was the earthly Kingdom of God,
destined to enter the world, to absorb the Roman Empire and
indeed all mankind, and to unite and take the place of the
various secular states.[3] This magnificent idea, which regards
the Church as κόσμος τοῦ κόσμου,[4] denoted indeed a complete
departure from the original theory of the subject, determined
by eschatological considerations; though we must not forget

(ὥστε εἶναι ἐπὶ τῶν ἁγίων συναθροιζομένων διπλῆν ἐκκλησίαν τὴν μὲν ἀνθρώπων, τὴν δὲ
ἀγγέλων). Nevertheless Origen does not assume two Churches, but, like Clement,
holds that there is only one, part of which is already in a state of perfection and
part still on earth. But it is worthy of note that the ideas of the heavenly hierarchy
are already more developed in Origen (de princip. I. 7). He adopted the old
speculation about the origin of the Church (see Papias, fragm. 6; 2 Clem. XIV.).
Socrates (H. E. III. 7) reports that Origen, in the 9th vol. of his commentary on
Genesis, compared Christ with Adam and Eve with the Church, and remarks that
Pamphilus' apology for Origen stated that this allegory was not new: ὃν πρῶτον
Ὠριγένην ἐπὶ ταύτην τὴν πραγματείαν ἐλθεῖν φασίν, ἀλλὰ τὴν τῆς ἐκκλησίας μυσ-
τικὴν ἑρμηνεῦσαι παράδοσιν. A great many more of these speculations are to be
found in the 3rd century. See, e.g., *the Acts of Peter and Paul* 29.

[1] De princip. IV. 2. 2; Hom. III. in Jesu N. 5: "nemo tibi persuadeat; nemo
semetipsum decipiat: extra ecclesiam nemo salvatur." The reference is to the
Catholic Church which Origen also calls τὸ ὅλον σῶμα τῶν συναγωγῶν τῆς ἐκκλησίας.

[2] Hermas (Sim. I.) has spoken of the "city of God" (see also pseudo-Cyprian's
tractate "de pascha computus"); but for him it lies in Heaven and is the complete
contrast of the world. The idea of Plato here referred to is to be found in his *Republic*.

[3] See c. Cels. VIII. 68—75.

[4] Comment. in Joh. VI. 38.

that Origen still demanded a really holy Church and a new polity. Hence, as he also distinguishes the various degrees of connection with the Church, [1] we already find in his theory a combination of all the features that became essential parts of the conception of the Church in subsequent times, with the exception of the clerical element. [2]

3. The contradictory notions of the Church, for so they appear to us, in Irenæus and Clement and still more in Tertullian and Origen, need not astonish any one who bears in mind that none of these Fathers made the Church the subject of a theological theory. [3] Hence no one as yet thought of questioning the old article: "I believe in a holy Church." But, at the same time, actual circumstances, though they did not at first succeed in altering the Church's belief, forced her to *realise* her changed position, for she had in point of fact become an association which was founded on a definite law of doctrine and rejected everything that did not conform to it. The identifying of this association with the ideal Church was a matter of course, [4] but it was quite as natural to take no immediate *theoretical* notice of the identification except in cases where it was absolutely necessary, that is, in polemics. In the latter case the unity of faith and hope became the unity of the doctrine of faith, and the Church was, in this instance, legitimised by the possession of the apostolic tradition instead of by the realising of that tradition in heart and life. From the principle that had been set

[1] Accordingly he often speaks in a depreciatory way of the ὄχλος τῆς ἐκκλησίας (the ignorant) without accusing them of being unchristian (this is very frequent in the books c. Cels., but is also found elsewhere).

[2] Origen, who is Augustine's equal in other respects also, and who anticipated many of the problems considered by the latter, anticipated prophetically this Father's view of the City of God—of course as a hope (c. Cels. viii. 68 f.). The Church is also viewed as τὸ κατὰ Θεον πολίτευμα in Euseb., H. E. V. Præf. § 4, and at an earlier period in Clement.

[3] This was not done even by Origen, for in his great work "de principiis" we find no section devoted to the Church.

[4] It is frequently represented in Protestant writers that the mistake consisted in this identification, whereas, if we once admit this criticism, the defect is rather to be found in the development itself which took place in the Church, that is, in its secularisation. No one thought of the desperate idea of an invisible Church; this notion would probably have brought about a lapse from pure Christianity far more rapidly than the idea of the Holy Catholic Church.

up it necessarily followed that the apostolic inheritance on which the truth and legitimacy of the Church was based, could not but remain an imperfect court of appeal until *living* authorities could be pointed to in this court, and until *every* possible cause of strife and separation was settled by reference to it. An empirical community cannot be ruled by a traditional written word, but only by persons; for the written law will always separate and split. If it has such persons, however, it can tolerate within it a great amount of individual differences, provided that the leaders subordinate the interests of the whole to their own ambition. We have seen how Irenæus and Tertullian, though they in all earnestness represented the *fides catholica* and *ecclesia catholica* as inseparably connected,[1] were already compelled to have recourse to bishops in order to ensure the apostolic doctrine. The conflicts within the sphere of the rule of faith, the struggles with the so-called Montanism, but finally and above all, the existing situation of the Church in the third century with regard to the world within her pale, made the question of organisation the vital one for her. Tertullian and Origen already found themselves face to face with episcopal claims of which they highly disapproved and which, in their own way, they endeavoured to oppose. It was again the Roman bishop[2] who first converted the proposition that the bishops are direct successors of the Apostles and have the same " locus magisterii " ("place of government ") into a theory which declares that *all* apostolic powers have devolved on the bishops and that these have therefore peculiar rights and duties in virtue of their office. [3] Cyprian added to this the corresponding theory of the Church.

---

1 Both repeatedly and very decidedly declared that the unity of faith (the rule of faith) is sufficient for the unity of the Church, and that in other things there must be freedom (see above all Tertull., de orat., de bapt., and the Montanist writings). It is all the more worthy of note that, in the case of a question in which indeed the customs of the different countries were exceedingly productive of confusion, but which was certainly not a matter of faith, it was again a bishop of Rome, and that as far back as the 2nd century, who first made the observance of the Roman practice a condition of the unity of the Church and treated nonconformists as heterodox (Victor; see Euseb., H. E. V. 24). On the other hand Irenæus says: ἡ διαφωνία τῆς νηστείας τὴν ὁμόνοιαν τῆς πίστεως συνίστησι.

2 On Calixtus see Hippolyt., Philos. IX. 12, and Tertull., de pudic.

3 See on the other hand Tertull., de monog., but also Hippol., l.c.

In one decisive point, however, he did not assist the secularising process which had been completed by the Roman bishop, in the interest of Catholicity as well as in that of the Church's existence (see the following chapter). In the second half of the third century there were no longer any Churches, except remote communities, where the only requirement was to preserve the Catholic faith; the bishops had to be obeyed. The idea of the one episcopally organised Church became the main one and overshadowed the significance of the doctrine of faith as a bond of unity. *The Church based on the bishops, the successors of the Apostles, the vicegerents of God, is herself the legacy of the Apostles in virtue of this her foundation.* This idea was never converted into a rigid theory in the East, though the reality to which it corresponded was not the less certain on that account. The fancy that the earthly hierarchy was the image of the heavenly was the only part that began to be taken in real earnest. In the West, on the other hand, circumstances compelled the Carthaginian bishop to set up a finished theory. [1] According to Cyprian, the Catholic Church, to which all the lofty predictions and predicates in the Bible apply (see Hartel's index under "ecclesia"), is the one institution of salvation outside of which there is no redemption

---

[1] Cyprian's idea of the Church, an imitation of the conception of a political empire, viz., one great aristocratically governed state with an ideal head, is the result of the conflicts through which he passed. It is therefore first found in a complete form in the treatise "de unitate ecclesiæ" and, above all, in his later epistles (Epp. 43 sq. ed. Hartel). The passages in which Cyprian defines the Church as "constituta in episcopo et in clero et in omnibus credentibus" date from an earlier period, when he himself essentially retained the old idea of the subject. Moreover, he never regarded those elements as similar and of equal value. The limitation of the Church to the community ruled by bishops was the result of the Novatian crisis. The unavoidable necessity of excluding orthodox Christians from the ecclesiastical communion, or, in other words, the fact that such orthodox Christians had separated themselves from the majority guided by the bishops, led to the setting up of a new theory of the Church, which therefore resulted from stress of circumstances just as much as the antignostic conception of the matter held by Irenæus. Cyprian's notion of the relation between the whole body of the Church and the episcopate may, however, be also understood as a generalisation of the old theory about the connection between the individual community and the bishop. This already contained an œcumenical element, for, in fact, every separate community was regarded as a copy of the one Church, and its bishop therefore as the representative of God (Christ).

(ep. 73. 21). She is this, moreover, not only as the community possessing the true apostolic faith, for this definition does not exhaust her conception, but as a harmoniously organised federation.[1] This Church therefore rests entirely on the episcopate, which sustains her,[2] because it is the continuance of the apostolic office and is equipped with all the power of the Apostles.[3] Accordingly, the union of individuals with the Church, and therefore with Christ, is effected only by obedient dependence on the bishop, i.e., such a connection alone makes one a member of the Church. But the unity of the Church, which is an attribute of equal importance with her truth, because this union is only brought about by love,[4] primarily appears in the unity of the episcopate. For, according to Cyprian, the episcopate has been from its beginning undivided and has continued to be

[1] We need only quote one passage here—but see also epp. 69. 3, 7 sq.: 70. 2: 73. 8—ep. 55. 24: "Quod vero ad Novatiani personam pertinet, scias nos primo in loco nec curiosos esse debere quid ille doceat, cum foris doceat; quisquis ille est et qualiscunque est, christianus non est, qui in Christi ecclesia non est." In the famous sentence (ep. 74. 7; de unit. 6): "habere non potest deum patrem qui ecclesiam non habet matrem," we must understand the Church held together by the *sacramentum unitatis*, i.e., by her constitution. Cyprian is fond of referring to Korah's faction, who nevertheless held the same faith as Moses.

[2] Epp. 4. 4 : 33. 1: "ecclesia super episcopos constituta"; 43. 5 : 45. 3: "unitatem a domino et per apostolos nobis successoribus traditam"; 46. 1 : 66. 8: "scire debes episcopum in ecclesia esse et ecclesiam in episcopo et si qui cum episcopo non sit in ecclesia non esse"; de unit. 4.

[3] According to Cyprian the bishops are the *sacerdotes* κατ᾽ ἐξοχήν and the *iudices vice Christi*. See epp. 59. 5 : 66. 3 as well as c. 4: "Christus dicit ad apostolos ac per hoc ad omnes præpositos, qui apostolis vicaria ordinatione succedunt: qui audit vos me audit." Ep. 3. 3: "dominus apostolos, i. e., episcopos elegit"; ep. 75. 16.

[4] That is a fundamental idea and in fact the outstanding feature of the treatise "de unitate". The heretics and schismatics lack love, whereas the unity of the Church is the product of love, this being the main Christian virtue. That is the *ideal* thought on which Cyprian builds his theory (see also epp. 45. 1 : 55. 24 : 69. 1 and elsewhere), and not quite wrongly, in so far as his purpose was to gather and preserve, and not scatter. The reader may also recall the early Christian notion that Christendom should be a band of brethren ruled by love. But this love ceases to have any application to the case of those who are disobedient to the authority of the bishop and to Christians of the sterner sort. The appeal which Catholicism makes to love, even at the present day, in order to justify its secularised and tyrannical Church, turns in the mouth of hierarchical politicians into hypocrisy, of which one would like to acquit a man of Cyprian's stamp.

so in the Church, in so far as the bishops are appointed and
guided by God, are on terms of brotherly intercourse and exchange, and each bishop represents the whole significance of
the episcopate. [1] Hence the individual bishops are no longer
to be considered primarily as leaders of their special communities, but as the foundation of the one Church. Each of these
prelates, however, provided he keeps within the association of
the bishops, preserves the independent right of regulating the
circumstances of his own diocese. [2] But it also follows that

[1] Ep. 43. 5:55. 24: "episcopatus unus episcoporum multorum concordi num-
erositate diffusus"; de unit. 5: "episcopatus unus est, cuius a singulis in solidum
pars tenetur." Strictly speaking Cyprian did not set up a theory that the bishops
were directed by the Holy Spirit, but in identifying Apostles and bishops and
asserting the divine appointment of the latter he took for granted their special
endowment with the Holy Spirit. Moreover, he himself frequently appealed to
special communications he had received from the Spirit as aids in discharging his
official duties.

[2] Cyprian did not yet regard uniformity of Church practice as a matter of
moment—or rather he knew that diversities must be tolerated. In so far as the
*concordia episcoporum* was consistent with this diversity, he did not interfere with
the differences, provided the *regula fidei* was adhered to. Every bishop who
adheres to the confederation has the greatest freedom even in questions of Church
discipline and practice (as for instance in the baptismal ceremonial); see ep. 59.
14: "Singulis pastoribus portio gregis est adscripta, quam regit unusquisque et
gubernat rationem sui actus domino redditurus"; 55. 21: "Et quidem apud antecessores nostros quidam de episcopis istic in provincia nostra dandam pacis mœchis
non putaverunt et in totum pænitentiæ locum contra adulteria cluserunt, non tamen
a co-episcoporum suorum collegio recesserunt aut catholicæ ecclesiæ unitatem
ruperunt, ut quia apud alios adulteris pax dabatur, qui non dabat de ecclesia
separaretur." According to ep. 57. 5 Catholic bishops, who insist on the strict
practice of penance, but do not separate themselves from the unity of the Church,
are left to the judgment of God. It is different in the case referred to in ep. 68,
for Marcion had formally joined Novatian. Even in the disputed question of
heretical baptism (ep. 72. 3) Cyprian declares to Stephen (See 69. 17: 73. 26;
Sententiæ episc., præfat.): "qua in re nec nos vim cuiquam facimus aut legem
damus, quando habeat in ecclesiæ administratione voluntatis suæ arbitrium liberum
unusquisque præpositus, rationem actus sui domino redditurus." It is therefore
plain wherein the unity of the episcopate and the Church actually consists; we
may say that it is found in the *regula*, in the fixed purpose not to give up the unity
in spite of all differences, and in the principle of regulating all the affairs of the
Church "ad originem dominicam et ad evangelicam adque apostolicam traditionem"
(ep. 74. 10). This refers to the New Testament, which Cyprian emphatically insisted
on making the standard for the Church. It must be taken as the guide, "si in
aliquo in ecclesia nutaverit et vacillaverit veritas"; by it, moreover, all false customs
are to be corrected. In the controversy about heretical baptism, the alteration of

the bishops of those communities founded by the Apostles themselves can raise no claim to any special dignity, since the unity
of the episcopate as a continuation of the apostolic office involves the equality of all bishops. [1] However, a special importance attaches to the Roman see, because it is the seat of the
Apostle to whom Christ first granted apostolic authority in
order to show with unmistakable plainness the unity of these
powers and the corresponding unity of the Church that rests
on them; and further because, from her historical origin, the
Church of this see had become the mother and root of the
Catholic Church spread over the earth. In a severe crisis which
Cyprian had to pass through in his own diocese he appealed
to the Roman Church (the Roman bishop) in a manner which
made it appear as if communion with that Church was in itself
the guarantee of truth. But in the controversy about heretical
baptism with the Roman bishop Stephen, he emphatically
denied the latter's pretensions to exercise special rights over
the Church in consequence of the Petrine succession. [2] Finally,

Church practice in Carthage and Africa, which was the point in question—for
whilst in Asia heretical baptism had for a very long time been declared invalid
(see ep. 75. 19) this had only been the case in Carthage for a few years—was
justified by Cyprian through an appeal to *veritas* in contrast to *consuetudo sine
veritate.* See epp. 71. 2, 3 : 73. 13, 23 : 74. 2 sq.: 9 (the formula originates with
Tertullian; see de virg. vel. 1—3). The *veritas*, however, is to be learned from the
Gospel and words of the Apostles: "Lex evangelii", "præcepta dominica", and
synonymous expressions are very frequent in Cyprian, more frequent than reference
to the *regula* or to the symbol. In fact there was still no Church dogmatic, there
being only principles of Christian faith and life, which, however, were taken from
the Holy Scriptures and the *regula*.

1 Cyprian no longer makes any distinction between Churches founded by Apostles,
and those which arose later (that is, between their bishops).

2 The statement that the Church is "super Petrum fundata" is very frequently
made by Cyprian (we find it already in Tertullian, de monog.); see de habitu
virg. 10; Epp. 59. 7 : 66. 8 : 71. 3 : 74. 11 : 73. 7. But on the strength of Matth. XVI.
he went still farther; see ep. 43. 5: "deus unus est et Christus unus et una ecclesia
et cathedra una super Petrum domini voce fundata"; ep. 48. 3 (ad Cornel.): "communicatio tua, id est catholicæ ecclesiæ unitas pariter et caritas"; de unit. 4: "super-
unum ædificat ecclesiam, et quamvis apostolis omnibus post resurrectionem suam
parem potestatem tribuat, tamen ut unitatem manifestaret, unitatis eiusdem originem
ab uno incipientem sua auctoritate disposuit"; ep. 70. 3: "una ecclesia a Christo
domino nostro super Petrum origine unitatis et ratione fundata" ("with regard to the
origin and constitution of the unity" is the translation of this last passage in the

although Cyprian exalted the unity of the organisation of the
Church above the unity of the doctrine of faith, he preserved
the Christian element so far as to assume in all his statements
that the bishops display a moral and Christian conduct in keeping with their office, and that otherwise they have *ipso facto*
forfeited it. [1] Thus, according to Cyprian, the episcopal office
does not confer any indelible character, though Calixtus and other
bishops of Rome after him presupposed this attribute. (For
more details on this point, as well as with regard to the contra-

"Stimmen aus Maria Laach," 1877, part 8, p. 355; but "ratio" cannot mean that);
ep. 73. 7: "Petro primum dominus, super quem ædificavit ecclesiam et unde unitatis
originem instituit et ostendit, potestatem istam dedit." The most emphatic passages
are ep. 48. 3, where the Roman Church is called "matrix et radix ecclesiæ catholicæ" (the expression "radix et mater" in ep. 45. 1 no doubt also refers to her),
and ep. 59. 14: "navigare audent et ad Petri cathedram atque ad ecclesiam prin-
cipalem, unde unitas sacerdotalis exorta est, ab schismaticis et profanis litteras ferre
nec cogitare eos esse Romanos, quorum fides apostolo prædicante laudata est (see
epp. 30. 2, 3 : 60. 2), ad quos perfidia habere non possit accessum." We can see
most clearly from epp. 67. 5 and 68 what rights were in point of fact exercised
by the bishop of Rome. But the same Cyprian says quite naïvely, even at the time
when he exalted the Roman cathedra so highly (ep. 52. 2), "quoniam *pro magnitudine sua* debeat Carthaginem Roma præcedere." In the controversy about heretical
baptism Stephen like Calixtus (Tertull., de pudic. 1) designated himself, on the
ground of the *successio Petri* and by reference to Matth. XVI., in such a way that
one might suppose he wished to be regarded as "episcopus episcoporum" (Sentent.
episc. in Hartel I., p. 436). He expressly claimed a primacy and demanded obedience
from the "ecclesiæ novellæ et posteræ" (ep. 71. 3). Like Victor he endeavoured to
enforce the Roman practice "tyrannico terrore" and insisted that the *unitas ecclesiæ*
required the observance of this Church's practice in all communities. But Cyprian
opposed him in the most decided fashion, and maintained the principle that every
bishop, as a member of the episcopal confederation based on the *regula* and the
Holy Scriptures, is responsible for his practice to God alone. This he did in a
way which left no room for any special and actual authority of the Roman see
alongside of the others. Besides, he expressly rejected the conclusions drawn by
Stephen from the admittedly historical position of the Roman see (ep. 71. 3): "Petrus
non sibi vindicavit aliquid insolenter aut adroganter adsumpsit, ut diceret se principatum tenere et obtemperari a novellis et posteris sibi potius oportere." Firmilian,
ep. 75, went much farther still, for he indirectly declares the *successio Petri* claimed
by Stephen to be of no importance (c. 17), and flatly denies that the Roman Church
has preserved the apostolic tradition in a specially faithful way. See Otto Ritschl,
l. c., pp. 92 ff., 110—141. In his conflict with Stephen Cyprian unmistakably took
up a position inconsistent with his former views as to the significance of the Roman
see for the Church, though no doubt these were ideas he had expressed at a critical
time when he stood shoulder to shoulder with the Roman bishop Cornelius.

[1] See specially epp. 65, 67, 68.

dictions that remain unreconciled in Cyprian's conception of
the Church, see the following chapter, in which will be shown
the ultimate interests that lie at the basis of the new idea of
the Church).

ADDENDUM I. The great confederation of Churches which
Cyprian presupposes and which he terms *the* Church was in
truth not complete, for it cannot be proved that it extended
to any regions beyond the confines of the Roman Empire or
that it even embraced all orthodox and episcopally organised
communities within those bounds. [1] But, further, the conditions
of the confederation, which only began to be realised in the
full sense in the days of Constantine, were never definitely formulated—before the fourth century at least. [2] Accordingly, the
idea of the one exclusive Church, embracing all Christians and
founded on the bishops, was always a mere theory. But, in
so far as it is not the idea, but its realisation to which Cyprian
here attaches sole importance, his dogmatic conception appears
to be refuted by actual circumstances. [3]

II. The idea of heresy is always decided by the idea of the
Church. The designation αἵρεσις implies an adherence to some-

[1] Hatch l.c., p. 189 f.

[2] The gradual union of the provincial communities into one Church may be
studied in a very interesting way in the ecclesiastical Fasti (records, martyrologies,
calendars, etc.), though these studies are as yet only in an incipient stage. See De
Rossi, Roma Sotter, the Bollandists in the 12th vol. for October; Stevenson, Studi
in Italia (1879), pp. 439, 458; the works of Nilles; Egli, Altchristl. Studien 1887
(Theol. Lit. Ztg. 1887, no. 13): Duchesne, Les sources du Martyrol. Hieron. Rome
1885, but above all the latter's study: Mémoire sur l'origine des diocèses épiscopaux
dans l'ancienne Gaule, 1890. The history of the unification of liturgies from the
4th century should also be studied.

[3] There were communities in the latter half of the 3rd century, which can be
proved to have been outside the confederation, although in perfect harmony with
it in point of belief (see the interesting case in Euseb., H.E. VII. 24. 6). Conversely,
there were Churches in the confederation whose faith did not in all respects correspond with the Catholic *regula* as already expounded. But the fact that it was
not the dogmatic system, but the practical constitution and principles of the Church,
as based on a still elastic creed, which formed the ultimate determining factor, was
undoubtedly a great gain; for a system of dogmatics developed beyond the limits
of the Christian *kerygma* can only separate. Here, however, all differences of faith
had of course to be glossed over, for the demand of Apelles: μὴ δεῖν ὅλως ἐξε-
τάζειν τὸν λόγον, ἀλλ' ἕκαστον, ὡς πεπίστευκε, διαμένειν· σωθήσεσθαι γὰρ τοὺς ἐπὶ
τὸν ἐσταυρωμένον ἠλπικότας κ.τ.λ., was naturally regarded as inadmissible.

thing self-chosen in opposition to the acknowledgment of something objectively handed down, and assumes that this is the particular thing in which the apostasy consists. Hence all those who call themselves Christians and yet do not adhere to the traditional apostolic creed, but give themselves up to vain and empty doctrines, are regarded as heretics by Hegesippus, Irenæus, Tertullian, Clement, and Origen. These doctrines are as a rule traced to the devil, that is, to the non-Christian religions and speculations, or to wilful wickedness. Any other interpretation of their origin would at once have been an acknowledgment that the opponents of the Church had a right to their opinions, [1] and such an explanation is not quite foreign to Origen in one of his lines of argument. [2] Hence the orthodox party were perfectly consistent in attaching no value to any sacrament [3] or acts esteemed in their own communion, when these were performed by heretics; [4] and this was a practical application of the saying that the devil could transform himself into an angel of light. [5]

[1] Hence we need not be surprised to find that the notion of heresy which arose in the Church was immediately coupled with an estimate of it, which for injustice and harshness could not possibly be surpassed in succeeding times. The best definition is in Tertull., de præscr. 6: "Nobis nihil ex nostro arbitrio indulgere licet, sed nec eligere quod aliquis de arbitrio suo induxerit. Apostolos domini habemus auctores, qui nec ipsi quicquam ex suo arbitrio quod inducerent elegerunt, sed acceptam a Christo disciplinam fideliter nationibus assignaverunt."

[2] See Vol. I., p. 224, note 1.

[3] We already find this idea in Tertullian; see de bapt. 15: "Hæretici nullum habent consortium nostræ disciplinæ, quos extraneos utique testatur ipsa ademptio communicationis. Non debeo in illis cognoscere, quod mihi est præceptum, quia non idem deus est nobis et illis, nec unus Christus, id est idem, ideoque nec baptismus unus, quia non idem; quem cum rite non habeant, sine dubio non habent, nec capit numerari, quod non habetur; ita nec possunt accipere quia non habent." Cyprian passed the same judgment on all schismatics, even on the Novatians, and like Tertullian maintained the invalidity of heretical baptism. This question agitated the Church as early as the end of the 2nd century, when Tertullian already wrote against it in Greek.

[4] As far as possible the Christian virtues of the heretics were described as hypocrisy and love of ostentation (see *e.g.*, Rhodon in Euseb., H. E. V. 13. 2 and others in the second century). If this view was untenable, then all morality and heroism among heretics were simply declared to be of no value. See the anonymous writer in Eusebius, H. E. V. 16. 21, 22; Clem., Strom. VII. 16. 95; Orig., Comm. ad Rom. l. X., c. 5; Cypr., de unit. 14, 15; ep. 73. 21 etc.

[5] Tertull., de præscr. 3—6.

But the Fathers we have named did not yet completely identify the Church with a harmoniously organised institution. For that very reason they do not absolutely deny the Christianity of such as take their stand on the rule of faith, even when these for various reasons occupy a position peculiar to themselves. Though we are by no means entitled to say that they acknowledged orthodox schismatics, they did not yet venture to reckon them simply as heretics. [1] If it was desired to get rid of these, an effort was made to impute to them some deviation from the rule of faith; and under this pretext the Church freed herself from the Montanists and the Monarchians. [2] Cyprian was the first to proclaim the identity of heretics and schismatics, by making a man's Christianity depend on his belonging to the great episcopal Church confederation. [3] But, both in East

---

[1] Irenæus definitely distinguishes between heretics and schismatics (III. 11. 9: IV. 26. 2; 33. 7), but also blames the latter very severely, "qui gloriosum corpus Christi, quantum in ipsis est, interficiunt, non habentes dei dilectionem suamque utilitatem potius considerantes quam unitatem ecclesiæ." Note the parallel with Cyprian. Yet he does not class them with those "qui sunt extra veritatem," *i.e.*, "extra ecclesiam," although he declares the severest penalties await them. Tertullian was completely preserved by his Montanism from identifying heretics and schismatics, though in the last years of his life he also appears to have denied the Christianity of the Catholics (?).

[2] Read, on the one hand, the Antimontanists in Eusebius and the later opponents of Montanism; and on the other, Tertull., adv. Prax.; Hippol., c. Noët; Novatian, de trinitate. Even in the case of the Novatians heresies were sought and found (see Dionys. Alex., in Euseb., H. E. VII. 8, where we find distortions and wicked misinterpretations of Novatian doctrines, and many later opponents). Nay, even Cyprian himself did not disdain to join in this proceeding (see epp. 69. 7 : 70. 2). The Montanists at Rome were placed by Hippolytus in the catalogue of heretics (see the Syntagma and Philosoph.). Origen was uncertain whether to reckon them among schismatics or heretics (see in Tit. Opp. IV., p. 696).

[3] Cyprian plainly asserts (ep. 3. 3): "hæc sunt initia hæreticorum et ortus adque conatus schismaticorum, ut præpositum superbo tumore contemnant" (as to the early history of this conception, which undoubtedly has a basis of truth, see Clem., ep. ad Cor. I. 44; Ignat.; Hegesippus in Euseb., H. E. IV. 22. 5; Tertull., adv. Valent. 4; de bapt. 17; Anonymus in Euseb; H. E. V. 16. 7; Hippolyt. ad. Epiphan. H. 42. 1; Anonymus in Eusebius, H. E. V. 28. 12; according to Cyprian it is quite the common one); see further ep. 59. 3: "neque enim aliunde hæreses obortæ sunt aut nata sunt schismata, quam quando sacerdoti dei non obtemperatur"; epp. 66. 5 : 69. 1: "item b. apostolus Johannes nec ipse ullam hæresin aut schisma discrevit aut aliquos speciatim separes posuit"; 52. 1 : 73. 2 : 74. 11. Schism and heresy are always identical.

and West, this theory of his became established only by very imperceptible degrees, and indeed, strictly speaking, the process was never completed at all. The distinction between heretics and schismatics was preserved, because it prevented a public denial of the old principles, because it was advisable on political grounds to treat certain schismatic communities with indulgence, and because it was always possible in case of need to prove heresy against the schismatics. [1]

III. As soon as the empiric Church ruled by the bishops was proclaimed to be the foundation of the Christian religion, we have the fundamental premises for the conception that everything progressively adopted by the Church, all her functions, institutions, and liturgy, in short, all her continuously changing arrangements were holy and apostolic. But the courage to draw all the conclusions here was restrained by the fact that certain portions of tradition, such as the New Testament canon of Scripture and the apostolic doctrine, had been once for all exalted to an unapproachable height. Hence it was only with slowness and hesitation that Christians accepted the inferences from the idea of the Church in the remaining directions, and these conclusions always continued to be hampered with some degree of uncertainty. The idea of the παράδοσισ ἄγραφος (unwritten tradition); i.e., that every custom, however recent, within the sphere of outward regulations, of public worship, discipline, etc., is as holy and apostolic as the Bible and the "faith", never succeeded in gaining complete acceptance. In this case, complicated, uncertain, and indistinct assumptions were the result.

[1] Neither Optatus nor Augustine take Cyprian's theory as the starting-point of their disquisitions, but they adhere in principle to the distinction between heretic and schismatic. Cyprian was compelled by his special circumstances to identify them, but he united this identification with the greatest liberality of view as to the conditions of ecclesiastical unity (as regards individual bishops). Cyprian did not make a single new article an "articulus stantis et cadentis ecclesiæ". In fact he ultimately declared—and this may have cost him struggle enough—that even the question of the validity of heretical baptism was not a question of faith.

# CHAPTER III.

CONTINUATION. THE OLD CHRISTIANITY AND THE NEW CHURCH.

1. THE legal and political forms by which the Church secured herself against the secular power and heresy, and still more the lower moral standard exacted from her members in consequence of the naturalisation of Christianity in the world, called forth a reaction soon after the middle of the second century. This movement, which first began in Asia Minor and then spread into other regions of Christendom, aimed at preserving or restoring the old feelings and conditions, and preventing Christendom from being secularised. This crisis (the so-called Montanist struggle) and the kindred one which succeeded produced the following results: The Church merely regarded herself all the more strictly as a legal community basing the truth of its title on its historic and objective foundations, and gave a correspondingly new interpretation to the attribute of holiness she claimed. She expressly recognised two distinct classes in her midst, a spiritual and a secular, as well as a double standard of morality. Moreover, she renounced her character as the communion of those who were sure of salvation, and substituted the claim to be an educational institution and a necessary condition of redemption. After a keen struggle, in which the New Testament did excellent service to the bishops, the Church expelled the Cataphrygian fanatics and the adherents of the new prophecy (between 180 and 220); and in the same way, during the course of the third century, she caused the secession of all those Christians who made the truth of the Church depend on a stricter administration of moral discipline. Hence, apart from the heretic and Montanist sects, there existed in the Empire, after the middle of the second

century, two great but numerically unequal Church confeder-
ations, both based on the same rule of faith and claiming the
title "ecclesia catholica", viz., the confederation which Constantine afterwards chose for his support, and the Novatian Catharist
one. In Rome, however, the beginning of the great disruption
goes back to the time of Hippolytus and Calixtus; yet the
schism of Novatian must not be considered as an immediate
continuation of that of Hippolytus.

2. The so-called Montanist reaction [1] was itself subjected to
a similar change, in accordance with the advancing ecclesiastical
development of Christendom. It was originally the violent
undertaking of a Christian prophet, Montanus, who, supported
by prophetesses, felt called upon to realise the promises held
forth in the Fourth Gospel. He explained these by the Apocalypse, and declared that he himself was the Paraclete whom
Christ had promised—that Paraclete in whom Jesus Christ himself, nay, even God the Father Almighty, comes to his own
to guide them to all truth, to gather those that are dispersed,
and to bring them into one flock. His main effort therefore
was to make Christians give up the local and civil relations
in which they lived, to collect them, and create a new undivided
Christian commonwealth, which, separated from the world, should
prepare itself for the descent of the Jerusalem from above. [2]

---

[1] See Ritschl, l. c.; Schwegler, Der Montanismus, 1841; Gottwald, De Montanismo
Tertulliani, 1862; Réville, Tertull. et le Montanisme, in the Revue des Deux Mondes
of 1st Novr. 1864; Stroehlin, Essai sur le Montanisme, 1870; De Soyres, Mont-
anism and the Primitive Church, 1878; Cunningham, The Churches of Asia, 1880;
Renan, Les Crises du Catholicisme Naissant in the Revue des Deux Mondes of 15th
Febr. 1881; Renan, Marc Aurèle, 1882, p. 208 ff.; Bonwetsch, Geschichte des
Montanismus, 1881; Harnack, Das Mönchthum, seine Ideale und seine Geschichte,
3rd. ed., 1886; Belck, Geschichte des Montanismus, 1883; Voigt, Eine verschollene
Urkunde des antimontanistischen Kampfes, 1891. Further the articles on Montanism
by Möller (Herzog's Real-Encyklopädie), Salmon (Dictionary of Christian Biography),
and Harnack (Encyclopedia Britannica). Weizsäcker in the Theologische Litter-
aturzeitung, 1882, no. 4; Bonwetsch, Die Prophetie im apostolischen und nach-
apostolischen Zeitalter in der Zeitschrift für kirchliche Wissenschaft und kirchliches
Leben, 1884, Parts 8, 9; M. von Engelhardt, Die ersten Versuche zur Aufrichtung
des wahren Christenthums in einer Gemeinde von Heiligen, Riga, 1881.

[2] In certain vital points the conception of the original nature and history of
Montanism, as sketched in the following account, does not correspond with that
traditionally current. To establish it in detail would lead us too far. It may be

The natural resistance offered to the new prophets with this extravagant message—especially by the leaders of communities, and the persecutions to which the Church was soon after subjected under Marcus Aurelius, led to an intensifying of the eschatological expectations that beyond doubt had been specially keen in Montanist circles from the beginning. For the New Jerusalem was soon to come down from heaven in visible form, and establish itself in the spot which, by direction of the Spirit, had been chosen for Christendom in Phrygia. [1] Whatever amount of peculiarity the movement lost, in so far as the ideal of an assembly of all Christians proved incapable of being realised or at least only possible within narrow limits, was abundantly restored in the last decades of the second century by the strength and courage that the news of its spread in Christendom gave to the earnest minded to unite and offer resistance to the ever increasing tendency of the Church to assume a secular and political character. Many entire commu-

noted that the mistakes in estimating the original character of this movement arise from a superficial examination of the oracles preserved to us and from the unjustifiable practice of interpreting them in accordance with their later application in the circles of Western Montanists. A completely new organisation of Christendom, beginning with the Church in Asia, to be brought about by its being detached from the bonds of the communities and collected into one region, was the main effort of Montanus. In this way he expected to restore to the Church a spiritual character and fulfil the promises contained in John. That is clear from Euseb., V. 16 ff. as well as from the later history of Montanism in its native land (see Jerome, ep. 41; Epiphan., H. 49. 2 etc.). In itself, however, apart from its particular explanation in the case of Montanus, the endeavour to detach Christians from the local Church unions has so little that is striking about it, that one rather wonders at being unable to point to any parallel in the earliest history of the Church. Wherever religious enthusiasm has been strong, it has at all times felt that nothing hinders its effect more than family ties and home connections. But it is just from the absence of similar undertakings in the earliest Christianity that we are justified in concluding that the strength of enthusiastic exaltation is no standard for the strength of *Christian* faith. (Since these words were written, we have read in Hippolytus' Commentary on Daniel [see Georgiades in the journal Ἐκκλ. ἀλήθεια, 1885, p. 52 sq.] very interesting accounts of such undertakings in the time of Septimius Severus. A Syrian bishop persuaded many brethren with wives and children to go to meet Christ in the wilderness; and another in Pontus induced his people to sell all their possessions, to cease tilling their lands, to conclude no more marriages etc., because the coming of the Lord was nigh at hand).

[1] Oracle of Prisca in Epiph. H. 49. 1.

nities in Phrygia and Asia recognised the divine mission of the prophets. In the Churches of other provinces religious societies were formed in which the predictions of these prophets were circulated and viewed as a Gospel, though at the same time they lost their effect by being so treated. The confessors at Lyons openly expressed their full sympathy with the movement in Asia. The bishop of Rome was on the verge of acknowledging the Montanists to be in full communion with the Church. But among themselves there was no longer, as at the beginning, any question of a new organisation in the strict sense of the word, and of a radical remodelling of Christian society. [1] Whenever Montanism comes before us in the clear light of history it rather appears as a religious movement already deadened, though still very powerful. Montanus and his prophetesses had set no limits to their enthusiasm; nor were there as yet any fixed barriers in Christendom that could have restrained them. [2] The Spirit, the Son, nay, the Father himself had appeared in them and spoke through them. [3] Imagination pic-

[1] Even in its original home Montanism must have accommodated itself to circumstances at a comparatively early date—which is not in the least extraordinary. No doubt the Montanist Churches in Asia and Phrygia, to which the bishop of Rome had already issued *literæ pacis*, were now very different from the original followers of the prophets (Tertull., adv. Prax. 1). When Tertullian further reports that Praxeas at the last moment prevented them from being recognised by the bishop of Rome, "falsa de ipsis prophetis et ecclesiis eorum adseverando", the "falsehood about the Churches" may simply have consisted in an account of the original tendencies of the Montanist sect. The whole unique history which, in spite of this, Montanism undoubtedly passed through in its original home is, however, explained by the circumstance that there were districts there, where all Christians belonged to that sect (Epiph., H. 51. 33; cf. also the later history of Novatianism). In their peculiar Church organisation (patriarchs, stewards, bishops), these sects preserved a record of their origin.

[2] Special weight must be laid on this. The fact that whole communities became followers of the new prophets, who nevertheless adhered to no old regulation, must above all be taken into account.

[3] See Oracles 1, 3, 4, 5, 10, 12, 17, 18, 21 in Bonwetsch, l.c., p. 197 f. It can hardly have been customary for Christian prophets to speak like Montanus (Nos. 3—5): ἐγὼ κύριος ὁ θεὸς ὁ παντοκράτωρ καταγινόμενος ἐν ἀνθρώπῳ, or ἐγὼ κύριος ὁ θεὸς πατὴρ ἦλθον, or ἐγὼ εἰμί ὁ πατὴρ καὶ ὁ υἱὸς καὶ ὁ παράκλητος, though Old Testament prophecy takes an analogous form. Maximilla says on one occasion (No. 11); ἀπέστειλέ με κύριος τούτου τοῦ πόνου καὶ τῆς συνθήκης καὶ τῆς ἐπαγγελίας αἱρετιστήν; and a second time (No. 12): διώκομαι ὡς λύκος ἐκ προβάτων· οὐκ εἰμὶ λύκος· ῥῆμά

tured Christ bodily in female form to the eyes of Prisca.[1]
The most extravagant promises were given.[2] These prophets
spoke in a loftier tone than any Apostle ever did, and they
were even bold enough to overturn apostolic regulations.[3] They
set up new commandments for the Christian life, regardless of
any tradition,[4] and they inveighed against the main body of

εἰμὶ καὶ πνεῦμα καὶ δύναμις. The two utterances do not exclude, but include, one
another (cf. also No. 10: ἐμοῦ μὴ ἀκούσητε ἀλλὰ Χριστοῦ ἀκούσατε). From James
IV. V. and Hermas, and from the Didache, on the other hand, we can see how the
prophets of Christian communities may have usually spoken.

[1] L.c., no. 9: Χριστὸς ἐν ἰδέᾳ γυναικὸς ἐσχηματισμένος. How variable must the
misbirths of the Christian imagination have been in this respect also! Unfortunately
almost everything of that kind has been lost to us because it has been suppressed.
The fragments of the once highly esteemed Apocalypse of Peter are instructive,
for they still attest that the existing remains of early Christian literature are not
able to give a correct picture of the strength of religious imagination in the first
and second centuries. The passages where Christophanies are spoken of in the
earliest literature would require to be collected. It would be shown what naïve
enthusiasm existed. Jesus appears to believers as a child, as a boy, as a youth, as
Paul etc. Conversely, glorified men appear in visions with the features of Christ.

[2] See Euseb., H. E. V. 16. 9. In Oracle No. 2 an evangelical promise is repeated
in a heightened form; but see Papias in Iren., V. 33. 3 f.

[3] We may unhesitatingly act on the principle that the Montanist elements, as
they appear in Tertullian, are, in all cases, found not in a strengthened, but a
weakened, form. So, when even Tertullian still asserts that the Paraclete in the
new prophets could overturn or change, and actually did change, regulations of
the Apostles, there is no doubt that the new prophets themselves did not adhere
to apostolic dicta and had no hesitation in deviating from them. Cf., moreover,
the direct declarations on this point in Hippolytus (Syntagma and Philos. VIII. 19)
and in Didymus (de trin. III. 41. 2).

[4] The precepts for a Christian life, if we may so speak, given by the new
prophets, cannot be determined from the compromises on which the discipline of
the later Montanist societies of the Empire were based. Here they sought for a
narrow line between the Marcionite and Encratite mode of life and the common
church practice, and had no longer the courage and the candour to proclaim the
"e sæculo excedere". Sexual purity and the renunciation of the enjoyments of
life were the demands of the new prophets. But it is hardly likely that they
prescribed precise "laws", for the primary matter was not asceticism, but the
realising of a promise. In later days it was therefore possible to conceive the
most extreme demands as regulations referring to none but the prophets themselves,
and to tone down the oracles in their application to believers. It is said of
Montanus himself (Euseb., H. E. V. 18. 2): ὁ διδάξας λύσεις γάμων, ὁ νηστείας
νομοθετήσας; Prisca was a παρθένος (l.c. § 3); Proculus, the chief of the Roman
Montanists, "virginis senectæ" (Tert., adv. Val. 5). The oracle of Prisca (No. 8)
declares that sexual purity is the preliminary condition for the oracles and visions

Christendom. [1] They not only proclaimed themselves as prophets, but as the last prophets, as notable prophets in whom was first fulfilled the promise of the sending of the Paraclete. [2] These Christians as yet knew nothing of the "absoluteness of

of God; it is presupposed in the case of every "sanctus minister". Finally, Origen tells us (in Titum, Opp. IV. 696) that the (older) Cataphrygians said: "ne accedas ad me, quoniam mundus sum; non enim accepi uxorem, nec est sepulcrum patens guttur meum, sed sum Nazarenus dei non bibens vinum sicut illi". But an express legal direction to abolish marriage cannot have existed in the collection of oracles possessed by Tertullian. But who can guarantee that they were not already corrected? Such an assumption, however, is not necessary.

[1] Euseb., V. 16. 9 : V. 18. 5.

[2] It will not do simply to place Montanus and his two female associates in the same category as the prophets of primitive Christian Churches. The claim that the Spirit had descended upon them in unique fashion must have been put forth by themselves with unmistakable clearness. If we apply the principle laid down on p. 98, note 3, we will find that—apart from the prophets' own utterances—this is still clearly manifest from the works of Tertullian. A consideration of the following facts will remove all doubt as to the claim of the new prophets to the possession of an unique mission. (1) From the beginning both opponents and followers constantly applied the title "New Prophecy" to the phenomenon in question (Euseb., V. 16. 4 : V. 19. 2; Clem., Strom. IV. 13. 93; Tertull., monog. 14, ieiun. 1, resurr. 63, Marc. III. 24 : IV. 22, Prax. 30; Firmil. ep. 75. 7; alii). (2) Similarly, the divine afflatus was, from the first, constantly designated as the "Paraclete" (Orac. no. 5; Tertull. passim; Hippol. passim; Didymus etc.). (3) Even in the third century the Montanist congregations of the Empire must still have doubted whether the Apostles had possessed this Paraclete or not, or at least whether this had been the case in the full sense. Tertullian identifies the Spirit and the Paraclete and declares that the Apostles possessed the latter in full measure—in fact as a Catholic he could not do otherwise. Nevertheless he calls Montanus etc. "prophetæ proprii" of the Spirit (pudic. 12; see Acta Perpet. 21). On the contrary we find in Philos. VIII. 19: ὑπὲρ δὲ ἀποστόλους καὶ πᾶν χάρισμα ταῦτα τὰ γύναια δοξάζουσιν, ὡς τολμᾶν πλεῖόν τι Χριστοῦ ἐν τούτοις λέγειν τινὰς αὐτῶν γεγονέναι. Pseudo-Tertullian says: "in apostolis quidem dicunt spiritum sanctum fuisse, paracletum non fuisse, et paracletum plura in Montano dixisse quam Christum in evangelio protulisse." In Didymus, l.c., we read: τοῦ ἀποστόλου γράψαντος κ.τ.λ., ἐκεῖνοι λέγουσιν τὸν Μοντανὸν ἐληλυθέναι καὶ ἐσχηκέναι τὸ τέλειον τὸ τοῦ παρακλήτου, τοῦτ' ἔστιν τὸ τοῦ ἁγίου πνεύματος. (4) Lastly, the Montanists asserted that the prediction contained in John XIV. ff. had been fulfilled in the new prophecy, and that from the beginning, as is denoted by the very expression "Paraclete."

What sort of mission they ascribed to themselves is seen from the last quoted passage, for the promises contained in it must be regarded as the enthusiastic carrying out of Montanus' programme. If we read attentively John XIV. 16—21, 23, 26 : XV. 20—26 : XVI. 7—15, 25 as well as XVII. and X.; if we compare the oracles of the prophets still preserved to us; if we consider the attempt of Montanus to gather the scattered Christians and really form them into a flock, and also a historically complete revelation of Christ as the fundamental condition of Christian consciousness;" they only felt a Spirit to which they yielded unconditionally and without reserve. But, after they had quitted the scene, their followers sought and found a kind of compromise. The Montanist congregations that sought for recognition in Rome, whose part was taken by the Gallic confessors, and whose principles gained a footing in North Africa, may have stood in the same relation to the original adherents of the new prophets and to these prophets themselves, as the Mennonite communities did to the primitive Anabaptists and their empire in Münster. The "Montanists" outside of Asia Minor acknowledged to the fullest extent the legal position of the great Church. They declared their adher-

his claim to be the bearer of the greatest and last revelations that lead to all truth; and, finally, if we call to mind that in those Johannine discourses Christ designated the coming of the Paraclete as his own coming in the Paraclete and spoke of an immanence and unity of Father, Son, and Paraclete, which one finds re-echoed in Montanus' Oracle No. V., we cannot avoid concluding that the latter's undertaking is based on the impression made on excited and impatient prophets by the promises contained in the Gospel of John, understood in an apocalyptic and realistic sense, and also by Matt. XXIII. 34 (see Euseb., V. 16. 12 sq.). The correctness of this interpretation is proved by the fact that the first decided opponents of the Montanists in Asia—the so-called " Alogi" (Epiph., H. 51)—rejected both the Gospel and Revelation of John, that is, regarded them as written by some one else. Montanism therefore shows us the first and—up till about 180—really the only impression made by the Gospel of John on non-Gnostic Gentile Christians; and what a remarkable one it was! It has a parallel in Marcion's conception of Paulinism. Here we obtain glimpses of a state of matters which probably explains why these writings were made innocuous in the canon. To the view advanced here it cannot be objected that the later adherents of the new prophets founded their claims on the recognised gift of prophecy in the Church, or on a prophetic succession (Euseb., H. E. V. 17. 4; Proculus in the same author, II. 25. 7 : III. 31. 4), nor that Tertullian, when it suits him, simply regards the new prophecy as a *restitutio* (*e.g.*, in Monog. 4); for these assumptions merely represent the unsuccessful attempt to legitimise this phenomenon within the Catholic Church. In proof of the fact that Montanus appealed to the Gospel of John see Jerome, Ep. 41 (Migne I. p. 474), which begins with the words: "Testimonia de Johannis evangelio congregata, quæ tibi quidam Montani sectator ingessit, in quibus salvator noster se ad patrem iturum missurumque paracletum pollicetur etc." In opposition to this Jerome argues that the promises about the Paraclete are fulfilled in Acts II., as Peter said in his speech, and then continues as follows: "Quodsi voluerint respondere et Philippi deinceps quattuor filias prophetasse **et** prophetam Agabum reperiri et in divisionibus spiritus inter apostolos et doctores et prophetas quoque apostolo scribente formatos, etc."

ence to the apostolic "regula" and the New Testament canon. [1] The organisation of the Churches, and, above all, the position of the bishops as successors of the Apostles and guardians of doctrine were no longer disputed. The distinction between them and the main body of Christendom, from which they were unwilling to secede, was their belief in the new prophecy of Montanus, Prisca, and Maximilla, which was contained, in its final form, in written records and in this shape may have produced the same impression as is excited by the fragments of an exploded bomb. [2]

In this new prophecy they recognised a *subsequent revelation* of God, which for that very reason assumed the existence of a previous one. This after-revelation professed to decide the practical questions which, at the end of the second century, were burning topics throughout all Christendom, and for which no direct divine law could hitherto be adduced, in the form of a strict injunction. Herein lay the importance of the new prophecy for its adherents in the Empire, and for this reason they believed in it. [3] The belief in the efficacy of the Para-

[1] We are assured of this not only by Tertullian, but also by the Roman Montanist Proculus, who, like the former, argued against heretics, and by the testimony of the Church Fathers (see, *e.g.*, Philos. VIII. 19). It was chiefly on the ground of their orthodoxy that Tertullian urged the claim of the new prophets to a hearing; and it was, above all, as a Montanist that he felt himself capable of combating the Gnostics, since the Paraclete not only confirmed the *regula*, but also by unequivocal utterances cleared up ambiguous and obscure passages in the Holy Scriptures, and (as was asserted) completely rejected doctrines like the Monarchian (see fuga 1, 14; corona 4; virg. vel. 1; Prax. 2, 13, 30; resurr. 63; pud. 1; monog. 2; ieiun. 10, 11). Besides, we see from Tertullian's writings that the secession of the Montanist conventicles from the Church was forced upon them.

[2] The question as to whether the new prophecy had or had not to be recognised as such became the decisive one (fuga 1, 14; coron. 1; virg. vel. 1; Prax. 1; pudic. 11; monog. 1). This prophecy was recorded in writing (Euseb., V. 18. 1; Epiph., H. 48. 10; Euseb., VI. 20). The putting of this question, however, denoted a fundamental weakening of conviction, which was accompanied by a corresponding falling off in the application of the prophetic utterances.

[3] The situation that preceded the acceptance of the new prophecy in a portion of Christendom may be studied in Tertullian's writings "de idolol." and "de spectac." Christianity had already been conceived as a *nova lex* throughout the whole Church, and this *lex* had, moreover, been clearly defined in its bearing on the faith. But, as regards outward conduct, there was no definite *lex*, and arguments in favour both of strictness and of laxity were brought forward from the Holy

clete, who, in order to establish a relatively stricter standard
of conduct in Christendom during the latter days, had, a few
decades before, for several years given his revelations in a
remote corner of the Empire, was the dregs of the original
enthusiasm, the real aspect of which had been known only to
the fewest. But the diluted form in which this force remained
was still a mighty power, because it was just in the generation
between 190 and 220 that the secularising of the Church had
made the greatest strides. Though the followers of the new
prophecy merely insisted on abstinence from second marriage,
on stricter regulations with regard to fasts, on a stronger
manifestation of the Christian spirit in daily life, in morals and
customs, and finally on the full resolve not to avoid suffering
and martyrdom for Christ's name's sake, but to bear them
willingly and joyfully, [1] yet, under the given circumstances,
these requirements, in spite of the express repudiation of everything " Encratite," [2] implied a demand that directly endangered
the conquests already made by the Church and impeded
the progress of the new propaganda. [3] The people who put
forth these demands, expressly based them on the injunctions
of the Paraclete, and really lived in accordance with them,
were not permanently capable of maintaining their position in
the Church. In fact, the endeavour to found these demands

Scriptures. No divine ordinances about morality could be adduced against the
progressive secularising of Christianity; but there was need of statutory commandments by which all the limits were clearly defined. In this state of perplexity the
oracles of the new prophets were gladly welcomed; they were utilised in order to
justify and invest with divine authority a reaction of a moderate kind. More than
that—as may be inferred from Tertullian's unwilling confession—could not be
attained; but it is well known that even this result was not reached. Thus the
Phrygian movement was employed in support of undertakings, that had no real
connection with it. But this was the form in which Montanism first became a
factor in the history of the Church. To what extent it had been so before, particularly as regards the creation of a New Testament canon (in Asia Minor and Rome),
cannot be made out with certainty.

[1] See Bonwetsch, l.c., p. 82—108.

[2] This is the point about which Tertullian's difficulties are greatest. Tatian is
expressly repudiated in de ieiun. 15.

[3] Tertullian (de monog.) is not deterred by such a limitation : " qui potest capere
capiat, inquit, id est qui non potest discedat."

on the legislation of the Paraclete was an undertaking quite as strange, in form and content, as the possible attempt to represent the wild utterances of determined anarchists as the programme of a constitutional government. It was of no avail that they appealed to the confirmation of the rule of faith by the Paraclete; that they demonstrated the harmlessness of the new prophecy, thereby involving themselves in contradictions; [1] that they showed all honour to the New Testament; and that they did not insist on the oracles of the Paraclete being inserted in it. [2] As soon as they proved the earnestness of their temper-

[1] It is very instructive, but at the same time very painful, to trace Tertullian's endeavours to reconcile the irreconcilable, in other words, to show that the prophecy is new and yet not so; that it does not impair the full authority of the New Testament and yet supersedes it. He is forced to maintain the theory that the Paraclete stands in the same relation to the Apostles as Christ does to Moses, and that he abrogates the concessions made by the Apostles and even by Christ himself; whilst he is at the same time obliged to reassert the sufficiency of both Testaments. In connection with this he hit upon the peculiar theory of stages in revelation—a theory which, were it not a mere expedient in his case, one might regard as the first faint trace of a historical view of the question. Still, this is another case of a dilemma, furnishing theology with a conception that she has cautiously employed in succeeding times, when brought face to face with certain difficulties; see virg. vel. 1; exhort. 6; monog. 2, 3, 14; resurr. 63. For the rest, Tertullian is at bottom a Christian of the old stamp; the theory of any sort of finality in revelation is of no use to him except in its bearing on heresy; for the Spirit continually guides to all truth and works wherever he will. Similarly, his only reason for not being an Encratite is that this mode of life had already been adopted by heretics, and become associated with dualism. But the conviction that all religion must have the character of a fixed *law* and presupposes definite regulations—a belief not emanating from primitive Christianity, but from Rome—bound him to the Catholic Church. Besides, the contradictions with which he struggled were by no means peculiar to him; in so far as the Montanist societies accepted the Catholic regulations, they weighed on them all, and in all probability crushed them out of existence. In Asia Minor, where the breach took place earlier, the sect held its ground longer. In North Africa the residuum was a remarkable propensity to visions, holy dreams, and the like. The feature which forms the peculiar characteristic of the Acts of Perpetua and Felicitas is still found in a similar shape in Cyprian himself, who makes powerful use of visions and dreams; and in the genuine African Acts of the Martyrs, dating from Valerian's time, which are unfortunately little studied. See, above all, the Acta Jacobi, Mariani etc., and the Acta Montani, Lucii etc. (Ruinart, Acta Mart. edit Ratisb. 1859, p. 268 sq., p. 275 sq.)

[2] Nothing is known of attempts at a formal incorporation of the Oracles with the New Testament. Besides, the Montanists could dispense with this because they distinguished the commandments of the Paraclete as "novissima lex" from the

ate but far-reaching demands, a deep gulf that neither side
could ignore opened up between them and their opponents.
Though here and there an earnest effort was made to avoid a
schism, yet in a short time this became unavoidable; for variations in rules of conduct make fellowship impossible. The lax
Christians, who, on the strength of their objective possession,
viz., the apostolic doctrine and writings, sought to live comfortably by conforming to the ways of the world, necessarily sought
to rid themselves of inconvenient societies and inconvenient
monitors; [1] and they could only do so by reproaching the latter
with heresy and unchristian assumptions. Moreover, the followers of the new prophets could not permanently recognise the
Churches of the "Psychical," [2] which rejected the "Spirit" and
extended their toleration so far as to retain even whoremongers
and adulterers within their pale.

In the East, that is, in Asia Minor, the breach between the
Montanists and the Church had in all probability broken out
before the question of Church discipline and the right of the
bishops had yet been clearly raised. In Rome and Carthage
this question completed the rupture that had already taken
place between the conventicles and the Church (de pudic. 1.21).
Here, by a peremptory edict, the bishop of Rome claimed the
right of forgiving sins as successor of the Apostles; and declared that he would henceforth exercise this right in favour of
repentant adulterers. Among the Montanists this claim was

"novum testamentum." The preface to the Montanist Acts of Perpetua and
Felicitas (was Tertullian the author?) showed indeed the high value attached to the
visions of martyrs. In so far as these were to be read in the Churches they were
meant to be reckoned as an "instrumentum ecclesiæ" in the wider sense.

[1] Here the bishops themselves occupy the foreground (there are complaints about
their cowardice and serving of two masters in the treatise de fuga). But it would
be very unjust simply to find fault with them as Tertullian does. Two interests
combined to influence their conduct; for if they drew the reins tight they gave
over their flock to heresy or heathenism. This situation is already evident in
Hermas and dominates the resolutions of the Church leaders in succeeding
generations (see below).

[2] The distinction of "Spiritales" and "Psychici" on the part of the Montanists
is not confined to the West (see Clem., Strom. IV. 13. 93); we find it very
frequently in Tertullian. In itself it did not yet lead to the formal breach with
the Catholic Church.

violently contested both in an abstract sense and in this application of it. The Spirit the Apostles had received, they said,
could not be transmitted; the Spirit is given to the Church;
he works in the prophets, but lastly and in the highest measure
in the new prophets. The latter, however, expressly refused
to readmit gross sinners, though recommending them to the
grace of God (see the saying of the Paraclete, de pud. 21;
"potest ecclesia donare delictum, sed non faciam"). Thus agreement was no longer possible. The bishops were determined
to assert the existing claims of the Church, even at the cost
of her Christian character, or to represent the constitution of
the Catholic Church as the guarantee of that character. At the
risk of their own claim to be Catholic, the Montanist sects resisted in order to preserve the minimum legal requirements for
a Christian life. Thus the opposition culminated in an attack
on the new powers claimed by the bishops, and in consequence
awakened old memories as to the original state of things, when
the clergy had possessed no importance. [1] But the ultimate
motive was the effort to stop the continuous secularising of the
Christian life and to preserve the virginity of the Church as a
holy community. [2] In his latest writings Tertullian vigorously

---

[1] A contrast to the bishops and the regular congregational offices existed in
primitive Montanism. This was transmitted in a weakened form to the later
adherents of the new prophecy (cf. the Gallic confessors' strange letter of recom-
mendation on behalf of Irenæus in Euseb., H. E. V. 4), and finally broke forth
with renewed vigour in opposition to the measures of the lax bishops (de pudic.
21; de exhort. 7; Hippolytus against Calixtus). The *ecclesia*, represented as *numerus episcoporum*, no longer preserved its prestige in the eyes of Tertullian.

[2] See here particularly, de pudicitia 1, where Tertullian sees the virginity of the
Church not in pure doctrine, but in strict precepts for a holy life. As will have
been seen in this account, the oft debated question as to whether Montanism was an
innovation or merely a reaction does not admit of a simple answer. In its
original shape it was undoubtedly an innovation; but it existed at the end of a
period when one cannot very well speak of innovations, because no bounds had
yet been set to subjective religiosity. Montanus decidedly went further than any
Christian prophets known to us; Hermas, too, no doubt gave injunctions, as a
prophet, which gave rise to innovations in Christendom; but these fell short of
Montanus' proceedings. In its later shape, however, Montanism was to all intents
and purposes a reaction, which aimed at maintaining or reviving an older state of
things. So far, however, as this was to be done by legislation, by a *novissima
lex*, we have an evident innovation analogous to the Catholic development. Whereas

defended a position already lost, and carried with him to the grave the old strictness of conduct insisted on by the Church.

Had victory remained with the stricter party, which, though not invariably, appealed to the injunctions of the Paraclete, [1] the Church would have been rent asunder and decimated. The great opportunist party, however, was in a very difficult position, since their opponents merely seemed to be acting up to a conception that, in many respects, could not be theoretic- ally disputed. The problem was how to carry on with caution the work of naturalising Christianity in the world, and at the same time avoid all appearance of innovation which, as such, was opposed to the principle of Catholicism. The bishops therefore assailed the form of the new prophecy on the ground of innovation; [2] they sought to throw suspicion on its content; in some cases even Chiliasm, as represented by the Montanists, was declared to have a Jewish and fleshly character. [3] They tried to show that the moral demands of their opponents were extravagant, that they savoured of the ceremonial law (of the Jews), were opposed to Scripture, and were derived from the worship of Apis, Isis, and the mother of the Gods. [4]  To the

in former times exalted enthusiasm had of itself, as it were, given rise to strict principles of conduct among its other results, these principles, formulated with exactness and detail, were now meant to preserve or produce that original mode of life. Moreover, as soon as the New Testament was recognised, the conception of a subsequent revelation through the Paraclete was a highly questionable and strange innovation. But for those who acknowledged the new prophecy all this was ultimately nothing but a means. Its practical tendency, based as it was on the conviction that the Church abandons her character if she does not resist gross secularisation at least, was no innovation, but a defence of the most elementary requirements of primitive Christianity in opposition to a Church that was always more and more becoming a new thing.

[1] There were of course a great many intermediate stages between the extremes of laxity and rigour, and the new prophecy was by no means recognised by all those who had strict views as to the principles of Christian polity; see the letters of Dionysius of Corinth in Euseb., H. E. IV. 23. Melito, the prophet, eunuch, and bishop, must also be reckoned as one of the stricter party, but not as a Montanist. We must judge similarly of Irenæus.

[2] Euseb., H. E. V. 16. 17. The life of the prophets themselves was subse- quently subjected to sharp criticism.

[3] This was first done by the so-called Alogi who, however, had to be repudiated.

[4] De ieiun. 12, 16.

claim of furnishing the Church with authentic oracles of God, set up by their antagonists, the bishops opposed the newly formed canon; and declared that everything binding on Christians was contained in the utterances of the Old Testament prophets and the Apostles. Finally, they began to distinguish between the standard of morality incumbent on the clergy and a different one applying to the laity, [1] as, for instance, in the question of a single marriage; and they dwelt with increased emphasis on the glory of the heroic Christians, *belonging to the great Church*, who had distinguished themselves by asceticism and joyful submission to martyrdom. By these methods they brought into disrepute that which had once been dear to the whole Church, but was now of no further service. In repudiating supposed abuses they more and more weakened the regard felt for the thing itself, as, for example, in the case of the so-called Chiliasm, [2] congregational prophecy and the spiritual independence of the laity. But none of these things could be absolutely rejected; hence, for example, Chiliasm remained virtually unweakened (though subject to limitations [3]) in the West and certain districts of the East; whereas prophecy lost its force so much that it appeared harmless and therefore died away. [4]

[1] Tertullian protested against this in the most energetic manner.

[2] It is well known that in the 3rd century the Revelation of John itself was viewed with suspicion and removed from the canon in wide circles in the East.

[3] In the West the Chiliastic hopes were little or not at all affected by the Montanist struggle. Chiliasm prevailed there in unimpaired strength as late as the 4th century. In the East, on the contrary, the apocalyptic expectations were immediately weakened by the Montanist crisis. But it was philosophical theology that first proved their mortal enemy. In the rural Churches of Egypt Chiliasm was still widely prevalent after the middle of the 3rd century; see the instructive 24th chapter of Eusebius' Ecclesiastical History, Book VII. "Some of their teachers," says Dionysius, "look on the Law and the Prophets as nothing, neglect to obey the Gospel, esteem the Epistles of the Apostles as little worth, but, on the contrary, declare the doctrine contained in the Revelation of John to be a great and a hidden mystery." There were even temporary disruptions in the Egyptian Church on account of Chiliasm (see Chap. 24. 6).

[4] "Lex et prophetæ usque ad Johannem" now became the motto. Churchmen spoke of a "completus numerus prophetarum" (Muratorian Fragment), and formulated the proposition that the prophets corresponded to the pre-Christian stage of revelation, but the Apostles to the Christian; and that in addition to this the apostolic age was also particularly distinguished by gifts of the Spirit. "Prophets and Apostles"

However, the most effective means of legitimising the present state of things in the Church was a circumstance closely connected with the formation of a canon of early Christian writings, viz., the distinction of an *epoch of revelation*, along with a corresponding classical period of Christianity unattainable by later generations. This period was connected with the present by means of the New Testament and the apostolic office of the bishops. This later time was to regard the older period as an ideal, but might not dream of really attaining the same perfection, except at least through the medium of the Holy Scriptures and the apostolic office, that is, the Church. The place of the holy Christendom that had the Spirit in its midst was taken by the ecclesiastic institution possessing the "instrument of divine literature" ("instrumentum divinæ litteraturæ") and the spiritual office. Finally, we must mention another factor that hastened the various changes; this was the theology of the Christian philosophers, which attained importance in the Church as soon as she based her claim on and satisfied her conscience with an objective possession.

3. But there was one rule which specially impeded the naturalisation of the Church in the world and the transformation of a communion of the saved into an institution for obtaining

now replaced "Apostles, prophets, and teachers," as the court of appeal. Under such circumstances prophecy might still indeed exist; but it could no longer be of a kind capable of ranking, in the remotest degree, with the authority of the Apostles in point of importance. Hence it was driven into a corner, became extinct, or at most served only to support the measures of the bishops. In order to estimate the great revolution in the spirit of the times let us compare the utterances of Irenæus and Origen about gifts of the Spirit and prophecy. Irenæus still expressed himself exactly like Justin (Dial. 39, 81, 82, 88); he says (II. 32. 4: V. 6. 1): καθὼς καὶ πολλῶν ἀκούομεν ἀδελφῶν ἐν τῇ ἐκκλησίᾳ προφητικὰ χαρίσματα ἐχόντων κ.τ.λ. Origen on the contrary (see numerous passages, especially in the treatise c. Cels.), looks back to a period after which the Spirit's gifts in the Church ceased. It is also a very characteristic circumstance that along with the naturalisation of Christianity in the world, the disappearance of charisms, and the struggle against Gnosticism, a strictly ascetic mode of life came to be viewed with suspicion. Euseb., H. E. V. 3 is especially instructive on this point. Here it is revealed to the confessor Attalus that the confessor Alcibiades, who even in captivity continued his ascetic practice of living on nothing but bread and water, was wrong in refraining from that which God had created and thus become a "τύπος σκανδάλου" to others. Alcibiades changed his mode of life. In Africa, however, (see above, p. 103) dreams and visions still retained their authority in the Church as important means of solving perplexities.

salvation, viz., the regulation that excluded gross sinners from
Christian membership. Down to the beginning of the third
century, in so far as the backslider did not atone for his
guilt [1] by public confession before the authorities (see Ep. Lugd.
in Euseb., H. E. V. 1ff.), final exclusion from the Church was
still the penalty of relapse into idolatry, adultery, whoredom,
and murder; though at the same time the forgiveness of God
in the next world was reserved for the fallen provided they
remained penitent to the end. In *theory* indeed this rule was
not very old. For the oldest period possessed no theories;
and in those days Christians frequently broke through what
might have been counted as one by appealing to the Spirit,
who, by special announcements—particularly by the mouth of
martyrs and prophets—commanded or sanctioned the readmission of lapsed members of the community (see Hermas). [2] Still,
the rule corresponded to the ancient notions that Christendom
is a communion of saints, that there is no ceremony *invariably*
capable of replacing baptism, that is, possessing the same value,
and that God alone can forgive sins. The practice must on
the whole have agreed with this rule; but in the course of the
latter half of the second century it became an established
custom, in the case of a first relapse, to allow atonement to be
made once for most sins and perhaps indeed for all, on condition of public confession. [3]  For this, appeal was probably made

---

[1] Tertullian, adv. Marc. IV. 9, enumerates "septem maculas capitalium delictorum," namely, "idololatria", "blasphemia", "homicidium", adulterium" "stuprum",
"falsum testimonium", "fraus". The stricter treatment probably applied to all these
seven offences. So far as I know, the lapse into heresy was not placed in the same
category in the first centuries; see Iren. III. 4. 2; Tertull., de præscr. 30 and, above
all, de pudic. 19 init.; the anonymous writer in Euseb., H. E. V. 28. 12, from which
passages it is evident that repentant heretics were readmitted.

[2] Hermas based the admissibility of a second atonement on a definite divine
revelation to this effect, and did not expressly discuss the admission of gross
sinners into the Church generally, but treated of their reception into that of the
last days, which he believed had already arrived. See particulars on this point in
my article "Lapsi", in Herzog's Real-Encyklopädie, 2 ed. Cf. Preuschen, Tertullian's Schriften de pænit. et de pudic. mit Rücksicht auf die Bussdisciplin, 1890;
Rolffs, Indulgenz-Edict des Kallistus, 1893.

[3] In the work de pænit. (7 ff.) Tertullian treats this as a fixed Church regulation.
K. Müller, Kirchengeschichte I. 1892, p. 114, rightly remarks: "He who desired
this expiation continued in the wider circle of the Church, in her "antechamber"

to Hermas, who very likely owed his prestige to the service
he here unwittingly rendered. We say "unwittingly," for he
could scarcely have intended such an application of his precepts,
though at bottom it was not directly opposed to his attitude.
In point of fact, however, this practice introduced something
closely approximating to a second baptism. Tertullian indeed
(de pænit. 12) speaks unhesitatingly of *two* planks of salvation. [1]
Moreover, if we consider that in any particular case the decision
as to the deadly nature of the sin in question was frequently
attended with great difficulty, and certainly, as a rule, was not
arrived at with rigorous exactness, we cannot fail to see that,
in conceding a second expiation, the Church was beginning to
abandon the old idea that Christendom was a community of

indeed, but as her member in the wider sense. This, however, did not exclude
the possibility of his being received again, even in this world, into the ranks of
those possessing full Christian privileges,—after the performance of penance or
*exhomologesis*. But there was no kind of certainty as to that taking place. Meanwhile this *exhomologesis* itself underwent a transformation which in Tertullian
includes a whole series of basal religious ideas. It is no longer a mere expression
of inward feeling, confession to God and the brethren, but is essentially performance.
It is the actual attestation of heartfelt sorrow, the undertaking to satisfy God by
works of self-humiliation and abnegation, which he can accept as a voluntarily
endured punishment and therefore as a substitute for the penalty that naturally
awaits the sinner. It is thus the means of pacifying God, appeasing his anger,
and gaining his favour again—with the consequent possibility of readmission into
the Church. I say the *possibility*, for readmission does not always follow. Participation in the future kingdom may be hoped for even by him who in this world is
shut out from full citizenship and merely remains in the ranks of the penitent.
In all probability then it still continued the rule for a person to remain till death
in a state of penance or *exhomologesis*. For readmission continued to involve the
assumption that the Church had in some way or other become *certain* that God
had forgiven the sinner, or in other words that she had power to grant this
forgiveness in virtue of the Spirit dwelling in her, and that this readmission therefore involved no violation of her holiness." In such instances it is first prophets
and then martyrs that appear as organs of the Spirit, till at last it is no longer
the inspired Christian, but the professional medium of the Spirit, viz., the priest,
who decides everything.

[1] In the 2nd century even endeavours at a formal repetition of baptism were
not wholly lacking. In Marcionite congregations repetition of baptism is said to
have taken place (on the Elkesaites see Vol. I. p. 308). One can only wonder that there
is not more frequent mention of such attempts. The assertion of Hippolytus
(Philos. IX. 12 fin.) is enigmatical: Ἐπὶ Καλλίστου πρώτω τετόλμηται δεύτερον αὐτοῖς βάπτισμα.

saints.  Nevertheless the fixed practice of refusing whoremongers, adulterers, murderers, and idolaters readmission to the Church, in ordinary cases, prevented men from forgetting that there was a boundary line dividing her from the world.

This state of matters continued till about 220. [1]  In reality the rule was first infringed by the peremptory edict of bishop Calixtus, who, in order to avoid breaking up his community, granted readmission to those who had fallen into sins of the flesh.  Moreover, he claimed this power of readmission as a right appertaining to the bishops as successors of the Apostles, that is, as possessors of the Spirit and the power of the keys. [2] At Rome this rescript led to the secession headed by Hippolytus.  But, between 220 and 250, the milder practice with regard to the sins of the flesh became prevalent, though it was not yet universally accepted.  This, however, resulted in no further schism (Cyp., ep. 55. 21).  But up to the year 250 no concessions were allowed in the case of relapse into idolatry. [3] These were first occasioned by the Decian persecution, since in many towns those who had abjured Christianity were more numerous than those who adhered to it. [4]  The majority of the bishops, part of them with hesitation, agreed on new principles. [5]

---

[1] See Tertull., de pudic. 12: "hinc est quod neque idololatriæ neque sanguini pax ab ecclesiis redditur." Orig., de orat. 28 fin; c. Cels. III. 50.

[2] It is only of whoremongers and idolaters that Tertullian expressly speaks in de pudic. c. I. We must interpret in accordance with this the following statement by Hippolytus in Philos. IX. 12: Κάλλιστος πρῶτος τὰ πρὸς τὰς ἡδονὰς τοῖς ἀνθρώποις συγχωρεῖν ἐπενόησε, λέγων πᾶσιν ὑπ' αὐτοῦ ἀφίεσθαι ἁμαρτίας. The aim of this measure is still clear from the account of it given by Hippolytus, though this indeed is written in a hostile spirit. Roman Christians were then split into at least five different sects, and Calixtus left nothing undone to break up the unfriendly parties and enlarge his own. In all probability, too, the energetic bishop met with a certain measure of success. From Euseb., H. E. IV. 23. 6, one might be inclined to conclude that, even in Marcus Aurelius' time, Dionysius of Corinth had issued lax injunctions similar to those of Calixtus. But it must not be forgotten that we have nothing but Eusebius' report; and it is just in questions of this kind that his accounts are not reliable.

[3] No doubt persecutions were practically unknown in the period between 220 and 260.

[4] See Cypr., de lapsis.

[5] What scruples were caused by this innovation is shown by the first 40 letters in Cyprian's collection. He himself had to struggle with painful doubts.

To begin with, permission was given to absolve repentant apostates on their deathbed. Next, a distinction was made between *sacrificati* and *libellatici*, the latter being more mildly treated. Finally, the possibility of readmission was conceded under certain severe conditions to all the lapsed, a casuistic proceeding was adopted in regard to the laity, and strict measures—though this was not the universal rule—were only adopted towards the clergy. In consequence of this innovation, which logically resulted in the gradual cessation of the belief that there can be only one repentance after baptism—an assumption that was untenable in principle—Novatian's schism took place and speedily rent the Church in twain. But, even in cases where unity was maintained, many communities observed the stricter practice down to the fifth century. [1] What made it difficult to introduce this change by regular legislation was the authority to forgive sins in God's stead, ascribed in primitive times to the inspired, and at a later period to the confessors in virtue of their special relation to Christ or the Spirit (see Ep. Lugd. in Euseb., H. E. V. 1ff.; Cypr. epp.; Tertull. de pudic. 22). The confusion occasioned by the confessors after the Decian persecution led to the non-recognition of any rights of "spiritual" persons other than the bishops. These confessors had frequently abetted laxity of conduct, whereas, if we consider the measure of secularisation found among the great mass of Christians, the penitential discipline insisted on by the bishops is remarkable for its comparative severity. The complete adoption of the episcopal constitution coincided with the introduction of the unlimited right to forgive sins. [2]

---

[1] Apart from some epistles of Cyprian, Socrates, H. E. V. 22, is our chief source of information on this point. See also Conc. Illib. can. 1, 2, 6—8, 12, 17, 18—47, 70—73, 75.

[2] See my article "Novatian" in Herzog's Real-Encyklopädie, 2nd ed. One might be tempted to assume that the introduction of the practice of unlimited forgiveness of sins was an "evangelical reaction" against the merciless legalism which, in the case of the Gentile Church indeed, had established itself from the beginning. As a matter of fact the bishops and the laxer party appealed to the New Testament in justification of their practice. This had already been done by the followers of Calixtus and by himself. See Philos. IX. 12: φάσκοντες Χριστὸν ἀφιέναι τοῖς εὐδοκοῦσι; Rom. XIV. 4 and Matt. XIII. 29 were also quoted. Before this Tertullian's opponents who favoured laxity had appealed exactly in the same way to

4. The original conception of the relation of the Church to salvation or eternal bliss was altered by this development. According to the older notion the Church was the sure communion of salvation and of saints, which rested on the forgiveness of sins mediated by baptism, and excluded everything unholy. It is not the Church, but God alone, that forgives sins, and, as a rule, indeed, this is only done through baptism, though, in virtue of his unfathomable grace, also now and then by special proclamations, the pardon coming into effect for repentant sinners, after death, in heaven. If Christendom readmitted gross sinners, it would anticipate the judgment of God, as it would thereby assure them of salvation. Hence it can only take back those who have been excluded in cases where their offences have not been committed against God himself, but have consisted in transgressing the commandments of the Church, that is, in venial sins. [1] But in course of time it was just in lay circles that faith in God's grace became weaker and trust in the Church stronger. He whom the Church abandoned was lost to the world; therefore she must not abandon him. This state of things was expressed in the new interpretation of the proposition, "no salvation outside the Church" ("extra ecclesiam nulla salus"), viz., *the Church alone saves from damnation which is otherwise certain.* In this conception the nature of the Church is depotentiated, but her powers are extended. If she is the institution which, according to Cyprian, is the indispensable preliminary condition of salvation, she can no longer be a sure communion of the saved; in other words, she becomes an institution from which proceeds the communion of saints; she includes both saved and unsaved. Thus her religious character consists in her being the indispens-

---

numerous Bible texts, *e.g.*, Matt. X. 23 : XI. 19 etc., see de monog, de pudic., de ieiun. Cyprian is also able to quote many passages from the Gospels. However, as the bishops and their party did not modify their conception of baptism, but rather maintained in principle, as before, that baptism imposes only obligations for the future, the "evangelical reaction" must not be estimated very highly; (see below, p. 117, and my essay in the Zeitschrift für Theologie und Kirche, Vol. I., "Die Lehre von der Seligkeit allein durch den Glauben in der alten Kirche."

[1] The distinction of sins committed against God himself, as we find it in Tertullian, Cyprian, and other Fathers, remains involved in an obscurity that I cannot clear up.

able medium, in so far as she alone guarantees to the individual
the *possibility* of redemption. From this, however, it immediately follows that the Church would anticipate the judgment
of God if she finally excluded anyone from her membership
who did not give her up of his own accord; whereas she could
never prejudge the ultimate destiny of a man by readmission.[1]
But it also follows that the Church must possess a means of
repairing any injury upon earth, a means of equal value with
baptism, namely, a sacrament of the forgiveness of sins. With
this she acts in God's name and stead, but—and herein lies the
inconsistency—she cannot by this means establish any final
condition of salvation. In bestowing forgiveness on the sinner
she in reality only reconciles him with herself, and thereby, in
fact, merely removes the certainty of damnation. In accordance with this theory the holiness of the Church can merely
consist in her possession of the means of salvation: *the Church
is a holy institution in virtue of the gifts with which she is
endowed.* She is the moral seminary that trains for salvation
and the institution that exercises divine powers in Christ's room.
Both of these conceptions presuppose political forms; both
necessarily require priests and more especially an episcopate.
(In de pudic. 21 Tertullian already defines the position of his
adversary by the saying, "ecclesia est numerus episcoporum.")
This episcopate by its unity guarantees the unity of the Church
and has received the power to forgive sins (Cyp., ep. 69. 11).

The new conception of the Church, which was a necessary
outcome of existing circumstances and which, we may remark,
was not formulated in contradictory terms by Cyprian, but by
Roman bishops,[2] was the first thing that gave a fundamental

---

[1] Cyprian never expelled any one from the Church, unless he had attacked the
authority of the bishops, and thus in the opinion of this Father placed himself
outside her pale by his own act.

[2] Hippol., Philos. IX. 12: Καὶ παραβολὴν τῶν ζιζανίων πρὸς τοῦτο ἔφη ὁ Κάλλιστος
λέγεσθαι· Ἄφετε τὰ ζιζάνια συναύξειν τῷ σίτῳ, τουτέστιν ἐν τῇ ἐκκλησίᾳ τοὺς
ἁμαρτάνοντας. Ἀλλὰ καὶ τὴν κιβωτὸν τοῦ Νῶε εἰς ὁμοίωμα ἐκκλησίας ἔφη γεγονέναι,
ἐν ᾗ καὶ κύνες καὶ λύκοι καὶ κόρακες καὶ πάντα τὰ καθαρὰ καὶ ἀκάθαρτα. οὕτω
φάσκων δεῖν εἶναι ἐν ἐκκλησίᾳ ὁμοίως· καὶ ὅσα πρὸς τοῦτο δυνατὸς ἦν συνάγειν
οὕτως ἡρμήνευσεν. From Tertull., de idolol. 24, one cannot help assuming that even
before the year 200 the laxer sort in Carthage had already appealed to the Ark.

*religious* significance to the separation of clergy and laity. The powers exercised by bishops and priests were thereby fixed and hallowed. No doubt the old order of things, which gave laymen a share in the administration of moral discipline, still continued in the third century, but it became more and more a mere form. The bishop became the practical vicegerent of Christ; he disposed of the power to bind and to loose. But the recollection of the older form of Christianity continued to exert an influence on the Catholic Church of the third century. It is true that, if we can trust Hippolytus' account, Calixtus had by this time firmly set his face against the older idea, inasmuch as he not only defined the Church as *essentially a mixed body (corpus permixtum)*, but also asserted the unlawfulness of deposing the bishop even in case of mortal sin. [1] But we do not find that definition in Cyprian, and, what is of more importance, he still required a definite degree of active Christianity as a *sine quâ non* in the case of bishops; and assumed it as a self-evident necessity. He who does not give evidence of this forfeits his episcopal office *ipso facto*. [2] Now if we consider

("Viderimus si secundum arcæ typum et corvus et milvus et lupus et canis et serpens in ecclesia erit. Certe idololatres in arcæ typo non habetur. Quod in arca non fuit, in ecclesia non sit"). But we do not know what form this took and what inferences they drew. Moreover, we have here a very instructive example of the multitudinous difficulties in which the Fathers were involved by typology: the Ark is the Church, hence the dogs and snakes are men. To solve these problems it required an abnormal degree of acuteness and wit, especially as each solution always started fresh questions. Orig. (Hom. II. in Genes. III.) also viewed the Ark as the type of the Church (the working out of the image in Hom. I. in Ezech., Lomm. XIV. p. 24 sq., is instructive); but apparently in the wild animals he rather sees the simple Christians who are not yet sufficiently trained—at any rate he does not refer to the whoremongers and adulterers who must be tolerated in the Church. The Roman bishop Stephen again, positively insisted on Calixtus' conception of the Church, whereas Cornelius followed Cyprian (see Euseb., H. E. VI. 43. 10), who never declared sinners to be a necessary part of the Church in the same fashion as Calixtus did. (See the following note and Cyp., epp. 67. 6; 68. 5).

[1] Philos., l.c,: Κάλλιστος ἐδογμάτισεν ὅπως εἰ ἐπίσκοπος ἁμάρτοι τι, εἰ καὶ πρὸς θάνατον, μὴ δεῖν κατατίθεσθαι. That Hippolytus is not exaggerating here is evident from Cyp., epp. 67, 68; for these passages make it very probable that Stephen also assumed the irremovability of a bishop on account of gross sins or other failings.

[2] See Cypr., epp. 65, 66, 68; also 55. 11.

HISTORY OF DOGMA       [Chap. III.

that Cyprian makes the Church, as the body of believers *(plebs credentium)*, so dependent on the bishops, that the latter are the only Christians not under tutelage, the demand in question denotes a great deal. It carries out the old idea of the Church in a certain fashion, as far as the bishops are concerned. But for this very reason it endangers the new conception in a point of capital importance; for the spiritual acts of a sinful bishop are invalid;[1] and if the latter, as a notorious sinner, is no longer bishop, the whole certainty of the ecclesiastical system ceases. Moreover, an appeal to the certainty of God's installing the bishops and always appointing the right ones[2] is of no avail, if false ones manifestly find their way in. Hence Cyprian's idea of the Church—and this is no dishonour to him—still involved an inconsistency which, in the fourth century, was destined to produce a very serious crisis in the Donatist struggle.[3] The view, however—which Cyprian never openly expressed, and which was merely the natural inference from his theory— that the Catholic Church, though the "one dove" ("una columba"), is in truth not coincident with the number of the elect, was clearly recognised and frankly expressed by Origen before him. Origen plainly distinguished between spiritual and fleshly members of the Church; and spoke of such as only belong to her outwardly, but are not Christians. As these are finally overpowered by the gates of hell, Origen does not hesitate to class them as merely seeming members of the Church. Conversely, he contemplates the possibility of a person being expelled from her fellowship and yet remaining a member in

[1] This is asserted by Cyprian in epp. 65. 4 and 67. 3; but he even goes on to declare that everyone is polluted that has fellowship with an impure priest, and takes part in the offering celebrated by him.

[2] On this point the greatest uncertainty prevails in Cyprian. Sometimes he says that God himself instals the bishops, and it is therefore a deadly sin against God to criticise them (*e.g.*, in ep. 66. 1); on other occasions he remembers that the bishops have been ordained by bishops; and again, as in ep. 67. 3, 4, he appears to acknowledge the community's right to choose and control them. Cf. the sections referring to Cyprian in Reuter's "Augustinische Studien" (Zeitschrift für Kirchengeschichte, Vol. VII., p. 199 ff.).

[3] The Donatists were quite justified in appealing to Cyprian, that is, in one of his two aspects.

the eyes of God. [1] Nevertheless he by no means attained to clearness on the point, in which case, moreover, he would have been the first to do so; nor did he give an impulse to further reflection on the problem. Besides, speculations were of no

[1] Origen not only distinguishes between different groups within the Church as judged by their spiritual understanding and moral development (Comm. in Matt. Tom. XI. at Chap. XV. 29; Hom. II. in Genes. Chap. 3; Hom. in Cantic. Tom. I. at Chap. I. 4: "ecclesia una quidem est, cum perfecta est; multæ vero sunt adolescentulæ, cum adhuc instruuntur et proficiunt"; Hom. III. in Levit. Chap. iii.), but also between spiritual and carnal members (Hom. XXVI. in Num. Chap. vii.) *i.e.*, between true Christians and those who only bear that name without heartfelt faith —who outwardly take part in everything, but bring forth fruits neither in belief nor conduct. Such Christians he as little views as belonging to the Church as does Clement of Alexandria (see Strom. VII. 14. 87, 88). To him they are like the Jebusites who were left in Jerusalem; they have no part in the promises of Christ, but are lost (Comm. in Matt. T. XII. c. xii.). It is the Church's task to remove such members, whence we see that Origen was far from sharing Calixtus' view of the Church as a *corpus permixtum*; but to carry out this process so perfectly that only the holy and the saved remain is a work beyond the powers of human sagacity. One must therefore content oneself with expelling notorious sinners; see Hom. XXI. in Jos., c. i. : "sunt qui ignobilem et degenerem vitam ducunt, qui et fide et actibus et omni conversatione sua perversi sunt. Neque enim possibile est, ad liquidum purgari ecclesiam, dum in terris est, ita ut neque impius in ea quisquam, neque peccator residere videatur, sed sint in ea omnes sancti et beati, et in quibus nulla prorsus peccati macula deprehendatur. Sed sicut dicitur de zizaniis: Ne forte eradicantes zizania simul eradicetis et triticum, ita etiam super iis dici potest, in quibus vel dubia vel occulta peccata sunt ... Eos saltem eiiciamus quos possumus, quorum peccata manifesta sunt. Ubi enim peccatum non est evidens, eiicere de ecclesia neminem possumus." In this way indeed very many wicked people remain in the Church (Comm. in Matt. T. X. at c. xiii. 47 f.: μὴ ξενιζώμεθα, ἐὰν ὁρῶμεν ἡμῶν τὰ ἀθροίσματα πεπληρωμένα καὶ πονηρῶν); *but in his work against Celsus Origen already propounded that empiric and relative theory of the Christian Churches which views them as simply "better" than the societies and civic communities existing alongside of them.* The 29th and 30th chapters of the 3rd book against Celsus, in which he compares the Christians with the other population of Athens, Corinth, and Alexandria, and the heads of congregations with the councillors and mayors of these cities, are exceedingly instructive and attest the revolution of the times. In conclusion, however, we must point out that Origen expressly asserts that a person unjustly excommunicated remains a member of the Church in God's eyes; see Hom. XIV. in Levit. c. iii. : "ita fit, ut interdum ille qui foras mittitur intus sit, et ille foris, qui intus videtur retineri." Döllinger (Hippolytus and Calixtus, page 254 ff.) has correctly concluded that Origen followed the disputes between Hippolytus and Calixtus in Rome, and took the side of the former. Origen's trenchant remarks about the pride and arrogance of the bishops of large towns (in Matth. XI. 9. 15: XII. 9—14: XVI. 8. 22 and elsewhere, *e.g.*, de orat. 28, Hom. VI. in Isai c. i., in Joh. X. 16), and his denunciation of such of them as, in order to

use here. The Church with her priests, her holy books, and
gifts of grace, that is, the moderate secularisation of Christendom corrected by the means of grace, was absolutely needed
in order to prevent a complete lapse into immorality. [1]

But a minority struggled against this Church, not with speculations, but by demanding adherence to the old practice with
regard to lapsed members. Under the leadership of the Roman
presbyter, Novatian, this section formed a coalition in the
Empire that opposed the Catholic confederation. [2] Their adherence to the old system of Church discipline involved a reaction against the secularising process, which did not seem to
be tempered by the spiritual powers of the bishops. Novatian's
conception of the Church, of ecclesiastical absolution and the
rights of the priests, and in short, his notion of the power of
the keys is different from that of his opponents. This is clear
from a variety of considerations. For he (with his followers)
assigned to the Church the right and duty of expelling gross
sinners once for all; [3] he denied her the authority to absolve

glorify God, assume a mere distinction of names between Father and Son, are also
correctly regarded by Langen as specially referring to the Roman ecclesiastics
(Geschichte der römischen Kirche I. p. 242). Thus Calixtus was opposed by the three
greatest theologians of the age—Tertullian, Hippolytus, and Origen.

[1] If, in assuming the irremovability of a bishop even in case of mortal sin,
the Roman bishops went beyond Cyprian, Cyprian drew from his conception of the
Church a conclusion which the former rejected, viz., the invalidity of baptism
administered by non-Catholics. Here, in all likelihood, the Roman bishops were
only determined by their interest in smoothing the way to a return or admission
to the Church in the case of non-Catholics. In this instance they were again
induced to adhere to their old practice from a consideration of the catholicity of
the Church. It redounds to Cyprian's credit that he drew and firmly maintained
the undeniable inferences from his own theory in spite of tradition. The matter
never led to a great *dogmatic* controversy.

[2] As to the events during the vacancy in the Roman see immediately before
Novatian's schism, and the part then played by the latter, who was still a member
of the Church, see my essay: "Die Briefe des römischen Klerus aus der Zeit. der
Sedisvacanz im Jahre 250" (Abhandl. f. Weizsäcker, 1892).

[3] So far as we are able to judge, Novatian himself did not extend the severer
treatment to all gross sinners (see ep. 55. 26, 27); but only decreed it in the case
of the lapsed. It is, however, very probable that in the later Novatian Churches
no mortal sinner was absolved (see, *e.g.*, Socrates, H. E. I. 10). The statement of
Ambrosius (de pænit. III. 3) that Novatian made no difference between gross and
lesser sins and equally refused forgiveness to transgressors of every kind distorts the

idolaters, but left these to the forgiveness of God who alone has the power of pardoning sins committed against himself; and he asserted: "non est pax illi ab episcopo necessaria habituro gloriæ suæ (scil. martyrii) pacem et accepturo maiorem de domini dignatione mercedem,"—"the absolution of the bishop is not needed by him who will receive the peace of his glory (*i.e.*, martyrdom) and will obtain a greater reward from the approbation of the Lord" (Cypr. ep. 57. 4), and on the other hand taught: "peccato alterius inquinari alterum et idololatriam delinquentis ad non delinquentem transire,"—"the one is defiled by the sin of the other and the idolatry of the transgressor passes over to him who does not transgress." His proposition that none but God can forgive sins does not depotentiate the idea of the Church; but secures both her proper religious significance and the full sense of her dispensations of grace: it limits her powers and *extent* in favour of her *content*. Refusal of her forgiveness under certain circumstances—though this does not exclude the confident hope of God's mercy—can only mean that in Novatian's view this forgiveness is the foundation of salvation and does not merely avert the certainty of perdition. To the Novatians, then, membership of the Church is not the *sine quâ non* of salvation, but it really secures it in some measure. In certain cases nevertheless the Church may not anticipate the judgment of God. Now it is never by exclusion, but by re-admission, that she does so. As the assembly of the baptised, who have received God's forgiveness, the Church must be a real communion of salvation and of saints; hence she cannot endure unholy persons in her midst without losing her essence. Each gross sinner that is tolerated within her calls her legitimacy in question. But, from this point of view, the constitution of the Church, *i.e.*, the distinction of lay and spiritual and the authority of the bishops, likewise retained nothing but the secondary importance it had in earlier times. For, according to those principles, the primary question as regards Church member-

---

truth as much as did the old reproach laid to his charge, viz., that he as "a Stoic" made no distinction between sins. Moreover, in excluding gross sinners, Novatian's followers did not mean to abandon them, but to leave them under the discipline and intercession of the Church.

ship is not connection with the clergy (the bishop). It is rather
connection with the community, fellowship with which secures
the salvation that may indeed be found outside its pale, but
not with certainty. But other causes contributed to lessen the
importance of the bishops: the art of casuistry, so far-reaching in its results, was unable to find a fruitful soil here, and
the laity were treated in exactly the same way as the clergy.
The ultimate difference between Novatian and Cyprian as to the
idea of the Church and the power to bind and loose did not
become clear to the latter himself. This was because, in regard
to the idea of the Church, he partly overlooked the inferences
from his own view and to some extent even directly repudiated
them. An attempt to lay down a principle for judging the case
is found in ep. 69. 7: "We and the schismatics have neither the
same law of the creed nor the same interrogation, for when
they say: 'you believe in the remission of sins and eternal life
through the holy Church', they speak falsely" ("non est una
nobis et schismaticis symboli lex neque eadem interrogatio;
nam cum dicunt, credis in remissionem peccatorum et vitam
æternam per sanctam ecclesiam, mentiuntur"). Nor did Dionysius of Alexandria, who endeavoured to accumulate reproaches
against Novatian, succeed in forming any effective accusation
(Euseb., H. E. VII. 8). Pseudo-Cyprian had just as little success
(ad Novatianum).

It was not till the subsequent period, when the Catholic
Church had resolutely pursued the path she had entered, that
the difference in principle manifested itself with unmistakable
plainness. The historical estimate of the contrast must vary
in proportion as one contemplates the demands of primitive
Christianity or the requirements of the time. The Novatian
confederation undoubtedly preserved a valuable remnant of the
old tradition. The idea that the Church, as a fellowship of
salvation, must also be the fellowship of saints (Καθαροί) corresponds to the ideas of the earliest period. The followers of
Novatian did not entirely identify the political and religious
attributes of the Church; they neither transformed the gifts of
salvation into means of education, nor confused the reality with
the possibility of redemption; and they did not completely lower

the requirements for a holy life. But on the other hand, in view of the minimum insisted upon, the claim *that they were the really evangelical party and that they fulfilled the law of Christ*[1] was a presumption. The one step taken to avert the secularising of the Church, exclusion of the lapsed, was certainly, considering the actual circumstances immediately following a great apostasy, a measure of radical importance; but, estimated by the Gospel and in fact simply by the demands of the Montanists fifty years before, it was remarkably insignificant. These Catharists did indeed go the length of expelling *all* so-called mortal sinners, because it was too crying an injustice to treat *libellatici* more severely than unabashed transgressors;[2] but, even then, it was still a gross self-deception to style themselves the "pure ones", since the Novatian Churches speedily ceased to be any stricter than the Catholic in their renunciation of the world. At least we do not hear that asceticism and devotion to religious faith were very much more prominent in

[1] The title of the evangelical life (evangelical perfection, imitation of Christ) in contrast to that of ordinary Catholic Christians, a designation which we first find among the Encratites (see Vol. I. p. 237, note 3) and Marcionites (see Tertull., adv. Marc. IV. 14: "Venio nunc ad ordinarias sententias Marcionis, per quas proprietatem doctrinæ suæ inducit ad edictum, ut ita dixerim, Christi, Beati mendici etc."), and then in Tertullian (in his pre-Montanist period, see ad mart., de patient., de pænit., de idolol.; in his later career, see de coron. 8, 9, 13, 14; de fuga 8, 13; de ieiun. 6, 8, 15; de monog. 3, 5, 11; see Aubé, Les Chrétiens dans l'empire Romain de la fin des Antonins, 1881, p. 237 ff.: "Chrétiens intransigeants et Chrétiens opportunistes") was expressly claimed by Novatian (Cypr., ep. 44. 3: "si Novatiani se adsertores evangelii et Christi esse confitentur"; 46. 2: "nec putetis, sic vos evangelium Christi adserere"). Cornelius in Eusebius, H. E. VI. 43. 11 calls Novatian: ὁ ἐκδικητὴς τοῦ εὐαγγελίου. This is exceedingly instructive, and all the more so when we note that, even as far back as the end of the second century, it was not the "evangelical", but the lax, who declared the claims of the Gospel to be satisfied if they kept God in their hearts, but otherwise lived in entire conformity with the world. See Tertullian, de spec. 1; de pænit. 5: "Sed aiunt quidam, satis deum habere, si corde et animo suspiciatur, licet actu minus fiat; itaque se salvo metu et fide peccare, hoc est salva castitate matrimonia violare etc."; de ieiun. 2: "Et scimus, quales sint carnalium commodorum suasoriæ, quam facile dicatur: Opus est de totis præcordiis credam, diligam deum et proximum tanquam me. In his enim duobus præceptis tota lex pendet et prophetæ, non in pulmonum et intestinorum meorum inanitate." The Valentinian Heracleon was similarly understood, see above Vol. I. p. 262.

[2] Tertullian (de pud. 22) had already protested vigorously against such injustice.

the Catharist Church than in the Catholic. On the contrary,
judging from the sources that have come down to us, we may
confidently say that the picture presented by the two Churches
in the subsequent period was practically identical.[1] As Novatian's adherents did not differ from the opposite party in doctrine
and constitution, their discipline of penance appears an archaic
fragment which it was a doubtful advantage to preserve; and
their rejection of the Catholic dispensations of grace (practice
of rebaptism) a revolutionary measure, because it had insufficient
justification. But the distinction between venial and mortal sins,
a theory they held in common with the Catholic Church, could
not but prove especially fatal to them; whereas their opponents,
through their new regulations as to penance, softened this distinction, and that not to the detriment of morality. For an
entirely different treatment of so-called gross and venial transgressions must in every case deaden the conscience towards
the latter.

5. If we glance at the Catholic Church and leave the
melancholy recriminations out of account, we cannot fail to see
the wisdom, foresight, and comparative strictness[2] with which
the bishops carried out the great revolution that so depotentiated
the Church as to make her capable of becoming a prop of
civic society and of the state, without forcing any great changes
upon them.[3] In learning to look upon the Church as a training

[1] From Socrates' Ecclesiastical History we can form a good idea of the state
of the Novatian communities in Constantinople and Asia Minor. On the later
history of the Catharist Church see my article "Novatian", l.c., 667 ff. The most
remarkable feature of this history is the amalgamation of Novatian's adherents in
Asia Minor with the Montanists and the absence of distinction between their manner of life and that of the Catholics. In the 4th century of course the Novatians
were nevertheless very bitterly attacked.

[2] This indeed was disputed by Hippolytus and Origen.

[3] This last conclusion was come to after painful scruples, particularly in the
East—as we may learn from the 6th and 7th books of Eusebius' Ecclesiastical
History. For a time the majority of the Oriental bishops adopted an attitude
favourable to Novatian and unfavourable to Cornelius and Cyprian. Then they
espoused the cause of the latter, though without adopting the milder discipline in
all cases (see the canons of Ancyra and Neocæsarea IV. sæc. init.). Throughout
the East the whole question became involved in confusion, and was not decided
in accordance with clear principles. In giving up the last remnant of her exclusiveness

school for salvation, provided with penalties and gifts of grace, and in giving up its religious independence in deference to her authority, Christendom as it existed in the latter half of the third century, [1] submitted to an arrangement that was really best adapted to its own interests. In the great Church every distinction between her political and religious conditions necessarily led to fatal disintegrations, to laxities, such as arose in Carthage owing to the enthusiastic behaviour of the confessors; or to the breaking up of communities. The last was a danger

(the canons of Elvira are still very strict while those of Arles are lax), the Church became "Catholic" in quite a special sense, in other words, she became a community where everyone could find his place, provided he submitted to certain regulations and rules. Then, and not till then, was the Church's pre-eminent importance for society and the state assured. It was no longer variance, and no longer the sword (Matt. X. 34, 35), but peace and safety that she brought; she was now capable of becoming an educative or, since there was little more to educate in the older society, a conservative power. At an earlier date the Apologists (Justin, Melito, Tertullian himself) had already extolled her as such, but it was not till now that she really possessed this capacity. Among Christians, first the Encratites and Marcionites, next the adherents of the new prophecy, and lastly the Novatians had by turns opposed the naturalisation of their religion in the world and the transformation of the Church into a political commonwealth. Their demands had progressively become less exacting, whence also their internal vigour had grown ever weaker. But, in view of the continuous secularising of Christendom, the Montanist demands at the beginning of the 3rd century already denoted no less than those of the Encratites about the middle of the second, and no more than those of the Novatians about the middle of the third. The Church resolutely declared war on all these attempts to elevate evangelical perfection to an inflexible law for all, and overthrew her opponents. She pressed on in her world-wide mission and appeased her conscience by allowing a twofold morality within her bounds. Thus she created the conditions which enabled the ideal of evangelical perfection to be realised in her own midst, in the form of monasticism, without threatening her existence. " What is monasticism but an ecclesiastical institution that makes it possible to separate oneself from the world and to remain in the Church, to separate oneself from the outward Church without renouncing her, to set oneself apart for purposes of sanctification and yet to claim the highest rank among her members, to form a brotherhood and yet to further the interests of the Church ? " In succeeding times great Church movements, such as the Montanist and Novatian, only succeeded in attaining local or provincial importance. See the movement at Rome at the beginning of the 4th century, of which we unfortunately know so little (Lipsius, Chronologie der römischen Bischöfe, pp. 250—255), the Donatist Revolution, and the Audiani in the East.

[1] It is a characteristic circumstance that Tertullian's de ieiun. does *not* assume that the great mass of Christians possess an actual knowledge of the Bible.

incurred in all cases where the attempt was made to exercise
unsparing severity. A casuistic proceeding was necessary as
well as a firm union of the bishops as pillars of the Church.
Not the least important result of the crises produced by the
great persecutions was the fact that the bishops in West and
East were thereby forced into closer connection and at the
same time acquired full jurisdiction ("per episcopos solos peccata
posse dimitti"). If we consider that the archiepiscopal constitution had not only been simultaneously adopted, but had also
attained the chief significance in the ecclesiastical organisation, [1]
we may say that the Empire Church was completed the moment
that Diocletian undertook the great reorganisation of his dominions. [2] No doubt the old Christianity had found its place in
the new Church, but it was covered over and concealed. In
spite of all that, little alteration had been made in the expression
of faith, in religious language; people spoke of the universal
holy Church, just as they did a hundred years before. Here
the development in the history of dogma was in a very special
sense a development in the history of the Church. Catholicism
was now complete; the Church had suppressed all utterances
of individual piety, in the sense of their being binding on

[1] The condition of the constitution of the Church about the middle of the 3rd
century (in accordance with Cyprian's epistles) is described by Otto Ritschl, l. c.,
pp. 142—237. Parallels to the provincial and communal constitution of secular
society are to be found throughout.

[2] To how great an extent the Church in Decius' time was already a state
within the state is shown by a piece of information given in Cyprian's 55th epistle (c. 9.): "Cornelius sedit intrepidus Romæ in sacerdotali cathedra eo tempore:
cum tyrannus infestus sacerdotibus dei fanda adque infanda comminaretur, cum
multo patientius et tolerabilius audiret adversus se æmulum principem quam
constitui Romæ dei sacerdotem." On the other hand the legislation with regard
to Christian flamens adopted by the Council of Elvira, which, as Duchesne (Mé-
langes Renier: Le Concile d'Elvire et les flamines chrétiens, 1886) has demonstrated,
most probably dates from before the Diocletian persecution of 300, shows how
closely the discipline of the Church had already been adapted to the heathen regulations in the Empire. In addition to this there was no lack of syncretist systems
within Christianity as early as the 3rd century (see the Κεστοί of Julius Africanus,
and other examples). Much information on this point is to be derived from Origen's
works and also, in many respects, from the attitude of this author himself. We
may also refer to relic- and hero-worship, the foundation of which was already laid
in the 3rd century, though the "religion of the second order" did not become a
recognised power in the Church or force itself into the official religion till the 4th.

Christians, and freed herself from every feature of exclusiveness. In order to be a Christian a man no longer required in any sense to be a saint. "What made the Christian a Christian was no longer the possession of charisms, but obedience to ecclesiastical authority," share in the gifts of the Church, and the performance of penance and good works. The Church by her edicts legitimised average morality, after average morality had created the authority of the Church. ("La médiocrité fonda l'autorité"). The dispensations of grace, that is, absolution and the Lord's Supper, abolished the charismatic gifts. The Holy Scriptures, the apostolic episcopate, the priests, the sacraments, average morality in accordance with which the whole world could live, were mutually conditioned. The consoling words: "Jesus receives sinners", were subjected to an interpretation that threatened to make them detrimental to morality. [1] And with all that the self-righteousness of proud ascetics was not excluded— quite the contrary. Alongside of a code of morals, to which any one in case of need could adapt himself, the Church began to legitimise a morality of self-chosen, refined sanctity, which really required no Redeemer. It was as in possession of this constitution that the great statesman found and admired her, and recognised in her the strongest support of the Empire. [2]

A comparison of the aims of primitive Christendom with those of ecclesiastical society at the end of the third century—a comparison of the actual state of things at the different periods is hardly possible—will always lead to a disheartening result; but the parallel is in itself unjust. The truth rather is that the correct standpoint from which to judge the matter was al-

---

[1] See Tertullian's frightful accusations in de pudic. (10) and de ieiun. (fin) against the "Psychici", *i.e.*, the Catholic Christians. He says that with them the saying had really come to signify "peccando promeremur", by which, however, he does not mean the Augustinian: "o felix culpa".

[2] The relation of this Church to theology, what theology she required and what she rejected, and, moreover, to what extent she rejected the kind that she accepted may be seen by reference to chap. 5 ff. We may here also direct attention to the peculiar position of Origen in the Church as well as to that of Lucian the Martyr, concerning whom Alexander of Alexandria (Theoderet, H.E. 1. 3) remarks that he was a ἀποσυνάγωγος in Antioch for a long time, namely, during the rule of three successive bishops.

ready indicated by Origen in the comparison he drew (c. Cels.
III. 29. 30) between the Christian society of the third century
and the non-Christian, between the Church and the Empire,
the clergy and the magistrates. [1] Amidst the general disorgan-
isation of all relationships, and from amongst the ruins of a
shattered fabric, a new structure, founded on the belief in one
God, in a sure revelation, and in eternal life, was being labor-
iously raised. It gathered within it more and more all the
elements still capable of continued existence; it readmitted the
old world, cleansed of its grossest impurities, and raised holy

---

[1] We have already referred to the passage above.  On account of its importance
we may quote it here:

"According to Celsus Apollo required the Metapontines to regard Aristeas as
a god; but in their eyes the latter was but a man and perhaps not a virtuous one…
They would therefore not obey Apollo, and thus it happened that no one believed
in the divinity of Aristeas.  But with regard to Jesus we may say that it proved
a blessing to the human race to acknowledge him as the Son of God, as God who
appeared on earth united with body and soul." Origen then says that the demons
counterworked this belief, and continues: "But God who had sent Jesus on earth brought
to nought all the snares and plots of the demons and aided in the victory of the Gospel of
Jesus throughout the whole earth in order to promote the conversion and ameliora-
tion of men; and everywhere brought about the establishment of Churches which
are ruled by other laws than those that regulate the Churches of the superstitious,
the dissolute and the unbelieving.  For of such people the civil population (πολιτευ-
όμενα ἐν ταῖς ἐκκλησίαις τῶν πολέων πλήθη) of the towns almost everywhere consists."
Αἰ δὲ τοῦ Θεοῦ Χριστῷ μαθητευθεῖσαι ἐκκλησίαι, συνεξεταζόμεναι ταῖς ὧν παροικοῦσι
δήμων ἐκκλησίαις, ὡς φωστῆρες εἰσιν ἐν κόσμῳ. τίς γὰρ οὐκ ἄν ὁμολογήσαι, καὶ τοὺς
χείρους τῶν ἀπὸ τῆς ἐκκλησίας καὶ συγκρίσει βελτιόνων ἐλάττους πολλῷ κρείττους
τυγχάνειν τῶν ἐν τοῖς δήμοις ἐκκλησιῶν; ἐκκλησία μὲν γὰρ τοῦ Θεοῦ, φέρ᾽ εἰπεῖν, ἡ
Ἀθήνησι πραεῖά τις καὶ εὐσταθής, ἅτε Θεῷ ἀρέσκειν τῷ ἐπὶ πᾶσι βουλομένη· ἡ
δ᾽Ἀθηναίων ἐκκλησία στασιώδης καὶ οὐδαμῶς παραβαλλομένη τῇ ἐκεῖ ἐκκλησίᾳ τοῦ
Θεοῦ· τὸ δ᾽αὐτὸ ἐρεῖς, περὶ ἐκκλησίας τοῦ Θεοῦ τῆς ἐν Κορίνθῳ καὶ τῆς ἐκκλησίας τοῦ
δήμου Κορινθίων· καὶ, φέρ᾽ εἰπεῖν, περὶ ἐκκλησίας τοῦ Θεοῦ τῆς ἐν Ἀλεξανδρείᾳ, καὶ
ἐκκλησίας τοῦ Ἀλεξανδρέων δήμου. καὶ ἐὰν εὐγνώμων ᾖ ὁ τούτου ἀκούων καὶ φιλαλήθως
ἐξετάζῃ τὰ πράγματα, θαυμάσεται τὸν καὶ βουλευσάμενον καὶ ἀνύσαι δυνηθέντα
πανταχοῦ συστήσασθαι ἐκκλησίας τοῦ Θεοῦ, παροικούσας ἐκκλησίαις τῶν καθ᾽ ἑκάστην
πόλιν δήμων οὕτω δὲ καὶ βουλὴν ἐκκλησίας Θεοῦ βουλῇ τῇ καθ᾽ ἑκάστην πόλιν συνε-
ξετάζων εὕροις ἄν ὅτι τινὲς μὲν τῆς ἐκκλησίας βουλευταὶ ἄξιοί εἰσι—εἴ τίς ἐστιν ἐν
τῷ παντὶ πόλις τοῦ Θεοῦ—ἐν ἐκείνῃ πολιτεύεσθαι οἱ δὲ πανταχοῦ βουλευταὶ οὐδὲν ἄξιον
τῆς ἐκ κατατάξεως ὑπεροχῆς, ἥν ὑπερέχειν δοκοῦσι τῶν πολιτῶν, φέρουσιν ἐν τοῖς ἑαυτῶν
ἤθεσιν· οὕτω δὲ καὶ ἄρχοντα ἐκκλησίας ἑκάστης πόλεως ἄρχοντι τῶν ἐν τῇ πόλει
συγκριτέον· ἵνα κατανοήσῃς, ὅτι καὶ ἐπὶ τῶν σφόδρα ἀποτυγχανομένων βουλευτῶν καὶ
ἀρχόντων ἐκκλησίας Θεοῦ, καὶ ῥαθυμοτέρων παρὰ τοὺς εὐτονωτέρως βιοῦντας οὐδὲν
ἧττόν ἐστιν εὑρεῖν ὡς ἐπίπαν ὑπεροχὴν τὴν ἐν τῇ ἐπὶ τὰς ἀρετὰς προκοπῇ παρὰ τὰ
ἤθη τῶν ἐν ταῖς πόλεσι βουλευτῶν καὶ ἀρχόντων

barriers to secure its conquests against all attacks. Within this
edifice justice and civic virtue shone with no greater brightness than they did upon the earth generally; but within it
burned two mighty flames—the assurance of eternal life, guaranteed by Christ, and the practice of mercy. He who knows
history is aware that the influence of epoch-making personages
is not to be sought in its direct consequences alone, as these
speedily disappear: that structure which prolonged the life of
a dying world, and brought strength from the Holy One to
another struggling into existence, was also partly founded on
the Gospel, and but for this would neither have arisen nor
attained solidity. Moreover, a Church had been created within
which the pious layman could find a holy place of peace and
edification. With priestly strife he had nothing to do, nor had
he any concern in the profound and subtle dogmatic system
whose foundation was now being laid. We may say that the
religion of the laity attained freedom in proportion as it became
impossible for them to take part in the establishment and
guardianship of the official Church system. It is the professional
guardians of this ecclesiastical edifice who are the real martyrs
of religion, and it is they who have to bear the consequences
of the worldliness and lack of genuineness pertaining to the
system. But to the layman who seeks from the Church nothing
more than aid in raising himself to God, this worldliness and
unveracity do not exist. During the Greek period, however,
laymen were only able to recognise this advantage to a limited
extent. The Church dogmatic and the ecclesiastical system
were still too closely connected with their own interests. It
was in the Middle Ages, that the Church first became a Holy
Mother and her house a house of prayer—for the Germanic
peoples; for these races were really the children of the Church,
and they themselves had not helped to rear the house in which
they worshipped.

## ADDENDA.

I. THE PRIESTHOOD. The completion of the old Catholic conception of the Church, as this idea was developed in the latter half of the third century, is perhaps most clearly shown in the attribute of priesthood, with which the clergy were invested and which conferred on them the greatest importance. [1] The development of this conception, whose adoption is a proof that the Church had assumed a heathen complexion, cannot be more particularly treated of here. [2] What meaning it has

[1] Ritschl, Entstehung der altkatholischen Kirche pp. 362, 368, 394, 461, 555, 560, 576. Otto Ritschl, l.c., pp. 208, 218, 231. Hatch "Organisation of the early Christian Church", Lectures 5 and 6; id., Art. "Ordination", "Priest", in the Dictionary of Christian Antiquities. Hauck, Art. "Priester" in Herzog's Real-Encyklopädie, 2nd ed. Voigt, l.c., p. 175 ff. Sohm, Kirchenrecht I. p. 205 ff. Louw, Het ontstaan van het Priesterschap in de christ. Kerk, Utrecht, 1892.

[2] Clement of Rome was the first to compare the conductors of public worship in Christian Churches with the priests and Levites, and the author of the Διδαχή was the first to liken the Christian prophets to the high priests. It cannot, however, be shown that there were any Christian circles where the leaders were directly styled "priests" before the last quarter of the 2nd century. We can by no means fall back on Ignatius, Philad. 9, nor on Iren., IV. 8. 3, which passage is rather to be compared with Διδ. 13. 3. It is again different in Gnostic circles, which in this case, too, anticipated the secularising process; read for example the description of Marcus in Iren., I. 13. Here, *mutatis mutandis*, we have the later Catholic bishop, who alone is able to perform a mysterious sacrifice to whose person powers of grace are attached—the formula of bestowal was: μεταδοῦναί σοι θέλω τῆς ἐμῆς χάριτος... λάμβανε ἀπ᾽ εμοῦ καὶ δι᾽ ἐμοῦ χάριν, and through whose instrumentality union with God can alone be attained: the ἀπολύτρωσις (I. 21.) is only conferred through the mystagogue. Much of a similar nature is to be found, and we can expressly say that the distinction between priestly mystagogues and laymen was of fundamental importance in many Gnostic societies (see also the writings of the Coptic Gnostics); it was different in the Marcionite Church. Tertullian (de bapt. 17) was the first to call the bishop "summus sacerdos", and the older opinion that he merely "played" with the idea is untenable, and refuted by Pseudo-Cyprian, de aleat. 2 ("sacerdotalis dignitas"). In his Antimontanist writings the former has repeatedly repudiated any distinction in principle of a particular priestly class among Christians, as well as the application of certain injunctions to this order (de exhort. 7: "nonne et laici sacerdotes sumus?... adeo ubi ecclesiastici ordinis non est consessus, et offers et tinguis et sacerdos es tibi solus, sed ubi tres, ecclesia est, licet laici."; de monog. 7). We may perhaps infer from his works that before about the year 200, the name "priest" was not yet universally applied to bishop and presbyters in Carthage (but see after this de præscr. 29, 41: sacer-

is shown by its application in Cyprian and the original of the
first six books of the Apostolic Constitutions (see Book II.).
The bishops (and also the presbyters) are priests, in so far as
they alone are empowered to present the sacrifice as representatives of the congregation before God[1] and in so far as they
dispense or refuse the divine grace as representatives of God
in relation to the congregation. In this sense they are also
judges in God's stead.[2] The position here conceded to the

dotalia munera; de pud. 1, 21; de monog. 12: disciplina sacerd.; de exhort. 7:
sacerdotalis ordo; ibid. 11: "et offeres pro duabus uxoribus, et commendabis illas
duas per sacerdotem de monogamia ordinatum; de virg. vel. 9: sacerdotale officium;
Scorp. 7: sacerdos). The latest writings of Tertullian show us indeed that the
name and the conception which it represents were already prevalent. Hippolytus
(Philos. praef.: ὧν ἡμεῖς διάδοχοι τυγχάνοντες τῆς τε αὐτῆς χάριτος μετέχοντες
ἀρχιερατείας καὶ διδασκαλίας, see also the Arabian canons) expressly claimed high
priesthood for the bishops, and Origen thought he was justified in giving the
name of "Priests and Levites" to those who conducted public worship among
Christians. This he indeed did with reserve (see many passages, e.g., Hom. II. in
Num., Vol. II. p. 278; Hom. VI. in Lev., Vol. II. p. 211; Comment. in Joh., Vol.
I. 3), but yet to a far greater extent than Clement (see Bigg, l.c., p. 214 f.). In
Cyprian and the literature of the Greek Church in the immediately following period
we find the designation "priest" as the regular and most customary name for the
bishop and presbyters. Novatian (Jerome. de vir. inl. 70) wrote a treatise *de
sacerdote* and another *de ordinatione*. The notable and momentous change of
conception expressed in the idea can be traced by us through its preparatory stages
almost as little as the theory of the apostolic succession of the bishops. Irenæus
(IV. 8. 3, 17. 5, 18. 1) and Tertullian, when compared with Cyprian, appear here
as representatives of primitive Christianity. They firmly assert the priesthood of
the whole congregation. That the laity had as great a share as the leaders of
the Churches in the transformation of the latter into Priests is moreover shown
by the bitter saying of Tertullian (de monog. 12): "Sed cum extollimur et inflamur
adversus clerum, tunc unum omnes sumus, tunc omnes sacerdotes, quia 'sacerdotes
nos deo et patri fecit'. Cum ad peræquationem disciplinæ sacerdotalis provocamur,
deponimus infulas."

[1] See Sohm, I. p. 207.

[2] The "deservire altari et sacrificia divina celebrare" (Cypr., ep. 67. 1) is the
distinctive function of the *sacerdos dei*. It may further be said, however, that *all*
ceremonies of public worship properly belong to him, and Cyprian has moreover
contrived to show that this function of the bishop as leader of the Church follows
from his priestly attributes; for as priest the bishop is *antistes Christi* (dei);
see epp. 59. 18: 61. 2: 63. 14: 66.5, and this is the basis of his right and duty to
preserve the *lex evangelica* and the *traditio dominica* in every respect. As *antistes
dei*, however, an attribute bestowed on the bishop by the apostolic succession and
the laying on of hands, he has also received the power of the keys, which confers
the right to judge in Christ's stead and to grant or refuse the divine grace. In

higher clergy corresponds to that of the mystagogue in heathen
religions, and is acknowledged to be borrowed from the latter. [1]
Divine grace already appears as a sacramental consecration of
an objective nature, the bestowal of which is confined to spiritual personages chosen by God. This fact is no way affected
by the perception that an ever increasing reference is made to
the Old Testament priests as well as to the whole Jewish ceremonial and ecclesiastical regulations. [2] It is true that there is
no other respect in which Old Testament commandments were
incorporated with Christianity to such an extent as they were
in this. [3] But it can be proved that this formal adoption every-

Cyprian's conception of the episcopal office the *successio apostolica* and the position
of vicegerent of Christ (of God) counterbalance each other; he also tried to
amalgamate both elements (ep. 55. 8: "cathedra sacerdotalis). It is evident that as
far as the inner life of each church was concerned, the latter and newer necessarily
proved the more important feature. In the East, where the thought of the apostolical succession of the bishops never received such pronounced expression as in
Rome it was just this latter element that was almost exclusively emphasised from
the end of the 3rd century. Ignatius led the way when he compared the bishop, in
his position towards the individual community, with God and Christ. He, however, is dealing in images, but at a later period the question is about realities
based on a mysterious transference.

[1] Soon after the creation of a professional priesthood, there also arose a class
of inferior clergy. This was first the case in Rome. This development was not
uninfluenced by the heathen priesthood, and the temple service (see my article in Texte
und Untersuchungen II. 5). Yet Sohm, l. c., p. 128 ff., has disputed this, and proposed
modifications, worth considering, in my view of the origin of the *ordines minores.*

[2] Along with the sacerdotal laws, strictly so called, which Cyprian already
understood to apply in a frightful manner (see his appeal to Deut. XVII. 12;
1 Sam. VIII. 7; Luke X. 16; John XVIII. 22 f.; Acts XXIII. 4—5 in epp. 3. 43,
59. 66), other Old Testament commandments could not fail to be introduced. Thus
the commandment of tithes, which Irenæus had still asserted to be abolished, was
now for the first time established (see Origen; Constit. Apost. and *my* remarks on
Διδ. c. 13); and hence Mosaic regulations as to ceremonial cleanness were adopted
(see Hippol. Canones arab. 17; Dionys. Alex., ep. canon.). Constantine was the
first to base the observance of Sunday on the commandment as to the Sabbath.
Besides, the West was always more hesitating in this respect than the East. In
Cyprian's time, however, the classification and dignity of the clergy were everywhere
upheld by an appeal to Old Testament commandments, though reservations still
continued to be made here and there.

[3] Tertullian (de pud. I.) sneeringly named the bishop of Rome "pontifex maximus",
thereby proving that he clearly recognised the heathen colouring given to the
episcopal office. With the picture of the bishop drawn by the Apostolic constitutions
may be compared the ill-natured descriptions of Paul of Samosata in Euseb., VII. 30.

where took place at a subsequent date, that is, it had practically no influence on the development itself, which was not legitimised by the commandments till a later period, and that often in a somewhat lame fashion.  We may perhaps say that the development which made the bishops and elders priests altered the inward form of the Church in a more radical fashion than any other.  "Gnosticism", which the Church had repudiated in the second century, became part of her own system in the third.  As her integrity had been made dependent on inalienable objective standards, the adoption even of this greatest innovation, which indeed was in complete harmony with the secular element within her, was an elementary necessity.  In regard to every sphere of Church life, and hence also in respect to the development of dogma [1] and the interpretation of the Holy Scriptures, the priesthood proved of the highest significance.  The clerical exposition of the sacred books, with its frightful ideas, found its earliest advocate in Cyprian and had thus a most skilful champion at the very first. [2]

II. SACRIFICE.  In Book I., chap. III., § 7, we have already shown what a wide field the idea of sacrifice occupied in primitive Christendom, and how it was specially connected with the celebration of the Lord's Supper.  The latter was re-

---

[1] Yet this influence, in a direct form at least, can only be made out at a comparatively late period. But nevertheless, from the middle of the 3rd century the priests alone are possessed of knowledge. As μάθησις and μυσταγωγία are inseparably connected in the mysteries and Gnostic societies, and the mystagogue was at once knowing one and priest, so also in the Catholic Church the priest is accounted the knowing one. Doctrine itself became a mystery to an increasing extent.

[2] Examples are found in epp. 1, 3, 4, 33, 43, 54, 57, 59, 65, 66. But see Iren., IV. 26. 2, who is little behind Cyprian here, especially when he threatens offenders with the fate of Dathan and Abiram. One of the immediate results of the formation of a priestly and spiritual class was that the independent "teachers" now shared the fate of the old "prophets" and became extinct (see my edition of the Διδαχή, prolegg. pp. 131—137). It is an instructive fact that Theoktistus of Cæsarea and Alexander of Jerusalem in order to prove in opposition to Demetrius that independent teachers were still tolerated, i.e., allowed to speak in public meetings of the Church, could only appeal to the practice of Phrygia and Lycaonia, that is, to the habit of outlying provinces where, besides, Montanism had its original seat. Euelpis in Laranda, Paulinus in Iconium, and Theodorus in Synnada, who flourished about 216, are in addition to Origen the last independent teachers (i.e., outside the ranks of the clergy) known to us in Christendom (Euseb., H. E. VI. 19 fin.).

garded as the pure (*i.e.*, to be presented with a pure heart), bloodless thank-offering of which Malachi had prophesied in I. 11. Priesthood and sacrifice, however, are mutually conditioned. The alteration of the concept "priest" necessarily led to a simultaneous and corresponding change in the idea of sacrifice, just as, conversely, the latter reacted on the former. [1] In Irenæus and Tertullian the old conception of sacrifice, viz., that prayers are the Christian sacrifice and that the disposition of the believer hallows his whole life even as it does his offering, and forms a well-pleasing sacrifice to God, remains essentially unchanged. In particular, there is no evidence of any alteration in the notion of sacrifice connected with the Lord's Supper. [2] But nevertheless we can already trace a certain degree of modification in Tertullian. Not only does he give fasting, voluntary celibacy, martyrdom, etc., special prominence among the sacrificial acts of a Christian life, and extol their religious value—as had already been done before; but he also attributes a God-propitiating significance to these performances, and plainly designates them as "merita" ("promereri deum"). To the best of my belief Tertullian was the first who definitely regarded ascetic performances as propitiatory offerings and ascribed to them the "potestas reconciliandi iratum deum." [3] But he himself was far from using

---

[1] See Döllinger, Die Lehre von der Eucharistie in den ersten drei Jahrhunderten, 1826. Höfling, Die Lehre der ältesten Kirche vom Opfer, p. 71 ff. Th. Harnack, Der christliche Gemeindegottesdienst im apostolischen und altkatholischen Zeitalter, p. 342 ff. Steitz, Art. "Messe" in Herzog's Real Encyklopädie, 2nd ed. It is idle to enquire whether the conception of the "sacerdotium" or that of the "sacrificium" was first altered, because they are correlative ideas.

[2] See the proof passages in Höfling, l. c., who has also treated in detail Clement and Origen's idea of sacrifice, and cf. the beautiful saying of Irenæus IV. 18. 3: "Non sacrificia sanctificant hominem; non enim indiget sacrificio deus; sed conscientia eius qui offert sanctificat sacrificium, pura exsistens, et præstat acceptare deum quasi ab amico" (on the offering in the Lord's Supper see Iren. IV. 17. 5, 18. 1); Tertull., Apolog. 30; de orat. 28; adv. Marc. III. 22 ; IV. 1, 35: adv. Jud. 5; de virg. vel. 13.

[3] Cf. specially the Montanist writings; the treatise *de ieiunio* is the most important among them in this case; see cc. 7, 16; de resurr. 8. On the use of the word "satisfacere" and the new ideas on the point which arose in the West (cf. also the word "meritum") see below chap. 5. 2 and the 2nd chap. of the 5th Vol. Note that the 2nd Ep. of Clement already contains the sayings : καλὸν ἐλεημοσύνη ὡς μετάνοια ἁμαρτίας· κρείσσων νηστεία προσευχῆς, ἐλεημοσύνη δὲ ἀμφοτέρων ... ἐλεη-

this fatal theory, so often found in his works, to support a lax
Church practice that made Christianity consist in outward forms.
This result did not come about till the eventful decades, prolific
in new developments, that elapsed between the persecutions of
Septimius and Decius; and in the West it is again Cyprian
who is our earliest witness as to the new view and practice. [1]  In
the first place, Cyprian was quite familiar with the idea of
ascetic propitiations and utilised it in the interest of the Catholicity of the Church; secondly, he propounded a new theory of
the offering in the cultus. As far as the first point is concerned,
Cyprian's injunctions with regard to it are everywhere based on
the understanding that even after baptism no one can be without sin (de op. et eleemos. 3); and also on the firm conviction
that this sacrament can only have a retrospective virtue. Hence
he concludes that we must appease God, whose wrath has been
aroused by sin, through performances of our own, that is,
through offerings that bear the character of "satisfactions". In
other words we must blot out transgressions by specially meritorious
deeds in order thus to escape eternal punishment. These deeds

μοσύνη γὰρ κούφισμα ἁμαρτίας γίνεται (16. 4; similar expressions occur in the
"Shepherd"). But they only show how far back we find the origin of these injunctions borrowed from Jewish proverbial wisdom. One cannot say that they had no
effect at all on Christian life in the 2nd century; but we do not yet find the idea
that ascetic performances are a sacrifice offered to a wrathful God. Martyrdom seems
to have been earliest viewed as a performance which expiated sins. In Tertullian's
time the theory, that it was on a level with baptism (see Melito, 12. Fragment
in Otto, Corp. Apol. IX. p. 418: δύο συνέστη τὰ ἄφεσιν ἁμαρτημάτα παρεχόμενα,
πάθος διὰ Χριστὸν καὶ βάπτισμα), had long been universally diffused and was also
exegetically grounded. In fact, men went a step further and asserted that the merits
of martyrs could also benefit others. This view had likewise become established long
before Tertullian's day, but was opposed by him (de pudic. 22), when martyrs abused
the powers universally conceded to them. Origen went furthest here; see exhort. ad
mart. 50: ὥσπερ τιμίῳ αἵματι τοῦ Ἰησοῦ ἠγοράσθημεν ... οὕτως τῷ τιμίῳ αἵματι
τῶν μαρτύρων ἀγορασθήσονταί τινες; Hom. X. in Num. c. II.: "ne forte, ex quo mar-
tyres non fiunt et hostiæ sanctorum non offeruntur pro peccatis nostris, peccatorum
nostrorum remissionem non mereamur." The origin of this thought is, on the one
hand, to be sought for in the wide-spread notion that the sufferings of an innocent
man benefit others, and, on the other, in the belief that Christ himself suffered in
the martyrs (see, e.g., ep. Lugd. in Euseb., H. E. V. 1. 23, 41).

[1] In the East it was Origen who introduced into Christianity the rich treasure
of ancient ideas that had become associated with sacrifices. See Bigg's beautiful
account in "The Christian Platonists of Alexandria," Lect. IV.—VI.

Cyprian terms "merita", which either possess the character of atonements, or, in case there are no sins to be expiated, entitle the Christian to a special reward (merces). [1] But, along with *lamentationes* and acts of penance, it is principally alms-giving that forms such means of atonement (see de lapsis, 35,36). In Cyprian's eyes this is already the proper satisfaction; mere prayer, that is, devotional exercises unaccompanied by fasting and alms, being regarded as "bare and unfruitful". In the work "de opere et eleemosynis" which, after a fashion highly characteristic of Cyprian, is made dependent on Sirach and Tobias, he has set forth a detailed theory of what we may call alms-giving as a *means of grace* in its relation to baptism and salvation. [2] However, this practice can only be viewed as a means of grace in Cyprian's sense in so far as God has accepted it, that is, pointed it out. In itself it is a free human act. After the Decian persecution and the rearrangement of ecclesiastical affairs necessitated by it, works and alms (opera et eleemosynæ) made their way into the absolution system of the Church, and were assigned a permanent place in it. Even

[1] Moreover, Tertullian (Scorp. 6) had already said: "Quomodo multæ mansiones apud patrem, si non pro varietate meritorum."

[2] See c. 1: Nam cum dominus adveniens sanasset illa, quæ Adam portaverit vulnera et venena serpentis antiqua curasset, legem dedit sano et præcepit, ne ultra iam peccaret, ne quid peccanti gravius eveniret; coartati eramus et in angustum innocentiæ præscriptione conclusi, nec haberet quid fragilitatis humanæ infirmitas adque imbecillitas faceret, nisi iterum pietas divina subveniens iustitiæ et misericordiæ operibus ostensis viam quandam tuendæ salutis aperiret, ut sordes postmodum quascumque contrahimus eleemosynis abluamus." c. 2: sicut lavacro aquæ salutaris gehennæ ignis extinguitur, ita eleemosynis adque operationibus iustus delictorum flamma sopitur, et quia semel in baptismo remissa peccatorum datur, adsidua et iugis operatio baptismi instar imitata dei rursus indulgentiam largiatur." 5, 6, 9. In c. 18 Cyprian already established an arithmetical relation between the number of alms-offerings and the blotting out of sins, and in c. 21, in accordance with an ancient idea which Tertullian and Minucius Felix, however, only applied to martyrdom, he describes the giving of alms as a spectacle for God and Christ. In Cyprian's epistles "satisfacere deo" is exceedingly frequent. It is almost still more important to note the frequent use of the expression "promereri deum (iudicem)" in Cyprian. See de unitate 15: "iustitia opus est, ut promereri quis possit deum iudicem: præceptis eius et monitis obtemperandum est, ut accipiant merita nostra mercedem." 18; de lapsis 31; de orat. 8, 32, 36; de mortal. 10; de op. 11, 14, 15, 26; de bono pat. 18; ep. 62. 2: 73. 10. Here it is everywhere assumed that Christians acquire God's favour by their works.

the Christian who has forfeited his Church membership by abjuration may ultimately recover it by deeds of sacrifice, of course under the guidance and intercessory coöperation of the Church. The dogmatic dilemma we find here cannot be more clearly characterised than by simply placing the two doctrines professed by Cyprian side by side. These are:—(1) that the sinfulness common to each individual can only be once extirpated by the power of baptism derived from the work of Christ, and (2) that transgressions committed after baptism, inclusive of mortal sins, can and must be expiated solely by spontaneous acts of sacrifice under the guidance of kind mother Church. [1] A Church capable of being permanently satisfied with such doctrines would very soon have lost the last remains of her Christian character. What was wanted was a means of grace, similar to baptism and granted by God through Christ, to which the *opera et eleemosynæ* are merely to bear the relation of *accompanying* acts. But Cyprian was no dogmatist and was not able to form a doctrine of the means of grace. He never got beyond his "propitiate God the judge by sacrifices after baptism" ("promereri deum judicem post baptismum sacrificiis"), and merely hinted, in an obscure way, that the absolution of him who has committed a deadly sin after baptism emanates from the same readiness of God to forgive as is expressed in that rite, and that membership in the Church is a condition of absolution. His whole theory as to the legal nature of man's (the Christian's) relationship to God, and the practice, inaugurated by Tertullian, of designating this connection by terms derived from Roman law continued to prevail in the West down to Augustine's time. [2] But, during this whole interval, no book was written by a Western Churchman which made the salvation of the sinful Christian dependent on ascetic offerings of atonement,

---

1 Baptism with blood is not referred to here.

2 With modifications, this has still continued to be the case beyond Augustine's time down to the Catholicism of the present day. Cyprian is the father of the Romish doctrine of good works and sacrifice. Yet is it remarkable that he was not yet familiar with the theory according to which man *must* acquire *merita*. In his mind "merits" and "blessedness" are not yet rigidly correlated ideas; but the rudiments of this view are also found in him; cf. de unit. 15 (see p. 134, note 3 ).

with so little regard to Christ's grace and the divine factor in the case, as Cyprian's work *de opere et eleemosynis*.

No less significant is Cyprian's advance as regards the idea of the sacrifice in public worship, and that in three respects. To begin with, Cyprian was the first to associate the specific offering, *i.e.*, the Lord's Supper [1] with the specific priesthood. Secondly, he was the first to designate the *passio dominis*, nay, the *sanguis Christi* and the *dominica hostia* as the object of the eucharistic offering. [2] Thirdly, he expressly represented the

---

[1] "Sacrificare", "sacrificium celebrare", in all passages where they are unaccompanied by any qualifying words, mean to celebrate the Lord's Supper. Cyprian has never called prayer a "sacrifice" without qualifying terms; on the contrary he collocates "preces" and "sacrificium", and sometimes also "oblatio" and "sacrificium". The former is then the offering of the laity and the latter of the priests.

[2] Cf. the whole 63rd epistle and above all c. 7: "Et quia passionis eius mentionem in sacrificiis omnibus facimus, passio est enim domini sacrificium quod offerrimus, nihil aliud quam quod ille fecit facere debemus"; c. 9.: "unde apparet sanguinem Christi non offerri, si desit vinum calici." 13; de unit. 17: "dominicæ hostiæ veritatem per falsa sacrificia profanare"; ep. 63. 4: "sacramentum sacrificii dominici". The transference of the sacrificial idea to the consecrated elements, which, in all probability, Cyprian already found in existence, is ultimately based on the effort to include the element of mystery and magic in the specifically sacerdotal ceremony of sacrifice, and to make the Christian offering assume, though not visibly, the form of a bloody sacrifice, such as secularised Christianity desired. This transference, however, was the result of two causes. The first has been already rightly stated by Ernesti (Antimur. p. 94) in the words: "quia eucharistia habet ἀνάμνησιν Christi mortui et sacrificii eius in cruce peracti, propter ea paullatim cœpta est tota eucharistia sacrificium dici." In Cyprian's 63rd. epistle it is still observable how the "calicem in commemorationem domini et passionis eius offerre" passes over into the "sanguinem Christi offerre", see also Euseb. demonstr. I. 13: μνήμην τῆς θυσίας Χριστοῦ προσφέρειν and τὴν ἔνσαρκον τοῦ Χριστοῦ παρουσίαν καὶ τὸ καταρτισθὲν αὐτοῦ σῶμα προσφέρειν. The other cause has been specially pointed out by Theodore Harnack (l.c., p. 409 f.). In ep. 63. 2 and in many other passages Cyprian expresses the thought "that in the Lord's Supper nothing else is done *by* us but what the Lord has first done *for* us." But he says that at the institution of the Supper the Lord first offered himself as a sacrifice to God the Father. Consequently the priest officiating in Christ's stead only presents a true and perfect offering when he imitates what Christ has done (c. 14: "si Christus Jesus dominus et deus noster ipse est summus sacerdos dei patris et sacrificium patri se ipsum obtulit et hoc fieri in sui commemorationem præcepit, utique ille sacerdos vice Christi vere fungitur, qui id quod Christus fecit imitatur et sacrificium verum et plenum tunc offert in ecclesia deo patri, si sic incipiat offerre secundum quod ipsum Christum videat obtulisse"). This brings us to the conception of the repetition of Christ's sacrifice by the priest. But in Cyprian's case it was still, so to speak, only a notion verging on that idea, that is, he only leads up to it,

celebration of the Lord's Supper as an incorporation of the
congregation and its individual members with Christ, and was
the first to bear clear testimony as to the special importance
attributed to commemoration of the celebrators ("vivi et defuncti"),
though no other can be ascertained than a specially strong
intercession.[1]  But this is really the essential effect of the sacrifice of the supper as regards the celebrators; for however
much the conceptions about this ceremony might be heightened,
and whatever additions might be made to its ritual, forgiveness
of sins in the strict sense could not be associated with it.
Cyprian's statement that every celebration of the Lord's Supper
is a repetition or imitation of Christ's sacrifice of himself, and
that the ceremony has therefore an expiatory value remains a
mere assertion, though the Romish Church still continues to

abstains from formulating it with precision, or drawing any further conclusions from
it, and even threatens the idea itself inasmuch as he still appears to conceive the
"calicem in commemorationem domini et passionis eius offerre" as identical with
it. As far as the East is concerned we find in Origen no trace of the assumption
of a repeated sacrifice of Christ. But in the original of the first 6 books of the
Apostolic Constitutions this conception is also wanting, although the Supper ceremonial has assumed an exclusively sacerdotal character (see II. 25: αἱ τότε (in the
old covenant) θυσίαι, νῦν εὐχαὶ καὶ δεήσεις καὶ εὐχαριστίαι. II. 53). The passage
VI. 23: ἀντὶ θυσίας τῆς δὶ αἱμάτων τὴν λογικὴν καὶ ἀναίμακτον καὶ τὴν μυστικήν,
ἥτις εἰς τὸν θάνατον τοῦ κυρίου συμβόλων χάριν ἐπιτελεῖται τοῦ σώματος αὐτοῦ καὶ
τοῦ αἵματος does not belong to the original document, but to the interpolator.
With the exception therefore of one passage in the Apostolic Church order (printed
in my edition of the Didache prolegg. p. 236) viz.: ἡ προσφορὰ τοῦ σώματος καὶ
τοῦ αἵματος, we possess no proofs that there was any mention in the East before
Eusebius' time of a sacrifice of Christ's body in the Lord's Supper. From this,
however, we must by no means conclude that the mystic feature in the celebration
of the sacrifice had been less emphasised there.

[1] In ep. 63. 13 Cyprian has illustrated the incorporation of the community with
Christ by the mixture of wine and water in the Supper, because the special aim
of the epistle required this: "Videmus in aqua populum intellegi, in vino vero
ostendi sanguinem Christi; quando autem in calice vino aqua miscetur, Christo
populus adunatur et credentium plebs ei in quem credidit copulatur et iungitur etc."
The special mention of the offerers (see already Tertullian's works: de corona 3,
de exhort. cast. 11, and de monog. 10) therefore means that the latter commend
themselves to Christ as his own people, or are recommended to him as such. On
the Praxis see Cyprian ep. 1. 2 "... si quis hoc fecisset, non offerretur pro eo nec
sacrificium pro dormitione eius celebraretur"; 62. 5: "ut fratres nostros in mente
habeatis orationibus vestris et eis vicem boni operis in sacrificiis et precibus
repræsentetis, subdidi nomina singulorum."

repeat this doctrine to the present day. For the idea that
partaking of the Lord's Supper cleansed from sin like the
mysteries of the Great Mother (magna mater) and Mithras, though
naturally suggested by the ceremonial practice, was counter-
acted by the Church principles of penance and by the doctrine
of baptism. As a sacrificial rite the Supper never became a
ceremony equivalent in effect to baptism. But no doubt, as far
as the popular conception was concerned, the solemn ritual
copied from the ancient mysteries could not but attain an
indescribably important significance. It is not possible, within
the framework of the history of dogma, to describe the development of religious ceremonial in the third century, and to show
what a radical alteration took place in men's conceptions with
regard to it (cf. for example, Justin with Cyprian). But, in
dealing with the history of dogma within this period, we must
clearly keep in view the development of the cultus, the new
conceptions of the value of ritual, and the reference of ceremonial usages to apostolic tradition; for there was plainly a
remodelling of the ritual in imitation of the ancient mysteries
and of the heathen sacrificial system, and this fact is admitted
by Protestant scholars of all parties. Ceremonial and doctrine
may indeed be at variance, for the latter may lag behind the
former and vice versâ, but they are never subject to entirely
different conditions.

III. MEANS OF GRACE, BAPTISM, and EUCHARIST. That which
the Western Church of post-Augustinian times calls sacrament
in the specific sense of the word (means of grace) was only
possessed by the Church of the third century in the form of
baptism.[1] In strict theory she still held that the grace once

---

[1] Much as the use of the word "sacramentum" in the Western Church from
Tertullian to Augustine (Hahn, Die Lehre von den Sacramenten, 1864, p. 5 ff.)
differs from that in the classic Romish use it is of small interest in the history of
dogma to trace its various details. In the old Latin Bible μυστήριον was translated
"sacramentum" and thus the new signification "mysterious, holy ordinance or
thing" was added to the meaning "oath", "sacred obligation". Accordingly Tertullian already used the word to denote sacred facts, mysterious and salutary signs
and vehicles, and also holy acts. Everything in any way connected with the Deity
and his revelation, and therefore, for example, the content of revelation as doctrine,
is designated "sacrament"; and the word is also applied to the symbolical which
is always something mysterious and holy. Alongside of this the old meaning

bestowed in this rite could be conferred by no holy ceremony of equal virtue, that is, by no fresh sacrament. The baptised Christian has no means of grace, conferred by Christ, at his disposal, but has his law to fulfil (see, *e.g.*, Iren. IV. 27. 2). But, as soon as the Church began to absolve mortal sinners, she practically possessed in absolution a real means of grace that was equally effective with baptism from the moment that this remission became unlimited in its application. [1] The notions as to this means of grace, however, continued quite uncertain in so far as the thought of God's absolving the sinner through the priest was qualified by the other theory (see above) which asserted that forgiveness was obtained through the penitential acts of transgressors (especially baptism with blood, and next in importance *lamentationes, ieiunia, eleemosynæ*). In the third century there were manifold holy dispensations of grace by the hands of priests; but there was still no theory which traced the means of grace to the historical work of Christ in the same way that the grace bestowed in baptism was derived from it. From Cyprian's epistles and the anti-Novatian sections in the first six books of the Apostolic Constitutions we indeed see that appeal was not unfrequently made to the power of for-

"sacred obligation" still remains in force. If, because of this comprehensive use, further discussion of the word is unnecessary, the fact that revelation itself as well as everything connected with it was expressly designated as a "mystery" is nevertheless of importance in the history of dogma. This usage of the word is indeed not removed from the original one so long as it was merely meant to denote the supernatural origin and supernatural nature of the objects in question; but more than this was now intended; "sacramentum" (*μυστήριον*) was rather intended to represent the holy thing that was revealed as something relatively concealed. This conception, however, is opposed to the Judæo-Christian idea of revelation, and is thus to be regarded as an introduction of the Greek notion. Probst (Sacramente und Sacramentalia, 1872) thinks differently. That which is mysterious and dark appears to be such an essential attribute of the divine, that even the obscurities of the New Testament Scriptures were now justified because these writings were regarded as altogether "spiritual". See Iren. II. 28. 1—3. Tert. de bapt. 2: "deus in stultitia et impossibilitate materias operationis suæ instituit."

[1] We have explained above that the Church already possessed this means of grace, in so far as she had occasionally absolved mortal sinners, even at an earlier period; but this possession was quite uncertain and, strictly speaking, was not a possession at all, for in such cases the early Church merely followed extraordinary directions of the Spirit.

giving sins bestowed on the Apostles and to Christ's declaration
that he received sinners; but, as the Church had not made up her
mind to repeat baptism, so also she had yet no theory that
expressly and clearly supplemented this rite by a *sacramentum
absolutionis*. In this respect, as well as in regard to the *sacramentum ordinis,* first instituted by Augustine, theory remained
far behind practice. This was by no means an advantage, for,
as a matter of fact, the whole religious ceremonial was already
regarded as a system of means of grace. The consciousness of
a personal, living connection of the individual with God through
Christ had already disappeared, and the hesitation in setting up
new means of grace had only the doubtful result of increasing
the significance of human acts, such as offerings and satisfactions,
to a dangerous extent.

Since the middle of the second century the notions of baptism [1] in the Church have not essentially altered (see Vol. I.
p. 206 ff.). The result of baptism was universally considered to
be forgiveness of sins, and this pardon was supposed to effect
an actual sinlessness which now required to be maintained. [2] We
frequently find "deliverance from death", "regeneration of
man", "restoration to the image of God", and "obtaining of
the Holy Spirit". ("Absolutio mortes", "regeneratio hominis",
"restitutio ad similitudinem dei" and "consecutio spiritus sancti")
named along with the "remission of sins" and "obtaining of
eternal life" ("remissio delictorum" and "consecutio æternitatis").
Examples are to be found in Tertullian [3] adv. Marc. I. 28 and
elsewhere; and Cyprian speaks of the "bath of regeneration
and sanctification" ("lavacrum regenerationis et sanctificationis").
Moreover, we pretty frequently find rhetorical passages where,
on the strength of New Testament texts, all possible blessings
are associated with baptism. [4] The constant additions to the

---

[1] Höfling, Das Sacrament der Taufe, 2 Vols., 1846. Steitz, Art. "Taufe" in Herzog's Real Encyklopädie. Walch, Hist. pædobaptismi quattuor priorum sæculorum, 1739.

[2] In de bono pudic. 2: "renati ex aqua et pudicitia," Pseudo-Cyprian expresses an
idea, which, though remarkable, is not confined to himself.

[3] But Tertullian says (de bapt. 6): "Non quod in aquis spiritum sanctum con-
sequamur, sed in aqua emundati sub angelo spiritui sancto præparamur."

[4] The disquisitions of Clement of Alexandria in Pædag. I. 6 (baptism and sonship)

baptismal ritual, a process which had begun at a very early
period, are partly due to the intention of symbolising these
supposedly manifold virtues of baptism, [1] and partly owe their
origin to the endeavour to provide the great mystery with fit
accompaniments. [2] As yet the separate acts can hardly be
proved to have an independent signification. [3] The water was

are very important, but he did not follow them up. It is deserving of note that
the positive effects of baptism were more strongly emphasised in the East than in
the West. But, on the other hand, the conception is more uncertain in the former
region.

[1] See Tertullian, de bapt. 7 ff.; Cypr., ep. 70. 2 ("ungi quoque necesse est eum
qui baptizatus est, ut accepto chrismate, *i.e.*, unctione esse unctus dei et habere in se
gratiam Christi possit"), 74. 5 etc.  "Chrism" is already found in Tertullian as well
as the laying on of hands. The Roman Catholic bishop Cornelius in the notorious
epistle to Fabius (Euseb., H. E. VI. 43. 15), already traces the rites which accompany
baptism to an ecclesiastical canon (perhaps one from Hippolytus' collection; see
can. arab. 19). After relating that Novatian in his illness had only received clinical
baptism he writes: οὐ μὴν οὐδὲ τῶν λοιπῶν ἔτυχε, διαφυγὼν τὴν νόσον, ὧν χρὴ
μεταλαμβάνειν κατὰ τὸν τῆς ἐκκλησίας κανόνα, τοῦ τε σφραγισθῆναι ὑπὸ τοῦ ἐπισκόπου.
It is also remarkable that one of the bishops who voted about heretic baptism
(Sentent. episcop., Cypr., opp. ed. Hartel I. p. 439) calls the laying on of hands a
sacrament like baptism: "neque enim spiritus sine aqua separatim operari potest
nec aqua sine spiritu male ergo sibi quidem interpretantur ut dicant, quod per manus
impositionem spiritum sanctum accipiant et sic recipiantur, cum manifestum sit
*utroque sacramento* debere eos renasci in ecclesia catholica." Among other particulars found in Tertullian's work on baptism (cc. 1. 12 seq.) it may moreover be
seen that there were Christians about the year 200, who questioned the indispens-
ability of baptism to salvation (baptismus non est necessarius, quibus fides satis
est). The assumption that martyrdom replaces baptism (Tertull., de bapt. 16; Origen),
is in itself a sufficient proof that the ideas of the "sacrament" were still uncertain
As to the objection that Jesus himself had not baptised and that the Apostles had
not received Christian baptism see Tert., de bapt. 11, 12.

[2] In itself the performance of this rite seemed too simple to those who sought
eagerly for mysteries. See Tertull., de bapt. 2: "Nihil adeo est quod obduret mentes
hominum quam simplicitas divinorum operum, quæ in actu videtur, et magnificentia,
quæ in effecta repromittitur, ut hinc quoque, quoniam tanta simplicitate, sine pompa,
sine apparatu novo aliquo, denique sine sumptu homo in aqua demissus et inter
pauca verba tinctus non multo vel nihilo mundior resurgit, eo incredibilis existimetur
consecutio æternitatis. Mentior, si non e contrario idolorum solemnia vel arcana
de suggestu et apparatu deque sumptu fidem at auctoritatem sibi exstruunt."

[3] But see Euseb., H. E. VI. 43. 15, who says that only the laying on of hands
on the part of the bishop communicates the Holy Spirit, and this ceremony *must*
therefore follow baptism. It is probable that confirmation as a specific act did not
become detached from baptism in the West till shortly before the middle of the
third century. Perhaps we may assume that the Mithras cult. had an influence here.

regarded both as the symbol of the purification of the soul and
as an efficacious, holy medium of the Spirit (in accordance with
Gen. I. 2; water and Spirit are associated with each other,
especially in Cyprian's epistles on baptism). He who asserted
the latter did not thereby repudiate the former (see Orig. in
Joann. Tom. VI. 17, Opp. IV. p. 133). [1] Complete obscurity
prevails as to the Church's adoption of the practice of child
baptism, which, though it owes its origin to the idea of this
ceremony being indispensable to salvation, is nevertheless a
proof that the superstitious view of baptism had increased. [2] In
the time of Irenæus (II. 22. 4) and Tertullian (de bapt. 18)
child baptism had already become very general and was founded
on Matt. XIX. 14. We have no testimony regarding it from
earlier times; Clement of Alexandria does not yet assume it.
Tertullian argued against it not only because he regarded conscious faith as a needful preliminary condition, but also because
he thought it advisable to delay baptism (cunctatio baptismi)
on account of the responsibility involved in it (pondus baptismi).
He says: "It is more advantageous to delay baptism, especially
in the case of little children. For why is it necessary for the
sponsors (this is the first mention of "godparents") also to be
thrust into danger?... let the little ones therefore come when
they are growing up; let them come when they are learning,
when they are taught where they are coming to; let them
become Christians when they are able to know Christ. Why
does an age of innocence hasten to the remission of sins?
People will act more cautiously in worldly affairs, so that one

---

[1] See Tertullian's superstitious remarks in de bap. 3—9 to the effect that water
is the element of the Holy Spirit and of unclean Spirits etc. Melito also makes
a similar statement in the fragment of his treatise on baptism in Pitra, Anal,
Sacra II., p. 3 sq. Cyprian, ep. 70. 1, uses the remarkable words: "oportet vero
mundari et sanctificari aquam prius a *sacerdote* (Tertull. still knows nothing of this:
c. 17: etiam laicis ius est"), ut possit baptismo suo peccata hominis qui baptizatur
abluere." Ep. 74. 5: "peccata purgare et hominem sanctificare aqua sola non potest,
nisi habeat et spiritum sanctum." Clem. Alex. Protrept. 10. 99: λάβετε ὕδωρ λογικόν.

[2] It was easy for Origen to justify child baptism, as he recognised something
sinful in corporeal birth itself, and believed in sin which had been committed in
a former life. The earliest justification of child baptism may therefore be traced
back to a philosophical doctrine.

who is not trusted with earthly things is trusted with divine.
Whoever understands the responsibility of baptism will fear its
attainment more than its delay." * To all appearance the
practice of immediately baptising the children of Christian families
was universally adopted in the Church in the course of the
third century. (Origen, Comment. in ep. ad Rom. V. 9, Opp.
IV. p. 565, declared child baptism to be a custom handed down
by the Apostles.) Grown up people, on the other hand, frequently postponed baptism, but this habit was disapproved. [1]

The Lord's Supper was not only regarded as a sacrifice, but
also as a divine gift. [2] The effects of this gift were not theoretically fixed, because these were excluded by the strict scheme [3]

* *Translator's note.* The following is the original Latin, as quoted by Prof.
Harnack: "Cunctatio baptismi utilior est, præcipue circa parvulos. Quid enim
necesse, sponsores etiam periculo ingeri . . . veniant ergo parvuli, dum adolescunt;
veniant dum discunt, dum quo veniant docentur; fiant Christiani, cum Christum
nosse potuerint. Quid festinat innocens ætas ad remissionem peccatorum? Cautius
agetur in sæcularibus, ut cui substantia terrena non creditur, divina credatur . . . Si
qui pondus intelligant baptismi, magis timebunt consecutionem quam dilationem."

[1] Under such circumstances the recollection of the significance of baptism in
the establishment of the Church fell more and more into the background (see
Hermas: "the Church rests like the world upon water"; Irenæus III. 17. 2: "Sicut
de arido tritico massa una non fieri potest sine humore neque unus panis, ita nec
nos multi unum fieri in Christo Iesu poteramus sine aqua quæ de cœlo est. Et
sicut arida terra, si non percipiat humorem, non fructificat: sic et nos lignum
aridum exsistentes primum, nunquam fructificaremus vitam sine superna voluntaria
pluvia. Corpora unim nostra per lavacrum illam quæ est ad incorruptionem unitatem acceperunt, animæ autem per spiritum"). The unbaptised (catechumens) also
belong to the Church, when they commit themselves to her guidance and prayers.
Accordingly baptism ceased more and more to be regarded as an act of initiation,
and only recovered this character in the course of the succeeding centuries. In
this connection the 7th (spurious) canon of Constantinople (381) is instructive:
καὶ τὴν πρώτην ἡμέραν ποιοῦμεν αὐτοὺς Χριστιανούς, τὴν δὲ δευτέραν κατηχουμένους,
εἶτα τὴν τρίτην ἐξορκίζομεν αὐτοὺς κ.τ.λ.

[2] Döllinger, Die Lehre von der Eucharistie in dem ersten 3 Jahrhunderten, 1826.
Engelhardt in der Zeitschrift für die hist. Theologie, 1842, I. Kahnis, Lehre vom Abendmahl, 1851. Rückert, Das Abendmahl, sein Wesen und seine Geschichte, 1856. Leimbach, Beiträge zur Abendmahlslehre Tertullian's, 1874. Steitz, Die Abendmahlslehre
der griechischen Kirche, in den Jahrbücher für deutsche Theologie, 1864—1868;
cf. also the works of Probst. Whilst Eucharist and love feast had already been
separated from the middle of the 2nd century in the West, they were still united
in Alexandria in Clement's time; see Bigg, l.c., p. 103.

[3] The collocation of baptism and the Lord's Supper, which, as the early Christian
monuments prove, was a very familiar practice (Tert., adv. Marc. IV. 34: sacra-

of baptismal grace and baptismal obligation. But in practice Christians more and more assumed a real bestowal of heavenly gifts in the holy food, and gave themselves over to superstitious theories. This bestowal was sometimes regarded as a spiritual and sometimes as a bodily self-communication of Christ, that is, as a miraculous implanting of divine life. Here ethical and physical, and again ethical and theoretical features were intermixed with each other. The utterances of the Fathers to which we have access do not allow us to classify these elements here; for to all appearance not a single one clearly distinguished between spiritual and bodily, or ethical and intellectual effects unless he was in principle a spiritualist. But even a writer of this kind had quite as superstitious an idea of the holy elements as the rest. Thus the holy meal was extolled as the communication of incorruption, as a pledge of resurrection, as a medium of the union of the flesh with the Holy Spirit; and again as food of the soul, as the bearer of the Spirit of Christ (the Logos), as the means of strengthening faith and knowledge, as a sanctifying of the whole personality. The thought of the forgiveness of sins fell quite into the background. This ever changing conception, as it seems to us, of the effects of partaking of the Lord's Supper had also a parallel in the notions as to the relation between the visible elements and the body of Christ. So far as we are able to judge no one felt that there was a *problem* here, no one enquired whether this relation was realistic or symbolical. The symbol is the mystery and the mystery was not conceivable without a symbol. What we now-a-days understand by "symbol" is a thing which is not that which it represents; at that time "symbol" denoted a thing which, in some kind of way, really is what it signifies; but, on the other hand, according to the ideas of that period, the really heavenly element lay either in or behind the visible form without being

---

mentum baptismi et eucharistiæ"; Hippol., can. arab. 38: "baptizatus et corpore Christi pastus"), was, so far as I know, justified by no Church Father on internal grounds. Considering their conception of the holy ordinances this is not surprising. They were classed together because they were instituted by the Lord, and because the elements (water, wine, bread) afforded much common ground for allegorical interpretation.

identical with it. Accordingly the distinction of a symbolic and realistic conception of the Supper is altogether to be rejected; we could more rightly distinguish between materialistic, dyophysite, and docetic conceptions which, however, are not to be regarded as severally exclusive in the strict sense. In the popular idea the consecrated elements were heavenly fragments of magical virtue (see Cypr., de laps. 25; Euseb., H. E. VI. 44). With these the rank and file of third-century Christians already connected many superstitious notions which the priests tolerated or shared.[1] The antignostic Fathers acknowledged that the consecrated food consisted of two things, an earthly (the elements) and a heavenly (the real body of Christ). They thus saw in the sacrament a guarantee of the union between spirit and flesh, which the Gnostics denied; and a pledge of the resurrection of the flesh nourished by the blood of the Lord (Justin; Iren. IV. 18. 4, 5; V. 2. 2, 3; likewise Tertullian who is erroneously credited with a "symbolical" doctrine[2]). Clement and Origen "spiritualise", because, like Ignatius, they assign a spiritual significance to the flesh and blood of Christ himself (summary of wisdom). To judge from the exceedingly confused passage in Pæd. II. 2, Clement distinguishes a spiritual and a material blood of Christ. Finally, however, he sees in the Eucharist the union of the divine Logos with the human spirit, recognises, like Cyprian at a later period, that the mixture of wine with water in the symbol represents the spiritual process, and lastly does not fail to attribute to the holy food a relationship to the body.[3]   It is true that Origen, the great

---

[1] The story related by Dionysius (in Euseb., l.c.) is especially characteristic, as the narrator was an extreme spiritualist. How did it stand therefore with the dry tree? Besides, Tertull. (de corona 3) says: "Calicis aut panis nostri aliquid decuti in terram anxie patimur". Superstitious reverence for the sacrament *ante et extra usum* is a very old habit of mind in the Gentile Church.

[2] Leimbach's investigations of Tertullian's use of words have placed this beyond doubt; see de orat. 6; adv. Marc. I. 14: IV. 40: III. 19; de resurr. 8.

[3] The chief passages referring to the Supper in Clement are Protrept. 12. 120; Pæd. I. 6. 43: II. 2. 19 sq.: I. 5. 15: I. 6. 38, 40; Quis div. 23; Strom. V. 10. 66: I. 10. 46: I. 19. 96: VI. 14. 113: V. 11. 70. Clement thinks as little of forgiveness of sins in connection with the Supper as does the author of the Didache or the other Fathers; this feast is rather meant to bestow an initiation into know-

mysteriosophist and theologian of sacrifice, expressed himself in
plainly "spiritualistic" fashion; but in his eyes religious mysteries
and the whole person of Christ lay in the province of the
spirit, and therefore his theory of the Supper is not "symbolical",
but conformable to his doctrine of Christ. Besides, Origen was
only able to recognise spiritual aids in the sphere of the intellect and the disposition, and in the assistance given to these
by man's own free and spontaneous efforts. Eating and drink-
ing and, in general, participation in a ceremonial are from
Origen's standpoint completely indifferent matters. The intelligent Christian feeds at all times on the body of Christ, that
is, on the Word of God, and thus celebrates a never ending
Supper (c. Cels. VIII. 22). Origen, however, was not blind to
the fact that his doctrine of the Lord's Supper was just as far
removed from the faith of the simple Christian as his doctrinal
system generally. Here also, therefore, he accommodated himself to that faith in points where it seemed necessary. This,
however, he did not find difficult; for, though with him everything is at bottom "spiritual", he was unwilling to dispense
with symbols and mysteries, because he knew that one must
be *initiated* into the spiritual, since one cannot learn it as one
learns the lower sciences.[1] But, whether we consider simple
believers, the antignostic Fathers or Origen, and, moreover,
whether we view the Supper as offering or sacrament, we everywhere observe that the holy ordinance had been entirely

ledge and immortality. Ignatius had already said, "the body is faith, the blood
is hope". This is also Clement's opinion; he also knows of a transubstantiation,
not, however, into the real body of Christ, but into heavenly powers. His teaching was
therefore that of Valentinus (see the Exc. ex. Theod. § 82, already given on Vol. i. p. 263)
Strom. V. 11. 70: λογικὸν ἡμῖν βρῶμα ἡ γνῶσις; I. 20. 46: ἵνα δὴ φάγωμεν λογικῶς;
V. 10. 66: βρῶσις γὰρ καὶ πόσις τοῦ θείου λόγου ἡ γνῶσίς ἐστι τῆς θείας οὐσίας.
Adumbrat. in epp. Joh.: "sanguis quod est cognitio"; see Bigg, l.c., p. 106 ff.

[1] Orig. in Matth. Comment. ser. 85: "Panis iste, quem deus verbum corpus
suum esse fatetur, verbum est nutritorium animarum, verbum de deo verbo procedens et panis de pane cœ'esti ... Non enim panem illum visibilem, quem tenebat
in manibus, corpus suum dicebat deus verbum, sed verbum, in cuius mysterio
fuerat panis ille frangendus; nec potum illum visibilem sanguinem suum dicebat,
sed verbum in cuius mysterio potus ille fuerat effundendus"; see in Matt. XI. 14;
c. Cels. VIII. 33. Hom. XVI. 9 in Num. On Origen's doctrine of the Lord's
Supper see Bigg, p. 219 ff.

diverted from its original purpose and pressed into the service of the spirit of antiquity. In no other point perhaps is the hellenisation of the Gospel so evident as in this. To mention only one other example, this is also shown in the practice of child communion, which, though we first hear of it in Cyprian (Testim. III. 25; de laps. 25), can hardly be of later origin than child baptism. Partaking of the Supper seemed quite as indispensable as baptism, and the child had no less claim than the adult to a magical food from heaven. [1]

----

In the course of the third century a crass superstition became developed in respect to the conceptions of the Church and the mysteries connected with her. According to this notion we must subject ourselves to the Church and must have ourselves filled with holy consecrations as we are filled with food. But the following chapters will show that this superstition and mystery magic were counterbalanced by a most lively conception of the freedom and responsibility of the individual. Fettered by the bonds of authority and superstition in the sphere of religion, free and self-dependent in the province of morality, this Christianity is characterised by passive submission in the first respect and by complete activity in the second. It may be that exegetical theology can never advance beyond an alternation between these two aspects of the case, and a recognition of their equal claim to consideration; for the religious phenomenon in which they are combined defies any explanation. But religion is in danger of being destroyed when the insufficiency of the understanding is elevated into a convenient principle of theory and life, and when the real mystery of the faith,

----

[1] The conception of the Supper as *viaticum mortis* (fixed by the 13th canon of Nicæa: περὶ δὲ τῶν ἐξοδευόντων ὁ παλαιὸς καὶ κανονικὸς νόμος φυλαχθήσεται καὶ νῦν, ὥστε εἴτις ἐξοδεύοι, τοῦ τελευταίου καὶ ἀναγκαιοτάτου ἐφοδίου μὴ ἀποστερεῖσθαι, a conception which is genuinely Hellenic and which was strengthened by the idea that the Supper was φάρμακον ἀθανασίας), the practice of benediction, and much else in theory and practice connected with the Eucharist reveal the influence of antiquity. See the relative articles in Smith and Cheetham's Dictionary of Christian Antiquities.

viz., how one becomes a new man, must accordingly give place to the injunction that we must obediently accept the religious as a consecration, and add to this the zealous endeavour after ascetic virtue. Such, however, has been the character of Catholicism since the third century, and even after Augustine's time it has still remained the same in its practice.

# EXCURSUS TO CHAPTERS II. AND III.

## CATHOLIC AND ROMAN. [1]

IN investigating the development of Christianity up till about the year 270 the following facts must be specially kept in mind: In the regions subject to Rome, apart from the Judæo-Christian districts and passing disturbances, Christianity had yet an undivided history in vital questions; [2] the independence of individual congregations and of the provincial groups of Churches was very great; and every advance in the development of the

---

[1] The fullest account of the "history of the Romish Church down to the pontificate of Leo I." has been given by Langen, 1881; but I can in no respect agree (see Theol. Lit. Ztg. 1891, No. 6) with the hypotheses about the primacy as propounded by him in his treatise on the Clementine romances (1890, see especially p. 163 ff). The collection of passages given by Caspari, "Quellen zur Geschichte des Taufsymbols," Vol. III., deserves special recognition. See also the sections bearing on this subject in Renan's "Origines du Christianisme," Vols. V.—VII., especially VII., chaps. 5, 12, 23. Sohm in his "Kirchenrecht" I. (see especially pp. 164 ff., 350 ff., 377 ff.) has adopted my conception of "Catholic" and "Roman", and made it the basis of further investigations. He estimates the importance of the Roman Church still more highly, in so far as, according to him, she was the exclusive originator of Church law as well as of the Catholic form of Church constitution; and on page 381 he flatly says: "The whole Church constitution with its claim to be founded on divine arrangement was first developed in Rome and then transferred from her to the other communities." I think this is an exaggeration. Tschirn (Zeitschrift für Kirchengeschichte, XII. p. 215 ff.) has discussed the origin of the Roman Church in the 2nd century. Much that was the common property of Christendom, or is found in every religion as it becomes older, is regarded by this author as specifically Roman.

[2] No doubt we must distinguish two halves in Christendom. The first, the ecclesiastical West, includes the west coast of Asia Minor, Greece, and Rome together with their daughter Churches, that is, above all, Gaul and North Africa. The second or eastern portion embraces Palestine, Egypt, Syria, and the east part of Asia Minor. A displacement gradually arose in the course of the 3rd century. In the West the most important centres are Ephesus, Smyrna, Corinth, and Rome, cities with a Greek and Oriental population. Even in Carthage the original speech of the Christian community was probably Greek.

communities at the same time denoted a forward step in their
adaptation to the existing conditions of the Empire. The first
two facts we have mentioned have their limitations. The further
apart the different Churches lay, the more various were the
conditions under which they arose and flourished; the looser
the relations between the towns in which they had their home
the looser also was the connection between them. Still, it is
evident that towards the end of the third century the development in the Church had well-nigh attained the same point
everywhere—except in outlying communities. Catholicism, essentially as we conceive it now, was what most of the Churches
had arrived at. Now it is an *a priori* probability that this
transformation of Christianity, which was simply the adaptation
of the Gospel to the then existing Empire, came about under
the guidance of the metropolitan Church, [1] the Church of
Rome; and that "Roman" and "Catholic" had therefore a
special relation from the beginning. It might *a limine* be objected to this proposition that there is no direct testimony in
support of it, and that, apart from this consideration, it is also
improbable, in so far as, in view of the then existing condition
of society, Catholicism appears as the *natural and only possible*
form in which Christianity could be adapted to the world. But
this is not the case; for in the first place very strong proofs
can be adduced, and besides, as is shown by the development
in the second century, very different kinds of secularisation
were possible. In fact, if all appearances are not deceptive,
the Alexandrian Church, for example, was up to the time of
Septimius Severus pursuing a path of development which, left
to itself, would *not* have led to Catholicism, but, in the most
favourable circumstances, to a parallel form. [2]

[1] Rome was the first city in the Empire, Alexandria the second. They were
the metropolitan cities of the world (see the inscription in Kaibel, No. 1561, p. 407:
θρέψε μ᾽ Ἀλεξάνδρεια, μέτοικον ἔθαψε δὲ Ῥώμη, αἱ κόσμου καὶ γῆς, ὦ ξένε, μητρο-
πόλεις). This is reflected in the history of the Church; first Rome appears, then
Alexandria. The significance of the great towns for the history of dogma and of
the Church will be treated of in a future volume. Abercius of Hieropolis, according
to the common interpretation (inscription V. 7 f.) designates Rome as "queen".
This was a customary appellation; see Eunap., vita Prohær. p. 90: ἡ βασιλεύουσα Ῥώμη.

[2] In this connection we need only keep in mind the following summary of facts.
Up to the end of the second century the Alexandrian Church had none of the

It can, however, be proved that it was in the Roman Church, which up to about the year 190 was closely connected with that of Asia Minor, that all the elements on which Catholicism is based first assumed a definite form.[1] (1) We know that the Roman Church possessed a precisely formulated baptismal confession, and that as early as the year 180 she declared this to be the apostolic rule by which everything is to be measured. It is, only in her case that we are really certain of this, for we can merely guess at it as regards the Church of Smyrna, that is, of Asia Minor. It was accordingly admitted that the Roman Church was able to distinguish true from false with special exactness;[2] and Irenæus and Tertullian appealed to her to decide the practice in Gaul and Africa. This practice, in its precisely developed form, cannot be shown to have existed in Alexandria till a later period; but Origen, who testifies to it, also bears witness to the special reverence for and connection with the Roman Church. (2) The New Testament canon, with its claim to be accounted catholic and apostolic and to possess

Catholic and apostolic standards, and none of the corresponding institutions as found in the Roman Church; but her writer, Clement, was also " as little acquainted with the West as Homer". In the course of the first half of the 3rd century she received those standards and institutions; but her writer, Origen, also travelled to Rome himself in order to see "the very old" church and formed a connection with Hippolytus; and her bishop Dionysius carried on a correspondence with his Roman colleague, who also made common cause with him. Similar particulars may also be ascertained with regard to the Syrian Church.

[1] See the proofs in the two preceding chapters. Note also that these elements have an inward connection. So long as one was lacking, all were, and whenever one was present, all the others immediately made their appearance.

[2] Ignatius already says that the Roman Christians are ἀποδιυλισμένοι ἀπὸ παντὸς ἀλλοτρίου χρώματος (Rom. inscr.); he uses this expression of no others. Similar remarks are not quite rare at a later period; see, for instance, the oft-repeated eulogy that no heresy ever arose in Rome. At a time when this city had long employed the standard of the apostolic rule of faith with complete confidence, namely, at the beginning of the 3rd century, we hear that a lady of rank in Alexandria, who was at any rate a Christian, lodged and entertained in her house Origen, then a young man, and a famous heretic. (See Euseb., H. E. VI. 2. 13, 14). The lectures on doctrine delivered by this heretic and the conventicles over which he presided were attended by a μυρίον πλῆθος οὐ μόνον αἱρετικῶν, ἀλλὰ καὶ ἡμετέρων. That is a very valuable piece of information which shows us a state of things in Alexandria that would have been impossible in Rome at the same period. See, besides, Dionys. Alex. in Euseb., H. E. VII. 7.

exclusive authority is first traceable in her; in the other communities it can only be proved to exist at a later period.  In
the great Antiochian diocese there was, for instance, a Church
some of whose members wished the Gospel of Peter read; in
the Pentapolis group of congregations the Gospel of the Egyptians was still used in the 3rd century; Syrian Churches of the
same epoch used Tatian's Diatessaron; and the original of the
first six books of the Apostolic Constitutions still makes no
mention of a New Testament canon. Though Clement of Alexandria no doubt testifies that, in consequence of the common
history of Christianity, the group of Scriptures read in the
Roman congregations was also the same as that employed in
public worship at Alexandria, he had as yet no New Testament canon before him in the sense of Irenæus and Tertullian.
It was not till Origen's time that Alexandria reached the stage
already attained in Rome about forty years earlier.  It must,
however, be pointed out that a series of New Testament books,
in the form now found in the canon and universally recognised,
show marks of revision that can be traced back to the Roman
Church. [1]  Finally, the later investigations, which show that after the third century the Western readings, that is, the Roman
text, of the New Testament were adopted in the Oriental MSS.
of the Bible, [2] are of the utmost value here; for the most natural

[1] I must here refrain from proving the last assertion. The possibility of Asia Minor
having had a considerable share, or having led the way, in the formation of the
canon must be left an open question (cf. what Melito says, and the use made of
New Testament writings in the Epistle of Polycarp). We will, however, be constrained to lay the chief emphasis on Rome, for it must not be forgotten that
Irenæus had the closest connection with the Church of that city, as is proved by
his great work, and that he lived there before he came to Gaul. Moreover, it is a
fact deserving of the greatest attention that the Montanists and their decided opponents in Asia, the so-called Alogi, had no ecclesiastical *canon* before them, though
they may all have possessed the universally acknowledged books of the Romish
canon, and none other, in the shape of *books read in the churches*.

[2] See the Prolegg. of Westcott and Hort (these indeed give an opposite judgment), and cf. Harris, *Codex Bezæ. A study of the so-called Western text of the
New Testament*, 1891. An exhaustive study of the oldest martyrologies has already
led to important cases of agreement between Rome and the East, and promises
still further revelations. See Duchesne, "Les Sources du Martyrologe Hieron." 1885.
Egli, "Altchristliche Studien, Martyrien und Martyrologieen ältester Zeit." 1887; the
same writer in the "Zeitschrift für wissenschaftliche Theologie", 1891, p. 273 ff.

explanation of these facts is that the Eastern Churches then received their New Testament from Rome and used it to correct their copies of books read in public worship. [1] (3) Rome is the first place which we can prove to have constructed a list of bishops reaching back to the Apostles (see Irenæus). [2] We know that in the time of Heliogabalus such lists also existed in other communities; but it cannot be proved that these had already been drawn up by the time of Marcus Aurelius or Commodus, as was certainly the case at Rome. (4) The notion of the apostolic succession of the episcopate [3] was first turned to account by the Roman bishops, and they were the first who definitely formulated the political idea of the Church in connection with this. The utterances and corresponding practical measures of Victor, [4] Calixtus (Hippolytus), and Stephen are the earliest of their kind; whilst the precision and assurance with which they substituted the political and clerical for the ideal conception of the Church, or amalgamated the two notions, as well as the decided way in which they proclaimed the sovereignty of the bishops, were not surpassed in the third century by Cyprian himself. (5) Rome was the first place, and

---

[1] On the relations between Edessa and Rome see the end of the Excursus.

[2] See my treatise "Die ältesten christlichen Datirungen und die Anfänge einer bischöflichen Chronographie in Rom." in the report of the proceedings of the Royal Prussian Academy of Science, 1892, pp. 617—658. I think I have there proved that, in the time of Soter, Rome already possessed a figured list of bishops, in which important events were also entered.

[3] That the idea of the apostolic succession of the bishops was first turned to account or appeared in Rome is all the more remarkable, because it was not in that city, but rather in the East, that the monarchical episcopate was first consolidated. (Cf. the Shepherd of Hermas and Ignatius' Epistles to the Romans with his other Epistles). There must therefore have been a very rapid development of the constitution in the time between Hyginus and Victor. Sohm, l.c., tries to show that the monarchical episcopate arose in Rome immediately after the composition of the First Epistle of Clement, and as a result of it; and that this city was the centre from which it spread throughout Christendom.

[4] See Pseudo-Cyprian's work "de aleat" which, in spite of remarks to the contrary, I am inclined to regard as written by Victor; cf. "Texte und Untersuchungen" V. 1; see c. 1 of this writing: "et quoniam in nobis divina et paterna pietas apostolatus ducatum contulit et vicariam domini sedem cælesti dignatione ordinavit et originem authentici apostolatus, super quem Christus fundavit ecclesiam, in superiore nostro portamus."

that at a very early period, to date occurrences according to
her bishops; and, even outside that city, churches reckoned, not
according to their own, but according to the Roman episcopate. [1]
(6) The Oriental Churches say that two bishops of Rome compiled the chief apostolic regulations for the organisation of the
Church; and this is only partially wrong. [2] (7) The three great
theologians of the age, Tertullian, Hippolytus, and Origen,
opposed the pretensions of the Roman bishop Calixtus; and
this very attitude of theirs testified that the advance in the
political organisation of the Church, denoted by the measures
of Calixtus, was still an unheard-of novelty, but immediately
exercised a very important influence on the attitude of other
Churches. We know that the other communities imitated this
advance in the succeeding decades. (8) The institution of lower
orders of clergy with the corresponding distinction of *clerici
maiores* and *minores* first took place in Rome; but we know
that this momentous arrangement gradually spread from that
city to the rest of Christendom. [3] (9) The different Churches
communicated with one another through the medium of Rome. [4]

[1] See report of the proceedings of the Royal Prussian Academy of Science, 1892,
p. 622 ff. To the material found there must be added a remarkable passage given
by Nestle (Zeitschrift für wissenschaftliche Theologie, 1893, p. 437), where the dates
are reckoned after Sixtus I.

[2] Cf. the 8th book of the Apostolic Constitutions with the articles referring to
the regulation of the Church, which in Greek MSS. bear the name of Hippolytus.
Compare also the Arabian Canones Hippolyti, edited by Haneberg (1870) and
commented on by Achelis (Texte und Untersuchungen VI. 4). Apart from the additions
and alterations, which are no doubt very extensive, it is hardly likely that the name
of the Roman bishop is wrongly assigned to them. We must further remember the
importance assigned by the tradition of the Eastern and Western Churches to one of
the earliest Roman "bishops", Clement, as the confidant and secretary of the
Apostles and as the composer and arranger of their laws.

[3] See my proofs in "Texte und Untersuchungen", Vol. II., Part 5. The canons
of the Council of Nicæa presuppose the distinction of higher and lower clergy for
the whole Church.

[4] We see this from the Easter controversy, but there are proofs of it elsewhere,
*e.g.*, in the collection of Cyprian's epistles. The Roman bishop Cornelius informs
Fabius, bishop of Antioch, of the resolutions of the Italian, African, and other
Churches (Euseb., H. E. VI. 43. 3: ἦλθον εἰς ἡμᾶς ἐπιστολαὶ Κορνηλίου Ῥωμαίων
ἐπισκόπου πρὸς... Φάβιον, δηλοῦσαι τὰ περὶ τῆς Ῥωμαίων συνόδου, καὶ τὰ δόξαντα
πᾶσι τοῖς κατὰ τὴν Ἰταλίαν καὶ Ἀφρικὴν καὶ τὰς αὐτόθι χώρας.. We must not

From these considerations we can scarcely doubt that the fundamental apostolic institutions and laws of Catholicism were framed in the same city that in other respects imposed its authority on the whole earth; and that it was the centre from which they spread, because the world had become accustomed to receive law and justice from Rome.[1] But it may be objected that the parallel development in other provinces and towns was spontaneous, though it everywhere came about at a somewhat later date. Nor do we intend to contest the assumption in this general sense; but, as I think, it can be proved that the Roman community had a direct and important share in the process and that, even in the second century, she was reckoned the first and most influential Church.[2] We shall give a bird's-eye view of the most important facts bearing on the question, in order to prove this.

No other community made a more brilliant entrance into Church history than did that of Rome by the so-called First Epistle of Clement—Paul having already testified (Rom. i. 8) that the faith of this Church was spoken of throughout the whole world. That letter to the Corinthians proves that, by the end of the first century, the Roman Church had already drawn up fixed rules for her own guidance, that she watched with motherly

forget, however, that there were also bishops elsewhere who conducted a so-called œcumenical correspondence and enjoyed great influence, as, *e.g.*, Dionysius of Corinth and Dionysius of Alexandria. In matters relating to penance the latter wrote to a great many Churches, even as far as Armenia, and sent many letters to Rome (Euseb., H. E. VI. 46). The Catholic theologian, Dittrich—before the Vatican Decree, no doubt—has spoken of him in the following terms (Dionysius von Alexandrien, 1867, p. 26): "As Dionysius participated in the power, so also he shared in the task of the primateship." "Along with the Roman bishop he was, above all, called upon to guard the interests of the whole Church."

This conception, as well as the ideas contained in this Excursus generally, is now entirely shared by Weingarten (Zeittafeln, 3rd. ed., 1888, pp. 12, 21): "The Catholic Church is essentially the work of those of Rome and Asia Minor. The Alexandrian Church and theology do not completely adapt themselves to it till the 3rd century. The metropolitan community becomes the ideal centre of the Great Church"... "The primacy of the Roman Church is essentially the transference to her of Rome's central position in the religion of the heathen world during the Empire: *urbs æterna urbs sacra.*"

[2] This is also admitted by Langen (l.c., 184 f.), who even declares that this precedence existed from the beginning.

care over outlying communities, and that she then knew how to
use language that was at once an expression of duty, love, and
authority. [1]  As yet she pretends to no legal title of any kind,
but she knows the "commandments and ordinances" ($\pi\rho\sigma\tau\acute{\alpha}\gamma\mu\alpha\tau\alpha$
and $\delta\sigma\kappa\alpha\iota\acute{\omega}\mu\alpha\tau\alpha$) of God, whereas the conduct of the sister Church
evinces her uncertainty on the matter; she is in an orderly
condition, whereas the sister community is threatened with dis-
solution; she adheres to the $\kappa\alpha\nu\grave{\omega}\nu$ $\tau\tilde{\eta}\varsigma$ $\pi\alpha\rho\alpha\delta\acute{\sigma}\sigma\varepsilon\omega\varsigma$, whilst the
other body stands in need of exhortation; [2] and in these facts
her claim to authority consists.  The Shepherd of Hermas also
proves that even in the circles of the laity the Roman Church
is impressed with the consciousness that she must care for the
whole of Christendom.  The first testimony of an outsider as
to this community is afforded us by Ignatius.  Soften as we
may all the extravagant expressions in his Epistle to the Romans,
it is at least clear that Ignatius conceded to them a precedence
in the circle of sister Churches; and that he was well acquainted
with the energy and activity displayed by them in aiding and
instructing other communities. [3]  Dionysius of Corinth, in his letter
to bishop Soter, affords us a glimpse of the vast activity manifested by the Christian Church of the world's metropolis on
behalf of all Christendom and of all brethren far and near;
and reveals to us the feelings of filial affection and veneration

[1] Cf. chaps. 59 and 62, but more especially 63.

[2] At that time the Roman Church did not confine herself to a letter; she sent
ambassadors to Corinth, $\sigma\acute{\iota}\tau\iota\nu\varepsilon\varsigma$ $\mu\acute{\alpha}\rho\tau\upsilon\rho\varepsilon\varsigma$ $\check{\varepsilon}\sigma\sigma\nu\tau\alpha\iota$ $\mu\varepsilon\tau\alpha\xi\grave{\upsilon}$ $\acute{\upsilon}\mu\tilde{\omega}\nu$ $\kappa\alpha\grave{\iota}$ $\acute{\eta}\mu\tilde{\omega}\nu$. Note
carefully also the position of the Corinthian community with which the Roman
one interfered (see on this point Wrede, Untersuchungen zum I Clemensbrief, 1891.)

[3] In Ignatius, Rom. inscr., the verb $\pi\rho\sigma\kappa\acute{\alpha}\theta\eta\mu\alpha\iota$ is twice used about the Roman
Church ($\pi\rho\sigma\kappa\acute{\alpha}\theta\eta\tau\alpha\iota$ $\grave{\varepsilon}\nu$ [to be un-rstood in a local sense] $\tau\acute{\sigma}\pi\omega$ $\chi\omega\rho\acute{\iota}\sigma\upsilon$ $\dot{P}\omega\mu\alpha\acute{\iota}\omega\nu$
—$\pi\rho\sigma\kappa\alpha\theta\eta\mu\acute{\varepsilon}\nu\eta$ $\tau\tilde{\eta}\varsigma$ $\grave{\alpha}\gamma\acute{\alpha}\pi\eta\varsigma=$ presiding in, or having the guardianship of, love).
Ignatius (Magn. 6), uses the same verb to denote the dignity of the bishop or
presbyters in relation to the community. See, besides, the important testimony in
Rom. II.: $\check{\alpha}\lambda\lambda\sigma\upsilon\varsigma$ $\grave{\varepsilon}\delta\iota\delta\acute{\alpha}\xi\alpha\tau\varepsilon$. Finally, it must be also noted that Ignatius presupposes an extensive influence on the part of individual members of the Church in
the higher spheres of government. Fifty years later we have a memorable proof
of this in the Marcia-Victor episode. Lastly, Ignatius is convinced that the
Church will interfere quite as energetically on behalf of a foreign brother as on
behalf of one of her own number. In the Epistle of Clement to James, c. 2, the
Roman bishop is called $\acute{\sigma}$ $\grave{\alpha}\lambda\eta\theta\varepsilon\acute{\iota}\alpha\varsigma$ $\pi\rho\sigma\kappa\alpha\theta\varepsilon\zeta\acute{\sigma}\mu\varepsilon\nu\sigma\varsigma$.

with which she was regarded in all Greece as well as in Antioch. This author has specially emphasised the fact that the Roman Christians are *Romans*, that is, are conscious of the particular duties incumbent on them as members of the metropolitan Church.[1] After this evidence we cannot wonder that Irenæus expressly assigned to the Church of Rome the highest rank among those founded by the Apostles.[2] His famous testimony has been quite as often under- as over-estimated. Doubtless his reference to the Roman Church is introduced in such a way that she is merely mentioned by way of example, just as he also adds the allusion to Smyrna and Ephesus; but there is quite as little doubt that this example was no arbitrary selection. The truth rather is that the Roman community *must* have been named, because its decision was already the most authoritative and impressive in Christendom.[3] Whilst giving a

---

[1] Euseb., H. E. IV. 23. 9—12; cf., above all, the words: Ἐξ ἀρχῆς ὑμῖν ἔθος ἐστὶ τοῦτο, πάντας μὲν ἀδελφοὺς ποικίλως εὐεργετεῖν, ἐκκλησίαις τε πολλαῖς ταῖς κατὰ πᾶσαν πόλιν ἐφόδια πέμπειν... πατροπαράδοτον ἔθος Ῥωμαίων Ῥωμαῖοι διαφυλάττοντες. Note here the emphasis laid on Ῥωμαῖοι.

[2] According to Irenæus a peculiar significance belongs to the old Jerusalem Church, in so far as all the Christian congregations sprang from her (III. 12. 5: αὖται φωναὶ τῆς ἐκκλησίας, ἐξ ἧς πᾶσα ἔσχηκεν ἐκκλησία τὴν ἀρχήν· αὖται φωναὶ τῆς μητροπόλεως τῶν τῆς καινῆς διαθήκης πολιτῶν). For obvious reasons Irenæus did not speak of the Jerusalem Church of his own time. Hence that passage cannot be utilised.

[3] Iren. III. 3. 1: "Sed quoniam valde longum est, in hoc tali volumine omnium ecclesiarum enumerare successiones, maximæ et antiquissimæ et omnibus cognitæ, a gloriosissimis duobus apostolis Paulo et Petro Romæ fundatæ et constitutæ ecclesiæ, eam quam habet ab apostolis traditionem et annuntiatam hominibus fidem, per successiones episcoporum pervenientem usque ad nos indicantes confundimus omnes eos, qui quoquo modo vel per sibiplacentiam malam vel vanam gloriam vel per cæcitatem et malam sententiam, præterquam oportet, colligunt. Ad hanc enim ecclesiam propter potentiorem principalitatem necesse est omnem convenire ecclesiam, hoc est, eos qui sunt undique fideles, in qua semper ab his, qui sunt undique, conservata est ea quæ est ab apostolis traditio." On this we may remark as follows: (1) The special importance which Irenæus claims for the Roman Church —for he is only referring to her—is not merely based by him on her assumed foundation by Peter and Paul, but on a combination of the four attributes "maxima", "antiquissima" etc. Dionysius of Corinth also made this assumption (Euseb., II. 25. 8), but applied it quite as much to the Corinthian Church. As regards capability of proving the truth of the Church's faith, all the communities founded by the Apostles possess *principalitas* in relation to the others; but the Roman Church has the *potentior principalitas*, in so far as she excels all the rest in her qualities of *ecclesia maxima et omnibus cognita* etc. Principalitas = "sovereign

formal scheme of proof that assigned the same theoretical value
to each Church founded by the Apostles, Irenæus added a reference to particular circumstance, viz., that in his time many
communities turned to Rome in order to testify their orthodoxy. [1]
As soon as we cease to obscure our vision with theories and
keep in view the actual circumstances, we have no cause for
astonishment. Considering the active intercourse between the
various Churches and the metropolis, it was of the utmost importance to all, especially so long as they required financial
aid, to be in connection with that of Rome, to receive support
from her, to know she would entertain travelling brethren, and
to have the power of recommending prisoners and those pining
in the mines to her influential intervention. The evidence of
Ignatius and Dionysius as well as the Marcia-Victor episode
place this beyond doubt (see above). The efforts of Marcion
and Valentinus in Rome have also a bearing on this question,
and the venerable bishop, Polycarp, did not shrink from the toil
of a long journey to secure the valuable fellowship of the
Roman Church; [2] it was not Anicetus who came to Polycarp,

authority," αυθεντία, for this was probably the word in the original text (see
proceedings of the Royal Prussian Academy of Science, 9th Nov., 1893). In common with most scholars I used to think that the "in qua" refers to "Roman
Church"; but I have now convinced myself (see the treatise just cited) that it
relates to "omnem ecclesiam", and that the clause introduced by "in qua" merely
asserts that every church, *in so far as she is faithful to tradition*, *i.e.*, *orthodox*,
must as a matter of course agree with that of Rome. (2) Irenæus asserts that every
Church, *i.e.*, believers in all parts of the world, must agree with this Church
("convenire" is to be understood in a figurative sense; the literal acceptation
"every Church must come to that of Rome" is not admissible). However, this
"must" is not meant as an imperative, but = ἀνάγκη = "it cannot be otherwise."
In reference to *principalitas* = ἀυθεντία (see I. 31. 1 : I. 26. 1) it must be remembered that Victor of Rome (l.c.) speaks of the "origo *authentici* apostolatus", and
Tertullian remarks of Valentinus when he apostatised at Rome, "ab ecclesia
*authenticæ* regulæ abrupit" (adv. Valent. 4).

[1] Beyond doubt his "convenire necesse est" is founded on actual circumstances.

[2] On other important journeys of Christian men and bishops to Rome in the
2nd and 3rd centuries see Caspari, l.c. Above all we may call attention to the
journey of Abercius of Hierapolis (not Hierapolis on the Meander) about 200 or
even earlier. Its historical reality is not to be questioned. See his words in the
epitaph composed by himself (V. 7 f.): εἰς Ῥώμην ὅς ἔπεμψεν ἐμὲν βασίληαν ἀθρῆσαι
καὶ βασίλισσαν ἰδεῖν χρυσόστολον χρυσοπέδιλον. However, Ficker raises very serious
objections to the Christian origin of the inscription.

but Polycarp to Anicetus. At the time when the controversy with Gnosticism ensued, the Roman Church showed all the rest an example of resolution; it was naturally to be expected that, as a necessary condition of mutual fellowship, she should require other communities to recognise the law by which she had regulated her own circumstances. No community in the Empire could regard with indifference its relationship to the great Roman Church; almost everyone had connections with her; she contained believers from all the rest. As early as 180 this Church could point to a series of bishops reaching in uninterrupted succession from the glorious apostles Paul and Peter [1] down to the present time; and she alone maintained a brief but definitely formulated *lex*, which she entitled the summary of apostolic tradition, and by reference to which she decided all questions of faith with admirable certainty. Theories were incapable of overcoming the elementary differences that could not but appear as soon as Christianity became naturalised in the various provinces and towns of the Empire. Nor was it theories that created the empiric unity of the Churches, but the unity which the Empire possessed in Rome; the extent and composition of the Græco-Latin community there; the security—and this was not the least powerful element—that accompanied the development of this great society, well provided as it was with wealth and possessed of an influence in high quarters already dating from the first century; [2] as well as the care which it displayed on behalf of all Christendom. *All these causes combined to convert*

---

[1] We cannot here discuss how this tradition arose; in all likelihood it already expresses the position which the Roman Church very speedily attained in Christendom. See Renan, Orig., Vol. VII., p. 70: "Pierre et Paul (réconciliés), voilà le chef-d'œuvre qui fondait la suprématie ecclésiastique de Rome dans l'avenir. Une nouvelle qualité mythique remplaçait celle de Romulus et Remus." But it is highly probable that Peter was really in Rome like Paul (see 1 Clem. V., Ignatius ad Rom. IV.); both really performed important services to the Church there, and died as martyrs in that city.

[2] The wealth of the Roman Church is also illustrated by the present of 200,000 sesterces brought her by Marcion (Tertull., de præsc. 30). The "Shepherd" also contains instructive particulars with regard to this. As far as her influence is concerned, we possess various testimonies from Philipp. IV. 22 down to the famous account by Hippolytus of the relations of Victor to Marcia. We may call special attention to Ignatius' Epistle to the Romans.

*the Christian communities into a real confederation under the
primacy of the Roman Church (and subsequently under the
leadership of her bishops).* This primacy cannot of course be
further defined, for it was merely a *de facto* one. But, from
the nature of the case, it was immediately shaken, when it was
claimed as a *legal* right associated with the person of the Roman
bishop.

That this theory is more than a hypothesis is shown by
several facts which prove the unique authority as well as the
interference of the Roman Church (that is, of her bishop). First,
in the Montanist controversy—and that too at the stage when
it was still almost exclusively confined to Asia Minor—the already sobered adherents of the new prophecy petitioned Rome
(bishop Eleutherus) to recognise their Church, and it was at
Rome that the Gallic confessors cautiously interfered in their
behalf; after which a native of Asia Minor induced the Roman
bishop to withdraw the letters of toleration already issued.[1] In
view of the facts that it was not Roman Montanists who were
concerned, that Rome was the place where the Asiatic members
of this sect sought for recognition, and that it was in Rome
that the Gauls interfered in their behalf, the significance of this
proceeding cannot be readily minimised. We cannot of course
dogmatise on the matter; but the fact can be proved that the
decision of the Roman Church must have settled the position
of that sect of enthusiasts in Christendom. Secondly, what is
reported to us of Victor, the successor of Eleutherus, is still
plainer testimony. He ventured to issue an edict, which we
may already style a peremptory one, proclaiming the Roman
practice with regard to the regulation of ecclesiastical festivals
to be the universal rule in the Church, and declaring that every
congregation, that failed to adopt the Roman arrangement,[2]

[1] See Tertullian, adv. Prax. 1; Euseb., H. E. V. 3, 4. Dictionary of Christian
Biography III., p. 937.

[2] Euseb., H. E. V. 24. 9: Ἐπὶ τούτοις ὁ μὲν τῆς Ῥωμαίων προεστὼς Βίκτωρ ἀθρόως
τῆς Ἀσίας πάσης ἅμα ταῖς ὁμόροις ἐκκλησίαις τὰς παροικίας ἀποτέμνειν ὡσὰν ἑτε-
ροδοξούσας, τῆς κοινῆς ἑνώσεως πειρᾶται, καὶ στηλιτεύει γε διὰ γραμμάτων, ἀκοινω-
νήτους πάντας ἄρδην τούς ἐκεῖσε ἀνακηρύττων ἀδελφούς. Stress should be laid on
two points here: (1) Victor proclaimed that the people of Asia Minor were to be
excluded from the κοινὴ ἕνωσις, and not merely from the fellowship of the Roman

was excluded from the union of the one Church on the ground of heresy. How would Victor have ventured on such an edict —though indeed he had not the power of enforcing it in every case—unless the special prerogative of Rome to determine the conditions of the "common unity" (κοινὴ ἕνωσις) in the vital questions of the faith had been an acknowledged and well-established fact? How could Victor have addressed such a demand to the independent Churches, if he had not been recognised, in his capacity of bishop of Rome, as the special guardian of the κοινὴ ἕνωσις?[1] Thirdly, it was Victor who formally excluded Theodotus from Church fellowship. This is the first really well-attested case of a Christian *taking his stand on the rule of faith* being excommunicated because a definite interpretation of it was already insisted on. In this instance the expression υἱὸς μονογενής (only begotten Son) was required to be understood in the sense of φύσει Θεός (God by nature). It was in Rome that this first took place. Fourthly, under Zephyrinus, Victor's successor, the Roman ecclesiastics interfered in the Carthaginian veil dispute, making common cause with the local clergy against Tertullian; and both appealed to the authority of predecessors, that is, above all, of the Roman bishops.[2] Tertullian, Hippolytus, Origen, and Cyprian were

---

Church; (2) he based the excommunication on the alleged heterodoxy of those Churches. See Heinichen, Melet. VIII., on Euseb., l.c. Victor's action is parallelled by that of Stephen. Firmilian says to the latter: "Dum enim putas, omnes abs te abstineri posse, solum te ab omnibus abstinuisti." It is a very instructive fact that in the 4th century Rome also made the attempt to have Sabbath fasting established as an *apostolic* custom. See the interesting work confuted by Augustine (ep. 36), a writing which emanates from a Roman author who is unfortunately unknown to us. Cf. also Augustine's 54th and 55th epistles.

[1] Irenæus also (l.c. § 11) does not appear to have questioned Victor's proceeding as such, but as applied to this particular case.

[2] See Tertull., de orat. 22: "Sed non putet institutionem unusquisque antecessoris commovendam." De virg. vel. I: "Paracletus solus antecessor, quia solus post Christum"; 2: "Eas ego ecclesias proposui, quas et ipsi apostoli vel apostolici viri condiderunt, et puto ante quosdam"; 3: "Sed nec inter consuetudines dispicere voluerunt illi sanctissimi antecessores". This is also the question referred to in the important remark in Jerome, de vir. inl. 53: "Tertullianus ad mediam ætatem presbyter fuit ecclesiæ Africanæ, invidia postea et contumeliis clericorum Romanæ ecclesiæ ad Montani dogma delapsus."

obliged to resist the pretensions of these ecclesiastics to authority outside their own Church, the first having to contend with Calixtus, and the three others with Stephen. [1] It was the Roman *Church* that first displayed this activity and care; the Roman bishop sprang from the community in exactly the same way as the corresponding official did in other places. [2] In Irenæus' proof from prescription, however, it is already the Roman *bishops* that are specially mentioned. [3]

[1] Stephen acted like Victor and excluded almost all the East from the fellowship of the Church; see in addition to Cyprian's epistles that of Dionysius of Alexandria in Euseb., H. E. VII. 5. In reference to Hippolytus, see Philosoph. l. IX. In regard to Origen, see the allusions in de orat. 28 fin.; in Matth. XI. 9, 15 : XII. 9—14 : XVI. 8, 22 : XVII. 14; in Joh. X. 16; Rom. VI in Isai. c. 1. With regard to Philosoph. IX. 12, Sohm rightly remarks (p. 389): "It is clear that the responsibility was laid on the Roman bishop not merely in several cases where married men were made presbyters and deacons, but also when they were appointed bishops; and it is also evident that he appears just as responsible when bishops are not deposed in consequence of their marrying. One cannot help concluding that the Roman bishop has the power of appointing and deposing not merely presbyters and deacons, but also bishops. Moreover, the impression is conveyed that this appointment and deposition of bishops takes place in Rome, for the passage contains a description of existent conditions in the Roman Church. Other communities may be deprived of their bishops by an order from Rome, and a bishop (chosen in Rome) may be sent them. The words of the passage are: ἐπὶ Καλλίστου ἤρξαντο ἐπίσκοποι καὶ πρεσβύτεροι καὶ διάκονοι δίγαμοι καὶ τρίγαμοι καθίστασθαι εἰς κλήρους· εἰ δὲ καὶ τις ἐν κλήρῳ ὢν γαμοίη, μένειν τὸν τοιοῦτον ἐν τῷ κλήρῳ ὡς μὴ ἡμαρτηκότα.

[2] In the treatise "Die Briefe des römischen Klerus aus der Zeit der Sedisvacanz im Jahre 250" (Abhandlungen für Weizsäcker, 1892), I have shown how the Roman clergy kept the revenue of the Church and of the Churches in their hands, though they had no bishop. What language the Romans used in epistles 8, 30, 36 of the Cyprian collection, and how they interfered in the affairs of the Carthaginian Church! Beyond doubt the Roman *Church* possessed an acknowledged primacy in the year 250; it was the primacy of active participation and fulfilled duty. As yet there was no recognised dogmatic or historic foundation assigned for it; in fact it is highly probable that this theory was still shaky and uncertain in Rome herself. The college of presbyters and deacons feels and speaks as if it were the bishop. For it was not on the bishop that the incomparable prestige of Rome was based—at least this claim was not yet made with any confidence,—but on the *city itself*, on the origin and history, the faith and love, the earnestness and zeal *of the whole Roman Church and her clergy*.

[3] In Tertullian, de præsc. 36, the bishops are not mentioned. He also, like Irenæus, cites the Roman Church as one amongst others. We have already remarked that in the scheme of proof from prescription no higher rank could be assigned to the Roman Church than to any other of the group founded by the Apostles. Tertullian

Praxeas reminded the bishop of Rome of the authority of his
predecessors ("auctoritates præcessorum eius") and it was in
the character of *bishop* that Victor acted. The assumption that
Paul and Peter laboured in Rome, that is, founded the Church
of that city (Dionysius, Irenæus, Tertullian, Caius), must have
conferred a high degree of prestige on her bishops, as soon as
the latter officials were elevated to the position of more or less
sovereign lords of the communities and were regarded as successors of the Apostles. The first who acted up to this idea was Calixtus.
The sarcastic titles of "pontifex maximus", "episcopus episcoporum", "benedictus papa" and "apostolicus", applied to him
by Tertullian in "de pudicitia" I. 13, are so many references to
the fact that Calixtus already claimed for himself a position of
primacy, in other words, that he associated with his own personal position as bishop the primacy possessed by the Roman
Church, which pre-eminence, however, must have been gradually
vanishing in proportion to the progress of the Catholic form
of organisation among the other communities. Moreover, that
is evident from the form of the edict he issued (Tert. l. c., I:
"I hear that an edict has been issued and that a decisive one",

continues to maintain this position, but expressly remarks that the Roman Church
has special authority for the Carthaginian, because Carthage had received its
Christianity from Rome. He expresses the special relationship between Rome and
Carthage in the following terms: "Si autem Italiæ adiaces habes Romam, unde
nobis quoque auctoritas præsto est." With Tertullian, then, the *de facto* position
of the Roman Church in Christendom did not lead to the same conclusion in the
scheme of proof from prescription as we found in Irenæus. But in his case also
that position is indicated by the rhetorical ardour with which he speaks of the
Roman Church, whereas he does nothing more than mention Corinth, Philippi,
Thessalonica, and Ephesus. Even at that time, moreover, he had ground enough
for a more reserved attitude towards Rome, though in the antignostic struggle he
could not dispense with the tradition of the Roman community. In the veil dispute
(de virg. vel. 2) he opposed the authority of the Greek apostolic Churches to that
of Rome. Polycarp had done the same against Anicetus, Polycrates against Victor,
Proculus against his Roman opponents. Conversely, Praxeas in his appeal to Eleutherus (c. I.: "præcessorum auctoritates"), Caius when contending with Proculus,
the Carthaginian clergy when opposing Tertullian (in the veil dispute), and Victor
when contending with Polycrates set the authority of Rome against that of the
Greek apostolic Churches. These struggles at the transition from the 2nd to the
3rd century are of the utmost importance. Rome was here seeking to overthrow
the authority of the only group of Churches able to enter into rivalry with her
those of Asia Minor, and succeeded in the attempt.

"audio edictum esse præpositum et quidem peremptorium "),
from the grounds it assigned and from the opposition to it on
the part of Tertullian.  From the form, in so far as Calixtus
acted here quite independently and, without previous consultation, issued a *peremptory* edict, that is, one settling the matter
and immediately taking effect; from the grounds it assigned,
in so far as he appealed in justification of his action to Matt.
XVI. 18 ff. [1]—the first instance of the kind recorded in history;
from Tertullian's opposition to it, because the latter treats it
not as local, Roman, but as pregnant in consequences for all
Christendom.  But, as soon as the question took the form of
enquiring whether the Roman *bishop* was elevated above the
rest, a totally new situation arose.  Even in the third century,
as already shown, the Roman community, led by its bishops,
still showed the rest an example in the process of giving a
political constitution to the Church.  It can also be proved that
even far distant congregations were still being bound to the
Roman Church through financial support, [2] and that she was
appealed to in questions of faith, just as the law of the city
of Rome was invoked as the standard in civil questions. [3]  It

---

[1] De pudic. 21 : "De tua nunc sententia quæro, unde hoc ius ecclesiæ usurpes.
Si quia dixerit Petro dominus: Super hanc petram ædificabo ecclesiam meam, tibi
dedi claves regni cælestis, vel, Quæcumque alligaveris vel solveris in terra, erunt
alligata vel soluta in cœlis, id circo præsumis et ad te derivasse solvendi et alligandi
potestatem?"  Stephen did the same; see Firmilian in Cyprian ep. 75.  With this
should be compared the description Clement of Rome gives in his epistles to James
of his own installation by Peter (c. 2).  The following words are put in Peter's
mouth: Κλήμεντα τοῦτον ἐπίσκοπον ὑμῖν χειροτονῶ, ᾧ τὴν ἐμὴν τῶν λόγων πιστεύω
καθέδραν ... διὸ αὐτῷ μεταδίδωμι τὴν ἐξουσίαν τοῦ δεσμεύειν καὶ λύειν, ἵνα περὶ
παντὸς οὗ ἄν χειροτονήσῃ ἐπὶ γῆς ἔσται δεδογματισμένον ἐν οὐρανοῖς. δήσει γὰρ ὅ
δεῖ δεθῆναι καὶ λύσει ὅ δεῖ λυθῆναι, ὡς τὸν τῆς ἐκκλησίας εἰδὼς κανόνα.

[2] See Dionysius of Alexandria's letter to the Roman bishop Stephen (Euseb.,
H. E. VII. 5. 2): Αἱ μέντοι Συρίαι ὅλαι καὶ ἡ 'Αραβία, οἷς ἐπαρκεῖτε ἑκάστοτε καὶ
οἷς νῦν ἐπεστείλατε.

[3] In the case of Origen's condemnation the decision of Rome seems to have
been of special importance.  Origen sought to defend his orthodoxy in a letter
written by his own hand to the Roman bishop Fabian (see Euseb., H. E. VI. 36;
Jerome, ep. 84. 10).  The Roman bishop Pontian had previously condemned him
after summoning a "senate"; see Jerome, ep. 33 (Döllinger, Hippolytus and Calixtus,
p. 259 f.).  Further, it is an important fact that a deputation of Alexandrian Christians,
who did not agree with the Christology of their bishop Dionysius, repaired to Rome

is further manifest from Cyprian's epistles that the Roman
Church was regarded as the *ecclesia principalis*, as the guardian
*par excellence* of the *unity* of the Church. We may explain
from Cyprian's own particular situation all else that he said in
praise of the Roman Church (see above p. 88, note 2) and
specially of the *cathedra Petri;* but the general view that she
is the "matrix et radix ecclesiæ catholicæ" is not peculiar to
him, and the statement that the "unitas sacerdotalis" originated
in Rome is merely the modified expression, necessitated by the
altered circumstances of the Church, for the acknowledged fact
that the Roman community was the most distinguished among
the sister groups, and as such had had and still possessed the
right and duty of watching over the unity of the whole. Cyprian
himself no doubt took a further step at the time of his correspondence with Cornelius, and proclaimed the special reference
of Matt. XVI. to the *cathedra Petri;* but he confined his theory
to the abstractions "ecclesia", "cathedra". In him the importance of this *cathedra* oscillates between the significance of a
once existent fact that continues to live on as a symbol, and
that of a real and permanent court of appeal. Moreover, he
did not go the length of declaring that any special authority
within the collective Church attached to the temporary occupant
of the *cathedra Petri.* If we remove from Cyprian's abstractions
everything to which he himself thinks there is nothing concrete
corresponding, then we must above all eliminate every prerogative of the Roman bishop for the time being. What remains
behind is the special position of the Roman Church, which indeed is represented by her bishop. Cyprian can say quite

---

to the *Roman* bishop Dionysius and formally accused the first named prelate. It
is also significant that Dionysius received this complaint and brought the matter up
at a Roman synod. No objection was taken to this proceeding (Athanas., de synod.).
This information is very instructive, for it proves that the Roman Church was ever
regarded as specially charged with watching over the observance of the conditions
of the general ecclesiastical federation, the κοινὴ ἕνωσις. As to the fact that in
circular letters, not excepting Eastern ones, the Roman Church was put at the head
of the address, see Euseb., H. E. VII. 30. How frequently foreign bishops came
to Rome is shown by the 19th canon of Arles (A.D. 314): "De episcopis pere-
grinis, qui in urbem solent venire, placuit iis locum dari ut offerant." The first
canon is also important in deciding the special position of Rome.

frankly: "owing to her magnitude Rome ought to have precedence over Carthage" ("pro magnitudine sua debet Carthaginem
Roma præcedere") and his theory: "the episcopate is one, and
a part of it is held by each bishop for the whole" ("episcopatus unus est, cuius a singulis in solidum pars tenetur"), virtually excludes any special prerogative belonging to a particular
bishop (see also "de unit." 4). Here we have reached the
point that has already been briefly referred to above, viz.,
that the consolidation of the Churches in the Empire after
the Roman pattern could not but endanger the prestige and
peculiar position of Rome, and did in fact do so. If we consider that each bishop was the acknowledged sovereign of his
own diocese—now Catholic, that all bishops, as such, were recognised to be successors of the Apostles, that, moreover, the
attribute of priesthood occupied a prominent position in the
conception of the episcopal office, and that the metropolitan
unions with their presidents and synods had become completely
naturalised—in short, that the rigid episcopal and provincial
constitution of the Church had become an accomplished fact,
so that, ultimately, it was no longer communities, but merely
bishops that had dealings with each other, then we shall see
that a new situation was thereby created for Rome, that is, for
her bishop. In the West it was perhaps chiefly through the
coöperation of Cyprian that Rome found herself face to face
with a completely organised Church system. His behaviour in
the controversy about heretical baptism proves that in cases of
dispute he was resolved to elevate his theory of the sovereign
authority of each bishop above his theory of the necessary
connection with the *cathedra Petri*. But, when that levelling
of the episcopate came about, Rome had already acquired
rights that could no longer be cancelled.[1] Besides, there was

---

[1] Peculiar circumstances, which unfortunately we cannot quite explain, are connected
with the cases discussed by Cyprian in epp. 67 and 68. The Roman bishop must
have had the acknowledged power of dealing with the bishop of Arles, whereas
the Gallic prelates had not this right. Sohm, p. 391 ff., assumes that the Roman
bishop alone—not Cyprian or the bishops of Gaul—had authority to exclude the
bishop of Arles from the general fellowship of the Church, but that, as far as the
Gallic Churches were concerned, such an excommunication possessed no legal effect,
but only a moral one, because in their case the bishop of Rome had only a

one thing that could not be taken from the Roman Church,
nor therefore from her bishop, even if she were denied
the special right to Matt. XVI., viz., the possession of Rome.
The site of the world's metropolis might be shifted, but Rome
could not be removed. In the long run, however, the shifting
of the capital proved advantageous to ecclesiastical Rome. At
the beginning of the great epoch when the alienation of East
from West became pronounced and permanent, an emperor,
from political grounds, decided in favour of that party in Antioch
"with whom the bishops in Italy and the city of the Romans
held intercourse" (οἷς ἂν οἱ κατὰ τὴν Ἰταλίαν καὶ τὴν Ῥωμαίων
πόλιν ἐπίσκοποι τοῦ δόγματος ἐπιστέλλοιεν [1]). In this instance the

spiritual authority and no legal power. Further, two Spanish bishops publicly appealed to the Roman see against their deposition, and Cyprian regarded this appeal
as in itself correct. Finally, Cornelius says of himself in a letter (in Euseb., H. E.
VI. 43. 10): τῶν λοιπῶν ἐπισκόπων διαδόχους εἰς τοὺς τόπους, ἐν οἷς ἦσαν, χειροτ-
ονήσαντες ἀπεστάλκαμεν. This quotation refers to Italy, and the passage, which
must be read connectedly, makes it plain (see, besides, the quotation in reference to
Calixtus given above on p. 162), that, before the middle of the 3rd century, the
Roman Church already possessed a legal right of excommunication and the recognised
power of making ecclesiastical appointments as far as the communities and bishops
in Italy were concerned (see Sohm, p. 389 ff.).

[1] Euseb., H. E. VII. 30. 19. The Church of Antioch sought to enter upon an
independent line of development under Paul of Samosata. Paul's fall was the victory
of Rome. We may suppose it to be highly probable, though to the best of my
belief there is for the present no sure proof, that it was not till then that the Roman
standards and sacraments, catholic and apostolic collection of Scriptures (see, on the
contrary, the use of Scripture in the Didaskalia), apostolic rule of faith, and apostolic
episcopacy attained supremacy in Antioch; |but that they began to be introduced
into that city about the time of Serapion's bishopric (that is, during the Easter
controversy). The old records of the Church of Edessa have an important bearing
on this point; and from these it is evident that her constitution did not begin to
assume a Catholic form till the beginning of the 3rd century, and that as the result
of connection with Rome. See the Doctrine of Addai by Phillips, p. 50: "Palut
himself went to Antioch and received the hand of the priesthood from Serapion,
bishop of Antioch. Serapion, bishop of Antioch, himself also received the hand
from Zephyrinus, bishop of the city of Rome, from the succession of the hand of
the priesthood of Simon Cephas, which he received from our Lord, who was there
bishop of Rome 25 years, (sic) in the days of the Cæsar, who reigned there 13 years."
(See also Tixeront, Édesse, pp. 149, 152.) Cf. with this the prominence given in the Acts
of Scharbil and Barsamya to the fact that they were contemporaries of Fabian, bishop of
Rome. We read there (see Rubens Duval, Les Actes de Scharbil et les Actes de
Barsamya, Paris, 1889, and Histoire d'Édesse, p. 130): "Barsamya (he was bishop of
Edessa at the time of Decius) lived at the time of Fabian, bishop of Rome. He had

interest of the Roman Church and the interest of the emperor coincided. But the Churches in the various provinces, being now completely organised and therefore seldom in need of any more help from outside, were henceforth in a position to pursue their own interest. So the bishop of Rome had step by step to fight for the new authority, which, being now based on a purely dogmatic theory and being forced to repudiate any empirical foundation, was inconsistent with the Church system that the Roman community more than any other had helped to build up. The proposition "the Roman Church always had the primacy" ("ecclesia Romana semper habuit primatum") and the statement that "Catholic" virtually means "Roman Catholic" are gross fictions, when devised in honour of the temporary occupant of the Roman see and detached from the significance of the Eternal City in profane history; but, applied to the *Church* of the imperial capital, they contain a truth the denial of which is equivalent to renouncing the attempt to explain the process by which the Church was unified and catholicised. [1]

received the laying on of hands from Abschelama, who had received it from Palut. Palut had been consecrated by Serapion, bishop of Antioch, and the latter had been consecrated by Zephyrinus, bishop of Rome." As regards the relation of the State of Rome to the Roman Church, that is, to the Roman bishop, who by the year 250 had already become a sort of *præfectus urbis*, with his district superintendents, the deacons, and in fact a sort of *princeps æmulus*, cf. (1) the recorded comments of Alexander Severus on the Christians, and especially those on their organisation; (2) the edict of Maximinus Thrax and the banishment of the bishops Pontian and Hippolytus; (3) the attitude of Philip the Arabian; (4) the remarks of Decius in Cyp. ep. 55 (see above p 124) and his proceedings against the Roman bishops, and (5) the attitude of Aurelian in Antioch. On the extent and organisation of the Roman Church about 250 see Euseb., H. E. VI. 43.

[1] The memorable words in the lately discovered appeal by Eusebius of Dory-læum to Leo I. (Neues Archiv., Vol. XI., part 2, p. 364 f.) are no mere flattery, and the fifth century is not the first to which they are applicable: "Curavit desuper et ab exordio consuevit thronus apostolicus iniqua perferentes defensare et eos qui in evitabiles factiones inciderunt, adiuvare et humi iacentes erigere, secundum possibilitatem, quam habetis; causa autem rei, quod sensum rectum tenetis et incon-cussam servatis erga dominum nostrum Iesum Christum fidem, nec non etiam indissimulatam universis fratribus et omnibus in nomine Christi vocatis tribuitis caritatem, etc." See also Theodoret's letters addressed to Rome.

## II. FIXING AND GRADUAL HELLENISING OF CHRISTIANITY AS A SYSTEM OF DOCTRINE.

_____

## CHAPTER IV.

### ECCLESIASTICAL CHRISTIANITY AND PHILOSOPHY.
### THE APOLOGISTS.

### 1. *Introduction.* [1]

THE object of the Christian Apologists, some of whom filled ecclesiastical offices and in various ways promoted spiritual progress,[2] was, as they themselves explained, to uphold the Christianity professed by the Christian Churches and publicly preached. They were convinced that the Christian faith was founded on revelation and that only a mind enlightened by God could grasp and maintain the faith. They acknowledged the Old Testament to be the authoritative source of God's revelation, maintained that the whole human race was meant to be

---

1 Edition by Otto, 9 Vols., 1876 f. New edition of the Apologists (unfinished; only Tatian and Athenagoras by Schwarz have yet appeared) in the Texte und Untersuchungen zur altchristlichen Litteratur-Geschichte, Vol. IV. Tzschirner, Geschichte der Apologetik, 1st part, 1805; id., Der Fall des Heidenthums, 1829. Ehlers, Vis atque potestas, quam philosophia antiqua, imprimis Platonica et Stoica in doctrina apologetarum habuerit, 1859.

2 It is intrinsically probable that their works directly addressed to the Christian Church gave a more full exposition of their Christianity than we find in the Apologies. This can moreover be proved with certainty from the fragments of Justin's, Tatian's and Melito's esoteric writings. But, whilst recognising this fact, we must not make the erroneous assumption that the fundamental conceptions and interests of Justin and the rest were in reality other than may be inferred from their Apologies.

reached by Christianity, and adhered to the early Christian eschatology. These views as well as the strong emphasis they laid upon human freedom and responsibility, enabled them to attain a firm standpoint in opposition to "Gnosticism", and to preserve their position within the Christian communities, whose moral purity and strength they regarded as a strong proof of the truth of this faith. In the endeavours of the Apologists to explain Christianity to the cultured world, we have before us the attempts of Greek churchmen to represent the Christian religion as a philosophy, and to convince outsiders that it was the highest wisdom and the absolute truth. These efforts were not rejected by the Churches like those of the so-called Gnostics, but rather became in subsequent times the foundation of the ecclesiastical dogmatic. The Gnostic speculations were repudiated, whereas those of the Apologists were accepted. The manner in which the latter set forth Christianity as a philosophy met with approval. What were the conditions under which ecclesiastical Christianity and Greek philosophy concluded the alliance which has found a place in the history of the world? How did this union attain acceptance and permanence, whilst "Gnosticism" was at first rejected? These are the two great questions the correct answers to which are of fundamental importance for the understanding of the history of Christian dogma.

The answers to these questions appear paradoxical. The theses of the Apologists finally overcame all scruples in ecclesiastical circles and were accepted by the Græco-Roman world, because they made Christianity *rational* without taking from, or adding to, its traditional historic material. The secret of the epoch-making success of the apologetic theology is thus explained: These Christian philosophers formulated the content of the Gospel in a manner which appealed to the common sense of all the serious thinkers and intelligent men of the age. Moreover, they contrived to use the positive material of tradition, including the life and worship of Christ, in such a way as to furnish this reasonable religion with a confirmation and proof that had hitherto been eagerly sought, but sought in vain. In the theology of the Apologists, Christianity, as the religious enlightenment directly emanating from God himself, is most sharply contrasted with all polytheism, natural religion, and ceremonial. They proclaimed it in the most emphatic manner as the religion of the spirit, of freedom, and of absolute morality. Almost the whole positive material of Christianity is embodied in the story which relates its entrance into the world, its spread, and the proof of its truth. The religion itself, on the other hand, appears as the truth that is surely attested and accords with reason—a truth the content of which is not primarily dependent on historical facts and finally overthrows all polytheism.

Now this was the very thing required. In the second century of our era a great many needs and aspirations were undoubtedly making themselves felt in the sphere of religion and morals. "Gnosticism" and Marcionite Christianity prove the variety and depth of the needs then asserting themselves within the space that the ecclesiastical historian is able to survey. Mightier than all others, however, was the longing men felt to free themselves from the burden of the past, to cast away the rubbish of cults and of unmeaning religious ceremonies, and to be assured that the results of religious philosophy, those great and simple doctrines of virtue and immortality and of the God who is a Spirit, were certain truths. He who brought the message that these ideas were realities, and who, on the strength of these realities, declared polytheism and the worship of idols to be obsolete, had the mightiest forces on his side; for the times were now ripe for this preaching. What formed the strength of the apologetic philosophy was the proclamation that Christianity both contained the highest truth, as men already supposed it to be and as they had discovered it in their own minds, and the absolutely reliable guarantee that was desired for this truth. To the quality which makes it appear meagre to us it owed its impressiveness. The fact of its falling in with the general spiritual current of the time and making no attempt to satisfy special and deeper needs enabled it to plead the cause of spiritual monotheism and to oppose the worship of idols in the manner most easily understood. As it did not require historic and positive material to describe the nature of religion and morality, this philosophy enabled the Apologists to demonstrate the worthlessness of the traditional religion and worship of the different nations.[1] The same cause, however, made them take up the conservative position with regard to the historical traditions of Christianity. These were not ultimately tested as to their content, for this was taken for granted, no matter how they might be worded; but they were used to give an assurance of the truth, and to prove that the religion of the spirit was not founded on human opinion, but on divine revelation. The only really important consideration in Christianity is that it is *revelation, real revelation.* The Apologists had no doubt as to what it reveals, and therefore any investigation was unnecessary. The result of Greek philosophy, the philosophy of Plato and Zeno, as it had further developed in the empires of Alexander the Great and the Romans, was to attain victory and permanence by the aid of Christianity. Thus we view the progress of this development to-day,[2] and Christianity really proved to be the force from which that religious philosophy, viewed as a theory of the world and system of morality, first received the courage to free itself from the polytheistic past and descend from the circles of the learned to the common people.

This constitutes the deepest distinction between Christian philosophers like Justin and those of the type of Valentinus. The latter sought for a *religion;* the former, though indeed they were not very clear about their own purpose, sought *assurance* as to a theistic and moral conception of the world which they already possessed. At first the complexus of Christian tradition, which must have possessed many features of attraction for them, was something foreign to both. The latter, however, sought to make this tradition intelligible. For the former it was enough that they had here a revelation before them; that this revelation

[1] That is, so far as these were clearly connected with polytheism. Where this was not the case or seemed not to be so, national traditions, both the true and the spurious, were readily and joyfully admitted into the *catalogus testimoniorum* of revealed truth.

[2] Though these words were already found in the first edition, Clemen (Justin 1890, p. 56) has misunderstood me so far as to think that I spoke here of conscious intention on the part of the Apologists. Such nonsense of course never occurred to me.

also bore unmistakable testimony to the one God, who was a
Spirit, to virtue, and to immortality; and that it was capable
of convincing men and of leading them to a virtuous life.
Viewed superficially, the Apologists were no doubt the conservatives; but they were so, because they scarcely in any respect
meddled with the contents of tradition. The " Gnostics", on
the contrary, sought to understand what they read and to investigate the truth of the message of which they heard. The
most characteristic feature is the attitude of each to the Old
Testament. The Apologists were content to have found in
it an ancient source of revelation, and viewed the book as a
testimony to the truth, *i.e.*, to philosophy and virtue; the Gnostics investigated this document and examined to what extent it
agreed with the new impressions they had received from the
Gospel. We may sum up as follows: The Gnostics sought to
determine what Christianity is as a religion, and, as they were
convinced of the absoluteness of Christianity, this process led
them to incorporate with it all that they looked on as sublime
and holy and to remove everything they recognised to be inferior. The Apologists, again, strove to discover an authority
for religious enlightenment and morality and to find the confirmation of a theory of the universe, which, if true, contained for
them the certainty of eternal life; and this they found in the
Christian tradition.

At bottom this contrast is a picture of the great discord
existing in the religious philosophy of the age itself (see p. 129,
vol. I.). No one denied the fact that all truth was divine, that
is, was founded on revelation. The great question, however,
was whether every man possessed this truth as a slumbering
capacity that only required to be awakened; whether it was
rational, *i.e.*, merely moral truth, or must be above that which
is moral, that is, of a religious nature; whether it must carry
man beyond himself; and whether a real redemption was necessary. It is ultimately the dispute between morality and religion,
which appears as an unsettled problem in the theses of the
idealistic philosophers and in the whole spiritual conceptions
then current among the educated, and which recurs in the contrast between the Apologetic and the Gnostic theology. And,

as in the former case we meet with the most varied shades
and transitions, for no one writer has developed a consistent
theory, so also we find a similar state of things in the latter; [1]
for no Apologist quite left out of sight the idea of redemption
(deliverance from the dominion of demons can only be effected by
the Logos, *i.e.*, God). Wherever the idea of freedom is strongly
emphasised, the religious element, in the strict sense of the
word, appears in jeopardy. This is the case with the Apologists
throughout. Conversely, wherever redemption forms the central
thought, need is felt of a suprarational truth, which no longer
views morality as the only aim, and which, again, requires
particular media, a sacred history and sacred symbols. Stoic
rationalism, in its logical development, is menaced wherever we
meet the perception that the course of the world must in some
way be helped, and wherever the contrast between reason and
sensuousness, that the old Stoa had confused, is clearly felt to
be an unendurable state of antagonism that man cannot remove by his own unaided efforts. The need of a revelation
had its starting-point in philosophy here. The judgment of
oneself and of the world to which Platonism led, the self-
consciousness which it awakened by the detachment of man
from nature, and the contrasts which it revealed led of necessity to that frame of mind which manifested itself in the craving
for a revelation. The Apologists felt this. But their rationalism gave a strange turn to the satisfaction of that need. It
was not their Christian ideas which first involved them in contradictions. At the time when Christianity appeared on the
scene, the Platonic and Stoic systems themselves were already
so complicated that philosophers did not find their difficulties
seriously increased by a consideration of the Christian doctrines.
As *Apologists*, however, they decidedly took the part of
Christianity because, according to them, it was the doctrine of
reason and freedom.

The Gospel was hellenised in the second century in so far
as the Gnostics in various ways transformed it into a Hellenic

---

[1] Note here particularly the attitude of Tatian, who has already introduced a
certain amount of the "Gnostic" element into his "Oratio ad Græcos", although,
he adheres in the main to the ordinary apologetic doctrines.

religion for the educated. The Apologists used it—we may
almost say inadvertently—to overthrow polytheism by maintaining
that Christianity was the realisation of an absolutely moral theism.
The Christian religion was not the first to experience this twofold
destiny on Græco-Roman soil. A glance at the history of the
Jewish religion shows us a parallel development; in fact, both
the speculations of the Gnostics and the theories of the Apologists were foreshadowed in the theology of the Jewish
Alexandrians, and particularly in that of Philo. Here also the
Gospel merely entered upon the heritage of Judaism. [1] Three centuries before the appearance of Christian Apologists, Jews, who
had received a Hellenic training, had already set forth the religion
of Jehovah to the Greeks in that remarkably summary and spiritualised form which represents it as the absolute and highest
philosophy, *i.e.*, the knowledge of God, of virtue, and of recompense in the next world. Here these Jewish philosophers had
already transformed all the positive and historic elements of the
national religion into parts of a huge system for proving the
truth of that theism. The Christian Apologists adopted this
method, for they can hardly be said to have invented it anew. [2]
We see from the Jewish Sibylline oracles how wide-spread it
was. Philo, however, was not only a Stoic rationalist, but a
hyper-Platonic religious philosopher. In like manner, the Christian
Apologists did not altogether lack this element, though in some
isolated cases among them there are hardly any traces of it.
This feature is most fully represented among the Gnostics.

This transformation of religion into a philosophic system would
not have been possible had not Greek philosophy itself happened
to be in process of development into a religion. Such a transformation was certainly very foreign to the really classical time
of Greece and Rome. The pious belief in the efficacy and
power of the gods and in their appearances and manifestations,
as well as the traditional worship, could have no bond of union

---

[1] Since the time of Josephus Greek philosophers had ever more and more
acknowledged the "philosophical" character of Judaism; see Porphyr., de abstin.
anim. II. 26, about the Jews: ἅτε φιλόσοφοι τὸ γένος ὄντες.

[2] On the relation of Christian literature to the writings of Philo, cf. Siegfried,
Philo von Alexandrien, p. 303 f.

with speculations concerning the essence and ultimate cause of things. The idea of a religious dogma which was at once to furnish a correct theory of the world and a principle of conduct was from this standpoint completely unintelligible. But philosophy, particularly in the Stoa, set out in search of this idea, and, after further developments, sought for one special religion with which it could agree or through which it could at least attain certainty. The meagre cults of the Greeks and Romans were unsuited for this. So men turned their eyes towards the barbarians. Nothing more clearly characterises the position of things in the second century than the agreement between two men so radically different as Tatian and Celsus. Tatian emphatically declares that salvation comes from the barbarians, and to Celsus it is also a "truism" that the barbarians have more capacity than the Greeks for discovering valuable doctrines. [1] Everything was in fact prepared, and nothing was wanting.

About the middle of the second century, however, the moral and rationalistic element in the philosophy and spiritual culture of the time was still more powerful than the religious and mystic; for Neoplatonism, which under its outward coverings concealed the aspiration after religion and the living God, was only in its first beginnings. It was not otherwise in Christian circles. The "Gnostics" were in the minority. What the great majority of the Church felt to be intelligible and edifying above everything else was an earnest moralism. [2] New and strange as the

[1] It is very instructive to find Celsus (Origen, c. Cels. I. 2) proceeding to say that the Greeks understood better how to judge, to investigate, and to perfect the doctrines devised by the barbarians, and to apply them to the practice of virtue. This is quite in accordance with the idea of Origen, who makes the following remarks on this point: "When a man trained in the schools and sciences of the Greeks becomes acquainted with our faith, he will not only recognise and declare it to be true, but also by means of his scientific training and skill reduce it to a system and supplement what seems to him defective in it, when tested by the Greek method of exposition and proof, thus at the same time demonstrating the truth of Christianity."

[2] See the section "Justin und die apostolischen Väter" in Engelhardt's "Christenthum Justin's des Märtyrers", p. 375 ff., and my article on the so-called 2nd Epistle of Clement to the Corinthians (Zeitschrift für Kirchengeschichte I. p. 329 ff.). Engelhardt, who on the whole emphasises the correspondences, has rather under-than over-estimated them. If the reader compares the exposition given in Book I., chap. 3, with the theology of the Apologists (see sub. 3), he will find proof of the intimate relationship that may be traced here.

undertaking to represent Christianity as a philosophy might seem at first, the Apologists, so far as they were understood, appeared to advance nothing inconsistent with Christian common sense. Besides, they did not question authorities, but rather supported them, and introduced no foreign positive materials. For all these reasons, and also because their writings were not at first addressed to the communities, but only to outsiders, the marvellous attempt to present Christianity to the world as the religion which is the true philosophy, and as the philosophy which is the true religion, remained unopposed in the Church. But in what sense was the Christian religion set forth as a philosophy? An exact answer to this question is of the highest interest as regards the history of Christian dogma.

## 2. *Christianity as Philosophy and as Revelation.*

It was a new undertaking and one of permanent importance to a tradition hitherto so little concerned for its own vindication, when Quadratus and the Athenian philosopher, Aristides, presented treatises in defence of Christianity to the emperor. [1] About a century had elapsed since the Gospel of Christ had begun to be preached. It may be said that the Apology of Aristides was a most significant opening to the second century, whilst we find Origen at its close. Marcianus Aristides expressly designates himself in his pamphlet as a *philosopher of the Athenians*. Since the days when the words were written: "Beware lest any man spoil you through philosophy and vain deceit" (Col. II. 8), it had constantly been repeated (see, as evidence, Celsus, passim) that Christian preaching and philosophy were things entirely different, that God had chosen the fools, and that man's duty was not to investigate and seek, but to

> [1] See Euseb., H. E. IV. 3. Only one sentence of Quadratus' Apology is preserved; we have now that of Aristides in the Syriac language; moreover, it is proved to have existed in the original language in the Historia Barlaam et Joasaph; finally, a considerable fragment of it is found in Armenian. See an English edition by Harris and Robinson in the Texts and Studies I. 1891. German translation and commentary by Raabe in the Texte und Untersuchungen IX. 1892. Eusebius says that the Apology was handed in to the emperor Hadrian; but the superscription in Syriac is addressed to the emperor Titus Hadrianus Antoninus.

believe and hope. Now a philosopher, as such, pleaded the cause
of Christianity. In the summary he gave of the content of
Christianity at the beginning of his address, he really spoke as
a philosopher and represented this faith as a philosophy. By
expounding pure monotheism and giving it the main place in
his argument, Aristides gave supreme prominence to the very
doctrine which simple Christians also prized as the most important. [1] Moreover, in emphasing not only the supernatural character of the Christian doctrine revealed by the Son of the Most
High God, but also the continuous inspiration of believers—the
new *race* (not a new *school*)—he confessed in the most express
way the peculiar nature of this philosophy as a divine truth.
According to him Christianity is philosophy because its content
is in accordance with reason, and because it gives a satisfactory
and universally intelligible answer to the questions with which
all real philosophers have concerned themselves. But it is no
philosophy, in fact it is really the complete opposite of this, in
so far as it proceeds from revelation and is propagated by the
agency of God, *i.e.*, has a supernatural and divine origin, on
which alone the truth and certainty of its doctrines finally depend.
This contrast to philosophy is chiefly shown in the unphilosoph-
ical form in which Christianity was first preached to the world.
That is the thesis maintained by all the Apologists from Justin
to Tertullian,[2] and which Jewish philosophers before them propounded and defended. This proposition may certainly be
expressed in a great variety of ways. In the first place, it is
important whether the first or second half is emphasised, and
secondly, whether that which is "universally intelligible" is to
be reckoned as philosophy at all, or is to be separated from it
as that which comes by "nature". Finally, the attitude to be
taken up towards the Greek philosophers is left an open question,
so that the thesis, taking up this attitude as a starting-point,
may again assume various forms. But was the contradiction
which it contains not felt? The content of revelation is to be

[1] See Hermas, Mand I.

[2] With reservations this also holds good of the Alexandrians. See particularly
Orig., c. Cels. I. 62.

rational; but does that which is rational require a revelation? How the proposition was understood by the different Apologists requires examination.

*Aristides.* He first gives an exposition of monotheism and the monotheistic cosmology (God as creator and mover of the universe, as the spiritual, perfect, almighty Being, whom all things need, and who requires nothing). In the second chapter he distinguishes, according to the Greek text, three, and, according to the Syriac, four classes of men (in the Greek text polytheists, Jews, Christians, the polytheists being divided into Chaldeans, Greeks, and Egyptians; in the Syriac barbarians, Greeks, Jews, Christians), and gives their origin. He derives the Christians from Jesus Christ and reproduces the Christian *kerygma* (Son of the Most High God, birth from the Virgin, 12 disciples, death on the cross, burial, resurrection, ascension, missionary labours of the 12 disciples). After this, beginning with the third chapter, follows a criticism of polytheism, that is, the false theology of the barbarians, Greeks, and Egyptians (down to chapter 12). In the 13th chapter the Greek authors and philosophers are criticised, and the Greek myths, as such, are shown to be false. In the 14th chapter the Jews are introduced (they are monotheists and their ethical system is praised; but they are then reproached with worshipping of angels and a false ceremonial). In the 15th chapter follows a description of the Christians, *i.e.,* above all, of their pure, holy life. It is they who have found the truth, because they know the creator of heaven and earth. This description is continued in chapters 16 and 17: "This people is new and there is a divine admixture in it." The Christian writings are recommended to the emperor.

*Justin.* [1] In his treatise addressed to the emperor Justin did not call himself a philosopher as Aristides had done. In es-

---

[1] Semisch, Justin der Märtyrer, 2 Vols., 1840 f. Aubé, S. Justin, philosophe et martyre, 2nd reprint, 1875. Weizsäcker, Die Theologie des Märtyrers Justin's in the Jahrbuch für deutsche Theologie, 1867, p. 60 ff. Von Engelhardt, Christenthum Justin's, 1878; id., "Justin", in Herzog's Real Encyklopädie. Stählin, Justin der Märtyrer, 1880. Clemen, Die religionsphilosophische Bedeutung des stoisch-christlichen Eudämonismus in Justin's Apologie, 1890. Flemming, zur Beurtheilung des Christenthums Justin's des Martyrers, 1893. Duncker, Logoslehre Justin's, 1848. Bosse, Der präexistente Christus des Justinus, 1891.

pousing the cause of the hated and despised Christians he represented himself as a simple member of that sect. But in the
very first sentence of his Apology he takes up the ground of
piety and philosophy, the very ground taken up by the pious
and philosophical emperors themselves, according to the judgment of the time and their own intention. In addressing them
he appeals to the λόγος σώφρων in a purely Stoic fashion. He
opposes the truth—also in the Stoic manner—to the δόξαις
παλαιῶν.[1] It was not to be a mere *captatio benevolentiæ*. In
that case Justin would not have added: "That ye are pious
and wise and guardians of righteousness and friends of culture,
ye hear everywhere. Whether ye are so, however, will be
shown."[2] His whole exordium is calculated to prove to the
emperors that they are in danger of repeating a hundredfold
the crime which the judges of Socrates had committed.[3] Like
a second Socrates Justin speaks to the emperors in the name
of all Christians. They are to hear the convictions of the wisest
of the Greeks from the mouth of the Christians. Justin wishes
to enlighten the emperor with regard to the life and doctrines
(βίος καὶ μαθήματα) of the latter. Nothing is to be concealed,
for there is nothing to conceal.

Justin kept this promise better than any of his successors.
For that very reason also he did not depict the Christian
Churches as schools of philosophers (cc. 61—67). Moreover,
in the first passage where he speaks of Greek philosophers,[4] he
is merely drawing a parallel. According to him there are bad
Christians and seeming Christians, just as there are philosophers
who are only so in name and outward show. Such men, too,
were in early times called "philosophers" even when they
preached atheism. To all appearance, therefore, Justin does
*not* desire Christians to be reckoned as philosophers. But it is
nevertheless significant that, in the case of the Christians, a

[1] Apol. I. 2, p. 6, ed. Otto.

[2] Apol. I. 2, p. 6, sq.

[3] See the numerous philosophical quotations and allusions in Justin's Apology
pointed out by Otto. Above all, he made an extensive use of Plato's Apology of
Socrates.

[4] Apol. I. 4. p. 16, also I. 7, p. 24 sq: I. 26.

phenomenon is being repeated which otherwise is only observed
in the case of philosophers; and how were those whom he was
addressing to understand him? In the same passage he speaks
for the first time of Christ. He introduces him with the plain
and intelligible formula: ὁ διδάσκαλος Χριστός ("the teacher
Christ").[1] Immediately thereafter he praises Socrates because
he had exposed the worthlessness and deceit of the evil demons,
and traces his death to the same causes which are now he says
bringing about the condemnation of the Christians. Now he
can make his final assertion. In virtue of "reason" Socrates
exposed superstition; in virtue of the same reason, this was
done by the teacher whom the Christians follow. *But this
teacher was reason itself; it was visible in him, and indeed it
appeared bodily in him.*[2]

Is this philosophy or is it myth? The greatest paradox the
Apologist has to assert is connected by him with the most
impressive remembrance possessed by his readers as philosophers. In the same sentence where he represents Christ as the
Socrates of the barbarians,[3] and consequently makes Christianity
out to be a Socratic doctrine, he propounds the unheard of
theory *that the teacher Christ is the incarnate reason of God.*

Justin nowhere tried to soften the effect of this conviction or
explain it in a way adapted to his readers. Nor did he conceal from them that his assertion admits of no speculative
demonstration. That philosophy can only deal with things
which ever are, because they ever were, since this world began,
is a fact about which he himself is perfectly clear. No Stoic
could have felt more strongly than Justin how paradoxical is the
assertion that a thing is of value which has happened only
once. Certain as he is that the "reasonable" emperors will
regard it as a rational assumption that "Reason" is the

---

[1] Apol. I. 4, p. 14.

[2] Apol. I. 5, p. 18 sq., see also I. 14 fin.: οὐ σοφιστὴς ὑπῆρχεν ἀλλὰ δύναμις
Θεοῦ ὁ λόγος αὐτοῦ ἦν.

[3] L. c.: οὐ γὰρ μόνον ἐν Ἕλλησι διὰ Σωκράτους ὑπὸ λόγου ἠλέγχθη ταῦτα, ἀλλὰ
καὶ ἐν βαρβάροις ὑπ' αὐτοῦ τοῦ λόγου μορφωθέντος καὶ ἀνθρώπου καὶ Ἰησοῦ Χριστοῦ
κληθέντος.

Son of God,[1] he knows equally well that no philosophy will bear him out in that other assertion, and that such a statement is seemingly akin to the contemptible myths of the evil demons. But there is certainly a proof which, if not speculative, is nevertheless sure. The same ancient documents, which contain the Socratic and super-Socratic wisdom of the Christians, bear witness through prophecies, which, just because they are predictions, admit of no doubt, that the teacher Christ is the incarnate reason; for history confirms the word of prophecy even in the minutest details. Moreover, in so far as these writings are in the lawful possession of the Christians, and announced at the very beginning of things that this community would appear on the earth, they testify that the Christians may in a certain fashion date themselves back to the beginning of the world, because their doctrine is as old as the earth itself (this thought is still wanting in Aristides).

The new Socrates who appeared among the barbarians is therefore quite different from the Socrates of the Greeks, and for that reason also his followers are not to be compared with the disciples of the philosophers.[2] From the very beginning of things a world-historical dispensation of God announced this reasonable doctrine through prophets, and prepared the visible appearance of reason itself. The same reason which created and arranged the world took human form in order to draw the whole of humanity to itself. Every precaution has been taken to make it easy for any one, be he Greek or barbarian, educated or uneducated, to grasp all the doctrines of this reason, to verify their truth, and test their power in life. What further importance can philosophy have side by side with this, how can one think of calling this a philosophy?

And yet the doctrine of the Christians can only be compared with philosophy. For, so far as the latter is genuine, it is also

[1] Celsus also admits this, or rather makes his Jew acknowledge it (Orig., c. Cels. II. 31). In Book VI. 47 he adopts the proposition of the "ancients" that the world is the Son of God.

[2] See Apol. II. 10 fin.: Σωκράτει οὐδεὶς ἐπείσθη ὑπὲρ τούτου τοῦ δόγματος ἀποθνήσκειν· Χριστῷ δὲ τῷ καὶ ὑπὸ Σωκράτους ἀπὸ μέρους γνωσθέντι ... οὐ φιλόσοφοι οὐδὲ φιλόλογοι μόνον ἐπείσθησαν.

guided by the Logos; and, conversely, what the Christians
teach concerning the Father of the world, the destiny of man,
the nobility of his nature, freedom and virtue, justice and
recompense, has also been attested by the wisest of the Greeks.
They indeed only stammered, whereas the Christians speak.
These, however, use no unintelligible and unheard-of language,
but speak with the words and through the power of reason.
The wonderful arrangement, carried out by the Logos himself,
through which he ennobled the human race by restoring its
consciousness of its own nobility, compels no one henceforth to regard the reasonable as the unreasonable or wisdom
as folly. But is the Christian wisdom not of divine origin?
How can it in that case be natural, and what connection can
exist between it and the wisdom of the Greeks? Justin bestowed
the closest attention on this question, but he never for a moment
doubted what the answer must be. Wherever the reasonable
has revealed itself, it has always been through the operation
of the *divine* reason. For man's lofty endowment consists in
his having had a portion of the divine reason implanted within
him, and in his consequent capacity of attaining a knowledge
of divine things, though not a perfect and clear one, by dint
of persistent efforts after truth and virtue. When man remembers
his real nature and destination, that is, when he comes to himself, the divine reason is already revealing itself in him and
through him. As man's possession conferred on him at the
creation, it is at once his most peculiar property, and the power
which dominates and determines his nature.[1] All that is reasonable

---

[1] The utterances of Justin do not clearly indicate whether the non-Christian
portion of mankind has only a σπέρμα τοῦ λόγου as a natural possession, or
whether this σπέρμα has in some cases been enhanced by the inward workings of
the whole Logos (inspiration). This ambiguity, however, arises from the fact that
he did not further discuss the relation between ὁ λόγος and τὸ σπέρμα τοῦ λόγου
and we need not therefore attempt to remove it. On the one hand, the excellent
discoveries of poets and philosophers are simply traced to τὸ ἔμφυτον παντὶ γένει
ἀνθρώπων σπέρμα τοῦ λόγου (Apol. II. 8), the μέρος σπερματικοῦ λόγου (ibid.)
which was implanted at the creation, and on which the human εὕρεσις καὶ θεωρία
depend (II. 10). In this sense it may be said of them all that they "in human fashion
attempted to understand and prove things by means of reason"; and Socrates is
merely viewed as the πάντων εὐτονώτερος (ibid.), his philosophy also, like all pre-
Christian systems, being a φιλοσοφία ἀνθρώπειος (II. 15). But on the other hand

is based on revelation. In order to accomplish his true destiny
man requires from the beginning the inward working of that
divine reason which has created the world for the sake of man,
and therefore wishes to raise man beyond the world to God.[1]

Apparently no one could speak in a more stoical fashion. But
this train of thought is supplemented by something which limits
it. Revelation does retain its peculiar and unique significance.
For no one who merely possessed the "seed of the Logos"
(σπέρμα τοῦ λόγου), though it may have been his exclusive guide
to knowledge and conduct, was ever able to grasp the whole
truth and impart it in a convincing manner. Though Socrates
and Heraclitus may in a way be called Christians, they cannot
be so designated in any real sense. Reason is clogged with
unreasonableness, and the certainty of truth is doubtful wherever
the whole Logos has not been acting; for man's natural endowment with reason is too weak to oppose the powers of evil and
of sense that work in the world, namely, the demons. We must

Christ was known by Socrates though only ἀπὸ μέρους; for "Christ was and is the
Logos who dwells in every man". Further, according to the Apologist, the μέρος
τοῦ σπερματικοῦ θείου λόγου bestows the power of recognising whatever is related
to the Logos (τὸ συγγενές II. 13). Consequently it may not only be said: ὅσα
παρὰ πᾶσι καλῶς εἴρηται ἡμῶν, τῶν Χριστιανῶν ἐστί (ibid.), but, on the strength of
the "participation" in reason conferred on all, it may be asserted that all who
have lived with the Logos (μετὰ λόγου) — an expression which must have been
ambiguous — were Christians. Among the Greeks this specially applies to Socrates
and Heraclitus (I. 46). Moreover, the Logos implanted in man does not belong to
his nature in such a sense as to prevent us saying ὑπὸ λόγου διὰ Σωκράτους ἠλέγχθη κ.τ.λ. (I. 5). Nevertheless αὐτὸς ὁ λόγος did not act in Socrates, for this
only appeared in Christ (ibid). Hence the prevailing aspect of the case in Justin
was that to which he gave expression at the close of the 2nd Apology (II. 15:
alongside of Christianity there is only *human* philosophy), and which, not without
regard for the opposite view, he thus formulated in II. 13 fin.: All non-Christian
authors were able to attain a knowledge of true being, though only darkly, by
means of the seed of the Logos naturally implanted within them. For the σπορά and
μίμημα of a thing, which are bestowed in proportion to one's receptivity, are quite
different from the thing itself, which divine grace bestows on us for our possession
and imitation."

1 "For the sake of man" (Stoic) Apol. I. 10 : II. 4, 5 ; Dial. 41, p. 260A, Apol I. 8:
"Longing for the eternal and pure life, we strive to abide in the fellowship of
God, the Father and Creator of all things, and we hasten to make confession, be-
cause we are convinced and firmly believe that that happiness is really attainable."
It is frequently asserted that it is the Logos which produces such conviction and
awakens courage and strength.

therefore believe in the prophets in whom the whole Logos spoke. He who does that must also of necessity believe in Christ; for the prophets clearly pointed to him as the perfect embodiment of the Logos. Measured by the fulness, clearness, and certainty of the knowledge imparted by the Logos-Christ, all knowledge independent of him appears as merely human wisdom, even when it emanates from the seed of the Logos. The Stoic argument is consequently untenable. Men blind and kept in bondage by the demons require to be aided by a special revelation. It is true that this revelation is nothing new, and in so far as it has always existed, and never varied in character, from the beginning of the world, it is in this sense nothing extraordinary. *It is the divine help granted to man, who has fallen under the power of the demons, and enabling him to follow his reason and freedom to do what is good. By the appearance of Christ this help became accessible to all men.* The dominion of demons and revelation are the two correlated ideas. If the former did not exist, the latter would not be necessary. According as we form a lower or higher estimate of the pernicious results of that sovereignty, the value of revelation rises or sinks. This revelation cannot do less than give the necessary assurance of the truth, and it cannot do more than impart the power that develops and matures the inalienable natural endowment of man and frees him from the dominion of the demons.

Accordingly the teaching of the prophets and Christ is related even to the very highest human philosophy as the whole is to the part,[1] or as the certain is to the uncertain; and hence also

---

[1] Justin has destroyed the force of this argument in two passages (I. 44. 59) by tracing (like the Alexandrian Jews) all true knowledge of the poets and philosophers to borrowing from the books of the Old Testament (Moses). Of what further use then is the σπέρμα λόγου ἔμφυτον? Did Justin not really take it seriously? Did he merely wish to suit himself to those whom he was addressing? We are not justified in asserting this. Probably, however, the adoption of that Jewish view of the history of the world is a proof that the results of the demon sovereignty were in Justin's estimation so serious that he no longer expected anything from the σπέρμα λόγου ἔμφυτον when left to its own resources; and therefore regarded truth and prophetic revelation as inseparable. But this view is not the essential one in the Apology. That assumption of Justin's is evidently dependent on a tradition, whilst his real opinion was more " liberal".

as the permanent is to the transient. For the final stage has
now arrived and Christianity is destined to put an end to
natural human philosophy. When the perfect work is there;
the fragmentary must cease. Justin gave the clearest expression
to this conviction. Christianity, *i.e.,* the prophetic teaching
attested by Christ and accessible to all, puts an end to the
human systems of philosophy that from their close affinity to
it may be called Christian, inasmuch as it effects all and more
than all that these systems have done, and inasmuch as the
speculations of the philosophers, which are uncertain and mingled
with error, are transformed by it into dogmas of indubitable
certainty.[1] The practical conclusion drawn in Justin's treatise
from this exposition is that the Christians are at least entitled
to ask the authorities to treat them as philosophers (Apol. I.
7, 20: II. 15). This demand, he says, is the more justifiable
because the freedom of philosophers is enjoyed even by such
people as merely bear the name, whereas in reality they set
forth immoral and pernicious doctrines.[2]

---

[1] Compare with this the following passages: In Apol. I. 20 are enumerated a
series of the most important doctrines common to philosophers and Christians. Then
follow the words: "If we then in particular respects even teach something similar
to the doctrines of the philosophers honoured among you, though in many cases
in a divine and more sublime way; and we indeed alone do so in such a way
that the matter is proved etc." In Apol. I. 44: II. 10. 13 uncertainty, error, and
contradictions are shown to exist in the case of the greatest philosophers. The
Christian doctrines are more sublime than all human philosophy (II. 15). "Our
doctrines are evidently more sublime than any human teaching, because the Christ who
appeared for our sakes was the whole fulness of reason" (τὸ λογικὸν τὸ ὅλον, II. 10).
"The principles of Plato are not foreign (ἀλλότρια) to the teaching of Christ, but
they do not agree in every respect. The same holds good of the Stoics" (II. 13).
"We must go forth from the school of Plato" (II. 12). "Socrates convinced no
one in such a way that he would have been willing to die for the doctrine proclaimed by him; whereas not only philosophers and philologers, but also artisans
and quite common uneducated people have believed in Christ" (II. 10). These are
the very people—and that is perhaps the strongest contrast found between Logos and
Logos in Justin—among whom it is universally said of Christianity: δύναμις ἐστὶ
τοῦ ἀρρήτου πατρὸς καὶ οὐχὶ ἀνθρωπείου λόγου κατασκευή (see also I. 14 and elsewhere.)

[2] In Justin's estimate of the Greek philosophers two other points deserve notice.
In the first place, he draws a very sharp distinction between real and nominal
philosophers. By the latter he specially means the Epicureans. They are no doubt
referred to in I. 4, 7, 26 (I. 14: Atheists). Epicurus and Sardanapalus are classed
together in II. 7; Epicurus and the immoral poets in II. 12; and in the conclusion of II. 15 the same philosopher is ranked with the worst society. But according

In the dialogue with the Jew Trypho, which is likewise meant for heathen readers, Justin ceased to employ the idea of the existence of a "seed of the Logos implanted by nature" (σπέρμα λόγου ἔμφυτον) in every man. From this fact we recognise that he did not consider the notion of fundamental importance. He indeed calls the Christian religion a philosophy;[1] but, in so far as this is the case, it is "the only sure and saving philosophy". No doubt the so-called philosophies put the right questions, but they are incapable of giving correct answers. For the Deity, who embraces all true being, and a knowledge of whom alone makes salvation possible, is only known in proportion as he reveals himself. True wisdom is therefore exclusively based on revelation. Hence it is opposed to every human philosophy,

---

to II. 3 fin. (ἀδύνατον Κυνικῷ, ἀδιάφορον τὸ τέλος προθεμένῳ, τὸ ἀγαθὸν εἰδέναι πλὴν ἀδιαφορίας) the Cynics also seem to be outside the circle of real philosophers. This is composed principally of Socrates, Plato, the Platonists and Stoics, together with Heraclitus and others. Some of these understood one set of doctrines more correctly, others another series. The Stoics excelled in ethics (II. 7) ; Plato described the Deity and the world more correctly. It is, however, worthy of note—and this is the second point—that Justin in principle conceived the Greek philosophers as a unity, and that he therefore saw in their very deviations from one another a proof of the imperfection of their teaching. In so far as they are all included under the collective idea "human philosophy", philosophy is characterised by the conflicting opinions found within it. This view was suggested to Justin by the fact that the highest truth, which is at once allied and opposed to human philosophy, was found by him among an exclusive circle of fellow-believers. Justin showed great skill in selecting from the Gospels the passages (I. 15—17), that prove the "philosophical" life of the Christians as described by him in c. 14. Here he cannot be acquitted of colouring the facts (cf. Aristides) nor of exaggeration (see, for instance, the unqualified statement: ἃ ἔχομεν εἰς κοινὸν φέροντες καὶ παντὶ δεομένῳ κοινωνοῦντες). The philosophical emperors were meant here to think of the "φίλοις πάντα κοινά". Yet in I. 67 Justin corrected exaggerations in his description. Justin's reference to the invaluable benefits which Christianity confers on the state deserves notice (see particularly I. 12, 17.) The later Apologists make a similar remark.

[1] Dialogue 8. The dialogue takes up a more positive attitude than the Apology, both as a whole and in detail. If we consider that both works are also meant for Christians, and that, on the other hand, the Dialogue as well as the Apology appeals to the cultured heathen public, we may perhaps assume that the two writings were meant to present a graduated system of Christian instruction. (In one passage the Dialogue expressly refers to the Apology). From Justin's time onward the apologetic polemic of the early Church appears to have adhered throughout to the same method. This consisted in giving the polemical writings directed against the Greeks the form of an introduction to Christian knowledge, and in continuing this instruction still further in those directed against the Jews.

because revelation was only given in the prophets and in Christ.[1]
The Christian is *the* philosopher,[2] because the followers of Plato
and the Stoics are virtually no philosophers.  In applying the
title "philosophy" to Christianity he therefore does not mean
to bring Christians and philosophers more closely together.  No
doubt, however, he asserts that the Christian doctrine, which is
founded on the knowledge of Christ and leads to blessedness,[3]
is in accordance with reason.

*Athenagoras.*  The petition on behalf of Christians, which
Athenagoras, "the Christian philosopher of Athens", presented
to the emperors Marcus Aurelius and Commodus, nowhere
expressly designates Christianity as a philosophy, and still less
does it style the Christians philosophers.[4]  But, at the very
beginning of his writing Athenagoras also claims for the Christian
doctrines the toleration granted by the state to all philosophic
tenets.[5]  In support of his claim he argues that the state punishes
nothing but practical atheism,[6] and that the "atheism" of the
Christians is a doctrine about God such as had been propounded
by the most distinguished philosophers—Pythagoreans, Platonists,
Peripatetics, and Stoics—who, moreover, were permitted to
write whatsoever they pleased on the subject of the "Deity".[7]
The Apologist concedes even more: " If philosophers did not
also acknowledge the existence of one God, if they did not
also conceive the gods in question to be partly demons, partly
matter, partly of human birth, then certainly we would be justly
expelled as aliens."[8]  He therefore takes up the standpoint that
the state is justified in refusing to tolerate people with completely new doctrines.   When we add that he everywhere assumes
that the wisdom and piety of the emperors are sufficient to test

---

[1] Dial. 2. sq. That Justin's Christianity is founded on theoretical scepticism is
clearly shown by the introduction to the Dialogue.

[2] Dial. 8: οὕτως δὴ καὶ διὰ ταῦτα φιλόσοφος ἐγώ.

[3] Dial., l. c.: πάρεστιν σοὶ τὸν Χριστὸν τοῦ Θεοῦ ἐπιγνόντι καὶ τελείῳ γενομένῳ
εὐδαιμονεῖν.

[4] See particularly the closing chapter.

[5] Suppl. 2,

[6] Suppl. 4.

[7] Suppl. 5—7.

[8] Suppl. 24 (see also Aristides c. 13).

and approve [1] the truth of the Christian teaching, that he merely
represents this faith itself as the *reasonable* doctrine, [2] and that,
with the exception of the resurrection of the body, he leaves
all the positive and objectionable tenets of Christianity out of
account, [3] there is ground for thinking that this Apologist differs
essentially from Justin in his conception of the relation of
Christianity to secular philosophy.

Moreover, it is not to be denied that Athenagoras views the
revelation in the prophets and in Christ as completely identical.
But in one very essential point he agrees with Justin; and he
has even expressed himself still more plainly than the latter, inasmuch as he does not introduce the assumption of a "seed
of the Logos implanted by nature" (σπέρμα λόγου ἔμφυτον). The
philosophers, he says, were incapable of knowing the full truth,
since it was not from God, but rather from themselves, that they
wished to learn about God. True wisdom, however, can only
be learned from God, that is, from his prophets; it depends
solely on revelation. [4] Here also then we have a repetition of
the thought that the truly reasonable is of supernatural origin.
Such is the importance attached by Athenagoras to this proposition, that he declares any demonstration of the "reasonable"
to be insufficient, no matter how luminous it may appear. Even
that which is most evidently true—*e.g.*, monotheism—is not
raised from the domain of mere human opinion into the sphere
of undoubted certainty till it can be confirmed by revelation,[5]
This can be done by Christians alone. Hence they are very
different from the philosophers, just as they are also distinguished
from these by their manner of life. [6] All the praises which
Athenagoras from time to time bestows on philosophers, particularly Plato, [7] are consequently to be understood in a merely

[1] Suppl, 7 fin. and many other places.
[2] *E. g.*, Suppl. 8. 35 fin.
[3] The Crucified Man, the incarnation of the Logos etc. are wanting. Nothing
at all is said about Christ.
[4] Suppl. 7.
[5] Cf. the arguments in c. 8 with c. 9 init.
[6] Suppl. 11.
[7] Suppl. 23.

relative sense. Their ultimate object is only to establish the
claim made by the Apologist with regard to the treatment of
Christians by the state; but they are not really meant to bring
the former into closer relationship to philosophers. Athenagoras
also holds the theory that Christians are philosophers, in so far
as the "philosophers" are not such in any true sense. It is only
the problems they set that connect the two. He exhibits less
clearness than Justin in tracing the necessity of revelation to
the fact that the demon sovereignty, which, above all, reveals
itself in polytheism,[1] can only be overthrown by revelation; he
rather emphasises the other thought (cc. 7, 9) that the necessary
attestation of the truth can only be given in this way.[2]

*Tatian's*[3] chief aim was not to bring about a juster treatment of the Christians.[4] He wished to represent their cause
as the good contrasted with the bad, wisdom as opposed to
error, truth in contradistinction to outward seeming, hypocrisy,
and pretentious emptiness. His "Address to the Greeks" be-

[1] Suppl. 18, 23—27. He, however, as well as the others, sets forth the demon
theory in detail.

[2] The Apology which Miltiades addressed to Marcus Aurelius and his fellow-
emperor perhaps bore the title: ὑπὲρ τῆς κατὰ Χριστιανοὺς φιλοσοφίας (Euseb., H. E. V.
17. 5). It is certain that Melito in his Apology designated Christianity as ἡ καθ'
ἡμᾶς φιλοσοφία (l. c., IV. 26. 7). But, while it is undeniable that this writer attempted,
to a hitherto unexampled extent, to represent Christianity as adapted to the Empire,
we must nevertheless beware of laying undue weight on the expression "philosophy".
What Melito means chiefly to emphasise is the fact that Christianity, which in former
times had developed into strength among the barbarians, began to flourish in the
provinces of the Empire simultaneously with the rise of the monarchy under Augustus,
that, as foster-sister of the monarchy, it increased in strength with the latter, and
that this mutual relation of the two institutions had given prosperity and splendour
to the state. When in the fragments preserved to us he twice, in this connection,
calls Christianity "philosophy", we must note that this expression alternates with
the other "ὁ καθ' ἡμᾶς λόγος", and that he uses the formula: "Thy forefathers held
this philosophy in honour along with the other cults" (πρὸς ταῖς ἄλλαις θρησκείαις).
This excludes the assumption that Melito in his Apology merely represented Christianity as philosophy (see also IV. 26. 5, where the Christians are called "τὸ τῶν
θεοσεβῶν γένος"). He also wrote a treatise περὶ κτίσεως καὶ γενέσεως Χριστοῦ. In
it (fragment in the Chron. Pasch.) he called Christ Θεοῦ λόγος πρὸ αἰώνων.

[3] See my treatise "Tatian's Rede an die Griechen übers.", 1884 (Giessener
Programm). Daniel, Tatianus, 1837. Steuer, Die Gottes- und Logoslehre des Tatian,
1893.

[4] But see Orat. 4 init., 24 fin., 25 fin., 27 init.

gins with a violent polemic against all Greek philosophers.
Tatian merely acted up to a judgment of philosophers and
philosophy which in Justin's case is still concealed.[1]  Hence it
was not possible for him to think of demonstrating analogies
between Christians and philosophers.  He also no doubt views
Christianity as "reasonable"; he who lives virtuously and follows
wisdom receives it;[2] but yet it is too sublime to be grasped
by earthly perception.[3]  It is a heavenly thing which depends
on the communication of the "Spirit", and hence can only be
known by revelation.[4]  But yet it is a "philosophy" with definite

---

[1] He not only accentuated the disagreement of philosophers more strongly than Justin,
but insisted more energetically than that Apologist on the necessity of viewing the
practical fruits of philosophy in life as a criterion; see Orat. 2, 3, 19, 25. Nevertheless Socrates still found grace in his eyes (c. 3).  With regard to other philosophers he listened to foolish and slanderous gossip.

[2] Orat. 13, 15 fin., 20. Tatian also gave credence to it because it imparts such
an intelligible picture of the creation of the world (c. 29).

[3] Orat. 12: τὰ τῆς ἡμετέρας παιδείας ἐστὶν ἀνωτέρω τῆς κοσμικῆς καταλήψεως.
Tatian troubled himself very little with giving demonstrations. No other Apologist
made such bold assertions.

[4] See Orat. 12 (p. 54 fin.), 20 (p. 90), 25 fin., 26 fin., 29, 30 (p. 116), 13 (p. 62),
15 (p. 70), 36 (p. 142), 40 (p. 152 sq.).  The section cc. 12—15 of the Oratio is
very important (see also c. 7 ff); for it shows that Tatian denied the natural immortality of the soul, declared the soul (the material spirit) to be something inherent
in all matter, and accordingly looked on the distinction between men and animals
in respect of their inalienable natural constitution as only one of degree. According
to this Apologist the dignity of man does not consist in his natural endowments;
but in the union of the human soul with the divine spirit, for which union indeed
he was planned. But, in Tatian's opinion, man lost this union by falling under
the sovereignty of the demons.  The Spirit of God has left him, and consequently
he has fallen back to the level of the beasts.  So it is man's task to unite the Spirit
again with himself, and thereby recover that religious principle on which all wisdom
and knowledge rest.  This anthropology is opposed to that of the Stoics and related
to the "Gnostic" theory.  It follows from it that man, in order to reach his
destination, must raise himself above his natural endowment; see c. 15: ἄνθρωπον
λέγω τὸν πόρρω μὲν ἀνθρωπότητος πρὸς αὐτὸν δὲ τὸν Θεὸν κεχωρηκότα.  But with
Tatian this conception is burdened with radical inconsistency; for he assumes that
the Spirit reunites itself with every man who rightly uses his freedom, and he
thinks it still possible for every person to use his freedom aright (11 fin., 13 fin.,
15 fin.)  So it is after all a mere assertion that the natural man is only distinguished
from the beast by speech. He is also distinguished from it by freedom. And further
it is only in appearance that the blessing bestowed in the "Spirit" is a *donum
superadditum et supernaturale*.  For if a proper spontaneous use of freedom infallibly leads to the return of the Spirit, it is evident that the decision and conse-

doctrines (δόγματα);[1] it brings nothing new, but only such blessings as we have already received, but could not retain[2] owing to the power of error, *i.e.*, the dominion of the demons.[3] Christianity is therefore the philosophy in which, by virtue of the Logos revelation through the prophets,[4] the rational knowledge that leads to life[5] is restored. This knowledge was no less obscured among the Greek philosophers than among the Greeks generally. In so far as revelation took place among the barbarians from the remotest antiquity, Christianity may also be called the barbarian philosophy.[6] Its truth is proved

quently the realisation of man's destination depend on human freedom. That is, however, the proposition which all the Apologists maintained. But indeed Tatian himself in his latter days seems to have observed the inconsistency in which he had become involved and to have solved the problem in the Gnostic, that is, the religious sense. In his eyes, of course, the ordinary philosophy is a useless and pernicious art; philosophers make their own opinions laws (c. 27); whereas of Christians the following holds good (c. 32): λόγου τοῦ δημοσίου καὶ ἐπιγείου κεχωρισμένοι καὶ πειθόμενοι Θεοῦ παραγγέλμασι καὶ νόμῳ πατρὸς ἀφθαρσίας ἐπόμενοι, πᾶν τὸ ἐν δόξῃ κείμενον ἀνθρωπίνῃ παραιτούμεθα.

[1] C. 31. init.: ἡ ἡμετέρα φιλοσοφία. 32 (p. 128): οἱ βουλόμενοι φιλοσοφεῖν παρ' ἡμῖν ἄνθρωποι. In c. 33 (p. 130) Christian women are designated αἱ παρ' ἡμῖν φιλοσοφοῦσαι. C. 35: ἡ καθ' ἡμᾶς βάρβαρος φιλοσοφία. 40 (p. 152): οἱ κατὰ Μωυσέα καὶ ὁμοίως αὐτῷ φιλοσοφοῦντες. 42: ὁ κατὰ βαρβάρους φιλοσοφῶν Τατιανός. The δόγματα of the Christians: c. 1 (p. 2), 12 (p. 58), 19 (p. 86), 24 (p. 102), 27 (p. 108), 35 (p. 138), 40, 42. But Tatian pretty frequently calls Christianity "ἡ ἡμετέρα παιδεία", once also "νομοθεσία" (12; cf. 40: οἱ ἡμέτεροι νόμοι), and often πολιτεία.

[2] See, *e.g.*, c. 29 fin.: the Christian doctrine gives us οὐχ ὑπερ μὴ ἐλάβομεν, ἀλλ' ὑπερ λαβόντες ὑπὸ τῆς πλάνης ἔχειν ἐκωλύθημεν.

[3] Tatian gave still stronger expression than Justin to the opinion that it is the demons who have misled men and rule the world, and that revelation through the prophets is opposed to this demon rule; see c. 7 ff. The demons have fixed the laws of death; see c. 15 fin. and elsewhere.

[4] Tatian also cannot at bottom distinguish between revelation through the prophets and through Christ. See the description of his conversion in c. 29. where only the Old Testament writings are named, and c. 13 fin., 20 fin., 12 (p. 54) etc.

[5] Knowledge and life appear in Tatian most closely connected. See, *e.g.*, c. 13 init.: "In itself the soul is not immortal, but mortal; it is also possible, however, that it may not die. If it has not attained a knowledge of that truth it dies and is dissolved with the body; but later, at the end of the world, it will rise again with the body in order to receive death in endless duration as a punishment. On the contrary it does not die, though it is dissolved for a time, if it is equipped with the knowledge of God."

[6] Barbarian: the Christian doctrines are τὰ τῶν βαρβάρων δόγματα (c. 1): ἡ

by its ancient date [1] as well as by its intelligible form, which enables even the most uneducated person that is initiated in it [2] to understand it perfectly. [3] Finally, Tatian also states (c. 40) that the Greek sophists have read the writings of Moses and the prophets, and reproduced them in a distorted form. He therefore maintains the very opposite of what Celsus took upon him to demonstrate when venturing to derive certain sayings and doctrines of Christ and the Christians from the philosophers. Both credit the plagiarists with intentional misrepresentation or gross misunderstanding. Justin judged more charitably. To Tatian, on the contrary, the mythology of the Greeks did not appear worse than their philosophy; in both cases he saw imitations and intentional corruption of the truth. [4]

καθ᾽ ἡμᾶς βάρβαρος φιλοσοφία (c. 35); ἡ βαρβαρικὴ νομοθεσία (c. 12); γραφαὶ βαρβαρικαί (c. 29); καινοτομεῖν τὰ βαρβάρων δόγματα (c. 35); ὁ κατὰ βαρβάρους φιλοσοφῶν Τατιανός (c. 42); Μωυσῆς πάσης βαρβάρου φιλοσοφίας ἀρχηγός (c. 31); see also c. 30, 32. In Tatian's view barbarians and Greeks are the decisive contrasts in history.

[1] See the proof from antiquity, c. 31 ff.

[2] C. 30 (p. 114): τούτων οὖν τὴν κατάληψιν μεμυημένος.

[3] Tatian's own confession is very important here (c. 26): "Whilst I was reflecting on what was good it happened that there fell into my hands certain writings of the barbarians, too old to be compared with the doctrines of the Greeks, too divine to be compared with their errors. And it chanced that they convinced me through the plainness of their expressions, through the unartificial nature of their language, through the intelligible representation of the creation of the world, through the prediction of the future, the excellence of their precepts, and the summing up of all kinds under one head. My soul was instructed by God and I recognised that those Greek doctrines lead to perdition, whereas the others abolish the slavery to which we are subjected in the world, and rescue us from our many lords and tyrants, though they do not give us blessings we had not already received, but rather such as we had indeed obtained, but were not able to retain in consequence of error." Here the whole theology of the Apologists is contained *in nuce*; see Justin, Dial. 7—8. In Chaps. 32, 33 Tatian strongly emphasises the fact that the Christian philosophy is accessible even to the most uneducated; see Justin, Apol. II. 10; Athenag. 11 etc.

[4] The unknown author of the Λόγος πρὸς Ἕλληνας also formed the same judgment as Tatian (Corp. Apolog., T. III., p. 2 sq., ed. Otto; a Syrian translation, greatly amplified, is found in the Cod. Nitr. Mus. Britt. Add. 14658. It was published by Cureton, Spic. Syr., p. 38 sq. with an English translation). Christianity is an incomparable heavenly wisdom, the teacher of which is the Logos himself. "It produces neither poets, nor philosophers, nor rhetoricians; but it makes mortals immortal and men gods, and leads them away upwards from the earth into super-Olympian regions." Through Christian knowledge the soul returns to its Creator: δεῖ γὰρ ἀποκατασταθῆναι ὅθεν ἀπέστη.

*Theophilus* agrees with Tatian, in so far as he everywhere appears to contrast Christianity with philosophy. The religious and moral culture of the Greeks is derived from their poets (historians) and philosophers (ad Autol. II. 3 fin. and elsewhere). However, not only do poets and philosophers contradict each other (II. 5); but the latter also do not agree (II. 4. 8: III. 7), nay, many contradict themselves (III. 3). Not a single one of the so-called philosophers, however, is to be taken seriously; [1] they have devised myths and follies (II. 8); everything they have set forth is useless and godless (III. 2); vain and worthless fame was their aim (III. 3). But God knew beforehand the "drivellings of these hollow philosophers" and made his preparations (II. 15). He of old proclaimed the truth by the mouth of prophets, and these deposited it in holy writings. This truth refers to the knowledge of God, the origin and history of the world, as well as to a virtuous life. The prophetic testimony in regard to it was continued in the Gospel. [2] Revelation, however, is necessary because this wisdom of the philosophers and poets is really demon wisdom, for they were inspired by devils. [3] Thus the most extreme contrasts appear to exist here. Still, Theophilus is constrained to confess that

---

1 Nor is Plato "ὁ δοκῶν ἐν αὐτοῖς σεμνότερον πεφιλοσοφηκέναι" any better than Epicurus and the Stoics (III. 6). Correct views which are found in him in a greater measure than in the others (ὁ δοκῶν Ἑλλήνων σοφώτερος γεγενῆσθαι), did not prevent him from giving way to the stupidest babbling (III. 16). Although he knew that the full truth can only be learned from God himself through the law (III. 17), he indulged in the most foolish guesses concerning the beginning of history. But where guesses find a place, truth is not to be found (III. 16: εἰ δὲ εἰκασμῷ, οὐκ ἄρα ἀληθῆ ἐστιν τὰ ὑπ᾽ αὐτοῦ εἰρημένα).

2 Theophilus confesses (I. 14) exactly as Tatian does: καὶ γὰρ ἐγὼ ἠπίστουν τοῦτο ἔσεσθαι, ἀλλὰ νῦν κατανοήσας αὐτὰ πιστεύω, ἅμα καὶ ἐπιτυχὼν ἱεραῖς γραφαῖς τῶν ἁγίων προφητῶν, οἳ καὶ προεῖπον διὰ πνεύματος Θεοῦ τὰ προγεγονότα ᾧ τρόπῳ γέγονεν καὶ τὰ ἐνεστῶτα τίνι τρόπῳ γίνεται, καὶ τὰ ἐπερχόμενα ποίᾳ τάξει ἀπαρτισθήσεται. Ἀπόδειξιν οὖν λαβὼν τῶν γινομένων καὶ προαναπεφωνημένων οὐκ ἀπιστῶ; see also II. 8—10, 22, 30, 33—35: III. 10, 11, 17. Theophilus merely looks on the Gospel as a continuation of the prophetic revelations and injunctions. Of Christ, however, he did not speak at all, but only of the Logos (Pneuma), which has operated from the beginning. To Theophilus the first chapters of Genesis already contain the sum of all Christian knowledge (II. 10—32).

3 See II. 8: ὑπὸ δαιμόνων δὲ ἐμπνευσθέντες καὶ ὑπ᾽ αὐτῶν φυσιωθέντες ἅ εἶπον δι᾽ αὐτῶν εἶπον.

truth was not only announced by the Sibyl, to whom his remarks
do not apply, for she is (II. 36): ἐν Ἕλλησιν καὶ ἐν τοῖς λοιποῖς
ἔθνεσιν γενομένη προφῆτις, but that poets and philosophers,
"though against their will", also gave clear utterances regarding the justice, the judgment, and the punishments of God, as
well as regarding his providence in respect to the living and
the dead, or, in other words, about the most important points
(II. 37, 38, 8 fin.). Theophilus gives a double explanation of
this fact. On the one hand he ascribes it to the imitation of
holy writings (II. 12, 37: I. 14), and on the other he admits
that those writers, when the demons abandoned them (τῇ ψυχῇ
ἐκνήψαντες ἐξ αὐτῶν), of themselves displayed a knowledge of
the divine sovereignty, the judgment etc., which agrees with
the teachings of the prophets (II. 8). This admission need not
cause astonishment; for the freedom and control of his own
destiny with which man is endowed (II. 27) must infallibly lead
him to correct knowledge and obedience to God, as soon as
he is no longer under the sway of the demons. Theophilus
did not apply the title of philosophy to Christian truth, this
title being in his view discredited; but Christianity is to him
the "wisdom of God", which by luminous proofs convinces the
men who reflect on their own nature. [1]

[1] The unknown author of the work *de resurrectione*, which goes under the
name of Justin (Corp. Apol., Vol. III.) has given a surprising expression to the
thought that it is simply impossible to give a demonstration of truth. (Ὁ μὲν
τῆς ἀληθείας λόγος ἐστὶν ἐλεύθερός τε καὶ αὐτεξούσιος, ὑπὸ μηδεμίαν βάσανον ἐλέγχου
θέλων πίπτειν μηδὲ τὴν παρὰ τοῖς ἀκούουσι δι᾽ ἀποδείξεως ἐξέτασιν ὑπομένειν. Τὸ
γὰρ εὐγενὲς αὐτοῦ καὶ πεποιθὸς αὐτῷ τῇ πέμψαντι πιστεύεσθαι θέλει). He inveighs
in the beginning of his treatise against all rationalism, and on the one hand
professes a sort of materialistic theory of knowledge, whilst on the other, for that
very reason, he believes in inspiration and the authority of revelation; for all
truth originates with revelation, since God himself and God alone is the truth. Christ
revealed this truth and is for us τῶν ὅλων πίστις καὶ ἀπόδειξις. But it is far from
probable that the author would really have carried this proposition to its logical
conclusion (Justin, Dial. 3 ff. made a similar start). He wishes to meet his adversaries "armed with the arguments of faith which are unconquered" (c. 1., p. 214),
but the arguments of faith are still the arguments of reason. Among these he
regarded it as most important that even according to the theories about the world,
that is, about God and matter, held by the "so-called sages", Plato, Epicurus,
and the Stoics, the assumption of a resurrection of the flesh is not irrational (c. 6,
p. 228 f.). Some of these, viz., Pythagoras and Plato, also acknowledged the im-

*Tertullian and Minucius Felix.* [1]  Whilst, in the case of the
Greek Apologists, the acknowledgment of revelation appears
conditioned by philosophical scepticism on the one hand, and
by the strong impression of the dominion of the demons on the
other, the sceptical element is not only wanting in the Latin
Apologists, but the Christian truth is even placed in direct opposition to the sceptical philosophy and on the side of philosophical
dogmatism, *i.e.*, Stoicism. [2] Nevertheless the observations of Tertullian and Minucius Felix with regard to the essence of Christianity, viewed as philosophy and as revelation, are at bottom
completely identical with the conception of the Greek Apologists,
although it is undeniable that in the former case the revealed
character of Christianity is placed in the background. [3] The
recognition of this fact is exceedingly instructive, for it proves

mortality of the soul. But, for that very reason, this view is not sufficient, "for
if the Redeemer had only brought the message of the (eternal) life of the soul
what new thing would he have proclaimed in addition to what had been made
known by Pythagoras, Plato, and the band of their adherents?" (c. 10, p. 246)
This remark is very instructive, for it shows what considerations led the Apologists
to adhere to the belief in the resurrection of the body. Zahn, (Zeitschrift für
Kirchengeschichte, Vol. VIII., pp. 1 f., 20 f.) has lately reassigned to Justin himself the fragment de resurr. His argument, though displaying great plausibility,
has nevertheless not fully convinced me. The question is of great importance for
fixing the relation of Justin to Paul. I shall not discuss Hermias' "Irrisio Gentilium
Philosophorum", as the period when this Christian disputant flourished is quite uncertain. We still possess an early-Church Apology in Pseudo-Melito's "Oratio ad
Antoninum Cæsarem" (Otto, Corp. Apol. IX., p. 423 sq.). This book is preserved
(written?) in the Syrian language and was addressed to Caracalla or Heliogabalus
(preserved in the Cod. Nitr. Mus. Britt. Add. 14658). It is probably dependent
on Justin, but it is less polished and more violent than his Apology.

[1] Massebieau (Revue de l'histoire des religions, 1887, Vol. XV. No. 3) has
convinced me that Minucius wrote at a later period than Tertullian and made use
of his works.

[2] Cf. the plan of the "Octavius". The champion of heathenism here opposed
to the Christian is a philosopher representing the standpoint of the middle Academy. This presupposes, as a matter of course, that the latter undertakes the
defence of the Stoical position. See, besides, the corresponding arguments in the
Apology of Tertullian, *e.g.*, c. 17, as well as his tractate: "de testimonio animæ
naturaliter Christianæ". We need merely mention that the work of Minucius is
throughout dependent on Cicero's book, "de natura deorum." In this treatise he
takes up a position more nearly akin to heathen syncretism than Tertullian.

[3] In R. Kühn's investigation ("Der Octavius des Min. Felix", Leipzig, 1882)
—the best special work we possess on an early Christian Apology from the point

that the conception of Christianity set forth by the Apologists was not an individual one, but the necessary expression of the conviction that Christian truth contains the completion and guarantee of philosophical knowledge. To Minucius Felix (and Tertullian) Christian truth chiefly presents itself as the wisdom implanted by nature in every man (Oct. 16. 5). In so far as man possesses reason and speech and accomplishes the task of the "examination of the universe" ("inquisitio universitatis"), conditioned by this gift, he has the Christian truth, that is, he finds Christianity in his own constitution, and in the rational order of the world. Accordingly, Minucius is also able to demonstrate the Christian doctrines by means of the Stoic principle of knowledge, and arrives at the conclusion that Christianity is a philosophy, *i.e.*, the true philosophy, and that philosophers are to be considered Christians in proportion as they have discovered the truth.[1] Moreover, as he represented Christian ethics to be the expression of the Stoic, and depicted the Christian bond of brotherhood as a cosmopolitan union of philosophers, who have become conscious of their natural similarity,[2] the revealed character of Christianity appears to be entirely given up. This religion is natural enlightenment, the revelation of a truth contained in the world and in man, the discovery of the one God from the open book of creation. The difference between him and an Apologist like Tatian seems here to be a radical one. But, if we look more closely, we find that Minucius—and not less Tertullian—has abandoned Stoic rationalism in vital points. We may regard his apologetic aim as his excuse for clearly drawing the logical conclusions from these inconsist-

of view of the history of dogma—based on a very careful analysis of the Octavius, more emphasis is laid on the difference than on the agreement between Minucius and the Greek Apologists. The author's exposition requires to be supplemented in the latter respect (see Theologische Litteratur-Zeitung, 1883, No. 6).

[1] C. 20: Exposui opiniones omnium ferme philosophorum..., ut quivis arbitretur, aut nunc Christianos philosophos esse aut philosophos fuisse jam tunc Christianos."

[2] See Minucius, 31 ff. A quite similar proceeding is already found in Tertullian, who in his *Apologeticum* has everywhere given a Stoic colouring to Christian ethics and rules of life, and in c. 39 has drawn a complete veil over the peculiarity of the Christian societies.

encies himself.   However, these deviations of his from the doctrines
of the Stoa are not merely prompted by Christianity, but rather
have already become an essential component of his philosophical
theory of the world.   In the first place, Minucius developed a
detailed theory of the pernicious activity of the demons (cc. 26,
27).   This was a confession that human nature was not what
it ought to be, because an evil element had penetrated it from
without.   Secondly, he no doubt acknowledged (I. 4 : 16. 5) the
natural light of wisdom in humanity, but nevertheless remarked
(32. 9) that our thoughts are darkness when measured by the
clearness of God.   Finally, and this is the most essential point,
after appealing to various philosophers when expounding his
doctrine of the final conflagration of the world, he suddenly
repudiated this tribunal, declaring that the Christians follow the
prophets, and that philosophers "have formed this shadowy picture
of distorted truth in imitation of the divine predictions of the
prophets" (34).   Here we have now a union of all the elements
already found in the Greek Apologists; only they are, as it
were, hid in the case of Minucius.   But the final proof that
he agreed with them in the main is found in the exceedingly
contemptuous judgment which he in conclusion passed on all
philosophers and indeed on philosophy generally [1] (34. 5 : 38. 5).
This judgment is not to be explained, as in Tertullian's case,
by the fact that his Stoic opinions led him to oppose natural
perception to all philosophical theory—for this, at most, cannot
have been more than a secondary contributing cause, [2] but by
the fact that he is conscious of following *revealed* wisdom. [3]

---

[1] Tertullian has done exactly the same thing; see Apolog. 46 (and de præscr. 7.)

[2] Tertull., de testim. I.: "Sed non eam te (animam) advoco, quæ scholis formata,
bibliothecis exercitata, academiis et porticibus Atticis pasta sapientiam ructas.
Te simplicem et rudem et impolitam et idioticam compello, qualem te habent qui
te solam habent... Imperitia tua mihi opus est, quoniam aliquantulæ peritiæ
tuæ nemo credit."

[3] Tertull., Apol. 46: "Quid simile philosophus et Christianus? Græciæ discipulus
et cœli?" de præscr. 7: "Quid ergo Athenis et Hierosolymis? Quid academiæ et
ecclesiæ?" Minuc. 38.5: "Philosophorum supercilia contemnimus, quos corruptores
et adulteros novimus... nos, qui non habitu sapientiam sed mente præferimus,
non eloquimur magna sed vivimus, gloriamur nos consecutos, quod illi summa
intentione quæsiverunt nec invenire potuerunt. Quid ingrati sumus, quid nobis
invidemus, si veritas divinitatis nostri temporis ætate maturuit?"

Revelation is necessary because mankind must be aided from without, *i.e.*, by God. In this idea man's need of redemption is acknowledged, though not to the same extent as by Seneca and Epictetus. But no sooner does Minucius perceive the teachings of the prophets to be divine truth than man's natural endowment and the speculation of philosophers sink for him into darkness. Christianity is the wisdom which philosophers sought, but were not able to find. [1]

We may sum up the doctrines of the Apologists as follows: (1) Christianity is revelation, *i.e.*, it is the divine wisdom, proclaimed of old by the prophets and, by reason of its origin, possessing an absolute certainty which can also be recognised in the fulfilment of their predictions. As divine wisdom Christianity is contrasted with, and puts an end to, all natural and philosophical knowledge. (2) Christianity is the enlightenment corresponding to the natural but impaired knowledge of man. [2] It embraces all the elements of truth in philosophy, whence it is *the* philosophy; and helps man to realise the knowledge with which he is naturally endowed. (3) Revelation of the rational was and is necessary, because man has fallen under the sway of the demons. (4) The efforts of philosophers to ascertain the right knowledge were in vain; and this is, above all, shown by the fact that they neither overthrew polytheism nor brought about a really moral life. Moreover, so far as they discovered the truth, they owed it to the prophets from whom they borrowed

[1] Minucius did not enter closely into the significance of Christ any more than Tatian, Athenagoras, and Theophilus; he merely touched upon it (9. 4 : 29. 2). He also viewed Christianity as the teaching of the Prophets; whoever acknowledges the latter must of necessity adore the crucified Christ. Tertullian was accordingly the first Apologist after Justin who again considered it necessary to give a detailed account of Christ as the incarnation of the Logos (see the 21st chapter of the Apology in its relation to chaps. 17—20).

[2] Among the Greek Apologists the unknown author of the work " de Monarchia ", which bears the name of Justin, has given clearest expression to this conception. He is therefore most akin to Minucius (see chap. I.). Here monotheism is designated as the καθολικὴ δόξα which has fallen into oblivion through bad habit; for τῆς ἀνθρωπίνης φύσεως τὸ κατ᾽ ἀρχὴν συζυγίαν συνέσεως καὶ σωτηρίας λαβούσης εἰς ἐπίγνωσιν ἀληθείας θρησκείας τε τῆς εἰς τὸν ἕνα καὶ πάντων δεσπότην. According to this, then, only an awakening is required,

it; at least it is uncertain whether they even attained a knowledge of fragments of the truth by their own independent efforts. [1]
But it is certain that many seeming truths in the writings of
the philosophers were imitations of the truth by evil demons.
This is the origin of all polytheism, which is, moreover, to some
extent an imitation of Christian institutions. (5) The confession
of Christ is simply included in the acknowledgment of the wisdom of the prophets; the doctrine of the truth did not receive
a new content through Christ; he only made it accessible to
the world and strengthened it (victory over the demons; special
features ackowledged by Justin and Tertullian). (6) The practical
test of Christianity is first contained in the fact that all persons
are able to grasp it, for women and uneducated men here become
veritable sages; secondly in the fact that it has the power of producing
a holy life, and of overthrowing the tyranny of the demons. In
the Apologists, therefore, Christianity served itself heir to antiquity,
*i.e.*, to the result of the monotheistic knowledge and ethics of the
Greeks: "Ὅσα οὖν παρὰ πᾶσι καλῶς εἴρηται, ἡμῶν τῶν Χριστιανῶν ἐστί"
(Justin, Apol. II. 13). It traced its origin back to the beginning of the
world. Everything true and good which elevates mankind springs
from divine revelation, and is at the same time genuinely human,
because it is a clear expression of what man finds within him
and of his destination (Justin, Apol. I. 46: οἱ μετὰ λόγου βιώσαντες
Χριστιανοί εἰσι, κἂν ἄθεοι ἐνομίσθησαν, οἷον ἐν Ἕλλησι μὲν Σωκράτης
καὶ Ἡράκλειτος καὶ οἱ ὅμοιοι αὐτοῖς, ἐν βαρβάροις δὲ Ἀβραὰμ κ.τ.λ.,
"those that have lived with reason are Christians, even though
they were accounted atheists, such as Socrates and Heraclitus
and those similar to them among the Greeks, and Abraham etc.
among the barbarians"). But everything true and good is
Christian, for Christianity is nothing else than the teaching of
revelation. No second formula can be imagined in which the
claim of Christianity to be the religion of the world is so powerfully expressed (hence also the endeavour of the Apologists to

---

[1] But almost all the Apologists acknowledged that heathendom possessed
prophets. They recognise these in the Sibyls and the old poets. The author of
the work "de Monarchia" expressed the most pronounced views in regard to this.
Hermas (Vis. II. 4), however, shows that the Apologists owed this notion also to
an idea that was widespread among Christian people.

reconcile Christianity and the Empire), nor, on the other hand, can we conceive of one where the specific content of traditional Christianity is so thoroughly neutralised as it is here. But the really epoch-making feature is the fact that the intellectual culture of mankind now appears reconciled and united with religion. The "dogmas" are the expression of this. Finally, these fundamental presuppositions also result in a quite definite idea of the essence of revelation and of the content of reason. The essence of revelation consists in its form: it is divine communication through a miraculous inward working. All the media of revelation are passive organs of the Holy Spirit (Athenag. Supplic. 7; Pseudo-Justin, Cohort. 8; Justin, Dialogue 115. 7; Apol. I. 31, 33, 36; etc.; see also Hippolytus, de Christo et Antichr. 2). These were not necessarily at all times in a state of ecstasy, when they received the revelations; but they were no doubt in a condition of absolute receptivity. The Apologists had no other idea of revelation. What they therefore viewed as the really decisive proof of the reality of revelation is the prediction of the future, for the human mind does not possess this power. It was only in connection with this proof that the Apologists considered it important to show what Moses, David, Isaiah, etc., had proclaimed in the Old Testament, that is, these names have only a *chronological* significance. This also explains their interest in a history of the world, in so far as this interest originated in the effort to trace the chain of prophets up to the beginning of history, and to prove the higher antiquity of revealed truth as compared with all human knowledge and errors, particularly as found among the Greeks (clear traces in Justin, [1] first detailed argument in Tatian). [2] If, however, strictly speaking, it is only the form and not the content of revelation that is supernatural in so far as this content coincides with that of reason, it is evident that the Apologists simply took the content of the latter for granted and stated it dogmatically. So, whether they expressed themselves in strictly Stoic fashion or not, they all essentially agree in the assumption that true religion

---

[1]  See Justin, Apol. I. 31, Dial. 7, p. 30 etc.

[2]  See Tatian, c. 31 ff.

and morality are the natural content of reason. Even Tatian
forms no exception, though he himself protests against the idea.

### 3. *The doctrines of Christianity as the revealed and rational religion.*

The Apologists frequently spoke of the doctrines or "dogmas"
of Christianity; and the whole content of this religion as philosophy is included in these dogmas. [1] According to what we have
already set forth there can be no doubt about the character of

---

[1] In the New Testament the content of the Christian faith is nowhere designated
as dogma. In Clement (I. II.), Hermas, and Polycarp the word is not found at all;
yet Clement (I. 20. 4, 27. 5) called the divine order of nature τὰ δεδογματισμένα
ὑπὸ Θεοῦ. In Ignatius (ad Magn. XIII. 1) we read: σπουδάζετε οὖν βεβαιωθῆναι
ἐν τοῖς δόγμασιν τοῦ κυρίου καὶ τῶν ἀποστόλων, but δόγματα here exclusively mean
the rules of life (see Zahn on this passage), and this is also their signification in
Διδαχή XI. 3. In the Epistle of Barnabas we read in several passages (I. 6: IX. 7:
X. 1, 9 f.) of "dogmas of the Lord"; but by these he means partly particular
mysteries, partly divine dispensations. Hence the Apologists are the first to apply
the word to the Christian faith, in accordance with the language of philosophy.
They are also the first who employed the ideas θεολογεῖν and θεολογία. The latter
word is twice found in Justin (Dial. 56) in the sense of "aliquem nominare deum".
In Dial. 113, however, it has the more comprehensive sense of "to make religio-
scientific investigations". Tatian (10) also used the word in the first sense; on the
contrary he entitled a book of which he was the author "πρὸς τοὺς ἀποφηναμένους
τὰ περὶ Θεοῦ" and not "πρὸς τοὺς θεολογοῦντας". In Athenagoras (Suppl. 10)
theology is the doctrine of God and of all beings to whom the predicate "Deity"
belongs (see also 20, 22). That is the old usage of the word. It was thus employed by Tertullian in ad nat. II. 1 (the threefold division of theology; in II. 2, 3
the expression "theologia physica, mythica" refers to this); Cohort. ad Gr. 3, 22.
The anonymous writer in Eusebius (H. E. V. 28. 4, 5) is instructive on the point.
Brilliant demonstrations of the ancient use of the word "theology" are found in
Natorp, Thema und Disposition der aristotelischen Metaphysik (Philosophische
Monatshefte, 1887, Parts 1 and 2, pp. 55—64). The title "theology", as applied to
a philosophic discipline, was first used by the Stoics; the old poets were previously
called "theologians", and the "theological" stage was the prescientific one which
is even earlier than the "childhood" of "physicists" (so Aristotle speaks throughout).
To the Fathers of the Church also the old poets are still οἱ παλαιοὶ θεολόγοι. But
side by side with this we have an adoption of the Stoic view that there is also a
philosophical theology, because the teaching of the old poets concerning the gods
conceals under the veil of myth a treasure of philosophical truth. In the Stoa arose
the "impossible idea of a 'theology' which is to be philosophy, that is, knowledge
based on reason, and yet to have positive religion as the foundation of its certainty."
The Apologists accepted this, but added to it the distinction of a κοσμικὴ and
θεολογικὴ σοφία.

Christian dogmas. *They are the rational truths, revealed by the prophets in the Holy Scriptures, and summarised in Christ* (Χριστὸς λόγος καὶ νόμος), *which in their unity represent the divine wisdom, and the recognition of which leads to virtue and eternal life.* The Apologists considered it their chief task to set forth these doctrines, and hence they can be reproduced with all desirable clearness. The dogmatic scheme of the Apologists may therefore be divided into three component parts. These are : (A) Christianity viewed as monotheistic cosmology (God as the Father of the world) ; (B) Christianity as the highest morality and righteousness (God as the judge who rewards goodness and punishes wickedness) ; (C) Christianity regarded as redemption (God as the Good One who assists man and rescues him from the power of the demons). [1] Whilst the first two ideas are expressed in a clear and precise manner, it is equally true that the third is not worked out in a lucid fashion. This, as will afterwards be seen, is, on the one hand, the result of the Apologists' doctrine of freedom, and, on the other, of their inability to discover a specific significance for the *person* of Christ within the sphere of revelation. Both facts again are ultimately to be explained from their moralism.

The essential content of revealed philosophy is viewed by the Apologists (see A, B) as comprised in three doctrines. [2] First, there is one spiritual and inexpressibly exalted God, who is Lord and Father of the world. Secondly, he requires a holy life. Thirdly, he will at last sit in judgment, and will reward the good with immortality and punish the wicked with death. The teaching concerning God, virtue, and eternal reward is traced to the prophets and Christ ; but the bringing about of a virtuous

[1] Christ has a relation to all three parts of the scheme, (1) as λόγος: (2) as νόμος, νομοθέτης, and κριτής ; (3) as διδάσκαλος and σωτήρ.

[2] In the reproduction of the apologetical theology historians of dogma have preferred to follow Justin ; but here they have constantly overlooked the fact that Justin was the most Christian among the Apologists, and that the features of his teaching to which particular value is rightly attached, are either not found in the others at all (with the exception of Tertullian), or else in quite rudimentary form. It is therefore proper to put the doctrines common to all the Apologists in the foreground, and to describe what is peculiar to Justin as such, so far as it agrees with New Testament teachings or contains an anticipation of the future tenor of dogma.

life (of righteousness) has been necessarily left by God to men
themselves ; for God has created man free, and virtue can only
be acquired by man's own efforts.  The prophets and Christ are
therefore a source of righteousness in so far as they are teachers.
But as God, that is, the divine Word (which we need not here
discuss) has spoken in them, Christianity is to be defined as the
Knowledge of God, mediated by the Deity himself, and as a
virtuous walk in the longing after eternal and perfect life with
God, as well as in the sure hope of this imperishable reward.
By knowing what is true and doing what is good man becomes
righteous and a partaker of the highest bliss.  This knowledge,
which has the character of divine instruction, [1] rests on faith in
the divine revelation.  This revelation has the nature and power
of redemption in so far as the fact is undoubted that without
it men cannot free themselves from the tyranny of the demons,
whilst believers in revelation are enabled by the Spirit of God
to put them to flight.  Accordingly, the dogmas of Christian
philosophy theoretically contain the monotheistic cosmology, and
practically the rules for a holy life, which appears as a renunciation of the world and as a new order of society. [2]  The goal
is immortal life, which consists in the full knowledge and contemplation of God.  The dogmas of revelation lie between the
cosmology and ethics; they are indefinitely expressed so far as
they contain the idea of salvation; but they are very precisely
worded in so far as they guarantee the truth of the cosmology
and ethics.

I.   The dogmas which express the knowledge of God and the
world are dominated by the fundamental idea that the world as the
created, conditioned, and transient is contrasted with something

---

[1]  Cicero's proposition (de nat. deor. II. 66. 167): "nemo vir magnus sine aliquo
afflatu divino unquam fuit," which was the property of all the idealistic philosophers of the age, is found in the Apologists reproduced in the most various forms
(see, *e.g.*, Tatian 29).  That all knowledge of the truth, both among the prophets
and those who follow their teaching, is derived from inspiration was in their eyes
a matter of certainty.  But here they were only able to frame a theory in the
case of the prophets; for such a theory strictly applied to all would have threatened
the spontaneous character of the knowledge of the truth.

[2]  Justin, Apol. I. 3: Ἡμέτερον οὖν ἔργον καὶ βίου καὶ μαθημάτων τὴν ἐπίσκεψιν
πᾶσι παρέχειν.

self-existing, unchangeable and eternal, which is the first cause
of the world. This self-existing Being has none of the attributes
which belong to the world; hence he is exalted above every name
and has in himself no distinctions. This implies, first, the unity
and uniqueness of this eternal Being; secondly, his spiritual
nature, for everything bodily is subject to change; and, finally,
his perfection, for the self-existent and eternal requires nothing.
Since, however, he is the cause of all being, himself being un-
conditioned, he is the fulness of all being or true being itself
(Tatian 5: καθὸ πᾶσα δύναμις ὁρατῶν τε καὶ ἀοράτων αὐτὸς ὑπόστασις ἦν, σὺν αὐτῷ τὰ πάντα). As the living and spiritual Being
he reveals himself in free creations, which make known his
omnipotence and wisdom, *i.e.*, his operative reason. These creations
are, moreover, a proof of the goodness of the Deity, for they
can be no result of necessities, in so far as God is in himself
perfect. Just because he is perfect, the Eternal Essence is also
the Father of all virtues, in so far as he contains no admixture
of what is defective. These virtues include both the goodness
which manifests itself in his creations, and the righteousness
which gives to the creature what belongs to him, in accordance
with the position he has received. On the basis of this train
of thought the Apologists lay down the dogmas of the monarchy
of God (τῶν ὅλων τὸ μοναρχικόν); his supramundaneness (τὸ ἄρρητον,
τὸ ἀνέκφραστον, τὸ ἀχώρητον, τὸ ἀκατάληπτον, τὸ ἀπερινόητον, τὸ
ἀσύγκριτον, τὸ ἀσυμβίβαστον, τὸ ἀνεκδιήγητόν; see Justin, Apol.
II. 6; Theoph. I. 3); his unity (εἷς Θεός); his having no beginning
(ἄναρχος, ὅτι ἀγένητος); his eternity and unchangeableness (ἀναλλοίωτος καθότι ἀθάνατος); his perfection (τέλειος); his need of
nothing (ἀπροσδεής); his spiritual nature (πνεῦμα ὁ Θεός); his
absolute causality (αὐτὸς ὑπάρχων τοῦ παντὸς ἡ ὑπόστασις, the
motionless mover, see Aristides c. 1); his creative activity
(κτίστης τῶν πάντων); his sovereignty (δεσπότης τῶν ὅλων); his
fatherhood (πατὴρ διὰ τὸ εἶναι αὐτὸν πρὸ τῶν ὅλων) his reason-
power (God as λόγος, νοῦς, πνεῦμα, σοφία); his omnipotence
(παντοκράτωρ ὅτι αὐτὸς τὰ πάντα κρατεῖ καὶ ἐμπεριέχει); his
righteousness and goodness (πατὴρ τῆς δικαιοσύνης καὶ πασῶν τῶν
ἀρετῶν χρηστότης). These dogmas are set forth by one Apologist
in a more detailed, and by another in a more concise form,

but three points are emphasised by all. First, God is primarily to be conceived as the First Cause. Secondly, the principle of moral good is also the principle of the world. Thirdly, the principle of the world, that is, the Deity, as being the immortal and eternal, forms the contrast to the world which is the transient. In the cosmology of the Apologists the two fundamental ideas are that God is the Father and Creator of the world, but that, as uncreated and eternal, he is also the complete contrast to it. [1]

These dogmas about God were not determined by the Apologists from the standpoint of the Christian Church which is awaiting an introduction into the Kingdom of God; but were deduced from a contemplation of the world on the one hand (see particularly Tatian, 4; Theophilus, I. 5, 6), and of the moral nature of man on the other. But, in so far as the latter itself belongs to the sphere of created things, the cosmos is the starting-point of their speculations. This is everywhere dominated by reason and order; [2] it bears the impress of the divine Logos, and that in a double sense. On the one hand it appears as the copy of a higher, eternal world, for if we imagine transient and changeable matter removed, it is a wonderful complex of spiritual forces; on the other it presents itself as the finite product of a rational will. Moreover, the matter which lies at its basis is nothing bad, but an indifferent substance created by God, [3] though indeed perishable. In its constitution the world is in every respect a structure worthy of God. [4] Nevertheless, according to the Apologists, the direct author of the world was not God, but the personified power of reason which they per-

---

[1] See the exposition of the doctrine of God in Aristides with the conclusion found in all the Apologists, that God requires no offerings and presents.

[2] Even Tatian says in c. 19: Κόσμου μὲν γὰρ ἡ κατασκευὴ καλή, τὸ δὲ ἐν αὐτῷ πολίτευμα φαῦλον.

[3] Tatian 5: Οὔτε ἄναρχος ἡ ὕλη καθάπερ ὁ Θεός, οὐδὲ διὰ τὸ ἄναρχον καὶ αὐτὴ ἰσοδύναμος τῷ Θεῷ· γεννητὴ δὲ καὶ οὐχ ὑπὸ τοῦ ἄλλου γεγονυῖα· μόνον δὲ ὑπὸ τοῦ πάντων δημιουργοῦ προβεβλημένη. 12. Even Justin does not seem to have taught otherwise, though that is not quite certain; see Apol. I. 10, 59, 64, 67: II. 6. Theophilus I. 4: II. 4, 10, 13 says very plainly: ἐξ οὐκ ὄντων τὰ πάντα ἐποίησεν.... τί δὲ μέγα, εἰ ὁ θεὸς ἐξ ὑποκειμένης ὕλης ἐποίει τὸν κόσμον;

[4] Hence the knowledge of God and the right knowledge of the world are most closely connected; see Tatian 27: ἡ Θεοῦ κατάληψις ἥν ἔχω περὶ τῶν ὅλων.

ceived in the cosmos and represented as the immediate source
of the universe. The motive for this dogma and the interest
in it would be wrongly determined by alleging that the Apologists purposely introduced the Logos in order to separate God
from matter, because they regarded this as something bad.
This idea of Philo's cannot at least have been adopted by them
as the result of conscious reflection, for it does not agree with
their conception of matter; nor is it compatible with their idea
of God and their belief in Providence, which is everywhere
firmly maintained. Still less indeed can it be shown that they
were all impelled to this dogma from their view of Jesus Christ,
since in this connection, with the exception of Justin and Tertullian, they manifested no specific interest in the incarnation
of the Logos in Jesus. The adoption of the dogma of the
Logos is rather to be explained thus: (1) The idea of God,
derived by abstraction from the cosmos, did indeed, like that of
the idealistic philosophy, involve the element of unity and spirituality, which implied a sort of personality; but the fulness of all
spiritual forces, the essence of everything imperishable were
quite as essential features of the conception; for in spite of the
transcendence inseparable from the notion of God, this idea was
neverthless meant to explain the world. [1] Accordingly, they
required a formula capable of expressing the transcendent and
unchangeable nature of God on the one hand, and his fulness
of creative and spiritual powers on the other. But the latter
attributes themselves had again to be comprehended in a unity,
because the law of the cosmos bore the appearance of a harmonious one. From this arose the idea of the Logos, and indeed the latter was necessarily distinguished from God as a
separate existence, as soon as the realisation of the powers
residing in God was represented as beginning. *The Logos is
the hypostasis of the operative power of reason, which at once
preserves the unity and unchangeableness of God in spite of the
exercise of the powers residing in him, and renders this very
exercise possible.* (2) Though the Apologists believed in the
divine origin of the revelation given to the prophets, on which

[1] The beginning of the fifth chapter of Tatian's Oration is specially instructive here.

all knowledge of truth is based, they could nevertheless not be
induced by this idea to represent God himself as a direct actor.
For that revelation presupposes a speaker and a spoken word;
but it would be an impossible thought to make the fulness of
all essence and the first cause of all things speak. The Deity
cannot be a speaking and still less a visible person, yet
according to the testimony of the prophets, a Divine Person
was seen by them. The Divine Being who makes himself known
on earth in audible and visible fashion can only be the Divine
Word. As, however, according to the fundamental view of the
Apologists the principle of religion, *i.e.*, of the knowledge of
the truth, is also the principle of the world, so that Divine
Word, which imparts the right knowledge of the world, must
be identical with the Divine Reason which produced the world
itself. In other words, the Logos is not only the creative Reason
of God, but also his revealing Word. This explains the motive
and aim of the dogma of the Logos. We need not specially
point out that nothing more than the precision and certainty
of the Apologists' manner of statement is peculiar here; the
train of thought itself belongs to Greek philosophy. But that
very confidence is the most essential feature of the case; for
in fact the firm belief that the principle of the world is also
that of revelation represents an important early-Christian idea,
though indeed in the form of philosophical reflection. To the
majority of the Apologists the theoretical content of the Christian faith is completely exhausted in this proposition. They required no particular Christology, for in every revelation of God
by his Word they already recognised a proof of his existence
not to be surpassed, and consequently regarded it as Christianity *in nuce*. [1] But the fact that the Apologists made a distinction *in thesi* between the prophetic Spirit of God and the
Logos, without being able to make any use of this distinction,

[1] According to what has been set forth in the text it is incorrect to assert that
the Apologists adopted the Logos doctrine in order to reconcile monotheism with
the divine honours paid to the crucified Christ. The truth rather is that the Logos
doctrine was already part of their creed before they gave any consideration to the
person of the historical Christ, and *vice versâ* Christ's right to divine honours was
to them a matter of certainty independently of the Logos doctrine.

is a very clear instance of their dependence on the formulæ of the Church's faith. Indeed their conception of the Logos continually compelled them to identify the Logos and the Spirit, just as they not unfrequently define Christianity as the belief in the true God and in his Son, without mentioning the Spirit. [1] Further their dependence on the Christian tradition is shown in the fact that the most of them expressly designated the Logos as the *Son* of God. [2]

The Logos doctrine of the Apologists is an essentially unanimous

---

[1] We find the distinction of Logos (Son) and Spirit in Justin, Apol. I. 5, and in every case where he quotes formulæ (if we are not to assume the existence of interpolation in the text, which seems to me not improbable ; see now also Cramer in the Theologische Studien, 1893. pp. 17 ff., 138 ff.). In Tatian 13 fin. the Spirit is represented as ὁ διάκονος τοῦ πεπονθότος Θεοῦ. The conception in Justin, Dial. 116, is similar. Father, Word, and prophetic Spirit are spoken of in Athenag. 10. The express designation τριάς is first found in Theophilus (but see the Excerpta ex Theodoto); see II. 15: αἱ τρεῖς ἡμέραι τύποι εἰσὶν τῆς τριάδος, τοῦ Θεοῦ καὶ τοῦ λόγου αὐτοῦ καὶ τῆς σοφίας αὐτοῦ; see II. 10, 18. But it is just in Theophilus that the difficulty of deciding between Logos and Wisdom appears with special plainness (II. 10). The interposition of the host of good angels between Son and Spirit found in Justin, Apol. I. 5 (see Athenag.), is exceedingly striking. We have, however, to notice, provided the text is right, (1) that this interposition is only found in a single passage, (2) that Justin wished to refute the reproach of ἀθεότης, (3) that the placing of the Spirit after the angels does not necessarily imply a position inferior to theirs, but merely a subordination to the Son and the Father common to the Spirit and the angels, (4) that the good angels were also invoked by the Christians, because they were conceived as mediators of prayer (see my remark on I. Clem. ad Corinth. LVI. 1); they might have found a place here just for this latter reason. On the significance of the Holy Spirit in the theology of Justin, see Zahn's Marcellus of Ancyra, p. 228: "If there be any one theologian of the early Church who might be regarded as depriving the Holy Spirit of all scientific *raison d'être* at least on the ground of having no distinctive(?) activity, and the Father of all share in revelation, it is Justin." We cannot at bottom say that the Apologists possessed a doctrine of the Trinity.

[2] To Justin the name of the Son is the most important; see also Athenag. 10. The Logos had indeed been already called the Son of God by Philo, and Celsus expressly says (Orig., c. Cels. II. 31); "If according to your doctrine the Word is really the Son of God then we agree with you;" but the Apologists are the first to attach the name of Son to the Logos as a proper designation. If, however, the Logos is intrinsically the Son of God, then Christ is the Son of God, not because he is the begotten of God in the flesh (early Christian), but because the spiritual being existing in him is the antemundane reproduction of God (see Justin, Apol. II. 6: ὁ υἱὸς τοῦ πατρὸς καὶ Θεοῦ, ὁ μόνος λεγόμενος κυρίως υἱός)—a momentous expression.

one.  Since God cannot be conceived as without reason, ἄλογος, but as the fulness of all reason,[1] he has always Logos in himself.  This Logos is on the one hand the divine consciousness itself, and on the other the power (idea and energy) to which the world is due ; he is not separate from God, but is contained in his essence.[2]  For the sake of the creation God produced (sent forth, projected) the Logos from himself, that is, he engendered[3] him from his essence by a free and simple act of will (Θεὸς ἐκ Θεοῦ πεφυκώς εξ ἑαυτοῦ. Dial. 61).  Then for the first time the Logos became a hypostasis separate from God, or, in other words, he first came into existence; and, in virtue of his origin, he possesses the following distinctive features :[4]

[1] Athenag., 10; Tatian, Orat. 5.

[2] The clearest expression of this is in Tatian 5, which passage is also to be compared with the following: Θεὸς ἦν ἐν ἀρχῇ, τὴν δὲ ἀρχὴν λόγου δύναμιν παρειλήφαμεν. Ὁ γὰρ δεσπότης τῶν ὅλων, αὐτὸς ὑπάρχων τοῦ παντὸς ἡ ὑπόστασις, κατὰ μὲν τὴν μηδέπω γεγενημένην ποίησιν μόνος ἦν· καθὸ δὲ πᾶσα δύναμις, ὁρατῶν τε καὶ ἀοράτων αὐτὸς ὑπόστασις ἦν, σὺν αὐτῷ τὰ πάντα· σὺν αὐτῷ διὰ λογικῆς δυνάμεως αὐτὸς καὶ ὁ λόγος, ὅς ἦν ἐν αὐτῷ, ὑπέστησε. Θελήματι δὲ τῆς ἁπλότητος αὐτοῦ προπηδᾷ λόγος· ὁ δὲ λόγος, οὐ κατὰ κενοῦ χωρήσας, ἔργον πρωτότοκον τοῦ πατρὸς γίνεται. Τοῦτον ἴσμεν τοῦ κόσμου τὴν ἀρχήν. Γέγονε δὲ κατὰ μερισμόν, οὐ κατὰ ἀποκοπήν· τὸ γὰρ ἀποτμηθὲν τοῦ πρώτου κεχώρισται, τὸ δὲ μερισθὲν οἰκονομίας τὴν αἵρεσιν προσλαβὸν οὐκ ἐνδεᾶ τὸν ὅθεν εἴληπται πεποίηκεν. Ὥσπερ γὰρ ἀπὸ μιᾶς δᾳδὸς ἀνάπτεται μὲν πυρὰ πολλὰ, τῆς δὲ πρώτης δᾳδὸς διὰ τὴν ἔξαψιν τῶν πολλῶν δᾳδῶν οὐκ ἐλαττοῦται τὸ φῶς, οὕτω καὶ ὁ λόγος προελθὼν ἐκ τῆς τοῦ πατρὸς δυνάμεως οὐκ ἄλογον πεποίηκε τὸν γεγεννηκότα. In the identification of the divine consciousness, that is, the power of God, with the force to which the world is due the naturalistic basis of the apologetic speculations is most clearly shown. Cf. Justin, Dial. 128, 129.

[3] The word "beget" (γεννᾶν) is used by the Apologists, especially Justin, because the name "Son" was the recognised expression for the Logos.  No doubt the words ἐξερεύγεσθαι, προβάλλεσθαι, προέρχεσθαι, προπηδᾶν and the like express the physical process more exactly in the sense of the Apologists. On the other hand, however, γεννᾶν appears the more appropriate word in so far as the relation of the essence of the Logos to the essence of God is most clearly shown by the name "Son".

[4] None of the Apologists has precisely defined the Logos idea. Zahn, l.c., p. 233, correctly remarks: "Whilst the distinction drawn between the hitherto unspoken and the spoken word of the Creator makes Christ appear as the thought of the world within the mind of God, yet he is also to be something real which only requires to enter into a new relation to God to become an active force. Then again this Word is not to be the thought that God thinks, but the thought that thinks in God.  And again it is to be a something, or an Ego, in

(1) The inner essence of the Logos is identical with the essence of God himself; for it is the product of self-separation in God, willed and brought about by himself. Further, the Logos is not cut off and separated from God, nor is he a mere modality in him. He is rather the independent product of the self-unfolding of God ($οἰκονομία$), which product, though it is the epitome of divine reason, has nevertheless not stripped the Father of this attribute. The Logos is the revelation of God, and the visible God. Consequently the Logos is really God and Lord, *i.e.*, he possesses the divine nature in virtue of his essence. The Apologists, however, only know of one kind of divine nature and this is that which belongs to the Logos. (2) From the moment when he was begotten the Logos is a being distinct from the Father; he is $ἀριθμῷ ἕτερόν τι, Θεὸς ἕτερος, Θεὸς δεύτερος$ ("something different in number, another God, a second God.") But his personality only dates from that moment. "Fuit tempus, cum patri filius non fuit," ("there was a time when the Father had no Son", so Tertullian, adv. Hermog. 3). The $λόγος προφορικός$ is for the first time a hypostasis distinct from the Father, the $λόγος ἐνδιάθετος$ is not.[1] (3) The Logos has an origin, the Father has not; hence it follows that in relation to God the Logos is a creature; he is the begotten, that is, the created God, the God who has a beginning. Wherefore in rank he is below God ($ἐν δευτέρᾳ χώρᾳ—δεύτερος Θεός$, "in the second place,

God's thinking essence, which enters into reciprocal intercourse with something else in God; occasionally also the reason of God which is in a state of active exercise and without which he would not be rational." Considering this evident uncertainty it appears to me a very dubious proceeding to differentiate the conceptions of the Logos in Justin, Athenagoras, Tatian, and Theophilus, as is usually done. If we consider that no Apologist wrote a special treatise on the Logos, that Tatian (c. 5) is really the only one from whom we have any precise statements, and that the elements of the conception are the same in all, it appears inadvisable to lay so great stress on the difference as Zahn, for instance, has done in the book already referred to, p. 232 f. Hardly any real difference can have existed between Justin, Tatian, and Theophilus in the Logos doctrine proper. On the other hand Athenagoras certainly seems to have tried to eliminate the appearance of the Logos in time, and to emphasise the eternal nature of the divine relationships, without, however, reaching the position which Irenæus took up here.

[1] This distinction is only found in Theophilus (II. 10); but the idea exists in Tatian and probably also in Justin, though it is uncertain whether Justin regarded the Logos as having any sort of being before the moment of his begetting.

and a second God "), the messenger and servant of God.  The
subordination of the Logos is not founded on the content of
his essence, but on his origin.  In relation to the creatures,
however, the Logos is the ἀρχή, i.e., not only the beginning but
the principle of the vitality and form of everything that is to
receive being.  As an emanation (the begotten) he is distinguished
from all creatures, for he alone is the Son; [1] but, as having a
beginning, he again stands on a level with them.  Hence the
paradoxical expression, ἔργον πρωτότοκον τοῦ πατρός (" first begotten work of the Father "), is here the most appropriate
designation.  (4) In virtue of his finite origin, it is possible
and proper for the Logos to enter into the finite, to act, to speak.
and to appear.  As he arose for the sake of the creation of the
world, he has the capacity of personal and direct revelation
which does not belong to the infinite God ; nay, his whole
essence consists in the very fact that he is thought, word, and
deed.  Behind this active substitute and vicegerent, the Father
stands in the darkness of the incomprehensible, and in the
incomprehensible light of perfection as the hidden, unchangeable
God. [2]

With the issuing forth of the Logos from God began the
realisation of the idea of the world.  The world as κόσμος
νοητός is contained in the Logos.  But the world is material
and manifold, the Logos is spiritual and one.  Therefore the

---

[1] Justin, Apol. II. 6., Dial. 61.  The Logos is not produced out of nothing, like
the rest of the creatures.  Yet it is evident that the Apologists did not yet sharply
and precisely distinguish between begetting and creating, as the later theologians
did; though some of them certainly felt the necessity for a distinction.

[2] All the Apologists tacitly assume that the Logos in virtue of his origin has
the capacity of entering the finite.  The distinction which here exists between
Father and Son is very pregnantly expressed by Tertullian (adv. Marc. II. 27):
"Igitur quæcumque exigitis deo digna, habebuntur in patre invisibili incongressibilique
et placido et, ut ita dixerim, philosophorum deo.  Quæcumque autem ut indigna
reprehenditis deputabuntur in filio et viso et audito et congresso, arbitro patris et
ministro."  But we ought not to charge the Apologists with the theologoumenon
that it was an inward necessity for the Logos to become man.  Their Logos hovers,
as it were, between God and the world, so that he appears as the highest creature,
in so far as he is conceived as the production of God; and again seems to be
merged in God, in so far as he is looked upon as the consciousness and spiritual
force of God.  To Justin, however, the incarnation is irrational, and the rest of the
Greek Apologists are silent about it.

Logos is not himself the world, but he is its creator and in a certain fashion its archetype. Justin and Tatian used the expression "beget" (γεννᾶν) for the creation of the world, but in connections which do not admit of any importance being attached to this use. The world was created out of nothing after a host of spirits, as is assumed by most Apologists, had been created along with heaven, which is a higher, glorious world. The purpose of the creation of the world was and is the production of men, *i.e.*, beings possessed of soul and body, endowed with reason and freedom, and therefore made in the image of God; beings who are to partake of the blessedness and perfection of God. Everything is created for man's sake, and his own creation is a proof of the goodness of God. As beings possessed of soul and body, men are neither mortal nor immortal, but capable either of death or immortality.[1] The condition on which men can attain the latter introduces us to ethics. The doctrines, that God is also the absolute Lord of matter; that evil cannot be a quality of matter, but rather arose in time and from the free decision of the spirits or angels; and finally that the world will have an end, but God can call the destroyed material into existence, just as he once created it out of nothing, appear in principle to reconcile the dualism in the cosmology. We have the less occasion to give the details here, because they are known from the philosophical systems of the period, especially Philo's, and vary in manifold ways. All the Apologists, however, are imbued with the idea that this knowledge of God and the world, the genesis of the Logos and cosmos, are the most essential part of Christianity itself.[2] This conception is really not peculiar to the Apologists: in the second century the great majority of Christians, in so far as they reflected at all, re-

---

[1] The most of the Apologists argue against the conception of the natural immortality of the human soul; see Tatian 13; Justin, Dial. 5; Theoph. II. 27.

[2] The first chapter of Genesis represented to them the sum of all wisdom, and therefore of all Christianity. Perhaps Justin had already written a commentary to the Hexaëmeron (see my Texte und Untersuchungen I. 1, 2, p. 169 f.). It is certain that in the second century Rhodon (Euseb., H. E. V. 13. 8), Theophilus (see his 2nd Book ad Autol.), Candidus, and Apion (Euseb., H. E. V. 27) composed such. The Gnostics also occupied themselves a great deal with Gen. I.—III.; see, *e.g.*, Marcus in Iren. I. 18.

garded the monotheistic explanation of the world as a main part
of the Christian religion.   The theoretical view of the world as
a harmonious whole, of its order, regularity and beauty; the
certainty that all this had been called into existence by an
Almighty Spirit; the sure hope that heaven and earth will pass
away, but will give place to a still more glorious structure,
were always present, and put an end to the bright and gor-
geously coloured, but phantastic and vague, cosmogonies and
theogonies of antiquity.

2.   Their clear system of morality is in keeping with their
relatively simple cosmology.   In giving man reason and freedom
as an inalienable possession God destined him for incorruptibility
(ἀθανασία, ἀφθαρσία), by the attainment of which he was to become
a being similar to God. [1]   To the gift of imperishability God,
however, attached the condition of man's preserving τὰ τῆς
ἀθανασίας ("the things of immortality"), *i.e.*, preserving the
knowledge of God and maintaining a holy walk in imitation of
the divine perfection.   This demand is as natural as it is just;
moreover, nobody can fulfil it in man's stead, for an essential
feature of virtue is its being free, independent action.   Man
must therefore determine himself to virtue by the knowledge
that he is only in this way obedient to the Father of the world
and able to reckon on the gift of immortality.   The conception
of the content of virtue, however, contains an element which
cannot be clearly apprehended from the cosmology; moral goodness consists in letting oneself be influenced in no way by the
sensuous, but in living solely, after the Spirit, and imitating the
perfection and purity of God. Moral badness is giving way to
any affection resulting from the natural basis of man. The
Apologists undoubtedly believe that virtue consists negatively in
man's renunciation of what his natural constitution of soul and
body demands or impels him to.   Some express this thought

---

[1] See Theophilus ad Aut. II. 27: Εἰ γὰρ ὁ Θεὸς ἀθάνατον τὸν ἄνθρωπον ἀπ᾽
ἀρχῆς πεποιήκει, Θεὸν αὐτὸν πεποιήκει· πάλιν εἰ θνητὸν αὐτὸν πεποιήκει ἐδόκει ἄν ὁ
Θεὸς αἴτιος εἶναι τοῦ θανάτου αὐτοῦ. Οὔτε οὖν ἀθάνατον αὐτὸν ἐποίησεν οὔτε μὴν
θνητόν, ἀλλὰ δεκτικὸν ἀμφοτέρων· ἵνα, εἰ ῥέψῃ ἐπὶ τὰ τῆς ἀθανασίας τηρήσας τὴν
ἐντολὴν τοῦ Θεοῦ, μισθὸν κομίσηται παρ᾽ αὐτοῦ τὴν ἀθανασίαν καὶ γένηται Θεός, εἰ δ᾽
αὖ τραπῇ ἐπὶ τὰ τοῦ θανάτου πράγματα παρακούσας τοῦ Θεοῦ, αὐτὸς ἑαυτῷ αἴτιος
ᾖ τοῦ θανάτου.

in a more pregnant and unvarnished fashion, others in a milder way.  Tatian, for instance, says that we must divest ourselves of the human nature within us; but in truth the idea is the same in all.  The moral law of nature of which the Apologists speak, and which they find reproduced in the clearest and most beautiful way in the sayings of Jesus, [1] calls upon man to raise himself above his nature and to enter into a corresponding union with his fellow-man which is something higher than natural connections.  It is not so much the law of love that is to rule everything, for love itself is only a phase of a higher law; it is the law governing the perfect and sublime Spirit, who, as being the most exalted existence on this earth, is too noble for the world.  Raised already in this knowledge beyond time and space, beyond the partial and the finite, the man of God, even while upon the earth, is to hasten to the Father of Light.  By equanimity, absence of desires, purity, and goodness, which are the necessary results of clear knowledge, he is to show that he has already risen above the transient through gazing on the imperishable and through the enjoyment of knowledge, imperfect though the latter still be.  If thus, a suffering hero, he has stood the test on earth, if he has become dead to the world, [2] he may be sure that in the life to come God will bestow on him the gift of immortality, which includes the direct contemplation of God together with the perfect knowledge that flows from it. [3] Conversely, the vicious man is given over to eternal death, and in this punishment the righteousness of God is quite as plainly manifested, as in the reward of everlasting life.

3.   While it is certain that virtue is a matter of freedom, it

---

[1] See Justin, Apol. I. 14 ff. and the parallel passages in the other Apologists.

[2] See Tatian, Orat. 11. and many other passages.

[3] Along with this the Apologists emphasise the resurrection of the flesh in the strongest way as the specific article of Christian anticipation, and prove the possibility of realising this irrational hope.  Yet to the Apologists the ultimate ground of their trust in this early-Christian idea is their reliance on the unlimited omnipotence of God and this confidence is a proof of the vividness of their idea of him.  Nevertheless this conception assumes that in the other world there will be a return of the flesh, which on this side the grave had to be overcome and regarded as non-existent.  A clearly chiliastic element is found only in Justin.

is just as sure· that no soul is virtuous unless it follows the will
of God, *i.e.*, knows and judges of God and all things as they
must be known and judged of; and fulfils the commandments
of God. This presupposes a revelation of God through the
Logos. A revelation of God, complete in itself and mediated
by the Logos, is found in the cosmos and in the constitution
of man, he being created in his Maker's image. [1] But experience has shown that this revelation is insufficient to enable
men to retain clear knowledge. They yielded to the seduction
of evil demons, who, by God's sufferance, took possession of the
world, and availed themselves of man's sensuous side to draw
him away from the contemplation of the divine and lead him
to the earthly. [2] The results of this temptation appeared in the
facts that humanity as a whole fell a prey to error, was subjected to the bonds of the sensuous and of the demons, and
therefore became doomed to death, which is at once a punishment and the natural consequence of want of knowledge of

---

[1] No uniform conception of this is found in the Apologists; see Wendt, Die
Christliche Lehre von der menschlichen Vollkommenheit 1882, pp. 8—20. Justin
speaks only of a heavenly destination for which man is naturally adapted. With
Tatian and Theophilus it is different.

[2] The idea that the demon sovereignty has led to some change in the psychological
condition and capacities of man is absolutely unknown to Justin (see Wendt, l. c.,
p. 11 f., who has successfully defended the correct view in Engelhardt's "Das Christenthum Justin's des Märtyrers" pp. 92 f. 151. f. 266 f., against Stählin, "Justin der
Märtyrer und sein neuester Beurtheiler" 1880, p. 16 f.). Tatian expressed a different opinion, which, however, involved him in evident contradictions (see above,
p. 191 ff.). The apologetic theology necessarily adhered to the two following propositions: (1) The freedom to do what is good is not lost and cannot be. This
doctrine was opposed to philosophic determinism and popular fatalism. (2) The
desires of the flesh resulting from the constitution of man only become evil when
they destroy or endanger the sovereignty of reason. The formal *liberum arbitrium*
explains the possibility of sin, whilst its actual existence is accounted for by the
desire that is excited by the demons. The Apologists acknowledge the universality
of sin and death, but refused to admit the necessity of the former in order not to
call its guilty character in question. On the other hand they are deeply imbued
with the idea that the sovereignty of death is the most powerful factor in the per-
petuation of sin. Their believing conviction of the omnipotence of God, as well as
their moral conviction of the responsibility of man, protected them in theory from
a strictly dualistic conception of the world. At the same time, like all who separate
nature and morality in their ethical system, though in other respects they do not
do so, the Apologists were obliged in practice to be dualists.

God.[1] Hence it required fresh efforts of the Logos to free men from a state which is indeed in no instance an unavoidable necessity, though a sad fact in the case of almost all. For very few are now able to recognise the one true God from the order of the universe and from the moral law implanted in themselves; nor can they withstand the power of the demons ruling in the world and use their freedom to imitate the virtues of God. Therefore the Almighty in his goodness employed new means through the Logos to call men back from the error of their ways, to overthrow the sovereignty of the demons upon earth, and to correct the disturbed course of the world before the end has yet come. From the earliest times the Logos (the Spirit) has descended on such men as preserved their souls pure, and bestowed on them, through inspiration, knowledge of the truth (with reference to God, freedom, virtue, the demons, the origin of polytheism, the judgment) to be imparted by them to others. These are his "prophets". Such men are rare among the Greeks (and according to some not found at all), but numerous among the barbarians, i.e., among the Jewish people. Taught by God, they announced the truth about him, and under the promptings of the Logos they also committed the revelations to writings, which therefore, as being inspired, are an authentic record of the whole truth.[2] To some of the most virtuous among them he himself even appeared in human form and gave directions. He then is a Christian, who receives and follows these prophetic teachings, that have ever been proclaimed afresh from the beginning of the world down to the present time, and are summed up in the Old Testament. Such a one

[1] Death is accounted the worst evil. When Theophilus (II. 26) represents it as a blessing, we must consider that he is arguing against Marcion. Polytheism is traced to the demons; they are accounted the authors of the fables about the gods; the shameful actions of the latter are partly the deeds of demons and partly lies.

[2] The Old Testament therefore is not primarily viewed as the book of prophecy or of preparation for Christ, but as the book of the full revelation which cannot be surpassed. In point of content the teaching of the prophets and of Christ is completely identical. The prophetical details in the Old Testament serve only to attest the *one* truth. The Apologists confess that they were converted to Christianity by reading the Old Testament. Cf. Justin's and Tatian's confessions. Perhaps Commodian (Instruct. I. 1) is also be understood thus.

is enabled even now to rescue his soul from the rule of the demons, and may confidently expect the gift of immortality.

With the majority of the Apologists "Christianity" seems to be exhausted in these doctrines; in fact, they do not even consider it necessary to mention *ex professo* the appearance of the Logos in Christ (see above, p. 189 ff.). But, while it is certain that they all recognised that the teachings of the prophets contained the full revelation of the truth, we would be quite wrong in assuming that they view the appearance and history of Christ as of no significance. In their presentations some of them no doubt contented themselves with setting forth the most rational and simple elements, and therefore took almost no notice of the historical; but even in their case certain indications show that they regarded the manifestation of the Logos in Christ as of special moment. [1] For the prophetic utterances, as found from the beginning, require an attestation, the prophetic teaching requires a guarantee, so that misguided humanity may accept them and no longer take error for truth and truth for error. The strongest guarantee imaginable is found in the fulfilment of prophecy. Since no man is able to foretell what is to come, the prediction of the future accompanying a doctrine proves its divine origin. God, in his extraordinary goodness, not only inspired the prophets, through the Logos, with the doctrines of truth, but has from the beginning put numerous predictions in their mouth. These predictions were detailed and manifold; the great majority of them referred to a more prolonged appearance of the Logos in human form at the end of history, and to a future judgment. Now, so long as the predictions had not yet come to pass, the teachings of the prophets were not sufficiently impressive, for the only sure witness of the truth is its outward attestation. In the history of Christ,

---

[1] The *Oratio* of Tatian is very instructive in this respect. In this book he has nowhere spoken *ex professo* of the incarnation of the Logos in Christ; but in c. 13 fin. he calls the Holy Spirit " the servant of God who has suffered ", and in c. 21 init. he says: "we are not fools and do not adduce anything stupid, when we proclaim that God has appeared in human form." Similar expressions are found in Minucius Felix. In no part of Aristides' Apology is there any mention of the pre-Christian appearance of the Logos. The writer merely speaks of the revelation of the Son of God in Jesus Christ.

however, the majority of these prophecies were fulfilled in the most striking fashion, and this not only guarantees the fulfilment of the relatively small remainder not yet come to pass (judgment, resurrection), but also settles beyond all doubt the truth of the prophetic teachings about God, freedom, virtue, immortality, etc. In the scheme of fulfilment and prophecy even the irrational becomes rational; for the fulfilment of a prediction is not a proof of its divine origin unless it refers to something extraordinary. Any one can predict regular occurrences which always take place, Accordingly, a part of what was predicted had to be irrational. Every particular in the history of Christ has therefore a significance, not as regards the future, but as regards the past. Here everything happened "that the word [of the prophet might be fulfilled." Because the prophet had said so, it had to happen. Christ's destiny attests the ancient teachings of the prophets. Everything, however, depends on this attestation, for it was no longer the full truth that was wanting, but a convincing proof that the truth was a reality and not a fancy. [1] But prophecy testifies that Christ is the ambassador of God, the Logos that has appeared in human form, and the Son of God. If the future destiny of Jesus is recorded in the Old Testament down to the smallest particular, and the book at the same time declares that this predicted One is the Son of God and will be crucified, then the paying of divine honours to this crucified man, to whom all the features of prophecy apply, is completely justified. The stage marked by Christ in the history of God's revelation, the content of which is always the same, is therefore the highest and last, because in it the "truth along with the proof" has appeared. This circumstance explains why the truth is so much more impressive and convinces more men than formerly, especially since Christ has also made special provision for the spread of the

---

1 We seldom receive an answer to the question as to why this or that particular occurrence should have been prophesied. According to the ideas of the Apologists, however, we have hardly a right to put that question; for, since the value of the historical consists in its having been predicted, its content is of no importance. The fact that Jesus finds the she-ass bound to a vine (Justin, Apol. 1. 32) is virtually quite as important as his being born of a virgin. Both occurrences attest the prophetic teachings of God, freedom, etc.

truth and is himself an unequalled exemplification of a virtuous
life, the principles of which have now become known in the
whole world through the spread of his precepts.

These statements exhaust the arguments in most of the Apologies; and they accordingly seem neither to have contemplated
a redemption by Christ in the stricter sense of the word, nor
to have assumed the unique nature of the appearance of the
Logos in Jesus. Christ accomplished salvation as a divine *teacher*,
that is to say, his teaching brings about the ἀλλαγή and ἐπα-
ναγωγή of the human race, its restoration to its original destination. This also seems to suffice as regards demon rule. Logically
considered, the individual portions of the history of Jesus (of
the baptismal confession) have no direct significance in respect
to salvation. Hence the teachings of the Christians seem to
fall into two groups having no inward connection, *i.e.*, the propositions treating of the rational knowledge of God, and the
predicted and fulfilled historical facts which prove those doctrines
and the believing hopes they include.

But Justin at least gave token of a manifest effort to combine
the historical statements regarding Christ with the philosophical
and moral doctrines of salvation and to conceive Jesus as
the Redeemer. [1] Accordingly, if the Christian dogmatic of
succeeding times is found in the connection of philosophical
theology with the baptismal confession, that is, in the " scientific
theology of facts", Justin is, in a certain fashion, the first framer
of Church dogma, though no doubt in a very tentative way.
(1) He tried to distinguish between the appearance of the Logos
in pre-Christian times and in Christ; he emphasised the fact
that the whole Logos appeared only in Christ, and that the
manner of this appearance has no counterpart in the past. (2)

---

[1] In Justin's polemical works this must have appeared in a still more striking
way. Thus we find in a fragment of the treatise πρὸς Μαρκίωνα, quoted by
Irenæus (IV. 6. 2), the sentence "unigenitus filius venit ad nos, suum plasma
in semetipsum recapitulans." So the theologoumenon of the *recapitulatio per
Christum* already appeared in Justin. (Vide also Dial. c. Tryph. 100.) If we
compare Tertullian's *Apologeticum* with his Antignostic writings we easily see how
impossible it is to determine from that work the extent of his Christian faith and
knowledge. The same is probably the case, though to a less extent, with Justin's
apologetic writings.

Justin showed in the Dialogue that, independently of the theologoumenon of the Logos, he was firmly convinced of the divinity
of Christ on the ground of predictions and of the impression
made by his personality.[1] (3) In addition to the story of the
exaltation of Christ, Justin also emphasised other portions of his
history, especially the death on the cross (together with baptism
and the Lord's Supper) and tried to give them a positive
significance.[2] He adopted the common Christian saying that
the blood of Christ cleanses believers and men are healed through
his wounds; and he tried to give a mystic significance to the
cross. (4) He accordingly spoke of the forgiveness of sins
through Christ and confessed that men are changed, through
the new birth in baptism, from children of necessity and ignorance
into children of purpose and understanding and forgiveness of
sins.[3] Von Engelhardt has, however, quite rightly noticed that
these are mere words which have nothing at all corresponding
to them in the general system of thought, because Justin remains
convinced that the knowledge of the true God, of his will, and
of his promises, or the certainty that God will always grant
forgiveness to the repentant and eternal life to the righteous,
is sufficient to convert the man who is master of himself. Owing
to the fundamental conviction which is expressed in the formulæ,
"perfect philosophy", "divine teacher", "new law", "freedom",
"repentance", "sinless life", sure hope", "reward", "immortality", the ideas, "forgiveness of sins", "redemption", "reconciliation", "new birth", "faith" (in the Pauline sense) must remain

[1] Christians do not place a man alongside of God, for Christ is God, though
indeed a second God. There is no question of two natures. It is not the divine
nature that Justin has insufficiently emphasised—or at least this is only the case
in so far as it is a second Godhead—but the human nature; see Schultz, Gottheit
Christi, p. 39 ff.

[2] We find allusions in Justin where the various incidents in the history of the
incarnate Logos are conceived as a series of arrangements meant to form part of
the history of salvation, to paralyse mankind's sinful history, and to regenerate
humanity. He is thus a forerunner of Irenæus and Melito.

[3] Even the theologoumenon of the definite number of the elect, which must be
fulfilled, is found in Justin (Apol. I. 28, 45). For that reason the judgment is put
off by God (II. 7). The Apology of Aristides contains a short account of the history of
Jesus; his conception, birth, preaching, choice of the 12 Apostles, crucifixion,
resurrection, ascension, sending out of the 12 Apostles are mentioned.

words, [1] or be relegated to the sphere of magic and mystery. [2] Nevertheless we must not on that account overlook the intention. Justin tried to see the divine revelation not only in the sayings of the prophets, but in unique fashion in the person of Christ, and to conceive Christ not only as the divine teacher, but also as the "Lord and Redeemer". In two points he actually succeeded in this. By the resurrection and exaltation of Jesus Justin proved that Christ, the divine teacher, is also the future judge and bestower of reward. Christ himself is able to give what he has promised—a life after death free from sufferings and sins, that is the first point. The other thing, however, which Justin very strongly emphasised is that Jesus is even now reigning in heaven, and shows his future visible sovereignty of the world by giving his own people the power to cast out and vanquish the demons in and by his name. Even at the present time the latter are put to flight by believers in Christ. [3] So the redemption is no mere future one; it is even now taking place, and the revelation of the Logos in Jesus Christ is not merely intended to prove the doctrines of the rational religion, but denotes a real redemption, that is, a new beginning, in so far as the power of the demons on earth is overthrown through Christ and in his strength. Jesus Christ, the teacher of the whole

---

[1] "To Justin faith is only an acknowledgment of the mission and Sonship of Christ and a conviction of the truth of his teaching. Faith does not justify, but is merely a presupposition of the justification which is effected through repentance, change of mind, and sinless life. Only in so far as faith itself is already a free decision to serve God has it the value of a saving act, which is indeed of such significance that one can say, 'Abraham was justified by faith.' In reality, however, this took place through μετάνοια." The idea of the new birth is exhausted in the thought: Θεὸς καλεῖ εἰς μετάνοιαν, that of the forgiveness of sins in the idea: "God is so good that he overlooks sins committed in a state of ignorance, if man has changed his mind." Accordingly, Christ is the Redeemer in so far as he has brought about all the conditions which make for repentance.

[2] This is in fact already the case in Justin here and there, but in the main there are as yet mere traces of it: the Apologists are no mystics.

[3] If we consider how largely the demons bulked in the ideas of the Apologists, we must rate very highly their conviction of the redeeming power of Christ and of his name, a power continuously shown in the victories over the demons. See Justin Apol. II. 6, 8; Dial. 11, 30, 35, 39, 76, 85, 111, 121; Tertull., Apol. 23, 27, 32, 37 etc. Tatian also (16 fin.) confirms it, and c. 12, p. 56, line 7 ff. (ed. Otto) does not contradict this.

truth and of a new law, which is the rational, the oldest, and
the divine, the only being who has understood how to call
men from all the different nations and in all stages of culture
into a union of holy life, the inspiring One, for whom his disciples
go to death, the mighty One, through whose name the demons
are cast out, the risen One, who will one day reward and punish
as judge, must be identical with the Son of God, who is the divine
reason and the divine power. In this belief which accompanies
the confession of the one God, creator of heaven and earth,
Justin finds the special content of Christianity, which the later
Apologists, with the probable exception of Melito, reproduced
in a much more imperfect and meagre form. One thing, however, Justin in all probability did not formulate with precision,
viz., the proposition that the special result of salvation, *i.e.*,
immortality, was involved in the incarnation of the Logos, in
so far as that act brought about a real secret transformation of
the whole mortal nature of man. With Justin, indeed, as with
the other Apologists, the " salvation " ($\sigma\omega\tau\eta\rho\iota\alpha$) consists essentially
in the apportioning of eternal life to the world, which has been
created mortal and in consequence of sin has fallen a prey to
the natural destiny of "death"; and Christ is regarded as the
bestower of incorruptibility who thus brings the creation to its
goal; but as a rule Justin does not go beyond this thought.
Yet we certainly find hints pointing to the notion of a physical
and magical redemption accomplished at the moment of the
incarnation. See particularly the fragment in Irenæus (already
quoted on page 220), which may be thus interpreted, and Apol.
I. 66. This conception, in its most complete shape, would have
to be attributed to Justin if the fragment V. (Otto, Corp. Apol. III.
p. 256) were genuine. [1]   But the precise form of the presentation

[1] Von Engelhardt, Christenthum Justin's, p. 432 f., has pronounced against its
genuineness; see also my Texte und Untersuchungen I. 1, 2, p. 158. In favour of
its genuineness see Hilgenfeld, Zeitschrift für wissenschaftliche Theologie, 1883,
p. 26 f. The fragment is worded as follows: Πλάσας ὁ Θεὸς κατ᾽ ἀρχὰς τὸν ἄνθρωπον τῆς γνώμης αὐτοῦ τὰ τῆς φύσεως ἀπηώρησεν ἐντολῇ μιᾷ ποιησάμενος τὴν
διάπειραν. Φυλάξαντα μὲν γὰρ ταύτην τῆς ἀθανάτου λήξεως πεποίηκεν ἔσεσθαι,
παραβάντα δὲ τῆς ἐναντίας. Οὕτω γεγονὼς ὁ ἄνθρωπος καὶ πρὸς τὴν παράβασιν εὐθὺς
ἐλθὼν τὴν φθορὰν φυσικῶς εἰσεδέξατο. Φύσει δὲ τῆς φθορᾶς προσγενομένης ἀναγκαῖον
ἦν ὅτι σῶσαι βουλόμενος ἦν τὴν φθοροποιὸν οὐσίαν ἀφανίσας. Τοῦτο δὲ οὐκ ἦν ἑτέρως

makes this very improbable. The question as to how, *i.e.*, in
what conceivable way, immortality can be imparted to the mortal
nature as yet received little attention from Justin and the Apologists: it is the necessary result of knowledge and virtue. Their
great object was to assure the belief in immortality. "Religion
and morality depend on the belief in immortality or the resurrection from the dead. The fact that the Christian religion, as
faith in the incarnate Son of God the creator, leads to the assurance
that the maker of all things will reward piety and righteousness
with the bestowal of eternal and immortal life, is the essential
advantage possessed by the Christian religion over all others.
The righteousness of the heathen was imperfect in spite of all
their knowledge of good and evil, because they lacked the certain
knowledge that the creator makes the just immortal and will
consign the unjust to eternal torment." The philosophical
doctrines of God, virtue, and immortality became through the
Apologists the certain content of a world-wide religion, which
is Christian because Christ guarantees its certainty. They made
Christianity a deistical religion for the whole world without
abandoning in word at least the old "teachings and knowledge"
(διδάγματα καὶ μαθήματα) of the Christians. They thus marked
out the task of "dogmatic" and, so to speak, wrote the prolegomena for every future theological system in the Church (see Von
Engelhardt's concluding observations in his "Christenthum Justin's"
pp. 447—490, also Overbeck in the Historische Zeitschrift,
1880, pp. 499—505.) At the same time, however, they adhered to the early-Christian eschatology (see Justin, Melito, and,
with reference to the resurrection of the flesh, the Apologists

γενέσθαι, εἰ μήπερ ἡ κατὰ φύσιν ζωὴ προσεπλάκη τῷ τὴν φθορὰν δεξαμένῳ, ἀφανίζ-
ουσα μὲν τὴν φθοράν, ἀθάνατον δὲ τοῦ λοιποῦ τὸ δεξάμενον διατηροῦσα. Διὰ τοῦτο
τὸν λόγον ἐδέησεν ἐν σώματι γενέσθαι, ἵνα (τοῦ θανάτου) τῆς κατὰ φύσιν ἡμᾶς φθορᾶς
ἐλευθερώσῃ. Εἰ γὰρ, ὡς φατε, νεύματι μόνον τὸν θάνατον ἡμῶν ἀπεκώλυσεν, οὐ προσῄει
μὲν διὰ τὴν βούλησιν ὁ θάνατος, οὐδὲν δὲ ἧττον φθαρτοὶ πάλιν ἦμεν, φυσικὴν ἐν
ἑαυτοῖς τὴν φθορὰν περιφέροντες.

---

[1] Schultz (Gottheit Christi, p. 41) very rightly points out that all the systems
of the post-Socratic schools, so far as they practically spread among the people,
invariably assume that knowledge, as such, leads to salvation, so that the bestowal
of the ἀφθαρσία need not necessarily be thought so naturalistic and mystic a process
as we are apt to imagine.

generally), and thus did not belie their connection with early Christianity. [1]

*Interpretation and Criticism, especially of Justin's Doctrines.*

1.  The fundamental assumption of all the Apologists is that there can only be one and the same relation on earth between God and free man, and that it has been conditioned by the creation. This thought, which presupposes the idea of God's unchangeableness, at bottom neutralises every quasi-historical and mythological consideration. According to it grace can be nothing else than the stimulation of the powers of reason existent in man; revelation is supernatural only in respect of its form, and the redemption merely enables us to redeem ourselves, just as this possibility was given at the creation. Sin, which arose through temptation, appears on the one hand as error which must almost of necessity have arisen so long as man only possessed the "germs of the Logos" (σπέρματα τοῦ λόγου), and on the other as the dominion of sensuousness, which was nearly unavoidable since earthly material clothes the soul and mighty demons have possession of the world. The mythological idea of the invading sway of the demons is really the only interruption of the rationalistic scheme. So far as Christianity is something different from morality, it is the antithesis of the service and sovereignty of the demons. Hence the idea that the course of the world and mankind require in some measure to be helped is the narrow foundation of the thought of revelation or redemption. The necessity of revelation and redemption was expressed in a much stronger and more decisive way by many heathen philosophers of the same period. Accordingly, not only did these long for a revelation which would give a fresh attestation to old truth, but they yearned for a force, a real redemption, a *præsens numen*, and some new thing. Still more powerful was this longing in the case of the

---

[1] Weizsäcker, Jahrbücher für deutsche Theologie, 1867, p. 119, has with good reason strongly emphasised this element. See also Stählin, Justin der Märtyrer, 1880, p. 63 f., whose criticism of Von Engelhardt's book contains much that is worthy of note, though it appears to me inappropriate in the main.

Gnostics and Marcion; compare the latter's idea of revelation
with that of the Apologists. It is probable indeed that the thought
of redemption would have found stronger expression among
them also, had not the task of *proof*, which could be best discharged by the aid of the Stoic philosophy, demanded religious
rationalism. But, admitting this, the determination of the highest good itself involved rationalism and moralism. For immortality is the highest good, in so far as it is perfect knowledge—
which is, moreover, conceived as being of a rational kind,— that
necessarily leads to immortality. We can only find traces of
the converse idea, according to which the change into the immortal condition is the *prius* and the knowledge the *posterius*.
But, where this conception is the prevailing one, moralistic intellectualism is broken through, and we can now point to a
specific, supernatural blessing of salvation, produced by revelation and redemption. Corresponding to the general development of religious philosophy from moralism into mysticism
(transition from the second to the third century), a displacement in this direction can also be noticed in the history of
Greek apologetics (in the West it was different); but this displacement was never considerable and therefore cannot be clearly
traced. Even later on under altered circumstances, apologetic
science adhered in every respect to its old method, as being
the most suitable (monotheism, morality, proof from prophecy),
a circumstance which is evident, for example, from the almost
complete disregard of the New Testament canon of Scripture
and from other considerations besides.

2. In so far as the possibility of virtue and righteousness
has been implanted by God in men, and in so far as—apart
from trifling exceptions—they can actually succeed in doing
what is good only through prophetic, *i.e.*, divine, revelations and
exhortations, some Apologists, following the early Christian
tradition, here and there designate the transformation of the
sinner into a righteous man as a work of God, and speak of
renewal and regeneration. The latter, however, as a real fact,
is identical with the repentance which, as a turning from sin
and turning to God, is a matter of free will. As in Justin, so
also in Tatian, the idea of regeneration is exhausted in the

divine call to repentance. The conception of the forgiveness of sins is also determined in accordance with this. Only those sins can be forgiven, *i.e.*, overlooked, which are really none, *i.e.*, which were committed in a state of error and bondage to the demons, and were well-nigh unavoidable. The blotting out of these sins is effected in baptism, " which is the bath of regeneration in so far as it is the voluntary consecration of one's own person. The cleansing which takes place is God's work in so far as baptism was instituted by him, but it is effected by the man who in his change of mind lays aside his sins. The name of God is pronounced above him who repents of his transgressions, that he may receive freedom, knowledge, and forgiveness of his previous sins, but this effects a change only denoting the new knowledge to which the baptised person has attained." If, as all this seems to show, the thought of a specific grace of God in Christ appears virtually neutralised, the adherence to the language of the cultus (Justin and Tatian) and Justin's conception of the Lord's Supper show that the Apologists strove to get beyond moralism, that is, they tried to supplement it through the mysteries. Augustine's assertion (de predest. sanct. 27) that the faith of the old Church in the efficacy of divine grace was not so much expressed in the *opuscula* as in the *prayers*, shows correct insight.

3. All the demands, the fulfilment of which constitutes the virtue and righteousness of men, are summed up under the title of *the new law*. In virtue of its eternally valid content this new law is in reality the oldest; but it is new because Christ and the prophets were preceded by Moses, who inculcated on the Jews in a transient form that which was eternally valid. It is also new because, being proclaimed by the Logos that appeared in Christ, it announced its presence with the utmost impressiveness and undoubted authority, and contains the promise of reward in terms guaranteed by the strongest proof—the proof from prophecy. The old law is consequently a new one because it appears now for the first time as purely spiritual, perfect, and final. The commandment of love to one's neighbour also belongs to the law; but it does not form its essence (still less love to God, the place of which is taken by faith, obedience, and imitation). The content of all moral demands is compre-

hended in the commandment of perfect, active holiness, which
is fulfilled by the complete renunciation of all earthly blessings,
even of life itself.  Tatian preached this renunciation in a specially powerful manner.  There is no need to prove that no remains of Judæo-Christianity are to be recognised in these ideas
about the new law.  It is not Judæo-Christianity that lies behind
the Christianity and doctrines of the Apologists, but Greek
philosophy (Platonic metaphysics, Logos doctrine of the Stoics,
Platonic and Stoic ethics), the Alexandrine-Jewish apologetics,
the maxims of Jesus, and the religious speech of the Christian
Churches.  Justin is distinguished from Philo by the sure conviction of the living power of God, the Creator and Lord of
the world, and the steadfast confidence in the reality of all the
ideals which is derived from the person of Christ.  We ought
not, however, to blame the Apologists because to them nearly
everything historical was at bottom only a guarantee of thoughts
and hopes.  As a matter of fact, the assurance is not less important than the content.  By dint of thinking one can conceive the highest truth, but one cannot in this way make out
the certainty of its reality.  No positive religion can do more
for its followers than faith in the revelation through Christ and
the prophets did for the Apologists.  Although it chiefly proved
to them the truth of that which we call natural theology and
which was the idealistic philosophy of the age, so that the
Church appears as the great insurance society for the ideas of
Plato and Zeno, we ought not at the same time to forget that
their idea of a divine spirit working upon earth was a far more
lively and worthy one than in the case of the Greek philosophers.

4.  By their intellectualism and exclusive theories the Apologists founded philosophic and dogmatic Christianity (Loofs:
"they laid the foundation for the conversion of Christianity into
a revealed doctrine."[1]  If about the middle of the second century

---

[1] Loofs continues: "The Apologists, viewing the transference of the concept
'Son' to the preëxistent Christ as a matter of course, enabled the Christological
problem of the 4th century to be started.  They removed the point of departure of
the Christological speculation from the historical Christ back into the preëxistence
and depreciated the importance of Jesus' life as compared with the incarnation

the short confession of the Lord Jesus Christ was regarded as
a watchword, passport, and *tessera hospitalitas (signum et vin-
culum)*, and if even in lay and uneducated circles it was conceived
as "doctrine" in contradistinction to heresy, this transformation
must have been accelerated through men, who essentially conceived Christianity as the "divine doctrine", and by whom all
its distinctive features were subordinated to this conception or
neutralised. As the philosophic schools are held together by
their "laws" (νόμοι) as the "dogmas" form the real bond between
the "friends", and as, in addition to this, they are united by
veneration for the founder, so also the Christian Church appeared
to the Apologists as a universal league established by a divine
founder and resting *on the dogmas of the perfectly known truth*,
a league the members of which possess definite laws, viz., the
eternal laws of nature for everything moral, and unite in common
veneration for the Divine Master. In the "dogmas" of the
Apologists, however, we find nothing more than traces of the
fusion of the philosophical and historical elements; in the main both
exist separately side by side. It was not till long after this that
intellectualism gained the victory in a Christianity represented by
the clergy. What we here chiefly understand by "intellectualism"
is the placing of the scientific conception of the world behind
the commandments of Christian morality and behind the hopes
and faith of the Christian religion, and the connecting of the
two things in such a way that this conception appeared as the
foundation of these commandments and hopes. Thus was created
the future dogmatic in the form which still prevails in the Churches
and which presupposes the Platonic and Stoic conception of the
world long ago overthrown by science. The attempt made at
the beginning of the Reformation to free the Christian faith from
this amalgamation remained at first without success.

They connected the Christology with the cosmology, but were not able to combine
it with the scheme of salvation. Their Logos doctrine is not a 'higher' Christology
than the prevailing form; it rather lags behind the genuine Christian estimate of
Christ. It is not God who reveals himself in Christ, but the Logos, the depotentiated God, who *as God* is subordinate to the supreme Deity."

# CHAPTER V.

THE BEGINNINGS OF AN ECCLESIASTICO-THEOLOGICAL INTER-
PRETATION AND REVISION OF THE RULE OF FAITH IN
OPPOSITION TO GNOSTICISM ON THE BASIS OF THE
NEW TESTAMENT AND THE CHRISTIAN PHILO-
SOPHY OF THE APOLOGISTS:
MELITO, IRENÆUS, TERTULLIAN, HIPPOLYTUS, NOVATIAN. [1]

I. *The theological position of Irenæus and the later
contemporary Church teachers.*

GNOSTICISM and the Marcionite Church had compelled orthodox
Christianity to make a selection from tradition and to make this
binding on Christians as an apostolical law. Everything that
laid claim to validity had henceforth to be legitimised by the
faith, *i.e.*, the baptismal confession and the New Testament canon
of Scripture (see above, chap. 2, under A and B). However, mere
" prescriptions " could no longer suffice here. But the baptismal
confession was no " doctrine "; if it was to be transformed into
such it required an interpretation. We have shown above that
the *interpreted* baptismal confession was instituted as the guide
for the faith. This interpretation took its *matter* from the sacred
books of *both* Testaments. It owed its guiding lines, however,

---

1 Authorities: The works of Irenæus (Stieren's and Harvey's editions), Melito
(Otto, Corp. Apol. IX.), Tertullian (Oehler's and Reifferscheid's editions), Hippolytus
(Fabricius', Lagarde's, Duncker's and Schneidewin's editions), Cyprian (Hartel's
edition), Novatian (Jackson). Biographies of Böhringer, Die Kirche Christi und
ihre Zeugen, 1873 ff. Werner, Der Paulinismus des Irenäus, 1889. Nöldechen,
Tertullian, 1890. Döllinger, "Hippolytus und Kallistus," 1853. Many monographs
on Irenæus and Tertullian.

on the one hand to philosophical theology, as set forth by the
Apologists, and on the other to the earnest endeavour to maintain
and defend against all attacks the traditional convictions and
hopes of believers, as professed in the past generation by the
enthusiastic forefathers of the Church.  In addition to this, certain
interests, which had found expression in the speculations of the
the so-called Gnostics, were adopted in an increasing degree
among all thinking Christians, and also could not but influence
the ecclesiastical teachers. [1]  The theological labours, thus initiated,
accordingly bear the impress of great uniqueness and complexity.
In the first place, the old Catholic Fathers, Melito, [2] Rhodon, [3]
Irenæus, Hippolytus, and Tertullian were in every case convinced
that all their expositions contained the universal Church faith
itself and nothing else.  Though the faith is identical with the
baptismal confession, yet every interpretation of it derived from
the New Testament is no less certain than the shortest formula. [4]
The creation of the New Testament furnished all at once a quite

[1]  The following exposition will show how much Irenæus and the later old
Catholic teachers learned from the Gnostics.  As a matter of fact the theology of
Irenæus remains a riddle so long as we try to explain it merely from the Apologists
and only consider its antithetical relations to Gnosis.  Little as we can understand
modern orthodox theology from a historical point of view—if the comparison be
here allowed—without keeping in mind what it has adopted from Schleiermacher
and Hegel, we can just as little understand the theology of Irenæus without taking
into account the schools of Valentinus and Marcion.

[2]  That Melito is to be named here follows both from Eusebius, H. E. V. 28. 5,
and still more plainly from what we know of the writings of this bishop; see
Texte und Untersuchungen zur Geschichte der altchristlichen Litteratur, I. 1, 2, p. 240 ff.).
The polemic writings of Justin and the Antignostic treatise of that "ancient" quoted
by Irenæus (see Patr. App. Opp. ed. Gebhardt etc. I. 2, p. 105 sq.) may in a certain
sense be viewed as the precursors of Catholic literature.  We have no material for
judging of them with certainty.  The New Testament was not yet at the disposal
of their authors, and consequently there is a gap between them and Irenæus.

[3]  See Eusebius, H. E. V. 13.

[4]  Tertullian does indeed say in de præscr. 14: "Ceterum manente forma regulæ
fidei in suo ordine quantumlibet quæras, et tractes, et omnem libidinem curiositatis
effundas, si quid tibi videtur vel ambiguitate pendere vel obscuritate obumbrari";
but the preceding exposition of the *regula* shows that scarcely any scope remained
for the "curiositas", and the one that follows proves that Tertullian did not
mean that freedom seriously.

unlimited multitude of conceptions, the whole of which appeared as "doctrines" and offered themselves for incorporation with the "faith".[1] The limits of the latter therefore seem to be indefinitely extended, whilst on the other hand tradition, and polemics too in many cases, demanded an adherence to the shortest formula. The oscillation between this brief formula, the contents of which, as a rule, did not suffice, and that fulness, which admitted of no bounds at all, is characteristic of the old Catholic Fathers we have mentioned. In the second place, these Fathers felt quite as much need of a rational proof in their arguments with their Christian opponents, as they did while contending with the heathen;[2] and, being themselves children of their time, they required this proof for their own assurance and that of their fellow-believers. The epoch in which men appealed to charisms, and "knowledge" counted as much as prophecy and vision, because it was still of the same nature, was in the main a thing of the past.[3] Tradition and reason had taken the place of charisms as courts of appeal. But this change had neither come to be clearly recognised,[4] nor was the right and scope of rational theology alongside of tradition felt to be a problem. We can indeed trace the consciousness of the danger in attempting to introduce new *termini* and regulations not prescribed by the Holy Scriptures.[5] The bishops themselves in fact encouraged this apprehension in order to

---

[1] The most important point was that the Pauline theology, towards which Gnostics, Marcionites, and Encratites had already taken up a definite attitude, could now no longer be ignored. See Overbeck's Basler Univ.—Programm, 1877. Irenæus immediately shows the influence of Paulinism very clearly.

[2] See what Rhodon says about the issue of his conversation with Appelles in Euseb., H. E. V. 13. 7 : ἐγὼ δὲ γελάσας κατέγνων αὐτοῦ, διότι διδάσκαλος εἶναι λέγων οὐκ ᾔδει τὸ διδασκόμενον ὑπ' αὐτοῦ κρατύνειν.

[3] On the old "prophets and teachers" see my remarks on the Διδαχή, c. 11 ff., and the section, pp. 93—137, of the prolegomena to my edition of this work. The διδάσκαλοι ἀποστολικοὶ καὶ προφητικοί (Ep. Smyrn. ap. Euseb., H. E. IV. 15. 39) became lay-teachers who were skilful in the interpretation of the sacred traditions.

[4] In the case of Irenæus, as is well known, there was absolutely no consciousness of this, as is well remarked by Eusebius in H. E. V. 7. In support of his own writings, however, Irenæus appealed to no charisms.

[5] See the passage already quoted on p. 63, note 1.

warn people against the Gnostics,[1] and after the deluge of
heresy, representatives of Church orthodoxy looked with distrust
on every philosophic-theological formula.[2] Such propositions
of rationalistic theology as were absolutely required, were, however, placed by Irenæus and Tertullian on the same level as
the hallowed doctrines of tradition, and were not viewed by
them as something of a different nature. Irenæus uttered most
urgent warnings against subtle speculations;[3] but yet, in the
naïvest way, associated with the faithfully preserved traditional
doctrines and fancies of the faith theories which he likewise
regarded as tradition and which, in point of form, did
not differ from those of the Apologists or Gnostics.[4] The

---

[1] Irenæus and Tertullian scoffed at the Gnostic terminology in the most bitter way.

[2] Tertullian, adv. Prax. 3: "Simplices enim quique, ne dixerim imprudentes et
idiotæ, quæ major semper credentium pars est, quoniam et ipsa regula fidei a pluribus
diis sæculi ad unicum et verum deum transfert, non intellegentes unicum quidem,
sed cum sua οἰκονομίᾳ esse credendum, expavescunt ad οἰκονομίαν." Similar remarks
often occur in Origen. See also Hippol., c. Nöet 11.

[3] The danger of speculation and of the desire to know everything was im-
pressively emphasised by Irenæus, II. 25—28. As a pronounced ecclesiastical pos-
itivist and traditionalist, he seems in these chapters disposed to admit nothing but
obedient and acquiescent faith in the words of Holy Scripture, and even to reject
speculations like those of Tatian, Orat. 5. Cf. the disquisitions II. 25. 3: "Si autem
et aliquis non invenerit causam omnium quæ requiruntur, cogitet, quia homo est
in infinitum minor deo et qui ex parte (cf. II. 28.) acceperit gratiam et qui nondum
æqualis vel similis sit factori; II. 26. 1: "Ἀμείνον καὶ συμφορώτερον, ἰδιώτας καὶ
ὀλιγομαθεῖς ὑπάρχειν, καὶ διὰ τῆς ἀγάπης πλησίον γενέσθαι τοῦ Θεοῦ ἢ πολυμαθεῖς
καὶ ἐμπείρους δοκοῦντας εἶναι, βλασφήμους εἰς τὸν ἑαυτῶν εὑρίσκεσθαι δεσπότην, and
in addition to this the close of the paragraph, II. 27. 1: Concerning the sphere within
which we are to search (the Holy Scriptures and "quæ ante oculos nostros occurrunt",
much remains dark to us even in the Holy Scriptures II. 28. 3); II. 28. 1 f. on the
canon which is to be observed in all investigations, namely, the confident faith in God
the creator, as the supreme and only Deity; II. 28. 2—7: specification of the great
problems whose solution is hid from us, viz., the elementary natural phenomena,
the relation of the Son to the Father, that is, the manner in which the Son was
begotten, the way in which matter was created, the cause of evil. In opposition to
the claim to absolute knowledge, i.e., to the complete discovery of all the processes
of causation, which Irenæus too alone regards as knowledge, he indeed pointed
out the limits of our perception, supporting his statement by Bible passages. But
the ground of these limits, "ex parte accepimus gratiam", is not an early-Christian
one, and it shows at the same time that the bishop also viewed knowledge as the
goal, though indeed he thought it could not be attained on earth.

[4] The same observation applies to Tertullian. Cf. his point blank repudiation

Holy Scriptures of the New Testament were the basis on which Irenæus set forth the most important doctrines of Christianity. Some of these he stated as they had been conceived by the oldest tradition (see the eschatology), others he adapted to the new necessities. The qualitative distinction between the *fides credenda* and theology was noticed neither by Irenæus nor by Hippolytus and Tertullian. According to Irenæus I. 10. 3 this distinction is merely quantitative. Here faith and theological knowledge are still completely intermixed. Whilst stating and establishing the doctrines of tradition with the help of the New Testament, and revising and fixing them by means of intelligent deduction, the Fathers think they are setting forth the faith itself and nothing else. Anything more than this is only curiosity not unattended with danger to Christians. Theology is interpreted faith. [1]

Corresponding to the baptismal confession there thus arose at the first a loose system of dogmas which were necessarily devoid of strict style, definite principle, or fixed and harmonious aim. In this form we find them with special plainness in Tertullian. [2] This writer was still completely incapable of inwardly connecting his rational (Stoic) theology, as developed by him for apologetic purposes, with the Christological doctrines of the *regula fidei*, which, after the example of Irenæus, he constructed and defended from Scripture and tradition in opposition to heresy. Whenever he attempts in any place to prove

of philosophy in de præsc. 7, and the use he himself nevertheless made of it everywhere.

[1] In point of form this standpoint is distinguished from the ordinary Gnostic position by its renunciation of absolute knowledge, and by its corresponding lack of systematic completeness. That, however, is an important distinction in favour of the Catholic Fathers. According to what has been set forth in the text I cannot agree with Zahn's judgment (Marcellus of Ancyra, p. 235 f.): "Irenæus is the first ecclesiastical teacher who has grasped the idea of an independent science of Christianity, of a theology which, in spite of its width and magnitude, is a branch of knowledge distinguished from others; and was also the first to mark out the paths of this science."

[2] Tertullian seems even to have had no great appreciation for the degree of systematic exactness displayed in the disquisitions of Irenæus. He did not reproduce these arguments at least, but preferred after considering them to fall back on the proof from prescription.

the *intrinsic* necessity of these dogmas, he seldom gets beyond rhetorical statements, holy paradoxes, or juristic forms. As a systematic thinker, a cosmologist, moralist, and jurist rather than a theosophist, as a churchman, a masterly defender of tradition, as a Christian exclusively guided in practical life by the strict precepts and hopes of the Gospel, his theology, if by that we understand his collective theological disquisitions, is completely devoid of unity, and can only be termed a mixture of dissimilar and, not unfrequently, contradictory propositions, which admit of no comparison with the older theology of Valentinus or the later system of Origen. [1] To Tertullian everything lies side by side; problems which chance to turn up are just as quickly solved. The specific faith of Christians is indeed no longer, as it sometimes seems to be in Justin's case, a great apparatus of proof for the doctrines of the only true philosophy; it rather stands, in its own independent value, side by side with these, partly in a crude, partly in a developed form; but inner principles and aims are nearly everywhere sought for in vain. [2] In spite of this he possesses inestimable importance in the history of dogma; for he developed and created, in a disconnected form and partly in the shape of legal propositions, a series of the most important dogmatic formulæ, which Cyprian, Novatian, Hosius, and the Roman bishops of the fourth century, Ambrosius and Leo I., introduced into the general dogmatic system of the Catholic Church. He founded the terminology both of the trinitarian and of the Christological dogma; and in addition to this was the first to give currency to a series of dogmatic concepts *(satisfacere, meritum, sacramentum, vitium originis etc., etc.).*

[1] The more closely we study the writings of Tertullian, the more frequently we meet with inconsistencies, and that in his treatment both of dogmatic and moral questions. Such inconsistencies could not but make their appearance, because Tertullian's dogmatising was only incidental. As far as he himself was concerned, he did not feel the slightest necessity for a systematic presentation of Christianity.

[2] With reference to certain articles of doctrine, however, Tertullian adopted from Irenæus some guiding principles and some points of view arising from the nature of faith; but he almost everywhere changed them for the worse. The fact that he was capable of writing a treatise like the de præscr. hæret., in which all proof of the intrinsic necessity and of the connection of his dogmas is wanting, shows the limits of his interests and of his understanding.

Finally it was he who at the very outset imparted to the type of dogmatic that arose in the West its momentous bias in the direction of *auctoritas et ratio*, and its corresponding tendency to assume a legal character (*lex*, formal and material), peculiarities which were to become more and more clearly marked as time went on. [1]   But, great as is his importance in this respect, it has no connection at all with the fundamental conception of Christianity peculiar to himself, for, as a matter of fact, this was already out of date at the time when he lived.   What influenced the history of dogma was not his Christianity, but his masterly power of framing formulæ.

It is different with Irenæus.   The Christianity of this man proved a decisive factor in the history of dogma in respect of its content.   If Tertullian supplied the future Catholic dogmatic with the most important part of its formulæ, Irenæus clearly sketched for it its fundamental idea, by combining the ancient notion of salvation with New Testament (Pauline) thoughts. [2] Accordingly, as far as the essence of the matter is concerned, the great work of Irenæus is far superior to the theological writings of Tertullian.   This appears already in the task, voluntarily undertaken by Irenæus, of giving a relatively complete exposition of the doctrines of ecclesiastical Christianity on the basis of the New Testament, in opposition to heresy. Tertullian nowhere betrayed a similar systematic necessity, which indeed, in the case of the Gallic bishop too, only made its appearance as the result of polemical motives.   But Irenæus to a certain degree succeeded in amalgamating philosophic theology and the statements of ecclesiastical tradition viewed as doctrines.   This result followed (1) because he never lost sight of a fundamental idea to which he tried to refer everything, and (2) because he was directed by a confident view of Christianity as a religion,

---

[1]    Further references to Tertullian in a future volume. Tertullian is at the same time the first Christian *individual* after Paul, of whose inward life and peculiarities we can form a picture to ourselves. His writings bring us near himself, but that cannot be said of Irenæus.

[2]   Consequently the *spirit* of Irenæus, though indeed strongly modified by that of Origen, prevails in the later Church dogmatic, whilst that of Tertullian is not to be traced there.

that is, a theory of its purpose. The first fundamental idea, in its all-dominating importance, was suggested to Irenæus by his opposition to Gnosticism. It is the conviction that the Creator of the world and the supreme God are one and the same.[1] The other theory as to the aim of Christianity, however, is shared by Irenæus with Paul, Valentinus, and Marcion. It is the conviction that Christianity is real redemption, and that this redemption was only effected by the appearance of Christ. The working out of these two ideas is the most important feature in Irenæus' book. As yet, indeed, he by no means really succeeded in completely adapting to these two fundamental thoughts all the materials to be taken from Holy Scripture and found in the rule of faith; he only thought with systematic clearness within the scheme of the Apologists. His archaic eschatological disquisitions are of a heterogeneous nature, and a great deal of his material, as, for instance, Pauline formulæ and thoughts, he completely emptied of its content, inasmuch as he merely contrived to turn it into a testimony of the oneness and absolute causality of God the Creator; but the repetition of the same main thoughts to an extent that is wearisome to us, and the attempt to refer everything to these, unmistakably constitute the success of his work.[2] God the Creator and the one Jesus Christ

---

[1] The supreme God is the Holy and Redeeming One. Hence the identity of the creator of the world and the supreme God also denotes the unity of nature, morality, and revelation.

[2] What success the early-Christian writings of the second century had is almost completely unknown to us; but we are justified in saying that the five books " adv. hæreses" of Irenæus were successful, for we can prove the favourable reception of this work and the effects it had in the 3rd and 4th centuries (for instance, on Hippolytus, Tertullian, Clement of Alexandria, Victorinus, Marcellus of Ancyra, Epiphanius, and perhaps Alexander of Alexandria and Athanasius). As is well known, we no longer possess a Greek manuscript, although it can be proved that the work was preserved down to middle Byzantine times, and was quoted with respect. The insufficient Christological and especially the eschatological disquisitions spoiled the enjoyment of the work in later times (on the Latin Irenæus cf. the exhaustive examination of Loof: "The Manuscripts of the Latin translation of Irenæus", in the "Studies of Church History" dedicated to Reuter, 1887). The old Catholic works written against heretics by Rhodon, Melito, Miltiades, Proculus, Modestus, Musanus, Theophilus, Philip of Gortyna, Hippolytus, and others have all been just as little preserved to us as the oldest book of this kind, the Syntagma of Justin against heresies, and the Memorabilia of Hegesippus. If we consider the criticism

are really the middle points of his theological system, and in this way he tried to assign an intrinsic significance to the several historical statements of the baptismal confession. Looked at from this point of view, his speculations were almost of an identical nature with the Gnostic.[1] But, while he conceives Christianity as an explanation of the world and as redemption, his Christocentric teaching was opposed to that of the Gnostics. Since the latter started with the conception of an original dualism they saw in the empiric world a faulty combination of opposing elements,[2] and therefore recognised in the redemption by Christ the separation of what was unnaturally united. Irenæus, on the contrary, who began with the idea of the absolute causality of God the Creator, saw in the empiric world faulty estrangements and separations, and therefore viewed the redemption by Christ as the reunion of things unnaturally separated—the "recapitulatio" (ἀνακεφαλαίωσις).[3] This speculative

to which Tatian's Christology was subjected by Arethas in the 10th century (Oratio 5; see my Texte und Untersuchungen I. 1, 2 p. 95 ff.), and the depreciatory judgment passed on Chiliasm from the 3rd century downwards, and if we moreover reflect that the older polemical works directed against heretics were supplanted by later detailed ones, we have a summary of the reasons for the loss of that oldest Catholic literature. This loss indeed makes it impossible for us to form an exact estimate of the extent and intensity of the effect produced by any individual writing, even including the great work of Irenæus.

[1] People are fond of speaking of the "Asia Minor" theology of Irenæus, ascribe it already to his teachers, Polycarp and the presbyters, then ascend from these to the Apostle John, and complete, though not without hesitation, the equation: John—Irenæus. By this speculation they win simply everything, in so far as the Catholic doctrine now appears as the property of an "apostolic" circle, and Gnosticism and Antignosticism are thus eliminated. But the following arguments may be urged against this theory: (1) What we know of Polycarp by no means gives countenance to the supposition that Irenæus learned more from him and his fellows than a pious regard for the Church tradition and a collection of historical traditions and principles. (2) The doctrine of Irenæus cannot be separated from the received *canon* of New Testament writings; but in the generation before him there was as yet no such compilation. (3) The presbyter from whom Irenæus adopted important lines of thought in the 4th book did not write till after the middle of the second century. (4) Tertullian owes his Christocentric theology, so far as he has such a thing, to Irenæus (and Melito?).

[2] Marcion, as is well known, went still further in his depreciatory judgment of the world, and therefore recognised in the redemption through Christ a pure act of grace.

[3] See Molwitz, De Ἀνακεφαλαιώσεως in Irenæi theologia potestate, Dresden, 1874.

thought, which involved the highest imaginable optimism in contrast to Gnostic pessimism, brought Irenæus into touch with certain Pauline trains of thought,[1] and enabled him to adhere to the theology of the Apologists. At the same time it opened up a view of the person of Christ, which supplemented the great defect of that theology,[2] surpassed the Christology of the Gnostics,[3] and made it possible to utilise the Christological statements contained in certain books of the New Testament.[4]

So far as we know at least, Irenæus is the first ecclesiastical theologian after the time of the Apologists (see Ignatius before that) who assigned a quite specific significance to the person of Christ and in fact regarded it as the vital factor.[5] That was possible for him because of his realistic view of redemption. Here, however, he did not fall into the abyss of Gnosticism, because, as a disciple of the "elders", he adhered to the early-Christian eschatology, and because, as a follower of the Apologists, he held, along with the realistic conception of salvation, the other dissimilar theory that Christ, as the teacher, imparts

---

[1] See, *e.g.*, the Epistle to the Ephesians and also the Epistles to the Romans and Galatians.

[2] But see the remark made above, p. 220, note 1. We might without loss give up the half of the Apologies in return for the preservation of Justin's chief Antignostic work.

[3] According to the Gnostic Christology Christ merely restores the *status quo ante*, according to that of Irenæus he first and alone realises the hitherto unaccomplished destination of humanity.

[4] According to the Gnostic conception the incarnation of the divine, *i.e.*, the fall of *Sophia*, contains, paradoxically expressed, the element of sin; according to Irenæus' idea the element of redemption. Hence we must compare not only the Gnostic Christ, but the Gnostic Sophia, with the Christ of the Church. Irenæus himself did so in II. 20. 3.

[5] After tracing in II. 14 the origin of the Gnostic theologoumena to the Greek philosophers Irenæus continues § 7: "Dicemus autem adversus eos: utramne hi omnes qui prædicti sunt, cum quibus eadem dicentes arguimini (Scil. "ye Gnostics with the philosophers"), cognoverunt veritatem aut non cognoverunt? Et si quidem cognoverunt, superflua est salvatoris in hunc mundum descensio. Ut (lege "ad") quid enim descendebat?" It is characteristic of Irenæus not to ask what is new in the revelations of God (through the prophets and the Logos), but quite definitely: Cur descendit salvator in hunc mundum?" See also lib. III. præf.: "veritas, hoc est dei filii doctrina", III. 10. 3: "Hæc est salutis agnitio quæ deerat eis, quæ est filii dei agnitio... agnitio salutis erat agnitio filii dei, qui et salus et salvator et salutare vere et dicitur et est." III. 11. 3: III. 12. 7: IV. 24.

to men, who are free and naturally constituted for fellowship
with God, the knowledge which enables them to imitate God,
and thus by their own act to attain communion with him.
Nevertheless to Irenæus the pith of the matter is already found
in the idea that Christianity is real redemption, *i.e.*, that the
highest blessing bestowed in Christianity is the deification of
human nature through the gift of immortality, and that this
deification includes the full knowledge and enjoying of God
(visio dei). This conception suggested to him the question as
to the cause of the incarnation as well as the answer to the
same. The question "cur deus—homo", which was by no
means clearly formulated in the apologetic writings, in so far
as in these "homo" only meant *appearance* among men, and
the "why" was answered by referring to prophecy and the
necessity of divine teaching, was by Irenæus made the central
point. The reasons why the answer he gave was so highly
satisfactory may be stated as follows: (1) It proved that the
Christian blessing of salvation was of a specific kind. (2) It was
similar in point of form to the so-called Gnostic conception of
Christianity, and even surpassed it as regards the promised
extent of the sphere included in the deification. (3) It harmonised with the eschatological tendency of Christendom, and at
the same time was fitted to replace the material eschatological
expectations that were fading away. (4) It was in keeping with
the mystic and Neoplatonic current of the time, and afforded
it the highest imaginable satisfaction. (5) For the vanishing trust
in the possibility of attaining the highest knowledge by the aid
of reason it substituted the sure hope of a supernatural transformation of human nature which would even enable it to
appropriate that which is above reason. (6) Lastly, it provided
the traditional historical utterances respecting Christ, as well as
the whole preceding course of history, with a firm foundation
and a definite aim, and made it possible to conceive a history
of salvation unfolding itself by degrees (οἰκονομία Θεοῦ). According to this conception the central point of history was no longer
the Logos as such, but Christ as the *incarnate God,* while at
the same time the moralistic interest was balanced by a really
religious one. An approach was thus made to the Pauline

theology, though indeed in a very peculiar way and to some extent only in appearance. A more exact representation of salvation through Christ has, however, been given by Irenæus as follows: Incorruptibility is a *habitus* which is the opposite of our present one and indeed of man's natural condition. For immortality is at once God's manner of existence and his attribute; as a created being man is only "capable of incorruption and immortality" ("*capax incorruptionis et immortalitatis*"); [1] thanks to the divine goodness, however, he is intended for the same, and yet is empirically "subjected to the power of death" ("sub condicione mortis"). Now the sole way in which immortality as a physical condition can be obtained is by its possessor uniting himself *realiter* with human nature, in order to deify it "by adoption" ("*per adoptionem*"), such is the technical term of Irenæus. The deity must become what we are in order that we may become what he is. Accordingly, if Christ is to be the Redeemer, he must himself be God, and all the stress must fall upon his birth as man. "By his birth as man the eternal Word of God guarantees the inheritance of life to those who in their natural birth have inherited death." [2]

---

[1] See II. 24. 3, 4: "Non enim ex nobis neque ex nostra natura vita est; sed secundum gratiam dei datur." Cf. what follows. Irenæus has in various places argued that human nature inclusive of the flesh is *capax incorruptibilitatis*, and likewise that immortality is at once a free gift and the realisation of man's destiny.

[2] Book V. pref.: "Iesus Christus propter immensam suam dilectionem factus est, quod sumus nos, uti nos perficeret esse quod et ipse": III. 6. 1: "Deus stetit in synagoga deorum... de patre et filio et de his, qui adoptionem perceperunt, dicit: hi autem sunt ecclesia. Hæc enim est synagoga dei," etc.; see also what follows. III. 16. 3: "Filius dei hominis filius factus, ut per eum adoptionem percipiamus, portante homine et capiente et complectente filium dei." III. 16. 6: "Dei verbum unigenitus, qui semper humano generi adest, unitus et consparsus suo plasmati secundum placitum patris et caro factus, ipse est Iesus Christus dominus noster... unus Iesus Christus, veniens per universam dispositionem et omnia in semetipsum recapitulans. In omnibus autem est et homo plasmatio dei, et hominem ergo in semetipsum recapitulans est, invisibilis visibilis factus, et incomprehensibilis factus comprehensibilis, et impassibilis passibilis, et verbum homo, universa in semetipsum recapitulans... in semetipsum primatum assumens... universa attrahat ad semetipsum apto in tempore." III. 18. 1: "Quando incarnatus est filius homo et homo factus longam hominum expositionem in se ipso recapitulavit, in compendio nobis salutem præstans, ut quod perdideramus in Adam id est secundum imaginem et similitudinem esse dei, hoc in Christo Iesu reciperemus." Cf. the whole 18th chapter where the deepest thoughts of the Pauline Gnosis of the death on the cross

But this work of Christ can be conceived as *recapitulatio* because God the Redeemer is identical with God the Creator; and Christ consequently brings about a final condition which existed from the beginning in God's plan, but could not be immediately realised in consequence of the entrance of sin.   It

are amalgamated with the Gnosis of the incarnation; see especially 18. 6, 7: "Ἤνωσεν οὖν τὸν ἄνθρωπον τῷ Θεῷ. Εἰ γὰρ μὴ ἄνθρωπος ἐνίκησεν τὴν ἀντίπαλον τοῦ ἀνθρώπου, οὐκ ἂν δικαίως ἐνικήθη ὁ ἐχθρός. Πάλιν τε, εἰ μὴ ὁ Θεὸς ἐδωρήσατο τὴν σωτηρίαν, οὐκ ἂν βεβαίως ἔσχομεν αὐτήν. Καὶ εἰ μὴ συνηνώθη ὁ ἄνθρωπος τῷ Θεῷ, οὐκ ἂν ἠδυνήθη μετασχεῖν τῆς ἀφθαρσίας. Ἔδει γὰρ τὸν μεσίτην Θεοῦ τε καὶ ἀνθρώπων διὰ τῆς ἰδίας πρὸς ἑκατέρους οἰκειότητος εἰς φιλίαν καὶ ὁμόνοιαν τοὺς ἀμφοτέρους συναγαγεῖν· καὶ Θεῷ μὲν παραστῆσαι τὸν ἄνθρωπον ἀνθρώποις δὲ γνωρίσαι τὸν Θεόν. Qua enim ratione filiorum adoptionis eius participes esse possemus, nisi per filium eam quæ est ad ipsum recepissemus ab eo communionem, nisi verbum eius communicasset nobis caro factum? Quapropter et per omnem venit ætatem, omnibus restituens eam quæ est ad deum communionem." The Pauline ideas about sin, law, and bondage are incorporated by Irenæus in what follows. The disquisitions in capp. 19—23 are dominated by the same fundamental idea. In cap. 19 Irenæus turns to those who hold Jesus to be a mere man, "perseverantes in servitute pristinæ inobedientiæ moriuntur,, nondum commixti verbo dei patris neque per filium percipientes libertatem ... privantur munere eius, quod est vita æterna: non recipientes autem verbum incorruptionis perseverant in carne mortali, et sunt debitores mortis, antidotum vitæ non accipientes. Ad quos verbum ait, suum munus gratiæ narrans: Ἐγὼ εἶπα, υἱοὶ ὑψίστου ἐστὲ πάντες καὶ θεοί· ὑμεῖς δὲ ὡς ἄνθρωποι ἀποθνήσκετε. Ταῦτα λέγει πρὸς τοὺς μὴ δεξαμένους τὴν δωρεὰν τῆς υἱοθεσίας, ἀλλ' ἀτιμάζοντας τὴν σάρκωσιν τῆς καθαρᾶς γεννήσεως τοῦ λόγου τοῦ Θεοῦ ... Εἰς τοῦτο γὰρ ὁ λόγος ἄνθρωπος et qui filius dei est filius hominis factus est, ἵνα ὁ ἄνθρωπος τὸν λόγον χωρήσας καὶ τὴν υἱοθεσίαν λαβὼν υἱὸς γένηται Θεοῦ. Non enim poteramus aliter incorruptelam et immortalitatem percipere, nisi adunati fuissemus incorruptelæ et immortalitati. Quemadmodum autem adunari possumus incorruptelæ et immortalitati, nisi prius incorruptela et immortalitas facta fuisset id quod et nos, ut absorberetur quod erat corruptibile ab incorruptela et quod erat mortale ab immortalitate, ut filiorum adoptionem perciperemus?" III. 21. 10: Εἰ τοίνυν ὁ πρῶτος Ἀδὰμ ἔσχε πατέρα ἄνθρωπον καὶ ἐκ σπέρματος ἐγεννήθη, εἰκὸς ἦν καὶ τὸν δεύτερον Ἀδὰμ λέγειν ἐξ Ἰωσὴφ γεγεννῆσθαι. Εἰ δὲ ἐκεῖνος ἐκ γῆς ἐλήφθη, πλάστης δὲ αὐτοῦ ὁ Θεός, ἔδει καὶ τὸν ἀνακεφαλαιούμενον εἰς αὐτὸν ὑπὸ τοῦ Θεοῦ πεπλασμένον ἄνθρωπον τὴν αὐτὴν ἐκείνῳ τῆς γεννήσεως ἔχειν ὁμοιότητα. Εἰς τὶ οὖν πάλιν οὐκ ἔλαβε χοῦν ὁ Θεός, ἀλλ' ἐκ Μαρίας ἐνήργησε τὴν πλάσιν γενέσθαι; Ἵνα μὴ ἄλλη πλάσις γένηται μηδὲ ἀλλὸ τὸ σωζόμενον ᾖ, ἀλλ' αὐτὸς ἐκεῖνος ἀνακεφαλαιωθῇ τηρουμένης τῆς ὁμοιότητος; III. 23. 1: IV. 38: V. 36: IV. 20: V. 16, 19—21, 22. In working out this thought Irenæus verges here and there on soteriological naturalism (see especially the disquisitions regarding the salvation of Adam, opposed to Tatian's views, in III. 23). But he does not fall into this for two reasons. In the first place, as regards the history of Jesus, he has been taught by Paul not to stop at the incarnation, but to view the work of salvation as only completed by the sufferings and death of Christ (See II. 20. 3: "dominus per passionem mortem destruxit et solvit errorem cor-is perhaps Irenæus' highest merit, from a historical and ecclesi-astical point of view, to have worked out this thought in preg-nant fashion and with the simplest means, *i.e.*, without the apparatus of the Gnostics, but rather by the aid of simple and essentially Biblical ideas. Moreover, a few decades later, he and Melito, an author unfortunately so little known to us, were already credited with this merit. For the author of the so-called "Little Labyrinth" (Euseb., H. E. V. 28. 5) can indeed boast with regard to the works of Justin, Miltiades, Tatian, Clement, etc., that they declared Christ to be God, but then continues: Τὰ Εἰρηναίου τε καὶ Μελίτωνος καὶ τῶν λοιπῶν τίς ἀγνοεῖ βιβλία, θεὸν καὶ ἄνθρωπον καταγγέλλοντα τὸν Χριστόν ("Who is ignorant of the books of Irenæus, Melito, and the rest, which proclaim Christ to be God and man"). The progress in theological views is very precisely and appropriately expressed in these words. The Apologists also professed their belief in the full revelation of God upon earth, that is, in revelation as the teaching which necessarily leads to immortality; [1] but Irenæus is the first to whom Jesus Christ, God and man, is the centre of history and faith. [2]

ruptionemque exterminavit, et ignorantiam destruxit, vitam autem manifestavit et ostendit veritatem et incorruptionem donavit"; III. 16. 9 : III. 18. 1—7 and many other passages), that is, to regard Christ as having performed a *work*. Secondly, alongside of the deification of Adam's children, viewed as a mechanical result of the incarnation, he placed the other (apologetic) thought, viz., that Christ, as the teacher, imparts complete knowledge, that he has restored, *i.e.*, strengthened the freedom of man, and that redemption (by which he means fellowship with God) therefore takes place only in the case of those children of Adam that acknowledge the truth proclaimed by Christ and imitate the Redeemer in a holy life (V. 1. 1.: "Non enim aliter nos discere poteramus quæ sunt dei, nisi magister noster, verbum exsistens, homo factus fuisset. Neque enim alius poterat enarrare nobis, quæ sunt patris, nisi proprium ipsius verbum ... Neque rursus nos aliter discere poteramus, nisi magistrum nostrum videntes et per auditum nostrum vocem eius percipientes, ut imitatores quidem operum, factores autem sermonum eius facti, communionem habe-amus cum ipso", and many other passages. We find a combined formula in III. 5. 3: "Christus libertatem hominibus restauravit et attribuit incorruptelæ hæreditatem."

[1] Theophilus also did not see further, see Wendt, l.c., 17 ff.

[2] Melito's teaching must have been similar. In a fragment attributed to him (see my Texte und Untersuchungen I. 1, 2 p. 255 ff.) we even find the expression "αἱ δύο οὐσίαι Χριστοῦ". The genuineness of the fragment is indeed disputed, but, as I think, without grounds. It is certainly remarkable that the formula is not found in Irenæus (see details below). The first Syriac fragment (Otto IX. p. 419) shows that Melito also views redemption as reunion through Christ.

Following the method of Valentinus, he succeeded in sketching a history of salvation, the gradual realising of the οἰκονομία Θεοῦ culminating in the deification of believing humanity, but here he always managed to keep his language essentially within the limits of the Biblical. The various acting æons of the Gnostics became to him different stages in the saving work of the one Creator and his Logos. His system seemed to have absorbed the rationalism of the Apologists and the intelligible simplicity of their moral theology, just as much as it did the Gnostic dualism with its particoloured mythology. Revelation had become history, the history of salvation; and dogmatics had in a certain fashion become a way of looking at history, the knowledge of God's ways of salvation that lead historically to an appointed goal. [1]

But, as this realistic, quasi-historical view of the subject was by no means completely worked out by Irenæus himself, since the theory of human freedom did not admit of its logical development, and since the New Testament also pointed in other directions, it did not yet become the predominating one even in the third century, nor was it consistently carried out by any one teacher. The two conceptions opposed to it, that of the early Christian eschatology and the rationalistic one, were still in vogue. The two latter were closely connected in the third century, especially in the West, whilst the mystic and realistic view was almost completely lacking there. In this respect Tertullian adopted but little from Irenæus. Hippolytus also lagged behind him. Teachers like Commodian, Arnobius, and Lactantius, however, wrote as if there had been no Gnostic movement at all, and as if no Antignostic Church theology existed. The immediate result of the work carried on by Irenæus and the Antignostic teachers in the Church consisted in the fixing of tradition and in the intelligent treatment of individual doctrines, which gradually became established. The most

---

[1] The conception of the stage by stage development of the economy of God and the corresponding idea of "several covenants" (I. 10. 3: III. 11—15 and elsewhere) denote a very considerable advance, which the Church teachers owe to the controversy with Gnosticism, or to the example of the Gnostics. In this case the origin of the idea is quite plain. For details see below.

important will be set forth in what follows. On the most vital point, the introduction of the philosophical Christology into the Church's rule of faith, see Chapter 7.

The manner in which Irenæus undertook his great task of expounding and defending orthodox Christianity in opposition to the Gnostic form was already a prediction of the future. The oldest Christian motives and hopes; the letter of both Testaments, including even Pauline thoughts; moralistic and philosophical elements, the result of the Apologists' labours; and realistic and mystical features balance each other in his treatment. He glides over from the one to the other; limits the one by the other; plays off Scripture against reason, tradition against the obscurity of the Scriptures; and combats fantastic speculation by an appeal sometimes to reason, sometimes to the limits of human knowledge. Behind all this and dominating everything, we find his firm belief in the bestowal of divine incorruptibility on believers through the work of the God-man. This eclectic method did not arise from shrewd calculation. It was equally the result of a rare capacity for appropriating the feelings and ideas of others, combined with the conservative instincts that guided the great teacher, and the consequence of a happy blindness to the gulf which lay between the Christian tradition and the world of ideas prevailing at that time. Still unconscious of the greatest problem, Irenæus with inward sincerity sketched out that future dogmatic method according to which the theology compiled by an eclectic process is to be nothing else than the simple faith itself, this being merely illustrated and explained, developed and by that very process established, as far as "stands in the Holy Scripture", and—let us add—as far as reason requires. But Irenæus was already obliged to decline answering the question as to how far unexplained faith can be sufficient for most Christians, though nothing but this explanation can solve the great problems, "why more covenants than one were given to mankind, what was the character of each covenant, why God shut up every man unto unbelief, why the Word became flesh and suffered, why the advent of the Son of God only took place in the last times etc." (I. 10. 3). The relation of faith and theological Gnosis was

fixed by Irenæus to the effect that the latter is simply a continuation of the former. [1] At the same time, however, he did
not clearly show how the collection of historical statements found
in the confession can of itself guarantee a sufficient and tenable knowledge of Christianity. Here the speculative theories
are as a matter of fact quite imbedded in the historical propositions of tradition. Will these obscurities remain when once
the Church is forced to compete in its theological system with
the whole philosophical science of the Greeks, or may it be
expected that, instead of this system of eclecticism and compromise, a method will find acceptance which, distinguishing
between faith and theology, will interpret in a new and speculative sense the whole complex of tradition? Irenæus' process
has at least this one advantage over the other method: according to it everything can be reckoned part of the faith, provid-
ing it bears the stamp of truth, without the faith seeming to
alter its nature. It is incorporated in the theology of facts
which the faith here appears to be. [2] The latter, however, imperceptibly becomes a revealed system of doctrine and history;
and though Irenæus himself always seeks to refer everything
again to the "simple faith" ($\psi\iota\lambda\grave{\eta}$ $\pi\acute{\iota}\sigma\tau\iota\varsigma$), and to believing simplicity, that is, to the belief in the Creator and the Son of God
who became man, yet it was not in his power to stop the
development destined to transform the faith into knowledge of
a theological system. The pronounced hellenising of the Gospel,

---

[1] It would seem from some passages as if faith and theological knowledge were
according to Irenæus simply related as the "is" and the "why". As a matter of
fact, he did express himself so without being really able to maintain the relationship thus fixed; for faith itself must also to some extent include a knowledge of
the reason and aim of God's ways of salvation. Faith and theological knowledge
are therefore, after all, closely interwoven with each other. Irenæus merely sought
for a clear distinction, but it was impossible for him to find it in his way. The
truth rather is that the same man, who, in opposition to heresy, condemned an
exaggerated estimate of theoretical knowledge, contributed a great deal to the
transformation of that faith into a monistic speculation.

[2] See I. 10. 2: Καὶ οὔτε ὁ πάνυ δυνατὸς ἐν λόγῳ τῶν ἐν ταῖς ἐκκλησίαις προεσ-
τώτων ἕτερα τούτων (scil. than the regula fidei) ἐρεῖ· οὐδεὶς γὰρ ὑπὲρ τὸν διδάσκαλον·
οὔτε ὁ ἀσθενὴς ἐν τῷ λόγῳ ἐλαττώσει τὴν παράδοσιν. Μιᾶς γὰρ καὶ τῆς αὐτῆς πίστεως οὔσης οὔτε ὁ πολὺ περὶ αὐτῆς δυνάμενος εἰπεῖν ἐπλεόνασεν, οὔτε ὁ τὸ ὀλίγον
ἠλαττόνησε.

brought about by the Gnostic systems, was averted by Irenæus and the later ecclesiastical teachers by preserving a great portion of the early Christian tradition, partly as regards its letter, partly as regards its spirit, and thus rescuing it for the future. But the price of this preservation was the adoption of a series of " Gnostic" formulæ. Churchmen, though with hesitation, adopted the adversary's way of looking at things, and necessarily did so, because as they became ever further and further removed from the early-Christian feelings and thoughts, they had always more and more lost every other point of view. The old Catholic Fathers permanently settled a great part of early tradition for Christendom, but at the same time promoted the gradual hellen-ising of Christianity.

## 2.  *The Doctrines of the Church.*

In the following section we do not intend to give a present-ation of the theology of Irenæus and the other Antignostic Church teachers, but merely to set forth those points of doctrine to which the teachings of these men gave currency in succeed-ing times.

Against the Gnostic theses [1] Irenæus and his successors, apart from the proof from prescription, adduced the following intrin-sic considerations: (1) In the case of the Gnostics and Marcion the Deity lacks absoluteness, because he does not embrace everything, that is, he is bounded by the *kenoma* or by the sphere of a second God; and also because his omnipresence, omniscience, and omnipotence have a corresponding limitation. [2] (2) The assumption of divine emanations and of a differentiated

---

[1] See Böhringer's careful reviews of the theology of Irenæus and Tertullian (Kirchengeschichte in Biographien, Vol. I. 1st section, 1st half (2nd ed.), pp. 378—612, 2nd half, pp. 484—739).

[2] To the proof from prescription belong the arguments derived from the novelty and contradictory multiplicity of the Gnostic doctrines as well as the proofs that Greek philosophy is the original source of heresy. See Iren. II. 14. 1—6; Tertull. de præscr. 7; Apolog. 47 and other places; the Philosophoumena of Hippolytus. On Irenæus' criticism of Gnostic theology see Kunze, Gotteslehre des Irenäus, Leipzig, 1891, p. 8 ff.

divine *pleroma* represents the Deity as a composite, *i.e.*, [1] finite
being; and, moreover, the personification of the divine qualities
is a mythological freak, the folly of which is evident as soon
as one also makes the attempt to personify the affections and
qualities of man in a similar way. [2] (3) The attempt to make out
conditions existing within the Godhead is in itself absurd and
audacious. [3] (4) The theory of the passion and ignorance of
Sophia introduces sin into the pleroma itself, *i.e.*, into the Godhead. [4] With this the weightiest argument against the Gnostic
cosmogony is already mentioned. A further argument against
the system is that the world and mankind would have been
incapable of improvement, if they had owed their origin to
ignorance and sin. [5] Irenæus and Tertullian employ lengthy
arguments to show that a God who has created nothing is in-

[1] See Irenæus II. 1. 2—4: II. 31. 1. Tertull., adv. Marc. I. 2—7. Tertullian
proves that there can be neither two morally similar, nor two morally dissimilar
Deities; see also I. 15.

[2] See Irenæus II. 13. Tertullian (ad Valent. 4) very appropriately defined the
æons of Ptolemy as "personales substantias extra deum determinatas, quas Valentinus in ipsa summa divinitatis ut sensus et affectus motus incluserat."

[3] See Irenæus, l.c., and elsewhere in the 2nd Book, Tertull. adv. Valent.
in several passages. Moreover, Irenæus still treated the first 8 Ptolemaic æons with
more respect than the 22 following, because here at least there was some appearance of a Biblical foundation. In confuting the doctrine of æons he incidentally
raised several questions (II. 17. 2), which Church theologians discussed in later
times, with reference to the Son and Spirit. "Quæritur quemadmodum emissi
sunt reliqui æones? Utrum uniti ei qui emiserit, quemadmodum a sole radii, an
efficabiliter et partiliter, uti sit unusquisque eorum separatim et suam figurationem
habens, quemadmodum ab homine homo... Aut secundum germinationem, quemadmodum ab arbore rami? Et utrum eiusdem substantiæ exsistebant his qui se
emiserunt, an ex altera quadam substantia substantiam habentes? Et utrum in eodem
emissi sunt, ut eiusdem temporis essent sibi?... Et utrum simplices quidam et
uniformes et undique sibi æquales et similes, quemadmodum spiritus et lumina
emissa sunt, an compositi et differentes"? See also II. 17. 4: "Si autem velut a
lumine lumina accensa sunt... velut verbi gratia a facula faculæ, generatione
quidem et magnitudine fortasse distabunt ab invicem; eiusdem autem substantiæ cum
sint cum principe emissionis ipsorum, aut omnes impassibiles perseverant aut et
pater ipsorum participabit passiones. Neque enim quæ postea accensa est facula,
alterum lumen habebit quam illud quod ante eam fuit." Here we have already a
statement of the logical reasons, which in later times were urged against the Arian
doctrine.

[4] See Iren. II. 17. 5 and II. 18.

[5] See Iren. II. 4. 2.

conceivable, and that a Demiurge occupying a position alongside of or below the Supreme Being is self-contradictory, inasmuch as he sometimes appears higher than this Supreme Being,
and sometimes so weak and limited that one can no longer
look on him as a God. [1] The Fathers everywhere argue on
behalf of the Gnostic Demiurge and against the Gnostic supreme
God. It never occurs to them to proceed in the opposite way
and prove that the supreme God may be the Creator. All
their efforts are rather directed to show that the Creator of the
world is the only and supreme God, and that there can be
no other above this one. This attitude of the Fathers is characteristic; for it proves that the apologetico-philosophical theology was their fundamental assumption. The Gnostic (Marcionite)
supreme God is the God of religion, the God of redemption;
the Demiurge is the being required to explain the world. The
intervention of the Fathers on his behalf, that is, their assuming
him as the basis of their arguments, reveals what was fundamental and what was accidental in their religious teaching.
At the same time, however, it shows plainly that they did not
understand or did not feel the fundamental problem that troubled
and perplexed the Gnostics and Marcion, viz., the qualitative
distinction between the spheres of creation and redemption.
They think they have sufficiently explained this distinction by
the doctrine of human freedom and its consequences. Accordingly their whole mode of argument against the Gnostics and
Marcion is, in point of content, of an abstract, philosophico-

---

[1] Tertullian in particular argued in great detail (adv. Marc. I. 9—19) that every
God must, above all, have revealed himself as a creator. In opposition to Marcion's
rejection of all natural theology, he represents this science as the foundation of all
religious belief. In this connection he eulogised the created world (I. 13) and at
the same time (see also the 2nd Book) argued in favour of the Demiurge, *i.e.*, of
the one true God. Irenæus urged a series of acute and weighty objections to the
cosmogony of the Valentinians (see II. 1—5), and showed how untenable was the
idea of the Demiurge as an intermediate being. The doctrines that the Supreme
Being is unknown (II. 6), that the Demiurge is the blind instrument of higher æons,
that the world was created against the will of the Supreme God, and, lastly, that
our world is the imperfect copy of a higher one were also opposed by him with
rational arguments. His refutation of the last conception is specially remarkable
(II. 7). On the idea that God did not create the world from eternal matter see
Tertull., adv. Hermog.

rational kind.[1] As a rule they do not here carry on their
controversy with the aid of reasons taken from the deeper views
of religion. As soon as the rational argument fails, however,
there is really an entire end to the refutation from inner grounds,
at least in the case of Tertullian; and the contest is shifted into
the sphere of the rule of faith and the Holy Scriptures. Hence,
for example, they have not succeeded in making much impression
on the heretical Christology from dogmatic considerations, though
in this respect Irenæus was still very much more successful than
Tertullian.[2] Besides, in adv. Marc. II. 27, the latter betrayed
what interest he took in the preëxistent Christ as distinguished
from God the Father. It is not expedient to separate the arguments advanced by the Fathers against the Gnostics from their
own positive teachings, for these are throughout dependent
on their peculiar attitude within the sphere of Scripture and
tradition.

Irenæus and Hippolytus have been rightly named Scripture
theologians; but it is a strange infatuation to think that this
designation characterises them as evangelical. If indeed we here
understand "evangelical" in the vulgar sense, the term may
be correct, only in this case it means exactly the same as
"Catholic". But if "evangelical" signifies "early-Christian",
then it must be said that Scripture theology was not the primary means of preserving the ideas of primitive Christianity ; for,
as the New Testament Scriptures were also regarded as *inspired*
documents and were to be interpreted according to the *regula,*
their content was just for that reason apt to be obscured. Both
Marcion and the chiefs of the Valentinian school had also been
Scripture theologians. Irenæus and Hippolytus merely followed
them. Now it is true that they very decidedly argued against
the arbitrary method of interpreting the Scriptures adopted by
Valentinus, and compared it to the process of forming the mosaic pic-

---

[1] But this very method of argument was without doubt specially impressive in
the case of the educated, and it is these alone of whom we are here speaking.
On the decay of Gnosticism after the end of the 2nd century, see Renan, Origines,
Vol. VII., p. 113 ff.

[2] See his arguments that the Gnostics merely *assert* that they have only one
Christ, whereas they actually possess several, III. 16. 1, 8 and elsewhere.

ture of a king into the mosaic picture of a fox, and the poems of Homer into any others one might choose; [1] but they just as decidedly protested against the rejection by Apelles and Marcion of the allegorical method of interpretation, [2] and therefore were not able to set up a canon really capable of distinguishing their own interpretation from that of the Gnostics. [3] The Scripture theology of the old Catholic Fathers has a twofold aspect. The religion of the Scripture is no longer the original form; it is the mediated, scientific one to be constructed by a learned process; it is, on its part, the strongest symptom of the secularisation that has begun. In a word, it is the religion of the school, first the Gnostic then the ecclesiastical. But it may, on the other hand, be a wholesome reaction against enthusiastic excess and moralistic frigidity; and the correct sense of the letter will from the first obtain imperceptible recognition in opposition to the "spirit" arbitrarily read into it, and at length banish this "spirit" completely. Irenæus certainly tried to mark off the Church use of the Scriptures as distinguished from the Gnostic practice. He rejects the accommodation theory of which some Gnostics availed themselves; [4] he emphasises more strongly than these the absolute sufficiency of the Scriptures by repudiating all esoteric doctrines; [5] he rejects all distinction between different kinds of inspiration in the sacred books; [6] he lays down the maxim that the obscure pas-

---

[1] See Iren., I. 9 and elsewhere; Tertull., de præscr. 39, adv. Valent. passim.

[2] See Tertull., adv. Marc. II. 19, 21, 22: III. 5, 6, 14, 19: V. 1.; Orig. Comm. in Matth., T. XV. 3, Opp. III., p. 655; Comm. in ep. ad Rom., T. II. 12. Opp. IV., p. 494 sq.; Pseudo-Orig. Adamantius, De recta in deum fide; Orig. I. pp. 808, 817.

[3] For this reason Tertullian altogether forbade exegetic disputes with the Gnostics, see de præscr. 16—19: "Ego non ad scripturas provocandum est nec in his constituendum certamen, in quibus aut nulla aut incerta victoria est aut parum certa."

[4] See Iren., III. 5. 1: III. 12. 6.

[5] See Iren., III. 14. 2: III. 15. 1; Tertull., de præscr. 25: "Scripturæ quidem perfectæ sunt, quippe a verbo dei et spiritu eius dictæ, nos autem secundum quod minores sumus et novissimi a verbo dei et spiritu eius, secundum hoc et scientia mysteriorum eius indigemus."

[6] See Iren. II. 35. 2: IV. 34, 35 and elsewhere. Irenæus also asserted that the translation of the Septuagint (III. 21. 4) was inspired. The repudiation of different kinds of inspiration in the Scriptures likewise involved the rejection of all the critical views of the Gnostics that were concealed behind that assumption. The Alexandrians were the first who again to some extent adopted these critical principles.

sages are to be interpreted from the clear ones, not vice versâ;[1] but this principle being in itself ambiguous, it is rendered quite unequivocal by the injunction to interpret everything according to the rule of faith[2] and, in the case of all objectionable passages, to seek the type.[3] Not only did Irenæus explain the Old Testament allegorically, in accordance with traditional usage;[4] but according to the principle: "with God there is nothing without purpose or due signification" ("nihil vacuum neque sine signo apud deum") (IV. 21. 3), he was also the first to apply the scientific and mystical explanation to the New Testament, and was consequently obliged to adopt the Gnostic exegesis, which was imperative as soon as the apostolic writings were viewed as a New Testament. He regards the fact of Jesus handing round food to those *lying* at table as signifying that Christ also bestows life on the long dead generations;[5] and, in the parable of the Samaritan, he interprets the host as the Spirit and the two denarii as the Father and Son.[6] To Irenæus and also to Tertullian and Hippolytus all numbers, incidental circumstances, etc., in the Holy Scriptures are virtually as significant as they are to the Gnostics, and hence the only question is what hidden meaning we are to give to them. "Gnosticism" is therefore here adopted by the ecclesiastical teachers in its full extent, proving that this "Gnosticism" is nothing else than the learned construction of religion with the scientific means of those days. As soon as Churchmen were forced to bring forward their proofs and proceed to put the same questions as the "Gnostics", they were obliged to work by their method. Allegory, however, was required in

---

[1] See Iren. II. 10. 1 : II. 27. 1, 2.

[2] See Iren. II. 25. 1.

[3] Irenæus appropriates the words of an Asia Minor presbyter when he says (IV. 31. 1): De his quidem delictis, de quibus ipsæ scripturæ increpant patriarchas et prophetas, nos non oportere exprobare eis ... de quibus autem scripturæ non increpant (scil. delictis), sed simpliciter sunt positæ, nos non debere fieri accusatores, sed typum quærere."

[4] See, *e.g.*, IV. 20. 12 where he declares the three spies whom Rahab entertained to be Father, Son, and Spirit.

[5] See Iren. IV. 22. 1.

[6] See Iren. III. 17. 3.

order to establish the continuity of the tradition from Adam down to the present time—not merely down to Christ—against the attacks of the Gnostics and Marcion. By establishing this continuity a historical truth was really also preserved. For the rest, the disquisitions of Irenæus, Tertullian, and Hippolytus were to such an extent borrowed from their opponents that there is scarcely a problem that they propounded and discussed as the result of their own thirst for knowledge. This fact not only preserved to their works an early-Christian character as compared with those of the Alexandrians, but also explains why they frequently stop in their positive teachings, when they believe they have confuted their adversaries. Thus we find neither in Irenæus nor Tertullian a discussion of the relation of the Scriptures to the rule of faith. From the way in which they appeal to both we can deduce a series of important problems, which, however, the Fathers themselves did not formulate and consequently did not answer. [1]

*The doctrine of God* was fixed by the old Catholic Fathers for the Christendom of succeeding centuries, and in fact both the methodic directions for forming the idea of God and their results remained unchanged. With respect to the former they occupy a middle position between the renunciation of all knowledge— for God is not abyss and silence—and the attempt to fathom the depths of the Godhead. [2] Tertullian, influenced by the Stoics, strongly emphasised the possibility of attaining a knowledge of God. Irenæus, following out an idea which seems to anticipate the mysticism of later theologians, made love a preliminary condition of knowledge and plainly acknowledged it as the principle of knowledge. [3] God can be known from revel-

---

[1] Justin had already noted certain peculiarities of the Holy Scriptures as distinguished from profane writings. Tertullian speaks of two *proprietates iudaicæ literaturæ* in adv. Marc. III. 5. 6. But the Alexandrians were the first to propound any kind of complete theories of inspiration.

[2] See above p. 233, note 2, Kunze, l.c.

[3] See Iren , II. 26. I, 13. 4: "Sic et in reliquis omnibus nulli similis erit omnium pater hominum pusillitati: et dicitur quidem secundum hæc propter delectionem, sentitur autem super hæc secundum magnitudinem." Irenæus expressly says that God cannot be known as regards his greatness, *i.e.*, absolutely, but that he can be known as regards his love, IV. 20. I: "Igitur secundum magnitudem non est

ation,[1] because he has really revealed himself, that is, both by the creation and the word of revelation. Irenæus also taught that a sufficient knowledge of God, as the creator and guide, can be obtained from the creation, and indeed this knowledge always continues, so that all men are without excuse.[2] In this case the prophets, the Lord himself, the Apostles, and the Church teach no more and nothing else than what must be already plain to the natural consciousness. Irenæus certainly did not succeed in reconciling this proposition with his former assertion that the knowledge of God springs from love resting on revelation. Irenæus also starts, as Apologist and Antignostic, with the God who is the First Cause. Every God who is not that is a phantom;[3] and every sublime religious state of mind which

cognoscere deum, impossibile est enim mensurari patrem; secundum autem dilectionem eius—hæc est enim quæ nos per verbum eius perducit ad deum—obedientes ei semper discimus quoniam est tantus deus etc."; in IV. 20. 4 the knowledge of God "secundum dilectionem" is more closely defined by the words "per verbum eius Iesum Christum." The statements in §§ 5 and 6 are, however, specially important: they who are pure in heart will see God. God's omnipotence and goodness remove the impossibility of man knowing him. Man comes to know him gradually, in proportion as he is revealed and through love, until he beholds him in a state of perfection. He must be in God in order to know God: ὥσπερ οἱ βλέποντες τὸ φῶς ἐντός εἰσι τοῦ φωτὸς καὶ τῆς λαμπρότητος αὐτοῦ μετέχουσιν, οὕτως οἱ βλέποντες τὸν Θεὸν ἐντός εἰσι τοῦ Θεοῦ, μετέχοντες αὐτοῦ τῆς λαμπρότητος. Καὶ διὰ τοῦτο ὁ ἀχώρητος καὶ ἀκατάληπτος καὶ ἀόρατος ὁρώμενον ἑαυτὸν ... τοῖς πιστοῖς παρέσχεν, ἵνα ζωοποιήσῃ τοὺς χωροῦντας καὶ βλέποντας αὐτὸν διὰ πίστεως. See also what follows down to the words: μετοχὴ Θεοῦ ἐστὶ τὸ γινώσκειν Θεὸν καὶ ἀπολαύειν τῆς χρηστότητος αὐτοῦ, et homines igitur videbunt deum, ut vivant, per visionem immortales facti et pertingentes usque in deum. Sentences of this kind where rationalism is neutralised by mysticism we seek for in Tertullian in vain.

[1] See Iren., IV. 6. 4: Ἐδίδαξεν ἡμᾶς ὁ κύριος, ὅτι Θεὸν εἰδέναι οὐδεὶς δύναται, μὴ οὐχὶ Θεοῦ διδάξαντος, τουτέστιν, ἄνευ Θεοῦ μὴ γινώσκεσθαι τὸν Θεόν· αὐτὸ δὲ τὸ γινώσκεσθαι τὸν Θεὸν θέλημα εἶναι τοῦ πατρός, Γνώσονται γὰρ αὐτὸν οἷς ἂν ἀποκαλύψῃ ὁ υἱός.

[2] Iren. II. 6. 1, 9. 1, 27. 2 : III. 25. 1 : "Providentiam habet deus omnium propter hoc et consilium dat: consilium autem dans adest his, qui morum providentiam habent. Necesse est igitur ea quæ providentur et gubernantur cognoscere suum directorem; quæ quidem non sunt irrationalia neque vana, sed habent sensibilitatem perceptam de providentia dei. Et propter hoc ethnicorum quidam, qui minus illecebris ac voluptatibus servierunt, et non in tantum superstitione idolorum coabducti sunt, providentia eius moti licet tenuiter, tamen conversi sunt, ut dicerent fabricatorem huius universitatis patrem omnium providentem et disponentem secundum nos mundum." Tertull., de testim. animæ; Apolog. 17.

[3] See Iren., IV. 6. 2 ; Tertull., adv. Marc. I, II.

does not include the feeling of dependence upon God as the Creator is a deception. It is the extremest blasphemy to degrade God the Creator, and it is the most frightful machination of the devil that has produced the *blasphemia creatoris.* [1] Like the Apologists, the early Catholic Fathers confess that the doctrine of God the Creator is the first and most important of the main articles of Christian faith; [2] the belief in his oneness as well as his absoluteness is the main point. [3] God is all light, all understanding, all Logos, all active spirit; [4] everything anthropopathic and anthropomorphic is to be conceived as incompatible with his nature. [5] The early-Catholic doctrine of God shows an advance beyond that of the Apologists, in so far as God's attributes of goodness and righteousness are expressly discussed, and it is proved in opposition to Marcion that

[1]  See Iren., V. 26. 2.

[2]  See Iren., II. 1. 1 and the Hymn II. 30. 9.

[3]  See Iren., III. 8. 3. Very pregnant are Irenæus' utterances in II. 34. 4 and II. 30. 9: "Principari enim debet in omnibus et dominari voluntas dei, reliqua autem omnia huic cedere et subdita esse et in servitium dedita" ... "substantia omnium voluntas dei;" see also the fragment V. in Harvey, Iren., Opp. II. p. 477 sq. Because everything originates with God and the existence of eternal metaphysical contrasts is therefore impossible the following proposition (IV. 2, 4), which is proved from the parable of the rich man and Lazarus, holds good: "ex una substantia esse omnia, id est Abraham et Moysem et prophetas, etiam ipsum dominum."

[4]  See Iren. II. 28. 4, 5: IV. 11. 2.

[5]  Tertullian also makes the same demand (*e.g.*, adv. Marc. II. 27); for his assertion "deum corpus esse" (adv. Prax. 7: "Quis enim negabit, deum corpus esse, etsi deus spiritus est? spiritus enim corpus sui generis in sua effigie") must be compared with his realistic doctrine of the soul (de anima 6) as well as with the proposition formulated in de carne 11: "omne quod est, corpus est sui generis; nihil est incorporale, nisi quod non est." Tertullian here followed a principle of Stoic philosophy, and in this case by no means wished to teach that the Deity has a human form, since he recognised that man's likeness to God consists merely in his spiritual qualities. On the contrary Melito ascribed to God a corporeal existence of a higher type (Eusebius mentions a work of this bishop under the title "ὁ περὶ ἐνσωμάτου Θεοῦ λόγος", and Origen reckoned him among the teachers who recognised that man had also a likeness to God in form (in body); see my Texte und Untersuchungen I. 1. 2, pp. 243, 248. In the second century the realistic eschatological ideas no doubt continued to foster in wide circles the popular idea that God had a form and a kind of corporeal existence. A middle position between these ideas and that of Tertullian and the Stoics seems to have been taken up by Lactantius (Instit. div. VII. 9, 21; de ira dei 2. 18.).

they are not mutually exclusive, but necessarily involve each other.[1]

In the case of the *Logos doctrine* also, Tertullian and Hippolytus simply adopted and developed that of the Apologists, whilst Irenæus struck out a path of his own. In the *Apologeticum* (c. 21) Tertullian set forth the Logos doctrine as laid down by Tatian, the only noteworthy difference between him and his predecessor consisting in the fact that the appearance of the Logos in Jesus Christ was the uniform aim of his presentation.[2]

---

[1] See Iren., III. 25. 2; Tertull., adv. Marc. I. 23—28: II. 11 sq. Hippolytus briefly defined his doctrine of God in Phil. X. 32. The advance beyond the Apologists' idea of God consists not only in the thorough discussion of God's attributes of goodness and righteousness, but also in the view, which is now much more vigorously worked out, that the Almighty Creator has no other purpose in his world than the salvation of mankind. See the 10th Greek fragment of Irenæus (Harvey, II. p. 480); Tertull., de orat. 4: "Summa est voluntatis dei salus eorum, quos adoptavit"; de pænit. 2: "Bonorum dei unus est titulus, salus hominum"; adv. Marc. II. 27: "Nihil tam dignum deo quam salus hominis." They had here undeniably learned from Marcion; see adv. Marc. I. 17. In the first chapters of the work de orat., however, in which Tertullian expounds the Lord's Prayer, he succeeded in unfolding the meaning of the Gospel in a way such as was never possible for him elsewhere. The like remark may be made of Origen's work de orat., and, in general, in the case of most authors who interpreted the Lord's Prayer in the succeeding period. This prayer kept alive the knowledge of the deepest meaning of the Gospel.

[2] Apol. 21: "Necesse et igitur pauca de Christo ut deo... Jam ediximus deum universitatem hanc mundi verbo et ratione et virtute molitum. Apud vestros quoque sapientes λόγον, id est sermonem et rationem, constat artificem videri universitatis." (An appeal to Zeno and Cleanthes follows). " Et nos autem sermoni atque rationi itemque virtuti, per quæ omnia molitum deum ediximus, propriam substantiam spiritum inscribimus, cui et sermo insit pronuntianti et ratio adsit disponenti et virtus præsit perficienti. Hunc ex deo prolatum didicimus et prolatione generatum et idcirco filium dei et deum dictum ex unitate substantiæ, nam et deus spiritus (that is, the antemundane Logos is the Son of God). Et cum radius ex sole porrigitur, portio ex summa; sed sol erit in radio, quia solis est radius nec separatur substantia sed extenditur (cf. adv. Prax. 8). Ita de spiritu spiritus et deo deus ut lumen de lumine accensum. Manet integra et indefecta materiæ matrix, etsi plures inde traduces qualitatis mutueris: ita et quod de deo profectum est, deus est et dei filius et unus ambo. Ita et de spiritu spiritus et de deo deus modulo alternum numerum, gradu non statu fecit, et a matrice non recessit sed excessit. Iste igitur dei radius, ut retro semper prædicabatur, delapsus in virginem quandam et in utero eius caro figuratus nascitur homo deo mixtus. Caro spiritu instructa nutritur, adolescit, adfatur, docet, operatur et Christus est." Tertullian adds: "Recipite interim hanc fabulam, similis est vestris." As a matter of fact the heathen must have viewed this statement as a philosophical speculation with a mythological conclusion. It is very instructive

He fully explained his Logos doctrine in his work against the Monarchian Praxeas. [1] Here he created the formulæ of succeeding orthodoxy by introducing the ideas " substance" and " person " and by framing, despite of the most pronounced subordinationism and a purely economical conception of the Trinity, definitions of the relations between the persons which could be fully adopted in the Nicene creed. [2] Here also the philosophical and cosmological interest prevails; the history of salvation appears only to be the continuation of that of the cosmos. This system is distinguished from Gnosticism by the history of redemption appearing as the natural continuation of the history of creation and not simply as its correction. The thought that the unity of the Godhead is shown in the *una substantia* and the *una dominatio* was worked out by Tertullian with admirable clearness. According to him the unfolding of this one substance into several heavenly embodiments, or the administration of the divine sovereignty by emanated *persons* cannot endanger the

to ascertain that in Hippolytus' book against Noëtus "the setting forth of the truth" (c. 10 ff.) he begins with the proposition: Θεός ἐβουλήθη κόσμον κτίσαι. The Logos whose essence and working are described merely went forth to realise this intention.

[1] See Hagemann, Die römische Kirche (1864), p. 172 ff.

[2] See my detailed exposition of the *orthodox* side of Tertullian's doctrine of the Trinity ("orthodox" in the later sense of the word), in Vol. IV. There it is also shown that these formulæ were due to Tertullian's *juristic* bias. The formulæ, " una *substantia*, tres *personæ* ", never alternates in his case with the others, "una *natura*, tres *personæ*"; and so it remained for a long time in the West; they did not speak of " natures " but of "substances" ("nature" in this connection is very rare down to the 5th century). What makes this remarkable is the fact that Tertullian always uses "substance" in the concrete sense "individual substance" and has even expressed himself precisely on the point. He says in de anima 32: "aliud est substantia, aliud natura substantiæ; siquidem substantia propria est rei cuiusque, natura vero potest esse communis. Suscipe exemplum: substantia est lapis, ferrum; duritia lapidis et ferri natura substantiæ est. Duritia (natura) communicat, substantia discordat. Mollitia lanæ, mollitia plumæ pariant naturalia eorum, substantiva non pariant... Et tunc naturæ similitudo notatur, cum substantiæ dissimilitudo conspicitur. Men and animals are similar *natura*, but not *substantia*." We see that Tertullian in so far as he designated Father, Son, and Spirit as one substance expressed their *unity* as strongly as possible. The only idea intelligible to the majority was a juristic and political notion, viz., that the Father, who is the *tota substantia*, sends forth officials whom he entrusts with the administration of the monarchy. The legal fiction attached to the concept "person" aided in the matter here.

unity; the "arrangement of the unity when the unity evolves
the trinity from itself" ("dispositio unitatis, quando unitas ex
semetipsa [trinitatem] derivat") does not abolish the unity, and,
moreover, the Son will some day subject himself to the Father,
so that God will be all in all.[1] Here then the Gnostic doctrine
of æons is adopted in its complete form, and in fact Hippolytus,
who in this respect agrees with Tertullian, has certified that the
Valentinians "acknowledge that the one is the originator of
all" ("τὸν ἕνα ὁμολογοῦσιν αἴτιον τῶν πάντων"), because with them
also, "the whole goes back to one" ("τὸ πᾶν εἰς ἕνα ἀνατρέχει").[2]
The only difference is that Tertullian and Hippolytus limit the
"economy of God" (οἰκονομία τοῦ Θεοῦ) to Father, Son, and
Holy Ghost, while the Gnostics exceed this number.[3] According to Tertullian "a rational conception of the Trinity constitutes truth, an irrational idea of the unity makes heresy" ("trinitas rationaliter expensa veritatem constituit, unitas irrationaliter
collecta hæresim facit") is already the watchword of the Christian
dogmatic. Now what he considers a rational conception is keeping in view the different stages of God's economy, and distinguishing between *dispositio, distinctio, numerus* on the one hand
and *divisio* on the other. At the beginning God was alone,
but *ratio* and *sermo* existed within him. In a certain sense then,

[1] See adv. Prax. 3: "Igitur si et monarchia divina per tot legiones et exercitus
angelorum administratur, sicut scriptum est: Milies centies centena milia adsistebant
ei, et milies centena milia apparebant ei, nec ideo unius esse desiit, ut desinat
monarchia esse, quia per tanta milia virtutum procuratur: quale est ut deus divi-
sionem et dispersionem pati videatur in filio et spiritu sancto, secundum et tertium
sortitis locum, tam consortibus substantiæ patris, quam non patitur in tot angelorum
numero?" (!!) c. 4: "Videmus igitur non obesse monarchiæ filium, etsi hodie apud
filium est, quia et in suo statu est apud filium, et cum suo statu restituetur patri a
filio." L.c.: Monarchia in tot nominibus constituta est, in quot deus voluit."

[2] See Hippol., c. Noëtum 11. According to these doctrines the unity is sufficiently preserved (1) if the separate persons have one and the same substance, (2)
if there is one possessor of the whole substance, *i.e.*, if everything proceeds from
him. That this is a remnant of polytheism ought not to be disputed.

[3] Adv. Prax. 8: "Hoc si qui putaverit, me προβολὴν aliquam introducere id est
prolationem rei alterius ex altera, quod facit Valentinus, primo quidem dicam tibi,
non ideo non utatur et veritas vocabulo isto et re ac censu eius, quia et hæresis
utitur; immo hæresis potius ex veritate accepit quod ad mendacium suum strueret";
cf. also what follows. Thus far then theologians had got already: "The economy
is founded on as many names as God willed" (c. 4).

he was never alone, for he thought and spoke inwardly.  If even
men can carry on conversations with themselves and make
themselves objects of reflection, how much more is this possible
with God. [1]  But as yet he was the only *person*. [2]  The moment,
however, that he chose to reveal himself and sent forth from
himself the word of creation, the Logos came into existence as
a real being, before the world and for the sake of the world.
For "that which proceeds from such a great substance and has
created such substances cannot itself be devoid of substance."
He is therefore to be conceived as permanently separate from
God "secundus a deo consititutus, perseverans in sua forma";
but as unity of substance is to be preserved ("*alius pater,
alius filius, alius non aliud*"—"*ego et pater unum sumus ad
substantiæ unitatem, non ad numeri singularitatem dictum est*"—
"*tres unum sunt, non unus*"—" the Father is one person and
the Son is another, different persons not different things", "*I
and the Father are one* refers to unity of substance, not to
singleness in number"—"the three are one thing not one person"), the Logos must be related to the Father as the ray to
the sun, as the stream to the source, as the stem to the root
(see also Hippolytus, c. Noëtum 10). [3]  For that very reason
"Son" is the most suitable expression for the Logos that has
emanated in this way (κατὰ μερισμόν).  Moreover, since he (as
well as the Spirit) has the same substance as the Father ("unius
substantiæ" = ὁμοούσιος) he has also the same *power* [4] as regards
the world.  He has all might in heaven and earth, and he has
had it *ab initio*, from the very beginning of time. [5]  On the
other hand this same Son is only a part and offshoot; the
Father is the whole; and in this the mystery of the economy
consists.  What the Son possesses has been given him by the
Father; the Father is therefore greater than the Son; the Son

[1] See adv. Prax. 5.

[2] Tertull., adv. Hermog. 3 : "fuit tempus, cum ei filius non fuit."

[3] Novatian (de trin. 23) distinguishes very decidedly between "factum esse" and
"procedere ".

[4] Adv. Prax. 2 : "Custodiatur οἰκονομίας sacramentum, quæ unitatem in trinitatem
disponit, tres dirigens, tres autem non statu, sed gradu, nec substantia, sed forma,
nec potestate, sed specie, unius autem substantiæ et unius status et potestatis."

[5] See the discussions adv. Prax. 16 ff.

is subordinate to the Father. [1] "Pater tota substantia est, filius vero derivatio totius et portio". [2] This paradox is ultimately based on a philosophical axiom of Tertullian: the whole fulness of the Godhead, *i.e.*, the Father, is incapable of entering into the finite, whence also he must always remain invisible, unapproachable, and incomprehensible. The Divine Being that appears and works on earth can never be anything but a part of the transcendent Deity. This Being must be a derived existence, which has already in some fashion a finite element in itself, because it is the hypostatised Word of creation, which has an origin. [3] We would assert too much, were we to say that Tertullian meant that the Son was simply the world-thought itself; his insistance on the "unius substantiæ" disproves this. But no doubt he regards the Son as the Deity depotentiated for the sake of self-communication; the Deity adapted to the world, whose sphere coincides witht he world-thought, and whose power is identical with that necessary for the world. From the standpoint of humanity this Deity is God himself, *i.e.*, a God whom men can apprehend and who can apprehend them; but from God's standpoint, which speculation can fix but not fathom, this Deity is a subordinate, nay, even a temporary one. Tertullian and Hippolytus know as little of an immanent Trinity

---

[1] Tertull., adv. Marc. III. 6: "filius portio plenitudinis." In another passage Tertullian has ironically remarked in opposition to Marcion (IV. 39) : "Nisi Marcion Christum non subiectum patri infert."

[2] Adv. Prax. 9.

[3] See the whole 14th chap. adv. Prax. especially the words: "Iam ergo alius erit qui videbatur, quia non potest idem invisibilis definiri qui videbatur, et consequens erit, ut invisibilem patrem intellegamus pro plenitudine maiestatis, visibilem vero filium agnoscamus pro modulo derivationis." One cannot look at the sun itself, but, "toleramus radium eius pro temperatura portionis, quæ in terram inde porrigitur." The chapter also shows how the Old Testament theophanies must have given an impetus to the distinction between the Deity as transcendent and the Deity as making himself visible. Adv. Marc. II. 27: Quæcunque exigitis deo digna, habebuntur in patre invisibili incongressibilique et placido et, ut ita dixerim, philosophorum deo. Quæcunque autem ut indigna reprehenditis, deputabuntur in filio et viso et audito et congresso, arbitro patris et ministro, miscente in semetipso hominem et deum in virtutibus deum, in pusillitatibus hominem, ut tantum homini conferat quantum deo detrahit." In adv. Prax. 29 Tertullian showed in very precise terms that the Father is by nature impassible, but the Son is capable of suffering. Hippolytus does not share this opinion; to him the Logos in himself is likewise ἀπαθής (see c. Noëtum 15).

as the Apologists; the Trinity only *appears* such, because the
unity of the substance is very vigorously emphasised; but in
truth the Trinitarian process as in the case of the Gnostics, is
simply the background of the process that produces the history
of the world and of salvation. This is first of all shown by
the fact that in course of the process of the world and of salvation the Son grows in his sonship, that is, goes through a
finite process;[1] and secondly by the fact that the Son himselt
will one day restore the monarchy to the Father.[2] These words
no doubt are again spoken not from the standpoint of man,
but from that of God; for so long as history lasts "the Son
continues in his form." In its point of departure, its plan, and
its details this whole exposition is not distinguished from the
teachings of contemporaneous and subsequent Greek philosophers,[3] but merely differs in its aim. In itself absolutely unfitted
to preserve the primitive Christian belief in God the Father and
the Lord Jesus Christ, its importance consists in its identification
of the historical Jesus with this Logos. By its aid Tertullian
united the scientific, idealistic cosmology with the utterances of
early Christian tradition about Jesus in such a way as to make
the two, as it were, appear the totally dissimilar wings of one
and the same building,[4] With peculiar versatility he contrived
to make himself at home in both wings.

[1] According to Tertullian it is certainly an *essential part of the Son's nature* to
appear, teach, and thus come into connection with men; but he neither asserted
the necessity of the incarnation apart from the faulty development of mankind, nor
can this view be inferred from his premises.

[2] See adv. Prax. 4. the only passage, however, containing this idea, which is
derived from 1 Cor. XV.

[3] Cf. specially the attempts of Plotinus to reconcile the abstract unity which is
conceived as the principle of the universe with the manifoldness and fulness of
the real and the particular (Ennead. lib. III.—V.). Plotinus employs the subsidiary
notion μερισμός in the same way as Tertullian; see Hagemann l.c. p. 186 f. Plotinus
would have agreed with Tertullian's proposition in adv. Marc. III. 15:"Dei nomen
quasi naturale divinitatis potest in omnes communicari quibus divinitas vindicatur."
Plotinus' idea of hypostasis is also important, and this notion requires exact examination.

[4] Following the baptismal confession, Tertullian merely treated the Holy Ghost
according to the scheme of the Logos doctrine without any trace of independent
interest. In accordance with this, however, the Spirit possesses his own "numerus"
—"tertium numen divinitatis et tertium nomen maiestatis",— and he is a person
in the same sense as the Son, to whom, however, he is subordinate, for the sub-

It is essentially otherwise with the Logos doctrine of Irenæus. [1] Whereas Tertullian and Hippolytus developed their Logos doctrine without reference to the historical Jesus, the truth rather being that they simply add the incarnation to the already existing theory of the subject, there is no doubt that Irenæus, as a rule, made Jesus Christ, whom he views as God and man, the *starting-point* of his speculation. Here he followed the Fourth Gospel and Ignatius. It is of Jesus that Irenæus almost always thinks when he speaks of the Logos or of the Son of God; and therefore he does not identify the divine element in Christ or Christ himself with the world idea or the creating Word or the Reason of God. [2] That

ordination is a necessary result of his later origin. See cc. 2, 8: "tertius est spiritus a deo et filio, sicut tertius a radice fructus a frutice, et tertius a fonte rivus a flumine et tertius a sole apex ex radio. Nihil tamen a matrice alienatur a qua proprietates suas ducit. Ita trinitas per consertos et connexos gradus a patre decurrens et monarchiæ nihil obstrepit et οἰκονομίας statum protegit"; de pudic. 21. In de præscr. 13 the Spirit in relation to the Son is called "vicaria vis". The element of personality in the Spirit is with Tertullian merely a result arising from logical deduction; see his successor Novatian de trin. 29. Hippolytus did not attribute personality to the Spirit, for he says (adv. Noët. 14): "Ἕνα Θεὸν ἐρῶ, πρόσωπα δὲ δύο, οἰκονομίᾳ δὲ τρίτην τὴν χάριν τοῦ ἁγίου πνεύματος· πατὴρ μὲν γὰρ εἷς, πρόσωπα δὲ δύο, ὅτι καὶ ὁ υἱός, τὸ δὲ τρίτον τὸ ἅγιον πνεῦμα. In his Logos doctrine apart from the express emphasis he lays on the creatureliness of the Logos (see Philos. X. 33: Εἰ γὰρ Θεόν σε ἠθέλησε ποιῆσαι ὁ Θεός, ἐδύνατο· ἔχεις τοῦ λόγου τὸ παράδειγμα) he quite agrees with Tertullian. See ibid.; here the Logos is called before his coming forth "ἐνδιάθετος τοῦ παντὸς λογισμός"; he is produced ἐκ τῶν ὄντων, *i.e.*, from the Father who then alone existed; his essence is "that he bears in himself the will of him who has begotten him" or " that he comprehends in himself the ideas previously conceived by and resting in the Father." Cyprian in no part of his writings took occasion to set forth the Logos doctrine in a didactic way; he simply kept to the formula: "Christus deus et homo", and to the Biblical expressions which were understood in the sense of divinity and preëxistence; see Testim. II. 1—10. Lactantius was still quite confused in his Trinitarian doctrine and, in particular, conceived the Holy Ghost not as a person but as "sanctificatio" proceeding from the Father or from the Son. On the contrary, Novatian, in his work *de trinitate*, reproduced Tertullian's views. For details see Dorner Entwickelungsgeschichte I. pp. 563—634, Kahnis, Lehre vom heiligen Geiste; Hagemann, l.c., p. 371 ff. It is noteworthy that Tertullian still very frequently called the preëxistent Christ *dei spiritus*; see de orat. I: "Dei spiritus et dei sermo et dei ratio, sermo rationis et ratio sermonis et spiritus, utrumque Iesus Christus." Apol. 21; adv. Prax. 26; adv. Marc. I. 10: III. 6, 16: IV. 21.

[1] See Zahn, Marcellus of Ancyra, pp. 235—244. Duncker, Des heiligen Irenäus Christologie, 1843.

[2] Zahn, l.c., p. 238.

he nevertheless makes Logos (μονογενής, πρωτότοκος, "only be-gotten", "first born") the regular designation of Christ as the preëxistent One can only be explained from the apologetic tradition which in his time was already recognised as authori-tative by Christian scholars, and moreover appeared justified and required by John I. 1. Since both Irenæus and Valentinus consider redemption to be the special work of Christ, the cosmo-logical interest in the doctrine of the second God becomes sub-ordinate to the soteriological. As, however, in Irenæus' system (in opposition to Valentinus) this real redemption is to be im-agined as *recapitulatio* of the creation, redemption and creation are not opposed to each other as antitheses; and therefore the Redeemer has also his place in the history of creation. In a certain sense then the Christology of Irenæus occupies a middle position between the Christology of the Valentinians and Mar-cion on the one hand and the Logos doctrine of the Apol-ogists on the other. The Apologists have a cosmological interest, Marcion only a soteriological, whereas Irenæus has both; the Apologists base their speculations on the Old Test-ament, Marcion on a New Testament, Irenæus on both Old and New.

Irenæus expressly refused to investigate what the divine element in Christ is, and why another deity stands alongside of the Godhead of the Father. He confesses that he here simply keeps to the rule of faith and the Holy Scriptures, and declines speculative disquisitions on principle. He does not ad-mit the distinction of a Word existing in God and one coming forth from him, and opposes not only ideas of emanation in general, but also the opinion that the Logos issued forth at a definite point of time. Nor will Irenæus allow the designation "Logos" to be interpreted in the sense of the Logos being the inward Reason or the spoken Word of God. God is a simple essence and always remains in the same state; besides we ought not to hypostatise qualities. [1] Nevertheless Irenæus, too, calls the preëxistent Christ the Son of God, and strictly maintains the personal distinction between Father and Son. What makes

[1] See Iren., II. 13. 8: II. 28. 4—9: II. 12. 2: II. 13. 2, and also the important passage II. 29. 3 fin.

the opposite appear to be the case is the fact that he does not utilise the distinction in the interest of cosmology. [1] In Irenæus' sense we shall have to say: The Logos is the revelation hypostasis of the Father, "the self-revelation of the self-conscious God", and indeed the eternal self-revelation. For according to him the Son *always* existed with God, *always* revealed the Father, and it was always the *full* Godhead that he revealed in himself. In other words, he is God in his specific nature, *truly* God, and there is no distinction of essence between him and God. [2] Now we might conclude from the strong

---

[1] A great many passages clearly show that Irenæus decidedly distinguished the Son from the Father, so that it is absolutely incorrect to attribute modalistic ideas to him. See III. 6. 1 and all the other passages where Irenæus refers to the Old Testament theophanies. Such are III. 6. 2 : IV. 5. 2 fin. : IV. 7. 4, where the distinction is particularly plain : IV. 17. 6 : II. 28. 6.

[2] The Logos (Son) is the administrator and bestower of the divine grace as regards humanity, because he is the revealer of this grace, see IV. 6 (§ 7 : "agnitio patris filius, agnitio autem filii in patre et per filium revelata"); IV. 5 : IV. 16. 7 : IV. 20. 7. He has been the revealer of God from the beginning and always remains so, III. 16. 6 : IV. 13. 4 etc.: he is the antemundane revealer to the angel world, see II. 30. 9: "semper autem coëxsistens filius patri, olim et ab initio semper revelat patrem et angelis et archangelis et potestatibus et virtutibus et omnibus, quibus vult revelari deus; he has always existed with the Father, see II. 30. 9 : III. 18. 1 : "non tunc cœpit filius dei, exsistens semper apud patrem"; IV. 20. 3, 7, 14. 1 : II. 25. 3 : "non enim infectus es, o homo, neque semper coëxsistebas deo, sicut proprium eius verbum." The Logos is God as God, nay, for us he is God himself, in so far as his work is the work of God. Thus, and not in a modalistic sense, we must understand passages like II. 30. 9 : "fabricator qui fecit mundum per semet-ipsum, hoc est per verbum et per sapientiam suam," or hymnlike statements such as III. 16. 6 : "et hominem ergo in semetipsum recapitulans est, invisibilis visibilis factus, et incomprehensibilis factus comprehensibilis et impassibilis passibilis et verbum homo" (see something similar in Ignatius and Melito, Otto, Corp. Apolog. IX, p. 419 sq.). Irenæus also says in III. 6. 2: "filius est in patre et habet in se patrem," III. 6. 1.: utrosque dei appellatione signavit spiritus, et eum qui ungitur filium et eum, qui ungit, id est patrem." He not only says that the Son has revealed the Father, but that the Father has revealed the Son (IV. 6. 3 : IV. 7. 7). He applies Old Testament passages sometimes to Christ, sometimes to God, and hence in some cases calls the Father the creator, and in others the Son ("pater generis humani verbum dei", IV. 31. 2). Irenæus (IV. 4. 2) appropriated the expression of an ancient "immensum patrem in filio mensuratum; mensura enim patris filius, quoniam et capit eum." This expression is by no means intended to denote a diminution, but rather to signify the identity of Father and Son. In all this Irenæus adhered to an ancient tradition; but these propositions do not admit of being incorporated with a rational system.

emphasis laid on "always" that Irenæus conceived a relationship of Father and Son in the Godhead, conditioned by the essence of God himself and existing independently of revelation. But the second hypostasis is viewed by him as existing from all eternity, just as much in the quality of Logos as in that of Son, and his very statement that the Logos has revealed the Father from the beginning shows that this relationship is always within the sphere of revelation. The Son then exists because he gives a revelation. Little interested as Irenæus is in saying anything about the Son, apart from his historical mission, naïvely as he extols the Father as the direct Creator of the universe, and anxious as he is to repress all speculations that lead beyond the Holy Scriptures, he could not altogether avoid reflecting on the problems: why there is a second deity alongside of God, and how the two are related to one another. His incidental answers are not essentially different from those of the Apologists and Tertullian; the only distinction is this incidental character. Irenæus too looked on the Son as "the hand of God", the mediator of creation; he also seems in one passage to distinguish Father and Son as the naturally invisible and visible elements of God; he too views the Father as the one who dominates all, the head of Christ, i.e., he who bears the creation and his Logos. [1] Irenæus had no opportunity of writing against

---

[1] Logos and Sophia are the hands of God (III. 21. 10: IV. 20): also IV. 6. 6: "Invisibile filii pater, visibile autem patris filius." Judging from this passage, it is always doubtful whether Irenæus, like Tertullian, assumed that transcendency belonged to the Father in a still higher sense than to the Son, and that the nature of the Son was more adapted for entering the finite than that of the Father (on the contrary see IV. 20. 7 and especially IV. 24. 2: "verbum naturaliter quidem invisibile"). But it ought not to have been denied that there are passages, in which Irenæus hints at a subordination of the Son, and deduces this from his origin. See II. 28. 8 (the knowledge of the Father reaches further than that of the Son and the Father is greater than the Son); III. 6. 1 (the Son *receives* from the Father the sovereignty); IV. 17. 6 (a very important passage: the Father owns the name of Jesus Christ as his, first, because it is the name of his Son, and, secondly, because he gave it himself); V. 18. 21, 3 ("pater conditionem simul et verbum suum portans"—"verbum portatum a patre"—"et sic unus deus pater ostenditur, qui est super omnia et per omnia et in omnibus; super omnia pater quidem et ipse est caput Christi"—"verbum universorum potestatem habet a patre"). "This is not a subordination founded on the nature of the second person, but an inequality that has arisen historically," says Zahn (l.c., p. 241); but it is doubtful whether such a distinction can be imputed to Irenæus.

the Monarchians, and unfortunately we possess no apologetic writings of his. It cannot therefore be determined how he would have written, if he had had less occasion to avoid the danger of being himself led into Gnostic speculations about æons. It has been correctly remarked that with Irenæus the Godhead and the divine personality of Christ merely exist beside each other. He did not want to weigh the different problems, because, influenced as he was by the lingering effects of an early-Christian, anti-theological interest, he regarded the results of this reflection as dangerous; but, as a matter of fact, he did not really correct the premises of the problems by rejecting the conclusions. We may evidently assume (with Zahn) that, according to Irenæus, "God placed himself in the relationship of Father to Son, in order to create after his image and in his likeness the man who was to become his Son;" [1] but we ought not to ask if Irenæus understood the incarnation as a definite purpose necessarily involved in the Sonship, as this question falls outside the sphere of Patristic thinking. No doubt the incarnation constantly formed the preëminent interest of Irenæus, and owing to this interest he was able to put aside or throw a veil over the mythological speculations of the Apologists regarding the Logos, and to proceed at once to the soteriological question. [2]

We have rather simply to recognise the contradiction, which was not felt by Irenæus because, in his religious belief, he places Christ on a level with God, but, as a theologian, merely touched on the problem. So also he shows remarkable unconcern as to the proof of the unity of God in view of the distinction between Father and Son.

[1] Irenæus very frequently emphasises the idea that the whole economy of God refers to mankind, see, e.g., I. 10. 3: ἐκδιηγεῖσθαι τὴν πραγματείαν καὶ οἰκονομίαν τοῦ Θεοῦ τὴν ἐπὶ τῇ ἀνθρωπότητι γενομένην, IV. 20. 7: Verbum dispensator paternæ gratiæ factus est ad utilitatem hominum, propter quos fecit tantas dispositiones." God became a creator out of goodness and love; see the beautiful expression in IV. 20. 7: "Gloria dei vivens homo, vita autem hominis visio dei," or III. 20. 2: "Gloria hominis deus, operationes vero dei et omnis sapientiæ eius et virtutis receptaculum homo." V. 29. 1: "Non homo propter conditionem, sed conditio facta est propter hominem."

[2] Irenæus speaks about the Holy Spirit in numerous passages. No doubt he firmly believes in the distinction of the Spirit (Holy Spirit, Spirit of God, Spirit of the Father, Spirit of the Son, prophetic Spirit, Wisdom) from the Father and Son, and in a particular significance belonging to the Spirit, as these doctrines are found

Nothing is more instructive than an examination of Irenæus'
views with regard to the *destination of man*, the *original state*,
the *fall*, and *sin;* because the heterogeneous elements of his
"theology", the apologetic and moralistic, the realistic, and the

in the *regula*. In general the same attributes as are assigned to the Son are everywhere applicable to him; he was always with the Father before there was any
creation (IV. 20. 3; Irenæus applies Prov. III. 19: VIII. 22 to the Spirit and not to
the Son); like the Son he was the instrument and hand of the Father (IV. pref. 4,
20. 1: V. 6. 1.). That Logos and Wisdom are to be distinguished is clear from
IV. 20. 1—12 and particularly from § 12: IV. 7. 4: III. 17. 3 (the host in the
parable of the Good Samaritan is the Spirit). Irenæus also tried by reference to
Scripture to distinguish the work of the Spirit from that of the Logos. Thus in
the creation, the guidance of the world, the Old Testament history, the incarnation,
the baptism of Jesus, the Logos is the energy, the Spirit is wisdom. He also alluded
to a specific ministry of the Spirit in the sphere of the new covenant. The Spirit
is the principle of the new knowledge in IV. 33. 1, 7, Spirit of fellowship with
God in V. 1. 1, pledge of immortality in V. 8. 1, Spirit of life in V. 18. 2. But
not only does the function of the Spirit remain very obscure for all that, particularly
in the incarnation, where Irenæus was forced by the canon of the New Testament
to unite what could not be united (Logos doctrine and descent of the Spirit upon
Mary—where, moreover, the whole of the Fathers after Irenæus launched forth into
the most wonderful speculations), but even the personality of the Spirit vanishes
with him, *e.g.*, in III. 18. 3: "unguentem patrem et unctum filium et unctionem,
qui est spiritus" (on Isaiah LXI. 1); there is also no mention of the Spirit in IV.
pref. 4 fin., and IV. 1. 1, though he ought to have been named there. Father, Son, and
Spirit, or God, Logos, and Sophia are frequently conjoined by Irenæus, but he
never uses the formula τριάς, to say nothing of the abstract formulæ of Tertullian.
In two passages (IV. 20. 5: V. 36. 2) Irenæus unfolded a sublime speculation, which
is inconsistent with his usual utterances. In the first passage he says that God
has shown himself prophetically through the Spirit (in the Old Testament), then
adoptively through the Son, and will finally show himself paternally in the kingdom
of heaven; the Spirit prepares man for the Son of God, the Son leads him to the
Father, but the Father confers on him immortality. In the other passage he adopts
the saying of an old presbyter (Papias?) that we ascend gradually through the
Spirit to the Son, and through the Son to the Father, and that in the end the Son
will deliver up everything to the Father, and God will be all in all. It is remarkable that, as in the case of Tertullian (see above), it is 1 Cor. XV. 23—28
that has produced this speculation. This is another clear proof, that in Irenæus the
equality of Father, Son, and Spirit is not unconditional and that the eternity of
Son and Spirit is not absolute. Here also we plainly perceive that the several
disquisitions in Irenæus were by no means part of a complete system. Thus, in
IV. 38. 2, he inverts the relationship and says that we ascend from the Son to the
Spirit: Καὶ διὰ τοῦτο Παῦλος Κορινθίοις φησί· γάλα ὑμᾶς ἐπότισα, οὐ βρῶμα, οὐδὲ
γὰρ ἠδύνασθε βαστάζειν· τουτέστι, τὴν μὲν κατὰ ἄνθρωπον παρουσίαν τοῦ κυρίου
ἐμαθητεύθητε, οὐδήπου δὲ τὸ τοῦ πατρὸς πνεῦμα ἐπαναπαύεται ἐφ' ὑμᾶς διὰ τὴν
ὑμῶν ἀσθένειαν. Here one of Origen's thoughts appears.

Biblical (Pauline), are specially apparent here, and the inconsistencies into which he was led are very plain. But these very contradictions were never eliminated from the Church doctrinal system of succeeding centuries and did not admit of being removed; hence his attitude on these points is typical.[1] The apologetic and moralistic train of thought is alone developed with systematic clearness. Everything created is imperfect, just from the very fact of its having had a beginning; therefore man also. The Deity is indeed capable of bestowing perfection on man from the beginning, but the latter was incapable of grasping or retaining it from the first. Hence perfection, *i.e.*, incorruptibility, which consists in the contemplation of God and is conditional on voluntary obedience, could only be the *destination* of man, and he must accordingly have been made *capable* of it.[2] That destination is realised through the guidance of God

---

[1] The opinions advanced here are, of course, adumbrations of the ideas about redemption. Nöldechen (Zeitschrift für wissenschaftliche Theologie, 1885, p. 462 ff): "Die Lehre vom ersten Menschen bei den christlichen Lehrern des 2 Jahrhunderts."

[2] Here the whole 38th chapter of the 4th Book is to be examined. The following sentences are perhaps the most important: Εἰ δὲ λέγει τις· οὐκ ἠδύνατο ὁ Θεὸς ἀπ᾽ ἀρχῆς τέλειον ἀναδεῖξαι τὸν ἄνθρωπον; Γνώτω, ὅτι τῷ μὲν Θεῷ, ἀεὶ κατὰ τὰ αὐτὰ ὄντι καὶ ἀγεννήτῳ ὑπάρχοντι, ὡς πρὸς ἑαυτόν, πάντα δυνατά· τὰ δὲ γεγονότα, καθὸ μετέπειτα γενέσεως ἀρχὴν ἰδίαν ἔσχε, κατὰ τοῦτο καὶ ὑστερεῖσθαι δεῖ αὐτὰ τοῦ πεποιηκότος· ὃ γὰρ ἠδύναντο ἀγέννητα εἶναι τὰ νεωστὶ γεγεννημένα. Καθὸ δὲ μή ἐστιν ἀγέννητα, κατὰ τοῦτο καὶ ὑστεροῦνται τοῦ τελείου. Καθὸ δὲ νεώτερα, κατὰ τοῦτο καὶ νήπια, κατὰ τοῦτο καὶ ἀσυνήθη καὶ ἀγύμναστα πρὸς τὴν τελείαν ἀγωγήν. The mother can no doubt give strong food to the child at the very beginning, but the child cannot stand it: ἄνθρωπος ἀδύνατος λαβεῖν αὐτό· νήπιος γὰρ ἦν, see also § 2—4: "Non ab initio dii facti sumus, sed primo quidem homines, tunc demum dii, quamvis deus secundum simplicitatem bonitatis suæ hoc fecerit, nequis eum putet invidiosum aut impræstantem. "Ego, inquit, "dixi, dii estis et filii excelsi omnes, nobis autem potestatem divinitatis baiulare non sustinentibus" ... Oportuerat autem primo naturam apparere, post deinde vinci et absorbi mortale ab immortalitate et corruptibile ab incorruptibilitate, et fieri hominem secundum imaginem et similitudinem dei, agnitione accepta boni et mali." Ibid.: ὑποταγὴ Θεοῦ ἀφθαρσία, καὶ παραμονὴ ἀφθαρσίας δόξα ἀγέννητος ... ὅρασις Θεοῦ περιποιητικὴ ἀφθαρσίας· ἀφθαρσία δὲ ἐγγὺς εἶναι ποιεῖ Θεοῦ. In this chapter Irenæus contemplates the manner of appearance of the Logos (as man) from the point of view of a συννηπιάζειν. His conception of the capacity and destination of man enabled him to develop his ideas about the progressive training of the human race and about the different covenants (see below). On this point cf. also IV. 20. 5—7. The fact that, according to this way of looking at things, the Good and Divine appeared only as the *destination* of man—which was finally to be reached through divine guidance—but not as his

and the free decision of man, for goodness not arising from
free choice has no value. The capacity in question is on the
one hand involved in man's possession of the divine image,
which, however, is only realised in the body and is therefore at
bottom a matter of indifference; and, on the other, in his likeness to God, which consists in the union of the soul with God's
Spirit, but only comes about when man is obedient to him.
Along with this Irenæus has also the idea that man's likeness
consists in freedom. Now, as man became disobedient immediately after the creation, this likeness to God did not become
perfect.[1] Through the fall he lost the fellowship with God to

---

*nature*, suggested both to Irenæus and Tertullian the distinction between "natura"
and "gratia" or between "substantia" and "fides et iustitia". In other words,
they were led to propound a problem which had occurred to the Gnostics long
before, and had been solved by them in a dualistic sense. See Irenæus II. 29. 1:
"Si propter substantiam omnes succedunt animæ in refrigerium, et superfluum est
credere, superflua autem et discessio salvatoris; si autem propter iustitiam, iam
non propter id, quod sint animæ sed quoniam sunt iustæ... Si enim natura et
substantia salvat, omnes salvabuntur animæ; si autem iustitia et fides etc. II. 34. 3:
"Non enim ex nobis neque ex nostra natura vita est, sed secundum gratiam dei
datur," II. 34. 4. Tertullian adv. Marc. III. 15: "Christi nomen non ex natura
veniens, sed ex dispositione." In Tertullian these ideas are not unfrequently opposed
to each other in this way; but the relationship between them has by no means
been made clear.

[1] On the psychology of Irenæus see Böhringer, p. 466 f., Wendt p. 22. The
fact that in some passages he reckoned the πνεῦμα in man as the latter's inalienable
nature (*e.g.* II. 33. 5), though as a rule (like Tatian) he conceives it as the divine
Spirit, is an evident inconsistency on his part. The εἰκών is realised in the body,
the ὁμοίωσις is not given by nature, but is brought about by the union with the
Spirit of God realised through obedience (V. 6. 1). The ὁμοίωσις is therefore subject to growth, and was not perfect at the beginning (see above, IV. 38. 4, where
he opposes Tatian's opinion). It is clear, especially from V. 12. 2, that it is only
the πνοή, not the πνεῦμα, that is to be conceived as an original possession. On
this point Irenæus appealed to 1 Cor. XV. 45. It is plain from the 37th chapter
of the 4th Book, that Irenæus also views everything as ultimately dependent on
man's inalienable freedom. Alongside of this God's goodness has scope for displaying itself in addition to its exercise at the creation, because it guides man's
knowledge through counsel; see § 1. On Matth. XXIII. 37 Irenæus remarks: " veterem
legem libertatis hominis manifestavit, quia liberum eum deus fecit ab initio, habentem
suam potestatem sicut et suam animam ad utendum sententia dei voluntarie et non
coactum a deo... posuit in homine potestatem electionis quemadmodum in angelis
(et enim angeli rationabiles), ut hi quidem qui obedissent iuste bonum sint possidentes,
*datum quidem a deo, servatum vero ab ipsis*." An appeal to Rome II. 4—7 (!)
follows. In § 2 Irenæus inveighs violently against the Gnostic doctrines of natural

which he was destined, *i.e.*, he is forfeit to death. This death was transmitted to Adam's whole posterity.[1] Here Irenæus followed sayings of Paul, but adopted the words rather than the sense; for, in the first place, like the Apologists, he very strongly emphasises the elements that palliate man's fall[2] and, secondly, he contemplates the fall as having a teleological significance. It is the fall itself and not, as in Paul's case, the

goodness and wickedness: πάντες τῆς αὐτῆς εἰσὶ φύσεως. In § 4 he interprets the Pauline: "omnia licent, sed non omnia expediunt," as referring to man's inalienable freedom and to the way in which it is abused in order to work evil (!): "liberæ sententiæ ab initio est homo et liberæ sententiæ est deus, cuius ad similitudinem factus est." § 5 : "Et non tantum in operibus, sed etiam in fide, liberum et suæ potestatis arbitrium hominis *servavit* (that is, respected) dominus, dicens: Secundum fidem tuam fiat tibi." § 4 : "deus consilium dat continere bonum, quod perficitur ex obedientia." § 3 : "Τὸ αὐτεξούσιον τοῦ ἀνθρώπου καὶ τὸ συμβουλευτικὸν τοῦ Θεοῦ μὴ βιαζομένου. IV. 4. 3 : "homo rationabilis et secundum hoc similis deo liber in arbitrio factus et suæ potestatis, ipse sibi causa est, ut aliquando quidem frumentum aliquando autem palea fiat."

[1] As a matter of fact this view already belongs to the second train of thought; see particularly III. 21—23. Here in reality this merely applies to the particular individuals who chose disobedience, but Irenæus almost everywhere referred back to the fall of Adam. See, however, V. 27. 2 : "Quicunque erga eum custodiunt dilectionem, suam his præstat communionem. Communio autem dei vità et lumen et fruitio eorum quæ sunt apud deum bonorum. Quicumque autem absistunt secundum sententiam suam ab eo, his eam quæ electa est ab ipsis separationem inducit. Separatio autem dei mors, et separatio lucis tenebræ, et separatio dei amissio omnium quæ sunt apud eum bonorum." V. 19. 1, 1. 3, 1. 1. The subjective moralism is very clearly defined in IV. 15. 2 : "Id quod erat semper liberum et suæ potestatis in homine semper servavit deus et sua exhortatio, ut iuste iudicentur qui non obediunt ei quoniam non obedierunt, et qui obedierunt et crediderunt ei, honorentur incorruptibilitate."

[2] Man's sin is thoughtlessness; he is merely led astray (IV. 40. 3). The fact that he let himself be seduced under the pretext of immortality is an excuse for him; man was *infans*, (See above; hence it is said, in opposition to the Gnostics, in IV. 38. 4 : "supergredientes legem humani generis et antequam fiant homines, iam volunt similes esse factori deo et nullam esse differentiam infecti dei et nunc facti hominis." The same idea is once more very clearly expressed in IV. 39. 3 ; "quemadmodum igitur erit homo deus, qui nondum factus est homo?" *i.e.*, how could newly created man be already perfect as he was not even man, inasmuch as he did not yet know how to distinguish good and evil?). Cf. III. 23. 3, 5 : "The fear of Adam was the beginning of wisdom; the sense of transgression led to repentance; but God bestows his grace on the penitent"... "eum odivit deus, qui seduxit hominem, ei vero qui seductus est, sensim paullatimque misertus est." The "pondus peccati" in the sense of Augustine was by no means acknowledged by Irenæus, and although he makes use of Pauline sayings, and by preference such as have a quite different sense, he is very far from sharing Paul's view.

consequences of the fall, that he thus views; for he says that
disobedience was conducive to man's development. Man had
to learn by experience that disobedience entails death, in order
that he might acquire wisdom and choose freely to fulfil the
commandments of God. Further, man was obliged to learn
through the fall that goodness and life do not belong to him
by nature as they do to God. [1] Here life and death are always
the ultimate question to Irenæus. It is only when he quotes
sayings of Paul that he remembers sin in connection with redemption; and ethical consequences of the fall are not mentioned
in this connection. "The original destination of man was not
abrogated by the fall, the truth rather being that the fall was
intended as a means of leading men to attain this perfection
to which they were destined." [2] Moreover, the goodness of God
immediately showed itself both in the removal of the tree of
life and in the sentence of temporal death. [3] What significance
belongs to Jesus Christ within this conception is clear: he is
the man who first realised in his person the destination of
humanity; the Spirit of God became united with his soul and
accustomed itself to dwell in men. But he is also the teacher
who reforms mankind by his preaching, calls upon them to
direct their still existing freedom to obedience to the divine
commandments, thereby restoring, i.e., strengthening, freedom,
so that humanity is thus rendered capable of receiving incorruptibility. [4] One can plainly see that this is the idea of Tatian

[1] See IV. 37. 7: "Alias autem esset nostrum insensatum bonum, quod esset
inexercitatum. Sed et videre non tantum nobis esset desiderabile, nisi cognovissemus
quantum esset malum non videre; et bene valere autem male valentis experientia
honorabilius efficit, et lucem tenebrarum comparatio et vitam mortis. Sic et cœleste
regnum honorabilius est his qui cognoverunt terrenum." The main passage is III.
20. 1, 2, which cannot be here quoted. The fall was necessary in order that man
might not believe that he was "naturaliter similis deo". Hence God permitted the
great whale to swallow man for a time. In several passages Irenæus has designated
the permitting of evil as kind generosity on the part of God, see, e.g., IV. 39. 1, 37. 7.

[2] See Wendt, l.c., p. 24.

[3] See III. 23. 6.

[4] See V. 1. 1: "Non enim aliter nos discere poteramus quæ sunt dei, nisi
magister noster, verbum exsistens, homo factus fuisset.... Neque rursus nos aliter
discere poteramus, nisi magistrum nostrum videntes," etc.; III. 23. 2, 5. 3 : " libertatem restauravit"; IV. 24. 1: "reformavit humanum genus"; III. 17. 1 : " spiritus

and Theophilus, with which Irenæus has incorporated utterances
of Paul. Tertullian and Hippolytus taught essentially the same
doctrine;[1] only Tertullian beheld the image and likeness of
God expressly and exclusively in the fact that man's will and
capacity are free, and based on this freedom an argument in
justification of God's ways.[2]

But, in addition to this, Irenæus developed a second train of
thought. This was the outcome of his Gnostic and realistic
doctrine of recapitulation, and evinces clear traces of the influence
of Pauline theology. It is, however, inconsistent with the moralistic teachings unfolded above, and could only be united with
them at a few points. To the Apologists the proposition: "it
is impossible to learn to know God without the help of God"
("impossibile est sine deo discere deum") was a conviction
which, with the exception of Justin, they subordinated to their
moralism and to which they did not give a specifically Christological signification. Irenæus understood this proposition in a
Christological sense,[3] and at the same time conceived the blessing of salvation imparted by Christ not only as the incorruptibility consisting in the beholding of God bestowed on obedience
IV. 20. 5—7: IV. 38, but also as the divine sonship which

sanctus in filium dei, filium hominis factum, descendit cum ipso assuescens habitare
in genere humano." III. 19. 1: IV. 38. 3: 39. 1, 2. Wendt's summary, l. c., p. 24:
"By the Logos becoming man, the type of the perfect man made its appearance,"
formulates Irenæus' meaning correctly and excludes the erroneous idea that he
viewed the Logos himself as the prototype of humanity. A real divine manhood
is not necessary within this train of thought; only a *homo inspiratus* is required.

[1] See Hippol. Philos. X. 33 (p. 538 sq.): Ἐπὶ τούτοις τὸν πάντων ἄρχοντα δημι-
ουργῶν ἐκ πασῶν συνθέτων οὐσιῶν ἐσκεύασεν, οὐ Θεὸν θέλων ποιεῖν ἔσφηλεν, οὐδὲ
ἄγγελον, ἀλλ' ἄνθρωπον. Εἰ γὰρ Θεόν σε ἠθέλησε ποιῆσαι, ἐδύνατο· ἔχεις τοῦ λόγου
τὸ παράδειγμα· ἄνθρωπον θέλων, ἄνθρωπόν σε ἐποίησεν· εἰ δὲ θέλεις καὶ Θεὸς γενέσθαι,
ὑπάκουε τῷ πεποιηκότι. The famous concluding chapter of the Philosophoumena
with its prospect of deification is to be explained from this (X. 34).

[2] See Tertull. adv. Marc. II. 4—11; his undiluted moralism appears with particular
clearness in chaps. 6 and 8. No weight is to be attached to the phrase in chapter 4
that God by placing man in Paradise really even then put him from Paradise into
the Church. This is contrary to Wendt's opinion, l.c., p. 67. ff., where the exposition
of Tertullian is *speciosior quam verior*. In adv. Marc. II. 4 ff. Wendt professes to
see the first traces of the scholastic and Romish theory, and in de anima 16, 41
the germ of the subsequent Protestant view.

[3] See IV. 5. 1, 6. 4.

has been won for us by Christ and which is realised in constant fellowship with God and dependence on him. [1] No doubt
he also viewed this divine sonship as consisting in the transformation of human nature; but the point of immediate importance here is that it is no longer human freedom but Christ
that he contemplated in this connection. Corresponding to this
he has now also a different idea of the original destination of
man, of Adam, and of the results of the fall. Here comes in
the mystical Adam-Christ speculation, in accordance with the
Epistles to the Ephesians and Corinthians. Everything, that is,
the "longa hominum expositio", was recapitulated by Christ in
himself; in other words he restored humanity *to what it originally was* and again included under one head what was divided.[2]
If humanity is restored, then it must have lost something before
and been originally in good condition. In complete contradiction
to the other teachings quoted above, Irenæus now says: "What
we had lost in Adam, namely, our possession of the image and
likeness of God, we recover in Christ. [3] Adam, however, is
humanity; in other words, as all humanity is united and renewed
through Christ so also it was already summarised in Adam.
Accordingly "the sin of disobedience and the loss of salvation
which Adam consequently suffered may now be viewed as belonging to all mankind summed up in him, in like manner as
Christ's obedience and possession of salvation are the property

---

[1] See IV. 14. 1 : "In quantum enim deus nullius indiget, in tantum homo indiget
dei communione. Hæc enim gloria hominis, perseverare et permanere in dei servitute." This statement, which, like the numerous others where Irenæus speaks of
the adoptio, is opposed to moralism, reminds us of Augustine. In Irenæus' great
work, however, we can point out not a few propositions which, so to speak, bear
the stamp of Augustine; see IV. 38. 3 : ὑποταγὴ Θεοῦ ἀφθαρσία.

[2] See the passages quoted above, p. 241 f.

[3] See III. 18. 1. V. 16. 1 is very remarkable: Ἐν τοῖς πρόσθεν χρόνοις ἐλέγετο
μὲν κατ᾽ εἰκόνα Θεοῦ γεγονέναι τὸν ἄνθρωπον, οὐκ ἐδείκνυτο δὲ, ἔτι γὰρ ἀόρατος ἦν
ὁ λόγος, οὗ κατ᾽ εἰκόνα ὁ ἄνθρωπος ἐγεγόνει. διὰ τοῦτο δὴ καὶ τὴν ὁμοίωσιν ῥᾳδίως
ἀπέβαλεν; see also what follows. In V. 1. 1 Irenæus even says: "Quoniam iniuste
dominabatur nobis apostasia, et cum natura essemus dei omnipotentis, alienavit nos
contra naturam diabolus." Compare with this the contradictory passage IV. 38 :
"oportuerat autem primo naturam apparere" etc. (see above, p. 268), where *natura
hominis* is conceived as the opposite of the divine nature.

of all mankind united under him as their head." [1] In the first
Adam we offended God by not fulfilling his commandments;
in Adam humanity became disobedient, wounded, sinful,
bereft of life; through Eve mankind became forfeit to death;
through its victory over the first man death descended
upon us all, and the devil carried us all away captive etc. [2]
Here Irenæus always means that in Adam, who represents all
mankind as their head, the latter became doomed to death. In
this instance he did not think of a hereditary transmission, but
of a mystic unity [3] as in the case of Christ, viewed as the

[1] See Wendt, l.c., p. 29, who first pointed out the two dissimilar trains of thought
in Irenæus with regard to man's original state, Duncker having already done so in
regard to his Christology. Wendt has rightly shown that we have here a real and
not a seeming contradiction; but, as far as the explanation of the fact is concerned,
the truth does not seem to me to have been arrived at. The circumstance that
Irenæus did not develop the mystic view in such a systematic way as the moralistic
by no means justifies us in supposing that he merely adopted it superficially (from
the Scriptures): for its nature admits of no systematic treatment, but only of a
rhetorical and contemplative one. No further explanation can be given of the
contradiction, because, strictly speaking, Irenæus has only given us fragments.

[2] See V. 16. 3 : ἐν τῷ πρώτῳ Ἀδὰμ προσεκόψαμεν, μὴ ποιήσαντες αὐτοῦ τὴν
ἐντολήν. IV. 34. 2 : "homo initio in Adam inobediens per mortem percussus est;"
III. 18. 7—23 : V. 19. 1 : V. 21. 1 : V. 17. 1 sq.

[3] Here also Irenæus keeps sin in the background; death and life are the essential
ideas. Böhringer l.c., p. 484 has very rightly remarked: "We cannot say that
Irenæus, in making Adam's conduct and suffering apply to the whole human race
had started from an inward, immediate experience of human sinfulness and a feeling
of the need of salvation founded on this." It is the thoughts of Paul to which
Irenæus tried to accommodate himself without having had the same feeling about
the flesh and sin as this Apostle. In Tertullian the mystic doctrine of salvation is
rudimentary (but see, e.g., de anima 40 : "ita omnis anima eo usque in Adam
censetur donec in Christo recenseatur," and other passages; but he has speculations
about Adam (for the most part developments of hints given in Irenæus; see the
index in Oehler's edition), and he has a new realistic idea as to a physical taint of
sin propagated through procreation. Here we have the first beginning of the doctrine
of original sin (de testim. 3 : "per diabolum homo a primordio circumventus, ut
præceptum dei excederet, et propterea in mortem datus exinde totum genus de suo
semine infectum suæ etiam damnationis traducem fecit." Compare his teachings in
de anima 40, 41, 16 about the disease of sin that is propagated "ex originis vitio "
and has become a real second nature). But how little he regards this original sin
as guilt is shown by de bapt. 18 : "Quare innocens ætas festinat ad baptismum? "
For the rest, Tertullian discussed the relationship of flesh and spirit, sensuousness
and intellect, much more thoroughly than Irenæus; he showed that flesh is not the seat
of sin (de anima 40). In the same book (but see Bk. V. c. 1) he expressly declared that in

second Adam. The teachings in III. 21. 10—23 [1] show what
an almost naturalistic shape the religious quasi-historical idea
assumed in Irenæus' mind. This is, however, more especially
evident from the assertion, in opposition to Tatian, that unless
Adam himself had been saved by Christ, God would have been
overcome by the devil. [2] It was merely his moralistic train of
thought that saved him from the conclusion that there is a
restoration of *all* individual men.

This conception of Adam as the representative of humanity
corresponds to Irenæus' doctrine of the God-man. The historical
importance of this author lies in the development of the Christology. At the present day, ecclesiastical Christianity, so far
as it seriously believes in the unity of the divine and human
in Jesus Christ and deduces the divine manhood from the work
of Christ as his deification, still occupies the same standpoint
as Irenæus did. Tertullian by no means matched him here;
he too has the formula in a few passages, but he cannot, like
Irenæus, account for its content. On the other hand we owe
to him the idea of the "two natures", which remain in their
integrity—that formula which owes its adoption to the influence

this question also sure results are only to be obtained from revelation. This
was an important step in the direction of secularising Christianity through "philosophy" and of emasculating the understanding through "revelation." In regard to
the conception of sin Cyprian followed his teacher. De op. et eleem. 1 reads indeed
like an utterance of Irenæus ("dominus sanavit illa quæ Adam portaverat vulnera");
but the statement in ep. 64. 5: "Recens natus nihil peccavit, nisi quod secundum
Adam carnaliter natus contagium mortis antiquæ prima nativitate contraxit" is
quite in the manner of Tertullian, and perhaps the latter could also have agreed
with the continuation: "infanti remittuntur non propria sed aliena peccata." Tertullian's proposition that absolutely no one but the Son of God could have remained
without sin was repeated by Cyprian (see, *e.g.*, de op. et eleem. 3).

[1] III. 22. 4 has quite a Gnostic sound... " eam quæ est a Maria in Evam
recirculationem significans; quia non aliter quod colligatum est solveretur, nisi ipsæ
compagines alligationis reflectantur retrorsus, ut primæ coniunctiones solvantur per
secundas, secundæ rursus liberent primas. Et evenit primam quidem compaginem a
secunda colligatione solvere, secundam vero colligationem primæ solutionis habere
locum. Et propter hoc dominus dicebat primos quidem novissimos futuros et novissimos primos." Irenæus expresses a Gnostic idea when he on one occasion plainly
says (V. 12. 3): Ἐν τῷ Ἀδὰμ πάντες ἀποθνήσκομεν, ὅτι ψυχικοί. But Paul, too,
made an approach to this thought.

[2] See III. 23. 1, 2, a highly characteristic statement.

of Leo I. and at bottom contradicts Irenæus' thought "the Son
of God became the Son of man", ("filius dei factus filius hominis"). Finally, the manner in which Irenæus tried to interpret
the historical utterances about Jesus Christ from the standpoint
of the Divine manhood idea, and to give them a significance in
regard to salvation is also an epoch-making fact.

"Filius dei filius hominis factus", "it is one and the same
Jesus Christ, not a Jesus and a Christ, nor a mere temporary
union of an æon and a man, but one and the same person,
who created the world, was born, suffered, and ascended"—this
along with the dogma of God the Creator is the cardinal doctrine of Irenæus:¹ "Jesus Christ truly man and truly God"
("Jesus Christus, vere homo, vere deus"). ² It is only the Church
that adheres to this doctrine, for "none of the heretics hold the
opinion that the Word of God became flesh" ("secundum nullam sententiam hæreticorum verbum dei caro factum est"). ³
What therefore has to be shown is (1) that Jesus Christ is really
the Word of God, *i.e.*, is God, (2) that this Word really became
man and (3) that the incarnate Word is an inseparable unity.
Irenæus maintains the first statement as well against the "Ebionites" as against the Valentinians who thought that Christ's
advent was the descent of one of the many æons.  In opposition to the Ebionites he emphasises the distinction between natural
and adopted Sonship, appeals to the Old Testament testimony in
favour of the divinity of Christ, ⁴ and moreover argues that we
would still be in the bondage of the old disobedience, if Jesus
Christ had only been a man. ⁵  In this connection he also discussed the birth from the virgin. ⁶ He not only proved it from
prophecy, but his recapitulation theory also suggested to him
a parallel between Adam and Eve on the one hand and Christ

¹ See, *e.g.*, III. 9. 3, 12. 2, 16. 6—9, 17. 4 and repeatedly 8. 2: "verbum dei,
per quem facta sunt omnia, qui est dominus noster Jesus Christus."

² See IV. 6. 7.

³ See III. 11. 3.

⁴ See III. 6.

⁵ See III. 19. 1, 2: IV. 33. 4: V. 1. 3; see also Tertullian against "Ebion"
de carne 14, 18, 24; de præscr. 10. 33.

and Mary on the other, which included the birth from the virgin. [1] He argues in opposition to the Valentinians that it was really the eternal Word of God himself, who was always with God and always present to the human race, that descended. [2] He who became man was not a being foreign to the world—this is said in opposition to Marcion—but the Lord of the world and humanity, the Son of God, and none other. The reality of the body of Christ, *i.e.*, the essential identity of the humanity of Christ with our own, was continually emphasised by Irenæus, and he views the whole work of salvation as dependent on this identity. [3] In the latter he also includes the fact that Jesus must

---

[1] See the arguments, l c., V. 19. 1 : " Quemadmodum adstrictum est morti genus humanum per virginem, salvatur per virginem, æqua lance disposita virginalis inobedientia per virginalem obedientiam," and other similar ones. We find the same in Tertull., de carne 17, 20. In this connection we find in both very extravagant expressions with regard to Mary (see, *e.g.*, Tertull., l.c. 20 fin. : "uti virgo esset regeneratio nostra spiritaliter ab omnibus inquinamentis sanctificata per Christum." Iren. III. 21. 7 : "Maria cooperans dispositioni (dei);" III. 22. 4 "Maria obediens et sibi et universo generi humano causa facta est salutis"... "quod alligavit virgo Eva per incredulitatem, hoc virgo Maria solvit per fidem"). These, however, have no doctrinal significance; in fact the same Tertullian expressed himself in a depreciatory way about Mary in *de carne* 7. On the other hand it is undeniable that the later Mariolatry has one of its roots in the parallel between Eve and Mary. The Gnostic invention of the *virginitas Mariæ in partu* can hardly be traced in Irenæus III. 21. 4. Tertullian (de carne 23) does not seem to know anything about it as yet, and very decidedly assumed the natural character of the process. The popular conception as to the reason of Christ's birth from a virgin, in the form still current to-day, but beneath all criticism, is already found in Tertullian *de carne 18* : "Non competebat ex semine humano dei filium nasci, ne, si totus esset filius hominis, non esset et dei filius, nihilque haberet amplius Salomone, ut de Hebionis opinione credendus erat. Ergo iam dei filius ex patris dei semine, id est spiritu, ut esset et hominis filius, cáro ei sola competebat ex hominis carne sumenda sine viri semine. Vacabat enim semen viri apud habentem dei semen." The other theory existing side by side with this, viz., that Christ would have been a sinner if he had been begotten from the semen, whereas he could assume sinless flesh from woman is so far as I know scarcely hinted at by Irenæus and Tertullian. The fact of Christ's birth was frequently referred to by Tertullian in order to prove Christ's kinship to God the Creator, *e.g.*, adv. Marc. III. 11. Hence this article of the *regula fidei* received a significance from this point of view also. An Encratite explanation of the birth from the Virgin is found in the old treatise *de resurr.* bearing Justin's name (Otto, Corp. Apol. III., p. 220.

[2] See, *e.g.*, III. 18. 1 and many other places. See the passages named in note, p. 276.

[3] So also Tertullian. See adv. Marc. III. 8: The whole work of salvation is destroyed by Docetism ; cf. the work *de carne Christi*. Tertullian exclaims to the

have passed through and been subjected to all the conditions
of a complete human life from birth to old age and death. [1]
Jesus Christ is therefore the Son of God who has really become
the Son of man; and these are not two Christs but one, in whom
the Logos is permanently united with humanity. [2] Irenæus called
this union "union of the Word of God with the creature"
("adunitio verbi dei ad plasma") [3] and "blending and communion of God and man" ("commixtio et communio dei et hominis") [4]

Docetist Marcion in c. 5: "Parce unicæ spei totius orbis." Irenæus and Tertullian
mean that Christ's assumption of humanity was complete, but not unfrequently
express themselves in such a manner as to convey the impression that the Logos
only assumed flesh. This is particularly the case with Tertullian, who, moreover,
in his earlier time had probably quite naïve Docetic ideas and really looked upon
the humanity of Christ as only flesh. See Apolog. 21 : "spiritum Christus cum
verbo sponte dimisit, prævento carnificis officio." Yet Irenæus in several passages
spoke of Christ's human soul (III. 22. 1 : V. 1.1) as also did Melito (τὸ ἀληθὲς καὶ
ἀφάνταστον τῆς ψυχῆς Χριστοῦ καὶ τοῦ σώματος, τῆς καθ' ἡμᾶς ἀνθρωπίνης φύσεως
Otto, l.c., IX, p. 415) and Tertullian (de carne 10 ff. 13; de resurr. 53). What we
possess in virtue of the creation was *assumed* by Christ (Iren., l.c., III. 22. 2.)
Moreover, Tertullian already examined how the case stands with sin in relation to
the flesh of Christ. In opposition to the opinion of the heretic Alexander, that the
Catholics believe Jesus assumed earthly flesh in order to destroy the flesh of sin in
himself, he shows that the Saviour's flesh was without sin and that it is not admissible
to teach the annihilation of Christ's flesh (de carne 16; see also Irenæus V. 14. 2, 3) :
"Christ by taking to himself our flesh has made it his own, that is, he has made
it sinless." It was again passages from Paul (Rom. VIII. 3 and Ephes II. 15) that
gave occasion to this discussion. With respect to the opinion that it may be with
the flesh of Christ as it is with the flesh of angels who appear, Tertullian remarks
(de carne 6) that no angel came to die; that which dies must be born; the Son of
God came to die.

[1] This conception was peculiar to Irenæus, and for good reasons was not repeated
in succeeding times; see II. 22 : III. 17. 4. From it also Irenæus already inferred the
necessity of the death of Christ and his abode in the lower world, V. 31. 1, 2.
Here we trace the influence of the recapitulation idea. It has indeed been asserted
(very energetically by Schultz, Gottheit Christi, p. 73 f.) that the Christ of Irenæus
was not a personal man, but only possessed humanity. But that is decidedly incorrect, the truth merely being that Irenæus did not draw all the inferences from the
personal humanity of Christ.

[2] See Iren. V. 31. 2 : "Surgens in carne sic ascendit ad patrem." Tertullian, de
carne 24 : "Bene quod idem veniet de cælis qui est passus ... et agnoscent qui
eum confixerunt, utique ipsam carnem in quam sævierunt, sine qua nec ipse esse
poterit et agnosci;" see also what follows.

[3] See Iren. IV. 33. 11.

[4] See Iren. IV. 20. 4; see also III. 19. 1.

without thereby describing it any more clearly.[1] He views
it as perfect, for, *as a rule,* he will not listen to any separation
of what was done by the man Jesus and by God the Word.[2]
The explicit formula of two substances or natures in Christ is
not found in Irenæus; but Tertullian already used it. It never

---

[1] He always posits the unity in the form of a confession without describing it.
See III. 16. 6, which passage may here stand for many. "Verbum unigenitus, qui
semper humano generi adest, unitus et consparsus suo plasmati secundum placitum
patris et caro factus ipse est Iesus Christus dominus noster, qui et passus est pro
nobis et ressurrexit propter nos … Unus igitur deus pater, quemadmodum ostendimus,
et unus Christus Iesus dominus noster, veniens per universam dispositionem et omnia
in semetipsum recapitulans. In omnibus autem est et homo plasmatio dei, ethominem
ergo in semetipsum recapitulans est, invisibilis visibilis factus, et incomprehensibilis
factus comprehensibilis et impassibilis passibilis et verbum homo." V. 18. 1 : "Ipsum
verbum dei incarnatum suspensum est super lignum."

[2] Here Irenæus was able to adopt the old formula "God has suffered" and the
like; so also Melito, see Otto l.c., IX. p. 416: ὁ Θεὸς πέπονθεν ὑπὸ δεξιᾶς Ἰσραη-
λιτιδος (p. 422): "Quidnam est hoc novum mysterium? iudex iudicatur et quietus
est; invisibilis videtur neque erubescit: incomprehensibilis prehenditur neque indig-
natur, incommensurabilis mensuratur neque repugnat; impassibilis patitur neque
ulciscitur; immortalis moritur, neque respondit verbum, cœlestis sepelitur et id fert."
But let us note that these are not "doctrines", but testimonies to the faith, as they
were always worded from the beginning and such as could, if need were, be adapted
to any Christology. Though Melito in a fragment whose genuineness is not universally admitted (Otto, l.c., p. 415 sq.) declared in opposition to Marcion, that
Christ proved his humanity to the world in the 30 years before his baptism; but
showed the divine nature concealed in his human nature during the 3 years of his
ministry, he did not for all that mean to imply that Jesus' divinity and humanity
are in any way separated. But, though Irenæus inveighed so violently against the
"Gnostic" separation of Jesus and Christ (see particularly III. 16. 2, where most
weight is laid on the fact that we do not find in Matth. : "Iesu generatio sic erat "
but "Christi generatio sic erat"), there is no doubt that in some passages he himself could not help unfolding a speculation according to which the predicates applying to the human nature of Jesus do not also hold good of his divinity, in fact he
actually betrayed a view of Christ inconsistent with the conception of the Saviour's
person as a perfect unity. We can indeed only trace this view in his writings in
the form of an undercurrent, and what led to it will be discussed further on. Both he
and Melito, as a rule adhered to the simple "filius dei filius hominis factus " and
did not perceive any problem here, because to them the disunion prevailing in the world
and in humanity was the difficult question that appeared to be solved through this
very divine manhood. How closely Melito agreed with Irenæus is shown not only
by the proposition (p. 419): "Propterea misit pater filium suum e cœlo sine corpore
(this is said in opposition to the Valentinian view), ut, postquam incarnatus esset in,
utero virginis et natus esset homo, vivificaret hominem et colligeret membra eius
quæ mors disperserat, quum hominem divideret," but also by the " propter hominem
iudicatus est iudex, impassibilis passus est?" (l.c.).

occurred to the former, just because he was not here speaking as a theologian, but expressing his belief. [1] In his utterances about the God-man Tertullian closely imitates Irenæus. Like the latter he uses the expression "man united with God" ("homo deo mixtus") [2] and like him he applies the predicates of the man to the Son of God. [3] B .t he goes further, or rather, in the interest of formal clearness, he expresses the mystery in a manner which shows that he did not fully realise the religious significance of the proposition, "the Son of God made Son of man" ("filius dei filius hominis factus"). He speaks of a "corporal and spiritual, *i.e.*, divine, substance of the Lord", ("corporalis et spiritalis [*i.e.*, divina] substantia domini") [4] of "either substance of the flesh and spirit of Christ" ("utraque substantia et carnis et spiritus Christi"), of the "creation of two substances which Christ himself also possesses", ("conditio duarum substantiarum, quas Christus et ipse gestat") [5] and of

---

[1] The concepts employed by Irenæus are *deus, verbum, filius dei, homo, filius hominis, plasma dei*. What perhaps hindered the development of that formula in his case was the circumstance of his viewing Christ, though he had assumed the *plasma dei*, humanity, as a personal man who (for the sake of the recapitulation theory) not only had a human nature but was obliged to live through a complete human life. The fragment attributed to Irenæus (Harvey II., p. 493) in which occur the words, τοῦ Θεοῦ λόγου ἑνώσει τῇ καθ᾽ ὑπόστασιν φυσικῇ ἑνωθέντος τῇ σαρκί, is by no means genuine. How we are to understand the words: ἵνα ἐξ ἀμφοτέρων τὸ περιφανὲς τῶν φύσεων παραδειχθῇ in fragment VIII. (Harvey II., p. 479), and whether this piece belongs to Irenæus, is uncertain. That Melito (assuming the genuineness of the fragment) has the formula of the two natures need excite no surprise; for (1) Melito was also a philosopher, which Irenæus was not, and (2) it is found in Tertullian, whose doctrines can be shown to be closely connected with those of Melito (see my Texte und Untersuchungen I. 1, 2, p. 249 f.). If that fragment is genuine Melito is the first Church teacher who has spoken of two natures.

[2] See Apol. 21: "verbum caro figuratus ... homo deo mixtus; adv. Marc. II. 27 : "filius dei miscens in semetipso hominem et deum;" de carne 15: "homo deo mixtus;" 18: "sic homo cum deo, dum caro hominis cum spiritu dei." On the Christology of Tertullian cf. Schulz, Gottheit Christi, p. 74 ff.

[3] De carne 5: "Crucifixus est dei filius, non pudet quia pudendum est; et mortuus est dei filius, prorsus credibile est, quia ineptum est; et sepultus resurrexit, certum est, quia impossibile est;" but compare the whole book; c. 5 init. : "deus crucifixus" "nasci se voluit deus". De pat. 3 : "nasci se deus in utero patitur." The formula: "ὁ γεννηθείς, ὁ μέγας Θεός is also found in Sibyll. VII. 24.

[4] De carne 1, cf. ad nat. II. 4: "ut iure consistat collegium nominis communione substantiæ."

[5] De carne 18 fin.

the "twofold condition not blended but united in one person—
God and man" ("duplex status *non confusus sed conjunctus* in
una persona—deus et homo".[1] Here we already have in a
complete form the later Chalcedonian formula of the two substances in one person.[2] At the same time, however, we can
clearly see that Tertullian went beyond Irenæus in his exposition.[3] He was, moreover, impelled to combat an antagonistic
principle. Irenæus had as yet no occasion to explain in detail
that the proposition "the Word became flesh" ("verbum caro

---

[1] Adv. Prax. 27: "Sed enim invenimus illum directo et deum et hominem
expositum, ipso hoc psalmo suggerente (Ps. LXXXVII. 5)... hic erit homo et filius
hominis, qui definitus est filius dei secundum spiritum... Videmus duplicem statum,
non confusum sed coniunctum in una persona deum et hominem Iesum. De Christo
autem differo. Et adeo salva est utriusque proprietas substantiæ, ut et spiritus res
suas egerit in illo, id est virtutes et opera et signa, et caro passiones suas functa
sit, esuriens sub diabolo... denique et mortua est. Quodsi tertium quid esset, ex
utroque confusum, ut electrum, non tam distincta documenta parerent utriusque substantiæ." In what follows the *actus utriusque substantiæ* are sharply demarcated:
"ambæ substantiæ in statu suo quæque distincte agebant, ideo illis et operæ et
exitus sui occurrerunt... neque caro spiritus fit neque spiritus caro: in uno plane
esse possunt." See also c. 29: "Quamquam cum duæ substantiæ censeantur in
Christo Iesu, divina et humana, constet autem immortalem esse divinam" etc.

[2] Of this in a future volume. Here also two *substances* in Christ are always
spoken of (there are virtually three, since, according to *de anima* 35, men have
already two substances in themselves). I know only one passage where Tertullian speaks of *natures* in reference to Christ, and this passage in reality proves
nothing; de carne 5: "Itaque utriusque substantiæ census hominem et deum exhibuit, hinc natum, inde non natum (!), hinc carneum, inde spiritalem" etc. Then:
"Quæ proprietas conditionum, divinæ et humanæ, æqua utique *naturæ* cuiusque
veritate disjuncta est."

[3] In the West up to the time of Leo I. the formula "deus et homo", or, after
Tertullian's time "duæ substantiæ", was always a simple expression of the facts
acknowledged in the Symbol, and not a speculation derived from the doctrine of
redemption. This is shown just from the fact of stress being laid on the unmixedness. With this was associated a theoretic and apologetic interest on the part
of theologians, so that they began to dwell at greater length on the unmixedness
after the appearance of that Patripassianism, which professed to recognise the *filius
dei* in the *caro*, that is in the *deus* so far as he is *incarnatus* or has *changed* himself into flesh. As to Tertullian's opposition to this view see what follows. In
contradistinction to this Western formula the monophysite one was calculated
to satisfy both the *salvation* interest and the understanding. The Chalcedonian
creed, as is admitted by Schulz, l.c., pp. 64 ff., 71 ff., is consequently to be explained
from Tertullian's view, not from that of the Alexandrians. Our readers will excuse
us for thus anticipating.

factum") denoted no transformation. That he excludes the idea
of change, and that he puts stress on the Logos' assumption
of flesh from the Virgin is shown by many passages. [1] Tertullian,
on the other hand, was in the first place confronted by (Gnostic)
opponents who understood John's statement in the sense of the
Word's transforming himself into flesh, and therefore argued
against the "assumption of flesh from the Virgin" ("assumptio
carnis ex virgine"); [2] and, in the second place, he had to do
with Catholic Christians who indeed admitted the birth from
the Virgin, but likewise assumed a change of God into flesh,
and declared the God thus invested with flesh to be the Son. [3]
In this connection the same Tertullian, who in the Church laid
great weight on formulæ like "the crucified God", "God con-
sented to be born" ("deus crucifixus", "nasci se voluit deus")
and who, impelled by opposition to Marcion and by his apologetic interest, distinguished the Son as capable of suffering from
God the Father who is impassible, and imputed to him
human weaknesses—which was already a further step,—sharply
emphasised the "distinct function" ("distincte agere") of the
two substances in Christ and thus separated the persons. With
Tertullian the interest in the Logos doctrine, on the one hand,
and in the real humanity, on the other, laid the basis of that
conception of Christology in accordance with which the unity
of the person is nothing more than an assertion. The "deus
factus homo" ("verbum caro factus") presents quite insuperable
difficulties, as soon as "theology" can no longer be banished.
Tertullian smoothed over these difficulties by juristic distinctions,

---

[1] "Quare," says Irenæus III. 21. 10—"igitur non iterum sumpsit limum deus
sed ex Maria operatus est plasmationem fieri? Ut non alia plasmatio fieret neque alia,
esset plasmatio quæ salvaretur, sed eadem ipsa recapitularetur, servata similitudine?"

[2] See de carne 18. Oehler has misunderstood the passage and therefore mis-
pointed it. It is as follows: "Vox ista (Joh. I. 14) quid caro factum sit contestatur,
nec tamen periclitatur, quasi statim aliud sit (verbum), factum caro, et non verbum ...
Cum scriptura non dicat nisi quod factum sit, non et unde sit factum, ergo ex alio,
non ex semetipso suggerit factum" etc.

[3] Adv. Prax. 27 sq. In de carne 3 sq. and elsewhere Tertullian indeed argues
against Marcion that God in contradistinction to all creatures can transform himself into anything and yet remain God. Hence we are not to think of a transformation in the strict sense, but of an *adunitio*.

for all his elucidations of "substance" and "person" are of this nature.

A somewhat paradoxical result of the defence of the Logos doctrine in the struggle against the "Patripassians" was the increased emphasis that now began to be laid on the integrity and independence of the human nature in Christ. If the only essential result of the struggle with Gnosticism was to assert the substantial reality of Christ's body, it was Tertullian who distinguished what Christ did as man from what he did as God in order to prove that he was not a *tertium quid*. The discriminating intellect which was forced to receive a doctrine as a problem could not proceed otherwise. But, even before the struggle with Modalism, elements were present which repressed the naïve confidence of the utterances about the God-man. If I judge rightly, there were two features in Irenæus both of which resulted in a splitting up of the conception of the perfect unity of Christ's person. The first was the intellectual contemplation of the perfect humanity of Jesus, the second was found in certain Old and New Testament texts and the tradition connected with these.[1] With regard to the first we may point out that Irenæus indeed regarded the union of the human and divine as possible only because man, fashioned from the beginning by and after the pattern of the Logos, was an image of the latter and destined for union with God. Jesus Christ is the realisation of our possession of God's image;[2] but this

---

[1] So I think I ought to express myself. It does not seem to me proper to read a twofold conception into Irenæus' Christological utterances under the pretext that Christ according to him was also the perfect man, with all the modern ideas that are usually associated with this thought (Böhringer, l.c., p. 542 ff., see Thomasius in opposition to him).

[2] See, *e.g.*, V. 1. 3. Nitzch, Dogmengeschichte I. p. 309. Tertullian, in his own peculiar fashion, developed still more clearly the thought transmitted to him by Irenæus. See adv. Prax. 12: "Quibus faciebat deus hominem similem? Filio quidem, qui erat induturus hominem... Erat autem ad cuius imaginem faciebat, ad filii scilicet, qui homo futurus certior et verior imaginem suam fecerat dici hominem, qui tunc de limo formari habebat, imago veri et similitudo." Adv. Marc. V. 8: "Creator Christum, sermonem suum, intuens hominem futurum, Faciamus, inquit, hominem ad imaginem et similitudinem nostram"; the same in de resurr. 6. But with Tertullian, too, this thought was a sudden idea and did not become the basis of further speculation.

thought, if no further developed, may be still united with the
Logos doctrine in such a way that it does not interfere with
it, but serves to confirm it. The case becomes different when
it is not only shown that the Logos was always at work in the
human race, but that humanity was gradually more and more
accustomed by him (in the patriarchs and prophets) to communion with God, [1] till at last the perfect man appeared in Christ.
For in this view it might appear as if the really essential element
in Jesus Christ were not the Logos, who has become the new
Adam, but the new Adam, who possesses the Logos. That
Irenæus, in explaining the life of Jesus as that of Adam according to the recapitulation theory, here and there expresses himself as if he were speaking of the perfect man, is undeniable:
If the acts of Christ are really to be what they seem, the man
concerned in them must be placed in the foreground. But how
little Irenæus thought of simply identifying the Logos with the
perfect man is shown by the passage in III. 19. 3 where he
writes: "ὥσπερ γὰρ ἦν ἄνθρωπος ἵνα πειρασθῇ, οὕτω καὶ λόγος ἵνα
δοξασθῇ. ἡσυχάζοντος μὲν τοῦ λόγου ἐν τῷ πειράζεσθαι καὶ σταυροῦσθαι
καὶ ἀποθνήσκειν, συγγινομένου δὲ τῷ ἀνθρώπῳ ἐν τῷ νικᾶν καὶ
ὑπομένειν καὶ χρηστεύεσθαι καὶ ἀνίστασθαι καὶ ἀναλαμβάνεσθαι"
("For as he was man that he might be tempted, so also he
was the Logos that he might be glorified. The Logos remained
quiescent during the process of temptation, crucifixion and death,
but aided the human nature when it conquered, and endured,
and performed deeds of kindness, and rose again from the dead,
and was received up into heaven"). From these words it is
plain that Irenæus preferred to assume that the divine and human
natures existed side by side, and consequently to split up the
perfect unity, rather than teach a mere ideal manhood which
would be at the same time a divine manhood. The "discrete
agere" of the two natures proves that to Irenæus the perfect
manhood of the incarnate Logos was merely an incidental
quality he possessed. In reality the Logos is the perfect man

[1] Iren. IV. 14. 2; for further particulars on the point see below, wher
Irenæus' views on the preparation of salvation are discussed. The views of Dorner,
l.c., 492 f., that the union of the Son of God with humanity was a gradual process,
are marred by some exaggerations, but are correct in their main idea.

in so far as his incarnation creates the perfect man and renders
him possible, or the Logos always exists behind Christ the
perfect man. But nevertheless this very way of viewing the
humanity in Christ already compelled Irenæus to limit the "deus
crucifixus" and to lay the foundation for Tertullian's formulæ.
With regard to the second point we may remark that there were
not a few passages in both Testaments where Christ appeared
as the man chosen by God and anointed with the Spirit. These
as well as the corresponding language of the Church were the
greatest difficulties in the way of the Logos Christology. Of
what importance is an anointing with the Spirit to him who is
God? What is the meaning of Christ being born by the power
of the Holy Ghost? Is this formula compatible with the other,
that he as the Logos himself assumed flesh from the Virgin etc.?
Irenæus no doubt felt these difficulties. He avoided them (III. 9. 3)
by referring the bestowal of the Spirit at baptism merely to the
*man* Jesus, and thus gave his own approval to that separation
which appeared to him so reprehensible in the Gnostics. [1] This
separation indeed rescued to future ages the minimum of humanity that was to be retained in the person of Christ, but at the
same time it laid the foundation of those differentiating speculations, which in succeeding times became the chief art and
subject of dispute among theologians. The fact is that one
cannot think in realistic fashion of the "deus homo factus"
without thinking oneself out of it.. It is exceedingly instructive

[1] "Secundum id quod verbum dei homo erat ex radice Iesse et filius Abrahæ,
secundum hoc requiescebat spiritus dei super eum... secundum autem quod deus
erat, non secundum gloriam iudicabat." All that Irenæus said of the Spirit in reference to the person of Christ is to be understood merely as an *exegetical* necessity
and must not be regarded as a theoretical *principle* (this is also the case with Tertullian). Dorner (l.c., p. 492 f.) has failed to see this, and on the basis of Irenæus'
incidental and involuntary utterances has attempted to found a speculation which
represents the latter as meaning that the Holy Ghost was the medium which gradually
united the Logos, who was exalted above growing and suffering, into one person
with the free and growing man in Jesus Christ. In III. 12. 5—7 Irenæus, in
conformity with Acts IV. 27: X. 38, used the following other formulæ about Christ:
ὁ Θεός, ὁ ποιήσας τὸν οὐρανὸν κ.τ.λ;, καὶ ὁ τούτου παῖς, ὃν ἔχρισεν ὁ Θεός—"Petrus
Iesum ipsum esse filium dei testificatus est, qui et unctus Spiritu Sancto Iesus dicitur."
But Irenæus only expressed himself thus because of these passages, whereas Hippolytus not unfrequently calls Christ παῖς Θεοῦ.

to find that, in some passages, even a man like Irenæus was
obliged to advance from the creed of the one God-man to the
assumption of two independent existences in Christ, an assumption which in the earlier period has only "Gnostic" testimony
in its favour. Before Irenæus' day, in fact, none but these
earliest theologians taught that Jesus Christ had two natures,
and ascribed to them particular actions and experiences. The
Gnostic distinction of the Jesus *patibilis* ("capable of suffering")
and the Christ ἀπαθής ("impassible") is essentially identical
with the view set forth by Tertullian adv. Prax., and this proves
that the doctrine of the two natures is simply nothing else than
the Gnostic, *i.e.*, scientific, adaptation of the formula: "filius dei
filius hominis factus". No doubt the old early-Christian interest still makes itself felt in the *assertion* of the one person.
Accordingly we can have no historical understanding of Tertullian's Christology or even of that of Irenæus without taking
into account, as has not yet been done, the Gnostic distinction of
Jesus and Christ, as well as those old traditional formulæ: "deus
passus, deus crucifixus est" ("God suffered, God was crucified").[1]

But beyond doubt the prevailing conception of Christ in

---

[1] On Hippolytus' views of the incarnation see Dorner, l.c., I. p. 609 ff.—an
account to be used with caution—and Overbeck, Quæst. Hippol. Specimen (1864),
p. 47 sq. Unfortunately the latter has not carried out his intention to set forth the
Christology of Hippolytus in detail. In the work quoted he has, however, shown
how closely the latter in many respects has imitated Irenæus in this case also. It
is instructive to see what Hippolytus has not adopted from Irenæus or what has
become rudimentary with him. As a professional and learned teacher he is at
bottom nearer to the Apologists as regards his Christology than Irenæus. As an
exegete and theological author he has much in common with the Alexandrians, just
as he is in more than one respect a connecting link between Catholic controver-
sialists like Irenæus and Catholic scholars like Origen. With the latter he moreover
came into personal contact. See Hieron., de vir. inl. 61: Hieron., ep. ad Damas.
edit. Venet. I., ep. 36 is also instructive. These brief remarks are, however, by no
means intended to give countenance to Kimmel's untenable hypothesis (de Hippol.
vita et scriptis, 1839) that Hippolytus was an Alexandrian. In Hippolytus' treatise c.
Noët. we find positive teachings that remind us of Tertullian. An important passage
is de Christo et Antichristo 3 f.: εἷς γὰρ καὶ ὁ τοῦ Θεοῦ παῖς (Iren.), δι' οὗ καὶ
ἡμεῖς τυχόντες τὴν διὰ τοῦ ἁγίου πνεύματος ἀναγέννησιν εἰς ἕνα τέλειον καὶ ἐπουράνιον ἄνθρωπον οἱ πάντες καταντῆσαι ἐπιθυμοῦμεν (see Iren.) Ἐπειδὴ γὰρ ὁ λόγος
τοῦ Θεοῦ ἄσαρκος ὢν (see Melito, Iren., Tertull.) ἐνεδύσατο τὴν ἁγίαν σάρκα ἐκ τῆς
ἁγίας παρθένου· ὡς νύμφιος ἱμάτιον ἐξυφάνας ἑαυτῷ ἦν τῷ σταυρικῷ πάθει (Irenæus
and Tertullian also make the death on the cross the object of the assumption of

Irenæus is the idea that there was the most complete unity between his divine and human natures; for it is the necessary consequence of his doctrine of redemption, that " *Jesus Christus factus est, quod sumus nos, uti nos perficeret esse quod et ipse* " [1]

the flesh), ὅπως συγκεράσας τὸ θνητὸν ἡμῶν σῶμα τῇ ἑαυτοῦ δυνάμει καὶ μίξας (Iren., Tertull.) τῷ ἀφθάρτῳ τὸ φθαρτὸν καὶ τὸ ἀσθενὲς τῷ ἰσχυρῷ σώσῃ τὸν ἀπολλύμενον ἄνθρωπον (Iren.). The succeeding disquisition deserves particular note, because it shows that Hippolytus has also borrowed from Irenæus the idea that the union of the Logos with humanity had already begun in a certain way in the prophets. Overbeck has rightly compared the ἀναπλάσσειν δι᾽ ἑαὑτοῦ τὸν Ἀδάμ, l.c., c. 26, with the ἀνακεφαλαιοῦν of Irenæus and l.c., c. 44, with Iren. II. 22, 4. For Hippolytus' Christology Philosoph. X. 33, p. 542 and c. Noët. 10 ff. are the chief passages of additional importance. In the latter passage it is specially noteworthy that Hippolytus, in addition to many other deviations from Irenæus and Tertullian, insists on applying the full name of Son only to the incarnate Logos. In this we have a remnant of the more ancient idea and at the same time a concession to his opponents who admitted an eternal Logos in God, but not a pre-temporal hypostasis of the Son. See c. 15 : ποῖον οὖν υἱὸν ἑαυτοῦ ὁ Θεὸς διὰ τῆς σαρκὸς κατέπεμψεν ἀλλ᾽ ἢ τὸν λόγον; ὃν υἱὸν προσηγόρευε διὰ τὸ μέλλειν αὐτὸν γενέσθαι. καὶ τὸ κοινὸν ὄνομα τῆς εἰς ἀνθρώπους φιλοστοργίας ἀναλαμβάνει ὁ υἱὸς (καίτοι τέλειος λόγος ὢν μονογενής). οὐδ᾽ ἡ σὰρξ καθ᾽ ἑαυτὴν δίχα τοῦ λόγου ὑποστῆναι ἠδύνατο διὰ τὸ ἐν λόγῳ τὴν σύστασιν ἔχειν. οὕτως οὖν εἰς υἱὸς τέλειος Θεοῦ ἐφανερώθη. Hippolytus partook to a much greater extent than his teacher Irenæus of the tree of Greek knowledge and he accordingly speaks much more frequently than the latter of the "divine mysteries" of the faith. From the fragments and writings of this author that are preserved to us the existence of very various Christologies can be shown; and this proves that the Christology of his teacher Irenæus had not by any means yet become predominant in the Church, as we might suppose from the latter's confident tone. Hippolytus is an exegete and accordingly still yielded with comparative impartiality to the impressions conveyed by the several passages. For example he recognised the woman of Rev. XII. as the Church and the Logos as her child, and gave the following exegesis of the passage (de Christo et Antichristo 61) : οὐ παύσεται ἡ ἐκκλησία γεννῶσα ἐκ καρδίας τὸν λόγον τὸν ἐν κόσμῳ ὑπὸ ἀπίστων διωκόμενον. "καὶ ἔτεκε", φησίν, "υἱὸν ἄρρενα, ὃς μέλλει ποιμαίνειν πάντα τὰ ἔθνη", τὸν ἄρρενα καὶ τέλειον Χριστόν, παῖδα Θεοῦ, Θεὸν καὶ ἄνθρωπον καταγγελλόμενον ἀεὶ τίκτουσα ἡ ἐκκλησία διδάσκει πάντα τὰ ἔθνη. If we consider how Irenæus' pupil is led by the text of the Holy Scriptures to the most diverse "doctrines", we see how the "Scripture" theologians were the very ones who threatened the faith with the greatest corruptions. As the exegesis of the Valentinian schools became the mother of numerous self-contradictory Christologies, so the same result was threatened here—" doctrinæ inolescentes in silvas iam exoleverunt Gnosticorum." From this standpoint Origen's undertaking to subject the whole material of Biblical exegesis to a fixed theory appears in its historical greatness and importance.

---

[1] See other passages on p. 241, note 2. This is also reëchoed in Cyprian. See, for example, ep. 58. 6 : " filius dei passus est ut nos filios dei faceret, et filius hominis (scil. the Christians) pati non vult esse dei filius possit."

("Jesus Christ became what we are in order that we might become what he himself is"). But, in accordance with the recapitulation theory, Irenæus developed the "factus est quod sumus nos" in such a way that the individual portions of the life of Christ, as corresponding to what we ought to have done but did not do, receive the value of saving acts culminating in the death on the cross. Thus he not only regards Jesus Christ as "salvation and saviour and saving" ("salus et salvator et salutare"),[1] but he also views his whole life as a work of salvation. All that has taken place between the conception and the ascension is an inner necessity in this work of salvation. This is a highly significant advance beyond the conception of the Apologists. Whilst in their case the history of Jesus seems to derive its importance almost solely from the fulfilment of prophecy, it acquires in Irenæus an independent and fundamental significance. Here also we recognise the influence of "Gnosis", nay, in many places he uses the same expressions as the Gnostics, when he sees salvation accomplished, on the one hand, in the mere appearance of Jesus Christ as the second Adam, and on the other, in the simple acknowledgment of this appearance.[2] But he is distinguished from them by the fact that he decidedly emphasises the personal acts of Jesus, and that he applies the benefits of Christ's work not to the "pneumatic" *ipso facto*, but in principle to all men, though practically only to those who listen to the Saviour's words and adorn themselves with works of righteousness.[3] Irenæus presented this work of Christ from various points of view. He regards it as

---

[1] See III. 10. 3.

[2] See the remarkable passage in IV. 36. 7: ἡ γνῶσις τοῦ υἱοῦ τοῦ Θεοῦ, ἥτις ἦν ἀφθαρσία. Another result of the Gnostic struggle is Irenæus' raising the question as to what new thing the Lord has brought (IV. 34. 1): "Si autem subit vos huiusmodi sensus, ut dicatis: Quid igitur novi dominus attulit veniens? cognoscite, quoniam omnem novitatem attulit semetipsum afferens, qui fuerat annuntiatus." The new thing is then defined thus: "Cum perceperunt eam quæ ab eo est libertatem et participant visionem eius et audierunt sermones eius et fruiti sunt muneribus ab eo, non iam requiretur, quid novius attulit rex super eos, qui annuntiaverunt adventum eius... Semetipsum enim attulit et ea quæ prædicta sunt bona."

[3] See IV. 36. 6: "Adhuc manifestavit oportere nos cum vocatione (*i.e.*, μετὰ τὴν κλῆσιν) et iustitiæ operibus adornari, uti requiescat super nos spiritus dei"— we must provide *ourselves* with the wedding garment.

the realisation of man's original destiny, that is, being in communion with God, contemplating God, being imperishable like
God; he moreover views it as the abolition of the consequences
of Adam's disobedience, and therefore as the redemption of men
from death and the dominion of the devil; and finally he looks
upon it as reconciliation with God. In all these conceptions
Irenæus fell back upon the *person* of Christ. Here, at the same
time, he is everywhere determined by the content of Biblical
passages; in fact it is just the New Testament that leads him
to these considerations, as was first the case with the Valentinians before him. How uncertain he still is as to their ecclesiastical importance is shown by the fact that he has no hesitation
in reckoning the question, as to why the Word of God became
flesh and suffered, among the articles that are a matter of consideration for science, but not for the simple faith (I. 10. 3).
Here, therefore, he still maintains the archaic standpoint according to which it is sufficient to adhere to the baptismal confession and wait for the second coming of Christ along with the
resurrection of the body. On the other hand, Irenæus did not
merely confine himself to describing the fact of redemption, its
content and its consequences; but he also attempted to explain
the peculiar nature of this redemption from the essence of God
and the incapacity of man, thus solving the question "cur deus
homo" in the highest sense. [1] Finally, he adopted from Paul
the thought that Christ's real work of salvation consists in his
death on the cross; and so he tried to amalgamate the two
propositions, *"filius dei filius hominis factus est propter nos"*
("the Son of God became Son of man for us") and "filius dei
passus est propter nos" ("the Son of God suffered for us") as
the most vital ones. He did not, however, clearly show which

---

[1] The incapacity of man is referred to in III. 18. 1: III. 21. 10; III. 21—23
shows that the same man that had fallen had to be led to communion with God;
V. 21. 3: V. 24. 4 teach that man had to overcome the devil; the intrinsic necessity of God's appearing as Redeemer is treated of in III. 23. 1: "Si Adam iam non
reverteretur ad vitam, sed in totum proiectus esset morti, victus esset deus et superasset
serpentis nequitia voluntatem dei. Sed quoniam deus invictus et magnanimis est,
magnanimem quidem se exhibuit etc." That the accomplishment of salvation must be
effected in a righteous manner, and therefore be as much a proof of the righteousness as of the immeasurable love and mercy of God, is shown in V. 1. 1: V. 21.

of these doctrines is the more important. Here the speculation of Irenæus is already involved in the same ambiguity as was destined to be the permanent characteristic of Church specula- tion as to Christ's work in succeeding times. For on the one hand, Paul led one to lay all the emphasis on the death on the cross, and on the other, the logical result of dogmatic thinking only pointed to the appearance of God in the flesh, but not to a particular work of Christ that had not been already in- volved in the appearance of the Divine Teacher himself. Still, Irenæus contrived to reconcile the discrepancy better than his successors, because, being in earnest with his idea of Christ as the second Adam, he was able to contemplate the whole life of Jesus as redemption in so far as he conceived it as a re- capitulation. We see this at once not only from his conception of the virgin birth as a fact of salvation, but also from his way of describing redemption as deliverance from the devil. For, as the birth of Christ from the Virgin Mary is the recapitulating counterpart of Adam's birth from the virgin earth, and as the obedience of the mother of Jesus is the counterpart of Eve's disobedience, so the story of Jesus' temptation is to him the recapitulating counterpart of the story of Adam's temptation. In the way that Jesus overcame the temptation by the devil (Matt. IV.) Irenæus already sees the redemption of mankind from Satan; even then Jesus bound the strong one. But, whereas the devil seized upon man unlawfully and deceitfully, no in- justice, untruthfulness, or violence is displayed in the means by which Jesus resisted Satan's temptation. [1] As yet Irenæus is quite as free from the thought that the devil has real rights upon man, as he is from the immoral idea that God accomplished his work of redemption by an act of deceit. But, on the strength of Pauline passages, many of his teachings rather view redemp- tion from the devil as accomplished by the *death* of Christ, and accordingly represent this death as a ransom paid to the "apostasy" for men who had fallen into captivity. He did not, however, develop this thought any further. [2]

---

[1] Irenæus demonstrated the view in V. 21 in great detail. According to his ideas in this chapter we must include the history of the temptation in the *regula fidei*.

[2] See particularly V. 1. 1: "Verbum potens et homo verus sanguine suo ratio-

His idea of the *reconciliation* of God is just as rudimentary,
and merely suggested by Biblical passages. He sometimes saw
the means of reconciliation solely in obedience and in the
"righteous flesh" as such, at other times in the "wood." Here
also the recapitulation theory again appears : through disobedience
at the tree Adam became a debtor to God, and through obedience at the tree God is reconciled.[1] But teachings as to vicarious suffering on the part of Christ are not found in Irenæus,

nabiliter redimens nos, redemptionem semetipsum dedit pro his, qui in captivitatem
ducti sunt ... dei verbum non deficiens in sua iustitia, iuste etiam adversus ipsam
conversus est apostasiam, ea quæ sunt sua redimens ab ea, non cum vi, quemadmodum
illa initio dominabatur nostri, ea quæ non erant sua insatiabiliter rapiens, sed
secundum suadelam, quemadmodum decebat deum suadentem et non vim inferentem,
accipere quæ vellet, ut neque quod est iustum confringeretur neque antiqua plasmatio
dei deperiret." We see that the idea of the blood of Christ as ransom does not
possess with Irenæus the value of a fully developed theory, but is suggestive of
one. But even in this form it appeared suspicious and, in fact, a Marcionite idea
to a Catholic teacher of the 3rd century. Pseudo-Origen (Adamantius) opposed it
by the following argument (De recta in deum fide, edid Wetstein 1673, Sectio I.
p. 38 sq. See Rufinus' translation in Caspari's Kirchenhistorische Anecdota Vol. I.
1883, p. 34 sq., which in many places has preserved the right sense): Τὸν πριω-
μενον ἔφης, εἶναι τὸν Χριστόν; ὁ πεπρακὼς τὶς ἐστιν; ἦλθεν εἰς σὲ ὁ ἁπλοῦς μῦθος·
ὅτι ὁ πωλῶν καὶ ὁ ἀγοράζων ἀδελφοί εἰσιν; εἰ κακός ὤν ὁ διάβολος τῷ ἀγαθῷ πέπρακεν,
οὐκ ἔστι κακὸς ἀλλὰ ἀγαθός· ὁ γὰρ ἀπ' ἀρχῆς φθονήσας τῷ ἀνθρώπῳ, νῦν οὐκ ἔτι
ὑπὸ φθόνου ἄγεται, τῷ ἀγαθῷ τὴν νομὴν παραδούς. ἔσται οὖν δίκαιος ὁ τοῦ φθόνου
καὶ παντὸς κακοῦ παυσάμενος. αὐτὸς γοῦν ὁ Θεὸς εὑρίσκεται πωλήσας· μᾶλλον δὲ
οἱ ἡμαρτηκότες ἑαυτοὺς ἀπηλλοτρίωσαν οἱ ἄνθρωποι διὰ τὰς ἁμαρτίας αὐτῶν· πάλιν
δὲ ἐλυτρώθησαν. διὰ τὴν εὐσπλαγχνίαν αὐτοῦ. τοῦτο γὰρ φήσιν ὁ προφήτης· Ταῖς ἁμαρτίαις ὑμῶν ἐπράθητε καὶ ταῖς ἀνομίαις ἐξαπέστειλα τὴν μητέρα ὑμῶν. Καὶ ἄλλος
πάλιν· Δωρεὰν ἐπράθητε, καὶ οὐ μετὰ ἀργυρίου λυτρωθήσεσθε. τὸ, οὐδὲ μετὰ ἀργυρίου·
δηλονότι, τοῦ αἵματος τοῦ Χριστοῦ. τοῦτο γὰρ φάσκει ὁ προφήτης (Isaiah, LIII. 5
follows). Εἰκὸς δὲ ὅτι κατὰ σὲ ἐπρίατο δοὺς ἑαυτοῦ τὸ αἷμα· πῶς οὖν καὶ ἐκ νεκρῶν
ἠγείρετο; εἰ γὰρ ὁ λαβὼν τὴν τιμὴν τῶν ἀνθρώπων, τὸ αἷμα, ἀπέδωκεν, οὐκέτι ἐπώλησεν.
Εἰ δὲ μὴ ἀπέδωκε, πῶς ἀνέστη Χριστός; οὐκέτι οὖν τό, Ἐξουσίαν ἔχω θεῖναι καὶ
ἐξουσίαν ἔχω λαβεῖν, ἵσταται; ὁ γοῦν διάβολος κατέχει τὸ αἷμα τοῦ Χριστοῦ ἀντὶ
τῆς τιμῆς τῶν ἀνθρώπων; πολλὴ βλασφήμιος ἄνοια! φεῦ τῶν κακῶν! Ἀπέθανεν, ἀνέστη
ὡς δυνατός· ἔθηκεν ὃ ἔλαβεν· αὕτη ποία πρᾶσις; τοῦ προφήτου λέγοντος· Ἀναστήτω
ὁ Θεὸς καὶ διασκορπισθήτωσαν οἱ ἐχθροὶ αὐτοῦ; Ὅπου ἀνάστασις, ἐκεῖ θάνατος!
That is an argument as acute as it is true and victorious.

[1] See Iren. V. 2, 3, 16. 3, 17—4. In III. 16. 9 he says : Christus per passionem
reconciliavit nos deo." It is moreover very instructive to compare the way in which
Irenæus worked out the recapitulation theory with the old proof from prophecy
("this happened that the Scripture might be fulfilled"). Here we certainly have an
advance; but at bottom the recapitulation theory may also be conceived as a
modification of that proof.

and his death is seldom presented from the point of view of
a sacrifice offered to God. [1] According to this author the reconciliation virtually consists in Christ's restoring man to communion and friendship with God and procuring forgiveness of
sins; he very seldom speaks of God being offended through
Adam's sin (V. 16. 3). But the incidental mention of the forgiveness of sins resulting from the redemption by Christ has
not the meaning of an *abolition* of sin. He connects the redemption with this only in the form of Biblical and rhetorical
phrases; for the vital point with him is the abolition of the
*consequences* of sin, and particularly of the sentence of death. [2]
Here we have the transition to the conception of Christ's work
which makes this appear more as a completion than as a restoration. In this connection Irenæus employed the following
categories: *restoring of the likeness of God in humanity; abolition of death; connection and union of man with God; adoption
of men as sons of God and as gods; imparting of the Spirit
who now becomes accustomed to abide with men;* [3] *imparting
of a knowledge of God culminating in beholding him; bestowal
of everlasting life.* All these are only the different aspects of
one and the same blessing, which, being of a divine order,
could only be brought to us and implanted in our nature by
God himself. But inasmuch as this view represents Christ not
as performing a reconciling but a perfecting work, his *acts* are

---

[1] See, *e.g.*, IV. 5. 4: προθύμως 'Αβραὰμ τὸν ἴδιον μονογενῆ καὶ ἀγαπητὸν παρα-
χωρήσας θυσίαν τῷ Θεῷ, ἵνα καὶ ὁ Θεὸς εὐδοκήσῃ ὑπὲρ τοῦ σπέρματος αὐτοῦ παντὸς
τὸν ἴδιον μονογενῆ καὶ ἀγαπητὸν υἱὸν θυσίαν παρασχεῖν εἰς λύτρωσιν ἡμετέραν.

[2] There are not a few passages where Irenæus said that Christ has annihilated
sin, abolished Adam's disobedience, and introduced righteousness through his
obedience (III. 18. 6, 7 : III. 20. 2 : V. 16—21); but he only once tried to explain
how that is to be conceived (III. 18. 7), and then merely reproduced Paul's thoughts.

[3] Irenæus has no hesitation in calling the Christian who has received the Spirit
of God the perfect, the spiritual one, and in representing him, in contrast to the
false Gnostic, as he who in truth judges all men, Jews, heathen, Marcionites, and
Valentinians, but is himself judged by no one; see the great disquisition in IV. 33
and V. 9. 10. This true Gnostic, however, is only to be found where we meet
with right faith in God the Creator, sure conviction with regard to the God-man
Jesus Christ, true knowledge as regards the Holy Spirit and the economy of
salvation, the apostolic doctrine, the right Church system in accordance with the
episcopal succession, the intact Holy Scripture, and its uncorrupted text and interpretation (IV. 33. 7, 8). To him the true believer is the real Gnostic.

thrust more into the background; his work is contained in his constitution as the God-man.   Hence this work has a universal significance for all men, not only as regards the present, but as regards the past from Adam downwards, in so far as they "according to their virtue in their generation have not only feared but also loved God, and have behaved justly and piously towards their neighbours, and have longed to see Christ and to hear his voice." [1]   Those redeemed by Jesus are immediately joined by him into a unity, into the true humanity, the Church, whose head he himself is. [2]   This Church is the communion of the Sons of God, who have attained to a contemplation of him and have been gifted with everlasting life.   In this the work of Christ the God-man is fulfilled.

In Tertullian and Hippolytus, as the result of New Testament exegesis, we again find the same aspects of Christ's work as in Irenæus, only with them the mystical form of redemption recedes into the background. [3]

[1] See IV. 22.  In accordance with the recapitulation theory Christ must also have descended to the lower world.   There he announced forgiveness of sins to the righteous, the patriarchs and prophets (IV. 27. 2).   For this, however, Irenæus was not able to appeal to Scripture texts, but only to statements of a presbyter. It is nevertheless expressly asserted, on the authority of Rom. III. 23, that these pre-Christian just men also could only receive justification and the light of salvation through the arrival of Christ among them.

[2] See III. 16. 6: "In omnibus autem est et homo plasmatio dei; et hominem ergo in semetipsum recapitulans est, invisibilis visibilis factus, et incomprehensibilis factus comprehensibilis et impassibilis passibilis, et verbum homo, universa in semetipsum recapitulans, uti sicut in supercælestibus et spiritalibus et invisibilibus princeps est verbum dei, sic et in visibilibus et corporalibus principatum habeat, in semetipsum primatum assumens et apponens semetipsum caput ecclesiæ, universa attrahat ad semetipsum apto in tempore."

[3] There are innumerable passages where Tertullian has urged that the whole work of Christ is comprised in the death on the cross, and indeed that this death was the aim of Christ's mission.  See, e.g., de pat. 3: "Taceo quod figitur; in hoc enim venerat"; de bapt. 11: "Mors nostra dissolvi non potuit, nisi domini passione, nec vita restitui sine resurrectione ipsius"; adv. Marc. III. 8: "Si mendacium deprehenditur Christi caro . . . nec passiones Christi fidem merebuntur. Eversum est igitur totum dei opus. Totum Christiani nominis et pondus et fructus, mors Christi, negatur, quam tam impresse apostolus demendat, utique veram, summum eam fundamentum evangelii constituens et salutis nostræ et prædictionis suæ, 1 Cor. XV. 3, 4; he follows Paul here.   But on the other hand he has also adopted from Irenæus the mystical conception of redemption—the constitution of

Nevertheless the *eschatology* as set forth by Irenæus in the fifth Book by no means corresponds to this conception of the work of Christ as a restoring and completing one; it rather appears as a remnant of antiquity directly opposed to the

Christ is the redemption—though with a rationalistic explanation. See adv. Marc. II. 27: "filius miscens in semetipso hominem et deum, ut tantum homini conferat, quantum deo detrahit. Conversabatur deus, ut homo divina agere doceretur. Ex æquo agebat deus cum homine, ut homo ex æquo agere cum deo posset." Here therefore the meaning of the divine manhood of the Redeemer virtually amounts to divine teaching. In de resurr. 63 Christ is called "fidelissimus sequester dei et hominum, qui et homini deum et hominem deo reddet." Note the future tense. It is the same with Hippolytus who in Philos. X. 34 represents the deification of men as the aim of redemption, but at the same time merely requires Christ as the lawgiver and teacher: "Καὶ ταῦτα μὲν ἐκφεύξῃ Θεὸν τὸν ὄντα διδαχθείς, ἕξεις δὲ ἀθάνατον τὸ σῶμα καὶ ἄφθαρτον ἅμα ψυχῇ, βασιλείαν οὐρανῶν ἀπολήψῃ, ὁ ἐν γῇ βιοὺς καὶ ἐπουράνιον βασιλέα ἐπιγνούς, ἔσῃ δὲ ὁμιλητὴς Θεοῦ καὶ συγκληρονόμος Χριστοῦ, οὐκ ἐπιθυμίαις ἢ πάθεσι καὶ νόσοις δουλούμενος. Γέγονας γὰρ Θεός· ὅσα γὰρ ὑπέμεινας πάθη ἄνθρωπος ὤν, ταῦτα ἐδίδου, ὅτι ἄνθρωπος εἶς, ὅσα δὲ παρακολουθεῖ Θεῷ, ταῦτα παρέχειν ἐπήγγελται Θεός, ὅτι ἐθεοποιήθης, ἀθάνατος γεννηθείς. Τουτέστι τὸ Γνῶθι σεαυτόν, επιγνοὺς τὸν πεποιηκότα Θεόν. Τὸ γὰρ ἐπιγνῶναι ἑαυτὸν ἐπιγνωσθῆναι συμβέβηκε τῷ καλουμένῳ ὑπ᾽ αὐτοῦ. Μὴ φιλεχθρήσητε τοίνυν ἑαυτοῖς, ἄνθρωποι, μηδὲ τὸ παλινδρομεῖν διστάσητε. Χριστὸς γὰρ ἐστιν ὁ κατὰ πάντων Θεός, ὃς τὴν ἁμαρτίαν ἐξ ἀνθρώπων ἀπολύειν προέταξε, νέον τὸν παλαιὸν ἄνθρωπον ἀποτελῶν, εἰκόνα τοῦτον καλέσας ἀπ᾽ ἀρχῆς, διὰ τύπου τὴν εἰς σὲ ἐπιδεικνύμενος στοργήν, οὗ προστάγμασιν ὑπακούσας σεμνοῖς, καὶ ἀγαθοῦ ἀγαθὸς γενόμενος μιμητής, ἔσῃ ὅμοιος ὑπ᾽ αὐτοῦ τιμηθείς. Οὐ γὰρ πτωχεύει Θεὸς καὶ σὲ Θεὸν ποιήσας εἰς δόξαν αὐτοῦ." It is clear that with a conception like this, which became prevalent in the 3rd cen‧tury, Christ's death on the cross could have no proper significance; nothing but the Holy Scriptures preserved its importance. We may further remark that Tertullian used the expression "satisfacere deo" about men (see, *e.g.*, de bapt. 20; de pud. 9), but, so far as I know, not about the work of Christ. This expression is very frequent in Cyprian (for penances), and he also uses it about Christ. In both writers, moreover, we find "meritum" (*e.g.*, Scorp. 6) and "promereri deum". With them and with Novatian the idea of "culpa" is also more strongly emphasised than it is by the Eastern theologians. Cf. Novatian de trin. 10: "quoniam cum caro et sanguis non obtinere regnum dei scribitur, non carnis substantia damnata est, quæ divinis manibus ne periret, exstructa est, sed sola carnis *culpa* merito reprehensa est." Tertullian de bapt. 5 says: "Exempto reatu eximitur et pœna." On the other hand he speaks of fasting as "officia humiliationis", through which we can "inlicere" God. Among these Western writers the thought that God's anger must be appeased both by sacrifices and corresponding acts appears in a much more pronounced form than in Irenæus. This is explained by their ideas as practical churchmen and by their actual experiences in communities that were already of a very secular character. We may, moreover, point out in a general way that the views of Hippolytus are everywhere more strictly dependent on Scripture texts than those of Irenæus. That many of the latter's speculations are not

speculative interpretation of redemption, but protected by the *regula fidei*, the New Testament, especially Revelation, and the material hopes of the great majority of Christians. But it would be a great mistake to assume that Irenæus merely repeated the hopes of an earthly kingdom just because he still found them in tradition, and because they were completely rejected by the Gnostics and guaranteed by the *regula* and the New Testament.[1]

found in Hippolytus is simply explained by the fact that they have no clear scriptural basis; see Overbeck, Quæst, Hippol., Specimen p. 75, note 29. On a superficial reading Tertullian seems to have a greater variety of points of view than Irenæus; he has in truth fewer, he contrived to work the grains of gold transmitted to him in such a way as to make the form more valuable than the substance. But one idea of Tertullian, which is not found in Irenæus, and which in after times was to attain great importance in the East (after Origen's day) and in the West (after the time of Ambrosius), may be further referred to. We mean the notion that Christ is the bridegroom and the human soul (and also the human body) the bride. This theologoumenon owes its origin to a combination of two older ones, and subsequently received its Biblical basis from the Song of Solomon. The first of these older theologoumena is the Greek philosophical notion that the divine Spirit is the bridegroom and husband of the human soul. See the Gnostics (*e.g.*, the sublime description in the Excerpta ex Theodoto 27); Clem. ep. ad Jacob. 4. 6; as well as Tatian, Orat. 13; Tertull., de anima 41 fin.: "Sequitur animam nubentem spiritui caro; o beatum connubium"; and the still earlier Sap. Sal. VIII. 2 sq. An offensively realistic form of this image is found in Clem. Hom. III. 27: νύμφη γὰρ εστὶν ὁ πᾶς ἄνθρωπος, ὁπόταν τοῦ ἀληθοῦς προφήτου λευκῷ λόγῳ ἀληθείας σπειρόμενος φωτίζηται τὸν νοῦν. The second is the apostolic notion that the Church is the bride and the body of Christ. In the 2nd Epistle of Clement the latter theologoumenon is already applied in a modified form. Here it is said that humanity as the Church, that is human nature (the flesh), belongs to Christ as his Eve (c. 14; see also Ignat. ad Polyc. V. 2; Tertull. de monog. 11, and my notes on Διδαχή XI. 11). The conclusion that could be drawn from this, and that seemed to have a basis in certain utterances of Jesus, viz., that the individual human soul together with the flesh is to be designated as the bride of Christ, was, so far as I know, first arrived at by Tertullian de resurr. 63: "Carnem et spiritum iam in semetipso Christus fœderavit, sponsam sponso et sponsum sponsæ comparavit. Nam et si animam quis contenderit sponsam, vel dotis nomine sequetur animam caro . . . Caro est sponsa, quæ in Christo spiritum sponsum per sanguinem pacta est"; see also de virg. vel. 16. Notice, however, that Tertullian continually thinks of all souls together (all flesh together) rather than of the individual soul.

[1] By the *regula* inasmuch as the words "from thence he will come to judge the quick and the dead" had a fixed place in the confessions, and the belief in the *duplex adventus Christi* formed one of the most important articles of Church belief in contradistinction to Judaism and Gnosticism (see the collection of passages in Hesse, "das Muratorische Fragment", p. 112 f.). But the belief in the return of

The truth rather is that he as well as Melito, Hippolytus, Tertullian, Lactantius, Commodian, and Victorinus lived in these
hopes no less than did Papias, the Asia Minor Presbyters and
Justin.[1] But this is the clearest proof that all these theologians
were but half-hearted in their theology, which was forced upon
them, in defence of the traditional faith, by the historical situation in which they found themselves. The Christ, who will
shortly come to overcome Antichrist, overthrow the Roman
empire, establish in Jerusalem a kingdom of glory, and feed
believers with the fat of a miraculously fruitful earth, is in fact
a quite different being from the Christ who, as the incarnate

Christ to this world necessarily involved the hope of a kingdom of glory under
Christ upon earth, and without this hope is merely a rhetorical flourish.

[1] Cf. here the account already given in Book I., chap. 3, Vol. I., p. 167 ff., Book I.,
chap. 4, Vol. I., p. 261, Book II., chap. 3, Vol. I., p. 105 f. On Melito compare the
testimony of Polycrates in Eusebius, H. E. V. 24. 5, and the title of his lost work
περὶ τοῦ διαβόλου καὶ τῆς ἀποκαλύψεως Ἰωάννου." Chiliastic ideas are also found in the
epistle from Lyons in Eusebius, H. E. V. 1 sq. On Hippolytus see his work
"de Christo et Antichristo" and Overbeck's careful account (lc., p. 70 sq.) of the
agreement here existing between Irenæus and Hippolytus as well as of the latter's
chiliasm on which unfounded doubts have been cast. Overbeck has also, in my
opinion, shown the probability of chiliastic portions having been removed at a
later period both from Hippolytus' book and the great work of Irenæus. The extensive fragments of Hippolytus' commentary on Daniel are also to be compared
(and especially the portions full of glowing hatred to Rome lately discovered by
Georgiades). With reference to Tertullian compare particularly the writings adv.
Marc. III., adv. Jud., de resurrectione carnis, de anima, and the titles of the subsequently suppressed writings de paradiso and de spe fidelium. Further see Commodian, Carmen apolog., Lactantius, Instit. div., l. VII., Victorinus, Commentary on
the Apocalypse. It is very remarkable that Cyprian already set chiliasm aside;
cf. the conclusion of the second Book of the Testimonia and the few passages in
which he quoted the last chapters of Revelation. The Apologists were silent about
chiliastic hopes, Justin even denied them in Apol. I. 11, but, as we have remarked,
he gives expression to them in the Dialogue and reckons them necessary to complete
orthodoxy. The Pauline eschatology, especially several passages in 1 Cor. XV.
(see particularly verse 50), caused great difficulties to the Fathers from Justin downwards. See Fragm. Justini IV. a Methodio supped. in Otto, Corp. Apol. III., p. 254,
Iren. V. 9, Tertull. de resurr. 48 sq. According to Irenæus the heretics, who
completely abandoned the early-Christian eschatology, appealed to 1 Cor. XV. 50.
The idea of a kind of purgatory—a notion which does not originate with the
realistic but with the philosophical eschatology—is quite plainly found in Tertullian,
e.g., in de anima 57 and 58 ("modicum delictum illuc luendum"). He speaks in
several passages of stages and different places of bliss; and this was a universally
diffused idea (e.g., Scorp. 6).

God, has already virtually accomplished his work of imparting perfect knowledge and filling mankind with divine life and incorruptibility. The fact that the old Catholic Fathers have both Christs shows more clearly than any other the middle position that they occupy between the acutely hellenised Christianity of the theologians, *i.e.*, the Gnostics, and the old tradition of the Church. We have indeed seen that the twofold conception of Christ and his work dates back to the time of the Apostles, for there is a vast difference between the Christ of Paul and the Christ of the supposedly inspired Jewish Apocalypses; and also that the agency in producing this conjunction may be traced back to the oldest time; but the union of a precise Christological Gnosis, such as we find in Irenæus and Tertullian, with the retention in their integrity of the imaginative series of thoughts about Antichrist, Christ as the warrior hero, the double resurrection, and the kingdom of glory in Jerusalem, is really a historical novelty. There is, however, no doubt that the strength of the old Catholic theology in opposition to the Gnostics lies in the accomplishment of this union, which, on the basis of the New Testament, appeared to the Fathers possible and necessary. For it is not systematic consistency that secures the future of a religious conception within a church, but its elasticity, and its richness in dissimilar trains of thought. But no doubt this must be accompanied by a firm foundation, and this too the old Catholic Fathers possessed—the church system itself.

As regards the details of the eschatological hopes, they were fully set forth by Irenæus himself in Book V. Apart from the belief that the returning Nero would be the Antichrist, an idea spread in the West during the third century by the Sibylline verses and proved from Revelation, the later teachers who preached chiliastic hopes did not seriously differ from the Gallic bishop; hence the interpretation of Revelation is in its main features the same. It is enough therefore to refer to the fifth Book of Irenæus. [1] There is no need to show in detail that

---

[1] Irenæus begins with the resurrection of the body and the proofs of it (in opposition to Gnosticism). These proofs are taken from the omnipotence and goodness of God, the long life of the patriarchs, the translation of Enoch and

chiliasm leads to a peculiar view of history, which is as much
opposed to that resulting from the Gnostic theory of redemption, as this doctrine itself forbids the hope of a bliss to be
realised in an earthly kingdom of glory. This is not the proper
place to demonstrate to what extent the two have been blended,

Elijah, the preservation of Jonah and of the three men in the fiery furnace, the
essential nature of man as a temple of God to which the body also belongs, and
the resurrection of Christ (V. 3—7). But Irenæus sees the chief proof in the incarnation of Christ, in the dwelling of the Spirit with its gifts in us (V. 8—16),
and in the feeding of our body with the holy eucharist (V. 2. 3). Then he discusses the defeat of Satan by Christ (V. 21—23), shows that the powers that be
are set up by God, that the devil therefore manifestly lies in arrogating to himself the lordship of the world (V. 24), but that he acts as a rebel and robber in
attempting to make himself master of it. This brings about the transition to
Antichrist. The latter is possessed of the whole power of the devil, sums up in
himself therefore all sin and wickedness, and pretends to be Lord and God. He is
described in accordance with the Apocalypses of Daniel and John as well as according
to Matth. XXIV. and 2nd Thessalonians. He is the product of the 4th Kingdom
that is, the Roman empire; but at the same time springs from the tribe of Dan
(V. 30. 2), and will take up his abode in Jerusalem etc. The returning Christ
will destroy him, and the Christ will come back when 6000 years of the
world's history have elapsed; for "in as many days as the world was made, in so
many thousands of years will it be ended" (V. 28. 3). The seventh day is then
the great world Sabbath, during which Christ will reign with the saints of the
first resurrection after the destruction of Antichrist. Irenæus expressly argued
against such "as pass for orthodox, but disregard the order of the progress of the
righteous and know no stages of preparation for incorruptibility" (V. 31). By this
he means such as assume that after death souls immediately pass to God. On the
contrary he argues that these rather wait in a hidden place for the resurrection
which takes place on the return of Christ, after which the souls receive back their
bodies and men now restored participate in the Saviour's Kingdom (V. 31. 2).
This Kingdom on earth precedes the universal judgment; "for it is just that they
should also receive the fruits of their patience in the same creation in which they
suffered tribulation"; moreover, the promise made to Abraham that Palestine
would be given to him and to his seed, i.e., the Christians, must be fulfilled
(V. 32). There they will eat and drink with the Lord in the restored body (V. 33. 1),
sitting at a table covered with food (V. 33. 2) and consuming the produce of the
land, which the earth affords in miraculous fruitfulness. Here Irenæus appeals to
alleged utterances of the Lord of which he had been informed by Papias (V. 33. 3, 4).
The wheat will be so fat that lions lying peacefully beside the cattle will be able
to feed themselves even on the chaff (V. 33. 3, 4). Such and similar promises are
everywhere to be understood in a literal sense. Irenæus here expressly argues
against any figurative interpretation (ibid. and V. 35). He therefore adopted the
whole Jewish eschatology, the only difference being that he regards the Church as
the seed of Abraham. The earthly Kingdom is then followed by the second resurrection, the general judgment, and the final end.

and how the chiliastic scheme of history has been emptied of its content and utilised in the service of theological apologetics. But the Gnostics were not the only opponents of chiliasm. Justin, even in his time, knew orthodox Christians who refused to believe in an earthly kingdom of Christ in Jerusalem, and Irenæus (V. 33 ff.), Tertullian, and Hippolytus [1] expressly argued against these. Soon after the middle of the second century, we hear of an ecclesiastical party in Asia Minor, which not only repudiated chiliasm, but also rejected the Revelation of John as an untrustworthy book, and subjected it to sharp criticism. These were the so-called Alogi. [2] But in the second century such Christians were still in the minority in the Church. It was only in the course of the third century that chiliasm was almost completely ousted in the East. This was the result of the Montanistic controversy and the Alexandrian theology. In the West, however, it was only threatened. In this Church the first literary opponent of chiliasm and of the Apocalypse appears to have been the Roman Presbyter Caius. But his polemic did not prevail. On the other hand the learned bishops of the East in the third century used their utmost efforts to combat and extirpate chiliasm. The information given to us by Eusebius (H. E. VII. 24), from the letters of Dionysius of Alexandria, about that father's struggles with whole communities in Egypt, who would not give up chiliasm, is of the highest interest. This account shews that wherever philosophical theology had not yet made its way the chiliastic hopes were not only cherished and defended against being explained away, but were emphatically regarded as Christianity itself. [3]    Cultured

---

[1] Hippolytus in the lost book ὑπὲρ τοῦ κατὰ Ἰωάννην εὐαγγελίου καὶ ἀποκαλύψεως. Perhaps we may also reckon Melito among the literary defenders of Chiliasm.

[2] See Epiph., H. 51, who here falls back on Hippolytus.

[3] In the Christian village communities of the district of Arsinoë the people would not part with chiliasm, and matters even went the length of an "apostasy" from the Alexandrian Church. A book by an Egyptian bishop, Nepos, entitled "Refutation of the allegorists" attained the highest repute. "They esteem the law and the prophets as nothing, neglect to follow the Gospels, think little of the Epistles of the Apostles, and on the contrary declare the doctrine set forth in this book to be a really great secret. They do not permit the simpler brethren among us to obtain

theologians were able to achieve the union of chiliasm and religious philosophy; but the "simplices et idiotæ" could only understand the former.  As the chiliastic hopes were gradually obliged to recede in exactly the same proportion as philosophic theology became naturalised, so also their subsidence denotes the progressive tutelage of the laity.  The religion they understood was taken from them, and they received in return a faith they could not understand; in other words, the old faith and the old hopes decayed of themselves and the *authority* of a mysterious faith took their place.  In this sense the extirpation or decay of chiliasm is perhaps the most momentous fact in the history of Christianity in the East.  With chiliasm men also lost the living faith in the nearly impending return of Christ, and the consciousness that the prophetic spirit with its gifts is a real possession of Christendom.  Such of the old hopes as remained were at most particoloured harmless fancies which, when allowed by theology, were permitted to be added to dogmatics.  In the West, on the contrary, the millennial hopes retained their vigour during the whole third century; we know of no bishop there who would have opposed chiliasm.  With this, however, was preserved a portion of the earliest Christianity which was to exercise its effects far beyond the time of Augustine.

Finally, we have still to treat of the altered conceptions regarding the Old Testament which the creation of the New produced among the early-Catholic Fathers.  In the case of Barnabas and the Apologists we became acquainted with a theory of the Old Testament which represented it as the Chris-

---

a sublime and grand idea of the glorious and truly divine appearance of our Lord, of our resurrection from the dead as well as of the union and assimilation with him; but they persuade us to hope for things petty, perishable, and similar to the present in the kingdom of God." So Dionysius expressed himself, and these words are highly characteristic of his own position and that of his opponents; for in fact the whole New Testament could not but be thrust into the background in cases where the chiliastic hopes were really adhered to. Dionysius asserts that he convinced these Churches by his lectures; but chiliasm and material religious ideas were still long preserved in the deserts of Egypt. They were cherished by the monks; hence Jewish Apocalypses accepted by Christians are preserved in the Coptic and Ethiopian languages.

tian book of revelation and accordingly subjected it throughout to an allegorical process. Here nothing specifically new could be pointed out as having been brought by Christ. Sharply opposed to this conception was that of Marcion, according to which the whole Old Testament was regarded as the proclamation of a Jewish God hostile to the God of redemption. The views of the majority of the Gnostics occupied a middle position between the two notions. These distinguished different components of the Old Testament, some of which they traced to the supreme God himself and others to intermediate and malevolent beings. In this way they both established a connection between the Old Testament, and the Christian revelation and contrived to show that the latter contained a specific novelty. This historico-critical conception, such as we specially see it in the epistle of Ptolemy to Flora, could not be accepted by the Church because it abolished strict monotheism and endangered the proof from prophecy. No doubt, however, we already find in Justin and others the beginning of a compromise, in so far as a distinction was made between the moral law of nature contained in the Old Testament—the Decalogue—and the ceremonial law; and in so far as the literal interpretation of the latter, for which a pedagogic significance was claimed, was allowed in addition to its typical or Christian sense. With this theory it was possible, on the one hand, to do some sort of justice to the historical position of the Jewish people, and on the other, though indeed in a meagre fashion, to give expression to the novelty of Christianity. The latter now appears as the *new* law or the law of freedom, in so far as the moral law of nature had been restored in its full purity without the burden of ceremonies, and a particular historical relation to God was allowed to the Jewish nation, though indeed more a wrathful than a covenant one. For the ceremonial regulations were conceived partly as tokens of the judgment on Israel, partly as concessions to the stiffneckedness of the people in order to protect them from the worst evil, polytheism.

Now the struggle with the Gnostics and Marcion, and the creation of a New Testament had necessarily a double consequence. On the one hand, the proposition that the "Father of

Jesus Christ is the creator of the world and the God of the
Old Testament" required the strictest adherence to the unity
of the two Testaments, so that the traditional apologetic view
of the older book had to undergo the most rigid development;
on the other hand, as soon as the New Testament was created,
it was impossible to avoid seeing that this book was superior
to the earlier one, and thus the theory of the novelty of the
Christian doctrine worked out by the Gnostics and Marcion had
in some way or other to be set forth and demonstrated. We
now see the old Catholic Fathers engaged in the solution of
this twofold problem; and their method of accomplishing it has
continued to be the prevailing one in all Churches up to the
present time, in so far as the ecclesiastical and dogmatic practice still continues to exhibit the inconsistencies of treating the
Old Testament as a Christian book in the strict sense of the
word and yet elevating the New above it, of giving a typical
interpretation to the ceremonial law and yet acknowledging that
the Jewish people had a covenant with God.

With regard to the first point, viz., the maintenance of the
unity of the two Testaments, Irenæus and Tertullian gave a
most detailed demonstration of it in opposition to Marcion,[1]
and primarily indeed with the same means as the older teachers
had already used. It is Christ that prophesied and appeared
in the Old Testament; he is the householder who produced
both Old and New Testaments.[2] Moreover, as the two have
the same origin, their meaning is also the same. Like Barnabas
the early-Catholic Fathers contrived to give all passages in the
Old Testament a typical Christian sense: it is the same truth
which we can learn from the prophets and again from Christ
and the Apostles. With regard to the Old Testament the watchword is: "Seek the type" ("Typum quæras").[3] But they went

[1] See Irenæus lib. IV. and Tertull. adv. Marc. lib. II. and III.

[2] It would be superfluous to quote passages here; two may stand for all. Iren.
IV. 9. 1: "Utraque testamenta unus et idem paterfamilias produxit, verbum dei,
dominus noster Iesus Christus, qui et Abrahæ et Moysi collocutus est." Both Testaments are "unius et eiusdem substantiæ." IV. 2. 3: "Moysis literæ sunt verba
Christi."

[3] See Iren. IV. 31. 1.

a step further still. In opposition to Marcion's antitheses and
his demonstration that the God of the Old Testament is a
petty being and has enjoined petty, external observances, they
seek to show in syntheses that the same may be said of the
New. (See Irenæus IV. 21—36). The effort of the older teachers
to exclude everything outward and ceremonial is no longer met
with to the same extent in Irenæus and Tertullian, at least
when they are arguing and defending their position against the
Gnostics. This has to be explained by two causes. In the first
place Judaism (and Jewish Christianity) was at bottom no longer
an enemy to be feared; they therefore ceased to make such
efforts to avoid the "Jewish" conception of the Old Testament.
Irenæus, for example, emphasised in the most naïve manner the
observance of the Old Testament law by the early Apostles
and also by Paul. This is to him a complete proof that they
did not separate the Old Testament God from the Christian
Deity. [1] In connection with this we observe that the radical
antijudaism of the earliest period more and more ceases. Irenæus and Tertullian admitted that the Jewish nation had a
covenant with God and that the literal interpretation of the Old
Testament was justifiable. Both repeatedly testified that the
Jews had the right doctrine and that they only lacked the
knowledge of the Son. These thoughts indeed do not attain
clear expression with them because their works contain no
systematic discussions involving these principles. In the second
place the Church itself had become an institution where sacred
ceremonial injunctions were necessary; and, in order to find
a basis for these, they had to fall back on Old Testament
commandments (see Vol. I., chap. 6, p. 291 ff.). In Tertullian we find this only in its most rudimentary form; [2] but in

---

[1] Iren. III. 12. 15 (on Gal. II. 11 f.): Sic apostoli, quos universi actus et
universæ doctrinæ dominus testes fecit, religiose agebant circa dispositionem legis,
qnæ est secundum Moysem, ab uno et eodem significantes esse deo"; see Overbeck "Ueber die Auffassung des Streits des Paulus mit Petrus bei den Kirchenvätern," 1877, p. 8 f. Similar remarks are frequent in Irenæus.

[2] Cf., e.g., de monog. 7: " Certe sacerdotes sumus a Christo vocati, monoga-
miæ debitores, ex pristina dei lege, quæ nos tunc in suis sacerdotibus prophetavit."
Here also Tertullian's Montanism had an effect. Though conceiving the directions
of the Paraclete as *new legislation*, the Montanists would not renounce the view

the course of the third century these needs grew mightily [1] and were satisfied. In this way the Old Testament threatened to become an authentic book of revelation to the Church, and that in a quite different and much more dangerous sense than was formerly the case with the Apostolic Fathers and the Apologists.

With reference to the second point, we may remark that just when the decay of antijudaism, the polemic against Marcion, and the new needs of the eccleciastical system threatened the Church with an estimate of the Old Testament hitherto unheard of, the latter was nevertheless thrust back by the creation and authority of the New Testament, and this consequently revived the uncertain position in which the sacred book was henceforth to remain. Here also, as in every other case, the development in the Church ends with the *complexus oppositorum*, which nowhere allows all the conclusions to be drawn, but offers the great advantage of removing every perplexity up to a certain point. The early-Catholic Fathers adopted from Justin the distinction between the Decalogue, as the moral law of nature, and the ceremonial law; whilst the oldest theologians (the Gnostics) and the New Testament suggested to them the thought of the (relative) novelty of Christianity and therefore also of the New Testament. Like Marcion they acknowledged the literal sense of the ceremonial law and God's covenant with the Jews; and they sought to sum up and harmonise all these features in the thought of an economy of salvation and of a history of salvation. This economy and history of salvation which contained the conception of a divine *accommodation and pedagogy*, and which accordingly distinguished between constituent parts of different degrees of value (in the Old Testament also), is the great result presented in the main work of Irenæus and accepted by Tertullian. It is to exist beside the proof from prophecy without modifying it; [2] and thus appears as something inter-

that these laws were in some way already indicated in the written documents of revelation.

[1] Very much may be made out with regard to this from Origen's works and the later literature, particularly from Commodian and the Apostolic Constitutions, lib. I.—VI.

[2] Where Christians needed the proof from prophecy or indulged in a devotional

mediate between the Valentinian conception that destroyed the
unity of origin of the Old Testament and the old idea which
neither acknowledged various constituents in the book nor recognised the peculiarities of Christianity. We are therefore justified in regarding this history of salvation approved by the
Church, as well as the theological propositions of Irenæus and
Tertullian generally, as a Gnosis "toned down" and reconciled
with Monotheism. This is shown too in the faint gleam of a
historical view that still shines forth from this "history of salvation" as a remnant of that bright light which may be recognised in the Gnostic conception of the Old Testament.[1]  Still,
it is a striking advance that Irenæus has made beyond Justin and
especially beyond Barnabas. No doubt it is mythological history
that appears in this history of salvation and the recapitulating
story of Jesus with its saving facts that is associated with it;
and it is a view that is not even logically worked out, but ever
and anon crossed by the proof from prophecy; yet for all that
it is development and history.

The fundamental features of Irenæus' conception are as
follow: The Mosaic law and the New Testament dispensation
of grace both emanated from one and the same God, *and were
granted for the salvation of the human race in a form appropriate to the times.*[2]  The two are in part different; but the
difference must be conceived as due to causes[3] that do not
affect the unity of the author and of the main points.[4]  We
must make the nature of God and the nature of man our point
of departure.  God is always the same, man is ever advancing
towards God; God is always the giver, man always the receiver;[5]

application of the Old Testament, everything indeed remained as before, and every
Old Testament passage was taken for a Christian one, as has remained the case
even to the present day.

[1] With the chiliastic view of history this newly acquired theory has nothing
in common.

[2] Iren. III. 12. 11.

[3] See III. 12. 12.

[4] No *commutatio agnitionis* takes place, says Irenæus, but only an increased
gift (IV. 11. 3); for the knowledge of God the Creator is "principium ʋangelii."
(III. 11. 7).

[5] See IV. 11. 2 and other passages, *e.g.*, IV. 20. 7 : IV. 26. 1 : IV. 37. 7 : IV. 38. 1—4.

God leads us ever to the highest goal; man, however, is not
God from the beginning, but is destined to incorruptibility,
which he is to attain step by step, advancing from the childhood stage to perfection (see above, p. 267 f.). This progress,
conditioned by the nature and destination of man, is, however,
dependent on the revelation of God by his Son, culminating in
the incarnation of the latter and closing with the subsequent
bestowal of the Spirit on the human race. In Irenæus therefore
the place of the many different revelation-hypostases of the
Valentinians is occupied by the one God, who stoops to the
level of developing humanity, accommodates himself to it, guides
it, and bestows on it increasing revelations of grace. [1]  The
fundamental knowledge of God and the moral law of nature, *i.e.*,
natural morality, were already revealed to man and placed in
his heart [2] by the creator. He who preserves these, as for
example the patriarchs did, is justified. (In this case Irenæus
leaves Adam's sin entirely out of sight). But it was God's will
to bring men into a higher union with himself; wherefore his
Son descended to men from the beginning and accustomed himself to dwell among them. The patriarchs loved God and re-
frained from injustice towards their neighbours; hence it was
not necessary that they should be exhorted with the strict letter
of the law, since they had the righteousness of the law in themselves. [3] But, as far as the great majority of men are concerned,
they wandered away from God and fell into the sorriest condition. From this moment Irenæus, keeping strictly to the Old
Testament, only concerns himself with the Jewish people. These

---

[1] Several covenants I. 10. 3; four covenants (Adam, Noah, Moses, Christ)
III. 11. 8; the two Testaments (Law and New Covenant) are very frequently mentioned.

[2] This is very frequently mentioned; see *e.g.*, IV. 13. 1: "Et quia dominus
naturalia legis, per quæ homo iustificatur, quæ etiam ante legisdationem custo-
diebant qui fide iustificabantur et placebant deo non dissolvit etc." IV. 15. 1.

[3] Irenæus, as a rule, views the patriarchs as perfect saints; see III. 11. 8:
"Verbum dei illis quidem qui ante Moysem fuerunt patriarchis secundum divini-
tatem et gloriam colloquebatur", and especially IV. 16. 3. As to the Son's having
descended from the beginning and having thus appeared to the patriarchs also,
see IV. 6. 7. Not merely Abraham but all the other exponents of revelation knew
both the Father and the Son. Nevertheless Christ was also obliged to descend to
the lower world to the righteous, the prophets, and the patriarchs, in order to
bring them forgiveness of sins (IV. 27. 2).

are to him the representatives of humanity. It is only at this period that the training of the human race is given to them; but it is really the Jewish *nation* that he keeps in view, and through this he differs very decidedly from such as Barnabas. [1] When righteousness and love to God died out in Egypt, God led his people forth so that man might again become a disciple and imitator of God. He gave him the written law (the Decalogue), which contains nothing else than the moral law of nature that had fallen into oblivion. [2] But when they made to themselves a golden calf and chose to be slaves rather than free men, then the Word, through the instrumentality of Moses, gave to them, as a particular addition, the commandments of slavery (the ceremonial law) in a form suitable for their training. These were bodily commandments of bondage which did not separate them from God, but held them in the yoke. The ceremonial law was thus a pedagogic means of preserving the people from idolatry; but it was at the same time a type of the future. Each constituent of the ceremonial law has this double signification, and both of these meanings originate with God, *i.e.*, with Christ; for "how is Christ the end of the law, if he be not the beginning of it?" ("quomodo finis legis Christus, si non et initium eius esset") IV. 12. 4. Everything in the law is therefore holy, and moreover we are only entitled to blame such portions of the history of the Jewish nation as Holy Scripture itself condemns. This nation was obliged to circumcise itself, keep Sabbaths, offer up sacrifices, and do whatever is related of it, so far as its action is not censured. All this belonged to the state of bondage in which men had a *covenant* with God and in which they also possessed

---

[1] On the contrary he agrees with the teachings of a presbyter, whom he frequently quotes in the 4th Book. To Irenæus the heathen are simply idolaters who have even forgotten the law written in the heart; wherefore the Jews stand much higher, for they only lacked the *agnitio filii*. See III. 5. 3 : III. 10. 3 : III. 12. 7 IV. 23, 24. Yet there is still a great want of clearness here. Irenæus cannot get rid of the following contradictions. The pre-Christian righteous know the Son and do not know him; they require the appearance of the Son and do not require it; and the *agnitio filii* seems sometimes a new, and in fact the decisive, *veritas*, and sometimes that involved in the knowledge of God the Creator.

[2] Irenæus IV. 16. 3. See IV. 15. 1: "Decalogum si quis non fecerit, non habet salutem".

the right faith in the one God and were taught before hand to
follow his Son (IV. 12, 5 ; "lex prædocuit hominem sequi oportere
Christum "). In addition to this, Christ continually manifested
himself to the people in the prophets, through whom also he
indicated the future and prepared men for his appearance. In
the prophets the Son of God accustomed men to be instruments
of the Spirit of God and to have fellowship with the Father in
them; and in them he habituated himself to enter bodily into
humanity. [1] Hereupon began the last stage, in which men, being
now sufficiently trained, were to receive the "testamentum libertatis" and be adopted as Sons of God. By the union of the
Son of God with the flesh the *agnitio filii* first became possible
to all; that is the fundamental novelty. The next problem was
to restore the law of freedom. Here a threefold process was
necessary. In the first place the Law of Moses, the Decalogue,
had been disfigured and blunted by the "traditio seniorum".
First of all then the pure moral law had to be restored; secondly,
it was now necessary to extend and fulfil it by expressly searching out the inclinations of the heart in all cases, thus unveiling
the law in its whole severity; and lastly the *particularia legis*,
*i.e.*, the law of bondage, had to be abolished. But in the latter

---

[1] As the Son has manifested the Father from of old, so also the law, and indeed
even the ceremonial law, is to be traced back to him. See IV. 6. 7 : IV. 12. 4 :
IV. 14. 2 : "his qui inquieti erant in eremo dans aptissimam legem . . . per omnes
transiens verbum omni conditioni congruentem et aptam legem conscribens ". IV.
4. 2. The law is a law of bondage; it was just in that capacity that it was
necessary; see IV. 4. 1 : IV. 9. 1 : IV. 13. 2, 4 : IV. 14. 3 : IV. 15 : IV. 16 : IV.
32 : IV. 36. A part of the commandments are concessions on account of hard-
ness of heart (IV. 15. 2). But Irenæus still distinguishes very decidedly between
the "people" and the prophets. This is a survival of the old view. The prophets
he said knew very well of the coming of the Son of God and the granting of a
new covenant (IV. 9. 3 : IV. 20. 4, 5 : IV. 33. 10); they understood what was
typified by the ceremonial law, and to them accordingly the law had only a typical signification. Moreover, Christ himself came to them ever and anon through
the prophetic spirit. The preparation for the new covenant is therefore found in
the prophets and in the typical character of the old. Abraham has this peculiarity, that both Testaments were prefigured in him: the Testament of faith, because he was justified before his circumcision, and the Testament of the law. The
latter occupied "the middle times", and therefore come in between (IV. 25. 1).
This is a Pauline thought, though otherwise indeed there is not much in Irenæus
to remind us of Paul, because he used the moral categories, *growth* and *training*,
instead of the religious ones, *sin* and *grace*.

connection Christ and the Apostles themselves avoided every transgression of the ceremonial law, in order to prove that this also had a divine origin. The non-observance of this law was first permitted to the Gentile Christians, Thus, no doubt, Christ himself is the end of the law, but only in so far as he has abolished the law of bondage and restored the moral law in its whole purity and severity, and given us himself.

The question as to the difference between the New Testament and the Old is therefore answered by Irenæus in the following manner. It consists (1) in the *agnitio filii* and consequent transformation of the slaves into children of God; and (2) in the restoration of the law, which is a law of freedom just because it excludes bodily commandments, and with stricter interpretation lays the whole stress on the inclinations of the heart. [1] But in

---

[1] The law, *i.e.*, the ceremonial law, reaches down to John, IV. 4. 2. The New Testament is a law of freedom, because through it we are adopted as sons of God, III. 5. 3 : III. 10. 5 : III. 12. 5 : III. 12. 14 : III. 15. 3 : IV. 9. 1, 2 : IV. 11. 1 : IV. 13. 2, 4 : IV. 15. 1, 2 : IV. 16. 5 : IV. 18 : IV. 32 : IV. 34. 1 : IV. 36. 2 Christ did not abolish the *naturalia legis*, the Decalogue, but extended and fulfilled them; here the old Gentile-Christian moral conception based on the Sermon on the Mount, prevails. Accordingly Irenæus now shows that in the case of the children of freedom the situation has become much more serious, and that the judgments are now much more threatening. Finally, he proves that the fulfilling, extending, and sharpening of the law form a contrast to the blunting of the natural moral law by the Pharisees and elders; see IV. 12. 1 ff.: "Austero dei præcepto miscent seniores aquatam traditionem". IV. 13. 1. f.: "Christus naturalia legis (which are summed up in the commandment of love) extendit et implevit... plenitudo et extensio... necesse fuit, auferri quidem vincula servitutis, superextendi vero decreta libertatis". That is proved in the next passage from the Sermon on the Mount: we must not only refrain from evil works, but also from evil desire. IV. 16. 5: "Hæc ergo, quæ in servitutem et in signum data sunt illis, circumscripsit novo libertatis testamento. Quæ autem naturalia et liberalia et communia omnium, auxit et dilatavit, sine invidia largiter donans hominibus per adoptionem, patrem scire deum... auxit autem etiam timorem: filios enim plus timere oportet quam servos". IV. 27. 2. The new situation is a more serious one; the Old Testament believers have the death of Christ as an antidote for their sins, "propter eos vero, qui nunc peccant, Christus non iam morietur". IV. 28. 1 f.: under the old covenant God punished "typice et temporaliter et mediocrius", under the new, on the contrary, "vere et semper et austerius"... as under the new covenant "fides aucta est", so also it is true that "diligentia conversationis adaucta est". The imperfections of the law, the "particularia legis", the law of bondage have been abolished by Christ, see specially IV. 16, 17, for the types are now fulfilled; but Christ and the Apostles did not transgress the law; freedom was first granted to the Gentile Christians (III. 12) and circumcision and foreskin united

these two respects he finds a real addition, and hence, in his
opinion, the Apostles stand higher than the prophets. He proves
this higher position of the Apostles by a surprising interpretation of 1 Cor. XII. 28, conceiving the prophets named in that
passage to be those of the Old Testament. [1] He therefore views
the two Testaments as of the same nature, but " greater is
the legislation which confers liberty than that which brings
bondage" ("maior est legisdatio quæ in libertatem, quam quæ
data est in servitutem"). Through the two covenants the accomplishment of salvation was to be hastened "for there is one
salvation and one God; but the precepts that form man are
numerous, and the steps that lead man to God are not a few ;
("una est enim salus et unus deus ; quæ autem formant hominem,
præcepta multa et non pauci gradus, qui adducunt hominem ad
deum"). A worldly king can increase his benefits to his subjects ;
and should it not also be lawful for God, though he is always
the same, to honour continually with greater gifts those who
are well pleasing to him? (IV. 9. 3). Irenæus makes no direct
statement as to the further importance which the Jewish people
have, and in any case regards them as of no consequence
after the appearance of the covenant of freedom. Nor does this
nation appear any further even in the chiliastic train of thought.
It furnishes the Antichrist and its holy city becomes the capital
of Christ's earthly kingdom; but the nation itself, which, according
to this theory, had represented all mankind from Moses to Christ,
just as if all men had been Jews, now entirely disappears. [2]

This conception, in spite of its want of stringency, made an
immense impression, and has continued to prevail down to the
present time. It has, however, been modified by a combination

(III. 5. 3). But Irenæus also proved how little the old and new covenants contradict each other by showing that the latter also contains concessions that have
been granted to the frailty of man; see IV. 15. 2 (1 Cor. VII.).

[1] See III. 11. 4. There too we find it argued that John the Baptist was not
merely a prophet, but also an Apostle.

[2] From Irenæus' statement in IV. 4 about the significance of the city of Jerusalem
we can infer what he thought of the Jewish nation. Jerusalem is to him the vine-
branch on which the fruit has grown ; the latter having reached maturity, the branch
is cut off and has no further importance.

with the Augustinian doctrine of sin and grace. It was soon
reckoned as Paul's conception, to which in fact it has a distant relationship. Tertullian had already adopted it in its essential features,
amplified it in some points, and, in accordance with his Montanist
ideas, enriched it by adding a fourth stage (ab initio—Moses—
Christ—Paraclete). But this addition was not accepted by the
Church.[1]

---

[1] No special treatment of Tertullian is required here, as he only differs from
Irenæus in the additions he invented as a Montanist. Yet this is also prefigured in
Irenæus' view that the concessions of the Apostles had rendered the execution of
the stern new law more easy. A few passages may be quoted here. De orat. 1 :
Quidquid retro fuerat, aut demutatum est (per Christum), ut circumcisio, aut sup-
pletum ut reliqua lex, aut impletum ut prophetia, aut perfectum ut fides ipsa. Omnia
de carnalibus in spiritalia renovavit nova dei gratia superducto evangelio, expunctore
totius retro vetustatis." (This differentiation strikingly reminds us of the letter of
Ptolemy to Flora. Ptolemy distinguishes those parts of the law that originate with
God, Moses, and the elders. As far as the divine law is concerned, he again
distinguishes what Christ had to complete, what he had to supersede and what he
had to spiritualise, that is, perficere, solvere, demutare). In the *regula fidei* (de
præscr. 13): "Christus prædicavit novam legem et novam promissionem regni cœlorum"; see the discussions in adv. Marc. II., III., and adv. Iud.; de pat. 6 : "am-
plianda adimplendaque lex." Scorp. 3, 8, 9; ad uxor. 2 ; de monog. 7 : "Et quoniam
quidam interdum nihil sibi dicunt esse cum lege, quam Christus non dissolvit, sed
adimplevit, interdum quæ volunt legis arripiunt (he himself did that continually),
plane et nos sic dicimus legem, ut onera quidem eius, secundum sententiam apostolorum, quæ nec patres sustinere valuerunt, concesserint, quæ vero ad iustitiam
spectant, non tantum reservata permaneant, verum et ampliata." That the new law
of the new covenant is the moral law of nature in a stricter form, and that the
concessions of the Apostle Paul cease in the age of the Paraclete, is a view we find
still more strongly emphasised in the Montanist writings than in Irenæus. In ad
uxor. 3 Tertullian had already said: "Quod permittitur, bonum non est," and this
proposition is the theme of many arguments in the Montanist writings. But the
intention of finding a basis for the laws of the Paraclete, by showing that they
existed in some fashion even in earlier times, involved Tertullian in many contradictions. It is evident from his writings that Montanists and Catholics in Carthage
alternately reproached each other with judaising tendencies and an apostasy to
heathen discipline and worship. Tertullian, in his enthusiasm for Christianity, came
into conflict with all the authorities which he himself had set up. In the questions
as to the relationship of the Old Testament to the New, of Christ to the Apostles,
of the Apostles to each other, of the Paraclete to Christ and the Apostles, he was
also of necessity involved in the greatest contradictions. This was the case not
only because he went more into details than Irenæus; but, above all, because the
chains into which he had thrown his Christianity were felt to be such by himself.
This theologian had no greater opponent than himself, and nowhere perhaps is
this so plain as in his attitude to the two Testaments. Here, in every question of

## 3. Results to ecclesiastical Christianity.

As we have shown, Irenæus, Tertullian, and Hippolytus had
no strictly systematised theology; they formulated theological
propositions because their opponents were theologians.   Hence
the result of their labours, so far as this was accepted by the
Western Church of the third century, does not appear in the
adoption of a systematic philosophical dogmatic, but in theological fragments, namely, the rule of faith fixed and interpreted
in an antignostic sense. [1]  As yet the rule of faith and theology
nowhere came into collision in the Western Churches of the
third century, because Irenæus and his younger contemporaries
did not themselves notice any such discrepancies, but rather
imagined all their teachings to be expositions of the faith itself,
and did not trouble their heads about inconsistencies.   If we

detail, Tertullian really repudiated the proposition from which he starts. In reference
to one point, namely, that the Law and the prophets extend down to John, see
Nöldechen's article in the Zeitschrift für wissenschaftliche Theologie, 1885,
p. 333 f. On the one hand, in order to support certain trains of thought, Tertullian
required the proposition that prophecy extended down to John (see also the
Muratorian Fragment: completus numerus prophetarum", Sibyll. I. 386: καὶ τότε
δὴ παῦσις ἔσται μετέπειτα προφητῶν, scil. after Christ), and on the other, as
a Montanist, he was obliged to assert the continued existence of prophecy.   In
like manner he sometimes ascribed to the Apostles a unique possession of the
Holy Spirit, and at other times, adhering to a primitive Christian idea, he denied
this thesis. Cf. also Barth " Tertullian's Auffassung des Apostels Paulus und seines
Verhältnisses zu den Uraposteln" (Jahrbuch für protestantische Theologie, Vol. III.
p. 706 ff.). Tertullian strove to reconcile the principles of early Christianity with
the authority of ecclesiastical tradition and philosophical apologetics. Separated from
the general body of the Church, and making ever increasing sacrifices for the
early-Christian enthusiasm, as he understood it, he wasted himself in the solution
of this insoluble problem.

[1] In addition to this, however, they definitely established within the Church the
idea that there is a "Christian" view in all spheres of life and in all questions
of knowledge. Christianity appears expanded to an immense, immeasurable breadth.
This is also Gnosticism.  Thus Tertullian, after expressing various opinions about
dreams, opens the 45th chapter of his work "de anima" with the words: "Tene-
mur hic de somniis quoque Christianam sententiam expromere".  Alongside of the
antignostic rule of faith as the "doctrine" we find the casuistic system of morality
and penance (the Church "disciplina") with its media of almsgiving, fasting, and
prayer; see Cypr, de op. et eleemos., but before that Hippol., Comm. in Daniel
('Εκκλ. 'Αληθ. 1886, p. 242): οἱ εἰς τὸ ὄνομα τοῦ Θεοῦ πιστεύοντες καὶ δι' ἀγαθοεργίας
τὸ πρόσωπον αὐτοῦ ἐξιλασκόμενοι.

wish to form a notion as to what ideas had become universally prevalent in the Church in the middle of the third century let us compare Cyprian's work "Testimonia", written for a layman, with Novatian's work "De Trinitate".

In the "Testimonia" the doctrine of the two Testaments, as developed by Irenæus, forms the framework in which the individual dogmas are set. The doctrine of God, which should have been placed at the beginning, has been left out in this little book probably because the person addressed required no instruction on the point. Some of the dogmas already belong to philosophical theology in the strict sense of the word; in others we have merely a precise assertion of the truth of certain facts. All propositions are, however, supported by passages from the two Testaments and thereby proved.[1] The theological counterpart to this is Novatian's work "De Trinitate". This first great Latin work that appeared in Rome is highly important. In regard to completeness, extent of Biblical proofs, and perhaps also its influence on succeeding times, it may in many respects be compared with Origen's work περὶ ἀρχῶν. Otherwise indeed it differs as much from that work, as the sober, meagre theology of the West, devoid of philosophy and speculation, differs in general from that of the East. But it sums up in classic fashion the doctrines of Western orthodoxy, the main features of which were sketched by Tertullian in his antignostic writings and the work against Praxeas. The old Roman symbol forms the basis of the work. In accordance with this the author gives a comprehensive exposition of his doctrine of God in the first eight chapters. Chapters 9—28 form the main portion; they establish the correct Christology in opposition to the heretics who look on Christ as a mere man or as the Father himself; the Holy Scriptures furnish the material for the proofs. Chapter 29 treats of the Holy Spirit. Chapters 30 and 31 contain the recapitulation and conclusion. The whole is based on Tertullian's treatise against Praxeas. No important argument in that work has escaped Novatian; but everything is extended, and made more systematic

---

[1] In the case of Irenæus, Hippolytus, and Tertullian we already find that they observe a certain order and sequence of books when advancing a detailed proof from Scripture.

and polished. No trace of Platonism is to be found in this dogmatic; on the contrary he employs the Stoic and Aristotelian syllogistic and dialectic method used also by his Monarchian opponents. This plan together with its Biblical attitude gives the work great outward completeness and certainty. We cannot help concluding that this work must have made a deep impression wherever it was read, although the real difficulties of the matter are not at all touched upon, but veiled by distinctions and for-mulæ. It probably contributed not least to make Tertullian's type of Christology the universal Western one. This type, how-ever, as will be set forth in greater detail hereafter, already approximates closely to the resolutions of Nicæa and Chalcedon.[1] Novatian adopted Tertullian's formulæ "one substance, three persons" ("una substantia, tres personæ"), "from the substance of God" ("ex substantia dei"), "always with the Father" ("semper apud patrem"), "God and man" ("deus et homo"), "two substances" ("duæ substantiæ"), "one person" ("una persona"), as well as his expressions for the union and separa-tion of the two natures adding to them similar ones and giving them a wider extension.[2] Taking his book in all we may see

---

[1] It is worthy of note that there was not a single Arian ecclesiastic of note in the Novatian churches of the 4th century, so far as we know. All Novatian's adherents, even those in the West (see Socrates' Ecclesiastical History), were of the orthodox Nicæan type. This furnishes material for reflection.

[2] Owing to the importance of the matter we shall give several Christological and trinitarian disquisitions from the work "de trinitate". The archaic attitude of this Christology and trinitarian doctrine is evident from the following consider-ations. (1) Like Tertullian, Novatian asserts that the Logos was indeed always with the Father, but that he only went forth from him at a definite period of time (for the purpose of creating the world). (2) Like Tertullian, he declares that Father, Son, and Spirit have one substance (that is, are ὁμοούσιοι., the *homoousia* of itself never decides as to equality in dignity); but that the Son is subordinate and obedient to the Father and the Spirit to the Son (cc. 17, 22, 24), since they derive their origin, essence, and function from the Father (the Spirit from the Son). (3) Like Tertullian, Novatian teaches that the Son, after accomplishing his work, will again become intermingled with the Father, that is, will cease to have an independent existence (c. 31); whence we understand why the West continued so long to be favourable to Marcellus of Ancyra; see also the so-called symbol of Sardika). Apart from these points and a few others of less consequence, the work, in its formulæ, exhibits a type which remained pretty constant in the West down to the time of Augustine, or, till the adoption of Johannes Damascenus' dogmatic. The sharp distinction between "deus" and "homo" and the use that

that he thereby created for the West a dogmatic *vademecum*,
which, from its copious and well-selected quotations from Scripture, must have been of extraordinary service.

The most important articles which were now fixed and trans-

is nevertheless made of "permixtio" and synonymous words are also specially
characteristic. Cap. 9: "Christus deus dominus deus noster, sed dei filius"; c. 11:
"non sic de substantia corporis ipsius exprimimus, ut solum tantum hominem illum
esse dicamus, sed ut divinitate sermonis in ipsa concretione permixta etiam deum
illum teneamus"; c. 11 Christ has *auctoritas divina.*, "tam enim scriptura etiam
deum adnuntiat Christum, quam etiam ipsum hominem adnuntiat deum, tam hominem descripsit Iesum Christum, quam etiam deum quoque descripsit Christum
dominum." In c. 12 the term "Immanuel" is used to designate Christ as God in
a way that reminds one of Athanasius; c. 13: "praesertim cum animadvertat,
scripturam evangelicam utramque istam substantiam in unam nativitatis Christi
foederasse concordiam"; c. 14: "Christus ex verbi et carnis coniunctione concre-
tus"; c. 16: "... ut neque homo Christo subtrahatur, neque divinitas negetur...
utrumque in Christo confoederatum est, utrumque coniunctum est et utrumque connexum est... pignerata in illo divinitatis et humilitatis videtur esse concordia...
qui mediator dei et hominum effectus exprimitur, in se deum et hominem sociasse
reperitur... nos sermonem dei scimus indutum carnis substantiam... lavit substantiam corporis et materiam carnis abluens, ex parte suscepti hominis, passione";
c. 17: "... nisi quoniam auctoritas divini verbi ad suscipiendum hominem interim
conquiescens nec se suis viribus exercens, deiicit se ad tempus atque deponit, dum
hominem fert, quem suscepit"; c. 18: "... ut in semetipso concordiam confibularet
terrenorum pariter atque caelestium, dum utriusque partis in se connectens pignora
et deum homini et hominem deo copularet, ut merito filius dei per assumptionem
carnis filius hominis et filius hominis per receptionem dei verbi filius dei effici
possit"; c. 19: "hic est enim legitimus dei filius qui ex ipso deo est, qui, dum
sanctum illud (Luke I. 35) assumit, sibi filium hominis annectit et illum ad se
rapit atque transducit, connexione sua et permixtione sociata praestat et filium illum
dei facit, quod ille naturaliter non fuit (Novatian's teaching is therefore like that
of the Spanish Adoptionists of the 8th century), ut principalitas nominis istius
"filius dei" in spiritu sit domini, qui descendit et venit, ut sequela nominis istius
in filio dei et hominis sit, et merito consequenter hic filius dei factus sit, dum non
principaliter filius dei est, atque ideo dispositionem istam anhelus videns et ordinem
istum sacramenti expediens non sic cuncta confundens, ut nullum vestigium dis-
tinctionis collocavit, distinctionem posuit dicendo. 'Propterea et quod nascetur ex
te sanctum vocabitur filius dei'. Ne si distributionem istam cum libramentis suis
non dispensasset, sed in confuso permixtum reliquisset, vere occasionem haereticis
contulisset, ut hominis filium qua homo est, eundum et dei et hominis filium pro-
nuntiare deberent... Filius dei, dum filium hominis in se suscepit, consequenter
illum filium dei fecit, quoniam illum filius sibi dei sociavit et iunxit, ut, dum
filius hominis adhaeret in nativitate filio dei, ipsa permixtionem foeneratum et mutuat-
um teneret, quod ex natura propria possidere non posset. Ac si facta est angeli
voce, quod nolunt haeretici, inter filium dei hominisque cum sua tamen sociatione
distinctio, urgendo illos, uti Christum hominis filium hominem intelligant quoque
dei filium et hominem dei filium id est dei verbum deum accipiant, atque ideo

ferred to the general creed along with the necessary proofs,
especially in the West, were: (1) the unity of God, (2) the
identity of the supreme God and the creator of the world, that
is, the identity of the mediators of creation and redemption, (3)

Christum Iesum dominum ex utroque connexum, et utroque contextum atque con-
cretum et in eadem utriusque substantiæ concordia mutui ad invicem fœderis con-
fibulatione sociatum, hominem et deum, scripturæ hoc ipsum dicentis veritate cog-
noscant ". c. 21: "hæretici nolunt Christum secundam esse personam post patrem,
sed ipsum patrem;" c. 22: "Cum Christus 'Ego' dicit (John X. 30), deinde patrem
infert dicendo, 'Ego et pater', proprietatem personæ suæ id est filii a paterna
auctoritate discernit atque distinguit, non tantummodo de sono nominis, sed etiam
de ordine dispositæ potestatis ... unum enim neutraliter positum, societatis concordiam, non unitatem personæ sonat ... unum autem quod ait, ad concordiam et
eandem sententiam et ad ipsam charitatis societatem pertinet, ut merito unum sit
pater et filius per concordiam et per amorem et per dilectionem. Et quoniam ex
patre est, quicquid illud est, filius est, manente tamen distinctione ... denique
novit hanc concordiæ unitatem est apostolus Paulus cum personarum tamen distinctione." (Comparison with the relationship between Paul and Apollos! "Quos
personæ ratio invicem dividit, eosdem rursus invicem religionis ratio conducit;
et quamvis idem atque ipsi non sint, dum idem sentiunt, ipsum sunt, et cum duo
sint, unum sunt"); c. 23: "constat hominem a deo factum esse, non ex deo pro-
cessisse; ex deo autem homo quomodo non processit, sic dei verbum processit".
In c. 24 it is argued that Christ existed before the creation of the world and that
not merely "predestinatione", for then he would be subsequent and therefore inferior to Adam, Abel, Enoch etc. "Sublata ergo prædestinatione quæ non est
posita, in substantia fuit Christus ante mundi institutionem"; c. 31: "Est ergo
deus pater omnium institutor et creator, solus originem nesciens(!), invisibilis, im-
mensus, immortalis, æternus, unus deus(!), ... ex quo quando ipse voluit, sermo
filius natus est, qui non in sono percussi aëris aut tono coactæ de visceribus vocis
accipitur, sed in substantia prolatæ a deo virtutis agnoscitur, cuius sacræ et divinæ
nativitatis arcana nec apostolus didicit ..., filio soli nota sunt, qui patris secreta
cognovit. Hic ergo cum sit genitus a patre, semper est in patre. Semper autem sic
dico, ut non innatum, sed natum probem; sed qui ante omne tempus est, semper
in patre fuisse discendus est, nec enim tempus illi assignari potest, qui ante tempus est; semper enim in patre, ne pater non semper sit pater: quia et pater illum
etiam præcedit, quod necesse est, prior sit qua pater sit. Quoniam antecedat
necesse est eum, qui habet originem, ille qui originem nescit. Simul ut hic minor
sit, dum in illo esse se scit habens originem quia nascitur, et per patrem quamvis
originem habet qua nascitur, vicinus in nativitate, dum ex eo patre, qui solus originem non habet, nascitur ..., substantia scilicet divina, cuius nomen est verbum ...,
deus utique procedens ex deo secundam personam efficiens, sed non eripiens illud
patri quod unus est deus ... Cuius sic divinitas traditur, ut non aut dissonantia
aut inæqualitate divinitatis duos deos reddidisse videatur ... Dum huic, qui est
deus, omnia substrata traduntur et cuncta sibi subiecta filius accepta refert patri,
totam divinitatis auctoritatem rursus patri remittit, unus deus ostenditur verus et
æternus pater, a quo solo hæc vis divinitatis emissa, etiam in filium tradita et
directa rursus per substantiæ communionem ad patrem revolvitur."

the identity of the supreme God with the God of the Old Testament, and the declaration that the Old Testament is God's book of revelation, (4) the creation of the world out of nothing, (5) the unity of the human race, (6) the origin of evil from freedom, and the inalienable nature of freedom, (7) the two Testaments, (8) Christ as God and Man, the unity of his personality, the truth of his divinity, the actuality of his humanity, the reality of his fate, (9) the redemption and conclusion of a covenant through Christ as the new and crowning manifestation of God's grace to all men, (10) the resurrection of man in soul and body. But the transmission and interpretation of these propositions, by means of which the Gnostic theses were overthrown, necessarily involved the transmission of the Logos doctrine; for the doctrine of the revelation of God and of the two Testaments could not have prevailed without this theory. How this hypothesis gained acceptance in the course of the third century, and how it was the means of establishing and legitimising philosophical theology as part of the faith, will be shown in the seventh chapter. We may remark in conclusion that the religious hope which looked forward to an earthly kingdom of Christ was still the more widely diffused among the Churches of the third century ; [1] but that the other hope, viz., that of being deified, was gaining adherents more and more. The latter result was due to men's increasing indifference to daily life and growing aspiration after a higher one, a longing that was moreover nourished among the more cultured by the philosophy which was steadily gaining ground. The hope of deification is the expression of the idea that this world and human nature do not correspond to that exalted world which man has built up within his own mind and which he may reasonably demand to be realised, because it is only in it that he can come to himself. The fact that Christian teachers like Theophilus, Irenæus, and Hippolytus expressly declared this to be a legitimate Christian hope and held out a sure prospect of its fulfilment

[1] If I am not mistaken, the production or adaptation of Apocalypses did indeed abate in the third century, but acquired fresh vigour in the 4th, though at the same time allowing greater scope to the influence of heathen literature (including romances as well as hagiographical literature).

through Christ, must have given the greatest impulse to the
spread and adoption of this ecclesiastical Christianity. But, when
the Christian religion was represented as the belief in the incarnation of God and as the sure hope of the deification of man, a
speculation that had originally never got beyond the fringe of
religious knowledge was made the central point of the system
and the simple content of the Gospel was obscured. [1]

[1] I did not care to appeal more frequently to the Sibylline oracles either in
this or the preceding chapter, because the literary and historical investigation of
these writings has not yet made such progress as to justify one in using it for the
history of dogma. It is well known that the oracles contain rich materials in
regard to the doctrine of God, Christology, conceptions of the history of Jesus,
and eschatology; but, apart from the old Jewish oracles, this material belongs to
several centuries and has not yet been reliably sifted.

# CHAPTER VI.

## THE TRANSFORMATION OF THE ECCLESIASTICAL TRADITION INTO A PHILOSOPHY OF RELIGION, OR THE ORIGIN OF THE SCIENTIFIC THEOLOGY AND DOGMATIC OF THE CHURCH.

### Clement and Origen.

THE Alexandrian school of catechists was of inestimable importance for the transformation of the heathen empire into a Christian one, and of Greek philosophy into ecclesiastical philosophy. In the third century this school overthrew polytheism by scientific means whilst at the same time preserving everything of any value in Greek science and culture. These Alexandrians wrote for the educated people of the whole earth; they made Christianity a part of the civilisation of the world. The saying that the Christian missionary to the Greeks must be a Greek was first completely verified within the Catholic Church in the person of Origen, who at the same time produced the only system of Christian dogma possessed by the Greek Church before John Damascenus.

1. *The Alexandrian Catechetical School. Clement of Alexandria.*[1]

"The work of Irenæus still leaves it undecided whether the form of the world's literature, as found in the Christian Church,

[1] Guericke, De schola, quæ Alex. floruit catechetica 1824, 1825. Vacherot, Hist. crit. de l'école d'Alex., 1846—51. Reinkens, De Clemente Alex., 1850. Redepenning, Origenes Thl. I. p. 57 ff. Læmmer, Clem. Al. de Logo doctrina, 1855. Reuter, Clem. theolog. moralis, 1853. Cognat, Clement d'Alex. Paris, 1859. Westcott, Origen

is destined only to remain a weapon to combat its enemies, or
is to become an instrument of peaceful labour within its own
territory." With these words Overbeck has introduced his examination of Clement of Alexandria's great masterpiece from the
standpoint of the historian of literature. They may be also applied
to the history of theology. As we have shown, Irenæus, Tertullian (and Hippolytus) made use of philosophical theology to
expel heretical elements; but all the theological expositions that
this interest suggested to them as necessary, were in their view
part of the faith itself. At least we find in their works absolutely
no clear expression of the fact that faith is one thing and theology
another, though rudimentary indications of such distinctions are
found. Moreover, their adherence to the early-Christian eschatology in its entirety, as well as their rejection of a qualitative
distinction between simple believers and 'Gnostics', proved that
they themselves were deceived as to the scope of their theological speculations, and that moreover their Christian interest was
virtually satisfied with subjection to the authority of tradition,
with the early-Christian hopes, and with the rules for a holy
life. But since about the time of Commodus, and in some cases
even earlier, we can observe, even in ecclesiastical circles, the

and the beginnings of Christian Philosophy (Contemporary Review, May 1879).
Winter, Die Ethik des Clemens von Alex., 1882. Merk, Cl. Alex. in seiner Ab-
hängigkeit von der griech. Philosophie, Leipzig, 1879 (see besides Overbeck, Theol.
Lit. Ztg., 1879. No. 20 and cf. above all his disquisitions in the treatise "Ueber.
die Anfänge der patristischen Litteratur," Hist. Ztschr. N. F., Vol. XII., pp. 455—472
Zahn, Forschungen, Vol. III. Bigg, The Christian Platonists of Alexandria, Oxford,
1886. Kremmer, De catal. heurematum, Lips. 1890. Wendland, Quæst. Musorianæ,
Berol. 1886. Bratke, Die Stellung des Clem. Alex. z. antiken Mysterienwesen
(Stud. u. Krit. 1888, p. 647 ff.). On Alexander of Jerusalem see Routh, Reliq. Sacr.
T. II. p. 161 sq.; on Julius Africanus see Gelzer, Sextus Jul. Afr. I. Thl., 1880,
p. 1 ff., Spitta, Der Brief des Jul. Afr. an Aristides, Halle 1877, and my article
in the Real-Encykl. On Bardesanes see Hilgenfeld, B., der letzte Gnostiker, 1864,
and Hort's article in the Dictionary of Christian Biography. On the labours in
scientific theology on the part of the so-called Alogi in Asia Minor and of the
Roman Theodotianists see Epiph. hær. 51, Euseb., H. E. V. 28 and my article
"Monarchianismus" in the R.-Encykl. f. protest. Theol. 2nd. ed., Vol. X., pp
183 ff., 188 ff. On the tendencies even of orthodox Christians to scientific theology
see Tertull., de præscr. hær. 8 ff. (cf. the first words of c. 8: "Venio itaque ad
illum articulum, quem et nostri prætendunt ad ineundam curiositatem. Scriptum est,
inquiunt, Quærite et invenietis" etc.).

growing independence and might of the aspiration for a scientific knowledge and treatment of the Christian religion, that is of Christian tradition. [1] There is a wish to maintain this tradition in its entirety and hence the Gnostic theses are rejected. The selection from tradition, made in opposition to Gnosticism — though indeed in accordance with its methods — and declared to be apostolic, is accepted. But there is a desire to treat the given material in a strictly scientific manner, just as the Gnostics had formerly done, that is, on the one hand to establish it by a critical and historical exegesis, and on the other to give it a philosophical form and bring it into harmony with the spirit of the times. Along with this we also find the wish to incorporate the thoughts of Paul which now possessed divine authority. [2] Accordingly schools and scholastic unions now make their appearance afresh, the old schools having been expelled from the Church. [3] In Asia Minor such efforts had already begun shortly before the time when the canon of holy apostolic tradition was fixed by the ecclesiastical authorities (Alogi). From the history of Clement of Alexandria, the life of bishop Alexander, afterwards bishop of Jerusalem, and subsequently from the history of Origen (we may also mention Firmilian of Cæsarea), we learn that there was in Cappadocia about the year 200 a circle of ecclesiastics who zealously applied themselves to scientific pursuits. Bardesanes, a man of high repute, laboured in the Christian kingdom of Edessa about the same time. He wrote treatises on philosophical theology, which indeed, judged by a Western standard, could not be accounted orthodox, and directed a theological school which maintained its ground in the third

[1] This manner of expression is indeed liable to be misunderstood, because it suggests the idea that something new was taking place. As a matter of fact the scientific labours in the Church were merely a continuation of the Gnostic schools under altered circumstances, that is, under the sway of a tradition which was now more clearly defined and more firmly fenced round as a *noli me tangere.*

[2] This was begun in the Church by Irenæus and Tertullian and continued by the Alexandrians. They, however, not only adopted theologoumena from Paulinism, but also acquired from Paul a more ardent feeling of religious freedom as well as a deeper reverence for love and knowledge as contrasted with lower morality.

[3] We are not able to form a clear idea of the school of Justin. In the year 180 the schools of the Valentinians, Carpocratians, Tatian etc. were all outside the Church.

322 HISTORY OF DOGMA [CHAP. VI.

century and attained great importance.[1] In Palestine, during
the time of Heliogabalus and Alexander (Severus), Julius Africanus composed a series of books on scientific theology, which
were specifically different from the writings of Irenæus and
Tertullian; but which on the other hand show the closest relationship in point of form to the treatises of the so-called Gnostics.
His inquiries into the relationship of the genealogies of Jesus
and into certain parts of the Greek Apocalypse of Daniel showed
that the Church's attention had been drawn to problems of
historical criticism. In his chronography the apologetic interest
is subordinate to the historical, and in his Κεστοί, dedicated to
Alexander Severus (Hippolytus had already dedicated a treatise
on the resurrection to the wife of Heliogabalus), we see fewer
traces of the Christian than of the Greek scholar. Alexander
of Ælia and Theoktistus of Cæsarea, the occupants of the two
most important sees in Palestine, were, contemporaneously with
him, zealous patrons of an independent science of theology. Even at
that early time the former founded an important theological library ;
and the fragments of his letters preserved to us prove that he
had caught not only the language, but also the scientific spirit
of the age. In Rome, at the beginning of the third century,
there was a scientific school where textual criticism of the Bible
was pursued and where the works of Aristotle, Theophrastus,
Euclid, and Galen were zealously read and utilised. Finally,
the works of Tertullian show us that, even among the Christians of Carthage, there was no lack of such as wished to
naturalise the pursuit of science within the Church; and Eusebius (H. E. V. 27) has transmitted to us the titles of a series
of scientific works dating as far back as the year 200 and
ascribed to ecclesiastics of that period.

Whilst all these phenomena, which collectively belong to the
close of the second and beginning of the third century, show

---

[1] On the school of Edessa see Assemani, Bibl. orient., T. III., P. II., p. 924;
Von Lengerke, De Ephraemi arte hermen., p. 86 sq.; Kihn, Die Bedeutung der
antiochenischen Schule etc., pp. 32 f. 79 f., Zahn, Tatian's Diatessaron, p. 54.
About the middle of the 3rd century Macarius, of whom Lucian the Martyr was a
disciple, taught at this school. Special attention was given to the exegesis of the
Holy Scriptures.

that it was indeed possible to suppress heresy in the Church, but not the impulse from which it sprang, the most striking proof of this conclusion is the existence of the so-called school of catechists in Alexandria. We cannot now trace the origin of this school, which first comes under our notice in the year 190,[1] but we know that the struggle of the Church with heresy was concluded in Alexandria at a later period than in the West. We know further that the school of catechists extended its labours to Palestine and Cappadocia as early as the year 200, and, to all appearance, originated or encouraged scientific pursuits there.[2] Finally, we know that the existence of this school was threatened in the fourth decade of the third century; but Heraclas was shrewd enough to reconcile the ecclesiastical and scientific interests.[3] In the Alexandrian school of catechists the whole of Greek science was taught and made to serve the purpose of Christian apologetics. Its first teacher, who is well known to us from the writings he has left, is *Clement of Alexandria*.[4] His main work is epoch-making. "Clement's intention is nothing

---

[1] Overbeck, l.c., p. 455, has very rightly remarked: "The origin of the Alexandrian school of catechists is not a portion of the Church history of the 2nd century, that has somehow been left in the dark by a mere accident; but a part of the well-defined dark region on the map of the ecclesiastical historian of this period, which contains the beginnings of all the fundamental institutions of the Church as well as those of the Alexandrian school of catechists, a school which was the first attempt to formulate the relationship of Christianity to secular science." We are, moreover, still in a state of complete uncertainty as to the personality and teaching of Pantænus (with regard to him see Zahn, "Forschungen" Vol. III., pp. 64 ff. 77 ff.). We can form an idea of the school of catechists from the 6th Book of Eusebius' Ecclesiastical History and from the works of Clement and Origen.

[2] On the connection of Julius Africanus with this school see Eusebius, VI. 31. As to his relations with Origen see the correspondence. Julius Africanus had, moreover, relations with Edessa. He mentions Clement in his chronicles. On the connection of Alexander and the Cappadocian circle with Pantænus, Clement, and Origen, see the 6th Book of Eusebius' Ecclesiastical History. Alexander and Origen were disciples of Pantænus.

[3] See my article "Heraklas" in the Real-Encyklopädie.

[4] We have the most complete materials in Zahn, "Forschungen" Vol. III. pp. 17—176. The best estimate of the great tripartite work (Protrepticus, Pædagogus, Stromateis) is found in Overbeck, l.c. The titles of Clement's remaining works, which are lost to us or only preserved in fragments, show how comprehensive his scientific labours were.

less than an introduction to Christianity, or, speaking more correctly and in accordance with the spirit of his work, an initiation
into it.  The task that Clement sets himself is an introduction
to what is inmost and highest in Christianity itself.  He aims,
so to speak, at first making Christians perfect Christians by
means of a work of literature.  By means of such a work he
wished not merely to repeat to the Christian what life has already
done for him as it is, but to elevate him to something still
higher than what has been revealed to him by the forms of
initiation that the Church has created for herself in the course
of a history already dating back a century and a half."  To
Clement therefore Gnosis, that is, the (Greek) philosophy of
religion, is not only a means of refuting heathenism and heresy,
but at the same time of ascertaining and setting forth what is
highest and inmost in Christianity.  He views it as such, however, because, apart from evangelical sayings, the Church tradition, both collectively and in its details, is something foreign to
him; he has subjected himself to its authority, but he can only
make it intellectually his own after subjecting it to a scientific
and philosophical treatment.¹  His great work, which has rightly
been called the boldest literary undertaking in the history of
the Church,² is consequently the first attempt to use Holy
Scripture and the Church tradition together with the assumption
that Christ as the Reason of the world is the source of all truth,
as the basis of a presentation of Christianity which at once
addresses itself to the cultured by satisfying the scientific demand
for a philosophical ethic and theory of the world, and at the
same time reveals to the believer the rich content of his faith.
Here then is found, in form and content, the scientific Christian
doctrine of religion which, while not contradicting the faith, does

¹ This applies quite as much to the old principles of Christian morality as to
the traditional faith.  With respect to the first we may refer to the treatise: "Quis
dives salvetur", and to the 2nd and 3rd Books of the Pædagogus.

² Clement was also conscious of the novelty of his undertaking; see Overbeck,
*l.c.*, p. 464 f. The respect enjoyed by Clement as a master is shown by the letters
of Alexander of Jerusalem. See Euseb., H. E. VI. 11 and specially VI. 14. Here
both Pantænus and Clement are called "Father", but whilst the former receives
the title, ὁ μακάριος ὡς ἀληθῶς καὶ κύριος, the latter is called: ὁ ἱερὸς Κλήμης,
κύριός μου γενόμενος καὶ ὠφελήσας με.

not merely support or explain it in a few places, but raises it
to another and higher intellectual sphere, namely, out of the
province of authority and obedience into that of clear knowledge
and inward, intellectual assent emanating from love to God.[1]
Clement cannot imagine that the Christian faith, as found in
tradition, can of itself produce the union of intellectual independence and devotion to God which he regards as moral perfection.
He is too much of a Greek philosopher for that, and believes
that this aim is only reached through knowledge. But in so far
as this is only the deciphering of the secrets revealed in the
Holy Scriptures through the Logos, secrets which the believer
also gains possession of by subjecting himself to them, all knowledge is a reflection of the divine revelation. The lofty ethical
and religious ideal of the man made perfect in fellowship with
God, which Greek philosophy had developed since the time of
Plato and to which it had subordinated the whole scientific
knowledge of the world, was adopted and heightened by Clement,
and associated not only with Jesus Christ but also with ecclesiastical Christianity. But, whilst connecting it with the Church
tradition, he did not shrink from the boldest remodelling of
the latter, because the preservation of its wording was to him
a sufficient guarantee of the Christian character of the speculation.[2]

In Clement, then, ecclesiastical Christianity reached the stage
that Judaism had attained in Philo, and no doubt the latter

---

[1] Strom. VI. 14, 109: πλέον ἐστὶν τοῦ πιστεῦσαι τὸ γνῶναι. Pistis is γνῶσις
σύντομος τῶν κατεπειγόντων (VII. 10. 57, see the whole chapter), Gnosis is
ἀπόδειξις τῶν διὰ πίστεως παρειλημμένων τῇ πίστει ἐποικοδομουμένη (l.c.), τελείωσις
ἀνθρώπου (l.c.), πίστις ἐπιστημονική (II. 11. 48).

[2] We have here more particularly to consider those paragraphs of the Stromateis where Clement describes the perfect Gnostic: the latter elevates himself by
dispassionate love to God, is raised above everything earthly, has rid himself of
ignorance, the root of all evil, and already lives a life like that of the angels.
See Strom. VI. 9. 71, 72: Οὐδὲ γὰρ ἐνδεῖ τι αὐτῷ πρὸς ἐξομοίωσιν τῷ καλῷ καὶ
ἀγαθῷ εἶναι· οὐδὲ ἄρα φιλεῖ τινὰ τὴν κοινὴν ταύτην φιλίαν, ἀλλ᾽ ἀγαπᾷ τὸν κτίστην
διὰ τῶν κτισμάτων, Οὔτ᾽ οὖν ἐπιθυμίᾳ καὶ ὀρέξει τινὶ περιπίπτει οὔτε ἐνδεής ἐστι
κατά γε τὴν ψυχὴν τῶν ἄλλων τινός συνὼν ἤδη δι᾽ ἀγάπης τῷ ἐραστῷ, ᾧ δὴ ᾠκεί-
ωται κατὰ τὴν αἵρεσιν καὶ τῇ ἐξ ἀσκήσεως ἕξει, τούτῳ προσεχέστερον συνεγγίζων,
μακάριος ὢν διὰ τὴν τῶν αγαθῶν περιουσίαν, ὥστε ἕνεκά γε τούτων ἐξυμοιοῦσθαι
βιάζεται τῷ διδασκάλῳ εἰς ἀπαθείαν. Strom. VII. 69—83: VI. 14, 113: οὕτως δύναμιν
λαβοῦσα κυριακὴν ἡ ψυχὴ μελετᾷ εἶναι Θεός, κακὸν μὲν οὐδὲν ἄλλο πλὴν ἀγνοίας
εἶναι νομίζουσα. The whole 7th Book should be read.

exercised great influence over him.[1] Moreover, Clement stands
on the ground that Justin had already trodden, but he has
advanced far beyond this Apologist. His superiority to Justin
not only consists in the fact that he changed the apologetic
task that the latter had in his mind into a systematic and positive
one; but above all in the circumstance that he transformed the
tradition of the Christian Church, which in his days was far
more extensive and more firmly established than in Justin's time,
into a real scientific dogmatic; whereas Justin neutralised the
greater part of this tradition by including it in the scheme of
the proof from prophecy. By elevating the idea of the Logos
who is Christ into the highest principle in the religious explanation of the world and in the exposition of Christianity, Clement
gave to this idea a much more concrete and copious content
than Justin did. Christianity is the doctrine of the creation,
training, and redemption of mankind by the Logos, whose work
culminates in the perfect Gnostics. The philosophy of the Greeks,
in so far as it possessed the Logos, is declared to be a counterpart of the Old Testament law;[2] and the facts contained in the
Church tradition are either subordinated to the philosophical
dogmatic or receive a new interpretation expressly suited to it.
The idea of the Logos has a content which is on the one hand
so wide that he is found wherever man rises above the level of
nature, and on the other so concrete that an authentic knowledge
of him can only be obtained from historical revelation. The
Logos is essentially the rational law of the world and the teacher;
but in Christ he is at the same time officiating priest, and the
blessings he bestows are a series of holy initiations which

---

[1] Philo is quoted by Clement several times and still more frequently made use
of without acknowledgment. See the copious citations in Siegfried, Philo von
Alexandrien, pp. 343—351. In addition to this Clement made use of many Greek
philosophers or quoted them without acknowledgment, e.g., Musonius.

[2] Like Philo and Justin, Clement also no doubt at times asserts that the Greek
philosophers pilfered from the Old Testament; but see Strom. I. 5. 28 sq.: πάντων
μὲν αἴτιος τῶν καλῶν ὁ Θεός, ἀλλὰ τῶν μὲν κατὰ προηγούμενον ὡς τῆς τε διαθήκης
τῆς παλαιᾶς καὶ τῆς νεάς, τῶν δὲ κατ᾽ ἐπακολούθημα ὡς τῆς φιλοσοφίας. τάχα δὲ
καὶ προηγουμένως τοῖς Ἕλλησιν ἐδόθη τότε πρὶν ἢ τὸν κύριον καλέσαι καὶ τοὺς
Ἕλληνας. ἐπαιδαγώγει γὰρ καὶ αὐτὴ τὸ Ἑλληνικὸν ὡς ὁ νόμος τοὺς Ἑβραίους εἰς
Χριστόν.

alone contain the possibility of man's raising himself to the divine life. [1] While this is already clear evidence of Clement's affinity to Gnostic teachers, especially the Valentinians, the same similarity may also be traced in the whole conception of the task (Christianity as theology), in the determination of the formal principle (inclusive of the recourse to esoteric tradition ; see above, p. 35 f.),[2] and in the solution of the problems. But Clement's great superiority to Valentinus is shown not only in his contriving to preserve in all points his connection with the faith of the main body of Christendom, but still more in his power of mastering so many problems by the aid of a single principle, that is, in the art of giving the most comprehensive presentation with the most insignificant means. Both facts are indeed most closely connected. The rejection of all conceptions that could not be verified from Holy Scripture, or at least easily reconciled with it, as well as his optimism, opposed as this was to Gnostic pessimism, proved perhaps the most effective means of persuading the Church to recognise the Christian character of a dogmatic that was at least half inimical to ecclesiastical Christianity. Through

[1]   See Bratke's instructive treatise cited above.

[2]   The fact that Clement appeals in support of the Gnosis to an esoteric tradition (Strom. VI. 7. 61 : VI. 8. 68 : VII. 10. 55) proves how much this writer, belonging as he did to a sceptical age, underestimated the efficacy of all human thought in determining the ultimate truth of things.  The existence of sacred writings containing all truth was not even enough for him; the content of these writings had also to be guaranteed by divine communication.  But no doubt the ultimate cause of this, as of all similar cases of scepticism, was the dim perception that ethics and religion do not at all come within the sphere of the intellectual, and that the intellect can produce nothing of religious value. As, however, in consequence of philosophical tradition, neither Philo, nor the Gnostics, nor Clement, nor the Neoplatonists were able to shake themselves free from the intellectual *scheme*, those things which— as they instinctively felt, but did not recognise—could really not be ascertained by knowledge at all received from them the name of *suprarational* and were traced to divine revelation.  We may say that the extinction or pernicious extravagancies to which Greek philosophy was subjected in Neoplatonism, and the absurdities into which the Christian dogmatic was led, arose from the fact that the tradition of placing the ethical and religious feelings and the development of character within the sphere of knowledge, as had been the case for nearly a thousand years, could not be got rid of, though the incongruity was no doubt felt.  Contempt for empiricism, scepticism, the extravagancies of religious metaphysics which finally become mythology, have their origin here.  Knowledge still continues to be viewed as the highest possession; it is, however, no longer knowledge, but character and feeling; and it must be nourished by the fancy in order to be able to assert itself as knowledge.

Clement theology became the crowning stage of piety, the highest
philosophy of the Greeks was placed under the protection and
guarantee of the Church, and the whole Hellenic civilisation was
thus at the same time legitimised within Christianity. The Logos
is Christ, but the Logos is at the same time the moral and
rational in all stages of development.   The Logos is the teacher,
not only in cases where an intelligent self-restraint, as understood
by the ancients, bridles the passions and instincts and wards
off excesses of all sorts; but also, and here of course the revelation is of a higher kind, wherever love to God alone determines
the whole life and exalts man above everything sensuous and
finite. [1]  What Gnostic moralists merely regarded as contrasts
Clement, the Christian and Greek, was able to view as stages;
and thus he succeeded in conceiving the motley society that
already represented the Church of his time as a unity, as the
humanity trained by one and the same Logos, the Pedagogue.
His speculation did not drive him out of the Church; it rather
enabled him to understand the multiplicity of forms she contained
and to estimate their relative justification; nay, it finally led him
to include the history of pre-Christian humanity in the system
he regarded as a unity, and to form a theory of universal history
satisfactory to his mind. [2]  If we compare this theory with the

---

[1] Clement was not a Neoplatonic mystic in the strict sense of the word. When
he describes the highest ethical ideal, ecstasy is wanting; and the freshness with
which he describes Quietism shows that he himself was no Quietist.  See on this
point Bigg's third lecture, l.c., particularly p. 98 f.  "... The silent prayer of the
Quietist is in fact ecstasy, of which there is not a trace in Clement. For Clement
shrank from his own conclusions.  Though the father of all the Mystics he is no
Mystic himself.  He did not enter the "enchanted garden", which he opened for
others.  If he talks of "flaying the sacrifice", of leaving sense behind, of Epop-
teia, this is but the parlance of his school.  The instrument to which he looks
for growth in knowledge is not trance, but disciplined reason.  Hence Gnosis,
when once obtained, is indefectible, not like the rapture which Plotinus enjoyed
but four times during his acquaintance with Porphyry, which in the experience of
Theresa never lasted more than half an hour.  The Gnostic is no Visionary, no
Theurgist, no Antinomian."

[2] What a bold and joyous thinker Clement was is shown by the almost audacious remark in Strom. IV. 22. 136: εἰ γοῦν τις καθ' ὑπόθεσιν προθείη τῷ γνωστικῷ
πότερον ἑλέσθαι βούλοιτο τὴν γνῶσιν τοῦ Θεοῦ ἢ τὴν σωτηρίαν τὴν αἰωνίαν, εἴη δὲ
ταῦτα κεχωρισμένα παντὸς μᾶλλον ἐν ταυτότητε ὄντα, οὐδὲ καθ' ὁτιοῦν διστάσας
ἕλοιτ' ἂν τὴν γνῶσιν τοῦ Θεοῦ.

rudimentary ideas of a similar kind in Irenæus, we see clearly
the meagreness and want of freedom, the uncertainty and narrowness, in the case of the latter. In the Christian faith as he
understood it and as amalgamated by him with Greek culture,
Clement found intellectual freedom and independence, deliverance
from all external authority. We need not here directly discuss
what apparatus he used for this end. Irenæus again remained
entangled in his apparatus, and much as he speaks of the *novum
testamentum libertatis*, his great work little conveys the impression that its author has really attained intellectual freedom.
Clement was the first to grasp the task of future theology.
According to him this task consists in utilising the historical
traditions, through which we have become what we are, and
the Christian communion, which is imperative upon us as being
the only moral and religious one, in order to attain freedom
and independence of our own life by the aid of the Gospel; and
in showing this Gospel to be the highest revelation by the Logos,
who has given evidence of himself whenever man rises above
the level of nature and who is consequently to be traced throughout the whole history of humanity.

But does the Christianity of Clement correspond to the Gospel?
We can only give a qualified affirmation to this question. For
the danger of secularisation is evident, since apostasy from the
Gospel would be completely accomplished as soon as the ideal
of the self-sufficient Greek sage came to supplant the feeling
that man lives by the grace of God. But the danger of secularisation lies in the cramped conception of Irenæus, who sets up
authorities which have nothing to do with the Gospel, and creates
facts of salvation which have a no less deadening effect though
in a different way. If the Gospel is meant to give freedom and
peace in God, and to accustom us to an eternal life in union
with Christ Clement understood this meaning. He could justly
say to his opponents : " If the things we say appear to some
people diverse from the Scriptures of the Lord, let them know
that they draw inspiration and life therefrom and, making these
their starting-point give their meaning only, not their letter "
(κἂν ἑτεροῖα τισι τῶν πολλῶν καταφαίνηται τὰ ὑφ' ἡμῶν λεγόμενα
τῶν κυριακῶν γραφῶν, ἰστέον ὅτι ἐκεῖθεν ἀναπνεῖ τε καὶ ζῇ καὶ τὰς

ἀφορμὰς ἀπ᾽ αὐτῶν ἔχοντα τὸν νοῦν μόνον, οὐ τὴν λέξιν, παριστᾶν ἐπαγγελλέται). [1]  No doubt Clement conceives the aim of the whole traditionary material to be that of Greek philosophy, but we cannot fail to perceive that this aim is blended with the object which the Gospel puts before us, namely, to be rich in God and to receive strength and life from him.   The goodness of God and the responsibility of man are the central ideas of Clement and the Alexandrians; they also occupy the foremost place in the Gospel of Jesus Christ.  If this is certain we must avoid that searching of the heart which undertakes to fix how far he was influenced by the Gospel and how far by philosophy.

But, while so judging, we cannot deny that the Church tradition was here completely transformed into a Greek philosophy of religion on a historical basis, nor do we certify the Christian character of Clement's "dogmas" in acknowledging the evangelical spirit of his practical position.  What would be left of Christianity, if the practical aim, given by Clement to this religious philosophy, were lost?  A depotentiated system which could absolutely no longer be called Christian.  On the other hand there were many valuable features in the ecclesiastical *regula* literally interpreted; and the attempts of Irenæus to extract an authoritative religious meaning from the literal sense of Church tradition and of New Testament passages must be regarded as conservative efforts of the most valuable kind.  No doubt Irenæus and his theological *confrères* did not themselves find in Christianity that freedom which is its highest aim; but on the other hand they preserved and rescued valuable material for succeeding times.  If some day trust in the methods of religious philosophy vanishes, men will revert to history, which will still be recognisable in the preserved tradition, as prized by Irenæus and the rest, whereas it will have almost perished in the artificial interpretations due to the speculations of religious philosophers.

The importance that the Alexandrian school was to attain in

---

[1] Strom. VII. 1. 1.  In several passages of his main work Clement refers to those churchmen who viewed the practical and speculative concentration of Church tradition as dangerous and questioned the use of philosophy at all.  See Strom. VI. 10. 80: πολλοὶ καθάπερ οἱ παῖδες τὰ μορμολυκεῖα, οὕτως δεδίασι τὴν ἑλληνικὴν φιλοσοφίαν, φοβούμενοι μὴ ἀπαγάγῃ αὐτούς. VI. 11. 93.

the history of dogma is not associated with Clement, but with his disciple Origen.[1] This was not because Clement was more heterodox than Origen, for that is not the case, so far as the Stromateis is concerned at least;[2] but because the latter exerted an incomparably greater influence than the former; and, with an energy perhaps unexampled in the history of the Church, already mapped out all the provinces of theology by his own unaided efforts. Another reason is that Clement did not possess the Church tradition in its fixed Catholic forms as Origen did (see above, chapter 2), and, as his Stromateis shows, he was as yet incapable of forming a theological system. What he offers is portions of a theological Christian dogmatic and speculative ethic. These indeed are no fragments in so far as they are all produced according to a definite method and have the same object in view, but they still want unity. On the other hand Origen succeeded in forming a complete system inasmuch as he not only had a Catholic tradition of fixed limits and definite type to fall back upon as a basis; but was also enabled by the previous efforts of Clement to furnish a methodical treatment of this tradition.[3] Now a sharp eye indeed perceives that Origen

[1] Eusebius, H. E. VI. 14. 8, tells us that Origen was a disciple of Clement.

[2] Clement's authority in the Church continued much longer than that of Origen See Zahn, "Forschungen" III. p. 140 f. The heterodox opinions advanced by Clement in the Hypotyposes are for the most part only known to us in an exaggerated form from the report of Photius.

[3] In ecclesiastical antiquity all systematising was merely relative and limited, because the complex of sacred writings enjoyed a different authority from that which it possessed in the following period. Here the reference of a theologoumenon to a passage of Scripture was of itself sufficient, and the manifold and incongruous doctrines were felt as a unity in so far as they could all be verified from Holy Scriptures. Thus the fact that the Holy Scriptures were regarded as a series of divine oracles guaranteed, as it were, a transcendental unity of the doctrines, and, in certain circumstances, relieved the framer of the system of a great part of his task. Hitherto little justice has been done to this view of the history of dogma, though it is the only solution of a series of otherwise insoluble problems. We cannot for example understand the theology of Augustine, and necessarily create for ourselves the most difficult problems by our own fault, if we make no use of that theory. In Origen's dogmatic and that of subsequent Church Fathers—so far as we can speak of a dogmatic in their case—the unity lies partly in the canon of Holy Scripture and partly in the ultimate aim; but these two principles interfere with each other. As far as the Stromateis of Clement is concerned, Overbeek (l.c.) has furnished the explanation of its striking plan. Moreover, how

personally no longer possessed such a complete and bold religious
theory of the world as Clement did, for he was already more
tightly fettered by the Church tradition, some details of which
here and there led him into compromises that remind us of
Irenæus; but it was in connection with his work that the development of the following period took place. It is therefore sufficient, within the framework of the history of dogma, to refer
to Clement as the bold forerunner of Origen, and, in setting
forth the theology of the latter, to compare it in important points
with the doctrines of Clement.

## 2. *The system of Origen.* [1]

Among the theologians of ecclesiastical antiquity Origen was
the most important and influential alongside of Augustine. He
proved the father of ecclesiastical science in the widest sense
of the word, and at the same time became the founder of that
theology which reached its complete development in the fourth
and fifth centuries, and which in the sixth definitely denied its
author, without, however, losing the form he had impressed on
it. Origen created the ecclesiastical dogmatic and made the
sources of the Jewish and Christian religion the foundation of
that science. The Apologists, in their day, had found everything
clear in Christianity; the antignostic Fathers had confused the
Church's faith and the science that treats of it. Origen recognised the problem and the problems, and elevated the pursuit
of Christian theology to the rank of an independent task by
freeing it from its polemical aim. He could not have become
would it have been conceivable that the riches of Holy Scripture, as presented to
the philosophers who allegorised the books, could have been mastered, problems
and all, at the first attempt.

[1] See the treatises of Huëtius (1668) reprinted by Lommatzsch. Thomasius, Origenes 1837. Redepenning, Origenes, 2 Vols. 1841—46. Denis, de la philosophie
d'Origène, Paris 1884. Lang, Die Leiblichkeit der Vernunftwesen bei Origenes,
Leipzig, 1892. Mehlhorn, Die Lehre von der menschlichen Freiheit nach Origenes
(Zeitschrift für Kirchengeschichte, Vol. II., p. 234 ff.). Westcott, Origenes, in the
Dictionary of Christian Biography Vol. IV Möller in Herzog's Real-Encyklopädie,
2nd ed., Vol. XI., pp. 92—109. The special literature is to be found there as
well as in Nitzsch, Dogmengeschichte I., p. 151, and Ueberweg, Grundriss der
Geschichte der Philosophie, 5th ed., p. 62 f.

what he did, if two generations had not preceded him in paving
the way to form a mental conception of Christianity and give
it a philosophical foundation. Like all epoch-making personalities,
he was also favoured by the conditions in which he lived, though
he had to endure violent attacks. Born of a Christian family
which was faithfully attached to the Church, he lived at a time
when the Christian communities enjoyed almost uninterrupted
peace and were being naturalised in the world; he was a member
of a Christian Church where the right of scientific study was
already recognised and where this had attained a fixed position
in an organised school.[1] He proclaimed the reconciliation of
science with the Christian faith and the compatibility of the
highest culture with the Gospel within the bosom of the Church,
thus contributing more than any other to convert the ancient
world to Christianity. But he made no compromises from shrewd
calculation: it was his inmost and holiest conviction that the
sacred documents of Christianity contained all the ideals of
antiquity, and that the speculative conception of ecclesiastical
Christianity was the only true and right one. His character was
pure, his life blameless; in his work he was not only unwearied,
but also unselfish. There have been few Fathers of the Church
whose life-story leaves such an impression of purity behind it as
that of Origen. The atmosphere which he breathed as a Christian
and as a philosopher was dangerous; but his mind remained
sound, and even his feeling for truth scarcely ever forsook him.[2]

[1] See his letter in Eusebius, H. E. VI. 19. 11 ff.

[2] In the polemic against Celsus it seems to us in not a few passages as if the
feeling for truth had forsaken him. If we consider, however, that in Origen's idea
the premises of his speculation were unassailable, and if we further consider into
what straits he was driven by Celsus, we will conclude that no proof has been
advanced of Origen's having sinned against the current rules of truth. These, however, did not include the commandment to use in disputation only such arguments
as could be employed in a positive doctrinal presentation. Basilius (Ep. 210 ad
prim. Neocaes) was quite ready to excuse an utterance of Gregory Thaumaturgus,
that sounded suspiciously like Sabellianism, by saying that the latter was not
speaking δογματικῶς, but ἀγωνιστικῶς. Jerome also (ad Pammach. ep. 48, c. 13),
after defending the right of writing γυμναστικῶς, expressly said that all Greek
philosophers "have used many words to conceal their thoughts, threaten in one
place, and deal the blow in another." In the same way, according to him, Origen,
Methodius, Eusebius, and Apollinaris had acted in the dispute with Celsus and

To us his theory of the world, surveyed in its details, presents various changing hues, like that of Philo, and at the present day we can scarcely any longer understand how he was able to unite the different materials; but, considering the solidity of his character and the confidence of his decisions, we cannot doubt that he himself felt the agreement of all essential parts of his system. No doubt he spoke in one way to the perfect and in another to the mass of Christian people. The narrow-minded or the immature will at all times necessarily consider such proceedings hypocrisy, but the outcome of his religious and scientific conception of the world required the twofold language. Orthodox theology of all creeds has never yet advanced beyond the circle first mapped out by his mind. She has suspected and corrected her founder, she has thought she could lop off his heterodox opinions as if they were accidental excrescences, she has incorporated with the simple faith itself the measure of speculation she was obliged to admit, and continued to give the rule of faith a more philosophic form, fragment by fragment, in order that she might thus be able to remove the gap between Faith and Gnosis and to banish free theology through the formula of ecclesiastical dogma. But it may reasonably be questioned whether all this is progress, and it is well worth investigating whether the gap between half theological, clerical Christianity and a lay Christianity held in tutelage is more endurable than that between Gnosis and Pistis, which Origen preserved and bridged over.

The Christian system of Origen [1] is worked out in opposition to the systems of the Greek philosophers and of the Christian Gnostics. It is moreover opposed to the ecclesiastical enemies of science, the Christian Unitarians, and the Jews. [2] But the

Porphyry. "Because they are sometimes compelled to say, not what they themselves think, but what is necessary for their purpose; they do this only in the struggle with the heathen."

[1] See, above all, the systematic main work "περὶ ἀρχῶν".

[2] Many writings of Origen are pervaded by arguments, evincing equal discretion and patience, against the Christians who contest the right of science in the Church. In the work against Celsus, however, he was not unfrequently obliged to abandon the simple Christians. C. Celsus III. 78: V. 14—24 are particularly instructive.

science of the faith, as developed by Origen, being built up with the appliances of Philo's science, bears unmistakable marks of Neoplatonism and Gnosticism. Origen speculated not only in the manner of Justin, but also in that of Valentinus and therefore likewise after the fashion of Plotinus; in fact he is characterised by the adoption of the methods and, in a certain sense, of the axioms current in the schools of Valentinus and traceable in Neoplatonism. But, as this method implied the acknowledgment of a sacred literature, Origen was an exegete who believed in the Holy Scriptures and indeed, at bottom, he viewed all theology as a methodical exegesis of Holy Writ. Finally, however, since Origen, as an ecclesiastical Christian, was convinced that the Church (by which he means only the perfect and pure Church) is the sole possessor of God's holy revelations with whose authority the faith may be justly satisfied, nothing but the two Testaments, as preserved by her, was regarded by him as the absolutely reliable divine revelation. [1] But, in addition to these, every possession of the Church, and, above all, the rule of faith, was authoritative and holy. [2] By acknowledging not only the relative correctness of the beliefs held by the great mass of simple Christians, as the Valentinians did, but also the indispensableness of their faith as the foundation of speculation, Origen like Clement avoided the dilemma of becoming a heterodox Gnostic or an ecclesiastical traditionalist. He was able to maintain this standpoint, because in the first place his Gnosis required a guaranteed sacred literature which he only found in

[1] In this point Origen is already narrower than Clement. Free judgments, such as were passed by Clement on Greek philosophy, were not, so far as I know, repeated by Origen. (See especially Clement, Strom. I. 5. 28—32 : 13. 57, 58 etc.); yet he also acknowledges revelations of God in Greek philosophy (see, *e.g.*, c. Cels. VI. 3), and the Christian doctrine is to him the completion of Greek philosophy (see the remains of Origen's lost Stromateis and Hom. XIV. in Genes. § 3; other passages in Redepenning II., p, 324 ff.).

[2] We must here content ourselves with merely pointing out that the method of scientific Scriptural exegesis also led to historico-critical investigations, that accordingly Origen and his disciples were also critics of the tradition, and that scientific theology, in addition to the task of remodelling Christianity, thus began at its very origin the solution of another problem, namely, the critical restoration of Christianity from the Scriptures and tradition and the removal of its excrescences: for these efforts, strictly speaking, do not come up for consideration in the history of dogma.

the Church, and because in the second place this same Gnosis
had extended its horizon far enough to see that what the heretical
Gnosis had regarded as contrasts were different aspects of the
same thing. The relative way of looking at things, an inheritance
from the best time of antiquity, is familiar to Origen, as it was
to Clement; and he contrived never to lose sight of it, in spite
of the absolute attitude he had arrived at through the Christian
Gnosis and the Holy Scriptures. This relative view taught him
and Clement toleration and discretion (Strom. IV. 22. 139: ἡ
γνῶσις ἀγαπᾷ καὶ τοὺς ἀγνοοῦντας διδάσκει τε καὶ παιδεύει τὴν
πᾶσαν κτίσιν τοῦ παντοκράτορος Θεοῦ τιμᾶν, "Gnosis loves and
instructs the ignorant and teaches us to honour the whole creation
of God Almighty"); and enabled them everywhere to discover,
hold fast, and further the good in that which was meagre and
narrow, in that which was undeveloped and as yet intrinsically
obscure. [1] As an orthodox traditionalist and decided opponent
of all heresy Origen acknowledged that Christianity embraces
a salvation which is offered to all men and attained by faith,
that it is the doctrine of historical facts to which we must adhere,
that the content of Christianity has been appropriately summarised
by the Church in her rule of faith, [2] and that belief is of itself
sufficient for the renewal and salvation of man. But, as an
idealistic philosopher, Origen transformed the whole content of
ecclesiastical faith into ideas. Here he adhered to no fixed
philosophical system, but, like Philo, Clement, and the Neoplatonists, adopted and adapted all that had been effected by the
labours of idealistic Greek moralists since the time of Socrates.
These, however, had long before transformed the Socratic saying
"know thyself" into manifold rules for the right conduct of life,
and associated with it a theosophy, in which man was first to
attain to his true self. [3] These rules made the true "sage"

[1] The theory that justified a twofold morality in the Church is now completely
legitimised, but the higher form no longer appears as Encratite and eschatological,
but as Encratite and philosophical. See, for example, Clement, Strom. III. 12. 82:
VI. 13. 106 etc. Gnosis is the principle of perfection. See Strom. IV. 7. 54:
πρόκειται δὲ τοῖς εἰς τελείωσιν σπεύδουσιν ἡ γνῶσις ἡ λογικὴ ἧς θεμέλιος ἡ ἁγία
τριὰς πιστίς, ἀγάπη, ἐλπίς.
See the preface to the work περὶ ἀρχῶν.
From the conclusion of Hippolytus' Philosophoumena it is also evident how

abstain from occupying himself in the service of daily life and "from burdensome appearance in public". They asserted that the mind "can have no more peculiar duty than caring for itself. This is accomplished by its not looking without nor occupying itself with foreign things, but, turning inwardly to itself, restoring its own nature to itself and thus practising righteousness."[1] Here it was taught that the wise man who no longer requires anything is nearest the Deity, because he is a partaker of the highest good through possession of his rich Ego and through his calm contemplation of the world; here moreover it was proclaimed that the mind that has freed itself from the sensuous[2] and lives in constant contemplation of the eternal is also in the end vouchsafed a view of the invisible and is itself deified. No one can deny that this sort of flight from the world and possession of God involves a specific secularisation of Christianity, and that the isolated and self-sufficient sage is pretty much the opposite of the poor soul that hungers after righteousness.[3] Nor, on the other hand, can any one deny that concrete examples of both types are found in infinite multiplicity and might shade off into each other in this multiplicity. This was the case with Clement and Origen. To them the ethical and religious ideal is the state without sorrow, the state of insensibility to all evils, of order and peace—but peace in God. Reconciled to the course of the world, trusting in the divine Logos,[4] rich in disinterested love to God and the brethen, reproducing the divine thoughts, looking up with longing to heaven its native city,[5] the created spirit

the Socratic Γνῶθι σεαυτόν was in that age based on a philosophy of religion and was regarded as a watchword in wide circles. See Clem. Pædag. III. 11. 1.

[1] See Gregory Thaumaturgus' panegyric on Origen, one of the most instructive writings of the 3rd century, especially cc. 11—18.

[2] Yet all excesses are repudiated. See Clem. Strom. IV. 22. 138: Οὐκ ἐγκρατὴς οὗτος ἔτι, ἀλλ᾽ ἐν ἕξει γέγονεν ἀπαθείας σχῆμα θεῖον ἐπενδύσασθαι ἀναμένων. Similar remarks are found in Origen.

[3] In many passages of Clement the satisfaction in knowledge appears in a still more pronounced form than in Origen. The boldest expression of it is Strom. IV. 22. 136. This passage is quoted above on p. 328.)

[4] See the beautiful prayer of the Christian Gnostic in Strom. IV. 23. 148.

[5] See Strom. IV. 26. 172: Origen's commentaries are continually interrupted by similar outbursts of feeling.

attains its likeness to God and eternal bliss. It reaches this by
the victory over sensuousness, by constantly occupying itself
with the divine—"Go ye believing thoughts into the wide field
of eternity"—by self-knowledge and contemplative isolation, which,
however, does not exclude work in the kingdom of God, that
is in the Church. This is the divine wisdom: "The soul practises
viewing herself as in a mirror: she displays the divine Spirit in
herself as in a mirror, if she is to be found worthy of this fellowship; and she thus discovers the traces of a mysterious way to
deification." [1] Origen employed the Stoic and Platonic systems
of ethics as an instrument for the gradual realisation of this ideal. [2]
With him the mystic and ecstatic as well as the magic and sacramental element is still in the background, though it is not wanting.
To Origen's mind, however, the inadequacy of philosophical
injunctions was constantly made plain by the following considerations. (1) The philosophers, in spite of their noble thoughts of
God, tolerated the existence of polytheism; and this was really
the only fault he had to find with Plato. (2) The truth did not
become universally accessible through them. [3] (3) As the result
of these facts they did not possess sufficient power. [4] In contrast
to this the divine revelation had already mastered a whole people
through Moses—"Would to God the Jews had not transgressed
the law, and had not slain the prophets and Jesus; we would
then have had a model of that heavenly commonwealth which
Plato has sought to describe" [5]—and the Logos shows his universal

---

[1] On deification as the ultimate aim see Clem., Strom. IV. 23. 149—155: VII.
10. 56, 13. 82, 16. 95: οὕτως ὁ τῷ κυρίῳ πειθόμενος καὶ τῇ δοθείσῃ δι' αὐτοῦ κατα-
κολουθήσας προφητείᾳ τελέως ἐκτελεῖται κατ' εἰκόνα τοῦ διδασκάλου ἐν σαρκὶ περι-
πολῶν Θεός. But note what a distinction Clement makes between ὁ Θεός and the
perfect man in VII. 15. 88 (in contradistinction to the Stoic identification); Origen
does this also.

[2] Gregory (l. c., c. 13) relates that all the works of the poets and philosophers were
read in Origen's school, and that every part of these works that would stand the
test was admitted. Only the works of atheists were excluded , "because these
overpass the limits of human thought." However, Origen did not judge philosophers in such an unprejudiced manner as Clement, or, to speak more correctly,
he no longer valued them so highly. See Bigg, l.c., p. 133, Denis l.c. Introd.

[3] See, for example, c. Cels. V. 43: VII. 47, 59 sq. He compared Plato and
other wise men to those doctors who give their attention only to cultured patients.

[4] See, for example, c. Cels. VI. 2.

[5] C. Cels. V. 43.

power in the Church (1) by putting an end to all polytheism, and (2) by improving everyone to the extent that his knowledge and capacity admit, and in proportion as his will is inclined to, and susceptible of, that which is good. [1]

[1] One of Origen's main ideas, which we everywhere meet with, particularly in the work against Celsus (see, for example, VI. 2) is the thought that Christ has come to improve all men according to their several capacities, and to lead some to the highest knowledge. This conception appears to fall short of the Christian ideal and perhaps really does so; but as soon as we measure it not by the Gospel but by the aims of Greek philosophy, we see very clearly the progress that has been attained through this same Gospel. What Origen has in his eye is mankind, and he is anxious for the amendment not merely of a few, but of all. The actual state of things in the Church no longer allowed him to repeat the exclamations of the Apologists that all Christians were philosophers and that all were filled with the same wisdom and virtue. These exclamations were naïve and inappropriate even for that time. But he could already estimate the relative progress made by mankind within the Church as compared with those outside her pale, saw no gulf between the growing and the perfect, and traced the whole advance to Christ. He expressly declared, c. Cels. III. 78, that the Christianity which is fitted for the comprehension of the multitude is not the best doctrine in an absolute, but only in a relative, sense; that the "common man", as he expresses himself, must be reformed by the prospect of rewards and punishments; and that the truth can only be communicated to him in veiled forms and images, as to a child. The very fact, however, that the Logos in Jesus Christ has condescended so to act is to Origen a proof of the universality of Christianity. Moreover, many of the wonderful phenomena reported in the Holy Scriptures belong in his opinion to the veiled forms and images. He is very far from doing violence to his reason here; he rather appeals to mysterious powers of the soul, to powers of divination, visionary states etc. His standpoint in this case is wholly that of Celsus (see particularly the instructive disquisition in I. 48), in so far as he is convinced that many unusual things take place between heaven and earth, and that individual names, symbols etc. possess a mysterious power (see, for example, c. Cels. V. 45). The views as to the relationship between knowledge and holy initiation or *sacramentum* are those of the philosophers of the age. He thinks, however, that each individual case requires to be examined, that there can be no miracles not in accordance with nature, but that on the contrary everything must fit into a higher order. As the letter of the precepts in both Testaments frequently contains things contrary to reason (see περὶ ἀρχῶν IV. 2. 8—27) in order to lead men to the spiritual interpretation, and as many passages contain no literal sense at all (l.c. § 12), so also, in the historical narratives, we frequently discover a mythical element from which consequently nothing but the idea is to be evolved (l.c. § 16 sq.: "Non solum de his, quæ usque ad adventum Christi scripta sunt, hæc Spiritus sanctus procuravit, sed ... eadem similiter etiam in evangelistis et apostolis fecit. Nam ne illas quidem narrationes, quas per eos inspiravit, absque huiuscemodi, quam supra exposuimus, sapientiæ suæ arte contexuit. Unde etiam in ipsis non parva promiscuit, quibus historialis narrandi ordo interpolatus, vel intercisus per

Not only, however, did Origen employ the Greek ethic in its varied types, but the Greek cosmological speculation also formed the complicated substructure of his religious system of morals. The Gnosis is formally a philosophy of revelation, that is a Scripture theology, [1] and materially a cosmological speculation. On the basis of a detailed theory of inspiration, which itself, moreover, originates with the philosophers, the Holy Scriptures are so treated that all facts appear as the vehicles of ideas and only attain their highest value in this aspect. Systematic theol-

impossibilitatem sui reflecteret atque revocaret intentionem legentis ad intelligentiæ interioris examen.") In all such cases Origen makes uniform use of the two points of view, that God wished to present something even to the simple and to incite the more advanced to spiritual investigations. In some passages, however, the former point of view fails, because the content of the text is offensive; in that case it is only the second that applies. Origen therefore was very far from finding the literal content of Scripture edifying in every instance, indeed, in the highest sense, the letter is not edifying at all. He rather adopted, to its widest extent, the critical method employed by the Gnostics particularly when dealing with the Old Testament; but the distinction he made between the different senses of Scripture and between the various legitimate human needs enabled him to preserve both the unity of God and the harmony of revelation. Herein, both in this case and everywhere else, lies the superiority of his theology. Read especially c. Celsum I. 9—12. After appealing to the twofold religion among the Egyptians, Persians, Syrians, and Indians—the mythical religion of the multitude and the mystery-religion of the initiated—he lays down exactly the same distinction within Christianity, and thus repels the reproach of Celsus that the Christians were obliged to accept everything without examination. With regard to the mythical form of Christianity he merely claims that it is the most suitable among religions of this type. Since, as a matter of fact, the great majority of men have neither time nor talent for philosophy, ποία ἂν ἄλλη βελτίων μέθοδος πρὸς τὸ τοῖς πολλοῖς βοηθῆσαι εὑρεθείη, τῆς ἀπὸ τοῦ Ἰησοῦ τοῖς ἔθνεσι παραδοθείσης (l.c., 9). This thought is quite in the spirit of antiquity, and neither Celsus nor Porphyry could have any fault to find with these arguments in point of form: all positive religions have a mythical element; the true religion therefore lies behind the religions. But the novelty which neither Celsus nor Porphyry could recognise lies in the acknowledgment that the one religion, even in its mythical form, is unique and divine, and in the demand that all men, so far as they cannot attain the highest knowledge, must subject themselves to this mythical religion and no other. In this claim Origen rejected the ancient contrast between the multitude and the initiated just as he repudiated polytheism; and in this, if I see rightly, his historical greatness consists. He everywhere recognised gradations tending in the same direction and rejected polytheism.

[1] Bigg (l.c., p. 154) has rightly remarked: "Origen in point of method differs most from Clement, who not unfrequently leaves us in doubt as to the precise Scriptural basis of his ideas."

ogy, in undertaking its task, always starts, as Clement and
Origen also did, with the conscious or unconscious thought of
emancipating itself from the outward revelation and community
of cultus that are the characteristic marks of positive religion.
The place of these is taken by the results of speculative cosmology, which, though themselves practically conditioned, do not
seem to be of this character. This also applies to Origen's
Christian Gnosis or scientific dogmatic, which is simply the
metaphysics of the age. However, as he was the equal of the
foremost minds of his time, this dogmatic was no schoolboy
imitation on his part, but was to some extent independently
developed and was worked out both in opposition to pantheistic
Stoicism and to theoretical dualism. That we are not mistaken
in this opinion is shown by a document ranking among the
most valuable things preserved to us from the third century;
we mean the judgment passed on Origen by Porphyry in Euseb.,
H. E. VI. 19. Every sentence is instructive, [1] but the culminating
point is the judgment contained in § 7 : κατὰ μὲν τὸν βίον Χρισ-
τιανῶς ζῶν καὶ παρανόμως, κατὰ δὲ τὰς περὶ τῶν πραγμάτων καὶ
τοῦ θείου δόξας Ἑλληνίζων καὶ τὰ Ἑλλήνων τοῖς ὀθνείοις ὑποβαλ-
λόμενος μύθοις. ("His outward life was that of a Christian and
opposed to the law, but in regard to his views of things and
of the Deity, he thought like the Greeks, inasmuch as he
introduced their ideas into the myths of other peoples.") We can
everywhere verify this observation from Origen's works and
particularly from the books written against Celsus, where he is
continually obliged to mask his essential agreement in principles
and method with the enemy of the Christians. [2] The Gnosis is
in fact the Hellenic one and results in that wonderful picture of
the world which, though apparently a drama, is in reality immovable, and only assumes such a complicated form here from its
relation to the Holy Scriptures and the history of Christ. [3] The

---

[1] Note, for example, § 8, where it is said that Origen adopted the allegorical
method from the Stoic philosophers and applied it to the Jewish writings. On
Origen's hermeneutic principles in their relation to those of Philo see Siegfried,
l.c., pp. 351—62. Origen has developed them fully and clearly in the 4th Book
of περὶ ἀρχῶν.

[2] See Overbeck, Theologische Literatur-Zeitung, 1878, Col. 535.

[3] A full presentation of Origen's theology would require many hundreds of

Gnosis neutralises everything connected with empiric history; and if this does not everywhere hold good with regard to the actual occurrence of facts, it is at least invariably the case in respect to their significance. The clearest proof of this is (1) that Origen raised the thought of the unchangeability of God to be the norm of his system and (2) that he denied the historical, incarnate Logos any significance for "Gnostics". To these Christ merely appears as the Logos who has been from eternity with the Father and has always acted from the beginning. He alone is the object of the knowledge of the wise man, who merely requires a perfect or, in other words, a divine teacher.[1] The Gospel too only teaches the "shadow of the secrets of Christ;" but the eternal Gospel, which is also the pneumatic one, "clearly places before men's minds all things concerning the Son of God himself, both the mysteries shown by his words, and the things of which his acts were the riddles" (σαφῶς παρίστησι τοῖς νοοῦσι τὰ πάντα ἐνώπιον περὶ αὐτοῦ τοῦ υἱοῦ τοῦ Θεοῦ, καὶ τὰ παριστάμενα μυστήρια ὑπὸ τῶν λόγων αὐτοῦ, τά τε πράγματα, ὧν αἰνίγματα ἦσαν αἱ πράξεις αὐτοῦ)[2] No doubt the true theology based on revela-

pages, because he introduced everything worth knowing into the sphere of theology, and associated with the Holy Scriptures, verse by verse, philosophical maxims, ethical reflexions, and results of physical science, which would require to be drawn on the widest canvas, because the standpoint selected by Origen allowed the most extensive view and the most varied judgments. The case was similar with Clement before him, and also with Tertullian. This is a necessary result of "Scripture theology" when one takes it up in earnest. Tertullian assumes, for example, that there must be a Christian doctrine of dreams. Why? Because we read of dreams in the Holy Scriptures.

[1] In c. Cels. III. 61 it is said (Lommatzsch XVIII., p. 337): ἐπέμφθη οὖν Θεὸς λόγος καθὸ μὲν ἰατρὸς τοῖς ἁμαρτωλοῖς, καθὸ δὲ διδάσκαλος θείων μυστηρίων τοῖς ἤδη καθαροῖς καὶ μηκέτι ἁμαρτάνουσιν. See also what follows. In Comment. in John I. 20 sq. the crucified Christ, as the Christ of faith, is distinguished from the Christ who takes up his abode in us, as the Christ of the perfect. See 22 (Lomm. I. p. 43): καὶ μακάριοι γε ὅσοι δεόμενοι τοῦ υἱοῦ τοῦ Θεοῦ τοιοῦτοι γεγόνασιν, ὡς μηκέτι αὐτοῦ χρῄζειν ἰατροῦ τοὺς κακῶς ἔχοντας θεραπεύοντος, μηδὲ ποιμένος, μηδὲ ἀπολυτρώσεως, ἀλλὰ σοφίας καὶ λόγου καὶ δικαιοσύνης, ἢ εἴ τι ἄλλο τοῖς διὰ τελειότητα χωρεῖν αὐτοῦ τὰ κάλλιστα δυναμένοις. Read also c. Cels. II. 66, 69: IV. 15, 18: VI. 68. These passages show that the crucified Christ is no longer of any account to the Gnostic, and that he therefore allegorises all the incidents described in the Gospels. Clement, too, really regards Christ as of no importance to Gnostics except as a teacher.

[2] Comment. in Joh. I. 9, Lomm. I. p. 20. The "mysteries" of Christ is the

tion makes pantheism appear overthrown as well as dualism, and here the influence of the two Testaments cannot be mistaken; but a subtle form of the latter recurs in Origen's system, whilst the manner in which he rejected both made the Greek philosophy of the age feel that there was something akin to it here. In the final utterances of religious metaphysics ecclesiastical Christianity, with the exception of a few compromises, is thrown off as a husk. The objects of religious knowledge have no history or rather, and this is a genuinely Gnostic and Neoplatonic idea, they have only a supramundane one.

This necessarily gave rise to the assumption of an esoteric and exoteric form of the Christian religion, for it is only behind the statutory, positive religion of the Church that religion itself is found. Origen gave the clearest expression to this assumption, which must have been already familiar in the Alexandrian school of catechists, and convinced himself that it was correct, because he saw that the mass of Christians were unable to grasp the deeper sense of Scripture, and because he realised the difficulties of the exegesis. On the other hand, in solving the problem of adapting the different points of his heterodox system of thought to the *regula fidei*, he displayed the most masterly skill. He succeeded in finding an external connection, because, though the construction of his theory proceeded from the top downwards, he could find support for it on the steps of the *regula fidei*, already developed by Irenæus into the history of salvation.[1] The system itself is to be, in principle and in every respect, monistic, but, as the material world, though created by God out of nothing, merely appears as a place of punishment and purification for souls, a strong element of dualism is inherent in the system, as far as its practical application is concerned.[2] The pre-

technical term for this theology and, at bottom, for all theology. For, in respect of the form given to it, revelation always appears as a problem that theology has to solve. What is revealed is therefore either to be taken as immediate authority (by the believer) or as a soluble problem. One thing, accordingly, it is not, namely, something in itself evident and intelligible.

[1] See Nitzsch, Dogmengeschichte, p. 136.

[2] To Origen the problem of evil was one of the most important; see Book III. of περὶ ἀρχῶν and c. Cels. VI. 53—59. He is convinced (1) that the world is not the work of a second, hostile God; (2) that virtues and the works arising from

vailing contrast is that between the one transcendent essence
and the multiplicity of all created things. The pervading ambiguity lies in the twofold view of the spiritual in so far as, on the
one hand, it belongs to God as the unfolding of his essence,
and, on the other, as being created, is contrasted with God.
This ambiguity, which recurs in all the Neoplatonic systems
and has continued to characterise all mysticism down to the
present day, originates in the attempt to repel Stoic pantheism

them are alone good in the proper sense of the word, and that nothing but the
opposite of these is bad; (3) that evil in the proper sense of the word is only
evil will (see c. Cels. IV. 66 : VI. 54). Accordingly he makes a very decided
distinction between that which is bad and evils. As for the latter he admits that
they partly originate from God, in which case they are designed as means of
training and punishment. But he saw that this conception is insufficient, both in
view of individual passages of Holy Scripture and of natural experience. There
are evils in the world that can be understood neither as the result of sin nor as
means of training. Here then his relative, rational view of things comes in, even
with respect to the power of God. There are evils which are a necessary consequence of carrying out even the best intentions (c. Cels. VI. 53: τὰ κακὰ ἐκ
παρακολουθήσεως γεγένηται τῆς πρὸς τὰ προηγούμενα): " Evils, in the strict sense,
are not created by God; yet some, though but few in comparison with the great,
well-ordered whole of the world, have of necessity adhered to the objects realised;
as the carpenter who executes the plan of a building does not manage without
chips and similar rubbish, or as architects cannot be made responsible for the
dirty heaps of broken stones and filth one sees at the sites of buildings; (l.c., c. 55).
Celsus also might have written in this strain. The religious, absolute view is here
replaced by a rational, and the world is therefore not the best absolutely, but the
best possible. See the Theodicy in περὶ ἀρχῶν III. 17—22. (Here, and also in
other parts, Origen's Theodicy reminds us of that of Leibnitz; see Denis, l.c.,
p. 626 sq. The two great thinkers have a very great deal in common, because
their philosophy was not of a radical kind, but an attempt to give a rational
interpretation to tradition.) But " for the great mass it is sufficient when they are
told that evil has not its origin in God" (IV. 66). The case is similar with that
which is really bad. It is sufficient for the multitude to know that that which is
bad springs from the freedom of the creature, and that matter which is inseparable
from things mortal is not the source and cause of sin (IV. 66, see also III. 42:
τὸ κυρίως μιαρὸν ἀπὸ κακίας τοιοῦτόν ἐστι. Φύσις δὲ σώματος οὐ μιαρά· οὐ γὰρ
ᾗ φύσις σώματός ἐστι, τὸ γεννητικὸν τῆς μιαρότητος ἔχει τὴν κακίάν); but a closer
examination shows that there can be no man without sin (III. 61) because error is inseparable from growth and because the constitution of man in the flesh makes
evil unavoidable (VII. 50). Sinfulness is therefore natural and it is the necessary
prius. This thought, which is also not foreign to Irenæus, is developed by Origen
with the utmost clearness. He was not content with proving it, however, but in
order to justify God's ways proceeded to the assumption of a Fall before time
began (see below).

and yet to preserve the transcendental nature of the human
spirit, and to maintain the absolute causality of God without
allowing his goodness to be called in question. The assumption
that created spirits can freely determine their own course is
therefore a necessity of the system; in fact this assumption is
one of its main presuppositions [1] and is so boldly developed as
to limit the omnipotence and omniscience of God. But, as from
the empirical point of view the knot is tied for every man at
the very moment he appears on earth, and since the problem
is not created by each human being as the result of his own
independent will, but lies in his organisation, speculation must
retreat behind history. So the system, in accordance with certain
hints of Plato, is constructed on the same plan as that of Valentinus, for example, to which it has an extraordinary affinity. It
contains three parts : (1) The doctrine of God and his unfoldings
or creations, (2) the doctrine of the Fall and its consequences,
(3) the doctrine of redemption and restoration. [2] Like Denis,

---

[1] See Mehlhorn, Die Lehre von der menschlichen Freiheit nach Origenes (Zeitschrift für Kirchengeschichte, Vol. II., p. 234 ff.)

[2] The distinction between Valentinus and Origen consists in the fact that the former
makes an aeon or, in other words, a part of the divine *pleroma*, itself fall, and that he
does not utilise the idea of freedom. The outline of Origen's system cannot be
made out with complete clearness from the work περὶ ἀρχῶν, because he endeavoured
to treat each of the first three parts as a whole. Origen's four principles are God,
the World, Freedom, Revelation (Holy Scripture). Each principle, however, is brought
into relation with Christ. The first part treats of God and the spirits, and follows
the history of the latter down to their restoration. The second part treats of the
world and humanity, and likewise closes with the prospect of the resurrection,
punishment in hell, and eternal life. Here Origen makes a magnificent attempt to
give a conception of bliss and yet to exclude all sensuous joys. The third book
treats of sin and redemption, that is, of freedom of will, temptation, the struggle
with the powers of evil, internal struggles, the moral aim of the world, and the
restoration of all things. A special book on Christ is wanting, for Christ is no
"principle"; but the incarnation is treated of in II. 6. The teachers of Valentinus'
school accordingly appear more Christian when contrasted with Origen. If we read
the great work περὶ ἀρχῶν, or the treatise against Celsus, or the commentaries
connectedly, we never cease to wonder how a mind so clear, so sure of the
ultimate aim of all knowledge, and occupying such a high standpoint, has admitted
in details all possible views down to the most naïve myths, and how he on the
one hand believes in holy magic, sacramental vehicles and the like, and on the
other, in spite of all his rational and even empirical views, betrays no doubt of
his abstract creations. But the problem that confronts us in Origen is that presented

however, we may also, in accordance with a premised theory of
method, set forth the system in four sections, viz., Theology,
Cosmology, Anthropology, Teleology. Origen's fundamental
idea is "the original indestructible unity of God and all spiritual
essence." From this it necessarily follows that the created spirit
after fall, error, and sin must ever return to its origin, to being
in God. In this idea we have the key to the religious philosophy
of Origen.

The only sources for obtaining a knowledge of the truth are
the Holy Scriptures of both Testaments. No doubt the speculations of Greek philosophers also contain truths, but these have
only a propædeutic value and, moreover, have no certainty to
offer, as have the Holy Scriptures, which are a witness to themselves in the fulfilment of prophecy. [1] On the other hand Origen
assumes that there was an esoteric deeper knowledge in addition to the Holy Scriptures, and that Jesus in particular imparted
this deeper wisdom to a few; [2] but, as a correct Church theologian, he scarcely made use of this assumption. The first

by his age. This we realise on reading Celsus or Porphyry (see Denis l.c., p. 613 :
"Toutes les théories d'Origène, même les plus imaginaires, représent l'état intel-
lectuel et moral du siècle où il a paru"). Moreover, Origen is not a teacher who,
like Augustine, was in advance of his time, though he no doubt anticipated the
course of ecclesiastical development. This age, as represented by its greatest men,
sought to gain a substructure for something new, not by a critical examination of
the old ideas, but by incorporating them all into one whole. People were anxious
to have assurance, and, in the endeavour to find this, they were nervous about
giving up any article of tradition. The boldness of Origen, judged as a Greek
philosopher, lies in his rejection of all polytheistic religions. This made him all
the more conservative in his endeavours to protect and incorporate everything else.
This conservatism welded together ecclesiastical Christianity and Greek culture into
a system of theology which was indeed completely heterodox.

    1 The proof from prophecy was reckoned by Origen among the articles belonging
to faith, but not to Gnosis (see for ex. c. Cels. II. 37); but, like the Apologists, he
found it of great value. As far as the philosophers are concerned, Origen always
bore in mind the principle expressed in c. Cels. VII. 46: πρὸς ταῦτα δ'ἡμεῖς φή-
σομεν οἱ μελετήσαντες μηδενὶ ἀπεχθάνεσθαι τῶν καλῶς λεγομένων· κἂν οἱ ἔξω τῆς
πίστεως λέγωσι καλῶς.  In that same place it is asserted that God in his love has
not only revealed himself to such as entirely consecrate themselves to his service, but
also to such as do not know the true adoration and reverence which he requires.
But as remarked above, p. 338, Origen's attitude to the Greek philosophers is much
more reserved than that of Clement.

    2 See, for ex., c. Cels. VI. 6, Comment in Johann. XIII. 59, Lomm. II., p. 9 sq.

methodical principle of his exegesis is that the faith, as professed
in the Church in contradistinction to heresy, must not be tampered with. [1]  But it is the carrying out of this rule that really
forms the task of the theologian. For the faith itself is fixed
and requires no particular presentation; it never occurred to
Origen to assume that the fixing of the faith itself could present
problems. It is complete, clear, easily teachable, and really leads
to victory over sensuality and sin (see c. Cels. VII. 48 and cf.
other passages), as well as to fellowship with God, since it rests
on the revelation of the Logos. But, as it remains determined
by fear and hope of reward so, as "uninformed and irrational
faith" ($\pi i\sigma\tau\iota\varsigma$ $i\delta\iota\omega\tau\iota\kappa\dot{\eta}$ and $\ddot{\alpha}\lambda o\gamma o\varsigma$) it only leads to a "somatic
Christianity" ($\chi\rho\iota\sigma\tau\iota\alpha\nu\iota\sigma\mu\dot{o}\varsigma$ $\sigma\omega\mu\alpha\tau\iota\kappa\dot{o}\varsigma$). It is the task of theology,
however, to decipher "spiritual Christianity".($\chi\rho\iota\sigma\tau\iota\alpha\nu\iota\sigma\mu\dot{o}\varsigma$
$\pi\nu\epsilon\upsilon\mu\alpha\tau\iota\kappa\dot{o}\varsigma$) from the Holy Scriptures, and to elevate faith to
knowledge and clear vision. This is effected by the method of
Scripture exegesis which ascertains the highest revelations of
God. [2] The Scripture has a threefold sense because, like the
cosmos, alongside of which it stands like a second revelation,
as it were, it must contain a pneumatic, psychic, and somatic
element. The somatic or historical sense is in every case the
first that must be ascertained. It corresponds to the stage of
mere faith and has consequently the same dignity as the latter.
But there are instances where it is to be given up and designated
as a Jewish and fleshly sense. This is to be assumed in all
cases where it leads to ideas opposed to the nature of God,
morality, the law of nature, or reason. [3] Here one must judge
(see above) that such objectionable passages were meant to
incite the searcher to a deeper investigation. The psychic sense
is of a moral nature: in the Old Testament more especially
most narratives have a moral content, which one can easily
find by stripping off the history as a covering; and in certain

---

[1] Περὶ ἀρχῶν preface.

[2] On Origen's exegetical method see Kihn, Theodor v. Mopsu. p. 20 ff., Bigg,
l.c. p. 131 ff. On the distinction between his application of the allegorical method
and that of Clement see specially p. 134 f. of the latter work.

[3] Origen noted several such passages in the very first chapter of Genesis
Examples are given in Bigg, p. 137 f.

passages one may content oneself with this meaning. The pneumatic sense, which is the only meaning borne by many passages, an
assertion which neither Philo nor Clement ventured to make in
plain terms, has with Origen a negatively apologetic and a
positively didactic aim. It leads to the ultimate ideas which,
once attained, are self-evident, and, so to speak, pass completely
over into the mind of the theologian, because they finally obtain
for him clear vision and independent possession.[1] When the
Gnostic has attained this stage, he may throw away the ladders
by which he has reached this height.[2] He is then inwardly united
with God's Logos, and from this union obtains all that he requires.
In most passages Origen presupposed the similarity and equal
value of all parts of the Holy Scriptures ; but in some he showed
that even inspiration has its stages and grades, according to the
receptivity and worthiness of each prophet, thus applying his
relative view of all matters of fact in such cases also. In Christ
the full revelation of the Logos was first expressed ; his Apostles
did not possess the same inspiration as he,[3] and among the
Apostles and apostolic men differences in the degrees of inspiration are again to be assumed. Here Origen set the example of
making a definite distinction between a heroic age of the Apostles
and the succeeding period. This laid the foundation for an
assumption through which the later Church down to our time
has appeased her conscience and freed herself from demands that
she could not satisfy.[4]

[1] Bigg, l.c., has very appropriately named Origen's allegorism "Biblical alchemy".

[2] To ascertain the pneumatic sense, Origen frequently drew analogies between
the domain of the cosmic and that of the spiritual. He is thus a forerunner of
modern idealistic philosophers, for example, Drummond: "To Origen allegorism is
only one manifestation of the sacramental mystery of nature (Bigg, p. 134).

[3] See Hom. in Luc. XXIX., Lomm. V., p. 193 sq.

[4] Since Origen does not, as a rule, dispute the literal meaning of the Scriptures,
he has also a much more favourable opinion of the Jewish people and of the
observance of the law than the earlier Christian authors (but see Iren. and Tertull.).
At bottom he places the observance of the law quite on the same level as the
faith of the simple Christians. The Apostles also kept the law for a time, and it
was only by degrees that they came to understand its spiritual meaning. They
were also right to continue its observance during their mission among the Jews. On
the other hand, he considers the New Testament a higher stage than the Old both
in its literal and its spiritual sense. See c. Cels. II. 1—4, 7, 75 : IV. 31 sq. : V. 10,
30, 31, 42 sq., 66: VII. 26.

THE DOCTRINE OF GOD AND HIS SELF-UNFOLDINGS OR CREA-
TIONS. [1] The world points back to an ultimate cause and the created
spirit to an eternal, pure, absolutely simple, and unchangeable
spirit, who is the original source of all existence and goodness,
so that everything that exists only does so in virtue of being
caused by that One, and is good in so far as it derives its
essence from the One who is perfection and goodness. This
fundamental idea is the source of all the conclusions drawn by
Origen as to the essence, attributes, and knowableness of God.
As the One, God is contrasted with the Manifold; but the order
in the Manifold points back to the One. As the real Essence,
God is opposed to the essences that appear and seem to vanish,
and that therefore have no real existence, because they have
not their principle in themselves, but testify: "We have not made
ourselves." As the absolutely immaterial Spirit, God is contrasted
with the spirit that is clogged with matter, but which strives to
get back to him from whom it received its origin. The One is
something different from the Manifold; but the order, the dependence, and the longing of that which is created point back to the One,
who can therefore be known relatively from the Manifold. In
sharpest contrast to the heretical Gnosis, Origen maintained the
absolute causality of God, and, in spite of all abstractions in
determining the essence of God, he attributed self-consciousness and
will to this superessential Essence (in opposition to Valentinus,
Basilides, and the later Neoplatonists). [2] The created is one thing
and the Self-existent is another, but both are connected together;

1 In opposition to the method for obtaining a knowledge of God, recommended
by Alcinous (c. 12), Maximus Tyr. (XVII. 8), and Celsus (by analysis [apophat.],
synthesis [kataphat.], and analogy), Origen, c. Cels. VII. 42, 44, appeals to the
fact that the Christian knows God better, namely, in his incarnate Son. But he
himself, nevertheless, also follows the synthetic method.

2 In defining the superessential nature of the One, Origen did not go so far
as the Basilidians (Philosoph. VII. 20, 21) or as Plotinus. No doubt he also regards the Deity as ἐπέκεινα τῆς οὐσίας (c. Cels. VII. 42—51; περὶ ἀρχῶν I. 1;
Clement made a closer approach to the heretical abstractions of the Gnostics inasmuch as he still more expressly renounced any designation of God; see Strom. V.
12, 13), but he is not βύθος and σιγή, being rather a self-comprehending Spirit,
and therefore does not require a hypostasis (the νοῦς) before he can come to himself. Accordingly the human intellect is not incapable of soaring up to God as
the later Neoplatonists assert; at least vision is by no means so decidedly opposed

as the created can only be understood from something self-existent, so the self-existent is not without analogy to the created. The Self-existent is in itself a living thing; it is beyond dispute that Origen with all his abstractions represented the Deity, whom he primarily conceived as a constant substance, in a more living, and, so to speak, in a more personal way than the Greek philosophers. Hence it was possible for him to produce a doctrine of the attributes of God. Here he did not even shrink from applying his relative view to the Deity, because, as will be seen, he never thinks of God without revelation, and because all revelation must be something limited. The omnipresence of God indeed suffers from no limitation. God is potentially every-where; but he is everywhere only potentially; that is, he neither encompasses nor is encompassed. Nor is he diffused through the universe, but, as he is removed from the limits of space, so also he is removed from space itself.[1] But the omniscience and omnipotence of God have a limit, which indeed, according to Origen, lies in the nature of the case itself. In the first place his omnipotence is limited through his essence, for he can only do what he wills;[2] secondly by logic, for omnipotence cannot produce things containing an inward contradiction: God can do

---

to thought, that is, elevated above it as something new, as is held by the Neopla-tonists and Philo before them. Origen is no mystic. In accordance with this conception Origen and Clement say that the perfect knowledge of God can indeed be derived from the Logos alone (c. Cels. VII. 48, 49 : VI. 65—73; Strom. V. 12. 85 : VI. 15. 122), but that a relative knowledge may be deduced from creation (c. Cels. VII. 46). Hence they also spoke of an innate knowledge of God (Pro-trept. VI. 68; Strom. V. 13. 78), and extended the teleological proof of God fur-nished by Philo (περὶ ἀρχῶν I. 1. 6; c. Cels. I. 23). The relatively correct predi-cates of God to be determined from revelation are his unity (c. Cels. I. 23), his absolute spirituality (πνεῦμα ἀσώματος, ἄϋλος, ἀσχημάτιστος)—this is maintained both in opposition to Stoicism and anthropomorphism; see Orig. περὶ ἀρχῶν I. 1, Origen's polemic against Melito's conception of God, and Clem., Strom. V. 11. 68 : V. 12. 82,—his unbegottenness, his immortality (this is eternity conceived as en-joyment; the eternity of God itself, however, is to be conceived, according to Clement, as that which is above time; see Strom. II. 2. 6), and his absolute caus-ality. All these concepts together constitute the conception of perfection. See Fischer, De Orig. theologia et cosmologia, 1840.

[1] Orig. περὶ αρχῶν II. 1. 3.

[2] C. Cels. V. 23.

nothing contrary to nature, all miracles being natural in the
highest sense [1]—thirdly, by the impossibility of that which is in
itself unlimited being comprehended, whence it follows that the
extent of everything created must be limited [2]—fourthly, by the
impossibility of realising an aim completely and without disturbing
elements. [3] Omniscience has also its corresponding limits; this is
specially proved from the freedom of spirits bestowed by God
himself. God has indeed the capacity of foreknowledge, but
he knows transactions beforehand because they happen; they do
not happen because he knows them. [4] That the divine purpose
should be realised in the end necessarily follows from the nature
of the created spirit itself, apart from the supporting activity of
God. Like Irenæus and Tertullian Origen very carefully discussed
the attributes of goodness and justice in God in opposition to
the Marcionites. [5] But his exposition is different. In his eyes
goodness and justice are not two opposite attributes, which can
and must exist in God side by side; but as virtues they are to
him identical. God rewards in justice and punishes in kindness.
That it should go well with all, no matter how they conduct
themselves, would be no kindness; but it is kindness when God
punishes to improve, deter, and prevent. Passions, anger, and
the like do not exist in God, nor any plurality of virtues; but,
as the Perfect One, he is all kindness. In other places, however,
Origen did not content himself with this presentation. In opposition to the Marcionites, who declared Christ and the Father
of Christ to be good, and the creator of the world to be just,
he argued that, on the contrary, God (the foundation of the world)

---

[1] L.c.

[2] Περὶ ἀρχῶν II. 9. 1: "Certum est, quippe quod præfinito aliquo apud se numero
creaturas fecit: non enim, ut quidam volunt, finem putandum est non habere creaturas; quia ubi finis non est, nec comprehensio ulla nec circumscriptio esse potest.
Quod si fuerit utique nec contineri vel dispensari a deo, quæ facta sunt, poterunt.
Naturaliter nempe quicquid infinitum fuerit, et incomprehensibile erit." In Matth.,
t. 13., c. 1 fin., Lomm. III., p. 209 sq.

[3] See above, p. 343, note 2.

[4] See c. Cels. II. 20.

[5] Clement also did so; see with respect to Origen περὶ ἀρχῶν II. 5, especially
§ 3 sq.

is good, but that the Logos-Christ, in so far as he is the peda-
gogus, is just.[1]

From the perfect goodness of God Origen infers that he reveals
or communicates himself, from his immutability that he *always*
reveals himself. The eternal or never beginning communication
of perfection to other beings is a postulate of the concept " God ".
But, along with the whole fraternity of those professing the same
philosophy, Origen assumed that the One, in becoming the
Manifold and acting in the interests of the Manifold, can only
effect his purpose by divesting himself of absolute apathy and
once more assuming a form in which he can act, that is, procuring
for himself an adequate organ—*the Logos*. The content of Origen's teaching about this Logos was not essentially different
from that of Philo and was therefore quite as contradictory;
only in his case everything is more sharply defined and the
hypostasis of the Logos (in opposition to the Monarchians) more
clearly and precisely stated.[2] Nevertheless the personal independ-

---

[1] See Comment. in Johann. I. 40, Lomm. I. p. 77 sq. I cannot agree that
this view is a *rapprochement* to the Marcionites (contrary to Nitzsch's opinion,
l.c., p. 285). The confused accounts in Epiph., H. 43. 13 are at any rate not to be
taken into account.

[2] Clement's doctrine of the Logos, to judge from the Hypotyposes, was perhaps
different from that of Origen. According to Photius (Biblioth. 109) Clement
assumed two Logoi (Origen indeed was also reproached with the same; see Pamphili Apol., Routh, Reliq. S., IV., p. 367), and did not even allow the second and
weaker one to make a real appearance on earth; but this is a misunderstanding
(see Zahn, Forschungen III., p. 144). Λέγεται μέν—these are said to have been
the words of a passage in the Hypotyposes—καὶ ὁ υἱὸς λόγος ὁμωνύμως τῷ πατρικῷ
λόγῳ, ἀλλ' οὐχ οὗτός ἐστιν ὁ σὰρξ γενόμενος, οὐδὲ μὴν ὁ πατρῷος λόγος, ἀλλὰ
δύναμίς τις τοῦ Θεοῦ, οἷον ἀπόρροια τοῦ λόγου αὐτοῦ νοῦς γενόμενος τὰς τῶν
ἀνθρώπων καρδίας διαπεφοίτηκε. The distinction between an impersonal Logos-
God and the Logos-Christ necessarily appeared as soon as the Logos was definitely hypostatised. In the so-called Monarchian struggles of the 3rd century the
disputants made use of these two Logoi, who formed excellent material for sophis-
tical discussions. In the Strom. Clement did not reject the distinction between a
λόγος ἐνδιάθετος and προφορικός (on Strom. V. 1. 6. see Zahn, l.c., p. 145 against
Nitzsch), and in many passages expresses himself in such a way that one can
scarcely fail to notice a distinction between the Logos of the Father and that
of the Son. "The Son-Logos is an emanation of the Reason of God, which
unalterably remains in God and is the Logos proper." If the Adumbrationes are
to be regarded as parts of the Hypotyposes, Clement used the expression ὁμοούσιος
for the Logos, or at least an identical one (See Zahn, Forschungen III., pp. 87—

ence of the Logos is as yet by no means so sharply defined as in the case of the later Arians. He is still the Consciousness of God, the spiritual Activity of God. Hence he is on the one hand the idea of the world existing in God, and on the other the product of divine wisdom originating with the will of God. The following are the most important propositions.[1] The Logos who appeared in Christ, as is specially shown from Joh. I. 1 and Heb. I. 1, is the perfect image[2] of God. He is the Wisdom

138 f.). This is the more probable because Clement, Strom. 16. 74, expressly remarked that men are not μέρος θεοῦ καὶ τῷ Θεῷ ὁμοούσιοι, and because he says in Strom. IV. 13. 91: εἰ ἐπὶ τὸ καταλῦσαι θάνατον ἀφικνεῖται τὸ διαφέρον γένος, οὐχ ὁ Χριστὸς τὸν θάνατον κατήργησεν, εἰ μὴ καὶ αὐτὸς αὐτοῖς ὁμοούσιος λεχθείη. One must assume from this that the word was really familiar to Clement as a designation of the community of nature, possessed by the Logos, both with God and with men. See Protrept. 10. 110: ὁ θεῖος λόγος, ὁ φανερώτατος ὄντως Θεός, ὁ τῷ δεσπότῃ τῶν ὅλων ἐξισωθείς). In Strom. V. 1. 1 Clement emphatically declared that the Son was equally eternal with the Father: οὐ μὴν οὐδὲ ὁ πατὴρ ἄνευ υἱοῦ· ἅμα γὰρ τῷ πατὴρ υἱοῦ πατήρ (see also Strom. IV. 7. 58: ἐν μὲν τὸ ἀγέννητον ὁ παντοκράτωρ, ἐν δὲ καὶ τὸ προγεννηθὲν δι᾿ οὗ τὰ πάντα ἐγένετο, and Adumbrat. in Zahn, l.c., p. 87, where 1 John I. 1 is explained: "principium generationis separatum ab opificis principio non est. Cum enim dicit "quod erat ab initio" generationem tangit sine principio filii cum patre simul exstantis." See besides the remarkable passage, Quis dives salv. 37: Θεῷ τὰ τῆς ἀγάπης μυστήρια, καὶ τότε ἐποπτεύσεις τὸν κόλπον τοῦ πατρός, ὃν ὁ μονογενὴς υἱὸς Θεὸς μόνος ἐξηγήσατο· ἔστι δὲ καὶ αὐτὸς ὁ Θεὸς ἀγάπη καὶ δι᾿ ἀγάπην ἡμῖν ἀνεκράβη· καὶ τὸ μὲν ἄρρητον αὐτοῦ πατήρ, τὸ δὲ ἡμῖν συμπαθὲς γέγονε μήτηρ· ἀγαπήσας ὁ πατὴρ ἐθηλύνθη, καὶ τούτου μέγα σημεῖον, ὃν αὐτὸς ἐγέννησεν ἐξ αὐτοῦ καὶ ὁ τεχθεὶς ἐξ ἀγάπης καρπὸς ἀγάπη, But that does not exclude the fact that he, like Origen, named the Son κτίσμα (Phot., l.c.). In the Adumbrat. (p. 88) Son and Spirit are called "primitivæ virtutes ac primo creatæ, immobiles existentes secundum substantiam". That is exactly Origen's doctrine, and Zahn (l.c., p. 99) has rightly compared Strom. V. 14. 89: VI. 7. 58; and Epit. ex Theod. 20. The Son stands at the head of the series of created beings (Strom. VII. 2. 5; see also below), but he is nevertheless specifically different from them by reason of his origin. It may be said in general that the fine distinctions of the Logos doctrine in Clement and Origen are to be traced to the still more abstract conception of God found in the former. A sentence like Strom. IV. 25. 156 (ὁ μὲν οὖν Θεὸς ἀναπόδεικτος ὢν οὐκ ἔστιν ἐπιστημονικός, ὁ δὲ υἱὸς σοφία τέ ἐστι καὶ ἐπιστήμη) will hardly be found in Origen I think. Cf. Schultz, Gottheit Christi, p. 45 ff.

[1] See Schultz, l.c., p. 51 ff. and Jahrbuch für protestantische Theologie I. pp. 193 ff. 369 ff.

[2] It is very remarkable that Origen περὶ ἀρχῶν I. 2. 1 in his presentation of the Logos doctrine, started with the person of Christ, though he immediately abandoned this starting-point "Primo illud nos oportere scire", so this chapter

of God, the reflection of his perfection and glory, the invisible image of God. For that very reason there is nothing corporeal in him [1] and he is therefore really God, not αὐτόθεος, nor ὁ Θεός, nor ἄναρχος ἀρχή ("beginningless beginning"), but the second God. [2] But, as such, immutability is one of his attributes, that is, he can never lose his divine essence, he can also in this respect neither increase nor decrease (this immutability, however, is not an independent attribute, but he is perfect as being an image of the Father's perfection). [3] Accordingly this deity is not a communicated one in the sense of his having another independent essence in addition to this divine nature; but deity rather constitutes his essence: ὁ σωτὴρ οὐ κατὰ μετουσίαν, ἀλλὰ κατ' οὐσίαν ἐστὶ Θεός [4] ("the Saviour is not God by communication, but in his essence"). From this it follows that he shares in the essence of God, therefore of the Father, and is accordingly ὁμοούσιος τῷ πατρί ("the same in substance with the Father") or, seeing that, as Son, he has come forth from the Father, is engendered from the essence of the Father. [5] But having

begins, "Quod aliud est in Christo deitatis eius natura, quod est unigenitus filius patris, et alia humana natura, quam in novissimis temporibus pro dispensatione suscepit. Propter quod videndum primo est, quid sit unigenitus filius dei."

[1] Περὶ ἀρχῶν I. 2. 2, 6.

[2] The expression was familiar to Origen as to Justin (see Dial. c. Tryph). See c. Cels. V. 39: Καὶ δεύτερον οὖν λέγωμεν Θεόν· ἴστωσαν, ὅτι τὸν δεύτερον Θεὸν οὐκ ἄλλο τι λέγομεν, ἢ τὴν περιεκτικὴν πασῶν ἀρετῶν ἀρετὴν καὶ τὸν περιεκτικὸν παντὸς οὑτινοσοῦν λόγου τῶν κατὰ φύσιν καὶ προηγουμένως γεγενημένων,

[3] Περὶ ἀρχῶν I. 2. 13 has been much corrupted by Rufinus. The passage must have been to the effect that the Son is indeed ἀγαθός, but not, like the Father, ἀπαραλλάκτως ἀγαθός

[4] Selecta in Psalm., Lomm. XIII., p. 134; see also Fragm. comm. in ep. ad Hebr., Lomm. V., p. 299 sq.

[5] L.c.: "Sic et sapientia ex deo procedens, ex ipsa substantia dei generatur. Sic nihilominus et secundum similitudinem corporalis aporrhœæ esse dicitur aporrhœa gloriæ omnipotentis pura quædam et sincera. Quæ utræque similitudines (see the beginning of the passage) manifestissime ostendunt communionem substantiæ esse filio cum patre. Aporrhœa enim ὁμοούσιος videtur, id est, unius substantiæ cum illo corpore, ex quo est vel aporrhœa vel vapor." In opposition to Heracleon Origen argues (in Joh. XIII. 25., Lomm. II., p. 43 sq.) that we are not homousios with God: ἐπιστήσωμεν δέ, εἰ μὴ σφόδρα ἐστὶν ἀσεβὲς ὁμοουσίους τῇ ἀγεννήτῳ φύσει καὶ παμμακαρίᾳ εἶναι λέγειν τοὺς προσκυνοῦντας ἐν πνεύματι τῷ Θεῷ. On the meaning of ὁμοούσιος see Zahn, Marcell., pp. 11—32. The conception decidedly excludes the possibility of the two subjects connected by it having a different essence; but it

proceeded, like the will, from the Spirit, he was always with God ;
there was not a time when he was not, [1] nay, even this expression is still too weak. It would be an unworthy idea to think
of God without his wisdom or to assume a beginning of his
begetting. Moreover, this begetting is not an act that has only
once taken place, but a process lasting from all eternity; the
Son is always being begotten of the Father. [2] It is the theology
of Origen which Gregory Thaumaturgus has thus summed up : [3]
εἷς κύριος, μόνος ἐκ μόνου, Θεὸς ἐκ Θεοῦ, χαρακτὴρ καὶ εἰκὼν τῆς
θεότητος, λόγος ἔνεργος, σοφία τῆς τῶν ὅλων συστάσεως περιεκτικὴ
καὶ δύναμις τῆς ὅλης κτίσεως ποιητική, υἱὸς ἀληθινὸς ἀληθινοῦ πατρός,
ἀόρατος ἀοράτου καὶ ἄφθαρτος ἀφθάρτου καὶ ἀθάνατος ἀθανάτου καὶ
ἀΐδιος ἀϊδίου. ("One Lord, one from one, God from God, impress
and image of Godhead, energetic word, wisdom embracing the
entire system of the universe and power producing all creation,
true Son of a true Father, the invisible of the invisible and incorruptible of the incorruptible, the immortal of the immortal,
the eternal of the eternal"). The begetting is an indescribable
act which can only be represented by inadequate images : it is
no emanation—the expression προβολή is not found, so far as I

says nothing about how they came to have one essence and in what measure they
possess it. On the other hand it abolishes the distinction of persons the moment
the essence itself is identified with the one person. Here then is found the Unitarian danger, which could only be averted by assertions. In some of Origen's
teachings a modalistic aspect is also not quite wanting. See Hom. VIII. in
Jerem. no. 2 : Τὸ μὲν ὑποκείμενον ἕν ἐστι, ταῖς δὲ ἐπινοίαις τὰ πολλὰ ὀνόματα ἐπὶ
διαφόρων. Conversely, it is also nothing but an appearance when Origen (for ex.
in c. Cels. VIII. 12) merely traces the unity of Father and Son to unity in feeling
and in will. The charge of Ebionitism made against him is quite unfounded (see
Pamphili Apol., Routh IV. p. 367).

[1] Οὐκ ἔστιν ὅτε οὐκ ἦν, de princip. I. 2. 9; in Rom. I. 5.

[2] Περὶ ἀρχῶν I. 2. 2—9. Comm. in ep. ad. Hebr. Lomm. V., p. 296: "Nunquam
est, quando filius non fuit. Erat autem non, sicut de æterna luce diximus, innatus,
ne duo principia lucis videamur inducere, sed sicut ingenitæ lucis splendor, ipsam
illam lucem initium habens ac fontem, natus quidem ex ipsa ; sed non erat quando
non erat." See the comprehensive disquisition in περὶ ἀρχῶν IV. 28, where we find
the sentence : "hoc autem ipsum, quod dicimus, quia nunquam fuit, quando non
fuit, cum venia audiendum est" etc. See further in Jerem. IX. 4, Lomm. XV.,
p. 212 : τὸ ἀπαύγασμα τῆς δόξης οὐχὶ ἅπαξ γεγέννηται, καὶ οὐχὶ γὲννᾶται ., . καὶ
ἀεὶ γεννᾶται ὁ σωτὴρ ὑπὸ τοῦ πατρός; see also other passages.

[3] See Caspari, Quellen, Vol. IV., p. 10.

know [1]—but is rather to be designated as an act of the will arising from an inner necessity, an act which for that very reason is an emanation of the essence. But the Logos thus produced is really a personally existing being; he is not an impersonal force of the Father, though this still appears to be the case in some passages of Clement, but he is the "sapientia dei substantialiter subsistens" [2] ("the wisdom of God substantially existing") "figura expressa substantiæ patris" (express image of the Father's substance"), "virtus altera in sua proprietate subsistens" (a second force existing in its own characteristic fashion"). He is, and here Origen appeals to the old Acts of Paul, an "animal vivens" with an independent existence. [3]  He is another person, [4] namely, the second person in number. [5] But here already begins Origen's second train of thought which limits the first that we have set forth. As a particular hypostasis, which has its "first cause" (πρῶτον αἴτιον) in God, the Son is "that which is caused" (αἴτιατόν), moreover as the fulness of ideas, as he who comprehends in himself all the forms that are to have an active existence, the Son is no longer an absolute *simplex* like the Father. [6] He is already the first stage of the transition from the One to the Manifold, and, as the medium of the world-idea, his essence has an inward relation to the world, which is itself without begin-

---

[1] In περὶ ἀρχῶν IV. 28 the *prolatio* is expressly rejected (see also I. 2. 4) as well as the "conversio partis alicuius substantiæ dei in filium" and the "procreatio ex nullis substantibus,"

[2] L.c. I. 2. 2.

[3] L.c. I. 2. 3.

[4] De orat. 15: "Ετερος κατ᾽ οὐσίαν καὶ ὑποκείμενον ὁ υἱός ἐστι τοῦ πατρός. This, however, is not meant to designate a deity of a hybrid nature, but to mark the personal distinction.

[5] C. Cels. VIII. 12.: δύο τῇ ὑποστάσει πράγματα. This was frequently urged against the Monarchians in Origen's commentaries; see in Joh. X. 21:II. 6 etc. The Son exists κατ᾽ ἰδίαν τῆς οὐσίας περιγραφήν. Not that Origen has not yet the later terminology οὐσία, ὑπόστασις, ὑποκείμενον, πρόσωπον. We find three hypostases in Joh. II. 6. Lomm. I., p. 109, and this is repeatedly the case in c. Cels.

[6] In Joh. I. 22, Lomm. I., p. 41 sq.: ὁ Θεὸς μέν οὖν πάντη ἕν ἐστι καὶ ἁπλοῦν ὁ δὲ σωτὴρ ἡμῶν διὰ τὰ πολλά. The Son is ἰδέα ἰδεῶν, σύστημα θεωρημάτων ἐν αὐτῶ (Lomm. I., p. 127).

ning. [1] As soon therefore as the category of causality is applied
—which moreover dominates the system—and the particular
contemplation of the Son in relation to the Father gives way
to the general contemplation of his task and destination, the Son
is not only called κτίσμα and δημιούργημα, but all the utterances
about the quality of his essence receive a limitation. We nowhere
find the express assertion that this quality is inferior or of a different
kind when compared with that of God; but these utterances
lose their force when it is asserted that complete similarity
between Father and Son only exists in relation to the world.
We have to acknowledge the divine being that appeared in Christ
to be the manifestation of the Deity; but, from God's standpoint,
the Son is the hypostasis appointed by and *subordinated* to
him. [2] The Son stands between the uncreated One and the
created Many; in so far as unchangeableness is an attribute of
self-existence he does not possess it. [3] It is evident why Origen
was obliged to conceive the Logos exactly as he did; it
was only in this form that the idea answered the purpose for
which it was intended. In the description of the essence of the
Logos much more heed continues to be given to his creative
than to his redeeming significance. Since it was only a teacher
that Origen ultimately required for the purpose of redemption,
he could unfold the nature and task of the Logos without thinking of
Christ, whose name indeed he frequently mentions in his disquisitions,
but whose person is really not of the slightest importance there. [4]

In order to comply with the rule of faith, and for this reason
alone, for his speculation did not require a Spirit in addition to the
Logos, Origen also placed the Spirit alongside of Father and Son.
All that is predicated about him by the Church is that he is
equal to the other persons in honour and dignity, and it was he that
inspired both Prophets and Apostles; but that it is still undecided

[1] See the remarks on the saying: " The Father is greater than I," in Joh. XIII. 25,
Lomm. II., p. 45 sq. and other passages. Here Origen shows that he considers the homoousia of the Son and the Father just as relative as the unchangeability of the Son.
[2] Περὶ ἀρχῶν II. 2. 6 has been corrupted by Rufinus; see Jerome ep. ad Avitum.
[3] See περὶ ἀρχῶν I. 2. 13 (see above, p. 354, note 3).
[4] Athanasius supplemented this by determining the essence of the Logos from
the redeeming work of Christ.

whether he be created or uncreated, and whether he too is to be
considered the Son of God or not.[1] As the third hypostasis, Origen
reckoned him part of the constant divine essence and so treated him
after the analogy of the Son, without producing an impressive
proof of the necessity of this hypostasis. He, however, became
the Holy Spirit through the Son, and is related to the latter as
the latter is related to the Father; in other words he is subordinate to the Son; he is the first creation of the Father through
the Son.[2] Here Origen was following an old tradition. Considered
quantitively therefore, and this according to Origen is the most
important consideration, the Spirit's sphere of action is the
smallest. All being has its principle in the Father, the Son
has his sphere in the rational, the Holy Spirit in the sanctified,
that is in the Church; this he has to rule over and perfect. Father, Son, and Spirit form a τρίας ("triad")[3] to which
nothing may be compared; they are equal in dignity and honour,
and the substance they possess is one. If the following is not
one of Rufinus' corrections, Origen said[4]: Nihil in trinitate maius
minusve dicendum est cum unius divinitatis fons verbo ac ratione
sua teneat universa"[5] ("nothing in the Trinity is to be called
greater or less, since the fountain of one divinity holds all his
parts by word and reason"). But, as in Origen's sense the union
of these only exists because the Father alone is the "source of
deity" (πηγὴ τῆς θεότητος) and principle of the other two hypostases, the Trinity is in truth no homogeneous one, but one which,
in accordance with a "subtle emanation idea", has degrees
within it. This Trinity, which in the strict sense remains a

---

[1] See περὶ ἀρχῶν præf. and in addition to this Hermas' view of the Spirit.

[2] Περὶ ἀρχῶν I. 3. The Holy Spirit is eternal, is ever being breathed out, but
is to be termed a creature. See also in Joh. II. 6, Lomm. I., p. 109 sq.: τὸ ἅγιον
πνεῦμα διὰ τοῦ λόγου ἐγένετο, πρεσβυτέρου (logically) παρ᾽ αὐτὸ τοῦ λόγου τυγ-
χάνοντος. Yet Origen is not so confident here as in his Logos doctrine.

[3] See περὶ ἀρχῶν I. 3, 5—8. Hence Origen says the heathen had known the
Father and Son, but not the Holy Spirit (de princip. I. 3: II. 7).

[4] L.c. § 7.

[5] See Hom. in Num. XII. 1, Lomm. X, p. 127: "Est hæc trium distinctio personarum in patre et filio et spiritu sancto, quæ ad pluralem puteorum numerum revo-
catur. Sed horum puteorum unum est fons. Una enim substantia est et natura
trinitatis."

Trinity of revelation, except that revelation belongs to the essence
of God, is with Origen the real secret of the faith, the mystery
beyond all mysteries. To deny it shows a Jewish, carnal feeling
or at least the greatest narrowness of conception.

The idea of createdness was already more closely associated
with the Holy Ghost than with the Logos. He is in a still
clearer fashion than the Son himself the transition to the series
of ideas and spirits that having been created by the Son, are
in truth the unfolding of his fulness. They form the next stage
after the Holy Spirit. In assuming the existence of such beings
as were required by his philosophical system, Origen appealed
to the Biblical doctrine of angels, which he says is expressly
acknowledged in the Church. [1] With Clement even the association
of the Son and Holy Ghost with the great angelic spirits is as
yet not altogether avoided, at least in his expressions. [2] Origen
was more cautious in this respect. [3] The world of spirits appears
to him as a series of well-arranged, graded energies, as the
representative of created reason. Its characteristic is growth,
that is, progress ($\pi\rho\omega\kappa\omega\pi\acute{\eta}$). [4] Growth is conditioned by freedom :
" *omnis creatura rationabilis laudis et culpæ capax : laudis, si
secundum rationem, quam in se habet, ad meliora proficiat, culpæ,
si rationem recti declinet* " [5] (" every rational creature is capable
of meriting praise or blame—praise, if it advance to better things
according to the reason it possesses in itself, blame, if it avoid
the right course "). As unchangeableness and permanence are

---

[1] Περὶ ἀρχῶν præf.

[2] From Hermas, Justin, and Athenagoras we learn how, in the 2nd century,
both in the belief of uneducated lay-Christians and of the Apologists, Son, Spirit,
Logos, and angels under certain circumstances shaded off into one another. To
Clement, no doubt, Logos and Spirit are the only unchangeable beings besides
God. But, inasmuch as there is a series which descends from God to men
living in the flesh, there cannot fail to be elements of affinity between Logos and Spirit
on the one hand and the highest angels on the other, all of whom indeed have
the capacity and need of development. Hence they have certain names and predicates in common, and it frequently remains uncertain, especially as regards the
theophanies in the Old Testament, whether it was a high angel that spoke, or the
Son through the angel. See the full discussion in Zahn, Forschungen, III., p. 98 f.

[3] Περὶ ἀρχῶν I. 5.

[4] So also Clement, see Zahn, l.c.

[5] Περὶ ἀρχῶν I. 5. 2.

characteristic of the Deity, so freedom is the mark of the created spirit.[1] In this thesis Origen goes beyond the assumption of the heretical Gnostics just as much as he does in his other proposition that the creaturely spirit is in no sense a portion of the divine (because it is changeable[2]); but in reality freedom, as he understands it, is only the capacity of created spirits to determine their own destiny *for a time*. In the end, however, they must turn to that which is good, because everything spiritual is indestructible. *Sub specie æternitatis*, then, the mere communication of the divine element to the created spirit[3] is *not* a mere communication, and freedom is no freedom; but the absolute necessity of the created spirit's developing itself merely appears as freedom. Yet Origen himself did not draw this conclusion, but rather based everything on his conception that the freedom of *naturæ rationabiles* consisted in the *possibilitas utriusque*, and sought to understand the cosmos, as it is, from this freedom. To the *naturæ rationabiles*, which have different *species* and *ordines*, human souls also belong. The whole of them were created from all eternity; for God would not be almighty unless he had always produced everything[4]; in virtue of their origin they are equal, for their original community with

---

[1] It was of course created before the world, as it determines the course of the world. See Comm. in Matth. XV, 27, Lomm. III., p. 384 sq.

[2] See Comm. in Joh. XIII. 25, Lomm. II., p. 45: we must not look on the human spirit as ὁμοούσιος with the divine one. The same had already been expressly taught by Clement. See Strom., II. 16. 74: ὁ Θεὸς οὐδεμίαν ἔχει πρὸς ἡμᾶς φυσικὴν σχέσιν ὡς οἱ τῶν αἱρέσεων κτίσται θέλουσιν. Adumbr., p. 91 (ed. Zahn). This does not exclude God and souls having *quodammodo* one substance.

[3] Such is the teaching of Clement and Origen. They repudiated the possession of any natural, essential goodness in the case of created spirits. If such lay in their essence, these spirits would be unchangeable.

[4] Περὶ ἀρχῶν I. 2. 10: "Quemadmodum pater non potest esse quis, si filius non sit, neque dominus quis esse potest sine possessione, sine servo, ita ne omnipotens quidem deus dici potest, si non sint, in quos exerceat potentatum, et deo ut omnipotens ostendatur deus, omnia subsistere necesse est." (So the Hermogenes against whom Tertullian wrote had already argued). "Nam si quis est, qui velit vel sæcula aliqua vel spatia transisse, vel quodcunque aliud nominare vult, cum nondum facta essent, quæ facta sunt, sine dubio hoc ostendet, quod in illis sæculis vel spatiis omnipotens non erat deus et postmodum omnipotens factus est." God would therefore, it is said in what follows, be subjected to a προκοπή, and thus be proved to be a finite being. III. 5. 3.

the Logos permits of no diversity [1]; but, on the other hand, they
have received different tasks and their development is consequently
different. In so far as they are spirits subject to change, they
are burdened with a kind of bodily nature, [2] for it is only the
Deity that is without a body. The element of materiality is a
necessary result of their finite nature, that is, of their being
created; and this applies both to angels and human souls. [3] Now
Origen did not speculate at all as to how the spirit world might
have developed in ideal fashion, a fact which it is exceedingly
important to recognise; he knows nothing at all about an ideal
development for all, and does not even view it as a possibility.
The truth rather is that as soon as he mentions the *naturæ
rationabiles*, he immediately proceeds to speak of their fall, their
growth, and their diversities. He merely contemplates them in
the given circumstances in which they are placed (see the exposition in περὶ ἀρχῶν II. 9. 2).

THE DOCTRINE OF THE FALL AND ITS CONSEQUENCES. All
created spirits must develop. When they have done so, they
attain perfection and make way for new dispensations and worlds. [4]
In the exercise of their freedom, however, disobedience, laxity,
laziness, and failure make their appearance among them in an
endless multiplicity of ways. [5] The disciplining and purifying

---

[1] Περὶ ἀρχῶν I. 8.

[2] Here, however, Origen is already thinking of the temporary wrong development, that is of growth. See περὶ ἀρχῶν I. 7. Created spirits are also of themselves immaterial, though indeed not in the sense that this can be said of God
who can never attach anything material to himself.

[3] Angels, ideas (see Phot. Biblioth. 109), and human souls are most closely
connected together, both according to the theory of Clement and Origen and also
to that of Pantænus before them (see Clem. eclog. 56, 57); and so it was taught
that men become angels (Clem. Strom. VI. 13. 107). But the stars also, which
are treated in great detail in περὶ ἀρχῶν I. 7, belong to the number of the angels.
This is a genuinely Greek idea. The doctrine of the preëxistence of human souls
was probably set forth by Clement in the Hypotyposes. The theory of the transmigration of souls was probably found there also (Phot. Biblioth. 109). In the
Adumbrat., which has been preserved to us, the former doctrine is, however, contested and is not found in the Stromateis VI. 16. 1. sq.

[4] Phot. Biblioth. 109: Κλήμης πολλοὺς πρὸ τοῦ Ἀδὰμ κόσμους τερατεύεται. This
cannot be verified from the Strom. Orig., περὶ ἀρχῶν II. 3.

[5] Περὶ ἀρχῶν I. 5 and the whole 3rd Book. The Fall is something that
happened before time began.

of these spirits was the purpose for which the material world
was created by God. [1] It is therefore a place of purification,
ruled and harmoniously arranged by God's wisdom. [2] Each
member of the world of spirits has received a different kind of
material nature in proportion to his degree of removal from the
Creator. The highest spirits, who have virtually held fast by
that which is good, though they too stand in need of restitution, guide the world, are servants of God (ἄγγελοι), and have
bodies of an exceedingly subtle kind in the form of a globe
(stars). The spirits that have fallen very deeply (the spirits of
men) are banished into material bodies. Those that have altogether
turned against God have received very dark bodies, indescribably
ugly, though not visible. Men therefore are placed between the
angels and demons, both of whom try to influence them. The
moral struggle that man has to undergo within himself is made
harder by the demons, but lightened by the angels, [3] for these
spiritual powers are at all times and places acting both upon

[1] The assumption of uncreated matter was decidedly rejected by Origen (περὶ
ἀρχῶν II. 1, 2). On the other hand Clement is said to have taught it in the
Hypotyposes (Phot., l.c.: ὕλην ἄχρονον δοξάζει); this cannot be noticed in the
Strom.; in fact in VI. 16. 147 he vigorously contested the view of the uncreated-
ness of the world. He emphasised the agreement between Plato and Moses in the
doctrine of creation (Strom. II. 16. 74 has nothing to do with this). According
to Origen, matter has no qualities and may assume the most diverse peculiarities
(see, e.g., c. Cels. III. 41).

[2] This conception has given occasion to compare Origen's system with Buddhism. Bigg. (p. 193) has very beautifully said: "Creation, as the word is com-
monly understood, was in Origen's views not the beginning, but an intermediate
phase in human history. Æons rolled away before this world was made; æons
upon æons, days, weeks, months and years, sabbatical years, jubilee years of æons
will run their course, before the end is attained. The one fixed point in this
gigantic drama is the end, for this alone has been clearly revealed," "God shall
be all in all." Bigg also rightly points out that Rom. VIII. and 1 Cor. XV. were
for Origen the key to the solution of the problems presented by creation.

[3] The popular idea of demons and angels was employed by Origen in the
most comprehensive way, and dominates his whole view of the present course of
the world. See περὶ ἀρχῶν III. 2 and numerous passages in the Commentaries
and Homilies, in which he approves the kindred views of the Greeks as well as of
Hermas and Barnabas. The spirits ascend and descend; each man has his guardian spirit, and the superior spirits support the inferior (περὶ αρχῶν I. 6). Accordingly they are also to be reverenced (θεραπεύεσθαι); yet such reverence as belongs
to a Gabriel, a Michael, etc., is far different from the adoration of God (c. Cels. VIII. 13).

the physical and the spiritual world. But everything is subject to the permission of the divine goodness and finally also to the guidance of divine providence, though the latter has created for itself a limit in freedom.[1] Evil, however, and it is in this idea that Origen's great optimism consists, cannot conquer in the end. As it is nothing eternal, so also it is at bottom nothing real; it is "nonexistent" (οὐκ ὄν) and "unreal" (ἀνυπόστατον).[2] For this very reason the estrangement of the spirits from God must finally cease; even the devil, who, as far as his *being* is concerned, resulted from God's will, cannot always remain a devil. The spirits must return to God, and this moment is also the end of the material world, which is merely an intermediate phase.[3]

According to this conception the doctrine of man, who in Origen's view is no longer the sole aim of creation to the same extent as he is with the other Fathers,[4] assumes the following form: The essence of man is formed by the reasonable soul, which has fallen from the world above. This is united with the body by means of the animal soul. Origen thus believes in a threefold nature of man. He does so in the first place,

---

[1] Clement wrote a special work περὶ προνοίας (see Zahn, Forschungen III., p. 39 ff.), and treated at length of προνοία in the Strom.; see Orig. περὶ ἀρχῶν III. 1; de orat. 6 etc. Evil is also subject to divine guidance; see Clem., Strom. I. 17. 81—87 : IV. 12. 86 sq. Orig. Hom. in Num. XIV., Lomm. X., p. 163: "Nihil otiosum, nihil inane est apud deum, quia sive bono proposito hominis utitur ad bona sive malo ad necessaria." Here and there, however, Origen has qualified the belief in Providence, after the genuine fashion of antiquity (see c. Cels. IV. 74).

[2] Περὶ ἀρχῶν II. 9. 2: "Recedere a bono, non aliud est quam effici in malo. Ceterum namque est, malum esse bono carere. Ex quo accidit, ut in quanta mensura quis devolveretur a bono, in tantam mensuram malitiæ deveniret." In the passage in Johann. II. 7, Lomm. I., p. 115, we find a closely reasoned exposition of evil as ἀνυπόστατον and an argument to the effect that τὰ πονηρά are—μὴ ὄντα.

[3] Περὶ ἀρχῶν I. 5. 3 : III. 6. The devil is the chief of the apostate angels (c. Cels. IV. 65). As a reasonable being he is a creature of God (l.c., and in Joh. II. 7, Lomm., l.c.).

[4] Origen defended the teleology culminating in man against Celsus' attacks on it; but his assumption that the spirits of men are only a part of the universal spirit world is, as a matter of fact, quite akin to Celsus' view. If we consider the plan of the work περὶ ἀρχῶν we easily see that to Origen humanity was merely an element in the cosmos.

because Plato holds this theory, and Origen always embraced
the most complicated view in matters of tradition, and secondly,
because the rational soul can never in itself be the principle of
action opposed to God, and yet something relatively spiritual
must be cited as the cause of this action. It is true that we
also find in Origen the view that the spirit in man has itself
been cooled down into a soul, has been, as it were, transformed
into a soul; but there is necessarily an ambiguity here, because
on the one hand the spirit of man is said to have chosen a
course opposed to God, and, on the other, that which is rational
and free in man must be shown to be something remaining
intact.[1] Man's struggle consists in the endeavour of the two
factors forming his constitution to gain control of his sphere of
action. If man conquers in this struggle he attains *likeness* to
God; the image of God he bears beyond danger of loss in his
indestructible, rational, and therefore immortal spirit.[2] Victory,
however, denotes nothing else than the subjugation of the instincts
and passions.[3] No doubt God affords help in the struggle, for
nothing good is without God,[4] but in such a way as not to
interfere with freedom. According to this conception sin is a

[1] The doctrine of man's threefold constitution is also found in Clement. See
Pædag. III. 1. 1; Strom V. 14. 94: VI. 16. 134. (quite in the manner of Plato).
Origen, who has given evidence of it in all his main writings, sometimes calls the
rational part spirit, sometimes ψυχὴ λογική, and at other times distinguishes two
parts in the one soul. Of course he also professes to derive his psychology from
the Holy Scriptures. The chief peculiarity of his speculation consists in his
assumption that the human spirit, as a fallen one, became as it were a soul, and
can develop from that condition partly into a spirit as before and partly into the
flesh (see περὶ ἀρχῶν III. 4. 1 sq.: II. 8. 1—5). By his doctrine of the preëxistence
of souls Origen excluded both the creation and traducian hypotheses of the origin
of the soul.

[2] Clement (see Strom. II. 22. 131) gives the following as the opinion of some
Christian teachers: τὸ μὲν κατ᾿ εἰκόνα εὐθέως κατὰ τὴν γένεσιν εἰληφέναι τὸν ἄνθρωπον, τὸ καθ᾿ ὁμοίωσιν δὲ ὕστερον κατὰ τὴν πελείωσιν μέλλειν ἀπολαμβάνειν. Orig.
c. Cels. IV. 30: ἐποίησε δ᾿ὁ Θεὸς τὸν ἄνθρωπον κατ᾿ εἰκόνα Θεοῦ, ἀλλ᾿ οὐχὶ καθ᾿
ὁμοίωσιν ἤδη.

[3] This follows from the fundamental psychological view and is frequently
emphasised. One must attain the σωφροσύνη.

[4] This is emphasised throughout. The goodness of God is shown first in his
having given the creature reason and freedom, and secondly in acts of assistance,
which, however, do not endanger freedom. Clem., Strom. VI. 12. 96: ἡμᾶς ἐξ ἡμῶν
αὐτῶν βούλεται σώζεσθαι.

matter of necessity in the case of fallen spirits; all men are met with as sinners and are so, for they were already sinners.[1] Sin is rooted in the whole earthly condition of men; it is the weakness and error of the spirit parted from its origin.[2] The idea of freedom, indeed, is supposed to be a feature which always preserves the guilty character of sin; but in truth it becomes a mere appearance[3] it does not avail against the constitution of man and the sinful habit propagated in human society.[4] All must be sinners at first,[5] for that is as much their destiny as is the doom of death which is a necessary consequence of man's material nature.[6]

### The Doctrine of Redemption and Restoration.

In the view of Clement and Origen the proposition: "God wishes us to be saved by means of ourselves" (ὁ Θεὸς ἡμᾶς ἐξ ἡμῶν αὐτῶν βούλεται σώζεσθαι) is quite as true as the other state-

---

[1] See above, p. 344, and p. 361, note 5. Origen continually emphasised the universality of sin in the strongest expressions:| c. Cels. III. 61—66 · VII. 50; Clem., Pæd. III. 12. 93 : τὸ ἐξαμαρτάνειν πᾶσιν ἔμφυτον.

[2] See Clem., Strom. VII. 16. 101 : μυρίων γοῦν ὄντων κατ᾽ ἀριθμὸν ἃ πράσσουσιν ἄνθρωποι σχεδὸν δύο εἰσὶν ἀρχαὶ πάσης ἁμαρτίας, ἄγνοια καὶ ἀσθένεια, ἄμφω δὲ ἐφ᾽ ἡμῖν, τῶν μήτε ἐθελόντων μανθάνειν μήτε αὖ τῆς ἐπιθυμίας κρατεῖν. Two remedies correspond to this (102) : ἡ γνῶσις τε καὶ ἡ τῆς ἐκ τῶν γραφῶν μαρτυρίας ἐναργὴς ἀπόδειξις and ἡ κατὰ λόγον ἄσκησις ἐκ πίστεώς τε καὶ φόβου παιδαγωγουμένη, or otherwise expressed: ἡ θεωρία ἡ ἐπιστημονική and ἡ πρᾶξις, which lead to perfect love.

[3] Freedom is not prejudiced by the idea of election that is found here and there, for this idea is not worked out. In Clem., Strom. VI. 9. 76, it is said of the friend of God, the true Gnostic, that God has destined (προώρισεν) him to sonship before the foundation of the world. See VII. 17. 107.

[4] C. Cels. III. 69.

[5] It is both true that men have the same freedom as Adam and that they have the same evil instincts. Moreover, Origen conceived the story of Adam symbolically. See c. Cels. IV. 40; περὶ ἀρχῶν IV. 16; in Levit. hom. VI. 2. In his later writings, after he had met with the practice of child baptism in Cæsarea and prevailed on himself to regard it as apostolic, he also assumed the existence of a sort of hereditary sin orginating with Adam, and added it to his idea of the preëxisting Fall. Like Augustine after him, he also supposed that there was an inherent pollution in sexual union; see in Rom. V. 9; VII. 4; in Lev. hom. VIII. 3; in Num. hom. 2 (Bigg, p. 202 f.).

[6] Nevertheless Origen assumes that some souls are invested with flesh, not for their own sins, but in order to be of use to others. See in Joh. XIII. 43 ad fin II. 24, 25; in Matth. XII. 30.

ment that no spirit can be saved without entering into fellowship with the Logos and submitting to his instruction. [1] They
moreover hold that the Logos, after passing through his various
stages of revealing activity (law of nature, Mosaic law), disclosed
himself in the Gospel in a manner complete and accessible to
all, so that this revelation imparts redemption and eternal happiness to all men, however different their capacities may be.
Finally, it is assumed that not only men but all spiritual creatures,
from the radiant spirits of heaven down to the dusky demons,
have the capacity and need of redemption; while for the highest
stage, the "spiritual Church", there is an *eternal Gospel* which
is related to the written one as the latter is to the law.  This
eternal Gospel is the first complete revelation of God's highest
intentions, and lies hidden in the Holy Scriptures. [2] These
elements compose Origen's doctrine of revelation in general and
of Christ in particular. [3] They presuppose the sighing of the
creature and the great struggle which is more especially carried
on upon earth, within the human breast, by the angels and
demons, virtues and vices, knowledge and passion, that dispute
the possession of man.  Man must conquer and yet he cannot do
so without help.  But help has never been wanting.  The Logos
has been revealing himself from the beginning.  Origen's teaching
corcerning the preparatory history of redemption is founded on
the doctrines of the Apologists; but with him everything takes
a more vivid form, and influences on the part of the heretical
Gnosis are also not lacking.  Pure spirits, whom no fault of their
own had caused to be invested with bodies, namely, the prophets,
were sent to men by the Logos in order to support the struggling
and to increase knowledge.  To prepare the way of salvation
the Logos chose for himself a whole people, and he revealed
himself among all men.  But all these undertakings did not yet
lead to the goal.  The Logos himself was obliged to appear and

---

[1] Origen again and again strongly urged the necessity of divine grace.

[2] See on this point Bigg, pp. 207 ff., 223 f.  Origen is the father of Joachim
and all spiritualists.

[3] See Knittel, Orig. Lehre von der Menschwerdung (Tübinger Theologische
Quartalschrift, 1872). Ramers, Orig. Lehre von der Auferstehung des Fleisches,
1851. Schultz, Gottheit Christi, pp. 51—62.

lead men back. But by reason of the diverse nature of the spirits, and especially of men, the redeeming work of the Logos that appeared could not fail to be a complicated one. In the case of some he had really to show them the victory over the demons and sin, a view which beyond dispute is derived from that of Valentinus. He had, as the " Godman," to make a sacrifice which represented the expiation of sin, he had to pay a ransom which put an end to the devil's sovereignty over men's souls, and in short he had to bring a redemption visible and intelligible to all. [1] To the rest, however, as divine teacher and hierophant

[1] With regard to this point we find the same explanation in Origen as in Irenæus and Tertullian, and also among the Valentinians, in so far as the latter describe the redemption necessary for the Psychici. Only, in this instance also, everything is more copious in his case, because he availed himself of the Holy Scriptures still more than these did, and because he left out no popular conception that seemed to have any moral value. Accordingly he propounded views as to the value of salvation and as to the significance of Christ's death on the cross, with a variety and detail rivalled by no theologian before him. He was, as Bigg (p. 209 ff.) has rightly noticed, the first Church theologian after Paul's time that gave a detailed theology of sacrifices. We may mention here the most important of his views. (1) The death on the cross along with the resurrection is to be considered as a real, recognisable victory over the demons, inasmuch as Christ (Col. II. 14) exposed the weakness of his enemies (a very frequent aspect of the matter). (2) The death on the cross is to be considered as an expiation offered to God. Here Origen argued that all sins require expiation, and, conversely, that all innocent blood has a greater or less importance according to the value of him who gives up his life. (3) In accordance with this the death of Christ has also a vicarious signification (see with regard to both these conceptions the treatise Exhort. ad martyr., as well as c. Cels. VII. 17: I. 31; in Rom. t. III. 7, 8, Lomm. VI., pp. 196—216 etc.). (4) The death of Christ is to be considered as a ransom paid to the devil. This view must have been widely diffused in Origen's time; it readily suggested itself to the popular idea and was further supported by Marcionite theses. It was also accepted by Origen who united it with the notion of a deception practised on the devil, a conception first found among the Basilidians. By his successful temptation the devil acquired a right over men. This right cannot be destroyed, but only bought off. God offers the devil Christ's soul in exchange for the souls of men. This proposal of exchange was, however, insincere, as God knew that the devil could not keep hold of Christ's soul, because a sinless soul could not but cause him torture. The devil agreed to the bargain and was duped. Christ did not fall into the power of death and the devil, but overcame both. This theory, which Origen propounded in somewhat different fashion in different places (see Exhort. ad martyr. 12; in Matth. t. XVI. 8, Lomm. IV., p. 27; t. XII. 28, Lomm. III., p. 175; t. XIII. 8, 9, Lomm. III., pp. 224—229; in Rom. II. 13, Lomm. VI., p. 139 sq. etc.), shows in a specially clear way the conservative method of this theologian, who would not positively abandon any idea-

he had to reveal the depths of knowledge, and to impart
in this very process a new principle of life, so that they might
now partake of his life and themselves become divine through
being interwoven with the divine essence. Here, as in the
former case, restoration to fellowship with God is the goal; but,
as in the lower stage, this restoration is effected through faith
and sure conviction of the reality of a historical fact—namely,
the redeeming death of Christ,— so, in the higher stage, it is
accomplished through knowledge and love, which, soaring upward beyond the Crucified One, grasp the eternal essence of
the Logos, revealed to us through his teaching in the eternal
Gospel.[1] What the Gnostics merely represented as a more or

No doubt it shows at the same time how uncertain Origen was as to the applica-
bility of popular conceptions when he was dealing with the sphere of the Psychici.
We must here remember the ancient idea that we are not bound to sincerity
towards our enemies. (5) Christ, the God who became flesh, is to be considered
as high priest and mediator between God and man (see de Orat. 10, 15). All the
above-mentioned conceptions of Christ's work were, moreover, worked out by
Origen in such a way that his humanity and divinity are necessary inferences
from them. In this case also he is characterised by the same mode of thought
as Irenæus. Finally, let us remember that Origen adhered as strongly as ever to
the proof from prophecy, and that he also, in not a few instances, regarded the
phrase, "it is written", as a sufficient court of appeal (see, for example, c. Cels.
II. 37). Yet, on the other hand, behind all this he has a method of viewing
things which considerably weakens the significance of miracles and prophecies. In
general it must be said that Origen helped to drag into the Church a great many
ancient (heathen) ideas about expiation and redemption, inasmuch as he everywhere found some Bible passage or other with which he associated them. While
he rejected polytheism and gave little countenance to people who declared:
εὐσεβέστεροί ἐσμεν καὶ Θεὸν καὶ τὰ ἀγάλματα σέβοντες (Clemens Rom., Hom.
XI. 12), he had for all that a principal share in introducing the apparatus of polytheism
into the Church (see also the way in which he strengthened angel and hero worship)

[1] See above, p. 342, note 1, on the idea that Christ, the Crucified One, is of no
importance to the perfect. Only the teacher is of account in this case. To Clement
and Origen, however, teacher and mystagogue are as closely connected as they are
to most Gnostics. Christianity is μάθησις and μυσταγωγία, and it is the one because
it is the other. But in all stages Christianity has ultimately the same object, namely,
to effect a reconciliation with God, and deify man. See c. Cels. III. 28: Ἀλλὰ
γὰρ καὶ τὴν καταβᾶσαν εἰς ἀνθρωπίνην φύσιν καὶ εἰς ἀνθρωπίνας περιστάσεις δύναμιν,
καὶ ἀναλαβοῦσαν ψυχὴν καὶ σῶμα ἀνθρώπινον, ἑώρων ἐκ τοῦ πιστεύεσθαι μετὰ τῶν
θειοτέρων συμβαλλομένην εἰς σωτηρίαν τοῖς πιστεύουσιν· ὁρῶσιν, ἀπ' ἐκείνου ἤρξατο
θεία καὶ ἀνθρωπίνη συννφαίνεσθαι φύσις· ἵν' ἡ ἀνθρωπίνη τῇ πρὸς τὸ θειότερον κοινωνίᾳ
γένηται θεία οὐκ ἐν μόνῳ τῷ Ἰησοῦ, ἀλλὰ καὶ πᾶσι τοῖς μετὰ τοῦ πιστεύειν ἀναλαμ-
βάνουσι βίον, ὃν Ἰησοῦς ἐδίδαξεν.

less valuable appearance — namely, the historical work of Christ
—was to Origen no appearance but truth.  But he did not view
it as *the* truth, and in this he agrees with the Gnostics, but as *a*
truth, beyond which lies a higher.  That historical work of
Christ was a reality; it is also indispensable for men of more
limited endowments, and not a matter of indifference to the
perfect; but the latter no longer require it for their personal
life.  Here also Origen again contrived to reconcile contradictions and thus acknowledged, outdid, reconciled, and united
both the theses of the Gnostics and those of orthodox Christians.
The object and goal of redemption are the same for all, namely,
the restoration of the created spirit to God and participation in
the divine life.  In so far as history is a struggle between spirits
and demons, the death of Christ on the cross is the turning-
point of history, and its effects extend even into heaven and hell. [1]

On the basis of this conception of redemption Origen developed
his idea of Christ.  Inasmuch as he recognised Christ as the
Redeemer, this Christ, the God-man, could not but be as many-
sided as redemption is.  Only through that masterly art of
reconciling contradictions, and by the aid of that fantastic idea
which conceives one real being as dwelling in another, could
there be any apparent success in the attempt to depict a homogeneous person who in truth is no longer a person, but the symbol
of the various redemptions.  That such an acute thinker, however, did not shrink from the monstrosity his speculation produced
is ultimately to be accounted for by the fact that this very
speculation afforded him the means of nullifying all the utterances
about Christ and falling back on the idea of the divine teacher as being
the highest one. The whole "humanity" of the Redeemer together
with its history finally disappears from the eyes of the perfect
one.  What remains is the principle, the divine Reason, which
became known and recognisable through Christ.  The perfect
one, and this remark also applies to Clement's perfect Gnostic,
thus knows no "Christology", but only an indwelling of the

---

[1] From this also we can very clearly understand Origen's aversion to the early
Christian eschatology.  In his view the demons are already overcome by the work
of Christ.  We need only point out that this conception must have exercised a most
important influence on his frame of mind and on politics.

Logos in Jesus Christ, with which the indwellings of this same
Logos in men began. To the Gnostic the question of the divinity
of Christ is of as little importance as that of the humanity. The
former is no question, because speculation, starting above and
proceeding downwards, is already acquainted with the Logos
and knows that he has become completely comprehensible in
Christ; the latter is no question, because the humanity is a
matter of indifference, being the form in which the Logos made
himself recognisable. But to the Christian who is not yet perfect
the divinity as well as the humanity of Christ is a problem, and
it is the duty of the perfect one to solve and explain it, and
to guard this solution against errors on all sides. To Origen,
however, the errors are already Gnostic Docetism on the one hand,
and the "Ebionite" view on the other.[1] His doctrine was
accordingly as follows: As a pure unchangeable spirit, the Logos
could not unite with matter, because this as μὴ ὄν would have
depotentiated him. A medium was required. The Logos did
not unite with the body, but with a soul, and only through the
soul with the body. This soul was a pure one; it was a created
spirit that had never fallen from God, but always remained in
faithful obedience to him, and that had chosen to become a soul
in order to serve the purposes of redemption. This soul then
was always devoted to the Logos from the first and had never
renounced fellowship with him. It was selected by the Logos
for the purpose of incarnation and that because of its moral dignity.
The Logos became united with it in the closest way; but this

---

[1] Clement still advocated docetic views without reservation. Photius (Biblioth.
109) reproached him with these (μὴ σαρκωθῆναι τὸν λόγον ἀλλὰ δόξαι), and they
may be proved from the Adumbrat, p. 87 (ed Zahn) : "fertur in traditionibus—
namely, in the Acta of Lucius—quoniam Iohannes ipsum corpus (Christi), quod erat
extrinsecus, tangens manum suam in profunda misisse et duritiam carnis nullo modo
reluctatam esse, sed locum manui præbuisse discipuli," and likewise from Strom. VI.
9. 71 and III. 7. 59. Clement's repudiation of the Docetists in VII. 17. 108 does
not affect the case, and the fact that he here and there plainly called Jesus a man,
and spoke of his flesh (Pæd. II. 2. 32 : Protrept. X. 110) matters just as little. This
teacher simply continued to follow the old undisguised Docetism which only admitted
the apparent reality of Christ's body. Clement expressly declared that Jesus knew
neither pain, nor sorrow, nor emotions, and only took food in order to refute the
Docetists (Strom. VI. 9. 71). As compared with this, Docetism in Origen's case
appears throughout in a weakened form; see Bigg, p. 191.

connection, though it is to be viewed as a mysteriously real union, continues to remain perfect only because of the unceasing effort of will by which the soul clings to the Logos. Thus, then, no intermixture has taken place. On the contrary the Logos preserves his impassibility, and it is only the soul that hungers and thirsts, struggles and suffers. In this, too, it appears as a real human soul, and in the same way the body is sinless and unpolluted, as being derived from a virgin; but yet it is a human one. This humanity of the body, however, does not exclude its capacity of assuming all possible qualities the Logos wishes to give it; for matter of itself possesses no qualities. The Logos was able at any moment to give his body the form it required, in order to make the proper impression on the various sorts of men. Moreover, he was not enclosed in the soul and body of Christ; on the contrary he acted everywhere as before and united himself, as formerly, with all the souls that opened themselves to him. But with none did the union become so close as with the soul, and consequently also with the body of Jesus. During his earthly life the Logos glorified and deified his soul by degrees and the latter acted in the same way on his body. Origen contrived to arrange the different functions and predicates of the incarnate Logos in such a way that they formed a series of stages which the believer becomes successively acquainted with as he advances in knowledge. But everything is most closely united together in Christ. This union (κοινωνία, ἕνωσις, ἀνακράσις) was so intimate that Holy Writ has named the created man, Jesus, the Son of God; and on the other hand has called the Son of God the Son of Man. After the resurrection and ascension the whole man Jesus appears transformed into a spirit, is completely received into the Godhead, and is thus identical with the Logos.[1]

---

[1] See the full exposition in Thomasius, Origenes, p. 203 ff. The principal passages referring to the soul of Jesus are de princip. II. 6: IV. 31 ; c. Cels. II. 9. 20—25. Socrates (H. E. III. 7) says that the conviction as to Jesus having a human soul was founded on a μυστική παράδοσις of the Church, and was not first broached by Origen. The special problem of conceiving Christ as a real θεάνθρωπος in contradistinction to all the men who only possess the presence of the Logos within them in proportion to their merits, was precisely formulated by Origen on many occasions. See περὶ ἀρχῶν IV. 29 sq. The full divine nature existed in Christ and yet, as before, the Logos operate! wherever he wished (l. c., 30): "non ita

In this conception one may be tempted to point out all possible
"heresies":—the conception of Jesus as a heavenly man—but
all men are heavenly;—the Adoptianist ("Ebionite") Christology
—but the Logos as a person stands behind it;—the conception

sentiendum est, quod omnis divinitatis eius maiestas intra brevissimi corporis claustra
conclusa est, ita ut omne verbum dei et sapientia eius ac substantialis veritas ac
vita vel a patre divulsa sit vel intra corporis eius coercita et conscripta brevitatem
nec usquam præterea putetur operata; sed inter utrumque cauta pietatis debet esse
confessio, ut neque aliquid divinitatis in Christo defuisse credatur et nulla penitus
a paterna substantia, quæ ubique est, facta putetur esse divisio." On the perfect
ethical union of Jesus' soul with the Logos see περὶ ἀρχῶν II. 6. 3: "anima Iesu
ab initio creaturæ et deinceps inseparabiliter ei atque indissociabiliter inhærens et
tota totum recipiens atque in eius lucem splendoremque ipsa cedens facta est cum
ipso principaliter unus spiritus;" II. 6. 5: "anima Christi ita elegit diligere iustitiam, ut pro immensitate dilectionis inconvertibiliter ei atque inseparabiliter inhæreret,
ita ut propositi firmitas et affectus immensitas et dilectionis inexstinguibilis calor
omnem sensum conversionis atque immutationis abscinderet, et quod in arbitrio erat
positum, longi usus affectu iam versum sit in naturam." The sinlessness of this
soul thus became transformed from a fact into a necessity, and the real God-man
arose, in whom divinity and humanity are no longer separated. The latter lies in
the former as iron in the fire II. 6. 6. As the metal *capax est frigoris et caloris*
so the soul is capable of deification. "Omne quod agit, quod sentit, quod intelligit,
deus est," "nec convertibilis aut mutabilis dici potest" (l.c.). "Dilectionis merito
anima Christi cum verbo dei Christus efficitur." (II. 6. 4). Τίς μᾶλλον τῆς Ἰησοῦ
ψυχῆς ἢ κἂν παραπλησίως κεκόλληται τῷ κυρίῳ; ὕπερ εἰ οὕτως ἔχει οὐκ εἰσὶ δύο ἡ
ψυχὴ τοῦ Ἰησοῦ πρὸς τὸν πάσης κτίσεως πρωτότοκον Θεὸν λόγον (c. Cels. VI. 47).
The metaphysical foundation of the union is set forth in περὶ ἀρχῶν II. 6. 2:
"Substantia animæ inter deum carnemque mediante—non enim possibile erat dei
naturam corpori sine mediatore miscere—nascitur deus homo, illa substantia media
exsistente, cui utique contra naturam non erat corpus assumere. Sed neque rursus
anima illa, utpote substantia rationabilis, contra naturam habuit, capere deum." Even
during his historical life the body of Christ was ever more and more glorified,
acquired therefore wonderful powers, and appeared differently to men according to
their several capacities (that is a Valentinian idea, see Exc. ex Theod. 7); cf. c.
Cels. I. 32—38: II. 23, 64: IV. 15 sq.: V. 8, 9, 23. All this is summarised in
III. 41: Ὅτι μὲν νομίζομεν καὶ πεπείσμεθα ἀρχῆθεν εἶναι Θεὸν καὶ υἱὸν Θεοῦ, οὗτος
ὁ αὐτολόγος ἐστὶ καὶ ἡ αὐτοσοφία καὶ ἡ αὐτοαλήθεια· τὸ δὲ θνητὸν αὐτοῦ σῶμα καὶ
τὴν ἀνθρωπίνην ἐν αὐτῷ ψυχὴν τῇ πρὸς ἐκεῖνον οὐ μόνον κοινωνίᾳ, ἀλλὰ καὶ ἑνώσει
καὶ ἀνακράσει, τὰ μέγιστά φαμεν προσειληφέναι καὶ τῆς ἐκείνου θεότητος κεκοινω-
νηκότα εἰς Θεὸν μεταβεβηκέναι. Origen then continues and appeals to the philosophical
doctrine that matter has no qualities and can assume all the qualities which the
Creator wishes to give it. Then follows the conclusion: εἰ ὑγιῆ τὰ τοιαῦτα, τί
θαυμαστόν, τὴν ποιότητα τοῦ θνητοῦ κατὰ τὸν Ἰησοῦν σώματος προνοίᾳ Θεοῦ βουλη-
θέντος μεταβαλεῖν εἰς αἰθέριον καὶ θείαν ποιότητα; The man is now the same as
the Logos. See in Joh. XXXII. 17, Lomm. II., p. 461 sq; Hom. in Jerem. XV. 6,
Lomm. XV., p. 288: εἰ καὶ ἦν ἄνθρωπος, ἀλλὰ νῦν οὐδαμῶς ἐστιν ἄνθρωπος.

of two Logoi, a personal and an impersonal; the Gnostic separation of Jesus and Christ; and Docetism. As a matter of
fact Origen united all these ideas, but modified the whole of
them in such a way that they no longer seem, and to some
extent are not, what they turn out to be when subjected to the
slightest logical analysis. This structure is so constituted that
not a stone of it admits of being a hair's-breadth broader or
narrower. There is only one conception that has been absolutely
unemployed by Origen, that is, the modalistic view. Origen is
the great opponent of Sabellianism, a theory which in its simplicity frequently elicited from him words of pity; otherwise he
made use of all the ideas about Christ that had been formed in
the course of two hundred years. This becomes more and more
manifest the more we penetrate into the details of this Christology.
We cannot, however, attribute to Origen a doctrine of two
natures, but rather the notion of two subjects that become
gradually amalgamated with each other, although the expression
"two natures" is not quite foreign to Origen. [1] The Logos
retains his human nature eternally, [2] but only in the same sense
in which we preserve our nature after the resurrection.

The significance which this Christological attempt possessed
for its time consists first in its complexity, secondly in the
energetic endeavour to give an adequate conception of Christ's
*humanity*, that is, of the moral freedom pertaining to him as a
creature. This effort was indeed obliged to content itself with a
meagre result: but we are only justified in measuring Origen's
Christology by that of the Valentinians and Basilidians, that is,
by the scientific one that had preceded it. The most important
advance lies in the fact that Origen set forth a scientific Christology in which he was able to find so much scope for the humanity
of Christ. Whilst within the framework of the scientific Christologies this humanity had hitherto been conceived as something

---

[1] In c. Cels. III. 28, Origen spoke of an intermingling of the divine and human
natures, commencing in Christ (see page 368, note 1). See I. 66 fin.; IV. 15,
where any ἀλλάττεσθαι καὶ μεταπλάττεσθαι of the Logos is decidedly rejected;
for the Logos does not suffer at all. In Origen's case we may speak of a *communicatio idiomatum* (see Bigg, p. 190 f.).

[2] In opposition to Redepenning.

indifferent or merely apparent, Origen made the first attempt
to incorporate it with the various speculations without prejudice
to the Logos, God in nature and person. No Greek philosopher
probably heeded what Irenæus set forth respecting Christ as
the second Adam, the *recapitulatur generis humani*; whereas
Origen's speculation could not be overlooked. In this case the
Gnosis really adopted the idea of the incarnation, and at the
same time tried to demonstrate the conception of the God-
man from the notions of unity of w:ll and love. In the treatise
against Celsus, moreover, Origen went the reverse way to work
and undertook to show, and this not merely by help of the
proof from prophecy, that the predicate deity applied to the
historical Christ.[1] But Origen's conception of Christ's person
as a model (for the Gnostic) and his repudiation of all magical
theories of redemption ultimately explain why he did not, like
Tertullian, set forth a doctrine of two natures, but sought to
show that in Christ's case a human subject with his will and
feelings became completely merged in the Deity. No doubt he
can say that the union of the divine and human natures had
its beginning in Christ, but here he virtually means that this
beginning is continued in the sense of souls imitating the example
of Christ. What is called the real redemption supposed to be
given in him is certainly mediated in the Psychic through his
*work*, but the *person* of Christ which cannot be known to any
but the perfect man is by no means identified with that real
redemption, but appears as a free moral personality, inwardly
blended with the Deity, a personality which cannot mechanically
transfer the content of its essence, though it can indeed exercise
the strongest impression on mind and heart. To Origen the
highest value of Christ's person lies in the fact that the Deity
has here condescended to reveal to us the whole fulness of his
essence, in the person of a man, as well as in the fact that a
man is given to us who shows that the human spirit is capable
of becoming entirely God's. At bottom there is nothing obscure

---

[1] This idea is found in many passages, especial in Book III., c. 22—43, where
Origen, in opposition to the fables about deification, sought to prove that Christ
is divine because he realised the aim of founding a holy community in humanity.
See, besides, the remarkable statement in III. 38 init.

and mystical here; the whole process takes place in the will and in the feelings through knowledge.[1] This is sufficient to settle the nature of what is called personal attainment of salvation. Freedom precedes and supporting grace follows. As in Christ's case his human soul gradually united itself with the Logos in proportion as it voluntarily subjected its will to God, so also every man receives grace according to his progress. Though Clement and Origen did not yet recommend actual exercises according to definite rules, their description of the gradations by which the soul rises to God already resembles that of the Neoplatonists, except that they decidedly begin with faith as the first stage. Faith is the first step and is our own work.[2] Then follows the religious contemplation of visible things, and from this the soul advances, as on the steps of a ladder, to the contemplation of the *substantiæ rationabiles*, the Logos, the knowable essence of God, and the whole fulness of the Deity.[3] She retraces her steps upwards along the path she formerly passed over as a fallen spirit. But, when left to her own resources, she herself is everywhere weak and powerless; she requires at every stage the divine grace, that is, enlightenment.[4]  Thus a

---

[1] A very remarkable distinction between the divine and human element in Christ is found in Clement Pæd. I. 3. 7: πάντα ὀνίνησιν ὁ κύριος καὶ πάντα ὠφελεῖ καὶ ὡς ἄνθρωπος καὶ ὡς Θεός, τὰ μὲν ἁμαρτήματα ὡς Θεὸς ἀφιείς, εἰς δὲ τὸ μὴ ἐξαμαρτάνειν παιδαγωγῶν ὡς ἄνθρωπος.

[2] "Fides in nobis; mensura fidei causa accipiendarum gratiarum" is the fundamental idea of Clement and Origen (as of Justin); "voluntas humana præcedit". In Ezech. hom. I. c. 11: "In tua potestate positum est, ut sis palea vel frumentum". But all growth in faith must depend on divine help. See Orig. in Matth. series 69, Lomm. IV., p. 372: "Fidem habenti, quæ est ex nobis, dabitur gratia fidei quæ est per spiritum fidei, et abundabit; et quidquid habuerit quis ex naturali creatione, cum exercuerit illud, accipit id ipsum et ex gratia dei, ut abundet et firmior sit in eo ipso quod habet"; in Rom. IV. 5, Lomm. VI., p. 258 sq.; in Rom. IX. 3, Lomm. VII., p. 300 sq. The fundamental idea remains: ὁ Θεὸς ἡμᾶς ἐξ ἡμῶν αὐτῶν βούλεται σώζεσθαι.

[3] This is frequent in Clement; see Orig. c. Cels. VII. 46.

[4] See Clem., Strom. V. 1. 7: χάριτι σωζόμεθα, οὐκ ἄνευ μέντοι τῶν καλῶν ἔργων. VII. 7. 48: V. 12. 82, 13. 83: εἴτε τὸ ἐν ἡμῖν αὐτεξούσιον εἰς γνῶσιν ἀφικόμενον τἀγαθοῦ σκιρτᾷ τε καὶ πηδᾷ ὑπὲρ τὰ ἐσκαμμένα, πλὴν οὐ χάριτος ἄνευ τῆς ἐξαιρέτου πτεροῦταί τε καὶ ἀνίσταται καὶ ἄνω τῶν ὑπερκειμένων αἴρεται ἡ ψυχή; The amalgamation of freedom and grace. Quis div. salv. 21. Orig. περὶ ἀρχῶν III. 2. 2: In bonis rebus humanum propositum solum per se ipsum imperfectum est

union of grace and freedom takes place within the sphere of
the latter, till the "contemplative life" is reached, that joyous
ascetic contemplativeness, in which the Logos is the friend,
associate, and bridegroom of the soul, which now, having become
a pure spirit, and being herself deified, clings in love to the
Deity. [1] In this view the thought of regeneration in the sense
of a fundamental renewal of the Ego has no place; [2] still
baptism is designated the bath of regeneration. Moreover, in
connection with the consideration of main Biblical thoughts (God
as love, God as the Father, Regeneration, Adoption, etc.) we
find in both Clement and Origen passages which, free from the
trammels of the system, reproduce and set forth the preaching
of the Gospel in a surprisingly appropriate way. [3] It is evident
that in Origen's view there can be no visible means of grace;
but it likewise follows from his whole way of thinking that the
symbols attending the enlightening operation of grace are not
a matter of indifference to the Christian Gnostic, whilst to the
common man they are indispensable. [4] In the same way he brought

---

ad consummationem boni, adiutorio namque divino ad perfecta quæque perlucitur.
III. 2. 5, I. 18; Selecta in Ps. 4, Lomm. XI., p. 450: τὸ τοῦ λογικοῦ ἀγαθὸν μικτόν
ἐστιν ἐκ τε τῆς προαιρέσεως αὐτοῦ καὶ τῆς συμπνεούσης θείας δυνάμεως τῷ τὸ κάλλιστα
προελομένῳ. The support of grace is invariably conceived as enlightenment; but
this enlightenment enables it to act on the whole life. For a more detailed account
see Landerer in the Jahrbücher für deutsche Theologie, Vol. II., Part 3, p. 500 ff.,
and Wörter, *Die christliche Lehre von Gnade und Freiheit bis auf Augustin,* 1860.

[1] This goal was much more clearly described by Clement than by Origen; but
it was the latter who, in his commentary on the Song of Solomon, gave currency
to the image of the soul as the bride of the Logos. Bigg (p. 188 f.): "Origen, the
first pioneer in so many fields of Christian thought, the father in one of his many
aspects of the English Latitudinarians, became also the spiritual ancestor of Bernard, the Victorines, and the author of the "De imitatione", of Tauler and
Molinos and Madame de Guyon."

[2] See Thomasius, Dogmengeschichte I., p. 467.

[3] See *e.g.*, Clem. Quis dives salv. 37 and especially Pædag. I. 6. 25—32 ; Orig.
de orat. 22 sq.—the interpretation of the Lord's Prayer. This exegesis begins with
the words : " It would be worth while to examine more carefully whether the so-called
Old Testament anywhere contains a prayer in which God is called Father by anyone ; for till now we have found none in spite of all our seeking ... Constant and
unchangeable sonship is first given in the new covenant."

[4] See above, p. 339 f.

into play the system of numerous mediators and intercessors
with God, viz., angels and dead and living saints, and
counselled an appeal to them. In this respect he preserved a
heathen custom. Moreover, Origen regards Christ as playing an
important part in prayer, particularly as mediator and high
priest. On prayer to Christ he expressed himself with great
reserve.

Origen's eschatology occupies a middle position between that
of Irenæus and the theory of the Valentinian Gnostics, but is
more akin to the latter view. Whilst, according to Irenæus,
Christ reunites and glorifies all that had been severed, though
in such a way that there is still a remnant eternally damned;
and, according to Valentinus, Christ separates what is illegitimately
united and saves the spirits alone, Origen believes that all spirits
will be finally rescued and glorified, each in the form of its
individual life, in order to serve a new epoch of the world when
sensuous matter disappears of itself. Here he rejects all sensuous
eschatological expectations. [1] He accepted the formula, "resurrection of the flesh", only because it was contained in the
doctrine of the Church; but, on the strength of I. Cor. XV. 44,
he interpreted it as the rising of a "corpus spirituale", which
will lack all material attributes and even all the members that
have sensuous functions, and which will beam with radiant light
like the angels and stars. [2] Rejecting the doctrine that souls
sleep, [3] Origen assumed that the souls of the departed immediately
enter Paradise, [4] and that souls not yet purified pass into a state
of punishment, a penal fire, which, however, like the whole world,
is to be conceived as a place of purification. [5] In this way also

---

[1] See περὶ ἀρχῶν II. 11.

[2] See περὶ ἀρχῶν II. 10. 1—3. Origen wrote a treatise on the resurrection,
which, however, has not come down to us, because it was very soon accounted
heretical. We see from c. Cels. V. 14—24 the difficulties he felt about the Church
doctrine of the resurrection of the flesh.

[3] See Eusebius, H. E. VI. 37.

[4] Orig., Hom. II. in Reg. I., Lomm. XI., p. 317 sq.

[5] C. Cels. V. 15: VI. 26; in Lc. Hom. XIV., Lomm. V., p. 136: "Ego puto,
quod et post resurrectionem ex mortuis indigeamus sacramento eluente nos atque
purgante". Clem., Strom. VII. 6. 34: φαμὲν δ᾽ ἡμεῖς ἁγιάζειν τὸ πῦρ, οὐ τὰ κρέα,
ἀλλὰ τὰς ἁμαρτωλοὺς ψυχάς, πῦρ οὐ τὸ παμφάγον καὶ βάναυσον, ἀλλὰ τὸ φρόνιμον

Origen contrived to reconcile his position with the Church
doctrines of the judgment and the punishments in hell; but, like
Clement, he viewed the purifying fire as a temporary and
figurative one; it consists in the torments of conscience. [1] In the
end all the spirits in heaven and earth, nay, even the demons, are
purified and brought back to God by the Logos-Christ, [2] after
they have ascended from stage to stage through seven heavens. [3]
Hence Origen treated this doctrine as an esoteric one: "for the
common man it is sufficient to know that the sinner is punished." [4]

This system overthrew those of the Gnostics, attracted Greek
philosophers, and justified ecclesiastical Christianity. If one
undertook to subject it to a new process of sublimation from
the standpoint given in the "contemplative life", little else would
be left than the unchangeable spirit, the created spirit, and the
ethic. But no one is justified in subjecting it to this process. [5]
The method according to which Origen preserved whatever
appeared valuable in the content of tradition is no less significant
than his system of ethics and the great principle of viewing
everything created in a relative sense. Supposing minds of a
radical cast, to have existed at the close of the history of ancient
civilisation, what would have been left to us? The fact of a
strong and undivided religious interest attaching itself to the
traditions of the philosophers and of the two Testaments was
the condition—to use Origen's own language—that enabled a
new world of spirits to arise after the old one had finished its
course.

During the following century Origen's theology at first acted
in its entirety. But it likewise attained this position of influence,
because some important propositions could be detached from

λέγοντες (cf. Heraclitus and the Stoa), τὸ διικνούμενον διὰ ψυχῆς τῆς διερχομένης τὸ
πῦρ. For Origen cf. Bigg, p. 229 ff. There is another and intermediate stage
between the punishments in hell and *regnum dei*.

[1] See περὶ ἀρχ. II. 10. 4—7; c. Cels. l.c.

[2] See περὶ ἀρχ. I. 6. 1—4: III. 6. 1—8; c. Cels. VI. 26.

[3] On the seven heavens in Clem. see Strom. V. 11. 77 and other passages.
Origen does not mention them, so far as I know.

[4] c. Cels. l.c.

[5] We would be more justified in trying this with Clement.

their original connection and fitted into a new one. It is one of the peculiarities of this ecclesiastical philosophy of religion that the most of its formulæ could be interpreted and employed *in utramque partem*. The several propositions could be made to serve very different purposes not only by being halved, but also by being grouped. With this the relative unity that distinguishes the system no doubt vanished; but how many are there who strive after unity and completeness in their theory of the world? Above all, however, there was something else that necessarily vanished, as soon as people meddled with the individual propositions, and enlarged or abridged them. We mean the frame of mind which produced them, that wonderful unity between the relative view of things and the absolute estimate of the highest good attainable by the free spirit that is certain of its God. But a time came, nay, had already come, when a sense of proportion and relation was no longer to be found.

In the East the history of dogma and of the Church during the succeeding centuries is the history of Origen's philosophy. Arians and orthodox, critics and mystics, priests who overcame the world and monks who shunned it but were eager for knowledge[1] could appeal to this system and did not fail to do so. But, in the main problem that Origen set for the Church in this religious philosophy of his, we find a recurrence of that propounded by the so-called Gnosticism two generations earlier. He solved it by producing a system which reconciled the faith of the Church with Greek philosophy ; and he dealt Gnosticism its death-blow. This solution, however, was by no means intended as the doctrine of the Church, since indeed it was rather based on the distinction between Church belief and theology, and consequently on the distinction between the common man and the theologian. But such a distinction was not permanently tenable in a Church that had to preserve its strength by the unity and finality of a revealed faith, and no longer tolerated fresh changes in the interpretation of its possession. Hence a further compromise was necessary. The Greek philosophy, or speculation, did not attain real and permanent recognition within

[1] See Bornemann, In investiganda monachatus origine quibus de causis ratio habenda sit Origenis. Gottingæ 1885.

the Church till a new accommodation, capable of being accounted both Pistis and Gnosis, was found between what Origen looked on as Church belief and what he regarded as Gnosis. In the endeavours of Irenæus, Tertullian, and Hippolytus were already found hesitating, nay, we may almost say naïve, attempts at such an accommodation; but ecclesiastical traditionalism was unable to attain complete clearness as to its own position till it was confronted with a philosophy of religion that was no longer heathen or Gnostic, bnt had an ecclesiastical colouring.

But, with this prospect, we have already crossed the border of the third century. At its beginning there were but few theologians in Christendom who were acquainted with speculation, even in its fragmentary form. In the course of the century it became a recognised part of the orthodox faith, in so far as the Logos doctrine triumphed in the Church. This development is the most important that took place in the third century; for it denoted the definite transformation of the rule of faith into the compendium of a Greek philosophical system, and it is the parallel of a contemporaneous transformation of the Church into a holy commonwealth (see above, chapter 3).

# HISTORY OF DOGMA

BY

## Dr. ADOLPH HARNACK

Volume III

# EDITOR'S PREFACE.

THE first chapter in this volume forms the concluding chapter of the First Volume of the German Work. It answers to the Seventh Chapter of the Second Book of the first great division of the subject, which has for its aim to shew the *origin of Ecclesiastical Dogma*. The First Book treats of the Preparation for Dogma; the Second of the Laying of the Foundation. This Second Book begins with the second volume of the English Translation, and closes with the first chapter of the third volume now published. Thereafter commences the Second Part of the Work, which deals with the *Development of Dogma*. The numbering of the chapters here begins anew, running on from I. to VI.

The Second Volume of the German Work commences with the Second Part, and tells the story of the Development of Dogma till the time of Augustine. Only a portion of it appears in this volume. The remainder will form the contents of the Fourth Volume. The author has prefixed to the volume two prefaces, one to the first, the other to the third Edition. These are here given.

The Appendix on Manichæism is the last of four which appear at the end of the first volume of the German Edition. The first three of these will be found at the end of the first volume of the English Edition.

A. B. BRUCE.

*Glasgow*, August, 1897.

## AUTHOR'S PREFACE TO FIRST EDITION OF VOLUME II. OF THE GERMAN WORK.

THE first half of the second part of the History of Dogma is here given apart and as the second volume, because it is complete in itself, and I shall be prevented from completing the work at once by other tasks.

The account contained in the following pages would have been shorter, if I could have persuaded myself of the correctness of the opinion, that a single, all-determining thought obtained its true development in the History of Dogma from the fourth to the eighth century. This opinion dominates, apart from a few monographs, all writings on the History of Dogma, and gives a uniform impress to the accounts of Protestants and Catholics. I share it within certain limits; but these very limits, which I have endeavoured to define, [1] have not yet received due attention. In the fourth century the formula that was correct, when judged by the conception of redemption of the ancient Church, prevailed; but the Fathers, who finally secured its triumph, did not give it the exposition which it originally demanded. In the fifth century, or the seventh, on the contrary, a formula that, measured by the same standard, was incorrect, prevailed; yet it was associated with an exposition that to some extent compensated for the incorrectness. In both cases, however, the imperfections of the conclusion, which are explained from various circumstances, became of the highest importance. For in them we find the reason why the phantom Christ did not wholly oust the historical; and, in order to overcome them, men turned anew to Philosophy, especially to Aristotle. The orthodox Church owes two things to the incorrect form in which the Trinitarian and Christological Dogma was finally stated: (1) contact with the Gospel, and (2) renewed contact with ancient science, *i.e.*, scholasticism.

[1] *Vide* pp. 167 ff. of this volume.

The account of these conditions demanded a more minute discussion of the process of the History of Dogma, than is usual in the ordinary text-books. Dogma developed slowly and amid great obstacles. No single step should be overlooked in the description, and, in particular, the period between the fourth and fifth Councils is not less important than any other. Political relationships, at no point decisive by themselves, yet everywhere required, as well as western influences, careful attention. I should have discussed them still more thoroughly, if I had not been restrained by considerations of the extent of the book. I have included the state of affairs and developments in the West, so far as they were related to, and acted upon, those in the East. In the following Book I shall begin with Augustine. The scientific theological expositions of the Fathers have only been brought under review, where they appeared indispensable for the understanding of Dogma. In any case I was not afraid of doing too much here. I am convinced that a shorter description ought not to be offered to students of Theology, unless it were to be a mere guide. The history of Christian Dogma— perhaps the most complicated history of development which we can completely review—presents the investigator with the greatest difficulties; and yet it is, along with the study of the New Testament, and in the present position of Protestantism, the most important discipline for every one who seeks really to study Theology. The theologian who leaves the University without being thoroughly familiar with it, is, in the most critical questions, helplessly at the mercy of the authorities of the day. But the royal way to the understanding of the History of Dogma, opened up by F. Chr. Baur, and pursued by Thomasius, does not lead to the goal; for by it we become acquainted with the historical matter only in the abbreviated form required for the defence of the completed Dogma.

The history of the *development* of Dogma does not offer the lofty interest, which attaches to that of its *genesis*. When we return from the most complicated and elaborate doctrinal formulas, from the mysticism of the Cultus and Christian Neoplatonism, from the worship of saints and ceremonial ritual of the seventh and eighth centuries, back to Origen and the third century, we are astonished to find that all we have mentioned was really in existence at the earlier date. Only it existed then amid a mass of different material, and its footing was insecure In many respects the whole historical development of Dogma from the fourth century to John of Damascus and Theodore of Studion was simply a vast process of reduction, selection, and definition. In the

East we are no longer called upon to deal in any quarter with new and original matter, but always rather with what is traditional, derivative, and, to an increasing extent, superstitious. Yet that to which centuries devoted earnest reflection, holding it to be sacred, will never lose its importance, as long as there still exists among us a remnant of the same conditions which belonged to those times. But who could deny that those conditions—in the Church and in learning—are still powerful among us? Therefore even the religious formulas are still in force which were created in the Byzantine age; nay, they are the dogmas κατ᾽ ἐξοχήν in all Churches, so that the popular idiom is nowise wrong which with the word "dogma" primarily designates the doctrines of the Trinity and the divine humanity of Christ. The inquirer who follows the development of these dogmas after the fourth century, and who, owing to the want of originality and freshness in his material, loses pleasure in his work, is ever and again reanimated, when he considers that he has to deal with matters which have gained, and still exercise, an immense power over the feelings and minds of men. And how much it is still possible for us to learn, as free Evangelical Christians, especially after generations of scholars have dedicated to this history the most devoted industry, so that no one can enter into their labours without becoming their disciples!

I know very well that it would be possible to treat the material reviewed in this book more universally than I have done. My chief purpose was to show how matters arose and were *in their concrete manifestation*. But the task of making dogma really intelligible in all its aspects within the limits of a History of Dogma, is after all as insoluble as any similar problem which isolates a single object from Universal History, and requires its investigation in and by itself. This limitation I need only recall. But something further has to be said. Dogmas, undoubtedly, admit of a process of refinement, which would bring them closer to our understanding and our feeling. But my powers are not equal to this lofty task, and even if I possessed the uncommon qualities of the psychologist and the religious philosopher, I should have hesitated about employing them in this book; for I did not wish to endanger the reliability of what I had to present by reflections, which must always remain more or less subjective. Thus I have limited myself to a few hints; these will only be found where the nature of the material itself induced me to seek for the far remote thought underlying the expression.

I have throughout striven in this volume, to give such an account as would demand to be read connectedly; for a work on the history of dogma, which is used only for reference, has missed its highest aim. I have believed that I could not dispense with the addition of numerous notes, but the text of the book is so written that the reader, if he prefers it, may disregard them.

*Marburg,* 14 June, 1887.

---

## PREFACE TO THE THIRD EDITION.

I HAVE subjected this volume to a thorough revision, and have sought to improve and strengthen it in not a few places. May this new edition also promote the study of a historical period whose products are still held by many among us to be incapable of reform.

*Berlin,* 28 May, 1894.                         ADOLF HARNACK.

# CONTENTS.

## FIRST PART: SECOND BOOK CONTINUED. [1]

[1] *Vide* Editor's Preface to this volume.

## SECOND PART.

### FIRST BOOK.

*The History of the Development of Dogma as the Doctrine of
the God-man on the basis of Natural Theology.*

# CHAPTER I.

THE DECISIVE SUCCESS OF THEOLOGICAL SPECULATION IN THE
SPHERE OF THE RULE OF FAITH, OR, THE DEFINING OF
THE NORM OF THE DOCTRINE OF THE CHURCH DUE
TO THE ADOPTION OF THE LOGOS CHRISTOLOGY.[1]

## 1. *Introduction.*

FROM the great work of Irenæus and the anti-gnostic writings
of Tertullian, it would seem as if the doctrine of the Logos,
or, the doctrine of the pre-existence of Christ as a distinct
person, was at the end of the second century an undisputed
tenet of Church orthodoxy, and formed a universally recognised
portion of the baptismal confession interpreted anti-gnostically,
*i.e.*, of the rule of faith. [2] But certain as it is that the Logos
Christology was in the second century not merely the property
of a few Christian philosophers, [3] it is, on the other hand, as
clear that it did not belong to the solid structure of the Catholic faith. It was not on the same footing as, *e.g.*, the doctrines
of God the Creator, the real body of Christ, the resurrection
of the body, etc. The great conflicts which, after c. A.D. 170,

---

[1] See Dorner, Entw.-Gesch. d. Lehre v. d. Person Christi, 1 Thl. 1845; Lange,
Gesch. u. Entw. der Systeme der Unitarier vor der nic. Synode, 1831; Hagemann,
Die römische Kirche und ihr Einfluss auf Disciplin und Dogma in den ersten drei
Jahrh. 1864, (the most important and most stimulating monograph on the subject);
and my art. 'Monarchianismus' in Herzog's R. E., 2nd ed., vol. X., pp. 178—213,
on which the following arguments are based.

[2] See Vol. II., pp. 20—38 and Iren. I. 10, 1; Tertull. De præscr. 13; Adv. Prax. 2.
In the rule of faith, De virg., vel. 1, there is no statement as to the pre-existence
of the Son of God.

[3] See Vol. I., p. 192, Note (John's Gospel, Revelation, Κήρυγμα Πέτρου, Ignatius,
and esp. Celsus in Orig. II. 31, etc.).

were waged for more than a century *within* the Catholic Church
rather show, that the doctrine only gradually found its way
into the creed of the Church.[1] But a higher than merely
Christological interest attaches to the gradual incorporation of
the Logos doctrine in the rule of faith. *The formula of the
Logos, as it was almost universally understood, legitimised speculation, i.e., Neo-platonic philosophy, within the creed of the
Church.*[2] When Christ was designated the incarnate Logos of
God, and when this was set up as His supreme characterisation,
men were directed to think of the divine in Christ as the
reason of God realised in the structure of the world and the
history of mankind. This implied a definite philosophical view
of God, of creation, and of the world, and the baptismal confession became a compendium of scientific dogmatics, *i.e.*, of a
system of doctrine entwined with the Metaphysics of Plato and
the Stoics. But at the same time an urgent impulse necessarily
made itself felt to define the contents and value of the Redeemer's life and work, not, primarily, from the point of view of
the proclamation of the Gospel, and the hopes of a future state,
but from that of the cosmic significance attaching to his
divine nature concealed in the flesh. Insomuch, however, as
such a view could only really reach and be intelligible to
those who had been trained in philosophical speculations, the
establishing of the Logos Christology within the rule of faith
was equivalent for the great mass of Christians to the setting up
of a mystery, which in the first place could only make an impression through its high-pitched formulas and the glamour of
the incomprehensible. But as soon as a religion expresses the

---

[1] The observation that Irenæus and Tertullian treat it as a fixed portion of the
rule of faith is very instructive; for it shows that these theologians were ahead of
the Church of their time. Here we have a point given, at which we can estimate
the relation of what Irenæus maintained to be the creed of the Church, to the
doctrine which was, as a matter of fact, generally held at the time in the Church.
We may turn this insight to account for the history of the Canon and the constitution, where, unfortunately, an estimate of the statements of Irenæus is rendered
difficult.

[2] By Neo-platonic philosophy we, of course, do not here mean Neo-platonism,
but the philosophy (in method and also in part, in results), developed before Neoplatonism by Philo, Valentinus, Numenius, and others.

loftiest contents of its creed in formulas which must remain mysterious and unintelligible to the great mass of its adherents, those adherents come under guardians. In other words, the multitude must believe in the creed; at the same time they no longer derive from it directly the motives of their religious and moral life; and they are dependent on the theologians, who, as professors of the mysterious, alone understand and are capable of interpreting and practically applying the creed. The necessary consequence of this development was that the mysterious creed, being no longer in a position practically to control life, was superseded by *the authority of the Church, the cultus, and prescribed duties*, in determining the religious life of the laity; while the theologians, or the priests, appeared alone as the possessors of an independent faith and knowledge. But as soon as the laity were actuated by a desire for religious independence, which produced a reaction, and yet was not powerful enough to correct the conditions out of which this state of matters arose, there made its appearance only an expedient of a conservative sort, viz., the order of the monks. As this order did not tamper with the prevailing system of the Church, the Church could tolerate it, and could even use it as a valve, by which to provide an outlet for all religious subjectivity, and for the energies of a piety that renounced the world. The history of the Church shows us, or, at any rate, lets us divine, this situation at the transition from the 3rd to the 4th century. On the one hand, we see—at least in the East—that the Christian faith had become a theology, which was regarded, to all intents without question, as the revealed faith, and only capable of being represented and expounded by "teachers". On the other hand, we find a lay Christendom tied to the priest, the cultus, the sacraments, and a ceremonial penitence, and revering the creed as a mystery. Between these arose with elemental force the order of the monks, which—apart from a few phenomena—did not attack the ecclesiastical system, and which could not be suppressed by priests and theologians, because it strove to realise on earth the object to which they themselves had subordinated the whole of theology, because it, as it were, sought to soar on wings to the same height, to which the steps of the long ladders constructed by theology were meant to conduct. [1]

Now the incorporation in the creed of philosophic (Platonic) speculation, *i.e.*, the Hellenising of the traditional doctrines, was not the only condition, but it was certainly one of the most important of the conditions, that led to the rise of this three-fold Christendom of clergy, laity, and monks, in the Church. That the Catholic Church was capable of accommodating these three orders in its midst is a proof of its power. That the combination forms up to the present day the signature of Catholic Churches is evidence, moreover, of the practical value attached by the Church to this unified differentiation. It, in fact, could not but best correspond to the different wants of men united to form a universal Church. So far as it was a consequence of the general conditions under which the Church existed in the third century, we must here leave its origin untouched, [2] but so far as it was due to the reception of philosophical speculation into the Church, its prior history must be presented. Yet it may not be superfluous to begin by noticing expressly, that the confidence with which first the Apologists identified the Logos of the philosophers and the Christ of faith, and the zeal with which the anti-gnostic Fathers then incorporated the Logos-Christ in the creed of believers, are also to be explained from a Christian interest. In their scientific conception of the world the Logos had a fixed place, and was held to be the "alter ego" of God, though at the same time he was also regarded as the representative of the Reason that operated in the Cosmos. Their conception of Christ as the appearance of the Logos in a personal form only proves that they sought to make the highest possible assertion concerning him, to justify worship being rendered him, and to demonstrate the absolute and unique nature of the contents of the Christian religion. The Christian religion was only in a position to gain the cultured, to conquer Gnosticism, and to thrust aside Polytheism in the Roman empire, because it had concluded an alliance with that intellectual potentate which already swayed the minds and hearts of the

[1] See my lecture on Monachism, 3rd ed. 1886.
[2] Yet see Vol. II., pp. 122—127.

best men, the philosophic-religious ethics of the age. This alliance found expression in the formula: Christ *is* word and law (Χριστὸς λόγος καὶ νόμος). The philosophic Christology arose, so to speak, at the circumference of the Church, and thence moved gradually to the centre of the Christian faith. The same is true of theology generally; its most concise description is philosophic Christology. A complete fusion of the old faith and theology, one that tranquillised the minds of the devout, was not consummated till the fourth, strictly speaking, indeed, till the fifth century (Cyril of Alexandria). Valentinus, Origen, the Cappadocians mark the stages of the process. Valentinus was very speedily ejected as a heretic. Origen, in spite of the immense influence which he exerted, was in the end unable to retain his footing in the Church. The Cappadocians almost perfected the complete fusion of the traditional faith of the Church conceived as mystery and philosophy, by removing Origen's distinction between those who knew and those who believed (Gnostics and Pistics); meanwhile they retained much that was comparatively free and looked on with suspicion by the traditionalists. Cyril's theology first marked the complete agreement between faith and philosophy, authority and specula- tion, an agreement which finally, in the sixth century, sup- pressed every independent theology. But from the end of the second century up to the closing years of the third, the fund- amental principle of philosophic theology had naturalised itself, in the very faith of the Church. This process in which, on the one hand, certain results of speculative theology became legitimised within the Church as revelations and mysteries, and on the other—as a sort of antidote—the freedom of theology was limited, is to be described in what follows.

It has been shown above (Vol. I., p. 190 ff.) that about the middle of the second century there existed side by side in the Churches chiefly two conceptions of the person of Christ. In the *Adoptian* view Jesus was regarded as the man in whom divinity or the spirit of God dwelt, and who was finally exalted to godlike honour. In the *Pneumatic* conception, Jesus was looked upon as a heavenly spirit who assumed an earthly body. The latter was adopted in their speculations by the Apologists.

The fixing of the apostolic tradition, which took place in opposition to the Gnostics, as also to the so-called Montanists, in the course of the second half of the second century, did not yet decide in favour of either view.[1] The Holy Scriptures could be appealed to in support of both. But those had decidedly the best of it, in the circumstances of the time, who recognised the incarnation of a special divine nature in Christ; and as certainly were the others in the right, in view of the Synoptic gospels, who saw in Jesus the man chosen to be his Son by God, and possessed of the Spirit. The former conception corresponded to the interpretation of the O. T. theophanies which had been accepted by the Alexandrians, and had proved so convincing in apologetic arguments;[2] it could be supported by the testimony of a series of Apostolic writings, whose authority was absolute;[3] it protected the O. T. against Gnostic criticism. It, further, reduced the highest conception of the value of Christianity to a brief and convincing formula: "*God became man in order that men might become gods;*" and, finally,—which was not least—it could be brought, with little trouble, into line with

[1] The points, which, as regards Christ, belonged in the second half of the second century to ecclesiastical orthodoxy, are given in the clauses of the Roman baptismal confession to which ἀληθῶς is added, in the precise elaboration of the idea of creation, in the εἰς placed alongside Χριστὸς Ἰησοῦς, and in the identification of the Catholic institution of the Church with the Holy Church.

[2] The Christian doctrine of the Son of God could be most easily rendered acceptable to cultured heathens by means of the Logos doctrine; see the memorable confession of Celsus placed by him in the lips of his "Jew" (II. 31): ὡς εἴγε ὁ λόγος ἐστὶν ὑμῖν υἱὸς τοῦ Θεοῦ, καὶ ἡμεῖς ἐπαινοῦμεν; see also the preceding: σοφίζονται οἱ Χριστιανοὶ ἐν τῷ λέγειν τὸν υἱὸν τοῦ Θεοῦ εἶναι αὐτολόγον.

[3] The conviction of the harmony of the Apostles, or, of all Apostolic writings, could not but result in the Christology of the Synoptics and the Acts being interpreted in the light of John and Paul, or more accurately, in that of the philosophic Christology held to be attested by John and Paul. It has been up to the present day the usual fate of the Synoptics, and with them of the sayings of Jesus, to be understood, on account of their place in the Canon, in accordance with the caprices of the dogmatics prevalent at the time, Pauline and Johannine theology having assigned to it the rôle of mediator. The "lower" had to be explained by the "higher" (see even Clemens Alex. with his criticism of the "pneumatic", the spiritual, Fourth Gospel, as compared with the first three). In older times men transformed the sense right off; nowadays they speak of *steps* which lead to the *higher* teaching, and they dress the old illusion with a new *scientific* mantle.

the cosmological and theological tenets which had been borrowed
from the religious philosophy of the age to serve as a foundation for a rational Christian theology. The adoption of the
belief in the divine Logos to explain the genesis and history
of the world at once decided the means by which also the
divine dignity and sonship of the Redeemer were alone to be
defined. [1] In this procedure the theologians themselves had no
danger to fear to their monotheism, even if they made the
Logos more than a product of the creative will of God. Neither
Justin, Tatian, nor any of the Apologists or Fathers show the
slightest anxiety on this point. For the infinite substance, resting behind the world,—and as such the deity was conceived—
could display and unfold itself in different subjects. It could
impart its own inexhaustible being to a variety of bearers,
without thereby being emptied, or its unity being dissolved
($\mu o \nu \alpha \rho \chi i \alpha$ $\kappa \alpha \tau$' $o i \kappa o \nu o \mu i \alpha \nu$, as the technical expression has it). [2]
But, lastly, the theologians had no reason to fear for the "deity'
of the Christ in whom the incarnation of that Logos was to be
viewed. For the conception of the Logos was capable of the
most manifold contents, and its dexterous treatment could be
already supported by the most instructive precedents. This conception could be adapted to every change and accentuation of
the religious interest, every deepening of speculation, as

[1] But the substitution of the Logos for the, otherwise undefined, spiritual being
($\pi \nu \epsilon \tilde{\upsilon} \mu \alpha$) in Christ presented another very great advantage. It brought to an end,
though not at once (see Clemens Alex.), the speculations which reckoned the heavenly
personality of Christ in some way or other in the number of the higher angels
or conceived it as one *Æon* among many. Through the definition of this " Spiritual
Being " as Logos his transcendent and unique dignity was firmly outlined and
assured. For the Logos was universally accepted as the *Prius* logically and tempor-
ally, and the *causa* not only of the world, but also of all powers, ideas, æons,
and angels. He, therefore, did not belong—at least in every respect—to their order.

[2] Augustine first wrought to end this questionable monotheism, and endeavoured
to treat seriously the monotheism of the living God. But his efforts only produced
an impression in the West, and even there the attempt was weakened from the start
by a faulty respect for the prevalent Christology, and was forced to entangle itself
in absurd formulas. In the East the accommodating Substance-Monotheism of
philosophy remained with its permission of a plurality of divine persons; and this
doctrine was taught with such naïvety and simplicity, that the Cappadocians, *e.g.*,
proclaimed the Christian conception of God to be the just mean between the
polytheism of the heathens and the monotheism of the Jews.

well as to all the needs of the Cultus, nay, even to new results
of Biblical exegesis.  It revealed itself gradually to be a variable quantity of the most accommodating kind, capable of being
at once determined by any new factor received into the theological ferment. It even admitted contents which stood in the most
abrupt contradiction to the processes of thought out of which
the conception itself had sprung, *i.e.*, contents which almost
completely concealed the cosmological genesis of the conception.
But it was long before this point was reached.  And as long
as it was not, as long as the Logos was still employed as the
formula under which was comprehended either the original idea
of the world, or the rational law of the world, many did not
entirely cease to mistrust the fitness of the conception to establish
the divinity of Christ.  For those, finally, could not but seek
to perceive the full deity in the Redeemer, who reckoned on
a deification of man.  Athanasius first made this possible to
them by his explanation of the Logos, but he at the same time
began to empty the conception of its original cosmological contents.  And the history of Christology from Athanasius to
Augustine is the history of the displacing of the Logos conception by the other, destitute of all cosmical contents, of the
Son,—the history of the substitution of the immanent and
absolute trinity for the economic and relative.  The complete
divinity of the Son was thereby secured, but in the form of a
complicated and artificial speculation, which neither could be
maintained without reservation before the tribunal of the science
of the day, nor could claim the support of an ancient tradition.

But the first formulated opposition to the Logos Christology
did not spring from anxiety for the complete divinity of Christ,
or even from solicitude for monotheism; it was rather called
forth by interest in the evangelical, the Synoptic, idea of Christ.
With this was combined the attack on the use of Platonic
philosophy in Christian doctrine.  The first public and literary
opponents of the Christian Logos-speculations, therefore, did not
escape the reproach of depreciating, if not of destroying, the
dignity of the Redeemer. It was only in the subsequent period,
in a second phase of the controversy, that these opponents of
the Logos Christology were able to fling back the reproach at

its defenders. With the Monarchians the first subject of interest was the man Jesus; then came monotheism and the divine dignity of Christ. From this point, however, the whole theological interpretation of the two first articles of the rule of faith, was again gradually involved in controversy. In so far as they were understood to refute a crude docetism and the severance of Jesus and Christ they were confirmed. But did not the doctrine of a heavenly æon, rendered incarnate in the Redeemer, contain another remnant of the old Gnostic leaven? Did not the sending forth of the Logos (προβολὴ τοῦ λόγου) to create the world recall the emanation of the æons? Was not ditheism set up, if two divine beings were to be worshipped? Not only were the uncultured Christian laity driven to such criticisms,—for what did they understand by the "economic mode of the existence of God"?—but also all those theologians who refused to give any place to Platonic philosophy in Christian dogmatics. A conflict began which lasted for more than a century, in certain branches of it for almost two centuries. Who opened it, or first assumed the aggressive, we know not. The contest engages our deepest interest in different respects, and can be described from different points of view. We cannot regard it, indeed, directly as a fight waged by theology against a still enthusiastic conception of religion; for the literary opponents of the Logos Christology were no longer enthusiasts, but, rather, from the very beginning their declared enemies. Nor was it directly a war of the theologians against the laity, for it was not laymen, but only theologians who had adopted the creed of the laity, who opposed their brethren.[1] We must

[1] The Alogi opposed the Montanists and all prophecy; conversely the western representatives of the Logos Christology, Irenæus, Tertullian and Hippolytus were Chiliasts. But this feature makes no change in the fact that the incorporation of the Logos Christology and the fading away of eschatological apocalyptic hopes went hand in hand. Theologians were able to combine inconsistent beliefs for a time; but for the great mass of the laity in the East the mystery of the person of Christ took the place of the Christ who was to have set up his visible Kingdom of glory upon earth. See especially the refutation of the Chiliasts by Origen (περὶ ἀρχ. II. 11) and Dionysius Alex. (Euseb. H. E. VII. 24, 25). The continued embodiment in new visions of those eschatological hopes and apocalyptic fancies by the monks and laymen of later times, proved that the latter could not make the received mystery of dogma fruitful for their practical religion.

describe it as the strenuous effort of Stoic Platonism to obtain
supremacy in the theology of the Church; the victory of Plato
over Zeno and Aristotle in Christian science; the history of
the displacement of the historical by the pre-existent Christ, of
the Christ of reality by the Christ of thought, in dogmatics;
finally, as the victorious attempt to substitute the mystery of
the person of Christ for the person Himself, and, by means of
a theological formula unintelligible to them, to put the laity with
their Christian faith under guardians—a state desired and indeed
required by them to an increasing extent.   When the Logos
Christology obtained a complete victory, the traditional view of
the Supreme deity as one person, and, along with this, every
thought of the real and complete human personality of the
Redeemer was in fact condemned as being intolerable in the
Church.  Its place was taken by "the nature" [of Christ],
which without "the person" is simply a cipher.  The defeated
party had right on its side, but had not succeeded in making
its Christology agree with its conception of the object and
result of the Christian religion.  This was the very reason of
its defeat.  A religion which promised its adherents that their
nature would be rendered divine, could only be satisfied by a
redeemer who in his own person had deified human nature. If,
after the gradual fading away of eschatological hopes, the above
prospect was held valid, then those were right who worked
out this view of the Redeemer.

    In accordance with an expression coined by Tertullian, we
understand by Monarchians the representatives of strict, not
economic, monotheism in the ancient Church.  In other words,
they were theologians who held firmly by the dignity of Jesus
as Redeemer, but at the same time would not give up the
personal, the numerical, unity of God; and who therefore
opposed the speculations which had led to the adoption of the
duality or trinity of the godhead.[1]  In order rightly to under-

---

[1] This definition is, in truth, too narrow; for at least a section, if not all, of
the so-called Dynamistic Monarchians recognised, besides God, the Spirit as eternal
Son of God, and accordingly assumed two Hypostases. But they did not see in
Jesus an incarnation of this Holy Spirit, and they were therefore monarchian in
their doctrine of Christ. Besides, so far as I know, the name of Monarchians was

stand their position in the history of the genesis of the dogmatics of the Church, it is decisive, as will have been already
clear from the above, that they only came to the front,
after the anti-gnostic understanding of the baptismal confession
had been substantially assured in the Church. It results from
this that they are, generally speaking, to be criticised as men
who appeared on the soil of Catholicism, and that therefore,
apart from the points clearly in dispute, we must suppose agreement between them and their opponents. It is not superfluous
to recall this expressly. The confusion to which the failure to
note this presupposition has led and still continually leads may
be seen, *e.g.*, in the relative section in Dorner's History of the
development of the doctrine of the Person of Christ, or in

not applied in the ancient Church to these, but only to the theologians who taught
that there was in Christ an incarnation of God the Father Himself. It was not
extended to the earlier Dynamistic Monarchians, because, so far as we know, the
question whether God consisted of one or more persons did not enter into the
dispute with them. In a wider sense, the Monarchians could be taken also to
include the Arians, and all those theologians, who, while they recognised the personal
independence of a divine nature in Christ, yet held this nature to have been one
*created* by God; in any case, the Arians were undoubtedly connected with Paul of
Samosata through Lucian. However, it is not advisable to extend the conception
so widely; for, firstly, we would thus get too far away from the old classification, and,
secondly, it is not to be overlooked that, even in the case of the most thorough-
going Arians, their Christology reacted on their doctrine of God, and their strict
Monotheism was to some extent modified. Hence, both on historical and logical
grounds, it is best for our purpose to understand by Monarchians those theologians
exclusively who perceived in Jesus either a man filled, in a unique way, with the
Spirit, or an incarnation of God the Father; with the reservation, that the former
in certain of their groups regarded the Holy Spirit as a divine Hypostasis, and were
accordingly no longer really Monarchians in the strict sense of the term. For the
rest, the expression "Monarchians" is in so far inappropriate as their opponents
would also have certainly maintained the "monarchia" of God. See Tertulli., Adv.
Prax. 3 f.; Epiphan. H. 62. 3: οὐ πολυθεΐαν εἰσηγούμεθα, ἀλλὰ μοναρχίαν κηρύττομεν.
They would even have cast back at the Monarchians the reproach that they were destroying the monarchy. " Ἡ μοναρχία τοῦ Θεοῦ " was in the second century a standing
title in the polemics of the theologians against polytheists and Gnostics—see the
passages collected from Justin, Tatian, Irenæus etc. by Coustant in his Ep. Dionysii
adv. Sabell. (Routh, Reliq. Sacræ III., p. 385 f.). Tertullian has therefore by no
means used the term "Monarchians" as if he were thus directly branding his
opponents as heretical; he rather names them by their favourite catch-word in a
spirit of irony (Adv. Prax 10; "vanissimi Monarchiani"). The name was therefore
not really synonymous with a form of heresy in the ancient Church, even if here
and there it was applied to the opponents of the doctrine of the Trinity.

Krawutzcky's study on the origin of the Didache.[1] The so-called Dynamistic Monarchians have had especially to suffer from this criticism, their teaching being comfortably disposed of as "Ebionitic". However, imperative as it certainly is, in general, to describe the history of Monarchianism without reference to the ancient pre-Catholic controversies, and only to bring in the history of Montanism with great caution, still many facts observed in reference to the earliest bodies of Monarchians that come clearly before us, seem to prove that they bore features which must be characterised as pre-Catholic, but not un-Catholic. This is especially true of their attitude to certain books of the New Testament. Undoubtedly we have reason even here to complain of the scantiness and uncertainty of our historical material. The Church historians have attempted to bury or distort the true history of Monarchianism to as great an extent as they passed over and obscured that of the so-called Montanism. At a very early date, if not in the first stages of the controversy, they read Ebionitism and Gnosticism into the theses of their opponents; they attempted to discredit their theological works as products of a specific secularisation, or as travesties, of Christianity, and they sought to portray the Monarchians themselves as renegades who had abandoned the rule of faith and the Canon. By this kind of polemics they have made it difficult for after ages to decide, among other things, whether certain peculiarities of Monarchian bodies in dealing with the Canon of the N. T. writings spring from a period when there was as yet no N. T. Canon in the strict Catholic sense, or whether these characteristics are to be regarded as deviations from an already settled authority, and therefore innovations. Meanwhile, looking to the Catholicity of the whole character of Monarchian movements, and, further, to the fact that no opposition is recorded as having been made by them to the N. T. Canon after its essential contents and authority appear to have been established; considering, finally, that the Montanists, and even the Marcionites and Gnostics, were very early charged with attempts on the Catholic Canon, we need no longer

[1] See Theol. Quartalschr. 1884, p. 547 ff. Krawutzcky holds the Didache to be at once Ebionitic and Theodotian.

doubt that the Monarchian deviations point exclusively to a time when no such Canon existed; and that other "heresies", to be met with in the older groups, are to be criticised on the understanding that the Church was becoming, but not yet become, Catholic. [1]

The history of Monarchianism is no clearer than its rise in the form of particular theological tendencies. Here also we have before us, at the present day, only scanty fragments. We cannot always trace completely even the settled distinction between Dynamistic—better, Adoptian—and Modalistic Monarchianism; [2] between the theory that made the power or Spirit of God dwell in the man Jesus, and the view that sees in Him the incarnation of the deity Himself. [3]

Certainly the common element, so far as there was one, of the Monarchian movements, lay in the form of the conception of God, the distinguishing feature, in the idea of revelation. But all the phenomena under this head cannot be classified with certainty, apart from the fact that the most numerous and important "systems" exist in a very shaky tradition. A really reliable division of the Monarchianism that in all its forms rejected the idea of a physical fatherhood of God, and only saw the Son of God in the *historical* Jesus, is impossible on the strength of the authorities up till now known to us. Apart from a fragment or two we only possess accounts by opponents. The chronology, again, causes a special difficulty. Much labour has been spent upon it since the discovery of the Philosophumena; but most of the details have remained very uncertain. The dates of the Alogi, Artemas, Praxeas, Sabellius, the Antiochian Synods against Paul of Samosata, etc., have not yet been firmly settled. The concise remarks on the subject in what follows rest on independent labours. Finally, we

[1] It is very remarkable that Irenæus has given us no hint in his great work of a Monarchian controversy in the Church.

[2] It was pointed out above, (Vol. I., p. 193) and will be argued more fully later on, that the different Christologies could pass into one another.

[3] We have already noticed, Vol. I., p. 195, that we can only speak of a naïve Modalism in the earlier periods; Modalism first appeared as an exclusive doctrine at the close of the second century; see under.

are badly informed even as to the geographical range of the
controversies. We may, however, suppose, with great probability,
that at one time or other a conflict took place in all centres of
Christianity in the Empire. But a connected history cannot be given.

## 2.  *The Secession of Dynamistic Monarchianism or Adoptianism.*

### (a).  The so-called Alogi in Asia Minor. [1]

Epiphanius [2] and Philastrius (H. 60) know, from the Syntagma
of Hippolytus, of a party to which the latter had given the
nickname of "Alogi". Hippolytus had recorded that its members rejected the Gospel and the Apocalypse of John, [3] attri-
buting these books to Cerinthus, and had not recognised the
Logos of God to whom the Holy Spirit had borne witness in
the Gospel. Hippolytus, the most prolific of the opponents of
the heretics, wrote, besides his Syntagma, a special work against
these men in defence of the Johannine writings; [4] and he per-

---

[1] Merkel, Aufklärung der Streitigkeiten der Aloger, 1782; Heinichen, De Alogis,
1829; Olshausen, Echtheit der vier Kanonischen Evangelien, p. 241 f.; Schwegler,
Montanismus, p. 265 ff. etc.; Volkmar, Hippolytus, p. 112 f.; Döllinger, Hippolytus
u. Kallistus, p. 229 f.; Lipsius, Quellenkritik des Epiphanius, p. 23 f., 233 f.;
Harnack in d. Ztschr. f. d. histor. Theol. 1874, p. 166 f.; Lipsius, Quellen der
ältesten Ketzergeschichte, p. 93 f., 214 f.; Zahn in d. Ztschr. für die histor. Theol.,
1875, p. 72 f.; Caspari, Quellen III., p. 377 f., 398 f., Soyres, Montanism, p. 49 f.;
Bonwetsch, Montanismus vv. ll.; Iwanzov-Platonov, Häresien und Schismen der
drei ersten Jahr. I, p. 233 f.; Zahn, Gesch. d. N. T. Kanons I., p. 220 ff.; Harnack,
das N. T. um d. J. 200, p. 38 ff.; Jülicher, Theol. Lit. Ztg., 1889, No. 7; Salmon
i. Hermathena, 1892, p. 161 ff.

[2] Hær. 51; after him Augustine H. 30, Prædest. H. 30 etc. The statement of
the Prædest. that a Bishop named Philo refuted the Alogi is worthless. Whether
the choice of the name was due to the Alexandrian Jew is unknown.

[3] Nothing is reported as to the Letters. Epiphanius is perhaps right in representing that they were also rejected (l.c. ch. 34); but perhaps they were not involved
in the discussion.

[4] See the list of writings on the statue of Hippolytus: υπερ του κατα ιωαν[ν]ην
ευαγγελιου και αποκαλυψεως; and Ebed Jesu, catal. 7 (Assemani, Bibl. Orient.
III. 1, 15): "Apologia pro apocalypsi et evangelio Johannis apostoli et evange-
listæ." Besides this Hippolytus wrote: "Capita adversus Caium," a Roman sym-
pathiser with the Alogi. Of this writing a few fragments have been preserved
(Gwynn, Hermathena VI., p. 397 f.; Harnack, Texte und Unters. VI. 3, p. 121 ff.;
Zahn, Gesch. des N. T. Kanons, II., p. 973 ff.

haps also attacked them in another work aimed at all Monarchians.[1] The character of the party can still be defined, in its
main features, from the passages taken by Epiphanius from
these writings, due regard being given to Irenæus III. 11, 9.
The Christological problem seems not to have occupied a foremost place in the discussion, but rather, the elimination of all
docetic leaven, and the attitude to prophecy. The non-descript,
the Alogi, were a party of the radical, anti-montanist, opposition in Asia Minor, existing within the Church—so radical that
they refused to recognise the Montanist communities as Christian.
They wished to have all prophecy kept out of the Church; in
this sense they were decided contemners of the Spirit (Iren. l.c.;
Epiph. 51, ch. 35). This attitude led them to an historical
criticism of the two Johannine books, the one of which contained Christ's announcement of the Paraclete, a passage which
Montanus had made the most of for his own ends, while the
other imparted prophetic revelations. They came to the conclusion, on internal grounds, that these books could not be
genuine, that they were composed "in the name of John"
(εἰς ὄνομα Ἰωάννου ch. 3, 18), and that by Cerinthus
(ch. 3, 4,); the books ought not therefore to be received in the

---

[1] It is certain that Epiphanius, besides the relative section of the Syntagma, also
copied at least a second writing against the "Alogi", and it is probable that this
likewise came from Hippolytus. The date of its composition can still be pretty
accurately determined from Epiphan. H. 31, ch. 33. It was written about A.D. 234;
for Epiphanius' authority closes the period of the Apostles 93 years after the
Ascension, and remarks that since that date 112 years had elapsed. Lipsius has
obtained another result, but only by an emendation of the text which is unnecessary
(see Quellen der ältesten Ketzergeschichte, p. 109 f.). Hippolytus treats his unnamed opponents as contemporaries; but a closer examination shows that he only
knew them from their writings—of which there were several (see ch. 33), and therefore knew nothing by personal observation of the conditions under which they
appeared. A certain criterion of the age of these writings, and therefore of the
party itself, is given by the fact that, at the time when the latter flourished, the
only Church at Thyatira was, from their own testimony, Montanist, while the
above-mentioned authority was already able to tell of a rising catholic Church, and
of other Christian communities in that place. A Christian of Thyatira, by name
Papylus, appears in the Martyrium Carpi et Papyli (see Harnack, Texte u. Unters.
III. 3, 4). The date when this movement in Asia Minor flourished can be discovered more definitely, however, by a combination, proved by Zahn to be justified,
of the statements of Hippolytus and Irenæus III. 11. 9. According to this, the
party existed in Asia Minor, A.D. 170—180.

Church (ch. 3: οὐκ ἄξια αὐτά φασιν εἶναι ἐν ἐκκλησία). The Gospel was charged with containing what was untrue; it contradicted the other Gospels, [1] and gave a quite different and, indeed, a notoriously false order of events; it was devoid of any sort of arrangement; it omitted important facts and inserted new ones which were inconsistent with the Synoptic Gospels; and it was docetic. [2] Against the Apocalypse it was alleged, above all, that its contents were often unintelligible, nay, absurd and untrue (ch. 32—34). They ridiculed the seven angels and seven trumpets, and the four angels by the Euphrates; and on Rev. II. 18, they supposed that there was no Christian community in Thyatira at the time, and that accordingly the Epistle was fictitious. Moreover, the objections to the Gospel must also have included the charge (ch. 18) that it favoured Docetism, seeing that it passed at once from the incarnation of the Logos to the work of the ministry of Christ. In this connection they attacked the expression "Logos" for the Son of God; [3] indeed, they scented Gnosticism in it, contrasted John I. with the beginning of Mark's Gospel, [4] and arrived at the result, that writings whose contents were partly docetic, partly sensuously Jewish and unworthy of God, must have been composed by Cerinthus, the gnosticising Judaist. In view of this fact it is extremely surprising to notice how mildly the party was criticised and treated by Irenæus as well as by Hippolytus. The former distinguishes them sharply from the declared heretics. He places them on a line with the Schismatics, who gave up communion with the Church on account of the hypo-

---

[1] Epiph. LI., ch. 4: φάσκουσι ὅτι οὐ συμφωνεῖ τὰ βιβλία τοῦ Ἰωάννου τοῖς λοιποῖς ἀποστόλοις, ch. 18: τὸ εὐαγγέλιον τὸ εἰς ὄνομα Ἰωάννου ψεύδεται … λέγουσι τὸ κατὰ Ἰωάννην εὐαγγέλιον, ἐπειδὴ μὴ τὰ αὐτὰ τοῖς ἀποστόλοις ἔφη, ἀδιάθετον εἶναι.

[2] Epiphanius has preserved for us in part the criticism of the Alogi on John I. II., and on the Johannine chronology (ch. 3, 4, 15, 18, 22, 26, 28, 29). In their conception the Gospel of John precluded the human birth and development of Jesus.

[3] Epiph. LI. 3, 28: τὸν λόγον τοῦ Θεοῦ ἀποβάλλονται τὸν διὰ Ἰωάννην κηρυχθέντα.

[4] Epiph. LI., ch. 6: λέγουσιν Ἰδοὺ δεύτερον εὐαγγέλιον περὶ Χριστοῦ σημαῖνον καὶ οὐδαμοῦ ἄνωθεν λέγον τὴν γέννησιν· ἀλλά, φησίν, Ἐν τῷ Ἰορδάνῃ κατῆλθε τὸ πνεῦμα ἐπ᾽ αὐτὸν καὶ φωνή· Οὗτός ἐστιν ὁ υἱὸς ὁ ἀγαπητός, ἐφ᾽ ὃν ηὐδόκησα.

crites to be found in it. He approves of their decided opposition
to all pseudo-prophetic nonsense, and he only complains that
in their zeal against the bad they had also fought against the
good, and had sought to eject all prophecy. In short, he feels
that between them and the Montanists, whom likewise he did
not look on as heretics, [1] he held the middle position maintained
by the Church. And so with Hippolytus. The latter, apart
from features which he could not but blame, confirms the conformity to the Church, claimed by the party itself (ch. 3), and
conspicuous in their insistence on the harmony of the Scriptures
($\sigma\nu\mu\phi\omega\nu\iota\alpha$ $\tau\tilde{\omega}\nu$ $\beta\iota\beta\lambda\tilde{\omega}\nu$). [2] He nowhere sets them on a line with
Cerinthus, Ebion, etc., and he has undoubtedly treated even
their Christological views, on which Irenæus had communicated
no information, more mildly, because he found so much in them
of an anti-docetic, anti-montanistic nature, with which he could
agree. But what was their teaching as to Christ? If Lipsius [3]
were correct in his opinion that the Alogi only saw in Jesus
a man naturally procreated, that they only pretended to hold
by the current doctrine, then the attitude to them of Irenæus
and Hippolytus would be incomprehensible. But our authority
gives no support to such a view. It rather shows plainly that
the Alogi recognised the first three Gospels, and consequently
*the miraculous birth* from the Holy Ghost and the virgin. They
placed, however, the chief emphasis on the human life of Jesus,
on his birth, baptism, and temptation as told by the Synoptics,
and for this very reason rejected the formula of the Logos, as
well as the "birth from above", *i.e.*, the eternal generation of
Christ. The equipment of Christ at his baptism was to them,
in view of Mark, ch. I., of crucial importance (see p. 16, Note 4)
and thus they would assume, without themselves making use
of the phrase "a mere man" ($\psi\iota\lambda\grave{o}\varsigma$ $\check{\alpha}\nu\theta\rho\omega\pi\sigma\varsigma$), an advancement

[1] This milder criticism—and neither Montanists nor Alogi stand in Irenæus'
catalogue of heretics—naturally did not prevent the view that those "unhappy
people" had got into an extremely bad position by their opposition to the prophetic
activity of the Spirit in the Church, and had fallen into the unforgivable sin against
the Holy Ghost.

[2] In Epiph. Ll., ch. 4: $\delta\sigma\kappa\sigma\tilde{\nu}\sigma\iota$ $\kappa\alpha\grave{\iota}$ $\alpha\grave{\upsilon}\tau\sigma\grave{\iota}$ $\tau\grave{\alpha}$ $\check{\iota}\sigma\alpha$ $\dot{\eta}\mu\tilde{\iota}\nu$ $\pi\iota\sigma\tau\epsilon\acute{\upsilon}\epsilon\iota\nu$.

[3] Quellen, p. 102 f., 112.

(προκοπή) of the Christ, ordained at his baptism to be Son
of God.[1]

The earliest opponents known to us of the Logos Christology were men whose adherence to the position of the
Church in Asia Minor was strongly marked. This attitude of
theirs was exhibited in a decided antagonism both to the Gnosticism, say, of Cerinthus, and to "Kataphrygian" prophecy. In
their hostility to the latter they anticipated the development of
the Church by about a generation; while rejecting all prophecy
and "gifts of the Spirit" (ch. 35), they, in doing so, gave the
clearest revelation of their Catholic character. Since they did
not believe in an age of the Paraclete, nor entertain materialistic hopes about the future state, they could not reconcile
themselves to the Johannine writings; and their attachment to
the conception of Christ in the Synoptics led them to reject
the Gospel of the Logos. An explicitly Church party could
not have ventured to promulgate such views, if they had been
confronted by a Canon already closed, and giving a fixed place
to these Johannine books. The uncompromising criticism, both
internal and external—as in the hypothesis of the Cerinthian
authorship—to which these were subjected, proves that, when
the party arose, no Catholic Canon existed as yet in Asia Minor,
and that, accordingly, the movement was almost as ancient as
that of the Montanists, which it followed very closely.[2] On this

---

[1] It is not quite certain whether we may appeal to the words in Epiph. LI.,
ch. 18 (20): νομίζοντες ἀπὸ Μαρίας καὶ δεῦρο Χριστὸν αὐτὸν καλεῖσθαι καὶ υἱὸν Θεοῦ,
καὶ εἶναι μὲν πρότερον ψιλὸν ἄνθρωπον, κατὰ προκοπὴν δὲ εἰληφέναι τὴν τοῦ Θεοῦ
προσηγορίαν.

[2] As regards the problem of the origin and gradual reception of the Johannine
writings, and especially of the Gospel, their use by Montanus, and their abrupt rejection
by the Alogi, are of the greatest significance, especially when we bear in mind the
Churchly character of the latter. The rise of such an opposition in the very region in
which the Gospel undoubtedly first came to light; the application to the fourth of a
standard derived from the Synoptic Gospels; the denial without scruple, of its apostolic
origin; are facts which it seems to me have, at the present day, not been duly
appreciated. We must not weaken their force by an appeal to the dogmatic character
of the criticism practised by the Alogi; the attestation of the Gospel cannot
have been convincing, if such a criticism was ventured on in the Church. But
the Alogi distinctly denied to John and ascribed to Cerinthus the Apocalypse as

understanding, the party had a legitimate place within the developing Catholic Church, and only so can we explain the criticism which their writings encountered in the period immediately succeeding. Meanwhile, the first express opposition with which we are acquainted to the Logos Christology was raised within the Church, by a party which, yet, must be conceived by us to have been in many respects specifically secularised. For the radical opposition to Montanism, and the open, and at the same time jesting, criticism on the Apocalypse, [1] can only be so regarded. Yet the preference of the Logos Christology to others is itself indeed, as Celsus teaches, a symptom of secularisation and innovation in the creed. The Alogi attacked it on this ground when they took it as promoting Gnosticism (Docetism). But they also tried to refute the Logos Doctrine and the Logos Gospel on historical grounds, by a reference to the Synoptic Gospels. *The representatives of this movement were, as far as we know, the first to undertake within the Church a historical criticism, worthy of the name, of the Christian Scriptures and the Church tradition.* They first confronted John's Gospel with the Synoptics, and found numerous contradictions; Epiphanius,—and probably, before him, Hippolytus,—called them, therefore, word-hunters (λεξιθηροῦντες H. 51, ch. 34). They and their opponents could retort on each other the charge of introducing innovations; but we cannot mistake the fact that the larger proportion of innovations is to be looked for on the side of the Alogi. How long the latter held their ground; how, when, and by whom they were expelled from the Church in Asia Minor, we do not know.

well as the Gospel. Of Cerinthus we know far too little to be justified in sharing in the holy horror of the Church Fathers. But even if the above hypothesis is false, and it is in fact very probable that it is, yet the very fact that it could be set up by Churchmen is instructive enough; for it shows us, what we do not know from any other source, that the Johannine writings met with, and had to overcome, opposition in their birth-place.

[1] The Roman Caius took over this criticism from them, as is shown by Hippolytus' Cap. adv. Caium. But, like Theodotus, to be mentioned presently, he rejected the view of the Alogi as regards John's Gospel.

**(b). The Roman Adoptians.—Theodotus the leather-worker
and his party: Asclepiodotus, Hermophilus, Apollonides,
Theodotus the money-changer, and also the
Artemonites.** [1]

Towards the end of the episcopate of Eleutherus, or at the
beginning of that of Victor (± 190) there came from Byzantium
to Rome the leather-worker Theodotus, who afterwards was

---

[1] See Kapp, Hist. Artemonis, 1737; Hagemann, Die römische Kirche in den drei
ersten Jahrh., 1864; Lipsius, Quellenkritik, p. 235 f.; Lipsius, Chronologie der
römischen Bischöfe, p. 173 f.; Harnack, in the Ztschr. f. d. hist. Theol., 1874,
p. 200; Caspari, Quellen III., pp. 318—321, 404 f.; Langen, Geschichte der römischen Kirche I., p. 192 f.; Caspari, Om Melchizedekiternes eller Theodotianernes
eller Athinganernes Laerdomme og om hvad de herve at sige, naar de skulle bline
optagne i. den kristelige Kirke, in the Tidsskr f. d. evang. luth. Kirke. Ny Raekke,
Bd. VIII., part 3, pp. 307—337. Authorities for the older Theodotus are; (1) the
Syntagma of Hippolytus according to Epiph. H. 54, Philaster H. 50. and Pseudo-
Tertull. H. 28; (2) the Philosophumena VII. 35, X. 23, IX. 3, 12, X. 27; (3) the
fragment of Hippolytus against Noëtus, ch. 3. 4) the fragments from the so-called
Little Labyrinth (in Euseb. H. E. V. 28), which was perhaps by Hippolytus, and
was written in the fourth decade of the third century, and after the Philosophumena.
This work was directed against Roman Dynamistic Monarchians under the leader-
ship of a certain Artemas, who are to be distinguished from the Theodotians.
(For the age and author of the Little Labyrinth, and for its connection with the
writings against the Alogi and against Noëtus; also for the appearance of Artemas,
which is not to be dated before ± 235: see Caspari, Quellen l.c., and my art.
"Monarchianismus", p. 186). Eusebius has confined his extracts from the Little
Labyrinth to such as deal with the Theodotians. These extracts and Philos. Lib. X.
are used by Theodoret (H. F. II. 4. 5); it is not probable that the latter had himself examined the Little Labyrinth. A writing of Theodotus seems to have been
made use of in the Syntagma of Hippolytus. As regards the younger Theodotus, his
name has been handed down by the Little Labyrinth, the Philosoph. (VII. 36) and
Pseudo-Tertull. H. 29 (Theodoret H. F. II. 6). The Syntagma tells of a party of
Melchizedekians, which is traced in the Philosoph. and by the Pseudo-Tertullian to
the younger Theodotus, but neither the party nor its founder is named. Very
mysterious in contents and origin is the piece, edited for the first time from Parisian
MSS. by Caspari (see above): περὶ Μελχισεδεκιανῶν καὶ Θεοδοτιανῶν καὶ Ἀθιγ-
γανῶν. The only controversial writing known to us against Artemas (Artemon) is
the Little Labyrinth. Unfortunately Eusebius has not excerpted the passages aimed
at him. Artemas is, again, omitted in the Syntagma and in the Philosoph. For this
reason Epiphanius, Pseudo-Tertull. and Philaster have no articles expressly dealing
with him. He is, however, mentioned prominently in the edict of the last Synod
of Antioch held to oppose Paul of Samosata (so also in the Ep. Alexandri in
Theodoret H. E. I. 3 and in Pamphilus' Apology Pro Orig. in Routh, Reliq. S. IV.
p. 367); therefore many later writers against the heretics have named him (Epiph.
H. 65. 1, esp. Theodoret H. F. II. 6. etc.). Finally, let it be noticed that the state-

characterised as the "founder, leader, and father of the God-denying revolt", *i.e.*, of Adoptianism. Hippolytus calls him a "rag" (ἀπόσπασμα) of the Alogi, and it is in fact not improbable that he came from the circle of those theologians of Asia Minor. Stress is laid on his unusual culture; "he was supreme in Greek culture, very learned in science" (ἐν παιδείᾳ Ἑλληνικῇ ἀκρός, πολυμαθὴς τοῦ λόγου); and he was, therefore, highly respected in his native city. All we know for certain of his history is that he was excommunicated by the Roman Bishop, Victor, on account of the Christology which he taught in Rome (Euseb. V. 28. 6: ἀπεκήρυξε τῆς κοινωνίας); *his is, therefore, the first case of which we are certain, where a Christian who took his stand on the rule of faith was yet treated as a heretic.*[1] As regards his teaching, the Philosophumena expressly testify to the orthodoxy of Theodotus in his theology and cosmology.[2] In reference to the Person of Christ he taught: that Jesus was a man, who, by a special decree of God, was born of a virgin through the operation of the Holy Spirit; but that we were not to see in him a heavenly being, who had assumed flesh in the virgin. After the piety of his life had been thoroughly tested, the Holy Ghost descended upon him in baptism; by this means he became Christ and received his equipment (δυνάμεις) for his special vocation; and he demonstrated the righteousness, in virtue of which he excelled all men, and was, of necessity, their authority. Yet the descent of the Spirit upon Jesus was not sufficient to justify the contention that he was now "God". Some of the followers of Theodotus represented

ments in the Synodicon Pappi, and in the Prædestinatus are worthless, and that the identification of the younger Theodotus with the Gnostic of the same name, extracts from whose works we possess, is inadmissable, not less so than the identification with Theodotus, the Montanist, of whom we are informed by Eusebius. In this we agree with Zahn (Forschungen III., p. 123) against Neander and Dorner. As an authority for the Roman Monarchians, Novatian, De Trinitate, also falls to be considered.

[1] It is significant that this took place in Rome. The Syntagma is further able to tell that Theodotus had denied Christ during the persecution in his native city before he came to Rome. See on this point my article on Monarchianism, p. 187.

[2] VII. 35: φάσκων τὰ περὶ μὲν τῆς τοῦ παντὸς ἀρχῆς σύμφωνα ἐκ μέρους τοῖς τῆς ἀληθοῦς ἐκκλησίας, ὑπὸ τοῦ Θεοῦ πάντα ὁμολογῶν γεγονέναι.

Jesus as having become God through the resurrection; others
disputed even this.[1] This Christology, Theodotus and his party
sought to prove from Scripture. Philaster says in general terms:
"they use the chapters of Scripture which tell of Christ as man,
but they avoid those which speak of him as God, reading and
by no means understanding" (Utuntur capitulis scripturarum
quæ de Christo veluti de homine edocent, quæ autem ut deo
dicunt ea vero non accipiunt, legentes et nullo modo intellegentes). Epiphanius has, fortunately, preserved for us fragments
of the biblical theological investigations of Theodotus, by the help
of the Syntagma. These show that there was no longer any
dispute as to the extent of the N. T. Canon; the Gospel of
John is recognised, and in this respect also Theodotus is Catholic. The investigations are interesting, however, because they
are worked out by the same prosaic methods of exegesis, adopted
in the above discussed works of the Alogi.[2]

[1] Philos. VII. 35: Θεὸν δὲ οὐδέποτε τοῦτον γεγονέναι θέλουσιν ἐπὶ τῇ καθόδῳ
τοῦ πνεύματος, ἕτεροι δὲ μετὰ τὴν ἐκ νεκρῶν ἀνάστασιν. The description in the
text is substantially taken from the Philos., with whose account the contents of the
Syntagma are not inconsistent. The statement that Theodotus denied the birth by
the virgin is simply a calumny, first alleged by Epiphanius. The account of the
Philos. seems unreliable, at most, on a single point, viz., where, interpreting Theodotus, it calls the Spirit which descended at the baptism "Christ" But possibly
this too is correct, seeing that Hermas, and, later, the author of the Acta Archelai
have also identified the Holy Spirit with the Son of God. (Compare also what
Origen [περὶ ἀρχ. pref.] has reported as Church tradition on the Holy Spirit.) In
that case we would only have to substitute the "Son of God" for " Christ", and to
suppose that Hippolytus chose the latter term in order to be able to characterise
the teaching of Theodotus as Gnostic (Cerinthian). On the possibility that the Theodotians, however, really named the Holy Spirit "Christ", see later on.

[2] Epiphanius mentions the appeal of the Theodotians to Deut. XVIII. 15; Jer.
XVII. 9; Isa. LIII. 2 f.; Mat. XII. 31; Luke I. 35; John VIII. 40; Acts II. 22;
1 Tim. II. 5. They deduced from Mat. XII. 31, that the Holy Spirit held a higher place
than the Son of Man. The treatment of the verses in Deut. and Luke is especially
instructive. In the former Theodotus emphasised, not only the "προφήτην ὡς ἐμέ",
and the "ἐκ τῶν ἀδελφῶν", but also the "ἐγερεῖ", and concluded referring the
passage to the Resurrection: ὁ ἐκ Θεοῦ ἐγειρόμενος Χριστὸς οὗτος οὐκ ἦν Θεὸς ἀλλὰ
ἄνθρωπος, ἐπειδὴ ἐξ αὐτῶν ἦν, ὡς καὶ Μωϋσῆς ἄνθρωπος ἦν—accordingly the resus-
citated Christ was not God. On Luke I. 35 he argued thus: "The Gospel itself says
in reference to Mary: 'the Spirit of the Lord will come upon thee'; but it does
not say: 'the Spirit of the Lord will be in thy body', or,'will enter into thee.'"—
Further, if we may trust Epiphanius, Theodotus sought to divide the sentence—
διὸ καὶ τὸ γεννώμενον ἐκ σοῦ ἅγιον κληθήσεται υἱὸς Θεοῦ—, from the first half of

Theodotus' form of teaching was, even in the life-time of its author, held in Rome to be intolerable, and that by men disposed to Modalism—*e.g.*, the Bishop himself, see under—as well as by the representatives of the Logos Christology. It is certain that he was excommunicated by Victor, accordingly before A.D. 199, on the charge of teaching that Christ was "mere man" (ψιλὸς ἄνθρωπος). We do not know how large his following was in the city. We cannot put it at a high figure, since in that case the Bishop would not have ventured on excommunication. It must, however, have been large enough to allow of the experiment of forming an independent Church. This was attempted in the time of the Roman Bishop Zephyrine (199—218) by the most important of the disciples of Theodotus, viz., Theodotus the money changer, and a certain Asclepiodotus. It is extremely probable that both of these men were also Greeks. A native, Natalius the confessor, was induced, so we are told by the Little Labyrinth, to become Bishop of the party, at a salary of 150 denarii a month. The attempt failed. The oppressed Bishop soon deserted and returned into the bosom of the great Church. It was told that he had been persuaded by visions and finally by blows with which "holy angels" pursued him during the night. The above undertaking is interesting in itself, since it proves how great had already become the gulf between the Church and these Monarchians in Rome, about A.D. 210; but still more instructive is the sketch given of the leaders of the party by the Little Labyrinth, a sketch that agrees excellently with the accounts given of the 'λεξιθηροῦντες' in Asia, and of the exegetic labours of the older Theodotus. [1]

the verse, as if the words "διὸ καὶ" did not exist, so that he obtained the meaning that the Sonship of Christ would only begin later,—subsequent to the test. Perhaps, however, Theodotus entirely deleted "διὸ καὶ", just as he also read "πνεῦμα κυρίου" for "πνεῦμα ἅγιον" in order to avoid all ambiguity. And since Hippolytus urges against him that John I. 14 did not contain "τὸ πνεῦμα σὰρξ ἐγένετο", Theodotus must at least have interpreted the word "λόγος" in the sense of "πνεῦμα"; and an ancient formula really ran: "Χριστὸς ὢν μὲν τὸ πρῶτον πνεῦμα ἐγένετο σάρξ" (2 Clem. IX. 5), where later "λόγος" was, indeed, inserted in place of "πνεῦμὰ". See the Cod. Constantinop.

[1] Euseb. (H. E. V. 28): "They falsified the Holy Scriptures without scruple, rejected the standards of the ancient faith, and misunderstood Christ. For they did not examine what the Scriptures said, but carefully considered what logical

The offence charged against the Theodotians was three-fold: the grammatical and formal exegesis of Holy Scripture, the trenchant textual criticism, and the thorough-going study of Logic, Mathematics, and the empirical sciences. It would seem at a first glance as if these men were no longer as a rule interested in theology. But the opposite was the case. Their opponent had himself to testify that they pursued grammatical exegesis " in order to prove their godless tenets," textual criticism in order to correct the manuscripts of the Holy Scriptures, and philosophy "in order by the science of unbelievers to support their heretical conception." He had also to bear witness to the fact that these scholars had not tampered with the inspiration of the Holy Scriptures, or the extent of the Canon (V. 28. 18). [1] Their whole work, therefore, was in the service of their theology. But the method of this work,—and we can infer it to have been also that of the Alogi and the older Theodotus—conflicted with the dominant theological method. Instead of Plato and

figure they could obtain from it that would prove their godless teaching. And if any one brought before them a passage from Holy Scripture, they asked whether a conjunctive or disjunctive figure could be made of it. They set aside the Holy Scriptures of God, and employ themselves, instead, with geometry, being men who are earthly, and talk of what is earthly, and know not what comes from above. Some of them, therefore, study the geometry of Euclid with the greatest devotion; Aristotle and Theophrastus are admired; Galen is even worshipped by some. But what need is there of words to show that men who misuse the sciences of the unbelievers to prove their heretical views, and falsify with their own godless cunning the plain faith of Scripture, do not even stand on the borders of the faith? They have therefore laid their hands so unscrupulously on the Holy Scriptures under the pretext that they had only amended it critically (διωρθωκέναι). He who will can convince himself that this is no calumny. For, if one should collect the manuscripts of any one of them and compare them, he would find them differ in many passages. At least, the manuscripts of Asclepiodotus do not agree with those of Theodotus. But we can have examples of this to excess; for their scholars have noted with ambitious zeal all that any one of them has, as they say, critically amended, i.e., distorted (effaced?). Again, with these the manuscripts of Hermophilus do not agree; and those of Apollonides even differ from each other. For if we compare the manuscripts first restored by them (him?) with the later re-corrected copies, variations are found in many places. But some of them have not even found it worth the trouble to falsify the Holy Scriptures, but have simply rejected the Law and the Prophets, and have by this lawless and godless doctrine hurled themselves, under the pretext of grace, into the deepest abyss of perdition.

[1] See under.

Zeno, the Adoptians revered the Empiricists; instead of the allegorical interpretation of Scripture, the grammatical was alone
held to be valid; instead of simply accepting or capriciously
trimming the traditional text, an attempt was made to discover
the original. How unique and valuable is this information!
How instructive it is to observe that this method struck the disciple of the Apologists and Irenæus as strange, nay, even as
heretical, that while he would have seen nothing to object to
in the study of Plato, he was seized with horror at the idea of
Aristotle, Euclid, and Galen, being put in the place of Plato!
The difference was, indeed, not merely one of method. In the
condition of the theology of the Church at that time, it could
not be supposed that religious conviction was especially strong
or ardent in men who depreciated the religious philosophy of
the Greeks. For whence, if not from this source, or from
Apocalyptics, did men then derive a distinctively pious enthusiasm?[2] It is also little to be wondered at that the attempt
made by these scholars to found a Church in Rome, was so
quickly wrecked. They were fated to remain officers without
an army; for with grammar, textual criticism, and logic one
could only throw discredit, in the communities, on the form of
Christological doctrine which held the highest place and had
been rendered venerable by long tradition. These scholars,
therefore, although they regarded themselves as Catholic, stood
outside the Church.[3] Of the works of these, the earliest exegetical scholars, nothing has come down to us.[4] They have gone

[1] See V. 28. 4, 5.

[2] The triumph of Neo-platonic philosophy and of the Logos Christology in
Christian theology is, in this sense, to be considered an advance. That philosophy,
indeed, in the third century, triumphed throughout the empire over its rivals, and
therefore the exclusive alliance concluded with it by Christian tradition was one
which, when it took place, could be said to have been inevitable. Suppose, however, that the theology of Sabellius or of Paul had established itself in the Church
in the 3rd century, then a gulf would have been created between the Church and
Hellenism that would have made it impossible for the religion of the Church to
become that of the empire. Neo-platonic tradition was the final product of antiquity;
it disposed, but as a living force, of the intellectual and moral capital of the past

[3] As "genuine" scholars—and this is a very characteristic feature—they took very
great care that each should have the credit of his own amendments on the text.

[4] The Syntagma knows of these; Epiph. H. 55. c. 1: πλάττουσιν ἑαυτοῖς καὶ
βίβλους ἐπιπλάστους,

without leaving any appreciable effect on the Church. Contrast
the significance gained by the schools of Alexandria and Antioch! The latter, which rose about 60 years later, took up again
the work of this Roman school. It, too, came to stand outside
the great Church; but it brought about one of the most important crises in the dogmatics of the Church, because in its philosophico-theological starting-point it was at one with orthodoxy.

The methodical and exegetical examination of the Holy
Scriptures confirmed the Theodotians in their conception of
Christ as the man in whom in an especial manner the Spirit
of God had operated, and had made them opponents of the
Logos Christology. The author of the Little Labyrinth does
not state wherein the doctrine of the younger Theodotus differed
from that of the older. When he says that some of the Theodotians rejected the law and the prophets προφάσει χάριτος, we
may well suppose that they simply emphasised—in a Pauline
sense, or because of considerations drawn from a historical
study of religion—the relativity of the authority of the O. T.; [1]
for there is as little known of any rejection of the Catholic
Canon on the part of the Theodotians, as of a departure from
the rule of faith. Now Hippolytus has extracted from the exegetical works of the younger Theodotus one passage, the discussion of Hebr. V. 6, 10; VI. 20f; VII. 3, 17; and out of
this he has made an important heresy. Later historians eagerly
seized on this; they ascribed to the younger Theodotus, as
distinguished from the older, a cultus of Melchizedek and invented a sect of Melchizedekians (= Theodotians). The money-
changer taught, it was said (Epiph. H. 55), that Melchizedek
was a very great power, and more exalted than Christ, the
latter being merely related to the former as the copy to the
original. Melchizedek was the advocate of the heavenly powers
before God, and the High Priest among men, [2] while Jesus as

---

[1] Even the great anti-gnostic teachers had come to this view (see Vol. II., p. 304)
without indeed drawing the consequences which the Theodotians may have deduced
more certainly.

[2] L.c. Δεῖ ἡμᾶς τῷ Μελχισεδὲκ προσφέρειν, φασίν, ἵνα δι' αὐτοῦ προσενεχθῇ ὑπὲρ
ἡμῶν, καὶ εὕρωμεν δι' αὐτοῦ ζωήν.

priest stood a degree lower. The origin of the former was completely concealed, because it was heavenly, but Jesus was born of Mary. To this Epiphanius adds that the party presented its oblations in the name of M. (εἰς ὄνομα τοῦ Μελχισεδέκ); for he was the guide to God, the prince of righteousness, the true Son of God. It is apparent that the Theodotians cannot have taught this simply as it stands. The explanation is not far to seek. There was a wide-spread opinion in the whole ancient Church, that Melchizedek was a manifestation of the true Son of God; and to this view many speculations attached themselves, here and there in connection with a subordinationist Christology.[1] The Theodotians shared this conception. Immediately after the sentence given above Epiphanius has (55, c. 8): And Christ, they say, was chosen that he might call us from many ways to this one knowledge, having been anointed by God, and chosen, when he turned us from idols and showed us the way. And the Apostle having been sent by him revealed to us that Melchizedek is great and remains a priest for ever, and behold how great he is; and because the less is blessed by the greater, therefore he says that he as being greater blessed Abraham the patriarch; of whom we are initiated that we may obtain from him the blessing.[2]

Now the Christological conception, formulated in the first half

---

[1] See Clem. Alex. Strom. IV. 25. 161; Hierakas in Epiph. H. 55, c. 5, H. 67, c. 3; Philast. H. 148. Epiph. has himself to confess (H. 55, c. 7), that even in his time the view to be taken of Melchizedek was still a subject of dispute among Catholic Christians: οἱ μὲν γὰρ αὐτὸν νομίζουσι φύσει τὸν υἱὸν τοῦ Θεοῦ ἐν ἰδέᾳ ἀνθρώπου τότε τῷ Ἀβραὰμ πεφηνέναι. Jerome Ep. 73 is important. The Egyptian hermit, Marcus, wrote, about A.D. 400, an independent work εἰς τὸν Μελχισεδὲκ κατὰ Μελχισεδεκειῶν, i.e., against those who saw in Melchizedek a manifestation of the true Son of God (see Photius, Biblioth. 200; Dict. of Christ. Biog. III. p. 827; Herzog's R. E., 2 Aufl. IX. p. 290); cf. the above described fragment, edited for the first time by Caspari; further Theodoret H. F. II. 6, Timotheus Presb. in Cotelier, Monum. Eccl. Græcæ III. p. 392 etc.

[2] Καὶ Χριστὸς μὲν, φασίν, ἐξελέγη, ἵνα ἡμᾶς καλέσῃ ἐκ πολλῶν ὁδῶν εἰς μίαν ταύτην τὴν γνῶσιν, ὑπὸ Θεοῦ κεχρισμένος καὶ ἐκλεκτὸς γενόμενος, ἐπειδὴ ἀπέστρεψεν ἡμᾶς ἀπὸ εἰδώλων καὶ ὑπέδειξεν ἡμῖν τὴν ὁδόν. Ἐξ οὗπερ ὁ ἀπόστολος ἀποςταλεὶς ἀπεκάλυψεν ἡμῖν, ὅτι μέγας ἐστὶν ὁ Μελχισεδέκ, καὶ ἱερεὺς μένει εἰς τὸν αἰῶνα, καὶ, Θεωρεῖτε πηλίκος οὗτος· καὶ ὅτι τὸ ἔλασσον ἐκ τοῦ μείζονος εὐλογεῖται, διὰ τοῦτο, φησί, καὶ τὸν Ἀβραὰμ τὸν πατριάρχην εὐλόγησεν ὡς μείζων ὤν· οὗ ἡμεῖς ἐσμὲν μύσται, ὅπως τύχωμεν παρ' αὐτοῦ τῆς εὐλογίας.

of this paragraph, was certainly not reported from an opponent.
It is precisely that of the Shepherd, [1] and accordingly very ancient in the Roman Church. [2] From this, and by a reference
to the controversial writing of Hippolytus (Epiph. l.c. ch. 9),
the "heretical" cultus of Melchizedek is explained. These Theodotians maintained, as is also shown by their exegesis on 1 Cor.
VIII. 6, [3] three points: First, that besides the Father the only
divine being was the Holy Spirit, who was identical with
the Son—again simply the position of Hermas; secondly, that
this Holy Spirit appeared to Abraham in the form of the King
of Righteousness—and this, as has been shown above, was no
novel contention; thirdly, that Jesus was a man anointed with
the power of the Holy Ghost. But, in that case, it was only
logical, and in itself not uncatholic, to teach that offerings and
worship were due, as to the true, eternal Son of God, to this
King of Righteousness who had appeared to Abraham, and
had blessed him and his real descendants, i.e., the Christians.
And if, in comparison with this Son of God, the chosen and
anointed servant of God, Jesus, appears inferior at first, precisely in so far as he is man, yet their position was no more
unfavourable in this respect than that of Hermas. For Hermas
also taught that Jesus, being only the adopted Son of God,
was really not to be compared to the Holy Spirit, the Eternal
Son; or, rather, he is related to the latter, to use a Theodotian
expression, as the copy to the original. Yet there is undoubtedly a great distinction between the Theodotians and Hermas.
They unmistakably used their speculations as to the eternal

[1] Cf. the striking agreement with Sim. V., especially ch. VI. 3 : αὐτὸς καθαρίσας
τὰς ἁμαρτίας τοῦ λαοῦ ἔδειξεν αὐτοῖς τὰς τρίβους τῆς ζωῆς.

[2] The theologico-philosophical impress which, as distinguished from Sim. V.,
marks the whole passage, is of course unmistakable. Notice what is said as to
Paul, and the expression "μύσται".

[3] The Theodotians seem to have taken Christ in this verse to mean not Jesus,
but the Holy Spirit, the eternal Son of God, deleting the name Jesus (Epiph.
H. 55, ch. 9). If that is so then the Philosophumena is right when it relates that
the Theodotians had also given the name of Christ to the pre-existent Son of God,
the Holy Ghost. Yet it is not certain whether we should regard the above
quoted chapter of Epiphanius at all as reporting the Theodotian interpretation
of 1 Cor. VIII. 6.

Son of God in order to rise to that Son from the man Jesus of history, and to transcend the historical in general as something subordinate.[1] There is not a word of this to be found in Hermas. Thus, the Theodotians sought, in a similar way to Origen, to rid themselves by speculation of what was merely historical, setting, like him, the eternal Son of God above the Crucified One. We have evidence of the correctness of this opinion in the observation that these speculations on Melchizedek were continued precisely in the school of Origen. We find them, and that with the same tendency to depreciate the historical Son of God, in Hieracas and the confederacy of Hieracite monks;[2] as also in the monks who held the views of Origen in Egypt in the fourth and fifth centuries.

We have accordingly found that these theologians retained the ancient Roman Christology represented by Hermas; but that they edited it theologically and consequently changed its intention. If, at that time, the "Pastor" was still read in the Roman Church, while the Theodotian Christology was condemned, then its Christology must have been differently interpreted. In view of the peculiar character of the book, this would not be difficult. We may ask, however, whether the teaching of the Theodotians is really to be characterised as Monarchian, seeing that they assigned a special, and as it seems, an independent role to the Holy Spirit apart from God. Meanwhile, we can no longer determine how these theologians reconciled the separate substance (hypostasis) of the Holy Ghost, with the unity of the Person of God. But so much is certain, that in their Christology the Spirit was considered by them only as a power, and that, on the other hand, their rejection of the Logos Christology was not due to any repugnance to the idea of a second divine being. This is proved by their teaching as to the Holy Spirit and His appearance in the Old Testament.

___

[1] Epiph. H. 55, ch. 8: εἰς ὄνομα δὲ τούτου τοῦ Μελχισεδὲκ ἡ προειρημένη αἵρεσις καὶ τὰς προσφορὰς ἀναφέρει, καὶ αὐτὸν εἶναι εἰσαγωγέα πρὸς τὸν Θεὸν καὶ δι᾽ αὐτοῦ, φησί, δεῖ τῷ Θεῷ προσφέρειν, ὅτι ἄρχων ἐστὶ δικαιοσύνης, ἐπ᾽ αὐτῷ τούτῳ καταστασθεὶς ὑπὸ τοῦ Θεοῦ ἐν οὐρανῷ, πνευματικός τις ὤν, καὶ υἱὸς Θεοῦ τεταγμένος .... c. 1: Χριστός, φησίν, ἐστὶν ἔτι ὑποδεέστερος τοῦ Μελχισεδέκ.

[2] See my art. in Herzog R. E., 2 Aufl. VI. p. 100 (Epiph. LV. 5; LXVII. 3).

But then the difference between them and their opponents does not belong to the sphere of the doctrine of God; they are rather substantially at one on this subject with a theologian like Hippolytus. If that is so, however, their opponents were undoubtedly superior to them, while they themselves fell short of the traditional estimate of Christ. In other words, if there was an eternal Son of God, or any one of that nature, and if He appeared under the old covenant, then the traditional estimate of Jesus could not be maintained, once he was separated from that Son. [1] The formula of the man anointed with the Spirit was no longer sufficient to establish the transcendent greatness of the revelation of God in Christ, and it is only a natural consequence that the O. T. theophanies should appear in a brighter light. We see here why the old Christological conceptions passed away so quickly, comparatively speaking, and gave place so soon in the Churches to the complete and essential elevation of Jesus to the rank of deity, whenever theological reflection awoke to life. It was, above all, the distinctive method of viewing the Old Testament and its theophanies that led to this.

In certain respects the attempt of the Theodotians presents itself as an innovation. They sought to raise a once accepted, but, so to speak, enthusiastic form of faith to the stage of theology and to defend it as the only right one; they expressly refused, or, at least, declared to be matter of controversy, the use of the title "God" (Θεός) as applied to Jesus; they advanced beyond Jesus to an eternal, unchangeable Being (beside God). In this sense, in consequence of the new interest which the representatives of the above doctrine took in the old formula, it is to be regarded as novel. For we can hardly attribute to pre-catholic Christians like Hermas, a special interest in the essential humanity of Jesus. They certainly believed that they gave full expression in their formulas to the highest possible estimate of the Redeemer; they had no other idea. These theologians, on the other hand, defended a lower conception of Christ against a higher. Thus we may judge them on their own ground; for they let the idea of a heavenly Son of God

[1] Hermas did not do this, in so far as in the language of religion he speaks only of *a* Son of God (Simil. IX.).

stand, and did not carry out the complete revision of the prevailing doctrine that would have justified them in proving their Christological conception to be the one really legitimate and satisfactory. They indeed supported it by Scriptural proof, and in this certainly surpassed their opponents, but the proof did not cover the gaps in their dogmatic procedure. Since they took their stand on the *regula fidei*, it is unjust and at the same time unhistorical to call their form of doctrine "Ebionitic", or to dispose of them with the phrase that Christ was to them *exclusively* a mere man (ψιλὸς ἄνθρωπος). But if we consider the circumstances in which they appeared, and the excessive expectations that were pretty generally attached to the possession of faith—above all, the prospect of the future deification of every believer—we cannot avoid the impression, that a doctrine could not but be held to be destructive, which did not even elevate Christ to divine honours, or, at most, assigned him an apotheosis, like that imagined by the heathens for their emperors or an Antinous. Apocalyptic enthusiasm passed gradually into Neo-platonic mysticism. In this transition these scholars took no share. They rather sought to separate a part of the old conceptions, and to defend that with the scientific means of their opponents.

Once more, 20 to 30 years later, the attempt was made in Rome by a certain Artemas to rejuvenate the old Christology. We are extremely ill informed as to this last phase of Roman Adoptianism; for the extracts taken by Eusebius from the Little Labyrinth, the work written against Artemas and his party, apply almost exclusively to the Theodotians. We learn, however, that the party appealed to the historical justification of their teaching in Rome, maintaining that Bishop Zephyrine had first falsified the true doctrine which they defended. [1] The relative correctness of this contention is indisputable, especially if we consider that Zephyrine had not dis-

---

[1] Euseb. H. E. V. 28. 3: φασὶ γὰρ τοὺς μὲν προτέρους ἅπαντας καὶ αὐτοὺς τοὺς ἀποστόλους, παρειληφέναι τε καὶ δεδιδαχέναι ταῦτα, ἃ νῦν οὗτοι λέγουσι, καὶ τετηρῆσθαι τὴν ἀλήθειαν τοῦ κηρύγματος μέχρι τῶν χρόνων τοῦ Βίκτορος . . . ἀπὸ δὲ τοῦ διαδόχου αὐτοῦ Ζεφυρίνου παρακεχαράχθαι τὴν ἀλήθειαν.

approved of the formula, certainly novel, that "the Father had suffered". The author of the Little Labyrinth reminds them that Theodotus had been already excommunicated by Victor, and of this fact they themselves cannot have been ignorant. When, moreover, we observe the evident anxiety of the writer to impose Theodotus upon them as their spiritual father, we come to the conclusion that the party did *not* identify themselves with the Theodotians. What they regarded as the point of difference we do not know. It is alone certain that they also refused to call Christ "God"; for the writer feels it necessary to justify the use of the title from tradition. [1] Artemas was still alive in Rome at the close of the 7th decade of the 3rd century, but he was completely severed from the great Church, and without any real influence. No notice is taken of him even in the letters of Cyprian. [2] Since Artemas was characterised as the "father" of Paul in the controversy with that Bishop (Euseb. H. E. VII. 30. 16), he had afterwards attained a certain celebrity in the East, and had supplanted even Theodotus in the recollection of the Church. In the subsequent age, the phrase: "Ebion, Artemas, Paulus (or Photinus)" was stereotyped; this was afterwards supplemented with the name of Nestorius, and in that form the phrase became a constant feature in Byzantine dogmatics and polemics.

(c). **Traces of Adoptian Christology in the West after Artemas.**

Adoptian Christology—Dynamistic Monarchianism—apparently passed rapidly and almost entirely away in the West. The striking formula, settled by the Symbol, "Christus, homo et deus", and, above all, the conviction that Christ had appeared in the O. T., brought about the destruction of the party. Yet,

[1] Euseb. H. E. V. 28. 4, 5.

[2] We know that he still lived about 270 from the document of the Synod of Antioch in the case of Paul of Samosata. We read there (Euseb. H. E. VII. 30. 17): "Paul may write letters to Artemas and the followers of A. are said to hold communion with him." We have probably to regard as Artemonites those unnamed persons, mentioned in Novatian De Trinitate, who explained Jesus to be a mere man (homo nudus et solitarius). Artemas is also named in Methodius Conviv. VIII. 10, Ed. Jahn, p. 37.

here and there—in connection, doubtless, with the reading of Hermas [1]—the old faith, or the old formula, that the Holy Spirit is the eternal Son of God and at the same time the Christ-Spirit, held its ground, and, with it, conceptions which bordered on Adoptianism. Thus we read in the writing " De montibus Sina et Sion " [2] composed in vulgar Latin and attributed wrongly to Cyprian, ch. IV: " The body of the Lord was called Jesus by God the Father; the Holy Spirit that descended from heaven was called Christ by God the Father, *i.e.*, anointed of the living God, the Spirit joined to the body Jesus Christ " (Caro dominica a deo patre Jesu vocita est; spiritus sanctus, qui de cælo descendit, Christus, id est unctus dei vivi, a deo vocitus est, spiritus carni mixtus Jesus Christus). Compare ch. XIII.: the H. S., Son of God, sees Himself double, the Father sees Himself in the Son, the Son in the Father, each in each (Sanctus spiritus, *dei filius*, geminatum se videt, pater in filio et filius in patre utrosque se in se vident). There were accordingly only two hypostases, and the Redeemer is the flesh (caro), to which the pre-existent Holy Spirit, the eternal Son of God, the Christ, descended. Whether the author understood Christ as "forming a person" or as a power cannot be decided; probably, being no theologian, the question did not occur to him. [3] We do not hear that the doctrine of Photinus, who was himself a Greek, gained any considerable approval in the West. But we learn casually that even in the beginning of the 5th century a certain Marcus was expelled from Rome for holding the heresy of Photinus, and that he obtained a following in Dalmatia. Incomparably more instructive, however, is the account given by Augustine (Confess. VII. 19. [25]) of his own and his friend Alypius' Christological belief, at a time when both stood quite near the Catho-

---

[1] Even Tertullian used the Christological formula of Hermas when he was not engaged in Apologetics or in polemics against the Gnostics.

[2] Hartel, Opp. Cypr. III., p. 104 sq.

[3] Hilary's work "De trinitate" also shows (esp. X. 18 ff., 50 ff.) what different Christologies still existed in the West in the middle of the 4th century. There were some who maintained : "quod in eo ex virgine creando efficax dei sapientia et virtus exstiterit, et in nativitate eius divinæ prudentiæ et potestatis opus intellegatur, sitque in eo efficientia potius quam natura sapientiæ.

lic Church, and had been preparing to enter it. At that time
Augustine's view of Christ was practically that of Photinus;
and Alypius denied that Christ had a human soul; *yet both had
held their Christology to be Catholic*, and only afterwards learned
better. [1] Now let us remember that Augustine had enjoyed a
Catholic education, and had been in constant intercourse with
Catholics, and we see clearly that among the laity of the West
very little was known of the Christological formulas, and very
different doctrines of Christ were in fact current even at the
close of the 4th century. [2]

## (d). The Ejection of the Adoptian Christology in the East,— Beryll of Bostra, Paul of Samosata, etc.

We can see from the writings of Origen that there were also
many in the East who rejected the Logos Christology. Those
were undoubtedly most numerous who identified the Father and
the Son; but there were not wanting such as, while they made a
distinction, attributed to the Son a human nature only, [3] and

---

[1] Augustine, l.c. ... Quia itaque vera scripta sunt (sc. the Holy Scriptures) totum
hominem in Christo agnoscebam; non corpus tantum hominis, aut cum corpore sine
mente animam, sed ipsum hominem, non persona veritatis, sed magna quadam naturæ
humanæ excellentia et perfectiore participatione sapientiæ præferri cæteris arbitrabar.
Alypius autem deum carne indutum ita putabat credi a Catholicis, ut præter deum
et carnem non esset in Christo anima, mentemque hominis non existimabat in eo
prædicari ... Sed postea hæreticorum Apollinaristarum hunc errorem esse cognos-
cens, catholicæ fidei collætatus et contemperatus est. Ego autem aliquanto posterius
didicisse me fateor, in eo quod "verbum caro factum est" quomodo catholica veritas
a Photini falsitate dirimatur.

[2] In the Fragment, only preserved in Arabic, of a letter of Pope Innocent I.
to Severianus, Bishop of Gabala (Mai, Spicileg. Rom. III., p. 702) we still read
the warning: "Let no one believe that it was only at the time when the divine
Word on earth came to receive baptism from John that this divine nature originated,
when, *i.e.*, John heard the voice of the Father from heaven. It was certainly
not so, etc."

[3] Orig. on John II. 2, Lomm. I., p. 92: Καὶ τὸ πολλοὺς φιλοθέους εἶναι εὐχο-
μένους ταράσσον, εὐλαβουμένους δύο ἀναγορεῦσαι θεούς, καὶ παρὰ τοῦτο περιπίπτοντας
ψευδέσι καὶ ἀσεβέσι δόγμασιν, ἤτοι ἀρνουμένους ἰδιότητα υἱοῦ ἑτέραν παρὰ τὴν τοῦ
πατρός, ὁμολογοῦντας Θεὸν εἶναι τὸν μέχρι ὀνόματος παρ' αὐτοῖς υἱὸν προσαγορευ-
όμενον, ἢ ἀρνουμένους τὴν θεότητα τοῦ υἱοῦ, τιθέντας δὲ αὐτοῦ τὴν ἰδιότητα καὶ τὴν
οὐσίαν κατὰ περιγραφὴν τυγχάνουσαν ἑτέραν τοῦ πατρός, ἐντεῦθεν λύεσθαι δύναται,
see also what follows. Pseudo-Gregor. (Apollinaris) in Mai (Nov. Coll. VII. 1,

accordingly taught like the Theodotians. Origen by no means
treated them, as a rule, as declared heretics, but as misled, or
"simple", Christian brethren who required friendly teaching.
He himself, besides, had also inserted the Adoptian Christology
into his complicated doctrine of Christ; for he had attached the
greatest value to the tenet that Jesus should be held a real man
who had been chosen by God, who in virtue of his free will,
had steadfastly attested his excellence, and who, at last, had
become perfectly fused with the Logos in disposition, will,
and finally also in nature (see Vol. II., p. 369 f.). Origen laid
such decided emphasis on this that his opponents afterwards
classed him with Paul of Samosata and Artemas,[1] and Pamphilus required to point out "that Origen said that the Son of
God was born of the very substance of God, $i.e.$, was ὁμοούσιος,
which means, of the same substance with the Father, but that
he was not a creature who became a son by adoption, but a
true son by nature, generated by the Father Himself" (quod
Origines filium dei de ipsa dei substantia natum dixerit, id est,
ὁμοούσιον, quod est, eiusdem cum patre substantiæ, et non esse
creaturam *per adoptionem* sed *natura* filium verum, ex ipso patre
generatum).[2] So Origen in fact taught, and he was very far
from seeing more in the Adoptian doctrine than a fragment of
the complete Christology. He attempted to convince the Adoptians of their error, more correctly, of their questionable one-
sidedness,[3] but he had seldom any other occasion to contend
with them.

p. 171) speaks of men who conceived Christ as being 'filled with divinity', but
made no specific distinction between Him and the prophets, and worshipped a man
with divine power after the manner of the heathens.

[1] Pamphili Apolog. in Routh, IV., p. 367; Schultz in the Jahrbb. f. protest
Theol. 1875, p. 193 f.   On Origen and the Monarchians, see Hagemann, l.c., p. 300 i.
[2] See l.c., p, 368.
[3] Orig. in Ep. ad Titum, Lomm. V., p. 287 "Sed et eos, qui hominem dicunt
dominum Iesum præcognitum et prædestinatum, qui ante adventum carnalem substantialiter et proprie non exstiterit, sed quod homo natus patris solam in se habuerit
deitatem, ne illos quidem sine periculo est ecclesiæ numero sociari." This passage,
undoubtedly, need not necessarily be applied to Dynamistic Monarchians, any more
than the description about to be quoted of the doctrine of Beryll. There may have
existed a middle type between Dynamistic and Modalistic Monarchianism, according
to which the humanity as well as the *deitas patris* in Jesus Christ was held to
be personal.

Perhaps we should here include the action against Beryll
of Bostra. This Arabian Bishop taught Monarchianism. His
doctrine aroused a violent opposition. The Bishops of the
province were deeply agitated and instituted many examinations
and discussions. But they appear not to have come to any
result. Origen was called in, and, as we are informed by
Eusebius, who had himself examined the acts of the Synods,
he succeeded in a disputation in amicably convincing the Bishop
of his error.[1] This happened, according to the common view,
in A.D. 244. We have to depend, for the teaching of Beryll,
on one sentence in Eusebius, which has received very different
interpretations.[2] Nitzsch says rightly,[3] that Eusebius missed
in Beryll the recognition of the separate divine personality
(hypostasis) in Christ and of his pre-existence, but not the recognition of his deity. However, this is not enough to class the
Bishop with certainty among the Patripassians, since Eusebius'
own Christological view, by which that of Beryll was here
gauged, was very vague. Even the circumstance, that at the
Synod of Bostra (according to Socrates) Christ was expressly
decreed to have a human soul, is not decisive; for Origen
might have carried the recognition of this dogma, which was

[1] Euseb. H. E. VI. 33. See also Socrates H. E. III. 7.

[2] L.c.: τὸν σωτῆρα καὶ κύριον ἡμῶν μὴ προϋφεστάναι κατ᾽ ἰδίαν οὐσίας περιγραφὴν πρὸ τῆς εἰς ἀνθρώπους ἐπιδημίας, μηδὲ θεότητα ἰδίαν ἔχειν, ἀλλ ἐμπολιτευο-
μένην αὐτῷ μόνην τὴν πατρικήν. The word περιγραφή is first found in the Excerpta
Theodoti 19, where κατὰ περιγραφήν is contrasted in the sense of personality with
the κατ᾽ οὐσίαν (τοῦ Θεοῦ). The latter was accordingly felt to be Modalistic: καὶ
ὁ λόγος σὰρξ ἐγένετο, οὐ κατὰ τὴν παρουσίαν μόνον ἄνθρωπος γενόμενος, ἀλλὰ καὶ
ἐν ἀρχῇ ὁ ἐν ταυτότητι λόγος κατὰ περιγραφὴν καὶ οὐ κατ᾽ οὐσίαν γενόμενος, ὁ υἱὸς ;
cf., ch. 10, where περιγράφεσθαι also expresses the personal existence, i.e., what was
afterwards termed ὑπόστασις. This word was not yet so used, so far as I know,
in the 3rd century. In Origen περιγραφή is likewise the expression for the strictly
self-contained personality; see Comm. on John I. 42, Lomm. I. 88: ὥσπερ οὖν
δυνάμεις Θεοῦ πλείονές εἰσιν, ὧν ἑκάστη κατὰ περιγραφήν, ὧν διαφέρει ὁ σωτήρ,
οὕτως ὁ λόγος—εἰ καὶ παρ᾽ ἡμῖν οὐκ ἔστι κατὰ περιγραφὴν ἐκτὸς ἡμῶν—νοηθήσεται
ὁ Χριστὸς κ.τ.λ. In our passage and Pseudo-Hippol. c. Beron. 1, 4, it means simply
"configuration".

[3] Dogmengesch. I., p. 202. See on Beryll, who has become a favourite of the
historians of dogma, apart from the extended historical works, Ullmann, de Beryllo,
1835; Theod. Stud. u. Krit., 1836; Fock Diss. de Christologia B. 1843; Rossel in
the Berliner Jahrbb., 1844, No. 41 f.; Kober in the Theol. Quartalschr., 1848, I.

of the highest importance to him, whatever the doctrine of
Beryll had been. That the Bishop rather taught Dynamistic
Monarchianism is supported, first, by the circumstance that
this form of doctrine had, as we can prove, long persisted in
Arabia and Syria; and, secondly, by the observation that Origen,
in the fragment of his commentary on the Ep. of Titus (see
above), has *contrasted* with the Patripassian belief [1] a kind of
teaching which seems to coincide with that of Beryll. Primitive
Dynamistic Monarchian conceptions must, however, be imputed also to those Egyptian Millenarians whom Dionysius of
Alexandria opposed, and whom he considered it necessary to
instruct "in the glorious and truly divine appearing of our
Lord" (περὶ τῆς ἐνδόξου καὶ ἀληθῶς ἐνθέου τοῦ κυρίου ἡμῶν
ἐπιφανείας. [2]

These were all, indeed, isolated and relatively unimportant
phenomena; but they prove that even about the middle of the
3rd century the Logos Christology was not universally recognised in the East, and that the Monarchians were still treated
indulgently. [3] Decisive action was first taken and Adoptianism was
ranked in the East with Ebionitism as a heresy, in the case of
the incumbent of the most exalted Bishopric in the East, Paul
of Samosata, Bishop of Antioch from 260, but perhaps a little
earlier. He opposed the already dominant doctrine of the
essential natural deity of Christ, and set up once more the old
view of the human Person of the Redeemer. [4] That happened

---

1 It is contained in the words of Origen given above, p. 35, note 3.

2 Euseb. H. E. VII. 24, 5. By the Epiphany we have to understand the future
appearing; but thorough-going Millenarians in the East, in the country districts,
hardly recognised the doctrine of the Logos.

3 The uncertainty which still prevailed in the 3rd century in reference to
Christology is seen whenever we take up works not written by learned theologians.
Especially the circumstance that, according to the Creed and the Gospel, the Holy
Ghost took part in the conception of Jesus, constantly prompted the most curious
phrases regarding the personal divinity of Christ, and the *assumptio carnis* of the
Logos, see, *e.g.*, Orac. Sibyll. VI. V. 6, where Christ is called "Sweet God whom
the Spirit, in the white plumage of the dove, begot."

4 Feuerlein, De hæresi Pauli Samosat., 1741; Ehrlich, De erroribus P.S., 1745;
Schwab, Diss. de P.S. vita atque doctrina, 1839; Hefele, Conciliengesch. 2 Aufl. I.,
p. 135; Routh, Reliq. S. III., pp. 286—367; Frohschammer, Ueber die Verwerfung
des ὁμοούσιος, in the Theol. Quartalschr. 1850, I.

at a time when, through Alexandrian theology, the use of the categories λόγος (word), οὐσία (being), ὑπόστασις (substance), ἐνυπόστατος (subsisting), πρόσωπον (person), περιγραφὴ οὐσίας (configuration of essence), etc., had almost already become legitimised, and when in the widest circles the idea had taken root that the Person of Jesus Christ must be accorded a background peculiar to itself, and essentially divine.

We do not know the circumstances in which Paul felt himself impelled to attack the form of doctrine taught by Alexandrian philosophy. Yet it is noticeable that it was not a province of the Roman Empire, but Antioch, then belonging to Palmyra, which was the scene of this movement. When we observe that Paul held a high political office in the kingdom of Zenobia, that close relations are said to have existed between him and the Queen, and that his fall implied the triumph of the Roman party in Antioch, then we may assume that a political conflict lay behind the theological, and that Paul's opponents belonged to the Roman party in Syria. It was not easy to get at the distinguished Metropolitan and experienced theologian, who was indeed portrayed by his enemies as an unspiritual ecclesiastical prince, vain preacher, ambitious man of the world, and wily Sophist. The provincial Synod, over which he presided, did not serve the purpose. But already, in the affair of Novatian, which had threatened to split up the East, the experiment had been tried A.D. 252 (253) of holding an Oriental general-council, and that with success. It was repeated. A great Synod—we do not know who called it—met in Antioch A.D. 264; Bishops from various parts of the East attended it, and, especially, Firmilian of Cæsarea. The aged Dionysius, Bishop of Alexandria, excused his absence in a letter in which he did not take Paul's side. The first Synod came to an end without result, because, it is alleged, the accused had cunningly concealed his false doctrines.[1] A second was also unsuccessful. Firmilian himself gave up the idea of a condemnation "because Paul promised to change his opinions." It was only at a third Synod, between 266 and 269, probably

[1] Eusebius speaks (H. E. VII. 28. 2) of a whole party (οἱ ἀμφὶ τὸν Σαμοσατέα) having been able to conceal their heterodoxy at the time.

268, at Antioch, Firmilian having died at Tarsus on his way
thither, that excommunication was pronounced on the Bishop,
and his successor Domnus was appointed. The number of the
members of Synod is stated differently at 70, 80, and 180;
and the argument against Paul was led by Malchion, a sophist
of Antioch and head of a high school, as also a presbyter of
the Church. He alone among them all was in a position to
unmask that "wily and deceitful man." The Acts of the discussion together with a detailed epistle, were sent by the Synod
to Rome, Alexandria, and all Catholic Churches. Paul, protected
by Zenobia, remained four years longer in his office; the Church
in Antioch split up: "there took place schisms among the
people, revolts among the priests, confusion among the pastors"
(ἐγένοντο σχίσματα λαῶν, ἀκαταστασίαι ἱερέων, ταραχὴ ποιμένων).[1]
In the year A.D. 272 Antioch was at last taken by Aurelian,
and the Emperor, to whom an appeal was brought, pronounced
on the spot the famous judgment, that the Church building was
to be handed to him with whom the Christian Bishops of Italy
and of Rome corresponded by letter. This decision was of course
founded on political grounds.[2]

[1] Basilius Diac., Acta Concilii Ephes., p. 427, Labb.

[2] The most important authorities for Paul's history and doctrine are the Acts
of the Synod of Antioch held against him, i.e., the shorthand report of the discussion between Paul and Malchion, and the Synodal epistle. These still existed
in the 6th century, but we now possess them only in a fragmentary form: in
Euseb. H. E. VII. 27—30 (Jerome de vir. inl. 71); in Justinian's Tract. c. Mono-
phys.; in the Contestatio ad Clerum C P.; in the Acts of the Ephesian Council; in
the writing against Nestor. and Eutych. by Leontius of Byzant.; and in the book
of Petrus Diaconus, "De incarnat. ad Fulgentium": all in Routh l.c. where the places
in which they are found are also stated. Not certainly genuine is the Synodal
epistle of six Bishops to Paul, published by Turrianus (Routh, l.c., p. 289 sq.); yet
its authenticity is supported by overwhelming reasons. Decidedly inauthentic is a
letter of Dionysius of Alex. to Paul (Mansi, I., p. 1039 sq.), also a pretended Nicene
Creed against him (Caspari, Quellen IV., p. 161 f.), and another found in the libel
against Nestorius (Mansi, IV., p. 1010). Mai has published (Vet. Script. Nova
Coll. VII., p. 68 sq.) five fragments of Paul's speeches: οἱ πρὸς Σαβῖνον λόγοι (not
quite correctly printed in Routh, l.c., p. 328 sq.) which are of the highest value,
and may be considered genuine, in spite of their standing in the very worst
company, and of many doubts being roused by them which do not admit of being
completely silenced. Vincentius mentions writings by Paul (Commonit. 35). In
the second grade we have the testimony of the great Church Fathers of the 4th
century, which rested partly on the Acts, partly on oral tradition: see, Athanas c.

The teaching of Paul was characterised by the Fathers as a
renewal of that of Artemas, but sometimes also as Neo-Jewish,
Ebionitic, afterwards as Nestorian Monothelite, etc. It was as
follows. God was simply to be regarded as one person. Father,
Son, and Spirit were the One God (ἓν πρόσωπον). In God a
Logos (Son) or a Sophia (Spirit) can be distinguished—both
can again according to Paul become identified—but they
are *qualities*.[1] God puts forth of Himself the Logos from
Eternity, nay, He begets him, so that he can be called Son
and can have being ascribed to him, but he remains an impersonal power.[2] Therefore it was absolutely impossible for
him to assume a visible form.[3] This Logos operated in the
prophets, to a still higher degree in Moses, then in many
others, and most of all (μᾶλλον καὶ διαφερόντως) in the Son of
David, born of the virgin by the Holy Ghost. The Redeemer
was by the constitution of his nature a man, who arose in time
by birth; he was accordingly "from beneath", but the Logos
of God inspired him from above.[4] The union of the Logos

Apoll. II. 3, IX. 3; de Synod. Arim. et Seleuc. 26, 43—45, 51, 93; Orat. c. Arian.
II., No. 43; Hilarius, De synod. §§ 81, 86, pp. 1196, 1200; Ephræm Junior in
Photius, Cod. 229; Gregor Nyss, Antirrhet. adv. Apoll., § 9, p. 141; Basilius, ep.
52 (formerly 300); Epiphan. H. 65 and Anaceph.; cf. also the 3 Antiochian formulas and the Form. Macrostich. (Hahn Biblioth. der Symbole, 2 Aufl. §§ 85, 89),
as also the 19 Canon of the Council of Nicæa, according to which Paul's followers
were to be re-baptised before reception into the Catholic Church. One or two
notes also in Cramer's Catena on S. John. pp. 235, 259 sq. Useful details are given
by Innocentius I., ep. 22; by Marius Mercator, in the Suppl. Imp. Theodos. et
Valentinian adv. Nestor. of the Deacon Basilius; by Theodorus of Raithu (see
Routh, l.c., pp. 327 sq. 357); Fulgentius, etc. In the later opponentsof the heretics
from Philaster, and in resolutions of Synods from the 5th century, we find nothing
new. Sozom. H. E. IV. 15 and Theodoret H. F. II. 8 are still of importance. The
Libellus Synodicus we must leave out of account.

1 Μὴ εἶναι τὸν υἱὸν τοῦ Θεοῦ ἐνυπόστατον, ἀλλὰ ἐν αὐτῷ τῷ Θεῷ—ἐν Θεῷ ἐπισ-
τήμῃ ἐνυπόστατος—εἷς Θεὸς ὁ πατὴρ καὶ ὁ υἱὸς αὐτοῦ ἐν αὐτῷ ὡς λόγος ἐν ἀνθρώπῳ.

2 Λόγος προφορικός—ὁ πρὸ αἰώνων υἱός—τὸν λόγον ἐγέννησεν ὁ Θεὸς ἄνευ παρθένου καὶ ἄνευ τινὸς οὐδενὸς ὄντος πλὴν τοῦ Θεοῦ· καὶ οὕτως ὑπέστη ὁ λόγος.

3 Σοφία οὐκ ἦν δυνατὸς ἐν σχήματι εὑρίσκεσθαι, οὐδὲ ἐν θέᾳ ἀνδρός· μείζων γὰρ
τῶν ὁρωμένων ἐστίν.

4 ᾽Λόγος μὲν ἄνωθεν, ᾽Ιησοῦς δὲ Χριστὸς ἄνθρωπος ἐντεῦθεν—Χριστὸς ἀπο Μαρίας
καὶ δεῦρό ἐστιν—ἄνθρωπος ἦν ὁ ᾽Ιησοῦς, καὶ ἐν αὐτῷ ἐνέπνευσεν ἄνωθεν ὁ λόγος· ὁ
πατὴρ γὰρ ἅμα τῷ υἱῷ (scil. τῷ λόγῳ) εἷς Θεός, ὁ δὲ ἄνθρωπος κάτωθεν τὸ ἴδιον
πρόσωπον ὑποφαίνει, καὶ οὕτως τὰ δύο πρόσωπα πληροῦνται—Χριστὸς ἐντεῦθεν τῆς
ὑπάρξεως τὴν ἀρχὴν ἐσχηκώς—λέγει ᾽Ιησοῦν Χριστὸν κάτωθεν.

with the man Jesus is to be represented as an indwelling [1] by
means of an inspiration acting from without, [2] so that the Logos
becomes that in Jesus which in the Christian is called by the
Apostle "the inner man"; but the union which is thus originated is a contact in knowledge and communion (συνάφεια κατὰ
μάθησιν καὶ μετουσίαν) a coming together (συνέλευσις); there does
not arise a being existent in a body (οὐσία οὐσιωμένη ἐν σώματι),
i.e., the Logos dwelt in Jesus not "in substance but in quality"
(οὐσιωδῶς, ἀλλὰ κατὰ ποιότητα). [3] Therefore the Logos is to be
steadily distinguished from Jesus; [4] he is greater than the
latter. [5] Mary did not bear the Logos, but a man like us in
his nature, and in his baptism it was not the Logos, but the
man, who was anointed with the Spirit. [6] However, Jesus was,
on the other hand, vouchsafed the divine grace in a special
degree, [7] and his position was unique. [8] Moreover, the proof
he gave of his moral perfection corresponded to his peculiar
equipment. [9] The only unity between two persons, accordingly
between God and Jesus, is that of the disposition and the will. [10]

[1] ῾Ως ἐν ναῷ—ἐλθόντα τὸν λόγον καὶ ἐνοικήσαντα ἐν Ἰησοῦ ἀνθρώπῳ ὄντι; in support of this Paul appealed to John XIV. 10: "sapientia habitavit in eo, sicut et
habitamus et nos in domibus"—

[2] Λόγον ἐνεργὸν ἐξ οὐρανοῦ ἐν αὐτῷ—σοφίας ἐμπνεούσης ἔξωθεν.

[3] Οὐ δίδως, says Malchion, οὐσιῶσθαι ἐν τῷ ὅλῳ σωτῆρι τὸν μονογενῆ.

[4] Ἄλλος γάρ ἐστιν Ἰησοῦς Χριστὸς καὶ ἄλλος ὁ λόγος.

[5] Ὁ λόγος μείζων ἦν τοῦ Χριστοῦ· Χριστὸς γὰρ διὰ σοφίας μέγας ἐγένετο.

[6] Μαρία τὸν λόγον οὐκ ἔτεκεν οὐδὲ γὰρ ἦν πρὸ αἰώνων ἡ Μαρία, ἀλλὰ ἄνθρωπον
ἡμῖν ἴσον ἔτεκεν—ἄνθρωπος χρίεται, ὁ λόγος οὐ χρίεται· ὁ Ναζωραῖος χρίεται, ὁ κύριος
ἡμῶν,

[7] Οὔκ ἐστιν ὁ ἐκ Δαβὶδ χρισθεὶς ἀλλότριος τῆς σοφίας.

[8] Ἡ σοφία ἐν ἄλλῳ οὐχ οὕτως οἰκεῖ—κρείττων κατὰ πάντα, ἐπειδὴ ἐκ πνεύματος
ἁγίου καὶ ἐξ ἐπαγγελιῶν καὶ ἐκ τῶν γεγραμμένων ἡ ἐπ᾽ αὐτῷ χάρις.

[9] Paul has even spoken of a διαφορὰ τῆς κατασκευῆς (συστάσεως) τοῦ Χριστοῦ.

[10] From this point we refer to the Λόγοι πρὸς Σαβῖνον of Paul. We give them
here on account of their unique importance: (1) Τῷ ἁγίῳ πνεύματι χρισθεὶς προσηγορεύθη Χριστός, πάσχων κατὰ φύσιν, θαυματουργῶν κατὰ χάριν· τῷ γὰρ ἀτρέπτῳ
τῆς γνώμης ὁμοιωθεὶς τῷ Θεῷ, καὶ μείνας καθαρὸς ἁμαρτίας ἡνώθη αὐτῷ, καὶ ἐνηργήθη
που ἐλέσθαι τὴν τῶν θαυμάτων δυναστείαν, ἐξ ὧν μίαν αὐτὸς καὶ τὴν αὐτὴν πρὸς τῇ
θελήσει ἐνέργειαν ἔχειν δειχθείς, λυτρωτὴς τοῦ γένους καὶ σωτὴρ ἐχρημάτισεν.—(2) Αἱ
διάφοροι φύσεις καὶ τὰ διάφορα πρόσωπα ἕνα καὶ μόνον ἑνώσεως ἔχουσι τρόπον τὴν
κατὰ θέλησιν σύμβασιν, ἐξ ἧς ἡ κατὰ ἐνέργειαν ἐπι τῶν οὕτως συμβιβασθέντων ἀλ-
λήλοις ἀναφαίνεται μονάς.—(3) Ἅγιος καὶ δίκαιος γεγενημένος ὁ σωτήρ, ἀγῶνι καὶ
πόνῳ τὰς τοῦ προπάτορας ἡμῶν κρατήσας ἁμαρτίας· οἷς κατορθώσας τῇ ἀρετῇ συνήφθη
τῷ Θεῷ, μίαν καὶ τὴν αὐτὴν πρὸς αὐτὸν βούλησιν καὶ ἐνέργειαν ταῖς τῶν ἀγαθῶν

Such unity springs from love alone; but love can certainly produce a complete unity, and only that which is due to love —not that attained by "nature"—is of worth. Jesus was like God in the unchangeableness of his love and his will, and became one with God, being not only without sin himself, but vanquishing, in conflict and labour, the sins of our ancestor. As he himself, however, advanced in the manifestation of goodness and continued in it, the Father furnished him with power and miracles, in which he made known his steadfast conformity to the will of God. So he became the Redeemer and Saviour of the human race, and at the same time entered into an eternally indissoluble union with God, because his love can never cease. Now he has obtained from God, as the reward of his love, the name which is above every name; God has committed to him the judgment, [1] and invested him with divine dignity, so that now we can call him "God [born] of the virgin". [2] So also we are entitled to speak of a pre-existence of Christ in the prior decree [3] and prophecy [4] of God, and

προκοπαῖς ἐσχηκώς· ἣν ἀδιαίρετον φυλάξας τὸ ὄνομα κληροῦται τὸ ὑπὲρ πᾶν ὄνομα, στοργῆς ἔπαθλον αὐτῷ χαρισθέν.—(4) Τὰ κρατούμενα τῷ λόγῳ τῆς φύσεως οὐκ ἔχει ἔπαινον· τὰ δὲ σχέσει φιλίας κρατούμενα ὑπεραινεῖται, μιᾷ καὶ τῇ αὐτῇ γνώμῃ κρατούμενα, διὰ μιᾶς καὶ τῆς αὐτῆς ἐνεργείας βεβαιούμενα, καὶ τῆς κατ᾽ ἐπαύξησιν οὐδέποτε παυομένης κινήσεως· καθ᾽ ἣν τῷ Θεῷ συναφθεὶς ὁ σωτὴρ οὐδέποτε δέχεται μερισμὸν εἰς τοὺς αἰῶνας μίαν αὐτὸς καὶ τὴν αὐτὴν ἔχων θέλησιν καὶ ἐνέργειαν, ἀεὶ κινουμένην τῇ φανερώσει τῶν ἀγαθῶν.—(5) Μὴ θαυμάσῃς ὅτι μίαν μετὰ τοῦ Θεοῦ τὴν θέλησιν εἶχεν ὁ σωτήρ· ὥσπερ γὰρ ἡ φύσις μίαν τῶν πολλῶν καὶ τὴν αὐτὴν ὑπάρχουσαν φανεροῖ τὴν οὐσίαν, οὕτως ἡ σχέσις τῆς ἀγάπης μίαν τῶν πολλῶν καὶ τὴν αὐτὴν ἐργάζεται θέλησιν διὰ μιᾶς καὶ τῆς αὐτῆς φανερουμένην εὐαρεστήσεως. Similar details are to be found in Theodorus of Mops.; but the genuineness of what is given here seems to me to be guaranteed by the fact that there is absolutely not a word of an ethical unification of the eternal Son of God (the Logos) with Jesus. It is God Himself who is thus united with the latter.

[1] Χρὴ δὲ γιγνώσκειν, we read in the Catena S. Joh., ὅτι ὁ μὲν Παῦλος ὁ Σαμ. οὕτω φησίν· ἔδωκεν αὐτῷ κρίσιν ποιεῖν, ὅτι υἱὸς ἀνθρώπου ἐστίν.

[2] Athanas.: Παῦλος ὁ Σαμ. Θεὸν ἐκ τῆς παρθένου ὁμολογεῖ, Θεὸν ἐκ Ναζαρὲτ ὀφθέντα.

[3] Athanas.: Ὁμολογεῖ Θεὸν ἐκ Ναζαρὲτ ὀφθέντα, καὶ ἐντεῦθεν τῆς ὑπάρξεως τὴν ἀρχὴν ἐσχηκότα, καὶ ἀρχὴν βασιλείας παρειληφότα, Λόγον δὲ ἐνεργὸν ἐξ οὐρανοῦ, καὶ σοφίαν ἐν αὐτῷ ὁμολογεῖ, τῷ μὲν προορισμῷ πρὸ αἰώνων ὄντα, τῇ δὲ ὑπάρξει ἐκ Ναζαρὲτ ἀναδειχθέντα, ἵνα εἷς εἴη, φησίν, ὁ ἐπὶ πάντα Θεὸς ὁ πατήρ. Therefore it is said in the letter of the six Bishops that Christ is God from eternity, οὐ προγνώσει, ἀλλ᾽ οὐσίᾳ καὶ ὑποστάσει.

[4] Προκαταγγελτικῶς. See p. 41, note 8.

to say that he became God through divine grace and his constant manifestation of goodness. [1] Paul undoubtedly perceived in the imparting of the Spirit at the baptism a special stage of the indwelling of the Logos in the man Jesus; indeed Jesus seems only to have been Christ from his baptism: "having been anointed with the Holy Spirit he was named Christ—the anointed son of David is not different from wisdom" (τῷ ἁγίῳ πνεύματι χρισθεὶς προσηγορεύθη Χριστός—ὁ ἐκ Δαβὶδ χρισθεὶς οὐκ ἀλλότριός ἐστι τῆς σοφίας)  The Bishop supported his doctrine by copious proofs from Scripture, [2] and he also attacked the opposite views. He sought to prove that the assumption that Jesus was by nature (φύσει) Son of God, led to having two gods, [3] to the destruction of Monotheism; [4] he fought openly, with great energy, against the old expositors, i.e., the Alexandrians, [5] and he banished from divine service all Church psalms in which the essential divinity of Christ was expressed. [6]

The teaching of Paul was certainly a development of the old doctrine of Hermas and Theodotus, and the Church Fathers had a right to judge it accordingly; but on the other hand we must not overlook the fact that Paul not only, as regards form, adapted himself more closely to the accepted terminology, but that he also gave to the ancient type of doctrine, already heterodox, a philosophical, an Aristotelian, basis, and treated it ethically and biblically. He undoubtedly learned much from Origen; but he recognised the worthlessness of the double personality construed by Origen, for he has deepened

[1] Κάτωθεν ἀποτεθεῶσθαι τὸν κύριον—ἐξ ἀνθρώπου γεγονέναι τὸν Χριστὸν Θεόν— ὕστερον αὐτὸν ἐκ προκοπῆς τεθεοποιῆσθαι.

[2] Vincentius, Commonit. 35—Athanasius (c. Ariam IV. 30) relates that the disciples of Paul appealed to Acts X. 36 in support of their distinction between the Logos and Jesus: τὸν λόγον ἀπέστειλεν τοῖς υἱοῖς Ἰσραὴλ εὐαγγελιζόμενος εἰρήνην διὰ Ἰησοῦ Χριστοῦ. They said that there was a distinction here like that in the O. T. between the word of the Lord and of the prophets.

[3] Epiphan. l.c., c. 3; see also the letter of the six Bishops in Routh, l.c., p. 291.

[4] On the supreme interest taken by Paul in the unity of God see p. 42, note 3, Epiph. l.c., ch. I.

[5] Euseb. H. E. VII. 30. 9.

[6] Euseb. l.c., § 10.

the exposition given by the latter of the personality of Christ, and seen that "what is attained by nature is void of merit" (τὰ κρατούμενα τῷ λόγῳ τῆς φύσεως οὐκ ἔχει ἔπαινον). Paul's expositions of nature and will in the Persons, of the essence and power of love, of the divinity of Christ, only to be perceived in the work of His ministry, because exclusively contained in unity of will with God, are almost unparalleled in the whole dogmatic literature of the Oriental Churches in the first three centuries. For, when such passages do occur in Origen, they at once disappear again in metaphysics, and we do not know the arguments of the Alogi and the Theodotians.[1] It is, above all, the deliberate rejection of metaphysical speculation which distinguishes Paul; he substituted for it the study of history and the determination of worth on moral grounds alone, thus reversing Origen's maxim: ὁ σωτὴρ οὐ κατ᾽ μετουσίαν, ἀλλὰ κατ᾽ οὐσίαν ἐστὶ θεός (the Saviour is God not by communion, but in essence). As he kept his dogmatic theology free from Platonism, his difference with his opponents began in his conception of God. The latter described the controversy very correctly, when they said that Paul "had betrayed the mystery of the Christian faith,"[2] i.e., the mystic conception of God and Christ due to natural philosophy; or[3] when they complained of Paul's denial that the difficulty of maintaining the unity of deity, side by side with a plurality of persons, was got

[1] The three fragments of "Ebion" given by Mai, l.c., p. 68, and strangely held by Hilgenfeld to be genuine (Ketzergeschichte, p. 437 f.), seem to me likewise to belong to Paul: at any rate they correspond to his doctrine: Ἐκ τῆς περὶ προφητῶν ἐξηγήσεως (1) Κατ᾽ ἐπαγγελίαν μέγας καὶ ἐκλεκτὸς προφήτης ἐστίν, ἴσως μεσίτης καὶ νομοθέτης τῆς κρείττονος διαθήκης γενόμενος· ὅστις ἑαυτὸν ἱερουργήσας ὑπὲρ πάντων μίαν ἐφάνη καὶ θέλησιν καὶ ἐνέργειαν ἔχων πρὸς τὸν Θεόν, θέλων ὥσπερ Θεὸς πάντας ἀνθρώπους σωθῆναι καὶ εἰς ἐπίγνωσιν ἀληθείας ἐλθεῖν τῆς δι᾽ αὐτοῦ τῷ κόσμῳ δι᾽ ὧν εἰργάσατο φανερωθείσης.—(2) Σχέσει γὰρ τῇ κατὰ δικαιοσύνην καὶ πόθῳ τῷ κατὰ φιλανθρωπίαν συναφθεὶς τῷ Θεῷ, οὐδὲν ἔσχεν μεμερισμένον πρὸς τὸν Θεόν, διὰ τὸ μίαν αὐτοῦ καὶ τοῦ Θεοῦ γενέσθαι τὴν θέλησιν καὶ τὴν ἐνέργειαν τῶν ἐπὶ τῇ σωτηρίᾳ τῶν ἀνθρώπων ἀγαθῶν.—(3) Εἰ γὰρ ἐθέλησεν αὐτὸν Θεὸς σταυρωθῆναι, καὶ κατεδέξατο λέγων. Μὴ τὸ ἐμόν, ἀλλὰ τὸ σὸν γενέσθω θέλημα, δῆλον ὅτι μίαν ἔσχεν μετὰ τοῦ Θεοῦ τὴν θέλησιν καὶ τὴν πρᾶξιν, ἐκεῖνο θελήσας καὶ πράξας, ὅπερ ἔδοξε τῷ Θεῷ. The second and third fragments may be by Theodorus of Mops., but hardly the first.

[2] In Euseb. H. E. VII. 30. 10.

[3] Epiph. l. c., ch. III.: Παῦλος οὐ λέγει μόνον Θεὸν διὰ τὸ πηγὴν εἶναι τὸν πατέρα.

over simply by making the Father their source. What is that but to admit that Paul started in his idea of God, not from the *substance*, but from the *person?* He here represented the interests of theism as against the chaotic naturalism of Platonism And in appreciating the character of Jesus he refused to recognise its uniqueness and divinity in his "nature"; these he found only in his disposition and the direction of his will. Therefore while Christ as a person was never to him "mere man" (ψιλὸς ἄνθρωπος), yet Christ's natural endowment he would not recognise as exceptional. But as Christ had been predestinated by God in a unique manner, so in conformity to the promises the Spirit and the grace of God rested on him exceptionally; and thus his work in his vocation and his life, with and in God, had been unique. This view left room for a human life, and if Paul has, ultimately, used the formula, that Christ had become God, his appeal to Philipp. II. 9 shows in what sense he understood the words.

His opponents, indeed, charged him with sophistically and deceitfully concealing his true opinion behind phrases with an orthodox sound. It is possible, in view of the fact, *e.g.*, that he called the impersonal Logos "Son", that there is some truth in this; but it is not probable. He was not understood, or rather he was misunderstood. Many theologians at the present day regard the theology of Hermas as positively Nicene, although it is hardly a whit more orthodox than that of Paul. If such a misunderstanding is possible to the scholars of to-day— and Hermas was certainly no dissembler,—why can Firmilian not have looked on Paul as orthodox for a time? He taught that there was an eternal Son of God, and that he dwelt in Jesus; he proclaimed the divinity of Christ, held there were two persons (God and Jesus), and with the Alexandrians rejected Sabellianism. On this very point, indeed, a sort of concession seems to have been made to him at the Synod. We know that the Synod expressly censured the term "ὁμοούσιος",[1] and this

---

[1] This was a well-known matter at the time of the Arian controversy, and the Semi-Arians, *e.g.*, appealed expressly to the decision at Ancyra. See Sozomen H. E. IV. 15; Athanas., De Synod. 43 sq.; Basilius, Ep. 52; Hilarius de synodis 81, 86; Routh, l.c., pp. 360—365. Hefele, Conciliengesch. I., 2, p. 140 f. : Caspari, Quellen IV., p. 170 f.

was done, Athanasius conjectures, to meet an objection of Paul. He is said to have argued as follows:—If Christ is not, as he taught, essentially human, then he is *ὁμοούσιος* with the Father. But if that be true then the Father is not the ultimate source of the deity, but Being (the *οὐσία*), and thus we have three *οὐσίαι*;[1] in other words the divinity of the Father is itself derivative, and the Father is of identical origin with the Son,— "they become brothers". This can have been an objection made by Paul. The Aristotelian conception of the *οὐσία* would correspond to his turn of thought, and so would the circumstance, that the possibility of a subordinate, natural, divinity on the part of the Son is left out of the question. The Synod again can very well have rejected *ὁμοούσιος* in the interests of anti-sabellianism.[2] Yet it is just as possible that, as Hilarius says, the Synod condemned the term because Paul himself had declared God and the impersonal Logos (the Son) to be *ὁμοούσιος, i.e.,* "of the same substance, of one substance".[3] However that may be, whenever Paul's view was seen through, it was at once felt by the majority to be in the highest degree heretical. No one was yet quite clear as to what sort of thing this "naturally—divine" element in Christ was. Even Origen had taught that he possessed a divinity to which prayer might not be offered.[4] But to deny the divine nature (physis) to the Redeemer, was universally held to be an attack on the Rule of Faith.[5] They correctly perceived the really weak point in Paul's Christology, his teaching, namely, that there were actually two Sons of God;[6] Hermas, however, had already preached

---

[1] Athanas. l.c.; *ἀνάγκη τρεῖς οὐσίας εἶναι, μίαν μὲν προηγουμένην, τὰς δὲ δύο ἐξ ἐκείνης.*

[2] This is also the opinion of Basilius (l.c.): *ἔφασαν γὰρ ἐκεῖνοι* (the Bishops assembled against Paul) *τὴν τοῦ ὁμοουσίου φωνὴν παριστᾶν ἔννοιαν οὐσίας τε καὶ τῶν ἀπ' αὐτῆς, ὥστε καταμερισθεῖσαν τὴν οὐσίαν παρέχειν τοῦ ὁμοουσίου τὴν προσηγορίαν τοῖς εἰς ἃ διῃρέθη.*

[3] Dorner's view (l.c. I. p. 513) is impossible because resting on a false interpretation of the word *ὁμοούσιος*; Paul held the Father and Jesus to be *ὁμοούσιοι* in so far as they were *persons*, and therefore the Synod condemned the term.

[4] See De orat. 15, 16.

[5] Euseb. H. E. VII. 30. 6, 16.

[6] See Malchion in Leontius (Routh, l.c., p. 312): *Παῦλος φησίν, μὴ δύο ἐπίστασθαι υἱούς· εἰ δὲ υἱὸς ὁ Ἰ, Χρ. τοῦ Θεοῦ, υἱὸς δὲ καὶ ἡ σοφία, καὶ ἄλλο μὲν ἡ σοφία,*

this, and Paul was not in earnest about the "eternal Son". Yet this was only a secondary matter. The crucial difference had its root in the question as to the divine nature (physis) of the Redeemer.

Now here it is of the highest interest to notice how far, in the minds of many Bishops in Palestine and Syria, the speculative interpretation of the Rule of Faith had taken the place of that rule itself. If we compare the letter of Hymenæus of Jerusalem and his five colleagues to Paul with the *regula fidei* —not, say, that of Tertullian and Irenæus—but the Rule of Faith with which Origen has headed his great work: περὶ ἀρχῶν, then we are astonished at the advance in the times. The Bishops explain at the opening of their letter, [1] that they desired to expound, "in writing, the faith which we received from the beginning, and possess, having been transmitted and kept in the Catholic Church, proclaimed up to our day by the successors of the blessed Apostles, who were both eye-witnesses and assistants of the Logos, from the law and prophets and the New Testament." (ἔγγραφον τὴν πίστιν ἣν ἐξ ἀρχῆς παρελάβομεν καὶ ἔχομεν παραδοθεῖσαν καὶ τηρουμένην ἐν τῇ καθολικῇ καὶ ἁγίᾳ ἐκκλησίᾳ, μέχρι τῆς σήμερον ἡμέρας ἐκ διαδοχῆς ἀπὸ τῶν μακαρίων ἀποστόλων, οἳ καὶ αὐτόπται καὶ ὑπηρέται γεγόνασι τοῦ λόγου, καταγγελλομένην, ἐκ νόμου καὶ προφητῶν καὶ τῆς καινῆς διαθήκης.) *But what they presented as "the faith" and furnished with proofs from Scripture, was the speculative theology*, [2] In no other writing can

---

ἄλλο δὲ ᾽Ι. Χρ., δύο ὑφίστανται υἱοί. See also Ephraem in Photius, Biblioth. cod. 229. Farther the Ep. II. Felicis II. papæ ad Petrum Fullonem.

[1] See Routh, l.c., p. 289 sq.

[2] The πίστις ἐξ ἀρχῆς παραληφθεῖσα reads (l.c.): "Οτι ὁ Θεὸς ἀγέννητος, εἷς ἄναρχος, ἀόρατος, ἀναλλοίωτος, ὃν εἶδεν οὐδεὶς ἀνθρώπων, οὐδὲ ἰδεῖν δύναται· οὗ τὴν δόξαν ἢ τὸ μέγεθος νοῆσαι ἢ ἐξηγήσασθαι καθώς ἐστιν ἀξίως τῆς ἀληθείας, ἀνθρωπίνῃ φύσει ἀνέφικτον· ἔννοιαν δὲ καὶ ὁπωσοῦν μετρίαν περὶ αὐτοῦ λαβεῖν, ἀγαπητόν, ἀποκαλύπτοντος τοῦ υἱοῦ αὐτοῦ ... τοῦτον δὲ τὸν υἱὸν γεννητόν, μονογενῆ υἱόν, εἰκόνα τοῦ ἀοράτου Θεοῦ τυγχάνοντα, πρωτότοκον πάσης κτίσεως σοφίαν καὶ λόγον καὶ δύναμιν Θεοῦ, πρὸ αἰώνων ὄντα, οὐ προγνώσει, ἀλλ᾽ οὐσίᾳ καὶ ὑποστάσει Θεὸν Θεοῦ υἱόν, ἔν τε παλαιᾷ καὶ νέᾳ διαθήκῃ ἐγνωκότες ὁμολογοῦμεν καὶ κηρύσσομεν. ὃς δ᾽ ἂν ἀντιμάχηται τὸν υἱὸν τοῦ Θεοῦ Θεὸν μὴ εἶναι πρὸ καταβολῆς κόσμου (δεῖν) πιστεύειν καὶ ὁμολογεῖν, φάσκων δύο θεοὺς καταγγέλλεσθαι, ἐὰν ὁ υἱὸς τοῦ Θεοῦ Θεὸς κηρύσσηται τοῦτον ἀλλότριον τοῦ ἐκκλησιαστικοῦ κανόνος ἡγούμεθα, καὶ πᾶσαι αἱ καθολικαὶ ἐκκλησίαι συμφωνοῦσιν ἡμῖν. The prehistoric history of the Son is now expounded,

we see the triumph in the sphere of religion of the theology
of philosophy or of Origen, *i.e.*, of Hellenism, so clearly, as in
this letter, in which philosophical dogmatics are put forward
as the faith itself. But further. *At the end of the third century
even the baptismal confessions were expanded in the East by
the adoption of propositions borrowed from philosophical theology;* [1] *or, to put it in another way,—baptismal confessions apparently now first formulated, were introduced in many Oriental
communities, which also now contained the doctrine of the Logos.*
Since these statements were directed against Sabellianism as
well as against "Ebionitism"; they will be discussed later on.

With the deposition and removal of Paul the historian's interest in his case is at an end. It was henceforth no longer
possible to gain a hearing, in the great forum of Church life,
for a Christology which did not include the personal pre-existence of the Redeemer: no one was permitted henceforth to
content himself with the elucidation of the divinely-human life
of Jesus in his work. It was necessary to believe in the divine
nature (physis) of the Redeemer. [2] The smaller and remote
communities were compelled to imitate the attitude of the
larger. Yet we know from the circular letter of Alexander of
Alexandria, A.D. 321, [3] that the doctrine of Paul did not by
any means pass away without leaving a trace. Lucian and his

and then it goes on: τὸν δὲ υἱὸν παρὰ τῷ πατρὶ ὄντα Θεὸν μὲν καὶ κύριον τῶν
γενητῶν ἁπάντων, ὑπὸ δὲ τοῦ πατρὸς ἀποσταλέντα ἐξ οὐρανῶν καὶ σαρκωθέντα ἐνηνθρωπηκέναι. διόπερ καὶ τὸ ἐκ τῆς παρθένου σῶμα χωρῆσαν πᾶν τὸ πλήρωμα τῆς
θεότητος σωματικῶς, τῇ θεότητι ἀτρέπτως ἥνωται καὶ τεθεοποίηται and at the close:
εἰ δὲ Χριστὸς Θεοῦ δύναμις καὶ Θεοῦ σοφία πρὸ αἰώνων ἐστίν· οὕτω καὶ καθὸ Χριστὸς ἓν καὶ τὸ αὐτὸ ὢν τῇ οὐσίᾳ· εἰ καὶ τὰ μάλιστα πολλαῖς ἐπινοίαις ἐπινοεῖται.
See also Hahn, Bibl. d. Symbol. 2 Aufl. § 82.

[1] The propositions are undoubtedly as a rule phrased biblically, and they are
biblical; but they are propositions preferred and edited by the learned exegesis of
the Alexandrian which certainly was extremely closely allied with philosophical
speculation.

[2] The followers of Paul were no longer looked upon as Christians even at the
beginning of the fourth century, and therefore they were re-baptised. See the 19
Canon of Nicæa: Περὶ τῶν Παυλιανισάντων, εἶτα προσφυγόντων τῇ καθολικῇ ἐκκλησίᾳ,
ὅρος ἐκτέθειται ἀναβαπτίζεσθαι αὐτοὺς ἐξάπαντος.

[3] Theodoret H. E. I. 4.

famous academy, the alma mater of Arianism, were inspired by
the genius of Paul. [1] Lucian—himself perhaps, a native of Samosata—had, during the incumbency of three Bishops of Antioch,
remained, like Theodotus and his party in Rome, at the head
of a school outside of the great Catholic Church. [2] In his
teaching, and in that of Arius, the foundation laid by Paul is
unmistakable. [3] But Lucian has falsified the fundamental thought
of Paul in yielding to the assumption of a Logos, though a
very subordinate and created Logos, and in putting this in the
place of the man Jesus, while his disciples, the Arians, have,
in the view sketched by them of the person of Christ, been
unable to retain the features Paul ascribed to it; though they
also have emphasised the importance of the will in Christ. We
must conclude, however, that Arianism, as a whole, is nothing
but a compromise between the Adoptian and the Logos Christology, which proves that after the close of the 3rd century,
no Christology was possible in the Church which failed to recognise the personal pre-existence of Christ.

Photinus approximated to Paul of Samosata in the fourth
century. Above all, however, the great theologians of Antioch
occupied a position by no means remote from him; for the
presupposition of the personal Logos Homousios in Christ,
which they as Church theologians had to accept simply, could
be combined much better with the thought of Paul, than the

---

[1] See my article "Lucian" in Herzog's R.E. 2 Aufl., Bd. VIII., p. 767 ff.

[2] See Theodoret l.c. : αὐτοὶ γὰρ Θεοδίδακτοι ἐστέ, οὐκ ἀγνοοῦντες ὅτι ἡ ἔναγχος
ἐπαναστᾶσα τῇ ἐκκλησιαστικῇ εὐσεβείᾳ διδασκαλία Ἐβίωνός ἐστι καὶ Ἀρτεμᾶ, καὶ
ζῆλος τοῦ κατ᾽ Ἀντιόχειαν Παύλου τοῦ Σαμοσατέως, συνόδῳ καὶ κρίσει τῶν ἀπαν-
ταχοῦ ἐπισκόπων ἀποκηρυχθέντος τῆς ἐκκλησίας—ὃν διαδεξάμενος Λουκιανὸς ἀποσυνάγωγος ἔμεινε τριῶν ἐπισκόπων πολυετεῖς χρόνους—ὧν τῆς ἀσεβείας τὴν τρύγα
ἐρροφηκότες (scil. Arian and his companions) νῦν ἡμῖν τὸ Ἐξ οὐκ ὄντων ἐπεφύησαν,
τὰ ἐκείνων κεκρυμμένα μοσχεύματα.

[3] See esp. Athanas. c. Arian I. 5. "Arius says that there are two wisdoms, one
which is the true one and at the same time exists in God; through this the Son arose
and by participation in it he was simply named Word and Wisdom; for wisdom, he
says, originated through wisdom according to the will of the wise God. Then he also
says that there is another Word apart from the Son in God, and through participation
therein the Son himself has been again named graciously Word and Son." This
is the doctrine of Paul of Samos., taken over by Arius from Lucian. On the
distinction see above.

Arian assumption of a subordinate god, with attributes half-
human, half-divine.  So also the arguments of Theodore of Mopsuestia as to the relation of the Logos and the man Jesus, as
to nature, will, disposition, etc., are here and there verbally identical with those of Paul; and his opponents, especially Leontius, [1]
were not so far wrong in charging Theodore with teaching like
Paul. [2] Paul was in fact condemned a second time in the great
scholars of Antioch, and — strangely—his name was once more
mentioned, and for the third time, in the Monothelite controversy.  In this case his statements as to the one will (μία
θέλησις sc. of God and Jesus) were shamefully misused, in order
to show to the opposition that their doctrine had been already
condemned in the person of the arch-heretic.

We possess, however, another ancient source of information,
of the beginning of the 4th century, the Acta Archelai. [3]  This
shows us that at the extreme eastern boundary of Christendom
there persisted even among Catholic clerics, if we may use here
the word Catholic, Christological conceptions which had remained
unaffected by Alexandrian theology, and must be classed with
Adoptianism.  The author's exposition of Christ consists, so
far as we can judge, in the doctrine of Paul of Samosata. [4]
Here we are shown clearly that the Logos Christology had, at
the beginning of the 4th century, not yet passed beyond the
borders of the Christendom comprehended in the Roman
Empire.

[1] See in Routh, l.c., p. 347 sq.

[2] See the careful and comprehensive collection of the arguments of Theodore
in reference to christology, in Swete, Theodori Episcopi Mopsuesteni in epp. B.
Pauli Commentarii, Vol. II. (1882), pp. 289—339.

[3] We have to compare also the treatises of Aphraates, written shortly before the
middle of the 4th century. He adheres to the designation of Christ as Logos
according to John I. 1; but it is very striking that in our Persian author there is
not even the slightest allusion in which one could perceive an echo of the Arian
controversies (Bickell, Ausgewählte Schriften der syr. Kirchenväter 1874, p. 15). See
tract 1, "On faith", and 17, "Proof that Christ is the Son of God."

[4] On the origin of the Acta Archelai see my Texte und Unters. I. 3, 137 ff.
The principal passages are to be found in ch. 49 and 50. In these the Churchman
disputes the view of Mani, that Jesus was a spirit, the eternal Son of God, perfect
by nature. "Dic mihi, super quem spiritus sanctus sicut columba descendit? Si
perfectus erat, si filius erat, si virtus erat, non poterat spiritus ingredi, sicut nec

### 3. Expulsion of Modalistic Monarchianism.

(a).  The Modalistic Monarchians in Asia Minor and in the
West: Noëtus, Epigonus, Cleomenes, Aeschines, Praxeas,
Victorinus (Victor), Zephyrinus, Sabellius, Callistus. [1]

The really dangerous opponent of the Logos Christology
in the period between A.D. 180 and 300 was not Adoptianism,
but the doctrine which saw the deity himself incarnate in Christ,
and conceived Christ to be God in a human body, the Father

regnum potest ingredi intra regnum. Cuius autem ei cælitus emissa vox testimonium detulit dicens: Hic est filius meus dilectus, in quo bene complacui? Dic age
nihil remoreris, quis ille est, qui parat hæc omnia, qui agit universa? Responde
itane blasphemiam pro ratione impudenter allegas, et inferre conaris?" The following
Christology is put in the lips of Mani : "Mihi pium videtur dicere, quod nihil eguerit
filius dei in eo quod adventus eius procuratur ad terras, neque opus habuerit columba, neque baptismate, neque matre, neque fratribus." On the other hand Mani
says in reference to the Church views: "Si enim hominem eum tantummodo ex
Maria esse dicis et in baptismate spiritum percepisse, ergo per profectum filius
videbitur et non per naturam. Si tamen tibi concedam dicere, secundum profectum
esse filium quasi hominem factum, hominem vere esse opinaris, id est, qui caro et
sanguis sit?" In what follows Archelaus says: "Quomodo poterit vera columba
verum hominem ingredi atque in eo permanere, caro enim carnem ingredi non
potest? sed magis si Iesum hominem verum confiteamur, eum vero, qui dicitur, sicut
columba, Spiritum Sanctum, salva est nobis ratio in utraque. Spiritus enim
secundum rectam rationem habitat in homine, et descendit et permanet et compe-
tenter hoc et factum est et fit semper... *Descendit spiritus super hominem dignum
se*... Poterat dominus in cælo positus facere quæ voluerat, si spiritum eum esse
et non hominem dices. Sed non ita est, quoniam exinanivit semetipsum formam
servi accipiens. *Dico autem de eo, qui ex Maria factus est homo.* Quid enim?
non poteramus et nos multo facilius et lautius ista narrare? sed absit, ut a veritate
declinemus iota unum aut unum apicem. Est enim qui de Maria natus est filius,
qui totum hoc quod magnum est, voluit perferre certamen Iesus. *Hic est Christus
dei, qui descendit super eum, qui de Maria est*... Statim (post baptismum) in
desertum a *Spiritu* ductus est *Iesus, quem cum diabolus ignoraret, dicebat ei: Si
filius est dei. Ignorabat autem propter quid genuisset filium dei* (scil. *Spiritus*), *qui
prædicabat regnum cælorum, quod erat habitaculum magnum,* nec ab ullo alio
parari potuisset; unde et affixus cruci cum resurrexisset ab inferis, *assumptus est
illuc, ubi Christus filius dei regnabat*... Sicut enim Paracleti pondus nullus alius
valuit sustinere nisi soli discipuli et Paulus beatus, *ita etiam spiritum,* qui de cælis
descenderat, per quem vox paterna testatur dicens: Hic est filius meus dilectus,
*nullus alius portare prævaluit, nisi qui ex Maria natus est super omnes sanctos
Iesus."* It is noteworthy that the author (in ch. 37) ranks Sabellius as a heretic
with Valentinus, Marcion, and Tatian.

[1] Döllinger, Hippolytus und Kallistus, 1853. Volkmar, Hippolyt. und die röm.
Zeitgenossen, 1855. Hagemann, Die römische Kirche, 1864. Langen, Gesch. d.
römischen Kirche I., p. 192 ff. Numerous monographs on Hippolytus and the

become flesh. Against this view the great Doctors of the
Church—Tertullian, Origen, Novatian, but above all, Hippolytus—
had principally to fight. Its defenders were called by Tertullian
"Monarchiani", and, not altogether correctly, "Patripassiani",
which afterwards became the usual names in the West (see *e.g.*,
Cypr., Ep. 73. 4). In the East they were all designated, after
the famous head of the school, "Sabelliani" from the second
half of the third century; yet the name of "Patripassiani"
was not quite unknown there also.¹ Hippolytus tells us in

origin of the Philosophumena, as also on the authorities for the history of the
early heretics, come in here. See also Caspari, Quellen III., vv. *ll.* The authorites
are for Noëtus, the Syntagma of Hippolytus (Epiph., Philaster, Pseudo-Tertull.), and
his great work against Monarchianism, of which the so-called Ὁμιλία Ἱππολύτου
εἰς τὴν αἵρεσιν Νοήτου τινός (Lagarde, Hippol. quæ feruntur, p. 43 sq.) may with
extreme probability be held to be the conclusion. Both these works have been
made use of by Epiph. H. 57. [When Epiph. (l.c. ch. 1) remarks that "Noëtus appeared
± 130 years ago", it is to be inferred that he fixed the date from his authority, the
anti-monarchian work of Hippolytus. For the latter he must have had a date, which
he believed he could simply transfer to the period of Noëtus, since Noëtus is
described in the book as οὐ πρὸ πολλοῦ χρόνου γενόμενος. But in that case his
source was written about A.D. 230—240, *i.e.*, almost at the same time as the so-
called Little Labyrinth. It is also possible, however, that the above date refers to the
excommunication of Noëtus. In that case the work which has recorded this event,
can have been written at the earliest in the fourth decade of the fourth century].
Most of the later accounts refer to that of Epiph. An independent one is the
section Philos. IX. 7 sq. (X. 27; on this Theodoret is dependent H. F. III. 3).
For Epigonus and Cleomenes we have Philos. IX. 7, 10, 11, X. 27; Theodoret
H. F. III. 3. For Æschines: Pseudo-Tertull. 26; Philos. VIII. 19, X. 26; for
Praxeas: Tertull. adv. Prax., Pseudo-Tertull. 30. The later Latin writers against
heretics are at this point all dependent on Tertullian; yet see Optat., de schism.
I. 9. Lipsius has tried to prove that Tertullian has used "Hippolytus against
Noëtus" in his work adv. Prax. (Quellen-kritik, p. 43; Ketzergeschichte, p. 183 f.;
Jahrbuch für deutsche Theologie, 1868, p. 704); but the attempt is not successful (see
Ztschr. f. d. hist. Theol., 1874, p. 200 f.). For Victorinus we have Pseudo-Tertull. 30.
For Zephyrinus and Callistus: Philos. IX. 11 sq. Origen has also had Roman
Monarchians in view in many of the arguments in his commentaries. On Origen's
residence in Rome and his relations with Hippolytus, see Euseb. H. E. VI. 14;
Jerome, De vir. inl. 61; Photius Cod. 121; on his condemnation at Rome, see
Jerome Ep. 33, ch. 4.

¹ Orig. in Titum, Lomm. V., p. 287 "... sicut et illos, qui superstitiose magis
quam religiose, uti ne videantur duos deos dicere, neque rursum negare salvatoris
deitatem, unam eandemque substantiam patris ac filii asseverant, id est, duo quidem
nomina secundum diversitatem causarum recipientes, unam tamen ὑπόστασιν subsistere, id est, unam personam duobus nominibus subiacentem, qui latine Patripassiani appellantur." Athanas., de synod. 7 after the formula Antioch. macrostich.

the Philosophumena, that at that time the Monarchian controversy agitated the whole Church, [1] and Tertullian and Origen
testified, that in their day the "economic" trinity, and the
technical application of the conception of the Logos to Christ,
were regarded by the mass of Christians with suspicion. [2]
Modalism, as we now know from the Philosoph., was for almost
a generation the official theory in Rome. That it was not an
absolute novelty can be proved; [3] but it is very probable, on

[1] IX. 6: μέγιστον τάραχον κατὰ πάντα τὸν κόσμον ἐν πᾶσιν τοῖς πιστοῖς ἐμ-
βάλλουσιν.

[2] Ad. Prax. 3 : Simplices quique, ne dixerim imprudentes et idiotæ, quæ maior
semper pars credentium est, quoniam et ipsa regula fidei a pluribus diis sæculi ad
unicum et verum deum transfert, non intelligentes unicum quidem, sed cum sua
οἰκονομία esse credendum, expavescunt ad οἰκονομίαν... Itaque duos et tres iam
iactitant a nobis prædicari, se vero unius dei cultores præsumunt,.. monarchiam
inquiunt tenemus." Orig., in Joh. II 3. Lomm. I. p. 95: "Ετεροι δὲ οἱ μηδὲν εἰδότες, εἰ μὴ 'Ιησοῦν Χριστὸν καὶ τοῦτον ἐσταυρωνένον, τὸν γενόμενον σάρκα λόγον τὸ
πᾶν νομίσαντες εἶναι τοῦ λόγου, Χριστὸν κατὰ σάρκα μόνον γιγνώσκουσι τοιοῦτον δέ
ἐστι τὸ πλῆθος τῶν πεπιστευκέναι νομιζομένων. Origen has elsewhere distinguished
four grades in religion: (1) those who worship idols, (2) those who worship angelic
powers, (3) *those to whom Christ is the entire God*, (4) those whose thoughts rise
to the unchangeable deity. Clement (Strom. VI. 10) had already related that there
were Christians who, in their dread of heresy, demanded that everything should
be abandoned as superfluous and alien, which did not tend directly to blessedness.

[3] See above (Vol. I., p. 195) where reference is made, on the one hand,
to the Modalism reflected in Gnostic and Enkratitic circles (Gosp. of the Egypt.,
and Acta Lenc., Simonians in Iren. I. 231); on the other, to the Church formulas
phrased, or capable of being interpreted, modalistically (see II. Ep. of Clement,
Ign. ad Ephes., Melito [Syr. Fragments]; and in addition, passages which speak
of God having suffered, died, etc.). It is instructive to notice that the development
in Marcionite Churches and Montanist communities moved parallel to that in the
great Church. Marcion himself, being no dogmatist, did not take any interest in the
question of the relation of Christ to the higher God. Therefore it is not right to
reckon him among the Modalists, as Neander has done (Gnost. Syxteme, p. 294,
Kirchengesch. I. 2, p. 796). But it is certain that later Marcionites in the West
taught Patripassianism (Ambros. de fide V. 13. 162, T. II., p. 579; Ambrosiaster
ad I. Cor. II. 2, T. II., App. p. 117). Marcionites and Sabellians were therefore
at a later date not seldom classed together. Among the Montanists at Rome there
were, about A.D. 200, a Modalistic party and one that taught like Hippolytus; at
the head of the former stood Æschines, at the head of the latter Proculus. Of
the followers of Æschines, Hippolytus says (Philos. X. 26) that their doctrine
was that of Noëtus: αὐτὸν εἶναι υἱὸν καὶ πατέρα, ὁρατὸν καὶ ἀόρατον, γεννητὸν καὶ
ἀγέννητον, θνητὸν καὶ ἀθάνατον. It is rather an idle question whether Montanus
himself and the prophetic women taught Modalism. They certainly used formulas
which had a Modalistic sound; but they had also others which could afterwards be

the other hand, that a Modalistic doctrine, which sought to
exclude every other, only existed from the end of the second
century. It was in opposition to Gnosticism that the first effort
was made to fix theologically the formulas of a naïve Modalism,
and that these were used to confront the Logos Christology in
order (1) to avert Ditheism, (2) to maintain the complete divinity of Christ, and (3) to prevent the attacks of Gnosticism. An
attempt was also made, however, to prove Modalism by exegesis. That is equivalent to saying that this form of doctrine,
which was embraced by the great majority of Christians, [1] was
supported by *scientific* authorities, from the end of the second
century. But it can be shown without difficulty, how hurtful
any contact with theology could not fail to be to the naïve
conception of the incarnation of the deity in Christ, and we may say
that it was all over with it—though of course the death-struggle
lasted long—when it found itself compelled to attack others or
to defend itself. When it required to clothe itself in a cloak
manufactured by a scientific theology, and to reflect on the
idea of God, it belied its own nature, and lost its *raison d'être*.
What it still retained was completely distorted by its opponents.
Hippolytus has in the Philosophumena represented the doctrine
of Noëtus to have been borrowed from Heraclitus. That

nterpreted and could not but be interpreted "economically". In the Test. of the
XII. Patriarchs many passages that, in the Jewish original, spoke of Jehovah's appearance among his people must now have received a Christian impress from their
Christian editor. It is remarkable that, living in the third century, he did not
scruple to do this, see Simeon 6: ὅτι ὁ κύριος ὁ Θεὸς μέγας τοῦ Ἰσραήλ, φαινόμε-
νος ἐπὶ γῆς ὡς ἄνθρωπος καὶ σώζων ἐν αὐτῷ τὸν Ἀδάμ ... ὅτι ὁ Θεὸς σῶμα λαβὼν
καὶ συνεσθίων ἀνθρώποις ἔσωσεν ἀνθρώπους; Levi 5, Jud. 22, Issachar. 7: ἔχοντες
μεθ᾽ ἑαυτῶν τὸν Θεὸν τοῦ οὐρανοῦ, συμπορευόμενον τοῖς ἀνθρώποις: Zebul. 9: ὄψεσθε
Θεὸν ἐν σχήματι ἀνθρώπου; Dan. 5; Naphth. 8: ὀφθήσεται Θεὸς κατοικῶν ἐν ἀνθρώποις ἐπὶ τῆς γῆς: Asher 7: ἕως οὗ ὁ ὕψιστος ἐπισκέψηται τὴν γῆν, καὶ αὐτὸς ἐλθὼν
ὡς ἄνθρωπος μετὰ ἀνθρώπων ἐσθίων καὶ πίνων; Benjamin 10. Very different Christologies, however, can be exemplified from the Testaments. It is not certain what
sort of party Philaster (H. 51) meant (Lipsius Ketzergesch., p. 99 f.). In the third
century Modalism assumed various forms, among which the conception of a
formal transformation of God into man, and a real transition of the one into the
other, is noteworthy. An exclusive Modalistic doctrine first existed in the Church
after the fight with Gnosticism.

[1] Tertull. l.c. and ch. I.: "simplicitas doctrinæ", ch. 9, Epiphan. H. 62. 2
ἀφελέστατοι ἢ ἀκέραιοι. Philos. IX. 7, 11: Ζεφυρῖνος ἰδιώτης καί ἀγράμματος, l.c.
ch. 6: ἀμαθεῖς.

is, of course, an exaggeration.  But once we grasp the whole
problem "philosophically and scientifically"—and it was so
understood even by some scientific defenders of Monarchianism—
then it undoubtedly resembles strikingly the controversy regarding the idea of God between the genuine Stoics and the Platonists.  As the latter set the transcendent, apathetic God of
Plato above the λόγος-θεός of Heraclitus and the Stoics, so
Origen, e.g., has charged the Monarchians especially with stop-
ping short at the God manifest, and at work, in the world,
instead of advancing to the "ultimate" God, and thus
apprehending the deity "economically".  Nor can it surprise
us that Modalistic Monarchianism, after some of its representatives had actually summoned science, i.e., the Stoa, to their
assistance, moved in the direction of a pantheistic conception of
God.  But this does not seem to have happened at the outset,
or to the extent assumed by the opponents of the school.  Not
to speak of its uncultured adherents, the earliest literary defenders of Modalism were markedly monotheistic, and had a real
interest in Biblical Christianity.  It marks the character of the
opposition, however, that they at once scented the God of
Heraclitus and Zeno--a proof of how deeply they themselves
were involved in Neo-platonic theology. [1]  As it was in Asia

---

[1] That the scientific defenders of Modalism adopted the Stoic method—just as
the Theodotians had the Aristotelian (see above)—is evident, and Hippolytus was
therefore so far correct in connecting Noëtus with Heraclitus, i.e., with the father
of the Stoa. To Hagemann belongs the merit (Röm. Kirche, pp. 354—371) of having
demonstrated the traces of Stoic Logic and Metaphysics in the few and imperfectly
transmitted tenets of the Modalists. (See here Hatch, The influence etc., p. 19 f. on
the συμπάσχειν and the substantial unity of ψυχή and σῶμα). We can still recognise, especially from Novatian's refutation, the syllogistic method of the Modalists,
which rested on nominalist, i.e., Stoic, logic. See, e.g., the proposition: Si unus
deus Christus, Christus autem deus, pater est Christus, quia unus deus; si non
pater sit Christus, dum et deus filius Christus, duo dii contra scripturas introducti
videantur." But those utterances in which contradictory attributes, such as visible —
invisible etc., are ascribed to God, could be excellently supported by the Stoic system
of categories. That system distinguished ἴδια (οὐσία, ὑποκείμενον) from συμβεβηκότα,
or more accurately (1) ὑποκείμενα (substrata, subjects of judgment); (2) ποιά
(qualitatives); (3) πὼς ἔχοντα (definite modifications) and (4) πρὸς τι πὼς ἔχοντα
(relative modifications). Nos. 2—4 form the qualities of the idea as a συγκεχυ-
ομένον; but 2 and 3 belong to the conceptual sphere of the subject itself, while 4
embraces the variable relation of the subject to other subjects. The designations

Minor that Adoptianism first entered into conflict with the
Logos Christology, so the Church of Asia Minor seems to
have been the scene of the first Modalistic controversy, while in
both cases natives of that country transferred the dispute to Rome.

Father and Son, visible and invisible etc., must be conceived as such relative,
accidental, attributes. The same subject can in one relation be Father, in another
Son, or, according to circumstances, be visible or invisible. One sees that this
logical method could be utilised excellently to prove the simple unreasoned propositions of the old Modalism. There are many traces to show that the system was
applied in the schools of Epigonus and Cleomenes, and it is with schools we have
here to deal. Thus, *e.g.*, we have the accusation which, time and again, Origen
made against the Monarchians, that they only assnme *one ὑποκείμενον*, and combine
Father and Son indiscriminately as modes in which it is manifested. (Hagemann
refers to Orig. on Matt. XVI. 14: οἱ συγχέοντες πατρὸς καὶ υἱοῦ ἔννοιαν; and on
John X. 21: συγχεόμενοι ἐν τῷ περὶ πατρὸς καὶ υἱοῦ τόπῳ—but συγχέειν is the
Stoic term). The proposition is also Stoic that while the one ὑποκείμενον is capable
of being divided (διαιρεῖν), it is only subjectively, in our conceptions of it (τῇ
ἐπινοίᾳ μόνῃ), so that merely ὀνόματα not differences καθ’ ὑπόστασιν, result. Further,
the conception of the Logos as a mere sound is verbally that of the Stoics, who
defined the φωνή (λόγος) as ἀὴρ πεπληγμένος ἢ τὸ ἴδιον αἰσθητὸν ἀκοῆς. Tertullian
adv. Prax. 7; "quid est enim, dices, sermo nisi vox et sonus oris et sicut *gram-
matici* tradunt, aër offensus, intelligibilis auditu, ceterum vacuum nescio quid et
inane et incorporale?" Hippolyt., Philos. X. 33: Θεὸς λόγον ἀπογεννᾷ, οὐ λόγον
ὡς φωνήν. Novatian, de trinit. 31: "sermo filius natus est, qui non in sono percussi aëris aut tono coactæ de visceribus vocis accipitur." The application of
Nominalist Logic and Stoic Methaphysics to theology was discredited in the
controversy with the Modalists under the names of "godless science", or "the
science of the unbelievers", just as much as Aristotelian philosophy had been in
the fight with the Adoptians. Therefore, even as early as about A.D. 250, one of
the most rancorous charges levelled at Novatian by his enemies was that he was
a follower of another, *i.e.*, of the Stoic, philosophy (Cornelius ap. Euseb. H. E. VI.
43. 16; Cypr. Ep. 55. 24, 60. 3). Novatian incurred this reproach because he opposed
the Monarchians with their own, *i.e.*, the syllogistic, method, and because he had
maintained, as was alleged, imitating the Stoics, "omnia peccata paria esse."
Now if the philosophy of Adoptian scholars was Aristotelian, and that of
Modalistic scholars was Stoic, so the philosophy of Tatian, Tertullian, Hippolytus, and Origen, in reference to the One and Many, and the *real* evolutions
(μερισμός) of the one to the many is unmistakably Platonic. Hagemann (l.c. pp.
182—206) has shown the extent to which the expositions of Plotinus (or Porphyry)
coincide in contents and form, method and expression—see especially the conception
of Hypostasis (substance) in Plotinus—with those of the Christian theologians mentioned,
among whom we have to include Valentinus. (See also Hipler in the östr. Vierteljahrsschr.
f. Kath. Theol. 1869, p. 161 ff., quoted after Lösche, Ztschr. f. wiss. Theol. 1884, p. 259).
When the Logos Christology triumphed completely in the Church at the end of
the third century, Neoplatonism also triumphed over Aristotelianism and Stoicism in
ecclesiastical science, and it was only in the West that theologians, like Arnobius,
were tolerated who in their pursuit of Christian knowledge rejected Platonism.

It is possible that Noëtus was not excommunicated till about A.D. 230, and, even if we cannot now discover his date more accurately, it seems to be certain that he first excited attention as a Monarchian, and probably in the last twenty years of the second century. This was perhaps in Smyrna, [1] his native place, perhaps in Ephesus. [2] He was excommunicated in Asia Minor, only after the whole controversy had, comparatively speaking, come to a close in Rome. [3] This explains why Hippolytus has mentioned him last in his great work against the Monarchians, while in the Philosoph. he describes him as the originator (IX. 6: ἀρχηγόν) of the heresy. [4] A disciple of his, Epigonus, came to Rome in the time of Zephyrinus, or shortly before (+ 200), and is said to have there diffused the teaching of his master, and to have formed a separate party of Patripassians. At first Cleomenes, the disciple of Epigonus, was regarded as the head of the sect, and then, from c. A.D. 215, Sabellius. Against these there appeared, in the Roman Church, especially the presbyter Hippolytus, who sought to prove that the doctrine promulgated by them was a revolutionary error. But the sympathies of the vast majority of the Roman Christians, so far as they could take any part in the dispute, were on the side of the Monarchians, and even among the clergy only a minority supported Hippolytus. The "uneducated" Bishop Zephyrine, advised by the prudent Callistus, was himself disposed, like Victor, his predecessor (see under), to the Modalistic views; but his main effort seems to have been to calm the contending parties, and at any cost to avoid a new

[1] Hippol. c. Noët. I., Philos. IX. 7.

[2] Epiph. l.c., ch. I.

[3] According to Hippol. c. Noët. I., he was not condemned after the first trial, but only at the close of a second,—a proof of the uncertainty that still prevailed. It is impossible now to discover what ground there was for the statement that Noëtus gave himself out to be Moses, and his brother to be Aaron.

[4] The fact that Noëtus was able to live for years in Asia Minor undisturbed, has evidently led Theodoret into the mistake that he was a later Monarchian who only appeared after Epigonus and Cleomenes. For the rest, Hippolytus used the name of Noëtus in his attack on him, simply as a symbol under which to oppose later Monarchians (see Ztschr. f. d. hist. Theol. 1874, p. 201); this is at once clear from ch. 2.

schism in the Roman Church, already sadly split up. After his
death the same policy was continued by Callistus (217—222),
now raised to the Bishopric. But as the schools now attacked
each other more violently, and an agreement was past hoping
for, the Bishop determined to excommunicate both Sabellius and
Hippolytus, the two heads of the contending factions.[1] The
Christological formula, which Callistus himself composed, was
meant to satisfy the less passionate adherents of both parties,
and this it did, so far as we may conjecture. The small party
of Hippolytus "the true Catholic Church", held its ground in
Rome for only about fifteen years, that of Sabellius probably
longer. The formula of Callistus was the bridge, on which the
Roman Christians, who were originally favourable to Monarchianism, passed over to the recognition of the Logos Christology,
following the trend of the times, and the science of the Church.
This doctrine must have already been the dominant theory in
Rome when Novatian wrote his work *De Trinitate,* and from
that date it was never ousted thence. It had been established in
the Capital by a politician, who, for his own part, and so far

---

[1] Philos. IX. 12 : Οὕτως ὁ Κάλλιστος μετὰ τὴν τοῦ Ζεφυρίνου τελευτὴν νομίζων
τετυχηκέναι οὗ ἐθηρᾶτο, τὸν Σαβέλλιον ἀπέωσεν ὡς μὴ φρονοῦντα ὀρθῶς, δεδοικὼς ἐμὲ
καὶ νομίζων οὕτω δύνασθαι ἀποτρίψασθαι τὴν πρὸς τὰς ἐκκλησίας κατηγορίαν, ὡς μὴ
ἀλλοτρίως φρονῶν. Hippolytus, whose treatment of Sabellius is respectful, compared
with his attitude to Callistus, says nothing of his own excommunication; it is therefore possible that he and his small faction had already separated from Callistus,
and for their part had put him under the ban. This cannot have happened under
Zephyrine, as is shown directly by Philos. IX. 11, and all we can infer from ch. 7
is that the party of Hippolytus had ceased to recognise even Zephyrine as Bishop ;
so correctly Döllinger, l.c., p. 101 f., 223 f.; a different view in Lipsius, Ketzergeschichte, p. 150. The situation was doubtless this: Epigonus and Cleomenes had
founded a real school (διδασκαλεῖον) in the Roman Church, perhaps in opposition
to that of the Theodotians, and this school was protected by the Roman bishops.
(s. Philos. IX. 7 : Ζεφυρῖνος [τῷ κέρδει προσφερομένῳ πειθόμενος] συνεχώρει τοῖς
προσιοῦσι τῷ Κλεομένει μαθητεύεσθαι ... Τούτων κατὰ διαδοχὴν διέμεινε τὸ διδασκαλεῖον κρατυνόμενον καὶ ἐπαῦξον διὰ τὸ συναίρεσθαι αὐτοῖς τὸν Σεφυρῖνον καὶ τὸν
Κάλλιστον). Hippolytus attacked the orthodoxy and Church character of the school,
which possessed the sympathy of the Roman community, and he succeeded, after
Sabellius had become its head, in getting Callistus to expel the new leader from
the Church. But he himself was likewise excommunicated on account of his Christology, his "rigourism" and his passionate agitations. At the moment the community of Callistus was no longer to him a Catholic Church, but a διδασκαλεῖον
(see Philos. IX. 12, p 458, 1; p. 462, 42).

as he took any interest at all in dogmatics, had been more inclined to the Modalistic theory.[1]

The scantiness of our sources for the history of Monarchianism in Rome,—not to speak of other cities—in spite of the discovery of the Philosophumena, is shown most clearly by the circumstance that Tertullian has not mentioned the names of Noëtus, Epigonus, Cleomenes, or Callistus; on the other hand, he has introduced a Roman Monarchian, Praxeas, whose name is not mentioned by Hippolytus in any of his numerous controversial writings. This fact has seemed so remarkable that very hazardous hypotheses have been set up to explain it. It has been thought that "Praxeas" is a nickname (= tradesman), and that by it we ought really to understand Noëtus,[2] Epigonus,[3] or Callistus.[4] The correct view is to be found in Döllinger[5] and Lipsius.[6] Praxeas[7] had come to Rome before Epigonus, at a date anterior to the earliest of Hippolytus' personal recollections, accordingly about contemporaneously with Theodotus, or a little earlier, while Victor was Bishop; according to Lipsius, and this is probable, even during the episcopate of Eleutherus.[8] He probably resided only a short time in Rome,

---

[1] The attempt has been made in the above to separate the historical kernel from the biassed description of Hippolytus in the Philos. His account is reproduced most correctly by Caspari (Quellen III., p. 325 ff.). Hippolytus has not disguised the fact that the Bishops had the great mass of the Roman community on their side (IX. 11), but he has everywhere scented hypocrisy, intrigues and subserviency, where it is evident to the present day that the Bishops desired to protect the Church from the *rabies theologorum*. In so doing, they only did what their office demanded, and acted in the spirit of their predecessors, in whose days the acceptance of the brief and broad Church confession was alone decisive, while beyond that freedom ruled. It is also evident that Hippolytus considered Zephyrine and the rest a set of ignorant beings (*idiotes*), because they would not accede to the new science and the "economic" conception of God.

[2] According to Pseudo-Tertull. 30, where in fact the name of Praxeas is substituted for Noëtus.

[3] De Rossi, Bullet. 1866, p. 170.

[4] So, *e g.*, Hagemann, l.c., p. 234 f., and similarly at an earlier date, Semler.

[5] L.c., p. 198.

[6] Jahrb. f. deutsche Theologie, 1868, H. 4.

[7] The name has undoubtedly not been shown elsewhere up till now.

[8] Chronol. d. röm. Bischöfe, p. 173 f.

where he met with no opposition; and he founded no school
in the city. When, twenty years afterwards, the controversy was
at its height in Rome and Carthage, and Tertullian found himself compelled to enter the lists against Patripassianism, the
name of Praxeas was almost forgotten. Tertullian, however,
laid hold of him because Praxeas had been the first to raise a
discussion in Carthage also, and because he had an antipathy
to Praxeas who was a decided anti-montanist. In his attack,
Tertullian has, however, reviewed the historical circumstances of
about the year A.D. 210, when his work Adv. Prax. was
written; nay, he manifestly alludes to the Roman Monarchians,
*i.e.*, to Zephyrinus and those protected by him. This observation contains what truth there is in the hypothesis that Praxeas
is only a name for another well-known Roman Monarchian.

Praxeas was a confessor of Asia Minor, and the first to bring
the dispute as to the Logos Christology to Rome.[1] At the
same time he brought from his birth-place a resolute zeal against
the new prophecy. We are here, again, reminded of the faction
of Alogi of Asia Minor who combined with the rejection of the
Logos Christology an aversion from Montanism; cf. also the
Roman presbyter Caius. Not only did his efforts meet with no
opposition in Rome, but Praxeas induced the Bishop, by giving
him information as to the new prophets and their communities
in Asia, to recall the *litteræ pacis*, which he had already sent
them, and to aid in expelling the Paraclete.[2] If this Bishop was
Eleutherus, and that is probable from Euseb. H. E. V. 4, then
we have four Roman Bishops in succession who declared themselves in favour of the Modalistic Christology, viz., Eleutherus,
Victor, Zephyrine, and Callistus; for we learn from Pseudo-
Tertullian that Victor took the part of Praxeas.[3] But it is also

---

[1] Adv. Prax.: Iste primus ex Asia hoc genus perversitatis intulit Romam, homo
et alias inquietus, insuper de iactatione martyrii inflatus ob solum et simplex et
breve carceris tædium.

[2] L.c.: Ita duo negotia diaboli Praxeas Romæ procuravit, prophetiam expulit et
hæresim intulit, paracletum fugavit et patrem crucifixit.

[3] Pseudo-Tertull.: Praxeas quidem hæresim introduxit quam Victorinus corrobo-
rare curavit. This Victorinus is rightly held by most scholars to be Bishop Victor;
(1) there is the name (on Victor = Victorinus, see Langen l c., p. 196; Caspari,
Quellen III., p. 323, n. 102); (2) the date; (3) the expression "curavit" which

possible that Victor was the Bishop whom Tertullian (Adv.
Prax.) was thinking of, and in that case Eleutherus has no
place here. It is at all events certain that when Dynamistic
Monarchianism was proscribed by Victor, it was expelled not
by a defender of the Logos Christology, but in the interests
of a Modalistic Christology. The labours of Praxeas did not
yet bring about a controversy in Rome with the Logos Doctrine;
he was merely the forerunner of Epigonus and Cleomenes there.
From Rome he betook himself to Carthage, [1] and strove against
the assumption of any distinction between God and Christ. But
he was resisted by Tertullian, who, at that time, still belonged
to the Catholic Church, and he was silenced, and even compelled to make a written recantation. With this ended the
first phase of the dispute. [2] The name of Praxeas does not again
occur. But it was only several years afterwards that the controversy became really acute in Rome and Carthage, and
caused Tertullian to write his polemical work. [3] Of the final
stages of Monarchianism in Carthage and Africa we know
nothing certain. Yet see under.

It is not possible, from the state of our sources, to give a
complete and homogeneous description of the doctrine of the
older Modalistic Monarchianism. But the sources are not alone
to blame for this. As soon as the thought that God Himself

points to a high position, and is exactly paralleled by the συναίρεσθαι used by
Hippolytus in referring to Zephyrine and Callistus (see p. 58, note 1); lastly,
the fact that Victor's successors, as we know definitely, held Monarchian views.
The excommunication of Theodotus by Victor proves nothing, of course, to the
contrary; for the Monarchianism of this man was of quite a different type from
that of Praxeas.

[1] This is definitely to be inferred from the words of Tertullian (l.c.): "Fructi-
caverant avenæ Praxeanæ hic quoque superseminatæ dormientibus multis in simplicitate doctrinæ"; see Caspari, l.c.; Hauck, Tertullian, p. 368; Langen, l.c., p. 199;
on the other side Hesselberg, Tertullian's Lehre, p. 24, and Hagemann, l.c.

[2] Tertullian, l.c.: Avenæ Praxeanæ traductæ dehinc per quem deus voluit (scil.
per me), etiam evulsæ videbantur. Denique caverat pristinum doctor de emendatione
sua, et manet chirographum apud psychicos, apud quos tunc gesta res est; exinde
silentium.

[3] Tertull., l.c. Avenæ vero illæ ubique tunc semen excusserant. Ita altquamdiu
per hypocrisin subdola vivacitate latitavit, et nunc denuo erupit. Sed et denuo
eradicabitur, si voluerit dominus.

was incarnate in Christ had to be construed theologically, very
various attempts could not fail to result.   These could lead,
and so far did lead, on the one hand, to hazardous conceptions
involving transformation, and, on the other, almost to the border
of Adoptianism; for, as soon as the indwelling of the deity of the
Father (*deitas patris*) in Jesus was not grasped in the strict sense
as an incarnation, as soon as the element that in Jesus constituted his personality was not exclusively perceived in the deity
of the Father, these Christians were treading the ground of the
Artemonite heresy.    Hippolytus also charged Callistus with
wavering between Sabellius and Theodotus, [1] and in his work
against Noëtus he alludes (ch. III.) to a certain affinity between
the latter and the leather-worker.  In the writings of Origen, moreover, several passages occur, regarding which it will always
be uncertain whether they refer to Modalists or Adoptians.  Nor
can this astonish us, for Monarchians of all shades had a common interest in opposition to the Logos Christology : *they represented the conception of the Person of Christ founded on the
history of salvation, as against one based on the history of his
nature.*

Among the different expositions of the doctrine of the older
Modalists that of Hippolytus in his work against Noëtus shows
us it in its simplest form.   The Monarchians there described
are introduced to us as those who taught that Christ is the
Father himself, and that the Father was born, suffered and
died. [2]  If Christ is God, then he is certainly the Father, or he
would not be God.   If Christ, accordingly, truly suffered, then
the God, who is God alone, suffered. [3]  But they were not only
influenced by a decided interest in Monotheism, [4] a cause which
they held to have been injured by their opponents, [5] whom

---

[1]   Philos. IX. 12, X. 27.   Epiph. H. 57. 2.

[2]   C. 1 : ἔφη τὸν Χριστὸν αὐτὸν εἶναι τὸν πατέρα καὶ αὐτὸν τὸν πατέρα γεγεννῆσθαι
καὶ πεπονθέναι καὶ ἀποτεθνηκέναι.

[3]   C. 2 : Εἰ οὖν Χριστὸν ὁμολογῶ Θεόν, αὐτὸς ἄρα ἐστὶν ὁ πατήρ, εἴ γε ἔστιν ὁ
Θεός. ἔπαθεν δὲ Χριστὸς, αὐτὸς ὢν Θεός, ἄρα οὖν ἔπαθεν πατήρ, πατὴρ γὰρ αὐτὸς ἦν

[4]   Φάσκουσιν συνιστᾶν ἕνα Θεόν (c. 2).

[5]   Hippolytus defends himself, c. 11. 14 : οὐ δύο θεοὺς λέγω, s. Philos. IX. 11,
fin. 12 : δημοσίᾳ ὁ Κάλλιστος ἡμῖν ὀνειδίζει εἰπεῖν· δίθεοί ἐστε. From c. Noët. 11 it

they called ditheists (δίθεοι), but they fought in behalf of the
complete deity of Jesus, which, in their opinion, could only be
upheld by their doctrine. [1] In support of the latter they appealed,
like the Theodotians, chiefly to the Holy Scriptures, and, indeed,
to the Catholic Canon; thus they quoted Exod. III. 6, XX. 2f.;
Isa. XLIV. 6, XLV. 5, 14 f.; Baruch. III. 36; John. X. 30,
XIV. 8f.; Rom. IX. 5. Even John's Gospel is recognised; but
this is qualified by the most important piece of information
which Hippolytus has given about their exposition of the Scriptures. They did not regard that book as justifying the introduction of a Logos, and the bestowal on him of the title Son
of God. The prologue of the Gospel, as well as, in general,
so many passages in the book, was to be understood allegorically. [2] The use of the category of the Logos was accordingly
emphatically rejected in their theology. We do not learn any
more about the Noëtians here. But in the Philosoph. Hippolytus has discussed their conception of God, and has presented
it as follows: [3] "They say that one and the same God was
creator and Father of all things; that he in his goodness
appeared to the righteous of olden times, although he is invisible; in other words, when he is not seen, he is invisible,
but when he permits himself to be seen, he is visible; he is
incomprehensible, when he wills not to be apprehended, comprehensible when he permits himself to be apprehended. So in
the same way he is invincible and to be overcome, unbegotten
and begotten, immortal and mortal." Hippolytus continues:

appears that the Monarchians opposed the doctrine of the Logos, because it led to
the Gnostic doctrine of Æons. Hippolytus had to reply: τὶς ἀποφαίνεται πλήθυν
Θεῶν παραβαλλομένην κατὰ καιρούς. He sought to show (ch. 14 sq.) that the μυστήριον οἰκονομίας of the Trinity taught by him was something different from the
doctrine of the Æons.

[1] Hippol. (c. Noët. I.) makes his opponent say, τὶ οὖν κακὸν ποιῶ δοξάζων τὸν
Χριστόν; see also ch. II. sq: Χριστὸς ἦν Θεὸς καὶ ἔπασχεν δι᾽ ἡμᾶς αὐτὸς ὢν πατήρ,
ἵνα καὶ σῶσαι ἡμᾶς δυνηθῇ, ἀλλο οὐ δυνάμεθα λέγειν; see again ch. IX. where Hippolytus says to his opponents that the Son must be revered in the way defined by
God in Holy Scriptures.

[2] S. c. 15: ἀλλ᾽ ἐρεῖ μοι τὶς· Ξένον φέρεις λόγον λέγων υἱόν. Ἰωάννης μὲν γὰρ
λέγει λόγον, ἀλλ᾽ ἄλλως ἀλληγορεῖ.

[3] L. IX. 10. See also Theodoret.

"Noëtus says, 'So far, therefore, as the Father was not made, he is appropriately called Father; but in so far as he passively submitted to be born, he is by birth the Son, not of another, but of himself.'" In this way he meant to establish the *Monarchia*, and to say that he who was called Father and Son, was one and the same, not one proceeding from the other, but he himself from himself; he is distinguished in name as Father and Son, according to the change of dispensations; but it is one and the same who appeared in former times, and submitted to be born of the virgin, and walked as man among men. He confessed himself, on account of his birth, to be the Son to those who saw him, but he did not conceal the truth that he was the Father from those who were able to apprehend it. [1] Cleomenes and his party maintain that "he who was nailed to the cross, who committed his spirit to himself, who died and did not die, who raised himself on the third day and rested in the grave, who was pierced with the lance and fastened with nails, was the God and Father of all." The distinction between Father and Son was accordingly nominal; yet it was to this extent more than nominal, that the one God, in being born man, *appeared* as Son; it was real, so far, from the point of view of the history of salvation. In support of the identity of the "manifested" and the invisible, these Monarchians referred to the O. T. theophanies, with as good a right as, nay, with a better than, the defenders of the Logos Christology. Now as regards the idea of God, it has been said that "the element of finitude was here potentially placed in God himself," and that these Monarchians were influenced by Stoicism, etc. While the former statement is probably unwarranted, the Stoic influence, on the contrary, is not to be denied. [2] But the foundation to which we have to refer them consists of two ancient liturgical

---

[1] We perceive very clearly here that we have before us not an unstudied, but a thought-out, and theological Modalism. As it was evident, in the speculations about Melchisedec of the Theodotians, that they, like Origen, desired to rise from the crucified Jesus to the eternal, godlike Son, so these Modalists held the conception, that the Father himself was to be perceived in Jesus, to be one which was only meant for those who could grasp it.

[2] See above (p. 55, note 1). In addition Philos. X. 27: τοῦτον τὸν πατέρα αὐτὸν υἱὸν νομίζουσι κατὰ καιροὺς καλούμενον πρὸς τὰ συμβαίνοντα.

formulas, used by Ignatius, the author of the II. Ep. of Clement, and Melito, [1] whom we include, although he wrote a work "Concerning the creation and genesis of Christ" (περὶ κτίσεως καὶ γενέσεως Χριστοῦ). Further, even Ignatius, although he held Christ to have been pre-existent, knew only of one birth of the Son, namely, that of God from the virgin. [2] We have here to recognise the conception, according to which, God, in virtue of his own resolve to become finite, capable of suffering etc., can and did decide to be man, without giving up his divinity. It is the old, religious, and artless Modalism, which has here been raised, with means furnished by the Stoa, to a theological doctrine, and has become exclusive. But in the use of the formula "the Father has suffered," we have undoubtedly an element of novelty; for it cannot be indicated in the post-apostolic age. It is very questionable, however, whether it was ever roundly uttered by the theological defenders of Modalism. They probably merely said that "the Son, who suffered, is the same with the Father."

We do not learn what conception these Monarchians formed of the human σάρξ (flesh) of Jesus, or what significance they attached to it. Even the Monarchian formulas, opposed by Tertullian in "Adv. Prax", and attributed to Callistus by Hippolytus, are already more complicated. We easily perceive that they were coined in a controversy in which the theological difficulties inherent in the Modalistic doctrine had become notorious. Tertullian's Monarchians still cling strongly to the perfect identity of the Father and Son; [3] they refuse to admit the Logos into their Christology; for the "word" is no substance, but

---

[1] See Ignat. ad Ephes. VII. 2: εἷς ἰατρός ἐστιν σαρκικός τε καὶ πνευματικός, γεννητὸς καὶ ἀγέννητος, ἐν σαρκὶ γενόμενος Θεός, ἐν θανάτῳ ζωὴ ἀληθινή, καὶ ἐκ Μαρίας καὶ ἐκ Θεοῦ, πρῶτον παθητὸς καὶ τότε ἀπαθής, Ἰησοῦς Χριστός; and see for Clement Vol. I., p. 186 ff.

[2] It is interesting to notice that in the Abyssinian Church of to-day there is a theological school which teaches a threefold birth of Christ, from the Father in eternity, from the virgin, and from *the Holy Ghost at the Baptism;* see Herzog, R. E., 2 Aufl., Bd. I., p. 70.

[3] C. 1: "Ipsum dicit patrem descendisse in virginem, ipsum ex ea natum, ipsum passum ipsum denique esse Iesum Christum." c. 2: "post tempus pater natus et pater passus, ipse deus, dominus omnipotens, Iesus Christus prædicatur"; see also c. 13.

merely a "sound"; [1] they are equally interested with the Noëtians in monotheism, [2] though not so evidently in the full divinity of Christ; like them they dread the return of Gnosticism; [3]
they hold the same view as to the invisibility and visibility of
God; [4] they appeal to the Holy Scriptures, sometimes to the
same passages as the opponents of Hippolytus; [5] but they find
themselves compelled to adapt their teaching to those proof-
texts in which the Son is contrasted, as a distinctive subject,
with the Father. This they did, not only by saying that
God made himself Son by assuming a body, [6] or that the Son
proceeded from himself [7]—for with God nothing is impossible: [8]
but they distinctly declared that the flesh changed the Father
into the Son; or even that in the person of the Redeemer the

---

[1] C. 7: "Quid est enim, dices, sermo nisi vox et sonus oris, et sicut gramma-
tici tradunt, aër offensus, intellegibilis auditu, ceterum vanum nescio quid."

[2] C. 2: "Unicum deum non alias putat credendum, quem si ipsum eundemque
et patrem et filium et spiritum s. dicat." c. 3: "Duos et tres iam iactitant a nobis
prædicari, se vero unius dei cultores præsumunt ... monarchiam, inquiunt, tenemus."
c. 13: "inquis, duo dii prædicuntur." c. 19: "igitur si propterea eundem et patrem
et filium credendum putaverunt, ut unum deum vindicent etc." c. 23: "ut sic duos
divisos diceremus, quomodo iactitatis etc."

[3] C. 8: "Hoc si qui putaverit me προβολὴν aliquam introducere," says Tertullian
"qnod facit Valentinus, etc."

[4] See c. 14. 15: "Hic ex diverso volet aliquis etiam filium invisibilem contendere, ut sermonem, ut spiritum ... Nam et illud adiiciunt ad argumentationem, quod
si filius tunc (Exod. 33) ad Moysen loquebatur, ipse faciem suam nemini visibilem
pronuntiaret, quia scil. ipse invisibilis pater fuerit in filii nomine. Ac per hoc si
eundem volunt accipi et visibilem et invisibilem, quomodo eundem patrem et filium ...
Ergo visibilis et invisibilis idem, et quia utrumque, ideo et ipse pater invisibilis, qua
et filius, visibilis ... Argumentantur, recte utrumque dictum, visibilem quidem
in carne, invisibilem vero ante carnem, ut idem sit pater invisibilis ante carnem,
qui et filius visibilis in carne."

[5] Thus to Exod. XXXIII. (ch. 14), Rev. I. 18 (ch. 17), Isa XXIV. 24 (ch. 19),
esp. John X. 30; XIV. 9, 10 (ch. 20), Isa. XLV. 5 (ch. 20). They admit that in
the Scriptures sometimes two, sometimes one, are spoken of; but they argued
(ch 18): "Ergo quia duos et unum invenimus, ideo ambo unus atque idem et
filius et pater."

[6] Ch. 10: "Ipse se sibi filium fecit."

[7] Ch. 11: "Porro qui eundem patrem dicis et filium, eundem et protulisse ex
semetipso facis."

[8] To this verse the Monarchians, according to ch. 10, appealed, and they quoted
as a parallel the birth from the virgin.

body (the man, Jesus) was the Son, but that the Spirit (God, Christ) was the Father.[1] For this they appealed to Luke I. 35. They conceived the Holy Spirit to be identical with the power of the Almighty, *i.e.*, with the Father himself, and they emphasised the fact that that which was *born*, accordingly the flesh, not the Spirit, was to be called Son of God.[2] The Spirit (God) was not capable of suffering, but since he entered into the flesh, he sympathised in the suffering. The Son suffered,[3] but the Father "sympathised"[4]—this being a Stoic expression. Therefore Tertullian says (ch. 23), "Granting that we would thus say, as you assert, that there were two separate (gods), it was more tolerable to affirm two separate (gods) than one dissembling (turn-coat) god" [Ut sic divisos diceremus, quomodo iactitatis, tolerabilius erat, duos divisos quam unum deum versipellem prædicare].

It is very evident that whenever the distinction between *caro* (filius) and *spiritus* (pater), between the flesh or Son and the Spirit or Father, is taken seriously, the doctrine approximates to the Artemonite idea. It is in fact changing its coat (versipellis). But it is obvious that even in this form it could not satisfy the defenders of the Logos Christology, for the personal identity between the Father and the Spirit or Christ is still retained. On the whole, every attempt made by Modalism to meet the demands of the Logos doctrine could not fail logically to lead to Dynamistic Monarchianism. We know definitely that the formulas of Zephyrine and Callistus arose out of attempts

[1] Ch. 27: "Æque in una persona utrumque distinguunt, patrem et filium, discentes filium carnem esse, id est hominem, id est Iesum, patrem autem spiritum, id est deum, id est Christum." On this Tertullian remarks: "et qui unum eundemque contendunt patrem et filium, iam incipiunt dividere illos potius quam unare; talem monarchiam apud Valentinum fortasse didicerunt, duos facere Iesum et Christum." Tertullian, accordingly, tries to retort on his opponents the charge of dissolving the Monarchia; see even ch. 4. The attack on the assumption of a transformation of the divine into the human does not, for the rest, affect these Monarchians (ch. 27 ff.).

[2] See ch. 26, 27: "propterea quod nascetur sanctum, vocabitur filius dei; caro itaque nata est, caro itaque erit filius dei."

[3] Ch. 29: "mortuus est non ex divina, sed ex humana substantia."

[4] L. c.: "Compassus est pater filio."

at a compromise,[1] though the charge of having two gods was
raised against Hippolytus and his party. Zephyrine's thesis
(IX. 11), "I know one God, Christ Jesus, and besides him no
other born and suffering," which he announced with the limiting
clause, "the Father did not die, but the Son,"[2] agrees with the
doctrines of "Praxeas", but, as is clear from the Philos., is also
to be understood as a formula of compromise. Callistus went
still further. He found it advisable after the excommunication
of Sabellius and Hippolytus, to receive the category of the Logos
into the Christological formula meant to harmonise all parties,
an act for which he was especially abused by Hippolytus, while
Sabellius also accused him of apostasy.[3] According to Zephyrine: God is in himself an indivisible Pneuma, which fills
all things, or, in other words, the Logos; as Logos he is
nominally two, Father and Son. The Pneuma, become flesh in
the virgin, is thus in essence not different from, but identical
with, the Father (John XIV. 11). He who became manifest, *i.e.*,
the man, is the Son, but the Spirit, which entered into the Son,
is the Father. "For the Father, who is in the Son, deified the
flesh, after he had assumed it, and united it with himself, and
established a unity of such a nature that now Father and Son
are called one God, and that henceforth it is impossible that
this single person can be divided into two; rather the thesis
holds true that the Father suffered in sympathy with the Son" —
not the Father suffered.[4]

---

[1] Philos. IX. 7, p. 440. 35 sq.; 11, p. 450. 72 sq.

[2] Ἐγὼ οἶδα ἕνα Θεὸν Χριστὸν Ἰησοῦν καὶ πλὴν αὐτοῦ ἕτερον οὐδένα γεννητὸν καὶ
παθητόν—οὐχ ὁ πατὴρ ἀπέθανεν, ἀλλὰ ὁ υἱός.

[3] L.c. IX. 12, p. 458, 78: ἀλλὰ καὶ διὰ τὸ ὑπὸ τοῦ Σαβελλίου συχνῶς κατηγο-
ρεῖσθαι ὡς παραβάντα τὴν πρώτην πίστιν. It is apparently the very formula "Compassus est pater filio" that appeared unacceptable to the strict Monarchians.

[4] Philos. IX. 12, p. 458, 80: Κάλλιστος λέγει τὸν λόγον αὐτὸν εἶναι υἱόν, αὐτὸν
καὶ πατέρα ὀνόματι μὲν καλούμενον, ἕν δὲ ὂν τὸ πνεῦμα ἀδιαίρετον. οὐκ ἄλλο εἶναι
πατέρα, ἄλλο δὲ υἱόν, ἓν δὲ καὶ τὸ αὐτὸ ὑπάρχειν, καὶ τὰ πάντα γέμειν τοῦ θείου
πνεύματος τά τε ἄνω καὶ κάτω· καὶ εἶναι τὸ ἐν τῇ παρθένῳ σαρκωθὲν πνεῦμα οὐχ
ἕτερον παρὰ τὸν πατέρα, ἀλλὰ ἓν καὶ τὸ αὐτό. Καὶ τοῦτο εἶναι τὸ εἰρημένον. John.
14. 11. Τὸ μὲν γὰρ βλεπόμενον, ὅπερ ἐστὶν ἄνθρωπος, τοῦτο εἶναι τὸν υἱόν, τὸ δὲ ἐν
τῷ υἱῷ χωρηθὲν πνεῦμα τοῦτο εἶναι τὸν πατέρα· οὐ γὰρ, φησίν, ἐρῶ δύο θεοὺς πατέρα
καὶ υἱόν, ἀλλ᾽ ἕνα. Ὁ γὰρ ἐν αὐτῷ γενόμενος πατὴρ προσλαβόμενος τὴν σάρκα ἐθεο-

Hippolytus discovered in this formula a mixture of Sabellian and Theodotian ideas, and he was right.¹ The approximation to the Christology founded on the doctrine of substances (hypostases), and the departure from the older Monarchianism, are, in fact, only brought about by Callistus having also made use of a Theodotian idea.² He still kept aloof from the Platonic conception of God; nay, it sounds like a reminiscence of Stoicism, when, in order to obtain a rational basis for the incarnation, he refers to the Pneuma (Spirit) which fills the universe, the upper and under world. But the fact that his formulas, in spite of this, could render valuable service in Rome in harmonising different views, was not only due to their admission of the Logos conception. It was rather a result of the thought expressed in them, that God in becoming incarnate had deified the flesh, and that the Son, in so far as he represented the essentially deified σάρξ, was to be conceived as a second person, and yet as one really united with God.³ At this point the ultimate Catholic interest in the Christology comes correctly to light, and this is an interest not clearly perceptible elsewhere in Monarchian theories. It was thus that men were gradually tranquillised in Rome, and only the few extremists of the Left and Right parties offered any resistance. Moreover, the formula was extraordinarily adapted, by its very vagueness, to set up among the believing people the religious Mystery, under whose protection the Logos Christology gradually made good its entrance.

The latter was elaborated in opposition to Modalism by Ter-

ποίησεν ἐνώσας ἑαυτῷ, καὶ ἐποίησεν ἕν, ὡς καλεῖσθαι πατέρα καὶ υἱὸν ἕνα Θεόν. καὶ τοῦτο ἓν ὂν πρόσωπον μὴ δύνασθαι εἶναι δύο, καὶ οὕτως τὸν πατέρα συμπεπονθέναι τῷ υἱῷ· οὐ γὰρ θέλει λέγειν τὸν πατέρα πεπονθέναι καὶ ἓν εἶναι πρόσωπον...

Here something is wanting in the text.

¹ Catholic theologians endeavour to give a Nicene interpretation to the theses of Callistus, and to make Hippolytus a ditheist; see Hagemann, l.c.; Kuhn, Theol. Quartalschrift, 1885, II.; Lehir, Études bibliques, II., p. 383; de Rossi and various others.

² This is also Zahn's view, Marcell., p. 214. The doctrine of Callistus is for the rest so obscure,—and for this our informant does not seem to be alone to blame—that, when we pass from it to the Logos Christology, we actually breathe freely, and we can understand how the latter simpler and compact doctrine finally triumphed over the laboured and tortuous theses of Callistus.

³ See the Christology of Origen.

tullian, Hippolytus, and Novatian in the West.[1] While Adoptianism apparently played a very small part in the development
of the Logos Christology in the Church, the Christological theses
of Tertullian and the rest were completely dependent on the
opposition to the Modalists.[2] This reveals itself especially in
the strict subordination of the Son to the Father. It was only
by such a subordination that it was possible to repel the charge,
made by opponents, of teaching that there were two Gods.
The philosophical conception of God implied in the Logos
theory was now set up definitely as the doctrine of the Church,
and was construed to mean that the unity of God was simply
to be understood as a "unicum imperium", which God could
cause to be administered by his chosen officials. Further, the
attempt was made to prove that Monotheism was satisfactorily
guarded by the Father remaining the sole First Cause.[3] But
while the reproach was thus repelled of making Father and Son
"brothers", an approach was made to the Gnostic doctrine of
Æons, and Tertullian himself felt, and was unable to avert, the
danger of falling into the channel of the Gnostics.[4] His arguments in his writing *Adv. Praxeas* are not free from half concessions and uncertainties, while the whole tenor of the work
contrasts strikingly with that of the anti-gnostic tractates. Tertullian finds himself time and again compelled in his work to
pass from the offensive to the defensive, and the admissions
that he makes show his uncertainty. Thus he concedes that
we may not speak of two Lords or two Gods, that in certain
circumstances the Son also can be called Almighty, or even
Father, that the Son will in the end restore all things to the
Father, and, as it would seem, will merge in the Father; finally,
and especially, that the Son is not only not *aliud a patre*
(different in substance from the Father), but even in some way

[1] See Vol. II., p. 256.

[2] This can be clearly perceived by comparing the Christology of Tertullian and
Hippolytus with that of Irenæus.

[3] See Tertullian adv. Prax. 3; Hippol. c. Noët. 11.

[4] Adv. Prax. 8, 13. It is the same with Hippolytus; both have in their attacks
on the Modalists taken Valentine, comparatively speaking, under their protection.
This is once more a sign that the doctrine of the Church was modified Gnosticism.

not *alius a patre*[1] (different in person etc). Yet Tertullian and his comrades were by no means at a disadvantage in comparison with the Monarchians. They could appeal (1) to the Rule of Faith in which the personal distinction between the Father and Son was recognised;[2] (2) to the Holy Scriptures from which it was, in fact, easy to reduce the arguments of the Monarchians *ad absurdum;*[3] (3) to the distinction between Christians and Jews which consisted, of course, in the belief of the former in the Son;[4] and lastly, and this was the most important point, they could cite the Johannine writings, especially in support of the doctrine of the Logos. It was of the highest importance in the controversy that Christ could be shown to have been called the Logos in John's Gospel and the Apocalypse.[5] In view of the way in which the Scriptures were then used in the Church, these passages were fatal to Monarchianism. The attempts to interpret them symbolically[6] could not but fail in the end, as completely as those, *e.g.*, of Callistus and Paul of Samasota, to combine the use of the expression "Logos" with a rejection of the apologetic conception of it based on Philo. Meanwhile Tertullian and Hippolytus did not, to all appearance, yet succeed in getting their form of doctrine approved in the Churches. The God of mystery of whom they taught was viewed as an unknown God, and their Christology did not correspond to the wants of men. The Logos was, indeed, to be held one in essence with God; but yet he was, by his being made the organ of the creation of the world, an inferior

[1] Ch. 18, in other passages otherwise.

[2] Tertull. adv. Prax. 2. Hippol. c. Noët. I.

[3] The Monarchian dispute was conducted on both sides by the aid of proofs drawn from exegesis. Tertullian, besides, in *Adv. Prax.*, appealed in support of the "economic" trinity to utterances of the Paraclete.

[4] See ad. Prax. 21: "Ceterum Iudaicæ fidei ista res, sic unum deum credere, ut filium adnumerare ei nolis, et post filium spiritum. Quid enim erit inter nos et illos nisi differentia ista? Quod opus evangelii, si non exinde pater et filius et spiritus, tres crediti, unum deum sistunt?"

[5] Πιστεύσωμεν, says Hippolyt. c. Noët. 17—κατὰ τὴν παράδοσιν τῶν ἀποστόλων ὅτι Θεὸς λόγος ἀπ' οὐρανῶν κατῆλθεν,—see already Tatian, Orat. 5 following Joh. I. 1: Θεὸς ἦν ἐν ἀρχῇ, τὴν δὲ ἀρχὴν λόγου δύναμιν παρειλήφαμεν.

[6] See above, p. 63.

divine being, or rather at once inferior and not inferior. This
conception, however, conflicted with tradition as embodied in
worship, which taught men to see God Himself in Christ, quite
as much as the attempt was opposed by doctrinal tradition, to
derive the use of the name "Son of God" for Christ, not from
His miraculous birth, but from a decree dating before the world. [1]
For the rest, the older enemies of Monarchianism still maintained
common ground with their opponents, in so far as God's evolving
of Himself in several substances (Hypostases) was throughout
affected by the history of the world (cosmos), and in this sense by
the history of revelation. The difference between them and at least
the later Monarchians was here only one of degree. The latter
began at the incarnation (or at the theophanies of the O. T.),
and from it dated a nominal plurality, the former made the
"economic" self-unfolding of God originate immediately before
the creation of the world. Here we have the cosmological interest coming once more to the front in the Church Fathers and
displacing the historical, while it ostensibly raised the latter to
a higher plane.

Wherever the doctrine of the Logos planted itself in the
third century the question, whether the divine being who appeared
on earth was identical with the Deity, was answered in
the negative. [2]  In opposition to this Gnostic view, which was
first to be corrected in the fourth century, the Monarchians
maintained a very ancient and valuable position in clinging to
the identity of the eternal Deity, with the Deity revealed on
earth. But does not the dilemma that arises show that the
speculation on both sides was as untenable as unevangelical?
Either we preserve the identity, and in that case defend the
thesis, at once absurd and inconsistent with the Gospel, that
Christ was the Father himself; or with the Gospel we retain
the distinction between Father and Son, but then announce a
subordinate God after the fashion of a Gnostic polytheism.
Certainly, as regards religion, a very great advance was arrived
at, when Athanasius, by his exclusive formula of Λόγος ὁμο-

[1] In the Symbolum the "γεννηθέντα ἐκ πνεύματος ἁγίου" is to be understood as
explaining τὸν υἱὸν τοῦ Θεοῦ.

[2] See *Adv. Prax.* 16.

οὐσιος (consubstantial Logos), negatived both Modalism and sub-ordinationist Gnosticism, but the Hellenic foundation of the whole speculation was preserved, and for the rational observer a second rock of offence was merely piled upon a first. How-ever, under the conditions of scientific speculation at the time, the formula was the saving clause by which men were once for all turned from Adoptianism, whose doctrine of a deification of Jesus could not fail, undoubtedly, to awaken the most question-able recollections.

## (b) The last stages of Modalism in the West, and the State of Theology.

Our information is very defective concerning the destinies of Monarchianism in Rome and the West, after the close of the first thirty years of the third century; nor are we any better off in respect to the gradual acceptance of the Logos Christ-ology. The excommunication of Sabellius by Callistus in Rome resulted at once in the Monarchians ceasing to find any follow-ers in the West, and in the complete withdrawal soon after-wards of strict and aggressive Modalism. [1] Callistus himself has, besides, not left to posterity an altogether clean reputation as regards his Christology, although he had covered himself in the main point by his compromise formula. [2] Hippolytus' sect had ceased to exist about A.D. 250; nay, it is not altogether improbable that he himself made his peace with the great Church shortly before his death. [3] We can infer from Novatian's im-portant work " De trinitate ", that the following tenets were recog-

---

[1] On these grounds the doctrine of Sabellius will be described under, in the history of Eastern Modalism.

[2] In forged Acts of Synod of the 6th century we read (Mansi, Concil. II., p. 621): "qui se Callistus ita docuit Sabellianum, ut arbitrio suo sumat unam per-sonam esse trinitatis." The words which follow later, "in sua extollentia separabat trinitatem" have without reason seemed particularly difficult to Döllinger (l.c., p. 247) and Langen (l.c., p. 215). Sabellianism was often blamed with dismembering the Monas (see Zahn, Marcell. p. 211.)

[3] See Döllinger, l.c., Hippolytus was under Maximinus banished along with the Roman Bishop Pontian to Sardinia. See the Catal. Liber. sub "Pontianus" (Lip-sius, Chronologic, pp. 194, 275).

nised in Rome about 250:[1] (1) Christ did not first *become* God. (2) The Father did not suffer. (3) Christ pre-existed and is true God and man.[2] But it was not only in Rome that these tenets were established, but also in many provinces. If the Roman Bishop Dionysius could write in a work of his own against the Sabellians, that "Sabellius blasphemed, saying that the Son was himself Father",[3] then we must conclude that this doctrine was then held inadmissible in the West. Cyprian again has expressed himself as follows (Ep. 73. 4): "Patripassiani, Valentiniani, Appelletiani, Ophitæ, Marcionitæ et ceteræ hæreticorum pestes" (—the other plagues of heretics), and we must decide that the strict Modalistic form of doctrine was then almost universally condemned in the West. Of the difficulties met with in the ejection of the heresy, or the means employed, we have no information. Nothing was changed in the traditional Creed— —a noteworthy and momentous difference from the oriental Churches! But we know of one case in which an important alteration was proposed. The Creed of the Church of Aquileia began, in the fourth century, with the words "I believe in God the Father omnipotent, invisible, and impassible" (Credo in deo patre omnipotente, *invisibili et impassibili*), and Rufinus, who

---

1 This writing shows, on the one hand, that Adoptians and Modalists still existed and were dangerous in Rome, and on the other, that they were not found within the Roman Church. On the significance of the writing see Vol. II., p. 313 f.

2 The Roman doctrine of Christ was then as follows: He has always been with the Father (sermo dei), but he first proceeded before the world from the substance of the Father (ex patre) for the purpose of creating the world. He was born into the flesh, and thus as *filius dei* and *deus* adopted a *homo*; thus he is also *filius hominis*. "Filius dei" and "filius hominis" are thus to be distinguished as two substances (substantia divina—homo), but he is one person; for he has completely combined, united, and fused the two substances in himself. At the end of things, when he shall have subjected all to himself, he will subject himself again to the Father, and will return to and be merged in him. Of the Holy Spirit it is also true, that he is a person (Paraclete), and that he proceeds from the substance of the Father; but he receives from the Son his power and sphere of work, he is therefore less than the Son, as the latter is less than the Father. But all three persons are combined as indwellers in the same substance, and united by love and harmony. Thus there is only one God, from whom the two other persons proceed.

3 Σαβέλλιος βλασφημεῖ, αὐτὸν τὸν υἱὸν εἶναι λέγων τὸν πάτερα. See Routh, Reliq. S. III., p. 373.

has preserved it for us, tells [1] that the addition was made, at any rate as early as the third century, in order to exclude the Patripassians.

But the exclusion of the strict Modalists involved neither their immediate end, nor the wholesale adoption of the teaching of Tertullian and Hippolytus, of the philosophical doctrine of the Logos. As regards the latter, the recognition of the name of Logos for Christ, side by side with other titles, did not at once involve the reception of the Logos doctrine, and the very fact, that no change was made in the Creed, shows how reluctant men were to give more than a necessary minimum of space to philosophical speculations. They were content with the formula, extracted from the Creed, "Jesus Christus, deus et homo", and with the combination of the Biblical predicates applied to Christ, predicates which also governed their conception of the Logos. In this respect the second Book of the Testimonies of Cyprian is of great importance. In the first six chapters the divinity of Christ is discussed, in terms of Holy Scripture, under the following headings. (1) Christum primogenitum esse et ipsum esse sapientiam dei, per quem omnia facta sunt; (2) quod sapientia dei Christus; (3) quod Christus idem sit et sermo dei; (4) quod Christus idem manus et brachium dei; (5) quod idem angelus et deus; (6) quod deus Christus. Then follows, after some sections on the appearing of Christ: (10) quod et homo et deus Christus. The later Nicene and Chalcedonian doctrine was the property of the Western Church from the third century, not in the form of a philosophically technical speculation, but in that of a categorical Creed-like expression of faith—see Novatian's "De trinitate", in which the doctrine of the Logos falls into the background. Accordingly the statement of Socrates (H. E. III. 7)

---

[1] Expos. Symboli Apost. ch. 19. The changes which can be shown to have been made on the first article of the Creed elsewhere in the West—see especially the African additions—belong probably at the earliest to the fourth century. Should they be older, however, they are all, it would seem, to be understood anti-gnostically; in other words, they contain nothing but explanations and comfirmatory additions. It is in itself incredible and incapable of proof that the Roman and after it the Western Churches should, at the beginning of the third century, have deleted, as Zahn holds, a ἕνα which originally stood in the first article of the Creed, in order to confute the Monarchians.

is not incredible, that the Western Churchman Hosius had already declared the distinction between οὐσία and ὑπόστασις (substantia and persona) before the Council of Nicæa. [1] The West
welcomed in the fourth century all statements which contained
the complete divinity of Christ, without troubling itself much
about arguments and proofs, and the controversy between the
two Dionysii in the middle of the third century (see under),
proves that a declared interest was kept up in the complete
divinity of Christ, as an inheritance from the Monarchian period
in Rome. [2] Nay, a latent Monarchian element really continued
to exist in the Western Church; this we can still study in the
poems of Commodian. [3] Commodian, again, was not yet acquainted
with speculations regarding the "complete" humanity of Jesus;
he is satisfied with the flesh of Christ being represented as a
sheath, (V. 224, "And suffers, as he willed, in our likeness"; [4]
on the other hand, V. 280, "now the flesh was God, in
which the virtue of God acted.") [5] But these are only symptoms

[1] See Vol. IV.

[2] We, unfortunately, do not know on what grounds the Roman Bishop approved
of the excommunication of Origen, or whether Origen's doctrine of subordination
was regarded in Rome as heretical.

[3] Here follow in the original illustrations which we relegate to this footnote.
Compare Instruct. II. 1 (Heading): " De populo absconso sancto omnipotentis Christi
dei vivi;" II. 1, p. 28. 22, ed. Ludwig): "omnipotens Christus descendit ad suos
electos;" II. 23, p. 43, 11 sq.: "Unde deus clamat: Stulte, hac nocte vocaris."
II. 39. 1, p. 52. Carmen apolog. 91 sq.: "Est deus omnipotens, unus, a semetipso
creatus, quem infra reperies magnum et humilem ipsum. Is erat in verbo positus,
sibi solo notatus, Qui pater et filius dicitur et spiritus sanctus;" 276: "Hic pater
in filio venit, deus unus ubique." (See also the following verses according to the
edition of Dombart): 285: "hic erat Omnipotens;" "334: "(ligno) deus pependit
dominus;" 353: "deum talia passum, Ut enuntietur crucifixus conditor orbis;"
359 sq.: "Idcirco nec voluit se manifestare, quid esset, Sed filium dixit se missum
fuisse a patre;" 398: "Prædictus est deus carnaliter nasci pro nobis;" 455: "quis
deus est ille, quem nos crucifiximus;" 610: "ipsa spes tota, deo credere, qui ligno
pependit;" 612: " Quod filius dixit, cum sit deus pristinus ipse;" 625: "hic erat
venturus, commixtus sanguine nostro, ut videretur homo, sed deus in carne latebat ...
dominus ipse veniet." 630, 764: "Unus est in cælo deus dei, terræ marisque, Quem
Moyses docuit ligno pependisse pro nobis;" etc. etc. Commodian is usually
assigned to the second half of the third century, but doubts have recently been
expressed as to this date. Jacobi, Commodian u. d. alt Kirchlich. Trinitätslehre,
in der deutschen Ztschr. f. Christl. Wissensch., 1853, p, 203 ff.

[4] Et patitur, quomodo voluit sub imagine nostra.

[5] Iam caro deus erat, in qua dei virtus agebat.

of a Christian standpoint which was fundamentally different from
that of oriental theologians, and which Commodian was by no
means the only one to occupy. He, Lactantius, and Arnobius [1]
are very different from each other. Commodian was a practical
Churchman; Arnobius was an empiricist and in some form also
a sceptic and decided opponent of Platonism; [2] while Lactantius
was a disciple of Cicero and well acquainted besides with the
speculations of Greek Christian theology. But they are all three
closely connected in the contrast they present to the Greek
theologians of the school of Origen; *there is nothing mystical
about them, they are not Neoplatonists.* Lactantius has, indeed,
expounded the doctrine of Christ, the incarnate Logos, as well
as any Greek; as a professional teacher it was all known and
familiar to him; [3] but as he nowhere encounters any problems
in his Christology, as he discusses doctrines with very few
theological or philosophical formulas, almost in a light tone, as
if they were mere matters of course, we see that he had no
interest of his own in them. He was rather interested in exactly
the same questions as Arnobius and Commodian, who again
showed no anxiety to go beyond the simplest Christological formulas — that Christ was God, that he had, however, also assumed
flesh, or united himself with a man, since otherwise we could
not have borne the deity: "And God was man, that he
might possess us in the future" (Et fuit homo deus, ut nos in
futuro haberet). [4] [5] The Christianity and theology which these

---

[1] See Francke's fine discussion, Die Psychologie und Erkentnisslehre des Arnobius (Leipzig, 1878).

[2] We recall the Theodotians of Rome.

[3] See Instit. IV. 6—30. The doctrine of the Logos is naturally worked out in
a subordinationist sense. Besides this, many other things occur which must have
seemed very questionable to the Latin Fathers 60 years afterwards: "Utinam," says
Jerome, "tam nostra confirmare potuisset quam facile aliena destruxit."

[4] Commod., Carmen apolog. 761.

[5] See the Christological expositions, in part extremely questionable, of Arnobius I. 39, 42, 53, 60, 62, and elsewhere. A. demands that complete divinity should
be predicated of Christ on account of the divine teaching of Christ (II. 60). In
his own theology many other antique features crop up; he even defends the view
that the supreme God need not be conceived as creator of this world and of men
(see the remarkable chap. 46 of the second book, which recalls Marcion and Celsus).
Many Church doctrines Arnobius cannot understand, and he admits them to be

Latins energetically supported against polytheism, were summed
up in Monotheism, a powerfully elaborated morality, the hope
of the Resurrection which was secured by the work of the God
Christ who had crushed the demons, and in unadulterated Chiliasm. [1]  Monotheism—in the sense of Cicero's " De natura deorum "—Moralism, and Chiliasm: these are the clearly perceived
and firmly held points, and not only for Apologetic purposes,
but also, as is proved especially by the second book of Commodian's " Instructiones ", in independent and positive expositions.
These Instructions are, along with the *Carmen Apolog.*, of the
highest importance for our estimate of Western Christianity in
the period A.D. 250—315.  We discover here, 100 years after
the Gnostic fight, a Christianity that was affected, neither by
the theology of the anti-gnostic Church Fathers, nor specially
by that of the Alexandrians, one which the dogmatic contentions
and conquests of the years 150—250 have passed over, hardly
leaving a trace. Almost all that is required to explain it by the
historian who starts with the period of Justin is to be found in
the slightly altered conditions of the Roman world of culture,
and in *the development of the Church system* as a practical
power, a political and social quantity. [2]  Even in the use of
Scripture this Christianity of the West reveals its conservatism.
The Books of the O. T. and the Apocalypse are those still
most in vogue. [3]  Commodian does not stand alone, nor are the
features to be observed in his "Instructiones" accidental.  And

puzzles whose solution is known to God alone (see *e.g.*, B. II. 74). Even in the
doctrine of the soul, which to him is mortal and only has its life prolonged by
receiving the doctrine brought by Christ, there is a curious mixture of antique
empiricism and Christianity. If we measure him by the theology of the fourth century,
Arnobius is heterodox on almost every page.

1 See the Carmen apolog. with its detailed discussions of the final Drama, Antichrist (Nero) etc.; Lactant IV. 12, VII. 21 sq.; Victorinus, Comm. on Revelation.

2 We can notice throughout in Commodian the influence of the' institution of
penance, that measuring-tape of the extent to which Church and World are
entwined.

3 The oldest commentary preserved, in part, to us is that of Victorinus of Pettan
on the Apocalypse.

we are not limited to the Apologists Arnobius and Lactantius for purposes of comparison. We learn much the same thing as to African Christianity from the works of Cyprian, or, even from the theological attitude of the Bishop himself, as we infer from Commodian's poems. And, on the other hand, Latin Church Fathers of the fourth century, *e.g.*, Zeno and Hilary, show in their writings that we must not look for the theological interests of the West in the same quarter as those of the East. *In fact the West did not, strictly speaking, possess a specifically Church "theology" at all.*[1] It was only from the second half of the fourth century that the West was invaded by the Platonic theology which Hippolytus, Tertullian, and Novatian had cultivated, to all appearance without any thorough success. Some of its results were accepted, but the theology itself was not. Nor, in some ways, was it later on, when the Western structure of Monotheism, energetic practical morality, and conservative Chiliasm fell a prey to destruction. The mystical tendencies, or the perceptions that led to them, were themselves awanting. Yet there is no mistake, on the other hand, as we are taught by the Institutiones of Lactantius as well as the Tractates of Cyprian, that the rejection of Modalism and the recognition of Christ as the Logos forced upon the West the necessity of rising from faith to a philosophical and, in fact, a distinctively Neoplatonic dogmatic. It was simply a question of time when this departure should take place. The recognition of the Logos could not fail ultimately to produce everywhere a ferment which transformed the Rule of Faith into the compendium of a scientific religion. It is hardly possible to conjecture how long and where Monarchians maintained their ground as independent sects in the West. It is yet most probable that there were Patripassians in Rome in the fourth century. The Western Fathers and opponents of heretics from the middle of the fourth century speak not infrequently of Monarchians—Sabellians; but they, as a rule, have simply copied Greek sources,

[1] The work of Arnobius is, in this respect, very instructive. This theologian did not incline as a theologian to Neoplatonism, at a time when, in the East, the use of any other philosophy in Christian dogmatics was *ipso facto* forbidden as heretical.

from which they have transferred the confusion that prevailed among the Greek representatives of Sabellianism, and to a still greater extent, we must admit, among the historians who were hostile to it. [1]

---

[1] Epiphanius (H. 62. 1) tells us that there were Sabellians in Rome in his time. Since he was acquainted with no other province or community in the West we may perhaps believe him. This information seems to be confirmed by a discovery made in A.D. 1742 by Marangoni. "He found at the Marancia gate on the road leading to S. Paolo a stair closed in his time which, as the discoverer believed, led to a cubiculum of S. Callisto, and in which were painted Constantine's monogram in very large letters, and, secondly, Christ sitting on a globe, between Peter and Paul. On the cover, in a mosaic of green stones, stood the inscription " Qui et filius diceris et pater inveniris" (Kraus, Rom. sott. 2 Aufl., p. 550). De Rossi, Kraus, and Schultze (Katakomben, p. 34) suppose that we have here the discovery of a burial place of Modalistic Monarchians, and that, as the monogram proves, of the fourth century. The sepulchre has again disappeared, and we have to depend entirely on Marangoni's account, which contains no facsimile. It is not probable that a Sabellian burial-place lay in immediate proximity to Domitilla's catacomb in the fourth century, or that the grave-yard of any sect was preserved. If we can come to any decision at all, in view of the uncertainty of the whole information, it seems more credible that the inscription belongs to the third century, and that the monogram was added to deprive it of its heretical character.

Whether Ambrosius and Ambrosiaster refer in the following quotations to Roman or say Western Monarchians living in their time is at least questionable. (Ambrosius, de fide V. 13. 162, Ed. Bened. II. p. 579 " Sabelliani et Marcionitæ dicunt, quod hæc futura sit Christi ad deum patrem subjectio, ut in patrem filius refundatur"; Ambrosiaster in Ep. ad Cor. II. 2, Ed. Bened. App. II., p. 117, "quia ipsum patrem sibi filium appellatum dicebant, ex quibus Marcion traxit errorem ").

Optatus (I. 9) relates that in the African provinces not only the errors, but even the names, of Praxeas and Sabellius had passed away ; in I. 10, IV. 5, V. 1 he discusses the Patripassians briefly, but without giving anything new. Nor can we infer from Hilary (de trinitate VII. 39 ; ad Constant. II. 9) that there were still Monarchians in his time in the West. Augustine says (Ep. 118 c. II. [12] ed. Bened. II., p. 498) dissensiones quæstionesque Sabellianorum silentur." Second-hand information regarding them is to be found in Augustine, Tract. in Joh. (passim) and Hær. 41. (The remarks here on the relation of Sabellius to Noëtus are interesting. Augustine cannot see why orientals count Sabellianism a separate heresy from Monarchianism).

Again we have similar notices in Aug. Prædest. H. 41—in H. 70 Priscillians and Sabellians are classed together; as already in Leo I—, in Isidor, H. 43, Gennadius, Eccl. Dogm. I. 4 (" Pentapolitana hæresis") Pseudo-hieron. H. 26 (" Unionita " etc., etc. In the Consult. Zacch. et Appollon. l. II. 11 sq. (Gallandi T. IX., p. 231 sq.)—a book written about 430—a distinction is made between the Patripassians and Sabellians. The former are correctly described, the latter confounded with the Macedonians. Vigilius Dial. adv. Arian. (Bibl. Lugd. T. VIII.).

## (c) The Modalistic Monarchians in the East: Sabellianism and the History of Philosophical Christology and Theology after Origen. [1]

After the close of the third century the name of "Sabellians" became the common title of Modalistic Monarchians in the East. In the West also the term was used here and there, in the same way, in the fourth and fifth centuries. In consequence of this the traditional account of the doctrines taught by Sabellius and his immediate disciples is very confused. Zahn has the credit of having shown that the propositions, especially, which were first published by Marcellus of Ancyra, were characterised by opponents as Sabellian because Monarchian, and in later times they have been imputed to the older theologian. But not only does the work of Marcellus pass under the name of Sabellius up to the present day, Monarchianism undoubtedly assumed very different forms in the East in the period between Hippolytus and Athanasius. It was steeped in philosophical speculation. Doctrines based on *kenosis* and transformation were developed.

[1] S. Schleiermacher in the Theol. Zeitschr. 1822, part 3; Lange in the Zeitschr. f. d. histor. Theol. 1832, II. 2. S. 17—46; Zahn, Marcell. 1867. Quellen: Orig., περὶ ἀρχ. I. 2; in Joh. I. 23, II. 2. 3, X. 21; in ep. ad Titum fragm. II; in Mt. XVI. 8, XVII. 14; c. Cels. VIII. 12, etc. For Sabellius, Philosoph. IX. is, in spite of its meagreness, of fundamental importance. Hippolytus introduces him in a way that shows plainly he was sufficiently well known at the time in the Roman Church not to need any more precise characterisation (see Caspari, Quellen III., p. 327). Epiphanius (H. 62) has borrowed from good sources. If we still possessed them, the letters of Dionysius of Alex. would have been our most important original authorities on S. and his Libyan party. But we have only fragments, partly in Athanasius (de sententia Dionysii), partly in later writers—the collection in Routh is not complete. Reliq S. III., pp. 371—403. All that Athanasius imparts, though fragmentary, is indispensable (espec. in the writings De synod.; de decret. synod. Nic. and c. Arian. IV. This discourse has from its careless use led to a misrepresentation of Sabellian teaching; yet see Rettberg, Marcell. Præf.; Kuhn, Kath. Dogmatik II. S. 344; Zahn, Marcell. S. 198 f.). A few important notices in Novatian, de trinit. 12 sq.; Method., Conviv. VIII. 10; Arius in ep. ad. Alex. Alexandriæ (Epiph., H. 69. 7); Alexander of Alex. (in Theodoret, H. E. I. 3); Eusebius, c. Marcell. and Præpar. evang.; Basilius, ep. 207, 210, 214, 235; Gregory of Nyssa, λόγος κατὰ Ἀρείου καὶ Σαβελλίου (Mai. V. P. Nova Coll. VIII. 2, p. I sq.)—to be used cautiously—; Pseudo-Gregor (Appollinaris) in Mai, l.c. VII. I., p. 170 sq.; Theodoret. H. F. II. 9; Anonymus, πρὸς τοὺς Σαβελλίζοντας (Athanas. Opp. ed. Montfaucon II., p. 37 sq.); Joh. Damascenus; Nicephorus Call., H. E. VI. 25. For Monarchianism we have a few passages in Gregorius Thaumaturg. The theologians after Origen and before Arius will be cited under.

And the whole was provided by the historians with the same label. At the same time these writers went on drawing inferences, until they have described forms of doctrine which, in this connection, in all probability never existed at all. Accordingly, even after the most careful examination and sifting of the information handed down, it is now unfortunately impossible to write a history of Monarchianism from Sabellius to Marcellus; for the accounts are not only confused, but fragmentary and curt. It is quite as impossible to give a connected history of the Logos Christology from Origen to Arius and Athanasius, although the tradition is in this case somewhat fuller. But the orthodox of the fourth and fifth centuries found little to please them in the Logos doctrine of those earlier disciples of Origen, and consequently they transmitted a very insignificant part of their writings to posterity. This much is certain, however, that in the East the fight against Monarchianism in the second half of the third century was a violent one, and that even the development of the Logos Christology (of Origen) was directly and lastingly influenced by this opposition. [1] The circumstance, that " Sabel-

---

[1] Emendations both to support and to refute Sabellianism were proposed in the valued works of the past; the N. T., as well as other writings belonging to primitive Christian literature, being tampered with. Compare Lightfoot's excursus on I. Clem. II., where Cod. A reads τοῦ Θεοῦ while C and S have τοῦ Χριστοῦ, the latter an emendation opposed to Monarchianism or Monophysitism (St. Clement of Rome, Appendix, p. 400 sq.). The old formulas τὸ αἷμα, τὰ παθήματα τοῦ Θεοῦ and others came into disrepute after the third century. Athanasius himself disapproved of them (c. Apoll. II. 13. 14, I., p. 758), and in the Monophysite controversy they were thoroughly distrusted. Thus in Ignatius (ad. Eph. I.) ἐν αἵματι Θεοῦ and (ad. Rom. VI.) τοῦ πάθους τοῦ Θεοῦ μου were corrected. On the other hand (II. Clem. IX.) the title of πνεῦμα for Christ was changed into λόγος. In the N. T. there are not a few passages where the various readings show a Monarchian or anti-Monarchian, a monophysite or dyophysite leaning. The most important have been discussed by Ezra Abbot in several essays in the " Bibliotheca Sacra " and the "Unitarian Review". But we can trace certain various readings due to a Christological bias as far back as the second century : thus especially the famous ὁ μονογενὴς υἱὸς for μονογενὴς Θεός John I. 18; on this see Hort., Two Dissertations I., on MONOΓΕΝΗΣ ΘΕΟΣ in Scripture and Tradition, 1878; Abbot in the Unitarian Review, June 1875. Since the majority of the important various readings in the N. T. belong to the second and third century, a connected examination of them would be very important from the standpoint of the history of dogma. For dogmatic changes in the western texts, the remarkable passage in Ambrosiaster on Rom. V. 14 falls especially to be noticed.

lianism" was almost the only name by which Monarchianism was known in the East, points, for the rest, to schisms having resulted only from, or, at any rate, after the appearance and labours of Sabellius in the East, therefore at the earliest since about 230—240. So long as Origen lived in Alexandria no schism took place in Egypt over the Christological question. [1]

Sabellius, perhaps by birth a Lybian from Pentapolis, [2] seems after his excommunication to have remained at the head of a small community in Rome. He was still there, to all appearance, when Hippolytus wrote the Philosophumena. Nor do we know of his ever having left the city,—we are nowhere told that he did. Yet he must have, at least, set an important movement at work abroad from Rome as his centre, and have especially fostered relations with the East. When, in Pentapolis, about A.D. 260, and several years after the death of Origen, the Monarchian doctrine took hold of the Churches there (Dionys., l.c.) —Churches which, it is significant, were to some extent Latin in their culture—Sabellius can hardly have been alive, yet it was under his name that the heresy was promoted. [3] But it would seem as if this prominence was given to him for the first time about A.D. 260. Origen at least had not, so far as I know, mentioned the name of Sabellius in his discussions of Monarchianism. These date from as early as A.D. 215. At the time, Origen was in Rome, Zephyrine being still Bishop. From the relations which he then entered into with Hippolytus, it has been rightly concluded that he did not hold aloof from the contentions in Rome, and took the side of Hippolytus. This attitude of Origen's may not have been without influence on his condemnation afterwards in Rome by Pontian, 231 or 232. Origen's writings, moreover, contain many sharp censures on Bishops who, in order to glorify God, made the distinction between Father and Son merely

---

[1] See Dionys. Alex. in Euseb. VII. 6. Dionysius speaks as if the appearance of Sabellian doctrine in his time in the Pentapolis were something new and unheard of.

[2] This information, however, first appears in Basil, then in Philaster, Theodoret. and Nicephorus; possibly, therefore, it is due to the fact that Sabellius' teaching met with great success in Libya and Pentapolis.

[3] Athanas de sententia Dionysii 5.

nominal. And this again seems to have been said not without
reference to the state of matters in Rome. The theology of
Origen made him an especially energetic opponent of the Modalistic form of doctrine; for although the new principles set up
by him—that the Logos, looking to the content of his nature,
possessed the complete deity, and that he from eternity was
created from the being of the Father—approached apparently
a Monarchian mode of thought, yet they in fact repelled it more
energetically then Tertullian and Hippolytus could possibly have
done. He who followed the philosophical theology of Origen
was proof against all Monarchianism. But it is important to
notice that in all places where Origen comes to speak about
Monarchians, he merely seems to know their doctrines in an
extremely simple form, and without any speculative embroid-
ery. They are always people who "deny that Father and Son are
two Hypostases" (they say: ἓν οὐ μόνον οὐσίᾳ, ἀλλὰ καὶ ὑπο-
κειμένῳ), who "fuse together" Father and Son (συγχέειν), who
admit distinctions in God only in "conception" and "name",
and not in "number", etc. Origen considers them therefore to
be untheological creatures, mere "believers". Accordingly, he
did not know the doctrine of Sabellius, and living in Syria and
Palestine had even had no opportunity of learning it.

That doctrine was undoubtedly closely allied, as Epiphanius
has rightly seen (H. 62. 1), to the teaching of Noëtus; it was
distinguished from the latter, however, both by a more careful
theological elaboration, and by the place given to the Holy
Ghost. [1] The opinion of Nitzsch and others, that we must distinguish between two stages in the theology of Sabellius, is unnecessary, whenever we eliminate the unreliable sources. The
central proposition of Sabellius ran that Father, Son, and Holy
Spirit were the same. Three names accordingly were attached to
one and the same being. It was his interest in monotheism that
influenced Sabellius. "What shall we say," urge his followers

[1] This appears also from our oldest witness, the letter of Dionysius, Eusebius
H. E. VII. 6: περὶ τοῦ νῦν κινηθέντος ἐν τῇ Πτολεμαΐδι τῆς Πενταπόλεως δόγματος,
ὄντος ἀσεβοῦς καὶ βλασφημίαν πολλὴν ἔχοντος περὶ τοῦ παντοκράτορος Θεοῦ πατρὸς
καὶ τοῦ κυρίου ἡμῶν Ἰησοῦ Χριστοῦ, ἀπιστίαν τε πολλὴν ἔχοντος περὶ τοῦ μονογενοῦς παιδὸς αὐτοῦ καὶ πρωτοτόκου πάσης κτίσεως, τοῦ ἐνανθρωπήσαντος λόγου, ἀναισ-
θησίαν δὲ τοῦ ἁγίου πνεύματος,

in Epiphanius (ch. 2), "have we one God or three Gods?" (τί
ἂν εἴπωμεν, ἕνα Θεὸν ἔχομεν, ἢ τρεῖς Θεούς;); and Epiphanius (ch. 3)
replies: "we do not propound polytheism" (οὐ πολυθεΐαν εἰσηγούμεθα). Whether Sabellius himself used the comparison between
the threefold nature of man and the sun remains a question
(one nature, three energies: τὸ Φωτιστικόν light giving, τὸ θάλπον
heat giving, τὸ σχῆμα the form). [1] The one being was also
called by Sabellius υἱοπάτωρ, [2] an expression which was certainly
chosen to remove any misunderstanding, to make it impossible
to suppose that two beings were in question. This υἱοπάτωρ
(son-father) was in Sabellius the ultimate designation for God
Himself, and not, say, merely for certain manifestations of a
μονάς (unit) resting in the background. Sabellius, however,
taught—according to Epiphanius and Athanasius—that God was
not at the same time Father and Son; but that he had, rather,
put forth his activity in three successive "energies"; first, in
the Prosopon (= form of manifestation, figure; not = Hypostasis)
of the Father as Creator and Lawgiver; secondly, in the
Prosopon of the Son as Redeemer, beginning with the incarnation and ending at the ascension; finally, and up till the present
hour, in the Prosopon of the Spirit as giver and sustainer of
life. [3] We do not know whether Sabellius was able strictly to
carry out the idea of the strict succession of the Prosopa, so
that the one should form the boundary of the other. It is

---

[1] Epiph., l. c.: Δογματίζει γὰρ οὗτος καὶ οἱ ἀπ᾽ αὐτοῦ Σαβελλιανοὶ τὸν αὐτὸν
εἶναι πατέρα, τὸν αὐτὸν υἱόν, τὸν αὐτὸν εἶναι ἅγιον πνεῦμα· ὡς εἶναι ἐν μιᾷ ὑποστάσει
τρεῖς ὀνομασίας, ἢ ὡς ἐν ἀνθρώπῳ σῶμα καὶ ψυχὴ καὶ πνεῦμα, Καὶ εἶναι μὲν τὸ
σῶμα ὡς εἰπεῖν τὸν πατέρα, ψυχὴν δὲ ὡς εἰπεῖν τὸν υἱόν, τὸ πνεῦμα δὲ ὡς ἀνθρώπου,
οὕτως καὶ τὸ ἅγιον πνεῦμα ἐν τῇ θεότητι. Ἡ ὡς ἐὰν ᾖ ἐν ἡλίῳ ὄντι μὲν ἐν μιᾷ
ὑποστάσει, τρεῖς δὲ ἔχοντι τὰς ἐνεργείας κ.τ.λ. Method. Conviv. VIII. 10 (ed. Jahn,
p. 37): Σαβέλλιος λέγει τὸν παντοκράτορα πεπονθέναι.

[2] Athanas., de synod. 16; Hilar., de trin. IV. 12.

[3] Epiph. H. 62, c. 1: Πεμφθέντα τὸν υἱὸν καιρῷ ποτέ, ὥσπερ ἀκτῖνα καὶ ἐργα-
σάμενον τὰ πάντα ἐν τῷ κόσμῳ τὰ τῆς οἰκονομίας τῆς εὐαγγελικῆς καὶ σωτηρίας
τῶν ἀνθρώπων, ἀναληφθέντα δὲ αὖθις εἰς οὐρανόν, ὡς ὑπὸ ἡλίου πεμφθεῖσαν ἀκτῖνα,
καὶ πάλιν εἰς τὸν ἥλιον ἀναδραμοῦσαν, Τὸ δὲ ἅγιον πνεῦμα πέμπεσθαι εἰς τὸν κόσμον,
καὶ καθεξῆς καὶ καθ᾽ ἕκαστα εἰς ἕκαστον τῶν καταξιουμένων κ.τ.λ. C. 3 Epiphanius
says: Οὐχ ὁ υἱὸς ἑαυτὸν ἐγέννησεν, οὐδὲ ὁ πατὴρ μεταβέβληται ἀπὸ τοῦ "πατήρ"
τοῦ εἶναι "υἱός" κ.τ.λ.... πατὴρ ἀεὶ πατήρ, καὶ οὐκ ἦν καιρὸς ὅτε οὐκ ἦν πατὴρ
πατήρ.

possible, indeed it is not improbable, that he could not fail to
recognise in nature a continuous energy of God as Father. [1] It
is self-evident that the Sabellians would approve of the Catholic
Canon; that they did, is confirmed by Epiphanius. They are
said to have appealed especially to passages like Deut. VI. 4,
Exod. XX. 3, Isa. XLIV. 6 and John X. 38. [2] But Epiphanius
remarks besides that the Sabellians derived their whole heresy
and its strength from certain Apocrypha, especially the so-called
Gospel of the Egyptians. [3] This note is instructive; for it not
only recalls to our recollection a lost literature of the second
century, especially the Gospel of the Egyptians, [4] but it also
shows that the use of an uncanonical Gospel had long continued
among Catholics in the Pentapolis, or at any rate in Egypt.[5]
Finally, it confirms the view that the Christology of Sabellius
cannot have been essentially different from the older, the so-
called Patripassian doctrine. It is distinguished from the latter
neither by the assumption of a transcendental Monas resting
behind the Prosopa, nor by the introduction of the category of
the Logos—which was made use of by Callistus, but not by
Sabellius; nor by a speculative theory, borrowed from the Stoa,
of the Deity, self-contained, and again unfolding itself; nor,
finally, by a doctrine of the Trinity constructed in any fashion
or by the expression $\upsilon i \sigma \pi \acute{\alpha} \tau \omega \rho$, which, as used by Sabellius, simply
affirmed the single personality of God. As to the doctrine of
the Trinity, a triad was distinctly out of the question in Sabellius. The only noteworthy and real differences are found in
these three points; first, in the attempt to demonstrate the succession of the Prosopa; secondly, as observed above, in the

[1] See Zahn, Marcell., p. 213.

[2] Epiph., l. c., c. 2.

[3] L. c.: Τὴν δὲ πᾶσαν αὐτῶν πλάνην καὶ τὴν τῆς πλάνης αὐτῶν δύναμιν ἔχουσιν
ἐξ Ἀποκρύφων τινῶν, μάλιστα ἀπο τοῦ καλουμένου Αἰγυπτίου εὐαγγελίου, ᾧ τινες
τὸ ὄνομα ἐπέθεντο τοῦτο. Ἐν αὐτῷ γὰρ πολλὰ τοιαῦτα ὡς ἐν παραβύστῳ μυστη-
ριωδῶς ἐκ προσώπου τοῦ σωτῆρος ἀναφέρεται, ὡς αὐτοῦ δηλοῦντος τοῖς μαθηταῖς τὸν
αὐτὸν εἶναι πατέρα, τὸν αὐτὸν εἶναι υἱόν, τὸν αὐτὸν εἶναι ἅγιον πνεῦμα.

[4] In the 2nd Ep. of Clement where it is frequently used, though this is disputed
by some, Modalistic formulas occur.

[5] Clemens Alex. knew it; see Hilgenfeld, Nov. Testam. extra can. recept., 2 ed.,
fasc. 4, p. 42 sq.

reference to the Holy Spirit; thirdly, in formally placing the Father on a parallel line with the two other Prosopa. The attempt mentioned above may be regarded as a return to the strict form of Modalism, which it was possible to hold was impugned by formulas like the *compassus est pater filio* (the Father suffered in sympathy with the Son). In the reference to the Holy Spirit, Sabellius simply followed the new theology, which was beginning to take the Spirit more thoroughly into account. Most important is the third point mentioned. For in ranging the Prosopon and energy of the Father in a series with the two others, not only was cosmology introduced into the Modalistic doctrine as a parallel to soteriology, but the preëminence of the Father over the other Prosopa was departed from in principle, and thus, in a curious fashion, the way was prepared for the Athanasian, and still more for the Western and Augustinian Christology. Here, undoubtedly, we have the decisive advance marked by Sabellianism within Monarchianism. It led up to the exclusive ὁμοούσιος (consubstantial); for it is probable that Sabellians employed this expression.[1] They could apply it with perfect right. Further, while up to this time no evident bond had connected cosmology and soteriology within Modalistic theology, Sabellius now made the histories of the world and salvation into a history of the God who revealed himself in them. In other words, this Monarchianism became commensurate in form with that theology which employed the conception of the Logos, and this fact may have constituted by no means the least part of the attractiveness which Sabellianism proved itself to possess in no small degree up to the beginning of the fourth century and even later.[2] However, it is not to be concealed that the teaching of Sabellius relative to the Prosopon of the Father is particularly obscure. The sentence attributed to him by Athanasius,[3] "as there are diversities of spiritual gifts, but

[1] See above, p. 45.

[2] There were still Sabellians in Neo-Cæsarea in the time of Basilius; Epiphanius knows of them only in Mesopotamia (H. 62 c. 1). The author of the Acta Archelai (c. 37) also became acquainted with them there; he treats them like Valentinians, Marcionites, and followers of Tatian as heretics.

[3] Orat. c. Arian IV. 25: ὥσπερ διαιρέσεις χαρισμάτων εἰσί, τὸ δὲ αὐτὸ πνεῦμα; οὕτω καὶ ὁ πατὴρ ὁ αὐτός μέν ἐστι, πλατύνεται δὲ εἰς υἱὸν καὶ πνεῦμα.

the same spirit, so also the Father is the same, but unfolds
himself in Son and Spirit"—seems at the first glance to contradict the details given above. Yet the different gifts are
certainly the Spirit himself, which so unfolds himself in them
that he does not remain an element behind them, but is completely merged in them. In the same way the Father unfolds himself in the Prosopa. The witnesses to the succession of the
Prosopa in Sabellius are too strong to allow us to infer from this
passage that the Father still remained Father after the unfolding
($\pi\lambda\alpha\tau\upsilon\sigma\mu\acute{o}\varsigma$) in the Son. But this passage shows that philosophical speculations could readily attach themselves to the simple
theory of Sabellius. Marcellus rejected his doctrine which he
knew accurately. What he missed in it was the recognition of
the Logos; therefore the idea of God had also not been correctly
apprehended by him. [1] But the form given to Monarchianism
by Marcellus [2] won few friends for that type of doctrine. Alexandrian theologians, or Western scholars who came to their
assistance, had already perfected the combination of Origen's
doctrine of the Logos with the Monarchian Ὁμοούσιος ; in other
words, they had turned the category used by Origen against
the λόγος κτίσμα conception (the Logos-created) of Origen himself. The saving formula, "the Logos of the same substance,
not made" (λόγος ὁμοούσιος οὐ ποιηθείς), was already uttered, and,
suspiciously like Monarchianism as it sounded at first, became
for that very reason the means of making Monarchianism superfluous in the Church, and of putting an end to it. [3]

But that only happened after great fights. One of these
we know, the controversy of the two Dionysii, a prelude to
the Arian conflict. [4] In the Pentapolis the Sabellian doctrine
had, soon after the death of Origen, won a great following even

[1] Euseb. c. Marcell., p. 76 sq.

[2] See on this Volume IV.

[3] Sabellius seems to have been held a heretic all over the West about A.D. 300;
see the Acta Archelai, Methodius etc.

[4] Hagemann, l.c., p. 411 ff.; Dittrich, Dion. d. Gr. 1867; Förster, in the Ztschr.
f. d. hist. Theol., 1871, p. 42 ff.; Routh, Reliq. S. III., pp. 373—403. The main
source is Athanasius de sentent, Dionysii, a defence of the Bishop, due to the appeal
of the Arians to him; see also Basilius de spiritu, p. 29; Athan. de synod. 43—45.

among the Bishops, "so that the Son of God was no longer
preached." Dionysius of Alexandria, therefore, composed various
letters in which he tried to recall those who had been misled,
and to refute Sabellianism. [1] In one of these, directed to Euphranor and Ammonius, he gave an extreme exposition of Origen's
doctrine of the subordination of the Son. This letter seemed
very questionable to some Christians—probably in Alexandria,
perhaps in Pentapolis. They lodged· a complaint, soon after
A.D. 260, against the Alexandrian Bishop with Dionysius in
Rome. [2] The latter assembled a synod at Rome, which disapproved of the expressions used by the Alexandrian, and himself despatched to Alexandria a didactic letter against the Sabellians and their opponents, who inclined to subordinationism. In
this letter the Bishop so far spared his colleague as not to
mention his name ; but he sent him a letter privately, calling for
explanations. The Alexandrian Bishop sought to justify himself
in a long document in four books (ἔλεγχος καὶ ἀπολογία), maintained
that his accusers had wickedly torn sentences from their context,
and gave explanations which seem to have satisfied the Roman
Bishop, and which Athanasius at any rate admitted to be thoroughly orthodox. But the letter of the Roman Bishop appears
to have had no immediate influence on the further development in
Alexandria (see under); the universal collapse of the Empire in
the following decades permitted the Alexandrian theologians

---

[1] Euseb., H. E. VII. 26. 1: Ἐπὶ ταύταις τοῦ Διονυσίου φέρονται καὶ ἄλλαι
πλείους ἐπιστολαί, ὥσπερ αἱ κατὰ Σαβελλίου πρὸς ᾿Αμμωνα τῆς κατὰ Βερενίκην ἐκκλησίας ἐπίσκοπον, καὶ ἡ πρὸς Τελέσφορον καὶ ἡ πρὸς Εὐφράνορα, καὶ πάλιν ᾿Αμμωνα
καὶ Εὔπορον. Συντάττει δὲ περὶ τῆς αὐτῆς ὑποθέσεως καὶ ἄλλα τέσσαρα συγγράμματα, ἃ τῷ κατὰ ῾Ρώμην ὁμωνύμῳ Διονυσίῳ προσφωνεῖ. Dionysius had already
called the attention of Sixtus II., the predecessor of the Roman Dionysius, to the
revolt in the Pentapolis.

[2] Hagemann maintains that they first turned to the Alexandrian Bishop himself,
and that he wrote an explanatory letter, which, however, did not satisfy them ;
but this cannot be proved (Athanasius de sentent. Dion. 13 is against it). The
standpoint of the accusers appears from their appeal to the Roman Bishop, from
the fact that he made their cause his own, and from the testimony of Athanasius.
who describes them as orthodox Churchmen (de sentent. Dion. 13)—they were
orthodox in the Roman sense. It is entirely wrong, with Dorner (Entwickelungs-
gesch. I., p. 748 f.) and Baur (Lehre v. d. Dreieinigkeit I., p. 313), to identify
the accusers with those heretics, who, according to Dionysius' letter, taught there
were three Gods; for the heretics meant were rather the Alexandrian theologians.

to continue their speculations, without needing to fear further immediate reproofs from Roman Bishops.

Two facts give a special interest to the controversy of the Dionysii. First, in spite of the acceptance of the sacred Triad, the Romans adhered simply, without any speculative harmonising, to the unity of the Deity, and decided that Origen's doctrine of subordination was Tritheism. Secondly, no scruple was felt at Alexandria in carrying out the subordination of the Son to the Father until it involved separation, though it was well known that such a view was supported, not by the tradition of the Church, but by philosophy alone. The accusers of the Alexandrian Dionysius charged him with separating Father and Son;[1] denying the eternal existence of the Son;[2] naming the Father without the Son and *vice versâ;*[3] omitting to use the world ὁμοούσιος;[4] and finally, with regarding the Son as a creature, related to the Father as the vine to the gardener, or the boat to the shipbuilder.[5] In these censures, which were not inaccurate, it is obvious that Dionysius, continuing the Neoplatonic speculations of his teacher, conceived the λόγος as *portio* and *derivatio* of the μονάς, thus, in order to meet Sabellianism, actually dividing him from the deity. Dionysius sought to excuse himself in his ἔλεγχος (Refutation), and emphasised exclusively the other side of Origen's doctrine, at the same time

---

[1] De sententia 10. 16.

[2] De sententia 14: οὐκ ἀεὶ ἦν ὁ Θεὸς πατήρ, οὐκ ἀεὶ ἦν ὁ υἱός, ἀλλ᾿ ὁ μὲν Θεὸς ἦν χωρὶς τοῦ λόγου, αὐτὸς δὲ ὁ υἱὸς οὐκ ἦν πρὶν γενηθῇ, ἀλλ᾿ ἦν ποτὲ ὅτε οὐκ ἦν, οὐ γὰρ ἀΐδιός ἐστιν, ἀλλ᾿ ὕστερον ἐπιγέγονεν.

[3] De sententia 16: πατέρα λέγων Διονύσιος οὐκ ὀνομάζει τὸν υἱόν, καὶ πάλιν υἱὸν λέγων οὐκ ὀνομάζει τὸν πατέρα, ἀλλὰ διαιρεῖ καὶ μακρύνει καὶ μερίζει τὸν υἱὸν ἀπὸ τοῦ πατρός.

[4] L. c. 18: προσφέρουσιν ἔγκλημα κατ᾿ ἐμοῦ ψεῦδος ὂν ὡς οὐ λέγοντος τὸν Χριστὸν ὁμοούσιον εἶναι τῷ Θεῷ.

[5] L. c. 18: πλὴν ἐγὼ γενητά τινα—says Dion. Alex.—καὶ ποιητά τινα φήσας νοεῖσθαι, τῶν μὲν τοιούτων ὡς ἀχρειοτέρων ἐξ ἐπιδρομῆς εἶπον παραδείγματα, ἐπεὶ μήτε τὸ φυτὸν ἔφην (τὸ αὐτὸ εἶναι) τῷ γεωργῷ, μήτε τῷ ναυπηγῷ τὸ σκάφος·— Ἕνα τῶν γενητῶν εἶναι—say the opponents of Dion.—τὸν υἱὸν καὶ μὴ ὁμοούσιον τῷ πατρί. The passage in the letter to Euphranor ran (c. 4): ποίημα καὶ γενητὸν εἶναι τὸν υἱὸν τοῦ Θεοῦ, μήτε δὲ φύσει ἴδιον, ἀλλὰ ξένον κατ᾿ οὐσίαν αὐτὸν εἶναι τοῦ πατρός, ὥσπερ ἐστὶν ὁ γεωργὸς πρὸς τὴν ἄμπελον καὶ ὁ ναυπηγὸς πρὸς τὸ σκάφος. καὶ γὰρ ὡς ποίημα ὢν οὐκ ἦν πρὶν γένηται.

admitting that in his incriminated writing he had incidentally
employed somewhat unsuitable similes.   Now he said that the
Father had always been Father, and that Christ had always
existed as the Logos and wisdom and power of God; that the
Son had his being from the Father, and that he was related
to the Father as the rays are to the light. [1] He explained that
while he had not used the word ὁμοούσιος, because it did not
occur in Holy Scripture, figures were to be found in his earlier
writings which corresponded to it; thus the figure of parents
and children, of seed or root and plant, and of source and
stream. [2]   The Father was the source of all good, the Son the
outflow; the Father the mind (νοῦς), the Son the word (λόγος)—
reminding us very forcibly of Neoplatonism—or the emanating
mind (νοῦς προπηδῶν), while the νοῦς itself remains "and is what
it was" (καὶ ἔστιν οἷος ἦν).   "But being sent he flew forth and
is borne everywhere, and thus each is in each, the one being
of the other, and they are one, being two ' (Ὁ δὲ ἐξέπτη
προπεμφθεὶς καὶ φέρεται πανταχοῦ καί οὕτως ἐστὶν ἑκάτερος ἐν
ἑκατέρῳ ἕτερος ὢν θατέρου, καὶ ἕν εἰσιν, ὄντες δύο). [3]   But he now
went further: any separation between Father and Son was to
be repudiated.   "I say Father, and before I add the Son, I
have already included and designated him in the Father."  The
same holds true of the Holy Spirit.   Their very names always
bind all three together inseparably.   "How then do I who use
these names think that these are divided and entirely separated
from each other? (πῶς οὖν ὁ τούτοις χρώμενος τοῖς ὀνόμασι μεμερ-
ίσθαι ταῦτα καὶ ἀφωρίσθαι παντελῶς ἀλλήλων οἴομαι;). [4]   In these
words the retreat was sounded; for what the Roman Bishop
rejected, but Alexandrian theology never ventured wholly to

[1] L. c. 15.

[2] L. c. 18.

[3] L. c. 23. The expositions of νοῦς and λόγος which were found both in the
2 and 4 books of Dionysius quite remind us of Porphyry: καὶ ἔστιν ὁ μὲν οἷον
πατὴρ ὁ νοῦς τοῦ λόγου, ὢν ἐφ' ἑαυτοῦ, ὁ δὲ καθάπερ υἱὸς ὁ λόγος τοῦ νοῦ. πρὸ
ἐκείνου μὲν ἀδύνατον, ἀλλ' οὐδὲ ἔξωθέν ποθεν, σὺν ἐκείνῳ γενόμενος, βλαστήσας δὲ
ἀπ' αὐτοῦ. οὕτως ὁ πατὴρ ὁ μέγιστος καὶ καθόλου νοῦς πρῶτον τὸν υἱὸν λόγον ἑρμηνέα
καὶ ἄγγελον ἑαυτοῦ ἔχει.

[4] L. c. 17.

discard, was the "dividing" (μερίζεσθαι). [1] The reservation lies
in the word "entirely" (παντελῶς). Dionysius added in conclusion: "Thus we unfold the unit into the triad without
dividing it, and we sum up the triad again into the unit without diminishing it," (οὕτω μὲν ἡμεῖς εἴς τε τὴν τριάδα τὴν μονάδα
πλατύνομεν ἀδιαίρετον, καὶ τὴν τριάδα πάλιν ἀμείωτον εἰς τὴν μονάδα συγκεφαλαιούμεθα). In this he has accommodated himself
to a mode of looking at things which he could only allege to
be his own under a mental reservation, as in the case of the
qualification "entirely" (παντελῶς). For the terms πλατύνειν and
συγκεφαλαιοῦσθαι were not those current in the school of Origen,
and admit of a different interpretation. Finally, Dionysius denied
the charge of the "sycophants" that he made the Father the
*Creator* of Christ. [2]

The letter of Dionysius of Rome falls midway between these
two manifestoes, which are so different, of the Alexandrian Bishop.
We have to regret very deeply that Athanasius has only preserved one, though a comprehensive, fragment of this document. [3]
It is extremely characteristic of the Roman Bishop, to begin
with, that it seeks to settle the sound doctrine by representing
it as the just mean between the false unitarian or Sabellian,
and the false trinitarian or Alexandrian doctrine. [4]   The second

---

[1] We see from the passages quoted by Basilius that Dionysius adhered to the
expression "τρεῖς ὑποστάσεις," but discarded the "μερισμένας εἶναι." while his
accusers must have attacked the former expression also: Εἰ τῷ τρεῖς εἶναι τὰς
ὑπαστάσεις μεμερισμένας εἶναι λέγουσι, τρεῖς εἰσί, κἂν μὴ θέλωσιν ἢ τὴν θείαν τριάδα παντελῶς ἀνελέτωσαν. This accordingly is to be translated: "if they maintain
that a separation is necessarily involved in the expression 'three Hypostases,' yet
there are three—whether they admit it or no—or they must completely destroy the
divine triad."

[2] L.c. 20, 21. It is very noteworthy, that Dionysius has not even brought himself to use the expression ὁμοούσιος in his ἔλεγχος. If he had Athanasius would
have given it in his extracts. For the rest, the attempt of Athanasius to explain
away the doubtful utterances of Dionysius, by referring them to the *human* nature
of Christ, is a makeshift born of perplexity.

[3] De decret. synod. Nic. 26 (see besides de sentent. Dion. 13).

[4] The attack on the latter has alone been preserved by Athanasius along with
the concluding argument; it is thus introduced: Ὅτι δὲ οὐ ποίημα οὐδὲ κτίσμα ὁ
τοῦ Θεοῦ λόγος, ἀλλ' ἴδιον τῆς τοῦ πατρὸς οὐσίας γέννημα ἀδιαίρετόν ἐστιν, ὡς
ἔγραψεν ἡ μεγάλη σύνοδος, ἰδοὺ καὶ ὁ τῆς Ῥώμης ἐπίσκοπος Διονύσιος γράφων κατὰ
τῶν τὰ τοῦ Σαβελλίου φρονούντων, σχετλιάζει κατὰ τῶν ταῦτα τολμώντων λέγειν
καὶ φήσιν οὕτως.

characteristic of the letter is that it regards the Alexandrian
doctrine as teaching that there are three Gods, and draws a parallel
between it and the Three principles of the Marcionites. *This
proves that the Roman Bishop did not trouble himself with the
speculation of the Alexandrians, and simply confined himself to
the result—as he conceived it—of three separate Hypostases.*[1]
Finally—and this is the third characteristic feature—the letter
shows that Dionysius had nothing positive to say, further
than that it was necessary to adhere to the ancient Creed,
definitely interpreting it to mean that the three, Father, Son,
and Spirit, were equally one. Absolutely no attempt is *made
to explain or to prove this paradox.*[2] But here undoubtedly

[1] Ἑξῆς δ᾽ ἂν εἰκότως λέγοιμι καὶ πρὸς τοὺς διαιροῦντας καὶ κατατέμνοντας καὶ
ἀναιροῦντας τὸ σεμνότατον κήρυγμα τῆς ἐκκλησίας τοῦ Θεοῦ, τὴν μοναρχίαν—thus
begins the fragment communicated by Athanasius,—εἰς τρεῖς δυνάμεις τινας καὶ
μεμερισμένας ὑποστάσεις καὶ θεότητας τρεῖς· πέπυσμαι γὰρ εἶναί τινας τῶν παρ᾽ ὑμῖν
κατηχούντων καὶ διδασκόντων τὸν θεῖον λόγον, ταύτης ὑφηγητὰς τῆς φρονήσεως· οἳ
κατὰ διάμετρον, ὡς ἔπος εἰπεῖν, ἀντίκεινται τῇ Σαβελλίου γνώμῃ· ὁ μὲν γὰρ
βλασφημεῖ, αὐτὸν τὸν υἱὸν εἶναι λέγων τόν πατέρα, καὶ ἔμπαλιν· οἱ δὲ τρεῖς θεοὺς
τρόπον τινὰ κηρύττουσιν, εἰς τρεῖς ὑποστάσεις ξένας ἀλλήλων, παντάπασι κε-
χωρισμένας, διαιροῦντες τὴν ἁγίαν μονάδα. ἡνῶσθαι γὰρ ἀνάγκη τῷ Θεῷ τῶν ὅλων
τὸν θεῖον λόγον, ἐμφιλοχωρεῖν δὲ τῷ Θεῷ καὶ ἐνδιαιτᾶσθαι δεῖ τὸ ἅγιον πνεῦμα, ἤδη
καὶ τὴν θείαν τριάδα εἰς ἕνα, ὥσπερ εἰς κορυφήν τινα (τὸν Θεὸν τῶν ὅλων τὸν παντοκράτορα λέγω) συγκεφαλαιοῦσθαί τε καὶ συνάγεσθαι πᾶσα ἀνάγκη. Μαρκίωνος γὰρ τοῦ
ματαιόφρονος δίδαγμα εἰς τρεῖς ἀρχὰς τῆς μοναρχίας τομὴν καὶ διαίρεσιν (διορίζει),
παίδευμα ὂν διαβολικόν, οὐχὶ δὲ τῶν ὄντως μαθητῶν τοῦ Χριστοῦ ... οὗτοι γὰρ τριάδα μὲν κηρυττομένην ὑπὸ τῆς θείας γραφῆς σαφῶς ἐπίστανται, τρεῖς δε θεοὺς οὔτε
παλαιὰν οὔτε καινὴν διαθήκην κηρύττουσαν According to Dionysius, then, some
Alexandrian teachers taught "τρόπον τινά"—this is the only limitation—a form of
Tritheism. The whole effort of the Bishop was to prevent this. We recognise here
the old Roman interest in the unity of God, as represented by Victor, Zephyrine,
and Callistus, but Dionysius may also have remembered, that his predecessors,
Pontian and Fabian, assented to the condemnation of Origen. Should we not
connect the angry reproach, levelled at the Alexandrian teachers, that they were
Tritheists, with the charge made by Callistus against Hippolytus, that he was a
Ditheist; and may we not perhaps conclude that Origen himself was also accused
of Tritheism in Rome?

[2] The positive conclusion runs: Οὔτ᾽ οὖν καταμερίζειν χρὴ εἰς τρεῖς θεότητας τὴν
θαυμαστὴν καὶ θείαν μονάδα, οὔτε ποιήσει κωλύειν τὸ ἀξίωμα καὶ τὸ ὑπέρβαλλον
μέγεθος τοῦ κυρίου· ἀλλὰ πεπιστευκέναι εἰς Θεὸν πατέρα παντοκράτορα καί εἰς Χριστὸν Ἰησοῦν τὸν υἱὸν αὐτοῦ καὶ εἰς τὸ ἅγιον πνεῦμα, ἡνῶσθαι δὲ τῷ Θεῷ τῶν ὅλων
τὸν λόγον· ἐγὼ γάρ, φησί. καὶ ὁ πατὴρ ἕν ἐσμεν. καὶ ἐγὼ ἐν τῷ πατρὶ καὶ ὁ πατὴρ ἐν
ἐμοί—these are the old Monarchian proof-texts—οὕτω γὰρ ἂν καὶ ἡ θεία τριὰς
καὶ τὸ ἅγιον κήρυγμα τῆς μοναρχίας διασώζοιτο. We see that Dionysius simply

lies the strength of the Roman Bishop's position. When we
compare his letter with that of Leo I. to Flavian and Agatho's
to the Emperor, we are astonished at the close affinity of these
Roman manifestoes. In form they are absolutely identical. The
three Popes did not trouble themselves about proofs or arguments, but fixed their attention solely on the consequences, or
what seemed to them consequences, of disputed doctrines.
Starting with these deductions they refuted doctrines of the
right and left, and simply fixed a middle theory, which existed
merely in words, for it was self-contradictory. This they grounded
formally on their ancient Creed without even attempting to argue
out the connection: one God—Father, Son and Spirit; one
Person – perfect God and perfect man; one Person—two wills.
Their contentment with establishing a middle line, which possessed
the attribute of that known in mathematics, is, however, a proof
that they had not a positive, but merely a negative, religious
interest in these speculations. Otherwise they would not have
been satisfied with a definition it was impossible to grasp; for
no religion lives in conceptions which cannot be represented
and realised. Their religious interest centred in the God Jesus,
who had assumed the *substantia humana*.

The letter of the Roman Bishop produced only a passing
impression in Alexandria. Its adoption would have meant the
repudiation of science. A few years afterwards the great Synod
of Antioch expressly rejected the term ὁμοούσιος (consubstantial)

---

places the "holy preaching of the Monarchy" and the "Divine Triad" side by
side: "stat pro ratione voluntas." Between this conclusion and the commencement
of the fragment preserved by Athanasius given in the preceding note, we have a
detailed attack on those who hold the Son to be a ποίημα like other creatures,
"while the Holy Scriptures witness to his having an appropriate birth, but not to
his being formed and created in some way." The attack on the ἦν ὅτε οὐκ ἦν
touches the fundamental position of the Alexandrian scholars as little as the opposition to three Gods; for Dionysius contents himself with arguing that God would
have been without understanding, if the Logos had not always been with him;
a thing which no Alexandrian doubted. The subtle distinction between Logos and
Logos Dionysius leaves wholly out of account, and the explanation of the Roman
Bishop on Proverbs VIII. 32 (κύριος ἔκτισέ με ἀρχὴν ὁδῶν αὐτοῦ): ἔκτισε ἐνταῦθα
ἀκουστέον ἀντὶ τοῦ ἐπέστησε τοῖς ὑπ' αὐτοῦ γεγονόσιν ἔργοις, γεγονόσι δὲ δι' αὐτοῦ
τοῦ υἱοῦ, must merely have caused a compassionate smile among the theologians
of Alexandria.

as being liable to misconstruction. [1] The followers of Origen in
his training school continued their master's work, and they were
not molested in Alexandria itself, as it seems, up till about
the close of the third century, If we review the great literary
labours of Dionysius, of which we, unfortunately, only possess
fragments, and observe his attitude in the questions debated in
the Church in his time, we see how faithfully he followed in
the track of Origen. The only difference lay in greater laxity
in matters of discipline. [2] He proved, in his work " On Promises "
(περὶ ἐπαγγελιῶν), that he possessed the zeal against all Chiliasm
and the dexterity in critical exegesis which characterised the
school of Origen; [3] and in his work "On Nature" (περὶ φύσεως)
he introduced, and endeavoured to carry out, a new task in
the science of Christian theology, viz., the systematic refutation of Materialism, i.e., of the Atomic theory. [4] Of the
later heads of the training school we know very little; but
that little is enough to let us see that they faithfully preserved the
theology of Origen. Pierius, who also led a life of strict asceticism,
wrote learned commentaries and treatises. Photius [5] testifies that
he taught piously concerning the Father and Son, "except that

[1] See above, page 45.

[2] See the letter to Fabius of Antioch, and the attitude of Dionysius in the
Novatian controversy, in which he sought at first to act as mediator precisely as
he did in the dispute over the baptism of heretics (Euseb. H. E. VI. 41, 42,
44—46, VII. 2—9).

[3] See the fragments in Euseb. H. E. VII. 24, 25. The criticism of the Apocalypse is a master-piece.

[4] See Euseb. H. E. VII. 26, 2; the fragments of the work in Routh, Reliq. S. IV.,
p. 393 sq. On this, Roch, die Schrift des Alex. Bischofs, Dionysius d. Gr. über
die Natur (Leipzig 1882) and my account of this dissertation in the Th. L. Z. 1883,
No. 2. Dionysius' work, apart from a few Biblical quotations which do not affect
the arguments, might have been composed by a Neo-platonic philosopher. Very
characteristic is the opening of the first fragment preserved by Eusebius. Πότερον
ἕν ἐστι συναφὲς τὸ πᾶν, ὡς ἡμῖν τε καὶ τοῖς σοφωτάτοις Ἑλλήνων Πλάτωνι καὶ
Πυθαγόρᾳ καὶ τοῖς ἀπὸ τῆς Στοᾶς καὶ Ἡρακλείτῳ φαίνεται; there we have in a
line the whole company of the saints with whom Epicurus and the Atomists were
confronted. We notice that from and after Justin Epicurus and his followers were
extremely abhorred by Christian theologians, and that in this abhorrence they felt
themselves at one with Platonists, Pythagoreans, and Stoics. But Dionysius was the
first Christian to take over from these philosophers the task of a systematic refutation.

[5] Photius Cod. 119.

he speaks of two "beings" and two natures; using the words
being and nature, as is plain from the context, in place of
Hypostasis, and not as those who adhere to Arius" (πλὴν ὅτι
οὐσίας δύο καὶ φύσεις δύο λέγει· τῷ τῆς οὐσίας καὶ φύσεως ὀνόματι,
ὡς δῆλον, ἔκ τε τῶν ἑπομένων καὶ προηγουμένων τοῦ χωρίου ἀντὶ τῆς
ὑποστάσεως καὶ οὐχ ὡς οἱ Ἀρείῳ προσανακείμενοι χρώμενος). This
explanation is hardly trustworthy; Photius himself is compelled
to add that Pierius held impious doctrines as to the Holy Ghost,
and ranked him far below the Father and Son. Now since he
further expressly testifies that Pierius, like Origen, held the pre-
existence of souls, and explained some passages in the O. T.
"economically", i.e., contested their literal meaning, it becomes
obvious that Pierius had not parted company with Origen; [1]
indeed, he was even called "Origen Junior". [2] He was the
teacher of Pamphilus, and the latter inherited from him his unconditional devotion to Origen's theology. Pierius was followed,
in Diocletian's time, by Theognostus at the Alexandrian school.
This scholar composed a great dogmatic work in seven books
called "Hypotyposes". It has been described for us by Photius, [3]
whose account shows that it was planned on a strict system,
and was distinguished from Origen's great work, in that the
whole was not discussed in each part under reference to one
main thought, but the system of doctrine was presented in
a continuous and consecutive exposition. [4] Thus Theognostus

---

[1] Routh, Reliq. S. III., pp. 425—435.

[2] Jerome, de vir. inl. 76; see also Euseb. H. E. VII. 32.

[3] Cod. 106.

[4] The first book dealt with the Father and Creator; the second, with the necessity
that God should have a son, and the Son; the third, took up the Holy Ghost;
the fourth, angels and demons; the fifth and sixth, the possibility and actuality of the
Son's incarnation; the seventh, God's creative work. From the description by Photius
it appears that Theognostus laid the chief stress on the refutation of two opinions,
namely, that matter was eternal, and that the incarnation of the Logos was an
impossibility. *These are, however, the two theses with which the Neo-platonic theologians of the 4th and 5th centuries confronted Christian science*, and in whose assertion
the whole difference between Neo-platonism, and the dogmatic of Alexandrian
churchmen at bottom consisted. It is very instructive to notice that even at the end
of the 3rd century the antithesis thus fixed came clearly to the front. If Theognostus,
for the rest, rejected the opinion that God created all things from a matter equally
eternal with himself, this did not necessarily imply his abandonment of Origen's

invented that form of scientific, Church dogmatic which was to
set a standard to posterity—though it was indeed long before
the Church took courage to erect a doctrinal structure of its
own. Athanasius had nothing but praise for the work of Theognostus, and has quoted a passage from the second book which
undoubtedly proves that Theognostus did full justice to the
Homoousian side of Origen's Christology.[1] But even the Cappadocians remarked certain affinities between Arius and Theognostus,[2] and Photius informs us that he called the Son a
"creature" (κτίσμα), and said such mean things about him that one
might perhaps suppose that he was simply quoting, in order
to refute, the opinions of other men. He also, like Origen,
taught heterodox views as to the Holy Spirit, and the grounds
on which he based the possibility of the incarnation were empty
and worthless. As a matter of fact, Theognostus' exposition of
the sin against the Holy Ghost shows that he attached himself
most closely to Origen. For it is based on the well-known
idea of the master that the Father embraced the largest, the
Son, the medium, and the Holy Spirit the smallest sphere; that
the sphere of the Son included all rational beings, inclusive of
the imperfect, while that of the Spirit comprehended only the perfect

principle of the eternity of matter; yet it is at any rate possible that in this point
he took a more guarded view of the master's doctrine.

[1] The fragment given by Athanasius (de decr. Nic. syn. 25) runs as follows:
Οὐκ ἔξωθέν τις ἐστιν ἐφευρεθεῖσα ἡ τοῦ υἱοῦ οὐσία, οὐδὲ ἐκ μὴ ὄντων ἐπεισήχθη· ἀλλὰ
ἐκ τῆς τοῦ πατρὸς οὐσίας ἔφυ, ὡς τοῦ φωτὸς τὸ ἀπαύγασμα, ὡς ὕδατος ἀτμίς· οὔτε
γὰρ τὸ ἀπαύγασμα οὔτε ἡ ἀτμὶς αὐτὸ τὸ ὕδωρ ἐστὶν ἢ αὐτὸς ὁ ἥλιος, οὔτε ἀλλό-
τριον· καὶ οὔτε αὐτός ἐστιν ὁ πατὴρ οὔτε ἀλλότριος ἀλλὰ ἀπόρροια τῆς τοῦ πατρὸς
οὐσίας, οὐ μερισμὸν ὑπομεινάσης τῆς τοῦ πατρὸς οὐσίας· ὡς γὰρ μένων ὁ ἥλιος ὁ
αὐτὸς οὐ μειοῦται ταῖς ἐκχεομέναις ὑπ' αὐτοῦ αὐγαῖς, οὕτως οὐδὲ ἡ οὐσία τοῦ πατρὸς
ἀλλοίωσιν ὑπέμεινεν, εἰκόνα ἑαυτῆς ἔχουσα τὸν υἱόν. Notice that the μερισμός is here
negatived; but this negative must have been limited by other definitions. At all
events we may perhaps regard Theognostus as midway between Pierius and
Alexander of Alexandria.

[2] See Gregory of Nyssa, c. Eunom. III. in Routh, l.c., p. 412; he proscribes the
proposition of Theognostus: τὸν Θεὸν βουλόμενον τόδε τὸ πᾶν κατασκευάσαι, πρῶτον
τὸν υἱὸν οἶόν τινα κανόνα τῆς δημιουργίας προϋποστήσασθαι. Stephanus Gobarus has
expressly noted it as a scandal that Athanasius should nevertheless have praised
Theognostus (in Photius, Cod. 282). Jerome did not admit him into his catalogue
of authors, and it is remarkable that Eusebius has passed him over in silence; this
may, however, have been accidental.

(τελειούμενοι), and that therefore the sin against the Holy Ghost, as the
sin of the "perfect", could not be forgiven. [1] The only novelty is
that Theognostus saw occasion expressly to attack the view "that
the teaching of the Spirit was superior to that of the Son" (τὴν
τοῦ πνεύματος διδασκαλίαν ὑπερβάλλειν τῆς τοῦ υἱοῦ διδαχῆς). Perhaps he did this to oppose another disciple of Origen, Hieracas,
who applied himself to speculations concerning Melchizedek, as
being the Holy Spirit, and emphasised the worship of the Spirit.[2]
This Copt, who lived at the close of the third and in the first half of
the fourth century, cannot be passed over, because, a scholar
like Origen, [3] he on the one hand modified and refined on certain
doctrines of his master, [4] and on the other hand, emphasised his
practical principles, requiring celibacy as a Christian law. [5]
Hieracas is for us the connecting link between Origen and the

---

[1] See Athanas. Ep. ad Serap. IV., ch. 11; Routh, l.c., pp. 407—422, where the
fragments of Theognostus are collected.

[2] See Epiph. H. 67. 3, 55. 5.

[3] Epiphanius (H. 67) speaks in the highest terms of the knowledge, learning,
and power of memory, possessed by Hieracas.

[4] H. understood the resurrection in a purely spiritual sense, and repudiated the
*restitutio carnis*. He would have nothing to do with a material Paradise; and
Epiphanius indicates other heresies, which H. tried to support by a comprehensive
scriptural proof. The most important point is that he disputed, on the ground
of 2 Tim. II. 5, the salvation of children who died even when baptised; "for
without knowledge no conflict, without conflict no reward." Epiphanius expressly
certifies his orthodoxy in the doctrine of the Trinity; in fact Arius rejected his
Christology along with that of Valentinus, Mani, and Sabellius, in his letter to
Alexander of Alex. (Epiph. H. 69. 7). From his short description of it (οὐδ ὡς
Ἱεράκας λύχνον ἀπὸ λύχνου, ἢ ὡς λαμπάδα εἰς δύο—these are figures already
employed by Tatian) we can only, however, conclude that H. declared the οὐσία of
the Son to be identical with that of the Father. He may have developed Origen's
Christology in the direction of Athanasius.

[5] See my Art. in Herzog's R. E. 2 Aufl. VI., p. 100 f. Hieracas recognised the
essential difference between the O. and N. T. in the commandments as to ἀγνεία,
ἐγκράτεια, and especially, celibacy. "What then did the Logos bring that was new?"
or what is the novelty proclaimed and instituted by the Only-begotten? The fear
of God? The law already contained that. Was it as to marriage? The Scriptures
(= the O. T.) had already dealt with it. Or as to envy, greed, and unrighteous-
ness? All that is already contained in the O. T. "Εν δὲ μόνον τοῦτο κατορθῶσαι
ἦλθε, τὸ τὴν ἐγκράτειαν κηρύξαι ἔν τῷ κόσμῳ καὶ ἑαυτῷ ἀναλέξασθαι ἀγνείαν καὶ
ἐγκράτειαν. Ἄνευ δὲ τούτου μὴ δύνασθαι ζῆν (Epiph. H. 67, ch. 1). He appealed
to 1 Cor. VII., Hebr. XII. 14, Math. XIX. 12, XXV. 21.

Coptic monks; the union of ascetics founded by him may mark
the transition from the learned schools of theologians to the
society of monks. But in his proposition that, as regards practice,
the suppression of the sexual impulse was the decisive, and
original, demand of the Logos Christ, Hieracas set up the great
theme of the Church of the fourth and following century.

In Alexandria the system of faith and the theology of Origen
were fused more and more completely together, and it cannot
be proved that the immediate disciples of Origen, the heads of
the training-school, corrected their master.[1] The first to do this
in Alexandria was Peter, Bishop and Martyr.[2] In his writings
"Concerning divinity" (περὶ θεότητος), "Concerning the sojourn
of our Saviour" (περὶ τῆς σωτῆρος ἡμῶν ἐπιδημίας), and especially
in his books "Concerning (the fact) that the soul does not pre-
exist, nor has entered this body after having sinned" (περὶ τοῦ
μηδὲ προϋπάρχειν τὴν ψυχὴν μηδὲ ἁμαρτήσασαν τοῦτο εἰς σῶμα
βληθῆναι), he maintains against Origen the complete humanity
of the Redeemer, the creation of our souls along with our
bodies, and the historical character of the events narrated in
Gen. III., and he characterises the doctrine of a pre-mundane
fall as a "precept of Greek philosophy which is foreign and alien
to those who desire to live piously in Christ" (μάθημα τῆς Ἑλληνικῆς
Φιλοσοφίας, ξένης καὶ ἀλλοτρίας οὔσης τῶν ἐν Χριστῷ εὐσεβῶς θελόντων
ζῆν).[3] This utterance proves that Peter had taken up a position definitely opposed to Origen;[4] but his own expositions show, on the
other hand, that he only deprived Origen's doctrines of their extreme
conclusions, while otherwise he maintained them, in so far as they
did not come into direct conflict with the rule of faith. The corrections on Origen's system were therefore not undertaken silently

---

[1] Procopius undoubtedly maintains (Comm. in Genes., ch. III., p. 76, in Routh,
Reliq. S. IV., p. 50) that Dionysius Alex., in his commentary on Ecclesiastes, contradicted the allegorical explanation of Gen. II., III; but we do not know in what
the contradiction consisted.

[2] Eusebius, H. E. IX. 6: Peter was made a martyr, probably in A.D. 311.

[3] See the fragments of Peter's writings in Routh, l.c., pp. 21—82, especially
pp. 46—50. Vide also Pitra, Analecta Sacra IV., p. 187 sq., 425 sq.

[4] Decidedly spurious is the fragment of an alleged Μυσταγωγία of Peter, in
which occur the words: τί δὲ εἴπω Ἡρακλᾶν καί Δημήτριον τοὺς μακαρίους ἐπισ-
κόπους, οἵους πειρασμοὺς ὑπέστησαν ὑπὸ τοῦ μανέντος Ὠριγένους, καὶ αὐτοῦ σχίσματα
βαλλόντος ἐν τῇ ἐκκλησίᾳ, τὰ ἕως σήμερον ταραχὰς αὐτῇ ἐγείραντα (Routh, l.c., p. 81).

even in Alexandria. A compromise took place between scientific theology, and the ancient antignostically determined Creed of the Church, or the letter of Holy Scripture, to which all the doctrines of Origen were sacrificed that contradicted the tenor of the sacred tradition. [1] But above all, the distinction made by him between the Christian science of the perfect and the faith of the simple was to be abolished. The former must be curtailed, the latter added to, and thus a product arrived at in a uniform faith which should be at the same time ecclesiastical and scientific. After theology had enjoyed a period of liberty, the four last decades of the third century, a reaction seems to have set in at the beginning of the fourth, or even at the end of the third century, in Alexandria. But the man had not yet risen who was to preserve theology from stagnation, or from being resolved into the ideas of the time. All the categories employed by the theologians of the fourth and fifth centuries were already current in theology, [2] but they had not yet received their definite impress and fixed value. [3] Even the Biblical texts which in those centuries were especially exploited *pro* and *contra*,

---

[1] We have unfortunately no more precise information as to Peter's attitude; we may determine it, however, by that of Methodius (see under).

[2] So μονάς—τριάς—οὐσία—φύσις—ὑποκείμενον—ὑπόστασις—πρόσωπον—περιγραφή—μερίζεσθαι—διαιρεῖν—πλατύνειν—συγκεφαλαιοῦσθαι—κτίζειν—ποιεῖν—γίγνεσθαι γεννᾶν—ὁμοούσιος—ἐκ τῆς οὐσίας τοῦ πατρός—διὰ τοῦ θελήματος—Θεὸς ἐκ Θεοῦ—φῶς ἐκ φωτός—γεννηθέντα οὐ ποιηθέντα—ἦν ὅτε οὐκ ἦν—οὐκ ἦν ὅτε οὐκ ἦν—ἦν ὅτε οὐκ ἦν—ἕτερος κατ᾽ οὐσίαν—ἄτρεπτος—ἀναλλοίωτος—ἀγέννητος—ἀλλότριος—πηγὴ τῆς θεότητος—δύο οὐσίαι—οὐσία οὐσιωμένη—ἐνανθρώπησις—θεάνθρωπος—ἕνωσις οὐσιώδης—ἕνωσις κατὰ μετουσίαν—συνάφεια κατὰ μάθησιν καὶ μετουσίαν—συγκρᾶσις—ἐνοικεῖν etc. Hipler in the Oesterr. Vierteljahrschrift für kathol. Theol. 1869, p. 161 ff. (quoted after Lösche, Ztschr. f. wiss. Theol. 1884, S. 259) maintains that expressions occurred in the speculations of Numenius and Porphyry as to the nature of God, which only emerged in the Church in consequence of the Nicene Council. Those technical terms of religio-philosophical speculation, common to the Neoplatonists of the 3rd century, the Gnostics and Catholic theologians, require reexamination. One result of this will be perhaps the conclusion that the philosophy of Plotinus and Porphyry was not uninfluenced by the Christian system, Gnostic and Origenistic, which they opposed. We await details under this head from Dr. Carl Schmidt.

[3] The meaning which was afterwards attached to the received categories was absolutely unthinkable, and corresponded perfectly to none of the definitions previously hit upon by the philosophical schools. But this only convinced men that Christianity was a revealed doctrine, which was distinguished from philosophical systems by mysterious ideas or categories.

had already been collected in the third. Dionysius of Alexandria had already given warning that the word ὁμοούσιος did not occur in Holy Scripture, and this point of view seems, as a rule, to have been thoroughly decisive even in the third century.[1]

We get an insight into the state of religious doctrine about the middle of the third century and afterwards from the works of Gregory,[2] the miracle-worker, who was one of the most eminent of Origen's disciples, and whose influence in the provinces of Asia Minor extended far into the fourth century. This scholar and Bishop who delivered the first Christian panegyric—one on Origen—and has in it given his autobiography, remained throughout his life an enthusiastic follower of Origen, and adhered, in what was essential, to his doctrine of the Trinity.[3] But Gregory felt compelled, in opposition to Christians whose conception of the Trinity was absolutely polytheistic, to emphasise the unity of the Godhead. He did this in his "Confession of faith",[4] and in a still greater degree, according to the testimony of Basilius, in his lost work διάλεξις πρὸς Ἀιλιανόν (Debate with Ailianus),[5] which contained a proposition, afterwards appealed to by Sabellians, and somewhat to the following effect, viz., Father and Son are two in thought, but one in substance (πατὴρ καὶ υἱὸς ἐπινοίᾳ μέν εἰσι δύο, ὑποστάσει δὲ ἕν). Gregory, on the other hand, described the Logos as creature (κτίσμα)

---

1 But we have not yet ascertained the method followed in the earlier period of collecting the verdicts of the older Fathers, and of presenting them as precedents; yet it is noteworthy that Irenæus and Clement already delighted in appealing to the πρεσβύτεροι, which meant for them, however, citing the Apostles' disciples, and that Paul of Samosata was accused in the epistle of the Synod of Antioch, of despising the ancient interpreters of the Divine Word (Euseb. VII. 30).

2 See Caspari IV., p. 10 ff.; Ryssel, Gregorius Thaumaturgus, 1880. Vide also Overbeck in the Th. L.—Z., 1881, No. 12, and Dräscke in the Jahrb. f. protest. Theol. 1881, H. 2. Edition by Fronto. Ducäus, 1621. Pitra, Analecta Sacra III.; also Loofs, Theol. L. Z., 1884, No. 23.

3 See Caspari's (l.c.) conclusions as to Gregory's confession of faith, whose genuineness seems to me made out. Origen's doctrine of the Trinity appears clearly in the Panegyric. The fragment printed by Ryssel, p. 44 f., is not by Gr. Thaumaturgus.

4 See Caspari, l.c., p. 10: τριὰς τέλεια, δόξῃ καὶ ἀϊδιότητι καὶ βασιλείᾳ μὴ μεριζομένη μηδὲ ἀπαλλοτριουμένη. Οὔτε οὖν κτιστόν τι ἢ δοῦλον ἐν τῇ τριάδι οὔτε ἐπείσακτον, ὡς πρότερον μὲν οὐχ ὕπαρχον, ὕστερον δὲ ἐπεισελθόν· οὔτε γὰρ ἐνέλιπέ ποτε υἱὸς πατρί, οὔτε υἱῷ πνεῦμα, ἄλλ' ἄτρεπτος καὶ ἀναλλοίωτος ἡ αὐτὴ τριὰς ἀεί.

5 Basil., ep. 210.

and created (ποίημα)—so Basilius tells us,—and this form of
expression can probably be explained by the fact that he thought
it necessary, in this way and aggressively (ἀγωνιστικῶς), to emphasise, on the basis of Origen's idea of the Homoousia of the
Son, the substantial unity of the deity, in opposition to a view
of the divine Hypostases which approximated to polytheism.
On the whole, however, we cannot avoid supposing, that at the
time when theology was introduced into the faith—a work
in which Gregory especially took part,—and in consequence
the worst confusions set in,[1] the tendency to heathen Tritheism
had grown, and theologians found themselves compelled to
maintain the "preaching of the monarchy" (κήρυγμα τῆς μοναρχίας)
to an increasing extent. This is proved by the correspondence
of the Dionysii, the theology of Hieracas, and the attitude of
Bishop Alexander of Alexandria; but we have also the evidence
of Gregory. True, the genuineness of the writing ascribed to
him, on the "essential identity"[2] (of the three Persons), is not
yet decided, but it belongs, at all events, to the period before
Athanasius. In this treatise the author seeks to establish the
indivisibility and uniqueness of God, subject to the hypothesis
of a certain hypostatic difference. In this he obviously approaches
Monarchian ideas, yet without falling into them. Further, the
very remarkable tractate, addressed to Theopompus, on the
incapability and capability of suffering,[3] treats this very subject,
without even hinting at a division between Father and Son
in this connection; on the other hand, the author certainly
does not call it in question. We can study in the works of
Gregory, and in the two treatises[4] just mentioned, which bear
his name, the state of theological stagnation, connected with
the indeterminateness of all dogmatic ideas, and the danger,

[1] It remained a matter of doubt in the East up to the beginning of the fourth
century, whether one ought to speak of three Hypostases (essences, natures), or one.

[2] Ryssel, p. 65 f., 100 f.; see Gregor. Naz., Ep. 243, Opp, p. II., p. 196 sq.,
ed. Paris, 1840.

[3] Ryssel, p. 71 f., 118 f. The genuineness of the tractate is not so certain as
its origin in the 3rd century; yet see Loofs, l.c.

[4] See also the *Sermo de incarnatione* attributed to Gregory (Pitra III., p. 144 sq ,
395 sq.)

then imminent, of passing wholly over to the domain of abstract philosophy, and of relaxing the union of speculation with the exegesis of Holy Scripture. The problems are strictly confined to the sphere of Origen's theology; but that theology was so elastic that they threatened to run wild and become thoroughly secular. [1] If, *e.g.*, we review the Christological tenets of Eusebius of Cæsarea, one of Origen's most enthusiastic followers, we are struck by their universal hollowness and emptiness, uncertainty and instability. While Monotheism is maintained with an immense stock of Bible texts and a display of all possible formulas, a created and subordinate God is, in fact, interposed between the deity and mankind.

But there was also in the East a theology which, while it sought to make use of philosophy, at the same time tried to preserve in their realistic form the religious truths established in the fight with Gnosticism. There were theologians who, following in the footsteps of Irenæus and Hippolytus, by no means despised science, yet found the highest truth expressed in the tenets handed down by the Church; and who therefore, refusing the claim of philosophical Gnosis to re-edit the principles of faith, only permitted it to support, connect, and interpret them. These theologians were necessarily hostile to the science of religion cultivated in Alexandria, and enemies of its founder Origen. We do not know whether, during his life-time, Origen came into conflict in the East with opponents who met him in the spirit of an Irenæus. [2] From his own statements we must suppose that he only had to deal with untrained disputants.

---

[1] Origen himself always possessed in his unconditional adherence to the Bible a kind of corrective against the danger of passing entirely over to philosophy. Though thoroughly versed in philosophical science, he sought never to be more than a scriptural theologian, and urged his disciples—witness his letter to Gregor. Thaum.—to give up their philosophical studies, and devote themselves wholly to the Bible. No professedly philosophical expositions occur in Origen himself, so far as I know, like those transmitted by his disciples. For the latter the comprehensive chapter of Eusebius (H. E. VII. 32) is very instructive. Here we meet with Bishops who seem to have been scholars first and clerics afterwards. This Eusebius (§ 22) has to tell of one: λόγων μὲν φιλοσόφων καὶ τῆς ἄλλης παρ᾽ Ἕλλησι παιδείας παρὰ τοῖς πολλοῖς θαυμασθείς, οὐχ ὁμοίως γε μὴν περὶ τὴν θείαν πίστιν διατεθειμένος.

[2] It is unknown who was the καλλίων ἡμῶν πρεσβύτης καὶ μακαριστὸς ἀνὴρ quoted by Epiph. (H. 64, ch. 8 and 67) as an opponent of Origen.

But in the second half of the third century, and at the beginning of the fourth, there were on the side of the Church antagonists of Origen's theology who were well versed in philosophical knowledge, and who not merely trumped his doctrine
with their ψιλὴ πίστις (bare faith), but protected the principles
transmitted by the Church from spiritualising and artificial interpretations, with all the weapons of science. [1]  The most important among them, indeed really the only one of whom we have
any very precise knowledge, besides Peter of Alexandria
(see above), is Methodius. [2] But of the great number of treatises
by this original and prolific author only one has been till now
preserved complete in the original—Conviv. decem virg., while
we have the greater part of a second—De resurr. [3]  The rest

[1] Besides these we have Eastern theologians, who, while they did not write
against Origen, show no signs in their works of having been influenced by Alexandrian theology, but rather resemble in their attitude Irenæus and Hippolytus
Here we have especially to mention the author of five dialogues against the Gnostics,
which, under the title " De recta in deum fide," bear the name of Adamantius ; see
the editio princeps by Wetstein, 1673, and the version of Rufinus discovered by Caspari
(Kirchenhistorische Anecdota, 1883; also Th. L.—Z. 1884, No. 8) which shows
that the Greek text is interpolated. The author, for whom we have perhaps to look
in the circle of Methodius, has at any rate borrowed not a little from him (and
also from the work of Theophilus against Marcion?). See Jahn, Methodii, Opp. I.,
p. 99, II. Nos. 474, 542, 733—749, 771, 777. Möller in Herzog's R. E., 2 Ed.,
IX., p. 725. Zahn, Ztschr. f. Kirchengesch., Vol. IX., p. 193 ff.: " Die Dialoge des
Adamantius mit den Gnostikern." The dialogues were written ± 300, probably
somewhere in East Asia Minor, or in West Syria, according to Zahn about 300
—313 in Hellenic Syria, or Antioch. They are skilfully written and instructive ; a
very moderate use is made of philosophical theology. Perhaps the Ep. ad Diogn. also
came from the circle of Methodius. Again, there is little philosophical theology to
be discovered in the original edition of the first six books of the apostolic Constitutions, which belongs to the third century. See Lagarde in Bunsen's Analecta
Ante-Nicæna T. II. The author still occupied the standpoint of Ignatius, or the old
anti-gnostic teachers. The dogmatic theology, in the longer recension of the work,
preserved in Greek, belongs entirely to the reviser who lived in or after the middle
of the 4th century (so App. Const. II. 24, VI. 11, 14, 41 [Hahn, Biblioth. der
Symbole, 2 Aufl., §§ 10, 11, 64] ; see my edition of the Διδαχὴ, p. 241 ff.  That
Aphraates and the author of the Acta Archelai were unaffected by Origen's theology
will have been clear from what was said above, p. 50 f.

[2] Jahn, S. Methodii Opp., 1865 ; Pars II. S. Methodius Platonizans, 1865 ;
Bonwetsch, M. von Olympus I. 1891. Vide also Pitra, Analecta Sacra T. III., IV.
(see Loofs, Th. L.—Z., 1884, No. 23, col. 556 ff.). Möhler, Patrologie, pp. 680—
700. Möller, l.c., p. 724 ff. Salmon Dict. of Christian Biogr. III. p. 909 sq.

[3] Besides smaller fragments are found, increased by Pitra.

has been preserved in the Slavic language, and only very lately
been rendered accessible. The personality of Methodius himself,
with his position in history, is obscure. [1] But what we do know
is enough to show that he was able to combine the defence of
the Rule of Faith as understood by Irenæus, Hippolytus, and
Tertullian, [2] with the most thorough study of Plato's writings
and the reverent appropriation of Plato's ideas. Indeed he lived
in these. [3] Accordingly, he defended " the popular conception of
the common faith of the Church" in an energetic counterblast
to Origen, and rejected all his doctrines which contained an
artificial version of traditional principles. [4] But on the other hand,
he did not repudiate the basis on which Origen's speculation
rested. He rather attempted with its presuppositions and method
to arrive at a result in harmony with the common faith.
There seems to be no doubt that he took the great work of
Irenæus as his model; for the manner in which Methodius has
endeavoured to overcome dualism and spiritualism, and to
establish a *speculative realism*, recalls strikingly the undertaking
of Irenæus. Like the latter, Methodius sought to demonstrate
the eternal importance of the natural constitution in spirit and
body of the creatures made by God; and he conceived salvation
not as a disembodying, not in any sense as a division and
separation, but as a transfiguration of the corporeal, and a union
of what had been unnaturally divided. He rejected the pessimism with which Origen had, like the Gnostics, viewed the world
as it is, the σύστασις τοῦ κόσμου, making it, if a well-ordered
and necessary prison, yet a prison after all. This he confronted
with the optimistic conviction, that everything which God has
created, and as he has created it, is capable of permanence and

[1] See Zahn, Ztschr. f. Kirchengesch. Vol. VIII., p. 15 ff. Place : Olympus in Lycia.

[2] He was ranked in later times with Irenæus and Hippolytus (see Andreas Cæs.
in præf. in Apoc., p. 2) and that as a witness to the inspiration of John's Apocalypse.

[3] See Jahn, l.c.

[4] See the long fragments of the writing *de resurrectione* which was directed
against Origen, as also the work περὶ τῶν γενητῶν. Methodius called Origen a
"Centaur" (Opp. I. 100, 101), *i.e.*, "Sophist," and compared his doctrine with the
Hydra (I. 86). See the violent attack on the new-fashioned exegetes and teachers
in De resurr. 8, 9 (Opp I. 67 sq.) and 20, (p. 74), where the ὀστᾶ νοητὰ and σάρκας
νοητάς of Origen's school are ridiculed ; ch. 21, p. 75 ; 39, p. 83.

transfiguration. ¹ Accordingly, he opposed Origen's doctrines of
the pre-existence of souls, the nature and object of the world
and of corporeality, the eternal duration of the world, a pre-
mundane Fall, the resurrection as a destruction of the body, etc.
At the same time he certainly misrepresented them, as, *e.g.*,
Origen's doctrine of sin, p. 68 sq. Like Irenæus, Methodius
introduced curious speculations as to Adam for the purpose
of establishing realism, *i.e.*, the maintenance of the literal truth
of sacred history. Adam was to him the whole of natural
humanity, and he assumed, going beyond Irenæus, that the
Logos combined the first man created (protoplast) with himself. ²

¹ See the short argument against Origen, De resurr. 28, p. 78: Εἰ γὰρ κρεῖττον
τὸ μὴ εἶναι τοῦ εἶναι τὸν κόσμον, διὰ τί τὸ χεῖρον ᾑρεῖτο ποιήσας τὸν κόσμον ὁ
Θεός; ἀλλ᾽ οὐδὲν ὁ Θεὸς ματαίως ἢ χεῖρον ἐποίει. οὐκοῦν εἰς τὸ εἶναι καὶ μένειν τὴν
κτίσιν ὁ Θεὸς διεκοσμήσατο. Wisdom I. 14 and Rom. VIII. 19 follow. The fight waged
by Methodius against Origen presents itself as a continuation of that conducted by
Irenæus against the Gnostics. It dealt in part with the same problems, and used
the same arguments and proofs. The extent to which Origen hellenised the Christian
tradition was in the end as little tolerated in the Church as the latitude taken by
the Gnostics. But while Gnosticism was completely ejected in two or three generations it took much longer to get rid of Origenism. Therefore, still more of Origen's theology passed into the "revealed" system of Church doctrine, than of the
theology of the Gnostics.

² See Conviv. III. 6 (p. 18 sq.): ταύτῃ γὰρ τὸν ἄνθρωπον ἀνείληφεν ὁ λόγος,
ὅπως δὴ δι᾽ αὐτοῦ καταλύσῃ τὴν ἐπ᾽ ὀλέθρῳ γεγονυῖαν καταδίκην, ἡττήσας τὸν ὄφιν.
ἥρμοζε γὰρ μὴ δι᾽ ἑτέρου νικηθῆναι τὸν πονηρὸν ἀλλὰ δι᾽ ἐκείνου, ὃν δὴ καὶ ἐκόμ-
παζεν ἀπατήσας αὐτὸν τετυραννηκέναι, ὅτι μὴ ἄλλως τὴν ἁμαρτίαν λυθῆναι καὶ τὴν
κατάκρισιν δυνατὸν ἦν, εἰ μὴ πάλιν ὁ αὐτὸς ἐκεῖνος ἄνθρωπος, δι᾽ ὃν εἴρητο τὸ "γῆ
εἶ καὶ εἰς γῆν ἀπελεύσῃ," ἀναπλασθεὶς ἀνέλυσε τὴν ἀπόφασιν τὴν δι᾽ αὐτὸν εἰς
πάντας ἐξενηνεγμένην. ὅπως, καθὼς ἐν τῷ Ἀδὰμ πρότερον πάντες ἀποθνήσκουσιν,
οὕτω δὴ πάλιν καὶ ἐν τῷ ἀνειληφότι Χριστῷ τὸν Ἀδὰμ πάντες ζωοποιηθῶσιν. Still
clearer is III. 4, where it is expressly denied that Adam is only a type of Christ:
φέρε γὰρ ἡμεῖς ἐπισκεψώμεθα πῶς ὀρθοδόξως ἀνήγαγε τὸν Ἀδὰμ εἰς τὸν Χριστόν,
οὐ μόνον τύπον αὐτὸν ἡγούμενος εἶναι καὶ εἰκόνα, ἀλλὰ καὶ αὐτὸ τοῦτο Χριστὸν καὶ
αὐτὸν γεγονέναι διὰ τὸ τὸν πρὸ αἰώνων εἰς αὐτὸν ἐγκατασκῆψαι λόγον. ἥρμοζε γὰρ
τὸ πρωτόγονον τοῦ Θεοῦ καὶ πρῶτον βλάστημα καὶ μονογενὲς τὴν σοφίαν τῷ πρωτο-
πλάστῳ καὶ πρώτῳ καὶ πρωτογόνῳ τῶν ἀνθρώπων ἀνθρώπῳ κερασθεῖσαν ἐνηνθρωπηκέναι,
τοῦτο γὰρ εἶναι τὸν Χριστόν, ἄνθρωπον ἐν ἀκράτῳ θεότητι καὶ τελείᾳ πεπληρωμένον
καὶ Θεὸν ἐν ἀνθρώπῳ κεχωρημένον· ἦν γὰρ πρεπωδέστατον τὸν πρεσβύτατον τῶν
αἰώνων καὶ πρῶτον τῶν ἀρχαγγέλων, ἀνθρώποις μέλλοντα συνομιλεῖν, εἰς τὸν πρεσβύτατον καὶ πρῶτον τῶν ἀνθρώπων εἰσοικισθῆναι τὸν Ἀδάμ. See also III. 7 8: προ-
γεγυμνάσθαι γὰρ... ὡς ἄρα ὁ πρωτόπλαστος οἰκείως εἰς αὐτὸν ἀναφέρεσθαι δύναται τὸν
Χριστόν, οὐκέτι τύπος ὢν καὶ ἀπείκασμα μόνον καὶ εἰκὼν τοῦ μονογενοῦς, ἀλλὰ καὶ αὐτὸ
τοῦτο σοφία γεγονὼς καὶ λόγος. δίκην γὰρ ὕδατος συγκερασθεὶς ὁ ἄνθρωπος τῇ σοφίᾳ
καὶ τῇ ζωῇ τοῦτο γέγονεν, ὅπερ ἦν αὐτὸ τὸ εἰς αὐτὸν ἐγκατασκῆψαν ἄκρατον φῶς

This union was conceived as a complete incorporation: "God embraced and comprehended in man;" and, starting from this incorporation, the attempt was made to explain redemption in terms of a mystical realism. Salvation was not consummated in knowledge (Gnosis), but it came to light, already achieved for mankind, in the constitution of the God-man.[1] But for this very reason Methodius borders, just like Irenæus, on a mode of thought which sees in the incarnation the necessary completion of creation, and conceives the imperfection of the first Adam to have been natural.[2] Adam, i.e., mankind, was before Christ still in a plastic condition, capable of receiving any impression and liable to dissolution. Sin, which had exclusively an external source, had therefore an easy task; humanity was first consolidated in Christ. In this way freedom is retained, but we easily see that Origen's idea of sin was more profound than that of Methodius.[3] The fantastic realism of the latter's view is carried out in his speculations on the transference of salvation from

[1] Yet see, under, the new turn given to the speculation.

[2] S. Conviv. III. 5: ἔτι γὰρ πηλουργούμενον τὸν Ἀδάμ, ὡς ἔστιν εἰπεῖν, καὶ τηκτὸν ὄντα ταὶ ὑδαρῆ, καὶ μηδέπω φθάσαντα δίκην ὀστράκου τῇ ἀφθαρσίᾳ κραταιωθῆναι καὶ παγιωθῆναι, ὕδωρ ὥσπερ καταλειβομένη καὶ καπαστάζουσα διέλυσεν αὐτὸ ἡ ἁμαρτία. διὸ δὴ πάλιν ἄνωθεν ἀναδεύων καὶ πηλοπλαστῶν τὸν αὐτὸν εἰς τιμὴν ὁ Θεός ἐν τῇ παρθενικῇ κραταιώσας πρῶτον καὶ πήξας μήτρᾳ καὶ συνενώσας καὶ συγκεράσας τῷ λογῳ, ἄτηκτον καὶ ἄθραυστον ἐξήγαγεν εἰς τὸν βίον, ἵνα μὴ πάλιν τοῖς τῆς φθορᾶς ἔξωθεν ἐπικλυσθεὶς ῥεύμασιν, τηκεδόνα γεννήσας διαπέσῃ. Methodius, like Irenæus, gave much study to Paul's Epistles, because they were especially quoted by Origen and his school (see ch. 51 fin., p. 90); on the difficulties which he felt see De resurr. 26, p. 77; 38, p. 83.

[3] The expositions of concupiscence, sin, and death, are distinguished very strongly from those of Origen. (For death as means of salvation see De resurr. 23, 49). They resemble the discussions of Irenæus, only Methodius maintains—a sign of the times—that sinlessness is impossible even to the Christian. See De resurr. 22 (I., p. 75): ζῶντος γὰρ ἔτι τοῦ σώματος πρὸ τοῦ τεθνήξεσθαι συζῆν ἀνάγκη καὶ τὴν ἁμαρτίαν, ἔνδον τὰς ῥίζας αὐτῆς ἐν ἡμῖν ἀποκρύπτουσαν, εἰ καὶ ἔξωθεν τομαῖς ταῖς ἀπὸ τῶν σωφρονισμῶν καὶ τῶν νουθετήσεων ἀνεστέλλετο, ἐπεὶ οὐκ ἂν μετὰ τὸ φωτισθῆναι συνέβαινεν ἀδικεῖν, ἅτε παντάπασιν εἰλικρινῶς ἀφῃρημένης ἀφ᾽ ἡμῶν τῆς ἁμαρτίας· νῦν δὲ καὶ μετὰ τὸ πιστεῦσαι καὶ ἐπὶ τὸ ὕδωρ ἐλθεῖν τοῦ ἁγνισμοῦ πολλάκις ἐν ἁμαρτίαις ὄντες εὑρισκόμεθα· οὐδεὶς γὰρ οὕτως ἁμαρτίας ἐκτὸς εἶναι ἑαυτὸν καυχήσεται, ὡς μηδὲ κἂν ἐνθυμηθῆναι τὸ σύνολον ὅλως τὴν ἀδικίαν. To this conception corresponds the view of Methodius that Christianity is a cultus of mysteries, in which consecration is unceasingly bestowed on the τελειούμενοι. Methodius also referred Rom. VII. 18 f. to those born again.

Christ to individuals. The deep sleep of the Protoplast is paralleled in the second Adam by the sleep of death. Now as Eve
was formed from, and was part of the being of sleeping Adam,
so the Holy Spirit issued from Christ lying in the sleep of death,
and was part of his being;[1] and from him the Church was
fashioned. " The Apostle has excellently applied the history of
" Adam to Christ. So we will require to say with him that the
" Church is of the bone and flesh of Christ, since for her sake
" the Logos left the Heavenly Father, and came down that he
" might cleave to his spouse; and he fell asleep unconscious
" of suffering, dying voluntarily for her, that he might present
" the Church to himself glorious and faultless, after he had purified
" her by the bath; so that she might receive the spiritual and
" blessed seed, which he himself, instilling and implanting, scatters
" into the depths of the Spirit, whom the Church receives and,
" fashioning, develops like a spouse, that she may bear and
" rear virtue. For in this way the word is also excellently ful-
" filled 'Grow and increase'; since the Church increases daily
" in greatness, beauty, and extent; because the Logos dwells
" with her, and holds communion with her, and he even now
" descends to us, and in remembrance (Anamnesis) of his suffering
" (continually) dies to himself. For not otherwise could the
" Church continually conceive believers in her womb, and bear
" them anew through the bath of regeneration, unless Christ
" were repeatedly to die, emptying himself for the sake of each
" individual, in order to find acceptance by means of his sufferings
" continuing and completing themselves; unless, descending from
" heaven, and united with his spouse, the Church, he imparted
" from his own side a certain power, that all who are edified
" in him should attain growth, those, namely, who, born again
" through baptism, have received flesh of his flesh, bone of his

---

1 The allegory receives another version Opp. I., p. 119: μή πως ἄρα αἱ τρεῖς
αὗται τῶν προγόνων κεφαλαὶ πάσης τῆς ἀνθρωπότητος ὁμοούσιοι ὑποστάσεις κατ'
εἰκόνα τινά, ὡς καὶ Μεθοδίῳ δοκεῖ—the passage occurs in Anastasius Sin. ap. Mai,
Script. Vet. N. Coll. IX. p. 619—τυπικῶς γεγόνασι τῆς ἁγίας καὶ ὁμοουσίου τριάδος, τοῦ μὲν ἀναιτίου καὶ ἀγεννήτου 'Αδὰμ τύπον καὶ εἰκόνα ἔχοντος τοῦ ἀναιτίου
καὶ πάντων αἰτίου παντοκράτορος Θεοῦ καὶ πατρός, τοῦ δὲ γεννητοῦ υἱοῦ αὐτοῦ
εἰκόνα προδιαγράφοντος τοῦ γεννητοῦ υἱοῦ καὶ λόγου τοῦ Θεοῦ, τῆς δὲ ἐκπορευτῆς
Εὕας σημαινούσης τὴν τοῦ ἁγίου πνεύματος ἐκπορευτὴν ὑπόστασιν.

"bone, *i.e*,, of his holiness and glory.  He, however, who calls
"bone and flesh wisdom and virtue, speaks truly; but the side
"is the Spirit of truth, the Paraclete, from whom the enlightened
"receiving their portion are born again, in a worthy manner, to
"immortality.  But no one can participate in the Holy Spirit,
"and be accounted a member of Christ, unless the Logos has
"first descended upon him, and, falling asleep, has 'emptied'
"himself, that he, rising again and rejuvenated, along with him
"who fell asleep for his sake, and re-fashioned in his own
"person, may participate in the Holy Spirit.  For the side ($\pi\lambda\varepsilon\nu\rho\alpha$)
"of the Logos is really the spirit of truth, the seven-formed
"of the prophet, from whom God, in accordance with the self-
"sacrifice of Christ, that is, the incarnation and suffering of Christ,
"takes away something, and fashions for him his spouse, in
"other words, souls fit for him and prepared like a bride." [1]
Methodius accordingly, starts in his speculations from Adam and
Eve as the real types of Christ and the Church; but he then
varies this, holding that the individual soul rather must become
the bride of Christ, and that for each the descent of the Logos
from heaven and his death must be repeated—mysteriously and
in the heart of the believer.

This variation became, and precisely through the instrumentality
of Methodius, of eminent importance in the history of dogma.[2]
We would not have had in the third century all the premises
from which Catholic Christianity was developed in the following
centuries, unless this speculation had been brought forward, or,
been given a central place, by a Christian theologian of the
earlier period.  *It marks nothing less than the tapering of the*
*realistic doctrinal system of the Church into the subjectivity of*
*monkish mysticism.*  For to Methodius, the history of the Logos-
Christ, as maintained by faith, was only the general background
of an inner history, which required to repeat itself in each believer: the Logos had to descend from heaven, suffer, die, and

[1]  Conviv. III. 8.

[2]  It was not altogether absent in earlier times, and on this see ch. V. § 2.  As
we have remarked above, individualism in this extreme form occurs also in Origen;
see, *e.g.*, "De orat." 17.: "He who has perceived the beauty of the bride whom
the Son of God loves as bridegroom, namely, the soul."

rise again for him.  Nay, Methodius already formulated his view
to the effect that *every believer must, through participation in
Christ, be born as a Christ.*[1]  The background was, however,
not a matter of indifference, seeing that what took place in the
individual must have first taken place in the Church.  *The Church,
accordingly, was to be revered as mother, by the individual
soul which was to become the bride of Christ.*  In a word : here
we have the theological speculation of the future monachism
*of the Church*, and we see why it could not but pair with the
loftiest obedience, and greatest devotion to the Church.

But the evidence that we have really here the fundamental
features of the monkish mysticism of the Church, is contained
in the correct perception of the final object of the work from
which the above details are taken.  The whole writing seeks to
represent the state of virginity as the condition of Christlikeness
(I. 5, p. 13).  Everything is directed to this end ; yet marriage
is not forbidden, but is admitted to possess a mystery of its
own.  Unstained virginity is ranked high above the married
state; towards it all Christians must strive; it is the perfectly
Christian life itself.  Yet Methodius succeeds in maintaining,
beside it, marriage and sin-stained birth from the flesh (II. 1 sq.).
He had already arrived at the position of Catholic monasticism;
the body belonging to the soul that would be the bride of
Christ must remain virgin.  The proper result of the work of
Christ is represented in the state of virginity of the believers
who still walk upon earth, and it is the bloom of imperishableness : "Exceedingly great and wonderful and glorious is virginity,
"and to speak plainly, following Holy Scripture, this most noble

---

[1] Conviv. VIII. 8: Ἐγὼ γὰρ τὸν ἄρσενα (Apoc. XII. 1 f.) ταύτῃ γεννᾶν εἰρῆ-
σθαι νομίζω τὴν ἐκκλησίαν, ἐπειδὴ τοὺς χαρακτῆρας καὶ τὴν ἐκτύπωσιν καὶ τὴν
ἀρρενωπίαν τοῦ Χριστοῦ προσλαμβάνουσιν οἱ φωτιζόμενοι, τῆς καθ᾽ ὁμοίωσιν μορφῆς
ἐν αὐτοῖς ἐκτυπουμένης τοῦ λόγου καὶ ἐν αὐτοῖς γεννωμένης κατὰ τὴν ἀκριβῆ γνῶσιν
καὶ πίστιν ὥστε ἐν ἑκάστῳ γεννᾶσθαι τὸν Χριστὸν νοητῶς· καὶ διὰ τοῦτο ἡ ἐκκλησία
σπαργᾷ καὶ ὠδίνει, μέχριπερ ἂν ὁ Χριστὸς ἐν ἡμῖν μορφωθῇ γεννηθείς, ὅπως ἕκαστος
τῶν ἁγίων τῷ μετέχειν Χριστοῦ Χριστος γεννηθῇ, καθ᾽ ὃν λόγον καὶ ἕν τινι γραφῇ
φέρεται " μὴ ἅψησθε τῶν Χριστῶν μου " οἱονεὶ Χριστῶν γεγονότων τῶν κατὰ μετουσίαν τοῦ πνεύματος εἰς Χριστὸν βεβαπτισμένων, συμβαλλούσης ἐνταῦθα τὴν ἐν τῷ
λόγῳ τράνωσιν αὐτῶν καὶ μεταμόρφωσιν τῆς ἐκκλησίας.  Even Tertullian teaches
(De pud. 22) that the martyr who does what Christ did, and lives in Christ, is
Christ.

"and fair practice is alone the ripe result, the flower and first
"fruits of incorruption, and therefore the Lord promises to admit
"those who have preserved their virginity into the kingdom of
"heaven ... for we must understand that virginity, while walking
"upon the earth, reaches the heavens" : μεγάλη τίς ἐστιν ὑπερφυῶς
καὶ θαυμαστὴ καὶ ἔνδοξος ἡ παρθενία, καὶ εἰ χρὴ φανερῶς εἰπεῖν
ἑπομένην ταῖς ἁγίαις γραφαῖς, τὸ οὖλαρ τῆς ἀφθαρσίας καὶ τὸ ἄνθος
καὶ ἡ ἀπαρχὴ αὐτῆς τοῦτο τὸ ἄριστον καὶ κάλλιστον ἐπιτήδευμα
μόνον τυγχάνει, καὶ δία ταῦτα καὶ ὁ κύριος εἰς τὴν βασιλείαν εἰσε-
λάσαι τῶν οὐρανῶν τοὺς ἀποπαρθενεύσαντας σφᾶς αὐτοὺς ἐπαγγελ-
λεται ..., παρθενίαν γὰρ βαίνειν μὲν ἐπὶ γῆς, ἐπιψαύειν δὲ τῶν
οὐρανῶν ἡγητέον (Conv. I. 1, p. 11).

Methodius started from other premises than the school of
Origen, and bitterly opposed the latter, but in the end he came
to the same practical result—witness the followers of Hieracas.
Their speculations also led to the depreciation of the objective
redemption, and to monachism. But the concrete forms were
very different. In Origen himself and his earliest disciples the
Church was by no means really the mother, or, if it were, it
was in a wholly different sense from that of Methodius. Asceticism and in particular virginity were not in themselves valuable,
an end in themselves, but means to the end. Finally, Gnosis
(knowledge) was different from Pistis (faith), and the ideal was
the perfect Gnostic, who is freed from all that is alien and
fleeting, and lives in the eternal and abiding. Methodius' teaching
was different. Pistis and Gnosis were related to each other as
theme and exposition: there is only one truth, which is the
same for all; but on the soil of the Church there is room for
the state of virginity, *which is the goal of the incarnation*, though
all may not yet reach it. The important and momentous
achievement of Methodius [1] consisted in subordinating a realistic
Church theology, which yet was not destitute of a speculative
phase, and even made a moderate use of the allegorical method,

---

[1] The theology of Methodius was in the Eastern Church, like Tertullian's in
the West, a prophecy of the future. His method of combining tradition and
speculation was not quite attained even by the Cappadocians in the 4th century.
Men like Cyril of Alexandria were the first to resemble him. *In Methodius we
have already the final stage of Greek theology.*

to the practical object of securing virginity, a life in which God
and Christ were imitated, (Conv. I. 5, p. 13: to imitate God
is to escape from corruption [ὁμοίωσις Θεῷ φθορᾶς ἀποφυγή];
Christ is not only arch-shepherd and arch-prophet [ἀρχιποιμήν-
ἀρχιπροφήτης], but also archetypal virgin [ἀρχιπαρθένος]). This
doctrine, as well as the practical attitude of Hieracas, and many
other features, as, *e.g.*, the considerably earlier Pseudo-Clementine
epistles "De virginitate," [1] prove that the great aspiration of
the time in the East was towards monachism, and Methodius
succeeded in uniting this with a Church theology. In spite of his
polemic against Origen he did not despise those phases of the
latter's theology, which were at all compatible with the traditional
comprehension of religious doctrine. Thus he accepted the
doctrine of the Logos implicitly in the form given to it by
Origen's school, without, of course, entangling himself in the
disputed terminology (see, *e.g.*, De creat. 11, p. 102); so far as
I know, he made no express defence of Chiliasm, in spite of the
high value he put on the Apocalypse. He is even said by
Socrates (H. E. VI. 13) to have admired Origen, in one of his
latest writings, "a sort of recantation" (ὡς ἐκ παλινῳδίας). However that may be, the future belonged not to Origen, nor to
the scientific religion that soared above faith, but to compromises,
such as those, stamped with monachism, which Methodius
concluded, to the combination of realistic and speculative elements,
of the objectivity of the Church and the mysticism of the
monks. [2] The great fight in the next decades was undoubtedly
to be fought out between two forms of the doctrine of the
Logos; the one, that of Lucian the martyr and his school,
which had adopted elements distinctive of Adoptianism, and the
other, professed by Alexander of Alexandria and the Western
theologians, which with Sabellianism held fast the unity of the
divine nature. But, in the case of the majority of Eastern

[1] See Funk, Patr. App. Opp. II., pp. 1—27, and Harnack, Sitzungsberichte d.
Preuss. Akad. d. Wissensch. 1891, p. 361 ff.

[2] On the authority of Methodius in later times, see the Testimonia Veterum in
Jahn, l. c. I., p. 6 sq. The defence of Origen against Methodius by Pamphilus and
Eusebius has unfortunately been preserved only to a very small extent. See Routh,
Reliq. S. IV., p. 339 sq.

Christians in the 4th century, the background or basis of these opposite views was formed, not by a theology purely Origenist, but by one of compromise, which had resulted from a combination of the former with the popular idea of the rules of faith, and which sought its goal, not in an absolute knowledge and the calm confidence of the pious sage, but in virginity, ecclesiasticism, and a mystical deification. Men like Methodius became of the highest consequence in the development of this theological genus, which, indeed, could not but gain the upper hand more and more, from the elemental force of factors existent in the Church.[1]

But while as regards Origen's theology reservations may have gradually grown stronger and more numerous in the course of the next decades, theological speculation aimed in the East, from about 250—320, at a result than which nothing grander or more assured could be imagined. In the West the old, short, Creed was retained, and, except in one case,[2] the Christological conflicts did not induce men to change it. *But in the leading Churches of the East, and during the given period, the Creeds were expanded by theological additions,*[3] *and thus exegetical and speculative theology was introduced into the Apostolic faith itself.*[4] Thus, in the Catholic Churches of the East, this

[1] It is instructive to notice how Athanasius has silently and calmly shelved those doctrines of Origen which did not harmonise with the wording of the rule of faith, or allegorised facts whose artificial interpretation had ceased to be tolerated.

[2] See above, p. 75.

[3] It is possible, and indeed probable, that Creeds were then set up for the first time in many Churches. The history of the rise of Creeds—further than the Baptismal formula—in the East is wholly obscure. Of course there always were detailed Christological formulas, but the question is whether they were inserted into the Baptismal formula.

[4] It has been already pointed out on p. 48, note 1, that the Biblical character of some of those additions cannot be used against their being regarded as theological and philosophical formulas. The theology of Origen—witness his letter to Gregory—was throughout exegetical and speculative; therefore the reception of certain Biblical predicates of Christ into the Creeds meant a desire to legitimise the speculation which clung to them as Apostolic. The Churches, however, by setting up theological Creeds only repeated a development in which they had been anticipated about 120 years before by the "Gnostics." The latter had theologically worked out Creeds as early as in the second century. Tertullian, it is true, says of the Valentinians (adv. Valent. I.) "*communem fidem affirmant,*" *i.e.*, they adapt

theology was for ever fused with the faith itself. A striking
example has been already quoted; those six Bishops who
wrote against Paul of Samosata in the seventh decade of the
third century, submitted a Rule of Faith, which had been elaborated philosophically and theologically, as the faith handed down

themselves to the common faith; but he himself relates (De carne, 20; see Iren. I. 7, 2)
that they preferred "διὰ Μαρίας" to "ἐκ Μαρίας"; in other words, of these two
prepositions, which were still used without question even in Justin's time, they, on
theological grounds, admitted only the one. So also they said "Resurrection from
the dead" instead of "of the body." Irenæus as well as Tertullian has spoken of
the "blasphemous" *regulæ* of the Gnostics and Marcionites which were always
being changed (Iren. I. 21 5, lII. 11 3, I. 31 3; II præf.; II. 19 8, III. 16, 1, 5;
Tertull., De præscr. 42; Adv. Valent. 4; Adv. Marc. I. 1, IV. 5, IV. 17). We can
still partly reconstruct these "Rules" from the Philosoph. and the Syntagma of
Hippolytus (see esp. the *regula* of Apelles in Epiphan. H. XLIV. 2). They have
*mutatis mutandis* the most striking similarity to the oriental confessions of faith
published since the end of the third century; compare, *e.g.*, the Creed, given under,
of Gregorius Thaumaturgus with the Gnostic rules of faith which Hippolytus had
before him in the Philosoph. There is, further, a striking affinity between them in
the fact that the ancient Gnostics already appealed in support of their *regulæ* to
secret tradition, be it of one of the Apostles or all, yet without renouncing the
attestation of these rules by Holy Scripture through the spiritual (pneumatic) method
of Exegesis. Precisely the same thing took place in the Eastern Churches of the
next age. For the tenor and phrasing of the new Creeds which seemed to be
necessary, the appeal to Holy Scripture was even here insufficient, and it was
necessary to resort to special revelations, as in the case alluded to, p. 115, note 3,
or to a παράδοσις ἄγραφος of the Church. That the new theology and Christology
had found their way into the psalms sung in the Church, can be seen from the
Synodal document on Paul of Samosata (Euseb. VII. 30, 11), where it is said of
the Bishop: ψαλμοὺς τοὺς μὲν εἰς τὸν κύριον ἡμῶν Ἰ. Χρ. παύσας ὡς δὴ νεωτέρους
καὶ νεωτέρων ἀνδρῶν συγγράμματα; *i.e.*, Paul set aside those Church songs which
contained the philosophical or Alexandrian christology. In this respect also the
Church followed the Gnostics: compare in the period immediately following, the
songs of Arius, on the one hand, and the orthodox hymns on the other; for we
know of Marcionite, Valentinian, and Bardesanian psalms and hymns. (See the close
of the Muratorian Fragment, further my investigations in the Ztschr. f. wissensch.
Theol., 1876, p. 109 ff.; Tertull., De Carne Chr. 17 ; Hippol., Philos. VI. 37; the
psalms of Bardesanes in Ephraim ; the Gnostic hymns in the Acts of John and
Thomas, in the Pistis Sophiæ, etc.). It is self-evident that these psalms contained
the characteristic theology of the Gnostics; this also appears from the fragments
that have been preserved, and is very clearly confirmed by Tertullian, who says of
Alexander the Valentinian (l. c.): "*sed remisso Alexandro cum suis syllogismis, etiam
cum Psalmis Valentini, quos magna impudentia, quasi idonei alicuius auctoris
interserit.*" The scholastic form of the Church was more and more complete in
the East in the second half of the third century, after one school, that of the
Alexandrian Catechists, had finally succeeded in partly insinuating its teaching into

in the holy Catholic Church. from the Apostles [1] But we possess numerous other proofs. Gregory of Nyssa tells us that from the days of Gregory Thaumaturgus till his own, the Creed of the latter formed the foundation of the instruction given to catechumens in Neo-Cæsarea. But this Creed [2] was neither more nor less than a compendium of Origen's theology, [3] which, here,

the Church. Where Valentine Basilides, etc., had absolutely failed, and Bardesanes partly succeeded, the School of Origen had been almost entirely successful. It is very characteristic that the ecclesiastical parties which opposed each other in the third century applied the term "school" (διδασκαλεῖον) as an opprobrious epithet to their antagonists. This term was meant to signify a communion which rested on a merely human, instead of a revealed doctrine. But the Church nearly approximated, in respect of doctrine, to the form of the philosophic schools, at the moment when her powerful organisation destroyed every analogy with them, and when the possession of the two Testaments marked her off definitely from them. Much might be said on "schola" and "ecclesia"; a good beginning has been made by Lange, Haus und Halle, 1885, p. 288 ff. See also v. Wilamowitz-Möllendorff, "Die rechtliche Stellung der Philosophenschulen," 1881.

[1] See also the document in Eusebius, H. E. VIII. 30, 6, where it is said of Paul: ἀποστὰς τοῦ κανόνος ἐπὶ κίβδηλα καὶ νόθα διδάγματα μετελήλυθεν.

[2] Caspari, l. c. IV., p. 10. 27. Hahn, § 114.

[3] It runs: Εἷς Θεός, πατὴρ λόγου ζῶντος, σοφίας ὑφεστώσης καὶ δυνάμεως καὶ χαρακτῆρος ἀϊδίου, τέλειος τελείου γεννήτωρ, πατὴρ υἱοῦ μονογενοῦς, Εἷς κύριος, μόνος ἐκ μόνου, Θεὸς ἐκ Θεοῦ, χαρακτὴρ καὶ εἰκων τῆς θεότητος, λόγος ἐνεργός, σοφία τῆς τῶν ὅλων συστάσεως περιεκτικὴ καὶ δύναμις τῆς ὅλης κτίσεως ποιητική, υἱὸς ἀληθινὸς ἀληθινοῦ πατρός, ἀόρατος ἀοράτου καὶ ἄφθαρτος ἀφθάρτου καὶ ἀθάνατος ἀθανάτου καὶ ἀΐδιος ἀϊδίου. Καὶ ἓν πνεῦμα ἅγιον, ἐκ Θεοῦ τὴν ὕπαρξιν ἔχον καὶ δι' υἱοῦ πεφηνὸς [δηλαδὴ τοῖς ἀνθρώποις], εἰκὼν τοῦ υἱοῦ, τελείου τελεία, ζωὴ ζώντων αἰτία, [πηγὴ ἁγία] ἁγιότης ἁγιασμοῦ χορηγός, ἐν ᾧ φανεροῦται Θεὸς ὁ πατὴρ ὁ ἐπὶ πάντων καὶ ἐν πᾶσι, καὶ Θεὸς ὁ υἱὸς ὁ διὰ πάντων-τριὰς τελεία, δόξῃ καὶ ἀϊδιότητι καὶ βασιλείᾳ μὴ μεριζομένη μηδὲ ἀπαλλοτριουμένη. Οὔτε οὖν κτιστόν τι ἢ δοῦλον ἐν τῇ τριάδι, οὔτε ἐπείσακτον, ὡς πρότερον μὲν οὐχ ὑπάρχον, ὕστερον δὲ ἐπεισελθόν· οὔτε γὰρ ἐνέλιπέ ποτε υἱὸς πατρί οὔτε υἱῷ πνεῦμα, ἀλλ' ἄτρεπτος καὶ ἀναλλοίωτος ἡ αὐτὴ τριὰς ἀεί. It ought to be distinctly noticed that the genuineness of this Creed is, in spite of Caspari's brilliant defence, not raised above all doubt. But the external and internal evidence in support of its authenticity seem to me overwhelming. According to Gregory of Nyssa it was said to have been revealed to Gregory Thaumaturgus immediately before entering on his Bishopric, by the Virgin Mary and the Apostle John. If this legend is old, and there is nothing to show it is not, then we may regard it as proving that this confession of faith could only be introduced into the Church by the use of extraordinary means. The abstract, unbiblical character of the Creed is noteworthy; it is admirably suited to a follower of Origen like Gregory; but it is less suited to a post-Nicene Bishop. Origen himself would hardly have approved of so unbiblical a Creed. It points to a time in which there was imminent danger of theological speculation relaxing its connection with the Books of Revelation.

was thus introduced into the faith and instruction of the
Church. Further, it is clear from the letter of Alexander of
Alexandria to Alexander of Constantinople, that the Church of
Alexandria possessed at that time a Creed which had been
elaborated theologically. [1] After the Bishop has quoted extensive
portions of it, which he describes as "the whole pious Apostolic
doctrine" (πᾶσα ἡ ἀποστολικὴ εὐσεβὴς δόξα), he closes with the
words "these things we teach and preach, that is the Apostolic
dogmas of the Church" (ταῦτα διδάσκομεν, ταῦτα κηρύττομεν,
ταῦτα τῆς ἐκκλησίας τὰ ἀποστολικὰ δόγματα). But these dogmas
belong to Origen's theology. Finally, we perceive from the
Nicene transactions, that many Churches then possessed Creeds,
which contained the Biblical theological formulas of Origen.
We may assert this decidedly of the Churches of Cæsarea,
Jerusalem, and Antioch. [2] The entire undertaking of the Fathers

[1] See Theodoret, H. E. I. 4; Hahn, l. c., § 65: Πιστεύομεν, ὡς τῇ ἀποστολικῇ
ἐκκλησίᾳ δοκεῖ, εἰς μόνον ἀγέννητον πατέρα, οὐδένα τοῦ εἶναι αὐτῷ τὸν αἴτιον
ἔχοντα... καὶ εἰς ἕνα κύριον Ἰησοῦν Χριστόν, τὸν υἱὸν τοῦ Θεοῦ τὸν μονογενῆ, γεννηθέντα οὐκ ἐκ τοῦ μὴ ὄντος, ἀλλ' ἐκ τοῦ ὄντος πατρός... πρὸς δὲ τῇ εὐσεβεῖ ταύτῃ
περὶ πατρὸς καὶ υἱοῦ δόξῃ, καθὼς ἡμᾶς αἱ θεῖαι γραφαὶ διδάσκουσιν, ἓν πνεῦμα ἅγιον
ὁμολογοῦμεν, τὸ καινίσαν τούς τε τῆς παλαιᾶς διαθήκης ἁγίους ἀνθρώπους καὶ τοὺς
τῆς χριματιζούσης καινῆς παιδευτὰς θείους. μίαν καὶ μόνην καθολικήν, τὴν ἀποστολικὴν ἐκκλησίαν, ἀκαθαίρετον μὴν ἀεί, κἂν πᾶς ὁ κόσμος αὐτῇ πολεμεῖν βουλεύηται...
Μετὰ τούτων τὴν ἐκ νεκρῶν ἀνάστασιν οἴδαμεν, ἧς ἀπαρχὴ γέγονεν ὁ κύριος ἡμῶν
Ἰ. Χρ., σῶμα φορέσας ἀληθῶς καὶ οὐ δοκήσει ἐκ τῆς θεοτόκου (one of the earliest
passages, of which we are certain, for this expression; yet it was probably already
used in the middle of the third century; a treatise was also written περὶ τῆς θεοτόκου by Pierius) Μαρίας, ἐπὶ συντελείᾳ τῶν αἰώνων, εἰς ἀθέτησιν ἁμαρτίας ἐ πιδημήσας
τῷ γένει τῶν ἀνθρώπων, σταυρωθεὶς καὶ ἀποθανών, ἀλλ' οὐ διὰ ταῦτα τῆς ἑαυτοῦ
θεότητος ἥττων γεγενημένος, ἀναστὰς ἐκ νεκρῶν, ἀναλημφθεὶς ἐν οὐρανοῖς, καθήμενος
ἐν δεξιᾷ τῆς μεγαλωσύνης.

[2] The Cæsarean Creed in Athanasius, Socrates, Theodoret and Gelasius, see
Hahn, § 116 and Hort, Two Dissertations, pp. 138, 139. It runs: Πιστεύομεν εἰς
ἕνα Θεὸν πατέρα παντοκράτορα, τὸν τῶν ἁπάντων ὁρατῶν τε καὶ ἀοράτων ποιητήν.
Καὶ εἰς ἕνα κύριον Ἰ Χρ., τὸν τοῦ Θεοῦ λόγον, Θεὸν ἐκ Θεοῦ, φῶς ἐκ φωτός, ζωὴν
ἐκ ζωῆς, υἱὸν μονογενῆ, πρωτότοκον πάσης κτίσεως, πρὸ πάντων τῶν αἰώνων ἐκ τοῦ
πατρὸς γεγεννημένον, δι' οὗ καὶ ἐγένετο τὰ πάντα· τὸν διὰ τὴν ἡμετέραν σωτηρίαν
σαρκωθέντα καὶ ἐν ἀνθρώποις πολιτευσάμενον, καὶ παθόντα, καὶ ἀναστάντα τῇ τρίτῃ
ἡμέρᾳ, καὶ ἀνελθόντα πρὸς τὸν πατέρα, καὶ ἥξοντα πάλιν ἐν δόξῃ κρῖναι ζῶντας καὶ
νεκρούς. Καὶ εἰς πνεῦμα ἅγιον. This Creed is also remarkable from its markedly
theological character. On the Creeds of Antioch and Jerusalem, which are at any
rate earlier then A.D. 325. see Hort, (l.c. 73) and Hahn, § 63. We cannot appeal,
as regards the phrasing, to the so-called Creed of Lucian (Hahn, § 115). Yet it is
extremely probable that it is based on a Creed by Lucian.

of the Nicene Council to set up a theological Creed to be observed by the whole Church, would have been impossible, had
not the Churches, or at least the chief Churches, of the East
already been accustomed to such Symbols. These Churches
had thus passed, in the generations immediately preceding
the Nicene, through a Creed-forming period, to which little
attention has hitherto been paid. In its beginning and its
course it is wholly obscure, *but it laid the foundation for
the development of theological dogmatics, peculiar to the
Church, in the fourth and fifth centuries.* It laid the foundation
—for the following epoch was distinguished from this one by
the fact that the precise definitions demanded by the doctrine
of redemption, as contained within the frame-work of Origen's
theology, were fixed and made exclusive. Thus the dangers
were guarded against, which rose out of the circumstance, that
the philosophical theory of God, and the idea of the Logos
which belonged to it, had been received into the system of
religion, *i.e.*, the Neo-platonic method and circle of ideas had
been legitimised, without the traditional tenets of the faith having
been sufficiently protected against them. In the new Creeds of
the period 260—325 we find the conditions to hand for a system
of religion based on the philosophical doctrine of God, a system
specifically belonging to the Church, completely expressed in
fixed and technical terms, and scientific. We find the conditions ready—but nothing more, or less. But it was also due to
the Creeds that in after times every controversy of the schools
necessarily became a conflict that moved and shook the Church
to its very depths. The men, however, who in the fourth and
fifth centuries made orthodox dogma, were undoubtedly influenced,
to a greater degree than their predecessors of from A.D. 260—
315, by specifically Church ideas; and their work, if we measure
it by the mixture of ideas and methods which they received
from tradition, was eminently a conservative *reduction* and
securing of tradition, so far as that was still in their possession.
It was really a new thing, a first step of immeasurable
significance, when Athanasius staked his whole life on the recognition of a single attribute—*the consubstantiality*—of Christ,
and rejected all others as being liable to pagan misinterpretation.

At the beginning of the fourth century, Rules of Faith and theology were differently related to each other in the Churches of the East and West. In the latter, the phraseology of the primitive Creed was strictly adhered to, and a simple antignostic interpretation was thought sufficient, by means of formulas like "Father, Son, and Spirit: *one God*"—"Jesus Christ, God and man "—"Jesus Christ, the Logos, wisdom, and power of God "— In the former, theological formulas were admitted into the Confession of Faith itself, which was thus shaped into a theological compendium ostensibly coming from the Apostles. But in both cases, the personal reality, and, with it, the pre-existence of the divinity manifested in Christ, were recognised by the vast majority;[1] they were included in the instruction given to Catechumens; they furnished the point of view from which men sought to understand the Person of Christ. And, accordingly, the accurate definition of the relation of the Deity to that other divine nature which appeared on earth necessarily became the chief problem of the future.

[1] See the interesting passage in Eusebius' letter to his Church, in which he (sophistically) so defends the rejection of the οὐκ ἦν πρὸ τοῦ γεννηθῆναι, as to fall back upon the universally recognised pre-existence of Christ (Theodoret, H. E. I. 12).

# DIVISION II.

## THE DEVELOPMENT OF THE DOGMA OF THE CHURCH.

---

## BOOK I.

### THE HISTORY OF THE DEVELOPMENT OF DOGMA AS THE DOCTRINE OF THE GOD-MAN ON THE BASIS OF NATURAL THEOLOGY.

Τὰ κρατούμενα τῷ λόγῳ τῆς φύσεως οὐκ ἔχει ἔπαινον,
τὰ δὲ σχέσει φιλίας κρατούμενα ὑπεραινεῖται.

PAUL OF SAMOSATA.

Ohne Autorität kann der Mensch nicht existiren,
und doch bringt sie ebensoviel Irrthum als
Wahrheit mit sich; sie verewigt im Einzelnen.
was einzeln vorübergehen sollte, lehnt ab und
lässt vorübergehen, was festgehalten werden
sollte, und ist hauptsächlich Ursache dass die
Menschheit nicht vom Flecke kommt.

# BOOK I.

## THE HISTORY OF THE DEVELOPMENT OF DOGMA AS THE DOCTRINE OF THE GOD-MAN ON THE BASIS OF NATURAL THEOLOGY.

### CHAPTER I.

#### HISTORICAL SITUATION. [1]

THE first main division of the history of dogma closed with the adoption of the Logos doctrine as the central dogma of the Church, and with the accompanying revision in the East of the old formulas of the faith under the influence of philosophical theology. The testament of primitive Christianity—the Holy Scriptures—and the testament of Antiquity—Neoplatonic speculation—were intimately and, as it seemed, inseparably connected in the great Churches of the East. The system of doctrine established by the Church in the third century corresponded to the Church whose structure appeared complete in the same period. As the political powers of the Roman Empire were conserved in the Catholic Church, so also were the spiritual forces of Antiquity in its faith. Both required to be invested with divine lustre in order to live through storms and amid universal ruin. [2] But Christianity was by no means completely Hellenised in Catholicism; that is proved, if we needed proof, by the attacks of

[1] Walch, Entw. einer vollst. Historie der Ketzereien, 1762 ff. Hefele, Koncilien-gesch., 2 Bd. I.—IV. Histories of the Roman Empire by Tillemont, Gibbon, Richter und Ranke (Weltgesch., Bd. IV. und V.). Réville, Die Religion z. Rom unter den Severern (German translation by Krüger, 1888). V. Schultze, Gesch. des Unter-gangs des griechisch-römischen Heidenthums, 2 Bde., 1887 f. Boissier, La fin du paganisme, 2 Bde. 1891. Dorner, Entw.-Gesch. d. L. v. d. Person Christi, II., 1853. H. Schultz, Die L. v. d. Gottheit Christi, 1881. Gass, Symbolik d. griech. Kirche, 1872. Kattenbusch, Lehrbuch d. vergleichenden Konfessionskunde. 1 Bd., 1890. Denzinger, Ritus Orientalium, 2 Bde. 1863 f.

[2] Tiele, Kompendium der Relig. Gesch. (German transl.), p. 283: "the Catholic Church is the secular Roman rule, modified and consecrated by Christian ideas."

Porphyry and Julian. Undoubtedly all the institutions and ideas felt to be necessary were included in the "Apostolic tradition" to an increasing extent. But since a place had been given in that tradition to the O. T. and the written memorials of primitive Christianity, these really furnished aids to the comprehension of the Gospel, which had certainly been obscured in the "*Gnosis*" as well as in the "*New Law*". The theology of Origen, in spite of some very earnest attacks upon it, was held in the East to be the pattern and the inexhaustible source of the theology of the Church, so far as a scientific system was desired. Even its opponents, like Methodius, could not escape its influence. From its rich store of formulas were more fully elaborated, in opposition to what was called Ebionitism and Sabellianism, those confessions which were employed in the cultus and instruction of the Church, and which, thus enriched, were then invested with some sort of Apostolic authority. [1] The West did not go so far; yet it was perfectly defenceless against the "advances" made by the Church in the Eastern half of the Empire; for certain theological and Christological conceptions to which it also clung, made any counter-movement impossible, though many teachers, preachers, and apologists went ways of their own, and in their doctrines of Christ and salvation mixed up obsolete Christian traditions with the popular philosophy of the West. Looking to theological metaphysics as wrapped up in the official formulas of the Church, the difference was finally only one of degree. It showed itself among those less interested and scholarly, who were therefore conservative in their instincts and looked with distrust on the theology of Origen; they thought with perfect simplicity that their own formulas: "Father, Son, and Spirit; one God", "Christ, the Logos, wisdom, and power of God", "*duæ substantiæ, una persona*", "Jesus Christ, God and man", constituted the "faith" which needed no explanation. The element of speculative philosophy was as a rule weak in the system of religion of the West. In place of it, the West of Tertullian possessed a series of juristic "plans" which were destined to have a great future.

In spite of many far-reaching differences in their practical and

[1] See above, p. 47 ff., 113 ff.

theoretical interests, in spite of the development in ecclesiastical affairs, Christians in East and West felt that they belonged to one united Church. The Novatian and Samosatian controversies ultimately resulted in strengthening the consciousness of unity,[1] even though a not altogether insignificant part of Christendom cast itself adrift. These controversies showed plainly that the Western and Eastern communities held substantially the same position in the world, and that both required to use the same means to maintain it. Communities everywhere adopted the character of the Church of the world. Their union preserved all the features of a political society, and, at the same time, of a disciplinary institution, equipped with sacred sanctions and dreadful punishments, in which individual independence was lost. [2] Of course, in proportion as this confederacy of Christians adapted itself to civic, national, and political relationships, in order to maintain and strengthen itself, the integrity of the Church was most gravely imperilled, when these very relationships lost their last shreds of unity in the collapse of the Empire. Above all, the great cleavage between the Eastern and Western halves of the Empire could not fail to be prejudicial to the Church. But about the close of the third century the latter, in spite of discontent in its midst, held more firmly together than the Empire, and its unity was still maintained after the fourth century by great Emperors and influential theologians. [3]

In addition to the episcopal constitution, uniformly and strictly carried out, the common basis of the Churches was due to the recognition of the same authorities and designs, the uniform appreciation of sacramental rites, and the strong tendency to asceticism for the sake of a future life. It was, at first, too stable for the different forces which threatened to shatter the Empire, and also, in consequence, beat upon the Imperial Church. But this basis was nevertheless insufficient. It can be easily shown that the elements composing it were as incapable ot

---

[1] See on this the correspondence between the oriental Bishops and Julius of Rome; Socr., H. E., II. 15; Ep. Julii ap Athan., Apolog. c. Arian, ch. 21 sq.

[2] See Vol. II., p. 122 f.

[3] Reuter, Augustinische Studien, in the Zeitschr. f. K.-Gesch. V., p. 349 ff., VI., p. 155 ff., 190.

guaranteeing the unity, as of protecting the Christianity, of the
Church, through a prolonged period.

Among the authorities the two Testaments, combined by the
evidence of prophecy and allegorical explanation, took the first,
indeed, strictly speaking, a unique place. But not only was their
extent not absolutely decided, but their interpretation was wholly
uncertain. In addition to this, the scope to be left to the "Apostolic tradition", *i.e.*, the illusion of "antiquity", and to the decision
of episcopal synods, was by no means defined; for the sufficiency
of Holy Scripture was placed, theoretically, beyond doubt.
But where elementary wants, felt by the great majority, were
to be satisfied, where a reassuring sanction was required for the
advancing secularisation, men did not rack their brains, if no
inconvenient monitors were in the way, to find precedents
in Holy Scripture for what was novel. They went right back
to the Apostles, and deduced from secret traditions what no
tradition ever possessed. Huge spheres of ecclesiastical activity
embracing new and extensive institutions—the reception of national customs and of the practices of heathen sects—were in
this way placed under "Apostolic" sanction, without any
controversy starting worth mention. This is true, *e.g.*, of the
ritual of worship and ecclesiastical discipline, "The sacred
canons" or "the apostolic canons" constituted from the close of
the third century, a court of appeal, which practically held the
same rank as the sacred writings, and which, especially in the
East, cast its protection to an increasing extent over national
customs and traditional morals in the face of attacks of every
kind. It is obvious that authorities so obtained were likely, in
the end, to divide the Churches of the different nations.

The crudest superstition was thus consecrated by "apostolic"
decrees, or legitimised, after the event, from the O. T.,[1] and
from the middle of the third century it ascended from the lower
strata of Christians to the upper, which had lost all spiritual
stability. And now in the fourth century, when Church and
State were fused into one, everything was assigned to the former
which had ever, or anywhere been regarded as venerable or
holy. As it had submitted to the Church, it demanded indulgent

[1] See my Edition of the Διδαχή, Prolegg. pp. 222 ff., 239 ff.

treatment. The religion of pure reason and of the strictest morality, the Christianity which the ancient apologists had once portrayed, had long changed into a religion of the most powerful rites, of mysterious means, and an external sanctity. The historical tradition of Christ and the founding of Christianity was turned into a romance, and this historical romance, which was interwoven with the religion, constantly received new chapters. The stream of the history of salvation ended in a waste swamp of countless and confused sacred tales, and in its course took in heathen fictions and the stories of gods and heroes. Every traditional holy rite became the centre of new sacred ceremonies, and every falling off in morality was covered by increasing the religious apparatus. The idea of forgiveness of sins was to many a cloak for frivolity and wickedness. Up to the middle of the third century, every Catholic Christian was, in all probability, a genuine monotheist. That can no longer be said of the generations who afterwards pressed into the Church. Polytheism had lost its name, indeed, but not its influence in the Church of the fourth century. Great masses preserved, in spite of their baptism, the piety to which they had been accustomed. Christian priests had to respect and adjust superstition, in order to keep the leadership in their hands, and theologians had no difficulty in finding, in the O. T. and in many views and usages of Christian antiquity, means of justifying what was most novel, alien, and absurd. Miracles were of everyday occurrence, and they were barbarous and detestable miracles, directed to meet the meanest instincts, and offensive to even moderately clear heads. [1] The Christian religion threatened to become a new

[1] Compare the criticism by Julian and his friends of the Christian religion and the worship paid to saints and relics, or read the writings in which Sulpicius Severus attempts to recommend Christianity to the refined society of Aquitania. We can study in the works of the historians Socrates and Sozomen the attitude of cultured Catholic Christians, after the complete triumph of the Church over paganism. Even Sozomen cannot be regarded as having reached the stage of the "dry tree," and yet into what a superstition the Christian faith is transformed in his pages! We see how paganism thrust itself into worship, in—to quote a well-known instance—August. Confess. VI. 2 ff. Let us, above all, remember that from the beginning of the fourth century special chapels and churches were built to the different saints. The saints took the place of the local deities; their festivals of the old provincial services of the gods. We have just begun to investigate the

paganism;[1] while, at the same time, making shipwreck of its
own unity and common character. For even if priests and
theologians were always to be in a position to keep the reins
in their hands, dissolution threatened the one undivided Church
which girt the Empire, if the local rites, customs, usages of
men were consecrated as Christian in every province, and might
establish themselves without any decided counterpoise.

But where was such a counterpoise to be found? In the
constitution? That was indeed a firm structure, binding Christendom
strongly together; but even it presented sides on which the
centrifugal forces, destructive of unity, found entrance. Love of
rule and ambition were encouraged by the episcopal chair. And
when the danger of dismemberment into independent bishoprics
was met by a rigid metropolitan leadership, the way was opened
up to that lofty ambition which desired the first place and the
highest influence in the province, and which sought to domineer
over the civil powers and to master neighbouring provinces.
The Patriarchs and Metropolitans who—to use an expression of

transformation of heathen tales of gods and heroes into legends of the saints, and
ancient light literature has contributed its quota in works of travel and adventure
by land and sea. These researches promise, if instituted critically and soberly, to
give interesting results; yet I doubt if the state of our materials will admit of
confident conclusions. Besides the worship of the saints, the cultus of the Emperor
threatened in the fourth century to intrude itself into the Church. Philostorgius
relates (H. E. II. 17) that Christians presented offerings to the picture of Constantine,
and honoured it with lanterns and incense; they also seem to have offered *vota*
to him that they might be protected from calamities.

[1] Besides the worship of saints, martyrs, and relics, we have to notice the new
forms of faith in demons. It would be impossible to believe more sincerely in
demons than Christians did in the second century. But that age was yet ignorant
of the fantastic tricks with them, which almost turned Christendom into a society
of deceived deceivers. (The expression was first applied to Christians by Plotinus:
see Vita Plot. by Porphyrius 16: ἐξηπάτων καὶ αὐτοὶ ἠπατημένοι). When we reflect
that the Vita Antonii was written by an Athanasius, nothing can again surprise
us. Spiritualism with all its absurdity, which we are once more conversant with in
the nineteenth century, had long been familiar in heathen circles, and then, as
now, it was connected with religious ideas on the one hand, and physical ex-
periments and speculations on the other. It forced its way into the Church, in spite
of all protests, from the third, still more, however, from the fourth century, after
it had long been wide-spread in "Gnostic circles." As a religious phenomenon it
signified a renaissance of the lowest forms of religion. But even the most enlightened
minds could not keep clear of it. Augustine proves this.

Socrates--played at being "hereditary lords" (Dynastai) no longer protected, but undermined the unity of the Church. The great Bishops of Rome and Alexandria, who sought to rule over the Church in order to preserve its unity and independence, entangled themselves in an ambitious policy, and produced division. The Emperors were really patrons of unity, and the supreme means at their disposal, the Œcumenical Synod, was their contrivance; in all cases it was a political institution, invented by the greatest of politicians, a two-edged sword which protected the endangered unity of the Church at the price of its independence.

But was not the bond of unity, the common ground, to be found in the common ideal, in the certain hope of a future life, and in asceticism? This bond was assuredly a strong one. The Church would hardly have succeeded in following out the free path opened up to it by Constantine had it not had in its midst, besides its transcendent promises, a power to which all, Greek and barbarian, polytheist and monotheist, learned and unlearned required ultimately, if reluctantly, to bow. And that power was the asceticism which culminated in monachism. The ancient world had arrived, by all the routes of its complicated development, at the bitterest criticism of and disgust at its own existence; but in no other faith was religion itself as effectively combined with asceticism, in none did the latter come so powerfully to the front, yet in none did it submit itself so pliably to Church government, as in Catholicism. A religion comprehended in a mere sacramental communion could not have gained the allegiance of the more clear-sighted and earnest. One that imposed on all, as an inalienable duty, the perfect fulfilment of the positive moral law, could not have held its ground. One that commanded all alike to renounce the world would have closed the world against it. But a religion which graded its members as priests, monks, and laity, embraced a threefold piety of initiated, perfect, and novices, and succeeded in the hardest task of all, that of reconciling priest with monk,[1] and of admitting the layman to a share in the

---

[1] The order of the monks had to pass through crises and conflicts before it was able to establish itself side by side with, and to influence a secularised priesthood; we possess the key to this struggle in the East in the writings of the forger who

blessings of both, was superior to all others, and possessed in its organisation, generally established, a strong bond of association.

Protestants at the present day can hardly form a conception of the hold which asceticism possessed over the mind in the fourth and fifth centuries, or of the manner in which it influenced imagination, thought, and the whole of life. At bottom only a single point was dealt with, abstinence from sexual relationships; everything else was secondary; for he who had renounced these, found nothing hard. Renunciation of the servile yoke of sin (servile peccati iugum discutere) was the watchword of Christians, and an extraordinary unanimity prevailed as to the meaning of this watchword, whether we turn to the Coptic porter or the learned Greek teacher, to the Bishop of Hippo, or Jerome, the Roman presbyter, or the biographer of Saint Martin. Virginity was the specifically Christian virtue, and the essence of all virtues: in this conviction the meaning of the evangelical law was summed up.[1]

composed the Apostolic constitutions and the longer recension of the Ignatian Epistles; in the West in the works, written from the opposite standpoint, of Sulpicius, as also in those of Jerome, Augustine, and the Gallican authors of the fifth century. Compare Hauck, K.-Gesch. Deutschlands, I., p. 49 ff. The order of the monks was imported into the West. It was not till about the middle of the fifth century that its opponents, inside and outside the ranks of the clergy, were silenced. For a time—at the end of the fourth century—it was in danger of being included in the condemnation of the Ascetics who held dualistic views.

[1] The Fathers of the fourth century could not proceed so consistently as Hieracas (see Vol. III., p. 98, n. 5) since they had to sanction the "lower" morality in the Church. The Eustathians who condemned marriage—see the decrees of the Synod of Gangra in Hefele, Concil. Gesch., I. 2, p. 777 ff.—were therefore opposed. But the numerous tractates "De virginitate" show how near the great Fathers of the Church came to the Eustathian view. We can hardly point to one who did not write on the subject. And the same thing is, above all, proved by Jerome's polemic against Jovinian, in spite of its limitation, in the Ep. (48) ad Pammachium. For the rest, Augustine did not differ from Jerome. His Confessions are pervaded by the thought that he alone can enjoy peace with God who renounces all sexual intercourse. Like Hieracas, Ambrose celebrated virginity as the real novelty in Christian morality; see De virginibus, I. 3 sq.: "Since the Lord wrapped himself in a bodily form, and consummated the marriage of deity with humanity, without the shadow of a stain, he has infused poor frail men with heavenly life over the whole globe. That is the race which the angels symbolised when they came to serve the Lord in the wilderness... That is the heavenly host which on that holy Christmas the exulting choirs of angels promised to the earth. We have the testimony of antiquity therefore from the beginning of time, but complete submission only since the word became flesh. This virtue is, in fact, our exclusive possession. The heathens had

But not only did the evangelical law culminate in virginity, but to it also belonged all promises. Methodius' teaching that it prepared the soul to be the bride of Christ, was from the fourth century repeated by everyone. Virginity lies at the root of the figure of bridegoom (Christ) and bride (the soul) which is constantly recurring in the greatest teachers of East and West, and it is the key to the corresponding exposition of the Song of Songs, in which often appear a surp'rising religious individualism and an impassioned love of Christ. [1]

it not; it is not practised by the still uncivilised barbarians; there are no other living creatures among whom it is to be found. We breathe the same air as they do, we share in all the conditions of an earthly life, we are not distinguished from them in birth, and so we only escape from the miseries of a nature otherwise similar to theirs through the virgin chastity, which, apparently extolled by the heathens, is yet, even if placed under the patronage of religion, outraged by them, which is persecuted by the barbarians, and is known to no other creatures." Compare with this Chrysostom's tractate on the state of virginity. Much thought was given after the middle of the fourth century to the relation of priest and monk, especially by those who wished to be monks and had to be priests. The virgin state (of the monks) was held by the earnest to be the easier and safer, the priestly condition the more perilous and responsible; yet in many respects it was regarded as also loftier, because the priest consummated the holy sacrifice and had to wield authority (Chrysostom de sacerdotio, esp. VI. 6—8 and III. 4—6, VI. 4). But the danger to which priests and bishops were subject of becoming worldly, was felt, not only by men like Gregory of Nasianzus and Chrysostom, but by countless earnest-minded Christians. A combination of the priestly (episcopal) office and professional asceticism was therefore early attempted and carried out.

[1] See Vols. II., p. 294, III., p. 109. The allegory of the soul of the Gnostic as the bride received its first lofty treatment in the Valentinian school. Thence Origen got it. The sources drawn upon by later writers were Origen's homilies and commentary on the Song of Songs (Lommatzsch. XIV., p. 233 sq.): the prologue of the latter in Rufinus begins with the words: "Epithalamium libellus hic, id est, nuptiale carmen, dramatis in modum mihi videtur a Salomone conscriptus, quem cecinit instar nubentis sponsæ, et erga sponsum suum, qui est sermo dei, cœlesti amore flagrantis. Adamavit enim eum, sive anima, quæ ad imaginem eius facta est, sive ecclesia." Jerome, who has translated the book, says that Origen surpassed himself in it. Methodius' writing "Convivium" in which the same thought often occurs, was also much read. The purest and most attractive form of the conception in the East appears in Gregory of Nyssa; see e.g., his homilies on the Song of Songs, and his description of the life of Macrina (Ed. Oehler, 1858, p. 172 sq.); we read p. 210 sq.: Διὰ τοῦτό μοι δοκεῖ τὸν θεῖον ἐκεῖνον καὶ καθαρὸν ἔρωτα τοῦ ἀοράτου νυμφίου. ὃν ἐγκεκρυμμένον εἶχεν ἐν τοῖς τῆς ψυχῆς ἀπορρήτοις τρεφόμενον, ἔνδηλον ποιεῖν τότε τοῖς παροῦσι καὶ δημοσιεύειν τὴν ἐν καρδίᾳ διάθεσιν, τὸ ἐπείγεσθαι πρὸς τὸν ποθούμενον, ὡς ἂν διὰ τάχους σὺν αὐτῷ γένοιτο τῶν δεσμῶν ἐκλυθεῖσα τοῦ σώματος. Besides Gregory we have to mention Macarius with his "Spiritual

But the ascetic ideal did not succeed in establishing itself, especially in the West, without severe conflicts, and it concealed within it dangers to the Church. Asceticism threatened to become an end in itself, and to depart from the historical foundation of the Christian religion. When the Church authorised

Homilies" (Migne T. XXXIV.; see Floss, Macarii Aegypt. epp. etc., 1850, German translation by Jocham, Kempten, 1878); compare especially the 15th homily which contains already the figure, repeated a hundred times afterwards, of the soul as the poor maiden who possesses nothing but her own body and whom the heavenly bridegroom loves. If she worthily cherishes chastity and love for him, then she becomes mistress of all the treasures of her Lord, and her transfigured body itself shares in his divinity. Further, Hom. IV., ch. 6 sq., 14 sq. Compare also Ep. 2. "A soul which has cast aside the ignominy of its outward form, which is no longer ruled by shameful thoughts or violated by evil desires, has manifestly become a partner of the heavenly bridegroom; for henceforth it has only one requirement. Stung by love to him it demands and, to speak boldly, longs for the immediate fulfilment of a spiritual and mysterious union that it may enter the indissoluble embrace of communion in sanctification." See Cyril Catech. III., ch. 16; καὶ γένοιτο πάντας ὑμᾶς ἀμώμως τῷ νοητῷ νυμφίῳ παραστάντας κ.τ.λ. Before this : ἡ γὰρ πρότερον δούλη ψυχὴ νῦν ἀδελφιδοῦν αὐτὸν τὸν δεσπότην ἐπεγράψατο, ὃς τὴν ἀνυπόκριτον ἀποδεχόμενος προαίρεσιν ἐπιφωνήσει· Ἰδοὺ εἶ καλὴ ἡ πλησίον μου, ἰδοὺ εἶ καλή· ὀδόντες σου ὡς ἀγέλαι τῶν κεκαρμένων (Cantic. 4, 1). διὰ τὴν εὐσυνείδητον ὁμολογίαν. We can point to very few Greek Fathers in whom the figure does not occur. All the greater is the contrast presented by the depreciatory verdict of Theodore of Mopsuestia on the Song of Songs (Kihn, Theodor v. M. 1880, p. 69 f.). It may be expressly noticed, besides, that Clement of Alex. as well as Methodius and Macarius had already transferred the figure of the bride to the married woman. Indeed, Macarius was conscious that he was acting boldly in doing so. Western nuns and monks were distinguished by lavishing those sexual feelings which were forbidden them on Christ (and Mary). Ambrose especially taught the West the conception of the soul as the bride of Christ; while Augustine was, apart from a few passages, more reserved, and Jerome wanted strength in sentiment and language. Not only in Ambrose's tractate "De Isaac et anima", really a commentary on the Song of Songs, but in innumerable passages in his works—even when it is least expected, as in the consolatory discourse on Valentinian's death (ch. 59 sq.)—the idea of a special tie between the virgin soul and Christ comes to the front. But Ambrose gave it a colouring of his own due to the deep sentiment of a great man, and his peculiar faculty of giving a warm expression to his personal love of Christ (see also Prudentius); compare passages like De pœnit. II. 8. We cannot appreciate too highly the important influence exerted on after times, and first on Augustine, by Ambrose's expression of his personal religion. The light that dawned in Augustine's confessions already shone from the works of Ambrose, and it was the latter, not the former, who conducted western piety to the specific love of Christ. On the mysticism of Macarius, who was in many respects allied to these western Christians, compare also the details in Förster (in the Jahrb. f. deutsche Theol. 1873, p. 439 f.). Bigg (the Christian Platonists of Alex., p. 188 f.) has very

the Christianity of 'the perfect', it really declared the great mass of its divine and apostolic institutions to be mere apparatus, meaningless to him who had resolved to renounce the world, and to prepare for eternity. Those settlers in Egypt, who sought to obtain redemption by torturing themselves, in the end imperilled religion not less than the great crowds who simply submitted to certain sacramental observances, and with the approval of the priests dragged into Christianity whatever pleased them. It was possible, and in fact the danger was imminent, for the ascetic ideal to lose any assured connection with Jesus Christ. Asceticism had also been proclaimed indeed by Greek science. But in that case the common character of religion disappeared; for a merely negative ideal of life, which at the same time was without a close dependence on history, could not form a lasting bond of connection among men.

Our information is exceptionally bad, and not from accident, as to the internal state of the Church, at the time when Constantine chose it to be the support of the Empire. But what we know is enough to establish the fact that the internal solidity by no means corresponded to the external. We may with greater propriety affirm that the Churches of the East were in danger of relapsing into worldliness, and that not only in the form of worldly modes of action. [1] The peril went deeper. Theology, the power which, as matters then were, could alone

rightly seen that Origen's homilies on the Song of Songs were at the root of Christian mysticism: "This book gave welcome expression to what after the triumph of Athanasius was the dominant feeling, and redeemed in some degree the name of its author, damaged by his supposed inclination to Arianism. And thus Origen, the first pioneer in so many fields of Christian thought, the father in one of his many aspects of the English Latitudinarians, became also the spiritual ancestor of Bernard, the Victorines, and the author of the De Imitatione, of Tauler, and Molinos and Mme. de Guyon."

[1] Church history has at this point in its investigations to collect the numerous data which prove how deeply members of the Church had become involved in heathen polytheistic morals, usages, customs, and conceptions, how strong reliance on sacred witchcraft, amulets, and sacramental vehicles had grown, and how far stability and peace of heart and mind had been lost. For the latter we can especially compare Eusebius (H. E. VIII. 1), (further the epitaph of Damasus on Euseb. the Roman Bishop, in Duchesne, Le liber Pontificalis, Tom. I., 1885, p. 167); of a later date, Cyril, Catech. 15, ch. 7. As regards syncretism, see the work on the Egyptian mysteries (ed. Parthey).

give an energetic protection to the distinctive character of religion, was at the point of dissolving it and abandoning it to the world.

We have already described in this volume the state of Eastern theology at the beginning of the fourth century. Conceptions of the faith which began and ended with the historical personality of Jesus Christ were equally condemned with the attempts, whether unstudied or philosophical, to identify the Person of Jesus with the Deity. [1] The realistic and eclectic theology of Irenæus had probably very few defenders in the West. The theology of the Apologists had triumphed, and all thinkers stood under the influence of Origen. But the genius of this great man was too powerful for the Epigoni. The importance of his system lay in a threefold direction: first, in the sharp distinction between Pistis and Gnosis, which he kept apart, and connected only by unity of aim; secondly, in the abundant material in his speculations, the conservatism that he showed in inweaving all that was valuable, and the balance which he knew how to preserve between the different factors of his system, relating them all to one uniform aim; thirdly, in the Biblical impress which he gave his theology by strict adherence to the text of Holy Scripture. In all these respects the Epigoni introduced changes. The most important in its consequences was the mingling of Pistis and Gnosis, of faith and theology. Origen had not published his system, in which the faith of the Church was reconciled with science, as Church doctrine. To him the distinction between the faith of the Church and the science of faith remained fixed. But in the next period — following the precedent of Methodius [2] and opposing Basil's principle — it was thought necessary to identify them. Reactionary and progressive tendencies met in these efforts. The Pistis

---

[1] See the short disclaimers in the fourth Catechism of Cyril of Jerusalem, (ch. 7. 8): Οὐχ, ὥς τινες ἐνόμισαν, ὁ υἱὸς μετὰ τὸ πάθος στεφανωθεὶς ὥσπερ ὑπὸ τοῦ Θεοῦ διὰ τὴν ὑπομονὴν ἔλαβε τὸν ἐν δεξιᾷ θρόνον, ἀλλ' ἀφ' οὗπέρ ἐστιν ἔχει τὸ βασιλικὸν ἀξίωμα... Μήτε ἀπαλλοτριώσῃς τοῦ πατρὸς τὸν υἱόν, μήτε συναλοιφὴν ἐργασάμενος υἱοπατρίαν πιστεύσῃς. Further, the 11th Catechism. So also Athanasius steadily disavows the heresy of the Adoptians as well as of the Sabellians.

[2] See Vol. III, p. 103.

(faith) was supplied with the formulas of Origen's theology, and Gnosis was to stop short at certain tenets of tradition, and to receive them without revision. The point was to find a new medium which should be at once tradition and speculation, Pistis and Gnosis. This endeavour was undoubtedly justified by an actual change accomplished before this and promoted by Origen himself, viz., the incorporation of the doctrine of the Logos in the faith of "the simple." These simple Christians already possessed a dogma which was shaped by exegesis and speculation, and confronted them as an external authority, a law of faith. This creation had forced its way from the circumference of the ecclesiastical system into its centre. Besides, the sharp distinction between a traditional doctrine of the Church and a science of religion contradicted the whole ecclesiastical tradition as established in the fight with Gnosticism. But the intermingling at first produced a kind of stagnation. It threatened to make faith lose its certainty, speculation its reasoning power, and the Church the unity of its confession. If we review the new religious formulas, which were brought into circulation about the year 300, and if we compare the theologies of the period—which unfortunately we only know in part—the theologies, namely, of the Alexandrian teachers, Gregory Thaumaturgus, Lucian, Methodius, Hieracas etc., we see a wealth of forms which, if blood-relations, are extremely different. How could the unity of the Church continue under their sway? and if it continued, was it Christianity after all that furnished the common element?

And this has brought us to the second point   Origen had recognised the full significance of the historical Christ for the stage of Pistis; while he directed the Gnostic to the eternal Logos. Now uncertainties arose here also. The historical Christ threatened to fall entirely into the background. We can observe this in the works of two of the Epigoni, which have no affinity to each other. Gregory Thaumaturgus has in his famous Symbol dealt only with the Logos "apart from the flesh" (λόγος ἄσαρκος), [1] and Methodius intended to declare the loftiest

---

[1] See Vol. III., p.115, the words run: εἷς κύριος, μόνος ἐκ μόνου, Θεὸς ἐκ Θεοῦ, χαρακτὴρ καὶ εἰκὼν τῆς θεότητος, λόγος ἐνεργός, σοφία τῆς τῶν ὅλων συστάσεως

truth when he demanded that Christ should be born in every man 'consciously' (νοητῶς), and that each must become a Christ by participation in Christ. [1] Further, in Origen the cosmological and soteriological interests balanced each other. We recognise this in his formulas which relate to the Logos. But here also a displacement was introduced, one that favoured cosmology. The word Ὁμοούσιος (consubstantial) was, indeed, retained by some, perhaps by many theologians; but as it was in itself ambiguous, so also it was no evidence of an interest in soteriology. The crowd of rhetorical and philosophical predicates heaped upon the Logos, did not serve to illustrate and establish the significance of the Logos as the principal factor in redemption; it was rather a term for the reason and order reigning in the universe, and for the spiritual forces with which humanity had been gifted. Men indeed held firmly, on all hands, to the incarnation; nay, it was regarded, as is proved by the great work of Theognostus, as being, next to the doctrine of the creation of matter, the feature that distinguished the speculation of the Church from that of the Neo-platonists. But the whole stress was laid on the question, what idea was to be formed of the constitution of the subject of which incarnation was predicated. A great school, that of Lucian of Antioch, distinguished, in the manner of Paul of Samosata, between wisdom proper, eternal, existent in God, and a created wisdom or Logos; and identified the latter alone with the incarnate Son— 'wisdom arose through wisdom according to the will of the wise God'. But in drawing this line, not only was the incarnation of the Deity rendered impossible, but every form of His personal activity on earth. The theological interest in Christ threatened to resolve itself entirely into cosmology and morality, or, as in Methodius, to be deprived of its meaning by a mystical alloy.

The liberty which theology enjoyed in the East up to the beginning of the fourth century, and the influence which it exerted on the Church in the same period, could not but produce complete confusion and loss of meaning. All the elements

περιεκτικὴ καὶ δύναμις τῆς ὅλης κτίσεως ποιητική, υἱὸς ἀληθινὸς ἀληθινοῦ πατρός, ἀόρατος ἀοράτου καὶ ἄφθαρτος ἀφθάρτου καὶ ἀθάνατος ἀθανάτου καὶ ἀίδιος ἀιδίου.

[1] See Vol. III., p. 110.

united by Origen in his vast system sought to establish themselves independently. Even tritheistic tendencies were not wanting; but, above all, the idea of a subordinate God and semidivine beings began to be familiar. The idea of the subordinate God is indeed as old as the theology of the Christian Church; even the Apologists shared it, and Origen, with all caution, adopted and justified it in working out his doctrine of the Son. But in the earlier period the *simplices et rudes* (the simple and uncultured) were still startled at the suggestion; theologians provided the idea with strong safe-guards, and Origen himself, who in many points bordered on Polytheism, on the other hand restored the Logos to the being of God, and united Father and Son as closely as possible. But opposition to 'Sabellianism' evidently rendered a later age much more careless. And it is indubitable that the idea of the created God, the God who came into being, coalesced with ancient polytheistic inclinations. The claims of Monotheism were considered to be satisfied by the effort to protect the supreme Deity, as against Modalism, from change and plurality; and the Logos and other beings entitled to worship were suffered calmly to spring up side by side with God; they could not, it was presumed, endanger Monotheism, because they belonged to the domain of the created. Add that theologians dealt in their speculations with a plethora of philosophical categories destitute of a fixed impress, or fixed value; [1] further, that this terminology, unsifted and uncontrolled, everywhere forced its way into the faith of the community, and we can form a conception of the danger which hovered over the Church. We find a Monotheism which did not exclude polytheism, a Logos-Christ, who, as a cosmological quantity, was of shifting nature and origin, ideas of the incarnation and redemption as designed to "enlighten" the human race, and to effect an incarnation of God in every individual soul. All this, too, was clothed in a rank growth of artificial philosophical expressions, identical with that used in contemporary science. And we may well ask whether such a theology was in a condition to protect even the scanty remains of the

[1] See Vol. III., p. 102.

evangelic tradition, above all, at the moment when the partition
between State and Church was torn down and the Church was
brought face to face with its greatest task. A deism—if the
term may be allowed—was at hand, surrounded by the shifting
forms of a speculation which had neither a settled boundary
nor an assured object. It almost seemed as if the special characteristics of the Christian religion were to be reduced to the
evidence of antiquity and prophecy, what Porphyry called
'foreign fables'. Yet even Scriptural proof was no longer everywhere called for and given with the zeal so noticeable in Origen;
although it was just the school of Lucian which neglected it
least. But what could Scripture avail against the method? If
a Bishop so capable and learned, and so well versed in tradition as Eusebius of Cæsarea was satisfied in his Christology
with the formulas we read there, if he could praise the religious
edicts and manifestoes of his Emperor, though they substantially
celebrated "God in nature", as brilliant specimens of his
Christian conviction, we must conclude that the Logos doctrine
settled in the Church was the strongest means of completely
effacing the figure of the historical Christ, and of resolving
everything into mist. [1] Even the rationalist, who in his study
of the history of religions always follows with sympathy the
progress to 'natural' religion, would require to restrain his
sympathy here. For the pure religion of humanity could not
have resulted from this development, but one that was wholly
indefinite, and therefore capable of being influenced from any
quarter, one in whose centre was throned that hollow and
helpless figment of thought, the ὄν, the πρώτη οὐσία (being—
primal being). And men would have gone on proclaiming this

_____

[1] On Eusebius' Christology see Dorner, Lehre v. d. Person Christi, I. (1845)
p. 792 ff. Lee, on the Theophan. 1843, Preliminary Dissert. The Christology of
Euseb. is that of the ancient apologists, approximating in its terms to Neoplatonic
speculations and richer in its phases on account of the many antitheses. In spite
of his dependence on Origen, Euseb. was chary of receiving all the ideas and
predicates which the former applied to the Son and to which orthodoxy afterwards
appealed. That is of consequence. Euseb. was more convinced than Origen that
the idea of deity was completely exhausted in that of the strictly one and unchangeable ὄν the πρώτη οὐσία; he separated the δεύτερος Θεός much further from
God than the Apologists; see Zahn, Marcell., p. 37 f.

religion to be Christianity, simply because they possessed in
Holy Scripture the means of proving it, and of dating it back
to the beginning of the world as the universal religion. And
they would have adopted sacred media, charms, and intermedi-
ary powers more and more boldly, because they were incapable
of understanding and applying either to God or to Jesus Christ
the tradition that God redeemed men through Jesus Christ.

The Bishops and theologians in the East about A.D. 320,
whose views were similar to those of Eusebius, had on their
side the strongest power to be found in an ecclesiastical communion—tradition: *they were the conservatives.* Conservative
theology, the theology that took its stand on Origen, limited
the idea of Deity to the primal being ($\pi\rho\acute{\omega}\tau\eta$ $o\dot{\nu}\sigma\acute{\iota}\alpha$), inoperative
and really incapable of being revealed, *i.e.*, to the Father. It
accordingly ignored the Logos and Christ in determining the
conception of God. Further, it deduced, like the Neoplatonists,
a second or third Ousia (being) from the first, and adorned the
Logos created by the will of the Father with the loftiest, yet
vacillating, predicates. It taught the incarnation of the Logos, and
celebrated its result, yet once more in indefinite, in high-sounding
and meaningless, Biblical phrases.   Finally, it subordinated
everything spiritual and moral to the thought of free-will and
human independence. Any attempt at precision could not fail,
on this domain, to be regarded as an innovation. Anything
might establish itself as long as it did not claim to be exclusive. [1]
There never did exist in the Church a general tendency to
form new dogmas—the terms 'new' and 'dogma' are mutually
exclusive; least of all did it exist in the East; there was either
indifference to philosophical speculation, or a desire that it
should have liberty, or it was regarded with suspicion. For the

---

[1] Gwatkin says very justly in Studies of Arianism (1882), p. 52: "In fact
Christendom as a whole was neither Arian nor Nicene. If the East was not Nicene,
neither was it Arian, but conservative: and if the West was not Arian, neither was
it Nicene, but conservative also. Conservatism, however, had different meanings in
East and West." In the East it was considered conservative to uphold the formulas
of Origen strengthened against Sabellianism. On the doctrine of the Logos and
Christ in Origen Bigg says very truly (The Christian Platonists of Alex., p. 182):
" What struck later ages as the novelty and audacity of Origen's doctrine was in
truth its archaism and conservatism."

rest, men reverenced in the cultus the mystery, *i.e.*, the complex of formulas whose origin had already become obscure.[1]

Nevertheless, there probably never was a time in the East
when a reaction did not exist against the development of the

[1] When theology is engaged in forming dogmas, it has never, as is really self-
evident, enjoyed the sympathy of any large section in the Church. There is nothing
to support the contention that the Christian Church passed through a period—
from Origen up to the Synod of Chalcedon or A.D. 431—during which there
prevailed universally, or even to a great extent, a supreme interest in the abstract
form of the contents of Religion, and an effort, with all the means at hand, to
expound it as exactly as possible. The great mass of Bishops, monks, and laity,
were then wholly occupied in satisfying themselves with what had been given.
This was the highest demand of the Catholic religion itself, which presupposed
the "Apostolic" as its foundation, which called everything else "heresy" (νεωτε-
ρισμός), and as an institution for worship did not permit changes.  Undoubtedly,
the period from Origen, or say, from Athanasius up to the Ephesian Council,
appears unique in the history of the Church. But that was an episode enacted in
opposition to the great body of Christians, and the theological leaders themselves,
in proportion to their piety, conceived their task to be compulsory, dangerous, and
ensnaring them in guilt.  To prove the former read Socrates' Church History (see
my discussion in Herzog R. E., Vol. XIV. p. 408 ff.).  This man was, on the one
hand, orthodox at every point, on the other, an enthusiastic partisan of Ἑλληνικὴ
παιδεία, full of veneration for the great Origen and his science, which he held
was to be fostered continually. But the production of dogma by scientific theology
was repugnant to him in every sense, *i.e.*, he accused and execrated dogmatic
controversies as much in the interest of a dogma fixed once for all as in that of
science. The Nicene Symbol belonged sufficiently to the past to be accepted by
him as holy and apostolical; but beyond this every new formula seemed to Socrates
pernicious, the controversies sometimes fights in the dark (nyktomachies), sometimes
an outflow of deceptive sophistry and ambitious rivalry: σιωπῇ προσκυνείσθω τὸ
ἄρρητον, *i.e.*, the mystery of the trinity. Had Socrates lived 100 years earlier, he
would not have been a Nicene, but a Eusebian Christian. He therefore passes very
liberal judgments on, and can make excuses for, the latest "heretics", *i.e.*, theologians
who have been recently refuted by the Church.  In this he stood by no means
alone. Others, even at a later date, went still further. Compare Evagrius (H. E. I. 11)
whose argument recalls Orig. c. Cels. III. 12.

Dogma has been created by the small number of theologians who sought for
precise notions, in the endeavour to make clear the characteristic meaning of the
Christian religion (Athanasius, Apollinaris, Cyril). That these notions, separated
from their underlying thought, fell into the hands of ambitious ecclesiastical
politicians, that the latter excited the fanaticism of the ignorant in their support,
and that the final decision was often due to motives which had nothing to do
with the case, is admittedly undeniable. But the theologians are not therefore to
blame, who opposed in the Church a lazy contentment with mystery, or an unlimited pursuit of scientific speculation. Their effort to make clear the essence of
Christianity, as they understood it, and at the same time to provide a λογικὴ
λατρεία, was rather, next to the zealous order of monks with whom they were intimately

Logos doctrine towards complete separation of the Son from the Father.[1] It sprang not only from Modalists, but also from disciples of Origen, and it celebrated at Nicæa an amazingly rapid triumph. In opposition to a school which had ventured too far forward, and had embroidered the doctrines of Paul of Samosata with questionable tenets of Origen, the term Ὁμοούσιος, once banned at Antioch, was successfully elevated to the dignity of the watchword of faith.

The importance of this rapid triumph for the history of dogma cannot be rated too highly. But procured as it was by the Emperor, the victory would have been resultless, had it not been for the man whose biography coincides with the history of dogma of the fourth century—Athanasius.

The second division of the history of dogma, the account of its development, opens with Athanasius, but his conception of the faith also dominated following centuries. Augustine alone surpassed him in importance; for Augustine was an Origen and Athanasius in one—and he was still more.[2] However, the connected, the sole great feature in the epoch. They set themselves to stem the *vis inertiæ* of the pious, and with the highest success. When indolence in the end held the field, an important result had at any rate been attained. The period from Athanasius till about the middle of the fifth century was in many respects the brilliant epoch of theology in the Church. Not even the age of Scholasticism can compare with it. That the work of the theologians became faith according to the Church—a thing Origen never thought of—involved its strength and weakness alike. The fanaticism of the masses for dogmatic and philosophical catch-words— see the amusing narrative of Gregory of Nyssa, Opp. ed. Paris, 1638, T. III. p. 466—affords no information as to the measure of their comprehension; for the dogmatic catch-word is merely a fetish in wide circles.

[1] Origen's doctrine of subordination was felt in the West simply to constitute ditheism; see Vol. III., p. 89 ff.

[2] See Ranke, Weltgeschichte Vol. IV. 1, p. 307: "Augustine's system is, if I mistake not, the second that arose in the Church; it set aside the peculiar characteristics of the first, that of Origen, and then made good its position." We can only admit that it held its ground in a modified sense. In fact we see here a parallel of the highest significance in the history of the world. The Church has produced two fundamental systems, Origen's and Augustine's. But the history of theology in the East is the history of the setting aside of Origen's system, and the same is to be said of the Augustinian in the Catholic West. Only the procedure in the East was more thorough-going and open than in the West. In the former Origen was condemned, in the latter Augustine was constantly celebrated as the greatest *Doctor ecclesiæ*. In both cases, however, the rejection of the theological system caused the loss of a coherent and uniform Christian conception of the world.

future course of history has yet to decide whether Athanasius' thought will not in the end live longer than the conceptions of Augustine. At the present day at least Augustine is given up sooner than Athanasius in the Churches.

But it is really not permissible to compare these great men. Augustine was a loftier genius, a man of inexhaustible wealth of ideas and sentiment; Athanasius' greatness consisted in *reduction*, in the energy with which, from a multitude of divergent speculations claiming to rest on tradition, he gave exclusive validity to those in which the strength of religion then lay. Augustine opened up a new view of the highest blessings and of human nature in the Church, he scattered a thousand germs for the future; Athanasius, like every reformer, *reduced*, he first secured a sphere of its own to the Christian religion on the soil, already won, of Greek speculation, and he referred everything to the thought of redemption. Augustine invented a new speculation, and the fascinating language of the deepest religious feeling, beyond which changed times and manners seem unable to go; Athanasius was unable to put forward either gifts of speculation or of eloquence on behalf of the thought in which he lived. His strength arose out of his conviction and his office.

Athanasius was a reformer, though not in the highest sense of the word. Behind and beside him existed a speculation which led on a shoreless sea, and the ship was in danger of losing its helm. [1] He grasped the rudder. We may compare the situation with that in which Luther found himself when confronting the mediæval Church and Scholasticism. It was not for a word, or a formula, [2] that he was concerned, but a crucial

---

[1] It might seem as if we ought to grant the same credit to Arius of having reduced and given fixity to vacillating and divergent speculations. But apart from the contents and value of his doctrine, Arius was always disposed to make concessions, and as semi-opponents defended him, so he unhesitatingly accepted half friends for complete allies. This very fact proves, however, that he would never have succeeded in clearing up the position.

[2] Athanasius always made a sparing use of the catch-word Ὁμοούσιος in his works. The formula was not sacred to him, but only the cause which he apprehended and established under cover of the formula. His conduct at the Synod of Alexandria shows that he laid no stress on words. For his theology he needed no Creed. The existence of one in the Nicene was valuable to him, but he was far from wor-

thought of his faith, the redemption and raising of humanity to divine life through the God-man. It was only from the certainty that the divinity manifest in Jesus Christ possessed the nature of the Deity (unity of being) and was for this reason alone in a position to raise us to divine life, that faith was to receive its strength, life its law, and theology its direction. But Athanasius in thus giving the chief place to faith in the God-man who alone delivers from death and sin, furnished practical piety, then almost exclusively to be found in monkish asceticism, with its loftiest motive. To speak briefly, this combined as closely as possible the Ὁμοούσιος (consubstantial), which guaranteed the deification of human nature, with monkish asceticism, and raised the latter from its still under-ground or, at least, insecure realm to the public life of the Church. While fighting against the phrase the created Logos (λόγος-κτίσμα) as heathen and as a denial of the power of the Christian religion, he at the same time as strenuously opposed worldly pursuits. He subordinated Scripture, tradition, and theology to the thought that the Redeemer was God by nature, but he also strove to work out the Christian life which received its motive from close communion with the God-Christ, [1] and the prospect of being invested both the divine nature. If we would do justice to Athanasius, both these facts must be kept in mind. He became the father of Catholic orthodoxy and the patron of ecclesiastical monachism, and that he never would have been, had he not also set the practical ideal of the piety of the time 'on the candlestick'. [2]

There is here nothing new in the common sense of the word; Athanasius had really on his side, the best part of the tradition of the Church, to which he also appealed. Irenæus had already given the central place to the object, nature, and accomplish-

shipping Symbols. While many of his friends sought support in the authority of the formula, he sought and found it solely in the cause.

[1] Bigg (l. c., p. 188) has very rightly called attention to the high value attached by orthodox Fathers after Athanasius' triumph to the Song of Songs in Origen's exposition.

[2] See the Vita Anton. of Athanasius and Gregory of Naz., Orat. 21. It is noteworthy that Paul of Samosata and the Eusebians were worldly Christians. On the other hand, the puritanism of Arius is, of course, famous.

ment of redemption in the categories: Logos, incarnation, God-man, deification, and sons of God. Athanasius could refer to a series of ideas in Origen and other Alexandrian catechists in support of his distinctive treatment of the Logos doctrine. New alone was *the fact*, the energy and exclusiveness of his view and action at a time when everything threatened to undergo dissolution.

Athanasius was no scientific theologian in the strict sense of the term; from theology he descended to piety, and found the exact word required. A man of authority, and attached to the tradition of his school, he was not in a position to disentangle the problem from the context in which the Apologists and Origen had set it. He was a disciple of Origen, but his attitude first to Marcellus, and then to the recent defenders of Ὁμοούσιος, the Cappadocians, proves that he was as destitute of scientific interest in a philosophical theory of life, as of the obstinacy of theologians. He had to deal with that which transcended theology. He was the first to raise to honour in the Church in all its force the old maxim that we must think of Christ as God (ὡς περὶ θεοῦ), and therefore he paved the way for the new principle, that we must think of God as in Christ (ὡς ἐν Χριστῷ).

In this he stood aloof from the rational thought of his time. While admitting its premises, he added an element, which neutral speculation was incapable of assimilating completely. Nothing certainly was more unintelligible to it, than the assumption of an essential unity of the quiescent and the active Deity. Athanasius fixed a gulf between the Logos of the philosophers, and the Logos whose redeeming work he proclaimed. What he said of the latter, declaring the mystery strongly and simply, and by no means committing himself to new distinctions, could not but appear to the Greeks 'an offence and folly'. But he did not shrink from reproach; with firm hand, though in awkward lines, he marked off a sphere of its own for the Christian faith. [1]

[1] The Cappadocians, theologians who reconciled the faith of Athanasius with the current philosophy, and apprehended it abstractly, did not retain his teaching pure and simple. This is especially shown by their doubtful contention that the Christian idea of God was the true mean between the Jewish and Greek. They

And this man respected science and its free development. We can observe this in his criticisms of Origen and the Alexandrian catechists. Undoubtedly it must have been important to him to obtain reliable witnesses (testes veritatis) for his doctrine, and the effort to do this explains frequently his practice of making the best of everything. But it does not entirely explain his conduct. Christian faith was in his view exhausted in faith in the God-man, the incarnation, and the redemption which constituted a divine nature; for this reason he permitted liberty in everything else. It would seem that he had no desire to abolish Origen's distinction between the Christian science of the perfect and the faith of the imperfect. He did not sit as a judge of heretics on Origen's doubtful tenets and correct them by the *regula fidei*, nor did he follow the course first taken by Bishop Peter, one of his predecessors, in Alexandria. [1] This is all the more remarkable, as for his own part he could hardly find a single point in the Gnostic heterodoxies of Origen with which he could agree.

Athanasius did not see beyond the horizon of his own time. He attributed the highest efficacy to the mysteries of the cultus. He regarded them as the personal legacy of Christ, immediate emanations of his life as God-man, and as containing the means of applying salvation. If in succeeding centuries the religious interest attached itself more and more closely to ritual, that did not imply any contradiction of the conception of the great Alexandrian. He also laboured on behalf of the dogma which was to obtain its practical and effective presentation in the

boldly characterised the plurality of Hypostases, *e.g.*, as a phase of truth preserved in Greek polytheism. Athanasius, therefore, did not take unmixed pleasure in their work. Cf. the λόγος κατηχητικός of Gregory of Nyssa (ch. 4, ed. Oehler): "Jewish dogma is refuted by adoption of the Word, and by faith in the Spirit, but the illusion of the Greeks (Ελληνίζοντες) in worshipping a multiplicity of Gods is dispelled by the (doctrine of the) unity of nature which destroys the extravagant opinion of a (divine) plurality. We must, in turn, retain the unity of being from the Jewish type of faith, and only the distinction of personal (divine) existences from the Greek; and by this means godless conceptions are met on the left and right in correspondingly salutary ways. For the trinity is a corrective for those who err as to unity, just as the doctrine of the unity (of God) is for those who have made shipwreck by belief in plurality."

[1] See Vol. III., p. 99 ff.

monks on the one hand, and in ritual on the other, until the transitory was exalted into the permanent.

*Athanasius' importance to posterity consisted in this, that he defined Christian faith exclusively as faith in redemption through the God-man who was identical in nature with God, and that thereby he restored to it fixed boundaries and specific contents.* [1] *Eastern Christendom has been able to add nothing up to the present day. Even in theory it has hit on no change, merely overloading the idea of Athanasius; but the Western Church also preserved this faith as fundamental. Following on the theology of the Apologists and Origen, it was the efficient means of preventing the complete Hellenising and secularisation of Christianity.*

The history of dogma in the East after the Nicene Council reveals two interlacing lines of development. First, the idea of the God-man from the point of view of the redemption and elevation of the human race to divine life, in other words, the faith of Athanasius, was elaborated on all sides. In this the history of dogma, in the strict sense of the term, exhausted itself, for dogma was faith in the God-man. But with this a second development was closely connected, one which dealt

---

[1] In the cleverly written introduction to his description of "Western Church architecture" (Stuttgart, 1884), Dehio works out the idea that the classical period of ancient Christian architecture, the fourth century, was distinguished not by the multiplicity of ideas and forms of construction, but rather by the simplification or reduction of the forms. The Church, confronted by the number of models in ancient architecture, laid hold of one of them, the Basilica, and transmitted it alone to the Middle Ages. That, however, meant not a loss, but an advance. "The genius of Christianity contributed nothing new to the architectural creations of Rome and Alexandria. The great revolution it evoked lay in another direction. It consisted in the reduction of the multiplicity of styles to one dominant and sole form, not so much by a metamorphosis of artistic feeling, as by making religion once more the central motive of life. It thus assigned to the future architecture of the Middle Ages conditions analogous to those which governed the beginnings of Greek art; and thus the birth of Gothic art was possible at the climax of the Middle Ages—for the second time in history, a true organic style, like that of the Greek temple." This observation is extremely instructive to the historian of dogma. The thought of Athanasius corresponds in theology to the meaning of the Basilica in the history of architecture in the fourth century. Both were happy simplifications from a wealth of ideas—reductions which concealed full and varied contents.

with the relations of dogma and theology. Here also one man can be named: it was the science that Origen had cultivated which formed the centre of interest. However, since his days the problem had become more complicated, for theological principles that penetrated deeply had been received into faith itself, and the great development up to the Council of Chalcedon, and still later, consisted in the incorporation of theological results and formulas in the general belief of the Church. The question, accordingly, was not merely whether a freer and more independent theology, like Origen's in spirit and method, could receive an acknowledged position and latitude in the Church; whether, in general, the phases of criticism and idealistic spiritualism, included in Origen's science, were to be tolerated. It was a much harder problem that arose, though one that from its nature was always half concealed. If the theological dogma, at the moment when it became a creed of the Church, received the value of an apostolic doctrine which had never been wanting in the Church, how were the theologians to be regarded who had really created it, and how were the most venerated men of the past to be looked upon who had either been wholly ignorant of the dogma, or had incidentally, or avowedly, contradicted it? The conclusion is clear. The former were to receive special honour as witnesses to, but not as creators of, the truth. The latter it was necessary to abandon, however real and constructive their labours may once have been, or their works were to be coloured, corrected, or even amended by the insertion of glosses. But how long will a theology receive room to work on dogma, if the work is again and again to be disguised and how long will theologians be found to continue the dangerous business? "Theology is the most thankless of sciences. It crushes its builders with the very stones which they have helped to erect." The relation of theology to dogma recalls the myth of Chronos. But here it is not the father who swallows his children, it is the creature that devours its creators up to the third and fourth generations. As, moreover, the age from the fourth to the sixth centuries is the classic period of all dogma, so in no other period does it so clearly exhibit to the historian its characteristic of demanding living sacrifices.

Accordingly we observe two phenomena in these centuries.
First, we have a continuous fight against the free theology of
Origen, against the heterodoxies which it embraced, its critical
phase, and its idealistic speculation. At any rate, more than two
centuries elapsed before it was finally refused all right of citizenship in the Church, and at the same time Ἑλληνικὴ παιδεία
(Greek culture) was deprived of any greater influence on dogma,
than what the latter required for its correct exposition and
justification. [1] But, in the second place, a traditionalism arose
which looked distrustfully on theology taking any share in the
work of the Church at the time, which substituted authority
for science, while it either exalted ancient teachers to heaven
as saints, or hurled them down to hell as heretics. It was due
to the secret logic of events that such a tendency gained
strength and finally triumphed; for if even the most capable
and independent theologians were compelled to live under the
delusion that what was new in their teaching could never be
true, or that the true could not possibly be new, it necessarily
followed that fewer and fewer would be found to undertake their
dangerous work. [2] Accordingly, after dogma had developed to

[1] The prestige of Origen in the Church was still in the first half of the fifth
century almost absolute and incomparable in wide circles. As we have above
remarked, the Church history of Socrates is in this respect particularly instructive.
The belittlers and enemies of this man were vain and ambitious obscurantists,
hero-levelling fellows; against them—Methodius, Eustathius, Apollinaris, and
Theophilus—he appealed to the testimony of Athanasius on behalf of Origen's
orthodoxy (VI. 13). Even the view that Origen's works and utterances required to
be sifted, appeared to him folly (VI. 17). He defended everything that the master
wrote. It was incomprehensible to him how the Arians could study and value
Origen, without becoming orthodox (VII. 6)—to the Arians the opposite was incomprehensible—and he declares with absolute conviction that Porphyry and Julian
would not have written what they did if they had read the great teacher (III. 23).
Further, Origen was once more quoted in the Monophysite controversies. Apart
from special uses of it, his name represented a great cause, namely, no less than
the right of science, Ἑλληνικὴ παιδεία, in the Church, a right contested by traditionalism in conjunction with the monks.

[2] It was pointed out above, p. 138, note 1, that even orthodox theological
leaders were not comfortable in their dogmatic work, so that the position from
the middle of the sixth century, the sovereign rule of traditionalism, was really
the goal desired from the beginning. The works of all prominent theologians
testify to this. Some deplored the fact that the mystery could not be worshipped
in silence, that they were compelled to speak; and the rest say explicitly, that the

a certain extent, held a certain number of conceptions capable of employing the intelligence, and was adapted to scholastic treatment, it became so sensitive that it ceased to tolerate a theology that would carry it further, even under all possible safe-guards. The theology that did independent work, that at no time professed to produce dogma, and therefore really had not existed, now came actually to an end. The date coincides with that at which Origen was condemned (the sixth century). The history of this process ran its course very gradually. On the other hand, there was no want of important actions in the history of the ejection of Origen's doctrine. We have here to mention the 'Origenist controversies', though we must not limit them, as has been customary, to a few decades. Along with them the opposition to the school of Antioch and its condemn-ation come before us. But we must not look at the victory of the creed of the Church over theological liberties merely from the point of view of a decline of science in the Church. We have rather to consider what a more liberal speculative and critical science had to offer at the time to the Church. In view of the way in which the pursuit of theology and the exposition of the faith were intertwined, there were gifts which the Church had to decline in order to maintain its tradition, *i.e.*, the stand-ard left to it of its Christianity. But the heterodoxies of the theologians presented neither an incentive to nor the means for a revision of the whole doctrine in its possession. Besides, the entire process of expelling the freer theology was carried out without crises worth mentioning, as if spontaneously. That is the strongest evidence of the weakness of the speculations and critical views which sought to hold their ground alongside the doctrine of the Church. The condition of affairs at the close, when we have (1) dogma (2) a theology of scholastic mysticism, and (3) antiquarian and formal science not confused with religion,

truth of their propositions lay in their negations alone. Hilary expresses himself per-haps most strongly (De trinit. II. 2): " Compellimur hæreticorum et blasphemantium vitiis illicita agere, ardua scandere, ineffabilia eloqui, inconcessa præsumere. Et cum sola fide explorari, quæ præcepta sunt, oporteret, adorare scilicet patrem et venerari cum eo filium, sancto spiritu abundare, cogimur sermonis nostri humilitatem ad ea, quæ inenarrabilia sunt extendere et in vitium vitio coarctamur alieno, ut, quæ contineri religione mentium oportuisset, nunc in periculum humani eloquii proferantur."

was in many respects an improvement, and the value of the product received its strongest attestation in the duration of the system. Leaving out of account a few oscillations, that had been actually attained, which the 'conservatives', *i.e.*, the great majority in all phases of violent dogmatic conflicts, had longed for, and had therefore always contemplated. A mysterious dogma had been arrived at, one elevated above the schools, which gave theologians liberty to be antiquarians, philologists, or philosophers; for what independent work was left in the pursuit of dogma was subject to the jurisdiction of these specialists, so far as it did not come under the review of the experts in mysteries and liturgies. But the great loss consisted in the fact that men no longer possessed a theological system complete in itself. Origen's was the only one that the Greek Church had produced. After its rejection there existed, besides dogma, a vast sum of incongruous fragments, bound artificially together by quotations from Scripture and tradition and from Aristotelian scholasticism. The great dogmatic work of John of Damascus only appears to be a logically connected system; it is in reality far from that.

As regards the periods, the dividing lines are formed by the Œcumenical Synods, namely, the so-called 2nd, then the 4th, 5th, 6th and 7th. But we can also use the names of Theodosius I., Pope Leo I., Justinian, and Pope Agatho. The unification of the Churches was rendered possible by the fact that they obtained a *forum publicum* (a public tribunal) in the universal Synods.[1] For the Creeds of the provincial Churches, which agreed only in the main points, and not even in all these, the Councils substituted a dogmatic confession whose proclamation, enactment, and extension excited the most violent conflicts. At the same time the confederation of the Churches

---

[1] But for Constantine the Nicene Council would not have been carried through, and but for the Emperor's uniform creeds would not been arrived at. They were Athanasius' best coadjutors. Nay, even the Emperors hostile to him helped him; for they used every effort to unite the Church on the basis of a fixed confession. It is therefore absurd to abuse the State Church, and yet to regard the establishment of the orthodox creed as a gain.

became a reality through the imperial policy, which sought to
come into touch with the strongest dogmatic currents, though
not infrequently it supported trivialities. The last traces of
independence possessed by individual communities were destroyed; along with unity, uniformity in doctrine, discipline, and
worship was almost re-established, and the constitution of the
Church, even in the higher ranks, was gradually so adapted to
that of the empire that the hierarchical organisation and administration of the Church corresponded to the order of the
State. But this re-arrangement required, in part, to be carried
out by force (τυραννίς of the Emperors and a few great Bishops),
and speaking strictly, was a reality for only a few decades. It
excited counter-movements; in opposition to it nationalistic feeling
first really gained strength, especially in the East, and the great
schisms of the national Churches there were also a consequence
of the absolutist attempts at unification.[1] In the West the State
collapsed under the storms of the tribal migration at the moment
when, in the East, the dismemberment of the imperial Church
into national Churches began. The attempts of the East Roman

---

[1] See Hatch, The Councils and the Unity of the Church, in his Social Constitution
of the Christian Churches, p. 172 ff.; he has given an excellent account of the
share of the State in this unity and its limitations; compare also my Analekten,
p. 253 ff. In the process by which Christendom was united externally and ecclesiastically, we can distinguish in the East three, and in the West four, epochs. The
first three were common to the Churches of both East and West. The first was
characterised by the recognition of the apostolic rule of faith in opposition to the
erroneous creeds of heretical associations, after a common ideal and a common
hope had united Christians up to the middle of the second century. The κανὼν
τῆς πίστεως became the basis of ἀδελφότης. The second epoch, in which organisation became already of supreme importance, was represented in the theory of the
episcopal office, and in the creation of the metropolitan constitution. While this
was struggling to establish itself amid violent crises, the State of Constantine
brought about the third epoch, in which the Church, by becoming completely
political, was united, and thus arrived at an external and uniform unity, so that
in it the essential nature of the Empire was continued. The Church became the
most solid organisation in the Empire, because it rested on the imperial order of
the ancient kingdom. It got no further than this organisation in the East; indeed,
several great provincial Churches soon separated from it; for the creation of Constantine concealed germs of dissolution; see Zahn, Konstantin d. Gr. 1876, p. 31 f. In
the West, on the contrary, the Roman Bishop began to engage in those enterprises
which, favoured by circumstances, succeeded in the course of centuries in substituting a new and distinctively ecclesiastical unity for that created by the state.

emperors to recover the Western half of the realm, or at least parts of it, more than once thwarted the oriental policy imperatively required of them, and are also, from the complications to which they led, of great importance for the history of dogma. While the Emperors of Byzantium were involved in a double task, which constituted an insoluble dilemma, the Roman Bishops served themselves heirs to the West Roman kingdom. In the revolution in political and social affairs, Christians and Latins were compelled to postpone their separate interests and to attach themselves closely to the most powerful defender of the old institutions. The Germans, who apparently broke up the Empire, brought about the internal unity of all that was Catholic and Latin, and strengthened the position of ecclesiastical Rome. The East, on the contrary, which had been less endangered actually did break up. In the Western Catholic Church the ancient Roman Empire was preserved after a fashion with its order and culture. This Church had no longer beside it a state similar in character and closely related to itself and thus its Bishop could train the new peoples to his service, and soon undertook an independent policy against the Western schemes of the East Roman Emperors. The internal separation between East and West was complete, when neither understood the language of the other. Yet the West still took an active interest in the controversy of the ' Three Chapters', and at the same time obtained, in the translation of the Antiochene and Persian *Instituta regularia divinæ legis,* and in the great works translated at the instigation of Cassiodorus, valuable gifts from the East which stand comparison with those made by Hilary, Ambrose, Rufinus, and Jerome. Even in the seventh century Rome and the East were for a time engaged in a lively correspondence. But the rule of Byzantium over Rome was felt to be that of the foreigner, and conversely the Roman spirit was alien to the Orientals. Their relations were forced. *Augustine hardly left a trace in the Eastern Church.* That was its greatest calamity. Of course it was less disposed by its past to understand him than the Western Church, and it was at no time really inclined to accept instruction from its rival.

The first period of the History of Dogma closes with the

Synods of Constantinople (381—383).  At them faith in the
complete divinity of the Redeemer was finally settled as the
creed of the Catholic Church, and his complete humanity was also
expressly acknowledged.  Next to Athanasius the chief part in
the decision was taken by the Cappadocians on the one hand,
and by the Roman Bishop and Ambrose on the other. It would
not have been arrived at, however, so early, if it had not been
carried through in Constantinople by a powerful ruler who came
from the West. The theologians, so far as any took part in it,
were men who were equipped with the full culture of the period,
and were also devoted to the ideals of monastic piety.  The
Cappadocians were still relatively independent theologians,
worthy disciples and admirers of Origen, using new forms to
make the faith of Athanasius intelligible to contemporary thought,
and thus establishing them, though with modifications, on a
secure basis. Beside them stood Apollinaris of Laodicea, a man
who anticipated the problems of the future, who was their equal
in scholarship, and surpassed them in many respects in theology.
But Arianism revealed its weakness by nothing more than its
rapid decline after it ceased to possess the imperial favour.
The impression made by it on the German nations, and its
prolonged popularity with them, must be described as an
'accident' in history. Catholicism was first made a reality by
Theodosius I.—'the idea of a communion which should unite
East and West in the same confession, beyond which no other
form of confession was recognised.' But Ranke remarks rightly [1]
that the Christian idea (of Nicene orthodoxy) gained the upper
hand over Hellenistic and heretical systems, not from the doctrine alone, but from the course of events.  The victory of the
Nicene Council was also decided at the Tigris by the defeat
of Julian, and at Adrianople by the death of Valens.  In this
first period the Christian Church was still in constant touch with
Hellenism, and adopted from it whatever it could use. But the
history of dogma can only give a very meagre view of these
relations.  Its boundaries gradually become altogether more
restricted. In the first three centuries it can hardly be separated

---

[1] Weltgeschichte IV. 1, p. 305 f.

from the universal history of the Church; in those following the
general life of the Church is less and less clearly reflected in
it. He who desires to become acquainted with that life, must
study the monachism, worship, ethics, and especially the theological science of the age. There is nothing in the history of
dogma to require us to portray a figure like that of Synesius,
and, if we define our task strictly, we can make little use of
the rich epistolary literature of the time.

The second period extends to the Council of Chalcedon
(451). Its first and longer half covers the time in which the
imperial Church, resting on the Nicene basis and directed by
emperor, priest, and monk, established itself. But after a time
of comparative peace,[1] the question again emerged as to the
relation of the divine and human in the person of the Redeemer.
The opposition between the school of Antioch and the new
Alexandrian theology, which felt itself to be the sole teaching
of the Church, culminated in this question, and the Alexandrian
Bishop succeeded in making it the centre of ecclesiastical interest.
The theologians of the school of Antioch still wrought in freedom; nay, even among their opponents there were to be found
men who defined the faith by its aim, and were not overawed
by traditionalism. Yet traditionalism grew more and more
powerful. Under the leadership of Epiphanius the great reaction against Origen began,[2] and not only the Alexandrian
Bishop, but the greatest scholar of the age took part in

---

[1] On these decades, which are to be described as in many respects the most
prosperous period of the Byzantine Church, see Herzog R. E., Vol. XIV., p. 403 ff.
Heathenism was then first completely overthrown, and the heretics, even finally the
Novatians, were hard pressed. The regime of Chrysostom seems to have been
especially signalised by the suppression of heretics in the patriarchate of Constantinople; see the account of Socrates. We know of other Bishops who were active
in extirpating heresy in the first half of the fifth century, a work in which Theodoret took part. The reigns of Gratian and Theodosius, on the one hand, the
indefatigable labours of Epiphanius on the other, laid the foundation. Their
programme was carried out from the end of the fourth century. But from about
the middle of the fifth century, when the last traces of the ancient Gnostics,
Novatians and Manichæans were substantially removed, great schisms began to
take place on the basis of the Chalcedonian decree.

[2] See before this Demetrius, Peter, Methodius, Eustathius, Marcellus, and
Apollinaris

it. [1]  To this was added another fact.  The constitution of the
Patriarchate began to reveal its effect in threatening the unity
of the Church.  The Cappadocian Churches of Asia Minor re-
ceded into the background simply because they possessed no
patriarch of their own, dogmatics began to constitute an instrument of provincial ecclesiastical policy, and the dogmatic formula to be a mark of the diocese and nationality.  In proportion
as this took place, the state was compelled to intervene.  Dogmatic questions became vital to it, and the appointment in the
capital to the Patriarchate, which it had fostered, was now a
political problem of the first rank; for the occupant of the chair
stood at the head of the spiritual affairs of the empire.  The
great controversy was not settled at the two Synods of Ephesus
(431, 449), but it was, ostensibly, at the Synod of Chalcedon
(451) by means of a long formula.  This formula was proposed
and dictated by the West in the person of Bishop Leo and
was approved by the Emperor; it was regarded in the West
as the simple and unchanged creed of the Fathers, in the East
as a compromise which was felt by some not to be sufficiently
orthodox, and by others to require interpretation.  Meanwhile
the East hardly possessed as yet the rudiments of a theology
capable of interpreting it.  Therefore the formula of Chalcedon
has not unjustifiably been called a 'national misfortune' for
the Byzantine Empire.  But even as regards the Church its
advantages no more than balanced its disadvantages.  During
this period the monks obtained the mastery over the Church.
Although their relations with the hierarchy were not infrequently
strained, they added very greatly to its strength.  The clergy
would have been completely eclipsed in the world and the state,
if they had not obtained a new support from the 'religiosi'
and 'religiosity'.  But while monachism became an important
element in the Church, the prestige of the state declined in the
minds of men; nothing was left to the Emperors but to adopt
certain monkish fashions for themselves, and along with the
state the life of social morality was depreciated in favour of
'religiosity' and a magical cultus.  For monachism merely pro-

---

[1] "Babylon is fallen, fallen,"—with these words of triumph did Jerome accompany the overthrow of Chrysostom in the Origenist controversy (Ep. 88).

motes itself and next to that a religion of idol-worship; it
quits the field where a vigorous morality arises. On the other
hand, however, the State was delivered at the close of this
period from its most powerful opponent, the Bishop of Alexandria, though at much too high a cost.

The third period extends up to the fifth Œcumenical Council
(Constantinople A.D. 553). The disadvantages of the Chalcedonian
formula made themselves felt in the first half of this century.
Great ecclesiastical provinces were in revolt, and threatened to
secede from the membership of the universal Church. Greek
piety everywhere showed itself to have been unsettled by the
decree of Chalcedon. Theology could not follow it; nay, it
appeared to be stifled by the decision, while in Monophysitism
life and movement prevailed. The perplexed Emperors were
at their wits' end, and tried provisionally to recall, or at
any rate to tone down, the formula, but in doing so they
prejudiced the union with the West. This was changed under
Justin I., but above all under Justinian I. As the reign of
the latter was signalised politically by the restoration of the
Byzantine supremacy, and the codification of its laws, it was
ecclesiastically distinguished by the restoration and establishment of the constitution and dogmatics of the Church. The
creed of Rome was recognised so far as its wording was concerned, but Rome itself was humbled; the Chalcedonian formula
remained in force, but it was interpreted in terms of Cyril's
teaching, and its future position was assured by the condemnation of the writings of the Antiochene schools on the one hand,
and of Origen on the other. Thus was the theology of the
past judged: 'solitudinem faciunt, pacem appellant'. The Justinian Church condemned the glorious Fathers, and the fifth Œcumenical Council blotted out the freer theological science. However, this measure was only possible because an orthodox
Church theology had developed in the first half of the sixth
century.[1] It presupposed the Chalcedonian formula, which had
become more venerable by age, and explained it by means of
the philosophy of Aristotle, which had then come once more

---

[1] See Loofs, Leontius von Byzanz in the "Texten und Unters. z. alt-christl.
Literaturgesch.," Vol. III., parts 1 and 2, p. 37 ff., 303 ff.

to the front, in order to reconcile it with the spirit of Cyril's theology, and to make it in some measure comprehensible. *Here we have the rise of ecclesiastical scholasticism* which now took its place beside the mystical Neo-platonic theology that had been most comprehensively stated by the Pseudo-areopagite, and which corrected and defined it, uniting with and balancing it. The effect of this development was extremely significant. Men now began for the first time to feel themselves at home on the ground of the Chalcedonian formula; piety also was reconciled to it. Productive dogmatic work ceased entirely; its place was taken by the mystical theology of scholasticism based on the inheritance from antiquity and the enumeration of authorities. Justinian in reality closed not only the school of Athens, but also that of Origen, the schools, *i.e.*, of productive theological science and criticism. [1] Henceforth theology only existed as a servant to the tradition of Justinian and Chalcedon. It was served in turn by the dialectic of Aristotle on the one hand, and the Neo-platonic mysticism of the Areopagite on the other. It did important work in the way of elaboration and adaptation; we are not warranted in passing a sweeping verdict of stultification and sleep; [2] but it made no further change in the creed of the Church and was bound hand and foot. [3]

[1] The closing of the school of Athens has been disputed. It was certainly not a great, formal action; see Krummacher, Gesch. d. Byzant. Litt., p. 4.

[2] See the works of Gass and Gelzer, especially the latter's interesting lecture: "Die politische und kirchliche Stellung von Byzanz.

[3] Noteworthy, but not surprising, is the parallel capable of being drawn between the history of theology and that of (heathen) philosophy during the whole period from Origen to Justinian. The history of Greek philosophy finds its limits in the middle of the fifth century, and again in the age of Justinian; the same is true of the science of the Church. In the general history of science Plato comes to be supplanted by Aristotle from the close of the fifth century; in dogmatics the influence of the Stagirite makes itself felt to an increased extent from the same date. Justinian's epoch-making measures, the codification of the law, the closing of the school of Athens, and the restoration of the Byzantine Church and Empire, point to an inner connection. This has not escaped Ranke. On account of the importance of the matter I give here his excellent discussion (Vol. IV. 2, p. 20 ff.): "Justinian closed the school of Athens ... An event of importance for the whole continued development of the human race; any further development in a direct line on the basis laid in classical antiquity was rendered impossible to the Greek

As regards the history of dogma the fourth period possesses no real independence. The dogmatic activity which characterised it was exclusively political; but since it created a new formula, we may here assume a special period. It ends with

spirit, while to Roman genius such an advance was left open and was only now rendered truly possible for after ages by means of the law-books. The philosophical spirit perished in the contentions of religious parties; the legal found a mode of expression which, as it were, concentrated it. The close of Greek philosophy recalls its beginning; nearly a thousand years had elapsed during which the greatest transformations in the history of the world had taken place. May I be permitted to add a general reflection, as to which I merely desire that it may not be rejected by the general feeling of scholars.

The Christian religion had risen upon earth in the conflict of religious opinions waged by nations, and had then in opposition to these developed into a Church. Christian theology which set itself to appropriate the mysterious and to come to terms with the intellect had grown up in constant contact, sometimes of a friendly, more often of a hostile kind, with Greek philosophy. That was the business of those centuries. Then appeared the great Christian theologians from Origen onwards; as we said in passing, they passed through, without exception, Greek or closely related Latin schools, and framed their doctrines accordingly. Greek philosophy had produced nothing comparable to them; it had, as regards public life, been thrust into the background and now it had perished. But it is striking that the great Christian theologians also came to an end. Never again do we find in later times men like Athanasius, the Gregories of Cappadocia, Chrysostom, Ambrose and Augustine. I mean that along with Greek philosophy the original development of Christian theology also came to a stand-still. The energy of the Church doctors, or the importance of the Church assemblies in these centuries cannot be paralleled by analogous phenomena belonging to later times. Different as they are in themselves we find a certain resemblance in the state of Roman law and of Christian theology. The old Roman jurisprudence now appeared as universally valid law in a redaction which while historical was yet swayed by the conditions of the day. At the same time, limits were set by the triumph of orthodoxy, especially of the dogmas declared in the Chalcedonian resolutions, to all the internal divisions of theology in which the divergent opinions were also defended with ability and thoroughness ... Justinian who reinstated orthodoxy, and gave the force of law to juridical conceptions, takes a high place in the rivalry of the centuries. Yet, while he raised his government to such a pinnacle of authority, he felt the ground shake momentarily under his feet." Greek science and the monkish view of the world, leagued as they were, dominated the spiritual life of the Church before as well as after the Justinian age; they were at bottom indeed far from being opposed, but possessed a common root. But how differently it was possible to combine them, what variations they were capable of! If we compare, e.g., Gregory of Nyssa with John of Damascus it is easy to see that the former still really thinks independently, while the latter confines himself to editing what is given. It is above all clear that the critical elements of theology had been lost. They only held their ground in the vagaries of mystical speculation; in all ages they are most readily tolerated there.

the sixth Œcumenical Council (A.D. 680). 'Justinian's policy of conquest was in the highest degree unstable, and went far beyond the resources of the Empire'. Whether his dogmatic policy was correct, which maintained union with the West at the cost of losing a large section of the Oriental Churches, is a question which may be debated. But whether an open and consistently monophysite policy was then still possible in Constantinople is very doubtful. Egypt, Syria, and Armenia were lost, not only to the state, but also to Greek language and culture. In order to keep them, or win them back from the Persians and Arabians, an energetic Emperor resolved to publish a monophysite rallying cry without prejudicing the wording of the Chalcedonian Creed. Monothelitism on the basis of the doctrine of the two natures is in itself no artificial creation; it is founded on the old consideration rising out of the doctrine of redemption; but at that time it had its origin in policy. Yet this still-born child of politics set the Eastern Church in an uproar for more than two generations. To prevent the loss not only of the East but of Italy also, the Emperor required the help of the Roman Bishop. Justinian's success in curbing the latter's authority had only continued for a little under his successors. The pontificate of Gregory I. still exerted an influence, and, at the sixth Council, Agatho, repairing the fault of one of his predecessors, dictated the formula, as Leo had done at Chalcedon. This bore the impress of the West, and did not correspond perfectly to the eastern conception. It further became manifest at the Council that, when it was a question of defining dogma, theology had been completely transformed into a rehearsal of authorities. Next to the older synodal decisions, the decisive precedent was formed by the immense, and frequently forged, collection of the *dicta patrum*.

After the sixth Council, orthodoxy and Monophysitism were definitively separated, though attempts were not wanting to harmonise them in the following centuries, in keeping with the monophysite tendencies, never wholly destroyed, of eastern orthodoxy. The mystery was firmly established, and obtained further definition; for the doctrine taught by John of Damascus of the enhypostasis of the human nature in the Logos) had been accepted, even in the age of Justinian, to be the correct interpretation of the doctrine of the two natures. The movement of thought in the Church passed accordingly to a new sphere; or, more correctly, the old absorbing interest of the Church in the mysteries of the cultus [1] now came to light undisguised, because the pursuit of theology, converted as it was into scholasticism, had become the business of scholars and experts in the mysteries, and it was only temporarily that a controversy springing out of it agitated the Church. Dogma, designed by the Nicene and Chalcedonian Creeds to be looked at and treated formally, henceforth revealed this its character thoroughly. The philosophy appropriate to it was found, or invented—that compound of Neoplatonism and Aristotelianism, with which no one could dispense who desired to unfold or comment on dogma orthodoxly. [2] He who passed over the philosophy of the Church stood in danger of becoming a heretic. [3]

---

[1] It is said of Polycarp in his Vita per Pionium (sæc. IV.): ἑρμηνεῦσαί τε ἱκανὸς μυστήρια, ἃ τοῖς πολλοῖς ἦν ἀπόκρυφα, οὕτω φανερῶς αὐτὰ ἐξετίθετο, ὥστε τοὺς ἀκούοντας μαρτυρεῖν, ὅτι οὐ μόνον ἀκούουσιν ἀλλὰ καὶ ὁρῶσιν αὐτά. That was accordingly the supreme thing; to be able also to see the mystery, the Christian possession of salvation.

[2] The fight between Platonism and Aristotelianism was accordingly acute among theologians in the following centuries; they often indeed made heretics of one another. Up till now we only know these disputes in part; they are important for the later conflicts in the West, but they do not belong to the history of dogma

[3] Even to-day simple-minded Catholic historians of dogma exist who frankly admit that he becomes necessarily a heretic who does not, e.g., use the conceptions "nature" and "person" correctly; and they even derive heresy from this starting-point. Thus Bertram (Theodoreti, Ep. Cyrensis, doctrina christologica, 1883) writes of Theodore of Mopsuestia: "Manifesto declarat, simile vel idem esse perfectam naturam et perfectam personam... Naturæ vox designat, quid sit aliqua res, vel essentiam vel quidditatem; hypostasis vero modum metaphysicum existendi monstrat. Ex quo patet, ad notionem perfectæ naturæ modum illum perfectum existendi non requiri. *Hac in re erravit Mopsuestenus, et hæresis perniciosa ex hoc errore nata est.* What a *quid pro quo!* The ignorance of the terminology, which was yet first created *ad hoc*, in order to escape Scylla and Charybdis, is held to be the real ground of the origin of the heresy. Such a view of things, which is as old as scholasticism, undoubtedly needed mysticism as its counterpoise, in order not to perish wholly from the religious sphere. Atzberger (Die Logoslehre d. h. Athan., 1880) has expressed himself still more unsophisticatedly, and therefore more instructively, on the relation of philosophy and dogma (p. 8, 29). But see also Hagemann (Röm Kirche, p. 361): "The Patripassians arrived at their doctrines of

But dogmatics, undoubtedly the foundation, did not dominate the Church as a living power. The conception of the natures of Christ found its continuation in that of the sacraments and sacramental things by which men became participators in Christ. The perceived (αἰσθητόν) thereby obtained side by side with the conceived (νοητόν) an ever loftier, and independent significance. Symbolism was more and more expunged; the mystery became more and more sensuous. But, in proportion as the latter was made operative in the cultus, the cultus itself was regarded, in all its setting and performance, in the light of the divino-human. [1] All its sensuous side, which was presented for his benefit to the worshipper, was regarded as deified and as promoting deification. Now in so far as the believer derived his life entirely from this cultus, a ritual system, to which the character of the divino-human attached, took the place of the God-man, Christ. Piety threatened to be submerged in a contemplation of wonders, the spiritual in the sensuous, and theology, in so far as not identified with scholasticism and polemics, in a science of mysteries. [2] From this point of view we can understand the worship of images and the reaction of icono-

God, his attributes, his creation, and incarnation, because they took their stand on Stoic logic and with it cherished the most extreme nominalism, and because they absolutely rejected the objective existence of ideas."

[1] For the history of the development of the Greek liturgy after the fourth century, Swainson's The Greek Liturgies, chiefly from original authorities (London 1884), is the standard work. For the doctrine of the mysteries cf. Steitz' Abhandlungen in the Lehrbb. f. deutsche Theol. 1864 ff.

[2] If we collect the fourth-century evidence of crude sensuous superstition intimately combined with Christian piety, we might believe that it could go no further. And yet it did go further from century to century, as anyone can easily convince himself by reading the tales of saints and relics, among which those of the oriental monophysites are the worst. But apart from this increase, we have to call attention to the fact that this barbarous superstition ascended into higher and more influential circles and was systematically cultivated by the monks, while the corrective of a more rational theology grew ever weaker. Theology became more defenceless, because it had to adapt itself to sacred ceremony. The worst gift bequeathed by moribund antiquity to the Church was the ritual of magic and the monstrous number of great and little aids in need and means of atonement. It is not the case that this state of matters was produced by the inrush of barbarian peoples; on the contrary, the decomposition of ancient culture and religion takes the first place in the process, and even the Neo-platonic philosophers are not free from blame. In view of this circumstance it is natural to conclude that the reforma-

clasm which opened the fifth period. But this explanation is
not complete; another factor coöperated. This was the relation
of Church and State which was also involved in the controversy
about images. There always were discords between them; but
these became more and more acute when the priesthood fell
completely under the sway of the monks. Even from the fifth
century the practice had begun of transferring monks to episcopal chairs, and it had almost become the rule in the following
centuries. But the monks both strove zealously to make the
Church independent and claimed sovereignty among the people,
and as a rule, though interested on behalf of the *nations,* they
also cherished a strong hostility to the *State:* in other words
they endangered the settlement of Church and State established
in the fifth and sixth centuries. Their most powerful instrument
was the sensuous cultus which had captivated the people, but
which undoubtedly, barbarous and mechanical as it was with
all its appliances and amulets, was yet connected with the ideal
forces still to be credited to the age, with science, art, and
especially piety. Here we have the miserable dilemma of the
period, and of the Church; the worship of images was barbarous,
but iconoclasm threatened to introduce an increased degree of barbarism. For the 'enlightened' (Aufklärung) were at the disposal of
an iron military despotism, and despised science, art, and religion.

tion of Athanasius bore little fruit, that it only checked for a time the polytheistic
under-current, and, in a word, that the Church could not have got into a worse
state than, in spite of Athanasius, it did, as regards the worship of Mary, angels,
saints, martyrs, images and relics, and the trickery practised with amulets. But even
if we were to go further and suggest that the later development of dogma itself, as
*e.g.,* in the worship of Mary and images, directly promoted religious materialism,
yet we cannot rate too highly the salutary importance of this dogma. For it kept
the worship of saints, images and the rest at the stage of a christianity of the
second order, invested with doubtful authority, and it prevented the monks from
cutting themselves wholly adrift from the *religio publica.* Finally, it is to be
pointed out that superstition has brought with it at all times ideas and conceptions
extremely questionable from the point of view of dogmatics, ideas which seem to be
affected by no amount of censure. Overbeck (Gött. Gel.- Auz. 1883, no. 28, p. 870)
has rightly described it as a phenomenon requiring explanation that the gnat-
straining centuries which followed Nicæa, could have swallowed such camels as,
*e.g.,* delighted the readers of the Acts of Thomas (even in the Catholic edition) or
of the numerous Apocalypses (see the edition of the Apoc. Apocal. by Tischendorf
and James, Apocrypha anecdota, 1893).

The Church of Byzantium was at that time engaged in a life and death struggle. Its existence was really at stake, and with it the existence of the old form of society and culture, in opposition to forces which as yet had no positive policy, but at first merely ruled by brute force. The priestly caste was arrayed against the military, the hosts of shaven monks against the standing army, which from the fourth century had played a great rôle, but now sought to be master in the state. These fearful fights ended in the restoration of the *status quo ante*, in so far as dogma and cultus were concerned, and the old order seemed all the more sacred after the attacks that had been made upon it. But on the political side, the state supported by the army carried off the victory—and this was not without consequences for the system and life of the Church. The monks were given a free hand in dogma, but their activity as ecclesiastical politicians was checked. The Emperor remained chief priest, in spite of some patriarchs who, until after the eleventh century, attempted to maintain an independent and equal position side by side with him. With the support of his army he resisted them. The independence of the Church was gone, in so far as it sought to rise above the level of an institution devoted to ritual and worship. Its activity was completely restricted to the mysteries and the preparation for death. It became an institution of the state, impressing it only by the unchangeableness of its doctrine and ceremonies. To the new peoples to whom this Church came, the Slavs, it was far more than to the Greeks an unchangeable, heavenly creation. A thousand years have passed away since the Slavs were hellenised; and they have not yet ventured, like the Germans, to think and feel freely and at their ease in the Church, although they recognise in it a main defence of their national characteristics against the West. From the West these 'Greek Slavs' were spiritually separated, after Augustine's ideas were admitted there. The external cleavage, though only complete in the eleventh century, began immediately after the image controversy. The states in the territory of the Greek Church still really stand under a military dictatorship: where this has fallen, as in the kingdom of Greece, a final stage has not yet been reached.

States like the former support an ecclesiastical department, but no Church.

The path into which Athanasius led the Church has not been abandoned; but the other forces of life completely restricted it. Orthodox dogma corresponds on the whole to the conception of Athanasius; but the balance which he held between the religious creed and the cultus has been disturbed to the disadvantage of the former. The creed still shows life when it is called in question, or when the nation it serves requires a flag. In other cases it lives in the science of scholastic mysticism, which has already become by degrees stereotyped and sacred, and in its presentation in public worship. Theology also is bound to the latter; it has thus received a standard of which Athanasius knew nothing. [1]

Our sources are the works of the Church Fathers and the Acts of Councils (Mansi). We still want a history of Greek ecclesiastical literature after Eusebius, capable of satisfying the most reasonable demands. Of more recent works on the subject that of Fessler is the best (Instit. Patrologiæ, 1850—52), Alzog's is the most familiar, and Nirschl's the newest.

[1] It is very characteristic as regards this, that while Cyril of Jerusalem described the Christian religion as μάθημα τῶν δογμάτων καὶ πράξεις ἀγαθαί, Photius defined it as μάθησις καὶ μυσταγωγία. From the fourth century interest was more and more transferred from the regulation of the whole life by religion, to its external consecration through the mysteries. The distinctions are indeed only gradual, but the descent was very significant. The Greek Church ultimately gave up the regulation of moral social life, and therewith renounced the power to determine private morality so far as the latter was not dominated by fear of death. The ultimate reason of this is to be sought in the order of the monks and the constitution of the Græco-Slavic states.

# CHAPTER II.

## THE FUNDAMENTAL CONCEPTION OF SALVATION AND GENERAL OUTLINE OF THE DOCTRINAL SYSTEM.

I. THE dogmatic conflicts in the East from the fourth up to the seventh century have this in common, that they centred almost entirely in Christology in the narrower sense, as well as in the incarnation of the Deity. Since men of all parties were meanwhile conscious that they were contending for the essence of Christianity, it follows that the conception of the salvation offered in the Christian religion is to be deduced from the formulas over which they fought, and which then made good their ground. This conclusion is, however, made further certain from the fact that the oriental Church took no interest in dogma, apart from those formulas, at least in the time of these conflicts. [1] Anything else, therefore, outside of the formulas, which was either fixed as *matter of course*, or maintained in ambiguous propositions in opposition to Manichæism, Fatalism, and Epicureanism, did not possess the value of a dog-

[1] Very instructive in this respect is the Church History of Socrates. A man's orthodoxy is completely decided for him by his attitude to the dogma of the Trinity (see H. E. III. 7, VI. 13, VII. 6, 11). The Cappadocians and the theologians after Socrates held similar views; see Gregory of Naz. Orat. XXVII. 10: "Philosophise about the world and worlds, matter, the soul, rational beings, good and bad alike, about resurrection, judgment, and retribution, and the sufferings of Christ. For if on these points you hit on the truth it is not without service, but if you fail, you can suffer no harm" (cf. Ullmann, Gregory of Naz., 1867, p. 217 f.). We have also to consider here the contents of the oriental symbols, creed-decalogues etc. The interest taken to an increasing extent from the fifth century in the tenets levelled against Origen was biblical and traditional. It only became dogmatic at a time when in theology and Christology the influence of "antiquity" had taken the place of that of dogma. On the place and importance of the doctrine of the Trinity in Gregory, see Ullman, p. 232 ff.

matic declaration in the strict sense. Remembering this, there
can be no doubt that the essence of the Christian religion, and
therefore the contents of its creed, are summed up in the
following proposition. *The salvation presented in Christianity
consists in the redemption of the human race from the state
of mortality and the sin involved in it, that men might attain
divine life, i.e., the everlasting contemplation of God, this redemption having already been consummated in the incarnation
of the Son of God, and being conferred on men by their close
union with him: Christianity is the religion which delivers
from death and leads to the contemplation of God.* [1] This proposition can be more precisely defined as follows: the highest
blessing bestowed in Christianity is adoption into the divine
sonship, which is assured to the believer, and is completed in
participation in the divine nature, or more accurately, in the
deification of man through the gift of immortality. This gift
includes the perfect knowledge and the lasting vision of God,
in a blessedness void of suffering, but it does not do away
with the interval between Christ and the believer. [2]   From this

---

[1] I share fully the view of Kattenbusch (Confessionskunde I., p. 296) that the
dogma was not merely supported by one idea, and that in the Greek Church of
to-day the idea of redemption held by the ancient Church no longer rules directly;
but this view does not contradict the exposition given in the text.

[2] The fact that the idea of deification was the ultimate and supreme thought
is not a discovery of recent times, but it is only in recent times that it has been
appreciated in all its importance. After Theophilus, Irenæus, Hippolytus, and Origen,
it is found in all the Fathers of the ancient Church, and that in a primary position.
We have it in Athanasius, the Cappadocians, Apollinaris, Ephraem Syrus, Epiphanius,
and others, as also in Cyril, Sophronius, and late Greek and Russian theologians.
In proof of it Psalm LXXXII. 6 is very often quoted—"I said ye are gods and all
sons of the most High." Just as often are θεοποίησις and ἀθανασία expressly combined.
Some Fathers feel the boldness of the formula; but that is very rare. I select
merely a few from my collection of passages: Athanas. de incarn. 54: "Αὐτὸς
ἐνηνθρώπησεν, ἵνα ἡμεῖς θεοποιηθῶμεν, καὶ αὐτὸς ἐφανέρωσεν ἑαυτὸν διὰ σώματος, ἵνα
ἡμεῖς τοῦ ἀοράτου πατρὸς ἔννοιαν λάβωμεν, καὶ αὐτὸς ὑπέμεινεν τὴν παρ᾽ ἀνθρώπου
ὕβριν, ἵνα ἡμεῖς ἀθανασίαν κληρονομήσωμεν, cf. Ep. ad Serap. I. 24, Orat. c. Arian. I.
38, 39, and often; Vita Antonii, c. 74, Ephraem, Comment. in Diatess., init. (ed.
Moesinger, p. 1): "Quare dominus noster carnem induit? Ut ipsa caro victoriæ
gaudia gustaret et dona gratiæ explorata et cognita haberet. Si deus sine carne
vicisset, quæ ei tribuerentur laudes? Secundo, ut dominus noster manifestum faceret,
se initio creationis nequaquam ex invidia prohibuisse, quominus homo fieret deus,
quia maius est, quod dominus noster in homine humiliabatur, quam quod in eo,

it follows: (1) *that redemption, as seen in its final effect, was conceived to be the abrogation of the natural state by a miraculous transformation of our nature;* that accordingly (2) the supreme good was definitely distinguished from the morally good; and that (3) an atonement was not included in it. For atonement can only be thought of where the division between God and man is regarded as an opposition of the will. But it further follows from this that this theology, in agreement with the apologetic and old Catholic doctrine, admitted no independent object to our present life. The work of the Christian consisted wholly in preparing for death (τὸ ἔργον τοῦ Χριστιανοῦ οὐδὲν ἄλλο

dum magnus et gloriosus erat, habitabat. Hinc illud: 'Ego dixi, dii estis'." Gregory of Nyss., Colloq. cum Macrina (ed. Oehler, p. 170): Τῶν οὖν τοιούτων ταῖς διὰ τοῦ πυρὸς ἰατρείαις ἐκκαθαρθέντων τε καὶ ἀφαγνισθέντων, ἕκαστον τῶν πρὸς τὸ κρεῖττον νοουμένων ἀντεισελεύσεται, ἡ ἀφθαρσία, ἡ ζωή; ἡ τιμή, ἡ χάρις, ἡ δόξα, ἡ δύναμις, καὶ εἴ τι ἄλλο τοιοῦτον αὐτῷ τε τῇ Θεῷ ἐπιθεωρεῖσθαι εἰκάζομεν. Gregory of Naz., Orat. 40, c. 45 (Decalogus fidei, ed Caspari, Alte und Neue Quellen, 1879, p. 21): πίστευε τὸν υἱὸν τοῦ Θεοῦ ... τοσοῦτον ἄνθρωπον διά σε, ὅσον σὺ γίνῃ δι' ἐκεῖνον Θεός. So also Orat. I. 5: " We become like Christ, since Christ also became like us; we become gods on his account, since he also became man for our sake." On the other hand, compare Orat. XLII. 17: μεθ' ἡμῶν τὸ κτίσμα, τῶν οὐ Θεῶν· εἰ κτίσμα δέ, οὐ Θεός, and XXXIX. 17: "How should he not be God, *to insert in passing a bold deduction,* by whom thou also dost become God?" Apollinaris Laod., Κατὰ μέρος πίστις (ed. Lagarde, p. 110): φαμὲν ἄνθρωπον γεγενῆσθαι τὸν τοῦ Θεοῦ λόγον, ἵνα τὴν ὁμοίωσιν τοῦ ἐπουρανίου λάβωμεν καὶ θεοποιηθῶμεν. Macar., hom. 39. Pseudo-hippolytus, Theophan. (ed. Lagarde, p. 41, 21): εἰ οὖν ἀθάνατος γέγονεν ὁ ἄνθρωπος, ἔσται καὶ θεός. Dionys. Areopag., sæpissime, *e.g.,* de cælesti hierar. c. 1: ἡ ἡμῶν ἀνάλογος θέωσις. Sophronius, Christmas Sermon (ed. Usener, Rhein. Mus. für Philologie, 1886, p. 505): θεωθῶμεν θείαις μεταβολαῖς καὶ μιμήσεσιν. Leo, Patriarch of Russia (Pawlow, p. 126): ἐθεώθημεν Θεοῦ τῇ μεταλήψει. Gennadius, Confess. (ed. Kimmel, p. 10): " dixit deus: Induam me carne ... et erit omnis homo tamquam deus non secundum naturam sed secundum participationem." We have, however, to notice that this deification, as understood by the Greek Church, did not by any means signify roundly "Becoming like God". The Greeks in the main did not connect any clear conception with the thought of the possession of salvation (felicity) further than the idea of imperishableness; and this very fact was their characteristic feature. It is the ineffable, the transcendent which may therefore be described as the θεία φύσις, because it is enjoyed for ever. The interval between Christ—who was born, and did not become, Son of God—and the sons by adoption is always very strongly emphasised; compare (the precise expositions in Augustine, De remiss. pace. II. 24) and above all, Athanasius' third discourse against the Arians ; further, Cyril Catech. II., ch. 4—7 and 19. Yet the θέωσις of Mary forms a kind of exception. The idea of deification is also found in Western writers, especially Augustine. But if I am not deceived Augustine himself brought it to an edifying end.

ἐστὶν ἢ μελετᾶν ἀποθνήσκειν). In the present there only existed
a preliminary possession of salvation. This was represented (1)
in the knowledge of God and of the accomplished incarnation of
the Son of God, and therewith in the certain hope of being
deified; (2) in power over demons; (3) in the call to salvation
and perfect acquaintance with the conditions of its reception;
(4) in certain communications of divine Grace which supported
believers in fulfilling those conditions—the forgiveness of sin in
baptism, the power of certain holy rites, and holy vehicles,
the example of the God-man etc.; and (5) in participation in
the mysteries—worship and the Lord's supper—and in the enjoyment of the consecration they imparted, as also, for ascetics,
in a foretaste of the future liberation from the senses and
deification. [1]

The certainty of faith in the future deification, however, because
its possibility and reality, rested exclusively on the fact of the
incarnation of the Son of God. The divine had already appeared
on earth and had united itself inseparably with human nature.

This conception formed the universal foundation for the
development - of dogmas in the fourth to the seventh century,
though all might not equally understand it or see its consequences clearly. Only thus can we comprehend how the Church
could perceive, define, and establish the nature of salvation in
the constitution of the incarnate Son of God. Faith simply
embraces the correct perception of the nature of the incarnate
Logos, because this perception of faith includes the assured
hope of a change of human nature analogous to the divinity
of Jesus Christ, and therewith everything worth striving for.
'We become divine through him, because for our sake he became man'. But the dogmatic formulas corresponding to this
conception only established their position after severe fights;
they never arrived at a perfectly exact expression; and they
never obtained the exclusive supremacy which they demanded.

---

[1] Athanasius (Ep. encycl. ad episc. Ægypt. et Lib. ch. I.) mentions as the gifts
of grace already possessed by Christians: (1) the type of the heavenly mode of
life, (2) power over demons, (3) adoption to be sons, (4) and what is exalted and
rises high above every gift—the knowledge of the Father and the Word himself
and the grant of the Holy Spirit. This list is not quite complete.

The reasons for this delay, inexactness, and failure to obtain supremacy are numerous and various. The most important deserve to be emphasised.

Firstly, every new formula, however necessary it might appear, had the spirit of the Catholic Church against it, simply because it was new; it could only gain acceptance by deceiving as to its character of novelty, and as long as the attempt to do so was unsuccessful, it was regarded by the pious with suspicion. [1] Secondly, the ability of the Catholic Fathers really to explain their faith, and to deduce dogmatic consequences, was extremely slight. Grown up in the schools of philosophy and rhetoric, they never clearly felt it to be their duty to give an abstract account of their faith, however they might understand it. Far from describing the system of doctrine as a statement of the nature and contents of Christian piety, and from evolving the latter from its distinctive conditions, they found it difficult even to make a simple inference from their conception of salvation to the person of Christ and *vice versa*. Their reasoning was always being disturbed by apologetic or other considerations foreign to it. Energetic men, to whom the matter of religion should be all in all, were accordingly required, if an advance were to take place in the work of formulating it. But such men have been extremely rare. There have been few in all periods of the history of dogma who clearly perceived and duly appreciated the final interests which moved themselves. This is true of the ancient Church, though then matters were a little better than in later centuries. Thirdly, the formulas required conflicted with every kind of philosophy; they amounted to an offence to the thought of the schools. This circumstance undoubtedly might afterwards prove an advantage; it was possible to show the divinity and sacredness of the formulas by referring to their inscrutability and therefore to the mystery that surrounded them. But as long as the formula was still new, this confirmation encountered doubts, and even afterwards, in spite of the 'mystery', it was impossible to do without a philosophy which should interpret it, and should restore confidence,

[1] See above, p. 137, f.

as to the contradictions, by new combinations of categories.
Now, as long as no such philosophy was created, faith was not satisfied, and the formula was not guaranteed permanence. Fourthly,
it was of the highest importance that by almost all the Fathers
their conception of the salvation procured by the God-man
(deification) was appended to, or bolstered up by, the system
of 'natural theology'. But under this system knowledge and
virtue were the highest blessings, and God was exclusively the
judge who rewarded the good and punished the wicked. Now,
it was undoubtedly possible so to combine these two lines of
thought that neither was prejudiced, and we will see that such
a combination alone corresponded to the ideas of those Christians, and was actually brought about. But it was impossible to
prevent natural theology from intruding more and more into
dogmatics, and from interfering with the success of the mystical
doctrine of redemption—for so we may well name it. Men were
not in a position to strike at the roots of those views of Christian salvation which did not definitely conceive the latter to be
distinctive, and which therefore did not sufficiently differentiate
it from virtue and the natural knowledge of God.

Fifthly, the complete acceptance of the mystical doctrine of
redemption was imperilled from another side, and this menace
also could never be completely averted. The picture of the
life of Jesus contained in the Gospels, in spite of all the arts
of exegesis, contradicted in a way it was impossible to disregard the Christological formulas called for by the doctrine.
The life even influenced the form given to the dogma of the
incarnation and its consequences [1] to an extent which, from the
standpoint of the theory of redemption, was questionable; and
it subsequently always accompanied the dogmatic formulas,

[1] In the introductory fourth Catechism in which Cyril summarises the main
points of the faith, he says (ch. IX.): πίστευε δὲ ὅτι οὗτος ὁ μονογενὴς υἱὸς τοῦ
Θεοῦ διὰ τὰς ἁμαρτίας ἡμῶν ἐξ οὐρανῶν κατῆλθεν ἐπὶ τῆς γῆς. (ch. X.): οὗτος ἐσταυ-
ρώθη ὑπὲρ τῶν ἁμαρτιῶν ἡμῶν. Nothing is said of the abolition of death. So also
in the Homilies of Chrysostom who generally tried to follow Paul, sin comes to
the front. The saying "Let us not fear death, but only sin," is often repeated with
variations by Chrysostom. Alexander of Alex. also in his letter to Alexander (Theodoret H. E. I. 4) gives as the only ground of the incarnation of the Son of God,
that he came εἰς ἀθέτησιν ἁμαρτίας, but he is unable to carry out the thought.

keeping alive in the Church the remnant of a conception of the Redeemer's personality which did not agree with them. The Church indeed never lost recollection of the human individuality of Jesus in its simple loftiness, its heart-winning love, and its holy earnestness; it never forgot the revelation of God in humanity. Scripture reading and, in part also, preaching preserved the memory, and with and by it thought was ever again led to the simplest and highest of facts, the love of God which is loftier than all reason, the rendering of service to our neighbour, sincere humility, and patience. But as the gospel prevented dogma from obtaining an exclusive supremacy, so also Pauline theology, and kindred views found in Holy Scripture, exerted an important influence, which maintained its ground side by side with the dogma, and often very strongly decided its exposition. That the work of Christ consisted in what he achieved, culminating in his sacrificial death, and signifying the overcoming and removal of guilt; that salvation accordingly consisted in the forgiveness, justification and adoption of men, are ideas absolutely wanting in none of the Church Fathers, and very prominent in a few, while in the majority they find their way into the exposition of the dogma of redemption. They do not agree with the latter, nay, in this combination can hardly be held to have deepened the conception in any point; for they rather menaced the finality of the fundamental dogmatic thought in which men lived. In fact they wrought mischief, i.e., they led to moral laxity, as in all cases where they are only allowed a secondary authority. But their existence must be expressly stated if our view is to be complete. New Testament reminiscences and thoughts and in general Biblical theological ideas of the most varied kind, always accompanied and impinged on dogma growing or full-grown. [1] They helped to delay its reduction into formulas, and prevented the mystical doctrine of redemption and its corresponding dogmas obtaining a completely exclusive supremacy in the Eastern Churches.

Sixthly and finally, the scheme of Christology, distinctive of the

[1] The contradictions and inconsistencies were not felt if it was possible to support the separate propositions by an appeal to Holy Scripture: see on this Vol. II., p. 331, n. 1.

West, forced on the Church by the policy of the emperors, brought a disturbing and confusing influence into the Eastern history of dogma. The Eastern Church, left to itself, could only, if it had simply given expression to its own idea of redemption, have raised to a dogma the one nature, made flesh, of God, the Logos (μία φύσις θεοῦ λόγου σεσαρκωμένη), and must have left the paradox standing that the humanity of Christ was consubstantial (ὁμοούσιος) with ours, and was yet from the beginning not only without sin, but free from any kind of corruption (φθορά). This dogma was condemned as heretical in the process, as we know, of forming an exclusive authoritative doctrine, and another was set up in its place which it required the most elaborate efforts of theologians to connect closely with the idea of redemption. Conversely, as regards the doctrine of the Trinity in the fourth century, while the correct formula—correct, *i.e.,* when gauged by the conception of redemption—triumphed, yet the consider-ations springing from natural theology and science were here so strong that the Eastern Church could only reconcile itself to the doctrine by the aid of a complicated theology, which in this case, however, was really heterodox, because it weakened the meaning of the formula. *In the fourth century the correct formula triumphed, but the triumph was procured by a theology really heterodox; in the fifth and up to the seventh an incorrect formula, if gauged by the idea of redemption, became supreme, but theology was able to treat it orthodoxly.* In view of these incongruities one is almost tempted to believe in the 'cunning of the idea'; for this development alone made possible, or demand-ed, the application of the whole apparatus of Platonic and Aristotelian philosophy to dogma. Neither the conception of the ὁμοούσιος (consubstantial) as given by Athanasius, nor the strictly Monophysite form of the incarnation dogma, would have conjured philosophy anew to its aid, and to a greater extent than was contained in the dogma itself. This happened and could not but happen, because men would not understand ομοούσιος as ταυτούσιος (of the same substance); and because they were forced to fit the two natures into their system. Dog-matics (the doctrines of the Trinity and the Incarnation) became the high school of Philosophy. By them the Middle Ages received all that they ever did of philosophical thought. And these facts were due to the circumstance that the idea of redemption was not expressed purely and absolutely in dogma, that rather in the doctrine of the Trinity, as well as in the Christology, the formula overlapped its support, or the support the formula, and therefore necessarily called for endless exertions. Where would Plato and Aristotle have been in the Church or the Middle Ages if the East had honoured Athanasius and Julian of Halicarnassus as the sole authoritative Fathers of the Church, and how nearly was this the case with both! How much the East owes to the interference of the West, and yet, on the other hand, how greatly did the same West disturb it! But it is to be described as a gain from another point of view, that the correct formulas—those which corresponded to the Greek idea of redemption—did not establish their position. *The evangelical conception of Christ was preserved to a greater degree in the Byzantine and Nestorian Church, based on the doctrine of the two natures, than in the Monophysite Churches.* The latter only prove that the consistent development of the materialistic idea of redemption reduces Christianity to barbarism. The Arabians taught Aristotle to the Nestorians and not to the Monophysites. But those Churches also show that the Christ who possessed one incarnate nature—that phantom—reduced the historical Christ almost to the vanishing point. All the features of the man Christ of history, which the Byzantine and Nestorian Church still kept alive in their communities, are so many evidences that the old idea of redemption was forced to submit to limitations.

But in spite of this the dogma of the God-man which sprang from the doctrine of redemption assumed a unique and predominant position and alone constituted dogma in the strict sense. Theology = the doctrine of the Trinity, Economy = the idea and realisation of the Incarnation. The course of development also shows by its inner logic, which indeed, as already pointed out, was not so stringent as more recent scholars would have us believe, that it was in this dogma that the strongest interest was taken. After Athanasius had proved the necessity and realisation of redemption through the incarnation of the

Son of God, the consubstantiality (Homoousia) of the Son
of God with God himself was first established. Then the
fact was emphasised that the Incarnate was constituted similarly
with man, and finally, the unity of deity and humanity in the
incarnate Son of God was settled. The historian of dogma has
here simply to follow the course of history. It is in this connection by no means clear how besides this the work of the
God-man is to be treated. As regards the work of Christ we
can only deal with 'conceptions' which are not firmly allied to the
dogma. But we have to remark finally, that not only in theory was
the dogma planned eschatologically, *i.e.*, with a view to the future
life, but that also in practice faith in the imminent approach of the
end of the world still influenced the pious. In a few Fathers this
faith undoubtedly held a subordinate place; but yet it formed
the rule, and the storms caused by the invasion of the tribes
as well as the political revolutions constantly gave it strength.

II. In relation to the blessing of salvation man is receptive
and passive. He receives it in this world in the hope of his
faith, and enjoys it in the other as a transcendently glorious
gift of grace. God alone can grant it, and no human effort
can deserve it. As we have already noticed, this religious blessing
of salvation is wholly different from moral goodness; for moral
goodness cannot be presented, but must be gained by our own
actions. On the other hand, Christianity as a religion cannot
take up a neutral attitude to moral goodness, but must rather
embrace the loftiest morality. That was also the universal conviction of the Greek Church and its theologians. The problem
which thus arose was solved without noteworthy vacillations,
and in the sense of the theology of the apologists and Origen.
It was assumed that freedom in the moral sphere corresponded
to receptivity in the domain of religion and the blessings of
salvation conferred by it; and that God attached the grant of
the religious blessing of salvation to the achievement of a
perfectly moral life, whose law, though not new, had first
found expression in the Christian religion as something perfect
and capable of being easily recognised. The scheme of nature
and grace current in the West since Augustine, was not
entirely unknown in the East, so far as words were concern-

ed.[1] But the latter already found "grace" in "nature", *i.e.*, in the inalienable natural disposition to freedom, and, on the other hand, conceived "grace" to be the communication of a higher nature. Hence the above scheme was not adapted to express Greek thought. Christianity was rather, on the one hand, the perfect law of goodness, and, on the other, a promise and sure pledge of immortality.[2] It was therefore holy living and correct faith. The convictions that God himself is the good; that he is the creator of the inalienable reason and freedom of man; that the perfect morality of man represents the only form of his similarity to God attainable in the sphere of the temporal and created; that the supreme law of goodness, hitherto obscured, has been once more revealed to men in the Christian religion, and that in the most impressive way imaginable—by the deity in a human form; finally, that the religious blessing of salvation procured by Christ contains the strongest motive to practise morality,[3] while it also includes mysterious forces which promote it: these convictions, according to the conception of Greek theologians, bound religion and morality together as closely as possible, and, since only the good man could receive salvation, guaranteed the character of Christianity as the moral religion. The monk Sophronius (seventh century) says in his Christmas Sermon: "Therefore the Son of God assumed human poverty, that he might make us gods by grace; and the divine father David sings in his psalms ... I said, ye are gods and all sons of the highest. God is in us; let us become gods by divine

---

[1] It occurs, *e.g.*, in the Homilies of Macarius. If elsewhere he speaks of χάρις, it is as a rule the substantial grace imparted in the sacraments (baptism) that is meant. The beginning of Cyril's first Catechism is very instructive: Καινῆς διαθήκης μαθηταὶ καὶ Χριστοῦ μυστηρίων κοινωνοί, νῦν μὲν τῇ κλήσει, μετ᾽ ὀλίγον δὲ καὶ τῇ χάριτι, καρδίαν ἑαυτοῖς ποιήσατε καινὴν καὶ πνεῦμα καινόν, ἵνα εὐφροσύνης ὑπόθεσις γένησθε τοῖς οὐρανοῖς.

[2] See Cyril, Catech. 4, c. 2: Ὁ τῆς θεοσεβείας τρόπος ἐκ δύο τούτων συνέστηκε, δογμάτων εὐσεβῶν καὶ πράξεων ἀγαθῶν. Καὶ οὔτε τὰ δόγματα χωρὶς ἔργων ἀγαθῶν εὐπρόσδεκτα τῷ Θεῷ, οὔτε τὰ μὴ μετ᾽ εὐσεβῶν δογμάτων ἔργα τελούμενα προσδέχεται ὁ Θεός ... μέγιστον τοίνυν κτῆμά ἐστι τὸ τῶν δογμάτων μάθημα.

[3] Cyril begins his 18th Catechism with the words "The root of every good action is the hope of the resurrection. For the expectation of obtaining a corresponding reward is a spur to incite the soul to practise good works." The way to morality is made easy by removal of the fear of death.

transformations and imitations" (Διὰ τοῦτο ὁ υἱὸς τοῦ Θεοῦ ἀνθρωπίνην πτωχείαν ἐνδύεται ἵνα θεοὺς ἡμᾶς ἀπεργάσηται χάριτι. καὶ
ταῦτα μελῳδῶν ὁ θεοπάτωρ Δαβίδ .... Ἐγὼ εἶπα· Θεοί ἐστε καὶ
υἱοὶ ὑψίστου πάντες. Θεὸς ἐν ἡμῖν· θεωθῶμεν θείαις μεταβολαῖς καὶ
μιμήσεσιν).[1] In the last phrase the Greek fundamental thought is
put into a classic form. Only we must not take "μεταβολαῖς"
and "μιμήσεσιν" to be equivalent. The former signifies the actual
process, the latter its condition and form; not the sufficient
reason, as is proved by "χάριτι."[2] There is, however, a form of
morality which does not appear to be merely subordinate to
religious faith and hope, but which anticipates the future blessings,
or puts man into the condition of being able to receive them
immediately. This is negative morality, or asceticism. It corresponds
in a true sense to the characteristic of the religious gift of salvation; it is also therefore no longer a mere adjunct to the latter,
but it is the adequate and essential disposition for the reception
of salvation. But in so far as ecstasy, intuition, and the power
of working miracles can be combined with it, it forms the anticipation of the future state. The ultimate rule of this conception
of Christianity may accordingly be compressed, perhaps, into the
saying: "Dost thou desire the supreme good, incorruption
(ἀφθαρσία), then divest thyself of all that is perishable." Side
by side with this we have the more general rule "Dost thou

---

[1] Ed. Usener, l. c. Once more we have to compare Cyril of Jerusalem. After
he has limited the "creed" to the ten sections of the Symbol he continues: μετὰ
δὲ τὴν γνῶσιν τῆς σεμνῆς καὶ ἐνδόξου ταύτης καὶ παναγίας πίστεως καὶ σεαυτὸν
γνῶθι λοιπὸν ὅστις εἶ. Accordingly, faith is that given from without, divine. Moral
self-knowledge and self-discipline are independent of it.

[2] The Greek Fathers speak not infrequently of the new birth in connection
with N. T. passages and it is to be admitted that some succeed in reproducing
the thought satisfactorily, but only—so far as I know—when they adhere closely to
the sacred texts. At all events we must not let ourselves be misled by the mere
title. This is shown most clearly by the closing chapters of Gregory of Nyssa's
Orat. catechet. (ch. 33 sq.). By regeneration Gregory understands the mysterious
birth in us of the divine *nature*, which is implanted by baptism. As the natural
man is born of moist seed, so the new undying man is born of water at the
invocation of the Holy Trinity. The new immortal nature is thus begun in germ
by baptism and is nourished by the Eucharist. That this conception has nothing
in common with the new birth of the New Test., since it has a physical process
in view, needs no proof. According to Cyril, regeneration only takes place after
man has voluntarily left the service of sin (see Catech. I., ch. 2).

desire the supreme good, then first be good and nourish the
new nature implanted in thee in Baptism by the Eucharist and
the other mysterious gifts." The extent to which all this was
connected with Christ is shown by the saying of Clemens Alex.
(Protrept. I. 7) — a saying which retained its force in after times:
" Appearing as a teacher he taught the good life, in order that afterwards as God he might grant everlasting life " (τὸ εὖ ζῆν ἐδίδαξεν
ἐπιφανεὶς ὡς διδάσκαλος, ἵνα τὸ ἀεὶ ζῆν ὕστερον ὡς Θεὸς χορηγήσῃ).

This whole conception of the importance of morality needed,
however, no doctrinal and specific description, any more than
the nature of morality and the principles of natural theology in
general. All that was already settled in its fundamental lines;
man knew it by his own reason; it formed the self-evident presupposition of the doctrine of redemption. The very freedom
used by the Church Fathers in dealing with details shows that
here they were treating matters generally recognised and only
called in question by Manichæans, Fatalists, etc., and that it
was therefore unnecessary to have recourse to revelation. In
describing the dogma of the Greek Fathers, therefore, we have
to consider their views of the nature of salvation, [1] of God as

---

[1] The fundamental conception of the nature of the blessing secured by salvation
is yet not wholly unknown to rational theology, since the latter supposed, though
with some uncertainty, that it could perceive a divine element in the original constitution of men (see, e g., Gregory of Nyssa). Even for the doctrine of the Trinity
recourse was had here and there to reason and the philosophers. But we must go
still farther. If the doctrine of redemption has been characterised above as mystical,
this does not exclude the fact that faith confers redemption in so far as it confers
a knowledge which in and by itself includes liberation. As long as men dealt independently with dogma, this conception was by no means wanting; indeed it
was really the hidden mystery in dogma which was clearly expressed by Clement
and Origen, but only dimly shadowed by later teachers. From this point, however,
faith and ethics were intimately combined; for ethics was also intellectual. No
later writer has stated and known the thought so clearly expressed by Clement of
Alex. (Strom. IV. 23, 149): Διόπερ ὁ Δημόκριτος εὖ λέγει "ὡς ἡ φύσις τε καὶ διδαχὴ
παραπλήσιον ἐστι" ... καὶ γὰρ ἡ διδαχὴ μεταρρυθμίζει τὸν ἄνθρωπον, μεταρρυθμί-
ζουσα δὲ φυσιοποιεῖ καὶ διήνεγκεν οὐδὲν ἢ φύσει πλασθῆναι τοιόνδε ἢ χρόνῳ καὶ
μαθήσει μετατυπωθῆναι· ἄμφω δὲ ὁ κύριος παρέσχηται, τὸ μὲν κατὰ τὴν δημιουργίαν,
τὸ δὲ κατὰ ἐκ τῆς διαθήκης ἀνάκτισίν τε καὶ ἀνανέωσιν. The whole matter gradually
became really mystical, i.e., indescribable and inconceivable in every sense in the
Fathers; the intellectual phase and intention almost disappeared. Conversely, the
reality of the blessing in salvation was thought of from the beginning as something
supernatural, surprising, and bestowed from without.

the Good and the Giver of salvation, of the state and duties of man, etc., on the one hand, as a kind of *a priori* presuppositions of the doctrine of redemption ; but, on the other, as individual conceptions, framed partly from contemporary philosophy, and partly from the Bible. They certainly have a right to a place in a description of the complete view taken by the ancient Church of Christianity; but as certainly they cannot be called dogmas; for dogmas are as essentially different from self-evident presuppositions as from fluctuating conceptions. Our only reason for discussing them in the history of dogma is that we may guard dogma from misunderstanding and correctly mark off the space due to it.[1] The Greek conception of Christianity has, like an ellipse, two centres: the doctrine of liberty, which embraces the whole of rational theology, Stoic and Platonic, and the doctrine of the actual redemption, which is supranatural. Supranatural as it was it admitted a relationship to natural theology, just as, conversely, freedom was regarded as a gift of divine grace. We find, indeed, that the two centres were first brought into the greatest possible proximity by the negative morality. Therefore from this point also the achievements of positive morality necessarily appear as a *minimum* to which the shadow of essential imperfection always clings.

It follows from the above exposition that the doctrines of God, the world, and man—with freedom and sin, are to be prefixed, as presuppositions and conceptions, to dogma, *i.e.*, the doctrines of the godman, while they are only to be discussed in so far as

---

[1] One might be disposed to assume that the dogmatic of the ancient Church also contained *articuli puri et mixti*, but this designation would be misleading. In the opinion of the Fathers, the gospel must have made *everything* clear; conversely, there is hardly anything in the dogmatics which able philosophers had not foreshadowed. The *realisation* was the mystery. Socrates says (H. E. III. 16): Πολλοὶ τῶν παρ' Ἕλλησι φιλοσοφησάντων οὐ μακρὰν τοῦ γνῶναι τὸν Θεὸν ἐγένοντο, καὶ γὰρ καὶ πρὸς τοὺς ἀπρονοησίαν εἰσάγοντας, οὔτε Ἐπικουρίους, ἢ ἄλλως ἐριστικούς, μετὰ τῆς λογικῆς ἐπιστήμης γενναίως ἀπήντησαν, τὴν ἀμαθίαν αὐτῶν ἀνατρέποντες, καὶ διὰ τούτων τῶν λόγων χρειώδεις μὲν τοῖς τὴν εὐσέβειαν ἀγαπῶσι κατέστησαν· οὐ μὴν τῆς κεφαλῆς τοῦ λόγου ἐκράτησαν, τοῦ μὴ γνῶναι τὸ ἀποκρυπτόμενον ἀπὸ τῶν γενεῶν καὶ ἀπὸ τῶν αἰώνων κατὰ Χριστὸν μυστήριον· Socrates had already in view violent opponents of the intrusion of Ἑλληνικὴ παιδεία into theology; but the dispute so passionately conducted never really weakened the confidence placed in natural theology. The actual position is correctly described in Eusebius' phrase (H. E. IV. 7, 14): ἡ καθ' ἡμᾶς ἐπὶ θείοις τε καὶ φιλοσόφοις δόγμασι διδασκαλία.

such discussion is required for the comprehension of dogma. But this does not complete the list of our tasks; the whole presentment of dogma must be prefaced by a chapter treating of the sources of our knowledge and our authorities, *i.e.*, Scripture, tradition, and the Church. So also we must at the close examine the mysterious application of redemption—the mysteries —and all that is connected with it.

The following arrangement of our material, in which a systematic exposition forms the basis of the historical, because the foundations of our view have not changed since the time of Origen, will thus be appropriate.

Ch. III.   Of the sources of knowledge and the authorities, or of Scripture, tradition, and the Church.

## A.   The Presuppositions of the Doctrine of Redemption, or Natural Theology.

Ch. IV.   The presuppositions and conceptions of God the Creator as bestower of salvation.

Ch. V.   The presuppositions and conceptions of man as recipient of salvation.

## B.   The Doctrine of Redemption in the Person of the God-man in its Historical Development.

Ch. VI.   The doctrine of the necessity and realisation of redemption through the incarnation of the Son of God.

Appendix.   The ideas of redemption from the devil and atonement through the work of the God-man.

Ch. VII.   The doctrine of the consubstantiality of the Son of God with God himself.

Appendix.   The doctrine of the Holy Spirit and the Trinity.

Ch. VIII.   The doctrine of the perfect similarity of constitution between the incarnate Son of God and humanity.

Ch. IX.   Continuation.   The doctrine of the personal unity of the divine and human nature in the incarnate Son of God.

## C. The Foretaste of Redemption.

Ch. X.   The mysteries and the like.

Ch. XI.   Conclusion.   Sketch of the history of the genesis of the orthodox system.

*Supplement* I.—The Greek conception of Christianity appears
undoubtedly to be exceedingly compact and clear, as long as
we do not look too deeply into the heart of it. The freeing
of dogmatics of all matters which do not fall within the scope
of the doctrine of redemption is very remarkable. But these
advantages are purchased, first, by abandoning any attempt to
establish an inner unity between the supreme notions of "moral
good" and "blessedness" (imperishableness); secondly, by the
depreciation of positive morality in favour of asceticism; thirdly,
by completely caricaturing the historical Christ. But the knowledge of the Christian faith possessed by the Fathers up to the
middle of the fifth century was still far from being in the deso-
late state in which theology makes no resolute attempt to
deduce the consequences of a doctrine, while it does not venture
to abandon it, but contents itself with perceiving "a profound
element of truth" in any or every theologoumenon brought to
it by tradition. The idea of the Greek Fathers, to which everything was subordinate, that Christianity is the religion which
delivers from perishableness and death, was derived from the
ancient Catholic Church. It presents itself as a specific limitation of primitive Christian hopes under the influence of views
held by the ancients. It is possible to express it in a grand
and awe-inspiring form, and this the Greek Fathers understood.
Further, where misery, mortality, and finitude are felt to be
the heaviest burdens laid upon men, the supreme good can
be nothing but endless, blessed rest. In so far as the Greek
Fathers perceived and firmly believed in this gift being conferred by the Christian religion, while they connected its bestowal
with Jesus Christ, they assigned to Christianity the highest conceivable significance, and to its founder the highest conceivable
dignity, within their range of vision. But the mood which
looked on Christianity from this point of view and regarded it
as consolatory, was that of the fall and ruin of the ancient
world, which no longer possessed the power to turn earnestly to
an energetic life. Without premising this the dogmatic developments are not intelligible. But we cannot retain the formulas
of the Greek faith without self-deception, if we change or refuse
to admit the validity of its premises. But if we are ready

honestly to retain them, then let us clearly understand to what Orthodoxy and Monophysitism came in the East. After they had piled one monstrosity on the top of the other, they were—to use a strong figure of Goethe's—almost choked in chewing the cud of moral and religious absurdities. Originally their doctrine was good for nothing in the world but for dying; afterwards they became deadly sick on this very doctrine.

*Supplement 2.*—If the conception of the supreme good may be regarded as a revised version, made by Greek philosophy, of the ancient Christian hopes of the future, yet this philosophy always rejected the idea of the incarnation of God, and therefore could not, in its definition of the supreme good, attain the certainty which was given in the Christian conception. In the fourth and fifth centuries, however, there were even Christian theologians—Synesius, for example—who would not admit the incarnation of God without revision, and yet held by the thought of deification; who accordingly approached, not rationalistic, but rather pantheistic views. At any rate, faith in the incarnation of God, along with the idea of creation, formed the dividing line between Greek philosophy and the dogmatics of the Church. "For what," says Athanasius, de incarn. 41, "is absurd or ridiculous in our teaching, except merely our saying that the Logos was made manifest in a human body?" (τί γὰρ ἄτοπον, ἢ τί χλεύης παρ᾽ ἡμῖν ἄξιον, ἢ πάντως ὅτι τὸν λόγον ἐν σώματι πεφανερῶσθαι λέγομεν;).[1] On the other hand, the Christian says (Cyril, Catech. 4, ch. 9): "If the incarnation was a dream, then salvation is also a dream." (Εἰ φάντασμα ἦν ἡ ἐνανθρώπησις, φάντασμα καὶ ἡ σωτηρία). That is the confession which in the Greek Church was the equivalent of 1 Cor. XV. 17 f.

*Supplement 3.*—In order to learn the classical form of Greek piety, the strongest root of dogma, it is necessary to study the literature of asceticism. For it seldom comes clearly to light in the dogmatic, apologetic, and polemical works, with the exception of the writings of Athanasius, and in the homiletic

---

[1] Compare Gregory Nyss., Orat. catech. 5: Τὸ μὲν εἶναι λόγον Θεοῦ καὶ πνεῦμα διά τε τῶν κοινῶν ἐννοιῶν ὁ "Ελλην καὶ διὰ τῶν γραφικῶν ὁ 'Ιουδαῖος ἴσως οὐκ ἀντιλέξει, τὴν δὲ κατὰ τὸν ἄνθρωπον οἰκονομίαν τοῦ Θεοῦ λόγου κατὰ τὸ ἴσον ἑκάτερος αὐτῶν ἀποδοκιμάσει ὡς ἀπίθανόν τε καὶ ἀπρεπῆ περὶ Θεοῦ λέγεσθαι.

literature, apart from Chrysostom, it is always greatly disguised
by rhetoric. But a distinction must be made even in ascetic
literature. The descriptions of the piety of monkish heroes lose
themselves as a rule in extravagance and eccentricity, and are
not typical because the writers set out to prove the already
supramundane character of those heroes. We have especially
to examine numerous writings on "the resurrection," "virginity,"
"perfection," and similar subjects, and also the practical homilies. We obtain perhaps the clearest and truest impression of
the piety of the Greek Church from reading the biography
of sister Macrina, by Gregory of Nyssa (Oehler, Biblioth. d.
KVV. I. 1, 1858, p. 172 ff.). The dying prayer put in her
lips (p. 213 f.) is given here because it expresses inimitably
the hopes and consolation of Greek Christianity, yet without
omitting the characteristic warmth of feeling which belonged to
its very essence.

"Her prayer was such that one could not doubt that she
was with God, and heard his voice. She said: Thou, Lord,
hast for us destroyed the fear of death. Thou hast made the end
of this earthly life the beginning of the true life. Thou makest
our bodies rest for a time in sleep, and dost awaken them again
with the last trumpet. Thou givest our clay, which Thou didst
fashion with Thy hands, to the earth to keep it, and Thou
takest again what Thou didst give, and dost transform into imperishableness and beauty that which was mortal and unseemly.
Thou hast snatched us from the curse and sin, having Thyself become both for us. Thou hast crushed the heads of the
dragon, which had grasped man with its jaw in the abyss of
disobedience. Thou hast paved the way of the resurrection
for us, having shattered the gate of Hades, and destroyed him
who had the power of death. Thou has given those who fear
Thee the image of Thy holy cross for a sign for the destruction of the adversary and the safety of our life. Eternal God,
to Whom I was dedicated from the womb, Whom my soul has
loved with all its power, to Whom I have consecrated my flesh
and my soul from my youth and till now! Place Thou an angel
of light by my side to lead me to the place of quickening
where is the source of rest in the bosom of the Holy Fathers.

Oh Thou who didst break the flaming sword, and didst restore
to Paradise the man crucified with Thee who begged Thy
mercy. Remember me, too, in Thy kingdom, because I also
am crucified with Thee, piercing my flesh with nails from fear
of Thee, and fainting in dread of Thy judgments! May the
awful abyss not divide me from Thine elect, nor the calumni-
ator block my way; may my sin not be found before Thine
eyes, if I, having failed through the weakness of our nature,
should have sinned in word, or deed, or thought! Thou who
hast power on earth to forgive sins, grant me forgiveness, that
I may be quickened, and when I put off my body may I be
found by Thee without stain in my soul, so that my soul,
spotless and blameless, may be received into Thy hands like
a sacrifice before Thy presence."

*Supplement* 4.—For centuries after the great work of Theognostus, which we only know very imperfectly, no complete system
of scientific theology was written in the East. The idea of a
system was in itself a philosophical one, and for its execution
all that was in existence were examples whose authority was
already shaken. Platonism only contributed to form a heterodox system. Aristotelianism with its formal logic, which triumphed
over all difficulties, first succeeded in creating an orthodox system. Systematic works, in the period up to Johannes Damascenus, fall into the following lists.

(1)  *On the incarnation of the Logos*—or Son of God. In these
works the central question of Greek dogma is discussed. The title
varies, or is more precise, according to the standpoint of each:
"On the two natures", "On not confounding the natures", etc.
Under this head come also the polemical, dogmatic tractates—
against Arius, Marcellus, Eunomius, Apollinaris, Nestorius, etc.—
as well as dogmatic monographs—on the Holy Ghost, the Trinity,
etc. We have to notice finally the *Expositiones veritatis* at the close
of the writings against the heretics, like those found, after the
precedent of Hippolytus, in, *e.g.*, Epiphanius and Theodoret.

(2)  *Exposition of Christian doctrines in catechetical form.*
Here Cyril's catechisms are especially important.[1] The catechism

[1] The plan of Cyril's catechisms is very instructive. First, there is in the preface
an inquiry as to the aim and nature of the instruction. It begins with the words

was always bound by the Symbol, but the Symbol necessitated
the treatment of the main points of Jesus' history as points of
doctrine, and the expiscation of their exact value for faith. Thus
dogma gained an important supplement from the exposition of
the Symbol. The decalogue of the creed by Gregory of Nazianzus
also falls to be mentioned here. In the great catechism of Gregory of Nyssa catechetic treatment is combined with apologetic.
Instructions how to pursue theological science came from the
Antiochene school and thence penetrated into the West—Junilius
—where Augustine had already written his work De doctrina
Christiana. So far as I know, the older Byzantine Church possessed no such instructions.

(3) *Apologetic works in reference to heathens and Jews.* In these,
natural theology—the monotheistic faith and doctrine of freedom
—is unfolded, and the Christian view of history, as well as the
proof of its antiquity, presented in opposition to polytheism and
ceremonial religions; so in several works by Eusebius, Apollinaris, Cyril of Alexandria, etc.

Ἤδη μακαριότητος ὀσμὴ πρὸς ὑμᾶς. Compare also ch. VI: Βλέπε μοι πηλίκην σοι
ἀξίαν ὁ Ἰησοῦς χαρίζεται ... μὴ νομίσῃς ὅτι μικρὸν πρᾶγμα λαμβάνεις· ἄνθρωπος
ὢν οἰκτρός, Θεοῦ λαμβάνεις προσηγορίαν ... τοῦτο προβλέπων ὁ Ψαλμῳδὸς ἔλεγεν ἐκ
προσώπου τοῦ Θεοῦ, ἐπειδὴ μέλλουσιν ἄνθρωποι Θεοῦ προσηγορίαν λαμβάνειν· Ἐγὼ
εἶπα, θεοί ἐστε καὶ υἱοὶ ὑψίστου πάντες, c. 12: ἐάν σε κατηχούμενος ἐξετάσῃ, τι
εἰρήκασιν οἱ διδάσκοντες, μηδὲν λέγε τῷ ἔξω· μυστήριον γάρ σοι παραδίδομεν καὶ
ἐλπίδα μέλλοντος αἰῶνος· τήρησον τὸ μυστήριον τῷ μισθαποδότῃ. Then follow three
Catechisms which impart information concerning sin, baptism, and penitence in
general, and are meant to awaken the right disposition. In the fourth a sketch is
given of the system of faith according to the Symbol. Ten systems are distinguished,
whose numbering, however, can no longer be established with certainty. The
exposition contained in Catechisms 5—18 do not agree with the sketch, seeing that
to the latter is appended a didactic section on the soul, the body, food, and clothing,
a section which is wanting in the exposition; the latter rather in the last catechism
deals with the Church, which is not mentioned in the sketch. The whole is concluded by five catechisms which explain the secret rites of the mysteries to the
baptised. The decalogue of the faith by Gregory contains, in the first commandment,
the doctrine of the Trinity; in the second, the creation out of nothing and the
providence of God; in the third, the origin of evil from freedom, not from an evil
matter or God; in the fourth, the doctrine of the incarnation and constitution of the
Redeemer; in the fifth, the crucifixion and burial; in the sixth, the resurrection and
ascension; in the seventh, the return of Christ in glory to act as judge; in the
eight and ninth, the general resurrection and retributive judgment; the tenth runs:
Δέκατον ἐργάζου τὸ ἀγαθὸν ἐπὶ τούτῳ τῷ θεμελίῳ τῶν δογμάτων, ἐπειδὴ πίστις
χωρὶς ἔργων νεκρά, ὡς ἔργα δίχα πίστεως.

(4) *Monographs on the work of the six days*, on the human soul, the body, the immortality of the soul, etc. In these, also, natural theology is developed and the scientific cosmology and psychology in the oldest sources of the Bible stated.

(5) *Monographs on virginity, monachism, perfection, the virtues, the resurrection.* Here the ultimate and supreme practical interests of piety and faith find expression.

(6) *Monographs on the mysteries, cultus and priesthood.* These are not numerous in the earlier period—yet instruction in the sacraments and their ritual was regularly attached to the training in the Symbol; see the Catechisms of Cyril which form a guide to the mysteries Their number, however, increased from the sixth century.

Copious, often intentionally elaborated, dogmatic material, finally, is also contained in scientific commentaries on the Biblical books and in the Homilies.

The right use for the history of dogma of these different kinds of sources is an art of method for which rules can hardly be given. The rhetorical, exegetical, philosophical, and strictly dogmatic expositions must be recognised as such and distinguished. At the same time we have to remember that this was an age of rhetoric which did not shrink from artifices and untruths of every kind. Jerome admits that in the works of the most celebrated Fathers one must always distinguish between what they wrote argumentatively (διαλεκτικῶς), and what they set down as truth. Basilius also (Ep. 210) was at once prepared to explain a heterodox passage in Gregory Thaumaturgus, by supposing that he had been speaking not dogmatically (δογματικῶς), but for the sake of argument (ἀγωνιστικῶς). So also Athanasius excuses Origen on the ground that he wrote much for the sake of practice and investigation (De decretis synod. Nic. 27, cf. ad Serap. IV. 9); and while completely defending the Christology of Dionysius Alex., he remarks that the latter in many details spoke from policy (κατ᾿ οἰκονομίαν). The same stock excuse was seized upon by the Fathers at Sardica in the case of Marcellus. According to this, how often must the great writers of the fourth and fifth centuries themselves have written for the sake of argument (ἀγωνιστικῶς)! Moreover, Gregory of Nazianzus speaks of a necessary and salutary οἰκονομηθῆναι τὴν ἀλήθειαν, *i.e.*, of the politic and prudent disguise and the gradual communication of the truth; and he appeals in support of this to God himself who only revealed the truth at the fitting time, οἰκονομικῶς (Orat. 41. 6, Ep. 26). Cyrus declares, in the monothelite controversy, that one must assume κατ' οἰκονομίαν a not altogether correct dogma, in order to attain something of importance.

Some, however, went much farther in this matter. As they did not hold themselves bound to stick to the truth in dealing with an opponent, and thus had forgotten the command of the gospel, so they went on in theology to impute untruthfulness to the Apostles, citing the dispute between Paul and Peter, and to Christ (he concealed his omniscience, etc.). They even charged God with falsehood in dealing with his enemy, the devil, as is proved by the views held by Origen, Gregory of Nyssa, and most of the later Fathers, of redemption from the power of the devil. But if God himself deceived his enemy by stratagem (*pia fraus*), then so also might men. Under such circumstances it cannot be wondered at that forgeries were the order of the day. And this was the case. We read even in the second century of numerous falsifications and interpolations made under their very eyes on the works of still living authors. Think of the grievances of the Church Fathers against the Gnostics, and the complaints of Dionysius of Corinth and Irenæus. But what did these often naïve and subjectively innocent falsifications signify compared with that spirit of lying which was powerfully at work even in official compositions in the third and fourth centuries? Read Rufinus' De adulterat. libr. Origenis, and weigh Rufinus' principles in translating the works of Origen. And the same spirit prevailed in the Church in the fifth and sixth centuries; see a collection of the means employed to deceive in my altchrist. Litt.-Gesch. I., p. xlii ff. In these centuries no one continued to put any trust in a documentary authority, a record of proceedings, or protocol. The letters by Bishops, of this period throng with complaints of forgeries; the defeated party at a Synod almost regularly raises the charge that the acts of Synod are falsified; Cyril and the great letter-writers complain that their letters are circulated in a corrupt form; the

epistles of dead Fathers—*e.g.*, that of Athanasius to Epictetus—
were falsified, and foreign matter was inserted into them; the followers of Apollinaris and Monophysites, *e.g.*, systematically corrupted the tradition. See the investigations of Caspari and Dräseke.
Conversely, the simplest method of defending an ancient Church
Father who was cited by the opposition, or on whose orthodoxy
suspicion was cast, was to say that the heretics had corrected
his works to suit themselves and had sown weeds among his
wheat. The official literature of the Nestorian and Monophysite
controversy is a swamp of mendacity and knavery, above which
only a few spots rise on which it is possible to find a firm
footing. Gregory I. (Ep. VI. 14) at once recalls in a given case
the forging of the acts of the Ephesian Synod. What was not
published as Nicene in later times, and to some extent very
soon! Much indeed was even then dismissed as mendacity and
deceit, much has been laid bare by the scholars of the seven-
teenth century. But if one considers the verdicts, anxieties,
and assertions of suspicion of contemporaries of those conflicts,
he cannot avoid the fear that present-day historians are still
much too confiding in dealing with this whole literature. The
uncertainties which remain in the study precisely of the most
important alterations of the history of dogma, and of the Church
of the Byzantine period, necessarily awaken the suspicion that
we are almost throughout more or less helpless in face of the
systematically corrupted tradition. All the same I would not
recommend so bold a handling of the sources as that formerly
practised by the Jesuits, and to-day by Vincenzi (Ketzertaufstreit,
Acten des 5 Concils, Honoriusfrage).

*Supplement* 5.—The form assumed by the substance of the
faith in the Greek Church shows very clearly the characteristic
point of view. First, namely, it was conceived—though, so far
as I know, seldom—as law; indeed Gregory of Nazianzus sketched
a decalogue of faith. This form must not be misunderstood.
The faith appears as law only in so far as its contents constitute a revealed ordinance of God to which man has to submit;
we must not let it suggest to us a parallel to the moral law.
Secondly, however, the creed is regarded in its formulas as a
mystery to be kept secret. Men were initiated into the faith

as they were initiated into the sacred rites. [1] Secrecy was,
according to ancient ideas, the necessary nimbus of all consecration. The conceptions of the creed as law and as mystery
have this in common, that in them the content of the faith
appears as something strictly objective, something given from
without. [2] But in so far as the authority of any formula whatever conflicts with original Christianity as much as this secrecy,
the dependence of the Greek Church on the practice of the
ancient mysteries and schools of philosophy is here manifest.

*Supplement* 6.—Ideas of the realisation of the supreme good
in the world beyond had to attach themselves to the phrases
of the creed known in the Symbols, and were not permitted to
disregard the numerous and diversified statements of Holy
Scripture. The motley and manifold conceptions which resulted
were owing to harmonising with primitive Christian eschatology
on the one hand, and Origen's doctrine of the consummation
on the other, subject to due regard for the sacred writings.
Origen's doctrine was more and more regarded as heretical from
the end of the fourth century, while previously recognised
theologians, like Gregory of Nyssa, had reproduced it in all its
main points. Its rejection marks the first decisive victory of
traditionalism—itself indeed impregnated with speculation—over
spiritualising speculation. In the fifth century, there were counted
as heretical, (1) the doctrine of apokatastasis (universalism) and
the possibility of redemption for the devil; [3] (2) the doctrine of
the complete annihilation of evil; (3) the conception of the
penalties of hell as tortures of conscience; (4) the spiritualising
version of the resuscitation of the body; and (5) the idea of

[1] See the investigations into the so-called Arcan-Disciplin, by Rothe, Th. Harnack, Bonwetsch, and Von Zezschwitz.

[2] Constantine delighted in applying the name "law" to the whole of the
Christian religion. This is western (nostra lex = nostra religio); it is rare in the
East. On the other hand, the whole Bible was not infrequently "the law" in the
one Church as well as in the other.

[3] Gregory of Nyssa still defended it, appealing to 1 Cor. XV. 28; see the
second half of his writing περὶ ψυχῆς καὶ ἀναστάσεως, and Orat. catech. 8, 35.
So also—for a time—Jerome and the older Antiochenes; even in the fifth century
it had numerous defenders in both East and West. It was definitively condemned
with the condemnation of Origen under Justinian. See under, ch. XI.

the continued creation of new worlds. On the other hand, the doctrines of Christ's reign on earth for a thousand years, and the double resurrection, etc., were in the East in part shelved, in part absolutely characterised as Jewish heresies.[1] The return of Christ, which was still described as imminent, though for many theologians it had lost its essential significance, the judgment of the world, the resurrection of the body,[2] the eternal misery (θάνατος ἐν ἀθανασίᾳ—undying death) of the wicked, were maintained, and even the conception of a transfiguration of heaven and this earth was not everywhere rejected. Retained accordingly were only those points enumerated in the symbols, and therefore no longer to be passed over. To these were added the expectation of Antichrist, which, however, only emerged, as a rule, during exceptional distress, as in the times of Arian emperors, Julian, barbarous nations, Mohammed, etc., and by no means now belonged to the solid substance of theological eschatology; (yet see Cyril, Catech. 15, ch. 11 f., the pseudo-hippolytan work περὶ συντελείας, and the late apocalypses of from the fourth to the seventh century). Blessedness was regarded as a state of freedom from suffering, of the perfect knowledge, and the intuitive and entrancing enjoyment, of God. Yet the majority recognised different degrees and stages of

[1] The last important theological representative of Chiliasm in the East was Apollinaris of Laodicea; see Epiph. H. 77, ch. 37, Jerome de vir. inl. 18. Jerome labours to prove (Ep. 129) that the *terra promissionis* was not Palestine, but a heavenly place. The Apocalypse was, as a rule, not included in the Canon in the East (in older times). With this state of matters is contrasted very strongly the fact that in the lower ranks of priests, monks, and laity apocalypses continued to be eagerly read, and new ones were ever being produced on the basis of the old.

[2] The doctrine of the resurrection of man in spirit and body still always formed a main point in Apologetic evidences, and was, as formerly,.proved from the omnipotence of God, from various analogical inferences, and from the essential importance of the body for human personality. The Cappadocians and some later Greek theologians still held, though in a much weakened form, to the spiritualistic version of the doctrine attempted by Origen. But, following Methodius, Epiphanius (H. 64, ch. 12 ff.) especially insisted that there was the most perfect identity between the resurrection body and our material body, and this faith, enforced in the West by Jerome, soon established itself as alone orthodox. There now arose many problems concerning the limbs and members of the future body, and even Augustine seriously considered these. He experimented on the flesh of a peacock, and confirmed his faith in the resurrection by the discovery of its preservation from decay.

blessedness, a conception in which we perceive the moralist
encroach upon the ground of religion, [1] since it put a high value
on special earthly achievements, such as asceticism and martyrdom. As regards the blessed dead, it was supposed in wide
circles that their souls waited in Hades, a subterranean place,
for the return of Christ; [2] there Christ had also preached the
gospel to the good who had died before him. [3] Not a few Fathers
of the fourth century maintained, following Origen, that the
souls of the pious at once enter Paradise, or come to Christ, [4]
and this opinion gained ground more and more. It was universal in regard to saints and martyrs. Besides, the conceptions
of the intermediate state, like everything else in this connection,
were altogether vague, since Greek theologians were only inter-

---

[1] The assumption of various degrees of blessedness (and damnation) must have
been almost universal; for the divergent opinion of Jovinian was felt to be heretical; see Jerome adv. Jovin. I. 3, II. 18—34. Still it excited more real interest in
the West than in the East (Augustine, De civitate, XXII., ch. 30). As regards the
idea of future existence, some Fathers supposed that men would positively become
angels, others that they would be like the angels.

[2] The different conceptions as to the relations of Hades, Hell, Paradise, the
bosom of Abraham, etc., do not come in here. According to Gregory of Nyssa,
Hades is not to be held a place, but an invisible and incorporeal state of the life
of the soul.

[3] This old theologoumenon (see Vol. I., p. 203) occurs in western and eastern
theologians. Those who would have become Christians if they had lived later, *i.e.*,
after Christ's appearance, were redeemed. The phrase *descendit ad inferna* came
into the Symbols from the fourth century. We find it in the West first, in the
Symbol of Aquileia, in the East in the formula of the fourth Synod at Sirmium
(359 εἰς τὰ καταχθόνια κατελθόντα). It is at least questionable whether it was
already in the Jerusalemite Symbol at the same date. Compare Hahn, Bibliothek
d. Symbole, 2 Aufl. §§ 24, 27, 34, 36, 37, 39—41, 43, 45, 46—60, 93, 94, 96,
108; Caspari, Ueber das Jerus. Taufbekenntniss in Cyrillus' Katechesen, with an
excursus: Hat das Jerus. Taufbekenntniss den *descensus ad inferos* enthalten, in
the norweg. Theol. Ztschr. Vol. I.

[4] With this it could be and, as a rule, was understood that their felicity up to
the last judgment was only preliminary. Two interests met here: those of a
spiritualising religion and of primitive Christian eschatology; see Vol. I., p. 129 f.
The latter required that blessedness should be attached to the return of Christ and
the last judgment; the former demanded that it should be complete as soon as the
believing soul had parted from the mortal body. Therefore, in spite of Jerome's
polemic against Vigilantius and Augustine's against Pelagius, no fixed Church
doctrine could be arrived at here, however much piety desired an absolute decision.
See for details Petavius and Schwane D. Gesch. d. patrist Zeit, p. 749 ff.

ested ultimately in the hope of deification.¹ In the West, on
the contrary, the entire primitive Christian eschatology was upheld pretty nearly intact during the fourth century, and even
the idea of Nero returning as Antichrist had numerous supporters. The reason of this lies in the fact that Neoplatonic speculation, and speculation generally, obtained at first no footing
here, and the specific import of Christianity at the same time
was still always expressed in the dramatically conceived eschatology. But the distinction between West and East goes at this
point much deeper. Strongly eschatological as was the aim of
the whole dogmatics of the East, it cannot be overlooked that
the heart of the matter—the thought of the judgment—had
been torn away from the eschatology since Origen. This thought
which expresses the fearful responsibility of every soul to the
God of holiness, and without which the forgiveness of sins
must remain an enigma and an empty word, dominated the gospel, and determined ancient Christianity. But "scientific"
theology had shelved it.² The name is not wanting in Origen's
system, but the thing had disappeared. In spite of all the emphasis laid on freedom, nothing exists but a cosmic process, in
which the many issues from the one, in order to return into
the one. In such a scheme the Judgment has been deprived
of its meaning. In subsequent times apokatastasis—universalism—was indeed condemned in the East, and Origen's system
was rejected; but any one who studies closely Greek Byzantine
dogmatics will see how profound was the attachment to this
most important point in Origenism and Neoplatonism. The
problems to which the creed gave birth in the fourth to the
seventh century, and which men laboured to solve, discounten-
ance any effective reference to the judgment. Again and again
we have deification as a hyperphysical and therefore physical

---

¹ Clement and Origen had assumed a purgatory in the shape of a cleansing fire
(see Vol. II., p. 377, n. 5); the Greek Fathers, however, have, so far as I know, dropped
the idea, with the exception of Gregory of Nyssa (περὶ ψυχῆς καὶ ἀναστάσεως,
Oehler, Vol. I., p. 98 f.). From Origen and Gregory the conception passed to
Ambrose who established it in the West, after the way had been prepared for it
by Tertullian. The Scriptural proof was 1 Cor. III. 13 f.; compare Augustine De
civitate dei, XXI. 23 sq. Enchir. 68 sq. (ignis purgatorius).

² It still lived in the popular views of Christianity held by the Orientals.

process, but dogmatics tell us little of the tenet that it is appointed unto man to die and after that the judgment. For this reason also the strict connection with morality was lost, and therefore in some regions even Islam was a deliverer. It was different in the West. What has been named the "Chiliasm" of the West, possessed its essential significance in the prospect of the judgment. If we compare West and East in the Middle Ages— the theologians, not the laity—no impression is stronger than that the former knew the fear of the judge to which the latter had become indifferent. It was the restless element in the life of faith of the West; it sustained the thought of forgiveness of sins; it accordingly made the reformation of Catholicism possible. And any reformation, if it should ever take place in the Greek Church, will begin by restoring the conviction of the responsibility of every individual soul, emphasising the judgment, and thus gaining the fixed point from which to cast down the walls of dogmatics.

*Literature.*—Hermann, Gregorii Nysseni sententiæ de salute adipiscenda, 1875. H. Schultz, Die Lehre von der Gottheit Christi, 1881. Kattenbusch, Kritische Studien der Symbolik, in the Studien und Kritiken, 1878, p. 94 ff. Ritschl, Die Christl. Lehre v. d. Rechtfertigung und Versöhnung, 2 Ed., Vol. I., pp. 3—21. Kattenbusch, Konfessionskunde I., p. 296 ff. On Monachism, especially in Russia, see Frank, Russ. Kirche, p. 190 ff.

# CHAPTER III.

## SOURCES OF KNOWLEDGE AND AUTHORITIES; OR, SCRIPTURE, TRADITION, AND THE CHURCH.

THE extent and authority of the Catholic authorities were already substantially fixed at the beginning of the fourth century, though their mutual relations and the manner of using them in detail were not. [1] Among the parties which contended over the correct definition of the dogma of redemption, they had to a certain degree become undoubtedly subjects of controversy. The great opposition between a more liberal theology and pure traditionalism was based upon a difference in the way of looking at the authorities. But this opposition never culminated in a clear contrast of principles. Consequently, theologians had no occasion to frame a special doctrine of the Church and the authorities—Scripture and tradition. The need was not, as in the case of the dogma of redemption, so pressing as to lead men to adopt the perilous and obnoxious course of formulating laws of faith anew. The petty skirmishes, however, with more or less obscure theologians and reformers, who point-blank objected to this or that portion of the traditional basis, did not come before the great tribunal of the Church, and the conflict with Manichæans, Paulicians, Euchites, and Bogomilians, has left no trace in the history of dogma. [2]

[1] See the account given in Vol. II., pp. 18—127, and elsewhere.

[2] The opposition to the Eustathians and Andians (see the Acts of the Synod of Gangra and Epiph. H. 70) does not belong to this section; for it arose from a different conception of the obligatoriness of the monk's life on Christians. On the contrary, it is noteworthy that Aërius, once a friend of Eustathius (Epiph. H. 75) not only maintained the original identity of bishops and presbyters—that had also been done, and supported from the N. T., by Jerome and the theologians of Antioch—

Still, changes took place in the period between Eusebius and
Johannes Damascenus. They followed simply the altered requirements of the Church. They gave utterance to the increased
traditionalism. Necessity became a virtue, *i.e.*, every new point
which was felt to be needed in order to preserve the unity of
the Church, or to adapt its institutions to the taste of the time,
was inserted in the list of authorities. This method was in
vogue even in the third century. It was now only further and
further extended. But it is hard to fix its results, since at that
time there was no fixity and there could be none, from the
nature of the principle that the state of the Church at any time
was to be declared as in every respect the traditional one. [1]

## 1. *Holy Scripture.* [2]

To the two Testaments a unique authority was ascribed.
They were the Holy Scriptures κατ᾽ ἐξοχήν; every doctrine had

but he made the question an *articulus stantis et cadentis ecclesiæ*. We cannot now
determine what motive influenced him. The attack of Marcellus of Ancyra on the
foundations of the prevalent theology, and his argument that the dogma was
essentially ἀνθρωπίνης βουλῆς τε καὶ γνώμης, are of incomparably greater significance
in principle. But his arguments were not understood, and produced no effect. Meanwhile, the basis of the whole structure of the Catholic Church in the East was at
no time left unassailed. The Church has never embraced everything which was,
and might be, named Christian. After the Marcionites and the older sects had
retired from the stage, or had fused with the Manichæans, Paulicians, Euchites, and
Bogomilians, etc., came upon the scene. These Churches contested the Catholic
foundations as the Marcionites and Manichæans had done; they accepted neither
the Catholic Canon, nor the hierarchical order and tradition. They succeeded, in
part, in creating lasting, comprehensive, and exclusive systems, and afforded work
to Byzantine theologians and politicians for centuries. But important as it is to
assert their existence, they have no place in the history of dogma; for at no time
had they any influence whatever on the formation of dogma in the East; they have
left no effect on the Church. Therefore general Church history has alone to deal
with them.

[1] The view held of the apostolate of the twelve first fully reached its Catholic
level in the fourth and fifth centuries. The Apostles were (1) missionaries who had
traversed the whole world and performed unheard of miracles, (2) the rulers of the
Churches, (3) teachers and law-givers in succession to Christ, having given in speech
and writing to the least detail all the regulations necessary to the Church for faith
and morals, (4) the authors of the order of worship, the liturgy, (5) heroic ascetics
and fathers of monachism, (6) though hesitatingly, the mediators of salvation.

[2] See histories of the Canon by Holtzmann, Schmiedel (in Ersch and Gruber
"Kanon"); Weiss, Westcott, and especially Zahn. Overbeck, Z. Gesch. des Kanons.

to be proved out of them, in other words, opinions that held something necessary to faith which did not occur in Scripture, had no absolute validity. Any one who declared that he took his stand on Scripture alone did not assume an uncatholic attitude. This view of the Holy Scriptures presupposed that their extent was strictly defined, and placed beyond all doubt. But this supposition was for centuries contradicted by the actual facts, which, however, were concealed, partly because men neither would nor dared look at them, partly because they really did not see them. The theologians of Antioch, and especially Theodore, criticised on internal and external grounds the contents of the Canon, as these were gradually being fixed; but in doing so even they were guided by an ecclesiastical tradition. Their criticism still had its supporters in the sixth century, and its influence extended not only to Persia, but even, through Junilius, to the West. But neither the spirit of the criticism nor its results ever made any impression whatever on the great Church. [1]

As regards the O. T., the oldest and most revered of the Greek Fathers followed Melito and Origen, and only recognised the 22—24 books of the Hebrew Canon, [2] according to the others in the Alexandrian Canon only a secondary validity, or none at all. While there was some hesitation about the Book of Esther, and that not only in Antioch, this decision obtained

1880. The controversy with the Jews as to the possession and exposition of the O. T. still continued in the Byzantine period; see on this McGiffert, Dialogue between a Christian and a Jew, entitled Ἀντιβολὴ Παπίσκου καὶ Φίλωνος κ.τ.λ. .... together with a discussion of Christian polemics against the Jews. New York, 1889.

[1] On the attitude of Theodore and his disciples to the Canon, see the thorough investigations of Kihn (Theodorus von Mopsuestia und Junilius Africanus, 1880). Theodore rejected from the O. T., Job, the Song of Songs, Chronicles, Ezra and Nehemiah, Esther, and the inscriptions of the Psalms; see Leontius Byz. Contra Nestor. et Eutych. L. III., ch. 13—17, Migne T. 86, p. 1365 sq. The fifth Synod expressly condemned Theodore's criticism and interpretation of Job and the Song of Songs, as well as his idea of inspiration in reference to Solomon's writings, and his exposition of some of the Psalms. On Theodore's prestige in Nisibis, see Kihn, p. 333 f.; on Junilius' dependence on him, l. c., 350—382. For the dependence of the Nestorian Canon on Theodore's, see Noeldeke in the Gött. Gel. Anz. 1868, St. 46, p. 1826 and Kihn, l. c., 336.

[2] Authoritative were especially the views of Athanasius, Cyril of Jerus. and Gregory of Nazianzus, who reckoned only 22 Books; see also the sixtieth Canon of the Council of Laodicea (363? inauthentic?).

in the Greek Churches, though divergences were not wanting
in provincial communities. But it was always in danger of
being disregarded, for the sacred books were continually transcribed from the LXX.; and so, as a rule, those writings, excluded in theory, were copied along with the others. The legend
of the genesis of the LXX., again, was always highly valued,
and it seemed to imply the sacredness of the whole translation.
Yet it was only in consequence of the attempts at union with
the Roman Church in the Middle Ages, and still more after
the ill-fated enterprise of Cyrillus Lucaris (17th century),
that the Greek Church was persuaded to give up the Hebrew
and adopt the Alexandrian and Roman Canon. But a binding,
official declaration never followed; the passiveness and thoughtlessness with which it changed, or upturned its position in so
important a question, is extraordinarily characteristic of the
modern Græco-Slavic Church. The question is not even yet
decided, and there are distinguished Russian theologians, who
regard the books of the Hebrew Canon as being alone strictly
canonical. They are, however, growing ever fewer. [1]  In the
Western Church a state of complete uncertainty still prevailed
in the fourth century as to the extent of the O. T. But the
Latin Bible, complete copies of which may not have been very
common, was a translation of the LXX. This fact was more
potent than the historical views which found their way into the
West from the East, in a disjointed form, and for whose
triumph Jerome had laboured. Augustine, who was ignorant of
Biblical criticism, held to the current Latin collection (see, *e.g.*,
his list in De doct. christ. II., 8), and at the Synods of Hippo,
A.D. 393 (can. 36), and Carthage, A.D. 397 (can. 47), the Alexandrian Canon was adopted. The decision that the Roman
Church was to be asked for a confirmation of this conclusion
does not seem to have been carried out. From that date the
Hebrew Canon was departed from in the West, though the
view of Athanasius, conveyed to it by Rufinus, and the decision
of Jerome, exerted a quiet influence, and even apart from this

---

[1] See Gass, Symbolik der griechischen Kirche, p. 97 ff.; Strack, Kanon des
A. T. in Prot. R.-E., Vol. VII. 2, p. 412 ff. The reader is referred to this article and
to Introductions to the O. T. for details. Kattenbusch, Confessionskunde I., p 292.

some uncertainty—*e.g.*, in the case of 4 Esra, the Pastor of Hermas, etc.,—still remained. [1] Cassiodorus seems to have taken a very important part in finally shaping the Latin Bible. But we cannot by any means describe the attitude of the West as uncritical. It only avoided the inconsistency into which scholars had fallen in extolling the LXX. as a divinely composed and authentic work, while they ranked the Hebrew Bible above it.

As regards the N. T., the Alexandrian Church accepted the Western collection in the time of Origen, and in the course of the third century most of the others, though not yet all, [2] seem to have followed its example. In so far as any reflection was given to their historical characteristics, the Scriptures were regarded as Apostolic-catholic, and were acknowledged to contain the real sources of evidence for Christian doctrine. But the principle of apostolicity could not be strictly carried out. In many national Churches apostolic writings were known and revered which were not found in the Western collection, and conversely, it was not always possible to perceive the Apostolic origin and Catholic recognition of a received book. Origen already therefore adopted the idea, consonant to the spirit of antiquity, that the collection embraced those books about whose title a general agreement had prevailed from the earliest times. Canonicity was decided by unanimous testimony. But even this principle did not meet the whole case; Origen himself violated it in forming the group of seven Catholic Epistles. Yet it became the established rule, and put an end to any consideration of the question based on criticism of the facts.

---

[1] Gregory I. (Moral XIX. 13) thought it necessary to excuse himself for arguing from Maccabees.

[2] Thus Syrian Churches still used Tatian's Diatessaron in the fourth century; and in a few circles among them there were retained in the Canon, the apocryphal correspondence of the Corinthians and Paul, the two Epp. of Clement, nay, even the Ep. of Clement de virginitate. On the other hand, some books were wanting. Not a few apocryphal writings held an undefined rank in the Syrian Patriarchate. In a word, the old Roman Canon, expanded in the course of the third century in Alexandria, did not get the length of being acknowledged in vast territories of the East proper. In spite of the association of the Apostolic Epistles with the Gospels, the higher rank peculiar to the latter was not done away with as late as the fourth century. Alexander of Alexandria (in Theodoret H. E. I. 4) describes the contents of Holy Scripture briefly as 'Law, Prophets, and Gospels.'

Eusebius, who was a very important authority, and who—if we are to understand the passage so—had been commissioned by the Emperor to prepare standard Bibles, followed the view of Origen; yet in the case of one book, the Apocalypse, he expressed his dislike in a way that ran counter to the principle of the Canon. The three, or four, categories, in which he required to arrange the books, show that men were struggling with a difficulty not to be solved in this way, which could only be solved by time with its power to hallow all inconsistencies. [1] If we collected statistically all the Eastern information we possess concerning the extent of the N. T. from the date of Eusebius up to the destruction of Constantinople—direct and indirect statements by Church Fathers, Synodal decisions, Bible manuscripts and indices from the Churches of various provinces, and especially Syria—we would be forced to the conclusion that complete confusion and uncertainty prevailed. [2] But this view would be erroneous. We have to multiply by hundreds the lists which enumerate 26 (27) books, *i.e.*, the *Acknowledged* and the *Disputed melioris notæ* of Eusebius.—Athanasius' Festival Epistle, A.D. 367, was of paramount importance in settling the complete equality of these two classes in the Patriarchates of Alexandria and Constantinople and in the West.—On the other hand, apart from the Syrian Churches, [3] the lists which diverge

[1] On the efforts of Eusebius to fix the extent of the N. T., see Texte und Untersuch. zur altchristl. Litteratur-Geschichte, Vol. II. 1, 2, p. 5 ff.

[2] Almost everything which was esteemed in quite different circumstances in the earliest period, is to be again found somewhere or other in the Byzantine age. Most instructive is the history of Clement's Epistles and Hermas. Conversely, the old doubts also remain and even new ones emerge (Philemon, see Jerome in his preface to the Epistle).

[3] The N. T. had a peculiar history in the Syrian Churches, which has not yet been written; see Nestle, 'Syrische Bibelübersetzungen' in the Prot. R.-E. Vol. XV.; Bäthgen's work on the Syrus Cureton. 1885, and my 'das N. T. um das Jahr 200' (1888). It is more than questionable whether Theodore of Mopsuestia did any independent criticism on the extent of the N. T. He, probably, simply adhered to the Canon of his Church, which then of the Catholic Epistles only admitted 1 Peter and 1 John, and rejected the Apocalypse; see Kihn, l. c., 65 ff. and the Canon of Chrysostom. While the whole Church was substantially agreed about the extent of the N. T., from the end of the fourth century, wide districts in the Patriarchate of Antioch retained their separate traditions. Only we must not forget

from the above owe their existence either to a badly applied scholarship, or to individual reminiscences, in rare cases to a divergent usage on the part of provincial Churches. From the end of the fourth century real unanimity prevailed, in the main, as to the contents of the N. T. and the authorship of the separate books, in Constantinople, Asia Minor, Alexandria, and the West. Apart from doubts of long standing, yet ineffectual and isolated, about the Catholic Epistles (and Philemon?), the one exception was John's Revelation, for which Eusebius' verdict was momentous.[1] But even in this case attempts to come to a decision were given up: the book was shelved, and re-emerged, from the circles in which it had maintained its ground, without exciting any controversy worth mentioning. The disquieting distinction between Acknowledged and Disputed books, abolished by Athanasius, was but very seldom of any consequence in practice; but scholars still recalled it here and there. When the collection was limited to 26 (27) books, the reading of others in the Church was, from the end of the fourth century, more strictly prohibited. But even at the beginning of the fifth, men in a position to know, like Jerome and Sozomen, can tell us that the prohibition was here and there unknown or disregarded. Some primitive Christian writings were thus in use in the Churches down to the fifth century and later; but the Monophysite Churches preserved, as a monkish protest against the spiritualism of Origen, Jewish Apocalypses revised by Christians and belonging to the earliest period, and the barbarism into which they fell spread a protective covering over these writings.[2]

The details are obscure of the way in which the Western

that the vast majority even of these had accepted the Roman Canon of undisputed books in the second half of the third century. But the agreement went no further; for from the fourth century they would take no more instruction from Alexandria.

[1] For the rest, Weiss has rightly shown (Einleitung in das N. T., p. 98) that the extent to which the Apocalypse was rejected, has been somewhat exaggerated. Extremely noteworthy is the view of Didymus on 2 Peter (Enarrat. in epp. cathol.): "Non est ignorandum præsentem epistolam esse falsatam, quæ licet publicetur non tamen in canone est."

[2] In the Byzantine Church also Apocalypses continued to be read, and new ones were constantly being produced.

Church obtained the Epistle of James, second Peter, and third
John. The Epistle to the Hebrews, not unknown to it from
the first, it received in the fourth century as a Pauline composition, from the East, through the famous intermediaries.
Those same men did away with all uncertainty at the close of
the fourth century on the ground of the decisions given by
Eusebius and Athanasius. The 27 books, *i.e.*, the Canon of
Athanasius, were alone recognised at the Synods of Hippo and
Carthage (397), and this result was confirmed by Augustine's
authority (see, *e.g.*, De doctr. christ. II. 8) without any general
declaration having been made. [1] But the sharper the line drawn
between the collection and all other writings, the more suspicious must those have appeared whose title could lead, or had
once admittedly led, to a claim for recognition as Catholic and
Apostolic. The category of "apocryphal" in which they had
formerly been placed, solely in order to mark the alleged or
real absence of general testimony in their favour, now obtained
more and more an additional meaning; they were of unknown
origin, or 'fabricated', and this was often supplemented by the
charge of being 'heretical'. But however great the gulf between
the canonical and uncanonical books, it is impossible to con-

[1] See also under this head the verdict, freer because dependent on Theodore,
which Junilius passed on the Catholic Epistles. Critical investigations have not yet
arrived at a final result regarding the Decretum Gelasii. Augustine himself has not
failed, besides, to notice the doubts that existed in his time; see Retractat. II. 4, 2.
In his De pecc. mer. I. 27, he still leaves the Ep. to the Hebrews unassigned. In
De doctr. christ. II. 8, he writes: "In canonicis autem scripturis ecclesiarum catho-
licarum quam plurimum auctoritatem sequatur, inter quas sane illæ sint, quæ
apostolicas sedes habere et epistolas accipere meruerunt." Accordingly, this principle
still holds. "Tenebit igitur hunc modum in scripturis canonicis, ut eas quæ ab
omnibus accipiuntur ecclesiis catholicis, præponat eis quas quædam non accipiunt;
in iis vero quæ non accipiuntur ab omnibus, præponat eas, quas plures gravioresque
accipiunt eis, quas pauciores minorisque auctoritatis ecclesiæ tenent. Si autem alias
invenerit a pluribus, alias a gravioribus haberi, quamquam hoc facile inveniri non
possit, æqualis tamen auctoritatis eas habendas puto." Since the older copies of
the Bible continued to be transcribed, uniformity had not been secured. It is true
we no longer possess western Bibles whose contents are limited to the earliest
Roman Canon—Gospels, Acts, 13 Pauline Ep., 1 and 2 John, 1 Peter, Jude, Revelation—but we have them with an Ep. to the Laodiceans, the Pastor (though in
the O. T.), and even with the apocryphal correspondence of the Corinthians and
Paul.

ceal the fact that the Church never published a general decision, excluding all doubt, on the extent of the Canon in ancient times. The Canon of Augustine was adopted by Pope Innocent I. (Ep. 6, ch. 7, ad Exsuperium).

With the complete elaboration of the conception of canonical books, every other description applied to them gave way to the idea of their divinity. [1] What could any predicate signify compared with the conviction that they had been composed by the Holy Ghost himself? Therefore the categories of canon- ical and inspired writings coincided, nay, inspiration in its highest sense was limited to the canonical books. The belief in inspiration was necessarily attended by the duty of pneu- matic or allegorical exegesis. This sacred art was then prac- tised by all, who were able thus to disregard the results of any other kind of exposition. The problems which pneumatic exegesis, praised even by cultured Hellenists, [2] had to solve, were mainly the following. It had (1) to demonstrate the agree- ment between the two Testaments, in other words; to christi- anise the O. T. completely, to discover prophecy every- where, to get rid of the literal meaning where it was ob- noxious, and to repel Jewish claims; [3] (2) to harmonise the statements of Holy Scripture with the prevailing dogmatics; (3) to furnish every text with a profound meaning, one valuable for the time. Exegesis became a kind of black art, and Augus- tine was not the only man who was delivered from Manichæan, by Biblical, Alchemy.

But while these tasks were generally fixed, a sure and un- varying method was still wanting. [4] Even the principles of

[1] The conception that the canonical books were solemnly set apart, occurs first in Athanasius; the Alexandrians, however, including Origen, had the idea and even the word before him (Orig. Prolog. in Cantic.). Athanasius writes in his Festival Ep. τὰ κανονιζόμενα καὶ παραδοθέντα πιστευθέντα τε θεῖα εἶναι βιβλία.

[2] The Neoplatonic opponents of the Church were not quite honest, they were rather talking διαλεκτικῶς, when they objected to the allegorical method of interpreting Holy Scripture. They treated their own sacred writings in exactly the same way.

[3] Sozomen says (H. E. V. 22) that the Jews were more readily seduced to heathenism, because they only interpreted Holy Scripture πρὸς ῥητόν, and not πρὸς θεωρίαν.

[4] Thus Arians and Orthodox sometimes appealed to the same texts. But the impossibility of drawing up a rule deciding how far the letter of Scripture was

Origen were not strictly retained.[1]  On the other hand, the
historical antiquarian interest, which he had awakened, in Holy
Scripture, continued to exert its influence.  It not only lasted
up to the fifth century,[2] but it also exerted a critical and re-
authoritative, caused more anxiety. Had God a human form, eyes, or voice; was
Paradise situated on the earth; did the dead rise with all their bodily members,
even with their hair, etc.?—to all these and a hundred similar questions there was
no sure answer, and consequently disputes arose between adherents of one and
the same confession. All had to allegorise, and, in turn, all had to take certain
texts literally. But what a difference existed between an Epiphanius and a Gregory
of Nyssa, and how many shades of belief there were between the crude anthropomorphists and the spiritualists! The latter, as a rule, had reason to dread the
arguments, and frequently the fists, of the former; they could not but be anxious about
their own orthodoxy, for the old *regula* was on the side of their opponents, and
the most absurd opinion had the prejudice that it was the most pious in its favour.
Ultimately, in the course of the fifth century, a sort of common sense established
itself, which could be taken as forming, with regard to the anthropomorphists, a
middle line between the exegetic methods of Chrysostom and Cyril of Alexandria,
and which had been anticipated by a few Fathers of the fourth century. Yet not
many concessions were made to the anthropomorphists. Even Antiochians like
Theodore had become suspected of an anthropomorphism incompatible with the
honour of God (see Johannes Philoponus, De creat. mundi, I. 22. in Gallandi XII.,
p. 496). He who did not rise from the *turpitudo litteræ ad decorem intelligentiæ
spiritalis* (Jerome ad Amos. 2) might come under suspicion of heresy. But, on the
other hand, the Cappadocians themselves opposed those who allegorised "too
much", and thus approximated too closely to heathen philosophers; and after a
part of Origen's expositions had passed into the traditional possessions of the
Church, the rest was declared heretical. Even before this Epiphanius had written
(H. 61, ch. 6): Πάντα τὰ θεῖα ῥήματα οὐκ ἀλληγορίας δεῖται, ἀλλὰ ὡς ἔχει, ἔχει;
θεωρίας δὲ δεῖται καὶ αἰσθήσεως. Origen's thorough-going principle that "God can
say and do nothing, which is not good and just", by which he criticised and
occasionally set aside the letter of Scripture, was too bold for the Epigoni with
their faith in authority. God had done what Scripture said of him, and what God
did was good. This principle not only ruined all lucid science, but also deprived
the Church of the intrinsic completeness of her creed. Yet we must not minimise
the result of the compromise made in the fourth and fifth centuries, between the
literal, allegorical, and typical methods of interpreting Scripture; for it has held
its ground up to the present day in a way really identical in all Churches, and
it seems to possess no small power to convince.

1  For Origen's principles see Vol. II., p. 346.

2  Origen, Eusebius, and Jerome are links in a chain of scholarly tradition and
work. The succession, however, marked a descent not only in point of time. The
attitude of Jerome and the conflicts in which he was involved show at the same
time that the age no longer tolerated independent scholarship in historical criticism.
Therefore it ceased after Jerome: such work was confined to registering antiquarian
notices, even doubtful ones, which were accepted without reflection, since, having
entered into the stock of tradition, they no longer roused criticism.

strictive influence on pneumatic exegesis [1]  This was the case among the scholars of Antioch. Diodorus and Theodore tried, following the precedent set by Lucian and Dorotheus, to form an inner connection between the pneumatic and the grammatico-historical exegesis. It cannot be held that this gave rise to a more rational method, or one more tenable from the critical standpoint. Yet in detail they followed sound principles. These again had been already pared down by Chrysostom and Theodoret in favour of the dominant method, but they lasted in the Nestorian Church and its schools as long as science existed there at all, and their influence extended into the West through Junilius. [2]

[1] Besides, when driven by necessity, *i.e.*, when brought face to face with inconvenient passages of Scripture, a way was found out of the difficulty in the demand that the historical occasion of the text must be carefully weighed. Thus Athanasius writes (Orat. c. Arian. I. 54), when setting himself to refute the Scriptural proofs of the Arians, and finding that he is in considerable straits: δεῖ δέ, ὡς ἐπὶ πάσης τῆς θείας γραφῆς προσήκει ποιεῖν καὶ ἀναγκαῖόν ἐστιν, οὕτω καὶ ἐνταῦθα, καθ᾽ ὃν εἶπεν ὁ ἀπόστολος καιρὸν καὶ τὸ πρόσωπον καὶ τὸ πρᾶγμα, διόπερ ἔγραψε, πιστῶς ἐκλαμβάνειν, ἵνα μὴ παρὰ ταῦτα ἢ καὶ παρ᾽ ἕτερόν τι τούτων ἀγνοῶν ὁ ἀναγιγνώσκων ἔξω τῆς ἀληθινῆς διανοίας γένηται. The same contention was often upheld in earlier times by Tertullian when driven into a corner by the exegesis of the Marcionites (see De præscr. adv. Marc. II.—V.). The exegetical "principle" of the Fathers gradually became the *complexus oppositorum*; *i.e.*, when the literal meaning was disturbing, then it was, in the words of Gregory of Nazianzus, (Orat. XXXI. 3): ἔνδυμα τῆς ἀσεβείας ἐστὶν ἡ φιλία τοῦ γράμματος: or men spoke of the *turpitudo litteræ*, the Jewish understanding of Scripture, the necessity of considering historical circumstances or the like. But if "advanced" theologians produced suspected allegorical explanations, then the cry was raised ὡς ἔχει, ἔχει, Holy Scripture is not to be understood according to Plato, etc.

[2] The distinction between Alexandrian—Origenistic—and Antiochene exegesis does not consist in the representatives of the latter having rejected wholesale the spiritual meaning. They rather recognised it, but they tried to determine it typically from the literal meaning. While the Alexandrians avowedly set aside the literal meaning in many passages, and attached the pneumatic sense to texts by some sort of device, the Antiochenes started from the literal meaning, seeking to discover it by all the means of a sound exegesis, and then showed that the narrative concerned was a σκιὰ τῶν μελλόντων, a type created by God, which had been fulfilled by Jesus Christ. They set up definite rules for the discovery of the literal meaning as well as for that of the typical and allegorical sense (θεωρία, not ἀλληγορία), which lay not in the words, but the realities, persons, and events designated by the words. The rules are strikingly like those of the Federal theologians—Cocceius—and the school of Hofmann; the method of the author of the Hebrews furnished their model. This procedure had various results. First, the

The West received through Hilary, Ambrose, Jerome, and
Rufinus, the erudite pneumatic method of the Greeks, as practised especially by the Cappadocians.  Before this, and for a
few decades afterwards, the exegesis of the West was mainly

method of Philo and Origen followed by the Alexandrians was strenuously opposed
both in independent treatises, and in connection with exegesis. Secondly, an effort
was made to give the literal meaning in all cases its due; thus Diodorus says in
the Catena of Nicephorus (Leipz. 1772, I. p. 524): τοῦ ἀλληγορικοῦ τὸ ἱστορικὸν
πλεῖστον ὅσον προτιμῶμεν. Thirdly, a real covenant was accordingly recognised
between God and the Jewish people, and that nation was accorded its significant
place in the history of salvation: the "history of salvation" which thus originated
differed essentially from that of Irenæus (see Vol. II., p. 305). Fourthly and finally,
the number of directly Messianic passages in the O. T. became extraordinarily
limited; while, according to pneumatic exegesis, everything in the O. T. was in a
sense directly Messianic, i.e., Christian, the Antiochenes only retained a few such
passages. The horizon of O. T. authors was more correctly defined. Theodore
decidedly disputed the presence of anything in the O. T. about the Son of God
or the Trinity. Further, the Antiochenes distinguished grades of inspiration, namely,
the spirit of prophecy, and that of wisdom, and they placed the former far above
the latter. Although the advance of this exegesis on the Alexandrian is obvious,
yet it is seriously defective in completeness and consistency in method. First, the
Antiochenes, in spite of their polemic against the older expositors—Hippolytus, Origen,
Eusebius, Apollinaris, Didymus, and Jerome—could not altogether divest themselves of the old principle of the authoritative interpretation of Scripture; "they
regarded the old traditional doctrine, the exposition given by the Fathers, and the
definitions of Synods, as the standard and touch-stone of agreement with the creed
of the Church, and they made of this rule what use they pleased"; from this source
their attitude became somewhat uncertain. Secondly, they only rarely succeeded in
criticising the literal meaning historically; where they did, they employed rationalistic interpretations, and accordingly their procedure approximated to Origen's
speculative exegesis, yet without following any fixed principle. Thirdly, their typolo-
gical exegesis also often bordered very closely on the allegorical, and since they assumed
a double sense in Scripture, they did not remove, but only disguised, the fundamental
error of current exegesis. Fourthly, they could not make clear the difference between the
O. T. and the N. T., because, in spite of their assumption of different degrees of
inspiration, they placed the O. T. prophets on a level with the Apostles; see
Theodore, Comment. on Neh. I. in Migne, T. LXVI., p. 402: τῆς αὐτῆς τοῦ ἁγίου
πνεύματος χάριτος οἵ τε πάλαι μετεῖχον καὶ οἱ τῷ τῆς καινῆς διαθήκης ὑπηρετούμενοι
μυστηρίῳ. Finally, by assuming directly Messianic passages in the O. T. they gave
up their own position, and placed themselves at the mercy of their opponents.

See later for the history of the school of Antioch, especially its relation to
Aristotle. Diestel, Gesch. des A. T. in der christl. Kirche, p. 126 ff. Fritzsche, de
Theod. Mops. vita et scriptis, Halae, 1836. Above all, the works of Kihn, Die
Bedeutung der Antioch. Schule a. d. exeget. Gebiete (1866), and Theodor von
Mopsuestia und Junilius als Exegeten (1880), where the older literature is given.
Swete, Theodori ep. Mops. in epp. Pauli Comment. Cambridge, 1880, 1881.

characterised by absence of system; along with reverence for
the letter we find all sorts of allegorical explanations, and in
turn a predilection for a dramatic close to earthly history.
Jerome was far from having fixed exegetic principles, since he
allegorised against his better knowledge wherever the orthodox
confession required it. In his time Tychonius, a Donatist, drew
up for the interpretation of Holy Scripture seven rules which
were to remove all difficulties (Augustine, De doctr. christ. III.
30 sq.).¹ These were adopted by Augustine in his work 'On
Christian Science', which, subject as it is to the errors of the
age, is a glorious memorial of the great Bishop's love of truth,
and evangelical feeling. Of evangelical feeling, in so far as
Augustine, in opposition to all biblicism, declared the study of
Holy Scripture to be merely the path towards love; he who
possessed love, no longer needed the Scripture, he lived with
Christ and God; accordingly he had ceased to require separate
'saving truths', for he lived in truth and love.²

¹ These rules are of material importance (for theology). The first treats of the
Lord and his body: i.e., we must and may apply the truth concerning the Lord
to the Church, and vice versa, since they form one person; only in this way do
we frequently get a correct sense. The second deals with the bi-partite body of
the Lord: we must carefully consider whether the true or the empirical Church is
meant. The third takes up the promises and the law, i.e., the spirit and letter;
the fourth treats of genus and species: we must observe the extent to which texts
apply; the fifth, of the dates: we must harmonise contradictory dates by a fixed
method, and understand certain stereotyped numbers as symbolical. The sixth
discusses repetition: i.e., we have frequently to refrain from assuming a chronological order, where such an order appears to exist, and the seventh deals with the
devil and his body, i.e., the devil and the godless, many things referring to the
latter which are said of the devil and vice versa—see the first rule.

² The thought wavers between that of Origen, who also elevates himself above
the historical Christ, and the genuinely evangelical idea that the Christian must
stop short at "means of salvation"; see De doctr. I. 34: "Nulla res in via (ad
deum) tenere nos debet, quando nec ipse dominus, in quantum via nostra esse
dignatus est, tenere nos voluerit, sed transire: ne rebus temporalibus, quamvis ab
illo pro salute nostra susceptis et gestis, hæreamus infirmiter, sed per eas potius
curramus alacriter etc." In ch. 35 love is held up as the exclusive goal: ch. 36
teaches that no one has understood Scripture who has not been led by it to love
God and his neighbour; but if he has been led to this love, then he loses nothing
by failing to hit on the correct sense of detached texts: in that case he is deceived,
but without guilt: "Quisquis in scripturis (I. 37) aliud sentit quam ille qui scripsit,

But this thought of the book does not give its prevailing colour; this is furnished, on the contrary, by the other ideas that Scripture is the only way by which to come to God and Christ, that it is to be interpreted by the rule of faith, that obscure passages are to be explained by clear ones, and that the literal meaning, where offensive, must yield to the deeper sense. The numerous hermeneutic rules set up by Augustine,[1] which are so many expedients and very like Origen's methodic principles, determined the nature of exegesis in later periods in the West. In connection with whatever else was derived from the East, the view that there was a triple and fourfold meaning in Scripture became a fixed doctrine.[2] The little book by Junilius which

illis non mentientibus fallitur; sed tamen, ut dicere cœperam, si ea sententia fallitur, qua ædificet caritatem, quæ finis præcepti est, ita fallitur ac si quisquam errore deserens viam, eo tamen per agrum pergat, quo etiam via illa perducit." Augustine says indeed (l. c.): "titubabit fides, si divinarum scripturarum vacillat auctoritas," but, on the other hand (I. 39): "Homo, fide, spe et caritate subnixus eaque inconcusse retinens, *non indiget scripturis nisi ad alios instruendos*. Itaque multi per hæc tria etiam in solitudine sine codicibus vivunt... Quibus tamen quasi machinis tanta fidei, spei et caritatis in eis surrexit instructio, ut perfectum aliquid tenentes, ea quæ sunt ex parte non quærant; perfectum sane, quantum in hac vita potest." This forcible way of assigning a practical purpose to the reading of Scripture and the understanding at the root of it, viz., that it was *the whole* that was of importance, is the opposite of the conception that Scripture embraces innumerable mysteries; but an affinity exists far down between them, inasmuch as Augustine seems to reserve to the monks the state in which Scripture is not required, and he borders on the belief of Origen (I. 34) that the Christ of history belongs to the past for him who lives in love. The whole conception is first found, besides, in the description by the Valentinian school of the perfect Gnostic; see Excerpta ex Theodoto, ch. 27: ποῦ δὲ ἔτι γραφῆς καὶ μαθήσεως κατόρθωμα τῇ ψυχῇ ἐκείνῃ τῇ καθαρᾷ γενομένῃ, ὅπου καὶ ἀξιοῦται πρόσωπον πρὸς πρόσωπον Θεὸν ὁρᾶν; besides Augustine expressly argued against those who supposed they could dispense with Scripture from the start, and appealed to an inner revelation (see the Præfat. to De doctr. christ.). He puts it beyond doubt that he who uses Scripture must bow to its authority even where he does not understand it.

[1] See the second and especially the third book of the work quoted. The second contains a short and precise review of all branches of knowledge which are collectively perceived to spring from heathenism, and it states which may and must be used by the Christian, and to what extent. The third book contains the hermeneutics proper.

[2] See Eucherius of Lyons, liber formularum spiritalis intelligentiæ ad Veranium filium, in Migne. Ser. lat. T. 50, p. 727. In later times the mnemonic formula was composed:     *Littera* gesta docet, quid credas *allegoria*,
          *Moralis* quid agas, quo tendas *anagogia*.

contained the Antiochene system of hermeneutics as handed
down at Nisibis, although much read, made few changes. But
it was exceedingly significant that Augustine, in spite of his
view that it was only a means, had placed the Bible on such
a pinnacle that all theologians who afterwards took their stand
upon it alone as against tradition, were able to appeal to him.
As a matter of fact Scripture held quite a different place in the
Church life of the West from that in the East: it came more
into the foreground. That also is to be explained, above all,
by the influence of Augustine,[1] and the deficiency of the
West in speculative ability.[2]

As the Church had never published a general decree, exclusive of all doubt, on the extent of Scripture, it had also
failed to publish one concerning its characteristics. Freedom
from error was generally deduced from inspiration, and it was,
as a rule, referred to the very words. But on the other hand,
an attempt was made here and there to leave room for the
individuality and historical limitation of the authors; minor inconsistencies were not wholly denied (see even Aug., De consensu evang.); and exegesis was often practised as if the strict
dogma of inspiration did not exist.[3] A clear idea of the suffi-

[1] The work "On Christian Science" points to Scripture as its sole object, and
does not discuss tradition at all. However, the latter receives its due inasmuch as
Augustine regards the propositions of the rule of faith—based on the Symbol—as
the *matters*, which constituted the essential contents of Scripture. In this definition
we find the reason why dogmatics never ceased to waver between Scripture and
the rule of faith. Yet we know that Augustine was by no means the first to hold
this view. Even the writer of the Muratorian fragment and Irenæus knew no better.

[2] Origen taught that Christian science was the science of Scripture; Augustine
stands upon his shoulders. But afterwards, in the East, the interest in dogmatic
formulas became uppermost, while in the West, the Bible remained pre-eminently
the direct source of knowledge of the faith.

[3] Even the men of Antioch, by whom, Chrysostom not excepted, human elements
were aknowledged to exist in the Bible, maintained the inspiration of other passages
*quoad litteram*, just like Origen and the Cappadocians. Augustine accepted this
freedom from error in its strictest sense; see Ep. 82. 3 (ad Hieron.): "Ego fateor
caritati tuæ, solis eis scripturarum libris, qui iam canonici appellantur, didici hunc
timorem honoremque deferre, ut nullum eorum auctorem scribendo aliquid errasse
firmissime credam. Ac si aliquid in eis offendero litteris, quod videatur contrarium
veritati, nihil aliud quam vel mendosum esse codicem, vel interpretem non assecu-
tum esse quod dictum est, vel me minime intellexisse non ambigam." In his
work *De consensu evang.*, which is particularly instructive as regards his whole

ciency of Scripture was certainly not reached; it was maintained
in general phrases, and was violated in generalities and in details. [1]
Finally, as regards the relation of the two Testaments to each
other, three views existed side by side. The Old Testament
was a Christian book as well as the New: it was throughout
the record of prophecy: it contained the true creed under certain limitations and imperfections, and led and still leads educa-
tionally to Christ. These points of view were adopted alternately as the occasion required. It was recognised that the
Jewish nation had possessed a covenant with God, yet the
consequences of this were far from being admitted. The same
method of employing the Bible was still upheld in apologetic
arguments as was followed by the Apologists of the second
century. [2] For the rest, even Cyril of Alexandria still brought
"heathen prophecy" to bear in this matter, while in other respects—speaking generally—the assumption of heathen 'prophets'
and inspired philosophers excited suspicion.

attitude to Holy Writ, he declares that the Apostles' writings make up sufficiently
for the absence of any by our Lord; for the Apostles were the Lord's hands, and
had written what he commanded. It is extremely surprising that this being the
view taken of the Bible—and even the translation of the LXX. was held to be
inspired—yet no one ever *ex professo* reflected on how the Canon was formed.
No miracle was assumed. Even Augustine quite naively stated, *sancti et docti
homines* had formed the N. T. (c. Faustum XXII. 79). Here the authority of the
Church comes in.

1 The early Catholic Fathers had already maintained the sufficiency of Holy
Scripture, as well as the necessity of proving everything out of it; see for the
latter point Orig. in Jerem., Hom. I. c. 7 (Lomm. XV. p. 115): Μάρτυρας δεῖ λαβεῖν
τὰς γραφάς. Ἀμάρτυροι γὰρ αἱ ἐπιβολαὶ ἡμῶν καὶ αἱ ἐξηγήσεις ἄπιστοί εἰσιν. Cyril
of Jerusalem has expressed himself similarly (Cat. 4, 17: Δεῖ γὰρ περὶ τῶν θείων
καὶ ἁγίων τῆς πίστεως μυστηρίων μηδὲ τὸ τυχὸν ἄνευ τῶν θείων παραδίδοσθαι γρα-
φῶν· καὶ μὴ ἁπλῶς πιθανότησι καὶ λόγων κατασκευαῖς παραφέρεσθαι. Μηδὲ ἐμοὶ
τῷ ταῦτα σοι λέγοντι, ἁπλῶς πιστεύσῃς· ἐὰν τὴν ἀπόδειξιν τῶν καταγγελλομένων
ἀπὸ τῶν θείων μὴ λάβῃς γραφῶν· Ἡ σωτηρία γὰρ αὕτη τῆς πίστεως ἡμῶν οὐκ ἐξ
εὑρεσιλογίας, ἀλλὰ ἐξ ἀποδείξεως τῶν θείων ἐστὶ γραφῶν); cf. Athanasius (Orat. adv.
gentes init.: Αὐτάρκεις μέν εἰσιν αἱ ἅγιαι καὶ θεόπνευστοι γραφαὶ πρὸς τὴν τῆς
ἀληθείας ἀπαγγελίαν). So also the Antiochenes, moreover Augustine De doctr. II. 9:
"In iis quæ aperte in scriptura posita sunt, inveniuntur illa omnia, quæ continent
fidem moresque vivendi, spem scilicet et caritatem." Vincent., Commonit. 2.

2 All the more did the use made of the O. T. for the constitution of the Church
differ from the apologetic view. Very many of the regulations of the O. T.
ceremonial law came once more to be highly valued by the Church, not as spiritually understood, but as directly applied to ecclesiastical institutions of every sort.

## 2. *Tradition.*

The authority of Holy Scripture frequently appears in the Fathers as something wholly abstract and despotic. It contained, in fact, a latent tendency to assert its independence of the conditions out of which it had arisen. But the revolution which was characterised by the isolation of the Bible, its deliverance from the authority of ecclesiastical tradition, and the annihilation of the latter, only took place in the sixteenth century, and even then it was, we know, not completely successful. In ecclesiastical antiquity, on the contrary, the bond was by no means severed which connected Scripture with the maternal organism of the Church. The Church, its doctrine, institutions, and constitution, were held, in and by themselves, to constitute the source of knowledge and the authoritative guarantee of truth. As the holy, Apostolic, and Catholic institution, it possessed nothing whatever untrue or capable of amendment either in its foundations or its development. Everything in it, rather, was apostolic, and the guidance of the Church by the Holy Ghost had preserved this apostolic fabric from any change. This thought was necessarily emphasised more and more strongly in consequence of the development undergone by Church affairs in the fourth and following centuries. Since at the same time, however, the independent authority and the sufficiency of the Bible were also emphasised, there arose difficulties, in part even manifest inconsistencies, which were never removed. [1] But they were not clearly felt, because men always possessed the power, when confronted by inconvenient monitors, to carry through ultimately, whether in the form of dogma, or in that of order, whatever was required. In face of traditions become obsolete an appeal was made to other traditions, or to the Bible; where written testimony was uncertain or awanting, recourse was had to tradition; *i.e.*, that was declared to be tradition which was

---

[1] The Orientals, especially the Antiochenes, but Cyril of Jerus. also, adhered more exclusively to Scripture; the Alexandrians, and even the Cappadocians relied more strongly on tradition. Yet the differences are only in degree. At any rate, the difference comes out more strongly on a comparison of Theodoret and Cyril of Alexandria.

not to be justified under another title. Hence it is already clear
that tradition never was and never could be systematised and
catalogued, that an authentic declaration never was and never
could be published as to its extent and scope. There was no
single deliverance on the application of tradition, which would
not, if consistently carried out, have thrown the Church into
confusion. If Augustine therefore (De bapt. c. Donat. II. 3, 4)
declared—certainly against his better knowledge—that ' canonical
Scripture was contained within fixed limits of its own ' (scriptura
canonica certis suis terminis continetur), yet it never occurred
to him or any one else to maintain as much about tradition.
The latter was in antiquity a wholly elastic category, as we see
when we look at its use in individual cases; in *summa* it was,
however, an extremely rigid and clear notion: meaning simply
that the Church was determined, in spite of all changes, to
regard itself as the unchangeable creation of the Apostles. It
derived its claim to this view partly from the divine promises,
partly from the organisation instituted for it, yet without alleging confidently any empirical factor within the Church which
should be the bearer of its infallibility. [1] The most important
consequences of this view held by the Church regarding itself
have been already stated in the second volume; but others
came to be added in the post-Constantinian period.

A.  The creed of the Church was always held to be the
most important part of its tradition. The anti-gnostic formulas
which the creed had preserved passed over in the East, along
with theorems, half biblical half speculative, and here and there
with purely philosophical or polemical discussions, into the
Symbols. [2] These Symbols, which had been adopted for use

[1] Reuter's excellent explanation of Augustine's position (Ztschrft. für K.-Gesch.
Vol. VIII., pp. 181 f., 186 f.) was then true of very wide circles: "The Episcopate,
and the Roman *sedes apostolica*, the whole relatively coördinated *sedes apostolicæ*,
the relative and the absolute plenary councils were held to be representations of
the (infallible) Church; but not one of these factors, not all of them combined,
formed the (infallible) representation of the (infallible) Church. The latter possessed
no indubitably sure institution or organs indubitably representative of it." The
decrees of councils were only placed on a complete equality with Scripture in the
East, after councils had ceased to be held, and when the latter therefore were
seen, like Scripture, in a nimbus of hoary antiquity.

[2] See Vol. II., p. 20 f. and III., pp. 48 ff., 111 ff.

in the Church, were regarded as apostolic testimonies. Their
phrasing was not considered in the East to be due to the
Apostles, but the honour paid them was justified from the
Apostles' preaching. [1] These Symbols of the provincial Churches
were supplanted in the period between the first and third (fourth)
Œcumenical Councils by the Nicene, or soon thereafter by the
so-called Constantinopolitan Symbol. [2] This confession [3] had
already been held at Chalcedon to be *the creed* pure and simple,
and it never lost this place of honour. If it had already been
constantly assumed that the doctrine of the Church was the
theme, or the matter, constituting the real contents of Scripture,
then this assumption was now definitely transferred to the
Nicene or the Constantinopolitan Symbol. All subsequent
dogmatic conclusions were accordingly regarded solely as explanations of this Symbol, [4] which was not maintained, however, to be of Apostolic origin—in its language. *Tradition, in
the strictest sense of the term, consisted in the contents of the
Symbol for the time being.* Cyril says of this (Cat. V. 12):
'In these few paragraphs the whole dogma of the faith (is)
comprised' (ἐν ὀλίγοις τοῖς στίχοις τὸ πᾶν δόγμα τῆς πίστεως

---

[1] The Symbol of Gregory Thaumaturgus was derived from a special revelation;
see Vol. III., p. 115.

[2] There were two symbol-constructing periods in the East before a universal
Confession was framed. The former of these embraced A.D. 250—325, the second,
A.D. 325 up to the beginning or the middle of the fifth century. In the latter
period the attempt was made either to transform the Nicene Creed into a baptismal
Confession, or to displace it by parallel formulas; sometimes the leading words of
the Nicene Symbol were inserted in those of the provincial Churches. See on the
history of this, the part played by the Bishops of Asia Minor in these develop-
ments, and the history of the so-called Constantinop. Symbol, my art. "Konstantinop.
Symbol" in Herzog's R.-E. 2, Vol. VIII.; Caspari's works, Hort's investigations,
Two Dissertations, Cambridge, 1876, and Kattenbusch, Confessionskunde I., p. 252 ff.

[3] It was originally the Baptismal Confession of the Church of Jerusalem, revised
soon after the middle of the fourth century, and furnished with a *regula fidei*
concerning the Holy Spirit; it came thus to be honoured first through the authority
of Epiphanius, and then through the energy of the Bishop of Constantinople, which
also led to its supplanting the Nicene Symbol.

[4] Monophysites and orthodox believers always professed to be able to read their
Christological formulas word for word in the Symbol. The Greek Church maintains
to the present day that the Nicene-Constantinopolitan Symbol contains everything
we require to believe.

περιλαμβανόμενον). As the Church had obtained in the Nicene Creed a complete and uniform Symbol, the view was transferred to it. There were two sides meanwhile to the relations of Scripture and Symbol. You might not believe the contents of the Symbol unless you could convince yourself of their truth from Scripture; [1] but on the other hand, your interpretation of Scripture had to be regulated by the creed laid down in the Symbol. [2] In the West a unique dignity was retained by the old Roman Symbol (or its parallel forms in the provincial Churches) which was regarded as being composed of twelve articles. From the fourth century at least it was held to be the *Apostolic Creed* in the strict sense of the term. [3] Its brevity and simplicity long preserved the Roman Church from extravagant theological speculations, but they could not barricade it against the theological development of the East. An industrious attempt was made, or at least professed, to derive the decision of dogmatic questions, as they emerged, from this Apostolic Symbol, and to rest upon it the whole of the ever increasing material of dogmatics. [4] It was only after the begin-

[1] So, above all, Cyril and the Antiochenes.

[2] No hesitation prevailed in the Church on this point; yet Synods simply forbade certain expositions of Scriptural texts as heretical. The Church alone furnished the *gubernaculum interpretationis* (see Vincent., Commonit. 2, 41) and that in its concise guide to faith, the Symbol. After the Constantinopolitan Symbol had been placed on an inaccessible height, we no longer find the blunt assertion that the creed is compiled from the Holy Scriptures. But this contention was also historically false. (For it see Cyril, Cat. V. 12): οὐ γὰρ ὡς ἔδοξεν ἀνθρώποις συνετέθη τὰ τῆς Πίστεως· ἀλλ᾽ ἐκ πάσης γραφῆς τὰ καιριώτατα συλλεχθέντα μίαν ἀναπληροῖ τὴν τῆς Πίστεως διδασκαλίαν. "Canon" was originally the rule of faith; the Scripture had in truth intervened, yet so that its authority had a support placed still further back, namely, the O. T. and the Lord's sayings.

[3] See my art. "Apostolisches Symbol" in Herzog's R.-E. 2 B. I. The opinion that the Apostles had composed the Symbol jointly (Rufinus) cannot be traced earlier than the middle of the fourth century, but it may be much older. Yet we must not date it too soon; for if the Churches of the western provinces had received the Symbol with this legend attached, they would hardly have ventured to propose changes on it. It was certainly not extolled even in Rome in the third century, so exuberantly as it was afterwards by Ambrose.

[4] This point falls to be discussed in the next book. Augustine had to rest his distinctive theology on the Symbol, though the latter was only imperfectly adapted for the purpose.

ning of the fifth century that the Constantinopolitan Symbol
supplanted the apostolic in Church use in Rome and the West, [1]
yet without the latter losing its prestige. This was of course
transferred in part to the new Symbol, but the old remained,
though latent, in force. [2] *The twelve articles of the Apostolic
Symbol, to be explained by the Constantinopolitan, constituted
in the West the ecclesiastical tradition* κατ᾽ ἐξοχήν. Justinian's
legislation confirmed this conception, though, indeed, that was
not needed. [3]

B. At the beginning of the fourth century there already
entered into the composition of the Church, not only its creed,
but a *cultus* fixed in its main features; there were further
*disciplinary* and *ceremonial provisions*—still differing, indeed, in
part in the various provincial Churches [4]—and finally, a settled
*constitution.* It was only in a very late period that the notion
of apostolicity was applied, in the strict sense, to the whole of
these elements; [5] but not only did the foundations of these
ordinances come to be characterised as apostolic, but as a rule,
and to an increasing extent, everything which there was a desire
to assure of permanence. Different methods were adopted,
however, of establishing the apostolic character of these institutions. First, it was maintained that regulations observed by the
whole Church required no proof that they were Apostolic. [6]

---

[1] See my art. on the Constantinop. Symbol, l. c.

[2] The history of the Apostolic Symbol between the fifth and sixth centuries
urgently requires investigation.

[3] Justinian's law-book is headed by the art. "De summa trinitate et de fide catholica
et ut nemo de ea publice contendere audeat"; but see also the famous decree of
the Emperors, Gratian, Valentinian and Theodosius, A.D. 380, with which the
law-book begins.

[4] See, *e.g.*, Socrates, H. E. V. 22.

[5] When this occurred a very exact distinction had already been made between
faith and disciplinary law. Apostolic faith was something different from and higher
than apostolic laws (διατάξεις, νόμοι, κανόνες ἐκκλησιαστικοὶ διὰ τῶν ἀποστόλων).
This corrected the equality apparently attributed to the two branches of tradition
by the common predicate "apostolic."

[6] See August., De bapt. c. Donat. II. 7, 12: "Multa, quæ non inveniuntur in
litteris apostolorum neque in conciliis posteriorum, et tamen quia per universam
custodiuntur ecclesiam, non nisi ab ipsis tradita et commendata creduntur." IV.
24. 31: "Quod universa tenet ecclesia, nec conciliis institutum sed semper retentum

Secondly, advantage was taken in the East, of the numerous
legends of the Apostles current in the Churches; they began
to be used in connection with the government and cultus of
the Churches in such a way that definite detailed regulations
were attributed to the Apostles, individually or collectively,
whenever they were required for the discipline or cultus of the
time. [1]  Thirdly, men began in the fourth century—not uninfluenced by Clement and Origen—to introduce the notion of
a παράδοσις ἄγραφος (unwritten tradition), in whose wholly undefined contents were even included dogmatic theories which
it was not everyone's business to understand; yet it dealt
extremely seldom with the trinitarian and Christological catch-
words. This idea of an 'unwritten tradition' crept in in a very
real sense; for it conflicted with more than one main point in
the fundamental positions of the Church. But it attained high
honour, and its existence absolutely became a dogma. But

est, non nisi auctoritate apostolica traditum rectissime creditur." V. 23. 31: " Multa,
quæ universa tenet ecclesia et ob hoc ab apostolis præcepta bene creduntur, quamquam scripta non reperiantur."

[1] The Apologists had exhibited Christianity as the worship of God in Spirit and
in truth, and as an alliance regulated by equality and fraternity. But there had gradually developed a complicated cultus round the mysteries, and a comprehensive and
detailed code of discipline had become necessary. For both of these appeal was
made to an increasing extent to apostolic authority. Compare the Apostolic Constitutions, the κανόνες ἐκκλησιαστικοί, the Apostolic Canons, in general the mass of
material, partly published, partly discussed, by Bickell, Pitra, and Lagarde; further,
the designation of the Liturgies of the provincial Churches as by Mark, James, etc.
The history, still partly unwritten, of these Eastern forgeries under apostolic names
is closely connected with the general history of the legends of the Apostles (see
Lipsius, Die apokryphen Apostelgesch.). The O. T. commandments were again
introduced into the Church by means of apostolic fictions, until the ancient awe of
Moses, the law-giver, was surmounted. After apostolic commandments of this sort
had been allowed to spring up luxuriantly for a time, the Church had no little
trouble to exorcise the spirits it had conjured. A sifting process began from the
sixth century—at least in the Byzantine Church—to which, e.g., the Constitutions fell
a victim. In the law books of the Monophysite and Nestorian Churches, much more
comprehensive matter had been preserved, under apostolic names, as possessed of
the value of law. Yet it did not receive the same honour as the Holy Scriptures.
In order to realise the possibility of such an unabashed invention of regulations
cloaked with the authority and name of the Apostles, we must remember that, from
the second century, writings bearing on discipline were in existence, called διδαχαὶ
or διατάξεις τῶν ἀποστόλων, and that these, having no individual impress, were
thoroughly adapted for constant remodelling and expansion.

because it really made all else unnecessary and was a dangerous drastic expedient, it was not defined, nor was its extent ever determined. And it did not banish Scriptural proof or the appeal to familiar and demonstrable tradition. *The existence was maintained of a tradition which dispensed with all criteria —and that was what the παράδοσις ἄγραφος was; but a prudent use was made of it.* Unwritten tradition was preferentially applied to the development of ritual and the sacramental performance of the mysteries, while the secret truths of the creed were based exclusively on Scripture and the Councils. [1]   But

[1] The assumption of a secret apostolic tradition—that is, the παράδοσις ἄγραφος —first appeared among the Gnostics, *i.e.*, among the first theologians, who had to legitimise as apostolic a world of notions alien to primitive Christianity. It then was found quite logically among the Alexandrians, and from them passed to Eusebius, who not only accepted it (H. E. II. 1, 4), but also vindicated it against Marcellus (lib. I. c. 1): ἐκκλησίας τὰς ἀπὸ τῶν θείων γραφῶν μαρτυρίας ἐξ ἀγράφου παραδόσεως σφραγιζομένης. But the Cappadocians first established it in their conflict with the Eunomians and Pneumatomachoi, yet the bold use made of it by them in defence of the dogma of the Trinity, was not afterwards parallelled. Basil (De spiritu sancto, 27) referred the orthodox doctrine of the Holy Ghost to the unwritten tradition, placing the latter on an equality with the public tradition; but he endeavoured at the same time to retain the old Alexandrian distinction between κήρυγμα and δόγμα, δόγμα being meant to embrace the theological formulation of the faith (τῶν ἐν τῇ ἐκκλησίᾳ πεφυλαγμένων δογμάτων καὶ κηρυγμάτων τὰ μὲν ἐκ τῆς ἐγγράφου διδασκαλίας ἔχομεν, τὰ δὲ ἐκ τῆς τῶν ἀποστόλων παραδόσεως διαδοθέντα ἡμῖν ἐν μυστηρίῳ παρεδεξάμεθα, ἅπερ ἀμφότερα τὴν αὐτὴν ἰσχὺν ἔχει πρὸς τὴν εὐσέβειαν ... ἄλλο γὰρ δόγμα, καὶ ἄλλο κήρυγμα, τὰ μεν γὰρ δόγματα σιωπᾶται, τὰ δὲ κηρύγματα δημοσιεύεται). The latter distinction was opposed to the tendency of the age, and remained without effect. (With that which Basil named dogma, the μυστικὴ παράδοσις was identical, of which Pamphilus and Eusebius speak, and by the aid of which they defended the orthodoxy of Origen; see Socrates III. 7.) But it is important that in order to prove the existence of a παράδοσις ἄγραφος, Basil appeals merely to matters of ritual—signs of the Cross, prayers of consecration, and baptismal rites. To these the unwritten tradition was in later times almost exclusively applied. Gregory of Nazianzus advanced in a different direction from Basil: he admitted to his opponents (Orat. 37) that tradition was defective in reference to the doctrine of the Spirit, but he believed he could assume a progressive development of the truth of revelation. But, as far as I know, he only once expressed himself so imprudently, and he found absolutely no imitators. His attempt only proves the difficulty caused by the defence of the dogma of the Trinity in the fourth century. In Cyril of Jerusalem (see his view so divergent from that of the Cappadocians, Cat. 16, ch. 2) and the older Antiochenes the παράδοσις ἄγραφος does not occur, but it does in Epiphanius (H. 61, ch. 6: δεῖ καὶ παραδόσει κεχρῆσθαι. οὐ γὰρ πάντα ἀπὸ τῆς θείας γραφῆς δύναται λαμβάνεσθαι· διὸ τὰ μὲν ἐν γραφαῖς, τὰ δὲ ἐν παραδόσεσιν παρέδωκαν οἱ ἅγιοι ἀπόστολοι). It is also found in Chrysostom,

this distinction was not sufficient, nor was it firmly held to be unalterable.

C. All conceptions of the authority of tradition, of which many Fathers—*e.g.*, Cyprian—described Scripture to be the main element, [1] were based ultimately on the conviction *that the Church had been invested with authority through its connection with the Holy Spirit himself.* [2] At this point two problems arose, which, though hardly ever clearly formulated, were yet felt, and which attempts were made to solve. I.—By whom and when did the Church speak? II.—How were novelties to be explained in the Church, especially in the sphere of doctrine, if the authority of the Church had its root exclusively in its apostolic character, that is, its ability to preserve the legacy of the Apostles?

As to I. It was a settled doctrine from the third century, that the representation of the Church was vested in the

---

Cyril of Alexandria, and others down to John of Damascus, who says plainly (De fide orthod. IV. ch. 12): ἄγραφός ἐστιν ἡ παράδοσις αὕτη τῶν ἀποστόλων, πολλὰ γὰρ ἀγράφως ἡμῖν παρέδοσαν (see details in Langen, Joh. von Damaskus, 1879, p. 271 ff.). So also the Greek Church of to-day teaches : διωρεῖται τὸ θεῖον ῥῆμα εἰς τε τὸ γραπτὸν καὶ ἄγραφον (see Gass, Symbolik der griech. Kirche, p. 107 ff.) Quotations are especially taken from Pauline texts in which παραδόσεις occur, and thus a sort of Scriptural proof is led in support of what does not occur in Scripture. The unwritten tradition is hardly again applied to the creed, since it was thought to be sufficiently supported by Scripture and the Symbol. In the West, Augustine was in the same doubtful position, with regard to certain theses which he defended against Donatists and Pelagians, as the Cappadocians were in reference to the orthodox doctrine of the Holy Ghost. Hence he derived, *e.g.*, the doctrine of original sin, which could not be otherwise proved out of tradition, from the rite of exorcism, declaring this to have been an apostolic tradition; (see c. Julian. VI. 5, 11): "Sed etsi nulla ratione indagetur, nullo sermone explicetur, verum tamen est quod antiquitus veraci fide catholica prædicatur et creditur per ecclesiam totam; quæ filios fidelium nec exorcizaret, nec exsufflaret, si non eos de potestate tenebrarum et a principe mortis erueret, etc.). So also he appealed against the Donatists in the controversy as to Baptism by Heretics (against Cyprian's authority) to the unwritten testimony of the whole Church (see note 6, p. 211).

[1] Cyprian calls Scripture "*divinæ traditionis caput et origo*" (Ep. 74, ch. 10). This designation is not common.

[2] The universal conviction is expressed in the famous sentence of Augustine (C. ep. Manich. 6) which he has given in various forms in the Confessions and elsewhere : *Ego vero evangelio non crederem, nisi me catholicæ ecclesiæ commoveret auctoritas.* Even Cyril of Jerusalem, who has emphasised most strongly the authority of Scripture, could not pass over that of the Church (Cat. IV., ch. 33).

Episcopate, though the strict conception of the latter, as first taught by Cyprian, that it was the main support of the Church, was for a long time not universally held. [1] We find, meanwhile, even, *e.g.*, from the plan of Eusebius' Church History, that the Bishops, the successors of the Apostles, were regarded as guarantors of the legitimacy of the Church. The conception never emerged that the Bishop was infallible as an individual; [2] but a certain inspiration was already—though not without differences of opinion—attributed to the provincial Synods. [3] Constantine was the first to form the idea of a universal Synod, [4] and he

[1] In his studies on Augustine, Reuter has shown that Augustine fell short of Cyprian (see his theses in the Ztschr. f. K.-Gesch., Vol. VIII., p. 184, and the relative discussions in Vol. VII.). In the East the compiler of Apostolic Constitutions took substantially the view of the Episcopate held by Ignatius, but not by Irenæus and Cyprian. Even Chrysostom's work, περὶ ἱερωσύνης, tends in the same direction as the Constitutions. It is very remarkable that Cyril of Jerusalem (Cat. XVIII., ch. 27) makes no mention of the hierarchy, but only of the Apostles, prophets, teachers and other office-bearers enumerated in the well-known passage in the Ep. to the Corinthians. That is a memorable archaism; yet see even Vincentius, Commonit. 40. He also says very little about Bishops, and nothing at all about the apostolic succession.

[2] On the contrary, the fallibility of individual bishops was always admitted from Irenæus down (III. 3, 1): "*Valde perfectos et irreprehensibiles in omnibus eos volebant esse (apostoli), quos et successores relinquebant, suum ipsorum locum magisterii tradentes, quibus emendate agentibus fieret magna utilitas, lapsis autem summa calamitas.*"

[3] Cyprian (Ep. LVII., ch. 5) introduces the decree of the provincial Council of Carthage with the words, "*Placuit nobis spiritu sancto suggerente.*" Acts XV. 28 certainly influenced this phrase. On the other hand, we must not allow it too much weight, for Cyprian often appeals to instructions given to him personally by the Holy Ghost. See also the Votum of Bishop Lucius of Ausafa, No. 73 of the sentent. episcoporum LXXXVII. at the Carthaginian Council: "*Secundum motum animi mei et spiritus sancti.*" The Synod of Arles, A.D. 314, also used the formula, "*Placuit ergo, præsente spiritu sancto et angelis eius*" (see Mansi, Collect. Concil. II. p. 469, and Hefele, Conciliengesch. I. 2, p. 204); and Constantine wished to have its decision regarded as "*cæleste iudicium*": this judgment by priests was to have the same honour as if it had been pronounced by the Lord himself (Mansi, l.c. p. 478). For the rest, we may here recall the fact that ἡ ἱερὰ σύνοδος had long been a technical term in common use among the Greeks (see also "holy senate" in Justin). On the origin of the ecclesiastical Synods see Sohm's excellent discussions in Kirchenrecht. I. p. 247 ff.

[4] This is now almost universally admitted; yet the idea was introduced by the great Oriental Synods in the cases of Novatian and Paul of Samosata, as well as by the Synod of Arles already indeed summoned by Constantine. The latter has

also supposed such a body to be under the special guidance
of the Holy Spirit, and therefore incapable of error. [1]  In the
course of the fourth century the idea that the Nicene Synod
possessed an infallible authority became slowly established; [2]
it was transferred in the following centuries to the Œcumenical Synods generally, yet so that one—the second—was
only subsequently stamped as Œcumenical. [3]  From the sixth

been looked on in the West as a General Council for more than a century, and can
also be regarded as such in many respects. On the Councils see Hatch's fine lecture
in his book "The Social Constitution of Christian Churches," p. 172 f.

[1]  See Constantine's letter to the Bishops after the Council of Nicæa (in Theodoret
H. E. I. 9 *fin*): "Whatever is determined in the holy assemblies of the Bishops,
may be attributed to the divine will." Further, Socrates H. E. I. 9, who contrasts
the recognition by the Emperor of the divine character of the Synod, with the
aspersions of Sabinus the Macedonian.

[2]  The orthodox party made use of the advantage presented by the decision of
a Synod which none could refuse to recognise as a wholly extraordinary event.
On the other hand, nothing but such an event could atone for the unusual forms
given to the creed, and thus attest a new theory.  For in spite of everything
which it had been hitherto possible to relate of Synods being under divine leadership, it was a novelty to raise the decision of a Synod to the level of an authority above discussion.  Of such a thing even Bishop Julius of Rome, *e.g.*, knew
nothing.  And it was all the more startling when the decision was supported
neither by the letter of Scripture, nor a clear tradition, nor even an analogy of
any sort.  But this very fact promoted the assumption of an absolute authority,—
though not yet in the case of Athanasius (see Gwatkin, Stud. of Arianism, p. 50);
a virtue was made of necessity.  With the first victory over Arianism, the view
arose that the dogma of the Trinity was a certain truth because it had been affirmed at Nicæa by 318 Bishops inspired by the Holy Ghost—thus the Cappadocians, Cyril of Alex. etc.  It is, however, extremely paradoxical, that even up to
the middle of the fourth century the Eusebians laid greater stress on the authority of Synodical decisions than the orthodox party.  In order to get the West to
accept the deposition of Athanasius, they continued to appeal to their Antiochene
Synod, and declared its decisions to be irreversible.  Although their tactics compelled them also to admit the validity of the Nicene Creed, they did so in the
hope that after the removal of Athanasius they would be able to carry an interpretation of it suitable to their own views.

[3]  The latter fact is admitted also by Hefele (l. c. Vol. I., p. 3). Besides, nothing
could be more incorrect than the opinion that the distinction between Œcumenical
and other Synods, as regards dogmatics, was established soon after the Nicene
Council. The greatest variety of opinion prevailed till past the middle of the fifth
century as to what Synods were œcumenical and might be ranked along with the
Nicene. Gregory of Nazianzus we know, *e.g.*, to have spoken very contemptuously
of the Constantinopolitan Synod, and, indeed, of Synods in general. Conversely,
a certain authority was still ascribed to Provincial Synods in dogmatic questions.

century there gradually ceased to be any doubt that the
resolutions of Œcumenical Synods possessed an absolute authority. [1] Whoever rebelled against them refused to admit that the
Synods in question were regular, but did not dispute the

Further, there is a passage in Augustine which infers not only a relatively binding authority on the part of Provincial Councils, but also uncertainty as to the
absolute authority of General Councils. The passage is extraordinarily characteristic of the unsteadiness of the whole structure of tradition. Meanwhile Reuter
(Zeitschr. f. K.-Gesch. VIII. p. 167, 173, 176, 186) has rightly decided that we
must keep steadily in view the special circumstances under which Augustine has
here written; De bap. c. Donat. II. 3, 4: "Quis nesciat sanctam scripturam canon-
icam tam veteris quam novi testamenti certis suis terminis contineri, eamque omnibus posterioribus episcoporum litteris ita præponi, ut de illa omnino dubitari et
disceptari non possit, utrum verum vel utrum rectum sit, quidquid in ea scriptum
esse constiterit: episcoporum autem litteras quæ post confirmatum canonem vel
scriptæ sunt vel scribuntur, et per sermonem forte sapientiorem cuiuslibet in ea re
peritioris, et per aliorum episcoporum graviorem auctoritatem doctioremque pruden-
tiam et per concilia licere reprehendi, si quid in eis forte a veritate deviatum est:
et ipsa concilia quæ per singulas regiones vel provincias fiunt, plenariorum conciliorum auctoritati quæ fiunt ex universo orbe Christiano, sine ullis ambagibus cedere:
ipsaque plenaria sæpe priora posterioribus emendari, cum aliquo experimento rerum
aperitur quod clausum erat, et cognoscitur quod latebat." *Emendari* can only
mean here actual emendation—not merely explanation, as Catholic historians of
dogma have to assume. It is also worthy of note, that Augustine assigned
Œcumenical rank to several Synods—*e.g.*, that of Arles—which afterwards were
not held to be Œcumenical. On the other hand, it is instructive that he himself
did not, like the Orientals, regard the Nicene decree as the foundation of the
doctrine of the Trinity; see Reuter's arguments on the relation of the work "De
trinitate" to the Nicene Symbol, (Ztschr. f. K.-Gesch. V. p. 375 ff.). The Council
of Chalcedon first put an end to dubiety as to the number, and the authority, of Œcumenical Councils in the East (even at the Robber Synod, A.D. 449,
only two had been recognised). Up till then the Nicene stood alone on an inaccessible height; moreover, in after times the uniqueness of this Council was still
remembered, though others were added beside it. For the rest, Roman Bishops
spoke very depreciatorily of, or even refused to recognise, many canons of later
councils; so Leo I. of the third of Constantinople (Ep. 106 [al. 80]), to say nothing
of the twenty-eighth of Chalcedon. But Leo did not recognise the second Council
as legitimate. Even Felix III. and Gelasius knew only of three Œcumenical Councils. General Synods Leo I. declared to be inspired (see Ep. 114, 2, to the Bishops
assembled at Chalcedon); but it is more than questionable whether he therefore
held all their resolutions to be absolutely irreversible.

[1] After the Council of Chalcedon, it was, above all, Justinian's legislation which
confirmed and popularised, even in the West, the view that there had been four
Œcumenical Councils: see his edict on the Three Chapters, 131: Οἱ ὑπὸ τῶν τεσσάρων
συνόδων, τῶν ἐν Νικαίᾳ καὶ Κωνσταντινουπόλει, ἐν Ἐφέσῳ καὶ ἐν Χαλκηδόνι τιθέντες
ὅροι νόμων τάξιν ἐχέτωσαν καὶ τὰ δόγματα αὐτῶν ὡς αἱ θεόπνευστοι τιμάσθωσαν

authority of regular Synods in general. After the seventh
Synod it was a settled principle in the orthodox Church of the
East that Scripture and the decisions of the seven Œcumenical
Councils formed the sources of the knowledge of Christian
truth. [1] They were characterised simply as the tradition, nay,
men spoke, and not infrequently speak and act up to the present
day, as if the Church possessed and required no other sources
of knowledge or authorities. As a rule, the παράδοσις ἄγραφος
is not included when Holy Scripture and the seven Councils
are spoken of.

This apparently simple, consistent development, seemingly
corresponding to all requirements, did not, however, solve all
difficulties, either after it had come to an end, or still less
during its course. But it had further to reckon with authorities,
some of which were of long standing, while others emerged in
the contemporary organisation of the Church. What position
was to be taken up in doctrinal controversies in which an Œcumenical Synod had not pronounced its decision? Must there not

γραφαί, Accordingly, this development was inaugurated by Constantine and closed
by Justinian. After him Gregory I. (Ep. L. I. 25) wrote: "Sicut sancti evangelii
quattuor libros, sic quattuor concilia suscipere et venerari me fateor." But this very
utterance proves that the West only slowly accepted this whole development; for
Gregory leaves out of account the fifth Œcumenical Council held meanwhile. Again,
the attitude of the North African Church in the sixth century proves that there the
dubiety felt by Augustine had not yet been wholly overcome. But the attempts of
the papal theologian Vincenzi to dispute the independent authority of the councils
generally—even for the above date—are thoroughly biassed, and carried out with
the most daring indifference to historical fact. See his "In St. Gregorii Nyss. et
Origenis scripta et doctrinam nova defensio", 5 T., 1865 f. and "De processione
spiritus s. ex patre et filio", 1878.

[1] This is taught without any variation by the later so-called Symbols of the
Greek Church and the most distinguished theologians up to the present day; see,
e.g., Damalas, Ἡ ὀρθόδοξος πίστις, Athens, 1877, p. 3 ff.: οὐδεὶς πιστεύει εἰς μίαν
ἐκκλησίαν ὁ μὴ ὁμολογῶν ὅτι τὰς ἐκπροσωπούσας ταύτην οἰκουμενικὰς συνόδους τὸ
πνεῦμα τὸ ἅγιον ὁδηγεῖ εἰς πᾶσαν ἀλήθειαν. καὶ ὅτι ἡ ἐκκλησία αὕτη δὲν δύναται
νὰ ἦ ἄλλη παρὰ τὴν ἐπῳκοδομημένην ἐπὶ τῆς μόνης ἑνοποιοῦ ἀρχῆς τῶν οἰκουμενικῶν
συνόδων· διότι ἡ ἀρχὴ τῶν μερικῶν ὑποχρεωτικῶν ὁμολογιῶν, ἣν καθιέρωσαν αἱ λοιπαὶ
ἐκκλησίαι, ἐστὶν ἡ μήτηρ τῆς διαιρέσεως . . . ἡ προμνημονευθεῖσα ἀναγνώρισις τῶν ἑπτὰ
οἰκουμενικῶν συνόδων ἐστὶ γεγονὸς ἱστορικόν, μηδεμίαν πλέον ἐκκλησιαστικὴν ανα-
ψηλάφησιν ἐπιδεχόμενον. According to present Greek ideas, the whole period of the
Councils belongs to the classical antiquity of the Church; this period has long run
its course.

be forthcoming in the Church *at any moment* a clear testimony
to the truth, solving all doubtful questions, and giving forth no
uncertain sound? What importance was due to the occupants
of the great episcopal chairs, the Bishops of the apostolic communities, and especially of Rome? Decisions were not reached
in all these questions, but a certain *common sense* arose. First,
the Church speaks also by a unanimous testimony, audible from
the earliest days, and this testimony never has been and never
for a moment is, lacking. What has been always, everywhere,
and by all, believed is inerrant tradition, even if it has not
been solemnly and formally attested, or laid down in primitive
authorities. This leads to a procedure similar to that followed
by Eusebius in settling the N. T., viz., that the antiquity,
unanimous attestation, and catholicity of a doctrine are to be
expiscated in order that it may be certified a doctrine of the
Church. The notion of 'antiquity' had now been extended
and shifted with the advance of the Church. In the fourth
century all the teachers held orthodox before Origen had been
regarded as ancient, or *vicini apostolorum* (neighbours of the
Apostles); the latter predicate especially had gradually been
extended to the beginning of the third century : men like Irenæus, Apollinaris of Hierapolis and Hippolytus even were called
γνώριμοι τῶν ἀποστόλων (friends of the Apostles). [1] Then the
whole period of the martyrs came to be considered sacred as the
ancient time. But the Church was compelled to recognise to
an increasing extent, that not much was to be gained for its
purposes from its theological 'witnesses' before Athanasius,
from those before as well as after Origen. Their names were
still held in sacred memory—with the exception of those who
seemed too greatly compromised, or had even fallen into bad
odour with their own contemporaries ; but their works disappeared
more and more, or gave place to forgeries. Accordingly, from
the fifth century, Athanasius and orthodox teachers of similar
views of the fourth century, appeared as the "Fathers" proper. [2]

[1] See as to this the Introduction to my History of Ancient Christian Literature
up to Eusebius, Vol. I. 1893.

[2] Athanasius was not indeed so frequently quoted as one would believe. His
works have been comparatively eclipsed by those of the Cappadocians, and the

When controversies arose, and soon even at Synods, the votes
of these men were *counted*. Doctrines were looked on as armed
with the testimony of antiquity, when they could be supported
from the Fathers from Athanasius to Cyril. Nor were forgeries
wanting here. The disciples of Apollinaris of Laodicea practised
these frauds to a vast extent, in order to rediscover their master's teaching in antiquity; they were afterwards imitated by
others. In any case, the tribunal of the 'Fathers' remained
an uncertain one; great as was the scope assigned to it, its
place and value were not dogmatically detailed. It was not
even really decided what relation the inspiration of the Councils
held to the *consensus patrum*, [1] (see under). Such a *consensus*
had often enough to be first restored; this was done by exegesis, or even by fabrications, because it was necessary to presuppose it. References of an opposite character remained of
no effect; but when needs must a want of accuracy (akribeia)
and detached errors were admitted in the case of individual
Fathers, without the general conception being modified by these
concessions. The Fathers were just read backwards—so to
speak—*i.e.*, from the standpoint of the dogma of the time being,
and their undeveloped or divergent doctrines were interpreted
in accordance with the principle of making the best of everything. [2]

final statement arrived at in the East, A.D. 381, of the dogma of the Trinity was
more favourable to them than to Athanasius. The Synod of Constantinople, A.D.
383, (see *in loco*) furnishes the first example of the authority of the Fathers being
made decisive, and of the Scriptures themselves being ignored. But the attempt
miscarried at the time.

[1] To the "teachers" the predicate "Θεόπνευστος" was also applied. Thus
Athanasius writes (De incarn. verbi 56): Αἱ γραφαὶ μὲν γὰρ διὰ θεολόγων ἀνδρῶν
παρὰ Θεοῦ ἐλαλήθησαν καὶ ἐγράφησαν. ἡμεῖς δὲ παρὰ τῶν αὐταῖς ἐντυγχανόντων
θεοπνεύστων διδασκάλων, οἳ καὶ μάρτυρες τῆς Χριστοῦ θεότητος γεγόνασι, μαθόντες
μεταδίδομεν καὶ τῇ σῇ φιλομαθίᾳ. Similarly, though very rhetorically, Arius in his
Thalia (Athanas. Orat. c. Arian I. 5): κατὰ πίστιν ἐκλεκτῶν Θεοῦ, συνετῶν Θεοῦ,
παίδων ἁγίων, ὀρθοτόμων, ἅγιον Θεοῦ πνεῦμα λαβόντων, τάδε ἔμαθον ἔγωγε ὑπὸ τῶν
σοφίης μετεχόντων, ἀστείων, θεοδιδάκτων, κατὰ πάντα σοφῶν τε.

[2] It would take us too far to give detailed instances of the points discussed
under this head. We only emphasise the following. (1) The attestation of a doctrine
by the Councils was often set side by side with that given by the "Fathers", the
"ancient" or "holy doctors", in such a way that the former seemed often to be
merely a special case of the latter. And this was quite natural. The Church

Secondly, a peculiar reverence was inherited from the past for Apostolic Churches or their bishops, entwined with the evidence based on history and dogmatics. Although the theory of Cyprian, which allowed no special importance to the Bishops

possessed no continuous testimony in the Councils; from its distinctive character, however, it required one. And this could only be furnished by the unbroken chorus of orthodox doctors. Even taken historically this court of appeal was the older. Irenæus and especially Clemens Alex. had already referred to deceased presbyters as authoritative teachers; and Eusebius' conception of Church History embraced the idea—see preface and outline—that side by side with the *successio episcoporum* there stood a series of witnesses who, in uninterrupted succession, had declared the true doctrine orally and in writing. (2) No definitions were arrived at of the manner in which the authority of the Bishops was related to that of the doctors. It was possible to shut one's eyes to this question, because in most cases the teachers were also bishops. As a rule, the Greeks spoke not of bishops, but the ancient doctors, when appealing to the witnesses to the truth. It was otherwise with the majority of the Latins after Cyprian (see p. 214). (3) As the usual procedure at the Councils was to set up no doctrinal tenet unless it was believed to have the support of the doctors, and as the claim was made that this course should always be adopted, the idea that the Councils were inspired was already abolished, and they were subordinated to the continuous testimony of the Church (see under). (4) The practice of consulting authorities began at the Ephesian Council; it played a more prominent part in every succeeding Synod. Athanasius and the Arians had undoubtedly disputed before this over passages in the Fathers, but their disputes were of slight importance compared with those that took place afterwards. (5) The notion of ecclesiastical antiquity gradually became more and more comprehensive; meanwhile the real ancient period of Christianity became more obscure, and bit by bit came to be forgotten. After the seventh the whole period of the Councils was looked on as the classical antiquity of the Church. If even in the fourth, nay, up to the middle of the fifth century, Councils were held to be an innovation, their absence was now considered a characteristic of the age of the Epigoni; indeed they were thought to be unnecessary, because everything was already settled. (6) The opinion held by faith that the "Fathers" had decided every disputed point before-hand, was a strong challenge to produce forgeries, and resulted in objective and and subjective falsehood. Caspari (Alte und neue Quellen, etc., 1879) has shown that the followers of Apollinaris were the first to forge on a large scale; but the Acts of Councils, and the examination of writings circulated under the names of celebrated Fathers, show that they had numerous imitators in the ranks of all parties. The practice of compiling collections of extracts, which was so much favoured after the middle of the fifth century, was, besides, especially adapted to conceal forgeries or inaccuracies. (7) But the limits, authority, and character of the Court of Appeal of the "Fathers" were never determined. It was taught that the orthodox Fathers agreed in all matters, nay, this theory was treated as a dogma. Stephen Gobarus' attempt (Photius, Cod. 232) to demonstrate the contradictions of the Fathers was felt to be profane, just as Eusebius had condemned as unchurchmanlike the attitude of Marcellus of Ancyra, who had censured the consultation, without

of Apostolic communities within the general authority of the Episcopate, had weakened this prestige, it still held its ground. Augustine still recalled it in the question of the extent of the Holy Scriptures. [1] But there now grew up, in consequence of

independent examination, of the "wisest" Fathers. But even John of Damascus had to admit that Fathers—otherwise orthodox—held divergent opinions on single points (De imag. I. 25), and Photius actually was more than once compelled, in the course of his learned studies, to notice mistakes committed by them (see his Bibliotheca). Therefore the question was never decided who constituted the orthodox Fathers. It became the custom to prefer (Athanasius), Gregory of Nazianzus, Chrysostom, Cyril, and afterwards also John of Damascus. In the fourth century the orthodox were much troubled by the fact that the Synod of Antioch (A.D. 268) rejected, while that of Nicæa accepted, the term Ὁμοούσιος. The treatment of this difficulty in Athanasius, "De synod." 43 sq., shows that no one had hit on the idea that the later decision made the earlier obsolete. It was rather held on the contrary: οἱ προλαβόντες ἀφανίζουσιν τοὺς μετὰ ταῦτα γενομένους. Therefore Athanasius sought and found evidences of the word Ὁμοούσιος before the Samostatian controversy. Ultimately, however, he had to adopt a different treatment of the whole question, i.e., to show that Ὁμοούσιος had only been rejected at Antioch as against Paul, in order not to admit a contradiction in the chorus of the Fathers. The same difficulty was caused about the middle of the fifth century by the term "δύο φύσεις", for it was hard to find an instance of that in antiquity. Of Eutyches the following expression is recorded (Mansi VI., p. 700): τὸ ἐκ δύο φύσεων ἐνωθεισῶν καθ᾽ ὑπόστασιν γεγεννῆσθαι τὸν κύριον ἡμῶν Ἰησοῦν Χριστὸν μήτε μεμαθηκέναι ἐν ταῖς ἐκθέσεσι τῶν ἁγίων πατέρων μήτε καταδέχεσθαι, εἰ τύχοι τι αὐτῷ τοιοῦτο παρά τινος ὑπαναγινώσκεσθαι, διὰ τὸ τὰς θείας γραφὰς ἀμείνονας εἶναι τῆς τῶν πατέρων διδασκαλίας. He afterwards disowned this expression as being distorted, his advocate corrected it in his name thus: "The Fathers have spoken in different ways, and I accept everything they say, but not as a rule of faith" (εἰς κανόνα δὲ πίστεως οὐ δέχομαι). That is very instructive. The words excited the greatest consternation in the assembly in which they were uttered, and the speaker felt himself compelled at once to excuse them on the ground of a momentary confusion.

[1] See above, Note 1, p. 198, and compare "De peccator. mer. et remiss." I., 50. Here the *auctoritas ecclesiarum orientalium* is mentioned (in reference to the Ep. to the Hebrews), and to Augustine this *auctoritas* was exalted, because Christianity had come from the Apostolic Churches, from the communities to which John and Paul had written, *above all, from Jerusalem* (*unde ipsum evangelium coepit prædicari*). The fact that the Donatists had been separated from Apostolic Churches proved to him that they were wrong; see especially the Liber ad Donat. post collat. c. 4, c. 29; also Ep. 52, c. 3 and c. Lib. Petil. l. II., c. 51 (Reuter in the Ztschr. f. K.-Gesch. V., p. 361 ff.). Optatus had already held the same view as Augustine; see the important details "De schism. Donat." II., 6, VI., 3. But even after the middle of the sixth century a Roman Pope, Pelagius I., singled out the fact in praise of Augustine, that he, "mindful of the divine teaching which founded the Church *on the Apostolic Chairs*, taught that those were schismatics who seceded from the doctrine and communion of *these Apostolic Chairs*" (Mansi, Concil. IX.,

the Metropolitan and Patriarchate form of government, a new aristocracy among the Bishops, which received its importance from the size and influence of the episcopal cities. Rome, Alexandria—the founding of whose Church by Mark was undisputed about A.D. 300—and Antioch were not affected by the rivalry involved in this new principle; for in these cases the special connection with the Apostles coincided with the greatness of the city. But the political factor prevailed so strongly that the Chairs of Corinth, Thessalonica, etc., and finally, even that of Ephesus, [1] lost all peculiar prestige—only that of Jerusalem, in spite of the political insignificance of the city, was ranked with those more distinguished [2]—but Constantinople was added to the list of the outstanding episcopates. In the East this was frankly justified by the political position of the city; [3] but this justification was so far insufficient as the chair, by its co-ordination with the Apostolic sees, participated in the attributes

p. 716). Pelagius even declared that when doubts as to the faith arose it was necessary to conform to *the Apostolic Chairs* (l. c. p. 732). This form of expression is all the more remarkable since the Roman Bishops of the fifth century spoke, as a rule, as if the designation *sedes apostolica* belonged peculiarly to their Chair.

[1] At the transition from the fourth to the fifth century; see Hefele II., pp. 77 ff., 495 f., 528 ff.

[2] See the 7th Canon of Nicæa, and in addition, Hefele's details, Vol. I., p. 403 f.; II., p. 213. Jerusalem was first raised to a Patriarchate at Chalcedon, see Hefele II., pp. 477, 502. Jerusalem became once more the 'holy city' in the fourth century; see Epiphanius and others.

[3] See the 3rd Canon of Constantinople, Hefele, II., p. 17 f. and the 28th of Chalcedon, Hefele, II., p. 527 f.; τῷ θρόνῳ τῆς πρεσβυτέρας ʽΡώμης διὰ τὸ βασιλεύειν τὴν πόλιν ἐκείνην, οἱ πατέρες εἰκότως ἀποδεδώκασι τὰ πρεσβεῖα, καὶ τῷ αὐτῷ σκοπῷ κινούμενοι οἱ ἑκατὸν πεντήκοντα θεοφιλέστατοι ἐπίσκοποι τὰ ἴσα πρεσβεῖα ἀπένειμαν τῷ τῆς νέας ʽΡώμης ἁγιωτάτῳ θρόνῳ, εὐλόγως κρίναντες, τὴν βασιλείᾳ καὶ συγκλήτῳ τιμηθεῖσαν πόλιν καὶ τῶν ἴσων ἀπολαύουσαν πρεσβείων τῇ πρεσβυτέρᾳ βασιλίδι ʽΡώμῃ, καὶ ἐν τοῖς ἐκκλησιαστικοῖς, ὡς ἐκείνην, μεγαλύνεσθαι πράγμασι, δευτέραν μετ᾽ ἐκείνην ὑπάρχουσαν. Constantinople was factitiously promoted to the place of Ephesus by reason of this unexampled act of legitimation. At the Robber Synod, nevertheless, it still held the fifth place. As regards the historical interpretation of the sixth Canon of Nicæa and the third of Constantinople, I agree substantially with the excellent arguments of Kattenbusch (l. c. I., p. 81 ff.); only it must be still more strongly emphasised that the Canons of A.D. 381 bore a clearly marked hostility to Alexandria. Even then it was considered necessary to suppress the authority of the Alexandrian Church, which was on the point of developing into the premier Church of the East.

which the latter possessed in virtue of their apostolic character. [1]
Such attributes continued to be ascribed to those chairs without
it being stated, however, in what they really consisted.  They
were nothing tangible, and yet they were held to exist. [2]  But
even in the view of Orientals they belonged in a preëminent
degree to Rome.  The works of the only western author before
Jerome who was also read in the East—*i.e.*, Cyprian—could
not fail to heighten the prestige of Rome. [3]  But that was
already great enough in itself.  As the ancient capital of the
Empire, as the city of the two chief Apostles, of the *Cathedra
Petri*, as the only apostolic community of the West, that which
had done more for the whole Church than any other, Rome
even in the East enjoyed a unique prestige. [4]  But as early as
the fourth century, and certainly from the fifth onwards, Rome
meant the Roman Bishop, with whose spiritual dignity were
fused the memories of the ancient city that had ruled the world.
These memories overhung the place, after the Emperor had
left, and the most of them clung to the Bishop.  In the
momentous Arian conflict the great Eastern sees, except Alexandria, became compromised or dishonoured; the orthodox
Orientals sought and found their support in Rome. [5]  The Emperor

[1] An energetic protest was admittedly raised, especially by Leo I. and his successors. Leo at the same time also advocated the rights of the Apostolic Churches
in general (Ep. 106). We cannot here follow out the controversy, although it
reflects the revivification of the Byzantine Church and State, and the attitude of
the Roman Bishops, which was purely ecclesiastical, though it did rest on fictions:
see Hefele II., pp. 408, 539 ff., 549 ff., and Sohm l. c. I., pp. 377—440. It was not
until the fourth Lateran Synod (Can. 5), when a Latin Patriachate existed at Constantinople (1215), that Rome recognised the 28th Canon of Chalcedon.

[2] Although all Bishops were held to be successors of the Apostles, yet Leo I.
singles out very distinctly those who had inherited the chairs of the Apostles; see
his letter to the Emperor Marcian (Ep. 104).

[3] Not only Eusebius, but also Theodore of Mopsuestia had read Cyprian's
Epistles. At the Council of Ephesus evidence taken from him was read; see Vincent, Commonit. 42. Of the Westerns, after Cyprian, Ambrose was especially
esteemed in the East. Augustine also possessed a certain authority.

[4] See Vol. II., p. 149 f.

[5] On the authority of the Roman Bishop in the fourth century, see Hauck, Der
römische Bischof in 4 Jahrh., 1881; Rade, Damasus, 1881; Langen, Gesch. der
römischen Kirche, 2 Vols., 1881, 1885; Sohm, l. c. In what follows we only discuss
Rome's prestige in the East. Even Hefele (l. c. I., p. 8) admits that the first eight

in Constantinople who brought the great controversy to an end
was a Western, full of veneration for Rome. The promotion
which he afterwards assigned to Constantinople was no equivalent—at first, at least,—for the advance in political power
secured to Rome by the Arian controversy.[1] The role of

Synods were not appointed and convoked by the Roman Bishops. His arguments
as to the presidency at the Synods are, however, biassed (pp. 29—44). It was at
Chalcedon that the legates of the Roman Bishop first occupied a special position.
The sixth Canon of Nicæa, when correctly interpreted, gives no preference to Rome,
but refers merely to the fact that it was the ecclesiastical metropolis for the Churches
of several provinces. It is credible that Julius I. uttered the principle (Socrates
H. E. II. 17): μὴ δεῖν παρὰ γνώμην τοῦ ἐπισκόπου Ῥώμης κανονίζειν τὰς ἐκκλησίας.
The peculiar authority of the Roman Chair showed itself in the fourth century in
the following facts. First, Constantine transferred to the Roman Bishop the duty
of presiding over the commission to examine the case of the Donatists. Secondly,
the oppressed adherents of the Nicene Symbol in the East turned to him for
protection (see even Langen, l. c. I., p. 425 f.). Thirdly, we have the request of
the Eusebians that Julius should decide the dogmatic question; it is true that very
soon—when they foresaw their defeat in Rome—they changed their tone. They
still conceded a peculiar dignity to Rome; it does not seem to me possible to
translate φιλοτιμίαν (Sozom. III. 8) with Langen by "ambition." Yet they pointed
out that Rome had received its Christianity from the East, and that it was as little
entitled to review the decision of a dogmatic question given in the East, as the
Oriental Bishops would have been to take up the Novatian affair after Rome had
spoken. (The letter is to be reconstructed from Sozom. III. 8, and Athanas. apolog.
c. Arian. 25—35.) Fourthly, we have evidence of Rome's position also in Julius'
epistle to the Orientals (Athanas. l. c.); fifthly, in Canons 3 and 5 of the Synod
of Sardica; and sixthly, in the request of the Antiochenes, or Jerome, to Damasus,
for a decision in the Antiochene schism (Ep. 16).

[1] Damasus' policy did not at once succeed in raising the prestige of the Roman
Chair in the East (see Rade, l. c., p, 137 f.), but the manner in which Theodosius I.
at first decided the Arian controversy there, did. "*Cunctos populos, quos clementiæ
nostræ regit temperamentum, in tali volumus religione versari, quam divinum
Petrum apostolum tradidisse Romanis religio usque ad nunc ab ipso insinuata
declarat,*" etc. Besides, the new style adopted by Damasus in his letter to the
Oriental Bishops (Theodoret H. E. V. 10) was not without effect in the East. He
calls them my "sons" instead of my "brethren," and he no longer speaks, like
other Bishops, as commissioned by the Synod—though the question at issue was
a decision of the Synod—or as representing the Western Church. On the contrary,
he addresses them in virtue of the authority of his "Apostolic Chair," which he
connects solely with Peter and without any reference to Paul. "The first rank is
due to the Holy Church, in which the Holy Apostle had his seat, and taught
how we should fitly guide the helm which we have undertaken to control." Rade
has, besides, here rightly conjectured (p. 136) that Jerome had a share in this letter,
which did a great deal to raise the influence of the Roman Chair in the East.

observer and arbiter, which the Roman Bishop was able to play
in the Christological controversies, made it possible for him to
maintain for a time the lofty position he had won. [1] (On the
aspirations of the Alexandrian Bishops, Athanasius, Peter, etc.,
and the successful opposition to them by Leo, see chap. IX.)
There can be no doubt that even in the eyes of the Orientals
there attached to the Roman Bishop a special something, which
was wanting to all the rest, a nimbus which conferred upon
him a peculiar authority. [2] Yet this nimbus was not sufficiently

[1] From and after Siricius I., the Roman Bishops maintained that it was their
province to care for all Churches (Constant., p. 659. Ep. 6, ch. 1). On the relation
of Leo I. to the East, and to the fourth Council, see Langen, l. c. II., pp. 10 f., 50 ff.
The phrase "our fatherly solicitude" occurs frequently even in the letters of his
predecessors to the East. The appeal of Cyril to Coelestine is very important in
its bearing on the dignity of the Roman Chair; compare the language of the
Roman legate at the Council of Ephesus (Mansi III., p. 1279 sq.).

[2] In the work "Der Papst und das Concil von Janus" (1869), p. 93, we find
this passage. "In the writings of the doctors of the Greek Church, Eusebius,
Athanasius, Basil the Great, the two Gregorys, and Epiphanius, not a word is to
be found of peculiar pregrogatives being assigned to a Roman Bishop. Chrysostom,
the most prolific of the Greek Fathers, is absolutely silent on the point, and so also
are the two Cyrils. Basil (Opp. ed. Bened. III. 301, Ep. 239 and 214) has expressed
his contempt for the writings of the Popes in the strongest terms [in the affairs of
Marcellus]: 'these proud and conceited westerns, who would only fortify heresy';
even if their letters descended from heaven, he would not accept them." It is true
that, seeing the now wide-spread view of the apostolic succession of all Bishops,
the prestige of the Roman Bishop is hardly perceptible in the East at the beginning of the fourth century, and that he had to fight, i.e., to wrest for himself
the position which had formerly belonged to the Roman Church. Therefore the
testimonies to a special dignity being possessed by the Roman Bishops in the East
in the fourth century are in fact comparatively scanty, But they are not wanting—
see, e.g., Greg. Naz., Carmen de vita sua T. II., p. 9, and Chrysostom, Ep. ad
Innocent I.—and from A.D. 380 this dignity bulked more largely in the eyes of
Orientals, though indeed, without receiving a definite and fixed meaning. Very
characteristic in this respect are the Church Histories of Socrates and Sozomen,
who on this point are free from partiality, and reflect the universal opinion. But
it does not occur to them to doubt that the Roman Bishop had a special authority
and a unique relation to the whole Church (see, e.g., Socrat. II. 8, 15, 17; Soz.
III. 8; also Theodoret's letter to Leo I.). Instructive here are the collections of Leo
Allatius and in the Innsbrucker Theol. Ztschr., 1877, p. 662 f.; see also three
treatises by the Abbé Martin: "Saint Pierre, sa venue et son martyre à Rome,"
in the Rev. des quest. historiq., 1873 (principally from oriental sources); "S. Pierre
et S. Paul dans l'église Nestorienne," Paris, 1875; "S. Pierre et le Rationalisme
devant les églises orientales," Amiens, 1876. These discussions, though in part uncritical, are very full of matter. Matt. XVI. 18, John XXI. 18, were undoubtedly

bright and luminous to bestow upon its possessor an unimpeach-
able authority; it was rather so nebulous that it was possible
to disregard it without running counter to the spirit of the
universal Church. And it gradually became fainter. The more
completely, after the middle of the fifth century, the internal
relations of West and East ceased, and the more strongly the
distinctively Byzantine spirit could assert itself in the diminished
Church of the East, so the more rapidly declined the prestige
of the Roman Bishop. Constantinople put an end to it in its
own midst, when the Roman Bishop set up claims which in the
fourth and fifth centuries had been palliated by actual circumstances and the necessities of the time, but which 500 years
afterwards could not fail to be felt as the intrusion of an alien
spirit. [1] Yet, in spite of this, the idea of the unity of the Church
still held its ground for a long time. After Synods ceased to
be held, the influence of the great Patriarchates throughout the
whole Church in the East increased [2]—though, indeed, the
orthodox Patriarchs of Alexandria, Antioch, and Jerusalem, had
lost their real importance; and theoretically the dignity of the

never referred in the East to the primacy of Rome (see Janus, p. 97). Still in any
case it is saying too little—even for the period about the year A.D. 380—to
remark as Rade does (l. c., p. 137). To the Orientals the Bishop of Rome was like
the rest, only, thanks to his situation, the natural representative of the Churches of
the western half of the Empire, acting, as it were, as correspondent in the name
of the Christians of the West.

[1] The prestige of the Roman Bishop in the East was accordingly on the increase from the beginning of the fourth till the middle of the fifth century, remained at its height till about the time of Justinian, when, however, it lost its
practical importance, and then, apart from the events about A.D. 680 and the next
decades, slowly declined, yet without ever being wholly destroyed. The Roman
Chair was now held to be schismatic; if not that, it would still have been the
first. Undoubtedly there was a strong inclination in later times to oppose it by
advancing the see of Jerusalem, the seat of James, but it was not possible to gain
any confidence in the claim of the latter to the first place. See on the criticism
of the papacy by the Greeks, Pichler, Gesch. der kirchl. Trennung zwischen Or.
u. Occ., 1864; Hergenröther, Photius, 3 Vols. 1867 ff; Gass, Symbolik, p. 216 ff.;
Kattenbusch, l. c., pp. 79—124. It was a settled doctrine of the Church in the East,
that the Church has no visible head.

[2] The terms τυραννίς and δυναστεία are first used, so far as I know, in reference
to Antioch, i.e., against Paul of Samos. (Eus. H. E. VII. 30), after Origen had already
complained of the ambition of the Great Bishops. Socrates has expressed himself
very frankly about this matter.

Roman Bishop as *primus inter pares,* though not unassailed,
was embraced in that of the great Eastern sees. But it was
never made clear how far the Patriarchs in their collective capacity really constituted an authority in dogma : there is not
even an explicit statement that they did form such an authority.
There was an uncertainty of opinion as to their position alongside of and in the Œcumenical Synods. [1] Here also there was
an absence of fixed definitions. The Church as it is, with its
graduated orders, crowned by the Patriarchs, constituted the
tradition and the authority. But the authority of no factor in
this system possessed, when isolated, any significance whatever.
It might not assert itself at the expense of the rest. Its dignity
was founded on its being a part of *antiquity.*

   As to II. This at once involves the answer to the second
question (see p. 214). The assumption that the Councils were
inspired did not imply any power on their part to deliver new
revelations to the Church. On the contrary, they proved their
peculiar possession of the Holy Spirit by their unfailing testimony to the ancient doctrinal tradition. [2] But in that case the
new formulas created by the Councils could not but cause

---

[1] The importance of the four Patriarchs—of Constantinople, Alexandria, Antioch,
and Jerusalem—was celebrated here and there in lofty expressions; it was especially
prominent in the later Symbols, so-called, of the Greek Church (see Gass, l. c.,
p. 222 f.). Their presence or that of their representative was even held to be
absolutely necessary at an Œcumenical Synod; but not only was the extent of their
authority never defined, but the essential equality of all Bishops was steadily maintained in the East; and the latest development of the Greek Church, *i.e.,* its disruption into perfectly independent National Churches, has thrown overboard the
whole 'Constitution of the Patriarchate', which in all ages was more a matter of
assertion than reality. The Bishop of Alexandria, undoubtedly, nearly succeeded
in becoming in the fifth century supreme Bishop of the East, but Leo and Pul-
cheria overthrew him. Kattenbusch (l. c. p. 357 ff.) furnishes further details as
to the "five Patriarchs as symbolical figures." Has the Patriarchate of Rome come
to an end in the view of the Greek Church? In the abstract, no; in the concrete,
yes.

[2] See above, p. 215 f. Augustine gives utterance to a very remarkable statement
in De bapt. c. Donat. II., 4, 5: "Quomodo potuit ista res (the baptism by heretics)
tantis altercationum nebulis involuta, ad plenarii concilii luculentam illustrationem
confirmationemque perduci, nisi primo diutius per orbis terrarum regiones multis
hinc atque hinc disputationibus et collationibus episcoporum pertractata constaret?"
Accordingly, only a matter which had already become ripe for decision through
frequent deliberations could be submitted to and decided by a Council.

offence. How far they did is shown by the history of the dogmatic controversies. Above all, the unbiblical catch-word 'consubstantial' ('Ομοούσιος), for a time directly rejected by the
Church, only won acceptance under great difficulties, even
among those who had little or no objection to the cause it
represented. These formulas had to be proved in some way or
other to have been anciently held. For 'Ομοούσιος it was of the
highest importance that a Council had made it an accomplished
fact. As the word gradually made good its ground, the Council lay far enough in the past to be itself regarded as belonging to antiquity. The evidence was got by reasoning in a
circle; the authority of the Council supported the word which
was anything but old, but the authority of any Council was
dependent on its rejection of all innovations. Numerous passages in the Fathers furnished material in confirmation of the
later formulas — which were never, so far as I know, bluntly
deduced from unwritten tradition (παράδοσις ἄγραφος); but a
strong preference was shown for understanding them as a repetition of the Nicene Symbol, the explication being disregarded,
just as Irenæus in his time had passed off the Symbol unfolded
in an antignostic sense, the *regula fidei*, for the Symbol itself,
*i.e.*, for the ancient repository of the truth. In spite of all novelties, it was thus contended that novelties were not forthcoming
in the Church. Nay, even the power of the Councils to *unfold*
doctrines authoritatively was not plainly asserted in the East;
on the other hand, a Western, Vincentius of Lerinum, did
maintain it, and essayed to furnish a theory on the subject.
After the uncertainties of the Greeks over the conception of
tradition, we really breathe freely when we study the attempt
of this man to introduce light and certainty into the question.
However, even in the East, the younger generation now and
then gave the older Fathers the benefit of looking at their
words as having been uttered at a time when dogma was
not yet explained, or sharply formulated. Strictly speaking,
this expedient was not tenable on Greek ground. Only a
very sparing use therefore was made of it there, [1] while the

---

[1] The more common way of putting it in the East was that the writer in
question had failed in the necessary "Akribeia" (exactness), *i.e.*, he could, and

Catholic West employs it to a great extent up to the present
day. [1]

The conception of tradition is accordingly quite obscure.
The hierarchical element does not *in theory* play the leading

should, have done it better (see, above all, the views of Photius). But it was
rarely admitted that the Church at the time referred to did not yet possess complete
*akribeia* in dogma. But we have further to notice here that a distinction was
still drawn both in East and West between questions of faith, in the strict sense
of the term, and theological doctrines, and that unity in the former was alone
demanded. But as this distinction was in itself obscure, since in fact questions of
faith had been transformed into theological and scientific ones, so in the East it became
more and more restricted, though it was never wholly effaced. Augustine, besides,
still laid great stress on this distinction, and accepted a whole group of theological doctrines in which differences did not endanger unity; the passages are given
in Reuter, Ztschr. f. K.-Gesch. V., p. 363 ff. But if "faith" is itself a doctrine,
where does it cease and the doctrine begin? Besides the excuse of want of accuracy, which, indeed, involves censure, that of ἁπλούστερον γεγραφέναι was asserted.
It involved no fault. Thus Athanasius writes (De Synod. 45) of the Fathers who
in A.D. 268 rejected the term Ὁμοούσιος at Antioch: περὶ τῆς τοῦ υἱοῦ θεότητος
ἁπλούστερον γράφοντες οὐ κατεγένοντο περὶ τῆς τοῦ ὁμουσίου ἀκρίβειας. Precisely
in the same way the Homoiousians at Nice excused the Nicene Fathers. Unique,
so far as I know, is the statement of Gregory of Naz. (Orat. 31. 28), which is only
explicable from the still wholly confused state of the doctrine of the Holy Ghost in his
time. "As the O. T. declared the Father clearly, but the Son more vaguely, so the
N. T. has revealed the Son, but only suggested the divinity of the Spirit" [compare
the contentions of the Montanists]. "Now, however, the Spirit reigns among us, and
makes himself more clearly known to us; for it was not advisable to proclaim the
divinity of the Son, so long as that of the Father was not recognised, or to impose
upon the former—if we may use such a bold expression—that of the Spirit, while
it (viz., the divinity of the Son) was not accepted." We may in this passage study
the distinction between Gregory the theologian and Athanasius.

[1] So, above all, Augustine, who excused Cyprian in this way, and further, set
up the general rule that as long as no unequivocal decisions had been given in a
question, the bond of unity was to be maintained among the dissentient Bishops
(De bapt. c. Donat. II. 4, 5). Augustine thus admitted that ecclesiastical tradition
did not at every moment solve all questions pending in the Church. The Donatist
and Pelagian controversy roused Western theologians to reflect on tradition. One
fruit of this reflection was the Commonitorium of Vincentius of Lerinum, unique,
because it deals professedly with the question of tradition. The arguments are
decisive of Western views, but the book did not extend its influence into the East;
there the ideas about tradition remained characteristically indefinite. A short analysis of the Commonitorium is necessary. Let it be noticed that it is ultimately
aimed at Augustine's doctrine of grace and predestination, but that a large part
of the rules are taken from that theologian.

After a preface, in which Vincentius remarks that he is only sketching out what
he had received from the past, he sets side by side the two foundations of the

part in it. The apostolical succession has in theory had no such thorough-going importance even in the West for the proof of tradition as one would expect. After the time of the Councils the authority of the Bishops as bearers of tradition was wholly

faith, the divine law (Holy Scripture) and the tradition of the Catholic Church (1). The former is sufficient by itself, but it requires the latter for its correct explanation (2). The latter embraces what had been believed *everywhere*, *at all times*, and *by all*—or, at least, by almost all priests and doctors (3). Accordingly, the following criteria were to be applied: (a) When a section of the Church renounced the communion of the Catholic faith, the Christian followed the great communion; (b) when a heresy threatened danger to the whole Church, he held by antiquity, "which, certainly, could not now be seduced"; (c) when he came upon heresy in antiquity itself, in a few men, or in a city or province, he followed the decision of a General Council; (d) if no such Council had spoken, he examined and compared the *orthodox* doctors and retained what—not two, or three—but all, had alike taught clearly, frequently, and persistently, in one and the same sense (4). These rules are illustrated by reference to the dangers, which had threatened the Church from Donatism, Arianism, and the Anabaptists (5—10). At this point, however, it is conceded that orthodox teachers might have and had fallen into error on one point; nevertheless they were blessed, but hell received the Epigoni, who, in order to start a heresy, took hold of the writings of one or other of the ancients (as the Donatists did of Cyprian's) which were composed in obscure language, and which, owing to the obscurity prevailing in them, seemed to coincide with their teaching. so that the views brought forward by these heretics bore not to have been maintained for the first time and exclusively by them. Such people were like Ham in uncovering the shame of their father (11). After this excursus the author adduces proofs from Paul's Epistles, that changes in the creed, in short, any kind of innovation, constituted the worst evil (12—14). In order to prove and tempt his own, God had permitted teachers belonging to the Church, and therefore not foisted in from without, to essay the setting up of new tenets in the Church; examples are taken from Nestorius, Photinus, and Apollinaris; their heresy is described, and contrasted with the true faith (15—22). But the greatest temptation of the Church was due to the innovations of Origen, who was so famous (23), and of the no less distinguished Tertullian (24). Here follows a detailed practical application; those who have been seduced by the great heretics should unlearn to their salvation, what they have learned to their destruction; they must apprehend as much of the doctrine of the Church as can be grasped by the mind, and believe what they cannot understand; all novelty is wickedness and folly; in making innovations ignorance cloaks itself under the 'scientific spirit', imbecility under 'enlightenment', darkness under 'light'. The pure science of the worship of God is only given in the Catholic, ancient, and harmonious tradition (25—27). Antiquity is really the thorough-going criterion of the truth.

This is followed by the second part, which contains the most original matter. It opens with the question whether there is any progress in the Church of Christ in religion. This is answered in the affirmative; the progress is 'very great'; but it consists in deepening, not in altering. It is *organic growth of knowledge* both on the part of individuals and the Church (28). In order to illustrate this,

spent on that proof. Yet even that is perhaps saying too much.
Everything was really obscure. So far, however, as the Greek
Church has not changed since John of Damascus, the Greek has at
present a perfectly definite sense of the foundation of religion.

use is made figuratively of the growth of the child and plants; religion is fortified
with years, expanded with time, and developed more subtly with age; yet everything remains really what it was, no innovation takes place, for a single novelty
would destroy everything (29—31). The Church is intent only on clearness, light,
a more subtle differentiation and invigoration of doctrine. What then did it ever
seek to attain by the decrees of Councils, except that simple belief should become
more definite, supine preaching be rendered more urgent, and that a wholly in-
dolent conduct of affairs should give place to a correspondingly anxious performance of duty? "Hoc inquam semper neque quidquam præterea, hæreticorum novitati-
bus excitata [that then is admitted], conciliorum suorum decretis catholica perfecit
ecclesia, nisi ut quod prius a majoribus sola traditione susceperat, hoc deinde posteris etiam per scripturæ chirographum consignaret, magnam rerum summam paucis
litteris comprehendendo *et plerumque propter intelligentiæ lucem non novum fidei
sensum novæ appellationis proprietate signando*" (32). As compared with this admission, the author attacks all the more vigorously the 'wicked verbal innovations'
practised by all heretics (33, 34). But it was still more necessary to be on one's
guard when heretics appealed to Scripture—as *e.g.*, the Arians did to predicates
taken from the Bible against the term ʽΟμοούσιος—for they were the real wolves
in sheeps' clothing, sons of the devil, for the devil also quoted the Bible (35—37).
All that was necessary to meet their exposition and obtain the correct sense, was
simply to apply the criteria given in ch. 4. (38). The last of these was the search
for the concordant views of many and great teachers, when a Council had not
yet decided the question concerned. Then follows a particular instruction which
betrays very clearly the uncertainty of that citerion. It was to be applied, not to
every unimportant question, but only, at least for the most part only, in the case
of the rule of faith; it was, further, only to be used when heresies had just arisen,
"before they had time to falsify the standards of the ancient creed, before they
could by a wider diffusion of the poison adulterate the writings of the forefathers.
Heresies already circulated and deeply rooted were not to be attacked in this
way, because in the long lapse of time they had had sufficient opportunity to pur-
loin the truth" (!!). Christians must try to refute these ancient heresies by the
authority of Scripture alone—accordingly the principle of tradition is declared in-
solvent; or they must simply be avoided as having been already condemned. But
even the principle of the *consensus* of the teachers is to be used with the greatest
caution; it is strictly guarded; it is only of weight when, as it were, a whole
Council of doctors can be cited (39). But in that case no one is entitled to disregard it, for the ancient doctors are the 'prophets and teachers' ranked by Paul
next to the Apostles, and described by him as presented to the Church by God.
He who despises them despises God. We must cling to the agreement of the holy
Churches, which are holy because they continue in the communion of the faith (40).

In the so-called second Commonitorium (ch. 41—43) there is first a recapitulation
in which the sufficiency of Scripture as source of truth is once more emphasised.

Besides Holy Scripture, tradition is the source of knowledge of,
the authority for, the truth; and tradition is the Church itself,
not, as in the West, governed by Rome, as a sovereign, living
power, but in its immovable, thousand-year-old doctrines and
orders. Even Scripture is to be explained by the tradition
which transmits it, although Scripture is itself to some extent
the *caput et origo traditionis*. But tradition still really presents
itself in two forms as it did among the earliest Alexandrians:
there is a perfectly official form—now that of the Councils,
and one more profound and indefinite—corresponding to the
'scientific tradition' (παράδοσις γνωστική) of the ancient Alexandrians.

### 3. *The Church*. [1]

Cyril of Jerusalem in his Catechisms portrays the Church
to his disciples as a spiritual communion. But in explaining the
predicate 'catholic' [2] he completely identifies this spiritual communion with the empirical Church. It is called Ἐκκλησία, because it summons all men together, and unites them with one
another. This it does at God's command; for after God had
rejected the first community as the 'synagogue of the wicked',

It is then shown that, at the Council of Ephesus held three years before, no
novelty was proposed, but decisions were based on the sayings of the Fathers.
The Fathers are named singly whose works were publicly read there (42). Vincentius therefore considered that the authority of the Council consisted wholly in
its strict adherence to the testimony of tradition. In the last chapter statements
follow to the same effect by the two last Roman Bishops. The authority of the
Roman Chair is appended 'that nothing may seem wanting to completeness'.
Perhaps the most notable feature in the whole of Vincentius' exposition is that
the Bishops as such—apart from the Council—play absolutely no part, and that,
in particular, no reference is made to their Apostolic succession as sharing in the
proof of doctrine. The ancient "teachers" are the court of appeal. We see that
Cyprian's influence was not so far-reaching, even in the West, as one should have
supposed. The proof of tradition was not really based on the hierarchy.

[1] Compare the statements of Kattenbusch, l. c., p. 330 ff. The East never arrived
at a definite theory of the nature and features of the Church.

[2] On this attribute see Vol. II., p. 75, n. 1. From the middle of the fourth
century the clause "καὶ [εἰς] μίαν ἁγίαν καθολικὴν ἐκκλησίαν" must have stood in
the Symbols of by far the most of the provincial Churches in the East. The εἰς
is to be referred also to the Church.

because they had crucified the Saviour, he built out of the heathen a second Church, on which his favour rests; that is the Church of the living God, pillar and foundation of the truth. To it alone belong the predicates one, holy, and catholic; the communities of the Marcionites, Manichæans, and other heretics are societies of godlessness. The Church, which was formerly barren, is the mother of us all; she is the Bride of Christ. In this second Church God has appointed Apostles, Prophets, and teachers, and miraculous gifts of every kind; he has adorned it with all virtues, proved it to be unconquerable in persecution, and made it an object of veneration even to kings, since its boundaries are wider than those of any secular kingdom. It is called Catholic because it extends over the whole globe, teaches all necessary dogmas to men universally and unceasingly, comprehends and leads to the true worship of God all men without respect of class, is able to cure all sins in soul and body, and possesses in its midst all virtues and all conceivable gifts of grace. [1]

These utterances of Cyril concerning the Church contain the quintessence of all that has ever been said of it by the Greeks. [2] They have adorned it with all conceivable attributes, applying to it all the O. T. passages descriptive of the people of Israel. [3] They glorified it as the communion of faith and virtue, and as a rule clung to this description of it in their catechetical and

---

[1] Cyril, Cat. XVIII., ch. 22—27.

[2] For Western doctrines of the Church see the next book. But they are not so different in theory from those of the East as some suppose.

[3] The Greeks spoke not infrequently of the "state" or "city" of God; Origen had already used the term, and it is common in Eusebius. On the other hand, the fine combination "Christ and the Church (as bride)" or "the Church as the body of Christ", which had been at a very early date reduced to the level of a homiletical or rhetorical view, was either thrust into the background, or superseded by the phrase "Christ and the individual soul." At a later date, the proposition, that Christ is the head of the Church, was often asserted against the Latins; but it was not very effective; for, seeing that the Greeks granted that the Church was a visible body in the common sense of the term, their thesis that this visible Church had none but an invisible head was beset with difficulties. Besides, Origen had been attacked as early as about A.D. 300, because he had explained Adam and Eve as referring to Christ and the Church (Socrates H. E. III. 7), though this allegory was supported by a very ancient tradition. Tychonius repeated it.

homiletical teaching. [1]  Indeed, their position was here so far
archaic, that they either did not mention the organisation of
the Church at all, or—what was even more significant—they
named in this connection the Apostles, Prophets, teachers and
the rest, in brief, the possessors and gifts of the Spirit (see
above in Cyril). We find the same teaching even in John ot
Damascus, who in his great work on dogma has given no
place at all to the Church, [2] and in the later so-called Symbols
of the Greek Church. [3] The difficult question, which Origen
first discussed, and which Augustine considered so thoroughly
in his fight with Donatism—the question about the Church as
*corpus verum* (the true body) and *corpus permixtum* (the mixed
body)—was hardly touched on in the East. [4]  When we read
Greek statements as to the Church—statements, besides, which
are altogether few in number—we not infrequently believe that
we are living in the second century, nay, before the Gnostic
controversy. We must not perceive in this attitude of the Greek
Fathers any sign of exceptional maturity. It was prescribed to
them, on the one hand, by natural theology, on the other, by
the narrowness of their view of the task of the Church. Redemption through Christ applied in intention to the whole
human race, which meanwhile was always simply conceived as
the sum of all individuals. In its result, it was limited by the
liberty of man to resist salvation through sin. The Church was
really, therefore, nothing but the sum of all individual believers
in heaven and upon earth. The view that the Church was the
mother of believers, a divine creation, the body of Christ, was
not properly carried out in dogma. Even the thought that
Christ had so assumed human nature that all it experienced in
him benefited mankind, was only applied—not to the Church—

[1] There are very numerous instances of this, and most of all in the influential
Chrysostom. Epiphanius' contention in the Expos. fid. cathol., ch. 3 is worthy of
notice: Ὁ Θεὸς, ὁ ἐπὶ πάντων, ἡμῖν Θεὸς ὑπάρχει τοῖς ἐκ τῆς ἁγίας ἐκκλησίας
γεννηθεῖσιν. This Jewish Christian regarded the Church as Israel, and its God as
the God of Israel; see what follows.

[2] Langen, Joh. Damascenus, p. 299 f.

[3] Gass, l. c., p. 205 f.

[4] It is treated in the later Symbols; see Gass, p. 206 f.

but to mankind as it existed, and the Eucharist itself did not help the Church to a special place in dogmatics. [1] In spite of the 'belief in one holy Catholic Church' (πιστεύειν εἰς μίαν ἁγίαν καθολικὴν ἐκκλησίαν) *the Church was no dogmatic conception* in the strict sense of the term. It did not form a link in the chain of the doctrines of redemption. And that is not surprising. Seeing the form given to the blessing of salvation, a *religious* conception of the Church could not be obtained. All was contained in the factors, God, mankind, Christ, the mysteries, and the individual.

But occasion was given to draw up definitions of the Church by (1) the O. T. and the spurious Jewish Church, (2) heresy and the actual organisation of the Church, (3) the administration of the mysteries, (4) and the fight against the Roman claims to the primacy. As regards the first point, all that was necessary had been said in the second and third centuries; there was nothing to add; it was repeated with greater or less animosity to Judaism, whose history appeared sometimes as the mysterious type of the Church, sometimes as its antitype. As to the second and third, there was no doubt that *the Church was the true teacher of the truth* [2] *and the legitimate administrator of the mysteries.* [3] It transmitted the μάθησις (learning) and it possessed the mysteries. Therefore—and of this there was no doubt—it was essential to her to have the organisation, which was crowned by Bishops and Councils, and priests who should present the sacrifices and judge in God's stead. Bishops and Councils we have spoken of above, the priests and their duties will be discussed in Chap. X. [4] It is remarkable, however, that the latter

1 Cyril of Alexandria frequently connects the Church with the incarnation and the Eucharist; but even he has not gone beyond the homiletic and edifying point of view.

2 Religious truth, however, really embraced all philosophy, see Anastasius Sin., Viæ dux (Migne, Patrol., Vol. 89, p. 76 sq.): Ὀρθοδοξία ἐστὶν ἀψευδὴς περὶ Θεοῦ καὶ κτίσεως ὑπόληψις ἢ ἔννοια περὶ πάντων ἀληθής, ἢ δόξα τῶν ὄντων καθάπερ εἰσίν.

3 Damalas has given a very pregnant summary of the old Patristic conception Ἡ ὀρθόδοξος πίστις (1877) p. 3: ἡ δὲ πίστις αὕτη εἰς τὴν μίαν ἁγίαν καθολικὴν καὶ ἀποστολικὴν ἐκκλησίαν ἐστὶ πεποίθησις, ὅτι αὕτη ἐστὶν ὁ φορεὺς τῆς θείας χάριτος τῆς ἐνδεικνυμένης εἰς δύο τινά, πρῶτον ὅτι αὕτη ἐστὶν ὁ ἀλάνθαστος διδάσκαλος τῆς χριστιανικῆς ἀληθείας καὶ δεύτερον ὁ γνήσιος τῶν μυστηρίων οἰκονόμος.

4 See Kattenbusch, l. c., pp. 346 ff., 357 ff., 393 ff.

is brought more to the front than the former. The Pseudo-areopagite was not the first to make his view of the Church depend essentially on the mysteries, and to regard the hierarchy primarily as performers of the sacred rites; he only completed what Ignatius, Clement, the first draft of the Apostolic Constitutions, Chrysostom *de sacerdotio*, [1] and many others had developed before or contemporaneously with him. The Church had been entrusted to the Bishops, because they constituted the living representation of God on earth, the vicars of Christ, participators in the activity of the Holy Spirit, and therefore the source of all sacraments. They were much less thought of as successors of the Apostles; the Church was the legacy not of the Apostles, but of Christ, and the dwelling place of the Holy Spirit. [2]

In the polemic against the Roman claims to supremacy, the view was strongly emphasised that Christ is the foundation and sole head of the Church, and this principle was opposed even to an exaggerated estimate of the Apostles in general and Peter in particular.

"He who secedes from the Church, withdraws himself at the same time from the influences of the Holy Spirit, and it is not easy to find a wise man among the heretics"; [3] but on what

---

[1] See Vol. III. 4—6, VI. 4; also the Homily on the day of his ordination as priest, Montfaucon I., p. 436 sq.

[2] Of course the Church was conscious of being, and called itself "apostolic." But it is perhaps not a mere accident that this predicate is not so stereotyped in the Symbols and other official manifestoes as the rest—unity, holiness and catholicity. The otherwise substantially identical expositions by the Greek Fathers of the word "catholic" have been collected by Söder, Der Begriff der Katholicität der Kirche und des Glaubens (1881), pp. 95 ff., 110 ff., 113 f., 115 f. "Catholic" was equivalent to orthodox even before Eusebius, as is shown by the interpolations of the word into the Martyrium Polycarpi. That this word was interpolated I have tried to prove in "The Expositor," 1885, Dec., p. 410 sq. It may be in place here to remark generally that the copyists are least to be trusted in the case of such predicates as were current at a later date—*e.g.*, as regards words like "bearer of God" "Homoousios", "Catholic" etc. The Monophysites especially made great efforts to introduce their catch-words into older writers. Even to-day the Armenians are not to be trusted.

[3] Heretics and Schismatics were more and more identified; see the so-called 6th Canon of Constantinople, A.D. 381 (it really dates from A.D. 382): αἱρετικοὺς λέγομεν τούς τε πάλαι τῆς ἐκκλησίας ἀποκηρυχθέντας καὶ τοὺς μετὰ ταῦτα ὑφ'

points the unity of the Church was based has not been made
clear. It first appears as if faith and virtue were sufficient, but
participation in the mysteries of the Church, and submission
to its organisation and tradition were added: indeed these in
practice took the first place. Yet the organisation of the Church
was not really carried higher than the Bishops, in spite of all
the empty words used about the Patriarchs: the Church was
orthodox and perfect, because it offered a security in its episcopal
and priestly constitution that it was the *ancient institution founded
by Christ*. In this conviction—we can hardly call it a doctrine—
the Church became more and more narrow; it made itself
a holy piece of antiquity. [1]

But after the close of the fifth century it ceased to be the
*one Church*. Tradition, which had been created to maintain the
unity of the Church, served in the end to split it up, because
national and local traditions, views, and customs had been
received into it to an increasing extent. The great cleavage into
Catholic and Novatian Catholic was not yet determined, or
supported by national considerations. The division into Græco-
Roman Catholicism and Germanic Arianism did owe its duration to opposite national tendencies. On the other hand, the
disruption of the Eastern Church into the Byzantine (Roman)
and the Oriental (Nestorian-Syrian, Jacobitish-Syrian, Coptic, and
Armenian) rested entirely on national antitheses, and, preserved
mainly by the monks who, in spite of all their renunciation of
the world, have always adopted a National Church attitude, has
continued up to the present day. Now, after the schism had
further taken place between the Byzantine (Neo-Roman) and the
Roman branches, the Church was divided into three (four) great
territories distinguished by their nationality: the Germano-Roman

ἡμῶν ἀναθεματισθέντας. πρὸς δὲ τούτοις καὶ τοὺς τὴν πίστιν μὲν τὴν ὑγιῆ προσ-
ποιουμένους ὁμολογεῖν, ἀποσχίσαντας δὲ καὶ ἀντισυνάγοντας τοῖς κανονικοῖς ἡμῶν
ἐπισκόποις.

[1] The question whether the holiness of Christians was founded on being members
in the Church—initiation into it—or depended on personal virtue was not decided
in the East, but it was never even definitely put. The cause of this vagueness existed
ultimately in the obscurity which prevailed among the Greeks in reference to the
relation of natural theology and dogma in general; see on this the following
chapters.

West (Rome), the countries on the Ægean sea (Constantinople), and the East split into Nestorianism and Monophysitism. Each had its own peculiar traditions and authorities. The Orientals, though rent asunder and quarrelling with each other, felt that they formed a unity compared with the two other sections, *i.e.*, the "Romans," and could, in reply to the "bragging of the Romans," point to a hundred marks which revealed the superiority of their Churches. They regarded their land as the cradle of the human race, their Church as the primitive home of religion; and if Jerusalem was no longer in their possession, yet they still had the ancient site of Paradise. [1] The Neo-Romans boasted of their Patriarchate, their unchanged faith, and their nation, which took no part in the crucifixion of Christ, in which the Romans and Barbarians had made common cause. The Romans, finally, had the chiefs of the Apostles, Peter and Paul, and the Pope, Peter's successor, with the secular power committed to him by Christ and Constantine. The common foundation of these Churches was not solid enough to resist the elements that were dissolving it. Nationality was stronger than religion.

*Literature.*—Jacobi, Die kirchliche Lehre von der Tradition u. heil. Schrift., Part I., 1847. Holtzmann, Kanon u. Tradition, 1859 (does not discuss to any extent the Church in antiquity). Söder, Der Begriff der Katholicität der Kirche, 1881. Seeberg, Studien zur Geschichte des Begriffs der Kirche, 1885. Kattenbusch, l. c. There is much material in Schwane, also in the writings which passed between Old Catholics and Roman Catholics after A.D. 186ç.

[1] See, *e.g.*, Elias of Nisibis, Proof of the truth of the faith (Ed. by Horst, 1886, p. 112 ff.).

A.—Presuppositions of the Doctrine of Redemption, or Natural Theology.

"Natural Theology" did not pass through any very thorough-going development in the Greek Church; but it reveals differences, according as Aristotelianism or Neoplatonism prevailed. By Natural Theology we are to understand the complex of conceptions that, according to the view then held, formed the self-evident and certain contents of the human mind, which was only held to be more or less darkened (see Chap. II.). These conceptions, however, arose in fact historically, and corresponded to the degree of culture at which the ancient world had arrived, especially through the work of the Greek Philosophers. We can divide them appropriately into doctrines concerning God and concerning man. But changes also took place in proportion to the growing influence exerted on these conceptions by the words of the Bible literally understood. Nevertheless the fundamental features remained in force; yet they were displaced and confused by foreign material during the period from Origen to John of Damascus.

## A.—*PRESUPPOSITION OF DOCTRINE OF REDEMP-TION OR NATURAL THEOLOGY.*

## CHAPTER IV.

PRESUPPOSITIONS AND CONCEPTIONS REGARDING GOD,
THE CREATOR, AS DISPENSER OF SALVATION.

### § 1. *The Doctrine of God. Its Method.*

THE main features of the doctrine of God were those familiar from the theology of the Apologists, as they were partly fixed and partly supplemented by the fight with Gnosticism. Speculations on the Deity as a Trinity ($\tau\rho\iota\grave{\alpha}\varsigma$) modified but little the general doctrine of God (yet see attempts in Augustine, De trinitate); for the unity, simplicity, indivisibility, and unchangeableness of God were at the same time maintained most definitely: in other words, the Father alone was almost always regarded as "root of the Deity" ($\dot{\rho}\dot{\iota}\zeta\alpha$ $\tau\tilde{\eta}\varsigma$ $\theta\varepsilon\acute{o}\tau\eta\tauο\varsigma$), where the Deity, in its essential being, was described in comparison with the world. The ultimate reason of this was that theology counted on a general intelligence for its general doctrine of God, and therefore had recourse to natural religion and theology, *i. e.,* to the results of Greek philosophy. It was indeed admitted by many Fathers (see esp. Athanasius, De incarn.) that men could know the Deity from creation only dimly, if at all; and that therefore the manifestation of God in Christ alone made it possible to recognise the nature of God as the undivided, spiritual and good Lord of the World. But, in fact, it was only a question of more or less as regards the natural knowledge of the spiritual and good God, the Creator. Other Fathers, especially those influenced by Aristotle, declared the knowledge of God in its whole extent to be innate (see Arnobius), or, a knowledge to be constantly tested by the observation of nature. No difference is here caused by the fact that some Fathers have described the existence of God and his distinctive nature as capable of proof, others, as incapable; for the latter only rejected the proof in so far as God could not be discovered by means of deduction from a *prius*. The psychological, cosmological,[1] and natural theological proofs were not despised by them in meeting Atheism, Polytheism, Manichæism, etc. We already find in Augustine suggestions of an ontological proof.[2] All these evidences were, indeed, given subject to the proviso, that all knowledge of God must be traced back to God himself, that it became indistinct in proportion to man's alienation from God, and that the revelation of Scripture first rendered everything clear and certain.

Further, it was expressly contended that God, as the infinite one, was, strictly speaking, incapable of being known, because his nature could not be described by any predicate. But this inscrutability, so far as represented in the avowal " whatever the creature is, that God is not," was held—and with this the Neoplatonists were agreed—to be the valuable and true knowledge (Athan. ad monach. 2: "even if it is not possible to comprehend what God is, it is possible to say what he is not:" καὶ εἰ μὴ δυνατὸν καταλαβέσθαι τί ἐστι Θεός, ἀλλὰ δυνατὸν εἰπεῖν, τί οὐκ ἐστιν).[3] The revelation through the Logos only

---

[1] The influence of Aristotle is first conspicuous in Diodore of Tarsus, who reproduced independently the cosmological proof of Aristotle (see Photius, Biblioth. 223). From the sixth century it is evident in the majority of the Fathers, and especially John of Damascus. See De fide orthod. I. 3 (12): Everything perceptible by the senses, as also the higher world of spirits, is subject to change; therefore it must have had a beginning, and been created. There must accordingly exist a being who created it, and that is God. Two other proofs are found in John of Dam.

[2] Augustine's line of argument was first to demonstrate rules of human thought, which accordingly transcended it. These rules—logical and ethical—he stated to be *truths*, their sum being *the truth*. This truth was a living power, accordingly it existed. Thus the way to the existence of God was given; see esp. De lib. arbitr. II. 3—15, but the thought is also suggested elsewhere in his writings, *e.g.*, the Confessions.

[3] In this the great majority of the Fathers were agreed. Augustine describes (De doctr. I. 6) the impossibility of declaring God, in a way that coincides word for word with the tenets of the Basilidians (Hippol., Philos. VII. 20). Augustine writes: "Diximusne aliquid et sonuimus aliquid dignum deo? Immo vero nihil me aliud quam dicere voluisse sentio; si autem dixi, non hoc est quod dicere volui. Hoc unde scio, nisi quia deus ineffabilis est, quod autem a me dictum est, si ineffabile

went beyond this in that it established this knowledge regarding the infinite Spirit and his inexpressible nature, and made it possible to perceive him in his likeness. [1] The Fathers influenced by Neoplatonism, however, assumed further that the contemplative ascetic, who was on the way to deification, could gain a direct vision of God in all his splendour, a conception which the Areopagite has combined with a scholastic theory of the knowableness of God by negation, eminence, causality. [2]

esset, dictum non esset? Ac per hoc ne ineffabilis quidem dicendus est deus, quia et hoc cum dicitur, aliquid dicitur. Et fit nescio quæ pugna verborum, quoniam si illud est ineffabile, quod dici non potest, non est ineffabile, quod vel ineffabile dici potest." Basilides: Ἔστι γὰρ, φησίν, ἐκεῖνο οὐχ ἁπλῶς ἄρρητον, ὃ ὀνομάζεται· ἄρρητον γοῦν αὐτὸ καλοῦμεν, ἐκεῖνο δὲ οὐδὲ ἄρρητον· καὶ γὰρ τὸ οὐδ᾽ ἄρρητον οὐκ ἄρρητον ὀνομάζεται, ἀλλὰ ἔστι, φησίν, ὑπεράνω παντὸς ὀνόματος ὀνομαζομένου. Men were therefore at the point already reached by Basilides' followers in the second century. Even Catechumens were taught this; see Cyril, Cat. VI., ch. 2: οὐ τὸ τί ἐστι Θεὸς ἐξηγούμεθα ... ἐν τοῖς περὶ Θεοῦ μεγάλη γνῶσις το τὴν ἀγνωσίαν ὁμολογεῖν. Similar teaching is very frequent in Plotinus. In the Vîta Plot. of Porphyry, ch. 23, the supreme God is thus defined: ὁ Θεὸς ὁ μήτε μορφὴν μήτε τινὰ ἰδέαν ἔχων, ὑπὲρ δὲ νοῦν καὶ πᾶν τὸ νοητὸν ἱδρύμενος.

[1] The Dogmatics of John of Damascus begin with John I. 18, Matt. XI. 17, and 1 Cor. II. 11.

[2] The striking contention of some disciples of Lucian (according to Philostorgius), and the most extreme Arians, Eunomius and Aëtius, but not Arius himself, that men could know the nature of God as well as God himself did, and as well as they knew themselves, is most closely connected with their Christology and their Aristotelianism. When the orthodox Fathers argued that the indescribable God could only be perceived in the Logos and through his work, and that God therefore would have been unknowable had not the Logos been his image, possessed of a like nature, those Arians had to meet the objection by emphasising even in the course of the christological controversy, the possibility of knowing God directly. In taking up this position they had of course to leave the nature of God out of the question, and to confine themselves to his will, as it had been clearly manifested in creation, and the preaching of the truth by the Logos. But this to them was no limitation; for they only attached importance in the first place to the knowledge of the divine will, and secondly to the renewed submission of men to the sovereignty of the divine will: (not to participation in the divine nature, unless in so far as that was already involved in the original equipment of man; see Socrates IV. 7; Epiph. H. LXXVI. 4, and the counter-observations of the Cappadocians). Their expositions are exceded by the Areopagite's completely Neoplatonic theology, from which, meanwhile, Augustine in one of his lines of thought was not far removed. The Areopagite already adopted the position that ruled for more than a thousand years, in which the contention that God—by reason of his splendour – was absolutely unknowable, was balanced by the mystical assumption of a sensuous, suprasensuous knowableness in virtue of the fusion of the mind of

## § 2.  *The Doctrine of God's Nature and Attributes.*

The Being of God was immortal substance and was primarily defined—as already results from the method of knowing God— by affirming that he was without beginning or end, that he was a spirit and the supreme First Cause, all which predicates were proved in connection with the proofs of his existence. The deity is the pneumatic Ὄν which, because it is not the world, is supramundane, simply governing the world, the one, indivisible, imperishable, unchangeable, supremely good and impassive being, to which, in the strict sense, a real existence alone belongs: the Fathers influenced by Aristotelianism emphasised especially the spiritual power which determined its own aims and the causality of the deity. God is the intelligible reality and infinite reason. So far as it is maintained of this being *(secundum hominem)* that he is good, the predicate affirms nothing but that he is perfect, *i. e.*, is completely self-sufficient and possesses blessedness in himself and therefore is not envious—see esp. Athanasius adv. pagan., also the Catechisms of Cyril. But the goodness of the Deity was also established from the fact of the revelation of God, first from creation, and here meant that God, since he is the gracious one, willed that creatures should participate in his blessedness, and carried out his intention under all circumstances.

Augustine broke through this natural conception of the goodness of God; for he understands by the Deity as *summum bonum* the power of love which takes hold of man, and leads him from worldliness and selfishness to peace and felicity. But even in Augustine this idea is intimately connected with the natural view.

As regards the divine attributes, the Fathers sought, while speaking of such, to keep clear of the idea of a plurality in

God with the mind of man. To him also we trace back the theology of affirmation and negation (kataphatic and apophatic)—the thing had, indeed, been very long in existence—*i.e.*, the method of making statements about God *via eminentiæ* and *via negationis;* see his Letters, the work, De divinis nominibus, and the beginning of the tractate, De mystica theologia. The importance of John of Damascus consists for posterity in his having united the Neoplatonic and Aristotelian elements in his doctrine of God; see De fide orthod. I. 1—4.

God, or conceptions of anything accidental. It is only for human thought that the absolute, perfect, homogeneous Being has attributes assigned to him, as varied representations of him in relation to the finite. The elevation above time and space presented itself as eternity and omnipresence; the latter attribute at the same time was the root of omniscience and omnipotence. Omnipotence was limited by the Fathers by two thoughts: it was circumscribed by the good will of God, and it left scope for human liberty. [1] Origen's thesis of the limitation of omniscience found no supporters in later times.

From the goodness (perfection) of God [2] all conceivable ethical qualities were deduced. But they did not obtain their due significance, because the abstract idea that God was the *requiter*, *i. e.*, rewarded the good and punished the wicked, formed, in spite of all Neoplatonic philosophy, the foundation of the whole conceptions of God, in so far as ethics were taken into account at all. This view, however, which was considered the "natural" one, readily became indifferent to the thought that men as God's creatures are dependent on him, that they are meant to form an inner unity, and that their life is conducted to a definite goal; in other words, it endangered the religious view of Christianity. It gave man complete independence in presence of God, and broke mankind up into a group of disconnected individuals. It descended from Judaism and the ancient world—the gods are *just*, because they reward and punish, the two facts being conceived in coördination. This view, further, was entitled to its place within the narrow

[1] Along with all fatalism and astrology the Greek Fathers also unanimously rejected the idea that God's prescience acted as fate and was the first cause of human actions, or that prophecy controlled the course of events. It was rather taught that prescience was consequent to the event perceived beforehand. But Augustine was not perfectly satisfied with this idea. He deepened it through the thought that the sum of all that happened was before God in an eternal *now*.

[2] But of this the saying of Gregory of Nyssa is true (περὶ ψυχ. κ. ἀναστασ· Oehler, p. 92): Παντὸς ἀγαθοῦ ἐπέκεινα ἡ θεία φύσις, τὸ δὲ ἀγαθὸν ἀγαθῷ φίλον πάντως, διὰ τοῦτο ἑαυτὴν βλέπουσα καὶ ὃ ἔχει θέλει καὶ ὃ θέλει ἔχει οὐδὲν τῶν ἔξωθεν εἰς ἑαυτὸν δεχομένη. Ἔξω δὲ αὐτῆς οὐδέν, ὅτι μὴ ἡ κακία μόνη, ἥτις, κἂν παράδοξον ᾖ, ἐν τῷ μὴ εἶναι τὸ εἶναι ἔχει. οὐ γὰρ ἄλλη τίς ἐστι κακίας γένεσις, εἰ μὴ ἡ τοῦ ὄντος στέρησις. Τὸ δὲ κυρίως ὂν ἡ τοῦ ἀγαθοῦ φύσις ἐστίν· ὃ οὖν ἐν τῷ ὄντι οὐκ ἔστιν, ἐν τῷ μὴ εἶναι πάντως ἐστίν.

horizon of the citizens of ancient communities, [1] but while it
could not be omitted from Christianity, it required to be subordinated to a higher thought. Accordingly, significant tendencies to correct the prevalent system of thought were not
wanting on the part of the Fathers. Origen had already tried
to regard the righteousness of God as a form of his loving
discipline; the conception that suffering is always bound up
with penal justice, had undoubtedly something to do with this
attempt. The continued fight with dualism—Manichæism—constantly made it necessary to demonstrate that power, goodness,
wisdom, and justice were combined in the Deity. [2] But in almost all the Fathers the attributes of goodness and justice
stood asunder. We can see the reason of this in the fact that
up to Augustine no serious effort was made to understand the
goodness of God as moral holiness, and this failure was in turn
due to the characteristic method of obtaining a knowledge of
God, the attempt to rise to the Deity from the notion of the
finite by means of sublimations. [3] The theory of God was beset
at this most important point with uncertainties, nay, inconsistencies. He was at once the impassive Being (Ὤν) and the
Judge who requited actions [4]—the latter conception, further, not
only including the coördination of goodness and justice, but
also the superiority of the former to the latter. The Alexandrians had grasped at the expedient, following Philo, [5] of
representing God as absolutely benevolent, but the Logos as the
Just; this, however, was to confess despair of solving the problem, showing once more very clearly that men could not think
without compunction (*affectiones humanæ*) of the (penal) justice

[1] See Leopold Schmidt, Die Ethik der alten Griechen, 2 Vols., 1882; further,
Ritschl in the Th. L. Z. 1883, Col. 6 f.

[2] These four attributes Gregory of Nyssa has particularised and sought to
harmonise in his great Catechism.

[3] This method, however, was by no means despised by Augustine himself.

[4] The doctrine of God came in this form to the theologians of the middle
ages. The nuances and inconsistencies of scholastic theology were caused by the
necessity of alternating between the two ideas of God as the intelligible Ὤν and
the Requiter. Some emphasised the one, others the other, more strongly. In certain
doctrines only the former, in others only the latter conception, could be used.

[5] See Bigg, The Christian Platonists of Alex. (1886), p. 12 f.

of which at most the Logos was capable; and it is interesting as a counterpart to the opposite idea adopted in later times. [1] But we see even here, why the doctrine of redemption could not become one of atonement in the ancient Church. If the distinctive form in which redemption was accomplished was to be justified, and its intrinsic necessity to be proved, then there must not only exist, but speculation must be founded on, the conviction that God's saving purpose transcended the thought of requital, and that he was morally holy. But that is out of the question where the Fathers are concerned. [2]

## § 3.  *The Cosmology.*

The Cosmological and allied anthropological problems were treated by the Fathers—who formally used Gen. I.—III. as their text—with the whole apparatus of contemporary philosophy, in this way satisfying their scientific craving for a rational conception of the world. The systems are therefore very different in details; but on the whole they existed peaceably side by side, showing that the differences presupposed a measure of agreement, sufficient for the solidarity of the doctrinal structure.

---

[1] In this view—in the Middle Ages—God appears rather as the strictly Just, Christ as the "good"; but the idea of goodness had changed.

[2] In the lower ranks of the communities, and among a few Oriental sects (Audians), anthropomorphic conceptions of God, the belief that he had a human shape, a body etc., held their ground. But they were retained also in some circles of monks (*e.g.*, those of the Scetian Desert), and even by a few Bishops. From the close of the fourth century, with the hostility to Origen's spiritualism was combined active resistance to this opposite view (Sozom. VIII. 11). The Stoic notion of God's corporeality had scarcely a defender after Tertullian; for Lactantius' view of the "figura" and "affectus" of God is not Stoic, but belongs to popular realism. In general, much that was anthropomorphic was retained in Western theology along with the realistic eschatology, and that by theologians who cherished a colourless eclectic moralism. Very instructive is Augustine's confession (Confess. V. *fin.*; VI. 3) that it was the sermons of Ambrose that first delivered him from the prejudice that the Catholic Church taught that the Deity was fashioned like man. If we reflect how much Augustine had mingled with Catholic Christians before his conversion, and how much he had heard of the Church, we cannot suppose he was the only one guilty of this prejudice. We need only recall the "apocryphal" writings of the Byzantine age, which were read to an extraordinary extent, to see how strong were anthropomorphism and the conceptions of a magic God.

These differences were slightest in the Cosmology proper. The task set the theologians of the fourth century was to bring Origen's cosmology more into harmony with the demands of the rule of faith, to adapt it more closely to the account given in Gen. I., and to defeat the Manichæan Cosmology. After the last decades of the fourth century, the slow course of development was hastened by violent opposition to Origen's cosmology, and the view of the Church, held before Origen, was substantially restored, though now as a scientific theory. [1] Yet the conception of an upper world of spirits, related to the present world as its ideal and type, continued to exist, and ever threw its shadow on the latter. [2] On the other hand, the Trinitarian

---

[1] See Justinian's edict against Origen, and the fifth Synod of Constantinople, Hefele, Concil. Gesch. II. 2, p. 780—797; at an earlier date, the attacks of Theophilus and Jerome on Origen.

[2] Origen held that the present world was only a place of punishment and purification. This view, which approximated very closely to the old Gnostic idea, was rejected; but the conception remained of an upper world of spirits, of which our world was the materialised copy. Where this conception was potent, a considerable part of the feeling which possessed Origen (after Plato) as he looked at our world must have endured. It was never wanting among the orthodox Fathers, and the Greeks of to-day have not lost it. "The world is a whole, but divided into two spheres of which the higher is the necessary *prius* and type of the lower": that is still the Greek view (see Gass, Symbolik, p. 143 f.). "God first and by his mere thought evoked out of non-existence all heavenly powers to exhibit his glory, and this intelligible world (κόσμος νοερός) is the expression of undisturbed harmony and obedient service." Man belongs to both worlds. The conception, as expounded by the Areopagite and established by John of Damascus (De fide orthod. II 2—12), that the world was created in successive stages, has not the importance of a dogma, but it has that of a wide-spread theologoumenon. It is Neoplatonic and Gnostic, and its publication and recognition show that the dissatisfaction felt by Origen with the account of the creation in Gen. I. was constantly shared by others. Men felt a living interest, not in the way plants, fishes, and birds came into being, but in the emanation of the spiritual from the Deity at the head of creation down to man. Therefore we have the κόσμος νοερός, the intelligible world, whose most characteristic feature consisted in its (3) gradations (διακοσμήσεις), which again fell into (three) orders, down to archangels and angels. (See Dionys. De divina hierarch. 6 sq., and John of Damascus, l.c., ch. III: πᾶσα ἡ θεολογία τὰς οὐρανίους οὐσίας ἐννέα κέκληκε. ταύτας ὁ Θεῖος ἱεροτελέστης εἰς τρεῖς ἀφορίζει τριαδικὰς διακοσμήσεις, Seraphim, Cherubim, thrones, dominions, powers, forces, principalities, archangels, and angels. We find a step in this direction as early as the App. Constit. VII. 35). In the creation, the system of spiritual powers was built from above downwards; while in sanctification by the mysteries, it was necessary to ascend the same series. The significant point was the union of the

conflicts led to a precise distinction being drawn between creating, making, begetting, and emanating, and thus the notion of creation out of nothing now first received its strict impress. But Neoplatonic ideas of the origin of the world lasted till after the beginning of the fifth century, even in the case of some Bishops, and side by side with it the Manichæan conception of the world spread secretly and found adherents among the clergy themselves up to the middle of it. The following proposition may be regarded as containing the quintessence of the orthodox Fathers from the fifth century, and at the same time as the presupposition that gave scope to all their further speculations. It can be stated thus: God from eternity bore in his own mind the idea of the world. In free self-determination he, in order to prove his goodness, created by the Logos, who embraces all ideas, this world, which has had a beginning and will have an end, in six days out of nothing, in accordance with the pattern of an upper world created by him.

The justification of divine providence and the production of Theodicies were called for by Manichæism and fatalism on the one hand, and the great political catastrophes and calamities on the other. It was taught that God constantly remained close to his creation, preserving and governing it. With this, rational beings were looked upon in their numerical sum total as the peculiar objects of divine providence. Providence was also defended in opposition to the loose and unstable form in which earlier and contemporary monotheistic philosophers had avowed it; it was recognised in principle to be a power pro-

conception of creation with the system of the cultus, or, better, the scheme which embodied the idea of creation in accordance with the line of progress laid down for asceticism and sanctification. This was retained by Greek theology in spite of all its disavowal of Origen, Neoplatonism, and Gnosticism. But even in the region of the material, incomparably greater interest was taken in warmth, cold, moisture, drought, in fire, air, earth, and water, in the four vital humours, than in the childish elements which the O. T. narrative of creation takes into account. Yet the whole was included under the title of the 'work of the six days', and the allegories of Origen were, in theory, rejected. The exegesis of Gen. I. became the doctoral problem proper among the Greek Fathers. The most important wrote works on the Hexaëmeron; among them that of Johannes Philoponus is scientifically the most advanced (περὶ κοσμοποιίας); it is dependent, not on Platonism, but on Aristotle, though it also opposes the latter.

tecting also the individual creature. Yet here Christian theologians themselves did not arrive at complete certainty. It was
admitted that providence was above human freedom in so far
as it was maintained that neither that freedom nor the evil
proceeding from it could hinder the divine intentions. But the
belief in providence was not definitely connected with redemption by Christ or with the Church, for it was considered a self-
evident presupposition of redemption and a piece of Natural
Theology. Therefore it was also destitute of any strict object.
The uncertainty of the ancient world as to the extent and
method of providence had left its influence, [1] and empirical
reflections on the objectlessness of certain institutions, or
phenomena in the world—e. g., of vermin—could not be
defeated by a view which had itself a naturalistic basis. Yet
in proportion as the sure and real knowledge of God was only
derived from the Christian religion, it was also recognised that
faith in providence was first made certain through Christ, and
that Christians were under the particular providence of God. [2]
The problem of the theodicy was solved (1) by proving that the
freedom of the creature was something appropriate and good,
the possibility of wickedness and evil, however, being necessarily combined with it; (2) by denying to wickedness any
reality in the higher sense of the term, since wickedness as it
was separated from God, the principle of all being, was held
to be not—being; [3] (3) by defending the *mala pœnæ* or evil as
fitting means of purification; and finally, (4) by representing
temporal sufferings as indifferent to the soul. Some older
Fathers, *e. g.*, Lactantius, emphasised, besides, even the necessity of wickedness in the interest of moralism: without it
virtue would be impossible. [4] But such opinions died out in the
fight with Manichæism. [5]

[1] For this reason a startling casuistry is to be noticed here and there, and
exceptions are laid down.

[2] Degrees of providence were generally distinguished.

[3] After Origen this Platonic proposition enjoyed the widest circulation: see esp.
Athanasius and the Cappadocians; but the Antiochians held no other view. Augustine
made use of it in a peculiar and characteristic way.

[4] Lactant. Instit. div. II., ch. 8, 12; V., ch. 7.

[5] See Vol. V., for the extent and form in which Augustine held such views.

In reference to the heavenly spirits which belonged to, and indeed formed, the upper world, the recognised Fathers were convinced of the following points. (1) They were created by God (see the Symb. Nic.). (2) They were endowed with freedom, but had no material bodies (ἐγγύτατα τοῦ ἀσωμάτου). (3) They had passed through a crisis after which a section had remained true to the good, while another had revolted. (4) The good spirits were instruments of the divine government of the world, their activity being useful and beneficial to men, even entering into the sacramental system by which grace was imparted. (5) The reality of wickedness in the world was to be attributed to the bad spirits, and especially to their head, the devil; they exercised an almost unbounded power on earth, not being able indeed to compel man, but only to induce him, to sin; they could also be scared away without fail by the name of Christ, the sign of the cross, and the Sacraments. [1] As regards the relation of the good angels to men, their superiority to men—in the

---

[1] No doubt existed of the necessity of believing in heavenly spiritual beings. Origen counted this belief a doctrine of the Church (De princip. præf. 10). The points numbered in the text may be regarded as the quintessence of what obtained generally. But such an agreement only made its appearance in the sixth century. Until then this point was a centre of contention between a form of Biblical "realism," and the Origenistic, i.e., the Greek philosophical, view as to the world of spirits. The treatment of the question by the Areopagite, and its approval by the Church, constituted a triumph of Neoplatonic mysticism over Biblicism. But that tendencies which went still farther in this direction had not been wholly destroyed, was shown by the Hesychastic controversy of the fourteenth century, or the assumption of an uncreated divine light, which was not the nature of God, but a specific energy, different from himself, and which could be seen. (See Engelhardt in Illgen's Ztschr., 1838, Part I., p. 68 ff.; Gass, Die Mystik des Nik. Kabasilas, 1849, p. 1 ff., and in Herzog's R.-E., 2nd Ed.). The Logos, accordingly, no longer satisfied, or rather, as Scholasticism had placed the Logos under an embargo, piety sought for a new mediator. He was to accomplish what the Logos no longer did: he was to be a visible revelation of God, himself and yet not himself; for God himself was simply quiescent being; accordingly he himself was conceived and realised in the form of an energy that could be traced. The theory of the Areopagite was, however, not satisfactory in this respect; for while the spirits might doctrinally be regarded as created beings, they were perceived as divine forces, emanations, rays of the perfect light, conceivable by degrees by man, and bringing him nearer to the deity. We have here a great difference from the western conception; in the East the Platonic and Gnostic doctrine of Æons had never been entirely abolished. In the West, while the gradation of angelic powers had been accepted, the pious impulse from which it originated had not.

present condition of the latter—was emphasised, but it was also taught on the other hand, that man after he was made perfect would be at least equal to them.  The former position gave rise to a sort of angel-worship, which nevertheless in earlier times was no proper part of religion.  The Synod of Laodicea, about A.D. 360, declared it in its thirty-fifth Canon to be idolatry. [1] And it was kept in check by the idea that Christ's work possessed also a mysterious significance for the upper world.  But the polytheistic cravings of man constantly influenced religious ideas, and as the Deity was farther and farther removed from ordinary Christian people by speculation, there gradually arose, along with the thought of the intercession of the angels, [2] a worshipping of them, which was indeed only settled ecclesiastically at the seventh Œcumenical Synod (A.D. 787).  There it was defined as adoration (προσκύνησις) in distinction from service (λατρεία). [3] Even Gregory I. had assigned the service of angels to the pre-christian stage of religion.  The points of doctrine which we have above grouped together became the bases of a great number of very different conceptions, which grew up in opposition to Origen's doctrine, or under its influence, or in dependence on exegesis (esp. of Gen. VI.), or, lastly, as a result of reminiscences of Greek folk-lore and philosophy.  Men speculated on the date of the creation of angels, and the method by which they were created, on their spirituality or higher corporeality, their functions—as guardian angels and genii, the manner in which the wicked angels fell, [4] the orders and

---

[1] There undoubtedly existed, even in the earliest time, a view which conjoined the angels with God, and thus made them also objects of worship, or, included them in the *fides, quæ creditur*.  We may here perhaps recall even 1 Tim. V. 21: διαμαρτύρομαι ἐνώπιον τοῦ Θεοῦ καὶ Χριστοῦ Ἰησοῦ καὶ τῶν ἐκλεκτῶν ἀγγέλων.  We can at any rate refer to Justin., Apol I. 6: (We worship God) καὶ τὸν παρ' αὐτοῦ υἱὸν... καὶ τὸν τῶν ἄλλων ἑπομένων καὶ ἐξομοιουμένων ἀγαθῶν ἀγγέλων στρατόν. Athenag. Suppl. 10, 24.

[2] This thought is undoubtedly extremely ancient, but at the earlier date it only existed in the outer circle of the faith.

[3] It had long—as early as the fourth century—been on the way; see the miraculous oratories of St. Michael; Sozom. II. 3, Theodoret on Coloss. T. III., p. 355 ff.

[4] On the devil, "the prince of the ranks encircling the earth," see the exposition by John of Dam., De fide orthod. II. 4.  The devil and the demons of their own free will turned away unnaturally from God.

divisions of angels, and much else. Here also the doctrine of
Origen, which culminated in the restoration of the revolted
spirits, was in the end expressly disowned. On the other hand,
the Neoplatonic conception of spirits and their orders, or the
Gnostic idea of the Æons as interpreters of the divine, was
more and more legitimised in the Church doctrine of angels,
and was combined by the Areopagite with the mystic system
of the illumination of the world, and the communication of the
divine to the creaturely. It was a very old idea—see Hebrews
and First Clement—that Christ was in Heaven the High Priest
and head (προστάτης) of believers in the presence of God.
Clement of Alex. had already worked out this conception,
following Philo's model, to the effect that Christ, in conjunction
with the angelic powers subject to him, conveyed to men the
energies of the heavenly sphere; that he ever offered himself
for men to the Father as a sacrifice without fire (θῦμα ἄπυρον);
that the Holy Spirit along with the angels kept the heavenly
and the earthly Church in constant contact. In short, the thought
of a graded hierarchy in heaven, with heavenly sacrifices,
intercessions, etc., as it also occurs among the Valentinians,
lay on the confines of the Alexandrian's speculation. These
thoughts are more fully matured in Origen: the sacrifice of
Christ applied also to the celestials, and the upper world,
brought into harmony, contributed to the redemption of the
lower. They were confirmed by the Neoplatonic philosophy of
religion. On the other hand, Ignatius conceived the governing body of the Church on earth as a hierarchy which represented the heavenly order, and put it in operation. The two
ideas—the Son, the Holy Ghost and the angelic hosts on the
one hand, and the earthly priesthood, on the other—only needed
to be combined, and a new stage of ecclesiastical theosophy
was reached. The Pseudo-areopagite was the first to gain it—
after, indeed, it had been already suggested clearly enough by
Clement of Alex.; see Strom. VI. 13, 107, and other passages.
Clement makes three dwellings in heaven correspond on one side to
the divisions of angels, and, again, to the threefold hierarchy on
earth. On the spread of this form of theosophy among the Syrian
Monophysite monks, see Frothingham, Stephen bar Sudaili, 1886.

This whole conception was after all, indeed, nothing but a timid expression of the thought that the plan of creation itself, extending down from the deity to man, included the means of redemption, and that, as alienation from the deity was due to the existence of graduated creations, so, at the same time. was the restoration to God. This conception, which contrasts abruptly with that of the Old Testament and Christianity, was compatible in principle neither with the idea of the creation, nor with the one historical redemption that took place once for all. It was Gnostic and Neoplatonic, *i. e.*, pagan. This its character was simply disguised by the retention of the creation so far as words went, and by the substitution for the Æons of Jesus Christ, the Holy Ghost, and angelic powers with Biblical names; and, further, of sacraments, sacrifices, and priests, whose existence and operations were derived from the work of Christ.

The root of this whole conception is ultimately found in the notion that the Logos, who was identified with the Son of God, continued to be conceived as the abode and bearer of all the ideas from which the world was evolved. Even Athanasius was not in a position thoroughly to correct this view,—see Atzberger, Die Logoslehre des heiligen Athanasius, 1880, p. 138 ff. Consequently, even the most clear-sighted of the Fathers were helpless against speculations which deduced redemption from the Cosmology. And thus a new Church Theosophy arose. A fantastic pantheism was introduced which had been created by the barbarous theosophy of expiring antiquity. It harmonised excellently with the religious barbarism which satisfied itself in the crudest and most daring myths and legends; nay, it kindled into fresh life with it. The living God, apart from whom the Soul possesses nothing, and the fervour of the saint threatened meanwhile to disappear. And side by side, nay, in cordial agreement, with these fantastic speculations, there existed a prosaic worship of the letter.

*Literature.*—See Nitzsch's account, here especially thorough, Dogmengesch. I. pp. 268—287, 328—347, and Schwane, Vol. II. pp. 15—108, 272—328.

# CHAPTER V.

## PRESUPPOSITIONS AND CONCEPTIONS REGARDING MAN AS THE RECIPIENT OF SALVATION.

### § 1. *Introductory.*

ACCORDING to the ideas of the Fathers, the doctrines of the condition and destiny of man belonged to Natural Theology. This appears from the fact that, starting from their Cosmology, they all strove to ascertain, from the original state of man, the nature of Christian redemption, in other words, the state of perfection. At the same time the reservation held good, that we should receive more than we could think or expect, and, in fact, that which was expected, and was deduced from the religious and ethical value which man had come to put upon himself in the course of history, was only carried back into his original state. The following propositions contain everything that can be stated as embodying a common conviction and common presupposition of all further conceptions, which in this matter turned out very different, in accordance with the speculative and empirical studies of the Fathers, and the object of their investigations for the time. *Man made in the image of God is a free self-determining being. He was endowed with reason by God, that he might decide for the good, and enjoy immortality. He has fallen short of this destiny by having voluntarily yielded and continuing to yield himself—under temptation, but not under compulsion – to sin, yet without having lost the possibility and power of a virtuous life, or the capacity for immortality. The possibility was strengthened and immortality restored and offered by the Christian revelation which came to the aid of the darkened reason with complete know-*

*ledge of God. Accordingly, knowledge decides between good and evil. Strictly taken, the will is morally nothing.* On this basis very different views were possible. It was asked, first, what was original endowment, and what destiny, in the case of man; secondly, in connection with this, how much was to be claimed as human *nature*, and how much as *a gift of grace* originally bestowed; and thirdly, in keeping with the above, how far and how deep the consequences of sin extended. The question was put, in the fourth place, whether bare freedom constituted man's character, or whether it did not correspond to his *nature* to be good. Fifthly, the philosophical question as to the constitution of man was here introduced and answered in various ways [dichotomically, trichotomically, the extent and scope of the flesh (σάρξ) in human nature, in its relation to the spirit (πνεῦμα) and to sin]. Sixthly, the relation of the creaturely spirit (πνεῦμα) to the divine, in other words, the origin of the human spirit, was discussed. Seventhly, lastly, and above all, men possessed two sources of knowledge: the account in Genesis with a realistic exposition, which seemed to pour scorn on all "spiritual" conceptions, but had nevertheless to be respected; and the relative section from Origen's theology, which was felt to an increasing extent to be intolerable to the Church, and which yet expressed the scientific, religious conviction of the Fathers, in so far as their thought was scientific. Under such circumstances different conceptions, compromises of all sorts, necessarily arose; but hardly anywhere was an advance made in the end on the views already presented by Irenæus. In the latest results, as they are to be found in the Dogmatics of John of Damascus, there is much that is more realistic than in Irenæus, but on the whole a type of doctrine is obtained which is more inadequate and confused, and less valuable. In what follows we intend to enter in detail only into the most important points.

## § 2. *The Anthropology.*

Since the end of the creation of the world was held to consist in the creation of rational beings, who could exhibit

the image of God and share in his blessedness, it followed that
the power of free self-determination and the capacity for immortality belonged to the notion of man, and that they were
therefore regarded as inalienable. All the doctors of the Church,
however, comprehended, in the idea of innate freedom, the
conceptions of the rational and moral plan of man's nature as
a whole, and they defined this natural disposition to be the
power to know God's will accurately, to follow it, and thus to
rise above nature. While it was left in doubt whether this
whole natural plan implied that man possessed bare freedom or
freedom directed to the good, it certainly characterised man as
a spiritual being, and for that very reason as an image of God.
Being such, man was independent as regards God. In other
words, the fact that he was an "image" did not directly
establish a lasting dependence on God, nor did it find expression in such a dependence. On the contrary, it established his
freedom in relation to God, so that man, being independent,
was now only subject to *the law of God*, *i.e.*, to that dispensation in virtue of which he was either rewarded or punished
according as he behaved. The connection with God was thus
exhausted in the noble constitution of man fixed once for all,
but was supremely valued and acutely felt as a gift of divine
grace, in the comparison with irrational animals. Meanwhile,
the Fathers differed from one another. Some—like Athanasius,
see even Tatian—assigned to human nature, in the strictest
sense of the term, only the creaturely and sensuous state of
being, in respect of which man is perishable, and they described everything else as a gift of divine grace inherent in
human nature. Others embraced in this nature the moral capacity, endowment of reason, and knowledge of God;—so the
majority; and very strenuously John of Damascus who repeatedly characterises the good as the natural: see De fide orthod.
II. 30, III. 14. The third class, finally, included even immortality, as a possession and not merely as a destiny, among the
natural attributes of the human soul. These distinctions, which,
however, are not particularly important for dogmatics, since all
ultimately held nature to be a gift of grace, and the gift of
grace to be a natural provision, were due partly to the differ-

ent psychological conceptions of the Fathers, partly to the standpoint from which they investigated the problems; they might —as *e.g.*, Athanasius—start from the doctrine of redemption or depend on moral, or empirical philosophical considerations. In psychology, the only point settled was that the fundamental form of human nature was twofold, spiritual and corporeal. This conception existed even where the soul itself was represented as something corporeal, or as only "as nearly as possible incorporeal" (ἐγγύτατα τοῦ ἀσωμάτου). Very many Greek Fathers, however, followed the view of Plato and Origen, according to which man consists of spirit, body, and soul—the soul uniting the other two. Consistently carried out, this opinion constantly led them back to the conception of Origen (Philo) that the spirit in man alone constituted his true nature, that it had its own, even a pretemporal, history, that in itself it belonged to the supernatural and divine sphere, and that the body was only a prison which had to be stripped off before the spirit could present itself in its true being. In order to escape these consequences, which were already discredited in the controversy with Neoplatonism and Manichæism, different methods were adopted. Among these occurred that already alluded to above, the conception of the spirit solely as a "super-added gift" (donum superadditum), a religious principle, to be found exclusively in the pious. But this expedient was seldom chosen; the whole question, so important and crucial, was rather stifled in a hundred questions of detail, tortured out of, or read into, the account in Genesis. The ever increasing restriction of the allegorical and spiritualising method of interpreting Gen. I. ff., led the Fathers *nolens-volens* to opinions remote from their scientific thought on religion The only passage in that account, moreover, which seemed to support the spiritualistic conception —"God breathed his own breath into man"—proved too much, and had therefore to be let alone. [1]  Origen's idea, that the

---

[1] Augustine's exposition in Ep. CCV. 19, was ultimately the opinion of most of the Greek Fathers, so far as they were not completely devoted to Neoplatonism. "Vis etiam per me scire, utrum dei flatus ille in Adam idem ipse sit anima. Breviter respondeo, aut ipse est aut ipso anima facta est. *Sed si ipse est, factus est ...* In hac enim quæstione maxime cavendum est, ne anima non a deo facta natura,

body was a prison of the soul, was contrasted with the other, also ancient, that man was rather a microcosm, having received parts from the two created worlds, the upper and under.[1] But this conception, the only one which contained a coherent theory of equal value formally with the doctrine of Origen, could not fail to remain a mere theory, for the ethics corresponding to it, or its ethical ideal, were not supported by the final aims of the dominant theology. When anthropological questions or the Biblical narrative were not directly taken into account, it becomes everywhere obvious, that the old Platonic antithesis of spirit and body was regarded by the Fathers as the antithesis between that which was precious and that which was to be mortified, and that the earthly and creaturely in man was felt to be a hampering barrier which was to be surmounted. Monachism and the eschatological prospect of deification are examples which show how thoroughly practical ideas and hopes were determined by the dualistic view, though its point had been blunted by the tenet of the resurrection of the body. Meanwhile the theoretical doctrines as to the nature of man continued to be beset by a profound inconsistency, and ultimately, in consequence of Biblicism, became aimless and barren.[2]

*Supplement.*—The different psychological views of the Fathers are reflected in the various theories as to the origin of individual souls. The oldest of these was the *traducian* theory of Tertullian, which was also represented by a few Greeks—Gregory of Nyssa, Anastasius Sinaita. According to

sed ipsius dei substantia tamquam unigenitus filius, quod est verbum eius, aut aliqua eius particula esse credatur, tamquam illa natura atque substantia, qua deus est quidquid est, commutabilis esse possit: quod esse animam nemo non sentit, qui se animam habere sentit." But the thought which underlay the last saying of the dying Plotinus (Porphyr., Vita Plot., ch. 2): πειρῶμαι τὸ ἐν ἡμῖν θεῖον ἀνάγειν πρὸς τὸ ἐν τῷ παντὶ θεῖον, was not entirely surmounted by many Greek Fathers.

1 Therefore the great controversy lasting for centuries, whether the skins with which God clothed Adam and Eve were real skins, or bodies. He who agreed with Origen taught the latter; he who looked on man as a microcosm, the former. Yet here also there were composite forms: *e.g.*, the skin meant only the fleshly body.

2 Scriptural proofs in support of the pre-existence of souls were not wanting: see John IX. 2. Jerome held to the doctrine for a time. Even Augustine was uncertain, and up to the time of Gregory the Great its flat rejection had not been determined on in the West (see Ep. VII. 53).

it the soul was begotten along with the body. Its extreme
opposite was Origen's idea of *pre-existence* which had still many
adherents in the fourth century, but fell more and more into
discredit, until, finally, it was expressly condemned at the
Synod of Constantinople, A. D. 553. According to this doctrine,
all souls were created at once by God along with the upper
world, and fell successively into the lower world, and into their
bodies. The middle view—an expedient of perplexity—was the
*creatian* which gradually gained ground all through the fourth
century, and can be characterised as the most wide-spread, at
least in the West, from the beginning of the fifth. It taught
that God was ever creating souls and planting them in the
embryos. The East contented itself with disowning Origen's
theory. Augustine, the greatest theologian of the West, was
unable to come to any fixed view regarding the origin of the soul.

   The different views of the Fathers are further reflected in
the different conceptions of the image of God in man. Religious
and moral speculation were to be harmonised at this point;
for the former was, indeed, never wholly wanting. Apart from
such theologians as saw the image of God, somehow or other,
even in the human figure, almost all were convinced that it
consisted in reason and freedom. But with this it was impossible
to remain perfectly satisfied, since man was still able to break
away from God, so as in fact to become unlike him, and to die.
On the other hand, theologians were certain that goodness and
moral purity never could be innate. In order to solve the
problem, different methods were adopted. Some abandoned
the premise that the possession of the divine image was
inalienable, and maintained that as it resided in the spirit that
had been bestowed it could be completely lost through sinful
sensuousness. The spirit returned to God, and the man relapsed
to the level of the beasts. But this solution seemed unsatisfactory, because it was necessary, in spite of it, to retain the
freedom that still, under all circumstances, existed to choose
the good. Accordingly, it was impossible to treat this theory
with any real seriousness. Others saw the possession of the
Divine image, resting on reason and freedom, in the destiny
of man to virtue and immortality, yet without stating what

change in that case was actually made by falling short of this destiny. The third section, finally, distinguished, after the example of Origen, between "image" (εἰκών) and "likeness" (ὁμοίωσις), and saw the former in the inalienable spiritual plan of man, the latter in moral similarity to God, which was, indeed, one always to be gained on the basis of natural endowments. The Fathers were unwilling, as this review shows, to rest content with the thought that the inalienable spiritual natural endowment of man constituted the divine image, but they found no means of getting beyond it. Their conception of moral goodness as the product of human freedom hindered them. All the more strongly did they emphasise and praise, as a kind of set-off, the goodness of God as Creator revealed in the natural constitution of man.

The different views of the Fathers are finally reflected in their conception of the primitive state. Christianity restores man to his state of ideal perfection. This state must, however, have already existed in some form at the beginning, since God's creation is perfect, and Genesis teaches, that man when created was good, and in a condition of blessedness (Paradise). On the other hand, it could not have been perfect, since man's perfection could not be attained except through freedom. The problem resolves itself into a complete contradiction, which, indeed, was already clearly to be found in Irenæus: the original condition of man must coincide with the state of perfection, and yet it must only have been preliminary. The Fathers tried various ways of solving this crucial and insoluble difficulty, in which again the empirical and moral philosophical conception combined with a religious one. An attempt was made by very many Fathers to limit somewhat the blessedness of the Paradisaical state, or to give a form to their conceptions of it different in quality—fanciful and material—from that of their ideas of the final perfection; accordingly, it was explained —by Gregory of Nyssa—that God himself, looking to the Fall, had not ordained the Paradisaical state to be perfect. By some, again, the inconsistencies were glossed over, while others determined, following Origen, wholly to abandon the historical interpretation of the state in Paradise, and to construct independently a primitive state for themselves. The last method had the advantage, in combination with the assumption of the pre-existence of souls, that it could transfer *all* men mystically into the original state. However, this radical solution conflicted too strongly with the letter of revelation, and the spirit of the Church tradition. It was rejected, and thus the problem remained in its obscurity. Therefore men contented themselves more and more with disregarding the main question : they set down incongruities side by side, and extracted separate points from the account in Genesis. To the latter belonged especially those which were believed to recommend virginity and as-ceticism, and to prove that these formed the mode of life *(habitus)* which corresponded to the true nature of man. Nor were opinions wanting that characterised asceticism as a salutary means of correcting the deterioration of the human state. "Asceticism and its toils were not invented to procure the virtue that comes from without, but to remove superinduced and unnatural vileness, just as we restore the natural brightness of iron by carefully removing the rust, which is not natural, but has come to it through negligence" (John of Damascus, De fide orth. III. 14).

The principles of ethics were, as a rule, discussed in con-nection with the original state of man. But even in reference to the blessedness enjoyed in that state no clear conception was reached ; for if man's distinctive nature was based on bare freedom, what sort of blessedness could there be for him? What could be bestowed on him which he did not possess already, or which, if bestowed, did not once more call in question the original possession? What could fall to his lot except an arbitrarily chosen reward? Again, as regards ethics, nothing certain could be established. While negative morality, asceticism, was conceived, as a rule, to be the natural and destined condition of man, yet an effort was made to construct an ideal of positive morality, in which the virtues of philoso-phy appeared in a rather superficial connection with those of religion. [1] Negative and positive morality each looked up, after

---

[1] See here even the Latins. Ambrosius learned the combination, as carried out by him in his De officiis, from the Cappadocians ; see also the remarkable opening

all, to a different supreme good, in the one case immortality, in the other the loftiest virtue. Therefore they could not be combined. The assumption of works of supererogation, which the Christian could accomplish while remaining in the world, formed the bridge between the two ethical ideals, but one which it must be admitted, contributed to flight from the one sphere to the other, rather than their connection. All attacks on the theory that ascetic achievements were especially valuable and meritorious were regarded as the outcome of moral laxity, and it is certain that in many cases they actually were.

## § 3. *Ethics. Sin.*

It was recognised by all the Fathers that the human race had turned from the good and thus degenerated from its origin, *i.e.,*—according to the view of the majority—from Adam. This universality of sin was throughout explained, not from an innate wicked power in man impelling him necessarily to sin, nor from matter in itself, still less from complicity on the part of the Deity.[1] Nor, on the other hand, was it as a rule ascribed to a direct inheritance of Adam's sin, for inherited sin is a contradiction in itself; Adam was the type, but not the ancestor, of sinners. The true explanation was found in the misuse of freedom, caused by the seductions of wicked demons, and the transmission of wicked customs. Along with this, the majority undoubtedly cherished the secret idea, which was not surmounted, that the incentive to revolt from God[2] came to a certain extent

of his work De pœnit. I. 1: "If the final and supreme aim of all virtue is to minister as far as possible to the spiritual benefit of our fellow-man, we may characterise benevolent moderation as one of the finest virtues." For the popular conceptions of Greek Christians, see Socr. H. E. III. 16, in connection with Rom. I. On the other hand, Augustine attempted to derive the philosophic virtues from man's dependence on God, from love; see, above all, the splendid exposition, Ep. CLV., ch. 12.

[1] Even the subtle way in which Origen justified evil as an element in the best possible world (see Vol. II., p. 343 f.) was seldom repeated. Yet see Augustine, De ordine II. 11 sq. (one of his oldest writings): "mala in ordinem redacta faciunt decorem universi."

[2] Sin was described as something negative not only by Augustine, but by all thinking Greeks before him. Their conception was undoubtedly based on a philo-

necessarily from the sensuous nature and creaturely infirmity
of man, and resulted from his composite constitution, and his
liability to death, whether that was acquired naturally or by
transgression, or inherited. Decay and death were especially
held to constitute an inducement to and cause of continuance in
sin. With natural sensuousness the fate of death was conjoined.
Both drove man from God. But in spite of this view the
assumption was retained of unaltered freedom. If on the one
hand stress was laid on sensuousness being a natural endowment of man, the unnaturalness of wickedness was emphasised
on the other, and thus bare freedom received a closer relation
to goodness, which, of course, was conceived as repressed by
sin. The good was the natural, but, again, in view of man's
sensuousness, unnatural evil was also natural to him. The essence
of sin, since wickedness was held to be something purely negative, was universally seen in alienation from God, being and
goodness; but all that this meant positively was that man had
subordinated his will to his sensuousness, and thereby lost the
feeling, desire, and knowledge of the divine. The consequences
of sin were held to be the following: First, by the majority,
the universal mortality which had prevailed from Adam, or the
loss of the true life;[1] secondly, the obscuration of the knowledge of God, and with it of religion in general. This darkening made it possible for the demons to seduce man from the
true God, to gain him to their own service, and the idolatry of
the creature, in the form of polytheism, and so even to exercise
an almost complete dominion over him, and the earth associated
with humanity. A third consequence of sin was found in a
certain weakening of freedom, which, though still existing, yet
only in rare cases succeeded, without new divine influences,
in reaching a morally good, perfect life.

sophical view that God was not only the originator of being, but really the sole
being. On the other hand, a distinction was made between the eternal being and
the creaturely, which came from God.

[1] The Antiochenes thought differently (see under), and so did the author of the
App. Const., who is exceedingly lax in his views; see, e.g., V. 7, p. 132 (Ed.
Lagarde). The latter regards death as an original divine institution, which makes
it possible for God to punish or reward. The resurrection was due to the rational
soul from God.

*Supplement.*—The view taken by Irenæus and Tertullian of the fundamental importance of the first Fall for the whole future race, was imperilled by Origen's theory of a fall on the part of spirits in their preëxistent state. It once more gradually won acceptance as an authoritative Biblical doctrine, but it never obtained the same certainty, clearness, or importance among the Greek Fathers as among the Latin (*i.e.*, after Ambrose); see Book II. of our description. The explanation which the theory of original sin furnished for the phenomenon of universal sinfulness was in form similar to Origen's, but was inferior to it in intelligibility, and was never unreservedly accepted by the Orientals. The later Greeks indeed, doubtless under the influence of the West, recognised original sin, but this only resulted in a contradiction; for the thought that each man was born *in puris naturalibus*, was, while no longer strictly formulated, never actually condemned. The old dilemma remained, that each man sinned either from a necessity of his nature or in virtue of his freedom; and the former opinion was at all times held in the East to be Manichæan. Inherited death, due to Adam, was taught as a rule; yet even in this matter certain views were never wholly obliterated which are only intelligible if death was regarded as something natural. From the point of view of the doctrine of redemption especially, it could seem more pertinent to hold death to be the natural destiny of man, from which, however, redemption delivered him. Accordingly, after Origen's theory had been abandoned on account of its want of Biblical support, all that was got in exchange for it was a contradiction: death was something natural and again unnatural. We cannot wonder at this contradiction; in the same way, no one really held the immortality assigned to the primitive state to be something indisputably natural, but neither was it regarded as absolutely supernatural.

## § 4. *The Fall and Original Sin. Doctrine of Redemption.*

This is the place to define more precisely the influence which this Natural Theology gained on Dogmatics, *i.e.*, on the conceptions of redemption through Jesus Christ. In so doing we

must keep firmly in mind, that, in spite of this influence, the
feeling remained uppermost that redemption was something
superlatively exalted, something unmerited, a pure gift of God
to humanity. This feeling was, however, more and more encouraged also by the fact that the simple tenets of Natural
Theology fell into confusion and became less impressive through
the enjoined and ever increasing attention to Biblical texts re-
alistically interpreted, and the necessity of repelling the system
of Origen. To this was added the constantly growing reluctance
to reflect independently at all, as well as the grand impressions
made by the divine dispensation which culminated in the incarnation of the Son of God, and was brought to view in the
mysteries.

In the first place, the conviction of the lofty and, at bottom,
inalienable dignity of man roused the idea that man receives
through redemption that which corresponds to his nature. If
adoption to the sonship of God and participation in the divine
nature appeared on the one hand as a gift above all reason
and expectation, yet it was looked at on the other as corresponding to the nature of man already fixed in his creation.
For man *is* God's image, and exalted as he is above the lower
animals by his constitution, rises as a spiritual being into the
heavenly sphere.

Secondly, the last word that Natural Theology has to say
of man is that he is a free and rational being, introduced into
the opposition of good and evil. Such a being has really to
do with God only in his capacity of *creator* and *rewarder*.
All other points of contact must necessarily always resolve into
that. Again, for such a being there can only exist one good,
that is knowledge, which includes virtue, and besides this certain rewards alone find a place; for his nature requires that he
should be independent in all his movements, nay, these only
possess any value through such independence. The Deity stands
at the beginning and the close of the history of free men as
the power that creates and rewards. But the intervening space
is not occupied by the Deity himself in order to govern man,
and to preserve his allegiance. On the contrary, man has to
deal solely with divine knowledge and rules in accordance with

which his freedom is meant to evince itself; for this freedom, while in itself a liberty of choice, was given to him that he might achieve, in a zealous pursuit of virtue based on rational knowledge, the moral perfection possessed by the Deity Himself. This whole view, which is familiar to us from the Apologists, was never completely lost by the Greek Fathers. Its first consequence was that henceforth the whole of religion could be,—as already in the case of the Apologists—and was, looked at from the point of view of *knowledge* and *law*. It appeared as a morality based on pure knowledge of God and the world, one to which nothing could be added. Along with freedom, the natural moral law was implanted in man, that is, the sure consciousness of the rules, by which he had to prove what was in him. The rules corresponded ultimately to the laws of the universe set in operation and maintained by God as supreme First Cause. This natural law, when it had been obscured in the mind of man, was repeated in the Decalogue by an external legislation, and, on account of the hard-heartedness of the Jews, was supplemented with burdens, temporary commandments; and it was finally reduced by Jesus Christ to the simplest of formulas, set in operation by the impressive preaching of rewards and punishments, and perfectly fulfilled by Jesus. He revealed the perfect knowledge of God, and restored the natural moral law—these two statements being really identical, for in both God appears as the supreme cause. [1] In this state-

---

[1] We perceive the Greek conception most clearly from the law in Apost. Const. VI. 19—24. The section begins with the words : γνόντες γὰρ Θεὸν διὰ Ἰησοῦ Χριστοῦ καὶ τὴν σύμπασαν αὐτοῦ οἰκονομίαν ἀρχῆθεν γεγενημένην, ὅτι δέδωκε νόμον ἁπλοῦν εἰς βοήθειαν τοῦ φυσικοῦ καθαρόν, σωτήριον, ἅγιον, ἐν ᾧ καὶ τὸ ἴδιον ὄνομα ἐγκατέθετο. The Decalogue is meant; it was given to the nation before its revolt, and God had no intention of adding sacrificial regulations, but tolerated sacrifices. After the revolt (of the golden calf) he himself, however, gave the ceremonial law: "He bound the people with irremovable fetters, and imposed heavy burdens and a hard yoke upon them, that they might abandon idolatry and turn again to that law which God had implanted by nature in all men" (ch. XX.). These "branding irons, lancets, and medicines" were, however, only for the sick. Christians who voluntarily believed in one God were delivered by him, above all, from the sacrificial service. Christ has fulfilled (κυρώσας) the law, but removed the additions, "if not all, yet the more irksome"; this is the opposite of Tertullian's opinion. He restored man's right of self-determination, and in doing so confirmed the natural law (τὸν φυσικὸν νόμον ἐβεβαίωσεν). More rigorous conditions are only

ment we have already mentioned the second consequence of the speculation: all grace can only possess the character of a support, of a rectification of knowledge. The whole of the operations of God's grace are in the end, crutches offered to feeble man. In offering them, God reveals a goodness which, after what he has already done in creation, is without any fixed limit. Grace is therefore not absolutely necessary for every man. [1] God, again, by no means reveals himself in it even as the blessing which man requires, but he simply imparts complete knowledge, and thus explains, and strengthens the motives for observing, the rules of conduct which man had long possessed. But in the third place, it follows from the speculation, that sin is nothing but the transgression, induced by imperfect knowledge, of those rules, whose observance does not exhibit man's dependence on God, but his independence and freedom. Sin subjects man to the judgment of God. Punishment is the gravest result of sin. But God would not be just, if he were not an indulgent judge. His goodness which supports man, has its counterpart in the indulgence which overlooks the time of ignorance of the individual, and leaves unpunished the sins of men whenever they feel penitent. [2] Since it is impossible in this whole

apparent. Just vengeance is even yet permitted, toleration is only better: οὐ τὰ φυσικὰ πάθη ἐκκόπτειν ἐνομοθέτησεν ἀλλὰ τὴν τούτων ἀμετρίαν (This is not the usual Greek view, but a conception peculiar to this lax author). But Christ himself abolished what had been "added" solely by fulfilling it first in his life and death, or by transforming the ceremonies into spiritual rites. The respect which Irenæus, as distinguished from the older teachers, had already entertained for the ceremonial law is shown even more clearly here.

[1] Yet see what is said below on Macarius.

[2] Forgiveness of sins was a conception which in this connection could hardly be carried out by the Fathers. The passing over of the time of ignorance and the acceptance of the reparation involved in penitence constituted forgiveness. Hardly another teacher from and after the fourth century, has expressed it so clearly as Clemens Alex.: τῶν προγεγενημένων Θεὸς δίδωσιν ἄφεσιν, τῶν δὲ ἐπιόντων αὐτὸς ἕκαστος ἑαυτῷ (Quis div. salv. 40, cf. Strom. II. 14, 58, and elsewhere); but the statement as to Christ in Pædag. I. 3, 7: τὰ μὲν ἁμαρτήματα ὡς Θεὸς ἀφιείς, εἰς δὲ τὸ μὴ ἐξαμαρτάνειν παιδαγωγῶν ὡς ἄνθρωπος, formed a part of the fundamental view of the following age. We cannot wonder at this. Between mechanical expiations and penitence there is in fact no third term, as soon as the forgiveness of sins is applied to individual cases. Only where faith in forgiveness is *the* faith itself, is it more than a word, and yet not magical.

question that there can be any suggestion of a restoration of man to that communion with God which he had forsaken, since on the contrary, the sole point was that man, to whom it was always possible to return, should not be impeded while striving and yet stumbling, the view was, in fact, inevitable that God remits punishment to every penitent. God would not appear just, but harsh and unloving, if he did not accept sincere penitence as an equivalent for transgressions. It was accordingly agreed that, although men are sinners, they become just in the sight of God through virtue and penitence, and redemption to eternal life through Christ can only benefit such as have acquired this righteousness through their independent efforts. The sacraments initiated men into this effort to obtain virtue, and they had also an indescribable influence upon it. But personal fulfilment of the law was still something thoroughly independent. Finally, it followed from this moral view, that it was impossible to gain a clear idea of the state of perfection. A state of freedom and a perfect virtue based on perfect knowledge cannot be raised higher than they are, and that which is given to reward the latter can never be intrinsically connected with it. The complete vacuity of the conceptions held of the final state, apart from the effect of the hope of an ever increasing knowledge, *i.e.*, vision of God, was accordingly also the natural consequence of the conviction that man, because he is free, is dependent on no one, and that he is always at the goal when he fulfils the law of God.

Thirdly, the rationalistic exposition of the doctrine of God and creation could not fail to impel apologists to expound the reasonableness of the doctrines of the Trinity, the resurrection of the body, etc. As a matter of fact the attempt was even made to prove the existence of a general agreement, a "common sense", as to the doctrine of the Trinity, and references were especially made to heathen philosophers, though, on the other hand, when it seemed expedient, the Greeks were denied any knowledge of the Trinity. Such references were all the more natural, since Neoplatonic philosophers, and at an earlier date Numenius, had constructed a kind of trinity. Cyril, again, in his Catechisms, supported

the resurrection of the body to a very large extent on rational
grounds, and others followed his example. For the extent to
which even the doctrine of the Incarnation was included in
Natural Theology, see following chapter.

Fourthly, from all this it followed, that man could ultimately
receive nothing from history which he could not, nay, had not
to, wrest for himself. But the Logos in the flesh (λόγος ἔνσαρκος)
belonged to history. Accordingly, it was impossible wholly to
get rid of the view that there was a standpoint for which the
historical Christ, since he was merely the edifying teacher,
meant nothing. This view was, as we know, expressed perfectly plainly by Origen (see Vol. II., p. 342, n. 1); and in
this he by no means stood alone. It was not only repeated
by half-heathen theologians, like Synesius, but it runs like a
hidden thread through the conceptions of all Greek theologians,
as long as they continued to think independently. It is the
negative complement of the idea that the knowledge accompanied by virtue, which transcends all that is visible, and therefore all that is historical, includes blessedness in itself, and
moreover, that it can be achieved from our own resources
through a direct *afflatus divinus*. But still further: even in
Augustine this view was not wholly surmounted. The man,
who perceived the Deity, and had gained faith, love, and hope,
stood beside the throne of God, and was with the Father of
light and his essential Word; the historical Christ lay beneath
him. [1] Further, even opponents of Origen, like Methodius and
his successors, the mystics, had arrived at the same conception
(see Vol. III., p. 110). For the ascetic mystic history passed
away along with the world; he might cast aside all crutches,
traversing independently the long, mysterious path from the
extreme outside to the inmost recess of the spiritual. At the
end of this path there stood, not Jesus Christ, but the unem-
bodied Logos (λόγος ἄσαρκος), since he was pure truth and pure
life. An incarnate Christ (ἔνσαρκος) was born in each who traversed this path. He in whom Christ was born, however, no
longer needed the historical Christ. [2]

[1] Augustine, De doctr. I. 34.

[2] See even Augustine, on John, tract. 21. n. 8: "Gratulemur et gratias agamus

Rationalism, or Christianity as the moral law which is freely fulfilled, and mysticism are regarded as opposites, and so they are before the tribunal of philosophy. But before that of positive religion they are not, they are rather akin, at least in the form in which they confront us in antiquity. [1] Mysticism of course embraces germs which when unfolded will resist rationalism. But at first it is nothing but rationalism applied to a sphere above reason (ratio). The admission that there was such a sphere formed the difference. It was mysticism as much as rationalistic moralism which secretly formed an opposition to the Christianity proclaimed by Jesus Christ to be *the way and the truth for all men and for every grade.* The most vital piety of the Greek Fathers, and the strenuous effort to make themselves at home in religion, insured them at least against losing the historical Christ.

But it was only a danger that here threatened. We may not say more. The Deity had come down to earth, God had become man, and that in the historical Jesus—faith in this stupendous fact, "the newest of the new, nay, the only new thing under the sun," limited all rationalism. It imperatively demanded the investigation, on the one hand, of the ground and cause, on the other, of the fruit and blessing, of this divine dispensation. It was necessary to find the relation of the latter to the mystery and horror of death. It was indeed impossible to make the "naturalness" of death credible; for all nature, higher and lower, rebelled against it. And the consciousness of a capacity for perfect knowledge and goodness underlay in practical life the sense of incapacity. Hence the conviction that man must be redeemed, and through Jesus Christ is redeemed. The doctrines of innate freedom, the law, and the independent achievement of virtue were not abandoned;

non solum nos Christianos factos esse, sed Christum ... admiramini gaudete: Christus facti sumus."

[1] Bigg (The Christian Platonists of Alex., 1886, p. 51 f.) has also correctly perceived this; he is speaking of the attitude of Clement and of the Alexandrians generally: "On one side Rationalist, on another Mystic." "Though there is in them a strong vein of Common Sense or Rationalism, they were not less sensible of the mystic supernatural side of the religious life than Irenæus. *The difference is that with them the mystical grows out of the rational.*"

but they were counterbalanced by faith in the necessity and reality of redemption. And this combination, unsatisfactory as it seems to us, was yet capable of forming men of Christian character. Such men were never wanting in any century of the older Greek Church after Athanasius and Chrysostom, although their theology lacked the confession of the Psalmist: "It is good for me to cleave to God" (Mihi adhærere deo bonum est). [1]

---

Instead of multiplying details we may here give the views on freedom, sin, and grace, of four eminent Greek Fathers, Athanasius, Gregory of Nyssa, Theodore of Mopsuestia, and John of Damascus.

(1) Athanasius.—The conceptions formed by Athanasius of the original state of man, of sin and grace, show especially his inability to distinguish between nature and grace. In his work "De incarnatione"[2] he strove to prove that the incarnation was a necessity on the part of God. Therefore he emphasises strongly the destiny of man, and distinguishes it sharply from his empirical condition; for this destiny sets God a task which he must carry out under all circumstances, if his goodness (ἀγαθότης) is to remain in force. Therefore, in many of the arguments of this work, human nature appears as the creaturely and sensuous constitution, while everything else, including the endowment of reason, takes the form of a *donum superadditum*, potentially given in the original state, and binding on God himself, a gift of grace, which was meant to rise to complete

[1] The text is indeed quoted by Macarius (Ep. I. *fin*) as the sum of all knowledge. But even to this theologian, who came nearest Western thought in some paraenetic remarks, and frequently drew the sharpest contrast between nature and grace (see Hom. I. 10, IV. 7—9), the "cleaving to God" meant nothing but the independent decision for God. The following passage (Hom. IV. 5) proves how remote Macarius was from Augustine: "How should God treat a man who, in the exercise of free will, devotes himself to the world, lets himself be seduced by its pleasures, or revels in dissipations? God only sends his help to him who renounces worldly pleasures, and preserves himself completely from the snares and traps of the sensuous world," etc. Here we see that the contrast between nature and grace was not so seriously meant. The same is the case with "law and gospel." No Greek Father was able to regard these as contrasted in the same way as we see them in the writings of Paul and Augustine.

[2] On its authenticity, see the next chapter.

knowledge of God through the free moral development of man
—for that was the goal. [Athanasius uses very different expressions for this in his writings: φαντασία περὶ Θεόυ (power
of conceiving God), γνῶσις (knowledge) κατανόησις (perception)
κατάληψις (comprehension) θεωρία τῶν θείων (theory of divine
things) θεωρία τῶν νοητῶν (—of the intelligible) θεωρία περὶ τοῦ
Θεοῦ (science of God) ἔννοια τῆς εἰς πατέρα γνώσεως (concept
of knowledge as to the Father)]. The change which took place
in man through sin, or through death, is accordingly conceived
as a loss of the divine. God is at the same time supremely
interested in preventing man, once destined to obtain perfect
divine knowledge, from becoming a prey to his lower nature,
and being destroyed. [1]

But even in the De incarn., and to a still greater extent
in his later anti-Arian writings, Athanasius defends the idea that
the rational spirit (ψυχὴ λογική—Athanasius being a dichotomist)
belongs to man's constitution, is immortal, and at bottom also
inalienable. This ψυχὴ λογικὴ can gradually recognise the Logos
and God from creation; it is, accordingly, not only an inalienable religious *talent*, but also an inalienable religious *factor*.
Its power extends so far that there have been holy men in all
ages (c. gent. 2; c. Arian. III. 33: πολλοὶ γὰρ οὖν ἅγιοι γεγόνασι
καθαροὶ πάσης ἁμαρτίας). The reconciliation of the two contradictory statements, that the higher endowment appears first as
grace, then as nature, is to be found in the following points.
(1) The ψυχὴ λογικὴ is only rational (logical) because it parti-
cipates in the Logos, is his image, possesses a shadow of him
(De incarn. 3), and retains its power only when steadfastly connected with him. For this reason it can be termed, although a
natural provision, an "external" (c. Arian. II. 68: "Adam was
outside before his transgression, having received grace and not
having had it adapted to his body"; ὁ Ἀδὰμ πρὸ τῆς παραβάσεως ἔξωθεν ἦν, λαβὼν τὴν χάριν καὶ μὴ συνηρμοσμένην ἔχων
αὐτὴν τῷ σώματι). (2) It is only in the apologetic arguments
of the treatise De incarn. that Adam's fall and its consequence
appear as forming a tremendous cleavage, and the state before

---

[1] De incarn. IV.: ἡ παράβασις τῆς ἐντολῆς εἰς τὸ κατὰ φύσιν αὐτοὺς ἐπέστρεψεν.
Accordingly, everything is supernatural which raises man above the level of nature.

and after the fall as a contrast. That was not the characteristic view of Athanasius,[1] as is shown by other arguments in the same writing, and the rest of the tractates. He contemplates not a loss once for all, but a gradual enfeeblement. Mankind has more and more lost, from generation to generation, the consciousness of God, *i.e.*, through the darkening of his mind. That which above all burdened humanity, however, was not sin, but the sentence of death pronounced by God on the sinner— see next chapter. The faculties for knowing God, and thus for attaining the goal, remained, but there was no corresponding power actually to reach the goal. A Catholic investigator has expressed this as follows:[2] "Sinful man gradually lost, according to Athanasius, what was supernatural in his prerogatives, and retained only what was natural. Supernatural were moral goodness on the one hand, the correct consciousness and due use of rationality and immortality on the other; while rationality and immortality generally were natural." The intrusion here of the modern Catholic categories of "natural and "supernatural" is incorrect; for the spiritual nature of man was held by all the Fathers to be supernatural. But the idea is correct. But we must go further. The difference here is exclusively quantitative; it is only qualitative from the fact that what remains of higher powers is as a rule of less than its initial value, *i.e.*, is no longer capable of reaching the goal. The same Catholic scholar is therefore perfectly correct, when —expressing himself with due caution—he finds (p. 159 f.) that Athanasius "does not seem to treat" the punishment of sin—better, sin — "with sufficient gravity". "He teaches, indeed, that the spiritual gifts of man were lost through sin, but he conceives this ruin as gradual in time and degree, depending on the extent to which men had turned from the contemplation of the spiritual and to the sensuous"; *i.e.*, Athanasius simply follows an empirical and natural line of thought, in virtue of which he finds in mankind very different grades of moral and intellectual position. That this was a consequence of human freedom con-

---

[1] Against Wendt, Die christl. Lehre von der menschlichen Volkommenheit (1880), p. 47 f.

[2] Atzberger, Die Logoslehre des h. Athanasius. (1880), p. 156.

stituted a sufficient explanation in itself and freed the Deity of
all blame. But it did not explain the universality of death,
and left out of account Gen. I.—III. The above empirical view,
which ultimately, indeed, cast a certain shadow on the Deity,
and these chapters of the Bible compelled him to secure, somehow or other, a historical beginning for the present condition
and therewith an original state of man. But the relations of
the present to that beginning are really exhausted in the continuance of the once pronounced sentence of death; [1] and the
primitive state, which is clearly enough described (c. gentes 2,
De incarn. 3, 4) as a destiny—Adam himself having not yet
attained what his endowments fitted him for, continued in this
sense; nay, it ultimately embraced the idea that God was under
the necessity of bringing the sentence of death to an end.

However, Athanasius did arrive at positive conclusions as to
the specific grace bestowed in the Christian redemption, in his
polemic against the Arians. It is not to be wondered at that
the discussion of grace in connection with creation and the
natural endowments of man only resulted, on the premises
stated by the Fathers, in tautologies. But against the Arians,
where Athanasius was not interested in cosmology, he shows
that we have received from grace what was by nature peculiar
to the Son, and he definitely distinguishes between grace in
creation and in redemption. Deut. XXXII. 6, 7, 18, where it
is said that God created and begot men, he interprets as follows:
" By creating, Moses describes the natural state of men, for
they are works and beings made; by begetting, he lets us see
the love of God to them after their creation" (c. Arian. II. 58).
Similarly on John I. 12, 13: "John makes use of the words
'to become' because they are called sons, not by nature, but
by adoption; but he has employed the word 'begotten', because
they in any case have received the name of son... The goodness of God consists in this, that he afterwards becomes, by
grace, the father of those whose creator he already is. He
becomes their father, however, when—as the Apostle says—
the men who have been created receive into their hearts the
Spirit of his Son, which calls, 'Abba, Father.' But the latter

[1] All men were lost in Adam's transgression," c. Arian. II. 61.

consist of all who have received the Word and have obtained power from him to become children of God. For since by nature they are creatures, they can only become sons by receiving the spirit of the natural and true Son. In order that this may happen the Word became flesh, that men might be made capable of receiving the Deity. This conception can also be found in the Prophet Malachi, who says: 'Did not one God create you? Have you not all one Father?' For here again he says in the first place 'created', and in the second 'father', in order similarly to show that we are first, and by nature, creatures, but afterwards are adopted as sons, God the creator becoming also our father," etc. (c. Arian. II. 59). These expositions are certainly worth noting, but we must not overestimate them; for in the same discourses against the Arians they are modified to the effect that our sonship depends on the Logos dwelling in us, *i.e.*, it receives a cosmological basis (see c. Arian. III. 10). In some passages it indeed looks as if the Logos only dwelt in us in consequence of the incarnation (see above and l. c. IV. 22); but it is quite clear in others that Athanasius thought of an indwelling before the incarnation, an indwelling wholly independent of it. With the recollection that there were sons of God in the O. T., Athanasius proves that the Logos was eternal. Accordingly, it is with him as with Clement of Alexandria: when the Fathers are not dealing with apologetic theology, and disregard the O. T., they are able to comprehend and describe the grace due to the historical Christ in its specific significance; but when they reason connectedly everything ultimately resolves into the natural endowment fixed once for all.

*Literature.*—See, besides the works quoted of Atzberger and Wendt, Möhler, Athanasius, I. p. 136 ff. Voigt, Athanasius, p. 104 ff., and Ritschl, Rechtfertigung und Versöhnung, 2 Ed. Vol. I. p. 8 ff.

(2) Gregory of Nyssa.—Gregory's theories also appear to be hampered by a contradiction because they are sketched from two different points of view. On the one hand he regards the nature of man in spirit and body as constituting his true being. To him, as opposed to Origen, the whole earthly world is

good, a mirror of divine wisdom and power, a place meant to
be pervaded by the divine. Before this could be possible "it
was necessary that a union should be effected between its
essential elements and the higher spiritual and divine nature,
whereby first the divine shone as through a glass into the earthly
world, after which the earthly, elevated with the divine, could
be freed from liability to decay, and be transfigured. This central significance, this part of constituting a bond between two
worlds in themselves opposed, was assigned to man, who stood
at the head of the ascending scale of earthly creatures, which
he comprehended like a microcosm, while he also as λογικὸν
ζῶον (a rational being) projected into the invisible world, in
virtue of his nature made in the image of God, *i.e.*, spiritual
and moral, and, especially, ethically free. This nature of man,
besides, being created, possessed nothing of itself, but only like
the sun-loving eye turned ever of its own accord to the eternal
light, living on it, and interpreting it to the earthly world
to which it essentially belonged."[1]   But on the other hand,
though Gregory rejected Origen's theories of the pre-existence
of souls, the pre-temporal fall, and the world as a place of
punishment (περὶ κατασκευῆς ἀνθρώπων, ch. 28, 29), regarding
them as Hellenic dogmas and therefore mythological, yet he
was dominated by the fundamental thought which led Origen
to the above view. The spiritual and the earthly and sensuous resisted each other. If man was, as Scripture says,
created in the image of God,[2] then he was a spiritual being,
and his being so constituted his nature (see l.c. ch. 16—18).
Man was a self-determining, but, because created, a changeable spirit, meant to share in all the blessings of God. So far
as he had a sensuous side, and was mortal, he was not an

---

[1] See Catech. mag. 5, 6, and the work, περὶ ψυχ. κ. ἀναστας., as also περὶ
κατασκ. ἀνθρωπ. 2 ff. 16. Möller in Herzog R.-E., 2 Ed. Vol. V., p. 401, and his work,
Gregorii Nyss. de natura hom. doctr. illustr. et cum Origeniana comparata, 1854.

[2] Orat. I. T. I., p. 150: Κατ᾽ εἰκόνα ἔχω τὸ λογικὸς εἶναι καθ᾽ ὁμοίωσιν δὲ γίνομαι
ἐν τῷ Χριστιανὸς γενέσθαι. The "image" cannot consist in the bodily. The latter
is at most a copy of the "image," see περὶ κατασκ. ἀνθρωπ. 8, 12. But the "image"
itself implies that it can only really be completely produced by free self-determination
on the part of man. "If any compulsion obtained, the image would not be realised."
(Catech. mag. 5).

image of God. Gregory now laid stress on man (homo)—as
he conceived it, humanity—having been first created, and then
having been fashioned into male and female. He concluded
from this that the earthly and sensuous side of man was
ἐπιγεννηματική, a subsequent creation, that, accordingly, the
spiritual in man was conceptually the primary, and his sensuous
and bodily nature the secondary, part of him.[1] He further
concluded that man was originally designed to live a sexless
life like the angels, that God would have multiplied men as
he did the angels by his power "in a noble fashion" (περὶ
κατασκ., 17), and that the proper and natural dwelling-place of
men was the pure and incorporeal future state.

But near as he was to consequences drawn by Origen,[2]
Gregory rejected them. The destiny of man sketched above
was an ideal one. In other words, God, looking to the Fall,
at once created and added the earthly and sensuous nature of
man; nay, this was not merely due to the Fall, but, as is
shown by the first line of thought given above, the earthly
nature of man had also, since it was possessed by divine energies
and transfigured, a lasting significance. But the Paradisaical
state in which men lived before the Fall, was not the highest;
for the body was not transfigured, though it had not yet been
stained by sexual intercourse. The highest state, in so far as
it was brought about by the resurrection (εἰς τὸ ἀρχαῖον τῆς
φύσεως ἡμῶν ἀποκατάστασις), was that which notionally preceded
the life in Paradise, but had never till now been concretely
realised. It was life in its incorporeal abode after the fashion
of the angels.[3] The incarnation of God had procured this state

---

[1] We have, however, to make a distinction here. As a creaturely spirit man
necessarily has a body, just as every picture has a material foundation, and every
mirror a back. This body, therefore, belonged, according to Gregory, to the notion
of man's nature; it was the phenomenon of the soul as the latter was the noumenon
of the body. But Gregory distinguishes this body from the sensuous and sexually
differentiated one.

[2] Gregory borders very closely upon them, not only in περὶ κατασκ., but also
in other writings. The fall does not, indeed, take the form of an event in the
experience of individual men actually to be found in a pre-existent state, but of a
kind of "intelligible collective deed of all humanity."

[3] See περὶ κατασκ. ἀνθρωπ. 16—18.

for all who, in virtue of their freedom, led a holy life, *i.e.*, who lived as man did in Paradise before the Fall; for that was possible to man even when on earth. In all this we must remember that Gregory's hold on the traditional dependence on Gen. I.—III. was very loose : he does not speak of Adam, but always of us. All men had the same freedom as Adam.¹ All souls really passed through Adam's history. Above all, no transference of sin took place, although Gregory is a Traducian (see περὶ κατ. ανθρ. ch. 29); every man sinned, because in virtue of his freedom he could sin, and by his sensuous nature (πάθη) was induced to sin. By this means a state of depravity and death was introduced—sin also being death—from which man in fact could not deliver himself. Nothing but the union of God with humanity procured redemption. Redemption was, in harmony with the speculations as to Adam, strictly objective, and the question as to its appropriation was therefore, at bottom, no question. A new condition was revealed for all men without any co-operation on their part, but it became real only to those who led a holy life, *i.e.*, who abstained entirely from sin.

*Literature.*—See, besides Möller's work, Wendt, l.c., p. 49 f.; Herrmann, Gregorii Nyss. sententiæ de salute adipiscenda, 1875; Bergades, De universo et de anima hominis doctrina Gregorii Nyss., Thessalonich, 1876; Stigler, Die Psychologie des hl. Gregor von Nyssa, Regensburg, 1857; Ritschl., l.c. Vol. I. p. 12 ff.; Hilt, Des hl. Gregor von Nyssa Lehre vom Menschen, Köln, 1890.

(3) Theodore.—Even in Irenæus² two inconsistent conceptions of the result of redemption stood side by side. It was held, on the one hand, to restore man to the original state from which he had fallen, and, on the other, to raise him from the primitive natural state of childhood to a higher stage. The

---

¹ Gregory here carries his speculation still further: God did not first create a single man, but the whole race in a previously fixed number; these collectively composed only one nature. They were really *one* man, divided into a multiplicity. Adam—that means all (περὶ κατασκ. 16, 17, 22). In God's prescience the whole of humanity was comprised in the first preparation.

² See Vol. II., p. 267 ff.

majority of the Greek Fathers were not in a position to decide
bluntly for either of these ideas; yet the former, under the
influence of Origen, prevailed. It was only in the school of
Antioch that it was really rejected, that the other view was
emphatically avowed, and thus the most decided attitude
adopted of opposition to Origen's theology. [1] The view of the
Antiochenes was teleological—but there was an entire absence of
any religious view of sin. In this respect it was directly opposed
to Augustine's system.

According to Theodore, [2] God's plan included from the
beginning two epochs ("Καταστάσεις"), the present and future
states of the world. The former was characterised by changeableness, temptation, and mortality, the latter by perfection,
immutability, and immortality. The new age only began with
the resurrection. of the dead, its original starting-point being
the incarnation of the Son of God. Further, there was a
spiritual and a sensuous. Man was composed of both, the
body having been created first, and the soul having then been
breathed into it. This is the opposite of Gregory of Nyssa's
view. Man was the connecting link between the two spheres;
he was designed to reveal the image of God in this world.
"Like a king, who, after building a great city and adorning
it with works of every kind, causes, when the whole is completed, a fine statue of himself to be erected, in which all the
inhabitants may gratefully revere the constructor, so the Creator
of the world, after he had elaborated his work, finally produced
man to be his own image, and all creatures find in him their
centre, and thus contribute to the due glorification of God." Now
although man is equipped with all the powers of reason and
of will, *yet, from the very nature of his present condition, he
is changeable, is defeated in the conflict, and is mortal.* Not till
the new principle of life was imparted by means of Christ

---

[1] It is instructive that Marcellus also thinks of a glory presented through
redemption, which is ὑπὲρ ἄνθρωπον.

[2] See Kihn, Theodor von Mops., p. 171 ff. Also the examples partly taken
from Theodore's commentaries on Genesis, Job, and Paul's epistles (see Swete, Theodori
in epp. Pauli comment. 1880, 1881), partly from fragments of other writings of
Theodore; cf. also Dorner, Theodori de imagine dei doctrina, 1844.

could the changeable nature be raised to immutability. Till then, accordingly, man was exposed to temptation, and as a being made up of spirit and body was *necessarily mortal*. The threat of death in Paradise did not mean that death was the consequence of sin—it was rather natural; but it was designed to inspire man with as great a hatred of sin, as if the latter were punished by death. Death, natural in itself, was a divine means of education, and accordingly salutary. "God knew that mortality would be beneficial to Adam, for if they had been invested with immortality, men, when they sinned, would have been exposed to eternal destruction." But even the permission of sin was salutary, and formed part of the divine plan of education. God gave a command, and thereby elicited sin, in order that he might, like a loving Father, teach man his freedom of choice and weakness. "Man was to learn that while he was in a state of moral changeableness, he would not be capable of sustaining an immortal existence. Therefore death was announced to him as the penalty of disobedience, although mortality was from the beginning an attribute of human nature." [1] No sin without a command, but also no knowledge of good and evil, of the possession of spiritual faculties, finally, no conflict. Accordingly, God gave the command in order to raise Adam above the stage of childhood, and it necessarily provoked conflict and defeat.

Adam is, however, to be thought of here, not as the ancestor, but as the type, of the human race. The law was given with the same object to all his descendants, to teach them to distinguish between good and evil, and to know their own powers and weakness. In the history of Adam we become acquainted with our own natural disposition. "In keeping with this we are under the necessity in our present life of rendering obedience to laws by which our natural power of making distinctions is awakened, we, meanwhile, being taught from what we ought to abstain and what to do, that the principles of reason may be active in us. Only when we find ourselves in the future state (Katastasis) will we be able with slight effort to perform what we recognise as good. Without law, therefore,

Kihn, l. c., p. 174.

we would have had no distinction between good and evil, and
no knowledge of sin, and like irrational animals we would
have done whatever occurred to us." In this state knowledge
and fighting are required to obtain the victory, but we are
constantly hampered by the body, the source of temptations.
Christ first gave us redemption from death, an immortal nature,
which, therefore, will obtain the victory without effort (on
Rom. V. 18).

Theodore was able to explain away the Pauline passages
which support a transmission of the death worked by sin, just
as he ignored the life of the first man in Paradise before the
Fall. All men died because of their own sinful actions; but
even this was meant figuratively. They died because of their
natural constitution, in which sin was latent. He opposed
Augustine's and Jerome's doctrine of original sin in an independent work, fragments of which have been preserved by Marius
Mercator. "Adam was created mortal whether he sinned or
not. For God did not say, 'Ye will be mortal,' but 'Ye
will die.'" Theodore quoted Ps. CIII. 15, and Rome. II. 6.
Against original sin he appealed to the case of saints like
Noah, Abraham, and Moses. If God had passed sentence of
death on all as the punishment of sin, he would not have made
Enoch immortal. Accordingly, Baptism did not, according to
Theodore, remove inherited sin, but initiated the believer into
sinless discipleship of Christ, and at the same time blotted out
the sins he had himself committed. In the former sense it had
its use even for children; for Baptism, like all grace emanating
from the incarnation, raised man to a new stage, elevated him
above his present nature, and prepared him for the future state
(Katastasis). This is most strongly emphasised by Theodore,
and here his teaching is distinguished from the doctrines of
Pelagius and Julian of Eclanum, [1] who subordinated redemption
through Christ completely to the rationalistic theory. That
Theodore did not do. While he was thoroughly convinced,
with Pelagius, that in the present state everything turned on
men's own actions which rested on knowledge, freedom, effort, and
heroic fighting, yet he was equally certain on the other hand,

---

[1] See Kihn, l. c., p. 179 f.

that human nature did not attain immutability, immortality, and sinlessness through this conflict—it was merely a condition—but only through redemption. For this reason Christ came. He did not restore, but produced a new, a higher state. He did not heal, but transfigured. [1]

Theodore's doctrine of man was strictly rationalistic and Aristotelian; it surpassed the theories of all the rest of the Greek Fathers in intelligibility and consistency. But for that very reason it did not correspond to all the ideas and desires embraced in the tradition of the Church.

(4) John of Damascus.—The doctrines taught by this dogmatist became final in the Greek Church, the later Symbols being substantially at one with them, [2] because he combined the conceptions of the Cappadocians with the Antiochene tradition, in the modified form assumed by the latter in Chrysostom, and at the same time did justice to the constantly increasing tendency to refrain as much as possible from allegorising Gen. I. ff. Briefly, John taught as follows: [3]—

Since God, "overflowing with goodness", was not satisfied with the contemplation of himself, but desired to have some one to whom he could do good, he created the universe, angels, and men. Even the angels were immortal, not by nature, but by grace; for everything which has a beginning has necessarily an end. But immortality being a gift became natural to spiritual beings, and therefore also to men. Men were created by God from nature, visible and invisible, in his own image, to be kings and rulers of the whole earth. Before their creation God had prepared Paradise for them to be as it were a royal castle, "set by his hands in Eden, a store-house of all joy and delight, situated to the East, and higher than the whole earth, but

---

[1] Chrysostom agrees entirely with Theodore in the opinion that man's free will takes the first step, which is then seconded by God with his power, in the appropriation of the good; see his notes on Rom. IX. 16, in Hom. 16; in ep. ad Heb., Hom. 12; in Ev. Joh., Hom. 17, etc. The passages are reproduced in Münscher, Lehrbuch der Dogmengeschichte (1832), p. 363 ff.

[2] See Gass, Symbolik d. griech. Kirche, p. 150 ff.

[3] De fide orthod. II. 2 ff., 11 ff. 24—30; III. 1, 14, 20; IV. 4, 11, 19—22, and the Homily in "ficum arefactum," as also the Dialogue against the Manichæans. Langen. l. c., p. 289 ff.; Wendt, l. c., p. 59 ff.

tempered and illumined by the finest and purest air, planted
with ever blossoming flowers, filled with perfume, full of light,
surpassing every idea of earthly grace and beauty, a truly
divine place."¹ But it was only with his body that man was
supposed to live in this material Paradise; he inhabited with
his spirit at the same time the "spiritual" Paradise, which is
indicated by the tree of life.² Of the tree of knowledge he
was not at first to eat; for knowledge, while good for the
perfect, is bad for the imperfect. The result of knowledge in
the case of the imperfect was to make man, instead of devot-
ing himself to the contemplation and praise of God, think of
himself: Adam, immediately after eating, noticed that he was
naked. "God intended that we should be free from desire and
care, and occupied solely with luxuriating in the contemplation
of himself." The eating "of all the trees" denoted the knowledge of God from the works of nature. In created man—the
union of visible and invisible nature—the *image* of God consisted in power of thought and freedom of will, *likeness* to him
in similarity in virtue, so far as that was possible. Soul and
body (as against Origen) were created together. Man was
originally innocent, upright, and adorned with all virtues;³ his
being so was a gift of grace; but so also was the fact that he
was spiritual. He was spiritual that he might endure and
praise his benefactor; corporeal, that he might be disciplined
by suffering and the recollection of suffering; he was too proud
of his greatness. Man was created a being who ruled in this
present life, and was transferred to another.⁴ He was finally
to be made divine by submission to God: his deification

¹ Accordingly we have here a recrudescence to some extent of what the older
Greek Fathers called "Judaism" or "earthly conceptions," cf. Peter's Apocalypse.

² Two traditional, inconsistent ideas are combined here: John was not quite
clear as to the tree of life. He gives different explanations of it in De fide II. 11
and IV. 11.

³ This is strongly emphasised by John (II. 12, IV. 4); but he has carefully
avoided stating how God could on his part adorn men with virtues. It cannot be
proved that this is to be attributed to the influence of the West. Such an assumption is not necessary, for we also find in the older Greek Fathers rhetorical
glorifications of the primitive state which do not harmonise with the system of
doctrine.

⁴ These are the two states (katastaseis) of the Antiochenes.

consisting in participation in the divine glory, not in a transformation into the divine essence.

Actually, *i.e.*, according to the logical development of the
system, the innocence of primitive man consisted in his power
to be innocent, and, with the support of divine grace, to abide
by and advance in goodness. A necessary converse of this was
the power to revolt; "for it is no virtue which is done under compulsion". Man, "that little world", retained, however, along with
his spiritual attributes, those of irrational nature; even in his soul
there was an irrational part, which was partly capable of submitting to the rational, but was partly independent of it (the
vital functions). The former embraced the desires, some of which
were within limits permitted, while the others were not. But,
the vital functions apart, over all was placed free will. It is in
our power to choose, and man decides on his own actions.
His origin alone is God's affair. "But error was produced by
our wickedness for our punishment and benefit  For God did
not make death, nor did he delight in the ruin of the living; on
the contrary, death was due to man, *i.e.*, to Adam's transgression, and so also were the other penalties." [1]  It was not right
to attribute everything to divine providence; "for that which
is in our power is not the affair of providence, but of our own
free will." God, certainly, in virtue of his omniscience, knows
everything from all eternity; he therefore assists by his grace
those who, he knows, will avail themselves of it. They alone
are also predestinated; their decision to be and do good is
known to God. Those are damned to whom all the supports
of grace are in vain. [2] With all this it remains true that all
virtue comes from God; for by him it was implanted in nature,
and by his support alone it is maintained. Accordingly, we
have once more the principle that nature, rational and free, is
a gift of grace; to be natural is to be virtuous, and conversion
is the return from the unnatural. [3]

[1] The significance of Adam's fall for his posterity is recognised (II. 28), but it
is noteworthy, only cursorily. John has no separate chapter on the Fall in his
great work. Even II. 30, only discusses it under a more general heading.

[2] See, l. c., II. 29, 30; IV. 22.

[3] II 30.

Man was created male. Woman was formed merely because God
foresaw the Fall, and in order that the race might be preserved
in spite of death. [1]  Man did not allow reason to triumph; he
mistook the path of honour, and preferred his lusts.  Consequently, instead of living for ever, he fell a prey to death and
became subject to tribulation and a miserable life.  For it was
not good that he should enjoy immortality untempted and
unproved, lest he should share the pride and condemnation of
the devil.  "Accordingly, man was first to attest himself, and,
made perfect by observance of the commandment when tempted,
was then to obtain immortality as the reward of virtue.  For,
placed between God and matter, he was to acquire steadfast-
ness in goodness, after he had abandoned his natural relation
to things, and become habitually united to God."  But, seduced
by the devil who enviously grudged man the possession which
he had himself lost, man turned to matter, and so, severed
from God, his First Cause, became subject to suffering, and
mortal, and required sexual intercourse.  (The fig-leaves denote
the tribulations of life, and the skins the mortal body).  Death,
come into the world through sin, henceforth, like a hideous
wild beast, made havoc of human life, although the liberty to
choose good as well as evil was never destroyed. [2]  But God
did not leave himself without a witness, and at last sent his
own Son, who was to strengthen nature, and to renew and
show and teach by his action the way of virtue which led from
destruction to eternal life.  The union of Deity with humanity
was "the newest of the new, the only new thing under the
sun." [3]  It applied, moreover, to the whole of human nature in
order to bestow salvation on the whole. [4]  This union resulted
in the *restitutio* to the original state, which was perfect in so
far as man, though not yet tested, was adorned with virtues.
Christ participated in the worst part of our nature in order, by
and in himself, to restore the form of the image and likeness,
and to teach us further by virtuous conduct, which by his aid

[1]  L. c., see Gregory of Nyssa.
[2]  II. 26 ff.
[3]  III. 1.
[4]  III. 6.

he made light for us. Then he overcame death, becoming the
first-fruits of our resurrection, and renewing the worn-out and
cast-off vessel. [1]

It has been pointed out above (p. 240) that natural theology
underwent no development in the Greek Church. We must
premise, however, that the course of the history of philosophy
is of greater moment for the development of the system, or
for systematic monographs. Without anticipating we may here
make the following remark. The Fathers of orthodox *dogma*
in the fourth and fifth centuries were Platonists. Aristotelianism
always led in this period to a heterodox form of dogma—
Lucian, the Arians, the Antiochenes, etc. But a theological
system constructed by the aid of Platonism could not fail at
that time to become equally heterodox. After Platonism had
done its work on dogma, and certain notions and conceptions
were generally fixed, an orthodox system could only be created
by means of Aristotelianism. Any further use of Platonism led
to questionable propositions.

[1] IV. 4, II. 12.

## B.—*THE DOCTRINE OF REDEMPTION IN THE PERSON OF THE GOD-MAN IN ITS HISTORICAL DEVELOPMENT.*

## CHAPTER VI.

### THE DOCTRINE OF THE NECESSITY AND REALITY OF REDEMPTION THROUGH THE INCARNATION OF THE SON OF GOD.

NATURAL theology was so wide in its scope as understood by the Greek Church, that, as indications in the preceding chapter will have already shown, only a historical fact absolutely unparalleled could make headway against it. The Greek Fathers knew of such a fact—"the newest of the new, yea, the only new thing under the sun"; it was the Incarnation of the Son of God. It alone balanced the whole system of natural theology, so far as it was balanced, and exerted a decisive influence upon it. But the incarnation could only be attached with complete perspicuity to that point in the natural system which seemed the more irrational, the more highly the value of human nature was rated—this point of contact being death. The dreadful paradox of death was destroyed by the most paradoxical fact conceivable. the incarnation of the Deity.

This at once implied that the fact could not but be capable of a *subsequent* explanation, nay, even of a kind of *a priori* deduction. But its glory, as an expression of the unfathomable goodness of God, was not thereby to be diminished. The necessity of redemption, whether that consisted in the restoration or the perfection of the human race, was based by the Fathers, as a rule, on the actual state of wretchedness of mankind under the dominion of death and sin. So far, however, as this condition was compared with the original state or destiny of man, redemption was already thought of as intrinsically necessary, and was no longer merely regarded as a postulate of man's need of salvation. In this connection the Fathers often lost sight of the capacity left to man of being and doing good. In innumerable passages they speak of the helplessness and irredeemableness of mankind, using expressions which could without difficulty be inserted in Augustine's doctrine of sin. But just as often a phrase occurs which betrays the fact that the whole view is nevertheless quite different; in other words, that the outward condition characterised by feebleness and death, and the sensuousness of corruptible human nature are thought of as the source of all evil and all sin. This state is accompanied by a darkening of knowledge which could not fail to subject man to the influence of the demons and lead him into idolatry.

The divine act of grace in Christ applied to death, the demonic rule, sin, and error. In Homilies, Biblical commentaries, and devotional writings, these points of view interchange, or are apparently regarded as equivalent. [1] But since natural theology formed the background of their conceptions, the absolute necessity of the form assumed by the act of grace in the incarnation could be demonstrated neither in relation to sin nor to error. The whole question turned here on support, example, and illumination, or, if this line was crossed, theology ceased to be systematic and consistent. The importance of Athanasius and the Cappadocians consisted in the strenuous emphasis laid by them on the impressive connection existing between the incarnation and the restoration of the human race

---

[1] Perhaps the most comprehensive passage is Eusebius, Demonstr. ev. IV. 12. But it also shows how far Eusebius still was from the thorough-going view of Athanasius: Τῆς οἰκονομίας οὐ μίαν αἰτίαν ἀλλὰ καὶ πλείους εὕροι ἄν τις ἐθελήσας ζητεῖν, πρώτην μὲν γὰρ ὁ λόγος διδάσκει, ἵνα καὶ νεκρῶν καὶ ζώντων κυριεύσῃ· δευτέραν δὲ ὅπως τὰς ἡμετέρας ἀπομάξοιτο ἁμαρτίας, ὑπὲρ ἡμῶν τρωθεὶς καὶ γενόμενος ὑπὲρ ἡμῶν κατάρα· τρίτην ὡς ἂν ἱερεῖον Θεοῦ καὶ μεγάλη θυσία ὑπὲρ σύμπαντος κόσμου προσαχθείη τῷ ἐπὶ πάντων Θεῷ· τετάρτην ὡς ἂν αὐτὸς τῆς πολυπλανοῦς καὶ δαιμονικῆς ἐνεργείας ἀπορρήτοις λόγοις καθαίρεσιν ἀπεργάσαιτο· πέμπτην ἐπὶ ταύτῃ, ὡς ἂν τοῖς αὐτοῦ γνωρίμοις καὶ μαθηταῖς τῆς κατὰ τὸν θάνατον παρὰ Θεῷ ζωῆς τὴν ἐλπίδα μὴ λόγοις μηδὲ ῥήμασιν καὶ φωναῖς ἀλλὰ αὐτοῖς ἔργοις παραστήσας, ὀφθαλμοῖς δὲ παραδοὺς τὴν διὰ τῶν λόγων ἐπαγγελίαν, εὐθαρσεῖς αὐτοὺς καὶ προθυμοτέρους ἀπεργάσαιτο καὶ πᾶσιν Ἕλλησιν ὁμοῦ καὶ βαρβάροις τὴν πρὸς αὐτοῦ καταβληθεῖσαν εὐσεβῆ πολιτείαν κηρύξαι.

to the divine life, and in their consequent escape to some extent
from the rationalistic scheme of doctrine; for the reference of
the incarnation to sin did not carry the Greeks beyond it.
The above combination had been made in the Church long
before this (see Irenæus), but in the theology of Origen it had
been subordinated to, and obscured by, complicated presuppositions.

Athanasius wrote a treatise "Concerning the incarnation of
the Logos" (περὶ ἐνανθρωπήσεως τοῦ λόγου), an early writing whose
value is so great because it dates before the outbreak of the
Arian controversy.[1] In this work he went a step further: for
he strove to prove that the redemption was a necessity on the
part of God. He based this necessity on the goodness (ἀγαθότης)
of God. This goodness, i.e., God's consistency and honour,
involved as they were in his goodness, were necessarily expressed in the maintenance and execution of decrees once formed
by him. His decrees, however, consisted, on the one hand, in
his appointment of rational creatures to share in the divine
life, and, on the other, in the sentence of death on transgressions. Both of these had to be established. God's intention
could not be allowed to suffer shipwreck through the wickedness of the devil and the sad choice of humanity. If it were,
God would seem weak, and it would have been better if he
had never created man at all. Then the transgression occurred.
"What was God now to do? Ought he to have demanded
penitence on the part of man? For one could have deemed
that worthy of God and said, that as men had become mortal
through the transgression, they should in like manner recover
immortality through repentance (change of mind). But repentance (in itself) did not retain the true knowledge as regards
God; God accordingly would in his turn have shown himself

[1] Draescke has attempted to show in a full discussion (Athanasiana i. d. Stud.
u. Krit., 1893, pp. 251—315 that the writings "Against the Greeks" and the "Incarnation of the Logos" belong, not to Athanasius, but to Eusebius of Emesa, and
were written A.D. 350. But after a close examination of his numerous arguments
I find none of them convincing, and I am rather confirmed in my belief
that no important objection can be raised against the authenticity of the two
tractates. An accurate analysis of "De incarn." is given by Kattenbusch, l. c. I.,
p. 297 ff.

untruthful, if death had not compelled men;[1] *nor did repentance deliver from the physical, but only put an end to sins. Therefore, if the transgression had alone existed, and not its consequence, mortality, repentance would have been all very well.* But when, the transgression having occurred, men were fettered to the mortality that had become natural to them, and were robbed of the grace which corresponded to their creation in the divine image, what else should have happened? Or what was needed for this grace and renewal except (the coming of) him who also in the beginning made all things of nothing, the Logos of God? For it was his part once more to restore the corruptible to incorruption."[2]

Athanasius shows that the Logos who originally created all things from nothing required to assume a body and thus to secure the restoration of man from corruptibility to incorruption (ἀφθαρσία). How this happened Athanasius discusses in various, to some extent inconsistent, lines of thought, in which he speaks especially of a removal of men's guilt through the death of Christ, as well as of an exhaustion of the sentence of death in the sacrifice of his body presented by the Logos. From these premises it follows that Athanasius had the death of Christ in view, whenever he thought of the incarnation of the Logos. "The Logos could not suffer τὴν τοῦ θανάτου κράτησιν ('the power of death' in mankind), and therefore took up the

---

1 This sentence does not seem to me quite clear; the meaning is probably: since repentance does not convey the true knowledge of God, but death resulted from loss of the latter, God would have broken his word if he had abolished death in consequence of mere repentance.

2 De incarn. 7: Τί οὖν ἔδει καὶ περὶ τούτου γενέσθαι ἢ ποιῆσαι τὸν Θεόν; μετάνοιαν ἐπὶ τῇ παραβάσει τοὺς ἀνθρώπους ἀπαιτῆσαι; τοῦτο γὰρ ἄν τις ἄξιον φήσειεν Θεοῦ, λέγων, ὅτι ὥσπερ ἐκ τῆς παραβάσεως εἰς φθορὰν γεγόνασιν, οὕτως ἐκ τῆς μετανοίας γένοιντο πάλιν ἂν εἰς ἀφθαρσίαν. Ἀλλ' ἡ μετάνοια οὔτε τὸ εὔλογον τὸ πρὸς τὸν Θεὸν ἐφύλαττεν· ἔμενε γὰρ πάλιν οὐκ ἀληθής, μὴ κρατουμένων ἐν τῷ θανάτῳ τῶν ἀνθρώπων· οὔτε δὲ ἡ μετάνοια ἀπὸ τῶν κατὰ φύσιν ἀποκαλεῖται, ἀλλὰ μόνον παύει τῶν ἁμαρτημάτων. Εἰ μὲν οὖν μόνον ἦν πλημμέλημα καὶ μὴ φθορᾶς ἐπακολούθησις, καλῶς ἂν ἦν ἡ μετάνοια· εἰ δὲ ἅπαξ προλαβούσης τῆς παραβάσεως, εἰς την κατὰ φύσιν φθορὰν ἐκρατοῦντο οἱ ἄνθρωποι, καὶ τὴν τοῦ κατ' εἰκόνα χάριν ἀφαιρεθέντες ἦσαν, τί ἄλλο ἔδει γενέσθαι; ἢ τίνος ἦν χρεία πρὸς τὴν τοιαύτην χάριν καὶ ἀνάκλησιν, ἢ τοῦ καὶ κατὰ τὴν ἀρχὴν ἐκ τοῦ μὴ ὄντος πεποιηκότος τὰ ὅλα τοῦ Θεοῦ λόγου; αὐτοῦ γὰρ ἦν πάλιν καὶ τὸ φθαρτὸν εἰς ἀφθαρσίαν ἐνεγκεῖν καὶ τὸ ὑπὲρ πάντων εὔλογον ἀποσῶσαι πρὸς τὸν πατέρα. Compare Orat. c. Arian. II. 68.

fight with death. He assumed a body and so became mortal.
This body he surrendered to death on behalf of all. His body
could not be really overcome, 'kept', by death. In it all
died, and for this very reason the law of death (νόμος τοῦ
Θανάτου) is now abrogated; its power was exhausted on the
body of the Lord (κυριακὸν σῶμα); it had no further claim on
his fellow-men (κατὰ τῶν ὁμοίων ἀνθρώπων)... The body assumed
by the Logos came to share in the universal meaning of the
Logos. The resurrection of the body and of the Logos guaranteed
the general resurrection and incorruption (ἀφθαρσία)." [1] Here
follows the place assigned to the sacrifice. It presented that
which was due (ὀφειλόμενον) to God in place of death. But
the pervading and prominent thought of Athanasius is that the
incarnation itself involved the Christian's passage from the fate of
death to incorruption (ἀφθαρσία), since the physical union of the
human with the divine nature in the midst of mankind raised the
latter to the region of divine rest and blessedness. [2] The result
of the incarnation consisted accordingly, first, in the eradication
of corruption (φθορά)—by the existence of the divine in its
midst, but, finally, by the death of Christ, in which the truth-
fulness of God was justified—and in the corresponding transformation into incorruptibility—renewal, or completion of the
divine image by participation in the nature, free from all suffering, of the Deity. [3] But, secondly, the incarnation also resulted,

[1] Kattenbusch, p. 298.

[2] L. c., ch. IX.: "Ὥσπερ μεγάλου βασιλέως εἰσελθόντος εἴς τινα πόλιν μεγάλην,
καὶ οἰκήσαντος εἰς μίαν τῶν ἐν αὐτῇ οἰκιῶν, πάντως ἡ τοιαύτη πόλις τιμῆς πολλῆς
καταξιοῦται, καὶ οὐκέτι τις ἐχθρὸς αὐτὴν οὔτε λῃστὴς ἐπιβαίνων καταστρέφει, πάσης
δὲ μᾶλλον ἐπιμελείας ἀξιοῦται διὰ τὸν εἰς μίαν αὐτῆς οἰκίαν οἰκήσαντα βασιλέα·
οὕτως καὶ ἐπὶ τοῦ πάντων βασιλέως γέγονεν. Ἐλθόντος γὰρ αὐτοῦ ἐπὶ τὴν ἡμετέραν
χώραν καὶ οἰκήσαντος εἰς ἓν τῶν ὁμοίων σῶμα, λοιπὸν πᾶσα ἡ κατὰ τῶν ἀνθρώπων
παρὰ τῶν ἐχθρῶν ἐπιβουλὴ πέπαυται, καὶ ἡ τοῦ θανάτου ἠφάνισται φθορὰ ἡ πάλαι
κατ' αὐτῶν ἰσχύουσα. Kattenbusch is right in considering Ritschl (l. c., I., p. 10,
11) to have gone too far in his assertion that "Athanasius' interpretation of the
death and resurrection of Christ is a particular instance of the main thought that
the Logos of God guarantees all redemptive work, using the human body in which
he dwells as the means." Athanasius certainly did not regard the death and resurrection as merely particular instances. They formed the object of the incarnation;
not that they were added or supplementary to it; they were bound up with it.

[3] Yet the view of Athanasius was not simply naturalistic; incorruptibleness
rather included the elements of goodness, love, and wisdom; a renewal affecting

as indeed had been long before held by the Apologists, in the
restoration of the correct knowledge of God, which embraced
the power of living rightly, through the incarnate Logos.  But
while Athanasius kept firmly in view this restoration of the
knowledge of God through the Logos, he was not thinking
merely of the new law, *i.e.*, the preaching of Christ; he held
it to have been given in the contemplation of the Person of
Christ.  In his work, that of a man, God came down to us.
The dullest eye was now in a position to perceive the one true
God—viz., in Christ—and to escape from the error of demon-
worship.  This thought is very significant; it had already been
expressed by Clement and Origen, having received a deeper
meaning from the latter, though he had not yet given it so
central a place in his system.  Athanasius expressly notes that
creation was not sufficient to let us perceive the Creator and
Father; we needed a man to live and work among us before
we could see clearly and certainly the God and Father of all. [1]

the inner nature of man was also involved. But it was not possible for Athanasius
to expound this systematically; therefore Schultz seems to me to have asserted too
much (Gottheit Christi, p. 80).

[1] The chief passages occur l. c., XIV—XVI., chap. XIV. *fin*: One might suppose
that the fitting way to know God was to recover our knowledge of him from the works
of creation.  It is not so, for men are no longer capable of directing their gaze
upward; they look down. "Therefore, when he seeks to benefit men, he takes up
his dwelling among us as man, and assumes a body like the human one, and
instructs men within their own lower sphere, *i.e.*, through the works of the body,
that those who would not perceive him from his care for all and his rule might
at least from the works of the body itself know the Logos of God in the body,
and through him the Father." C. 15: Ἐπειδὴ οἱ ἄνθρωποι ἀποστραφέντες τὴν πρὸς
τὸν Θεὸν θεωρίαν, καὶ ὡς ἐν βύθῳ βυθισθέντες κάτω τοὺς ὀφθαλμοὺς ἔχοντες, ἐν γενέσει
καὶ τοῖς αἰσθητοῖς τὸν Θεὸν ἀνεζήτουν, ἀνθρώπους θνητοὺς καὶ δαίμονας ἑαυτοῖς θεοὺς
ἀνατυπούμενοι· τούτου ἕνεκα ὁ φιλάνθρωπος καὶ κοινὸς πάντων σωτήρ, ὁ τοῦ Θεοῦ
λόγος, λαμβάνει ἑαυτῷ σῶμα καὶ ὡς ἄνθρωπος ἐν ἀνθρώποις ἀναστρέφεται καὶ τὰς
αἰσθήσεις πάντων ἀνθρώπων προσλαμβάνει, ἵνα οἱ ἐν σωματικοῖς νοοῦντες εἶναι τὸν
Θεόν, αφ᾽ ὧν ὁ κύριος ἐργάζεται διὰ τῶν τοῦ σώματος ἔργων, ἀπ᾽ αὐτῶν νοήσωσι
τὴν ἀλήθειαν, καὶ δι᾽ αὐτοῦ τὸν πατέρα λογίσωνται. The sequel shows, indeed,
that Athanasius thought above all of Jesus' miraculous works. He has summarised
his whole conception of the result of redemption in the pregnant sentence (ch. XVI.):
Ἀμφότερα γὰρ ἐφιλανθρωπεύετο ὁ σωτὴρ διὰ τῆς ἐνανθρωπήσεως, ὅτι καὶ τὸν θάνατον
ἐξ ἡμῶν ἠφάνιζε καὶ ἀνεκαίνιζεν ἡμᾶς· καὶ ὅτι ἀφανὴς ὢν καὶ ἀόρατος διὰ τῶν ἔργων
ἐνέφαινε καὶ ἐγνώριζεν ἑαυτὸν εἶναι τὸν λόγον τοῦ πατρός, τὸν τοῦ παντὸς ἡγεμόνα
καὶ βασιλέα. Origen had already laid stress on the perception of God in Christ,
and set it above philosophical knowledge (analytic, synthetic, and analogical, against

When Athanasius placed the knowledge of God side by side
with the deliverance from death, the transition was obtained
from the fact of redemption to the doctrine of the appropriation,
and to the explanation of the particular result, of the work of
love done by the Logos. This only benefited those who
voluntarily appropriated the divine knowledge made accessible
by the incarnate Logos, and who regulated their conduct by
the standards and with the power thus given them. [1] In any
case the transformation of the corruptible into the incorruptible
(the Theopoiesis) remained under this conception the ultimate
and proper result of the work of the Logos, being ranked
higher than the other, the knowledge of God. [2] But here we
find the greatest difference between Athanasius and like-minded
theologians on the one hand, and Arius, the Eusebians, etc.,
on the other. The elements contained in their views are the
same; but the order is different. For these " conservative "
theologians saw the work of the Logos primarily in the communication of the true and complete knowledge which should
be followed by a state of perfection. But Athanasius made every-

Alcinous, Maximus of Tyre, and Celsus): see c. Cels. VII. 42, 44; De princip. I. 1.
For Clement see Protrept. I. 8: ὁ λόγος ὁ τοῦ Θεοῦ ἄνθρωπος γενόμενος, ἵνα δὴ καὶ
σὺ παρὰ ἀνθρώπου μάθῃς, πῇ ποτὲ ἄρα ἄνθρωπος γένηται Θεός.

[1] Parallel with this view and intertwined with it we undoubtedly have the other,
that eternal life is mystically appropriated by means of sacred rites and the holy
food. In this conception, which is extremely ancient, Christianity seems degraded
to the level of the nature-religions of the East or the Græco-oriental mysteries
(see Schultz, Gottheit Christi, p. 69). But as even the earliest Alexandrians (also
Ignatius) constantly resolved the naturalistic view into a spiritual and moral one,
so also hardly any one of the theologians of the following centuries can be named
who would have purely and simply defended the former.

[2] See esp. Orat. c. Arian. II. 67—70, where the final designs of Athanasius'
Christianity are revealed. It is at the same time to be noted that while redemption
meant restoration, it was the transference into a still higher grace. We experience
all that was done to the body of Christ. We are baptised, as Christ was in Jordan,
we next received the Holy Spirit, and so also our flesh has died, and been renewed,
sanctified and raised to eternal life in his resurrection. Accordingly, Athanasius
sums up at the close of his work, ch. 54: Αὐτὸς γὰρ ἐνηνθρώπησεν, ἵνα ἡμεῖς θεο-
ποιηθῶμεν· καὶ αὐτὸς ἐφανέρωσεν ἑαυτὸν διὰ σώματος, ἵνα ἡμεῖς τοῦ ἀοράτου πατρὸς
ἔννοιαν λάβωμεν· καὶ αὐτὸς ὑπέμεινε τὴν παρ' ἀνθρώπων ὕβριν, ἵνα ἡμεῖς ἀθανασίαν
κληρονομήσωμεν. ἐβλάπτετο μὲν γὰρ αὐτὸς οὐδέν, ἀπαθὴς καὶ ἄφθαρτος καὶ αὐτολόγος
ὢν καὶ Θεός· τοὺς δὲ πάσχοντας ἀνθρώπους, δι' οὓς καὶ ταῦτα ὑπέμεινεν, ἐν τῇ ἑαυτοῦ
ἀπαθείᾳ ἐτήρει καὶ διέσωζε.

thing tend to this consummation as the restoration and the communication of the divine nature.  Accordingly, it was to him a vital theological question how the incorruptible was constituted which was represented in the Logos, and what kind of union it had formed with the corruptible.  But while he put the question he was sure of the answer. His opponents, however, could not at all share in his interest in this point, since their interest in Christ as the supreme teacher did not lead them directly to define more precisely the kind of heavenly manifestation which he represented even for them.  When they did give such definitions, they were influenced by theoretical, or exegetical considerations, or were engaged in refuting the propositions of their opponents by setting up others.

The Trinitarian and Christological problems which had occupied the ancient Church for more than three centuries here rise before us.  That their decision was so long delayed, and only slowly found a more general acceptance, was not merely due to outward circumstances, such as the absence of a clearly marked tradition, the letter of the Bible, or the politics of Bishops and Emperors.  It was, on the contrary, owing chiefly to the fact that large circles in the Church felt the need of subordinating even the doctrine of redemption to rational theology, or of keeping it within the framework of moralism.  The opposite conviction, that nature was transformed through the incarnate Logos, resulted here and there in a chaotic pantheism; [1] but that was the least danger. The gravest hindrance to the acceptance of the view of Athanasius consisted in the paradoxical tenets which arose regarding the Deity and Jesus Christ. Here his opponents found their strength; they were more strongly supported by the letter of Scripture and tradition, as well as by reason.

*Supplement I.*—No subsequent Greek theologian answered the question, why God became man, so decidedly and clearly as Athanasius. But all Fathers of unimpeached orthodoxy followed in his footsteps, and at the same time showed that his doctrinal

[1] Not in Athanasius himself—Kattenbusch says rightly (p. 299): The θεοποίησις is for A. an enhancement of human life physically and morally; his idea of it does not look forward to man being pantheistically merged in God, but to the renewal of man after his original type.

ideas could only be held on the basis of Platonism. This is at once clear in the case of Gregory of Nyssa, who in some points strengthened the expositions given by Athanasius. Yet his model was Methodius rather than Athanasius. [1]

Gregory sought, in the first place, to give a more elaborate defence of the method of redemption—by means of the incarnation,—but in doing so he obscured Athanasius' simple combination of the incarnation and its effect. According to Gregory, God is boundless might, but his might was never divorced from goodness, wisdom, and righteousness. He next shows in detail (Catech. magn. 17—26) against Jews and heathens — as Anselm did afterwards—that the incarnation was the *best* form of redemption, because the above four fundamental attributes of God came clearly to light in it. Especially interesting in these arguments is the emphasis laid on God's treatment of those who had passed over to his enemies, his respect for their freedom in everything, and his redemption of men without wronging the devil, their master, who possessed a certain claim upon them. This account of the matter indeed had strictly an apologetic purpose. [2] In the second place, Gregory, while following Athanasius, still more strongly identified the state from which God has delivered us with death. The state of sin was death. He taught, with the Neoplatonists, that God alone was Being. Therefore all revolt from God to the sensuous, *i.e.*, to not-being, was death. Natural death was not the only death; it might rather mean deliverance from the bonds of the body become brutal (l. c., ch. 8). Sensuousness was death. In the third place, although he also saw the redemption in the act of incarnation, Gregory held that it was not perfected until the resurrection of Jesus. That is, he was more thoroughly influenced than Athanasius by the conviction that the actual redemption presupposed renunciation of the body. We are first

---

[1] See Vol. III., p. 104 ff.

[2] The Apologetic argument also includes the treatment of the question, why the redemption was not accomplished sooner. Apologists from Justin to Eusebius and Athanasius had put it and attempted to answer it. Gregory also got rid of it by referring to the physician who waits till illness has fully developed before he interferes (Catech. magn., ch. 29 ff.).

redeemed, when we share in the resurrection which the human
nature assumed by Christ experienced through the resurrection
(l. c., ch. 16). The mystery of the incarnation only becomes
clear in this resurrection. The Deity assumed human nature,
in order by this union to exhaust, until it had wholly disappeared, that which was liable to death in this nature, *viz.*, evil.
This result was only perfected in the resurrection of the human
nature of Christ; for in it that nature was first shown completely
purified and rendered capable of being possessed of eternal life. [1]
In the fourth place, Gregory was able to demonstrate the application of the incarnation more definitely than Athanasius could
with his figure of the king and the city. But he does so by
the aid of a thoroughly Platonic idea which is only slightly
suggested in Athanasius, and is not really covered by a Biblical
reference (to the two Adams; see Irenæus). Christ did not
assume the human nature of an individual person, but human
nature. Accordingly, all that was human was intertwined with
the Deity; the whole of human nature became divine by intermixture with the Divine. Gregory conceives this as a strictly
physical process: the leaven of the Deity has pervaded the whole
dough of humanity, through and in Christ; for Christ united with
himself the whole of human nature with all its characteristics. [2]
This conception, which was based on the Platonic universal

[1] L. c., ch. 16. For, since our nature in its regular course changed also in him
into the separation of body and soul, he reunited that which had been divided by
his divine power as if by a kind of cement, and rejoined in an indissoluble union
the severed parts (comp. Irenæus and Methodius). And that was the resurrection,
viz., the return after dissolution and division of the allies to an indissoluble union,
both being so bound together, that man's original state of grace was recalled, and
we return to eternal life, after the evil mingled with our nature has been removed
by our dissolution (!); just as it happens with liquids, which, the vessel being
broken, escape and are lost, because there is nothing now to hold them. But as
death began in one man and from him passed to the whole of nature and the
human race, in the same way the beginning of the resurrection extended through
one man to the whole of humanity."

[2] See conclusion of the preceding note, and Herrmann, Gregorii Nyss. sententias
de salute adipis., p. 16 ff. Underlying all the arguments of the "Great Catechism"
we have the thought that the incarnation was an *actus medicinalis* which is to be
thought of as strictly natural, and that extends to all mankind. See Dorner (Entwick.-
Gesch. d. L. v. d. Person Christi, I., p. 958 f.), who, besides, regards Gregory's
whole conception as strictly ethical.

notion "humanity", differed from that of Origen; but it also
led to the doctrine of Apokatastasis (universalism), which Gregory
adopted. Meanwhile, in order to counterbalance this whole
"mystical", *i.e.*, physical, conception, he emphasised the personal
and spontaneous fulfilment of the law as a condition, in the same
way as the later Antiochenes. The perfect fulfilment of the law
was, however, according to Gregory, only possible to ascetics.[1]

In the fifth place, Gregory set the sacraments in the closest
relation to the incarnation, recognising (l. c., ch. 33—40) Baptism and the Lord's Supper as the only means by which
mortal man was renewed and became immortal. It undoubtedly appears superfluous to a rigorous thinker to require
that something special should happen to the individual when
all mankind has been deified in the humanity assumed
by Christ. But the form given to his ideas by Gregory
was in keeping with the thought of his time, when mysterious rites were held to portray and represent that which was
inconceivable. Sixthly, and lastly, Gregory gave a turn to
the thought of the incarnation in which justice was done to
the boldest conception of Origen, and "the newest of the new"
was subordinated to a cosmological and more general view.
Origen had already, following the Gnostics, taught—in connection with Philipp. II. 10 and other texts—that the incarnation
and sacrificial death of Christ had an importance that went
beyond mankind. The work of Christ extended to wherever there
were spiritual creatures; wherever there was alienation from
God, there was restoration through Christ. He offered himself
to the Father for angels and æons (see Valentine). To all
orders of spiritual beings he appeared in their own shape. He
restored harmony to the whole universe. Nay, Christ's blood
was not only shed on earth at Jerusalem "for sin" (pro peccato);
but also "for a gift on the high altar which is in the heavens"
(pro munere in superno altari quod est in cœlis).[2] Gregory took
up this thought. The reconciliation and restitution extend to
all rational creation.[3] Christ came down to all spiritual crea-

---

[1] See Herrmann, l. c., p. 2 sq.

[2] Passages in Bigg, l. c., p. 212 f.

[3] See περὶ ψυχ. κ. ἀναστάσ., p. 66 sq., ed. Oehler. Orat. cat. 26.

tures, and adopted the forms in which they lived, in order to
bring them into harmony with God: οὐ μόνον ἐν ἀνθρώποις ἄνθρωπος γίνεται, ἀλλὰ κατὰ τὸ ἀκόλουθον πάντως καὶ ἐν ἀγγέλοις
γινόμενος πρὸς τὴν ἐκείνων φύσιν ἑαυτὸν συγκατάγει. [1] This thought,
far from enriching the work of the historical Christ, served
only, as in the case of the Gnostics, to dissipate it. And, in
fact, it was only as an apologist of Catholic Christianity that
Gregory held closely to the historical personality of Christ.
When he philosophised and took his own way, he said little
or nothing of the Christ of history. [2] It is almost with him as
with Origen. He also reveals a supreme view of the world,
according to which that which alienates the Kosmos from God
forms part of its plan as much as that which restores it to
him, the Kosmos being, from its creation, full of God, and,
because it *is*, existing in God. The incarnation is only a
particular instance of the universal presence of the divine in creation. Gregory contributed to transmit to posterity the pantheistic
conception, which be himself never thought out abstractly, or
apart from history. A real affinity existed between him and
the pantheistic Monophysites, the Areopagite, and Scotus
Erigena, and even modern "liberal" theology of the Hegelian
shade may appeal to him. In the "Great Catechism" (ch. XXV.),
which was meant to defend the historical act of the incarnation,
he has an argument which is in this respect extremely significant. [3] "The assumption of our nature by the deity should,
however, excite no well-founded surprise on the part of those
who view things (τὰ ὄντα) with any breadth of mind, (not too

---

[1] Orat. in ascens. Christi in Migne T. XLVI., p. 693; on the other hand, Didymus (De trinit. II. 7, ed. Mingarelli, p. 200): ὁ Θεὸς λόγος οὐ διὰ τοὺς ἀμαρτή-
σαντας ἀγγέλους ἄγγελος· ἀλλὰ διὰ τοὺς ἐν ἀμαρτίᾳ ἀνθρώπους ἄνθρωπος ἀτρέπτως,
ἀσυγχύτως, ἀναμαρτήτως, ἀφράστως. Yet in other places he has expressed himself
like Origen. The latter was attacked by Jerome and Theophilus on account of this
doctrine. The Synod of Constantinople condemned it.

[2] Compare the whole dialogue with Macrina on the soul and the resurrection,
where the historical Christ is quite overlooked.

[3] To Athanasius also it was not unknown; see De incarn. 41: τὸν κόσμον σῶμα
μέγα φασὶν εἶναι οἱ τῶν Ἑλλήνων φιλόσοφοι καὶ ἀληθεύουσι λέγοντες. Ὁρῶμεν γὰρ
αὐτὸν καὶ τὰ τούτου μέρη ταῖς αἰσθήσεσι ὑποπίπτοντα. Εἰ τοίνυν ἐν τῷ κόσμῳ σώματι
ὄντι ὁ τοῦ Θεοῦ λόγος ἐστί, καὶ ἐν ὅλοις καὶ τοῖς κατὰ μέρος αὐτῶν πᾶσιν ἐπιβέβηκε.
τί θαυμαστὸν ἢ τί ἄτοπον εἰ καὶ ἐν ἀνθρώπῳ φαμὲν αὐτὸν ἐπιβεβηκέναι κ.τ.λ., c. 42.

μικροψύχως). For who is so weak in mind as not to believe
when he looks at the universe that the divine is in everything,
pervading and embracing it, and dwelling in it? For everything depends on the existent, and it is impossible that there
should be anything not having its existence in that which is.
Now, if all is in it and it in all, why do they take offence at
the dispensation of the mystery taught by the incarnation of
God, of him who, we are convinced, is not even now outside
of mankind? For if the form of the divine presence is not now
the same, yet we are as much agreed that God is among us
to-day as that he was in the world then.   Now he is united
with us as the one who embraces nature in his being, but then
he had united himself with our being, that our nature, snatched
from death, and delivered from the tyranny of the Adversary,
might become divine through intermixture with the divine. For
his return from death was for the mortal race the beginning
of return to eternal life." The pantheistic theory of redemption appeared in after times in two forms. In one of these the
work of the historical Christ was regarded as a particular
instance, or symbol, of the universal, purifying and sanctifying operations continuously carried out through sanctifying
media—the sacraments--by the Logos in combination with, as
in their turn on behalf of, the graded orders of supersensuous
creatures; this was the view of Dionysius the Areopagite. The
other form of the theory included in the very idea of the
incarnation the union of the Logos with those individual believing souls in whom he was well pleased. The latter conception
which was already prominent in Methodius is especially marked
in Macarius. In Homily IV. *e.g.*, (ch. 8, 9), his first words
lead us to expect an exposition of the one historical incarnation.
Instead of that we read: "Thus in his love the infinite, inscrut-
able God humbled himself and assumed the members of our bodily
nature ... and transformed in love and benevolence to men he
incorporates and unites himself with the holy and faithful souls
in whom he is well pleased, etc." In each a Christ is born. [1]

[1] A third form of the pantheistic conception of the incarnation can be perceived
in the thesis, that the humanity of Christ was heavenly; in other words, that the
Logos had always borne humanity in himself, so that his body was not of later

The thought that Christ assumed the general concept of humanity occurs, though mingled with distinctive ideas, in Hilary, who was dependent on Gregory.[1] We find it also in Basil,[2] Ephræm,[3] Apollinaris,[4] Cyril of Alexandria, etc. Throughout these writers the conception is clearly marked that in Christ our nature is sanctified and rendered divine, that what it has experienced benefits us, as a matter of course, in our

origin than his divinity. This Gnostic view, which, however, is not necessarily pantheistic, had supporters, e.g., in Corinth in the time of Athanasius, who himself opposed it. (Ep. ad Epictetum Corinth.: see Epiphan.. p. 77, c. Dimoeritas). They said that the body born of Mary was ὁμοούσιον τῇ τοῦ λόγου θεότητι, συναίδιον αὐτῷ διὰ παντὸς γεγενῆσθαι, ἐπειδὴ ἐκ τῆς οὐσίας τῆς Σοφίας συνέστη. They taught, accordingly, that humanity itself sprang from the Logos; he had for the purpose of his manifestation formed for himself by metamorphosis a body capable of suffering. He had, therefore, on one side of his being given up his immutability, departed from his own nature (ἠλλάγη τῆς ἰδίας φύσεως) and transformed himself into a sensuous man. The point of interest here was the perfect unity of Christ. Those whom Hilary opposed (De trinit. X. 15 sq.) did not maintain the heavenly and eternal humanity of the Logos. On the other hand, this thesis occurs in Apollinaris, in whom, however, it is not to be explained pantheistically, although pantheistic inferences can hardly be averted. The heavenly humanity of Christ is also opposed by Basil in Ep. ad Sozopol. (65); it re-emerged in the circles of the most extreme Monophysites; but it was at the same time openly affirmed there by Stephen Bar Sudaili: "everything is of one nature with God"; "all nature is consubstantial with the divine essence" (Assem., Biblioth. II. 30, 291); see Dorner, l. c., II., p. 162 f., and Frothingham, Stephen Bar Sudaili (1886) who has printed, p. 28 sq., the letter of Xenaias which warns against the heresy "that assimilates the creation to God." Finally, a kind of subtilised form of this phenomenon is found in the old-catholic conception, that the Son of God came down to men immediately after the Fall, that he repeatedly dwelt among them, and thus accustomed himself to his future manifestation (see Irenæus' conception, Vol. II., p. 236). In the later Fathers, when they were not writing apologetically, this old conception does not, so far as I know, occur often, or, it is very strictly distinguished from the incarnation; see, e.g., Athan., Orat. III. 30.

[1] See, e.g., Hilary, Tract. in Ps. LI, ch. 16: "Ut et filius hominis esset filius dei, naturam in se universæ carnis assumpsit, per quam effectus vera vitis genus in se universæ propaginis tenet." Ps. LIV. ch. 9 : "Universitatis nostræ caro est factus." Other passages are given in Dorner, Entw-Gesch. der Lehre v. d. Person Christi, I., p. 1067, and Ritschl, l. c., I. p. 15.

[2] Hom. 25, T. I., p. 504 sq. This exposition coincides completely with Gregory's thought.

[3] Dorner, l. c., p. 961.

Dorner, l. c., the κατὰ μέρος πίστις. See besides the passage given in Vol. II., p. 223, n. 1.

individual capacity, and that we in a very real way have risen
with Christ.

Even in the Antiochenes passages occur which are thus to be
interpreted—exegesis led them to this view; [1] but they exist, so
far as I know, even in Chrysostom,[2] and they are so phrased
in general as to show that according to them this suffering and
dying with Christ, as an independent fact, was not merely a
supplementary condition of the actual union with Christ, but
the only form in which it was accomplished. In them the
general concept of humanity does not occur; accordingly, the
humanity of Christ is conceived much more concretely. He is
really a fighting, striving man who reaches victory through
free-will. [3] As this man himself is united morally with the
deity, the moral element must never be left out of account in
our union with him. But in so far as the incarnation of Christ
produces a new state (Katastasis), one not included in the plan
of humanity, it undoubtedly results in our glorification, a state
not involved in the moral element *per se*.

When we come to John of Damascus we no longer find any
definitive conception of the incarnation. The clear intention
assigned to it by Athanasius has escaped him; even of the ideas
of Gregory of Nyssa only a part, and that the apologetic part,
are reproduced (De fide Orth. III. 1, 6). At this point also
the attempt to unite the Aristotelian tradition of the school of
Antioch with the Alexandrian only led to a combination of
fragments. Yet the sentence, "Christ did not come to this or
that one, but to our common nature", [4] never wholly became
a dead letter in the Greek Church. But everything taught in
that Church as to the incarnation is already to be found either
developed, or in germ, in Irenæus; not the simple exposition
of Athanasius, but a mixture of the thought of the historical

---

[1] See Theodore on Rom. VI. 6: τῷ Χριστῷ, φησίν, ἐσταυρωμένῳ ὥσπερ ἅπασα
ἡμῶν ἡ ὑπὸ τὴν θνητότητα κειμένη φύσις συνεσταυρώθη, ἐπειδὴ καὶ πᾶσα αὐτῷ συναν
έστη, πάντων ἀνθρώπων αὐτῷ συμμετασχεῖν ἐλπιζόντων τῆς ἀναστάσεως· ὡς ἐντεῦθεν συναφανισθῆναι μὲν τὴν περὶ τὸ ἁμαρτάνειν ἡμῶν εὐκολίαν, διὰ τῆς ἐπὶ τὴν ἀθανασίαν τοῦ σώματος μεταστάσεως.

[2] Förster, Chrysostomus, p. 126 ff.

[3] See Kihn, Theodor., p. 180 ff.

[4] Χριστὸς οὐ πρὸς ἕνα καὶ δεύτερον ἦλθεν, ἀλλὰ πρὸς τὴν κοινὴν φύσιν.

with that of the mystical redemption, is to be traced in the majority of the Fathers. It is the Christ in us, the cosmical Christ, as we already saw in Methodius.

*Supplement II.*—Those Fathers, and they were in the majority, who found the cause of the incarnation in the intention of God to rehabilitate the human race, knew of no necessity for the incarnation apart from the entrance of sin. While they almost all explained that what Christ conferred was more and greater than what man had lost, yet they did not use this idea in their speculations, and they attached as a rule no special significance to it. But even Irenæus had also looked at the incarnation as the final and supreme means of the divine economy by which God gradually brought the original creation, at first necessarily imperfect, to completion. [1] Where this idea occurred, it also involved the other, that Christ would have come even if there had been no sin. Accordingly, those Fathers who laid no special stress on sin, seeing it appeared to them to be more or less natural, and who conceived redemption rather as a perfecting than restitution, maintained the necessity of the incarnation even apart from sin: so Theodore of Mopsuestia, Pelagius and others. [2] The incarnation was regarded by them as forming the basis of the life in which man is raised above his nature and common virtue, that is, the ascetic and angelic life. Clement of Alex., starting from quite different premises, expressed the same thought. Abstinence from evil was the perfection that had been attained even by Greeks and Jews; on the other hand, the perfect Gnostic, only possible after the complete revelation of the Logos, found perfection in the ascetic life of intuition, a life resting on faith, hope, and love. [3] Therefore in order to institute this life, the complete revelation of the Logos was required; it was unnecessary to bring sin into the question. However, the proposition that Christ would have come even if Adam had not sinned was, so far as I know, bluntly asserted by no Greek theologian; the combination of Adam and Christ in the Bible stood in the way.

*Supplement III.*—On the ground of Biblical texts like Matt.

---

[1] See Vol. II., p. 272, 307; the thought is not wanting in Tertullian.
[2] See Dorner, l. c. II., p. 432 ff. Kihn, Theodor., p. 179 f.
[3] Strom. VI. 7, 60.

XXV. 24, Eph. I. 3—5, 11, II. Tim. I. 8—10, the Greeks have
also spoken (*e.g.*, Athan. c. Arian. II. 75—77) of an election
of believers in Christ before the foundation of the world, and
of the decree of redemption framed by God, with reference
already to sin, before the creation. Athanasius even says that
our future eternal life in Christ is conditioned by the fact that
our life was founded on Christ even before time was. But the
idea of predestination, like the thought that Christ is the head
of his Church, is confined to the lines of a Biblical doctrine,
which for that very reason is true. Neither the doctrine of the
work of Christ, nor of the appropriation of his work, is influenced
by those conceptions. As a rule, however, the idea of predestination takes the form that God having foreseen men's attainments
in virtue elected them. This version is especially clear in the
school of Antioch, and even enters into their Christology; but
it is the opposite of what Paul meant.

# APPENDIX TO CHAPTER VI.

## THE IDEAS OF REDEMPTION FROM THE DEVIL, AND OF ATONEMENT THROUGH THE WORK OF THE GOD-MAN.

### § 1. *Christ's Death as Ransom and Sacrifice.*

THE Greek Fathers did not go beyond, nor could they give a more consistent form to, the views on this subject already expounded by Irenæus and Origen. [1] The fact of the incarnation was so closely and exclusively connected, at least in the East, with the conception of the *result* of redemption, that everything else had to yield in importance to the latter. Of course at all times and in all directions the attempt was made, after the example of Irenæus and the indications of Holy Scripture, to insert the facts of Jesus' history in the work of redemption. This can be seen especially in Athanasius and the two Cyrils—"Whatever happened to his humanity has happened to us." Again, the death of Christ was frequently recalled when the forgiveness of sins was taken into account; but it is difficult here to draw the line between exegesis, rhetoric, and dogmatics. As a rule, we obtain the impression that theology could have dispensed with all the facts of Christ's life. [2] On the other hand, the death of Christ always appeared so tragic and wonderful an event, that men were compelled to attribute a special

[1] See Vol. II., pp. 286 ff., 365 ff.

[2] The two Cappadocians doubted, not without reserve, the necessity of Christ's death. G. of Nazianzus says that the divine Logos could also have redeemed us θελήματι μόνον, and G. of Nyssa (Orat. cat. 17) thought that the method of redemption was to be considered as arbitrary as the remedies of physicians. In other places, indeed, they expressed themselves differently, and Athanasius connected the death of Christ closely with the incarnation (see above).

saving value to it. But just as it was not represented in art up to the fifth century, so the majority of the Greeks really regarded it, along with Christ's whole passion, as a sacred mystery, and that not only in the intellectual sense. Here thought yielded to emotion, and imposed silence on itself. Goethe said towards the close of his life, "We draw a veil over the sufferings of Christ simply because we revere them so deeply; we hold it to be reprehensible presumption to play and trifle with and embellish those profound mysteries in which the divine depths of suffering lie hidden, never to rest until even the noblest seems mean and tasteless." That exactly represents the Greek feeling. It also gives the key to the saying of Gregory of Nazianzus (Orat. XXVII. 10) that the appreciation of the sufferings of Christ was one of those points on which it was possible to make a mistake with impunity (cf. Iren. I. 10). By this he meant, not only that the specific result of the passion was uncertain, but also that it was inexpressible. [1] It was reserved for the Middle Ages and our modern times to cast off all modesty and reverence here.

Yet a few theologians and exegetes could not refrain from speculating about the death of Christ, though they did not yet use frivolous arithmetical sums. The death of Christ was, in the first place, connected, following Rom. VIII. 3, with the condemnation of sin—death—in the flesh ($\varkappa \alpha \tau \alpha \varkappa \rho i\nu \epsilon \iota \nu$ $\tau \grave{\eta}\nu$ $\grave{\alpha}\mu\alpha\rho$-$\tau i\alpha\nu$ $(\tau \grave{o}\nu$ $\theta \acute{\alpha}\nu\alpha\tau o\nu)$ $\grave{\epsilon}\nu$ $\tau \tilde{\eta}$ $\sigma\alpha\rho\varkappa i)$. That constituted the strongest connection of Ensarkosis (embodiment in the flesh), death, resurrection, and redemption, reached within the Greek Church. In Christ's final agony *the Ensarkosis first came to some extent to its end*, for by death the flesh was purified from sin and mortality, and was presented in Christ's resurrection pure, holy, and incorruptible. This thought was worked out in various ways by Athanasius, Gregory of Nyssa, and Cyril of Jerusalem, as well as, especially, by Apollinaris. [2] But in later times the conception of the complete hypostatic union forbade the vanquish-

---

[1] See the great importance laid already by Justin on the Cross, an importance which it still has for the piety of the Greek Church.

[2] Apollinaris who was the strictest dogmatist of the fourth century, substantially limited the significance of Christ's death, so far as I know, to this effect.

ing of corruption ($\Phi\theta o\rho\dot{\alpha}$) and death being dated a moment later than the assumption of human nature. Therefore it was held that Christ had even at the incarnation destroyed corruption and death (the penalty of sin) from the flesh; but his death was wholly voluntary and *economic*.

In the second place Irenæus had already, in a connected argument, emphasised the necessity of tracing the incarnation of the Logos and his passion to the goodness and righteousness of God, and he further insisted that Christ had delivered us not from a state of infirmity, but from the power of the devil, redeeming those estranged from God, and unnaturally imprisoned, not by force, but with due regard to justice. Origen, however, was the first to explain the passion and death of Christ with logical precision under the points of view of *ransom* and *sacrifice*. With regard to the former he was the first to set up the theory that the devil had acquired a legal claim on men, and therefore to regard the death of Christ (or his soul) as a ransom paid to the devil. This Marcionite doctrine of price and barter was already supplemented by Origen with the assumption of an act of deceit on the part of God. It was, in spite of an energetic protest, taken up by his disciples, and afterwards carried out still more offensively. It occurs in Gregory of Nyssa who (Catech. 15—27), in dealing with the notion of God, treats it broadly and repulsively. We find it in Ambrose, who speaks of the *pia fraus*, in Augustine and Leo I. It assumes its worst form in Gregory I.: the humanity of Christ was the bait; the fish, the devil, snapped at it, and was left hanging on the invisible hook, Christ's divinity. It proves that the Fathers had gradually lost any fixed conception of the holiness and righteousness of God; but on the other hand, it expresses the belief that the devil's power will not first be broken by the future appearing of Christ, but has been already shattered by his death. In this sense it is the epitaph of the old dogmatics which turned on eschatology.[1] For the rest, Gregory of Nazi-

[1] Irenæus held that men were God's debtors, but in the power (unjustly) of the devil. Origen held a different view. The devil had a claim on men, and Christ paid him his soul as the price, but the devil could not keep it. The devil acted unjustly to Christ, he was not entitled to take possession of one who was sinless;

anzus [1] and John of Damascus felt scruples about admitting God
and the devil to have been partners in a legal transaction.
With reference to the sacrifice of Christ, Origen was of
epoch-making importance. On the one hand, he started from
Rom. III. 25 and similar texts, on the other, he was strongly
influenced by the Græco-oriental expiatory mysteries, and was
the first to introduce into the Church, following the precedent
set by the Gnostics, a theology of sacrifice or propitiation
based on the death of Christ. He thereby enriched, but at the
same time confused, Greek theology. He taught that all sins
required a holy and pure sacrifice in order to be atoned for,
in other words, to be forgiven by God; this sacrifice was the
body of Christ, presented to the Father. This thought which,
as expounded, approximates to the idea of a vicarious suffering
of punishment, was adopted by Athanasius who combined it
with the other ideas that God's veracity required the threat of
death to be carried out, and that death accordingly was accepted
by Christ on behalf of all, and by him was destroyed. [2] The
idea that only the sacrificial death of God could vanquish death
which was decreed by him, and thus conciliate God, occurs also

see passages given in Münscher, p. 428 ff. Leo I, following Ambrose, gives the
deception theory in a crude form.

[1] See Ullman, Gregor, p. 318 f.

[2] De incarnat. 9: Συνιδὼν γὰρ ὁ λόγος, ὅτι ἄλλως οὐκ ἂν λυθείη τῶν ἀνθρώπων
ἡ φθορά, εἰ μὴ διὰ τοῦ πάντως ἀποθανεῖν, οὐχ οἷόν τε δὲ ἦν τὸν λόγον ἀποθανεῖν,
ἀθάνατον ὄντα καὶ τοῦ πατρὸς υἱόν, τούτου ἕνεκεν τό δυνάμενον ἀποθανεῖν ἑαυτῷ
λαμβάνει σῶμα, ἵνα τοῦτο τοῦ ἐπὶ πάντων λόγου μεταλαβόν, ἀντὶ πάντων ἱκανὸν
γένηται τῷ θανάτῳ καὶ διὰ τὸν ἐνοικήσαντα λόγον ἄφθαρτον διαμείνῃ, καὶ λοιπὸν ἀπὸ
πάντων ἡ φθορὰ παύσηται τῇ τῆς ἀναστάσεως χάριτι· ὅθεν ὡς ἱερεῖον καὶ θῦμα
παντὸς ἐλεύθερον σπίλου, ὃ αὐτὸς ἑαυτῷ ἔλαβε σῶμα προσάγων εἰς θάνατον, ἀπὸ
πάντων εὐθὺς τῶν ὁμοίων ἠφάνιζε τὸν θάνατον τῇ προσφορᾷ τοῦ καταλλήλου. We
see how the conceptions of the vicarious endurance of punishment, and of a sacrifice, meet here; indeed, generally speaking, it was difficult to keep them apart.
Athanasius throughout lays greater stress on the former; Origen, as a Hellenist,
on the latter; see Athan., l. c., 6—10, but esp. Ch. XX: ὠφείλετο πάντας
ἀποθανεῖν... ὑπὲρ πάντων τὴν θυσίαν ἀνέφερεν, ἀντὶ πάντων τὸν ἑαυτοῦ ναὸν εἰς
θάνατον παραδιδούς, ἵνα τοὺς μὲν πάντας ἀνυπευθύνους καὶ ἐλευθέρους τῆς ἀρχαίας
παραβάσεως ποιήσῃ... ὁ πάντων θάνατος ἐν τῷ κυριακῷ σώματι ἐπληροῦτο καὶ ὁ
θάνατος καὶ ἡ φθορὰ διὰ τὸν συνόντα λόγον ἐξηφανίζετο. θανάτου γὰρ ἦν χρεία, καὶ
θάνατον ὑπὲρ πάντων ἔδει γενέσθαι, ἵνα τὸ παρὰ πάντων ὀφειλόμενον γένηται, c.
Arian. I. 60, II. 7, 66 sq.

in other Greek Fathers of the fourth century.[1] Following the estimate formed of the infinite value of the final passion of the God-man,[2] we constantly find in them also traces, sometimes more, sometimes less, distinct, of the thought of substitution in connection with satisfaction; but it remains obscure,[3] nay, it is frequently again withdrawn. In other words, it was sometimes twisted, as already in Irenæus, into the idea of example pure and simple. Thus the Antiochene school especially, who held his death to have been a natural event, considered that Christ's final passion influenced our freely-formed resolutions, but this version is not entirely wanting in any Greek Father. Others, *e.g.*, Gregory of Nazianzus, explained that God did not demand the sacrifice—or ransom—but received it δι' οἰκονομίαν.[4] In this case, as much as in earlier times, δι' οἰκονομίαν meant "that the Scriptures might be fulfilled"; that is, it was tantamount to abandoning a direct explanation of the fact itself. In any case Cyril of Alexandria shows most clearly the vicarious idea of the passion and death of the God-man in connection with the whole Christological conception.[5] Eusebius'

---

[1] See esp. Cyril, Catech. XIII. 33, but also the Cappadocians; cf. Ullmann, l. c., p. 316 ff.

[2] Even Cyril of Jerusalem says, l. c.: οὐ τοσαύτη ἦν τῶν ἁμαρτωλῶν ἡ ἀνομία, ὅση τοῦ ὑπεραποθνήσκοντος ἡ δικαιοσύνη. οὐ τοσοῦτον ἡμάρτομεν, ὅσον ἐδικαιοπράγησεν ὁ τὴν ψυχὴν ὑπὲρ ἡμῶν τεθεικώς. Similarly Chrysostom in the Ep. ad Rom., Hom. 10, T. X., p. 121. But the idea is emotional, and not the starting-point of a philosophical theory. It is different with the Westerns.

[3] The expiation of our guilt is more infrequently thought of than the taking over of sin's punishment; that is, guilt is only indirectly referred to.

[4] See Ullmann, l. c., p. 319.

[5] The idea of sacrifice falls into the background, which was only to be expected in the case of this energetic spokesman of genuine Greek Christian theology. Substitution passed naturally into, or rather grew out of, the idea of mystical mediation. Because all human nature was purified and transfigured really and physically in Christ, he could, *regarded as an individual*, be conceived as substitute or ἀντίλυτρον; see Cyril on John I. 29 and Gal. III. 13. Meanwhile Cyril also says that Christ outweighed all in merit. For the rest, he does not venture to affirm that Christ became a curse, but explains that he endured what one burdened with a curse must suffer. Compare also the exposition in the Orat. de recta fide ad reginas (Mansi IV., p. 809). The points of *voluntariness* and *substitution* were emphasised more strongly by orthodox theologians after Cyril, in order not to compromise the perfectly hypostatic deification—from the moment of the incarnation—of Christ's human nature

method of formulating the idea comes nearest Paul's, but it is
only a paraphrase;¹ and the inability of theologians to recognise,
expose and dispute the differences in their divergent conceptions is the strongest proof that they were not clearly aware of
the bearing and weight of their own propositions.

## § 2. *Christ as man the Mediator.*

The West, which had a scheme of its own in Christology,
(see below) also possessed characteristic features in its conception
of the work of Christ.² Here, as in almost all departments of
activity in the Latin Church, it was of the highest moment
that Tertullian, the jurist, and Cyprian, the ecclesiastical ruler,
were the first Latin theologians. Disinclined for philosophical
and strictly religious speculation, and dominated by a prosaic
but powerful moralism, the Latins were possessed from the
first of an impulse to carry religion into the legal sphere. The
sacred authorities, or the Symbol, were regarded as the "law"
(*lex*) of God; divine service was the place where the censure of
God was pronounced; the deity was thought of as judge.
Father, Son, and Spirit were held to be "*personæ*" who
possessèd a common property ("*substantia*" not "*natura*").
Christ as the "*persona*" who controlled a two-fold "property,"
one inherited from his Father (his divinity) and one from his
mother (his humanity). Christ required to be obedient to God,
and—as Tertullian first said³ and Cyprian repeated—had to
satisfy God (*deo satisfacere*).⁴ In this phrase everything was
comprised: man—the Christian—was to give God that which
he owed him, *i.e.*, he was to satisfy God's legal claims. After
this came the "promereri deum", *i. e.*, rendering services to
God, gaining God's favour by our merits. But in Tertullian

---

¹ Demonstr. X. I: ὑπὲρ ἡμῶν κολασθεὶς καὶ τιμωρίαν ὑποσχών, ἣν αὐτὸς μὲν οὐκ
ὤφειλεν, ἀλλ᾽ ἡμεῖς τοῦ πλήθους ἕνεκεν τῶν πεπλημμελημένων, ἡμῖν αἴτιος τῆς τῶν
ἁμαρτημάτων ἀφέσεως κατέστη ... τὴν ἡμῖν προστετιμημένην κατάραν ἐφ᾽ ἑαυτὸν
ἑλκύσας, γενόμενος ὑπὲρ ἡμῶν κατάρα.

² See fuller details in next book. Here we only give a sketch. Comp. Wirth,
Der verdienstbegriff bei Tertullian, 1892.

³ See Vol. II., p. 294.

⁴ This notion was afterwards one of the most common in the West.

and Cyprian "satisfacere deo" meant more precisely to atone
for wrongs inflicted on God by acts of penitence, and to appease
him *(placare deum, satisfacere deo per hostias*: Arnobius).
Further *"promereri"* was applied above all to *bona opera*, works
(fasting) and alms-giving (Cypr., De oper. et eleemos.). Even
from the middle of the third century an ecclesiastical system was
drawn out in the Latin West of works to be rendered to God
(order of penance);[1] and this system gradually took in, like a
net, all man's relations to God. It was throughout governed
by the idea that the magnitude of transgressions and that of
the works rendered to God, the penitential offerings, were to
have a strictly legal relation, and, similarly, that what a man's
merits entitled him to from God had a fixed and regulated
value. It is not the case, as has been supposed, that this idea
first arose in the Church in the Romano-German period, and
is therefore to be described as a result of German criminal
law. On the contrary, the idea of *satisfactiones* and *merita*
already belonged in its entirety to the Roman age, and during
it was strictly worked out. From the days of Tertullian and
Cyprian the Latins were familiar with the notion that the
Christian had to propitiate God, that cries of pain, sufferings,
and deprivations were means, sacrificial means, of expiation,
that God took strict account of the *quantity* of the atonement,
and that, where there was no guilt to be blotted out, those
very means were represented as *merits*. All those trivial
definitions, which betray a low state of legal and moral views,
and which one would gladly attribute to barbarous nations,
had become the property of the Church before the incursion
of the Germans; and Anselm's principle, "Every sin must be
followed either by satisfaction or punishment",[2] can be already
shown in Sulpicius Severus,[3] and corresponds to the thought
of Cyprian and his successors.[4]

[1] It occurs already in Tertullian; but we do not yet perceive its full extent in
the Church in his time; it has not even the full significance that it possesses in
Cyprian.
[2] Necesse est ut omne peccatum satisfactio aut pœna sequatur.
[3] See Sulp. Sev., Dial. II. 10: Fornicatio deputetur ad pœnam, nisi satisfactione
purgetur.
[4] For fuller details see a later Vol.

But Cyprian also applied the "*satisfacere deo*" to Christ himself. As in the Middle Ages the most questionable consequences of the theory and practice of penance reacted on the conception of Christ's work, so from the time of Cyprian the latter was influenced by the view taken of human acts of penitence. His suffering and death constituted a sacrifice presented by Christ to God in order to propitiate him. This thought, started by Cyprian, was never afterwards lost sight of in the West. The angry God whom it was necessary to propitiate and of whom the Greeks knew so little, became more and more familiar in the West. Jewish and Pauline traditions here joined with those of Roman law. Hilary is especially clear in combining the sacrifice of Christ with the removal of guilt and of punishment. [1] This combination was repeated by Ambrose, [2] Augustine, and the great popes of antiquity; [3] least certainly, perhaps, by August-

---

[1] On Ps. LIII. 12: "passio suscepta voluntarie est, officio ipsa satisfactura pœnali"; Ch. 13: "maledictorum se obtulit morti, ut maledictionem legis solveret, hostiam se ipsum voluntarie offerendo." Along with this Hilary has the mystical realistic theory of the Greeks.

[2] A few passages are given in Förster, Ambrosius, pp. 136 ff., 297 f. The "*redimere a culpa*" is for Ambrose the decisive point. In his work De incarn. dom. he is never tired of answering the question as to the motive of the incarnation with the phrase: "*ut caro, quæ peccaverat, redimeretur,*" frequently adding "*a culpa.*" He also uses very often the word "*offerre*" (applied to the death of Christ). In Ps. XLVIII., exp. 17, we read: "quæ maior misericordia quam quod pro nostris flagitiis se præbuit immolandum, ut sanguine suo mundum levaret, cuius peccatum nullo alio modo potuisset aboleri." See Deutsch, Des Ambrosius Lehre von der Sünde und Sündentilgung, 1867.

[3] There are many striking passages in Leo I. in which death is described as an expiatory sacrifice which blots out guilt. See, further, Gregory I., Moral. XVII. 46: "delenda erat culpa, sed nisi per sacrificium deleri non poterat. Quærendum erat sacrificium, sed quale sacrificium poterat pro absolvendis hominibus inveniri? Neque etenim iustum fuit, ut pro rationali homine brutorum animalium victimæ cæderentur . . . Ergo requirendus erat homo . . . qui pro hominibus offerri debuisset, ut pro rationali creatura rationalis hostia mactaretur. Sed quid quod homo sine peccato inveniri non poterat, et oblata pro nobis hostia quando nos a peccato mundare potuisset, si ipsa hostia peccati contagio non careret? Ergo ut rationalis esset hostia, homo fuerat offerendus: ut vero a peccatis mundaret hominem, homo et sine peccato. Sed quis esset sine peccato homo, si ex peccati commixtione descenderet. Proinde venit propter nos in uterum virginis filius dei, ibi pro nobis factus est homo. Sumpta est ab illo natura, non culpa. Fecit pro nobis sacrificium, corpus suum exhibuit pro peccatoribus, victimam sine peccato, quæ et humanitate mori et iustitia mundare potuisset."

ine, who being a Neoplatonic philosopher and profound Christian thinker, was also familiar with other and more productive points of view. [1] The distinctive nature, however, of this Latin view of the work of Christ, as the propitiation of an angry God by a sacrificial death, was characteristically expressed in the firmly established thought that Christ performed it as man, therefore, by means, not of his divine, but of his human attributes.[2] The Latins were shut up to this conclusion. Their views regarding the work of Christ had been influenced by the works of penance enjoined by the Church, and on the other hand, the latter owed their value to the voluntary acceptance of suffering. Again, "sacrifices" in general were something human—God does not render, but receives sacrifices. Finally, mankind was in God's debt. From all this it necessarily followed that Christ in presenting himself as a sacrifice did so as *man*. But with this conclusion the Latins severed themselves from the supreme and final interests of Greek piety—for this rather required that the deity should have assumed with human nature all the "*passiones*" of the latter and made them its own. If the rigid Greek con-

[1] Whatever occurs in Ambrose is to be found also in Augustine; for the latter has not, so far as I know, omitted to use a single thought of the former; he only adds something new.

[2] See Ambrose, De fide III. 5: "Idem igitur sacerdos, idem et hostia, et sacerdotium tamen et sacrificium humanæ condicionis officium est. Nam et agnus ad immolandum ductus est et sacerdos erat secundum ordinem Melchisedech." This thought recalls Cyprian, although Ambrose has hardly taken it from him; Cypr. Ep. LXIII. 14: "Christus Iesus dominus et deus noster ipse est summus sacerdos dei patris et sacrificium patri se ipsum obtulit." The same idea is repeated in contents and form, but rendered more profound, by Augustine (Confess. X. 68, 69, see Ritschl, l. c., I., p. 38): "In quantum enim homo, in tantum mediator; in quantum autem verbum, non medius, quia æqualis deo . . . pro nobis deo victor et victor et victima, et ideo victor quia victima; pro nobis deo sacerdos et sacrificium; et ideo sacerdos quia sacrificium;" see De civit. dei IX. 15: "Nec tamen ab hoc mediator est, quia verbum, maxime quippe immortale et maxime beatum verbum longe est a mortalibus miseris; sed mediator per quod homo." Accordingly, not only was that which Christ presented in sacrifice human—Ambrose, De incarn. VI.: "ex nobis accepit quod proprium offeret pro nobis ... sacrificium de nostro obtulit"; but Christ as priest and mediator was man. He had to represent man, and that again only a man could do. Very pregnant is the sentence of Ambrose (in Luc. exp. IV. 7) "ut quia solvi non queunt divina decreta, persona magis quam sententia mutaretur." That is the genuine idea of substitution. Ambrose does not even shrink from saying "quia peccata nostra suscepit, peccatum dictus est" (Expos. in Ps. CXIX., X. 14).

ception, which, indeed, in after times was full of gaps and inconsistencies, represented Christ's sufferings as a whole to be not voluntary, but the complete acceptance of the Ensarkosis (life in the flesh), yet God is always the subject. [1] On the whole, therefore, the conception of sacrifice is really alien in the view of the Greeks to the strict theory of Christ's significance. It found its way in through exegesis and the mysteries, and threatened the compactness of the dogmatic conception, according to which everything that Christ did was summed up in the *complete assumptio carnis* (assumption of the flesh). Nor was the alien view able to shake the fundamental conception that the God-Logos was the *subject* in all that pertained to Christ. Among the Latins, on the other hand, the idea of the atoning sacrifice *plus* substitution is genuine, and has no general theory

---

[1] The subtle distinction between East and West is accordingly to be defined as follows. Both held that the human nature of Christ suffered, for the divine was incapable of suffering; but the East taught that the deity suffered through the human nature which he had made his own, the West that the man suffered and presented his human nature as a sacrifice in death; the latter, however, obtained an infinite value, for the deity was associated with it. From this we have two consequences. First, the idea of substitution could take root on Greek ground only superficially, and in an indefinite form; for the dying *God*-man really represented no one, but rather received all really into the plenitude of his divinity; it was different in the West. Secondly, the method of computing the value of Christ's mortal agony could similarly find no footing in the East; for the deity was the subject of the transaction, and precluded all questioning and computing. The striking utterances of Orientals as to the supreme value of Christ's work are really therefore only rhetorical (see above). If, on the other hand, the means of atonement under discussion, and the substitution are human, the question, of course, arises what value these possess, or what value is lent them by the divinity that is behind this sacrifice and this priest. We must take the statements of the Latin Fathers more literally. Ambrose confesses "Felix ruina quæ reparatur in melius" and "Amplius nobis profuit culpa quam nocuit: in quo redemptio quidem nostra divinum munus invenit. Facta est mihi culpa mea merces redemptionis, per quam mihi Christus advenit... Fructuosior culpa quam innocentia; innocentia arrogantem me fecerat—and here indeed the paradox becomes nonsensical—culpa subjectum reddidit." (Numerous passages are given in Deutsch, l. c., see also Förster, l. c,, pp. 136, 297). Augustine often repeats and varies this thought, and other Western writers reproduce it from him. "Felix culpa quæ tantum et talem meruit habere redemptorem." Lastly, Leo I. preaches (Serm. LXI. 3): "validius donum factum est libertatis, quam debitum servitutis." Sayings like these, apart from the special pleading in which Western writers have always delighted since Tertullian, are to be taken much more seriously than if they had come from the East. And in fact momentous speculations were certainly instituted by them.

against it; for they never were able to rise perfectly to the contemplation of Christ's work as the *assumptio carnis*, an expression of the loftiest piety among the Greeks. Those of the latter who, like the Antiochenes, either did not share or only imperfectly shared the realistic idea of redemption, referred, it is worth remarking, the work of Christ, like the Latins, to the human side of his personality. [1]

Great as are the distinctions here—the West did not possess in antiquity a definite dogmatic theory as to the atoning work of Christ. Greek views exerted their influence; [2] and, besides, Western Christians were not yet disposed, with a very few exceptions, to trouble themselves with thoughts that had no bearing on practical life.

[1] An affinity exists between the theology of the Antiochenes and Latins— esp. pre-Augustinian; but it is greater to a superficial than to a more exact observer. The Antiochene conception always had the Alexandrian for a foil; it never emancipated itself sufficiently from the latter to set up a perfectly compact counter-theology; it was in a sense Greek piety and Greek theology *watered down*. The Latins did not possess this foil. Their theology must not be gauged by Origen and Neoplatonism as if they furnished its starting-point.

[2] So from Hilary down to Augustine. The most important of the Western Fathers accepted the Greek idea of the purchase from the devil, although it flatly contradicted their own doctrine of the atonement; and this proves how uncertain they were. The grotesque conception of the role played by the devil at the death of Christ, had nevertheless something good about it. It reminded men that every knave is a stupid devil, and that the devil is always a stupid knave.

# APPENDIX ON MANICHÆISM.

THREE great religious systems confronted each other in Western Asia and Southern Europe from the close of the third century: Neoplatonism, Catholicism and Manichæism. All three may be characterised as the final results of a history, lasting for more than a thousand years, of the religious development of the civilised peoples from Persia to Italy. In all three the old national and particular character of religions was laid aside ; they were world-religions of the most universal tendency, and making demands which in their consequences transformed the whole of human life, public and private. For the national cultus they substituted a system which aspired to be theology, theory of the universe and science of history, and at the same time embraced a definite ethics, and a ritual of divine service. Formally, therefore, the three religions were alike, and they were also similar in that each had appropriated the elements of different older religions. Further, they showed their similarity in bringing to the front the ideas of revelation, redemption, ascetic virtue, and immortality. But Neoplatonism was natural religion spiritualised, the polytheism of Greece transfigured by Oriental influences and developed into pantheism. Catholicism was the monotheistic world-religion based on the O. T. and the Gospel, but constructed by the aid of Hellenic speculation and ethics. Manichæism was the dualistic world-religion resting on Chaldæism,[1] but interspersed with Christian, Parsi, and perhaps Buddhist thoughts. To Manichæism the Hellenic element was wanting, to Catholicism the Chaldee and Persian. These three world-religions

[1] See Brandt, Die mandäische Religion, 1889 (further, Wellhausen in the deutsch. Litt.-Ztg., 1890, No. 41).

developed in the course of two centuries (c. A.D. 50—250), Catholicism coming first and Manichæism last. Catholicism and Manichæism were superior to Neoplatonism for the very reason that the latter possessed no founder; it, therefore, developed no elemental force, and never lost the character of being an artificial creation. Attempts which were made to invent a founder for it naturally failed. But, even apart from the contents of its religion, Catholicism was superior to Manichæism, because its founder was venerated not merely as the bearer of revelation, but as the Redeemer in person and the Son of God. The fight waged by Catholicism with Neoplatonism had been already decided about the middle of the fourth century, although the latter continued to hold its ground in the Greek Empire for almost two centuries longer. As against Manichæism the Catholic Church was certain of victory from the beginning; for at the moment when Manichæism disputed its supremacy, it became the privileged State Church. But its opponent did not suffer itself to be annihilated; it lasted till far into the Middle Ages in East and West, though in various modifications and forms.

*Authorities—(a) Oriental.*

1. Mohammedan.—Among our sources for the history of Manichæism the Oriental are the most important; of these the Mohammedan, though comparatively late, are distinguished by the excellence of the tradition and their impartiality, and must be given the first place, since in them old Manichæan writings are employed, and we possess no other originals of this sort belonging to the third century, except a few short and rather unimportant fragments. At the head stands Abulfaragius, Fihrist (c. 980), see the edition by Flügel and the work of the latter: "Mani, seine Lehre und seine Schriften," 1862; further, Shahrastâni, Kitâb al-milal wan-nuhal (12th century), see edition by Cureton and German translation by Haarbrücker, 1851; some notes and extracts in Tabari (10th century), al-Birunî (11th century), Ibn al-Murtada (see Kessler, Mani, I., p. 346 ff.), and other Arabian and Persian historians.

2. Christian.—Of Eastern Christians we learn most from

Ephraem Syrus (+373) in various writings, and in a tractate on
the subject edited by Overbeck; from Esnîk, the Armenian (see
Zeitschr. f. d. hist. Theol., 1840, II.; Langlois, Collection, etc.,
II., p. 395 sq.), who wrote in the fifth century against Marcion
and Mani; and from the Alexandrian Patriarch Eutychius (+916)
who composed a chronicle (ed. by Pococke, 1628). Besides this,
separate pieces of information occur in Aphraates (4th century),
Barhebraeus (Arab. and Syr. 13th century) and others.

### (b) Greek and Latin.

The earliest mention of the Manichæans in the Roman or
Greek empire occurs in an edict of Diocletian (see Hänel, Cod.
Gregor. tit. XV.), which is held by some not to be genuine,
and by others is dated A.D. 287, 290, 296, or 308 (so Mason,
The Persec. of Dioclet., p. 275 sq.). Eusebius gives a brief
account (H. E. VII. 31). The main authority, however, for
Greek and Roman writers was the Acta Archelai, which though
not what they pretended to be, namely, an account of a disputation between Mani and Bishop Archelaus of Cascar in
Mesopotamia, yet contain much that is reliable, esp as to the
doctrine of Mani, and also embrace Manichæan fragments.
The Acts, which for the rest consist of various documents,
originated at the beginning of the fourth century (in Edessa?).
Jerome maintains (De vir. inl. 72) that they were originally
composed in Syria (so also Kessler); but Nöldeke (Ztschr. d.
deutsch. morgenl. Gesellsch. vol. 43, p. 537 ff.) and Rahlfs have
disproved Kessler's arguments (Gött. Gel. Anz., 1889, No. 23).
They have made it very probable that the Acts, while they may
have been based on Syrian sources, were originally written in
Greek. They were soon afterwards translated into Latin. We
only possess this version (Edited by Zacagni, 1698; Routh,
Reliq. S. Vol. V., 1848); of the Greek version small fragments
have been preserved (see on the Acta Archelai the discussions
by Zittwitz in the Zeitschr. f. die histor. Theol., 1873, and the
Dissertation by Oblasinski. Acta disp. Arch. et Manetis, 1874.
In the form in which we now have them, they are a compilation
largely edited on the pattern of the Clementine Homilies). The

Acta were made use of by Cyril of Jerusalem (Catech. VI.), Epiphanius (Hær. 66) and very many others. All Greek and Latin students of heresy have put the Manichæans in their catalogues; but they only rarely give any original information about them (see Theodoret Hær. fab. I. 26).

Important matter occurs in the decrees of Councils from the fourth century (see Mansi, Acta Concil., and Hefele, Concilien-geschichte, Vols. I.—III.), and in the controversial writings of Titus of Bostra (4th century, in Syriac after a MS. of A.D. 411) πρὸς Μανιχαίους (edit. by de Lagarde, 1859), and Alexander of Lycopolis, Λόγος πρὸς τὰς Μανιχαίου δόξας (edit. by Combefis.). Of Byzantines, John of Damascus (De hæres and Dial.) and Photius (cod. 179 Biblioth.) deserve special mention; see also the Manichæan form of oath in Tollii insignia itiner. ital. p. 126 sq., and in Cotelier, P. P. App. Opp. I. p. 543; further, Rahlfs, l.c. The controversy with the Paulicians and Bogomilians, who were frequently identified with the Manichæans, renewed the interest in the latter. In the West the works of Augustine are the great repository for our knowledge of the Manichæans:— "Contra epistolam Manichæi, quam vocant fundamenti", "Contra Faustum Manichæum", "Contra Fortunatum", "Contra Adimantum", "Contra Secundinum", "De actis cum Felice Manichæo", "De genesi c. Manichæos", "De natura boni", "De duabus animabus", "De utilitate credendi", "De moribus eccl. Cathol. et de moribus Manichæorum", "De vera religione", "De hæres." But the more complete the view of Manichæism to be obtained from these writings, the more cautious we must be in our generalisations; for the Manichæism of the West undoubtedly received Christian elements which were wanting in its original and oriental form.

## Mani's Life.

Mani (Μάνης; Manes, Μανιχαῖος, Manichæus—the name has not yet been explained; it is not even known whether it is of Persian or Semitic origin) is said, as the Acta Archelai inform us, to have been originally called "Cubricus". Nothing reliable was ever known as to his life in the Romano-Greek empire; for the account in the Acta Archelai is wholly biassed and untrustworthy. Even if criticism succeeded in pointing out the sources from which it was derived, in discovering the tendencies that were at work, and in thus sifting out portions that were tenable, yet it could only do so by depending on the comparatively trustworthy Oriental Mohammedan tradition. We must therefore examine the latter alone. According to it, Mani was a Persian of distinguished birth belonging to Mardin. The date of his birth is uncertain; Kessler holds the statement in Bîrunî to be reliable, that he was born in anno 527 of the era of the Babylonian astronomers, *i.e.*, A.D. 215—216. He received a careful education from his father Fâtàk (Πατέκιος) at Ctesiphon. Since the father afterwards adhered to the confession of the "Moghtasilah", the Baptists, in southern Babylonia, the son was also brought up in their religious doctrines and practices. The Baptists (see the Fihrist) were probably not unconnected with the Elkesaites and Hemerobaptists, and were in any case allied to the Mandæans. It is not improbable that this Babylonian sect had adopted Christian elements. The boy accordingly became early acquainted with very different forms of religion. If even a small proportion of the narratives about his father rest on truth—the greater number being certainly only Manichæan legends—he had already introduced his son into the religious medley, out of which the Manichæan system arose. Manichæan tradition tells us that Mani received revelations, and took up a critical attitude towards religious instruction, even when a boy. But it is all the less trustworthy, as it also relates that he was forbidden to ventilate publicly his new religious knowledge. It was only when he was from 25 to 30 years of age that he began to preach his new religion at the court of the Persian king, Sapores I.—on the day, it is stated, of the king's coronation, A.D. 241—242. A Persian tradition says that he was previously a Christian presbyter, but this, in any case, is wrong. Mani did not remain long in Persia, but undertook long journeys for the purpose of spreading his religion, and he also sent out disciples. According to the Acta Archelai, his missionary activity extended into the West, into the territory of the Christian Church; but it is certain from Oriental sources that his work was rather carried on in Transoxania, Western China, and southwards into India. His labours met with success there as well as in Persia. Like Mohammed after him, and the founder of the Elkesaites before him, he proclaimed himself the last and greatest of the prophets, whose revelation of God surpassed all that had been given till then, the latter being allowed only a relative value. He instituted the absolute religion. In the last years of the reign of Sapores I. (c. A.D. 270) Mani returned to the Persian capital, and gained adherents even at the court. Naturally, however, the ruling priestly caste of the Magi, on whom the king was compelled to lean, were hostile to him, and after a few successes Mani was taken prisoner and driven into exile. The successor of Sapores, Hormuz (272—273), seems to have been favourable to him, but Bahrâm I. abandoned him to the fanaticism of the Magi, and had him crucified at the capital, A.D. 276—277. His dead body was skinned; and his adherents were dreadfully persecuted by Bahrâm.

## Mani's Writings.

Mani himself composed very many writings and epistles, of which a large proportion were still known to the Mohammedan historians, but which are now all lost. The later heads of the Manichæan Churches also wrote religious tractates, so that the ancient Manichæan literature must have been very extensive. According to the Fihrist, Mani made use of the Persian and Syriac languages; he invented, however, like the Oriental Marcionites before him, an alphabet of his own which the Fihrist has transmitted to us. In this alphabet the sacred works of the Manichæans were afterwards written. The Fihrist enumerates seven principal works by Mani, six in Syriac and one in Persian; as to some of them we possess statements also in Titus of Bostra, Epiphanius, Augustine, and Photius, as well as in the oath-formula and the Acta Archelai. We have (1) The Book of mysteries: see Acta Archelai; it contained discussions with the Christian sects which were spreading in the East, especially the Marcionites and Bardesanians, as well as with

their conception of the Old and New Testaments. (2) The
Book of Giants (demons? probably in connection with Gen. VI.).
(3) The Book of Regulations for the hearers,—apparently identical with the "epistula fundamenti" of Augustine and the
"Book of the Chapters" of Epiphanius and the Acta Archelai.
It was the most extensively circulated and popular of Manichæan works, and was also translated into Greek and Latin—
being a brief summary of the whole fundamentally authoritative
doctrine. (4) The Book Schâhpûrakân. Flügel was unable to
explain this title; according to Kessler, it means "Epistle to
King Sapores". This tractate contained eschatological teaching.
(5) The Book of quickening. It is identified by Kessler with
the "Thesaurus (vitæ)" of the Acta Archelai, Epiphanius, Photius, and Augustine; in that case it was also in use among the
Latin Manichæans. (6) The Book πραγματεία—contents unknown. (7)—In the Persian language; a book whose title is not
stated in the Fihrist, as we have it, but which is probably
identical with the "Holy Gospel" of the Manichæans; see the
Acta Archelai and many witnesses. This was the work set up
by the Manichæans in opposition to the Gospels of the Church.
Besides these main works, Mani wrote a great number of shorter
tractates and letters. The epistolography was then established
by his successors. These Manichæan treatises were also familiar
in the Græco-Roman empire and existed in collections—see the
βιβλίον ἐπιστολῶν in the oath-formula; and an "epistula ad virginem Menoch" in Augustine. Fabricius has collected the Greek
fragments of Manichæan epistles in the Bibliotheca Græca VII. 2,
p. 311 sq. There also existed a Manichæan Book of "memoirs"
and one of "prayers" in the Greek language, as well as many
others (e.g., the "Canticum Amatorium" cited by Augustine),
all of which, however, were destroyed by Christian Bishops in
alliance with the magistracy. A Manichæan Epistle to one
Marcellus has been preserved to us in the Acta Archelai. Zittwitz supposes that this letter was much fuller in its original
form, and that the author of the Acts has borrowed from it
the material for the speeches which he makes Mani deliver in
the discussion. The same scholar refers the account of Turbo
in the Acts and their historical statements (in section 4) to the

writing of a Turbo of Mesopotamia, a Manichæan renegade and Christian. But on this point it is at least possible to hold a different opinion.

### Mani's Doctrine. The Manichæan System.

Clearly as the main features of the Manichæan doctrine can be presented even at the present day, and certain as it is that Mani himself published a complete system, yet many details are uncertain, being differently described in different places, and it often remains doubtful what the original doctrinal view of the founder was.

The Manichæan system of religion was a consistent and uncompromising dualism, in the form of a fanciful view of nature. No distinction was drawn between the physical and ethical: in this respect the character of the system was thoroughly materialistic; for Mani's identification of the good with light, and the bad with darkness, was not merely figurative. The light was really the only good, and darkness the only bad. Hence it followed, that religious knowledge could be nothing but the knowledge of nature and its elements, and that redemption consisted exclusively in a physical deliverance of the fractions of light from darkness. But under such circumstances, ethics became a doctrine of abstinence from all elements arising from the realm of darkness.

The self-contradictory character of the present world formed for Mani the starting-point of his speculation. But the inconsistency appeared to him to be primarily elemental, and only secondarily ethical, in so far as he regarded the material side of man as an emanation from the bad parts of nature. From the self-contradictory character of the world he inferred two beings, originally wholly separate from each other,—light and darkness. Both were, however, to be thought of after the analogy of a kingdom. The light appeared as the good Primeval Spirit - God, shining in the ten (twelve) virtues of love, faith, fidelity, magnanimity, wisdom, gentleness, knowledge, intelligence, mystery, and insight. It also manifested itself in the heaven and earth of light with their guardians, the

glorious Æons. The darkness, similarly, was a spiritual realm:
more correctly, it was represented in a spiritual, or feminine,
personification; but it had no "God" at its head. It embraced
an "earth of darkness". As the earth of light had five, distinguishing features—the gentle breeze, cooling wind, bright
light, cheering fire, and clear water—so also the earth of
darkness had five—fog, fiery heat, burning wind, darkness, and
damp. Satan with his demons was born from the realm of
darkness. From eternity the two realms stood opposed. They
came into contact on one side, but they did not mingle. Then
Satan began to storm, and made an attack on the realm, the
earth, of light. The God of light, with his Syzygos (mate) "the
spirit of his right hand", now generated the Primeval man, and
sent him, equipped with the five pure elements, to fight against
Satan. But Satan proved himself the stronger. Primeval man
was defeated for a moment. Now indeed the God of light
himself marched forth, utterly defeated Satan by the help of
new Æons—the spirit of life, etc.—and delivered the Primeval
man. But a part of the light of the latter had already been
robbed by darkness, the five dark elements had already mingled with the generations of light. The Primeval man could
only descend into the abyss and hinder the increase of the
dark "generations" by cutting off their roots; but the elements
once mixed he could never again separate. The mixed elements
were the elements of the present visible world. This was
fashioned out of them at the command of the God of light;
the formation of the world was itself the first step in the
redemption of the imprisoned portions of light. The world
itself was represented as an ordered chain of different heavens
and different earths, which was borne and supported by the
Æons, the angels of light. In sun and moon, which from their
nature were almost wholly pure, it possessed great reservoirs,
in which the rescued portions of light were stored. In the sun
Primeval man himself dwelt along with the holy spirits, who
pursued the work of redemption; in the moon the Mother of
life was throned. The twelve signs of the zodiac constituted
an artificial machine, a great wheel with buckets which poured
the portions of light delivered from the world into the moon

and sun, the illuminating vessels swimming in space. There
they were purified anew, and finally reached God himself in
the realm of pure light. The later Manichæans of the West
designated the portions of light scattered in the world—in
elements and organisms—and waiting for redemption, "Jesus
patibilis."

Now it is characteristic of the materialistic and unhuman
character of the system, that while the construction of the world
is regarded as the work of the good spirits, the creation of man
is referred to the princes of darkness. The first man, Adam,
was begotten by Satan in conjunction with "sin," "greed" and
"lust." But the spirit of darkness conjured into him all the
portions of light which he had robbed, in order to make more
certain of his power to rule over them. Adam was accordingly
a divided being, created in the image of Satan, but bearing the
stronger spark of light within him. Eve was associated with him
by Satan. She was seductive sensuousness, although even she
had a tiny spark of light in her. If the first human beings thus
stood under the rule of Satan, yet from the very first the glorious
spirits took an interest in them. These sent Æons—e.g., Jesus—
down to them, who instructed them as to their nature, and
warned Adam especially against the senses. But the first man
fell a victim to sexual lust. Cain and Abel, indeed, were not
sons of Adam, but of Satan and Eve; but Seth was the light-
possessed offspring of Adam and Eve. Thus arose mankind,
among whose individual members light was very variously dis-
tributed. It was always stronger, however, in men than women.
Now the demons sought in the course of history to bind men
to themselves through sensuality, error, and false religions, which
included above all the religion of Moses and the prophets, while
the spirits of light continued their process of distillation, in order
to obtain the pure light in the world. But they could only
deliver men by giving the true Gnosis as to nature and its
powers, and by recalling them from the service of darkness and
sensuousness. For this purpose prophets, preachers of the true
knowledge, were sent into the world. Mani himself appears, in
accordance with the example set by Gnostic Jewish Christians,
to have held Adam, Noah, and Abraham, and perhaps Zoroaster

and Buddha to have been such prophets.  Probably Jesus was also considered by him to have been a prophet come down from the world of light; not, however, the historical Jesus, but a contemporary, seemingly human, Jesus who neither suffered nor died (Jesus impatibilis). Some Manichæans taught that Primeval man himself, as Christ, spread the true Gnosis. But in any case Mani was held, as he claimed, to be the last and greatest prophet, having taken up the work of " Jesus impatibilis," and of Paul, who is also recognised, and having been the first to bring complete knowledge. He was the " guide," the "ambassador of the light," the " Paraclete." Only by his labours and those of his "imitators, the Elect," was the separation of light from darkness accomplished.  The process by which the unfettered parts of light finally ascend to the God of light himself are very fancifully elaborated.  He who has not succeeded in becoming elect in his life-time, has not completely redeemed himself, has to pass through severe purifications in the future state, until he also is gathered to the blessedness of the light.  A doctrine of transmigration of souls has, however, been erroneously imputed to the Manichæans. Bodies fall naturally, like the souls of un-redeemed men, to the powers of darkness.  But those souls, according at least to the oldest conception, contain no light at all; a later view, adapted to the Christian, taught that the parts of light existing in them were really lost.  Finally, when the elements of light are delivered—completely, or as far as possible—the end of the world takes place. All glorious spirits assemble, the God of light himself appears, accompanied by the Æons and the perfectly righteous. The angels who uphold the world withdraw from their burden, and everything collapses.  An enormous conflagration destroys the world: once more the two powers are completely severed: high above is the realm of light restored to its perfect state, low down is the darkness (now powerless?).

## Ethics, Social Constitution and Cultus of the Manichæans.

The only possible ethics based on this doctrine of the world were dualistic and ascetic.  But as it was not only considered necessary to escape from darkness, but also to cherish, strengthen, and purify the parts of light, the ethics were not merely negative. They aimed not at suicide, but at preservation. Yet in practice they assumed a thoroughly ascetic form. The Manichæan had to abstain above all from sensuous enjoyment. He was to deny himself to it by means of three seals: the *signaculum oris, manus, and sinus* (the seal of the mouth, hand, and breast). The *signaculum oris* forbade any use of unclean food, as well as impure talk; unclean were all animal flesh, wine etc.; vegetable food was permitted, because plants contained more light; but the destruction of plants, even the plucking of fruits or breaking of twigs, was not allowed. The *sign. manus* prevented any occupation with things, in so far as they contained elements of darkness. Finally, the *sign. sinus* forbade especially any satisfaction of sexual desire, and therefore prohibited marriage. Besides, life was regulated by an extremely rigorous list of fasts. Fast-days were selected in obedience to certain astronomical conjunctures. Moreover, men fasted, *i.e.,* held holiday, regularly on Sunday, and generally also on Monday. The number of fast-days amounted almost to a quarter of the year. Times of prayer were appointed just as exactly. Four times a day had the Manichæan to utter prayers; and these were preceded by ablutions. He who prayed turned to the sun or moon, or to the North as the seat of light. Yet the inference that the Manichæans worshipped the sun and moon themselves is wrong. The Fihrist has preserved some Manichæan forms of prayer. They were directed to the God of light, the whole realm of light, the glorious angels and Mani himself, who is addressed in them as "the great tree in whom is all healing." According to Kessler, these prayers are closely allied to the Mandæan and ancient Babylonian hymns.

An asceticism so minute and strict as that demanded by Manichæism, [1] could only be practised thoroughly by a few. The religion would, therefore, have been compelled to forego an extensive propaganda, had it not conceded a morality of two kinds. A distinction was accordingly drawn within the

---

[1] It also professed imitation of the apostolic life; see Raumer's note on Confess. Aug. VI. 7 (12).

community between the "Electi" (perfecti), the perfect Manichæans, and the Catechumeni (auditores), the secular Manichæans. Only the former submitted to all the demands imposed
by the religion; for the latter the regulations were relaxed.
They required to avoid idolatry, witchcraft, greed, lying,
fornication, etc.; above all, they must kill no living creature—
keeping Mani's ten commandments. They were to renounce
the world as far as possible; but they lived in fact very much
like their fellow-citizens of other faiths. We have here,
accordingly, substantially the same state of matters as in the
Catholic Church, where a twofold morality also prevailed, viz.,
that of the religious orders and of the secular Christians. The
only difference was that the position of the Electi was still
more distinguished than that of the monks. For the Christian
monks never wholly forgot that redemption was a gift of God
through Christ, while the Manichæan Electi were really themselves redeemers; therefore it was the duty of the Auditores to
pay the deepest veneration and render the greatest services to
the Electi. These perfect beings, as they languished away in
their asceticism, were admired and cherished most devotedly.
Analogous is the reverence paid by Catholics to the saints,
and by Neoplatonists to the "philosophers," but the prestige
of the Manichæan Electi surpassed that of both. Foods were
brought to them in abundance; by using them the Electi
delivered the parts of light from the plants. They prayed for
the Auditores, they blessed and interceded for them, thereby
abbreviating the purgatory through which the latter had to
pass after death. And the Electi alone possessed complete
knowledge of religious truths—it was otherwise in Catholicism.

The distinction between Electi and Auditores did not, however, constitute the whole idea of the Manichæan Church; it
possessed a hierarchy also. This fell into three grades, so that
altogether there were five in the religious constitution. In its
fivefold division the social order was conceived to be a copy
of the numbers of the realm of light. At the head stood the
Teachers ("the sons of gentleness" = Mani and his successors);
these were followed by the Administrators (" sons of knowledge "
= the Bishops); then the Elders ("sons of understanding" = the

presbyters); the Electi ("sons of mystery"); and finally the Auditores ("sons of insight"). The number of Electi was at all times small. According to Augustine, there were twelve Teachers and seventy-two Bishops. One of the Teachers appears to have stood as president at the head of the whole Manichæan Church. At least Augustine speaks of such an one, and the Fihrist also knows of a supreme head over all Manichæans. The constitution accordingly had here also a monarchical head.

The cultus of the Manichæans must have been very simple, and have consisted essentially of prayers, hymns, and ceremonies of adoration. This simple divine service promoted the secret spread of the doctrine. Besides, the Manichæans seem, at least in the West, to have adhered to the Church's order of festivals. The Electi celebrated special festivals; but the chief one common to all was the "Bema" (Βῆμα), the festival of the "doctoral chair," in memory of the death of Mani, in the month of March. Believers prostrated themselves before a decorated, but vacant chair, erected on a pedestal with five steps. Long fasts accompanied the festival. Christian and Mohammedan writers were able to learn little concerning the mysteries and "sacraments" of the Manichæans; the Christians therefore raised the charge that obscene rites and repulsive practices were observed. But it may be held certain that the later Manichæan mysteries were solemnised after the style of Christian Baptism and the Lord's Supper. They may have been based on old rites and ceremonies instituted by Mani himself, and descended from natural religion.

## The Historical Position of Manichæism.

In the present state of the inquiry it is made out, and the account given above will also have shown, that Manichæism did not rise on the soil of Christianity. We would even be better justified if we were to call Mohammedanism a Christian sect; for Mohammed approaches the Jewish and Christian religions incomparably more closely than Mani. Kessler has the credit of having shown that the ancient Babylonian religion, the original source of all the Gnosis of Western Asia, was the foundation of the Manichæan system. The opinion formerly held is accord-

ingly wrong, viz., that Manichæism was a reformation on the
ground of Parsiism, a modification of Zoroastrianism under the
influence of Christianity. It was rather a religious creation *belonging to the circle of Semitic religions:* it was the Semitic
nature-religion lifted out of national limitations, modified by
Christian and Persian elements, raised to the level of Gnosis,
and transforming human life by strict rules. But when we have
perceived this, we have only obtained a very general explanation of the origin of Manichæism. The question rises, through
what means and to what extent Mani adopted Persian and
Christian elements, and further, in which form the nature-religion
of ancient Babylonia was made use of by him.

Now as regards the latter point, it is well known that the
Semitic nature-religions had been taken up, centuries before
Mani, by isolated enthusiastic or speculative heads, had been
philosophically deepened and remodelled into "systems", in
support of which missions were conducted by means of mysterious cults. Mani's enterprise was accordingly nothing new, but
was rather the last in a long series of similar attempts. Even
the earlier ones, from Simon Magus the Samaritan down, had
adopted Christian elements to a greater or less extent, and the
Christian Gnostic scholastic sects of Syria and Western Asia
all pointed back to ancient Semitic nature-religions, which were
transformed by them into a philosophy of the world and of life.
But in particular the doctrines of the Babylonian sect of Moghtasilah, which were indeed influenced also by Christianity, seem
to have afforded Mani material for his religio-philosophical speculation. The religion of this sect was not, however, purely Semitic (see the treatise by Kessler on the Mandæans in the Real-
Encyklopædia für prot. Theol. u. Kirche, 2 Ed., Vol. IX.,
p. 205 ff.; the Mandæans were allied to the Moghtasilah, Brandt,
l. c.). From this source sprang the rigid dualism on which Mani's
system was based; for the ancient Persian religion was not in
principle dualistic, but in its ultimate foundation Monistic, since
Ahriman was created by Ormuzd. However, ancient Persian
theologoumena were employed by Mani. Even the designation
of the antitheses as "light" and "darkness" was hardly independent of Parsiism, and elsewhere in Manichæism there occur

technical terms taken from the Persian religion. Whether Mani's idea of redemption goes back to the ancient Babylonian religion or to Zoroastrianism, I do not venture to decide ; the idea of the "Prophet" and the "Primeval man" is at all events Semitic.

It is very difficult to determine how far Mani's acquaintance with Christianity went, and how much he borrowed from it ; further, through what agencies Christian knowledge reached him. In any case, in those regions where Manichæism was settled and where it came more closely into contact with Christianity, it was at a later stage influenced by the latter. Western Manichæans of the fourth and fifth centuries were much more "Christian" than those of the East. In this respect the system passed through the same development as Neoplatonism. As regards Mani himself, it is safest to suppose that he held Judaism as well as Christianity to be entirely false religions. But if he not only characterised himself as the Paraclete—and it is probable that he originated this use of the title—but also admitted "Jesus" to so high a role in his system, we can hardly explain this otherwise than by supposing that he distinguished between Christianity and Christianity. The religion which emanated from the historical Christ was to him as objectionable as that Christ himself and as Judaism; i.e., Catholicism was to him a diabolical religion. But he distinguished the Jesus of darkness from the Jesus of light, who wrought contemporaneously with the other, This distinction agrees as strikingly with that of the Gnostic Basilides, as the criticism of the O. T. conducted by Manichæism with that of the Marcionites; (see even the Acta Archelai in which Marcion's antitheses are placed in Mani's lips). Finally, Manichæan doctrines show agreement with those of the Christian Elkesaites; yet it is possible, nay, probable, that the latter are to be derived from the common ancient Semitic source, and therefore they do not come further into consideration. Mani's historical relation to Christianity will therefore be as follows: from Catholicism, with which in all probability he was not very accurately acquainted, Mani borrowed nothing, rejecting it rather as a devilish error. On the other hand, he regarded Christianity in the form which it had assumed in the Basilidian and Marcionite sects (also among the Barde-

sanians?) as a relatively valuable and correct religion. But from
them, as also from the Persians, he took hardly anything but
names, and perhaps, besides, what criticism he had of the O. T.
and Judaism. His lofty estimate of Paul (and his epistles?),
as well as his express rejection of the Acts of the Apostles,
also point to influences due to Marcionitism. He seems to have
recognised and to have interpreted in accordance with his own
teaching a part of the historical matter of the Gospel.

Finally, the question further rises whether Buddhistic elements
are not to be observed in Manichæism. The majority of later
scholars since F. Chr. Baur have answered this question in the
affirmative. According to Kessler, Mani used Buddha's teaching,
at least for his ethics. There is no doubt that he took long
journeys to India, and was familiar with Buddhism. The occurrence of the name of Buddha (Budda) in the legend about Mani
and perhaps in his own writings points to the fact that the
founder of this religion concerned himself with Buddhism. But
what he borrowed from it for his own doctrine must have been
very unimportant. On a closer comparison we find that the difference between the two faiths is in all their main doctrines very
great, and that the resemblances are almost always merely
accidental. This is true even as regards morality and asceticism.
There is no point in Manichæism for whose explanation we need
have recourse to Buddhism. Under such circumstances any
relationship between the two religions remains a bare possibility;
nor has the investigation of Geyler raised this possibility to a
probability (Das System des Manichäismus und sein Verhältniss
zum Buddhismus, Jena 1875).

How are we to explain the fact, that Manichæism spread so
rapidly and really became a world-religion? The answer has
been given that it was because it was the complete Gnosis, the
fullest, most consistent, and most artistic system based on the
ancient Babylonian religion (so Kessler). This explanation is not
sufficient, for no religion makes an impression mainly by its
doctrinal system, however complete that may be. But it is also
incorrect, for the older Gnostic systems were not more meagre
than the Manichæan. What rather gave Manichæism its strength
was, above all, *the combination of ancient mythology and a rigid*

*materialistic dualism with an extremely simple, spiritual cultus, and a strict morality;* this was supplemented by the personality of the founder (of which indeed we know little enough). If we compare it with the Semitic nature-religions, it is obvious that it retained their mythologies, transformed into "doctrines," but did away with the whole sensuous cultus, substituting a spiritual worship as well as a strict morality. Thus it was capable of satisfying the new wants of an old world. It offered revelation, redemption, moral virtue, and immortality, spiritual blessings, on the ground of nature-religion. Further, the simple and yet firm constitution calls for attention which Mani himself gave to his institution. The learned and the ignorant, the enthusiast and the man of the world, could here find a welcome, no one had more laid upon him than he could and would bear; moreover, each was attracted and secured by the prospect of reaching a higher stage, while those who were gifted were besides promised that they would require to submit to no authority, but would be led by pure reason to God. As this religion was thus adapted, perhaps beforehand, to individual needs, it was also capable of continuously appropriating what was foreign. Furnished from the first with fragments of different religions, it could increase or diminish its store, without breaking its own elastic structure. But a great capacity for adaptation was quite as necessary to a world-religion, as a divine founder in whom men could see and venerate the supreme revelation of God himself. While Manichæism in fact knew of no redeemer, although it gave Mani this title; while it only recognised a physical and Gnostic process of redemption; yet in Mani it possessed the chief prophet of God.

If we notice, finally, that Manichæism presented a simple, apparently profound, and yet easy, solution of the problem of good and evil, which had become especially burdensome in the second and third centuries, we have named the most important phenomena which explain its rapid extension.

## Sketch of the History of Manichæism.

Manichæism first got a firm footing in the East, in Persia, Mesopotamia, and Transoxania. The persecutions which it had to endure did not hinder its extension. The seat of the Mani-

chæan Pope was for centuries in Babylon, and afterwards in
Samarcand. Even after Islam had conquered the East, Manichæism held its ground; it even seems to have spread still
further owing to the Mohammedan conquest, and it gained
secret adherents among the Mohammedans themselves. The
doctrine and discipline of the Manichæan Church underwent
little change in the East, it especially did not there approach
much nearer the Christian religion. But it experienced attempts
at reform several times; for, as was natural, its "Auditores"
readily became secularised. These attempts also led temporarily
to schisms and the formation of sects. At the close of the
tenth century, the time when the Fihrist was written, the Manichæans had been already expelled from the cities in Mesopotamia and Persia, and had withdrawn into the villages. But in
Turkestan and up to the borders of China, there existed numerous Manichæan communities, nay, even whole tribes which had
adopted the religion of Mani. Probably the great Mongolian
migrations first put an end to Manichæism in Central Asia.
But in India, on the coasts of Malabar, there were Manichæans
even in the fifteenth century, side by side with Thomist Christians (see Germann, Die Thomaschristen, 1875). Manichæism first
penetrated into the Græco-Roman Empire about A.D. 280, in
the time of the Emperor Probus (see Eusebius. Chronicon). If
we may hold Diocletian's edict against the Manichæans to be
genuine, they already had a firm footing in the West at the
beginning of the fourth century; but Eusebius did not know
the sect accurately as late as about A.D. 325. It was only
after about A.D. 330 that the religion spread rapidly in the
Roman Empire. Its adherents were recruited, on the one hand,
from the ancient Gnostic sects, especially the Marcionites,
Manichæism having, besides, strongly influenced the development of the Marcionite Churches in the fourth century. On the
other hand, it gained followers from the great number of the
"cultured", who sought for a "rational" and yet to some extent Christian, religion, and who had exalted "free inquiry"—
esp. as regards the O. T.—into a battle-flag. Criticism on Catholicism, and polemics, were now the strong point of Manichæism, esp.
in the West. It admitted the stumbling-blocks which the O. T.

presented to every thinker, and gave itself out as a Christianity without the O. T. Instead of the subtle Catholic theories about divine predestination and human freedom, and the difficult Theodicy, it offered an extremely simple conception of sin and goodness. It did not preach the doctrine of the incarnation, which was particularly repugnant to those who were passing from the ancient cults to the Universal Religion. In its rejection of this doctrine, it coincided with Neoplatonism. But while the latter, with all its attempts to accommodate itself at various points to Christianity, found no formula that would introduce into its midst the special veneration of Christ, the Western Manichæans succeeded in giving their doctrine a Christian colouring. Of the Manichæan mythology all that became popular was the rigid physical dualism; its barbarous portions were prudently disguised as "mysteries"; nay, they were even frankly disavowed here and there by the adepts. The farther Manichæism pushed into the West, the more Christian and philosophical it became; in Syria it kept itself comparatively pure. It found its most numerous adherents in North Africa, where it had secret followers even among the clergy; this may perhaps be explained by the Semitic origin of a part of the population. Augustine was an "Auditor" for nine years, while Faustus was at the time the most distinguished Manichæan teacher in the West. In his later writings against Manichæism Augustine chiefly discusses the following problems: (1) the relations of knowledge and faith, reason and authority; (2) the nature of good and evil, and the origin of the latter; (3) the existence of free-will, and its relation to divine omnipotence; (4) the relation of evil in the world to the divine government.

The Christian Byzantine and Roman Emperors from Valens onwards issued strict laws against the Manichæans. But at first these bore little fruit. The "Auditores" were difficult to detect, and really gave slight occasion for a persecution. In Rome itself the doctrine had a large following, especially among the scholars and professors, between A.D. 370 and 440, and it made its way among the mass of the people by means of a popular literature, in which even the Apostles played a prominent part ("Apocryphal Acts of the Apostles"). Manichæism also experienced attempts at reform in the West; but we know little about them. Leo the Great, in alliance with the civil power, was the first to adopt active measures against Manichæism. Valentinian III. sentenced its adherents to banishment, Justinian made the penalty death. It seems to have been extinguished in North Africa by the persecution of the Vandals. It really died out nowhere else, either in the Byzantine Empire, or in the West; for it gave an impulse to the formation of new sects which were allied to it in the early part of the Middle Ages. If it has not been proved that the Spanish Priscillians had been already influenced by Manichæism in the fourth century, still it is undoubted that the Paulicians and Bogomilians, as well as the Cathari, are to be traced back to it (and Marcionitism). Thus, if not the system of Mani the Persian, yet Manichæism modified by Christianity accompanied the Catholic Church of the West on into the thirteenth century.

*Literature.*—Beausobre, Hist. critique de Manichée et du Manichéisme, 2 vols. 1734 sq. Too great prominence is given in this work to the Christian elements in Manichæism. Baur, Das manichäische Religionssystem, 1831. Manichæan speculation is here presented speculatively. Flügel, Mani, 1862; an investigation based on the Fihrist. Kessler, Unters. z. Genesis des manich. Religionssystems, 1876; by the same author, "Mani, Manichäer" in the R.-Encykl. f. protest Theol. u. Kirche, 2 Ed., Vol. IX., p. 223—259; the account given above is based in several of its expositions on this article. Kessler has since published a work, "Mani, Forschungen über die manich. Relig. Ein Beitrag z. vergleichenden Religionsgeschichte des Orients. I. Bd. Voruntersuchungen und Quellen, 1889;" see on this the acute reviews of Rahlfs (Gött Gel. Anz. 1889, No. 23), Nöldeke (Zeitschrift d. deutschen morgenl. Gesellsch. Vol. XLIII., p. 535 ff.) and August Müller (Theol. Lit.-Ztg., 1890, No. 4). The older accounts may be mentioned of Mosheim, Lardner, Walch, and Schröckh, as also the monograph of Trechsel, Ueber Kanon, Kritik und Exegese der Manichäer, 1832, and A. Newmann's Introductory Essay on the Manichæan heresy, 1887.

# THE MYSTERIES OF MITHRA
## by Franz Cumont

This is the definitive coverage of a great ideological struggle between the west and the orient in the first centuries of the Christian era. At this time, Mithraism, a mystery religion originating in Persia, spread rapidly through the Roman Empire, and achieved such strength that Europe almost became Mithraic. Dr. Cumont, the world's greatest authority on aspects of classical religions, here discusses the origins of this colorful oriental religion, and its association with the Roman army. Then utilizing fragmentary monuments and texts, in one of the greatest feats of scholarly detection, he reconstructs the mystery teachings and secret doctrines, the hidden organization and cult of Mithra. Mithraic art is discussed, analyzed, and shown in 70 illustrations. 239pp. 5⅜ x 8.

Paperbound **$1.50**

# CHRISTIAN AND ORIENTAL PHILOSOPHY OF ART
## by Ananda K. Coomaraswamy

The late A. K. Coomaraswamy was a unique fusion of art historian, philosopher, orientalist, linguist, expositor. Here he discusses the true function of aesthetics in art, the importance of symbolism, the importance of intellectual and philosophic background for the artist. He analyzes the role of a traditional culture in enriching art, and demonstrates that modern abstract art and primitive art, despite superficial resemblances, are completely divergent. Other topics discussed are the common philosophy which pervades all truly great art; the beauty inherent in such forms of activity as mathematics; the union of traditional symbolism and individual portraiture in premodern cultures.

2 illustrations. Bibliography for the study of medieval and oriental art. 114 bibliographic notes. 148pp. 5⅜ x 8.

T378 Paperbound $1.25

# PRIMITIVE MAN AS PHILOSOPHER
## by Paul Radin

This standard anthropological work considers aspects of primitive thought from such typical primitive peoples as the Winnebago, Oglala Sioux, Maori, Baganda, Batak, Buin of Melanesia, Polynesians of Tahiti and Hawaii, Zuni, Ewe and many others. It examines both the conditioning of thought which each society places upon the individual, and the freedom which the individual has either to deviate from group belief or to form group belief. Intensive discussion is given to such methodological problems as determining cultural standards.

It covers primitive thought on such topics as the relation of a man to his fellows, the purpose of life, marital relations, freedom of thought, death, resignation, and analyzes intensively folk wisdom from many primitive peoples. It also considers more abstract aspects of thought such as the nature of reality, the structure of the ego, human personality, the systematization of ideas, the concept of gods, belief, and similar matters.

It is not a simple compendium of traits, ripped out of context, but a brilliant interpretation of myth and symbolism in terms of the meaning assigned to them in each culture. It is factual in approach, and quotes original primitive documents extensively. It does not tear ideas from their matrix, nor does it seek far-fetched interpretations in terms of preconceived psychological theories.

Throughout most of this interesting book, primitive men are allowed to speak for themselves. Most of the supporting data were obtained at first hand, much of it by the author himself in his contacts with primitive peoples.

Bibliography. Index. xviii $+$ 402pp. 5⅜ x 8.

T392 Paperbound $1.95

# THE IDEA OF PROGRESS
## by J. B. Bury

Written by one of the greatest historians of our generation, this unusual volume describes the birth and growth of one of the most important basic ideas of our civilization: progress, or the concept that men are advancing in a definite and desirable direction.

This idea is so much a part of our mental background that we never consider that it is purely a modern idea, and that it was not held by the Greeks or Romans or Medieval and Renaissance Europeans. It first arose in the rationalistic philosophy of the Enlightenment.

Dr. Burry does not attempt to evaluate the "truth" of the idea of progress. He does, however, demonstrate how important this idea has been as a motivating force in modern history. He relates it to the writings end actions of such men as Montesquieu, Condorcet, Darwin, Descartes, Diderot, Gibbon, Kant, Louis XIV, Malthus, Marx, Turgot, Voltaire, and Locke. He draws examples from such widely different fields as literature, philosophy, history, economics, political science, physics, biology, and music.

Unabridged reissue. Introduction by Charles A. Beard. Index. xl + 375pp. 5⅜ x 8.

T40 Paperbound $1.95

# SCEPTICISM AND ANIMAL FAITH
## by George Santayana

In SCEPTICISM AND ANIMAL FAITH, Santayana analyzes the nature of the knowing process and demonstrates by means of clear, powerful arguments how we know and what validates our knowledge. The central concept of his philosophy is found in a careful discrimination between the awareness of objects independent of our perception and the awareness of essences attributed to objects by our mind, or, what Santayana calls the realm of **existents** and the realm of **subsistents**. Since we can never be certain that these attributes actually inhere in a substratum of existents, scepticism is established as a form of belief but animal faith is shown to be a necessary quality of the human mind. Without this faith there could be no rational approach to the necessary problem of understanding and surviving in this world.

Santayana derives this practical philosophy from a wide and fascinating variety of sources. He considers critically the positions of such philosophers as Descartes, Euclid, Hume, Kant, Parmenides, Plato, Pythagoras, Schopenhauer, and the Buddhist school as well as the assumptions made by the ordinary man in everyday situations. Such matters as the nature of belief, the rejection of classical idealism, the nature of intuition and memory, symbols and myth, mathematical reality, literary psychology, the discovery of essence, sublimations of animal faith, the implied being of truth, and many others are given detailed analyses in individual chapters.

Unabridged reissue with a preface by the author. Index. xii + 314pp. 5⅜ x 8.

T236 Paperbound **$1.50**

# TRANSFORMATION OF NATURE IN ART

## by A. N. Coomaraswamy

An unabridged reissue of a basic work on Asiatic religious art and philosophy of religion by one of the greatest Indologists of the century. With vast erudition, Coomaraswamy analyzes the community of theory behind medieval European and Asiatic art, and demonstrates that both differ radically from post-Renaissance European art because of a basic philosophic orientation on the part of the medieval and oriental artist.

The author's first paper considers the theory of religious art in Asia, with references to Chinese and Indian theory; the second analyzes mystical religious art interpretation in the medieval European mystic Meister Eckhart. Further papers consider Indian medieval aesthetic manuals, the interpretation of symbolic language in aesthetics, the origin and use of images in India. This is a book not only for the orientalist, the art historian, the philosopher, but also for the artist who realizes, with Dante, that "Who paints a figure, if he cannot be it, cannot draw it."

Glossaries of Sanskrit and Chinese terms. Bibliography. 41pp of notes. v + 245pp. 5⅜ x 8.

T368 Paperbound **$1.75**